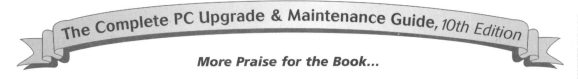

The Complete PC Upgrade & Maintenance Guide, 10th Edition

More Praise for the Book...

I am a student at UC Santa Barbara as well as a computer enthusiast/geek/nerd/addict and have to say, your book KICKS ASS! ...the amount of information in it, as well as your own personal suggestions and experiences is outstanding.

Jason Brooks
Student
UC Santa Barbara

I read the first chapter and couldn't put it down! I read it from cover to cover. I now own three computers (two PCs and one laptop). One of the PCs (a 486), I bought ($20) from a friend that told me it was totally fried. He had taken it to the local PC shop and they told him it was useless. I took it apart, cleaned it up, and put it back together step by step with your book. When I turned on the power switch, it booted right up! It's still going with no problems today. (My son thanks you!) Anyway, I now have fixed several of my friends computers (Plug and Play my FOOT!!!), and believe that there is nothing that I can't fix on a computer.... I can't thank you enough. I tell everyone about your book.... Again, thanks for opening my eyes and taking the fear out of my favorite hobby.

Sergeant Derrick Ball
Loadmaster on the C-130 aircraft in the U.S. Marine Corps

I am just sending you this note to thank you. I used three of your books, *The Complete PC Upgrade and Maintenance Guide*, *Troubleshooting Windows 3.1*, and [another book] in preparing for my A+ certification exam. Well, I am glad to say that I passed with well over 90% in each exam and owe it in no small part I feel to your excellent books. They really gave me an edge and there was very little on the exam that stumped me. I am a big fan of your writing and find all of your articles and books very entertaining and easy to understand.

Arthur Cramer
Certified A+ Technician

The Complete PC Upgrade & Maintenance Guide was chosen by Heathkit Educational Systems as part of their PC Servicing and A+ Certification Preparation courses. Quite frankly, we use it because it is the best book on the subject available today.

Douglas M. Bonham
Heathkit Educational Systems

Congratulations on your excellent book, *The Complete PC Upgrade & Maintenance Guide*. We pride out PC service and repair center as being one of the best in western Pennsylvania, and your book is an integral part of our success. Not only is it required reading for every PC technician that we employ, it is the most important reference tool in our shop. The advice in the hard drive chapters alone has saved us hundreds of hours of troubleshooting throughout the years.

Anthony J. Pugliese
President, PCE Computers

It is witty, easy reading, and very informative. I find most books boring and tedious..., but this book was actually fascinating to me. I read it for hours at a time and the amazing thing is it's a technical book.... I now use it as my PC bible.

Brett Havener
Computer Tech, Proprieter
Q-Point

The Complete PC Upgrade & Maintenance Guide

Tenth Edition

Mark Minasi

SYBEX®

San Francisco • Paris • Düsseldorf • Soest • London

Associate Publisher: Gary Masters
Developmental Editor: Brenda Frink
Editor: Linda Lambeth Orlando
Project Editor: Benjamin Tomkins
Technical Editors: James Kelly and Rima Regas
Book Designer: Kris Warrenburg
Graphic Illustrators: Tony Jonick and Jerry Williams
Electronic Publishing Specialist: Cyndy Johnsen
Project Team Leader: Leslie Higbee
Proofreaders: Nancy Riddiough, Catherine Morris, and
Sachi Guzman
Companion CD: Ginger Warner
Beta and Licensing Specialist: Heather O'Connor
Publishing Intern: Chad Mack
Indexer: Ted Laux
Cover Designer: Design Site
Cover Illustration: Design Site

First edition copyright ©1991 SYBEX Inc.
Second edition copyright ©1993 SYBEX Inc.
Third edition copyright ©1994 SYBEX Inc.
Fourth edition copyright ©1995 SYBEX Inc.
Fifth edition copyright ©1996 SYBEX Inc.
Sixth edition copyright ©1996 SYBEX Inc.
Seventh edition copyright ©1996 SYBEX Inc.
Eighth edition copyright © 1997 SYBEX Inc.
Ninth edition copyright © 1998 SYBEX Inc.

Library of Congress Card Number: 99-63820
ISBN: 0-7821-2606-5

Manufactured in the United States of America

10 9 8 7 6 5 4 3 2 1

To the people who have helped me and continue to help me over the years, the people who gave me a chance or gave me a hand: Ludwig Braun, Andy Kydes, Nancy Denkhe, Pete Moulton, John, Doug, Julie, and the other Data-Tech folks, Maureen Quinn, all of the thousands of students who've read this book and helped make it better, Fred Langa, Steve Levy, Wayne Rash, the Sybex gang (Dianne, Rudy, Rodnay, Gary, Neil, Guy, Barbara, and many others), Donna Cook, Stan Altman, and everyone else I've overlooked. Thank you all very much!

ACKNOWLEDGMENTS

Since this book's first incarnation in 1986, I've had help from many people. I can't thank them all here, but let me mention a few. My apologies to anyone I miss.

Big thanks for the tenth edition updates to John Heilborn.

Thanks to Joe Jorden, Bruce Jones, and David Groth for their able contributions to the ninth edition.

Thanks to Glenn Hartwig for updating this book for the eighth edition. He provided a much needed new chapter on laptop and notebook computers (Chapter 26) as well as several new and revised topics.

Thanks to Christa Anderson for updating this book for the seventh edition. Her work was tireless, and I appreciate it.

Our artist-in-residence (even though she's no longer in residence), Elizabeth Creegan, and one of our long-time Troubleshooting instructors, Terry Keaton, did the original versions of the illustrations. They both excel in a world in which I've never exceeded apprentice status—the visual arts—and they've always been patient with my sometimes muddy requests. Thanks to them both, and (how could I forget?) thanks also to Doug Zimmer, instructor emeritus, for the original versions of the SCSI cable diagrams.

My associate, Paula Longhi, wrote the initial draft of the CD-ROM chapter, and I thank her for that.

Over the years, I've gotten plenty of editorial assistance and suggestions from Sheila Walsh, the biggest, baddest Tae Kwon Do black belt to ever open up a PC; Pete Moulton, my old partner and good buddy; and Rob Oreglia and Scott Foerster, more instructors emeriti. I continue to get good feedback from the staff of Tech Teach International: Kris Ashton, Peter Brondos, Shawn Caison, Patrick Campbell, David Costow, Eric Christiansen, Bob Deyo, Ceen Dowell, Brandi Dunnegan, Paul Eve, Scot Hull, Lisa Justice, Andrew McGoff, Ellen O'Day, Nicole Price, Holliday Ridge, David Sheridan, Marc Spedden, Frederick Thornton, and Steven Wright. And you, too, can give me feedback at help@minasi.com on the Internet.

And speaking of my e-mail address, thanks to all of you who have taken a few minutes to tell me how much you liked the book.

These books don't get into your hands unless some publisher who thinks they're worth it puts them there. The first such person was Stephen Levy, the publisher of the first version of this book, and my thanks go to him. Dianne King at Sybex arranged for Sybex to start publishing this; Dianne's goofing off somewhere, but we miss her. Gary Masters, the Maxwell Perkins of the computer press, remains this book's guardian angel. Thanks also to this and the previous edition's Developmental Editors, Brenda Frink and Neil Edde. Thanks go also to past and present editors Linda Lambeth Orlando, Doug Robert, Peter Weverka, Vivian Perry, and Anamary Ehlen; all the Project Editors and Production Coordinators for all the editions, because a book like this is a monster on the production side: Project Editors Ben Tomkins, Linda Good, Lee Ann Pickrell, Emily Smith, Malcolm Faulds, and Dann McDorman; Technical Editors Jim Kelly, Rima Regas, Mike Hanna, Aaron Kushner, Maryann Brown, and Kim Ringer; Electronic Publishing Supervisor Kate Kaminski; Electronic Publishing Specialists Cyndy Johnsen, Tony Jonick, and Bill Gibson; Project Team Leader Leslie Higbee; Production Coordinators Shannon Murphy, Theresa Gonzalez, Kimberley Askew, Dave Nash, and Blythe Woolston; Publishing Intern Chad Mack; CD Technician Ginger Warner; Beta and Licensing Specialist Heather O'Connor; Graphic Illustrators Tony Jonick and Jerry Williams;

Proofreaders Nancy Riddiough, Catherine Morris, Sachi Guzman, Eryn Osterhaus, and Duncan Watson; and of course, Indexer Ted Laux.

Thanks also to the folks at Adaptec and Creative Labs, Inc. who graciously allowed us to excerpt their documentation for this book. Kudos also to Dale Palovich and his team, who put together the new videos for the tenth edition.

CONTENTS AT A GLANCE

TABLE OF CONTENTS

4 Avoiding Service: Preventive Maintenance   **241**

19   Modems and Serial Interfaces

INTRODUCTION

This new edition brings tons of new information. Over the years, each edition has seen chapters yanked out and completely rewritten, and that's true in this edition, in spades.

What's New in the 10th Edition

In some ways, the PC hardware world doesn't change much. After 12 years, VGA is still the baseline video standard and floppies still hold only 1.44MB of data. But in other ways, it's moving all the time, and that's motivated this latest overhaul of *The Complete PC Upgrade & Maintenance Guide*.

The two hard disk standards that held nearly all of the PC disk market in the '80s, ST506 and ESDI, are all but gone now, replaced by EIDE and, to a lesser extent, SCSI. As a result, the hard disk chapters have been completely reworked. Roughly every two years sees a newer and faster kind of memory, so the memory section has seen serious revisions. I think every single edition of this book has required expansion of the CPU section, as Intel's not letting any moss grow under its feet, and this edition is no exception, with added Pentium III coverage.

CD-ROMs became as common on new systems as floppy drives back around 1995, but more and more systems nowadays have writeable CD-R drives, and you'll find that our coverage on that topic has been revised and expanded.

Many of you have written me to tell me that you've found the videos useful. But they were starting to show signs of age, so we shot a whole new bunch, which you can find on your CD-ROM. I hope you find them helpful!

But those sections are just the start. You'll find more on video, laptops, power, and more. But I've gotta run, just thought of something I need to add to the *11th* edition...

Why This Book?

I've been programming computers since 1973. But for years, I wasn't a "hardware guy." After moving from mainframe programming to the early PCs that came out in the mid-'70s, I watched the microcomputer market, waiting for the computer that was useful and didn't require any soldering to get it up and running.

That's why I liked the IBM PC from the very beginning. Just take it out of the box, plug some stuff together, and *voila*! A completely usable computer—and *no soldering*.

That was, of course, until I'd had it for nine months. Then, right in the middle of doing some work, all of a sudden, the floppy drive light came on for no apparent reason, the system rebooted itself, and the number 601 appeared on the screen. Nothing else happened—the machine refused to do any more. I turned it on and off again, and it did the same thing.

"What now?" I thought. It was 1982. Replacing *everything* was expensive. Floppy drives cost $500 apiece. A PC motherboard cost $1,400. A floppy controller cost $275. Of course, all of this happened shortly *after* the warranty on my PC ran out. I had an all-IBM machine, but some of the parts came from a dealer who was not an authorized IBM dealer, so IBM wouldn't even talk to me. I went to a service department of a large computer store chain seeking help. I looked at their hourly rates and *knew* from their high prices that they must know what they're doing (I was younger and dumber), so I confidently left my machine with them. They kept the machine for two months, said they couldn't find anything wrong with it, and charged me $800.

The problem, of course, persisted. I was scared. I mean, I'd just spent some big bucks for this computer, and then add to that $800 on some non-repairs, and it still didn't work. So I figured, "What the heck, I can't make it any worse," and took the top off.

What I saw was that the drive was connected with a ribbon cable to a circuit board, a board I later found was called the "floppy controller board." The controller board was new, the drive was new (the repair shop had already replaced them)—but what about the cable? You guessed it; $35 bought a new cable from a local computer supply place, and the problem went away forever.

I found out that I wasn't the only person with PC repair needs. On average, seven out of ten PCs suffer a breakdown of some kind. It takes an average of five days to fix, and the fix costs an average of $257. (This is according to a survey from the Business Products Consulting Group. The results were based on a survey of 500 business users. Besides, it was about time to throw in a statistic.) Even if you pay a maintenance company lots of money to keep your machines in shape, you should *still* do whatever repairs you can. That's because the big cost of machine failures isn't the cost of the machine—it's the cost of the lost employee time, as employees must wait in line to use machines or forgo the services of a PC altogether. You may have to wait four hours for a service person, only to find that the fix was a simple five-minute operation. The result: four hours of lost employee time. Furthermore, and perhaps more important, service bureaus don't repair hard disks; they throw them away—along with your data. It's not hard to bring dead hard drives back to life, as you'll learn in this book.

Emboldened by my success, I read what few references existed about microcomputer repair, and I tried fixing a lot of things. Some things got fixed, some got "smoked." I asked a lot of questions and made a lot of mistakes, and finally got to the point where at worst I didn't do any damage and usually met with success. I'd like to accelerate *you* to that point with this book. (But you'll still "smoke" the occasional device—everybody does.) Once I figured out how simple it was to fix PCs, I developed a series of seminars on PC repair that I and my coworkers conduct in the United States, Canada, and Europe. By 1994, more than 30,000 people had attended those seminars.

That's why you're reading this. (Unless you're thumbing through it in the bookstore. If you are, then *buy* the silly thing. Hundreds of thousands of people already have, so it's a good bet that you'll like it.)

This course won't teach you to fix *all* problems. Not all problems *can* be fixed—for instance, leaving your hard disk out in the rain will probably render your erstwhile data storage medium usable for little more than a paperweight. Nevertheless, even if you've never opened up a PC or installed an expansion board, this book can help you.

It will also help with terminology. Part of your job may involve talking to technical types. Some of those folks are good at talking to ordinary mortals, but there are some (and I'm sure you know a few of them) who can't seem to speak a single sentence without a liberal sprinkling of TLAs (you know, Three-Letter Acronyms). A thorough reading of this book will enable you to speak fluent "PC-ese," and the index will point you to definitions of most PC terms.

You'll also see a fair amount about installation in this book. Installation of new equipment often brings headaches: how to do it, why doesn't it work once installed, testing the new equipment, ensuring that it doesn't adversely affect already installed equipment. And I'll talk about how to take a tired old PC and soup it up to get better performance from it.

In the process of working with IBM PCs since 1981 and microcomputers since 1976, I have picked up or written a number of very useful utilities that assist in the diagnosis of PC problems. I'll discuss them in this book, and you'll find the programs on the book's CDs.

Who Is This Book For?

I'm writing this for the needy and the curious. Some of you *must* understand the machines that you depend on so much so that you can better keep them in top shape. Others may just wonder what's going on under the hood. Whoever you are, dig in and try something!

So don't let that useful little gray box on your desk control *you* when it goes down. Take control of *it*. (Remember who's supposed to be boss.) Even if you never take the machine apart (coward!), you'll still learn a lot about what goes on under the hood of your machine, and how to make it work faster and live longer.

Terminology

There are so many machines that it's hard to know how to refer generically to PCs. So here's the informal convention that I'll use in this book: when I say *PC* in this text, I include all PC-compatible machines—anything from an 8088 CPU to a Pentium II/Xeon, a laptop to a desktop, big to small, unless otherwise specified. Where necessary, I'll use *XT* to refer to XTs and XT clones—the 8088-based machines that you may still have hanging around. I'll use *AT* to refer to 286, 386, 486, Pentium, or Pentium Pro/II machines in general. More specifically, an *AT-type machine* is a desktop machine using a processor of 286 or later vintage. Most nowadays use a combination of expansion slots called "ISA" and "PCI" slots, but you may come across other kinds like EISA and VESA bus slots (and don't worry, I'm going to explain what those are in greater detail in Chapter 3, "Inside the PC: Pieces of the Picture"). Examples of those machines include not only the common clone, but also big names like Compaq, HP, Dell, Gateway, and Packard Bell.

Back in 1987, IBM decided to go its own way in the PC market, so I'll usually be specific about discussing IBM machines. *PS/2* refers to the Micro Channel-based (again, another Chapter 3 term) PS/2s, the ones numbered from 50 up. They're not making them any more (to my knowledge), but you'll probably come across Micro Channel machines now and then. Currently IBM's focusing on building machines pretty much like others', basically souped-up AT architectures.

My goal in developing this book is to include material of use to "techies" as well as to those who've never even opened up a PC. I'm not going to try to make an electrical engineer out of you; I'm not one myself. All it takes to do most PC maintenance is a screwdriver and some patience. I've made every effort to keep the jargon to a minimum and to define unusual PC terms when I use them. I *am* going to use jargon, however, as it will get you used to the "industry-speak;" that will equip you to read industry journals, Web sites, and other books.

Structure of This Book

First, we'll take a minute to survey the machines out on the market and look at the features that separate one type of PC from another. Then we'll look under the hood and see what's inside a PC. After that we'll step back and examine some preventive maintenance techniques and troubleshooting approaches. Next we'll look in detail at circuit boards, fixing dead machines, and PC memory. Then you'll learn all about hard disks: how they work, how to install them, how to do data recovery on them, and everything you could ever need to know about viruses and virus prevention. The book then takes a look at floppy disks, printers, and multimedia essentials (CD-ROMs, sound cards, and video capture boards). There's even a whole chapter on tapping into the vast sea of resources and information available on the Internet. The "This Old Computer" chapter is designed for those of you with legacy equipment and the "Building the Ultimate Computer" chapter provides step-by-step instructions for assembling a cutting-edge PC. Finally, we wrap up neatly with a buyer's guide, and an extensive hardware dictionary for easy reference.

Safety Notes and Cautions

Before we get started, a few words of disclaimer:

Please heed the warnings that you'll see in the text. Read *all* of a chapter before trying surgery. The reason for this is simple. If I've put something in an order that isn't clear, you could damage the computer or yourself.

I mention many products in this text. I am not endorsing these products. Where I make note of them, they have been of value to me. However, manufacturer quality can vary, and goods can be redesigned.

In general, it's pretty hard to hurt yourself with a PC, short of dropping it on your toe. But there are a few exceptions.

- Power Supply: There's a silver or black box with a fan in it in the back of your machine. It's the power supply; it converts AC from the wall socket into DC for the PC's use. You can't miss the label, in five languages, that says, "If you open me, I'll kill you." Do not open it.

  If you were to open the top of the power supply while the machine was plugged in, or even if the power was off, you could get a full 120 volts (220–240 for those of you on the other side of the Atlantic) through you if you touched the wrong things. Even if it's not plugged in, there are power-storing devices called *capacitors* that can give you a good shock even after the machine has been unplugged and turned off. The same, by the way, goes for monitors: don't open them up.

WARNING   Let me reiterate this: do not open the power supply or the monitor. Under the wrong circumstances *it could kill you.* There's always somebody who doesn't pay attention to the important stuff, but PAY ATTENTION TO THIS WARNING.

- It is certainly safe to *replace* a power supply, although when doing such a replacement, again, be double sure that it is unplugged before removing the original power supply. More important, why go into the power supply in the first place? The only possible user repair I can imagine is to replace the fuse in the box, and again, don't even think of trying it unless you know how to discharge large capacitors safely.

- Another power supply item. Never connect a power supply to the wall socket and turn it on *when it is not connected to a PC motherboard.* Only turn on a power supply when the motherboard power connectors are in place.

  Why? Back in the original PC days, some of the power supplies on the market would literally *explode* if you ran them like this (called "running it without a load"). Power supplies aren't glamorous things; no one touts the quality of their power supplies when selling PCs. Result? The cheapest power supplies possible get put into PCs. Your modern power supply is almost certainly not one of the explosive kinds, but I'd avoid the risk, myself. Besides, there isn't anything that you can test with a power supply just standing alone.

- Unless it's an emergency procedure, BACK UP your data before doing anything drastic. What if something goes wrong and the machine never comes back?

- You can damage circuit boards by removing them with the power on. Don't do it. Turn the machine off before removing a circuit board.

- Take static electricity precautions; they're discussed in Chapter 4, "Avoiding Service: Preventive Maintenance."

The rest of the things you'll find in the PC are safe, but don't ignore these warnings.

Having said all of that, welcome! Let's get to know your PC better and have some fun in the process.

CHAPTER

ONE

Five Easy Pieces:
PC Hardware in a Nutshell

- CPUs, peripherals, and controllers

- Buses and interfaces

- Additional features

- What distinguishes one PC from another

If you have any experience with buying, using, or fixing PCs, you've no doubt heard a bushel of strange terms—RAM, CPU, USB, PCI, Pentium, you name it. And believe me, it's not going to get any better, because this business *loves* jargon. And besides, if this stuff ever got *easy*, we "expert" types would have to go out and get jobs…oops, sorry, skip that! (I just hate it when this voice recognition software gets confused about what to transcribe and what not to transcribe.)

Seriously, PC hardware *can* be confusing because there are so many parts to a PC. I wish I could write this book so as to completely avoid the geeky details like "the standard keyboard port uses I/O addresses 60 hex through 64 hex and IRQ 1," but ultimately you'll *have* to know that stuff or you won't really be effective as a buyer, upgrader, or fixer. (A "keyboard port," by the way, is the connector and circuitry in the computer that makes it possible for you to attach a keyboard to your PC. And until they get those direct neural interfaces working in the next century or two, keyboards will remain kinda essential. I'll explain that "IRQ" and "I/O" stuff in Chapter 6, "Installing New Circuit Boards (without Creating New Problems to Troubleshoot)." Simply jumping in at that level, however, would probably convince the average reader that perhaps quantum physics would be a simpler course of study.

What we need, then, is some structure, and a bird's-eye view of PC hardware. It's a lot easier to understand some new term if you've got a classification system. What I'm going to explain in this chapter is the mental model that I use to understand PC hardware. It's not perfect—not *everything* will fit into this model—but I think you'll find it useful in your hardware education.

CPUs, Peripherals, and Controllers

Basically, PC hardware boils down to three kinds of devices: the *central processing unit* (*CPU*) (or, as more and more machines offer multi-processor capabilities, the *CPUs*), *peripherals* (the input, output, and storage devices that it needs to do actual work), and in-between devices that I'll generically call *controllers* or *adapters*.

For example, consider what makes it possible for the PC to put images on your video monitor. Every PC has a video monitor, and every PC also has a chip inside it called the CPU, or *processor*, which is essentially the "engine" of the PC. When you hear someone say that she's got a "Pentium II computer," she's describing the particular model name of the CPU around which her computer is built. Common CPU names you might hear are Celeron, Pentium Pro, Pentium, Pentium II, or Pentium III. These are all names for CPUs made by Intel. Other processors that are commonly used today are made by Cyrix and AMD, who market CPU chips with names like M II, 686, K6, or 586.

In between the CPU and the monitor is a kind of "diplomatic" device—a circuit that knows how to talk to both the CPU and the video monitor—called the *video adapter* or *video controller*. If you ever see a reference to an S3 graphics adapter, a super VGA (SVGA) adapter, or a 3D adapter, then you're reading references to *video adapters*. Video adapters contain memory that they use to retain the current video image, as well as on-board electronics that know how to do many useful graphical tasks like drawing lines, circles, and polygons. In fact, one of the most important specifications today for 3D video cards is the number of polygons they can draw in a second (measured in millions of polygons per second). Companies such as Diamond, ATI, STB, Creative Laboratories, Cirrus, Trident, and S3 build video controllers, as well as the components for video controllers produced by many other manufacturers, some of which are now actually integrated on the motherboard.

You'll see this CPU-adapter or controller-peripheral connection all throughout PC hardware:

- Figures 1.1 and 1.2 show speaker connections on the motherboard and a Creative Labs Sound Blaster sound card. By the way, there are two kinds of speakers used on computers today. One is the small PC speaker that's attached directly to your motherboard. The other one is attached to special stereo sound circuitry that may also be built on the motherboard or may be on a separate circuit board that you plug into your motherboard.

FIGURE 1.1:

The PC speaker and its connection on the motherboard

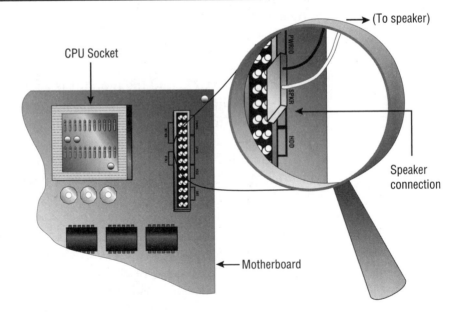

FIGURE 1.2:

A Creative Labs Sound Blaster sound card

- Most motherboards today have built-in circuitry to control EIDE hard drives and CD-ROMs. In fact, 80–85% of all drives being used in PCs today use the EIDE interface.

NOTE If you want to connect another kind of drive to your system like a *Small Computer System Interface (SCSI)* controller, for example, you'll need to install a special SCSI adapter in one of the I/O slots on your motherboard.

- To connect a printer to the PC, you'll need a parallel port adapter.

Those are just a few examples; you'll see tons more in this book.

Buses and Interfaces

But wait, we're not done yet. We've got three parts of my PC model down—CPUs, peripherals, and controllers/adapters. I'd better explain two more pieces that I've already mentioned: *buses* and *interfaces*.

You're talking to a friend who has just bought a new computer. Lapsing into fluent computerese, your friend says, "Hey, I just got this 500 megahertz Pentium III with 128 megabytes of RAM, an 8-gig hard disk, and AGP video." Notice how your friend described the computer—the first thing mentioned was a "500 megahertz Pentium III." As you've already read, "Pentium III" describes the central processing unit or CPU, the chip around which the entire computer is built. Some people compare it to a car's engine, not a terrible analogy, and megahertz is vaguely analogous to horsepower—but we'll take up CPUs in greater detail in Chapter 3, "Inside the PC: Pieces of the Picture."

The next part of the statement—"128 megabytes of RAM, 8-gig hard disk, and AGP video"—refers to hardware *other than* the CPU; hardware that helps to make the computer useful. *RAM* is the computer's memory, a bunch of electronic chips that the CPU uses to store the program and data it's currently working on. RAM, by the way, stands for *random-access memory,* and no, it's not a very useful acronym. What we ought to call it is "chips that the CPU can both store data to and read data from," but I suppose that would make for far too long an acronym. We'll take up RAM in some detail in Chapter 3 as well as Chapter 9, "Power Supplies and Power Protection." "Eight-gig hard disk?" Eight *gigs* (*gigabytes,* or billion bytes) describes the amount of data storage space the computer has on its hard drive. This is memory that will remain intact even after the computer has been shut down. Many explanations of computers show simple block diagrams that look something like Figure 1.3.

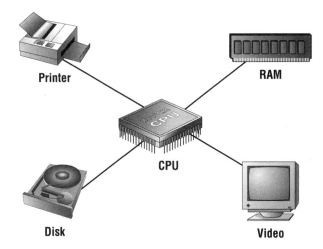

Printer   **RAM**

CPU

Disk   **Video**

In order for PCs to be easily upgraded, PC manufacturers put empty electronic connectors inside each PC; most people call them *expansion slots*. The expansion slots are the easily visible part of the *bus*, a standard way to communicate with a CPU. Over the years, several bus types have become popular. The most common bus nowadays is PCI; don't worry about what "PCI" stands for—we'll take it up in detail in Chapter 3. Most motherboards today have at least two kinds of expansion slots, PCI, and ISA. Figure 1.4 shows a motherboard with both of these kinds of slots. Notice which is which—you can really run into trouble if you try to plug an expansion board into the wrong kind of slot.

Why are there PCI and ISA bus connectors in this computer? So there is a standard that computer system designers and computer expansion board designers can agree on. *That's* important because it means you can buy your PC from one vendor and your sound card, display board, or an internal modem (to name just a few examples) from another vendor and be pretty sure that it'll work on your PC. Just as the standard electrical sockets in your house's walls make it easy for you to buy appliances with electrical plugs and immediately use those appliances, a standard bus connector like PCI or ISA means you can buy a PC from one vendor and a network card from another vendor and be pretty sure they'll play nicely together. (The mildly tentative tone of that last sentence reflects the fact that hardware compatibility in the PC world is sadly not a sure thing, and even the biggest names in the PC business sometimes sell hardware that just plain doesn't do what it's supposed to.) Some of the other bus names you may come across besides PCI and ISA are *Video Electronic Standards Association* (*VESA*), and *Micro Channel Architecture* (*MCA*). We'll cover the newer buses (current and coming) in Chapter 3 and we'll look at the older ones like VESA in Chapter 28, "This Old Computer."

FIGURE 1.4:

Notice the PCI and ISA expansion slots on this typical Pentium motherboard.

While most current video boards connect to the CPU through a PCI interface, one of the main things that drives innovation in the computer business is speed: the faster the CPU and the video controller can blast pictures onto the screen, the more popular the computer is likely to be. But PCI's top speed was too slow in the eyes of some, making PCI the bottleneck in your PC's video subsystem. Intel's answer? Add another bus to the computer to use instead of a PCI for graphics boards only. The new bus is called an *Advanced Graphics Port* (*AGP*). Thus, when you read an ad saying that a computer has "AGP video," it means there's a connector inside the PC that is designed to offer higher speed than PCI, and the system uses an AGP-compatible video controller. We've seen CPUs, peripherals, controllers, and buses; now what about interfaces? Just as standard buses like PCI make it easy for one vendor to offer a PC and another a disk controller, there's also a standard interface between the disk controller and the disk. For historical reasons, there is more than one way to connect a disk to a disk controller. Most PC systems nowadays use a disk interface called the *Enhanced Integrated Drive Electronics* (*EIDE*). EIDE is so popular, in fact, that virtually all new motherboards have EIDE controller circuitry built right in. Typically, you'll find two EIDE connectors, each of which can accommodate up to two EIDE drives (either hard drives or CD-ROMS). How are CPUs, buses, adapters, interfaces, and peripherals connected? Does one have to go with another? For example, will you find that SCSI adapters are available only for PCI? Not at all. As far as I know, SCSI adapters are available for every bus around, with the exception of AGP. Five easy pieces, then: CPUs, buses, controllers/adapters, interfaces, and peripherals. The CPU does the thinkin', the peripherals do the doin', and the controllers/adapters help them communicate. Buses and interfaces are just the "glue" that sticks them all together.

Actually, There's a Sixth Piece

Buying all of this hardware is of no value if you can't make it all work. As you probably know, computer hardware is of no value if there isn't *software* to control it. So in a sense there's a *sixth* piece to my five-piece model: software designed to control specific pieces of hardware. These pieces of software are called *drivers*.

The best hardware in the world is no good if your operating system and applications don't support it. The question of whether or not a particular piece of hardware has drivers for, say, Windows 95, Windows 98, Windows NT, or Linux is of vital importance when you're buying new hardware. So check with your software vendor before falling in love with some new doodad.

Typical PC Components and Issues

At this point, you may be thinking, "Yes, I've heard of Pentium II, megahertz, EIDE, and AGP, but that's not *all* I've heard of—what about BIOS, or Ethernet, or Zip drives?" The intention of this chapter is to give you a very brief introduction to almost all basic PC terms, to help you start to organize the concepts of PC hardware in your mind—but first I needed to explain the five-part model. Now that I've got you basically comfortable with the terms CPU, bus, adapter/controller, interface, and peripheral, I can round out the chapter with a five-second explanation of what I see as the most significant PC terms. (We'll take most of these on in greater detail in the rest of the book.)

What you'll see in Table 1.1 is a PC feature followed by a few common examples and a brief bit of "why you care." Following the table, Figure 1.5 identifies some of the connectors you'll see on the back of your PC.

T A B L E 1 . 1 : PC Pieces

FEATURE	TYPICAL EXAMPLES	BRIEF DESCRIPTION
CPU type	Pentium, Pentium Pro, Xeon, Pentium II, Pentium III, Celeron, K5, K6, Alpha	The CPU determines how much memory the system can address, what kind of software it can run, and how fast it can go. The main difference in modern processors is speed—but newer ones add other capabilities like better graphics handling and multiprocessor support.

Continued on next page

TABLE 1.1 CONTINUED: PC Pieces

FEATURE	TYPICAL EXAMPLES	BRIEF DESCRIPTION
CPU speed	100–550MHz and beyond!	Megahertz (MHz) is a very rough measure of system speed. All other things being equal, a 10MHz processor would run twice as fast as a 5MHz processor. Generally, though, all things are rarely equal.
Bus type	PCI, PC Card (also known as PCMCIA), CardBus, PC bus (8-bit ISA), AT bus (16-bit ISA), Proprietary 32-bit, 16- or 32-bit Micro Channel Architecture (MCA), EISA, Local or VESA bus, AGP	The bus determines what kind of expansion circuit boards will work in the machine. As with a CPU, a major bus characteristic is speed. Boards built for one bus generally will not work on other buses, so the second main bus characteristic is compatibility. (Having a PC with the fastest bus in the world is no good if no one makes boards that work in that bus.) PC Card and CardBus are mainly used only in laptops; most current desktops use PCI or ISA, or possibly AGP. You'll find that most controllers come in versions for any kind of bus.
AGP bus	Your system either has it or it doesn't.	This is a relatively new bus designed only for use with very fast video boards.
BIOS manufacturer	American Megatrends, Inc. (AMI), IBM, Compaq, Phoenix, Award	The *basic input/output system (BIOS)* is the most basic control software for your computer. The BIOS is what makes a PC IBM-compatible. It tells the computer how to look at the bus, memory, and floppy drive, and how to read other programs. The BIOS isn't a plug-in card, it's a chip that's mounted right on the motherboard.
Plug-and-Play compatibility	Either a PC system *is* PnP compatible, or it isn't. Unfortunately, many are "almost."	*Plug-and-Play (PnP)* is a standard that allows a computer to automatically identify and configure devices that you want to add to the system. Trouble is, many PCs that claim to be are not quite PnP compatible because they incorporate some older hardware (older is cheaper) that isn't PnP compatible.
Hard disk/storage adapter	IDE, EIDE, SCSI	The interface controller that allows your computer to communicate with your hard drive and CD-ROM. Most systems today use EIDE because it is inexpensive, easy to install, and fast. EIDE uses a 40-pin cable to interface with drives.

Continued on next page

TABLE 1.1 CONTINUED: PC Pieces

FEATURE	TYPICAL EXAMPLES	BRIEF DESCRIPTION
CD-ROM speed, interface	EIDE or SCSI	CD-ROMs are the basic means for distributing programs and data today. For less than $2/disc, a vendor can provide the equivalent of about 600 books' worth of text. CD-ROM drives are the peripherals that make it possible to read those discs. With a CD-ROM, speed is a relative thing. If you're using it to read text files or load software, a slower drive (around 16x by today's standards) will do. But if you're using it to play games, then you want the fastest CD drive you can get (50x plus today).
DVD (digital versatile disc)	Primarily used for movies today, DVD discs are starting to be used as the distribution medium for software as well.	Basically, the next step after CD-ROM. DVD discs look like CD-ROM discs, but DVDs can store more than 26 times as much data as CD-ROMs. While current CD-ROMs can store around 650MB, DVD drives can store as much as 17GB, depending on the model drive and disc you use.
Video board	Current manufacturers: ATI, Diamond, STB, Matrox, S3, Cirrus, Chips & Technologies Types/standards: Video Graphics Array (VGA), Super Video Graphics Array (SVGA), 8514 Adapter, Extended Graphics Array (XGA)	The video board determines how images are displayed on your monitor. This in turn affects what kind of software you can run and how quickly data can get on the screen. Video boards vary by the number of colors and pixels (the dots on the screen) that they can display. Most important in modern video boards, however, is whether they hold video data as a simple "dumb frame buffer," which requires that the CPU do all the video work, or contain circuitry that can help with the grunt work of graphical screens; boards like that are called "bitblitter" boards.

The main issues in video nowadays are speed, resolution, and color depth (the number of colors the system can display at one time). The interface between most video boards and their monitors is called an "analog RGB interface," where RGB just stands for Red, Green, and Blue. And although some of the newer video boards today interface with the new flat panel displays with analog boards, more and more of the new flat panel displays use a faster, digital interface. |

Continued on next page

TABLE 1.1 CONTINUED: PC Pieces

FEATURE	TYPICAL EXAMPLES	BRIEF DESCRIPTION
Parallel port	Unidirectional, Bidirectional, Enhanced Parallel Port (EPP), and Enhanced Capabilities Port (ECP)	The parallel port is the basic adapter for printers and external drives (like Zip and R/W CD-ROMs). The interface uses a connector called a Centronics connector at the printer end and a DB-25 on the computer end. In its simplest form, the parallel port is unidirectional (data goes from the computer to the printer). Most current parallel ports now also support bi-directional data flow (data can go back and forth between the computer and the parallel device) and higher data transmission speeds.
Serial port	COM1, 2, 3, 4	Serial ports are adapters that support a wide variety of low-speed peripherals including modems, serial mice, digital cameras, Personal Digital Assistants like the 3Com Palm Pilot, and some kinds of scanners. They connect to peripherals using an interface called RS-232, which most commonly uses a male DB-25 or DB-9 connector.
Serial port UART	8250, 16450, 16550	The Universal Asynchronous Receiver/Transmitter (UART) is the main chip around which a serial port or internal modem is built. The 16550 UART is the fastest of the lot, and is essential for high-speed communications and communications in multi-tasking environments. Software supports fast serial ports through a FIFO (First-In, First-Out) buffer.
Universal Serial Bus	Available as a built-in port or an add-on interface card	This adapter (also called USB) was first introduced in 1995. It features both speed and flexibility; one USB interface can support up to 127 devices at speeds of up to 12 million bits per second. Keyboards, mice, scanners, digital cameras, and modems are examples of devices that USB can support. Problems: only Windows 95 & 98 do a good job of supporting it; Windows NT and OS/2 lag behind. USB adapters use a small proprietary connector as their interface to USB-compliant peripherals.
Main memory RAM	16, 32, 48, 64, 96, 128, 256, 512MB	This is the workspace PCs use for the software they're currently processing. Newer software generally requires more RAM than older software.

Continued on next page

TABLE 1.1 CONTINUED: PC Pieces

FEATURE	TYPICAL EXAMPLES	BRIEF DESCRIPTION
Amount of L2 static cache	256K, 512K, 1MB	Main memory is slower than most CPUs, making memory speed an important system bottleneck. Faster memory exists, but it's expensive. PCs compromise by including just a small amount of this faster memory called *cache*.
Type of RAM	DRAM, EDO, SDRAM	While main memory *is* slower than most CPUs, memory chip vendors have been working hard to try to bridge that gap. The fastest current kind of main memory is called *synchronous dynamic random access memory (SDRAM)*. It is preferable in new systems. By the way, memory usually connects to the CPU through a proprietary bus, rather than PCI or some other standard.
System clock/calendar	Built in on the motherboard or added on an expansion board	Though the time and date clock on computers was rarely considered important in the past, there's a lot of concern today about the date in computers. People are worried about something that's being called the "Y2K bug." The problem: Some programs in PCs and other computers use only a 2-digit year format, which could cause some minor system failures. But the truth is, the Y2K bug is more bark than bite. The only thing we really need to worry about is that people may panic and cause problems. For the most part, computers will have few or no serious problems.
Keyboard	Key layouts vary	Keyboards have a controller on the PC's main board and use either a mini-DIN (PS/2) or a full-sized DIN interface. Most new keyboards are compatible, and you've got your choice about what kind of shape, color, size, and ergonomics you prefer.
Floppy disks	5¼": 1.2MB; 3½": 1.44MB, 2.88MB (unusual)	*Floppy disks* (also called *floppies*) are low-capacity removable media used to make your data portable. Today, since files are getting larger and larger, many computers are equipped with both a floppy drive and a Zip drive or some other high-capacity drive. The most common floppy drive today holds 1.44MB (just under a million and a half) bytes of data. Zip drives, by contrast, hold 100 million bytes—about the same as 70 floppy diskettes. Floppies are driven by circuits called (not surprisingly) *floppy controllers,* and they interface with these controllers through a standard 40-wire connector.

Continued on next page

TABLE 1.1 CONTINUED: PC Pieces

FEATURE	TYPICAL EXAMPLES	BRIEF DESCRIPTION
Cartridge storage devices	Iomega Jaz, Zip drives, Shark drive, Syquest drives	These work like hard disks but are usually a bit slower. Their main feature is that they're reasonably priced backup devices. Some attach to a parallel port, some to EIDE, others to SCSI.
Number of expansion slots	3–10	The more, the merrier. Many big-name computers sport only three expansion slots. Look instead for the eight-slot models.
Configuration method	Switches configuration (CMOS) memory	Computers won't work until you tell them about themselves, or *configure* them. Today, virtually all computers configure themselves using built-in software in the BIOS. In some cases, you may need to set a few jumpers to configure CPU voltage levels, bus frequency, and cache memory on the motherboard.
Number of interrupts (IRQ levels) supported	8 or 16	In order for the computer to use its peripheral devices, it needs to know when a device has information for it. For example, if you press a key on the keyboard, the keyboard has to have a way to get that information to the computer. In the past, computers would get this information by "polling" their external devices (looking first at one device, then the next, and so on, repeating the process, many times per second). Trouble is, this takes up a lot of computing time, and early microcomputers had little power to spare. So instead, the engineers that developed the microcomputer changed to a new system that uses interrupts. Interrupts (also called IRQs) are associated with the external devices. When a device has information for the computer, it signals the CPU through its interrupt line. The problem is, generally no two devices can share an interrupt. So when configuring your system, you need to make sure that you don't assign the same interrupt to two or more devices. Doing so will cause the two devices to have a conflict, and can make the system crash—or at least not recognize the devices.

Continued on next page

TABLE 1.1 CONTINUED: PC Pieces

FEATURE	TYPICAL EXAMPLES	BRIEF DESCRIPTION
Number of direct memory access (DMA) channels supported	4 or 8	Usually, the only thing talking to your memory is the CPU. Information stored in RAM is read by the CPU and the CPU uses RAM to store information. Some devices, however, like hard drives, take a (relatively) long time to move data back and forth. And if the computer needs to act as the go-between for this data, the CPU can get bogged down in the process. DMA (direct memory access) allows certain devices to communicate directly with RAM (main memory), allowing the CPU to attend to other processes while the hard drive, for instance, transfers data to RAM. Using DMA to handle data transfer between many of the external devices and RAM really improves the overall processing speed of your computer.
Sound card	8-bit, 16-bit, or 32-bit FM, MIDI, and/or wavetable audio interface	Sound cards support music and sound reproduction on your PC, but music and sound are represented in either an 8-bit or a 16-bit format. 32-bit is better, but takes more space. The sounds are recorded and reproduced either with FM synthesis, MIDI control, or wavetables. Additionally, a sound card in combination with a CD-ROM can play music on your PC, with the right audio interface cable.
LAN board	Ethernet, Token Ring, FDDI, ATM, and ARCNet	*Local area networks (LANs)* allow PCs to communicate with each other and share data and printers. To do this, each PC on a LAN needs a *network interface card, (NIC)*. There are several types of NICs, including Ethernet, Token Ring, Fiber Distributed Data Interface (FDDI), and Asynchronous Transfer Mode (ATM). Ethernet is the most common. Most businesses have LANs, and more and more homes are adding LANs as they acquire two or more PCs.
Printer control language	Epson codes, HPPCL (LaserJet commands), PostScript, others	Printer control languages tell your printer how to underline words, put pictures on the page, and change typefaces.

The connectors you'll
see on the back of your
computer

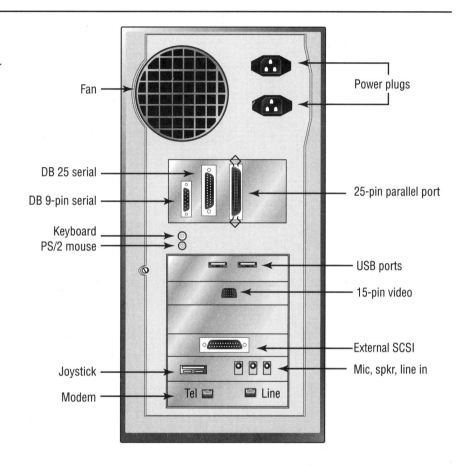

Fan

Power plugs

DB 25 serial

DB 9-pin serial

25-pin parallel port

Keyboard
PS/2 mouse

USB ports

15-pin video

External SCSI

Joystick

Mic, spkr, line in

Modem

Tel

Line

   Whew! Looks like a lot of stuff? Well, of course, it *is* a lot of
stuff! If there weren't a whole bunch of things to learn in PC
hardware this would be a pretty short book, right? But fear not,
I promise we'll take it all, nice and easy. First, though, let's get
comfy with the inside of the PC in the next chapter.

Disassembling the PC

- Tools to use, tools to avoid

- Some general disassembly advice

- Hints for successful reassembly

- Common reassembly mistakes

In this chapter we'll take a look at how to disassemble a PC so it can be reassembled. Now, it might seem that I ought to spend a few chapters just *talking* about PCs and PC repair before actually taking the thing apart. But that's *not* what we're going to do. You see, I've found in teaching PC repair to thousands of people that understanding PC repair and upgrade requires two *kinds* of knowledge.

The first kind of knowledge is a sort of "how it all fits together" knowledge; an understanding of things like how extended memory is different from conventional memory or what a superscalar CPU is. It's knowledge of the components and interfaces—the connections between those components—that enables you to diagnose a problem or select the correct upgrade part. You'll learn about this kind of "microcomputer anatomy and physiology" throughout most of the rest of the book—in fact, the extended/ expanded and superscalar stuff is in the next chapter.

The second sort of knowledge that you'll need is a different kind; a familiarity with tools and with some simple rules of disassembly. Perhaps it's my personal bias, but I prefer to teach these skills before getting into the concepts of Chapter 3, "Inside the PC: Pieces of the Picture." It may be that I do that because I'm kind of clumsy personally: I'm the kind of guy who forgets to put the plug in the bottom of the oil pan before I start refilling the engine with oil, so this has been hard-won knowledge. That won't be true for all of you—if you're already someone who's comfortable with tools, then you probably *don't* have to be reminded that screwdrivers go "lefty loosey, righty tighty"—but us klutzes do, at least sometimes, and that's what this chapter is about. There are right ways to take a machine apart and wrong ways; this chapter shows you one of the right ways.

Choose Your Weapons: PC Repair Tools

Most PC problems can be fixed with nothing more complex than a screwdriver. But if you do a *lot* of PC work, then there are other tools that you will no doubt want to add to your toolkit.

What's the best kind of PC? Ask me at different times and I'll give you different answers. But if I'm in the process of fixing a PC when you ask me, then I'll tell you, "A PC sitting on the middle of a table, which is sitting in the middle of a room on a nice, low-static wood floor." Fixing PCs is actually a lot of fun; getting at the PC to work on it, however, is usually a pain. Computers are frequently shoved into corners—dark corners—connectors, if they are labeled at all, are labeled in the smallest print possible, and the machines get more and more tightly packed inside. (You'll find that PCs get darker inside and the lettering on the connectors gets smaller every year, for some strange reason. Maybe it's the same thing that makes my father claim that snow gets heavier and more difficult to shovel every year; he's always speculated that it was due to variations in gravity.)

One of the best tools to add to your toolkit is a little flashlight, like the Mini-Maglite. And for seeing those hard-to-see places, a small dental mirror is great.

Screwdrivers

The basic tool. They come in straight-slot, Phillips, and Torx varieties. You may also occasionally need a tool called a nut driver, which is a sort of screwdriver that has a hex drive at the end instead of a blade. The most common size nut driver for computers is ¼ inch. The straight-slot screw has, as its name implies, a single metal slot across its top. Be careful with these—it's easy for the screwdriver to slip from the slot, making it hard to bear down on a straight-slot screw and easy to jab yourself in the hand.

That's probably why Phillips screws were invented. Phillips screws have two slots at right angles to one another that taper in toward the center of the two slots. A corresponding peak in the Phillips screwdriver's tip fits nicely into that indentation, helping the screwdriver to stay centered and not slip as easily.

Or at least that's the idea.

There are two problems with Phillips screws, at least in the PC business. First, the screws that PC makers use are often made of some kind of soft, presumably cheap steel. And to make matters worse, the slots aren't very deep, making it very easy to strip the heads of the screws. So be careful when removing Phillips screws from your computer. The second problem is related to the first. It seems that half of the computers that I work on have previously been worked by Ignatz the Strong Man, apparently on loan from the circus. People tighten PC case screws as if their data will leak out of the seams otherwise. It's a dumb practice for two reasons—first, it's unnecessary and second, you'll strip the heads on the screws. Tighten to a snug fit; don't cinch it down like it'll be subjected to a vibration test. And another thought along those lines: there are several sizes of Phillips screwdrivers. I'm aware of size 000, 00, 0, 1, 2, and 3, but I'm sure there are more. Most PC screws are size 1. However, you may come across a case screw (one of the screws that secures the case to the chassis) that's a No. 2. The important point is to use the correct size screwdriver for the screw you're working with. Don't try to remove a No. 2 with a No. 1 Phillips; again, you'll strip the head. By the way, if you should happen to come across a screw that HAS a stripped slot, get out the ¼" nut driver I mentioned earlier. You can screw it in (or out) with that, since virtually all PC screws these days also have hex heads instead of round heads. See Figure 2.1.

FIGURE 2.1:

The typical hex-head/ Phillips-head PC screw can be turned with either a Phillips screwdriver or a 1/4" nut driver.

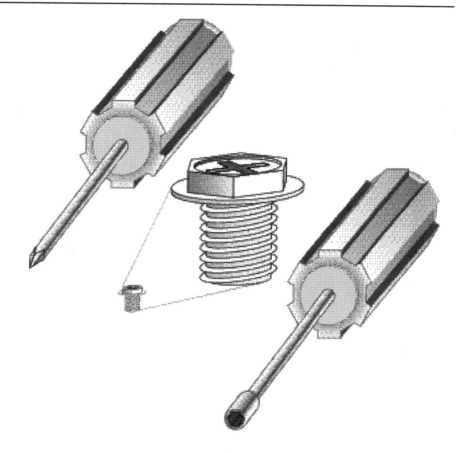

Personally, I like electric screwdrivers. The Black and Decker that I got for Christmas was just about the most useful present I ever received. (And remember, it's made in the United States!)

Compaq computers usually use a third type of screw, called a *Torx screw*. The Torx uses a six-sided, star-shaped hole in the head of the screw. Torx screwdrivers come in at least 15 sizes, which is a major pain for support people. You'll probably use only sizes T-10 and T-15. Why do manufacturers use Torx screwdrivers? Well, it's certainly not because of convenience—whatever they are, they are not *convenient*. I think it's because until about 10 years ago, most people couldn't easily buy Torx screwdrivers. The idea was probably that a computer company that used Torx screws could keep casual users from attempting to work on their computers. This was, however, a dumb idea. Things sometimes go wrong with PCs. Also, you may want to upgrade yours or replace a battery. If you can't get inside it, it can become useless junk before its time. Fortunately, anyone who's ever had to change the headlights on a GM car already *has* a set of Torx screwdrivers.

While I'm on this topic, let me tell you a quick story. Years ago, I bought a number of PCs from a PC configuration/sales company. We'd specified on the bid that we wanted 100 percent IBM components, as this was 1983 and the clone stuff was a bit iffy on compatibility. The company delivered the PC with seals on the back of the box. When I had trouble installing software on the computer, I broke the seals, took the cover off, and discovered that the video board, floppy controller, and hard disk controller *weren't* IBM products. I called the vendor and explained that he had not fulfilled the contract when he sent us the non-IBM parts. His answer: that I'd violated the warranty on the computer by removing the seals. (I suppose he would have used Torx fasteners if he'd thought of it.) My answer: after I thanked him for the first really good laugh I'd had in a while, I told him to either take the PCs back or outfit them correctly. He agreed to rebuild them with IBM components. Now, the moral of the story is *not* that IBM makes the best parts (although they're often quite good). The moral *is* that you should specify what you want in your PC and then make sure that you get it. And if you buy a computer and the vendor tries to keep you out of it, be suspicious.

Anti-Static Wrist Straps

Repairing your PC can do more harm than good if you're not careful. I'll say this again in Chapter 4, "Avoiding Service: Preventive Maintenance," but it's worthwhile mentioning it here (even if it *will* end up being a bit redundant). Remember that:

- Static electricity can damage chips.

- You generate static all the time.

- In order for you to *feel* a static charge, it must be in excess of 2,000 volts.

- You can destroy a chip with less than 35 volts!

We're all aware of static electricity on dry winter days, when walking across a carpet and touching a metal doorknob results in an annoying shock. But you're probably not aware that you generate static almost all of the time, static that you don't even feel. It's entirely possible that you can reach over and pick up a board or a chip, not feel any tingle at all—and destroy the board or chip.

The answer is an anti-static wrist strap. It's an elastic fabric band that fits over your wrist and then attaches to an electrical ground.

Some anti-static wrist straps attach to ground by plugging into a wall socket; they've actually got a plug on them! Since it *is* possible that a severely badly wired outlet could shock you, don't plug yourself in until you've read Chapter 9, "Power Supplies and Power Protection." In it, you'll find information about an outlet-wiring tester that you can use to check an outlet before hooking yourself up to it. Other anti-static wrist straps have alligator clips on them, which you connect to a piece of unpainted metal on your computer's case.

No matter what kind of anti-static strap you get, be sure to get *something*. Or you could end up breaking more things than you fix.

NOTE   Interestingly, although newer computers use smaller and denser components, most current components are actually less susceptible to static damage than older ones because they are designed with buffers on the input and output lines. Although this can save you if you happen to make a mistake, don't use it as an excuse to be careless with your system and components—they can still be destroyed by static.

Retrieving Tools

Here's the scenario. You're putting a PC back together, and you're mostly done. You're threading one of the last screws into the back of an expansion board, and the screw slips…and drops into the bowels of the PC. Arggh.

What do you do? Well, one approach is to pick up the PC, hold it upside-down, and give it a shake. C'mon, admit it—you've done it. (*I* have.) But it's not a good idea. First of all, the silly screw will end up hitting the floor and rolling under something, so you'll never find it. Second, you'll probably rearrange something inside the cabinet of the PC.

Some people have screwdrivers with magnetic tips, that they use to retrieve lost screws. This method works, but I'm awfully leery of having magnets around PCs. It's far too easy to forget that the screwdriver is magnetic and to lay it on top of a floppy disk or a tape cassette. Doing any of those things might erase data on the disk or tape.

Instead, pick up a little gadget called a retrieving tool (also known as a *pickup tool* or a *multi-finger* tool). They look kind of like giant hypodermic needles, with a button or a plunger at one end and a set of little spring-loaded fingers on the other end. Push the plunger and the fingers pop out like a tiny hand; let go of the plunger and the little fingers retract, grabbing anything within their grasp. Retrieving tools come in different sizes ranging from the "too short" version, which doesn't quite reach as far as you need it to, and the "way too long" version, usable for oil refinery part retrieval, presumably. (See Figure 2.2.) There are also versions with flexible shafts to aid with retrieval in hard-to-reach corners. You can find them in hardware stores.

FIGURE 2.2:

Retrieving tools: too short, too long, flexible

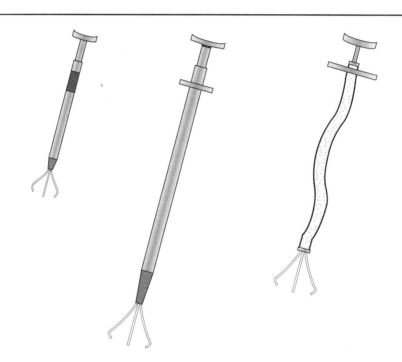

Hemostats

Some people call these "forceps"; they look somewhat like a pair of skinny pliers. Their tips are narrow, allowing you to grab things in hard-to-get-to spaces (like the extractors, mentioned above). Additionally, this tool has a little clamp, so you can use it to hold things together. And if you went to college in the early

'70s, as I did, then hey, you may even have one of these around from those days.

The extractor is smaller, so it can get into a wider range of places. On the other hand, hemostats can grip better, making them ideal for removing things jammed into the wrong place, like the narrow space between your internal CD-ROM and disk drives.

Pliers and Diagonal Cutters

Extractors, hemostats, and pliers make a kind of hierarchy. Pliers are not nearly as good at getting to difficult places as the other two are, but their gripping power is wonderful. And one more incredibly useful tool is known to techies as a "diagonal cutter" or, for reasons I've never heard explained, "dikes." This tool is shaped a bit like a pair of pliers, but it has diagonal cutters at the business end instead of grippers. So when someone says that they're going to "dike that chip off the board," they're not talking about water control devices, they're just saying that they'll use the diagonal cutters to remove a chip. (See Figure 2.3.)

FIGURE 2.3:

Pliers and diagonal cutters (dikes)

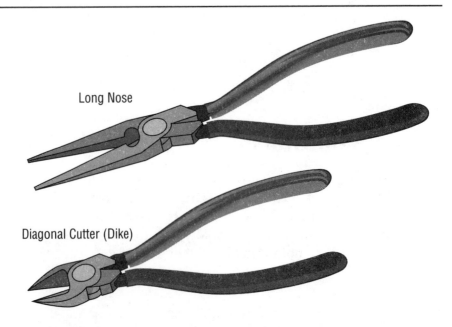

Long Nose

Diagonal Cutter (Dike)

Chip Extractors (PLCC and PGA)

As you'll learn in the next chapter, there are many types of integrated circuits (chips). Some are rectangular in shape, and others are square. The square chips come in two varieties. One is called a *Plastic Leadless Chip Carrier* (*PLCC*) and the other is called a *Pin Grid Array* (*PGA*). The PLCCs are pretty tough to remove from their sockets without breaking them unless you've got the right tool. Pulling out a PLCC requires a special extractor. Most socketed PGAs (like Pentium processors) are in zero insertion force (ZIF) sockets today and don't require a tool. All you do is lift the locking lever and lift out the chip. For the older PGAs you'll need a different extractor than for the PLCCs.

Where do you get those tools? JDR has a PLCC extractor for around $14 (Part No. EXT-PLCC). I haven't been able to find a source of 273-pin PGA extractors; they're the type that you use to remove some of the older Pentiums. Jensen Tools does carry an any-size PGA extraction/inserter for $225, however. Fortunately, the Pentium II and III are large (and the Xeon's even larger), and they are quite easy to insert or remove without special tools—but for those with "ancient" machines, chip extractors can be wonderful. The JDR PLCC extractor is shown in Figure 2.4.

FIGURE 2.4:

JDR Microdevices
PLCC Extractor

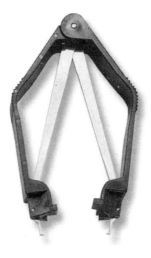

Tools to Avoid

Many PC repair types start their tool collections with one of those 10-piece sets that you can pick up at computer stores for 10 bucks or so. They're not a bad start, and usually contain a few straight-slot, Phillips, and Torx screwdrivers, as well as a multi-finger retrieving tool—and the "chip-mangler twins"—chip extractors and chip inserters. The manufacturers of these devices think they are useful extraction/insertion tools, but they are not. If you get them in a kit, throw them away. They do more damage than good. These tools to avoid are shown in Figure 2.5.

FIGURE 2.5:

IC Extraction/
Insertion Kit

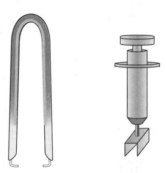

Common rectangular-shaped chips are called DIP chips, or Dual Inline Pin chips. The *chip extractor* has two hooks that you snag under the DIP chip, then you pull up to remove the chip. The first problem with these tools is their inaccuracy. It's just as easy to yank a chip's socket off the motherboard as it is to yank the chip itself. The second problem is the lack of control that they offer. When removing a DIP chip with this extractor, you end up grabbing the tool like you would a pair of pliers, a hand/muscle configuration better suited to pulling *teeth* than to pulling delicate chips. You'll get the chip out, all right—or, at least, you'll get *most* of it out. It is better to use a flat blade screwdriver to remove DIP chips. Just pry up one end of the chip a bit, then go to the other end of the chip and pry up the other end a bit, then return to the first end, and so on. Gradually work it out of the socket, and it'll come out whole and re-usable.

The *chip inserter* is a small cylindrical tool with a plunger in it. The idea is that you put a chip into the slot at the end of this tool, position the tool over the chip socket, push the plunger, and the chip slides right into the socket. The reality is that the chip smashes against the socket, mashing all of the chip's legs and generally rendering the chip unusable. *Stay away from this tool.*

Now that you've got the right tools (and gotten rid of the wrong ones), let's see what to do with them.

General PC Disassembly Advice

Keep a few basics in mind when disassembling computers.

Be Sure That Disassembly Is Necessary

New troubleshooters are always trigger-happy with their electric screwdrivers, but, as I'll discuss in Chapter 5, "Troubleshooting PC Problems," the vast majority of PC problems *aren't* hardware problems.

Even if you *do* have a hardware problem, you should stop before opening the machine, and ask yourself a very important troubleshooter's question: Is this thing still under warranty? If you can make the problem SEP (Somebody Else's Problem), then by all means do. If you're sure it's a printer that's dead out of the box, don't try to fix it—just send it back. Stuff that's dead right out of the box usually can't be fixed because it never worked to begin with. (There *are* a few exceptions to that rule, but it's true in general.) Always ask: "Is this trip necessary?"

Make Sure You Have Adequate Workspace

You will need a lot of room—most of a tabletop would be good; all of it would be better. Reduce the potential for static electricity. Raise the air humidity to 50 percent or so, use a commercial anti-static remedy, or just touch something metal before you touch any PC component. (See Chapter 4 for more ideas on handling static electricity.)

Keep the Small Parts Organized

Get a cup or a bag to store screws and small pieces of hardware. If you just leave the screws on the table, you'll eventually end up accidentally sweeping the screws off the table and onto the floor, where they'll roll down a floor register or under the heaviest object available. I knew a guy who kept the screws in the vent on top of the power supply—the one just above the fan. One day, he forgot they were there and turned the machine on. Power supply fans can *really* sling screws around!

> **NOTE**   An important goal of good PC maintenance is to end up without any spare parts.

Since there will be at least two kinds of screws, it's not a bad idea to steal a page from car mechanics' books and use an egg carton to store them. Screws to secure the case, for example, tend to be a different size from the rest of the screws in the system, and sometimes you'll run across hard disks or CD-ROMs that require short screws. Anyway, egg cartons have a bunch of compartments, and you can label each compartment to correspond to the screw(s) you put there. Or if you want something even more secure, many hardware and sporting good stores sell small plastic compartmentalized boxes with hinged lids. They aren't very expensive, and you can close the lid on each compartment as you fill it. That way you'll know what goes where when you go to put the computer back together.

Or use yet another approach: Once you've removed a part, put all of the screws into the holes they came out of. You'll have to remove them again before replacing the part in its original location, so there's a bit of extra work with this method, but the chances of losing screws are much slimmer this way. This is particularly true because now and then you'll see a drive mounted in some kind of bracket in such a way that you've *got* to use the very short screws that came with the drive and bracket. If you instead use standard-length PC mounting screws, you'll end up driving the screw into the housing of the drive itself, making the drive unusable.

Remember that the plan here is to end up without any spare parts.

Back Up the Configuration

Every post-XT computer (which means virtually every modern PC) stores a small bit of vital configuration information in a special memory chip called *CMOS memory*. That memory chip can't work—to be more specific, it "forgets"—unless it's hooked up to a working battery. If you end up removing the battery, the system will complain about not being configured when you reassemble it.

Let's take a minute and be sure that you understand what I'm talking about here, because there's a pretty common error that you may see when you reassemble your PC. When your computer's CMOS memory loses its information, your computer announces that with an error message on bootup. The message *will* say something like "I've lost my configuration information, so I don't know what kind of hardware I've got. Please reload the setup information in my CMOS."

On some older computers you'll see some pretty cryptic messages, ranging from "162" and two beeps (on a PS/2) to "Invalid CMOS information—run SETUP" and the like. I'll cover this later, in Chapter 6, "Installing New Circuit Boards (without Creating New Problems to Troubleshoot)," but the SETUP program is usually built into your computer and is accessed with different combinations of keystrokes. For example, on a computer with an AMI BIOS, you press the delete key (Del) while the computer is booting. On an Award or Phoenix BIOS, you usually start up SETUP by pressing Ctrl+Alt+Esc while the system boots; it's Ctrl+Alt+Ins for some other machines. You make a Dell computer run SETUP by pressing Ctrl+Alt+Enter at any time. Some computers (such as Compaq) flash a rectangular-shaped cursor in the upper-right or upper-left corner of the screen for a brief period while booting up; if you press F1 or F10 (depending on the computer model) during that time, then the computer will enter its SETUP. By the way, do you see the extreme variation in methods of accessing SETUP? That's only the first of many, many reasons why it's essential to keep your computer's documentation someplace handy, something I'll end up harping on throughout this book.

No matter how you get into SETUP, seeing this error message is pretty unsettling for first-time PC explorers. Relax; if you end up getting this message when you reassemble your system, it's probably not something that you did wrong. More than likely, your computer lost its CMOS because you disconnected the battery while disassembling, or it may just be that the battery was failing. All you've got to do is run SETUP and restore the PC's values.

In general, a PC that's lost its CMOS information can make pretty good guesses about what the correct values for the CMOS parameters should be. In many cases, it will beep at you and make you look over what it comes up with, and you'll be content with its choices. But one place where the computer might need a bit of help is in identifying your hard disk. This is more true on earlier systems, because post-1995 PCs are pretty good at figuring out what kind of hard disk or disks they have, but even the newest PC might get confused, so it's a good idea to note the hard disk information on your PC before disassembling it. Run your PC's SETUP program and look in the "basic configuration" screen; you'll see information on up to four disks there.

TIP

In an effort to be "idiot-proof," some PCs don't let you set a drive type at all. By doing this, the designers of these PCs have severely limited the range of drives that you use in their computers—but maybe that was the idea, unfortunately. In any case, if you run across a computer that just plain won't let you examine or modify its drive information, then relax—you've got nothing to worry about. The system will configure itself automatically if you clear the CMOS while disassembling it.

It may be obvious, but I'll say it anyway: do this *before* you disassemble the PC. In the basic configuration screen on some systems, hard disk type is represented as a number between 1 and 47. Some of the newer systems are able to auto-detect the hard drive type. One those systems, you may be able to just boot up and the computer will auto-detect the hard drive(s) during bootup. On others you may need to go into the BIOS setup and select the auto-detect option. Whatever your system does, it's a good idea to write down the drive type (if present) and the drive parameters (cylinders, heads, and sectors per track). Also consider these two special conditions:

- SCSI hard disks are sufficiently unusual that the basic software that's built into the PC can't handle them. As a result, these unusual drives have their own built-in software (it's called a BIOS) to support themselves. However, because the basic BIOS that comes with the PC is of no use, you must tell the PC's BIOS to not worry about the hard disk. That leads to this seeming paradox: If you have a SCSI disk drive, then your computer's SETUP program will probably indicate that you have no hard disks.

- If your disk is of drive type 47, then it may be a user-definable type. That means you've got to write down some extra information: the number of heads, cylinders, and sectors; the write precompensation cylinder; and the landing zone of the drive. Again, we'll get into all of those things later in the book.

If you've got all of that written down, then you'll be set in case you find that the CMOS data has dissolved. If you own Norton Utilities, then take a look at the utility named DISKTOOL; among other things, it will save CMOS information to a file as part of making what it calls a *rescue disk*.

Again, recording the CMOS information is important; you never know when you're going to need this information.

Turn the PC and Associated Peripherals Off

This should be a relatively straightforward step. Leave the PC plugged in, for reasons I'll get to in a minute.

Take the Monitor off the PC and Set It Aside

If you haven't got much work space, it's not a bad idea to put the monitor on the floor *with the tube facing into the room*. This might seem like exactly the wrong thing to do, since you might think that you could accidentally kick in the picture tube. In fact, just the opposite is true. It's very difficult to kick in the front of a picture tube. The glass in front is usually between ½ and ¾ of an inch thick! Kick the front and you're more likely to break your foot than the picture tube. The most vulnerable part of a monitor is the little stem that's at the rear of the picture tube. It's usually protected by only a thin wall of plastic, and the glass stem is only about 1/16 of an inch or so thick.

Unplug the Computer and Remove the Cover

Now, I don't know about you, but whenever I look at the back of a PC that I'm trying to disassemble for the first time, all I see are screws.

The problem then becomes knowing which screws help me get the top off the computer and which screws will, when loosened, cause something in the computer to go "thunk!" (if the screw was supporting something big) or "dink!" (if the screw was supporting something small). You'll see case support screws on the back and sometimes on the side of PC cases. There are typically two to four screws on the back of a PC that don't hold the cover in place—they fasten the power supply to the inside of the PC. So look carefully and make sound decisions when removing PC screws.

I can't detail how to get into every kind of PC case, but let's take a look at two common case types: the desktop and the tower. Let's start with a desktop case. Take a look at Figures 2.6 and 2.7.

FIGURE 2.6:

Typical desktop case

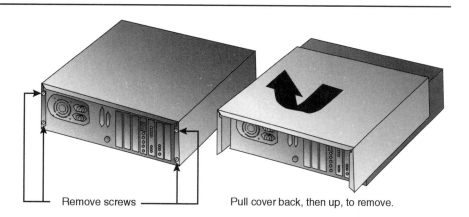

Remove screws   Pull cover back, then up, to remove.

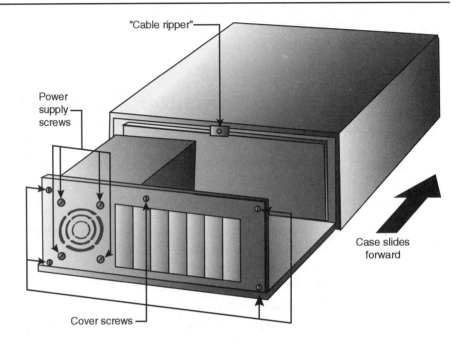

Older "cable ripper" desktop case

"Cable ripper"

Power supply screws

Case slides forward

Cover screws

These figures depict typical desktop PC cases. Note that on the back of the PC in Figures 2.6 and 2.7, there are four to six screws that hold the case in place, and four others that hold the power supply in place. When you remove the screws, remember that you've got to keep track of them somehow, so remove them and store them in one of the ways I recommended earlier (or use your own storage method if you're feeling adventuresome). Be careful not to knock the screws over onto the floor. (If you're as clumsy as I am, you'll wait until there are more small screws and hardware.) Some models save you some trouble by using thumbscrews, which are attached to the case so they can't get lost.

If you have a case like the one shown in Figure 2.7, slide the cover carefully forward and set it aside. And I mean *carefully*—don't rip the thin ribbon cables when you remove the top. The part of the case that mates with the middle screw is often a piece of unsmoothed sheet metal, and those of us who've met it before know it as the "cable ripper." So be careful, because it is *very easy* to scratch a cable with the ripper. Just a nick can make your floppy or hard disk (the peripherals that use these cables) misbehave. I once saw a cable that had gotten the "rip the top open and scratch the cable" treatment and it caused floppies to read and write fine but refuse to format.

Now let's take a look at how to remove the cover on a tower case, like the one in Figure 2.8.

FIGURE 2.8:

Typical tower case

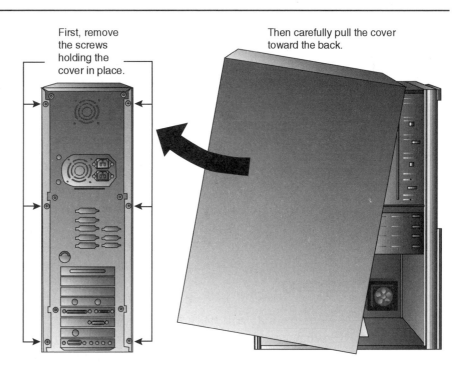

First, remove the screws holding the cover in place.

Then carefully pull the cover toward the back.

Now, this is a full size tower. There are also mid-towers and mini-towers. They all come apart basically the same way. You remove some screws from the back and swing the cover off. Note that the power supply screws are on the inside of the back of the computer. The case screws, in contrast, sit outside of the metal lip that runs around the outside of the back of the computer.

It's usually tougher getting the cover back onto a tower than it is removing the cover in the first place, so keep an eye on how the cover comes *off*, so that you can figure out how it goes back *on*. Expect that the worst part of reassembling the computer will be convincing the cover to fit nicely on the case.

Now that you've got the top off, take this opportunity to write your name on the inside of the case with an indelible marker, as a small extra bit of security. By the way, in desktop cases, the most important screw in the back is the top center screw—it holds the weight of the monitor. In normal usage, it is best to ensure that all five screws are in place. However, if you're going to be lazy, the one screw that *you must have* in place is the center screw. When you're reassembling, however, *don't* be lazy. Every one of those screws has a job. Look, PC companies are cheap, believe me. If they could save five cents on a screw, then they would. Those screws are in that case for a good reason.

By the way, should you need to replace the case screws on most PC-type systems, they're type 6-32 3/8-inch hex head/Phillips screws. The circuit boards and some drives are secured with type 4-40 3/8-inch screws.

Diagram!

Ensure that you have some paper and a pen so you can diagram what you disassemble. What order were the boards in? When you unplug something, it may not be simple to see how to reconnect it *unless* you have a good diagram. If there is no distinct marking on a cable, take a marker and *make* one. These machines aren't library books—it's okay to write on them. Remember that the game plan is that you should at least leave the machine the way you found it. You may not be able to fix the system, but you certainly don't want to leave it any *worse off* than you found it. If you're new in the business, pay special attention to the problem sources discussed in the following sections.

Ribbon Cables   *Ribbon cables* (also called *data cables*) are flat cables connected to upright pins on circuit boards. There is a definite "correct" way to put them on a connector. As you can see in Figure 2.9, the ribbon cables have a dark stripe on one edge (usually red). By the way, some manufacturers have begun using fine red speckles along one edge of the ribbon cables, so look carefully if you don't see the stripe at first.

FIGURE 2.9:

Ribbon cable

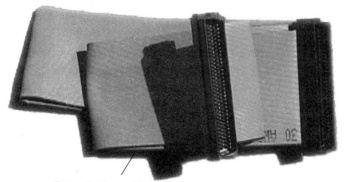

Dark red stripe on this edge

The stripe on the ribbon cable corresponds to the position of pin number one on the connector. Trouble is, often the connector you're plugging the cable into will not be labeled. Therefore, it's a good idea to take a close look at how the cable is connected to the board/device. A few landmarks can be very useful. For example, does that dark stripe go up on the board? Down? Toward the speaker? Toward the power supply? (Note that I didn't say "left" or "right"—those can get you into trouble.) Make sure to note the current position of the cables in your diagram.

And while you're diagramming cables and cable placement, remember to not only diagram what cables are there; diagram what cables are *not* there. I know this sounds sort of like a Zen koan, but what I mean is this: Suppose there is a ribbon connector on one of your computer's circuit boards, but you're not using it. For example, many sound cards nowadays have a connector on them for a proprietary CD-ROM interface. If you're not using the interface—for instance, if you don't have a CD-ROM, or if you've got a SCSI CD-ROM—then you probably won't notice the connector when you disassemble the computer. When you reassemble the computer, however, you'll say to yourself, "Hmmm...a connector. I wonder what goes on it..."—and then you get creative, usually with bad results. (Plugging a floppy drive into a CD-ROM interface will toast the floppy drive. It might even toast the CD-ROM interface.)

I recently removed a motherboard from a system that had two rows of 15 pins on the corner of the motherboard. Small wires connected to the pins for power control, reset, status lights, and the like, as normal. But the connectors seemed to have been put on randomly: one connector sat across three pins, then four pins were unused, then another connector covered two pins, then six pins were unused in the first row. The second row was just as bad. Now, if I hadn't written these connections down, try to imagine how many different possibilities I'd have had to try—it boggles the mind. So remember: Noting which connections are *unused* is as important as noting which connections are *used*.

Board and Cable Placement Students often ask, "Does it matter which slot you put a board into?" Well, it depends, but in general, when you pull a board from a slot, you should replace it in that slot when you reassemble. Additionally, as you'll learn in the next chapter, there may be several different *types* of slots on your motherboard. You've got to put boards of type X into slots of type X. For example, one kind of slot on the motherboard is called an ISA slot, and another is called a PCI slot—again, they're both defined in the next chapter. Not only won't an ISA board work electronically in a PCI slot, but the connectors don't match.

Furthermore, more advanced bus types require that you note which slot you took a board from, and restore the board to that slot. Plug a board into the wrong slot and the PC will either emit lots of error messages or may fail to work altogether when you put it back together. In other words, if you took a board out of the second slot over from the power supply, then put the board back into the third slot over from the power supply, you may encounter problems.

Some boards require that you return them to their original slot for electronic reasons. Other boards require that you return them to their original slot for more pedestrian reasons: Their slot may be the only slot that they fit in. You may not be able to get cables routed to and from the boards unless you put the boards in particular slots. Or a board may sit a mite higher than the others, and only one slot offers enough vertical clearance to accommodate that board; or some slots may be effectively truncated by memory modules, rendering them useless for longer boards. And speaking of cables, you should be able to tuck cables out of the way when reassembling—take note of how it is done on the machine before you take it apart.

DIP Switches   Before you remove a board, look to see if the board has any DIP switches. If it does, it never hurts to make a note of the DIP switch settings (Figure 2.10). I've spent 20 minutes setting a DIP switch bank only to find that I've set the *wrong* bank! Now I've messed up a perfectly good configuration and made my reassembly task all the more difficult. Besides, there are DIP switch gremlins who move the switches when you're not looking. (Honest, there *are*—I can think of no other explanation, and I don't have kids or cats.)

FIGURE 2.10:

Typical DIP switches

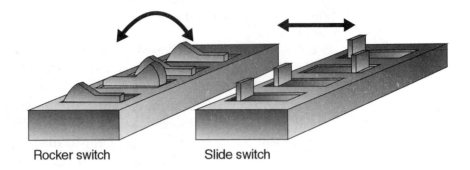

Rocker switch   Slide switch

Jumpers These have the same story as DIP switches. Write them down, take a picture of them, try putting the board on a copying machine, whatever works—but document the things.

Motherboard Connections Once you've got the case open, you'll see the main circuit board, (the motherboard). It'll have a bunch of things connected to it:

- **Power supply connections.** There are often two white plastic connectors labeled P8 and P9; some computers use only one big connector, rather than two smaller ones, but the majority of PCs use the two-connector method introduced by IBM in the PC back in the Neolithic year of 1981. Whether they're labeled or not, mix 'em up when you reassemble the machine and poof! goes the system. Fortunately, all you need to do is remember two simple rules, and you'll never install the power plugs in incorrectly. (1) Keep the black wires together. (2) Never force the plugs onto the connectors. That's it! Look at the illustration in Figure 2.11. See the piece of plastic that fits beside the plug? That's there to make it very hard to push the plugs on backwards. So if you don't force the plugs on, you can't put them on backward. Now the only thing you can do incorrectly is switch the left and right plugs. But if you always keep the black wires together, you won't make that mistake either.

FIGURE 2.11:

The dual power connectors labeled P1 and P2 (labeling may vary from vendor to vendor)

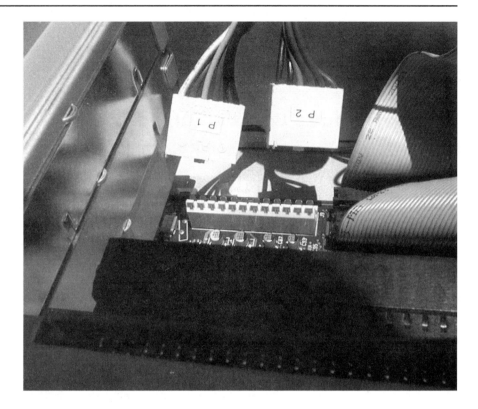

- **Speaker connection.** This connects the timer (which generates the sound signal) to the speaker. It's generally a connector with yellow and black wires.

- **Keylock connection.** On systems with front panel keylocks, a set of wires (two on some systems, four on others) connects the motherboard to the keylock. Fail to reconnect it, and the keylock feature won't work.

- **Power connection.** Some PCs have "soft power" switches to allow software to control whether the computer is powered up or not. There's a button on the front of the PC that tells the power management software that it's okay to completely power up the computer. But the button must be connected to the motherboard for that to happen. Forget to reconnect the button and the PC will look awfully dead, and that sort of thing can panic your clients (or you, if it's your PC and it's the first time you're disassembling it).

Remove Boards Correctly

If you have never removed a circuit board, take a look at Figure 2.12.

First, detach all connectors from the board. When you do that, again, please be sure to diagram which connector went where. Be very careful about forcing anything open or off. Remove the board's retaining screw (put the screw in the cup, remember) and grasp the board front and back with two hands. Rock the board back and forth (*not side to side!*) and it'll come out. *Don't* touch the gold edge connectors on the bottom part of the board—keep your finger gunk off the edge connectors.

FIGURE 2.12:

Removing a circuit board

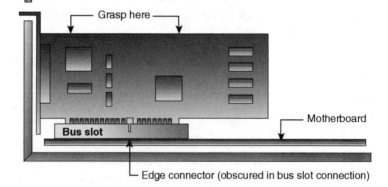

1. Remove any connectors (diagramming them first).
2. Remove the board's mounting screw.
3. Grasp the board along its top edge and rock it *gently* up and out.
4. Once the board is out of its slot, avoid touching the edge connector.

Grasp here

Motherboard

Bus slot

Edge connector (obscured in bus slot connection)

Now that you've got those boards out, you may be noticing how very similar boards are. How do you keep track of the fact that *this* green-and-black circuit board with lots of jumpers goes into the first slot, but *that* green-and-black circuit board with lots of jumpers goes into the *third* slot? Take a look at Figure 2.13 for some hints.

FIGURE 2.13:

Various identification marks on boards

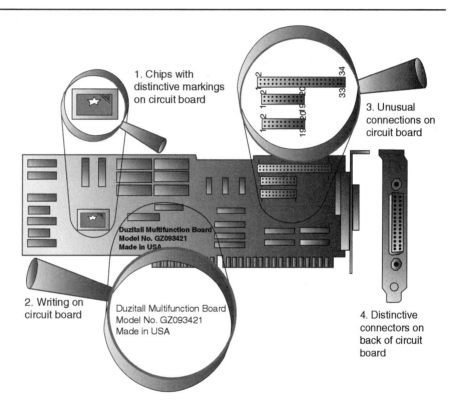

1. Chips with distinctive markings on circuit board

3. Unusual connections on circuit board

Duzitall Multifunction Board
Model No. GZ093421
Made in USA

2. Writing on circuit board

Duzitall Multifunction Board
Model No. GZ093421
Made in USA

4. Distinctive connectors on back of circuit board

When you get started in the PC disassembly business, all boards look the same. But after a while, you'll see that they have quite distinguishable characteristics.

As you know, circuit boards are covered with chips. And those chips may have a distinctive look, like a company logo or the like. It's hard, for example, to miss Intel's logo on their CPUs.

Boards may also have some kind of writing on them. Sometimes it's a copyright or patent notice, or the logo of the board designer. Sometimes it's even a label on the board that actually tells you what the thing does. Use these things to distinguish various boards.

Other boards have connectors that stand out, either on the board's face or on the back of the board. Use them, chip logos, and writing on the board to differentiate boards. You don't have to know yet what a board does; you've only got to be able to document where it came from and what it was connected to.

Of course, if there's no other way to differentiate boards, you can always just put a paper label on the boards—printer-ready mailing labels are just fine.

Remove the Drives

After you've removed the boards, you may want to take a bit of a breather—you've done some real work there if it's your first time. As a matter of fact, in some classes we stop here, put the boards back in, power the system up, and verify that it still works. A gradual approach to exploration isn't a bad idea. (Remember, we *did* orbit the Earth for practice for eight years before going to the Moon...)

When you *are* ready to remove some drives, you'll find up to five main types of drives in your computer:

- Floppy disk drives
- Hard disk drives

- CD-ROM drives

- Tape drives

- Removable cartridge storage drives (Zip, Jaz, SuperDisk)

Of course, you may not have all five types. But no matter what kind of drive you've got, they all come out roughly the same way:

- They're secured to the chassis in some way.

- They get power from the power supply.

- They're connected to a board in the computer.

Removing Drive Screws

First, free the drives from the PC's chassis. Most drives come out something like the diagram in Figure 2.14.

FIGURE 2.14:

Removing the hard drive

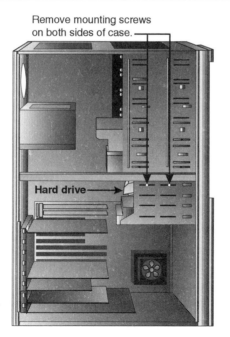
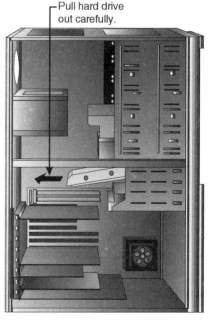

Remove mounting screws on both sides of case.

Hard drive

Pull hard drive out carefully.

Part of the PC chassis is usually a metal cradle with holes drilled on either side of it. Screws threaded through the holes secure the drive to the chassis. There are usually four screws holding a drive in place, two on either side (there are exceptions, but most computers work this way). Remove the screws, and you'll be able to move the drive around; that'll make removing the cables easier. Notice that most modern hard drives remove from the back. The floppy drives and CD-ROMs on most machines can be removed from the front or the back. Take a look at Figure 2.15. You can remove a floppy drive from the front or the rear of the computer. Once you have removed the screws, pull out the cables from the back of the drive and remove the drive.

FIGURE 2.15:

Removing a 3-1/2" floppy drive

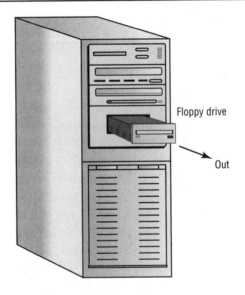

Floppy drive

Out

Disconnect the Cables

Your drive will have a power cable and a data cable connected to it. Your CD-ROM drive will probably also have an audio cable. Remove those next. (Are you remembering to add this to your diagram?)

The first, and easier, cable to find and remove is the power cable. Power cables extend, as you'd imagine, from the power supply (the silver box with the big thick power cable on the back of it) to the drive. You'll see one of two types of power connectors, as you see in Figure 2.16.

FIGURE 2.16:

Two types of power connectors

Molex connector   Berg connector

Most drives use the larger, more common Molex connector (named for the company that makes them). It's a milky white plastic connector with four relatively thick wires extending from its back; it has one yellow, one red, and two black wires. Just work the connector from side to side to remove it. 3-½" floppy drives use the smaller Berg connector. On some machines, the drive power cables are labeled P10, P11, or P12. Remove them from the drive's circuit board *carefully*, as the connector tends to be a bit balky about coming loose from some drives. Now and then I see some would-be Hercules end up breaking the connector right off the drive altogether. Just grasp the power connector and gently rock it from side to side. It'll come loose.

Once you've got the power connector off, get the data cables off. These are usually flat ribbon cables. Floppy drives and tape drives have 34-wire cables. IDE CD-ROMs (the most common type) have 40-wire cables, as do IDE hard disks. SCSI drives have 50-wire cables. Again, diagramming is important. Replace one of these cables backwards, and you could permanently damage something. In my experience, one of the top two or three mistakes that troubleshooting tyros make is to blithely remove cables without first noting where they should go upon reassembly, or in what configuration—red line up, red line down, or whatever. Every cable's layout looks obvious when it's removed, I know. But it's often *not* obvious when the time comes to replace it. (End of sermon.)

Remove the Power Supply

By now, the boards are out of the machine, and the drives are also gone. That'll make getting the power supply out simple. At this point, the power supply's drive connections are detached, so you needn't worry about them. What you *haven't* yet detached, however, are the power connections to the motherboard. Some computers have two motherboard power connectors that must be detached. Others (those with advanced power management abilities) have just one big power connector.

The Three Basic Power Supply Types

How do you know whether or not you've got advanced power management? Simple. Look at the back of the computer. Is there a rocker switch for the system's power? Now look at the front of the computer. Is there a "power" button? Most computers before around 1990 had a power switch only on the back of the computer. The power switch was inconvenient there, but it was simple for the PC designers: the power supply was back there, and it was just easier to put the switch on the power supply.

Around 1990, PC designers decided that people wanted power switches on the front of their computers, so they routed a big thick cable from inside the power supply to the front of the PC, and the switch controlled that. It's a bit cumbersome for anyone building a new PC (as you'll read in a bit), but the switch was in a convenient place.

Around 1997, PCs got a whole new level of power management. If you're running Windows 98 or a late version of Windows 95, then the computer can shut down your system or sort of put it into a light sleep when you're not using it. (Yes, I know, this isn't news in the laptop world, but it's sort of new for desktops.) These computers *also* have a power switch on their front panels—but it's not a *real* power switch. Follow the wires from the "power" switch and you'll see that it doesn't go to the power supply; it connects to the motherboard. The front power switch is a kind of "soft" power switch. You can power up your computer with it, or you can turn the computer off—but it doesn't *really* go off. It goes into a low-power suspended state. That way, when you turn on your computer, it doesn't have to go through the entire boot process; it needs only to "wake itself up" and it's ready to go. The *real* power switch is on the back of the PC.

So the quick and easy to way to figure out if you've got an advanced power management PC is to look at the power switches. If there's one on the back, it's old. If there's one on the front, it's medium-old. If there's one on the back *and* the front, it's relatively new, with advanced power management. And by the way, the computers with advanced power management have only *one* connector to the motherboard, rather than two as with the older systems.

Removing the Power Supply with a Rear Power Switch

Once you've removed the power connectors to the motherboard, you're ready to pull the power supply. Remove the four screws in the back of the chassis that hold the power supply in place. Then, if the power supply comes free, great, if not, try pushing it forward a bit to disengage it.

Again, be sure to diagram the power connectors! They look almost exactly the same… but put them on the motherboard backwards, and you'll smoke that motherboard. You can see the typical power supply connections in Figure 2.17. Remember, keep the black wires together as shown in the illustration.

FIGURE 2.17:

Power supply connectors

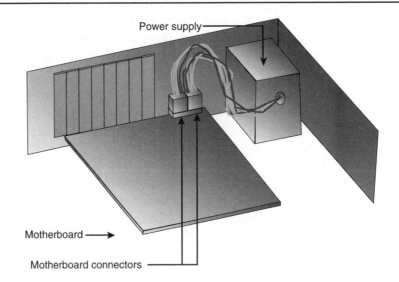

Removing a Power Supply with a Front Power Switch

If you have one of those PCs with only one power switch, located in the front as I described earlier, you'll use a slightly different approach. Take a look at Figure 2.18 to see how.

FIGURE 2.18:

Removing the power supply from a PC with a front power switch

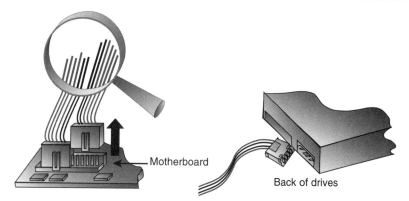

Motherboard

Back of drives

Unplug all connections to the computer's hardware.

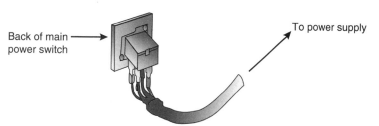

Back of main power switch

To power supply

Unplug the connection to the main power switch.

As before, remove any connections, and remove the power supply case. But there's a middle step that doesn't exist on the power supplies with rear switches. There's a thick, black cable that extends from inside the power supply all the way to the front switch. There are four wires inside the thick black cable: a black, a blue, a white, and a brown wire. Now, AC power doesn't include positive and negative wires—there's a *hot* wire and a *return* wire instead. Ordinarily, the black is the hot, and the white is the return; older power supplies just ran a white and black into the power supply from the wall socket, and that was all that was needed—but the needs of the new power supply's front panel switches change all that. In order to build a front-panel switch, power supply/case makers decided to drag both the hot *and* the return out to the *front* of the case, and then send the hot and return *back* into the power supply.

- The *black* wire connects the *hot* side of the wall outlet to the switch.

- The *brown* wire connects the *hot* side of the power supply's power input to the power switch. When you push the switch on, you connect white and brown, providing a *hot* AC connection for the power supply.

- The *white* wire connects the *return* side of the wall to the power switch.

- The *blue* wire connects the *return* side of the power supply's power input to the power switch. When you push the switch on, you connect black and blue, providing a return AC connection for the power supply.

If you disconnect the black, blue, white, and brown wires from the front panel switch, you should be able to see from the previous discussion how important it is to diagram your connections. This is one case where if you reconnect things backwards, then you could end up directly connecting *hot* from the wall socket right into *return* from the wall socket. That would cause a short circuit that could make your computer catch fire!

If you look at the front panel switch, then you'll see four flat connection points called *spade lugs* where you can connect or disconnect the white, black, brown, or blue wires. You'll notice a very low ridge on the connector and that there are two spade lugs on either side of the ridge. Before disconnecting the wires from the switch, notice that the black and the blue are on one side of the ridge, and the white and the brown are on the other side. The ridge is just a "reminder" about which wires go with which other wires. Just keep the white and the brown on one side, and the black and the blue on the other side, and all will be well. The way I remember it is that one side is "black and blue."

I've been beating the drum of "diagram" for the entire chapter, but there is no more important place where you must diagram than this. Put simply, these wires run directly from the AC line current to the power supply. Mix them up when you put them back together and you will create a direct short circuit on your house or office wiring. If you don't diagram this, don't put it back together. (Unless, of course, you need a reason for a fire drill...)

Handling Advanced Power Management PCs

If you've got a PC with two power switches, then removing the power supply is actually quite like removing a power supply with a single rear switch. The power supply itself is held to the chassis with four screws. Take out the first three, and support the power supply a bit as you remove the fourth one. When you remove the last screw, the power supply just falls out of the case, which can be bad if it falls onto something delicate, like the motherboard.

The front-panel power switch is really just a software-driven switch, and you'll notice that the wires from the motherboard to the front-panel switch are pretty small—which would be another clue to the fact that it's not a real power switch. It'll be connected to the motherboard with a Berg connector. Diagram it and remove it.

Remove the Motherboard

Finally, the motherboard comes out. (Recall that the motherboard is the circuit board lying flat on the bottom of the case.)

Before you remove it, look on the motherboard for small wires and flat rectangular connectors; they usually lead to the keylock, speaker connections, status LEDs, a reset switch, and perhaps (with a new system) the front panel power switch, if you haven't removed it already. Take these connectors off but again, be *very, very, very sure* to diagram those connections before removing them.

Drawer-Type Cases

If you have a system with the drawer-type case, look around the back of the case near the peripheral connections and see if you can find the latch that holds the drawer in place. It's usually a sheet metal tab you can slide to the side and then smoothly slide out the motherboard. "Smoothly" if you've remembered to disconnect everything, that is—keep a watchful eye out for wires you've forgotten; it's easy to sever them with the often-sharp edges of the sheet metal of the PC case. If you're replacing the motherboard, you unbolt it from the drawer and bolt the new one in.

You can remove the motherboard from the drawer by removing two to six screws. They attach the motherboard to the drawer with metal standoffs.

Standard Cases

With standard PC cases, you'll have to unbolt the motherboard from the bottom of the PC case to remove it (or the side if you have a tower case). You'll see from one to five small plastic connectors, depending on the make of the case. Most systems have a speaker cable and a keylock connector with four wires on a five-pin connector. You may also find a turbo LED and switch connectors, a reset switch connector, and a hard disk activity light connector (on motherboards that have integral IDE controllers). On most motherboards these days, the connections are labeled, as are the plugs on the ends of the cables.

You could remove the battery from the motherboard (assuming it has one), but if possible, remove the motherboard with the battery attached. It saves you the trouble of reconfiguring the system when you reassemble it. In Figure 2.19, I've diagrammed a motherboard.

FIGURE 2.19:

Pentium motherboard with detail showing connection points

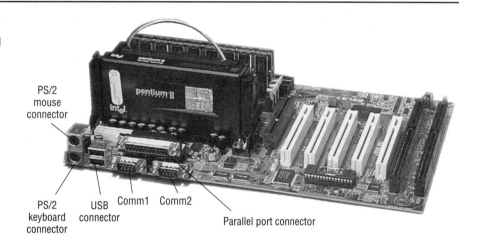

PS/2 mouse connector

PS/2 keyboard connector

USB connector

Comm1   Comm2

Parallel port connector

Different motherboards are held in place in different ways, but the most common method involves a couple of screws and some plastic spacers.

Note that the motherboard is usually held down by only two screws. Remove them and store them. Your motherboard may be held in place with more than two screws, but two is most common.

Once you've removed the screws, you still won't be able to just pull out the motherboard. It is held off the metal case with some plastic spacers. In most cases you don't need to remove the spacers. Instead, grab the board and carefully move it away from the power supply. The motherboard should slide over and out of the case.

NOTE   Some motherboards are too wide to slide over and out of the channels that hold the plastic spacers. With these boards, you'll need to use a pair of needle-nose pliers to pinch the tips of the spacers in the motherboard. This releases them, allowing you to pull the motherboard up and off the spacers. Figure 2.20 shows how to release the spacers.

FIGURE 2.20:

Pinching the spacers to release them from the motherboard

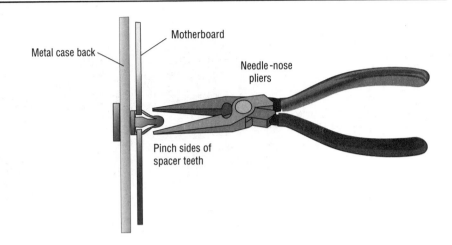

Metal case back

Motherboard

Needle-nose pliers

Pinch sides of spacer teeth

Some motherboards use metal standoffs instead of plastic spacers. In that case, you'll remove from three to six screws, and the motherboard will lift right out of the case.

Did you get this far? Then congratulations! You've completely disassembled a PC. (And you've remembered to diagram everything, right?)

Reassembly Hints

A rock climber friend once explained to me some of the ins and outs of rock climbing. The thing that surprised me most was the fact that people get into the most trouble when climbing *down* mountains, not *up*. I guess that shouldn't have been all that surprising, though since PC disassembly is pretty similar. It's during the reassembly that the mistakes get made.

Basically, when reassembling machines, just reverse the order of disassembly. Plan ahead. Don't be afraid to pull some things out and start over if you're in a corner. The important thing is to *take your time*. Here are a few tips on putting your computer back together.

Connecting Cables and Edge Connectors: The Pin 1 Rule

Expansion boards in the PC are often controller boards for external devices like disk drives or displays. Cables connect the boards to the displays. A common short cable type is a ribbon cable.

Most ribbon connectors can plug in either of two ways. Plugging in a connector upside down will usually not damage the device or the controller board but it will keep it from working. Many cables are "keyed"—that is, a connector is modified so that it cannot be plugged in incorrectly. However, many aren't, so the following bit of information is valuable.

A ribbon cable consists of many small wires laid out flat in parallel to form a flat cable, hence the "ribbon" name. One of the wires on the extreme outside of the cable will be colored differently than the others. For instance, ribbon cables are usually blue, white, or gray. The edge wire's color is often darker, like dark blue or red. This wire connects to pin 1 of the connector. (Some cables are multicolored, looking like small rainbows. Use the brown wire for pin 1 there.) This information has saved me more times than I care to recount. I learned it after incinerating a hard disk. (If you're going to make mistakes, you might as well learn from them.)

How do you find pin 1 on the circuit board? Many labels are stenciled right onto the board—very nice. Others label only pin 2, as pin 1 is on the back of the board. So look for a "1," and if you can't find it use "2." If you can't find either, turn the circuit board over. Notice the round blobs of solder where chips are secured to the circuit board. These are called "solder pads." On some circuit boards, all of the solder pads are round except for the pin 1s—they're square. Take a look at Figure 2.21, which illustrates a circuit board with pin 1 labelled.

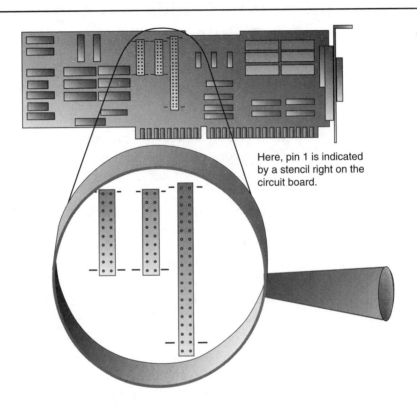

Here, pin 1 is indicated by a stencil right on the circuit board.

You'll find pin 1 on the circuit board of a hard or floppy disk, on disk controllers, or anywhere a ribbon cable connects to a circuit board.

Like most other convenient rules, there are exceptions. You may not find any indication of pin 1. Not all boards are labeled. Sadly, there are no "Pin 1 Police." That's why diagrams are so important.

With ribbon cables comes one of the most common—and most dangerous—reassembly mistakes; you can see it in Figure 2.22.

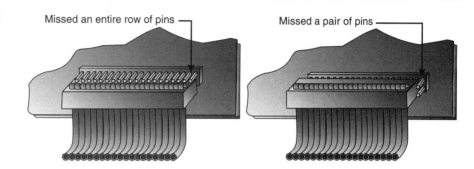

Missed an entire row of pins

Missed a pair of pins

Unfortunately, it's remarkably easy to put a ribbon cable back on and accidentally offset it by one pin or a row of pins, either vertically or horizontally. On one motherboard that I worked with, offsetting the pins by one destroyed the motherboard.

The diagram in Figure 2.22 shows the missed pins as being nicely visible; but bear in mind that it's just as easy to leave the naked pins *below* the connector, where it'll take close inspection to find them. So check your pin header connections closely.

Common Reassembly Mistakes

In general, all you need for a good reassembly is patience and a good diagram. But here's what people tend to do wrong. Most of this stuff isn't fatal to your system *in the long term*, but it'll make you sweat until you figure it out. And if you take it to a repair shop to get it "fixed," the repair people will know who caused the problem (heh, heh).

Bad Motherboard Seating

Pay special attention when reseating the motherboard on its plastic spacers. Notice that the spacers are designed with a top disk and a bottom disk, and a bit of space between. Then notice that the motherboard has raised metal slots with a V shape. The spacers are supposed to sit so that the V is between the upper and lower disks. Get a flashlight and check the spacers. Another way to test motherboard seating is to insert a circuit board—if it doesn't fit right, your motherboard is probably seated wrong.

In a related issue, make sure that the motherboard isn't sitting right on the metal case; there must be a bit of airspace between it and the case, or you'll short-circuit the board for sure. I tend to come across a lot of cheap cases whose screw holes don't line up exactly right, and I worry that some stray piece of metal on the (cheap) case will short out the (expensive) motherboard. So I tuck a sheet of cardboard between the motherboard and the case, punching holes in the cardboard to allow the screws and plastic spacers to pass through.

Reversed Data or Control Cables

"Let's see, which side *does* this blue line go on?" Very common. If you don't diagram carefully, you may find yourself having trouble trying to figure out how a ribbon cable connects to, say, a drive. Well, if you didn't diagram carefully, use the Pin 1 Rule to help you.

Mishandled Boards

Don't stack boards. Lay them out separately. Occasionally, rough handling can scratch and remove a circuit board trace. This can be repaired by soldering a short (*as short as possible!*) wire across the cut in the trace. If unsure (traces can be faint or thin to begin with), use your ohmmeter. Set to low ohms (Rx1 on the dial), then put the probes on either side of the suspected cut. The meter should read "0" if everything's okay.

Forgetting to Attach Power

This one's good for a heart attack. You forget to attach that Molex or Berg power connector to the hard disk, and—arggh!—you get disk boot failure.

Neglecting to Plan Cabling

Novice troubleshooters stuff the cables any which way to get them in the box. Then, the next time they open the box, the cables pop up and get caught on the tab for the center screw. Cables rip and bend, teardrops flow—you get the picture. Stuffed cables also impede airflow in the case and heat up the inside of the machine.

Put the drives part way in, then attach their cables, then look and ask: How can I route these cables so they'll be out of the way? Sometimes the best way is to move the drives around, so don't hesitate to be creative.

Forgetting the Speaker Connection, Keylock Connection, and Battery

The first two are minor, the last annoying. Forget to reconnect the battery, and your computer won't remember the configuration you set up. This can be very frustrating since the system will run when you set it up, but the next time you try to boot, it will give you the `INVALID CONFIGURATION` error.

Panicking When It Doesn't Power Up Immediately

I've seen students do this sometimes. They can't get the computer to boot up, so they tear it apart again, ripping cables and forcing boards out before removing their screws. Stay calm. No matter how important the machine is, you cannot fix it by rushing.

Quick Review

Before leaving this chapter, let's take a quick review of the finer points of safe open-PC surgery.

- Always ask yourself, "Is this trip necessary?" Other useful questions are, "Is the problem someone else's? And are you sure that it's a hardware problem?"

- Work with sufficient space.

- Use the right tool for each job.

- Back up the configuration and document jumper and DIP switch settings.

- Don't force things. If something won't come out, stop and look again.

- Keep screws and other small things organized.

- Be careful that you don't rip cables when removing the top.

- Diagram!

Well, now that you've figured out how to get inside and look around, what do you have? In the next chapter, we'll figure out what you've found.

CHAPTER

THREE

3

Inside the PC:
Pieces of the Picture

- The motherboard

- CPU specifications and applications

- PC Memory

- PC expansion buses

- Common interfaces (disk, display, network, other peripherals)

Essential Upgrade #1

Installing a CPU

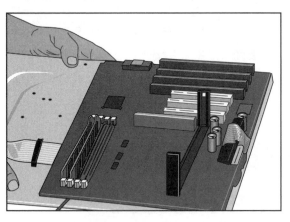

1 Black plastic guides help you slide the CPU cartridge into its slot.

2 Front view of the Pentium II. Note the fan power connector.

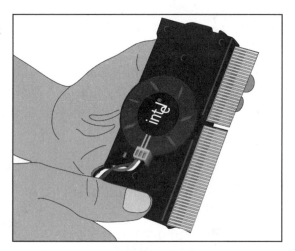

3 Back view of the Pentium II. Don't touch the gold edge connectors when handling or installing.

gold edge connectors

4 Insert the cartridge between the plastic guides and into the CPU slot.

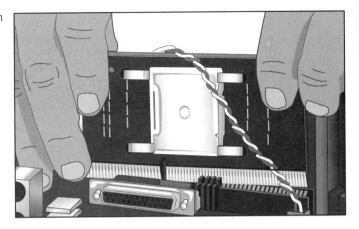

5 Connect the cartridge fan's power cord to the power connector on the motherboard behind the CPU slot.

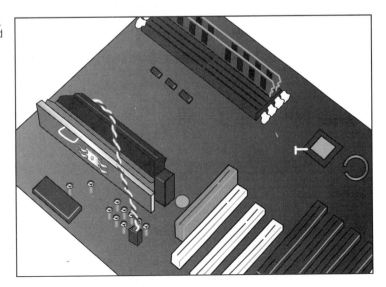

6 An installed Pentium II, with the fan power cord connected.

Got it apart? Excellent. Now let's see what's in there.

The PC is a modular device—that is, it consists of a number of standard modules like video cards, disk drives, and so on. This modularity is convenient to both users and manufacturers because it allows computer systems to be both compatible with each other and (as a result of standardization) inexpensive.

For our purposes, the PC's modularity also makes troubleshooting and repair much easier for normal people without thousands of dollars' worth of test equipment. Fixing PCs is much more tractable than, say, repairing your TV. (Also, your PC lacks the large *capacitors* that make the TV dangerous to fool around with even when unplugged.) If the problem's really bad, you may have to open the machine to fix it—but remember that most PC problems involve broken software or "broken" users, not hardware. Many repairs just require finding and replacing the faulty component. (Also, being able to go to a strange machine and identify the components impresses the heck out of a skeptical audience, such as those folks who question your troubleshooting abilities.) So the first step is to identify what's in the box.

A PC is composed of just a few components:

- A system board or motherboard; this usually contains:
    - Central Processing Unit (CPU)
    - Main memory (DRAM, EDO, SDRAM)
    - Expansion slots attached to PCI, ISA bus connectors
    - System clock/calendar
    - Keyboard adapter (interface)
    - Mouse adapter (interface)

- Floppy disk controller

- Primary Enhanced Integrated Drive Electronics (EIDE) interface, mainly for hard disks and CD-ROMs

- Secondary EIDE interface

- Many motherboards also contain these:

  - Heat sink unit

  - Serial port (RS-232C) or "COM" port

  - Parallel (printer) port

  - Static cache memory

  - Universal Serial Bus (USB) connections (usually two, sometimes just one)

- Sound card (a few systems build this into the motherboard)

- Power supply

- Floppy disk drive(s)

- Hard disk drive(s)

- CD-ROM drive(s)

- Cooling fan(s)

The System Board/Motherboard

Since their creation in 1971, microcomputers of all kinds have usually included most of their essential electronics on a single printed circuit board, called the *motherboard*. There are other ways of designing a computer, but the put-most-of-it-on-one-board approach is most popular, although even that goes through fads.

The first IBM PC in 1981 had a relatively simple motherboard and lots of expansion boards; modern computers tend to have more complex motherboards and a smaller number of expansion boards. Eventually, the majority of PCs will have no expansion boards at all, because the functions that most of us need will be completely incorporated on the motherboard. In fact, that's the case with some laptops like the Digital HiNote Ultra 2000, whose motherboard includes a 56K modem, a 10/100 megabit Ethernet card, 16-bit sound, a joystick interface, and video. I have kind of mixed feelings about these heavily integrated motherboards: on the one hand, they're tremendously convenient, but on the other hand, there's a "take it or leave it" aspect to them. For example, the Digital laptop *does* have a built-in Ethernet circuit, freeing me from having to buy, install, and configure—all very nice things. On the other hand, the built-in Ethernet card is a Xircom card and, while I like Xircom cards just fine, I would have preferred to use a 3Com card, because it's easier to find drivers for 3Com stuff.

The 1981 motherboards had room for a processor chip, 64K of memory, a keyboard connection, and some expansion slots. The 1998 motherboards on the common clone desktop also include a clock/calendar, serial port, parallel port, hard and floppy drive interfaces, mouse port, quite a bit more memory (512MB on some models), and a couple of Universal Serial Bus ports. And *that's* for a clone; proprietary models from firms like Compaq go even further and put sound and video on the motherboard as well.

Now and then, however, the industry will decide to basically shrink the motherboard down to nothing and adopt a so-called "backplane" design. In the backplane design, the basic computer has *only* expansion slots, and the CPU sits on one of them. When vendors go through these backplane phases, they claim that it makes their PCs "modular." By that, they mean that you'd upgrade your PC's CPU simply by removing the circuit board that contains the PC and replacing it with a new CPU board—a five-minute bit of brain surgery that instantly transforms your PC from, say, a Pentium to a Pentium II computer. Sounds good, yes, but the reality is less attractive: since the board that the machine's CPU is on is not built to any kind of standard, you can't just buy a faster CPU board from anyone—you've got to buy it from the original vendor. And in my experience, those vendors price their proprietary CPU upgrade boards quite high, often more expensive than just buying a whole new *faster* system!

If you want modularity, take my advice: the ultimate "upgradable" computer is a generic clone. It's based on a standard-sized motherboard that fits in a standard-sized case and takes standard boards and drives. When I want to upgrade it, all I do is buy a new motherboard and swap it out for the old one. For example, I recently upgraded a 100MHz Pentium computer to a 233MHz Pentium II computer for $350—all I needed was a new motherboard. (I'll have more to say on the whole idea of buying generic throughout the book.)

Now, I've been calling this board a "motherboard," but some vendors have used different names for it; over the years, IBM has called it a "system board" or a "planar board," so don't be surprised if you hear those terms. I've also seen clone motherboard manufacturers call their boards "mainboards."

But enough talking about them—what do they look like? Following are a number of diagrams of motherboards of old and new machines.

Figures 3.1 and 3.2 are diagrams of Pentium, Pentium II, Pentium III, and Xeon motherboards.

FIGURE 3.1:

Pentium motherboard

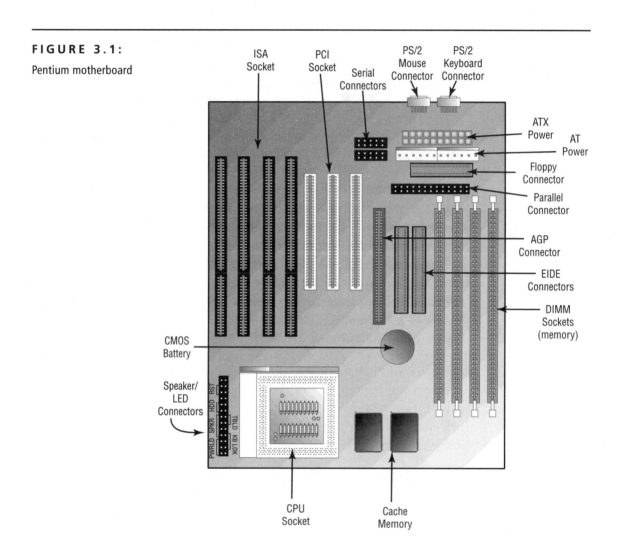

FIGURE 3.2:

Pentium II
motherboard

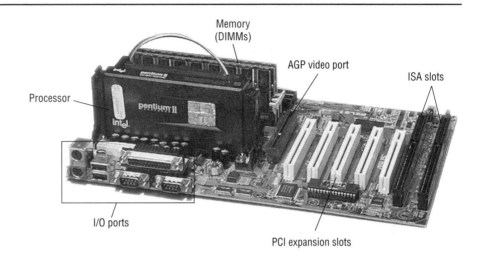

Central Processing Unit (CPU)

There are a lot of chips on those motherboards, and they all kind
of look alike, don't they? They may look equal, but some are more
equal than others are. The big boss is the CPU. It's the part of the
computer that knows how to do mathematics (and it's pretty smart;
it can even do logarithms and cosines and that sort of thing) and
logic, the two parts of all computer programs.

Since the first IBM PC in 1981, most PCs have been built around
CPUs designed by Intel Corporation. Today, there are two other
manufacturers whose microprocessors have made considerable
inroads into the PCs we buy: Advanced Micro Devices (AMD)
and Cyrix. But both of these manufacturer's chips are based upon
the processors that Intel developed. Since all of these processors
are able to run Microsoft Windows, they have been nicknamed
"Wintel" computers. In truth, though, they are also able to run
other operating systems like DOS, Unix, and Linux, a variation of

Unix that has been gaining more and more popularity recently. Intel has designed and created many microprocessors over the years, but the ones that interest us here are members of a family of chips starting with the 8086 and progressing to the Pentium III chips. Why is there a family? Why aren't we still using the 8086? In a word, performance. CPU performance determines, in large part, computer performance. A modern Pentium III is *hundreds* of times faster than the original 8086, and differences of speed on that order change how you use computers. Back in the early 1980s, people started using spreadsheet programs, and those programs strained the power of then-contemporary chips like the 8088. It wasn't unusual for a complex spreadsheet to require *hours* to recalculate. Nowadays, even the cheapest PC is so fast that I can't remember the last time I waited for a spreadsheet to recalculate.

Intel has been improving CPU performance in two main ways. First, they improve some things quantitatively, by just taking an old circuit and making it run faster. Simple CPU speed, measured in "megahertz" (defined in a page or two), is an example. The second way that CPUs get snappier is through qualitative improvements, such as new manufacturing techniques that improve chip quality.

Whether improvements come quantitatively or qualitatively, CPUs vary in several ways that affect their performance. These variations are introduced in Table 3.1, which shows CPU properties. Take a minute now and look over this section so that later you'll understand where a lot of PC limitations come from.

T A B L E 3 . 1 : CPU Properties

PROPERTY	DESCRIPTION
CPU speed	How many operations can be done per second?
Microcode efficiency	How many steps are required (for example) to multiply two numbers?

Continued on next page

TABLE 3.1 CONTINUED: CPU Properties

PROPERTY	DESCRIPTION
Word size	What is the largest number that can be operated on in one operation?
Numeric coprocessor	Can the CPU directly perform floating point numerical computations?
Number of instruction pipelines	How many processes can run simultaneously on this chip?
Pipeline management	How does the CPU "look ahead" to future instructions so as to make the best of its power?
Internal cache RAM	How much internal high-speed memory does this chip include?
Data path	What is the largest number that can be transported into the chip in one operation?
Maximum memory	How much memory can the chip use?

CPU Speeds (Megahertz)

Computers are a little like clockwork devices. A clock strikes a beat, and a certain small amount of work gets done. Just like a beginning piano player plays to the beat of a metronome, computers run to the beat of a clock (although it's an electronic clock). If you set the metronome too fast for the beginning piano player, he/she will become confused and the music won't come out right; the player won't have enough time to find the next piano key, and the rendition will probably fall apart. Similarly, if you set the clock rate of a CPU too high, it will malfunction, but the result isn't discordant music; it's a system crash.

Normally, running a CPU too fast won't damage the chip; the computer just won't function properly. Part of the design of a computer like the PC includes determining a clock rate.

In some ways, the clock on a computer is like the coxswain on a rowing team. The coxswain is the person who holds up the megaphone, exhorting the rowers "Stroke! Stroke! Stroke!" If he tells them to stroke too fast, they get out of sync and the boat slows down or stops. The coxswain is restricted to telling the team to stroke *no faster than the slowest rower.* In a PC, many chips all work to the beat of the computer's clock. That means that the computer's clock can't run any faster than the slowest computer component. CPU clocks generally "tick" millions of times per second. A clock that ticks at exactly one million times per second is said to be a one megahertz clock (1MHz). The Apple II used a 2MHz clock. The early PCs and XTs used a 4.77MHz clock. IBM followed the PC with the AT, whose original model used a 6MHz clock, and later IBM offered a version that ran at 8MHz; modern systems are up to 550MHz or faster.

Since the speed of a computer is used as a means of measuring how well it operates, the megahertz value of a computer is used as an important measure of its power. It's similar to looking at horsepower as an approximate measure of a car's power. All other things being equal, a faster clock means faster execution and better performance.

It's worth mentioning, however, that all things usually *aren't* equal. The CPU is only part of what makes a computer fast. A really fast CPU paired with an amazingly slow hard disk would turn in a mediocre performance. I once benchmarked a circa-1983 XT against a 1994 Pentium and found that the Pentium's hard disk and graphic boards were about 10 times faster than the XT's, but the CPU was almost *three hundred* times faster. A Pentium seems quick compared to an XT, of course, but not anywhere near 300 times faster, mostly because of the slower peripherals. If a computer were about 30 times faster than an XT in its disk, graphics board, and CPU, then it would probably feel faster than the Pentium system I benchmarked. My advice, then—and I'll repeat it throughout this book—is this: when buying a computer on a budget, you may have to choose between a faster CPU or faster peripherals. I'd take the faster peripherals.

Having said that, however, I should also mention that Intel and other CPU manufacturers tend to stop making any but the fastest CPUs at any given time, so you probably won't have the option to buy a really out-of-date, slow CPU anyway.

Nowadays, the slowest computer you're likely to come across will be 66MHz or 100MHz. The fastest speeds you'll hear may get up around 550MHz or faster.

Megahertz Revisited: Hot Chips, Clock Doublers, Triplers, Quintuplers, and In-Between

For many years, the maximum possible CPU speed determined a lot about the rest of the computer. Usually a PC manufacturer would design the entire motherboard to operate at the same speed as the CPU. When CPUs rose in speed from 5MHz to 8MHz, motherboards changed in speed from 5MHz to 8MHz. All of the chips on the motherboard, including complex chips like memory chips, had to be 8MHz to support an 8MHz motherboard. At the time, this turned out to be impossible for speeds beyond 8MHz, so since about 1984, motherboards have been designed so that different parts of them could run at different speeds. Coupling slowpoke components with speed demons means that some of the speed demons' power is wasted, but it's the only way to build economical systems.

From 1984 on, the section of the motherboard that supported memory was decoupled from the rest of the motherboard, speed-wise, as were the expansion slots or "bus slots"—you'll read more about memory and bus slot speeds a bit later in this chapter. But memory and bus slots constituted only a fraction of the motherboard real estate. Most of the chips and circuits on the motherboard of mid-to-late-'80s motherboards had to match the CPU's speed, so every time Intel came out with a faster chip, the motherboard designers had to go back to the drawing boards and design faster motherboards.

But building faster and faster motherboards is like climbing a mountain that gets steeper and steeper as you climb. Moving from 5MHz to 8MHz was easy; from 8MHz to 12MHz was harder. And 12MHz to 20MHz was even harder, as was the move around 1989 to motherboards that ran most of their components at 33MHz. In the closing months of the '80s, however, Intel started talking about producing 50MHz and 66MHz chips. Building motherboards *that* fast must have seemed just about impossible at the time.

Clock Doubler Chips

Intel needed to address several issues with their 50+MHz chips in 1989/1990. First was the motherboard question: what good is a 66MHz chip if no one knows how to build a motherboard that can use it? The second question came from the owners of existing systems. Weary of buying systems that seemed obsolete as soon as they were purchased, people wanted the ability to upgrade their systems without major surgery. So Intel came up with an alternative way to speed up CPUs: *clock doublers.*

The original clock doubler was a special 80486 (a processor we'll introduce later, but for the moment, understand that it was Intel's flagship processor between 1989 and 1993) that could plug right into a CPU socket on a 25MHz motherboard. The motherboard was a normal 25MHz motherboard designed to accommodate a 25MHz 80486DX—but the 80486 wasn't a normal 80486DX. Instead, it was designed to operate at 25MHz from the motherboard's point of view, but to operate internally at *twice* that rate—50MHz. Any internal action in the CPU, like numeric calculations or moving data from one internal area to another, was accomplished at 50MHz. But external instructions, like loading data from memory or storing data to memory, happened more slowly, at 25MHz.

NOTE   Intel has names for these two clock rates, by the way. The external speed (25MHz, in the case of the previous example) is called the *system bus frequency*. The internal clock rate (50MHz, in the above example) is called the *processor core frequency*.

Now, given that this chip ran at 25MHz for external instructions and 50MHz for internal instructions, what should Intel have called this chip—a 25MHz chip or a 50MHz chip? It's a bit of a conundrum, until you realize that the folks making the decision were, well, more oriented to the *marketing* side of Intel than the engineering side of Intel. So the new chip got the name 80486DX2-50—the "2" referring to the clock doubling, the "50" referring to its higher speed. They also offered an 80486DX2-66, a chip that plugged into a 33MHz motherboard but ran at 66MHz internally.

At the time, Intel made an 80486DX-25 (a chip that ran both inside and out at 25MHz), an 80486DX-50 (a chip that ran both inside and out at 50MHz), and an 80486DX2-50. People often asked, "How fast is the DX2 *really*—is it more like the 'straight 25' or the 'straight 50'?" The answer was that it depended on what you were doing. Very CPU-intensive operations like calculating spreadsheets or doing complex graphics probably looked more like 50MHz than 25MHz, and input/output-oriented programs like databases probably looked more like 25MHz than 50MHz. An in-between application like a word processor fell somewhere in between. And, remember, Intel *also* offered the 80486DX-50, a 50MHz chip that ran 50MHz both inside and out. Many people *thought* they were buying 50MHz DX but actually bought a "50MHz" DX2, and the difference in performance was significant.

Clock Tripler Chips

In 1994, Intel introduced yet another variation on the 486 line, an 80486DX that was a *clock tripler*. Offered in a 75MHz and a 100MHz version, these chips operated on motherboards that were 25MHz and 33MHz, respectively. (Why does 33MHz tripled equal 100MHz? Why not 99MHz? Marketing reality again. After all, round up 99MHz and you get 100MHz...well, kind of. Hey, maybe they used one of those Pentiums with the floating point bug to do the calculation, hmm?) Intel also took the opportunity to spruce up the internal workings of this new 486, and they added a bit more very fast internal memory (it's called internal cache, and we'll get to it soon), raising the amount inside the chip from 8K (which the 80486 previously contained) to 16K. That small amount of internal memory did indeed speed up the computer a bit in addition to the clock tripling, leading Intel to explore new realms of salesmanship by calling the new chip the *DX4*. That name is just DX4, by the way; there's no "80486" in the name. There's also a clock-tripled Pentium 200MHz chip that runs on a 66MHz motherboard.

Clock "One and a Halfers" and Some *Really* Hot Chips

We've seen clocks doubled and tripled. Are there clock-quadrupled chips? Yes, and quintupled chips: the 333MHz Pentium II runs 66MHz externally, and 333 internally, a five-fold increase. While figuring out how to build the 4x and 5x systems, Intel started playing around with non-integer multiples. Some CPUs have their clocks increased by *50 percent*, kind of a "one and a half clock." The original Pentium models were offered in speeds of 60MHz and 66MHz. Later Pentium chips code-named the "P54C" by Intel were rated at 90 and 100MHz. They used 60MHz and 66MHz motherboards and just increased their internal clock rates by half.

Before leaving megahertz behind, it's worth quickly discussing exactly *why* there were originally two Pentium models with two clock rates so close. Why bother offering both a 60MHz and a 66MHz model?

The Pentium was a really tough chip to design. Every Intel chip design team is extremely limited in that no matter what the new chip's able to do, the one thing that it *must* do is run old software. This demand for backward compatibility makes for complex chips. Complex means lots of little components go into the chip, or, as insiders would say, the backward compatibility "needs a lot of silicon." Now, all that silicon generates heat. Put too much silicon in too small a place, and it starts to damage itself. Make the clock run faster, and the silicon gets even hotter. The Intel folks were just plain running up against some physical design barriers.

The Pentium showed its heat requirements in its technical specifications. According to Intel, the 60 and 66MHz Pentium should be expected to generate heat enough to bring the chip to 85 degrees. *Centigrade.*

That's about 185 degrees Fahrenheit. Good grief, you could toast marshmallows on that thing! Intel tried its hardest to make a 66MHz Pentium chip work, but it was just so difficult that they ended up making Pentium chips that were mostly rejects. They *weren't* rejects, however, if they ran at a somewhat slower, *cooler*, rate, like 60MHz. So the 60MHz chips are, unfortunately, the rejects; Intel just lowered the standards to make them sellable.

Besides clock speed, however, another determining factor in chip heat is in the voltage that it operates on. The heat created by a chip is related to the square of the voltage. For a long time, most CPUs ran at 5 volts.

Intel decided to build the clock one-and-a-half P54C chips with 3.3-volt power supplies. Five squared is 25, 3.3 squared is about 11. A 3.3-volt chip runs a lot cooler, which is why Intel uses 3.3 volts for the DX4, the newer Pentiums, and some later chips. Pentium Pros use 1.5 volts.

The fact that the DX4 is a 3.3-volt chip means that, paradoxically, it was the fastest 80486 chip, but was also the coolest.

Clock "Two and a Halfers": The Pentium OverDrive

I know that all of these chip speed permutations are getting a bit bizarre, but we're not done yet. Intel markets a Pentium OverDrive chip, a chip that upgrades some existing 486 systems to Pentium-level speed.

A couple of caveats about this: first, this won't work on all 486s; you've got to have a 486 system that was designed with an extra-large socket. The extra-large socket has extra pins and was designed for the Pentium OverDrive chip. Second, it's kind of dubious how much like a Pentium the Pentium OverDrive can be, because the OverDrive is a 32-bit chip, where the true Pentium is a 64-bit chip.

But enough bad news. The *good* news is that the Pentium OverDrive increases the internal speed of the OverDrive chip to two and a half times the speed of the motherboard. A Pentium OverDrive for a 25MHz 486 system runs internally at 63MHz. The OverDrive for a 33MHz system runs internally at 83MHz.

When shopping for the OverDrive chip, remember that you choose the chip based on the speed of your computer's motherboard. If you've got a 486DX2-66, then remember that your computer's motherboard runs at 33MHz, because the DX2 is a clock doubler.

So What *Is* the Fastest Chip?

In mid-1998, Intel released two new Pentium II systems, the 350MHz and 400MHz chips. Intel was able to make the higher speed work by using smaller components in a process first tested on the 333MHz chip, a design code-named "Deschutes." (It was expensive to design, and Intel feared they were throwing all that research money down Deschutes... no, that's not true. Deschutes is a river in the West; that's where Intel gets its names for design projects, don't ask me why.) Since the 300MHz and 333MHz systems both use a 66MHz system bus speed, the performance difference between a 300MHZ system and a 333MHz system is quite small. The 350MHz and faster systems, however, have a system bus speed of 100MHz. The difference between a 333MHz (a 66 multiplied by 5) and a 350MHz (a 100 multiplied by 3.5) is quite significant, not so much because of the processor speed, but because the rest of the system runs at 100MHz versus 66MHz. One downside to the extra speed you get with the 100MHz bus, however, is that it runs a lot hotter than the 66MHz systems. The heat problem is actually one reason for the newest version of the Pentium Pro, the "Pentium II Xeon" chip. One of the Xeon's new features is a built-in thermometer that monitors the chip's temperature. If the temperature gets above a safe level, the Xeon can safely shut the system down.

A Word on Overclocking and Matching Clock Speeds

Clock rates on chips and clock rates on motherboards are connected. If the motherboard is built for 66MHz, then you should get a CPU that can handle a 66MHz clock. (Note I'm talking about the external or "system bus frequency," not the internal rate.) Similarly, it's not a good idea to get a chip that's designed to run at a higher clock rate than the motherboard. The fit between motherboard and chip should be "just right."

Why is this true? Well, consider what happens if you get a chip that's too slow for the motherboard. For example, the Intel Pentium 150MHz chip had an external clock rate of 50MHz and was tripled. If you put it on a motherboard that is designed to provide a 66MHz clock signal to the processor, then the processor will not be able to keep up with that rate. The result is that the chip will fail and overheat, possibly permanently damaging it. In the reverse situation, suppose you had a motherboard that put out a 66MHz-clock signal, and you installed a 400MHz Xeon, which can handle an external clock rate of 100MHz. You wouldn't be driving the "400MHz" chip at 100MHz, you'd be driving it at 66MHz. It's a clock quadrupler, so the chip would dutifully quadruple that value, giving you a 266MHz Xeon. That would be a waste of money.

This underscores a general point about chips and sockets: put a chip in that's too slow and it will overheat and fail. Install a chip that's too fast and it will work fine, but you're throwing your money away.

That all sounds logical, but some people point out that the difference between slow chips and fast chips is often luck anyway, because chip manufacturers just build a few thousand chips and then test them to see which ones are fast and which are slow. When testing, chip makers are conservative, goes the argument, so they might rate a chip at xMHz that could actually work at $1.3x$ or the like. Modern motherboards let you dial in any clock rate you want, so people buy a middle-rated chip and dial up a high clock rate. If the system doesn't crash immediately, they figure they've gotten lucky and bought a fast chip for the price of a slow one. This is called "overclocking." I don't recommend it, and basically here's why: Intel gets to charge more money for faster chips, and Intel's profit ratio indicates to me that they have no aversion to a healthy ROI (return on investment, that is). Yes, I suppose there's a few that slip through the cracks, but in general a chip rated at X is no better than X. Overclocking can also cause other problems, as you'll read later in the section on buses.

Microcode Efficiency and Pipelines

As you just read, one way to make a chip faster is to simply drive it faster, by running up its clock in some way. Another way is to design the chip to make better use of each clock cycle.

Microcode Improvements

Microcode improvements have been an important part of Intel's strategy for ever-faster chips over the years; for example, the 8088 chip was succeeded by the 80188 chip, a chip that seems to do all of the same things that the 8088 does. Where's the difference?

In the case of the 8088 versus the 80188 (and, actually, in the case of the 80386 versus the 80486), a lot of the difference lies in its *microcode efficiency*. Put simply, microcode efficiency just means: "How many clock ticks does it take a CPU to get a particular thing done?" For example, an 8088 can calculate an integer division—that is, a division without any decimal places; divide 7 by 2 on an 8088 and you get 3, not 3.5. And to make matters worse, it can take the 8088 up to 70 clock cycles to get that done. The 80188, in contrast, can do it in only 25 clock cycles. Compare two machines that are identical except that one runs an 80188 and the other runs an 8088, and the 80188 will be able to do some things faster than an 8088.

The 80386 and 80486 are also similar in many ways, as you'll learn later in this chapter, but they differ in microcode efficiency. The simplest useful instruction that you can do with an 80386 is the MOV AX, BX, an assembly-language command that invokes a microcode instruction that moves data from a storage area inside the microcomputer called BX to another storage area inside the microcomputer called AX. Technically, it's called a register-to-register transfer. All register operations on an 80386 require at least two clock cycles. The 80486 was designed so that all of the two-cycle register instructions on the 80386 run in just one clock cycle on the 80486. One of the places that Intel is always looking to improve its chips is via the chip's microcode.

Pipelining Instructions

By now, the folks at Intel had squeezed a lot of the "juice" out of improving microcode efficiency. So they needed some other tricks to continue to beat better speed out of newer chips. So starting with the Pentium, Intel has designed CPUs with smarter and smarter *pipelines*. What's a pipeline? Well, if you peek inside the workings of a CPU, you'll see that it looks somewhat like an assembly line—I'll get specific about what happens in that line in a moment, but for now just visualize an assembly line like one that builds cars or TVs. Instead of turning out cars or TVs, however, CPUs turn out executed instructions, and they don't call it an assembly line; they call it a pipeline. With pipelining, a bit of data goes to the first station in the pipeline; then when that bit moves on to the next station, another bit takes its place at the first station. With pipelining, there's a bit along every station of the process. So instead of each bit of data having to wait for the preceding bit to go through the entire pipeline before starting off, a bit moves to each station along the way immediately after its predecessor leaves.

Now, if you wanted to assemble more cars per hour, you could approach it in two ways. The obvious way is to just try to get each of the workers to do their jobs faster, allowing you to run the assembly line faster. That would be like taking an existing CPU and increasing its clock rate, upping its megahertz. It's not a bad approach to speed, but there's another way. Instead of just trying to do the same old thing, only faster, you could re-engineer the entire process, streamlining the steps along the way.

What happens along a CPU's pipeline? It varies from chip to chip, but basically you can break down the execution of any instruction into five basic steps:

- **Fetch.** Get the next instruction, either from random access memory (RAM) outside the CPU (on CPUs before the 486) or from the CPU's "instruction cache" memory (on 486 and later chips).

- **Decode.** Instructions differ in length; some are one byte long, some are several bytes long. A given instruction, like a Move command, may come in several different flavors: move from one location inside the CPU chip to a location outside the CPU chip, move from one place in the CPU to another place inside the CPU, and so on. Even though the instruction differences are subtle, they're important. The decode section handles that.

- **Get the operands.** Most instructions require data to work on. Simply saying "Move" means nothing; the CPU must know *what* you want to move *where*. The *what* and *where* are operands. Similarly, if you tell the CPU, "Add 34 and 22," then *34* and *22* are the operands.

- **Execute.** As the Nike guys say, just do it. Whatever the instruction said to do—add, move, divide, compare, or whatever—now's the time to get it done.

- **Write back results.** Once the operation has been done, the results of the operation—both the values created and any status information—get written to registers inside the computer.

By breaking up the task of executing an instruction into smaller subtasks, chipmakers can divide up the job of chip design into smaller chunks, and that in turn makes it possible to build these subsystems faster and faster. In other words, it's easier to build a CPU made up of five fast subpieces than it is to build a CPU out of one fast piece. This process of fetch-decode-get operands-execute-write back is called the *CPU pipeline*. Some CPUs put multiple pipelines in a CPU, but we'll discuss that in a few pages.

Some of Intel's competitors try to outdo Intel in the speed department by changing the structure of a pipeline. Cyrix makes a chip called the M1 that uses seven substeps rather than five. Advanced Micro Devices (AMD) makes a CPU called the K5 with six substeps, and NexGen makes an Nx586 with seven substeps. Intel even outdid itself with the Pentium Pro/Pentium II/Celeron/Xeon, which divides its pipelines into 14 steps!

Ultimately, Intel has stated a goal that some future member of the *x*86 family will execute each of its instructions in just one clock cycle. (Then again, world peace and funding Social Security are two goals that the government doesn't seem to be getting too far on, so don't hold your breath on the one-cycle promise either.)

Word Size

Every computer uses internal work areas, kind of like workbenches. These workbenches are called *registers*.

Any computer can be programmed to manipulate any size number, but the bigger the number, the longer it takes. The largest number that the computer can manipulate in one operation is determined by its *word size*. This is 8, 16, or 32 bits.

Think of it this way: if I ask you, "What is 5 times 6," you'd answer, "30," immediately—you did it in one operation. If I ask, "What is 55 times 66," you will do a series of steps to arrive at the answer. 55 is larger than your word size; 5 isn't. If you had a bigger "workbench," a bigger word size, then you could get complex calculations done in fewer steps and therefore more quickly. That's one reason why a 386, with 32-bit registers, is faster than a 286, with 16-bit registers.

The 8088 through 80286 chips used 16-bit words. The 80386 through Pentium II/Pentium Pro/Celeron/Xeon systems use 32-bit words. And future processors will most probably use 64, 128, and even larger word lengths.

Data Path

No matter how large the computer's word size, the data must be transported into the CPU. This is the width of the computer's "loading door." It can also be 8, 16, or 32 bits. Obviously, a wider door will allow more data to be transported in less time than will a narrower door. Consider, for example, an 8MHz 8088 versus an 8MHz 8086. The *only difference* between the 8088 and the 8086 is that the 8088 has an 8-bit data path, and the 8086 has a 16-bit data path. Now, both the 8088 and the 8086 have 16-bit registers, so a programmer would issue the same command to load 16 bits into either one—the command MOV AX,0200 will move the 16-bit value 200 hex into a 16-bit register called AX. That will take twice as long on the 8088 as it would on the 8086, because the 8086 can do it in one operation while the 8088 takes two. Note what's going on—although they're both 8MHz computers, the 8088 machine computes more slowly for some operations.

Now, you can see that the 8086 is a faster, more powerful chip than the 8088. But did you know that the 8088 was released *later* than the 8086? It's true; here's why.

When the 8086 was first released in 1977, it was one of the first microprocessors with a 16-bit data path. Almost every popular microprocessor-based computer available at the time was based on a CPU with an 8-bit data path. (*Almost* because the LSI-11 microprocessor had a 16-bit data path, and a few Heathkit computers used the LSI-11.) Because the CPUs all expected 8 bits whenever they *read* data and provided 8 bits when they *wrote* data, the motherboards of computers in those days contained enough circuitry to transport 8 bits around.

Now, the 8086 was a neat-looking chip, because its 16 bits seemed just the stuff to build a powerful microcomputer around. But consider the *bad* side of a 16-bit CPU: it requires a 16-bit motherboard. An 8086's motherboard must contain enough circuitry to transport *16* bits around, so it could be *twice* as expensive as an 8-bit motherboard of the same type. That put the 8086 at an economic disadvantage. (It may seem like a trivial matter now, but in the late '70s, hardware was more expensive, and an 8086-based motherboard was significantly more expensive than an 8-bit motherboard.)

So the folks at Intel said to themselves, "How can we offer the power of the 8086 and still keep motherboard prices down?" And so they built the 8088, a year after the 8086's release. Inside, the 8088 is identical to the 8086. The only difference is in the size of its "front door"—the path that the 8088 uses to transport data into and out of the chip. Because it is only 8 bits wide, motherboard designers could easily adapt existing designs to the new chip. As a result, the 8088 enjoyed a moderate amount of success from 1979 to 1981. Of course, after IBM released the PC in 1981 based on the 8088, moderate eventually changed to amazing.

History repeated itself in 1988 with the 80386SX. The original 80386 was introduced in 1985—Intel's next-generation chip with a 32-bit data path. The 386 did fairly well fairly quickly, but not quickly enough for Intel. The 286 sold well also, but the 286 had a problem as far as Intel was concerned: Intel didn't *own* the 286. By that, I mean that while Intel invented the 286, it had also licensed several vendors to make the 286, so many 286s being sold were lining the pockets of Advanced Micro Devices, Fairchild, Siemens, and a number of other chip builders. Intel wanted *all* of the profit from the 386, however, so they refused to license the 386 to any other company.

The 286 was not only a cheap chip, it was also a 16-bit chip, and a pure 16-bit chip at that—both word size and data path. That meant that 286 PCs could be built around 16-bit motherboards, and 32-bit motherboards were going to be just plain expensive. Therefore, 286-based PCs would be *tons* cheaper than 386 PCs, so more 286s would sell than 386s; Intel didn't like that. So they embarked on a campaign of what has to be characterized as chip infanticide. They ran a huge advertising campaign advising people to stay away from the 286 and to buy 386-based PCs. They *also* answered the manufacturer's concerns about the costs of building a 32-bit motherboard by offering the 80386SX.

The 80386SX was an 80386 with one difference: its "front door" was 16 bits, not 32 bits. Vendors liked that because they could take their old 16-bit 80286 motherboards, modify their design a bit, and voilà! They could offer "386 technology." After a year, it became clear that the original 80386 needed a name, so it became known as the 80386DX.

The 80486 line of chips also included an 80486SX, but was it a 16-bit chip? No. It *was* a chip with reduced functionality, but the reduction was not due to changes in data path. Instead, the 486SX was different from the 486DX in the way that it calculated arithmetic, and that leads us to a discussion of numeric coprocessors, as you'll learn in the upcoming section "Numeric Coprocessors."

The Pentium, MMX, Pentium Pro, Pentium II, Celeron, and Xeon chips actually have a data path *larger* than the word size; these chips have a 64-bit data path and 32-bit word sizes. What good is it having a front door that's twice the size of the workbench? Again, Pentium and later chips aren't so much faster because of higher megahertz, but because of internal design—to use an old phrase, you might say that they don't work *harder*, they work *smarter*. Once Intel figured that it could only do so much with a single 32-bit system, they decided to speed up the process by essentially giving the Pentium a *second* workbench, a second pipeline, as you'll read in a few pages. That second pipeline needs feeding, hence the value of a larger data path.

The early Pentium line of chips also included an SX-like chip called the "Pentium OverDrive" chip. The Pentium uses a 64-bit data path, but 486 manufacturers wanted to include Pentium compatibility on their motherboards. However, 486 motherboards are 32-bit in nature. How, then, to offer Pentium compatibility? Simple. This is where Intel's Pentium OverDrive chip, which features a 32-bit data path, came in. Kind of a Pentium SX, you might say. Was it a good idea? Sure, if your 486 motherboard could accommodate it (a few could). But, again, that'll all make sense when we get to the discussion of instruction pipelines, coming soon. But first, let's look at yet another way to speed up your computer: give it a little shot of super-fast memory, *internal cache*.

Internal Cache Memory

When we talk of RAM on a computer, we're talking about chips that the CPU uses to store its programs and data as it works, chips external to the CPU. But the increasing speed of CPUs has driven a corresponding need for faster RAM.

The Memory Tradeoff: SRAM versus DRAM

RAM is commonly designed to be *dynamic* RAM, a simpler and cheaper design than its alternative, *static* RAM. I'll discuss static versus dynamic RAM in more detail in Chapter 8, "Semiconductor Memory," but for now, just understand that RAM presents a very fundamental tradeoff to system designers. Those designers can either build computers to use dynamic RAM or static RAM, and here's the tradeoff:

- Dynamic RAM (DRAM) is relatively cheap, but it is also relatively slow. In fact, no one makes DRAM that's fast enough to match speeds with modern CPUs.

- Static RAM (SRAM) is fast—it can be as fast as any of Intel's chips. But it's expensive, up to 10 to 20 times as expensive for a given amount of memory as DRAM.

At this point, the only way to build RAM that is as fast as the CPU is to populate the entire PC with static RAM, but that would be much too expensive. So PCs use a lot of dynamic RAM, which unfortunately sacrifices speed. To get back some of that speed, Intel puts a small amount of fast static RAM right into the CPU.

That way, oft-used data needn't be accessed via the relatively slow DRAM; instead, the CPU can keep the most important data right by its side, in this small "cache" of storage. In fact, that's what it's called—cache RAM. It first appeared in some of the faster 386-based systems, because designers included space on the motherboards of high-performance systems for a bit of SRAM.

L1 Cache, L2 Cache, and the 80486 Family

Many computers designed since around 1987 have included cache RAM on their motherboards. The 80486 took the idea of cache a step further, however, in that the 80486 line of chips was the first in the x86 family to include cache RAM right on the CPU. With the exception of the DX4, they all contain 8K of internal cache. The DX4 doubled that amount to 16K. But even that small amount of extra fast memory significantly improved CPU performance. Of course, while a few K of cache is *nice*, it'd be nicer to have even more.

Most desktop motherboards add from 64K to 1024K more static RAM cache to the motherboard. That's not *internal* cache, however, because it's not internal to the CPU. It's *external* cache and it's commonly called *L2 cache*. (The meaning of "external" when it comes to L2 cache gets a bit stretched with the Pentium II, as you'll see in a minute.) The internal cache in the 80486 and later processors is called L1 cache. *L1 cache* is built into the processor and usually runs at a speed nearly equaling or equaling the internal processor speed (the "core processor frequency" in Intel-ese).

Some Systems Are "Broke"

L2 cache is terrific for speed, but notice that I said most *desktop* PCs include cache. That's *very* important to anyone trying to compare the power of laptop computers to desktops. For example, right at the moment I'm writing on an "ancient" (late 1995)

166MHz clone Pentium. Sitting next to it on my desk is a 266MHz Digital Ultra HiNote 2000, a laptop. The HiNote is a wonderful machine, but put it next to the 166MHz desktop and they seem to be about the same speed; if anything, the 166 often seems faster. Why? Because the 166 has 256K of L2 static cache on its motherboard. The HiNote, like most laptops, has no L2 cache. That doesn't stop manufacturers from misleading buyers, however. Recall that all 486 and later chips have a smidgen of *internal* L1 cache. I always cringe when I see ads for laptops trumpeting, "16K internal cache RAM!"

Basically, most laptop designs are "broke," by which I mean that they have no *cache*. Okay, sorry, 40 lashes for the bad pun...

Pentium Cache

Speaking of the Pentium, by the way, part of how it turned out better-than-486 performance was through its cache. The Pentium's cache system is better than the 486's in four ways. First, the Pentium has twice as much cache, with two 8K caches—one for data, one for program code. (A later variation of the Pentium, the MMX chip, had double that amount, a 16K instruction and a 16K data cache.) Second, the cache's method of organizing its cached data is more efficient, using a "write-back" algorithm. The opposite of a write-back algorithm, a "write-through" algorithm, forces data written to the SRAM cache memory to be immediately written to the slower DRAM memory. That means that memory *reads* can come out of the cache quickly, but memory *writes* must always occur at the slower DRAM time. Reasoning that not every piece of information written to memory *stays* in memory very long, the Pentium's cache algorithm puts off writing data from SRAM to DRAM for as long as possible, unlike the 486, which uses a write-through cache. Third, the cache controller wastes time in searching to see if an item is in the cache—the Pentium reduces that time by dividing the cache into smaller caches, each of which can be searched more quickly; that technique is called a *two-way set-associative cache*.

To explain the fourth way in which the Pentium's cache is better than the 486's, I've got to first make an important point about what a cache must do. Recall that a cache must guess what data and program code the CPU will need soon, and then go get that data before the CPU asks for it. But guessing what the CPU will need isn't a straightforward task, particularly when there are decisions to be made. For example, suppose the cache sees that the CPU is currently executing some instructions that mean, "Compare value A with value B. If A is greater than B, then set the value *maximum* to A; otherwise, set the value *maximum* to B." That simple statement boils down to a bunch of instructions, instructions in memory that had better be in the cache if the Pentium is going to be able to continue running without delays. But since the cache controller can't know whether the CPU will take the "A was greater than B" or "B was greater than A" fork in the road, it doesn't know which result's code to go grab and put in the cache. For years, *mainframe* cache controllers have used a technique called *branch prediction* to guess which way the CPU will go, and now PC chips—the Pentium and later chips—have cache controllers built into them with branch prediction capabilities. So that's *four* ways that the Pentium makes better use of your memory than the 486 did.

The Pentium Pro, Pentium II, and Xeon Caches

What about the Pentium Pro and its cousins, the Pentium II, Celeron, and Xeon chips? Well, there's some good news and some bad news.

With the Pentium Pro, Intel introduced the revolutionary step of making a sort of double-sized chip, a chip that looked kind of like two Pentium chips side by side. The second "chip," however, was a 512K L2 memory, a built-in cache RAM. This cache was terrific in that it could talk to the CPU at half of the CPU's full internal speed (the "core processor frequency"), not the external bus speed. Motherboards could be designed with even more external cache, however, and some Pentium Pro systems sold with as much as 1024K of external cache, a mix of the built-in L2 cache and some chips on the motherboard. As any chips on the motherboard can communicate with the processor only at the external bus speed rather than the internal speed, you might call that on-motherboard cache a sort of level 3 cache. The Pentium Pro has 16K of L1 cache, as did the original Pentium.

With the Pentium II, Intel created a larger rectangular package called a Single Edge Cartridge (SEC), which no longer allows external cache. You can see a Pentium II in Figure 3.3.

FIGURE 3.3:

Pentium II in SEC package

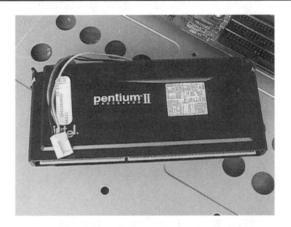

The result is that you can't design a motherboard for a Pentium II that contains any cache. The Pentium II has its built-in 512K of L2 cache, but that's it. (The Pentium II also has more L1 cache than the Pentium Pro, 16K of data and 16K of instruction cache, for a total of 32K.) And that leads to an interesting comparison of the older Pentium Pro versus the Pentium II. Some of the Pro motherboards had room for 1M (one thousand bytes) of cache (I say this in past tense because Pros have become scarcer than hen's teeth). Therefore, one can benchmark a Pentium Pro at 200MHz (the fastest that they were built) versus a Pentium II at

333MHz—the Pentium Pro can actually be faster, because it's got 1024K of cache versus the Pentium II's half megabyte of cache!

The Pentium II Xeon chip addresses that problem and offers considerably improved performance for two reasons. First, the Xeon communicates between its built-in L2 cache and its processor at full core processor speed—a 400MHz Xeon talks to its L2 cache at a full 400MHz. Second, the Xeon comes with up to 1024K of built-in L2 cache. As you can buy the Xeon in up to 400MHz speeds, it's the ideal platform for playing Quake…

But I haven't mentioned the Celeron. What kind of L2 cache does it come with? Originally it had none. But Intel's customers weren't very happy about the Celeron's missing cache, so current models of the Celeron also have cache memory.

Numeric Coprocessors

Look at an early PC or XT, and next to the 8088 is an empty socket. From 1981 to 1983, IBM wouldn't say officially for what the socket on the PC was intended. But then they announced what everyone already knew: it was for the Intel 8087, a special purpose microprocessor. The 8087 is a microprocessor that is only good for one class of tasks: floating point numeric operations.

Since then, all succeeding Intel CPUs offered some way of incorporating a floating point computation unit. In fact, all of the current processors have a built-in *floating-point processor unit* (*FPU*).

The MMX: A Matrix Math Coprocessor

By the time the Pentium arrived, it seemed like there wasn't much to say anymore about coprocessors, because even the lowliest Pentium had the coprocessor circuitry built in.

But then a newer form of the Pentium arrived, the *MMX* (MMX, by the way, is purportedly not an acronym, because it doesn't officially stand for anything, but it basically means "multimedia extensions"). MMX technology is an enhancement to Intel CPUs, designed to make PCs faster and more colorful when they're handling multimedia applications (interactive video, virtual reality, and high-quality 3D) and communications applications. The enhancement is provided by MMX versions of Intel chips, which, in addition to their regular features, respond to 57 instructions that are oriented to highly parallel operations with multimedia and communications data types. Multimedia apps do lots of computation, lots of things in parallel, and tend to use small integer data types. The 57 new microcode instructions that constitute MMX technology were designed to help speed up the core algorithms and thus improve overall application performance. Having the MMX instructions in a Pentium chip makes it easier to build code to do multimedia things like simultaneous, real-time activities. An example would be multiple channels of audio, near–TV quality video or animation, and Internet communication all running in the same application. And, in fact, MMX computers that I've worked on that have video capture boards can capture much higher-quality video than comparable non-MMX computers can with the same video capture hardware.

The 57 instructions use a technique known as *Single Instruction, Multiple Data* (*SIMD*), which means that a single instruction operates on multiple pieces of data in parallel. For example, with a single MMX instruction, up to eight integer pairs can be added together in parallel. This parallel operation uses 64-bit registers. Depending on the operation, these are defined as eight 8-bit bytes, four 16-bit words, two 32-bit double words, or one 64-bit quad word.

MMX technology was designed to simplify writing things that must manipulate matrix-oriented data, applications like:

• Video capture programs

- Graphical manipulation programs like Paint Shop Pro
- Graphical oriented games
- 2D and, to a lesser extent, 3D graphics
- Speech recognition
- Data compression

The MMX represents a very specific policy goal for Intel: *let the system processor do all the computing*. Years ago, Intel sought to build terrific video capture boards around special-purpose chips designed to do one and only one thing: convert an analog video signal into a digital signal quickly. But Intel realized that they'd rather sell 100 million Pentium II chips a year than sell 50 million Pentium II chips, 5 million video capture chips, 10 million sound chips, and so on. So they started encouraging multimedia vendors to build cheaper boards that offload more and more of their work onto the main processor. The result is, of course, that people want faster and faster processors. The MMX's 57 new commands were added to the Pentium to make it easier for the processor to get those jobs done.

Does any software *require* the MMX? There are quite a few, but most of them are video games. Thus, if someone asks, "Is Windows 98 (or NT) MMX-compatible?" the answer is, "Yes." MMX CPUs have all the same opcodes as older CPUs, and the operating systems mentioned here have not been written to require the MMX opcodes.

What this means, of course, is that the new MMX-type processors should run all your old applications just fine. It doesn't mean, however, that you, personally, can somehow add MMX technology to your current 486 or Pentium chip. MMX instructions are new instructions directly incorporated into the processor, and this can only be accomplished when the chip is manufactured.

Which CPUs are MMX-compatible? The first MMX-capable CPU was *called* the MMX. It was a modified Pentium. But the Pentium chip didn't have enough room to be able to handle both the floating point numeric coprocessor support as well as the matrix MMX support at the same time, so unfortunately when you're running MMX-specific software on an MMX, the floating point support is disabled. That's too bad, because whenever you're doing matrix-specific calculations, you're likely to be also doing complex math (logs, sines, exponentials). The job still gets done, but without the floating point coprocessor, complex math takes longer to do. Thus, the MMX gets faster on matrix operations but gets slower on floating point. Is it a good tradeoff? Sorry, there's just no good answer to this one; it all depends upon the software you're running.

The next MMX was the Pentium II. The Pentium II is just a Pentium Pro with MMX circuits added. The good news is that the Pentium II has the power to simultaneously run both the MMX commands and the floating point command—very cool! Clearly Intel regretted releasing a chip that made software choose between matrix and floating point, leading some to wonder if the correct name of the Pentium II should really be the *Repent*ium chip. In any case, the Pentium II was soon joined by a lower-priced model (the Celeron) and a higher-priced model (the Xeon), both close cousins—so close, in fact, that they have MMX circuitry as well.

Superscalar and Instruction Pipelines

Remember I said earlier that the Pentium and later chips try to "work smarter, not harder?" I'll explain that in a bit more detail here. As time goes on, Intel tries to speed up their CPUs. But they're greatly hampered by the need for backward compatibility. So they use another way to make the Pentium faster: basically, they put two CPUs into it.

The Pentium Pipeline Structure

As you've read earlier, the circuitry that constitutes a CPU—registers, instruction decoders, and arithmetic/logic units—are all called *instruction pipelines* by CPU designers. All of the Intel CPUs that we've discussed, up to and including the 486 family, had just one pipeline in each chip, which is a techie way of saying, "The 486 and predecessors could do only one thing at a time."

In contrast, there are essentially two CPUs in the Pentium chip. The first one is like a 486DX, a CPU with floating point capabilities built right into it. The second is a 486SX, lacking a floating point unit. (Why didn't they put two floating point units in? It would have made the thing bigger, hotter, and more expensive.) That means that the Pentium is essentially a parallel-processing CPU, with the ability to do two things at once. Those two CPUs-within-a-CPU are called the *U and V pipelines*, and the fact that the Pentium has more than one pipeline makes it a *superscalar* CPU. (Why not parallel processing or multiprocessing or dual processing, I don't know—superscalar is the buzzword.)

The neat part of this dual pipelining is that the Pentium uses both pipelines *automatically*. It takes a simple non–Pentium-aware program, reads it, and divides it up into two pipelines. Now, that's not always possible, because some programs contain internal *dependencies*, but the Pentium does the best that it can.

For example, consider these three commands:

A = 3

B = 2

C = A + B

The first two commands—A = 3 and B = 2—are *not* dependent. You can manipulate A and manipulate B, and there's no interaction. Once they're done, then you're set to do C = A + B. As a result, A = 3 could go over the U pipeline while B = 2 goes over the V pipeline, and then C = A + B could run on the U pipeline once A = 3 was done. But now consider this sequence:

A = 1

A = A + 2

The second command can't be executed until the first command is done. Therefore, in this case, the Pentium would be forced to put the first command—A = 1—into one of the pipelines and then wait for it to finish before executing A = A + 2.

You'll see programs advertised as "designed for the Pentium" or "optimized for the Pentium." That means the instructions have been arranged so that the Pentium can keep both pipelines stuffed and busy. So-called "Pentium programs" will run fine on a 486 and even, on a 386, except that they'll run more slowly, because (among other things) those processors have only one pipeline.

The Pentium Pro/II/Celeron/Xeon Pipeline Structure

If two pipelines sound like a lot, then hold onto your hat, because the Pentium Pro/Pentium II/Celeron/Xeon chips contain an even more complex system with (depending on how you look at it) three or five pipelines. How does it work?

Think of the Pentium Pro pipelines as being organized in three major pieces:

- Decode
- Execute
- Clean up

The "decode" section works as it does on earlier chips, just mainly fetching an instruction and figuring out what it needs to do—integer math, floating point math, a memory read or write, or something else. There are three decoding pipelines, which means that the Pentium Pro can get three instructions ready at the same time. There aren't any interdependency problems with the decode phase.

The second phase executes the actual instruction. As this takes the most time, Intel included *five* execution pipelines. Any one of them can perform very simple operations, but for more demanding (or time-consuming) tasks, there are specialists. Two of the pipelines can only do integer computations, like the V pipeline on a Pentium. Two of the pipelines can do both integer computations and floating point computations, like the U pipeline on a Pentium. And one of the pipelines specializes in transferring data to and from memory. As with the Pentium's two-pipeline system, there's no guarantee that all five pipelines will remain active at all times, because interdependent code may, once again, make that impossible.

Recall that the older Pentium had to examine the incoming stream of program instructions and determine the dependencies within that stream; the Pentium Pro and later chips have the same need. For non-optimized code, the Pentium Pro family has often proven to be fast but not amazingly so. In fact, in February 1996, *BYTE* magazine reported that the Pentium Pro ran 16-bit applications (including the 16-bit parts of Windows 95) *slower* than the Pentium did, because the Pentium Pro was "tuned" to run 32-bit applications better than the Pentium. That's why if you're running Windows 3.1 or DOS programs, *or* if you're running a lot of those older programs under Windows 95/98 or Windows NT, then you may not see particularly impressive behavior. You need *truly* 32-bit code (and code optimized for the Pentium Pro family) to see the performance improvements in the Pentium Pro, the Pentium II, the Celeron, and the Xeon (although the Celeron's lack of cache makes it a pretty lame performer no matter what you do). And it's sadly true that there's not all that much code around that's really tuned to use 32 bits; even "new" 32-bit software like Office 97 still contains a lot of old 16-bit code. In my experience, the programs that are best tuned to use 32 bits are the high-end stuff—SQL database engines and file/print servers—and what some might call the low end: games. Personal productivity programs don't seem to be a priority for performance tuning; instead, the vendors seem more intent on adding thousands of features.

A final thought on superscalar architecture: it's now possible to take a second look at the Pentium OverDrive chip, the Pentium chip that fits on specially designed 486 motherboards. Is it a good idea? Well, consider what the Pentium really is: two 32-bit chips. As long as there are 64 bits feeding it, then the Pentium makes sense. But taking two 32-bit pipelines and forcing them to share a single 32-bit data path seems likely to end up creating a chip that only performs like a single 32-bit chip. (Maybe that's why Intel took so long to finally release it.)

Memory Addressable by a CPU

Megabytes are a unit of storage size—just about the amount of space needed to store a million characters. We use this term to talk about the size of primary memory—RAM, the kind of memory that goes in expansion boards, the kind of memory that Lotus can run out of if you've got a large spreadsheet—as well as secondary memory, which are disk drives. When most people say "memory," they are talking about *primary* memory, so memory means chips or RAM. Folks usually just say "disk" memory when that's what they mean, rather than secondary memory.

Disk memory is also not *volatile*, which means that when you shut it off, it retains its data. Remove power from a memory chip (which happens whenever you turn the machine off), and it forgets whatever it contained. That's why you have to save your work to disk before shutting off the machine.

But the fact that both disks and memory get measured in megabytes confuses people. I'll say, "I work with a Pentium II with 128MB of memory," and they'll think, "What good is *that*? Even I've got *six gigabytes* (6 billion bytes) on my PC." I was talking about primary memory—128MB of RAM. I didn't say anything at all about how much hard disk space I've got. *They* were thinking of hard disk space, and didn't tell me how much memory their PC has. (I hope it would be at the very least 32MB, and I wouldn't outfit a computer nowadays with less than 64MB.) End of digression.

You can't just keep adding memory to your PC indefinitely. A particular chip can only *address* a certain size of memory. For the oldest CPUs, this amount was 16,384 bytes—a 16K memory. The original IBM PC's CPU can address 1024K, or 1M. Other, newer chips can address even more. The 80386, 80486, Pentium, and Pentium Pro families can address gigabytes.

Details on CPU Chips

While I've talked a lot about various CPU chips in this part of the chapter, there are a few odds and ends that I haven't covered yet. I'll tie up those things here. Let's start off by listing all the Intel CPUs (and Intel-compatible CPUs) around, summarizing their characteristics. Table 3.3 summarizes the PC CPUs (organized under abbreviated headings explained in the key that follows the table).

TABLE 3.3: CPU Specifications and Applications

MODEL	ECF	ICF	WS	DP	IP	M	MC	IC	V	MMX	COMP
Intel											
8088	8	8	16	8	1	1	no	0	5	N	
8086	8	8	16	16	1	1	no	0	5	N	
80c86	8	8	16	16	1	1	no	0	5	N	
80186	16	16	16	16	1	1	no	0	5	N	
80286	20	20	16	16	1	16	no	0	5	N	
80386DX	40	40	32	32	1	4096	no	0	5	N	
80386SX	25	25	32	16	1	16	no	0	5	N	
80486SLC	25 33	25 33	32	32	1	64	no	8	5	N	
80486DX	25 33 50	25 33 50	32	32	1	4096	yes	8	5	N	
80486SX	20 25 33	20 25 33	32	32	1	4096	no	8	5	N	
80486DX2	20 25 33	40 50 66	32	32	1	4096	yes	8	5	N	
80486DX4	25 33	75 100	32	32	1	4096	yes	16	5	N	
Pentium	60 66	100 133 150 166 200	32	64	2	4096	yes	16	5 and 3.3	N	
MMX	66	200 233 266	32	64	2	4096	yes	32	1.5	Y	
Pentium Pro	60 66	166 200	32	64	3	65536	yes	32	1.5	N	

Continued on next page

TABLE 3.3 CONTINUED: CPU Specifications and Applications

MODEL	ECF	ICF	WS	DP	IP	M	MC	IC	V	MMX	COMP
Pentium II	66 100	233 266 300 333 350 400	32	64	3	65536	yes	32	1.5	Y	
Celeron	66	233 266 300	32	64	3	65536	yes	32	1.5	Y	
Xeon	100	350 400	32	64	3	65536	yes	32	2	Y	
NEC											
V20	10	10	16	8	1	1	no	0	5		8088
V30	10	10	16	16	1	1	no	0	5		8086
Cyrix											
80486SLC	25 33	25 33	32	32	1	16	no	1	5		386SX
80486SLC	25	50	32	32	1	16	no	1	5		386SX
80486DLC	33	33	32	32	1	4096	no	1	5		386DX
80486DX	33 40 50	33 40 50	32	32	1	4096	yes	8	5		486DX
80486DX2	25 33 40	50 66 80	32	32	1	4096	yes	8	5		486DX2
586		100 120	32	64	1	4096	yes	16	3.45–5		Pentium
6x86	75 66 60 55 50	150 133 120 110 100	32	64	2	4096	yes	16	3.3–5		Pentium

Continued on next page

T A B L E   3 . 3   C O N T I N U E D : CPU Specifications and Applications

MODEL	ECF	ICF	WS	DP	IP	M	MC	IC	V	MMX	COMP
AMD											
386SE	25 33	25 33	32	16	1	16	no	0	3–5		386SX
386DE	33 40 33 40	33 40	32	32	1	4096	no	0	3–5		386DX
486DXLV	33	33	32	32	1	4096	yes	8	3.0–3.6		486DX
486SXLV	33	33	32	32	1	4096	no	8	3.0–3.6		486SX
486DX	33 40	33 40	32	32	1	4096	yes	8	5		486DX
486SX	33 40	33 40	32	32	1	4096	no	8	5		486SX
486DX2	25 33	50 66	32	32	1	4096	yes	8	5		486DX2
486DX2-80	40	80	32	32	1	4096	yes	8	5		486DX2
486DXL2	25 33	50 66	32	32	1	4096	yes	8	5		486DX2
486SX2-50	25	50	32	32	1	4096	yes	8	5		486SX
Am5x86	33	133				4096	yes	16	3.45		Pentium 75

KEY TO TABLE 3.3:

EFC = External clock frequency (in MHz)

ICF = Internal clock frequency (in MHz)

WS = Word size (in bits)

DP = Data path (in bits)

IP = Instruction pipelines (how many)

M = Memory (in bytes)

MC = Math coprocessor

IC = Internal cache (in K)

V = Voltage (in volts)

Comp = Intel compatibility

Some of these chips are more powerful or less powerful. Some can actually allow you to improve the throughput of your existing PC. For instance, if you have a 386 system, you can speed it up with a 486DLC, which is not really a 486...but I'm getting ahead of myself. You'll see a bit of repetition in this section, but I left that in because I've thrown an awful lot of concepts at you so far; the intent in this section is to tie up all the CPU concepts before progressing on to memory, buses, and other hardware topics.

The 8088

The 8088 is the "Grand Old Man" of PC CPUs. It comes in what is called a 40-pin DIP package, which means a rectangular plastic case with two rows of 20 pins. *DIP* stands for *Dual Inline Package*. Older 8088s were called 8088-1s, because they could run at only low speeds (5MHz or slower). Turbo PC/XT clones ran at 6.66, 7.16, or 8.0MHz. To do this, they used the 8088-2, which is rated at up to 8MHz. The 8088 is the equivalent of about 29,000 transistors.

The 8086

The 8086 predates the 8088 by a year and is actually more powerful than it, but the 8086 is not as well known. The 8086 is different from the 8088 in that the 8086 not only has internal 16-bit registers (a 16-bit word) but also a 16-bit data path, the doorway to the outside world. Because that required 16-bit motherboards, however, the 8086 never really caught on. The 8088 is essentially a hobbled 8086, because it has only an 8-bit data path. But that made for a cheaper motherboard, so IBM went with the 8088—and the rest is history. But a few clone makers opted for 8086-based systems because the 8086 was 100-percent compatible with the 8088 *and* faster; one example was Compaq, with a tremendously successful computer called the Deskpro.

The 80186 and 80188

You don't hear much about these chips, but they were souped-up versions of the 8086 and 8088. They didn't really have much in the way of new capabilities, they were just a kind of polished version of the old chips, sort of similar to the way that the 80486 is not a big leap from the 80386, but rather is a mildly improved version. The main differences were that the 186 and the 188 were manufactured in a PGA package (see the 80286 for more on this), and had more efficient microcode. Tandy sold a computer called the Tandy 2000 that was 80186-based. It could have been a high-performance competitor to the Deskpro, but Tandy unwisely opted to make it only about 60-percent compatible with the IBM PC, forcing Tandy 2000 users to buy special versions of software. There weren't too many titles developed for the Tandy 2000, and it went nowhere.

The 80186 was the last member of what might be called the first family of PC CPUs, a family that started with the 8086.

The 80286

The 80286, introduced in 1981, was a major step forward for *x*86 technology. Its package is a square of ceramic called a *Pin Grid Array* (*PGA*) package. It also comes in a cheaper package called a *Plastic Leadless Chip Carrier* (*PLCC*). The PLCC is the more durable of the two, and is mainly found in laptops, due to its lower profile. The PGA package has an inner and an outer square of solid pins; the PLCC has curved-under legs around its perimeter. The PGA "stands" on its legs. The PLCC is surrounded by its legs. You can see chip types in Figure 3.4.

FIGURE 3.4:

Chip package types

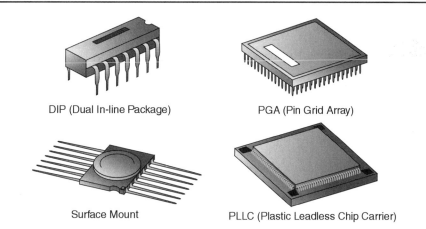

DIP (Dual In-line Package)   PGA (Pin Grid Array)

Surface Mount   PLLC (Plastic Leadless Chip Carrier)

The 286 packs a lot more power into a small package than the 8088 does: the 80286 is the equivalent of about 130,000 transistors in about the same volume. Because of this, the 80286 ran hotter, and some models required extra cooling provisions such as a heat sink. Heat sinks are small metal caps with metal cooling fins that fit on top of a chip and enable the chip to better dissipate the heat that it generates. You see them on modern CPUs, like Pentiums, which produce even greater amounts of heat.

The 80286 is the sole member of the second family of PC-compatible CPUs. In many ways, it was a rough draft for the 386 family, the third and current family of PC CPUs.

The 80386DX and 80386SX

The 80386, or as it is officially called by Intel, the 80386DX, was another quantum leap for the *x*86 family. Introduced in 1985, it came in a PGA package and was the equivalent of about 250,000 transistors. It incorporated a wealth of programming features, including the ability to multitask DOS programs with the help of operating systems like Windows. The 32-bit data path speeds data access, leading to the design of buses like the Micro Channel, EISA, VESA, and PCI buses (see the upcoming section on buses). It also differed from previous *x*86 designs in that it could address 4096M of RAM.

The 386SX is identical to the 386DX except that it has a 16-bit data path to allow it to be more easily incorporated into AT-type hardware designs (recall that the AT's 286 has a 16-bit data path also). It is contained in a PLCC package.

The 80386 family brought a new set of instruction codes and a 32-bit programming model to PC CPUs that is essentially unchanged to this day. Look at the most modern PC programs, and 99 percent of them will run on a circa-1985 386-based system, albeit slowly.

The 80386SL

The SL was part of a two-chip set that was basically a combination of a 386SX and a motherboard. The two chips together constituted almost all of what's needed to build an SX computer. What made it particularly interesting was that the chip set included power management. For example, the SL system could shut down the CPU between keystrokes, saving power. The SL mainly appeared in laptops; they were in PLCC packages.

The 80486DX

The 80486 (officially the 80486DX) was sort of an upgraded 386. Code-named during development "P4," it combined a tuned-up 386 with two chips that sped up a 386 system: the 385 cache controller and the 387 numeric coprocessor. The microcode was larger and faster—there were the equivalent of 1.25 *million* transistors in this chip. Depending upon what the computer was doing, a 25MHz 386 with a 385 and a 387 (CPU and external math coprocessor) would sometimes execute only half as many instructions per second as a 25MHz 486.

Better yet, the 486 chip was actually cheaper than a 386, 385, and 387 together, so eventually 486 computers were cheaper than fully loaded 386 machines. The DX appeared in PGA packages.

The 80486SX

The 80486SX was more of a marketing tool than a new chip. Intel took the 486DX chips that failed the math coprocessor during product testing and sold them in a new package they called a 486SX. It had a specified maximum clock speed of 20MHz and no math coprocessor. Intel then offered a math coprocessor called the 487SX that was, believe it or not, a fully functional 486DX—a CPU chip with coprocessor and all. Once the 487SX was planted in its socket, it instructed the 486SX to just go to sleep; the 487SX then handled everything including both general computing and numeric coprocessing, just as if it were a normal 486DX system running at 20MHz.

The 80486DX2, DX4, and the OverDrive Chip

The 80487SX, as it turns out, was a mere harbinger of the wide variety in CPUs that was to follow. With the 486, Intel first started experimenting with product diversification, taking a basically good product (the 486DX) and repackaging it in a variety of ways.

Recall that the 80487SX was *not* a floating point coprocessor. It was a fully functional 80486DX, but packaged a bit differently—the pins on the bottom of the chip were arranged differently from the way they were arranged on the 80486DX, so you couldn't just pop an 80486DX in the 80487SX socket. Furthermore, unlike the floating point coprocessors of yore (the 8087, 187, 287, and 387 families), the 80487SX didn't work with the erstwhile main processor—it *took* *over alto*gether, effectively disconnecting the 80486SX. A bit of clever marketing, eh? Buy a "cheap" 486SX and then end up buying a whole 486DX disguised as a coprocessor, with the result that Intel gets to sell more chips than if you'd bought a 486DX in the first place.

Next stop in the 486-marketing universe was the original Over-Drive chip. ("Original" because the phrase "overdrive" has since been recycled by Intel a number of times.) The OverDrive chip was a 486DX built for a 487SX socket, as usual, *except* that they made it a clock doubler like the 486DX2.

The net effect was that the OverDrive chip did everything at least as quickly as a 25MHz 80486DX, and many operations *twice* as fast! So the OverDrive chip would speed up your PC by about one-third to one-half. Was it worth it? An OverDrive chip cost around $300, not a small amount, but then not a budget-buster either.

Intel then took on the market of folks who had a 486DX and wanted more speed by offering the clock doubler 486DX2. Recall that the 80486DX2, like the OverDrive chip, ran outwardly at *x*MHz, but worked internally at 2*x*MHz. Thus, a so-called 66MHz 80486DX2 worked in a motherboard designed for a 33MHz chip, but ran internally at 66MHz. The value was, again, that a PC vendor needed only take one of its already existing 33MHz 80486DX models, replace the 33MHz 80486DX processor with a 66MHz 80486DX processor, and it instantly got a "66MHz 486."

The last in the Intel 486 line was the DX4, a 486 that clock tripled and contained power management right on the chip, combining 386SL-like technology and clock tripling to produce a very nice processor. Its main role was in laptops, where it functioned extremely well.

The 486SLC and 486DLC

This one wasn't an Intel chip. It wasn't even a 486. A 486SLC is a 386SX (no numeric coprocessor, recall) with just *1K of cache* and, of course, a *16-bit data path*. The resulting chip was somewhere between a 386SX and a 486SX in performance. The 1K was pretty measly, so you'd have to say that the performance was closer to the 386SX than to the 486. There's also a 486DLC, a 386DX with 1K of cache memory added, and no coprocessor. These chips were pin-compatible with the 386SX and 386DX, not the 486 line. My main gripe with them was the marketing baloney that went with them: people were told they were getting 486 technology when they bought one of these chips, but they actually got only 386 technology.

Micro technology improvement, macro sales pitches. Yup, you can always tell when a technological industry matures: the guys in the wheelhouse are marketing guys rather than engineers.

The 386DRU2

Another Intel competitor. It was an odd-looking name, but that was internal designation. This Cyrix chip was a 386 clone, save that it was a clock doubler: you could make a 25MHz 386 into a 50MHz 386 with one of these.

That, in general, has been Cyrix's modus operandi: take what Intel does and do it better. It's not served them badly.

The Pentium

In March of 1993, Intel introduced the processor they'd code-named "P5," known now as the Pentium processor. In some ways, it was just a souped-up 486. In other ways, it was much more, as you've seen from the earlier parts of this chapter. Here's a quick look at Pentium features besides the ones we've already examined.

Greater Raw Speed   The Pentium comes in a variety of flavors: 60, 66, 75, 90, 100, 125, 133, 150, and 166MHz, and, in its newer MMX flavor, is available up to 266MHz. Intel offers an Over-Drive upgrade for chips 100MHz and under that increases the chip's speed by about half.

The 120/133MHz OverDrive processor upgrade is designed to reduce the voltage used by the 60MHz and 66MHz chips from 5 volts to the 3.3 used by the more recent chips that take advantage of Intel's Voltage Reduction Technology.

NOTE   Counterintuitively, you may get better performance from a 133 than a 150, because the 133 is a doubled 66MHz chip and the 150 is a two-and-a-halved 60.

The Pentium is difficult to make because, for one thing, it's much bigger than the 486. The 486 contains 1.2 million transistors; the Pentium contains 3.1 million—over two and a half times as many.

That's an important contributing factor to the extreme heat, and it doesn't get any better with the Pentium Pro; as a laptop user, I look forward to a Hexium notebook that will serve double duty as both a fast computer and a portable hot plate for us road warrior types. (Just kidding.)

Seriously, though, I'd avoid the 60 and 66, and go straight to the 90 and 100 chips, because they're actually cooler (lower voltage, remember).

Fault Tolerance   The Pentium is designed to be linked with another Pentium on a motherboard designed for fault tolerance. The second Pentium constantly monitors the first; if the main Pentium malfunctions, the other one jumps right in and takes up without skipping a beat. Another purpose for two CPUs on one motherboard is symmetric multiprocessing (SMP). Most dual CPU implementations are for SMP and not for fault tolerance.

First MMX Implementation Another Pentium first is the so-called multimedia support, the matrix functions in the MMX. The MMX is just a Pentium with MMX instructions included and a larger cache. The Pentium's a hot chip, in more ways than one. So hot, in fact, that you should recall that if you're still running older 16-bit apps then you won't be all that impressed with its successors, the Pentium Pro family. So don't feel that you absolutely *must* upgrade your existing 166MHz system. In actual fact, simply adding RAM to your system may make it produce the performance you're looking for.

The Pentium II

The Pentium II (PII) made some impressive improvements to the original Pentium processor. Ranging in speeds from 233MHz to 450MHz, the PII improves not only speed, but also performance. The PII incorporates a 100MHz "front bus" interface (for the 350MHz, 400MHz, and 450MHz chips), allowing the processor to achieve greater speeds in interfacing with system resources.

The PII also has MMX technology built into the processor, thereby satisfying the new demands by users and software for faster graphics. The original PII came with 32KB of level 1 cache (16KB for data and 16KB for instructions) and 512KB of level 2 cache.

Pentium II XEON

The PII processor was further enhanced by the creation of the XEON family. The XEON PII is designed for business applications and high-speed processing; up to eight processors can be combined to work together. The processor functions at 400MHz or 450MHz and can handle higher level 2 cache. The 400MHz and 450MHz are available with 512KB or 1MB of level 2 cache, but the 450MHz can handle up to a whopping 2MB.

Intel Celeron Processor

The Intel Celeron processor has become quite popular with home PC users. The reason for its increase in sales is due to its cost. Intel made a decision to lower processor costs (which in turn lowered PC costs) by making some changes to its existing processor families.

Recall that the new standard Pentium chips have 32KB of level 1 cache and 512KB of level 2 cache. The level 2 cache is the expensive kind, so it makes sense that if you reduce its size you could reduce the cost of the processor, right? Well, that's what Intel did. The Celeron processor comes in speeds ranging from 300MHz to 466MHz (which operate at 66MHz bus speed and still have 32KB of level 1 cache). But these processors come with only 128KB of level 2 cache. Although this is a drastic cut in level 2 cache size, the reduction in price for the processor and the PCs that use it make it a very favorable choice for buyers looking to save money on a new PC. Check out the Celeron chip on Intel's web site at `http://www.intel.com/celeron`.

Pentium III

Intel released its newest Pentium processor with a marketing blitz no one will soon forget. But is the new chip worth all the hype? Let's see.

First, the speeds offered by the Pentium III are getting higher. 450MHz, 500MHz, and 550MHz speeds are available, and the chips also come with the MMX technology. 512KB of level 2 cache is standard. But other than the increase in speed, what's the big deal? Well, the Pentium III's strength lies in its ability to handle graphics faster and smoother than previous chips. Remember

MMX? The Pentium III does MMX processing 70 instructions better! These new instructions are designed for real-time video, streaming video, and better graphic capabilities.

There's a lot more to the Pentium III. You can go read the technical details for yourself at `http://www.intel.com/PentiumIII`.

Pentium Challengers: M1, Nx586, and K5

For many years, chip companies competed with Intel by making clones of its chips. But the Pentium was a different story, because its difference from the 486 was not tremendous—it's a fast chip, but it's not staggeringly faster than a 486. Add that to Intel's public relations disaster back in November 1994 over the Pentium's floating point division problems, and computer manufacturers soon became more open to putting a non-Intel chip in their computers.

That was the opening needed to create Cyrix's M1, NexGen's Nx586, and AMD's K5. All three of these chips are intended to be "what the Pentium should have been." They're backward-compatible with 486 software, so they run Windows 95/98, DOS, Windows NT, and the like. But they all depart from the Pentium in slightly different ways.

The Cyrix 6x86

In October 1995, Cyrix announced the shipment of its rival to the Pentium, the 6x86 (formerly the M1). Although the 6x86 is a two-pipeline superscalar chip like the Pentium, the 6x86 offers a number of other features that are also offered by the Pentium Pro (released after the 6x86). However, the Cyrix 5x86, formerly known as the M1sc, is not a rival to the Pentium, although the numbering scheme makes it sound like it is. 5x86s are pin-compatible with an Intel 486, 6x86s with a Pentium. The 6x86 features:

- **Superpipelining.** Instead of the Pentium's five stages, the 6x86 uses a seven-stage pipeline to avoid lags in the execution process and increase the flow of information.

- **Register renaming.** Provides temporary data storage for instant data availability without waiting for the CPU to access the on-chip cache or main system memory.

- **Data dependency removal.** Provides instruction results to both pipelines simultaneously so that neither pipeline is stalled while waiting for the results of calculations.

- **Multi-branch prediction.** Boosts processor performance by predicting with high accuracy the next instructions needed.

- **Speculative execution**. Allows the pipelines to continuously execute instructions following a branch without stalling the pipelines.

- **Out-of-order completion.** Can process instructions out of order, making it possible to get faster-to-process instructions out of the way before spending time on the longer ones. This feature applies to the Execute and Write-Back portions of the calculation process.

The 6x86 is a clock doubler or tripler (depending on the model). It stores calculation instructions and their results in a 16KB cache so that they can be called back into memory quickly if necessary. Cyrix also has released the MII processors, which are supposed to rival the Intel's Celeron processor line in power.

NOTE The 6x86 has received mixed reviews about its Windows NT compatibility, so check Microsoft's Hardware Compatibility List before buying non-Intel systems for Windows NT use.

AMD's K5

The K5 is a fifth-generation processor offered by AMD. The K5 is distinct from AMD's 5x86, a souped-up version of the 486. The K5, a 64-bit version more like the Pentium, started shipping as of June 1996. The K5's most salient feature is its four instruction pipelines (twice as many as the Pentium).

The biggest difference between the K5 and the Cyrix 6x86 is that the Cyrix chip is a *CISC* (*Complex Instruction Set Chip,* an older approach to designing CPUs), whereas the K5 is a *RISC* (*Reduced Instruction Set Chip,* a newer approach) chip. As such, it must translate the complex instructions it receives to simpler ones that can be executed more quickly.

NexGen's Nx586

This chip is the oddball of the crowd. First of all, it does not support floating point operations, making it incompatible even with some programs that run on an 80486DX. Second, it is not pin-compatible with the Pentium, requiring designers to create a whole new motherboard to use it. Third, it runs at four volts, in comparison to the other two, which match the Pentium's 3.3-volt requirement.

It runs two instruction pipelines and can handle instructions out of order. NexGen rates chips not by their speed, but by equivalent speeds for the Pentium. The other non-Intel manufacturers do likewise. For example, the 6x86 that is rated at 100MHz actually runs at 93MHz, but Cyrix claims that it performs equally to a Pentium at that speed, and some benchmarks bear it out. The Nx586 was the first of the three to ship commercially; AMD now owns NexGen.

The Pentium Pro family (described next) of chips does well sales-wise, but it's not entirely clear that it's because of their performance; more likely, it's a matter of their big megahertz numbers. The fact that the Pentium Pro line isn't really all that much faster than the Pentium line underscores that fact that the task of speeding up CPUs is getting tougher and tougher. It's not enough to provide more megahertz, more raw speed. The winner in the CPU races will be the one that uses its time most wisely, with multiple pipelines, out-of-order instruction, data bypassing, and the like.

Intel's Pentium Pro Family

Last in the Intel lineup to be designed entirely by Intel (the P7 and P8, which are under development right now, will be joint ventures with Hewlett-Packard), the "P6" line of chips (Pentium Pro, Pentium II, Celeron, and Xeon chips) differ from their predecessors for many reasons. But are they *faster* chips? Well, yes, kind of—but, like their predecessors, the P6 family is largely limited by its heritage: it's got to be *x*86 compatible.

Just looking at the P6 family shows how they're different. With the exception of the Celeron, the P6s are fairly large chips, because they contain lots of memory. The Pentium Pro chip, for example, is actually *two* chips. Inside the Pentium Pro, there is one chip (*die* is the actual word; it refers to the silicon wafer that is the actual electronics of a chip), which is the main processor. It has about 5.5 million transistors. Alongside it is a built-in 256K external or L2 cache, about 15 million transistors' worth of static memory. You can see that in Figure 3.5.

FIGURE 3.5:

L2 cache on the
Pentium Pro chip

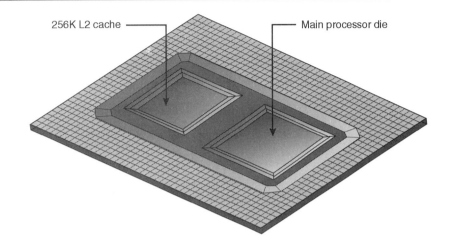

256K L2 cache ─────┐   ┌───── Main processor die

The Pentium Pro incorporates three pipelines, rather than the two of the Pentium. By breaking up instruction execution into 14 steps, Intel has made it possible to do what they call *dynamic execution*. Explained earlier in the discussion of superscalar architectures, dynamic execution works by using three parallel units to fetch and decode instructions; once prepared for execution, those instructions are tossed into a "pool" of waiting instructions. There's not much waiting, however, because the P6s have five different execution units working side by side to try to shove instructions through at top speed. That helps because the Pentium Pro can handle groups of instructions *out of their original order*, which keeps as many of the fetch/decode and execution units working at the highest capacity possible.

Oddly enough, the Pentium Pro has an L1 cache of only 16K, the same as the standard Pentium, and in fact less than the Pentium MMX chips. That is offset by the large L2 cache incorporated into the chip. By putting the L2 cache on the chip, the Pentium

Pro can more quickly access that memory, making it a faster "external" cache than the external caches found on Pentium and earlier chips. But 20 million transistors! That sucker is a mite toasty, so make sure there's a decent CPU fan on your Pentium Pro. Most come with a fan, as you see in Figure 3.6.

The other P6ers—Celeron, Xeon, and Pentium II—all have 32K of L1 cache and can also suffer from heat exhaustion (the Xeon even has a sensor on-chip to detect overheating).

The later P6s' heat problems weren't as terrible as they could be, however, because Intel has again reduced the size of the transistors that make up the chip. Where the Pentium was built with 0.8-micron and 0.6-micron components, the Xeon is built with 0.25 micron. That will help make the Xeon work at a decent reliability factor when running at 400MHz.

400MHz. And to think my first PC ran at 4.77MHz....

Speed demons that they are, depending on which operating system you're running, the P6s may not be the best choice. Recall that Intel decided to bite the bullet and sacrifice some backward compatibility with 16-bit applications in order to get better speed from 32-bit ones. Unfortunately, this means that 16-bit operating systems (including parts of Windows 95 and 98) don't run very well on the Pentium Pro. In fact, they may run more slowly on the Pentium Pro than the Pentium. This chip might be a better choice for those planning to run full 32-bit operating systems, such as Windows NT Workstation.

The new Pentium III processors are very similar to the Pentium IIs; however, the IIIs run faster (450–550MHz), support 70 new instructions, and run on the new 100MHz-system bus.

FIGURE 3.6:

Pentium II package
with fan

PC Memory

The PC, like all computers, must have *main memory*. Main memory's job is to be the place where the PC stores the programs and data that it is working on right now. It needs to be able to access these programs and data in *nanoseconds* (billionths of seconds), rather than—as in the case of secondary memory such as hard disks—*milliseconds* (thousandths of seconds).

The other name for main memory, which we've talked about before, is RAM, an acronym for the particularly unhelpful name *random access memory*. I say it's unhelpful because "random access" just means that it's as easy to get to the 1,000,000th location as it is to get to the first location. By contrast, with *sequential access*, like a tape drive, you've got to fast forward or rewind the tape to get to a particular location—the data is sequential. "Random" tells us very little because there's another kind of memory you'll meet later named *ROM*, for *read-only memory*. That too is sequential; the only difference between RAM and ROM is that you can both write data to RAM and read data from it, and you can only read data from ROM. Heck, even disk drives are random access. So a better name for RAM would probably be read/write memory or RWM, but you can't pronounce RWM. You *can* pronounce RAM, so the term caught on.

How Memory Is Packaged: DIPs, SIMMs, and DIMMs

Most modern RAM modules are circuits, small circuit boards with chips on them. On some systems, it's a group of eight or nine small chips (you see that on some video boards and on most pre-1988 motherboards), or more likely, it's a mini-circuit board with several square chips mounted on it, called a *Single Inline Memory Module (SIMM)*. Memory is always organized into banks—either eight or nine discrete chips, or a SIMM. Most motherboards have room for four banks of memory. Some of the newer machines have no memory on the motherboard at all, but instead have a large circuit board with room for megs and megs of memory. You'll also see *Dual Inline Memory Modules*, or *DIMMs*; they're just small circuit boards with chips on *both* sides of them, to pack more memory onto the package.

Over the years, memory packaging has changed. Before the late '80s, you'd buy memory as a bunch of small chips (called "DIPs" because that's the type of package used), and you'd plug them into chip sockets on the computer's motherboard or an add-in daughtercard. Depending on the processor type, you'd have to add memory in increments of 8, 9, 16, 18, 32, or 36 chips. Those minimum increments are called "banks" of memory. Soon, the first generation of SIMMs appeared. Known as "30-pin SIMMs," one SIMM was the equivalent of eight or nine DIPs, and for a time most motherboards had sockets for 30-pin SIMMs. Around 1992, a newer SIMM package that was the equivalent of 32 or 36 DIPs became more popular; this package is known as a "72-pin SIMM," and most modern motherboards' memory sockets are 72-pin SIMM sockets. Computers built around Pentium-class or Pentium Pro–class processors require that when you upgrade memory, you do it with pairs of 72-pin SIMMs. Since 1996, a kind of main memory called a synchronous dynamic RAM (SDRAM) has appeared on the market. It too is a 72-pin SIMM, but it works differently and so requires yet another socket type. Many motherboards nowadays have both sockets for old-style 72-pin SIMMs and sockets for SDRAM modules. You can see two kinds of SIMMs in Figure 3.7.

FIGURE 3.7:

Single Inline Memory Modules (SIMMs)

30-pin SIMM

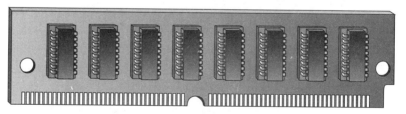

72-pin SIMM

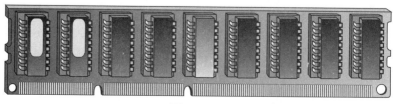

168-pin DIMM

Solving the Memory Speed Problem: DRAM, Fast Page, EDO, Burst EDO, and SDRAM

You read earlier in this chapter that it would be nice to have memory that ran as quickly as the processor, but that no one makes inexpensive, fast memory. It would seem, then, that slow memory speed is an important pothole in the road to maximum speed, and the smart PC buyer should be sure to spend all available money on the latest, fastest memory. And PC hardware vendors have been eager to separate PC buyers from that money. Fast memory *can*, in fact, lead to a faster computer, but not that much faster.

Originally, main memory was simple dynamic RAM (DRAM), a good, inexpensive memory design that you don't see anymore. Recall that there *is* fast memory around called SRAM—static RAM. But it's too expensive to use for all system memory, so most PCs try to strike a balance by using a lot of cheap memory for main system memory and add a little bit of the expensive SRAM to act as a memory cache. So PCs in the mid-to-late '80s tended to be a mix of a lot of DRAM and a bit of SRAM.

Memory makers wanted to build a DRAM that was faster (closer to SRAM speed), without making it too much more expensive. And that's when DRAM designers hit upon a couple of important concepts:

- It's impossible to make DRAM able to just grab data from any old location quickly.

- But once a DRAM has accessed a piece of data in *one* location, it is possible to design the DRAM so that it can quickly access data that is *nearby*.

A memory called static column RAM appeared in 1986 that used this information, and Compaq used it in their Compaq Deskpro 386 to squeeze good performance out of their computer. The early '90s saw another "read nearby data fast" approach called Fast Page Mode memory, which was followed by Extended Data Out or EDO memory, which was followed by a slightly faster approach called Burst Extended Data Out memory. Each memory type was faster than its predecessors were, but they all shared the same basic characteristic: once a piece of data was read from a chip, nearby data could be read quickly. How near "nearby data" had to be varied from design to design, but it meant that at some point you'd exceed the "neighborhood" of the original data read. So, for example, let's assume that a "neighborhood" for a bit of data in a memory is 2048 bytes long. (Assume there's no static cache in this example.) It's the first thing in the morning, and the CPU's about to access its very first byte of the day. Because that's a DRAM access that's not near the previous access (since there *was* no previous access), that first access is pretty slow. But suppose that the next thing the CPU needs is the byte right after that first byte (which is a quite reasonable assumption). It's "nearby" to the first byte and so its access is fast. Assuming that the CPU keeps requesting data sequentially, it'll find fast response for the next 2046. But after that, access gets slow again as the CPU enters another "neighborhood."

The latest kind of popular RAM solves that problem. It's called, as I mentioned earlier, synchronous DRAM or SDRAM. How it works is interesting. The CPU tells it, "Go get some data at location 10,455," and the SDRAM goes to do that. That initial access takes a bit of time, as with earlier DRAM. But what the SDRAM does next is really interesting: it just starts pumping data out of the memory sequentially until the CPU tells it to stop. After the data in location 10,455, it gets 10,456, then 10,457, and so on, and *all at SRAM speeds*! Basically, the memory just goes on "autopilot" and shotguns data sequentially at the CPU. Now, *if the CPU needs a big hunk of sequential data*, then this can be quite fast, and that's why if you look at current PC advertisements, they all trumpet how much SDRAM you get, as if it really made a difference in your system's performance. But the fact is, SDRAM or any other kind of RAM really *won't* affect system speed tremendously. You can see two SDRAM SIMMs in Figure 3.8.

FIGURE 3.8:

SDRAM (with Pentium II cartridge socket in background)

More RAM Is Better Than Faster RAM

To see why variations in system RAM type won't affect your PC's performance a lot, let's return to the notion of the static cache RAM. The idea with this 256K–1024K of memory cache is that it's obviously fast to access. So if the CPU needs the data from location X in main memory *and* the cache happens to already *have* that data, then the CPU can read the data from cache with almost no delay at all. If the data for location X isn't in the cache, that's fine—there's no hardware failure or anything like that—but it's slower, because the request for the data will have to go out to the slower main memory. But consider: if a system has, say, 256K of cache and 32MB of main memory, then the cache has room for copies of only a small percentage of the data in the main memory. What determines which data are kept in cache and which data isn't? A memory controller circuit, either on the motherboard (in older systems) or the CPU (in modern systems). A cleverly built memory controller can get a lot of mileage out of a small amount of cache memory.

The key, then, to building a system that's both fast memory-wise and easy on the wallet is to add a small amount of expensive, fast memory as cache and then add a clever memory controller to get the most out of it. And that's what virtually every modern computer does (save for laptops, which generally don't have cache).

NOTE   In modern computers, well over 95 percent of the CPU's memory requests are satisfied by the static cache.

Let's do a little math to consider what that means *vis-à-vis* performance. Assume that about 25 percent of what the CPU does requires memory accesses. A slow memory system, then, could affect only 25 percent of the CPU's performance for good or ill. (This is a rough analysis and isn't completely accurate, it's just a back-of-the-envelope look at how memory affects performance.) But 95 percent of those memory accesses are satisfied by the nearly instantaneous static memory cache, so slow main memory could only affect 5 percent of the 25 percent of the CPU's tasks that are memory-oriented; in other words, *main memory speed affects about 1.25 percent of CPU tasks!* It may be that by the time you read this, some other new whiz-bang kind of memory has appeared to unseat SDRAM as the "fastest" memory technology, and you can be sure that its price tag will reflect its "latest and greatest" nature. But I'd suggest that rather than spending all kinds of money on faster memory, I'd just spend that money on *more* memory. A PC with 16MB of blindingly fast memory would run Windows 98 far more slowly than a PC with 64MB of run-of-the-mill RAM.

Self-Healing RAM: ECC Memory

As we buy more and more memory, however, our PCs become more fragile, because every memory byte is a circuit, and every circuit is something that can go wrong. A PC with 256K of RAM has millions fewer failure points than does a PC with 64MB of RAM. This is not to suggest that you should buy PCs with 256K of RAM; in fact, I'm not sure you *can* buy a machine with that little RAM. I think my microwave oven has a couple of megs these days...

From the original 1981 machines onward, PCs have been able to detect memory errors through a system called "parity." Parity couldn't fix the error, it just knew that it was there. Once the parity error detection circuitry detected a memory error, it made a sort of abrupt response to the problem: it just stopped the computer cold. That made people ask the question, "What good is parity if it just locks the system up—how is that better than just continuing to run with faulty memory?" which is not a bad question. Parity also required a bit more memory. Early systems either used 8-bit SIMMs or 9-bit SIMMs—the difference was that the 9-bit SIMMs had parity. The same thing appears today with 72-pin SIMMs; they come in "32-bit" or "36-bit" varieties. The 36-bit variety includes parity.

Many systems nowadays opt not to use parity, and it's a shame, because parity has finally come into its own. Pentium II-based systems with parity memory can not only detect an error, they can *correct* that error. This process is called Error Correcting Code or ECC memory. ECC memory's been around for mainframes and minis for years, but not for PCs save for a few expensive machines. With modern machines, however, all you need do is make sure that you buy parity memory (36-bit SIMMs rather than 32-bit SIMMs) and configure the system to use the memory for ECC—it's usually a software setting of some kind—and you get mainframe memory power for pennies. The shame is that many hardware vendors don't tell their customers about it.

Types of Memory

So far, we've probably covered many of the terms that you come across when reading computer ads or tips on "powering up" your PC. But another bunch of terms remains—conventional memory, extended memory, and expanded memory. These are more software-oriented terms than hardware-oriented, but they're worth going over in case you're trying to configure software that starts asking questions about how much memory you've got.

Why so many kinds of memory? Mainly because of unfortunate planning: nobody ever thought the PC would need more than 640K of memory. (There's a famous Bill Gates quote from the early '80s along the lines of "No one will ever need more than 640K of memory on a personal computer.")

The familiar first 640K of a PC's memory is called *conventional memory*. It is supplemented by *reserved areas* containing ROM, read-only memory, and bits of RAM on expansion boards; all of those RAM and ROM areas are called the *upper memory area*. The 286 and later machines can address memory beyond that called *extended memory*. And a small-but-important number of applications can use special memory called *expanded memory*, or, as it is also known, *LIM memory*. Let's look at these in turn.

Let me note here that the introduction of memory managers into DOS since DOS 5.0 complicates things a bit, but I'm afraid that I'm going to have to tiptoe around the subject of memory managers. The fact of the matter is that memory management is a very large topic, and I haven't got room here to do it justice. If you'd like to learn more about memory management under DOS, take a look at Chapter 3 of my book, *Troubleshooting Windows,* also published by Sybex.

You probably know that there are many kinds of memory these days. While you may not have heard of all of them, the three most common areas are:

- Conventional

- Extended—Windows 95, 98, and NT do most of their work with this type of memory

- Expanded, also called *Expanded Memory Specification* (*EMS*) or *Lotus-Intel-Microsoft* (*LIM*), mainly used by some programs written in the late '80s and even used by some modern games, oddly

Why so many kinds of memory? It's worth noting something before we go any further:

Nobody planned this. It just kind of "growed up that way."

We discussed the difference between RAM and disk memory earlier in this chapter. Just remember these three things, and you shouldn't have any problem distinguishing between them:

- RAM is volatile, meaning that it does not hold data when you turn a PC off, but disk drives retain the data stored on them even if the power is turned off.

- PCs tend to have a lot more disk space than they've got RAM space.

- As mentioned before, RAM is a lot faster than disk memory.

Designing a Computer's Memory: Zoning the First Megabyte

Many of the constraints that we face today have their roots in the past, a past over 17 years ago. Trust me, this isn't just a history lesson—some things IBM decided in the summer of 1980 affect how Windows 95, 98, and NT work today.

In the summer of 1980, IBM commenced the PC development project. The goal of the small design team was to build a "home computer" (that's what we called them in those days) that could compete with the Apple II. The PC had a good start in that it was based around a much more powerful chip than the Apple's. The chip that IBM selected was, of course, the Intel 8088, and one of the powerful features was that the 8088 could address ("talk to") up to 1024K—1M, or 1,048,576 bytes—of RAM. That limit shaped DOS, the need for DOS compatibility shaped Windows 3.x, and Windows 3.x compatibility constrained much of the Windows 95/98 architecture. (Think of it as "The Curse of Backward Compatibility.")

Planning a new computer is kind of like planning a new community. Before breaking ground on a new planned community, a zoning board or planning board determines what use will be made of all of the land space. Thus, the planners of a new community start from some unused land, perhaps fallow farmland. After acquiring the land, the next step is to plot it out into lots and then determine which lots will hold residential buildings, which ones commercial buildings, industrial buildings, local government, and so on. We could say that before any buildings are built, a planner must allocate addresses. Before any buildings get built, the planner decides that any buildings built on address X must be residential, and any on a given address Y must be commercial.

Interrupt Vectors and DOS

The bottom 1K is an area used by the CPU as a kind of "table of contents" of hardware support programs called software interrupts; the table of contents is composed of pointers to those programs called *interrupt vectors*. This is a fixed size of 1024 bytes—400 in hexadecimal. One interrupt points to the program that controls your disk drives, another to the video board, and so on. That 1K is reserved for the interrupt vector table no matter what operating system you're running, and no matter which

CPU you're using. Above that is DOS itself. I can't say exactly how much space DOS takes up in memory, simply because first of all, there are many versions of DOS and second, different CONFIG.SYS options use more or less space, and that space adds to the DOS space requirements.

Device Drivers

Directly above DOS loads a special class of programs called device drivers. Virtually every DOS-using computer uses at least one of these. (Under Windows, they're called "Windows drivers" and they are files with an extension of either .386 for Windows 3.x or .VXD for Windows 95/98.)

Device drivers are programs that either allow DOS to support a new piece of hardware or add new capabilities to an existing piece of hardware. Device drivers are loaded in the CONFIG.SYS file with the DEVICE= statement. Some examples of device drivers include:

- A driver to support a SCSI hard disk, a Zip drive, or a CD-ROM drive

- A mouse driver, like MOUSE.SYS, that enables your system to recognize and control your mouse

- The memory manager drivers that many people use, HIMEM.SYS and EMM386.EXE, which make your previously useless memory above 640K into a useful resource for your software

Sometimes the order in which you load device drivers is important in DOS. In any case, device drivers change the way that your system reacts to information from your system's hardware. When you're trying to track down a problem, it's always a good idea to boot with as few device drivers as possible, whether talking about DOS, Windows, or Windows NT.

Command Shell

Every operating system has a program that accepts inputs from users and reformulates them in a manner that the operating system can understand. In the case of DOS, the most common command shell was COMMAND.COM. It loaded after the device drivers, but before TSRs.

TSR or Memory Resident Programs

Under DOS, *terminate and stay resident* (*TSR*) programs did much the same thing as device drivers, but they were loaded from AUTOEXEC.BAT, so they loaded after any device drivers. (TSRs are no longer used—Windows handles multiple applications differently.) Here are a few examples of TSR programs:

- The program to use a 3270 or 5250 emulation board, hardware that attached your system to a mainframe

- A small utility that came with DOS called DOSKEY that remembered the last 20-or-so commands that you typed, so if you made a mistake, you could recall a previous command, edit it, and resubmit it to the PC

- Many virus and anti-virus programs

- Network shells and protocol stacks

- Many disk cache programs that speed up disk access

- Disk compression programs, like Stacker or DOS's Drive-Space, which were memory resident through either a device driver or TSR format

DOS relied upon TSRs and device drivers, but they came with a price: they took up your precious 640K conventional space that you needed to run DOS programs.

User Programs

Above the TSRs, you find the currently loaded program—Lotus 1-2-3 in the simple example I'm illustrating here. The remaining memory was then available for 1-2-3 worksheets. Again, the top address is 640K minus 1, rather than 640K, because we started counting at *zero, not one.*

The vast majority of DOS programs claimed that they could run only in the low 640K of your PC's memory, and that's largely true. That's why the 640K conventional memory area is so important; if your program can live only in conventional memory and the conventional memory is full, getting more memory won't help. One of my users once said of her computer, which had only 4MB of RAM at the time, "We need to buy more memory for my PC—I'm running out of memory." She was indeed running out of memory, but with an old application that couldn't use any more memory than 640K. As far as that application was concerned, the memory beyond 640K didn't even exist.

Many Windows users may be feeling smug at this point, thinking that they are no longer the prisoner of that silly 640K limitation. Unfortunately, Windows 3.1/Windows for Workgroups 3.11 are still pretty needy of conventional memory—they won't run without a certain amount of it. Windows 95 and 98 are less dependent on the bottom 640K *unless* you are running old Windows 3.1 and/or DOS programs; when that happens, Windows 95 and 98 revert to their old Windows 3.1 ways and get needy of lower memory space. To be completely free of the need for conventional memory, you'd have to be running Windows NT.

Video RAM

People used to say that DOS and DOS programs had a "640K barrier" or "640K limitation," but that's not actually true. DOS programs were almost all written to run on the 8088 chip (and, of course, its successors, the 286 and later). Any 8088 program can address up to 1024K of memory—in theory. There's nothing about DOS or the 8088 (or the Pentium II, for that matter) that requires the story end at 640K. Nevertheless, 640K is a very real barrier for most systems. Why?

The blame for 640K can be laid at the feet of those 1980 PC designers.

As used in the IBM world, the video board—the circuit board that acts as an interface between the CPU and the monitor—must have some memory on it. That memory is then shared between the circuitry on the video board and the CPU. The CPU "puts data on the screen" by putting data into this video RAM. The video circuitry sees the data in the memory and interprets it as graphical or textual information.

Video memory is memory used by video boards to keep track of what's to be displayed on the screen. When a program puts a character on the screen, or draws a circle on the screen, it is actually making changes to this video memory. IBM set aside 128K for video memory, but most video boards don't actually need or use that much memory space. The answer to the original question, however ("Where does the 640K limit come from?") is that the video RAM must go somewhere, and the original PC designers placed it from 640K through 768K. Even if there were more memory for user programs above 768K, most programs could not use that memory, and *here* we see the DOS limitation: in general, DOS programs needed *contiguous blocks of memory*.

Thus, DOS programs could start grabbing memory just above DOS itself and then keep going until they hit a pothole of some kind—and in this case, that pothole is the video memory—at which point they stop looking for memory. In general, DOS programs aren't smart enough to use fragmented memory. That's not true for Windows 3.1, Windows 95/98, and Windows NT programs.

We'll see later that a small workaround for this problem is to load TSRs and device drivers above 768K—a major reason to use memory managers.

You may be saying, "Why doesn't someone just build a PC with the video addresses higher up? Then there'd be more space for conventional memory." Unfortunately, that would not work. The reason is that a large number of programs are designed to directly manipulate the video hardware, and those programs are all written assuming that the video is where it's supposed to be—between 640K and 768K.

The current standard SVGA still uses the addresses from 640K through 768K, (A0000–BFFFF).

Used memory address space differs from total memory on board because video board manufacturers use a technique called *paging* (explained in the upcoming section "Video Memory and Paging"). Paging allows them to put lots of memory on the video board—lots of memory means better video—without taking up a lot of the CPU's total 1024K memory address space. I'll explain "ROM on board" in the upcoming section on the reserved area.

Note that the video board can be convinced to disable memory usage from B0000 to B1000, the addresses that the MDA uses. That's so your system could run two monitors. Although it's not a common use, some debugging systems for programmers let you test-run your program with program output going to a VGA monitor while displaying debugging information on a monochrome MDA monitor.

Newer PCI-based video boards are quite a bit smarter about using memory, so you can put multiple PCI-based video cards into a single computer.

Video Memory Layout The 128K set aside for video memory isn't just laid out as one big 128K block; rather, there are three separate and distinct video memory areas, as seen in Figure 3.9.

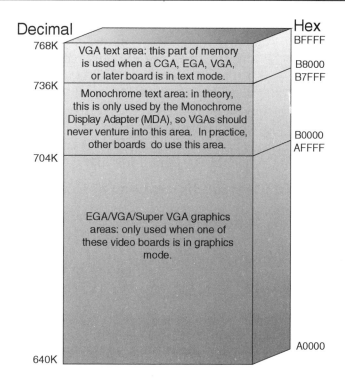

On current graphics boards, graphics activity takes place in the bottom 64K of the video area. This is accessed only when in graphics mode. The 32K from B0000 through B7FFF was designated for the Monochrome Display Adapter (MDA), although IBM MDAs used only memory from B0000 through B0FFF, a 4K area. Later MDA improvements like the Hercules Graphics Controller and clones used the entire 32K region.

Video Memory and Paging   As you look at the VGA graphics area, a question may be forming in your mind. Anyone who's bought a video board has heard of video boards with a megabyte or two or four of memory. Where does this memory go, given that there's only 64K of addresses set aside for VGA graphics? The answer is in a technique called *paging*. Recall that the video RAM is not on the motherboard, but rather on the video board. (Of course, if the VGA is integrated into the motherboard, the video RAM will be also.) Paging hardware on the VGA board allows the video board to present only 64K of its 256K (the amount of memory found on a normal VGA) to the CPU at a time. There are then four 64K pages on a standard VGA and, as it turns out, they each have a job. One page governs the blue part of the screen, another the red, another the green, and the final one the intensity of an image. The actual process of generating a complete VGA graphics screen looks something like the following:

1. Issue the command to bring in (page in) the blue 64K.

2. Draw the blue part of the screen in the blue memory page.

3. Issue the command to page in the green page.

4. Draw the green part of the image.

5. Issue the command to page in the red 64K page.

6. Draw the red part of the screen.

7. Issue the command to page in the intensity page.

8. Designate the areas that need high intensity and low intensity.

NOTE   Paging is a process used commonly in the computer world to shoe-horn a lot of memory into just a few addresses.

You'll see this notion of paging in many places in the computer world. Now that you've got a little insight into what's involved to make *one small change* to what's visible on a VGA screen, it's easy to understand why Windows—or any graphical program—can run slowly even on a fast machine. There's just so darn much housekeeping that's got to be done every time you do so much as move the mouse! That's why a graphics accelerator (discussed in Chapter 21, "Video Adapters and Displays,") makes so much sense for today's software; in fact, most current video boards are accelerators.

The System Reserved Area

In addition to device drivers, user programs, and video, the PC needs to steal from the CPU's memory address space for the following:

- Small amounts of memory called *buffers* or *frames* used by some expansion boards

- Special memory containing system software called ROM (read-only memory)

ROM (Read-Only Memory) We've talked so far about memory and RAM as if they were identical notions. As mentioned earlier, another kind of memory exists, which is not used as much as RAM, but is important nonetheless. Unlike RAM, which the CPU can both write data to and read data from, this other kind of memory cannot be altered. It can only be read, so it is called read-only memory. This is memory that someone (the computer manufacturer, usually) loads just once with a special device called a PROM blaster, EPROM programmer, or the like. So you can read information from ROM, but you can't write new information. (Well, you *can* write the information, but the ROM will ignore you. Think of ROM as a chip that can *give* advice, but can't *take* it.)

Why have a memory chip that you can only store information in *once*? Well, unlike normal RAM, the ROM has the virtue that it doesn't lose its memory when you turn the machine off—techie types would say that it is *nonvolatile*. We use ROM to store software that won't change. In essence, we can say that ROM on a circuit board contains the software that tells the system how to use a circuit board.

ROM chips are found on expansion boards like LAN, video, or scanner interface cards, to name a few examples. It is also found on the system board. The ROM on the system board contains a piece of software called BIOS, the basic input/output system. You may recall from earlier in this chapter that BIOS is a set of low-level programs that directly manipulate your hardware. Those programs are called "software interrupts" and are pointed to by the interrupt vectors at the bottom of RAM memory. DOS relies on BIOS in that DOS doesn't communicate directly with your hardware; rather, it issues commands through BIOS. Thus, when DOS reads your floppy, it does it by calling on the BIOS routine that reads your floppy drive. That's why the BIOS is so important: the BIOS determines in large measure how compatible your PC is.

As you'd expect, IBM's BIOS is *the* standard of compatibility. Back in the early '80s, the first cloners developed BIOS software that conformed in varying degrees to the IBM standard; so the question, "Does it run Lotus 1-2-3 and Microsoft Flight Simulator?" was the acid test of compatibility. Nowadays, I suppose it is "Does it run Windows NT?" Three companies—Phoenix Software, Award Software, and American Megatrends, Incorporated (AMI)—derive large incomes from their main business of writing *very* compatible BIOS software for clone makers. This has simplified the business of cloning considerably.

I've said that ROM contains software. As you know, software changes from time to time. Occasionally a problem can be fixed by "upgrading the ROM"—getting the latest version of the ROM-based software from the manufacturer. On older systems, it means opening up the system boxes and replacing a chip. On newer systems, it's easier—all you've got to do is to run a program that rewrites the ROM. You do need to be careful about this though, because the BIOS on some systems may be designed to run some specific hardware that is present on that computer only. If you replace the BIOS on a system like that, some of the devices on the computer may not function correctly (or at all).

For this reason, you've got to know exactly what version of software is in the ROM chips in the computers that you are responsible for. In a maintenance notebook, keep track of the serial numbers or dates on the labels pasted on the backs of the ROM chips in your PCs, or look at the PC when it boots up for an opening message from the BIOS including the software version of the BIOS. Whenever you install a board, note any ROM identifying marks. It will save you from having to pop the top to find out when you call for service.

ROM chips can usually be easily identified because they are generally larger chips (24- or 28-pin DIP chips), they are socketed (so they can be easily changed), and they often have a paper label pasted on them with a version number or some such printed on it. ROM chips are memories, albeit inflexible ones, so they require a place in the memory addresses in the reserved area from 640K to 1024K.

Flash RAM   Upgrading ROM is actually a bit different for most modern PCs. They store their BIOS on a special kind of memory chip called a flash RAM or, as the chips were once more commonly known, an electrically erasable programmable read-only memory (EEPROM, pronounced "double-E-PROM").

A flash RAM is the same as a BIOS, with the one very important exception that it is possible for a *program* to modify the BIOS. BIOS upgrades can then be done by just running a BIOS update program.

Flash RAM modules are a great convenience on laptops, because laptops are so crowded inside that prying them apart to change a BIOS chip is an enormous hassle. With a flash RAM, however, it's child's play: just run a BIOS update program supplied by the laptop manufacturer, and the new BIOS is installed.

Buffers and Frames You've seen that video boards require memory to hold the current video image. They're not the only boards that use memory addresses, however; other boards also need a little memory space reserved for them. A LAN board, for example, may require some storage space. Here are a few examples:

- Token Ring LAN boards have 16K of ROM that contains a sort of network-level BIOS. They also have a RAM buffer that can be adjusted to be as small as 8K or as large as 64K.

- Many Ethernet boards these days have a 32K RAM buffer on them; that RAM buffer must have an address within the CPU's address range.

- Some old ARCNet cards (it's an acronym for *Attached Resource Computer Network*) have up to 64K of ROM on them.

- Older VGA boards had 24K of ROM on them, but super VGA boards usually have 32K or 40K of ROM.

- Many hard disk controllers have ROM, particularly hard disk controllers that offer some kind of high performance or unusual capabilities, like SCSI or enhanced IDE host adapters.

- Scanner interface cards like the one supplied with the old Hewlett-Packard ScanJet included some ROM.

- It's going to be described later, but a kind of memory board called an expanded or LIM memory board contains from 16K to 64K of page frame memory space to buffer transfers into and out of LIM memory.

All of those memory pieces must fit somewhere in the reserved area from 640K to 1024K in the PC memory address space.

Before we leave this section, let's add reserved areas to our memory map, as in Figure 3.10.

FIGURE 3.10:

Memory map with
reserved areas
displayed

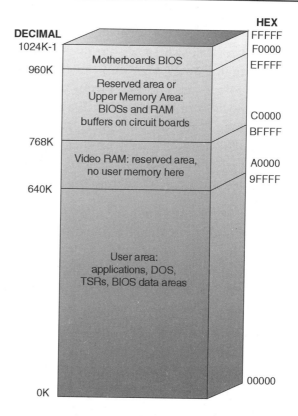

That's how the original PC designers laid out the first PC. The layout of that first 1024K became a standard that no software or hardware designer dared violate, at the cost of 100-percent PC compatibility. But with more complex PCs came more memory—and a chance to get to more space.

Believe it or not, we've only gotten as far as the 8088 in this review of how software uses memory. But don't worry, the rest goes more quickly!

Extended Memory

Not content with the 8088/8086, Intel began in 1978 to develop processor chips with power rivaling that of minicomputers and mainframes. One thing micros lacked (then) that more powerful computers had was larger memory address space. So from the 80286's introduction in 1981 onward, Intel chips could address megabytes and megabytes. An 80286 can actually talk to ("address") 16MB. An 80386 or later can talk to 4GB (1GB is 1024MB) of RAM. The term for normal RAM above the 1MB level is *extended* memory.

Why does memory above 1024K get a completely new name? Largely because the 286 and later chips have "split personalities": they can either address memory beyond 1024K *or* run DOS programs. To use memory above 1024K, the 286 and later chips must shift to a new processor mode called *protected mode*. Protected mode has lots of virtues, but one big flaw: when a chip is in protected mode, it's incompatible with an older 8088 or 8086.

You see, most early CPUs used in microcomputers were more glorified calculator chips than computers—the 4004, 8008, 8080, 8085, 8086, 8088, 80188, and 80186 all fall into this category. Intel intended that the 80286 should have some powers that were mainframe-like, and in particular should be able to talk to more memory, and to *protect* that memory.

You're probably familiar with the notion that large mainframe computers can run multiple programs at the same time. Basically, the memory space of the computer gets parceled out to the applications ("Okay, text editor, you get 120K, and database, you get 105K, and spreadsheet, you get 150K—no, you may *not* have more!"), and everyone's expected to stay in their places. But what about the odd program that accidentally strays from its area? If the text editor stretches a bit, it overwrites the database's area—

what to do? Or, worse yet, suppose your computer were acting as a server on a LAN, and one program (a virus, or the like) tried to peek into the memory of the LAN server program itself—the *program that contains the system passwords*?

NOTE   The 8088, 8086, and earlier chips cannot ever address memory above 1024K, so they can never have extended memory.

That's why memory protection is a good idea, and why mainframes have memory protection. The mainframe CPU has hardware built into it that keeps track of what application gets to use what memory. It's as if the CPU can put a "force field" around each program. As long as the program stays within its force field, it's okay. But if it tries to reach out of that area, it is stopped by the force field, and the CPU's "security system" is alerted that a protection violation was attempted. The operating system can then terminate the application (with extreme prejudice…). In less colorful terms, if an application tries to reach out of its space, the protection hardware senses this and stops the application, probably by ending the program and informing the user.

This memory protection is essential for any multitasking operating systems, and Linux, Windows NT, and Windows 95/98 multitask. Furthermore, they work with extended memory, so you'd think that they would exploit these "force fields."

They do, but in varying ways. The oddest approach to memory protection is the one that Windows 3.x used. You see, all this placing of "force fields" must be controlled by some program, which means that there's got to be some control over who gets to set up force fields and who doesn't. That leads to the notion in the Intel world of privilege rings, as you see in Figure 3.11.

FIGURE 3.11:

Privilege rings

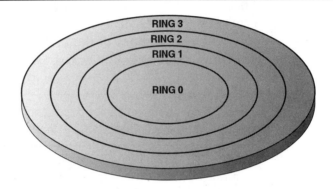

Programs in ring 0 can control anything. Programs in ring 1 can control other ring 1, 2, or 3 programs. Ring 2 programs only control ring 2 or 3 programs, and ring 3 programs can only affect other ring 3 programs. Logically, then, the operating system should be ring 0, and the applications should be ring 3. That's the way that most operating systems are built.

Sadly, Windows 3.x didn't do that. Under that operating system, all programs were granted ring 0 privileges. *All* programs. That meant that while all programs had memory protection, all programs also had the ability to override the memory protection. No Windows 3.x program was safe from any other Windows 3.x program, leading to an unfortunately familiar error called a *general protection fault* (*GPF*). Other operating systems, including Windows 95, are built better, but Windows 95 really only works protection-wise when you use programs written for Windows 95; older Windows applications still aren't protected.

Anyway, back to the history: until 1981, none of the Intel CPUs had this built-in memory protection, but the 286 and later chips all have the feature. These chips can also address memory beyond 1024K, but *only* while in protected mode. Again, the 8088, 8086, and earlier chips cannot under any circumstances address memory beyond 1024K, so they cannot ever have extended memory.

Basically, programs that run while in protected mode don't try to do *anything* with memory without first requesting memory blocks from the operating system. Then, once the OS has granted them an area in memory, the programs load their data into their spaces, and stay there.

And *that's* the problem.

Remember the basic problem with multitasking DOS programs—the idea that "DOS programs are spoiled children"? This whole notion of first asking the operating system—DOS—for permission before using memory is totally unknown in the DOS world. Programs written for DOS pretty much assume that they're the only program in the system, so they just take whatever they want without asking for it. So for the 286 to have memory protection, it would not only have to be a *different* chip, it would have to be an *incompatible* chip—incompatible with DOS and DOS programs, in particular.

Now, designing and releasing a new chip that was totally incompatible with any previous Intel offerings would be suicidal. So Intel gave the 286 and subsequent chips split personalities: when they boot up, they act just like an 8088, except faster. They can talk to 1024K, and no more: this 8088 emulation mode is called real mode. You'll sometimes hear people refer to DOS programs (when speaking of Windows) as "real mode" programs. That just means they were built for the 8088. Of course, despite the fact that no one buys 8088s any more, software is still written for the 8088 every day because of DOS's popularity. With a few instructions, it can shift over to protected mode and talk to lots of memory beyond 1024K. But, again, once the 286 or later chip is in protected mode, it can't run programs designed for real mode—DOS and DOS programs, that is.

You may be wondering, why don't they just write an operating system that uses this protected mode? As I suggested earlier, they have—that's the whole idea of Windows 3.x, Windows NT, and Unix. Windows 3.x programs can address 16MB; some Windows programs—the ones that use Win32s—can address even more than that, although they require a 386 or 486 computer to do so.

Does that mean that DOS programs absolutely cannot use extended memory? By no means. There is a class of DOS programs that use software called a *DOS extender* to allow them to use extended memory. Basically, a DOS extender is a tiny operating system that unlocks the door to extended memory and provides tools that programmers can exploit to use that memory. Examples include 1-2-3 version 3.x, AutoCAD, and many database programs. This use of extended memory explains why, for example, 8088-based machines could run 1-2-3 version 3.

As XT-type machines were based on 8088/8086 chips, they *couldn't* have extended memory. ATs and later machines *can*. When you see your computer count up to 16MB or 32MB or 64MB during the Power On Self Test, you've got some extended memory.

Let's take a simple example—an old 286 with 1024K of memory. There is 1024K of RAM, all of which must be given addresses. You recall from the earlier part of this chapter that the addresses from 0 to 640K are intended to be filled so that conventional memory space exists. Addresses 640K through 1024K must be left alone, because they're intended for memory from other sources, such as the video board and add-in cards. So, of the 1024K, 640K gets put in the 0–640K range. That leaves 1024K – 640K, or 384K. Where does that memory get placed? It goes in the extended memory addresses, making it extended memory.

Figure 3.12 shows how it would look on our memory map.

FIGURE 3.12:

Memory map with
extended memory
included

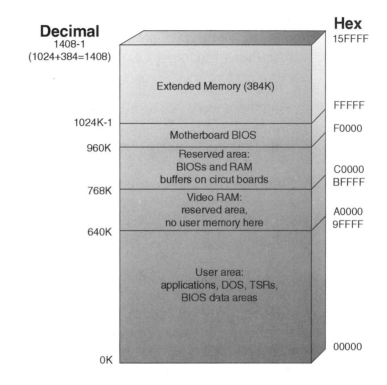

Decimal
1408-1
(1024+384=1408)

Hex
15FFFF

Extended Memory (384K)

FFFFF

1024K-1

F0000

Motherboard BIOS

960K

Reserved area:
BIOSs and RAM
buffers on circut boards

C0000
BFFFF

768K

Video RAM:
reserved area,
no user memory here

A0000
9FFFF

640K

User area:
applications, DOS, TSRs,
BIOS data areas

00000

0K

Not to belabor the point, but this breaking up of memory causes
a lot of confusion for users, so let me emphasize again why the
memory gets allocated this way.

The key to understanding the answer is in understanding that
there's a difference between *memory* and *memory addresses*.

Remember my analogy in the beginning of this section about
designing a computer versus designing a town? Well, let's suppose we're designing a town built on 1024 one-acre lots (conveniently enough). Suppose we zone the first 640 lots for residential

use, the next 128 for industrial, and the remaining 256 for commercial buildings. We now have addresses, and purposes for those addresses, but nothing *in* those addresses. Sure, there's now a lot called "200 First Avenue," but it's only a muddy rectangle of ground: send mail there, and it just sits outside and rots.

Once the town has been zoned, we start putting houses in the residential addresses—filling our PC with memory. But suppose a vendor of prefabricated houses shows up with 1024 houses? That's the situation that a computer designer is faced with when building a computer with 1024K of RAM. First, she plunks down houses in the first 640 lots, filling our "conventional" addresses. But the zoning board (that is, the requirements of PC hardware compatibility) precludes her from putting any of the houses in the top 384 addresses. (Here, the computer designer plays both the roles of the planning board and the prefabricated house vendor.) The top 384 lots do not have normal system RAM (houses) in them; rather, they have special RAM. That area is filled in for a PC with some RAM physically located on the video board, and perhaps some ROM located on the motherboard or add-in boards. That, too, is worth stressing: the memory in the video area isn't taken from the system's main memory; when you buy a PC with 1024K of memory, none of that memory is ROM or video RAM. A PC with 1024K of RAM actually has a fair amount *more* than 1024K of RAM, if you count the RAM on the video board and the ROM and RAM buffers on the expansion boards—and that memory is *not* counted when your system does its power-up memory count. There is simply nowhere to put the extra 384 houses, which is why XTs and PCs—8088-based computers—don't have more than 640K of system RAM.

Now let's move along to the 286 and later chips. They have memory limitations of 16MB or more, so now we've got to zone the addresses above 1024K. Continuing the town planning analogy, suppose that we've had our town operating for 30 years, when a community springs up outside our original 1024 lots. We'd call that a suburb of the town; it might have a different tax rate, be governed differently, and have different levels of access to the privileges accorded town residents. For example, suburbanites might have to pay a fee to use the town parks, whereas the town residents might be able to use the parks for free. So it is with extended memory; the addresses above 1024K are not accessible to the vast majority of DOS programs, as you've seen earlier in this discussion.

Return to the case of the vendor of prefab houses who finds herself with 1024 houses as she shows up in our new town. Again, she puts houses on the first 640 spaces and is then told that she cannot put houses on the top 384 addresses. "What will I do with these extra 384 houses?" she wails. "Take them out to the suburbs," she's told. So she puts the remaining 384 houses in the *extended* addresses, because the 384 addresses that she skipped from 640 to 1024 will be filled with buildings from another source.

So, getting back to the original question: what's happening with a 286 computer that counts up to 1024K on power-up? First, understand that 1024K is a count only of program memory. There is more memory in the computer—video RAM on the video board, system BIOS ROM on the motherboard, and ROM and perhaps small RAM buffers on add-in cards in the system—*that is not counted*. The 1024K fills up the first 640K and cannot fill up any of the addresses between 640K and 1024K, or the PC will have program memory in the same addresses as video memory or ROM. Just as you can't put two houses on the same lot, so also two separate memories wired to the same address would both malfunction. So the extra 384K of RAM gets addressed starting at 1024K and going up to 1408K.

TIP

You do not have to fill a lower memory address before filling a higher address; that's why you can have extended memory before filling the system's reserved area.

One more point that hangs some people up: I've said that the reserved area from 640K to 1024K contains memory, but it's not completely full. You'll usually find that there are plenty of unused addresses between 768K and 1024K, a fact that created the memory manager market in the first place. Many people seem to feel that all of the addresses from 0 through 1024K must be filled by *something* before any addresses above 1024K can be filled. But that's not true; you *could* build a computer with 128K of conventional memory, video RAM between 640K and 768K, ROM between 768K and 1024K, and 6MB of extended memory above 1024K. (You'd have trouble finding software that would run on it, but you could do it.)

Extended memory is simple for programmers to use, provided those programmers have a DOS extender or an operating environment that supports extended memory. The tremendous memory demands of programs today have made use of extended memory a necessity for many programs built in the '90s. But extended memory wasn't always easy to work with, which led to *expanded* memory.

EMS, LIM, Paged, Expanded Memory

In 1985, Lotus 1-2-3 version 1A was the best-selling software package in history. People used Lotus for everything. And Parkinson's Law ("work expands to fill all available resources") seemed to become an iron rule—more and more users found the 640K limitation a chafing one. Not as chafing, however, as the 1-2-3 copy protection scheme. Copy protection was a common practice among software vendors until around 1986. 1-2-3's copy protection required that you insert a key disk into your A: drive *whenever* you wanted to run 1-2-3. No key disk, no Lotus.

So, when Lotus announced 1-2-3 version 2, people were excited. At $495 a copy, it seemed a mite pricey; but Lotus made its users an upgrade offer. "Send us $125 and your version 1A key disk, and we'll send you 2," they offered. Well, at $125, that was hard to turn down. The downside was that you had to send in the key disk, which meant that you couldn't use 1-2-3 1A *or* 2 until the upgrade arrived; but Lotus FedExed the upgrades, and people only saw a day or so of downtime. (In case you're wondering, the world was a much different place then, and people didn't rely on PCs as heavily as they do today. Nowadays, of course, an upgrade offer that took a PC out of action for a day or two would be laughed off the market.) So hundreds of thousands of users got the 2 upgrade.

This is when it became clear that there was just one little problem: 1-2-3 version 2 took up more memory space than version 1A. Which meant that any spreadsheets that packed the memory up to the 640K rafters—and there were plenty—would not run under 2 for love or money. Worse yet, the users couldn't revert to 1A (they'd turned in their 1A key disks), leaving them stranded. "Golly," those users said. (Well, they didn't actually say, "Golly," but this book is rated "G" for general audiences.) Lotus realized that they'd better do something *fast*, so they called up Intel, the chip designers, and asked what could be done. Lotus and Intel developed a paged memory system (recall paging in the video discussion) that they called expanded memory. It involved buying a new kind of memory board that Intel built called an *AboveBoard*. (I'll explain the details on how it works in a bit.)

Let's finish our memory map by adding expanded memory off to the side of the normal memory column, as in Figure 3.13.

FIGURE 3.13:

Memory map with
expanded memory

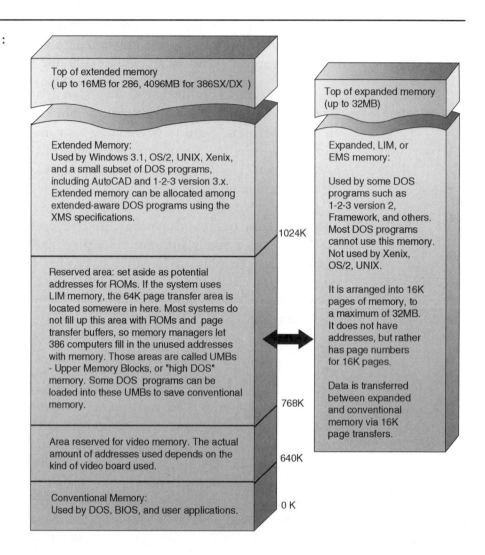

Top of extended memory
(up to 16MB for 286, 4096MB for 386SX/DX)

Top of expanded memory
(up to 32MB)

Extended Memory:
Used by Windows 3.1, OS/2, UNIX, Xenix,
and a small subset of DOS programs,
including AutoCAD and 1-2-3 version 3.x.
Extended memory can be allocated among
extended-aware DOS programs using the
XMS specifications.

1024K

Expanded, LIM, or
EMS memory:

Used by some DOS
programs such as
1-2-3 version 2,
Framework, and others.
Most DOS programs
cannot use this memory.
Not used by Xenix,
OS/2, UNIX.

Reserved area: set aside as potential
addresses for ROMs. If the system uses
LIM memory, the 64K page transfer area is
located somewere in here. Most systems do
not fill up this area with ROMs and page
transfer buffers, so memory managers let
386 computers fill in the unused addresses
with memory. Those areas are called UMBs
- Upper Memory Blocks, or "high DOS"
memory. Some DOS programs can be
loaded into these UMBs to save conventional
memory.

768K

It is arranged into 16K
pages of memory, to
a maximum of 32MB.
It does not have
addresses, but rather
has page numbers
for 16K pages.

Data is transferred
between expanded
and conventional
memory via 16K
page transfers.

Area reserved for video memory. The actual
amount of addresses used depends on the
kind of video board used.

640K

Conventional Memory:
Used by DOS, BIOS, and user applications.

0 K

On 8088 and most 80286 computers, you needed a specific
memory board to support LIM: two common examples of this
kind of memory board were, again, the Intel AboveBoard and the
AST RAMPage cards. On 386 and later machines, you can achieve
LIM compatibility with just software. That means that a 386 can
make extended memory behave software-wise like expanded

memory. Part of what Windows 3.1, Windows 95/98, and Windows NT can do for DOS programs is to provide them with some extended memory that behaves like expanded memory. (The motherboards of some 286s could do that also, but not many.)

So now we've seen conventional, extended, and expanded memory. Let's review what we know so far:

- Conventional memory:

  - Available to all PCs.

  - Limited to 640K.

  - Virtually every program can use this memory.

  - By default, DOS, device drivers, and TSRs loaded in conventional memory.

- Extended memory:

  - Only possible with machines based on 286 and later chips; was impossible with XTs.

  - A class of DOS programs could use it.

  - Used by Unix, Linux, Windows (3.*x*, 95/98, and NT).

- Expanded memory:

  - Also called Lotus-Intel-Microsoft (LIM) memory or Expanded Memory Specification (EMS) memory.

  - Could be used with PCs, XTs, ATs—any PC machine.

  - Useful under DOS *with programs that can use it*, such as Lotus version 2.*x* and WordPerfect 5.1.

  - 386+ computers can make their extended memory act like expanded, as can a few 286-based machines.

The only problem remaining is how to tell them apart. I always remember extended versus expanded by pronouncing the latter "ex*P*anded," so I can remember that it is "*P*aged."

PC Expansion Buses

"Pentium 32MB system with 4GB drive and AGP video for sale," reads a computer ad. The Pentium part is clearly the processor. The 32MB is the RAM part, as you've just read, and everybody (well, anybody reading *this* book) knows what a hard disk is. But what's AGP? AGP is the name of one kind of *expansion bus*. What exactly an expansion bus *is*, why you want one, and why you've got to worry about buses is the topic of this section.

What Is a Bus?

In order to be useful, the CPU must talk to memory, expansion boards, coprocessor (if the system has an external coprocessor), keyboard, and the like. It communicates with other devices on the motherboard via metal *traces* in the printed circuit, the copper lines that you'll see running around a board. That's how the SIMMs that probably live on your computer's motherboard communicate with the CPU, which is *also* probably on your computer's motherboard—they talk back and forth by shooting electrons along these thin metal traces

But how can *expansion boards*, which aren't part of the motherboard, be connected to the CPU, the memory, and so on? Through the *bus*, or rather, through one of the buses, the expansion bus or *buses*—modern computers may have multiple expansion buses.

Back in the early days of microcomputers, some computers didn't allow easy expansion. Take, for example, the early Macintosh computers. To expand a 128K or 512K Mac, you had to do some extensive engineering—which is why most people didn't mess around inside those computers. Any circuit boards that you wanted to add usually had to be mounted haphazardly inside the Mac's case; installing a hard disk actually involved disassembling the computer, soldering connections onto the Mac motherboard, and reassembling the machine. Making modifications difficult puts the user at the mercy of the modifier, because virtually all such modifications are done at the expense of the manufacturer's warranty and service agreement, if any—and they're expensive, because they require a technician.

You don't have to do such brain surgery on a PC, thankfully. PCs have expansion slots that allow easy upgrade. (By the way, today's Macs also have expansion slots, fortunately; in fact, Macs built after 1995 actually have the same bus as some PCs, the PCI bus that we'll discuss soon.)

Another disadvantage of the old Macintosh approach is that the average Joe/Jane can't do the modifications him/herself. This would be like you having to cut a hole in the wall of your house to find a main power line every time you want to use an appliance. Without standard interface connectors (that is, an outlet), you would have to find the power line, then splice the appliance into it to get power for the appliance.

This scenario, as we know, is silly, because we have standard outlet plugs. But it wasn't always unthinkable; when electricity first arrived, adding every new appliance involved some fancy wiring work. (Kind of like adding a station to a LAN today.) Nowadays, however, we have a nice standard way to add appliances. Any manufacturer who wants to sell me a device requiring electrical power needs only to ensure that the device takes standard U.S. current, and add a two-prong or three-prong plug. "Upgrading" my house, then (adding the new appliance) is a simple matter: just "plug and play." Many computers adopt a similar approach. Such computers have published a connector standard: any vendor desiring to offer an expansion board for this computer need only follow the connector specifications, and the board will work in the computer. Even the earliest computers included such a connector, first called the "omnibus connector," because it gave access to virtually all important circuits in the computer. "Omnibus" was quickly shortened to "bus," and bus it has remained.

So a bus is a communication standard, an agreement about how to build boards that can work in a standard PC. For various reasons, however, there are over a half-dozen such different standards in the PC world.

The First "PC" Bus

The PC wasn't the first computer based on a chip, not by about eight years. The first commercially available microcomputer was a computer called the Altair. It consisted of a case and a row of expansion slots. It was a backplane computer, with even the CPU on an expansion card. The bus that the Altair used became a standard in the industry for years, and in fact is still used in some machines: it was called the S-100 or Altair bus.

Although it was a standard, it wasn't ever true that every microcomputer used the S-100. The Apple II used a bus of its own, called the "Apple bus." The original 1981 PC model used yet another bus, with 62 lines. It came to be known as (you can see that this is something of a pattern, although a dull one) the PC bus.

The 62 lines mentioned above are offered to the outside world through a standard connector, as mentioned previously. These connectors are also called "expansion slots," because expansion boards must plug into these slots. Some PCs have had no slots at all, so they weren't expandable; other machines have three, and most clone-type machines have eight slots. Some machines offer 10 slots. The more slots, the better: expansion slots equal flexibility and "upgradability." (I know it's not a word, but you get the idea.) Let's take a minute, however, and look at what those 62 lines do.

Data Path

Now, remember that the original PC and XT were based on the 8088 chip. The 8088 had a data path (the "front door," recall?) of just 8 bits, so the PC bus only includes eight data lines. That means this bus is "8 bits wide," and so data transfers can only occur in 8-bit chunks on this bus. Expansion slots on a computer with this bus are called "8-bit" slots. Eight of the 62 wires, then, transport data around the computer.

Consider the importance of data path in bus design. The 8 data bits supported by the original PC bus would be pretty inadequate for a Pentium-based system; recall that the Pentium uses a 64-bit data path.

Could someone actually *build* a Pentium computer with 8-bit expansion slots? Sure. But every time that the Pentium wanted to do a full 64-bit read of data, it would have to chop that request up into eight separate 8-bit reads. *Really* slow. But it could be done, and in fact there are, as you'll learn later, designs almost as bad: most P5- and P6-based systems (which incorporate a 16-bit bus to this day), and the ISA bus you'll read about in a page or two, in addition to a 32-bit bus called PCI.

Memory Size

The original PC bus included 20 wires to address memory. What's that mean to us normal user types? Well, given that each one of those address wires can carry either a 0 or a 1 signal, then each wire can carry only one of two possible values. Since there are 20 of the address lines, the total number of possibilities is $2 \times 2 \times 2...20$ times. That's 2 to the 20th power, or just over one million. However, in a sense, you already knew that, because the 8088 can only address 1MB of RAM. All of those address lines are duplicated on the PC bus, accounting for another 20 of the 62 bus lines.

Memory or I/O Address?

The 20 address lines actually do double duty, because there are two kinds of addresses: the memory's addresses and *input/output addresses*. I'll discuss I/O addresses in greater detail in Chapter 6, "Installing New Circuit Boards (Without Creating New Problems to Troubleshoot)." However, at this point I'll mention that the computer must be able to tell when the address lines are transmitting a memory address versus when the address lines are transmitting an I/O address; one line on the bus designates which one it is.

Additionally, there are several other lines on the bus that tell whether the data on the bus has been read from memory (or an I/O device), or whether data is to be written to memory or I/O.

Electronic Overhead

Some bus wires just transport simple electric power; there are +5 volts, –5 volts, +12 volts, and electric ground lines as part of the bus. Why are those lines there? Simple: to power a board plugged into a bus slot.

There are also a few control lines, like Reset (which, as you'd imagine, resets the processor), clock signals, and Refresh, which controls memory refresh (more on that in Chapter 8).

Interrupts and Direct Memory Access Channels

Add-in cards sometimes need to demand the attention of the CPU; they do that via hardware interrupts or IRQ (interrupt request) levels. There are six IRQ levels on the PC bus, labeled IRQ 2 through IRQ 7. Each gets a wire on the bus. There are also IRQ 0 and IRQ 1, but they're not available on the bus.

Some of those add-in cards also need to transfer data to the system's memory quickly; they can do that via a direct memory access (DMA) channel. There are three DMA channels on the bus, labeled DMA 1 through DMA 3. There is also DMA channel 0, but, like IRQs 0 and 1, it's not accessible through the bus.

DMA and IRQs are both *extremely* important topics in PC upgrades, and I'm going to cover them in detail in Chapter 6.

We took a somewhat in-depth look into the first PC bus so that you're ready to see why the many buses that followed are improvements on the original PC bus, and to help you decide which bus is right for any of the machines that you buy.

The first enhancement to the PC bus came with the IBM AT; let's take a look at that bus.

The AT (ISA) Bus

When developing the AT, IBM saw that it had to upgrade the bus. One reason was because the 80826 is a chip with a 16-bit data path. They certainly *could* have designed the AT with an 8-bit bus, but it'd be a terrible shame to make a 286 chip transfer data 8 bits at a time over the bus, rather than utilize its full 16-bit data path. So they thought that it'd be nice to have a 16-bit bus.

On the other hand, there was backward compatibility with the PC and XT to think of: it would be tough to sell a lot of ATs if they couldn't use the hardware (and software) of the existing, established PC/XT world. So IBM came up with a fairly good solution: they kept the old 62-line slot connectors and *added* another 36-wire connector, placing it in line with the older 62-line connector to provide some of these features:

- Eight more data lines, bringing the data bus to 16 bits in width.

- Four more address lines, bringing the address bus to 24 bits in width. Two to the 24th power is around 16 million, so the AT's 16-bit slots could support up to 16MB of RAM, in theory.

- Four more DMA channels, 4 through 7.

- Five more IRQ levels: IRQ 10, 11, 12, 14, and 15. I'm getting a little ahead of myself, but I know that some of you will have an immediate question. You may know—and if not, you'll learn in Chapter 6—that there are *eight* more IRQs on a machine of this type; so why do we see only five on this newer bus slot? First, IRQ 9 is wired where IRQ 2 previously was, saving a bus line. What about IRQ 2? It's off the bus now because it's the line that makes possible the new IRQ lines. Second, IRQ 13 is dedicated to the math coprocessor, so there's no point in giving it any of the bus's wires. Finally, IRQ 8 is connected to the system's clock/calendar, so it also does not require a line on the bus.

These two-part connectors are called, as you'd expect, 16-bit slots. You can see these two kinds of connectors in Figure 3.14.

FIGURE 3.14:

8-bit and 16-bit bus slots

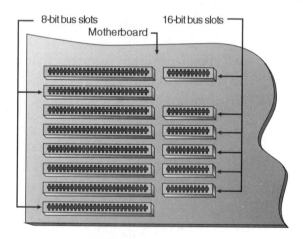

For a while, this 16-bit bus was called the *AT bus*, and you'll still hear some people use that name. Since 1988, however, most people have referred to these types of bus slots as *Industry Standard Architecture (ISA)* slots. You can tell the difference between an 8-bit and a 16-bit ISA board by looking at the edge connector on the bottom of it. Take a look at an 8-bit board, as you see in Figure 3.15.

FIGURE 3.15:

8-bit board

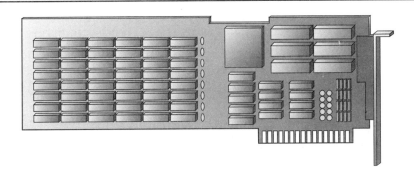

Notice that it has a single edge connector on the bottom. In contrast, look at a 16-bit board, like the one in Figure 3.16.

FIGURE 3.16:

16-bit board

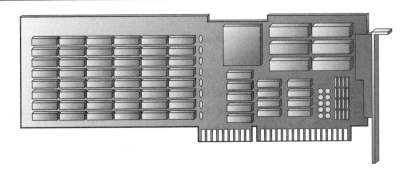

Since the 16-bit slots are just a superset of the 8-bit bus, 8-bit boards work just fine in 16-bit slots, which is a good thing—no modern PCs that I know of have the simple 8-bit slots. However, almost all *do* have the 16-bit slots, making 8-to-16 compatibility good in the unlikely case that you have an old 8-bit board around that you want to use.

Years ago, you would sometimes see a motherboard with both 8-bit slots and 16-bit slots. If the 16-bit slots can use 8-bit boards, why have any 8-bit slots on an AT-type machine at all? The reason is not an electrical reason, but a physical reason. Some older 8-bit boards have a *skirt* that extends down and back on the circuit board, making it physically impossible to plug an 8-bit board with a skirt into a 16-bit connector. You can see a board with a skirt in Figure 3.17.

FIGURE 3.17:

8-bit board with a skirt

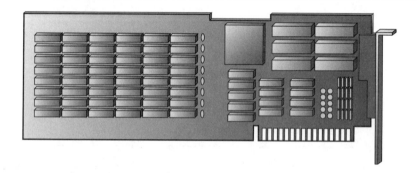

Just How Fast Is That Bus?

You learned back in the CPU section that different CPUs run at different speeds. You can't take a CPU rated to run at 25MHz and run it at 66MHz; it'll fail. (You can *try*—recall that it's called "overclocking"—but it's not a good idea.)

Buses have clocks, as well, and those clocks drive the boards inserted into their expansion slots. That suggests a question: how is it that any board pretty much works in any kind of computer?

Why does an ISA video board built for a 12MHz computer still work in a 400MHz Pentium II?

Part of the answer, you'll recall, is that the 400MHz Pentium II looks like a 100MHz chip from the motherboard's point of view; the 400MHz part is internal to the CPU chip. So the fastest bus you'd need for a 400MHz Pentium would be 100MHz. But for the rest of the story, let's return to 1985.

Early Buses Equaled Clock Rates

Prior to 1985, buses ran at the same speed as their CPUs. The PC ran at 4.77MHz, and so did the PC bus. "Turbo" XT clones that ran at 7.16MHz had buses that ran at 7.16MHz. When IBM released the 6MHz AT, then its bus ran at 6MHz, and so on.

But all of this variation in bus speeds led to a major headache for expansion board buyers. A board designed for the 4.77MHz PC might not (and often *did* not) work in the faster machines. Part of a PC upgrader's job was to know which PC bus speeds a particular board would work in.

Compaq Tries Not to Miss the Bus

Then Compaq released its Deskpro 286/12.

In 1985, IBM was selling the AT, as you've already read. The fastest version ran at 8MHz. Compaq, as the number one IBM cloner, decided to seriously outpace IBM with their new Deskpro 286/12—the 12 stood for 12MHz.

Now, okay, 12MHz isn't such a big deal nowadays. But back then, it was like Compaq today offering a Pentium that runs at 800MHz. Nobody else even came close. But what to do about the bus? If they built a 12MHz 286 computer with a 12MHz bus, then in all probability no existing boards would work. Who'd buy a fast computer that wouldn't work with any of the add-in boards on the market?

Compaq's answer: decouple the main clock from the bus clock. They ran the CPU and much of the motherboard at 12MHz, but ran the bus at only 8MHz. Expansion boards sitting in slots would see only an 8MHz environment, so the new Deskpro could be both fast *and* compatible. And ever since, that's how everybody builds their ISA slots, at 8MHz. That's why you've never got to worry about whether your computer is too slow for a particular board; from the board's point of view, every computer—including yours—runs at 8MHz. This *sounds* good, but…

The big drawback in having the expansion bus run at a separate clock speed than the external CPU bus is that some boards *should* run at CPU speed, like memory boards. Imagine that you've got a 100MHz Pentium. It communicates with its motherboard at 66MHz, because it's a clock-and-a-halfer. Suppose you want to put more memory on this system, so you buy an ISA memory card. (Please *don't* do this; this is just an example.) You pop it into one of the computer's 16-bit slots, and you'll have extended your memory, but *all memory accesses will be at 8MHz, not 66MHz*; every time you access memory on that board, your system will slow down to 8MHz. Yuck. And many of us use ISA boards on a daily basis to talk to our hard disks, video monitors, and local area networks. This is a major reason why we need something other than the ISA bus as a standard, and why there are so many different kinds of alternative buses available.

ISA's Not Enough: Mesozoic Local Bus

The first folks to try to set a new bus standard were, again, Compaq, a year later.

In 1986, Compaq introduced one of the first 80386-based desktop computers. Because the 80386DX is a 32-bit chip, Compaq wanted to exploit that power with a new bus slot. Remember, *they* were the guys who saddled us with the 8MHz bus slots in the first place. Standard-speed bus slots were still a good idea, but how to offer memory expansion boards that were 32-bit in data path and 16MHz (the computer's clock rate) in speed, unless by building an entirely new bus?

Compaq decided to just include a new 32-bit slot on the motherboard, a slot solely for use with a specific memory card that Compaq (and later, third-party vendors) sold. Some 386 cloners adopted this new bus format, but it never really caught on. Instead, each vendor developed its *own* 32-bit "standard." Intel had one it pushed for a while in the late '80s, AT&T had another, Micronics a fourth, and so on.

These buses all had several things in common:

- They had a 32-bit data path.

- They ran at the clock speed of the 386 computer—usually 16MHz, 20MHz, 25MHz, or 33MHz.

- They only supported one particular board, sold by the motherboard's manufacturer.

These buses came to be known as *private* buses or, later, *local* buses, because they were "local" to the processor, since there was no extra clock circuitry between them and the CPU. From 1986 to 1991, the main value of local bus boards and slots was, again, to accommodate memory for their specific computer. These were the remote ancestors of what we now call the *VESA Local Bus* (*VLB*) standard—what I think of as the "Mesozoic" version of VLB. I suppose that if you used one of these on a hard disk controller, you'd "Jurassic *park*" the heads on your drive. (Yeah, it was a lousy pun. But stick around; they get worse.) Discussion of VLB, by the way, is coming up in a bit; I just wanted to keep this discussion in at least moderately chronological order.

The PS/2 Bus: Micro Channel Architecture (MCA)

Not to be outdone by Compaq in the trendsetting department, IBM attempted to change the rules again on April 2, 1987 when they announced the PS/2 line. The PS/2 Models 50 to 80 (*not* the 25 or 30) got a new bus called the *Micro Channel Architecture* (*MCA*) bus, in order to facilitate faster data transfer within the computer, and to lower noise levels. (ISA is a *very* noisy standard, which is another reason why it hasn't gotten faster over the years.) It didn't catch on, but IBM pushed it doggedly for years before surrendering in the mid-'90s.

Introducing a new bus was a bold move (although perhaps not a very bright one), in that the MCA bus was completely incompatible with the old ISA bus. ISA expansion boards didn't (and *don't*) work in the PS/2 line. PS/2 buyers must be sure when buying a board that it's an MCA board, not an ISA board, because the ISA boards are completely useless in MCA machines.

What prompted this bold move? Well, some of the things that we've already discussed and a few others. MCA never really caught on that strongly (and we'll talk about why that's true in a minute), but some of the features that it offered have become essential for any advanced bus.

Better Speed and Data Path

As you'd expect, MCA tried to better ISA by hitting its weak points. MCA runs at 10MHz, not 8MHz. Not a great improvement, but an improvement.

MCA also supported either a 16-bit data path or a 32-bit data path. It actually has a "streaming" mode, wherein it can transfer 64 bits at a time.

Software Board Configuration

Anyone who's installed an older ISA board (installation of boards is, again, our main topic for Chapter 6) has almost certainly struggled with small DIP switches and jumpers. These are small hardware devices used to configure older ISA boards. They're a pain in the neck, because they're often hard to change around, and you've got to remove the PC's cover to get to them in the first place.

Micro Channel boards, in contrast, are software configurable—no jumpers, and no DIP switches. You just run one central configuration program, and you can set up a computer by clicking things with the mouse, rather than rooting around in the machine. This is a feature that was nice when it came out, but it's *essential* now—which is why Plug-and-Play hardware is becoming more and more ubiquitous.

Boards Can Share Interrupts

Once you start configuring boards, you'll find that the thing you're running out of most is interrupt levels. You can't put a mouse card on the same IRQ level as your local area network board, or your network connection could crash the first time that you move the mouse. That's because of how ISA was designed.

With MCA, it was *possible* to design a board that shares its interrupts with other boards. Very few Micro Channel boards *did* share interrupts, but it's possible. Why? Blame the people who write drivers. Despite the fact that several buses now support interrupt sharing, it's still almost unheard of, even in the most modern systems.

Bus Mastering Improves upon DMA

While I haven't explained *Direct Memory Access* (*DMA*) in detail yet, it's basically a way for expansion boards to quickly transfer data from themselves to the system's RAM, or from the RAM to the boards.

DMA's main goal in life is speed: it makes the PC faster.

DMA can't do one thing, however. Boards can transfer data directly to RAM, or RAM to boards, but *not* boards to boards. That's handled by a kind of "super" DMA called *bus mastering*. Bus mastering was not really supported by ISA (I say "not really supported" because you can have one, but only one, bus master card in an entire ISA machine), but MCA supported bus mastering.

Bus mastering is another one of those features that first appeared with MCA, but is *de rigeur* for any modern advanced bus.

MCA was neat because it was cleaner, as I said before, so it could transfer data at higher speeds than the current ISA machines. (I said "could" because it has the capability, but that capability never became important in its market.) It also included something called *Programmable Option Select* (*POS*). It allowed circuit boards to be a lot smarter about how they interact with the computer. For one thing, DIP switch and configuration problems lessen considerably. More on this in Chapter 6.

EISA (Extended Industry Standard Architecture)

The MCA turned out to be pretty unimportant in the market mainly because IBM locked it up six ways to Sunday, patent-wise. Companies couldn't clone the MCA without paying a Draconian 5 *percent* of their *gross* to IBM as fealty (oops, that's supposed to be "royalties") for use of MCA. Five percent of gross is probably more than most companies are making as *profits*. For the 5 percent, you didn't even get the plans for MCA. What's supposed to happen is *first* you spent hundreds of thousands of dollars figuring out how to clone MCA—IBM offered no help—*then* you got to pay Big Blue the 5 percent.

So Compaq talked eight other compatible makers (a group called "Watchzone"—Wyse, AST, Tandy, Compaq, Hewlett-Packard, Zenith, Olivetti, NEC, and Epson) into forming a joint venture to respond to MCA. They created yet another new bus, one called the *Extended Industry Standard Architecture* (*EISA*), which was intended to have MCA's good features, without sacrificing compatibility with the old AT (ISA) bus. Presumably building with it cost less than 5 percent of profits. It appeared in 1989 and still shows up on the motherboards of some systems that include both PCI and EISA slots. (PCI's coming up.)

EISA never got amazingly popular, but it was a kind of well-designed, solid bus that found its way into a lot of high-end servers. It was gaining some momentum around the mid-'90s, but it was overtaken by the newer, more powerful PCI standard.

What about EISA's features? Summarized, they include:

- 32-bit data path

- Enough address lines for 4GB of memory

- More I/O addresses, 64K of them

- Software setup capability for boards, so no jumpers or DIP switches—similar to POS

- 8MHz clock rate (unfortunately)

- No more interrupts or DMA channels

- Supports cards that are physically large, making them cheaper to build (smaller cards cost more to design)

- Bus mastering

Note that EISA is *not* a local bus, because it runs at 8MHz. It runs at that poky speed because it must be, recall, hardware compatible with ISA, hence the need for slow bus slots. EISA will also run DMA at higher speeds than will ISA. The lack of local bus means, however, that EISA memory boards aren't a possibility. EISA machines either need enough SIMM space on the motherboard for sufficient memory, or the motherboard vendor must design a proprietary expansion slot for a proprietary memory card.

Local Bus

In the XT and AT days, you expanded memory just by buying a memory expansion card, putting memory chips on it, and inserting the card into one of the PC's expansion slots. But by the time that PCs got to 12MHz, that easy answer disappeared. As I've already said, no matter how fast your PC is—20MHz, 25MHz, 33MHz—the expansion slots still only run at 8MHz.

Now, I've been kind of beating up on slow buses, but they're not all *that* bad, in reality. Most boards in expansion slots communicate with things that are fairly slow anyway, like floppy drives, printer ports, modems, and the like.

There are really only a handful of boards that benefit from really high speeds. I've mentioned memory. Another board that really needs to be able to blitz data around is a video graphics board. Take a moment and calculate how many pixels (dots on the screen) you've got on a 1024×768 video screen. Then consider that the CPU must shove them around perhaps dozens of times per second, and you can see that having fast access to the video board is a good thing.

Hard disk interfaces benefit from high speed, and in particular SCSI hard disk interfaces. Video capture boards are another type of fast board, and local area network cards are yet another candidate for local busing.

There are two main kinds of local bus around these days: the VLB bus and the PCI bus.

VESA Local Bus

As I've already told you, the local bus grew out of a sort of non-standard. Some manufacturers designed a special high-speed slot for the motherboard that will only accommodate a memory board. That was the first local bus.

A bit later on, vendors started including local bus slots for video cards and then selling you the video cards that fit into those slots. The problem was one of non-compatibility: the local bus video card on one machine was incompatible with the local bus video card on another machine.

Since the lack of cross-compatibility was getting in the way of video board sales, an industry group promulgated and promoted a local bus standard called VESA after the group's name—*Video Electronic Standards Association.* It saw some moderate popularity for a bit in the early '90s but died out around 1993. It's not likely you'll run across a VESA motherboard with a Pentium or later chip on it; VESA's heyday was in the 486 days.

The VESA Local Bus (VLB) was an important step in the evolution of computers—having a 33MHz bus was cool!—but it wasn't enough. VLB is really just a 32-bit, high-speed extension of the older, dumb ISA architecture. Sometimes I describe VLB as a "big, dumb bus."

VLB actually hurt the PC world, in a way. When I say that, I mean that VLB offered improved speed, but no better ways of *using* that speed: it just perpetuated the old PC approach of doing everything in a fast, brute force manner. Brute force here refers to the fact that the VLB did not offer most of the attractive features of the Micro Channel and EISA buses; it did not offer software setup of boards or bus mastering. VLB systems were still saddled with jumper-setting installations, and the CPU must baby-sit every single data transfer over the VLB bus. Forcing the CPU to manage each and every transfer keeps the CPU squarely in the middle of the system, making it a bottleneck to system performance.

PCI: Today's Bus

The PC world needed a better bus, because without a better bus there wasn't all that much sparkle in new CPUs. Intel was aware of this and was worried. Less sparkly new systems means fewer new systems *sold*, and that meant fewer CPUs sold. Whatever hurts the PC world hurts Intel sales, so Intel designed an even newer, faster bus slot called PCI, short for Peripheral Component Interconnect. (Obviously, Intel believes in clinging to at least *one* PC tradition—dumb acronyms.) PCI is a good bus for a number of reasons. You can see a PCI board in Figure 3.18 and a PCI bus slot in Figure 3.19. The smaller and lighter-colored slots are the PCI slots, the larger and older slots next to them are ISA slots.

FIGURE 3.18:

PCI board

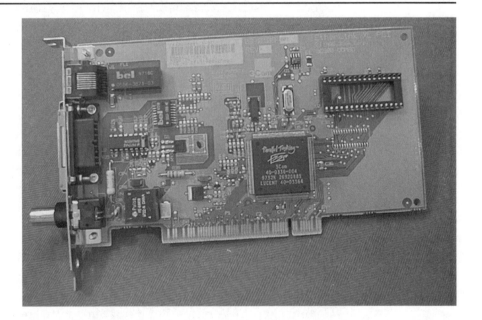

PCI and ISA bus slots

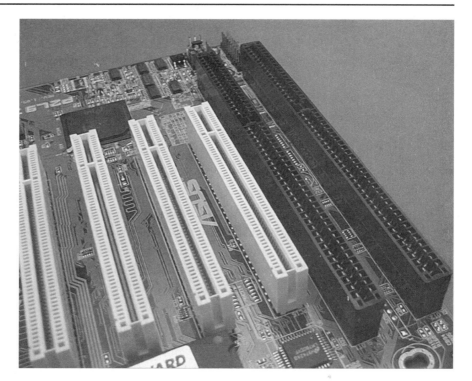

Processor Independence

The PCI bus doesn't directly interface with the CPU. Rather, it communicates with the CPU via a "bridge circuit" that can act as a buffer between the specifics of a particular CPU and the bus.

What does that mean? It means really good news for non-PC computer users. Macintosh PCs and RISC-based machines like the DEC Alpha are now coming out with PCI slots. That means a bigger market for PCI boards and an avenue for board makers to reach the PC, Mac, and RISC markets with a single board.

Wider Data Path

PCI distinguishes itself first because it is a 64-bit bus. PCI supports a data path appropriate for the newer Pentium-based computers, which require 64 bits at each clock cycle. PCI also supports a 32-bit data path, however, so it could be used in 486 systems in theory, although I don't know of any that used PCI.

High Speed

Like VLB, PCI runs to 33MHz. The net throughput of a PCI bus can be as large as 132MBps with a 32-bit board, or 264MBps with a 64-bit board. In theory one can run PCI at 66MHz, but I don't know of any chipsets that support that. Also, people whom I've talked to inside Intel are skeptical about how successful it'll be.

Backward Compatibility

Although ISA or EISA boards cannot fit in PCI slots, the common chipsets that support PCI also support ISA and EISA. That means it's easy to build a PC with PCI, ISA, and EISA slots all on the same motherboard. Typical motherboard configurations either support PCI and ISA or PCI and EISA. For some reason, the PCI/ISA motherboards support only a single processor, and in general the PCI/EISA motherboards support multiple processors. There's no engineering reason for that; it's just that the Intel chipsets for single processor systems support PCI/ISA and the Intel chipsets for multiprocessor systems support PCI/EISA. Nowadays, almost all motherboard makers use the Intel chipsets.

Bus Mastering

Like EISA and Micro Channel—and *unlike* VLB—PCI supports bus master adapter boards, paving the way for the "community of processors" that I referred to earlier.

Non–bus mastered data transfers require a lot of the CPU's time. For example, one author reports that a file transfer via an Ethernet network required over 40 percent CPU utilization when the Ethernet card was ISA, but only 6 percent with a similar setup and a PCI Ethernet card. Bus mastering is a good idea, and it's discussed in more detail in Chapter 6.

Software Setup

PCI supports the Plug-and-Play standard developed in 1992 by hardware vendors. There are, in general, no jumpers or DIP switches on PCI boards. There usually isn't even a board-specific configuration program. PCI setup is terrific on a Plug-and-Play system, but it can be a bit challenging on a non–Plug-and-Play system. There's an extensive discussion of that in Chapter 6.

PCI is a good architecture, and it is relatively cheap to build PCI boards. That's no doubt why it has become the premier PC bus.

Accelerated Graphics Processing (AGP): Local Bus Returns

The original 33MHz bus was the VLB bus. And what created the driving need for a fast bus? Video. The two things that *always* seem to drive demand for faster buses are memory and video. 33MHz was a pretty fast speed for a video board back when CPUs ran at 50MHz and 66MHz. Of course, they soon ran faster than that, so it shouldn't be any surprise that video is again screaming for more speed.

This time, however, Intel wanted to be out in front and so, before some competitor could come up with a faster bus for graphics, Intel did. They call it the *Accelerated Graphics Processing* (*AGP*) bus. (Note that the A stands for *accelerated*—PC Magazine and some others seem to want to rename AGP *Advanced* Graphics Processing.) It accomplishes two things:

- It is four times faster than PCI for transferring data. CPUs on systems with AGP video boards can, then, blast video images to their video board pretty quickly.

- It allows a video board to supplement its own video memory with some system memory.

Think of Accelerated Graphics Processing as just the latest local bus. In addition to speed, AGP allows a CPU to put a bitmap into regular old system memory and then be able to directly use and display that bitmap for the video board. You can see an AGP bus slot in Figure 3.20. The AGP slot is the one that's darker and slightly "offset" from the other, lighter PCI slots.

FIGURE 3.20:

Accelerated graphics processing slot

Intel clearly wants this new bus to be a very special-purpose bus. AGP motherboards only have one AGP slot, and as far as I can see, the chipsets only allow one AGP board. That's kind of a shame. In the past, new local buses *started* out as video or memory buses, but then SCSI host adapter vendors or other clever folks used the faster slots to do new and interesting things. More and more "interesting things" created a demand for faster buses, and soon large manufacturers responded with a new general-purpose bus. (That's how PCI appeared.) Because there's only one AGP slot essentially by definition, I suppose AGP won't turn out to be an intermediate step to a faster general-purpose bus.

PC Card (PCMCIA): The Portable Bus

Laptop computers are an absolute must for traveling professionals; I have personally owned *15* of them in the past 10 years. Laptops are great because they're almost 100-percent software compatible with their bigger cousins, the desktop machines. But until around 1995, laptops had an Achilles' heel: add-in circuit boards. I've felt for a good long time now that eventually laptops will be *all* that we'll buy, because they're portable and don't take up as much office space as do other types of computer cases. Currently, relatively low-quality video and a lack of expandability hampers laptop market penetration. However, PCMCIA (or the PC Card, as it was re-dubbed in 1995) removes the second objection. And the new 14.5-inch LCD screens on laptops like the IBM ThinkPads and the Digital Ultra HiNote 2000 take a serious bite out of the first.

Over the years, it's been customary to add two kinds of hardware to laptops: an internal modem and more memory. But, because laptops never had standard expansion slots, laptop owners had to go to the laptop vendors and buy their proprietary memory—often an expensive proposition. But cost wasn't the worst part of this lack of a standard bus; in fact, cost was less important than the fact that lack of a standard bus led to the lack of a *market* for add-in boards for laptops.

Japanese vendors of memory products tried to address this problem in the late '80s by founding the *Personal Computer Memory Card Industry Association,* or, in its hard-to-remember acronym, *PCMCIA.* (The head of the group once said, "If we'd have known how important the acronym would be, we would have picked another name. Some people just remember *People Can't Memorize Computer Industry Acronyms.*") After a few years of apologetic wincing, the association renamed the bus the PC Card bus; people still say PCMCIA, however, so you'll hear both names. A PC Card/PCMCIA board is about the size of a credit card, but a mite thicker. You can see some PC Cards in Figure 3.21.

FIGURE 3.21:

PC Cards

Type 1, Type 2, and Type 3 PC Card Slots

The standard proved extremely popular—so popular, in fact, that hardware vendors said to the PCMCIA, "Why not also support modems or hard disks?" So the memory card interface became a "PC Card Type 1 slot." A Type 1 (or "release 1," in some references) slot is 3.3mm thick, with a 68-pin connector. Again, most Type 1 cards are memory cards, either normal RAM or "flash" memory cards loaded with a piece of software (for example, 1-2-3 and WordPerfect are available on these cards).

The need for internal modems drove the Type 2 slots. While developing Type 2, an important software standard called Card Services and Socket Services was developed—more on that later. Type 2 cards can be designed to act as an object placed directly into the PC's memory address space. Why is this different from Type 1 cards? If you bought a software-on-a-card Type 1 card, like the WordPerfect example that I just gave, then the PC would have to copy the data from the Type 1 card into the PC's memory before it could run the software on the card. That took time, *and* used up some of the PC's memory. With Type 2, that's not necessary, making startup faster and increasing the amount of free memory available. Type 2 cards are 5mm thick, allowing more space for more complex circuitry. Type 1 cards will work in Type 2 slots.

Shortly after, the PCMCIA defined a Type 3 specification, one flexible enough to support removable hard disks. The main difference of Type 3 is that it's a lot thicker—Type 3 cards can be 10.5mm thick. Most laptops have room for either two Type 2 cards or a single Type 3. When purchasing Type 3 cards, be sure that what you're buying meets the standard—there are so-called "Type 3" hard disks that are 13mm thick. Xircom has also made a very cool combination modem/Ethernet card that actually has the connectors right on it. The connectors made it thicker, so they went to a Type 3 form factor. Yes, it takes up both slots, but it's very nice not to have to carry cables around to attach to the card.

Socket and Card Services

The PC Card standard supports the ability to remove and install a PC Card "on the fly." All other buses require that you power down the computer before installing or removing a card, but PC Card supports *hot swap*—the ability to swap out a card while the computer is running. The computer supports this capability with two levels of software support.

Socket services is the PCMCIA name for the BIOS-like software that handles the low-level hardware calls to the card. They are loaded like a device driver. While cards can be swapped without powering down, changes in cards *do* require a reboot. (PC Card version 2.01 is the most recent version, but it is rumored that version 3 will allow changes without reboots.)

Card services is a higher-layer set of routines that manage how the PC Card memory areas map into the CPU's memory area. They also provide a high-level interface supporting simple commands that are common to almost all PCMCIA cards, commands like erase, copy, read, and write data.

In Windows 3.x and Windows NT, you've usually got to reboot in order to enable or disable a PC Card. In Windows 95/98, however, you can change most PC Card cards at will, using them and removing them without rebooting. DOS requires a separate third-party set of programs to provide card and socket services; Windows 95/98 and Windows NT 3.51 and 4 have built-in card and socket services.

PC Card Features

Let's compare PC Card to the other buses that we've discussed, feature for feature.

- **Memory address space.** PC Card supports a 64MB addressing ability. (This is because the bus uses 26 bits for addressing, and two to the 26th power is around 64 million.) This will be adequate for current machines, but will look sparse in a few years, as more demanding operating systems like Windows NT become more popular.

- **Bus mastering.** PC Card does not support bus mastering or DMA.

- **Plug-and-Play setup.** PC Card allows—*requires*—that hardware setups be done with software. Because of the physical size of a PC Card, you'll never see jumpers or DIP switches.

- **Number of PCMCIA slots possible in a single system.** Most of the other buses support no more than 16 slots. The PC Card standard can, theoretically, support *4080* PC Card slots on a PC. In reality, most laptops only have two Type 2 slots. Some, like Digital's HiNote 2000 laptop, have four slots (yet another reason why I own one).

- **Data path.** The data path for PC Card is only 16 bits, a real shame but one that is fixed in a later version of PC Card called CardBus.

- **Speed.** Like other modern bus standards, PC Card is limited to a 33MHz clock rate.

Years ago, it seemed to me that the smaller size of PC Card cards, coupled with their low power usage, made the new bus quite attractive not only for laptops, but also for the so-called "green" PCs, desktop computers designed to use as little power as possible. I figured that for that reason, PC Card could become an important *desktop* standard as well as a laptop standard. That didn't happen in the desktop world, *but* in the laptop world be *sure* that whatever new laptop you buy has at least two Type 2 PC Card slots.

Or, even better, if it's a relatively new laptop, make sure it's got two *CardBus* slots.

CardBus

First specified back in 1994, this is PC Card: The Next Generation. CardBus slots' main claim to fame is that they have a 32-bit data path rather than a 16-bit data path. They're also backward-compatible: a CardBus slot can accommodate a PCMCIA card without trouble. Other features include the following:

- They run at lower voltage—3.3 volts and lower, compared to 5 volts and lower for PC Cards.

- They can transfer data at up to 133Mbps (megabytes per second)—they're 4 bytes wide and run up to 33MHz.

- In theory, you can do bus mastering and actually have a CPU on the CardBus card, although I haven't seen that in any cards yet.

If your laptop supports CardBus, buy CardBus cards when possible. I've run 100 megabit Ethernet with both PC Card and CardBus boards, and the CardBus is noticeably faster. But be sure your operating system supports CardBus. That's the hard part—only some CardBus cards work under Windows NT 4.0. Just about all CardBus cards work under Windows 98.

Table 3.5 summarizes the differences between the buses.

TABLE 3.5: Bus Types

Bus Type	Maximum Speed	Number of Data Bits	Number of Address Bits	Software Setup?	Bus Master?
PC bus	10MHz (on some clones)	8	20	No	No
ISA bus	8MHz, faster on some clones	16	24	No	Only on one board
MCA	8MHz	32	32	Yes	Yes
VESA	33MHz	32	32	No	No
EISA	8MHz	32	32	Yes	Yes
PC Card	33MHz	16	26	Yes	No
PCI	33MHz	32	32	Yes	Yes
CardBus	33MHz	32	32	Yes	Yes
AGP	66MHz	32	32	Yes	Yes

FireWire/IEEE 1394

I think that FireWire (IEEE 1394) gets the award for "Best Name of an Emerging Standard." FireWire is a new kind of serial bus. It was designed to replace serial ports, parallel ports, SCSI ports, and any other port that you'd use to connect a device to your computer, with a universal 6-wire connector (two power, four data) that will work for any of these.

Like the Universal Serial Bus (discussed later in this chapter), FireWire is based on a daisy-chain physical topology, meaning that devices will be able to cascade from hubs attached to the card in the computer. FireWire supports 63 devices, however, instead of the 127 that its cousin interface, Universal Serial Bus, supports.

Although it's not required that this card be PCI, the couple of early 1394 cards that I've seen on the market are PCI. When the cards are commercially available, it's probable that they will be PCI to take advantage of the local bus. This bus will need all the speed it can get, because it's intended to work with devices that will require a lot of bandwidth, such as scanners, video cameras, and the like. Although, as I said, it's designed to replace all other ports, FireWire is designed to cope with devices that require high and variable amounts of bandwidth. The standard is designed to support speeds of 100Mbps, 200Mbps, and 400Mbps, varying the path that the signal takes in order to avoid traffic problems.

Configuring sounds simple, but how about *powering* those dozens of devices? Well, two of the six wires in the cable are power lines, so your add-in devices can technically use your computer's main power supply. However, it will probably be a good idea to get many devices with their own power supplies in order to keep the strain on the system power supply to a minimum.

That's about all there is to say for a standard that's neither finished nor implemented. FireWire looks like a good bet. It should certainly simplify the process of adding or removing drives and other devices to your system, and it's meant to be fast. However, it's a little early to tell how it's going to work in practice. The standard is out, and there are few devices with an IEEE 1394 interface. Windows 98 was *supposed* to have 1394 support built in but doesn't seem to. Watch this space as more happens…

System Clock

The system clock, mentioned before, is the "metronome" for the computer system. It was implemented on the early PCs on a chip called the 8284A. The 8284A was located near the 8088 on the system board of most XTs. The early AT-class machines had an 82284 chip.

Why would you care where the clock chip on your computer is? Well, in the old days, you could install a reset switch using the clock chip. Nowadays, however, modern PCs have the clock circuit integrated with other chips on the motherboard.

Well, we've taken a good long look at what's on the PC's motherboard; now let's look at the other things inside your machine.

Power Supply

U.S. line current is 120 volts *alternating current* (*AC*). The PC, like most digital devices, is set up to use *direct current* (*DC*) at 5 and 12 volts. The conversion process is done by a *power supply*. The power supply is the silver or black box to the rear and right of the inside of the PC case. Power supplies are rated by the amount of power that they can handle: the earliest PCs used 63.5-Watt power supplies, and some servers ship with 375-Watt power supplies. Your power supply determines in part how many peripherals you can put into a PC. Chapter 9, "Power Supplies and Power Protection," discusses selecting, replacing, and installing a power supply. The power supply can't always cope with environmental conditions, so that chapter also discusses add-on products: surge suppressors, spike isolators, and uninterruptible power supplies. You can see a power supply in Figure 3.22.

FIGURE 3.22:

The power supply

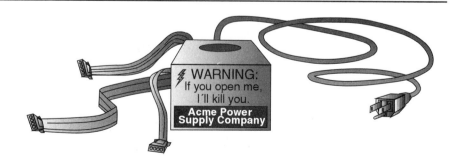

As I mentioned, the power supply is easy to find in the system: it's the silver or black box in the back of the chassis that has a label on it that warns you, in five languages, not to open the power supply.

Keyboard

The PC is useless without an input device, and the keyboard is one of the two input devices (the other being a mouse) used by most of us. The keyboard is subject to a number of hazards, however, so it needs maintenance—and sometimes replacement. The PC's keyboard actually contains a microprocessor of its own, called the Intel 8041, 8042, or 8048. Taking apart a keyboard isn't hard—but reassembling it *is*, and truthfully there's little point in it nowadays, because keyboards are very cheap. You can get a regular 101-key enhanced keyboard for under $20, or an ergonomic "broken" keyboard for under $75. PS/2 and "standard" keyboards are electronically identical. The only difference is the connector. Most new keyboards have either a PS/2 connector and an adapter for the larger DIN connector, or the larger DIN connector and an adapter for the PS/2.

Mouse

Nearly every computer is equipped with a *mouse*, an input device used for pointing and selecting. The *graphical user interfaces* (*GUIs*) on modern operating systems can work with just a keyboard, but they are cumbersome without some kind of dedicated pointing device, and the most common is a mouse.

Mice come in the mechanical and optical variety. The mechanical is the more popular type, and mice interface either via a serial port, PS/2 port (which is also serial), a "bus mouse" port, or with a cordless (usually serial) interface.

Controllers in Your Computer

Other than the motherboard, power supply, and outside peripherals, the only things left—important things—are the expansion boards in your computer. With the exception of memory boards—and the majority of modern computers don't use memory boards, they put all of their memory on the motherboard—most of the boards in your system are *controllers* of some kind.

What's a Controller?

Every peripheral device, whether internal or external, needs something to handle communications between it and the computer. Sometimes these items are called controllers, interfaces, ports, or adapters. For example, a hard disk needs a hard disk controller, the keyboard needs a keyboard controller, and the video display needs a video adapter (controller). The main reason that there are controllers is that they do these things:

- Allow for well-defined industry standards (well, *fairly* well-defined industry standards) by creating a specification that all controller boards are designed to fit and operate in

- Match data transfer speeds between peripherals and the CPU

- Convert data from the CPU's format to what the peripheral uses, as well as amplify the electronic signals between CPU and peripheral

Adaptec's 2942W PCI SCSI bus mastering host adapter is as different from IBM's original XT-type hard drive controller as a Corvette is from a Chevette, yet 99 percent of the software that was written to work with the latter works just fine (or better) with the former. The underlying hardware is a lot better, and a lot *different*, so you'd imagine there would be big compatibility problems, but the hardware has been housebroken to respond to CPU requests in the same manner (although faster) as the old Xebec-designed IBM controller. Ditto video controllers designed by ATI or Paradise: they respond to the same software as IBM's original CGA, EGA, or VGA, but are cheaper and generally work faster. Using controllers with well-defined interfaces makes building compatible hardware possible.

Remember that notion of well-defined interfaces: together, all of these interfaces define what is called "PC compatible."

You can understand the value of well-defined interfaces and modularity by looking at an automobile. Perhaps (if you're my age) you learned to drive in an old '60s car, or, if you're my Dad's age, you learned to drive in a car from the '40s. Both of us now drive cars designed and built in the '80s. The old '67 Country Squire station wagon (okay, so now you know I grew up in the suburbs) was a radically different car from the Honda that I now drive. The Hudson my dad drove in the '40s was even more radically different from his current Toyota truck. But despite our education on different cars, we're both as well prepared to drive a '90s car as someone who's only driven '80s cars, because the *interfaces* are the same. Because I don't interact directly with the car, but rather with the dashboard gauges and controls, I don't need to know the innards of the motor. If somebody stole into my backyard tomorrow and replaced my internal combustion engine under the hood with an engine that runs on air, I wouldn't know the difference.

Most peripherals are considerably slower than the CPU in transferring data. Even the hard disk, for example, is thousands of times slower than the CPU. Most microcomputers (like the PC) have been designed to control everything in their systems, to do *all* of the computing work, but that's not necessary. One of the first examples of that appeared with a company named Cogent Data Systems. Years ago, they made a hard disk controller for AT-class machines with memory and a microprocessor right on it: the main CPU just makes a request of the hard disk controller, then (with the right software) goes off to do something else while waiting for the controller to do the job. Eventually, the controller informs the CPU that it's finished with the data request and that in fact the controller has already transferred the data into the CPU's memory. Truthfully, the "speed matching" benefits of controllers haven't been really exploited in the PC world yet, because intra-PC "distributed computing" doesn't really exist—again, *yet*. The power of advanced buses like PCI was supposed to change that, but the change is coming slowly—partially because board designers tend to keep doing the same thing over and over again, and partially because Intel encourages people to put work on the CPU's shoulders. That way, consumers will demand faster and faster CPUs or multi-CPU systems.

Another controller function is simple amplification. The CPU speaks its own electrical language to other chips on the motherboard. But it's a language without too much power—a CPU wouldn't be able to "shout" loudly enough to be heard any appreciable distance on a LAN. Devices like video monitors need signals massaged into forms that they can use. Again, controllers serve this function.

A typical system will have a keyboard controller, a video controller, controllers for the floppy and hard disks, and interface controllers for LAN, mouse, parallel, and serial ports.

Controllers Aren't Always Separate Boards

Here's a common misconception: a controller must be on a board all its own.

Not at all. The keyboard controller is generally not a board; it's just a chip on the motherboard. The hard and floppy disk controllers *used* to reside on separate boards in XT-type machines. Then, the earliest AT-class machines put the hard disk controller and the floppy controller on the same board. Another board held the parallel port, another the serial ports, yet another the joystick, and so on. Nowadays, motherboards incorporate all of those functions and more in a single extremely integrated circuit board. These "integrated motherboards" are terrific price/performance values.

For Those Who've Read Earlier Editions...

You may be raising your eyebrows at that last comment. What am I doing singing the praises of integrated motherboards? Didn't I once warn readers away from them? Yes, that's true: I *used* to be very much opposed to putting everything on the motherboard. So why the change? Well, I *like* integrated motherboards now for the same reason that I disliked them before: compatibility. Nowadays there is an informal standard for these "do-it-all" motherboards; you can easily find a replacement motherboard for your Apex Clones computer from Acme Clones. My old objection stemmed from the fact that the folks who used integrated motherboards (Compaq, Dell, Gateway, and those folks) all built integrated motherboards that were not interchangeable. Hence, if a Dell motherboard went bad, you were stuck buying a replacement from Dell, at a higher price than you would have paid had the motherboard been a more generic item. New manufacturing techniques have improved the quality of these motherboards, reducing the risk of failure of one or more of the integrated components.

Let's take a quick look at the common controllers in the system.

Video Adapter

To allow the computer to communicate with a display monitor, a display adapter must be inserted in one of the PC's expansion slots.

The basic kind of video board you find in the PC world even to this day is an enhancement of an old 1987 video standard called the *Video Graphics Array,* or *VGA.* It can display information either in a text-only form or in a graphical form.

Why is a 10-plus-year-old standard still current? Mainly because of the lack of a market leader. For years, graphical standards were created by IBM, video boards with names like MDA, CGA, PGA, 8514, EGA, and the now-common VGA. You can see a video board in Figure 3.23.

FIGURE 3.23:

Generic video adapter

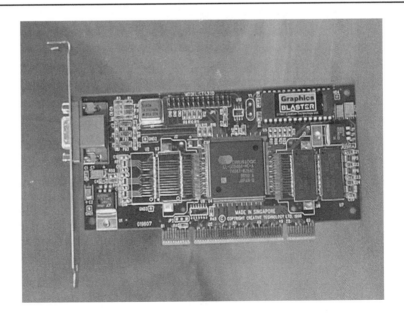

But the lack of industry centralization has left us with no new standards; instead, there are a lot of video boards that exceed VGA's capabilities, boards generically called "super VGA" boards. Even though they're all lumped under the name super VGA, they're all different, making it difficult sometimes to find *drivers* (the software that controls the video board) for a particular board.

Despite their variation, video boards all have several distinct components, as you see in Figure 3.24.

FIGURE 3.24:

Video board components

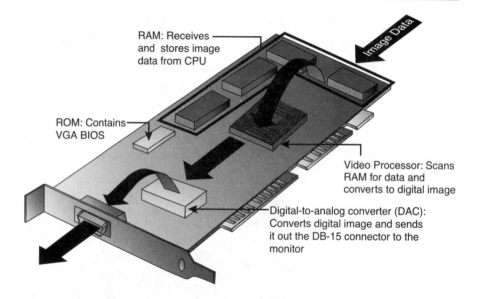

The video board contains video memory, as you learned earlier in the discussion on memory. The CPU places the video image into the video memory. A video chip on the video board then examines the data in the video memory and creates a digital image signal. That digital signal is then converted to an analog signal by a chip called the DAC, the Digital-to-Analog Converter, another chip on the video board, and the resultant signal goes out the connector on the back of the board and into your monitor.

Video boards are distinguished by their *resolution*, which is the number of dots (pixels) that they can put on the video screen and their *color depth* (the number of colors they can display at one time). More dots means sharper pictures. They're also distinguished by how many different colors they can display on those dots and by how much work the CPU must do in order to create images.

You see, on older video boards, the CPU had to do all of the work of picture creation; it had to place each and every one of the pixels on the computer's screen. Nowadays, however, video boards include special circuitry called *accelerator* or *bitblitter* chips that can speed up video operations considerably. Many video boards also have hardware support for 3D rendering, allowing games to have a real-time realism that quite literally could not have happened in an under-$1,000,000 machine 10 years ago. Other video boards include TV tuner support and/or video capture hardware. You'll learn more about video in Chapter 21.

SCSI Host Adapter

The *small computer systems interface* (*SCSI*) is a general-purpose interface that allows you to install just one circuit board in your system and use it to act as the "manager" for hard disks, tape drives, optical disks, CD-ROMs, digital cameras, scanners, and even a few kinds of printers. As you'll learn in Chapter 16, "Understanding and Installing SCSI Devices," SCSI can support up to seven devices.

Floppy Disk Controller and Disk Drives

The floppy disk drive is an essential peripheral, if an ancient one. The 1.44MB format has existed since the mid-'80s and has improved not a whit since then. Why? As with video, there's no market leader in the PC hardware area that can simply put a stake in the ground and say, "This *is* the new floppy standard." There are some great floppy technologies that store upward of 250MB on a floppy, including the popular Zip drives, but none has really "caught on" and created a critical mass. And sadly, there may *never* be an industry consensus about high-capacity floppy drives, because most modern machines can boot from CD-ROM, allowing firms to bypass floppies altogether for distribution purposes and ship CDs instead, even in cases like operating systems when the distribution media must be bootable.

Since they are peripherals, floppies require an interface. This interface is called a floppy disk controller. These will, in general, not give you many problems. They *do* fail occasionally, however, so you need to know how to recognize this and address it, since virtually all PCs have the floppy drive circuitry on the motherboard. In the case of a floppy drive controller failure, you'd have to either get a new motherboard (the excuse you've been looking for to upgrade to a newer processor!) or disable the floppy controller circuit and try to find a stand-alone board that can act as a floppy controller. (More info in Chapter 15, "Understanding, Installing, and Repairing Floppy Drives.")

The much more fertile ground for failure lies in the floppy disks and floppy disk drives themselves. Floppy drives can require speed adjustment, head alignment, and head cleaning. Speed adjustment and head cleaning can be done simply and cheaply. Alignment can require some specialized equipment and is not always cost effective, but it will be discussed later. Floppy drives are so very cheap these days that it's usually pointless to do anything but replace them, but it never hurts to know a bit about a component's innards.

Beyond adjustment is the problem of compatibility among drive types. There are three kinds of 3.5-inch floppies, something you'll need to know if you're working with old floppies. Almost all new floppies you'll come across are the 1.44MB floppies. Chapter 15 talks about floppy installation and the kinds of maintenance that you can do on a floppy drive.

CD-ROM Drive

Once a nice add-on, a CD-ROM drive is now a necessity for any home machine and a recommended peripheral for a business machine. (Why don't all business machines need CDs? Because most businesses have networks, and CD-ROM drives can be networked, lessening the need for every machine on the network to have a CD-ROM drive.)

CD-ROM drives are essential because virtually every software package today is distributed only on CD-ROM. Chapter 24, "An Overview of CD-ROM," examines these issues and explains how to choose and install a CD-ROM drive.

DVD Drives

Digital Versatile Disk (DVD) drives are the next technology level for CD-ROMs. Where CD-ROMs can store up to 630MB on a 4¾" disk, DVDs can store up to 17GB (17 *billion* bytes).

DVDs use the same kind of interfaces as CD-ROMs, either EIDE (as is most common) or SCSI. They are backward-compatible, which means you can read CD-ROMs in DVD drives.

Hard Disks and Hard Disk Interfaces

Most of your system's software and most of the data that you've created lives on your system's *hard disk.*

Years ago, you bought a hard disk by its size and by its interface. Normal-duty hard drives used an interface called ST-506. High-performance drives used a drive interface called the *Enhanced Small Device Interface,* or *ESDI.*

Nowadays, you still choose a hard disk by its size (see, some things never change) and by its interface; but the interface will either be the SCSI or the *Enhanced Integrated Drive Electronics* (*EIDE*) interface. The vast majority of PCs currently use EIDE, since virtually all PC motherboards have not one but *two* EIDE interfaces built right on them. Each EIDE interface can support two drives. As there are two EIDE interfaces, then, the average PC can support four drives right out of the box. Most folks have at least one CD-ROM drive and a hard disk drive, so they've got two "openings." Good candidates to fill those openings are perhaps more hard disk drives, a DVD drive, or perhaps a tape drive or Zip drive for backups.

When a hard disk fails, your main concern shouldn't be the hard disk. Hard disks are easy to replace and install, as you'll learn in the chapters on hard disks. Your main worry should be the *data* on your drive. Data recovery is the subject of Chapter 14, "Recovering Data and Fixing Hard Disks."

Older disk subsystems used hard disk controllers—ST506 and ESDI interface boards were controllers—but the newer SCSI and

EIDE interfaces do not use controllers; rather, they call them "host adapters" because their job is much simpler than the job of a controller. Basically, a host adapter just rearranges the data so that it can be accepted by the bus. Much of the circuitry that once sat on the controller now lives on the disk drive itself.

Some hard disk failures—precipitous drops in speed or loss of data—can be addressed at either the controller or the drive level. Problems like head crashes can be avoided with some simple techniques explained in Chapter 13, "Preventive Maintenance for Your Hard Disk." Even the ultimate disaster—a reformatted hard disk—can be reversed in some cases. Chapter 14 provides more information.

Tape Drives and Other Backup Devices

Thinking about skipping this part and going on to parallel ports, eh? It amazes me how many people don't have tape drives on their systems. It's quite common for PCs to sport 8GB or 11GB hard disks, but no tape drive. Once you bought that 8GB drive, how did you plan to back it up, anyway—with floppies? (Let's see, now; 8192MB divided by 1.44MB per floppy equals... too many floppies.)

If your computer doesn't have a backup device, then ask yourself: can I really afford to lose all of this data? If the answer is no, then think about getting a tape drive. Tape drives install in the same kind of slot that you'd put a floppy drive into, and they have one of three kinds of controllers. Some tape drives run off a SCSI host adapter; others connect to the floppy disk controller; and a few have their own proprietary controller. Or consider the Jaz drive from Iomega, a tool I like and use quite a bit. It's a backup system that uses removable hard disk cartridges. The benefit to this drive is that if you have a hard disk failure, you can reboot with any drive and actually run your programs and read your data directly from the Jaz drive the same way you would with a hard drive. We'll discuss backups more in Chapters 10 through 14.

Parallel (Centronics) Interfaces/IEEE 1284

The most common method of attaching a printer to a computer is through a very simple interface called the *Centronics* interface. The interface was named after Centronics, the company that invented it in 1976. It's more commonly known today as the "parallel port." Another way to connect printers to PCs is through a serial port, and I'll cover them in the very next section.

PCs can support up to three parallel ports. They are named LPT1, LPT2, and LPT3; the name refers to Line PrinTer one, two, or three.

Originally, parallel ports were unidirectional. They transported data only from the PC to the printer. There were *control* lines that led status information from the printer back to the PC, but data only flowed in one direction. For years, some parallel ports have had the option to move data backward, from the printer to the PC. That's important for two reasons:

- New printers can now send textual status information to the PC. Thus, it is possible with some printers for the printer to tell the PC, "I'm low on toner," or "I am a LaserJet 6."

- Modern PCs put things on the parallel port that aren't printers. Removable media drives and CD-ROM drives are two examples of things that can have parallel port options.

Some parallel ports not only support bidirectional data flow, they also support increased data transfer speed. These ports are called *enhanced* parallel ports, or EPP interfaces. Some parallel ports shanghai a direct memory access (DMA, explained in Chapter 6) channel and become *Enhanced Capability Ports* (*ECPs*), offering even more speed. The IBM PC's parallel port was originally a proprietary interface, but it's become so widely used that there is now an "official" standard describing it, IEEE 1284. You'll sometimes see parallel ports or parallel cables referred to not as "parallel" but as "IEEE 1284 compliant."

Most printers only require a simple unidirectional parallel port. But if you've got a bidirectional, EPP, or ECP port, then those more advanced ports work fine with any kind of printer.

Parallel ports themselves won't usually pose much of a problem, once you've got them installed and configured. But the printers themselves, well, that's another story.

The actual printer is the greater source of failures: printers employ a large number of moving parts. While printers are much more reliable nowadays than they were in the bad old days of daisy wheel printers, there's always the odd paper feed or "black page" problems.

Worse yet, as printers get more powerful, their software gets more complex. It's a shame that so many people fail to exploit the full power of their computers simply because WordPerfect or Word isn't programmed to do the exploiting.

Modems and Communication Ports

Besides parallel ports, the other common printer interface is the serial port. Serial ports are also known as async ports, comm ports, or RS-232 ports. They are bidirectional interfaces for low to medium speed data transfer; most serial ports can't transfer data faster than 115,000 bits per second, but there are some serial ports that can transfer data at 345,000 bits per second.

A serial port's main job isn't usually printers, however. The two most common uses for serial ports are to attach mice or modems to your PC. Modems allow your PC to communicate remotely with other computers via phone lines and to act as a fax machine.

The DOS names for the communications ports are COM1 and COM2. It's theoretically possible to have COM3 and COM4, but they're limited in their usefulness. (More on that in Chapter 6.)

RS-232 is a source of many cable problems: either the wrong cable is configured, or environmental problems (electronic noise) cause communication errors. Figure 3.25 depicts an IBM RS-232 adapter. Data communications troubleshooting is an entire book in itself—several books, in fact—but I cover the essentials in Chapter 19, "Modems and Serial Interfaces."

FIGURE 3.25:

IBM RS-232 adapter

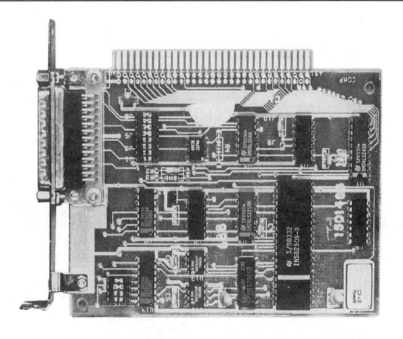

Serial ports are the PC's general-purpose input/output devices. Hand-held machines like the PalmPilot attach to the PC via serial ports; digital cameras do; some scanners do, modems, mice, printers… it seems on many systems that there are too many things to attach to a serial port and not enough serial ports. *That's* why they invented USB.

The Universal Serial Bus (USB)

It's far too easy to run out of serial ports. For instance, say you have a serial mouse and a modem. No problem, right? The mouse goes on COM1, the modem on COM2. But what happens when you add a smart UPS, a device that can communicate with your computer for diagnostics and software control, to the mix? At this point, you have the choice of either losing your modem (it's possible to navigate a graphical operating system with the arrow and Tab keys, but it's no fun), losing some of the UPS's capabilities, or adding another COM port with an add-in card and hoping that one set of software will function with a non-standard interrupt. If you don't set up COM3 to use another interrupt, then it will conflict with COM1, but not all software is prepared to deal with that.

It's a puzzle, and the problems associated with adding serial ports could keep people from using some devices that need them. But the picture has started changing, albeit slowly. It's possible that soon you won't need to worry about the number of serial or parallel ports that you have because devices are slowly being designed that use another interface called the *Universal Serial Bus* (*USB*). If you've purchased a PC since 1997, you *probably* have one or two USB ports on your computer. If the USB standard takes hold, it could make using the plethora of new PC-related devices a little easier. But before it works, we need three things: PCs with USB ports, operating system software that supports USB, and USB-ready peripherals. We've got the first already (new PCs mainly have USB), so the first condition's in place. Windows 98 supports USB but Windows NT *doesn't*, so we're halfway there on the second condition. But there are very few USB devices around so far. I'm hopeful that will change soon, however. But I'm getting ahead of myself—what is USB, anyway?

What Is USB?

The USB, developed by Microsoft, Compaq, National Semiconductor, and 25 other USB members, is intended to take the place of the keyboard port, parallel ports, game port, and serial ports by replacing them with a single connection from which you can daisy-chain *more than a hundred* USB-compatible devices. This single connection is even simpler than a nine-pin serial port, since it has only four pins. Physically, it looks either like one device (such as a keyboard) plugged into the computer, and then everything else plugged into a hub on the keyboard, or a hub plugged into the computer and then everything plugged into the hub. As in SCSI, each device can be plugged into up to seven devices and/or hubs at a time. You can see a USB connector and cable in Figure 3.26.

FIGURE 3.26:
USB cable

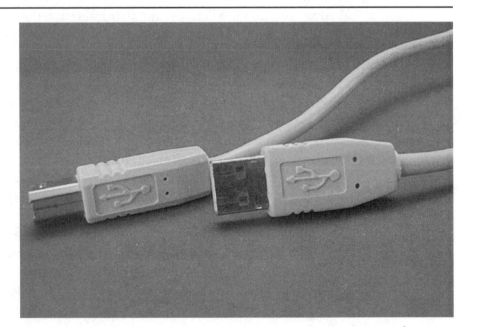

Either way, it is designed to be much simpler to put together; rather than installing cards for many of these devices, you plug them into a hub and call it a day. If they're true Plug-and-Play devices (as many are planned to be) then a PnP OS should recognize them with very little help from you.

NOTE   Windows 98 has (and future versions of Windows NT will have) USB support with device drivers built into them.

USB is designed to be faster than serial ports as well. The standard describes an interface that can transmit up to 12 megabits per second, as opposed to the 100+ kilobits per second of a serial interface. The speed is meant to keep up with telephony applications, such as low-resolution video conferencing. (For higher resolution video, you'd need IEEE 1394.)

USB recognizes four types of data transfer, divided by the type of peripheral device that uses them: bulk, interrupt, asynchronous, and control. Printers, scanners, and digital cameras, which must send a great deal of information to the PC at one time, are bulk transmitters. Keyboards and joysticks, which people use to sporadically transmit small amounts of data that must be processed immediately, use interrupt transmittal. Telecom applications use asynchronous transmissions, which must be delivered in a steady stream and in a certain order.

The hub determines which devices are plugged into it at any given time, and from that it deduces how much bandwidth each needs, based on the kind of data transmittal the device is trying to perform.

Who Needs It?

Just about anyone should be able to benefit from the new interface, once appliances that are pin-compatible with USB become available. The ability to plug in a number of devices with only one port will be particularly useful to laptop owners, since laptops have limited real estate into which to plug additional devices. You don't need lots of available ports, and the hub should be easier to get to than the back of your computer. It's intended to work for just about anything that you can plug into a port in your computer: speakers, modems, keyboards, and the like.

What's Available?

As I said before, USB ports are present on most new machines, even laptops (my Digital Ultra HiNote 2000 includes such a port, and Toshiba and IBM have notebooks with USB as well). As for devices to plug into USB ports, I've only seen a few. Intel sells an inexpensive videoconference camera that's connected via USB. Kodak sells a digital camera that can download its data to a PC with USB. Logitech has a page scanner that's USB. I've worked with those three devices and found that they work quite well under Windows 98. I'm told there are USB keyboards as well, but I haven't tried them. Altec Lansing sells an interesting set of speakers with sound generation circuits inside them that attach to a PC via USB that seem to work quite well.

System Clock/Calendar and Configuration (CMOS) Chip

The system clock/calendar keeps the date and time even when the unit is turned off. Older XT-type systems required a separate board to support a clock/calendar, but virtually every modern computer has the feature built right into its motherboard as standard equipment.

The Clock/Calendar and CMOS Battery Issues

The clock/calendar is built on the same chip as the configuration memory circuit. Configuration memory, more commonly called the CMOS, is a small amount of memory that holds information that the computer needs in order to get started in the morning.

When you first turn your computer on, it must figure out what hardware it contains so that it can control that hardware. There's a list of the hardware in your system in the configuration memory. Most memory, however, is *volatile*, a 75-cent word meaning, "When you remove power from the memory, the memory forgets whatever was sitting in it." That's why the memory has a battery attached to it, so that the memory doesn't lose power, so it can remember while the rest of the PC slumbers.

Of course, with time, that battery will run down in power, the configuration memory will forget what kind of hardware is in your system, and the clock/calendar will no longer keep correct time. You'll have to install a new battery, of course, to fix the problem; but here's a common question about batteries and the clock.

People will tell me that their computer can no longer remember its configuration information, forcing them to re-enter the configuration information into the computer every time that they turn the computer on. (They should just replace the battery but, for whatever reason, they haven't.) I explain that they've got to replace the battery, but they disagree, saying, "No, the battery's fine."

"How do you know that?" I ask.

"Because the computer keeps correct time," they respond. They're arguing that because the clock circuit still runs, the configuration memory circuit should still run. It's a good argument, but it misses the fact that running the clock requires less power *by far* than does running the configuration memory. As you may have learned from painful experience, it's possible for your car's battery to have enough power to run the interior lights and the radio, but not to crank the starter.

The vast majority of the time, the only problem from the clock will be with (1) the battery or (2) the software to use it.

The battery causes problems, of course, when it runs down and no longer keeps time. Replacement is no problem, save for some clock/calendar boards that *solder* the battery on the board. You kind of have to wonder if the people who designed this either (1) have parents who are first cousins or (2) want to be able to charge you $120 three years later to replace the battery. Many motherboard manufacturers nowadays have a soldered battery, but that may not be terrible news, because some of those motherboards also support a standard external battery; you just move a jumper on the motherboard to disable the soldered battery and enable the connection for the external battery. (More on CMOS and batteries in Chapter 6.)

By the way, don't confuse the clock/calendar that I've discussed here with the clock that raps out the beat that the PC dances to—the one I mentioned a few pages back based on the 8284 or 82284 chip. They're different circuits. The CPU clock doesn't run when the power is off to the PC, in contrast to the clock/calendar, which continues to run all of the time, courtesy of its battery.

PC BIOS/CMOS and Year 2000

Clock/calendar circuits are fairly simple devices, so you'd never suspect that they could paralyze a computer—but some can. Many PC BIOS programs and clock circuits are not Year 2000 (Y2K) compliant. That means that come January 1, 2000, some PCs will start behaving strangely. In most cases, "strange" just means that they'll be unable to recognize dates after 1999 and so will be forever stuck in some incorrect year: they'll think the year after 1999 is 1900. (Others will think it's 1981, the earliest year most BIOS programs can represent.) But there's a group of PCs built in the 1993–1995 time frame that have a much more severe problem. You see, first the clock will change the year from 1999 to 1900. But *then* the BIOS will see the year 1900 and know that it's wrong and so assume that the PC is having a major breakdown *and refuse to boot at all*. If you've got one of these lucky ones, check with the manufacturer of your BIOS—either Award, AMI, or Phoenix. For information on identifying a BIOS with Y2K problems, contact the companies at their Web sites:

- `www.ami.com/y2k/`

- `www.phoenix.com/year2000/`

Last year Award and Phoenix merged, so you can find information about either BIOS at the Phoenix Web site. To get information on the Y2K issue you may need to poke around their Web site a bit since, like all Web sites, things have a tendency to move around. By the way, should you decide that you do need a BIOS upgrade, you'll need to contact your system or motherboard manufacturer to obtain it—Phoenix doesn't sell directly to end users.

Local Area Network (LAN) Adapters

Put more than two PCs into an office, and soon you see the urge to merge: PC networks are everywhere. (Got one in your home yet? No? Don't worry; you will soon.)

Networks make it easy to share data, printers, modems, and access to the Internet. But the first step in networking your computer is to put a LAN board in every PC. They come in several flavors. The most popular kind of network is called Ethernet, and there are Ethernet boards for all of the PC buses. Second is Token Ring; Token Ring boards are usually about two to three times more expensive than Ethernet boards, and you tend to see them in large companies more than in smaller firms. Oldest in the network world of the big three is *ARCNet*, something that's pretty much dying out, but you may see one or two of them around.

There's an awful lot to say about networks, but I'm afraid I can't cover them in this book, save to offer advice on installing LAN boards as boards *per se*; you'll find that advice in Chapter 6. For extensive coverage of network troubleshooting, take a look at *The Complete Network Upgrade and Maintenance Guide*, also from Sybex.

Sound Boards

Years ago, Creative Laboratories introduced the Sound Blaster, a board that allowed your PC to emit squeaks, squawks, squeals, and explosions. What good was that? Well, games, mostly. But sound cards have come a long way since then. Nowadays, you can buy sound cards that can actually produce quality superior to that of a CD player.

Sound cards are more than just a plaything. Multimedia in PCs is becoming a business tool—it's already an education tool. For many applications, clicking on the OK button will bring up an animated window of a teacher explaining how to use a program's feature, rather than just the simple text screens that we used to see in older systems.

That will be a bit friendlier, but *understanding* what the person in the animation is saying in the first place requires good sound equipment. The wrong sound card/speaker combination can make voices sound like broadcasts from bad AM radios; the right combination can provide the audio version of virtual reality.

NOTE	Chapter 22, "Play It Loud: Sound Cards," discusses sound cards in detail.

Other Common Boards

That's about it for the most commonly found boards. You may also see the following boards:

- **3270 or 5250 emulation cards**. Despite improvements in IBM's *SNA* (*Systems Network Architecture*) in the past few years, it's probably easiest to get your PC to talk to the mainframe by making it look like a dumb 3270 terminal, the familiar IBM "green screens" that you see in offices around the world. ("Dumb" in terminal parlance means it lacks stand-alone processing power.) Attachmate, DCA (the IRMA guys), and others do a nice business filling this need. Plug one into your system and your PC can hook up to the same old coaxial cable that's been serving IBM mainframe users for years. Just because you're attached to your company's AS/400, however, doesn't mean that you've got an emulation board. Another way to get to your firm's mainframe or mainframes is over the LAN. In that case, your LAN has a machine on it acting as a *gateway*.

- **Tape controllers**. If you want to install a tape drive for backup to your system, you'll need a controller of some kind. Many tape drives can use the floppy controller, but it's not recommended—such tapes are painfully slow, and remember that you bought the tape to quickly back up the hard disk. Some tapes are internal, some external. I'd recommend external because then you can buy a tape controller board for *all* of your machines, then only buy a few of the expensive tape drives themselves, and let the users share the occasional use of a tape drive. (That's "occasional" only when compared to the frequency of use for the hard disk. Backups should be near daily if you generate work of any importance at all. Yes, I know it's a pain, but can you *really* afford to lose a whole day's work? And are you sure you'd be able to recreate it if you did?) The higher-capacity tape drives all run off SCSI, but some cheaper tapes attach to the EIDE interface on your system.

- **Scanner interface cards**. Graphical and character scanners are becoming more and more popular. And with good reason—desktop publishing really shines with graphics. Today's audience demands lots of visuals. Scanners offer a way to add pictures to text in a computer-readable form. Character scanners allow easier entry of text in computer-readable form. Some scanners run off a SCSI host adapter (the preferable alternative, because there are no new boards to install once you've already got SCSI), but many scanners still use proprietary interface cards.

Finding Your Way around inside Your PC

Well, now you've learned some things about how your PC's put together. You know the names of some of the pieces in your system. But how do you take apart *your* computer and figure out what's where? It can be tremendously disorienting to try to figure out what's in a computer the first time. Here's my approach.

Once you get the top of the computer off, find the easy stuff. What do I mean when I say "easy?" These things:

- The power supply
- The fan

- The floppy drives

- The hard disk or disks

- The CD-ROM and tape drives, if present

Once you've figured those out, only the boards are left. Figuring out the boards doesn't seem so difficult once the rest of the system has been identified.

Finding the Easy Stuff

The power supply is easy to find. It's a silver or black box with a fan on it, and it's attached to the power switch. As I've noted before, it probably has a label on it that says in five languages, "If you open me, I'll kill you."

The floppy drives should be simple to locate: just look at the slots in the front of the computer. The hard disk will be a box that whirs and has no slot in the front of it. CD-ROMs are, I hope, also simple to find; they're usually well marked. (Although there's an apocryphal story about a tech support person who was called by a user because the user had broken his "cup holder." You know, the retractable one that CDs also happen to fit into.) Tape drives are likewise usually labeled.

That leaves the tougher-to-identify components: the circuit boards. Have you started drawing your diagram yet? If not, get cracking on it. It's really simple to screw up a computer by taking it apart and not being able to put it back together.

Locating Things on the Motherboard

Your system's motherboard, once you remove it, will have a few points of note. I'll use a typical Pentium II motherboard for examples.

The Power Connection

Be sure to note where the power cables from the power supply go to the motherboard, as I mentioned in the last chapter. Putting them back together backward will smoke the motherboard. You see the power connection in Figure 3.27.

FIGURE 3.27:

Motherboard power connection

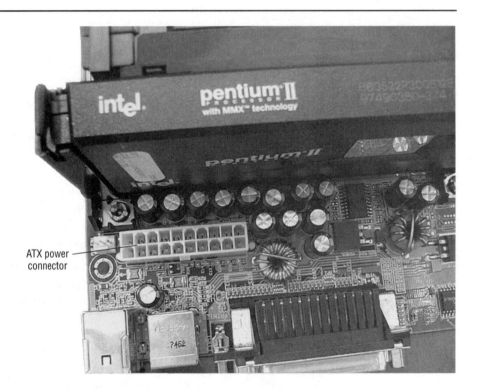

ATX power connector

Finding the CPU

The CPU on your system is often easily identifiable because many of them have a prominent Intel logo painted on them. Look also for the distinctive names 80386, 80486, Pentium, and the like.

Nowadays, finding a Pentium II or a Xeon is a snap; they're sitting upright in black plastic cases. You usually can't see the actual CPU, though, because it's surrounded by metal fins. Those fins are the heat sink that helps keep the chip from catching fire. (No, I'm not kidding.) You can see the processor in Figure 3.28.

FIGURE 3.28:

Pentium II processor on motherboard

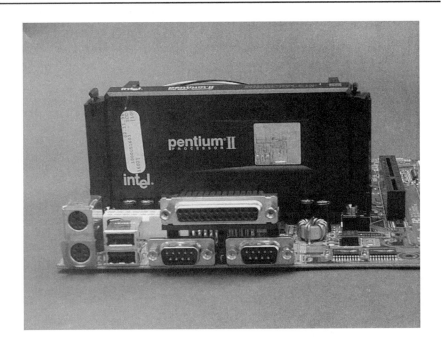

Older CPUs are also often socketed, and most Intel-type CPUs are in PGA packages. No matter what generation of PC you own, one good method for finding the CPU is to look for the largest chip in the box; that's often it.

Remembering the Memory

Your PC's motherboard has both RAM and ROM on it.

RAM memory is usually easy to spot, because it is normally in the form of a SIMM. If you've got an older computer that uses separate chips, then the memory looks like uniform rows of small socketed chips. You see the memory in Figure 3.29.

FIGURE 3.29:

SDRAM in Pentium II motherboard

ROM memory is usually a large chip or pair of chips in sockets, *often with a label on the top* indicating a software version number. Newer systems don't have socketed ROM, because they're flash memory and should not need physical replacing—you can just download new versions of the BIOS programs.

Slots

The only other things that you will be sure to want to find are the expansion slots in the computer. They're obvious, in that they're relatively long, narrow electrical connectors. Refer to the bus discussion earlier in this chapter to get an idea about the differences between the different bus slot types. Figure 3.30 shows (from left to right) two ISA slots, five PCI slots, and an AGP slot.

FIGURE 3.30:

Expansion slots on a motherboard

CMOS Battery

Keep a computer long enough, and you'll have to replace the battery or it won't be able to hold its configuration. Figure 3.31 shows that this motherboard uses a coin-type battery.

FIGURE 3.31:

CMOS battery on a
motherboard

Drive Interface Cables

Every motherboard I know of these days has the floppy drive
controller and two EIDE host adapters integrated into its electronics. You'll have to attach and detach drive ribbon cables, so it's a
good idea to locate the floppy and EIDE connectors, as you see in
Figure 3.32.

FIGURE 3.32:

Floppy and EIDE
connectors on
motherboard

Floppy   EIDE
connector   connectors

Identifying Circuit Boards

This is going to sound silly, but I use two basic approaches to identifying strange circuit boards.

The first "rule" is the "What is it connected to?" rule. Suppose you're trying to figure out what a board does. You notice that the back of the board is connected to a cable that goes to the video monitor. Heck, even a non-physicist like me can figure out that the board must have something to do with video, so it's probably a video adapter.

Now, at this moment, you're saying, "Hey, wait a minute; I've disassembled the machine. Nothing's attached to it right now, so I have no idea what the board *used* to be attached to." Remember in the last chapter when I said that diagramming was essential? Here's an example of why that's true. (I hope at this stage in your

PC exploration that this comment falls in the category of cautionary tale, rather than "I told you so....")

The second "rule" of board identification is the "What kind of connectors does it have on the back?" rule. There are different kinds of connectors on the back of a PC. Let's take a minute and get familiar with them.

Actually, with modern PCs, the issue is often not "What does this board do?" because most new systems have pretty integrated motherboards. Most new systems have *everything* on the motherboard save for a video board and (possibly) a LAN card and/or a modem. The more important question is, "What does this *connector* on my integrated motherboard do?" Well, again, a little organization, documentation, and observation can answer those questions.

The D Shell Connector

The D shell connector is called that because if you look at the right way, it looks like a capital D. You can see a D shell connector in Figure 3.33.

FIGURE 3.33:

A D shell connector

D shell connectors come in male and female varieties. They also vary by the number of pins or sockets in their connectors. You'll see DB9 (9 pins or sockets), DB15, DB25, and DB37 connectors.

They're used in serial ports, parallel ports, video adapters, joystick interfaces, and some LAN interfaces.

HP or Miniature D Shell Connector

The miniature D or HP connector looks a lot like a D shell connector, but the pins are all placed next to one another. The HP connector puts 50 pins in the same space that a normal D shell puts only 25 pins. You can see an HP connector in Figure 3.34.

FIGURE 3.34:

An HP connector

As I said, it looks like a D shell connector. The main application that I've seen for HP connectors is in SCSI interfaces. A 50-pin version shows up on SCSI-2 interfaces, and SCSI-3 (a later version of the SCSI standard) uses a 68-pin HP connector.

Sometimes you'll hear people call the 50-pin HP connector a SCSI-2 connector, and the 68-pin HP connector a SCSI-3 connector. Not everybody knows the HP name.

Centronics Connector

Made popular by its first big use in an interface created by a company of the same name, the Centronics connector looks like the drawing in Figure 3.35.

FIGURE 3.35:

A Centronics connector

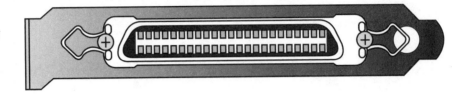

Don't confuse the Centronics connector with the Centronics interface, another name for the parallel port. The connector, which looks like an edge connector surrounded by a metal shell, is used on printers and in SCSI devices. In addition to parallel ports, Centronics connectors are used by some SCSI host adapters.

BNC Connector

A *BNC connector,* or *Bayonet Naur connector* (Bayonet is what they supposedly look like and Naur is the guy who invented them), looks like a cylinder about 1 centimeter across with a thin tube down its center, and two small bumps on its periphery. You can see several BNC connectors in Figure 3.36.

FIGURE 3.36:

BNC connectors

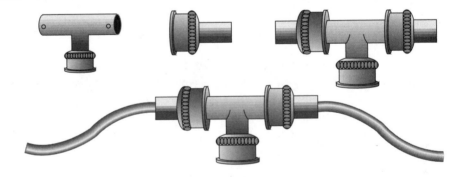

In Figure 3.36, you see (clockwise, from upper left) a T connector, used to connect a single BNC connector to two other BNC connectors. Next, you see a BNC plug, and then a T connector with two plugs. At the bottom of the diagram, you see two cables with BNC plugs connected to a T connector. The T connector would then be attached to a BNC connector on the back of a circuit board.

BNCs are most commonly used in a kind of LAN called Ethernet. Ethernet attaches in several different ways, known as *thick* net, *thin* net, and *10BaseT*. It is the thin net implementation of Ethernet that uses BNC connectors. Thin net is also known as *10Base2*.

BNC connectors have also been used in ARCNet (another kind of LAN) and 3270 (a mainframe terminal interface) connectors.

RJ-45 or RJ-13 Connector

These connectors look like the so-called "modular jacks" that you use to plug a phone into an answering machine or a wall jack. As a matter of fact, the connector that you use for a normal phone is called an RJ-11, or Registered Jack type 11 connector. Some networks use the slightly larger RJ-45 connector, which looks similar. The RJ-11 has four wires in it. The RJ-45 has eight wires in it.

RJ-45 is used in 10BaseT Ethernet connections, as well as LocalTalk connectors such as you'd see in a Macintosh network.

DIN Connector

The *DIN connector* comes from Germany; roughly translated, its name means "German national connector." The DIN connector is a round, notched connector about an inch across, with from three to seven pins in it.

DIN connectors are most commonly used in the PC world to connect keyboards to a motherboard.

Miniature DIN Connector

As the name implies, these are smaller versions of DIN connectors. You see a couple of variations on this in Figure 3.37.

You'll see these used for bus mouse interfaces, InPort mouse interfaces, some keyboard interfaces, and some serial port applications.

Miniplug

A *miniplug* connector is the kind of connection that allows a set of headphones to attach to a Sony Walkman. You see these on CD-ROM players or on the backs of sound cards, for microphone inputs or line input or output.

RCA Plug

RCA plugs are the kind of connectors that you might see on the back of your VCR labeled "Audio in" or "Video in." They were used years ago for simple video output on an old kind of video board called the Color/Graphics Adapter and a later board called the Enhanced Graphics Adapter. Nowadays, you usually only see them for sound inputs or outputs on some sound cards, or for video inputs on a video capture board.

USB Connector

Universal Serial Bus systems have a *USB connector*—a kind of flat connector with a tongue in its middle, as you see in Figure 3.38.

FIGURE 3.38:

USB Connector (in center; mini DINs on left, D shells on right)

Boards and Connectors

Now let's put all of this information together into some diagrams of common boards and connectors. Take a look at Figure 3.39.

FIGURE 3.39:

Common boards and connectors

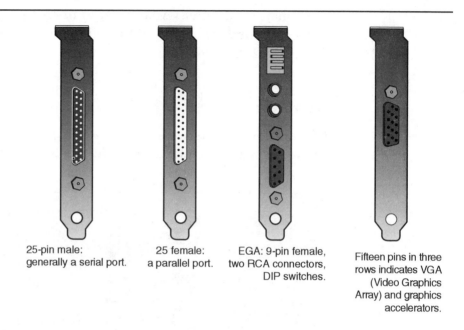

25-pin male: generally a serial port.

25 female: a parallel port.

EGA: 9-pin female, two RCA connectors, DIP switches.

Fifteen pins in three rows indicates VGA (Video Graphics Array) and graphics accelerators.

In Figure 3.39, you see the backs of some common interface boards. As I said earlier, note the extensive use of D shell connectors.

Originally, video boards used a female DB9 connector to pipe out either color images, via what was called an RGB connector, or high-resolution monochrome images, via a digital monochrome video interface. That led to confusion, because it was possible to plug an RGB color monitor into a digital output; when that happened, little wisps of smoke would soon issue from atop the color monitor, and it would cease to function. Color video boards also output a kind of signal called *composite video,* which you can read more about in Chapter 23, "You Oughta Be in Pictures: Video Capture." If you see a female DB9 on a modern system, the board is most likely a Token Ring network card.

Nowadays, however, virtually all video adapters use a D shell that is the same size as the old DB9, except that this D shell has *three* rows of pins, not two, housing 14 or 15 pins. I say "14 or 15" because there is room for 15 pins, but some boards fill in one of the holes. You'll see those connectors on just about every video board, and *very* rarely you'll see a video board with several RCA connectors on the back; such a board is sending video out in multiple signals as is done on some high-end video equipment.

The parallel port usually employs a 25-socket female D shell connector. I say "usually" because Tandy used a DIN connector for their parallel port for a while. And, just to confuse the issue a bit, some older SCSI host adapters use a female DB25 for attaching external SCSI devices.

Serial ports also use D shell connectors—two kinds, in fact. Some serial ports use a male DB25. Others use a male DB9 connector. Note that oddity: most connectors you'll find on a PC are *not* male connectors, so the fact that serial ports use either 9-pin or 25-pin males is unusual. (My old girlfriend Sheila—she's mentioned in the acknowledgments—told me that she remembered that male 25s and male 9s were serial ports because most serial killers were male. A rather graphic way of remembering, for sure, but then again, Sheila was six foot one and rated number one in the country in Tae Kwon Do, so I didn't argue with her about the little things, if you know what I mean.)

Why are most connectors on a PC female? Well, designers of some kinds of interfaces have to put a connector of one gender on the PC and a connector of the opposite gender on the cable that the interface uses. Male connectors have a bunch of little pins, and pins break. Female connectors have a bunch of little sockets, and sockets don't, in general, break. Now, in the case of pin breakage, would you rather have to replace a cable ($) or an interface board ($$$)? *That's* why the female connectors go on the PC side rather than the cable side.

Let's look at some more boards, as you see in Figure 3.40.

A BNC connector helps give this away as an Ethernet LAN board. Here, the female 15-pin connector is for Thick Ethernet cable, not games.

A 10baseT Ethernet card has an RJ-45 connector with a few LEDs. Some combination Ethernet boards include BNC and 15-pin connectors, too.

Two RJ-11 phone jacks: an internal modem.

Joysticks and standard Ethernet (Thicknet) use 15-pin connectors. This may be a game card or an Ethernet LAN board.

Not all mice use a 9-pin serial connection; PS/2s use a round 6-pin mouse port.

A round port with nine holes identifies this as a bus mouse interface card.

As I mentioned earlier, Ethernet comes in three guises: thick net, thin net, and twisted-pair versions. Thick net is the oldest variety of Ethernet, and it's also called "10Base5 Ethernet." It interfaces via a DB15 female connector, and is sometimes called an *AUI* (*Adapter Unit Interface*) or *DIX* (*DEC-Intel-Xerox*) connector. Thin net uses a BNC connector; in the board pictured in Figure 3.40, you can use either the thick net connector or a thin net connector. The board next to it shows the third kind of Ethernet connection, a twisted-pair or 10BaseT connection, with an RJ-45 connector.

Next to that board is a modem. Modems have RJ-13 jacks for interfacing to phone lines, and the RJ-13s look like RJ-45s, so it might be easy to confuse an Ethernet card with a modem card. But modems have two connectors, and Ethernet cards often have an LED or two on their backs.

Below those cards is a VGA, mentioned earlier, a joystick interface (a female DB15), and two types of miniature DIN connectors used to create a mouse interface.

Let's wrap up our look at the backs of common boards with a third group of boards, shown in Figure 3.41.

The top three boards in Figure 3.41 are varieties of SCSI interfaces, as I've mentioned earlier. Video capture boards take video inputs and convert them into digital data, and they can accept either simple composite video (like the kind that comes out the back of common VCRs), or they'll usually take the higher-quality "super VHS" type connector, a miniature DIN. Below them are some backsides of some sound cards. Note that many sound cards have a joystick interface built right onto them.

FIGURE 3.41:

Common boards

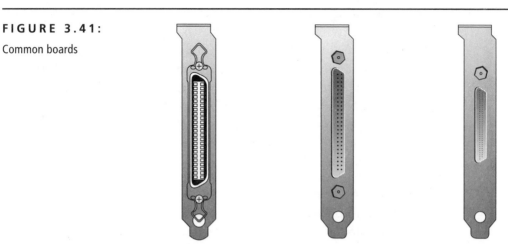

Centronics 50, 50 HP, and 68 HP connectors are all used for SCSI host adapters.

| Sound cards typically have a joystick port, volume control, and audio input/output jacks. | Playback-only sound cards have headphone output jacks, line-out jacks, and volume control. | Interface cards for add-in CD-ROM drives have two audio output jacks for speakers. |

Well, that was a long chapter, but now you're a certified "micro-biologist." The next chapter's a bit lighter, so don't stop now: turn the page and see how to keep all this stuff working!

CHAPTER
FOUR

Avoiding Service: Preventive Maintenance

- The menace of heat

- Electromagnetism

- Electrostatic discharge

- Damage caused by water and liquids

The most effective way to cut down your repair bills is by good, preventive maintenance. There are things in the PC environment—some external, some created in ignorance by you through inattention—that can drastically shorten your PC's life.

Now, some of the things that affect your PC's life are common-sense things; I don't really imagine that I've got to tell you not to spill soft drinks (or, for that matter, hard drinks) into the keyboard. But there are other PC gremlin sources that aren't quite so obvious; so, obvious or not, we'll get to all the environmental hazards in this chapter. A few factors can endanger your PC's health:

- Excessive heat
- Dust
- Magnetism
- Stray electromagnetism
- Power surges, incorrect line voltage, and power outages
- Water and corrosive agents

Heat and Thermal Shock

Every electronic device carries within it the seeds of its own destruction. More than half of the power given to chips is wasted as heat—but heat destroys chips. One of an electronic designer's main concerns is to see that an electronic device can dissipate heat as quickly as it can generate it. If it cannot, heat slowly builds up until the device fails.

There are several ways you can help control your PC's heat problem:

- Install an adequate fan in the power supply or add an auxiliary fan.

- Install a heat sink.

- Adjust your box design for better ventilation.

- Run the PC in a safe temperature range.

Removing Heat with a Fan

In general, laptops don't require a fan, because enough heat dissipates from the main circuit board all by itself. But most desktop and tower PCs will surely fail without a fan.

When designing a fan, engineers must trade off noise for cooling power. Years ago, power supplies were quite expensive, running in the $300 range for the cheapest power supply, so great care was exercised in choosing the right fan for protection. Nowadays, power supplies cost under $25, and I doubt that most engineers at PC companies could even tell you what kind of fan is sitting in their machines, any more than they could tell you who makes the case screws.

Now, that's a terrible shame, because the $3 fan that's sitting in most PC power supplies is a vital part. If it dies, your PC will cook itself in just a few hours.

And they *do* die.

The more stuff that's in your PC, the hotter it runs. The things that make PCs hot inside include:

- Chips, memory chips, and CPUs in particular, because they have the greatest number of transistors inside them.

- Drive motors in hard disks, floppies, and CD-ROMs. Some CD-ROMs run quite warm, like the Plexor 4-Plex models. Large hard disks run *extremely* hot. I've seen an old Maxtor 660MB ESDI drive run so hot that it almost burned my fingers; I've seen the same thing more recently on my 1.7GB Fujitsu drive. Newer drives in the 3½ " half-height or third-height format run much cooler. Some circuit boards can run quite hot, depending on how well (or how poorly) they're designed.

Truthfully, heat buildup inside a PC is much less of a problem than it was in the mid-1980s. In those days, every drive was a full-height drive, and every computer had 640K of memory built up from 90 separate 64K chips. Add one of those early hot 8087 coprocessors, and it was common to find the inside of a PC running 30 degrees F (16 degrees C) warmer inside its box than in the outside room.

Removing Heat with a Heat Sink

For years, electronic designers have had to struggle with hot components on circuit boards. Sometimes a fan just isn't enough, so they need more help cooling an infernal chip. They do it with a *heat sink*. A heat sink is a small piece of metal, usually aluminum, with fins on it. The heat sink is glued or clamped to the hot chip. The metal conducts heat well, and the fins increase the surface area of the heat sink. The more area on the heat sink, the more heat that can be conducted off to the air and thereby removed from the PC.

The standard Pentium II and Xeon processor packages have a heat sink and a fan integrated with the chip. The idea is that the heat sink pulls the heat off and the fan disperses it. The Celeron doesn't come with a heat sink, but that doesn't mean that it's not a good idea to think about putting one on a hot chip. You can find heat sinks in electronics supply catalogs.

Adding a fan can really increase the heat sink's ability to cool its chip. I've noticed that many modern motherboards have connections to power a couple of auxiliary fans, and you can buy fans that attach to those connections from PC clone parts places (look in the back of *Computer Shopper* for them).

Good and Bad Box Designs

It's frustrating how totally unaware of heat problems many computer manufacturers are. The first tower computer I purchased was from a company named ACMA, and they put together an impressive machine. There were two fans in the case—a very nice touch—as well as a CPU fan. I've got to say that they spoiled me. A later (1994) purchase, from an outfit called Systems Dynamics Group, was somewhat less enjoyable. The back of the PC chassis had room for two fans, but there was only one fan in the system. There's nothing intrinsically wrong with that, except that the cutout for the second fan—which is right next to the first fan— was left empty. The result was that the fan just sucked in air from the cutout a few inches away from it, and blew it back out. Made the fan happy, I suppose, but didn't do much for the CPU.

I noticed this pointless ventilation system pretty quickly, so I took some tape and covered up the extraneous cutout. Within seconds, the air being pumped out the back of the Pentium got 10 degrees warmer. If I'd left the extra cutout uncovered, then the only ventilation that my Pentium system would have gotten was just the simple convection from the heated boards and drives. Even at that, however, the Pentium system—which included a 1GB drive, 80MB of RAM, a CD-ROM, video capture board, video board, SCSI host adapter, and Ethernet card—only ran 10 degrees hotter inside the box than outside the box.

Things could have been a bit worse if the case was like some I've seen, with the fan *on the bottom of the tower*! This is not too common, fortunately, but it's worth asking so you can avoid it when purchasing a PC. This setup puts the circuit boards on the top of the tower, and the fan on the bottom. I have no idea who designed this case, but it's nice to know that the banjo player kid from *Deliverance* finally has someone to look down upon. The point I'm making here is, take a minute and look at the airflow in the box. Of course, even if you have a good box, you can still run into heat problems.

Dead Fans

Years ago (around 1995), I installed Freelance Graphics on my system. Pulling the first floppy out of my A: drive, I noticed that the floppy was warm. My memory flashed back to 1982, when something similar had happened—so I knew what was going on. My system's fan had died.

Fortunately, I found the problem early and shut down the computer. I had to travel to Europe for a few weeks to teach classes and consult, but I figured, no problem—I'll just leave the computer off.

Unfortunately, while I was gone, one of my employees helpfully started up the computer—reasoning that I always leave my computers on all the time, so what the hey? So, despite the "do not turn it on" sign I'd left on it, the computer merrily melted itself down while I lectured in Amsterdam. By the time I returned, the hard disk had self-destructed, as had the Ethernet card in it.

It's actually pretty amazing what *didn't* die in the system. The CPU (a 50 MHz 486DX) ran for a couple of years afterward (until it became too slow to be of value) and the Adaptec 1742 SCSI host adapter is still in service in an old server.

Heat Sensor Devices

Now, I could have avoided this problem altogether with a 110 Twinalert from a company called PC Power and Cooling Systems. They're a name to know when you're buying power supplies. The 110 Twinalert is a circuit board about the size of a business card that plugs into a floppy power connector. When the PC's internal temperature gets to 110 degrees F, it starts making an annoying squealing noise. At 118 degrees F, it just shuts the computer down. The device is under $50, and every network server should have one.

While I'm on the subject of PC Power and Cooling, I should mention that this company also makes an interesting variety of power products for the PC, including power supplies with very quiet fans, power supplies with built-in battery backup, and high-quality PC cases. I use their stuff when I want to increase the odds that my PC will be running when I need it.

My introduction to PC Power and Cooling came with a hot 386. When I say "hot," I mean that this PC ran 25 degrees warmer inside than the temperature outside. PC Power and Cooling sells the Turbo Cool, a power supply that claimed at the time to cool your PC by 35 to 40 degrees (all Fahrenheit). Now, obviously, my 386 could not be cooled by 35 degrees, because it is only 25 degrees over ambient—the best that a fan can do is to lower the temperature inside the machine to the surrounding temperature. However, buying PC Power and Cooling Systems' Turbo Cool cooled my machine from 25 degrees over ambient to only *four* degrees over ambient. You can find PC Power and Cooling Systems' address in the Vendors' Guide (Appendix A).

Safe Temperature Ranges for PCs

Electronic components have a temperature range within which they are built to work. IBM suggests that the PC, for instance, is built to work in the range of 60 to 85 degrees F. This is because the circuit boards can run as hot as 125 degrees, but a typical machine may be as much as 40 degrees hotter *inside* than outside. And 125 minus 40 yields 85 degrees, the suggested maximum temperature.

Obviously, if you've got a good fan, the acceptable range of room temperatures expands considerably. If you had a really good fan, the inside of the machine would be close to the same temperature as the outside. You don't want the inside of the PC to get any hotter than 110 degrees—hard disks can fail at that point, although, again, circuit boards can function in higher temperatures than that.

Since the temperature inside the PC is the ambient temperature plus some constant, there are two ways to cool the inside of the PC—either lower the constant with a good fan or lower the ambient temperature. Keep the room cooler and the PC will be cooler.

Heat also aids the corrosion process. Corrosion is a chemical process, and inside a computer, corrosion can roughly *double* in speed when the temperature of the process is raised by 10 degrees C (about 18 degrees F). Chips slowly deteriorate, the hotter the faster.

How do you measure temperature and temperature changes in your PC? Simple—get a *digital temperature probe*. Radio Shack markets one for around $30. Or you can buy one from Edmund Scientific Corp., whose address is listed in Appendix A.

The easy way to use the probe is to tape it over the exit vents by the fan's power supply. An indoor/outdoor switch lets you quickly view the PC's inside temperature and the ambient temperature.

Duty Cycles

We said before that a device should get rid of heat as quickly as it creates it. Not every device is that good, however. Devices are said to have a *duty cycle*. This number—expressed as a percentage—is the proportion of the time that a device can work without burning up. For example, a powerful motor may have a 50 percent duty cycle. This means that it should be active only 50 percent of the time. A starter motor on a car, for example, must produce a tremendous amount of power. Powerful motors are expensive to produce, so instead, cars use a motor that can produce a lot of power for a very short time. If you crank the engine on your car for several minutes at a stretch, then you will likely damage or destroy the car's starter motor. Floppy disk drive motors are a similar example: run a floppy motor continuously and you'll likely burn out the motor. *Hard* disk motors, on the other hand, run continuously and must be designed with a 100 percent duty cycle.

Duty cycle is used to describe active versus inactive time for many kinds of devices, although this definition could be misleading, since it implies that all devices can be continually active without problems. Not all devices are designed to be active all of the time. Some desktop laser printers, for example, will not run well if they are required to print continuously.

Thermal Shock

Because a PC is warmer inside than outside, changes in room temperature can become multiplied inside a PC.

This problem leads to a hazard called *thermal shock*. Thermal shock comes from subjecting components to rapid and large changes in temperature. It can disable your computer due to expansion/contraction damage. The most common scenario for thermal shock occurs when the PC is turned on Monday morning after a winter's weekend. Many commercial buildings turn the temperature down to 55 degrees over the weekend: your office may contain some of that residual chill early Monday morning. Inside the PC, though, it may still be 55. Then you turn the machine on. Within 30 minutes some PCs can warm up to 120 degrees. This rapid, 65-degree rise in temperature brings on thermal shock.

This is an argument for leaving the PC on 24 hours a day, seven days a week. (We'll see some more reasons to do this soon.) The temperature inside the PC will be better regulated. By the way, you can't leave portable PCs on all the time, but you should be extra careful with portables to avoid thermal shock. If your laptop has been sitting in the trunk on a cold February day, be sure to give it some time to warm up before trying to use it. And give it some time in a *dry* place, or water vapor will condense on the cold disk platters. Water on the disk platters is a surefire way to reduce your drive's life.

Sunbeams

Another heat effect is caused by sunbeams. Direct sunlight isn't a good thing for electronic equipment. A warm sunbeam feels nice for a few minutes, but sit in one for an hour and you'll understand why PCs don't like them. Direct sunlight is also, of course, terrible for floppy disks. Find a shadowy area, or use drapes.

Dealing with Dust

Dust is everywhere. It consists of tiny sand granules, fossil skeletons of minuscule creatures that lived millions of years ago, dead skin, paper particles, and tiny crustaceans called dust mites that live off the other pieces. Dust is responsible for several evils.

First, it sticks to the circuit boards inside your computer. As dust builds up, an entire board can become coated with a fine insulating sheath. That would be fine if the dust was insulating your house, but thermal insulation is definitely a bad thing for computers. You seek, as we have seen, to minimize impediments to thermal radiation from your computer components. To combat this, remove dust from inside the computer and from circuit boards periodically. A good period between cleaning is a year in a house and six months in an office. A simpler approach is to use the "while I'm at it" algorithm—when you need to disassemble the machine for some other reason, clean the insides while you're at it. A tool that can assist you is a can of compressed air. Just as effective for the case and inside support assemblies is a dust-free cloth wetted with a little water and ammonia (just a few drops). Don't use the cloth on circuit boards—get a can of compressed air and blow the dust off.

Actually, *compressed air* isn't actually compressed air, but some kind of compressed gas. Take a second look when you buy this stuff: a lot of it is Freon or some other chlorinated fluorocarbon (CFC), which enlarges the hole in the ozone layer. Rather than using one of these, choose one of the "ozone-friendly" alternatives, such as the one marketed by Chemtronics.

This should be obvious, but when you blow dust off boards, be aware of where it is going: if you can, have the vacuum cleaner nearby, or take the board to another area, then you'll have better luck. *Please* don't hold the board over the PC's chassis and blow off the dust with compressed air—all it does is move the dust, not *remove* the dust.

The second dust evil is that dust can clog spaces, like:

- The air intake area to your power supply or hard disk

- The space between the floppy disk drive head and the disk

To combat the floppy drive problem, some manufacturers offer a floppy dust cover that you put in place when the machine is turned off. The sad part of this is that you really need the cover when the machine is on. CRT displays have an unintended, unexpected, unpleasant, and unavoidable side effect—they attract dust. Turn your screen on, and all of the dust in the area drops everything (what would dust particles drop, I wonder?) and heads straight for the display. Some of the particles get sidetracked and end up in the floppy drives.

One place that creates and collects paper dust is, of course, the printer. Printers should be vacuumed or blown out periodically, *away* from the computer (remember, dust goes somewhere when blown away).

By the way, another fertile source of dust is ash particles. Most of us don't burn things indoors, *unless* we are smokers. If you smoke, fine: just don't do it near the computer. Years ago, I ran across a study by the U.S. Government Occupation Safety and Hazard Administration (OSHA), which estimated that smoke at a computer workstation cuts the computer's life by 40 percent. That's $1200 on a $3000 workstation. (Alas, I saw that back in 1985, and didn't note the information in detail—I wish I had!—so I can't cite the particular study.)

Magnetism

Magnets—both the permanent and electromagnetic type—can cause permanent loss of data on hard or floppy disks. Most often, the magnetism found in an office environment is produced by electric motors and electromagnets. A commonly overlooked electromagnet is the one in phones that ring using a real bell (not common these days). The clapper is forced against the bell (or buzzer, if the phone has one of those) in the phone by powering an electromagnet. If you absent-mindedly put such a phone on top of a stack of floppy disks, and the phone rings, you will probably have unrecoverable data errors on at least the top one.

Don't think you have magnets around? How about:

- Magnets to put notes on a file cabinet
- A paper clip holder with a magnet
- A word processing copy stand with a magnetic clip
- A magnetic screw extractor

Another source of magnetism is, believe it or not, a CRT. I have seen disk drives refuse to function because they were situated inches from a CRT. X-ray machines in airports similarly produce some magnetism, although there is some controversy here. Some folks say, "Don't run floppies through the X-ray—walk them through." Others say the X-ray is okay, but the metal detector zaps floppies. Some people claim to have been burned at both. Personally, I walk through an average of three to four metal detectors per week carrying 3.5-inch floppy disks, and have never (knock wood) had a problem. My laptops have been through X-ray machines everywhere, and I've never lost a byte on the hard disk because of it.

Airport metal detectors should be sufficiently gentle for floppies. Magnetism is measured in a unit called *gauss*. Metal detectors *in the U.S.* (notice the emphasis) emit far less gauss than that necessary to affect disks. I'm not sure about Canada and Europe, but I notice that the fillings in my teeth seem to set off the metal detectors in the Ottawa airport.

What about preventive maintenance? For starters, get a phone with a ringer that is not a real bell, to minimize the chance of erasing data inadvertently. Another large source of magnetism is the motor in a printer—generally, it is not shielded (the motors on the drives don't produce very much magnetism, in case you're wondering).

Do you (or someone that you assist) work in a word processing pool? Many word processors (the people kind, not the machine kind) use a copy stand that consists of a flexible metal arm and a magnet. The magnet holds the copy to be typed on the metal arm. The arm can sit right in front of the operator's face, so that he or she can easily type the copy.

The problem arises when it's time to change the copy. I watched a word processing operator remove the magnet (so as to change the copy), and slap the magnet on the side of the computer. It really made perfect sense—the case was steel, and held the magnet in a place that was easy to access. The only bad part of the whole operation was that the hard disk on that particular PC chassis was mounted on the extreme right-hand side of the case, right next to the magnet. You can start to see why I hate magnets.... A few years ago, I was a keynote speaker at a conference held in San Antonio, next to the Alamo. As part of the "thank you" package that the conference organizers put together, we speakers got a refrigerator magnet in the shape of the Alamo. After almost placing my wallet (with my credit cards in it) on the magnet, almost laying demonstration floppies that I'd gotten at the conference on it, and almost storing the Alamo magnet in my laptop case (you know, next to the laptop's hard disk and any floppies that I had in the case), I finally gave up and threw the magnet away before I had a chance to *really* do some damage.

Oh, and by the way, *speakers* have magnets in them. Years ago, a friend purchased a home entertainment system: a VCR, a stereo, and some monster speakers. That's when I noticed that he had stacked his videotapes on top of the speakers. I almost didn't have the heart to tell him, but I eventually advised him that his videos were history—and, sad to say, they *were*. Modern multimedia PCs all have speakers that claim to have shielded magnets; but I've got a Sony woofer/satellite speaker system that makes my monitor's image get wobbly when I put the speakers too near the monitor. No matter what the manual says, I think I'll just keep the floppies away from there.

My advice is to go on an anti-magnet crusade. Magnets near magnetic media are disasters waiting to happen.

A sad story: a large government agency's data center bought a hand-held magnetic bulk floppy eraser. (I'm not sure why—they weren't a secret shop, and thus did not have the need.) The PC expert in the shop tested it on a few junk floppies, then turned it off and didn't think about it. The next day, he remembered that he had left it on top of a plastic floppy file drawer. This meant that the eraser, even though turned off, was about an inch from the top of the floppies. He spent the next day testing each of the floppies, one by one. Most were dead. They got rid of the bulk eraser. I'm not sure what they did with the PC expert.

Stray Electromagnetism

Stray electromagnetism can cause problems for your PC and, in particular, for your network. Here, I'm just referring to any electromagnetism that you don't want. It comes in several varieties.

- Radiated *electromagnetic interference* (*EMI*)

- Power noise and interruptions
- *Electrostatic discharge* (*ESD*)—static electricity

Electromagnetic Interference

EMI is caused when electromagnetism is radiated or conducted somewhere that we don't want it to be. I discuss two common types—crosstalk and RFI—in the next two sections.

Crosstalk

When two wires are physically close to each other, they can transmit interference between themselves called *crosstalk*. We're not talking about short circuits here: the insulation can be completely intact. The problem is that the interfering wire contains electronic pulses. Electronic pulses produce magnetic fields as a side effect. The wire being interfered with is touched or crossed by the magnetic fields. Magnetic fields crossing or touching a wire produce electronic pulses as a side effect. (Nature is, unfortunately, amazingly symmetrical at times like this.) The electronic pulses created in the second wire are faint copies of the pulses (the signal) from the first wire. These pulses interfere with the signal that we're trying to send on the second wire.

Crosstalk is not really a problem when applied to power lines, although I have heard of cases where the alternating current in power lines creates a hum on a communications line through crosstalk. The larger worry is when bundles of wires are stored in close quarters, and the wires are data cables.

There are five solutions to crosstalk:

- Move the wires farther apart (not always feasible).
- Use twisted pair cable (varying the number of twists reduces crosstalk).

- Use shielded cable (the shield reduces crosstalk—don't even think of running ribbon cables for distances over six feet).

- Use fiber optic cable—it's not electromagnetic, it's photonic (is that a great word, or what? It means that they use light instead of electricity to transmit data), so there's no crosstalk.

- Don't run cables over fluorescent lights. The lights are noise emitters.

I once helped troubleshoot a network that had been installed in a classroom. The contractor had run the wires through the ceiling, but the network seemed to not work. (Ever notice how often the words "network" and "not work" end up in the same sentence? A Russian friend calls them "nyetworks.") I pushed aside the ceiling tiles and found that the cable installer had saved himself some time and money by foregoing cable trays, instead wrapping the cables around the occasional fluorescent lamp. So, on a hunch, I said to the people that I was working with, "Start the network up again," and I turned off the lights. Sure enough, it worked.

Radio Frequency Interference

Radio Frequency Interference (*RFI*) is high-frequency (10 kHz) radiation. It's a bad thing for computer communications. Sources are:

- High-speed digital circuits, like the ones in your computer

- Nearby radio sources

- Cordless telephones

- Keyboards

- Power-line intercoms (intercoms that use the power line's 60Hz as the carrier wave)

- Motors

Worse yet, your PC can be a *source* of RFI. If this happens, the FCC police come to your place of business and take your PC away. (Well, not really. But they *will* fine you.)

RFI is bad because it can interfere with high-speed digital circuits. Your computer is composed of digital circuits. RFI can seem sinister because it seems to come and go mysteriously. Like all noise, it is an unwanted signal. How would we go about receiving a *wanted* RF signal? Simple—construct an antenna. Suppose we want to receive a signal of a given frequency? We design an antenna of a particular length. (Basically, the best length is one quarter of the wavelength. A 30-meter wavelength is best picked up by a 7.5-meter antenna. But it's not important that you know that—to learn more about it, pick up an amateur radio book.) Now suppose there is some kind of RFI floating around. We're safe as long as we can't receive it. But suppose the computer is connected to the printer with a cable that, through bad luck, happens to be the correct length to receive that RFI? The result: printer gremlins. Fortunately, the answer is simple: shorten or lengthen the cable.

Electric motors are common RFI-producing culprits. I recently saw a workstation in Washington where the operator had put an electric fan (to cool *herself*, not the workstation) on top of the workstation. When the fan was on, it warped the top of the CRT's image slightly. Electric can openers, hair dryers, electric razors, electric pencil sharpeners, and printers are candidates. Sometimes it's hard to determine whether the device is messing up the PC simply by feeding back noise onto the power line or whether it is troubling the PC with RFI. The answer either way is to put the devices on separate power lines.

Your PC also *emits* RFI, which can impair the functioning of other PCs, televisions, and various sensitive pieces of equipment. By law, a desktop computer cannot be sold unless it meets "Class

B" specifications. The FCC requires that a device 3 meters from the PC must receive no more than the RFI shown in Table 4.1.

TABLE 4.1: Permissible RF Output (FCC Class B Specification)

FREQUENCY	MAXIMUM FIELD STRENGTH (microvolts/meter)
30–88 MHz	100
89–216 MHz	150
217–1000 MHz	200

RFI became an issue with personal computers when the PC came out because IBM had shielded its PC line and sought to make life a little tougher on the clonemakers. By pushing the FCC to get tough on PCs, IBM had a bit of a jump on the market. Unfortunately, getting Class B certification isn't that hard, and just about every PC qualifies these days: clonemakers now say that their machines are "FCC Class B Certified." This has caused the reverse of IBM's original intent, because the FCC certification seems a mark of legitimacy. In reality, FCC certification is not a measure of good design, quality components, or compatibility; it just means that the equipment doesn't produce excessive amounts of electromagnetic interference.

Protecting your PC from the devices around it and protecting the devices from your PC are done in the same way. If the PC doesn't leak RFI, then it's less likely to pick up any stray RFI in the area. Any holes in the case provide entry/exit points. Use the brackets that come with the machine to plug any unused expansion slots. To prevent unplanned air circulation paths, it is also a good idea to plug unused expansion slots. Ensure that the case fits together snugly and correctly. If the case includes cutouts for interface connectors, find plates to cover the cutouts or simply use metal tape.

A simple AM radio can be used to monitor RFI field strength. A portable radio is ideal, because it has light headphones and a small enough enclosure to allow fairly local signal strength monitoring. A cheap model is best—you don't want sophisticated noise filtering. Tune it to an area of the dial as far as possible from a strong station. Lower frequencies seem to work best. You'll hear the various devices produce noises. I first noticed these noises when working ages ago on a clone computer with an XT motherboard, a composite monitor, an external hard disk, and a two-drive external Bernoulli box. The quietest part of the system was the PC: the hard disk screamed and buzzed, the Bernoulli made low frequency eggbeater-like sounds, and the monitor produced a fairly pure and relatively loud tone.

The PC sounded different, depending on what it was doing. When I typed, I heard a machine-gun–like sound. When I asked for a text search, the fairly regular search made a "dee-dee-dee" sound. It's kind of fun (okay, I guess I don't get out much), and you might pop the top on your system and do a little "radio astronomy" on it.

I've also used the radio in a number of other ways. Once, I received a new motherboard, a 486 that I was going to use to upgrade a 286 system. I installed it, and nothing happened. No beeps, no blinking cursor, nothing but the fan. So I removed the motherboard and placed it on a cardboard box (no electrical short fears with a cardboard box). Then I placed a power supply next to it, plugged in the P8/P9 connectors, and powered up. I ran the radio over the motherboard and got no response, just a constant hum. Placing the radio right over the CPU got nothing. I reasoned that what I was hearing was just the clock circuit. I felt even more certain of my guess when I noticed that the CPU had been inserted backwards into its socket. One dead motherboard, back to the manufacturer.

Power Noise

Your wall socket is a source of lots of problems. They basically fall into these three categories:

- Overvoltage and undervoltage
- No voltage at all—a power blackout
- Transients—spikes and surges

I'll consider these categories of problems in Chapter 9, "Power Supplies and Power Protection." Right now, however, let's look at the fourth kind of power noise, the one that *you* cause: *power-up power surges*.

In the process of discussing how to fix this, I'll have to weigh in on The Great PC Power Switch Debate.

Leave Your Machines On 24 Hours a Day

I'd like to discuss one power-related item here: user-induced power surges. What user-induced power surges, you say? Simple: every time you turn on an electrical device, you get a power surge through it. Some of the greatest stresses that electrical devices receive are when they are turned on or turned off. When do light bulbs burn out? Think about it—they generally burn out when you first turn them on or off. One study showed that when a device is first turned on, it draws as much as four to six times its normal power for less than one second. (This phenomenon is called *inrush current* in the literature. I found this bit of information on page 27 of *Computer Electric Power Requirements* by Mark Waller, published by Sams in 1987.) For that brief time, your PC may be pulling 600 to 900 watts—not a prescription for long PC life.

The answer? Leave your PCs on 24 hours a day, seven days a week. We've done it at my company for years. Turn the monitor off, or turn the screen intensity down, or use one of those annoying automatic screen savers so the monitor doesn't get an image burned into it. Turn the printer off also. Leaving the machines on also regulates temperature and reduces a phenomenon called chip creep that I'll discuss in the next chapter.

What? You're still not convinced? I know, it seems non-intuitive—most people react that way. But it really does make sense. First of all, consider the things that you keep on all the time, like these:

- Digital clocks, which obviously run continuously, incorporate some of the same digital technology as microcomputers, and they're pretty reliable.

- Calculators—I've seen accountants with calculators that are on all the time.

- Mainframes, minis, and your phone PBX never go off.

- TVs (part of the TV is powered up all the time so that it can "warm up" instantly, unlike older sets).

- Thermostats—the temperature-regulating device in your home or business is a circuit that works all the time.

Most of the things that I just named are some of the most reliable, never-think-about-them devices that you work with.

In addition to the things I've already said, consider the hard disk. All disks incorporate a motor to spin them at high speeds (depending upon the drive, they may spin at speeds ranging from 3600 to 10,000 rpm). You know from real life that it's a lot harder to get something moving than it is to keep it moving. (Ever push a car?) The cost, then, of turning hard disk motors on and off is that sometimes they just won't be able to get started.

For example, back in 1984 I bought my first hard disk, an external 32MB drive. It cost $929, and while it's dead and buried now, for years I was loathe to stop using it, because nine hundred bucks is a lot of money. For a long time I kept it attached to a server and constantly running. This illustrates the don't-turn-it-off point of view. The drive required a "jumpstart" when it was turned off overnight: if the thing didn't want to work, we just removed it from the system, took off the hard disk's circuit board to expose the motor, and gave the motor a spin. After a couple of spins, we reassembled it, and it would start up fine. (No, I didn't put anything important on it, but it was a great demonstration tool. And it kept data just fine.)

Here's the point: as long as we didn't turn the system off, the hard drive worked quite well, at least as well as old 32MB hard drives work. This applies to hard disks in general, and in fact to anything with a motor. Yes, the motor's life is shortened when continuously on, but even then the expected life of the motor is beyond the reasonable life of a hard disk.

Leaving your computer on all the time heads off thermal shock, which is yet another reason to leave it on. Machines should never be power cycled quickly. I've seen people fry their power supplies by turning their computers on and off several times in a 30-second period "to clear problems" and end up creating bigger problems.

A final word of caution. Leaving the machine on all the time is a good idea only if:

- Your machine is cooled adequately. If your machine is 100 degrees inside when the room is 70 degrees, it'll overheat when the room goes to 90 degrees on summer weekends when the building management turns off the cooling in your building. Make sure your machine has a good enough fan to handle higher temperatures.

- You have adequate surge protection. Actually, you should not run the machine at all unless you have adequate surge protection.

- You have fairly reliable power. If you lose power three times a week, there's no point in leaving the machines on all the time—the power company is turning them off and on for you. Even worse, the power just after a power outage is noise-filled.

Before moving on, let's take a quick peek at the other kinds of power problems, the ones we'll tackle in greater detail in Chapter 9.

Transients

A *transient* is any brief change in power that doesn't repeat itself. It can be an undervoltage or an overvoltage. Sags (momentary undervoltage) and surges (momentary overvoltage) are transients. Being brief, the transient may be of a high enough frequency that it slips right past the protective capacitors in your power supply and punches holes in your chips. (No, they're not holes you can see, at least not without some very good equipment.) Transients have a cumulative effect—the first 100 may do nothing. Eventually, however, enough chickens come home to roost that your machine decides, one day, to go on vacation. (You might say that if enough chickens come home to roost, the machine "buys the farm." Permanently.) We'll talk about protection against these things in Chapter 9.

Overvoltage

You have an *overvoltage* condition when you get more than the rated voltage for a period of greater than 2.5 seconds. Such a voltage measurement is done as a moving average over several seconds.

Chronic overvoltage is just as bad for your system as transient overvoltage: the chips can fail as a result of it.

Undervoltage

Summer in much of the country means air conditioners are running full blast, and the power company is working feverishly to meet the power demands that they bring. Sometimes it can't meet the full needs, however, so announces a reduction in voltage called a *brownout*.

Brownouts are bad for large motors, like the ones you'd find in a compressor for refrigeration. Brownouts make your TV screen look shrunken, and they confuse power supplies. A power supply tries to provide continuous power to the PC. Power equals voltage times current. If the voltage drops and you want constant power, what do you do? Simple: draw more current. But drawing more current through a given conductor heats up the conductor. The power supply and the chips get hot, and may overheat.

Surge protectors can't help you here. A power conditioner can— it uses a transformer to compensate for the sagging voltage. We'll discuss them in greater detail in Chapter 9.

Electrostatic Discharge

ESD—or, as you probably know it, *static electricity*—is annoyingly familiar to anyone who has lived through a winter indoors. The air is very dry (winter and forced hot-air ducts bring relative humidity to around 20 percent in my house, for example) and is an excellent insulator. You build up a static charge and keep it (until you touch something like a metal doorknob—or much worse, your computer). On the other hand, in the summer, when relative humidity can be close to 100 percent (until 1998 I lived in a suburb of Washington, D.C., a city built over a swamp), you build up static charges also, but they leak away quickly due to the humidity of the air. Skin resistance also has a lot to do with dissipating charges. The resistance of your skin can be as little as 1,000 ohms when wet and 500,000 ohms when dry. (This fun fact is courtesy of Jearl Walker's *Flying Circus of Physics*, published by John Wiley in 1977.)

You know how static electricity is built up. Static can damage chips if it creates a charge of 200 volts or more. If a static discharge is sufficient for the average person to notice it, it is at least 2,000 volts.

Scuffing across a shag rug in February can build up 50,000 volts. This is an electron "debt" which must be paid. The next metal item you touch (metal gives up electrons easily) pays the debt with an electric shock. If it's 50,000 volts, why doesn't it electrocute you when you touch the metal? Simple, the amperage(which is the volume of electricity) is tiny. This is because even though the voltage is high, the resistance is up in the millions of ohms and 50,000 volts divided by millions of ohms is a tiny amount of current. (As my physics professor used to tell us, "Twinkle, twinkle, little star; power equals I squared R." And people say physics is dull.) Different materials generate more or less static. Many people think that certain materials are static-prone, while others are not. As it turns out, materials have a triboelectric value. Two materials rubbed together will generate static in direct proportion to how far apart their triboelectric values are.

Some common materials, in order of their triboelectric values, are:

- Air
- Human skin
- Asbestos
- Rabbit fur
- Glass
- Human hair
- Nylon

- Wool

- Fur

- Lead

- Silk

- Aluminum

- Paper

- Cotton

- Steel wool

- Hard rubber

- Nickel and copper

- Brass and silver

- Gold and platinum

- Acetate and rayon

- Polyester

- Polyurethane

- Polyvinyl

- Chloride

- Silicon

- Teflon

Once an item is charged, the voltage potential between it and another object is proportional to the distance between it and the other item on the table. For instance, suppose I charge a glass rod with a cotton cloth. The glass will attract things below it on this list, like paper, but will attract more strongly things listed below paper.

Why does static damage PC components? The chips that largely comprise circuit boards are devices that can be damaged by high voltage, even if at low current. The two most common families of chips are CMOS (Complementary Metal Oxide Semiconductor) chips, (which include NMOS [Negative Metal Oxide Semiconductor], PMOS [Positive Metal Oxide Semiconductor] and an assortment of newer devices that seem to appear on an almost daily basis), and TTL (Transistor-Transistor Logic) chips. TTLs are an older family. TTLs are faster–switching chips—so potentially faster chips (memories, CPUs, and such) could be designed with TTL. Ah, but TTL has a fatal flaw: it draws a lot of power. TTL chips need much more electricity than CMOS chips, so they create more heat, and so, while fast TTL CPUs could be constructed, CPUs are tough because densely packed TTLs produce so much heat that they would destroy themselves. One common family of TTL chips has ID numbers starting with 74, as in 7400, 7446, 74LS128, and the like. Actually, the LS in the middle of the ID means it is a variant on TTL called Low power Schottky, hence the LS.

CPUs and memories are generally CMOS chips. CMOS has a lower theoretical maximum speed, but it runs on a lot less power. Sadly, they are also more subject to static electricity damage. TTL chips can withstand considerably more static electricity than CMOS chips. By the way, CPUs and memories are all CMOS.

Even if static doesn't destroy a chip, it can shorten its life. Static is, then, something to be avoided if possible. Another effect occurs when the static is discharged. When the fat blue spark jumps from your finger to the doorknob, a small electromagnetic pulse (EMP) is created. This isn't too good for chips, either. (It's the thing you've heard about that could cause a single nuclear explosion to destroy every computer in the country, except a lot smaller.) The easiest way I get rid of my static is to discharge the static buildup on something metal that is not the computer's case. A metal desk or table leg is good.

For your business, however, you may want something a trifle more automatic. The options are:

- Raise the humidity with a humidifier (evaporative, not ultra-sonic—ultrasonic creates dust).

- Raise the humidity with plants, or perhaps an aquarium.

- Install static-free carpet.

- Put anti-static "touch me" mats under the PCs.

- Make your own anti-static spray (see below).

From the point of view of comfort, I recommend the first option strongly. Your employees don't feel dried-out, and the static problem disappears. Raise humidity to just 50 percent and the problem will go away.

You can make inexpensive, homemade anti-static spray. Just get a spray pump bottle and put about an inch of fabric softener in it. Fill it the rest of the way with water, shake it well, and you've got a spray for your carpets to reduce static. Just spritz it on the rug, and the rug will smell nice, and everyone will know that you've been busy. (I hear you asking, "How long does it last?" Don't worry, you'll know.)

In a similar vein, a person from a temporary services agency once told me that they tell their word processing operators to put a sheet of Bounce under the keyboard to reduce static. While this may make the area smell nice, it will have no effect on static around the computer.

Technicians who must work with semiconductors all of the time use a ground strap to minimize ESD. The idea with a ground strap is that you never create a spark—and therefore EMP—because you've always got a nice ground connection that's draining off your charges. A good ground strap is an elastic wristband with a metal plate built into it to provide good electrical connection, attached to a wire with an alligator clip. You put the clip on something grounded—the power supply case is the most common place—and put the strap around your wrist. As you're connected to a ground, you continuously drain off your charges. A resistor in the ground strap slows down the discharge process a bit (from a microsecond to a few milliseconds), so you don't end up with one of the dangerous sparks that we've discussed before. If you do a lot of board work in a dry place, ground straps are essential. Several Silicon Valley defense-contracting firms have a policy of firing employees for not wearing their ESD wrist straps when working on high tech equipment such as satellites and military equipment.

When you must handle electronic components, take these precautions:

- Get an anti-static strap.

- Reduce the amount of static that you transfer to a chip with a ground strap, or remember the high-tech equivalent of knocking wood—touch unpainted metal periodically. One member of my staff has suggested handling chips only while naked on a wooden floor. While this might be entertaining to some of the staff, it would not, unfortunately, prevent static charges from building up, since on a very dry day, even the movement of your hair can build up a charge.

- Get an anti-static strap. They're cheap.

- Don't handle components in areas having high static potential. For example, avoid carpets unless they are anti-static or in high humidity environments. Don't wear an acrylic sweater when changing chips. Get leather-soled shoes. If your work environment allows it, you can really avoid static by removing your shoes and socks.

- Don't handle chips any more than is necessary. If you don't touch them, you won't hurt them.

- Use anti-static protective tubes and bags to transport and store chips.

- If possible, pick up components by their bodies. Don't touch the pins any more than necessary.

- Have I mentioned yet that you should have an anti-static strap and use an anti-static mat?

Use the proper precautions, and your PC won't get a big "charge" out of being touched by you.

Avoiding Water and Liquids

Water is an easy hazard to detect and avoid. You don't need any sophisticated detection devices. Shielding is unnecessary—you just keep the computer away from water.

Water and liquids are introduced into a computer system in one of several ways:

- Operator spills

- Leaks

- Flooding

Spills generally threaten the keyboard. One remedy—the one recommended by every article and book I've ever read on maintenance—is to forbid liquids near the computer. In most shops, this is unrealistic. Some people use clear flexible plastic covers on the keyboard, kind of like what Burger King uses on their cash registers. They've got normal cash registers, but they have a plastic skin over the keys that allows the user to spill "special sauce" all over the keyboard without harming it. Use the plastic covers, and they can just hose down the keyboard. (Just kidding.) With one of these keyboard "skins," you might say that you can "practice safe typing."

SafeSkin is offered by Merritt Computer Products in Dallas. Their address is listed in Appendix A. They offer versions for the various odd keyboards in the PC world.

A similar disaster, flooding, sometimes occurs. Don't assume that flooded components are destroyed components. Disassemble the computer and clean the boards by cleaning the contacts and edge connectors. You can buy connector cleaner fluids, or some people use a hard white artist's eraser—do not use pencil erasers! (A Texas Instruments study showed that they contain acids that do more harm than good to connectors.) Blow out crevices with compressed air. (And if you do disassemble, clean, dry, and reassemble your computer, and then find that it works, write the manufacturer a letter; they might put your face in an advertisement.)

Avoid floods by thinking ahead. Don't store any electrical devices directly on the floor; they'll be damaged when the floor is cleaned. Generally, flooding indoors is under six inches. Be aware of flooding from improper roofing; when installing PCs, don't put one in directly under the suspicious stain on the ceiling. ("Oh, that—it was fixed two years ago. No problem now.")

Corrosion

Liquids (and gases) can accelerate corrosion of PCs and PC components. Corrosive agents include:

- Salt sweat in skin oils

- Water

- Airborne sulfuric acid, salt spray, and carbonic acid

Your fear here is not that the PC will fall away to rust; the largest problem that corrosion causes is oxidation of circuit contacts. When a device's connector becomes oxidized, it doesn't conduct as well, and so the device does not function, or—worse—malfunctions sporadically. Salt in sweat can do this, so be careful when handling circuit boards; don't touch edge connectors unless you have to. This is why some firms advertise that they use gold edge connectors; gold is resistant to corrosion.

You don't believe that you have detectable traces of finger oils? Try this simple experiment. Pour a glass of soda or beer into a very clean glass—preferably a plastic cup that has never been used before. There will be a noticeable "head" on the drink. (Diet soda seems particularly fizzy.) Now put your finger into the center of the head, just for a second. The head will rapidly dissolve, because the oils damage the surface tension required to support the head. It's the quickest way to eliminate a large head so you can pour a larger glass of beer. Or you could try buying a nice new 20-inch color computer monitor and see how many of your colleagues fail to understand that it is not a touch-screen device. You will end up with numerous thick, oily smudge marks on your monitor that are very visible and annoying when a dark background is displayed on it.

Carbonated liquids include carbonic acid, and coffee and tea contain tannic acids. The sugar in soda is eaten by bacteria that leave behind conductive excrement—like hiring some germs to put new traces on your circuit board. Generally, try to be very careful with drinks around computers.

Don't forget cleaning fluids. Be careful with that window cleaner that you're using to keep the display clean. If your PC is on a pedestal on the floor, and the floor is mopped each day, some of the mopping liquid gets into the PC. Cleaning fluids are very corrosive.

You can clean edge connectors with either hard white erasers (remember, don't use the pink erasers—they're acidic!) or connector cleaner products. One of the best-known vendors of these products is Texwipe. You can get a catalog of their products by writing to them at their address, listed in Appendix A.

Making the Environment "PC Friendly"

Let's sum up what we've seen in this chapter. Protect your PC by doing the following:

- Check power considerations:
    - No heating elements (Mr. Coffee, portable heaters) in the same outlet as a PC
    - No large electric motors (refrigerators, air conditioners) on the same line as the PC
    - Some kind of power noise protection
- Check temperature ranges:
    - Maximum 110 degrees F (43 degrees C)
    - Minimum 65 degrees F (18 degrees C)

The minimum temperature can actually be considerably lower, as long as the computer remains *on* all of the time.

- Prevent dust buildup—you can buy (from PC Power and Cooling) power supplies with a filtered fan that suck air in through the *back* rather than the usual approach of pulling it in through the front.
- Make sure there isn't a vibration source like an impact printer on the same table as the hard disk.

- Make sure you're familiar with or (if you're a support person) teach your users about:

    - Leaving the machines on all the time

    - Keeping cables screwed in and out of the way

    - Basic "don't do this" things in DOS, like formatting the hard disk

- Protect against static electricity.

A Sample Preventive Maintenance Program

Although this chapter has discussed some preventive maintenance (PM) concerns, I've mainly talked about environmental problems PCs face. The fact is, if you're a PC support person, you're probably too overworked to do actual preventive maintenance.

PM implies that you take a machine off a person's desk at regular intervals, perhaps as often as every six months, and move it to your "shop" to give it a good going-over so that you'll anticipate problems.

If you actually have the support staff to do this, here's the PM procedure I use. If you have only one machine, it's particularly important. These steps should take about two hours.

1. Pick up the PC at its worksite. (Yes, this takes more time than having it delivered to your workplace, but you'll learn a lot just from observing its working environment.) Examine:

    - Are the connectors screwed in?

    - Have screws disappeared from the back of the machine?

    - What else is plugged into the PC's outlet? No Mr. Coffees?

- Is the PC on a rickety table?

- Is the PC near a window? Is it in a location that can get direct sun at some point in the day?

2. Ask if the machine is doing anything strange.

3. Ensure that the hard disk (if any) is backed up.

4. Run the machine's diagnostics. It is a good idea to run Scandisk to see what percent of the user's drive consists of "lost clusters."

5. If it's a DOS computer, examine the AUTOEXEC.BAT and CONFIG .SYS files for any obvious problems—lack of a BUFFERS command, for example. If it's a Windows machine, look at the .INI files for obvious tampering. If it's running Windows 95/98 or Windows NT, just run the computer a bit to ensure that it isn't obviously misconfigured.

6. Disassemble the PC.

7. Clean the edge connectors with a connector cleaner and a lint-free cloth or a hard white artist's eraser.

8. Push the chips back into their sockets (discussed in the next chapter).

9. Use canned air to remove dust from circuit boards—don't forget the circuit board under the hard disk.

10. Reassemble the PC. Ensure that all of the cables are securely in place.

11. Rerun the diagnostics.

12. Ensure that all screws are present. If they are not, add screws.

By now, your PC is shined to a high gloss. But what happens when something goes wrong? For that, turn to the next chapter.

5

Troubleshooting PC Problems

- General rules of thumb

- Seven steps to success

- The importance of checking your software

- IBM Diagnostic Error Code tables

Okay, suppose you dust out your PC fortnightly. You clean and adjust your disk drives semi-annually. You have a robot that shoots anyone coming within 50 feet of your PC with food or drink. But, one day, WordPerfect refuses to print your purple prose. How do you proceed?

You might say that this is a chapter about religion. I want you to develop a process for dealing with computer repairs that you follow as dutifully as a zealot follows a religion.

Why get religious? Because people who fix PCs day in and day out—people who fix *anything* day in and day out, for that matter— have learned to do it by following some repeatable procedures and step-by-step methods. The alternative method is to attack each problem in a haphazard way.

Now, I'm somebody who's tried both the religious way and the haphazard way. As such, you might say that I'm uniquely qualified to offer you some advice on how to choose that approach to take.

If you find that you're plagued with too much free time, time you've got to spend with the spouse and kids; if you just can't sleep at night, and need something to fill those insomniac hours; if Saturdays and Sundays are painful tedium broken only by the occasional *Three Stooges* rerun—then by all means, adopt the haphazard method. You'll be able to tackle all kinds of fascinating problems, most of which you created yourself while noodling around trying to fix the original problem. And, since the true haphazard fixer never takes notes, you'll get to experience the joy of problem-solving over and over, even when it's the same problem.

If, on the other hand, you want to do something with your days other than futzing around with balky PCs, then think about getting religion.

Don't get me wrong; there's nothing wrong with futzing around with a PC—you'll get some of your deepest insights and "ohhh… *that's* how it works" kind of knowledge of PCs through that kind of experimentation. All I'm saying is to keep the experiments and the fixing as separate as possible. And when you *must* experiment, then make sure that all of your experiments are repeatable ones; taking notes should be gospel.

General Troubleshooting Rules

These rules have kept me out of trouble for a long time. I know they'll be of use to you.

Don't Panic

I Will Win

Write Everything Down

Do the Easy Stuff First

Reboot and Try Again

Simplify Your Configuration and Reboot

Draw a Picture

Separate the Parts into Components and Test Components

Never Assume Something Is Good

Trust No One: The Documentation Sometimes Lies

Observe Like Sherlock Holmes

Wish for Luck

While some of these suggestions are a bit tongue-in-cheek, there's a nugget of advice in every one, and they're all part of the philosophy of troubleshooting.

Remember "Don't Panic" and "I Will Win"

You've got to have confidence in yourself as a troubleshooter. Look, this stuff isn't that hard. My technical training is as a Ph.D. economist rather than as a computer scientist or engineer, I've got 10 thumbs, and people pay *me* to fix machines—you can do it too. There's not that much to these machines. When it comes right down to it, the only thing that you really can't replace for (at most) a hundred dollars or so is your data, and you can protect that with frequent backups.

If you don't go in there *knowing* that you're going to win, you're going to get beaten—these machines can *smell* fear. An old girl-friend, a black belt in Tae Kwon Do, told me once that an important tenet of Tae Kwon Do is to "have an indomitable spirit." Sounds good to me—practice some *Tech* Kwon Do, and don't forget that indomitable spirit.

Write Everything Down

If you read Chapter 2, "Disassembling the PC" (and if you didn't, go do it), then you've already read about the hazards of not documenting. I tend not to write things down when I'm pretty sure that the operation will be simple (it almost never is), or if it's sufficiently traumatic that I'm certain that I couldn't forget (there's always another, bigger trauma waiting). I've found that I'm more likely to write things down if I keep my notebook (the paper kind) handy. As a bonus, writing things down in your notebook means that you'll be able to find them later.

Do the Easy Stuff First

I am, by nature, a lazy person. That's why I got interested in computers: they were machines that could free me from some drudgery. The *inexperienced* and lazy troubleshooter tries to save time by not making notes, by acting before thinking, and *swapping* when he ought to be *stopping*… stopping to consider his next move.

What I've eventually figured out is that well-planned laziness is a virtue. An *experienced* lazy person looks ahead and says, "Oh, heck, what if I *can't* fix this thing? I don't want to create any more trouble for myself than necessary." And so the lazy person keeps diagrams and writes down everything that she does so she doesn't have to tear out her hair trying to put the thing back together.

The *experienced* lazy person does the easy stuff first: if it's a video problem, and it's not software, then there are four things that could be swapped: the motherboard, the video board, the cable, or the monitor. What gets swapped first? The easy thing: the cable.

Reboot and Try Again

Your computer is affected by fluctuations in the power supply of as brief a duration as four milliseconds. That means that if your power disappeared for only 1/200 of a second, you wouldn't see the lights flicker, the microwave would still work, and the TV wouldn't skip a beat, even the digital clocks wouldn't start blinking. But several bytes of your computer's memory (not a lot of the memory, or you'd see a memory error message of some kind) get randomized. The result is that a program that has always worked pretty well all of a sudden stops dead. You'll never find out why it locked up that one time in a thousand. Maybe everybody in the building was running their photocopiers at the same time. Maybe radiation from a solar storm assaulted your memory chips (yes, that can happen, although it's unlikely; when a technician blames something on "cosmic rays," she's being facetious). It doesn't matter; the quick answer to this problem is just to start over and reboot the machine.

Now, don't get too trigger-happy with the reboot if you're in the middle of an application. It's usually a really bad idea to reboot out of Windows 95/98 or Windows NT—try everything you can to get the machine to respond and let you do a graceful shutdown. If you reboot in the middle of an application, the application may have left files "open," and any such files will be lost if you reboot before the application has "closed" the files. (Such half-finished files lead to a phenomenon you may have seen called "lost clusters." More on that when we discuss hard disks in Chapters 10 through 14.)

Simplify, Simplify, Simplify!

The average PC has about a bazillion screen savers, applications, background communications programs (like fax receive programs), applications, and of course driver programs for sound boards, network cards, video boards, and the mouse, to name just a few. It's really hard to determine the source of a problem when there are innumerable interactions between hardware and software.

That means that it's a good idea to eliminate as much as you can from a PC before trying to diagnose it. Boot without the network. If you're running Windows 95 or 98, wait for the Starting Windows... message and press F8. That gives you the chance to boot Windows in "safe" mode. In Windows NT, you can choose a configuration with a simple video driver at startup, and then you can use the Control Panel, under Services, to stop any unnecessary services.

We've seen this in the DOS world time and time again. Memory resident or TSR (Terminate and Stay Resident, referring to the fact that they remain in memory) programs can interfere with system functions. It may just be that the reason your drive E: will not format is because you've got your LAN software loaded. Don't ask me why—just try it. Remove all those pop-ups by rebooting without them and see if the problem goes away. Software troubleshooting is just like hardware troubleshooting: divide and conquer. Each piece of software that you're running is a piece of the system, and you want to minimize the number of pieces that you have to deal with. TSRs are the easiest part to remove.

Draw a Picture, Separate into Components, and Test

This is a true story. A friend was once a PC troubleshooter type for a county government in Virginia, where I live. She tells this story about another PC troubleshooter type—let's call him Ignatz. One day, their help desk got a phone call.

"Ignatz," the caller said, "WordPerfect isn't printing with the new laser printer!"

Now, an experienced lazy person listens and says, "Gosh—how can I fix this without leaving my chair?" Many of us would probably zero in on that word, *new*. As in "*new* laser printer." The next question might be something like, "What kind of printer did you have before the new laser printer?" "Have you ever seen Word-Perfect print on this laser printer before?" (Probably not.) "Have you reinstalled WordPerfect for the laser printer?" (A confused "What?" is the probable answer.)

Ignatz, on the other hand, attacked the problem by first swapping the motherboard on the PC that was attached to the laser printer.

Yes, that's right—you read that correctly. It even kind of fixed the problem, as Iggie figured that he'd reload the user's software while he was at it. Yeah, we can observe that Ignatz is, umm, shall we say, "a couple sandwiches short of a picnic" when it comes to troubleshooting. But I see people do less extreme (but just as unnecessary) things all the time. Heck, I still do a lot of dumb things myself, playing Macho Man with a Screwdriver. But I hope to get better at remembering to be lazy when troubleshooting.

Now, if old Ig had stopped to think, then he could have diagrammed the whole system. Simplified, you could say that the laser printer is attached to a cable, which attaches to a parallel port, which is connected to the motherboard, which runs the software. That kind of divides up the problem into: laser printer, cable, parallel port, motherboard, and software. Each of those components can then be isolated and tested. "Testing" most hardware just means swapping it, as most of us lack the very expensive equipment needed to test hardware. But software can be played with in many ways, the most fruitful of which is usually in its setup and configuration. I'd look at the software first. I always look at the software before I go after the hardware. Why? Simple: I've got a much better chance of finding the answer in software.

Never Assume

It's far too easy to assume that something is blameless. "How could the problem be the new version of ThunderWord? It's been clean for the last five versions!" Subject everything to your scrutiny, *including* the documentation. And while we're on the subject…

Be Prepared to Believe that the Documentation Lies

Years ago, I bought my first VGA board. It was made by Compaq, and it wasn't cheap, but I'd bought it from Compaq because I knew that they'd make a compatible, high-quality product. Since it was in the early days of the VGA, many clones were kinda wobbly compatibility-wise, so I was playing it safe.

When I went to install the board, I took the time to read the documentation. About half of the booklet that came with the board discussed installation. In particular, there were several pages about how to properly set the three jumpers that were clearly marked and even presented in black-and-white photos in the booklet. Before even removing the board from its anti-static bag, I studied the documentation and figured out how to set the three jumpers. Donning my anti-static wrist strap, I removed the board from its bag.

But it had only one jumper on it.

I looked and looked and *looked*, but there was only one jumper on the %$#@! thing. I picked up the manual again—and a lone piece of paper fluttered from between its pages. It basically said, "Your VGA is a new and improved model. It's got only one jumper. Set it like this." Frustrating, yes, but at least Compaq provided the right documentation, albeit hidden. Jumpers are usually not the real nightmare, however: the documentation is. Almost every one of these things is badly translated from some Pacific Rim nation's language to English and, worst of all, it's usually wrong. The jumper setting for the parallel port is usually off, and I've seen incorrect documentation for the serial port jumpers as well. I've often wondered if the documentation's author didn't have a sense of humor, however: this three-by-eight-inch piece of paper is *copyrighted*.

If you're wondering, by the way, how I figured out the correct settings, then I'm afraid that there's no trick that I can share with you. When I run into one of these boards, I check my notes to see if I've run into this particular model before. If I have, great; if not, all I can do is trial and error.

Observe Like Sherlock Holmes

In Arthur Conan Doyle's tales of the Great Detective, Holmes sometimes exclaims about some new piece of evidence. He's obviously excited about it, but when Watson asks him *why* he's excited, Holmes gives nothing away. "Not yet, Watson," he demurs. "It's too early for theories."

What Holmes knew was that problem solving involves making theories, and then proving or disproving the theories with facts. But suppose Holmes had advanced an early theory aloud, perhaps in the company of the beleaguered Inspector Lestrade? Lestrade would like nothing better than to witness his harasser Holmes brought down by a faulty theory. Now, Holmes also knows that, so he's got a subconscious aversion to finding any facts that disprove this ill-uttered supposition. By keeping his mouth shut until he's got enough facts, he can offer a theory that he feels confident about.

You'll see this in your everyday troubleshooting life. Someone stands over your shoulder as you peer inside a disemboweled PC carcass. "What do you think it is?" he says.

This is a crucial moment. Learn to say automatically, "I don't know—there's not enough information yet." Otherwise, you'll find that now the game you're playing is no longer "fix the machine;" unconsciously, you're now playing a game called "prove you're right." So hang onto the theories until you've got the facts.

When you open up a machine, you expose the machine to a certain risk that you'll do something dumb to it. PC troubleshooting differs from, say, automotive troubleshooting, in that the thing that's most commonly broken is the user. If you separate out the "user is broken" stuff, like they forgot to turn it on or the like, software is the next most common. Honest-to-God hardware problems are actually quite uncommon compared to user and software problems. That leads me to the seven specific troubleshooting steps.

Six Steps to Troubleshooting Success

The smart troubleshooter makes the troubleshooting job tractable by breaking down problems into steps. Don't panic, and remember to be methodical; otherwise you will thrash helplessly about and get frustrated. Once you are frustrated, you are *lost*, and you start creating new problems.

Following is the method that I use. It looks a lot like methods suggested by other people, but it's not the only method. You certainly don't have to use *my* method, but find one you like, and stick to it. It's the "this'll take only five minutes" repairs that get me in trouble. (You know—like when someone gives you directions, saying, "You can't miss it." I *know* I'm in trouble then.) I'll assume for this discussion that you are interacting with someone else (the person with the PC problem), but you can just as easily interview yourself.

Before opening up the computer, do the following:

1. Check the nut behind the keyboard.

2. Check that everything is plugged in: power, monitor, phone lines, printer, modem, and so on.

3. Check the software.

4. Check external signs. Make notes of them.

5. Run the diagnostics disk.

Only then, if you still haven't solved the problem:

6. Disassemble the machine, clean the connectors, push the socketed chips back into their sockets, and put the machine back together.

Notice that the first six steps *aren't* hardware steps; let's take a closer look at all seven.

Check for Operator Error

Operator error is responsible for 93.3 percent of PC failures. (That's a made-up statistic. But it got your attention and probably isn't far from the truth.) There are lots of things that an operator can do wrong.

There are three main sources of problems for PCs: hardware, software, and users. Guess which one is the most likely? Users. Software's second. Hardware is a distant third. Why are there so many people problems in the computer business? Mainly because the user interfaces still stink, even the "good" ones.

For example, when I used to teach hands-on dBase classes, I'd regularly see a student looking bewildered at the screen. "It didn't work," they say. I'd ask, "Did you type in exactly what I told you to?" "Yes," they'd say. I'd look at their screen. They *did*, indeed, type in exactly what I told them to *this time*. Three commands back, however, they miskeyed something and ignored the resulting error message. These are intelligent people: they're just under some stress (they have to pay attention to me *and* the computer), and they miss a detail. It's easy to do.

The language of computers confuses people. You've heard the stories about users doing goofy things; well, they're true. I've seen them. I once watched a user follow the dBase III 1.0 installation instructions: "Insert System Disk 1 in drive A: and close the door." He inserted the disk in the drive, then got up (looking a little puzzled, I'll give him that), and closed the door to his office. If I hadn't been there to actually see it, I probably wouldn't have believed it. But before you giggle too loudly, consider: where was the "door?" Have you seen a "door" on a floppy drive lately? No, there's never been one, really—just a little latch across it or a small shutter. I mean, if you hired me to put a door on your house, and instead I installed a little plastic latch, then you'd sue me, and you'd *win*.

When teaching those same dBase classes, now and then I'd get some guy staring at the keyboard in puzzlement.

"What's wrong?" I'd ask.

"I'm looking for a key," he'd reply.

"Which one? I'll point it out," I would offer.

"The 'any' key," he'd say, still puzzled. I would look at the screen, where dBase was prompting, "Press any key to continue...." I had just gotten finished with my "pay attention to what the computer is doing" lecture, and so this poor soul was trying his hardest to follow my directions. (Nowadays, there is an answer for the "any key" searchers. Egghead Software sells an "any key" kit: it's a keytop sticker that says, "ANY KEY." You install it on...well, any key.)

I've seen users "copy a floppy" with a photocopier. They're not dumb—they saw the "double-sided" sticker on the floppy, so they copy both sides. I once saw a bank organize their backup floppies by punching holes in them so they would go into a small binder. True stories, all of them.

A friend at Microsoft tells the story of being called by someone who couldn't get Windows to do anything. "I've got my foot on the pedal," he said, "and it's not doing anything!" Well, mice are often found on the floor, but...

Even worse, sometimes users will (horrors!) prevaricate slightly. "I didn't do anything. It just stopped working." Please note: I'm not one of those techie types whose motto is, "Assume that the user is lying," but sometimes it happens. More often, it's not that they lie. It's just that they don't know what's important, or they're embarrassed to tell you what they really did.

People feel defensive calling a support person (such as you). You want to collect as much information as possible. If you make them feel defensive, they'll misremember, or withhold information. Here's a trick that telemarketers are told: smile when you're on the phone with someone. It works. (As Sam Kinison said, "It creates the illusion that you care.") Being a support person can be wearing. There's a tendency to feel like "these people must get up early in the morning to think up dumb things to ask," but you can't let it get you down. Remember, these folks can't be too dumb—after all, the same company that hired them hired you, too. (Heh, heh.)

Again, think *lazy*. How can you collect enough information while on the phone to fix the problem right over the phone? The key is to not act like so many support people, the ones who don't even let you get your question out before they break in with, "Are you sure your computer is plugged in?" Stop and think how idiotic this phrasing is. Who's going to answer "No"? It's roughly equivalent to saying "Oh! Look at that. It's not plugged in. I *am* an idiot. Sorry to bother you."

Now, don't get me wrong: you've got to ask the question—that's why it's step two in our seven steps. But there's a right way, and a wrong way. One right way is the "bureaucracy" approach. "I'm sorry that's happening to you. That must be really frustrating; I'll do whatever I can for you. But first, you know how it is here at XYZ Corp.; we've got a form for everything. Forgive me, but I've got to ask some dumb-sounding questions. Can you just double-check for me that the PC is plugged in..." Another good approach is to couch it in a self-deprecating way. "My asking you if the PC is plugged in reminded me of something dumb I did the other day. The PC was plugged into the surge protector, and the surge protector was plugged into the wall. It took me 15 minutes to figure out that the surge protector was turned off! Can you believe that I did something that stupid?" If the next sound you hear is, "Ummm, can I call you back? Someone just walked into my office," then you can be pretty sure you've just engineered another fixed PC.

Best of all, however, that's a PC that your user just fixed. He's now had a success, so he'll remember that particular problem/solution combination. (Psychology tells us that people learn better with positive reinforcement than with negative reinforcement.) He'll probably end up feeling more capable, more likely to tackle the problem himself next time. "Success is a habit," said Vince Lombardi.

Another source of operator error is with inexperienced operators. The PC isn't exactly the simplest thing in the world to master. The author of a book titled *Computer Wimp: 100 Things I Wish I'd Known Before I Bought My First Personal Computer* observes in that book that learning to use a computer system may be the most difficult learning endeavor that a person will undertake in his/her post-school life. (Things like raising kids are undoubtedly tougher, but they're different kinds of learning experiences.) It doesn't take a genius to recognize that most PC hardware and software manuals aren't the easiest things to comprehend. The answer? Good education. There are tons of good books, videos, college courses, and professional seminars on PCs, one for every budget. "If you think education is expensive," they say, "try ignorance."

Is Everything Plugged In?

I know this sounds stupid, but we've all done it. A friend bought a modem and couldn't get it to work. It accepted commands all right, but could not dial out. The phone line was tested with a regular phone and worked fine. He was quite puzzled until he realized that he'd plugged the phone line into the "out" jack in the modem (intended to be connected to a phone so that a phone line can be shared between the modem and a phone), rather than the "in" jack. Another time, I ran the IBM diagnostic disk on my PC and kept getting "bad address mark" errors on my disk drives. I was all set to spend a lot of money for new drives until I realized that the disk that I was using was not formatted. (The drives were fine.)

As I just said, when you ask the user, "Is it plugged in?" be diplomatic. (Don't you hate when tech support people ask *you* that question?) But be firm.

- Is the PC plugged into some kind of multi-outlet strip?

- Is the strip on? Did the user kick off the power switch?

- Can the user actually see that the power strip is plugged into the wall?

- Are the other devices plugged into the power strip working? Try having the user plug a desk lamp or fan into the power strip and see if it works.

- Is the outlet on the wall switched?

I know of a large communications company that kept sending technicians to try to determine why a LAN server kept dying at strange hours of the night. They'd set up the software at the user site, leave it running, and then eventually get called back to the site because after a day or two all kinds of files had been trashed. The techs would always ask, "Has this been turned off in the middle of an operation?" The users would solemnly (and annoyingly—this tech guy wasn't going to weasel out of fixing his company's buggy software *that* easily, they thought) shake their heads no. Finally this large company sent their SuperTech—the guy who'd seen it all. He looked over the server and listened to the users' stories.

Now, this guy *knew* from the symptoms that the server was getting shut down improperly. (Remember that indomitable spirit. On the other hand, save the spirit for the machine—don't get snotty with the users.) So he looked for easy ways to turn the machine off accidentally. Noticing two light switches on the wall and only one fluorescent ceiling panel, he flipped both switches. You guessed it—the server was plugged into a switched outlet. The security staff, in making the rounds each night, would shut off the lights.

- Are the peripherals plugged in? Are they plugged *into the computer*?

Not only is everything plugged in, but is everything in *tight*? Multiple pin connectors slowly bend under gravity unless the mounting screws are tightened. As someone stretches his/her legs under the desk, a loose power cord could be moved enough to disconnect it, or disconnect and reconnect it. Connectors on the floor take a lot of abuse.

I think the reason that people don't properly secure connectors is that it can't be done without one of those small straight-slot screwdrivers that are smaller than the one you've got in the kitchen tool drawer, but larger than the one you have to adjust the screws in your glasses. (Of course, we true PC repair warriors are never without our small screwdriver with the pocket clip on it and the logo of some company on its side, but normal humans…) Nowadays, you can find a remedy: many cables are sold with big plastic screws that are easily hand-turnable. (Many folks call those screws "thumbscrews," and I guess it's as good a term as any, but I find it a bit medieval.) Whenever possible, get cables with hand-turnable screws. They'll pay for themselves in the long run.

I'm one of the worst offenders in the cable screws department. As I install and reinstall things a lot, I tend to just push my serial and video cables into their sockets, not bothering with the screwdriver (I don't have the little screwdriver with the pocket clip when I don't happen to have my pocket protector around. You know: sometimes I want to work undercover, so I leave the pocket protector behind.) A few years ago, I had myself convinced that my serial port or modem was fried, as I was getting terrible error rates on my communications sessions all of a sudden. As I'd just gotten finished doing a lecture on lightning damage to serial ports, and it was T-storm season in Washington, I figured ruefully that I'd just lost a serial port. "But," I thought, "Who knows? Maybe when lightning toasted the port, it burned some chips up—I can at least take some pictures." So I got ready to take my PC apart. Of course, one of the first things I did was to remove the cables, and that's when I noticed that the serial cable just about fell off the back of the PC when I touched it. So I returned the cables to their interfaces—making sure they were secured tightly—and, as you've already guessed, the problems went away.

Check the Software

Remember I said that more problems are software problems than hardware problems? Software problems arrive in several guises:

- Operator error

- Keyboard/screen/disk/timer conflicts with memory resident software

- Software that doesn't clean up after itself

- Software that requires hardware that isn't connected or activated

- Buggy applications

- Buggy driver programs

Software troubleshooting could be a book in itself, and in fact all of the books out there on supporting Windows 95/98, Novell NetWare, Windows NT, and the like are software troubleshooting books. But let's tackle some of the broad causes of software problems.

Dynamic Link Libraries (DLLs) and Virtual Device Drivers (VxDs)

Modern operating systems like Windows 95/98 and Windows NT are built in a kind of layer-cake fashion. The application programs sit atop the cake—they're the frosting. But they sit atop layers of cake and filling, layers that they need—heck, frosting all by itself is a bit much, right? Two important parts are Dynamic Link Libraries (DLLs) and Virtual Device Drivers (VxDs).

The bottom layer of the cake is the hardware. In some senses, you can summarize the job of an operating system this way: the application programs (the word processor, the e-mail program, the spreadsheet, or Mortal Kombat) need things done for them by the hardware (the video board, the network card, the hard disk). But if every application tries to use a piece of hardware at the same time, nothing works; what you need is a kind of traffic cop between the apps and the hardware. The OS is that cop, the piece in between that routes hardware requests between applications and hardware, keeping traffic jams to a minimum and "crashes" nonexistent (well, in theory, anyway).

The lowest level of system software is the set of programs that are customized to particular pieces of hardware. These programs, called *drivers*, attach in a modular fashion to the main body of the OS (called the *kernel*). For example, in order to get Windows to recognize and use your Hewlett-Packard LaserJet model 5P, you must load a driver for that printer, adding it to the Windows system software.

Drivers can pose a bit of a problem for software stability. Most of the operating system is designed by a close-knit software development team; for example, most of the code in Windows NT was written by a few individuals working together at Microsoft. But most Windows drivers aren't written by Microsoft. Instead, the burden of writing driver programs usually falls to the hardware vendors: Diamond writes drivers for its Viper video boards, HP writes drivers for its laser printers, and so on. Programmers working at these companies don't get the same kind of support that they'd have as IBM or Microsoft employees, and so as a result they can't always write driver programs that are well-integrated into an operating system. This is not a slap at programmers at Diamond, Hewlett-Packard, or any other hardware vendor; it's just a reality that the guy on Microsoft's Windows programming team who writes the Calculator code probably plays softball on the same team as the woman who writes the Windows kernel code. And that has to mean that he'll get better answers to sticky programming questions than would someone from outside Microsoft.

Because of the way that drivers work in modern operating systems, they're usually called *virtual* device drivers. In the Windows world, the acronym for that is *VxD*. VxDs are sometimes designed to plug into a particular operating system (which means, for example, that you might not want to waste your time trying to use a Windows 95 VxD under Windows NT, unless you know that the driver will work in either of those operating systems).

The bottom line is that driver programs are often a weak link in an operating system. Windows 98 may run fine for weeks, and then you install a new version of the driver for your ATI Mach 64 video card. You try to enter print preview mode from your favorite word processor, and something happens, whether it's an outright lockup or some garbage on the screen. It's most likely to be that new driver.

While this isn't gospel, most operating system designers do much of their initial development on "lowest common denominator" hardware, like VGA for video. Keep those plain-Jane drivers around and use them when possible as a kind of "known good" baseline configuration.

And a final tip about device drivers: when a new version comes along, *keep the old one around for a while*! "Latest" isn't always "greatest" when it comes to drivers. Do what a friend of mine does, and use the "baby food" method of testing new drivers. The first time she mentioned this to me, I looked puzzled.

"The *baby food* method?" I asked her. (I'm an excellent straight man.)

"Sure," she replied. "When a baby starts eating solid food, you don't know what he's going to be allergic to. So, suppose you want to see if he's allergic to carrots. You start feeding him carrots; if a few days go by and he hasn't swollen up, then carrots are probably okay."

"I do that with device drivers. I just pop 'em into the system, try out all my applications to make sure that none of them break, and then just live with the thing for a week to see if anything new and unpleasant happens to my system. If not, I keep the driver. If I get troubles, then I document the troubles, restore the old device driver, and see if those troubles go away."

Good advice. But I'd add one thing to it. When you swap drivers on a piece of hardware, be sure to power down the system completely before restarting it. Some video drivers in particular don't work quite right unless you power down and restart after installing a new driver.

Another term you'll see turn up when doing software troubleshooting is *DLL*, short for *Dynamic Link Library*. A library is a file containing a bunch of small programs that get a particular thing done. It's called a library for two reasons: first, there are usually many of those small programs in a particular library, and, second, the library file resembles a library in that it is publicly available; the programs in it are available to any application. For example, the program that tells Windows how to change the color of a part of the screen is almost certainly part of a library.

Now, the question of how a program finds a library is called *linking*. For most of the history of computer programming, libraries get linked when a program called the *link editor* makes a copy of the desired library routines, and incorporates those routines directly into the program. This is called *static* linking. Static linking is bad because (1) if you are running three programs that all know how to print (for example), then you're wasting RAM because you've now got three copies of the print routine resident in memory; and (2) if the way that the OS wants an application to print (to continue the example) changes, then every application would have to be rebuilt.

Operating systems in use since the early '80s incorporate a different kind of linking called *dynamic linking*. Under dynamic linking, a dynamic link library is relinked every time the application calls for one of its library routines. Taking the example of printing, under static linking a program gets the whole library program inserted into it. A program linked dynamically to a library contains only a note that says, in essence, "When you need this routine, go out to PRINT.DLL, load it up, and link the routine before going any further." A DLL can also be shared; once one program has PRINT.DLL in memory, any other program needing PRINT.DLL gets the one copy that's already in memory, rather than loading another one.

What's this got to do with troubleshooting? Well, sometimes an incorrectly installed program may crash, complaining of a lack of a DLL. That may be fixable by simply adding the DLL's directory to a "path" statement of some kind, or the DLL may have been accidentally erased.

Or it could have been replaced.

Whenever you click File, then Open in Windows 95/98 or Windows NT, your program calls up a DLL that contains a routine that knows how to put a File/Open dialog box on the screen. (In Windows, it's called COMMDLG.DLL.) Now and then, I've installed programs that actually replaced the comes-in-the-Windows-box version of COMMDLG.DLL with their own, "improved" versions.

How do you find out whether you've got a cowbird DLL in the nest? One simple way is to just compare the dates of the *other* DLLs that shipped with the OS to the suspect one. Or, as is more frequently the solution, you can simply re-install the OS; it's often a more timesaving solution than poking through DLLs looking for the "pretender."

A number of mysteries can be linked to software that doesn't recover well from disabled or nonexistent hardware.

- Trying to print to a nonexistent printer.
- Trying to print a non-PostScript formatted file to a PostScript printer.
- Trying to print to a printer that is offline.
- Trying to display graphics data on a monochrome monitor.

- Some older programs have copy protection built into them. Unfortunately, this sometimes means that they won't run on a computer faster than 8MHz. (Yes, you read that right.) You may have to try slowing down the system, if you've got a speed setting for your PC.

- Running a program that needs more memory than the PC contains.

But here's my favorite hardware-induced software error. The PS/2s insist on being properly configured before they'll do any work for you. If they are configured wrong—they boot up and find that they have more or less memory than they expected, or more or fewer disk drives, or the like—they print a 162 error on the screen, and wait patiently for an F1 to continue.

If you have an external floppy disk drive on a PS/2, it has its own power supply and power switch. If you forget to turn on the external floppy before booting up the PS/2, you'll get a scary-looking 162 error. Just turn the floppy drive on and reboot. Do *not* re-run the configuration program found on the Reference Diskette: it will sense (assuming the floppy is still off) that there isn't an external floppy any more, and will stop looking for it. Then when you *do* turn the external floppy on, the PS/2 won't talk to it. Argggh. (By the way, there are a number of PS/2 motherboards floating around that just plain won't hold a configuration for very long— that's another problem altogether.)

Faulty Software

Sometimes the problem is just plain buggy software. Even the most popular programs can misbehave when faced with a full disk, insufficient memory, or some situation that the designer didn't anticipate or didn't test.

Try to make the bug reproducible. If it is a suspected bug in a compiler product, trim off as much of the other code as is possible while retaining the bug. Ideally, a program no longer than 10 lines of code should demonstrate the problem. Then report it to the manufacturer and other users in your company.

Check External Signs

If the computer has indicator lights, what do they indicate? Are all of the lights glowing on the modem? Does the printer indicate "ready"? Is the hard disk squealing or grinding? Does the monitor image look bent? Your drives and other peripherals produce hums, whirrs, and clicks. After a while, these noises become familiar, and any variation in them signals a problem. Pay attention to these signs.

The first step in successful troubleshooting is in isolating the problem component. These signs can point the way.

It is very important to note any signs here. Document what lights are on and off, the positions of switches, etc.

Run Diagnostic Programs

Many PC-type machines come with diagnostic programs that can help pinpoint a problem (assuming, of course, that the computer is functioning well enough to run them in the first place). Other computers, like some "no-name" clones, do not. Various public domain diagnostic programs exist.

There are some very good third-party diagnostic programs, and I'm going to talk about them in a few pages.

Truthfully, diagnostic programs are not so valuable in helping to *locate* errors. They mainly make you feel confident that there is nothing wrong with the PC. As I suggested earlier, they're of limited value. After all, what must be running in order to run these programs? Well, the system board must be running, the video must run so you can see the screen, the keyboard must be active to accept commands, and the floppy must work so the program can load. Merely loading the program (or any other program, for that matter) tells you some things about the system. So when I talk to vendors I question the value (in a nice way, of course) of their software.

An additional bonus of running diagnostics is that they are visually attractive; by that, I mean that they're not beautiful—but they look technical as heck. My friend Dave Stang says that if nothing else, running a diagnostic on a customer's machine buys you a few minutes to think about what's actually wrong. Whenever possible, diagnostic programs should be run from write-protected floppies to eliminate viruses as culprits.

Third-Party Diagnostic Software

In addition to the diagnostic software offered by PC hardware vendors, there is also an entire portion of the software business whose major occupation is writing and marketing diagnostic software.

- **Inventory.** These programs display and inventory what they can detect in your system. That can be useful not as inventory in and of itself; its greater value is in inventorying what the system can *see.* If you know darn well that you installed the mouse interface, but it doesn't show up on the system inventory, then you've got a problem. Before looking *too* hard for the answer, however, ask yourself first: is the driver for the mouse loaded? Diagnostic programs, like DOS and application programs, usually can't detect an unusual piece of hardware unless the driver for that program is loaded.

- **Burn-in.** When you first get a computer, it's a good idea to "burn it in." This means to run it continuously for at least three days, running some kind of diagnostic software over and over again. Some PC manufacturers even offer a "burn-in" when buying a new PC. Simple diagnostics are no good for this kind of thing for two reasons. First, most simple diagnostics insist on informing you of any errors, then *requiring* you to press a key to acknowledge that you've seen the error message. Higher quality diagnostic programs allow you to run the diagnostic in a "logging" mode whereby any error messages are saved to a logging file, and do not require confirmation of an error. Second, good diagnostics let you run the diagnostic in a "continuous" mode, whereby it runs over and over and over until you tell it to stop. Burn-in is not an unimportant step, so don't ignore it! Of the last 10 computers I've installed, two didn't fail until after four days of continuous testing. If I'd not done a burn-in on them, I probably would have ended up with a mysterious error appearing at a no-doubt inopportune time (Mr. Murphy and his law seem to have taken up residence in my office).

- **Interrupt/DMA/input/output address summary.** As you'll learn in the next chapter, the hardest thing about installing a new circuit board is adjusting some things called the input/output port address, the DMA channel, the IRQ level, and the ROM address. (Don't sweat if you don't know what they are—they're all explained in the next chapter.) The reason that you adjust these things is to make sure that they don't conflict with the port/DMA/IRQ/ROM of any other boards. For example, if you're putting a board in the system, and that board must use either interrupt number 5 or interrupt number 7, but there's already a board in your system that uses interrupt number 7, then you can't let the new board use interrupt number 7. But the question arises, how do you find out what interrupts are currently in use on your system? Diagnostic procedures *try* to report these things. I say "try" because they unfortunately can't be trusted in this task, not due to inadequacies on the part of their programmers but because of a simple fact: there's no way to reliably detect ports, DMAs, IRQs, or ROM addresses. How *do* you find out this information? You can look at the devices in your system by checking "System" in your Control Panel if you are using Windows 95/98 or Windows NT.

- **Diagnostics.** A diagnostic program should provide you with a way to give your hardware a workout. It will test your computer's memory thoroughly, test every possible data pattern on your hard disk, run your serial port at its maximum speed—in short, a good diagnostic program should be a sort of cybernetic boot camp for your computer.

- **Setup.** Some of these programs do things associated more with setup responsibilities than diagnostic ones. For example, most of these programs will low-level format a hard disk, an important step in setting up an older type of hard disk. Others may have a built-in system setup program that sets up the CMOS chip in a computer.

If you read those bullets carefully, you no doubt noticed a lot of "shoulds," as in "a good diagnostic program should...." All of this equivocation has a purpose, believe me: most diagnostic programs are junk. Look carefully before you spend the ton of money that you can easily spend on a diagnostic package. It is said that one time the science fiction author Theodore Sturgeon was approached by a literary critic who said, "Ted, you write such good stuff; why do you waste your time writing science fiction?" Sturgeon asked," What's wrong with science fiction? "The critic answered, "Ninety percent of science fiction is crap." (Well, he didn't actually say "crap," but this book is rated for general audiences.) Sturgeon is reported to have replied archly, "Ninety percent of *everything* is crap." I'm afraid that this truism, dubbed "Sturgeon's Law" by generations of science fiction fans, applies well to the diagnostics world. Let me then not waste ink beating up on this chaff; let's look at the wheat.

- **Checkit** from Touchstone Software. Checkit is a nice, inexpensive (compared to most diagnostic programs) package that is largely inexpensive because it leaves out some of the hardware that you need to do a system checkout. That's not meant to be a negative assessment; I like Checkit and use it quite a bit. But Checkit does not include a few diagnostic tools, including a loopback plug for the parallel port, a loop-back plug for the serial port, or a digital diagnostic test disk for the floppy drive. My guess as to *why* they didn't include those things is that they can be found elsewhere, and Touch-stone wanted to offer an inexpensive package—adding the extra doodads can double the price. There are two things I really like about Checkit: it's got a good set of motherboard checkout routines (DMA, timer, IRQ and the rest) as well as one of the better memory testers.

- **QAPlus/PRO** from DiagSoft is another good package in the same market niche as Checkit. No loopbacks or other doo-dads, just a good system inventory and memory tester.

- **PC-Technician** is an industrial-strength package from Wind-sor Technologies. I first looked at PC-Technician back in 1988, and I must truthfully say that I didn't think much of it then. But it's quickly matured into a nice general inventory/setup/deep diagnostic routine. It's a bit pricier than the previous two—$195 when last I checked—but it's a complete package. There are the test disks, the loopbacks, a nice manual, and a carrying case for your tools. (Just make sure you don't put any magnetic screwdrivers next to the disks in the case!) Windsor also sells a program that will put your PC printer through its paces, as well as a plug-in BIOS POST code checker like the ones discussed elsewhere in this section. The features that I like best about PC-Technician are the memory test—again, a good one in the same league as QAPlus's and Checkit's—and the serial and parallel tests. All in all, PC Technician is the best all-in-one tester, but it's pricey.

- **DisplayMate** from Sonera Technologies checks only one thing—your display. But it does an extremely thorough job, testing aspects of your monitor that you probably didn't know were testable—"pincushioning," for example. The accompanying manual is a tutorial on monitor problems and solutions. It won't test your memory or your printer, but it deserves a place on your diagnostic shelf.

One word of advice when running a diagnostic: although I told you to load all drivers before running the diagnostics, *don't* run your memory manager; it just confuses a memory test. As I've suggested, you can spend a *lot* of money on these programs, so it's a good idea to take advantage of the option that many computer dealers provide today whereby you can buy software and return it within a few weeks.

Under the Hood: Troubleshooting Step 6

Assuming that you've performed steps 1 through 5, you may actually have a circuit board problem. Many circuit board problems can be handled simply and without any fancy equipment. Step 6 just says:

- Take the PC apart.
- Clean any connectors with an artist's eraser or connector cleaner.
- Push all socketed chips back into their sockets.
- Reassemble the PC.

As we saw in the chapter on preventive maintenance, edge connectors get dirty and make circuit boards fail. Sometimes "dead" boards will do the Lazarus trick if you clean their edge connectors.

If you examine most circuit boards, you'll see that most chips are soldered right onto the board. Soldering is a process wherein the chip is bonded to the printed circuits on the board by heating a mixture of tin and lead to the point where it is molten, then allowing the tin/lead mixture to flow over the printed circuit and chip leg and finally solidify. Soldering is a great technique for mass-producing electronic components. The downside is that when you must fix soldered components, you must *first* de-solder the components. This isn't much fun, and most people don't have soldering skills.

Not all chips are soldered to boards, however. Some are put in *sockets*. A typical board might have 30 soldered chips and four socketed ones. Chips are socketed either because they've been voted "most likely to fail," or because the designer wanted to put off a decision until the last minute, or because the chip will likely have to be replaced periodically because it contains software that changes over time—remember ROM? So socketing chips makes our jobs as troubleshooters easier.

On the other hand, heating and cooling of systems make these socketed chips "creep" out of their sockets. That's why you should push socketed chips back into their sockets when inspecting a board for whatever reason. One particularly persnickety tech that I know actually takes the socketed chips out of their sockets, cleans their chip legs with connector cleaner, *then* puts the chips back in the sockets.

This should be obvious, but let me point it out anyway. Don't push *soldered* chips. The best that it can do is nothing. The worst it can do is to damage a board and maybe a chip. When you push socketed chips back into a board, be sure that you are supporting the *back* of the board. If you just put a board on a table, then push down on the chips, you can end up bending and damaging the board.

I know that advice like "take it apart, clean the connectors, push the chips back in the sockets, and reassemble" doesn't sound very dazzling. But, darn it, *it works*! Buying a board to replace a defective one is a pretty rare event for me as a troubleshooter, and I don't do much soldering. And besides, it impresses the people whose machines you're fixing—all they see you do is basically touch the boards. Eventually, you get the reputation as a person who can just "lay hands upon the board… and make it *whole!*" (With apologies to the evangelists in the crowd.)

Installing New Circuit Boards (Without Creating New Problems)

■ Configuring new circuit boards

■ Understanding I/O addresses, IRQs, DMA, and bus mastering

■ Resolving installation conflicts

■ Working with Plug and Play

Circuit boards and chips are fairly reliable, as long as you keep them above water and don't subject them to the ol' 110-volt torture test. So most boards that you handle won't be defective boards. You'll much more often be doing upgrades to existing machines, like replacing a video board with a faster, more powerful one, adding a sound card, or adding a LAN board to a machine that isn't yet on your company's network.

Putting a new board into your system and making it work involves four steps:

- **Installation**. Put it in the system and make sure the cables are all on right.

- **Configuration**. Make sure the board and the rest of the system communicate.

- **Testing**. Weed out the boards that either don't work or will soon stop working.

- **Loading and configuring drivers**. Load the software that will help the PC use the hardware.

Getting those four things done will be the focus of this chapter. But I see some of you are thinking about skipping this, so let's answer the question...

But I Have Plug and Play, So I Don't Have to Worry about This, Right?

For a few years now, PC manufacturers have attempted to make our lives easier by designing PCs around a specification called *Plug and Play (PnP)*. If you've got a PC built after 1996, it's almost certainly a PnP system. PnP's designers intended for PnP systems to configure themselves automatically, as you no doubt guessed from the name "Plug and Play." You just pop a new board into your system, boot up the computer, and your PC automatically loads the drivers that it needs to use the new board. In seconds, you're using your new hardware.

PnP sometimes *does* work as advertised, but only if your PC meets some fairly specific criteria—the right hardware, the right drivers, and the right operating system. If you *don't* have all those pieces in place, however, then you'll find that PnP systems can actually be *harder* to configure than older systems. In fact, let's say that again, with emphasis.

WARNING PnP needs both hardware *and* software. So if you're not running Windows 95/98, your PC is not PnP, and hardware configuration can still be a real pain no matter *whose* PnP hardware you've bought.

As many of us are running PnP hardware with a non-PnP operating system (like DOS, Windows 95/98, or Windows NT 4), there's a special section later in this chapter on living with PnP's Dark Side. (In that section, you'll also learn about exactly *what* are the "right" hardware, drivers, and operating system you need to make PnP happy.)

Installing boards in a PC of any kind isn't the toughest task in the world, but getting them to work once they're installed is made a bit difficult by a few different things. Some of the things that can make the process of installing new boards more...shall we say, "interesting," are: bad board documentation (and there's no shortage of that), insufficient information about the computer that you're installing the board into (that's usually *your* fault), having to know what an I/O address, DMA channel, IRQ level, ROM address, or RAM address is, and finally, PnP woes.

That's what this chapter is all about. You'll learn what all of those things are and what you need to know in order to get new circuit boards into your system and make them work. It's not difficult stuff, but it *does* need some explaining, and I promise that

I'll make the whole thing as understandable as possible. As an extra bonus, understanding I/O, DMA, IRQ, and the like, constitutes a big step forward in understanding your PC's guts.

Configuring New Circuit Boards

Most circuit boards are fully functional when you take them out of the box. But most of those circuit boards seem not to work when you install them in a PC. Why? The main reason is that the new board may *conflict* with existing boards or, more specifically, some resource on the board.

Put simply, you can't have two boards in a system that claim to be the same thing. If you were to insert two identical sound cards into the same system, then neither one would work, even if both boards were in working order before you put them into the PC.

Configuration consists of:

- Resolving device conflicts
- Providing software support (BIOS and/or device drivers)

On older upgrade boards, configuration involves setting jumpers or DIP switches. Newer boards almost always accomplish these settings through software—either automatically or through drivers that you install in your computer. While no board requires all of these, the items that require configuration are:

- Telling a memory expansion board how much memory is on the board (older boards only)
- Telling a new modem which COM port to use (COM1, COM2, COM3, or COM4, or higher)

- Telling a printer port whether it is LPT1, LPT2, or LPT3 (older boards only)

- Selecting DMA channels on a board (more on this later)

- Selecting IRQ lines on a board (more later)

- Selecting I/O addresses on a board (ditto)

- Selecting RAM and/or ROM addresses on a board (still ditto)

- Loading a driver for the board and telling the driver what I/O address you *set* the board to use (again, covered later in this chapter)

In many cases, the board is pre-configured at the factory to the correct settings, but not always. That's because it's usually impossible for the manufacturer to know what the proper settings should be for I/O addresses, DMA channels, IRQ lines, RAM addresses, and ROM addresses *in your particular machine.* And, as you'll see, unfortunately *some* boards are "hard-wired" to a particular configuration that you can't change. The inflexible nature of those boards may mean that you can't get them to work in your PC.

Solving Real-Life Configuration Conflicts

What does a hardware conflict *look* like? Here are a few common examples of installation woes.

Scenario 1

You install an internal modem in a PC; the modem refuses to work. Worse, your mouse, which used to work, doesn't work anymore. What do you do?

Scenario 2

You install a sound card in your system, and it seems to work pretty well. But now you can't print from inside Windows without crashing. What do you do?

Scenario 3

You're installing an Ethernet local area network card in a system, and it doesn't work. So you try an identical one. It doesn't work either. As you watch the *fourth* identical board fail, you begin to suspect a pattern. What's going on?

Scenario 4

You want to install a video capture board into your brand-spanking-new 500MHz PnP Pentium III system, but then you realize that all of the boards in your system have already used up all the IRQs. You need another IRQ (which I'll define later, but for now just understand it's a scarce thing). You realize that you've got an internal modem in your system that you don't use, and that it takes up an IRQ. So you remove the internal modem, install the video capture board, and fire up your computer. After Windows 98 starts, it tells you that there's no way you can use the video capture board, because there are not enough IRQs to accommodate the board. Clearly, Windows 98 is delusional, so how do you medicate it properly?

Each of these problems is caused by *resource conflicts*. Here are some explanations of what caused the problems.

In Scenario 1, modern computers all come with two serial ports, named COM1 and COM2. But internal modems also need a communications (comm) port—in fact, they have serial interface hardware right on them, meaning that when you install an internal modem, you're *also* installing an extra comm port.

Now, that comm port built into the internal modem is probably set up at the factory to act like COM2, but you've already *got* a COM2 on your system. That means that the comm port will conflict with the existing COM2 on your system—and if your mouse isn't working any more, then it's likely that your mouse is a serial mouse on, as you've guessed by now, COM2.

What's the answer? There are two basic approaches. First, you could disable one of the serial ports that came with your PC. The second possibility is to configure the new comm port that's incorporated into the internal modem to be a third comm port. Basically you do that by assigning a spare IRQ (trust me, I'll explain IRQs soon) to the comm port. But that can be a problem, either because you've run out of IRQs (an easy thing to do) or the communications software that you're running is too dumb to be able to work with anything but good old vanilla COM1 and COM2. That happens *less* with Windows 95/98 and Windows NT software than it did with DOS software, but it happens.

Now, I hear you asking, "*How* do I disable one of the comm ports on my computer, or assign a 'spare' IRQ to this internal modem?" The answer is the basis of configuration: you move a jumper (see Figure 6.1), move a DIP switch (see Figure 6.2), or run a program to reassign the board's function from COM1 to COM2 or to shut it off altogether. Whether it's a DIP switch, a jumper, or a program depends on the particular machine. Most modern systems configure all of the I/O ports in the BIOS. They don't use jumpers any more for basic system configuration. But you never know, even the latest systems still have one or two jumpers for setting things like the bus speed and processor voltages. (I'll have more to say about this in a minute, but I didn't want to leave you hanging.)

FIGURE 6.1:

Jumpers and how
they work

Jumpers tend to be arranged by manufacturers in one of two ways. In the situation above, you see three sets of jumper pins. Moving from left to right, you see a jumper above the three pairs of pins, then conecting the leftmost pair, then connecting the middle pair. This might be interpreted as "jumper leftmost pins—enable BIOS," jumper middle pins—disable BIOS.

The alternative use of the jumpers is in triples. Here, you select an option by either jumpering pins 1 and 2, or 2 and 3. Above, you see the jumper above the pins, then jumpering pins 2 and 3, and finally jumpering pins 1 and 2. For example, jumpering pins 1 and 2 might mean "enable BIOS" and jumpering 2 and 3 might mean "disable BIOS."

FIGURE 6.2:

Jumper and DIP
switches example

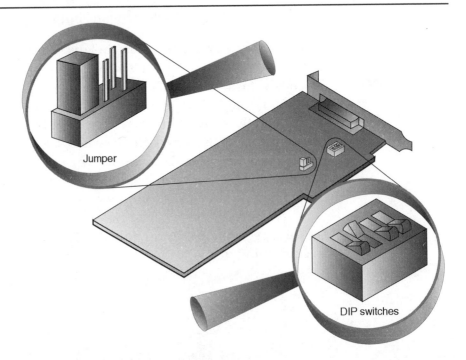

Jumper

DIP switches

Note the symptom in that first example: you installed a new internal modem, and all of a sudden the mouse stopped working.

NOTE   Clue to device conflicts: if you've installed a new board, and it doesn't work, don't just pull it out. Test the rest of the system, with the new board in place. Does something that worked yesterday not work today? That's your clue that (1) the board is probably not broken, but is conflicting with something and (2) you now know what it's conflicting with, so it's easier to track down exactly what you've got to change to make the thing work.

In Scenario 2, the sound card needed something called an interrupt, or *IRQ* (which is an acronym for *Interrupt ReQuest*). Many sound cards are set to use IRQ 7, but IRQ 7 is preassigned to the first parallel port, LPT1. Under an operating system like Windows 95/98 or Windows NT, you can't build a conflict like this into your system, because the OS notices the conflict from the beginning and attempts to correct it during installation. In contrast, DOS and Windows 3.1 don't worry about interrupt conflicts and will simply fail. The answer? Set the sound card to another interrupt. The answer to "how do I do *that*?" is coming.

In Scenario 3, the Ethernet card has a bit (16K) of memory on it, memory that must sit somewhere in the bottom 1024K of memory addresses. When you install the Ethernet card, you tell it where to place that 16K of memory—and if you don't tell it where to put the memory, it just uses a default value. If a whole boatload of these cards don't work, then it could be due to one of three things. First, all of your Ethernet cards could be faulty. Second, it may be that the default location of the memory is the same location that some *other* memory in your system is using; for example, you might have a SCSI host adapter that uses those memory addresses for its BIOS. In that case, you've just got to find another location for the Ethernet card's memory. Third, if you're using DOS on your system, then you may be using a memory manager like EMM386.EXE, and it may have grabbed the same address range for itself. If that happens, then you've got a software conflict rather than a hardware conflict, but it all boils down to the same thing: a nonfunctional board. The answer in that case is to tell the memory manager to stay the heck away from the LAN board's territory with an exclude statement (again, the answer to "how?" is coming). Fourth, if you're running Windows 95/98 or Windows NT, then the network card driver may be looking for that 16K window in the wrong place: in actual fact, the board's working fine, it's just the driver software that needs adjustment. You usually adjust drivers in a program called the Control Panel in Windows 95/98 or Windows NT.

Scenario 4 illustrates why PnP is sometimes called "Shrug and Pray." (It's also a bit technical, so if you don't follow it now, don't worry, we'll return to this a bit later in the chapter.) You freed up an IRQ by removing the internal modem, which, by the way, was configured to behave as COM2. That freed up the IRQ associated with COM2, IRQ 4. So why didn't PnP automatically assign the newly freed IRQ 4 to the video capture board? Because the PnP system was designed to overlook IRQ 4 when searching for IRQs, since all computers have a COM2 (which uses IRQ 4 by default) and, therefore, IRQ 4 must be occupied. How to solve it? Use the Windows 98 Device Manager to force the computer to use IRQ 4 for the video capture board, reboot, and the video capture board works fine.

And, in case you're wondering, yes, all four of these scenarios *are* true stories. Sadly.

Resolving Device Conflicts

The simplest kind of installation problem is a conflict with the easy stuff, like COM1 or LPT1 (by the way, *LPT* is an acronym for *Line PrinTer*). In most cases, you can't get away with two floppy controllers for the same reason.

You are *not*, however, allowed multiple COM ports with the same designation. For example, you can't have more than one COM1. But you can have a COM1, COM2, COM3, and so on. You can also have an LPT1, LPT2, and LPT3, although this is far less common.

Again, a COM or LPT conflict arises when two boards have the same COM or LPT name. If two boards both use COM1, then reconfigure them. You can reconfigure a board in one of several ways.

On older systems:

Alter the position of a jumper, as shown in Figure 6.1.

- Alter the settings of a DIP switch, covered in the next section.

- Run a program to adjust the board's "soft" switch, settings. They operate just like physical switches, but are modified via software, rather than by physically moving them around.

On newer systems:

- PnP systems attempt to take software setup a step further and do it automatically—you don't even have to run a setup program. The setup happens automatically every time you boot up your computer, and it usually works.

Plug and Play

By the way, if you are using a PnP board under Windows 95 or 98 and it won't configure automatically, you may have to remove the board from the system (logically) and let Windows reinstall it for you (hopefully correctly this time). To do this, open the Control Panel by selecting Settings from the Start menu (in the lower-left corner of your screen). Then, in the Control Panel, double-click the icon called System. This will open a window labeled System Properties. Click on the tab labeled Device Manager. Then find the device that isn't working correctly, select it (by clicking once on it), and then click the Remove button at the bottom of the window. Then exit and restart your computer. When your computer reboots it should reinitialize the device correctly.

But that really begs the tougher, more common question: how do you know what switch to move? I'm afraid there's no simple answer here; you've just gotta look at the documentation. People don't seem to believe this; they'll bring me a circuit board and ask me, "What does this do?" while pointing to a jumper. I just shrug my shoulders. There's no way to know without the documentation, so here's one of the best pieces of troubleshooting advice you'll ever get: become a documentation packrat—but more on documentation later.

Configuration Tools: A Word about DIP Switches

Since we're discussing configuration, here are a few points about DIP switches. There are two basic types, diagrammed in Figure 6.3: the slide switch and the rocker switch.

FIGURE 6.3:

Types of DIP switches

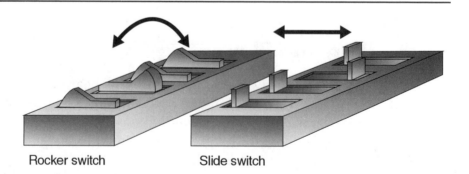

Rocker switch   Slide switch

DIP switches are chip-sized things that contain between four and twelve small plastic switches. You'll see them even on some of the most modern PnP compatible systems. In a Perfect World, DIP switches are easy to access and labeled On or Off. Sadly, that's not always true; some say Open or Closed. If they do, just remember that Open = Off and Closed = On. Sometimes they say 1 or 0 —1 = On, 0 = Off. Sometimes (grrrr…) they don't say anything at all. In this case, play around with them until you figure it out, then write it in your notebook.

Second, if you have set the switches correctly, but the PC refuses to recognize the settings, be aware that sometimes DIP switches are defective. (It's happened to me.) To test this, remove the system board and test the switches for continuity with an ohmmeter.

Finally, remember that sometimes manufacturers mislabel DIP switches, or install them upside down. It *does* happen—rarely, but it happens.

Software Switch Setup Advice

More and more boards are being designed without DIP switches, and their manufactures instead use software setup. Software setup has a good side and a bad side. The good side is that you can change settings on a board (such as making it COM1 rather than COM2) without having to open up the PC and mess with jumpers—you just run a program and you're done. The bad side is that now *you have to keep the setup program around forever*. What's that you say? You're not that organized? You can barely keep track of the software long enough to get the board installed once? Okay, one solution is to get a big envelope and tape it to the side of your computer. Then put all of your setup disks in that envelope so that you'll always have them if you ever need them.

Still think you might lose your diskettes? Okay, okay, maybe you don't HAVE to keep the diskette around forever, but it's a real good idea since you'll need the software that it contains to reinstall the board again if your system ever fails.

So what do you do if you DO lose the diskette? Your first course of action would be to check the manufacturer's Web site. Almost every board manufacturer maintains a database of the installation software for their boards online. As long as the company is around, you should be able to get the software from there. And by the way, it might be a good idea to check that site once in a while anyway, since the companies often provide upgraded drivers there, too. Who knows, you might be able to improve your system's performance. At one time, for example, US Robotics actually had a software upgrade for their 28K modems. All you had to do was download the new software for their 28K modem and it would become a 33K modem!

Understanding I/O Addresses, DMA, IRQs, RAM, and ROM Addresses

I've been promising to explain those "IRQ" things in detail, and if you made it this far, you've been patiently waiting for me to keep that promise. The time has come, this is the place...

When I was a kid, there was a kind of standing joke about Christmas Eve. Parents would buy their kids all kinds of stuff, and the stuff would come in boxes, arranged in a way that no one could ever duplicate: once you took the pieces of the toy out of the box, you'd never be able to repack it the way it came. The really fun part, however, was the incredibly bad documentation that came with the toys. There was, for example, the story about one poor father who, when following the instructions for assembling a new bicycle, wound up building the kids a new swing set out of the parts instead. "Daddy," the son asked, the day after Christmas, "where's my new bicycle?" (I think a couple of comedians in the early '60s made a living parodying these "assembly instructions.")

The folks that made all that toy documentation needed somewhere to go as the years wore on, so they moved to circuit board documentation. They all assume that you understand five pretty important things. Those five things are:

- **I/O addresses:** Addresses the circuit board uses to communicate with the CPU.

- **DMA channels:** Used to speed up I/O to and from the system's memory, but your system is severely limited in how many boards can be hooked up to use DMA channels.

- **IRQ levels:** Hardware components must interrupt the CPU to force it to service them in some time-critical fashion.

- **ROM addresses:** Many boards include some of their low-level control software in ROM. The ROM requires a memory address, which cannot conflict with other ROMs or any RAM in the system.

- **RAM buffers:** Some add-in cards maintain a little (8K–64K) RAM on board to hold data temporarily. That RAM should not conflict with any other RAM or ROM in your system.

Here's the scoop on these obscure-sounding resources.

I/O Addresses

Stop and think for a minute about how the CPU talks to a piece of hardware like a serial port, a disk controller, or a keyboard controller. You already know how the CPU talks to one kind of hardware—the memory. You know that the CPU can determine which part of what memory chip it's talking to because each location in memory has its own unique *memory address*.

Other hardware components have addresses as well, and although they're not memory addresses, the computer talks to them in more or less the same way it talks to memory. First, the computer puts the address of the device it wants to talk to on its bus, and then it either reads data from that location or writes data to that location. The address locations that the computer uses to talk to these devices are called *I/O* (*Input/Output*) addresses.

There are fewer I/O addresses than there are memory addresses, a lot fewer: any computer built with a 386 or later processor can address 4096MB of RAM, but only 64K of I/O addresses. That's not a serious limitation, however, since most of us won't be attaching (for example) even *one* thousand keyboards to a single PC.

I/O addresses allow a CPU to tell its peripherals apart, as you can see in Figure 6.4.

FIGURE 6.4:

Distinguishing peripherals with I/O addresses

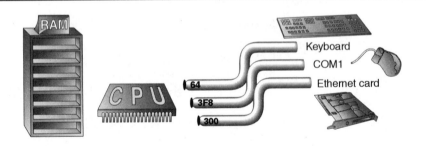

The CPU communicates with the RAM using memory addresses. It communicates with other peripherals—a keyboard controller, a serial port with a mouse on it, and an Ethernet LAN card, in this simplified example—via their I/O addresses. The keyboard controller sits at address 64, the serial port at 3F8—there's an F in the number because it's a hex number, which I'll get to in a minute—and the Ethernet card is at address 300.

What this means is that when the CPU wants to send some data to the Ethernet card, it drops it down the tube labeled 300, rather than the one labeled 3F8 or 64. (There aren't really tubes in a computer, of course; I just like the imagery of the CPU communicating with its minions via old-fashioned pneumatic tubes.)

It's Hex, but There Are No Spells

A quick word on the hex notation: you'll see that both memory addresses and I/O addresses tend to be reported in hexadecimal, an alternative way of writing numbers. There's no especially good reason for this; it's just something that techies prefer. If you've really got to understand the gory details of hex, then take a look at Appendix B, "A Short Overview on Reading Hexadecimal."

Briefly, though, hex is just another way to represent numbers. We're all comfortable with counting in the decimal system—the "normal" way of numbering: 0, 1, 2, 3, 4, 5, 6, 7, 8, 9…but what comes next? Well, we're used to the next number being a 10, which is the first number—0—with a 1 stuck on the front of it. The next one is the next number, 1, except that 1 is still stuck on the front of it to produce 11, and so on.

Decimal has 10 single-character number symbols, which is why it's called "base 10." Hexadecimal is based not on 10, but on 16. Why do we use hexadecimal? Because it's a lot easier for programmers to use than binary (100110110011110111011010101010101's) which is the way computers actually "think." Anyway, hex starts off with the familiar zero through nine, so it's got the first 10. But after nine comes the letter A—hex uses the letter A to represent its eleventh digit. As you'd imagine, B comes next, and so on to F. You count in hex, then, like so: 0, 1, 2, 3, 4, 5, 6, 7, 8, 9, A, B, C, D, E, F... and then 10. See, hex has a 10 just like decimal, but it arrives later.

For example, suppose I were to tell you that the COM1 serial port uses an address range from 3F8 through 3FF. (I can hear Ford Prefect of *The Hitchhiker's Guide to the Galaxy* answer, "Why? Do you think you're likely to tell me that?") How many addresses does COM1 then take up? Well, you know that 3F8 is the first address. After 3F8 comes 3F9. Just like all the numbers you've ever known, the rightmost digit is the one that changes as the number gets bigger; nine comes after eight, so 3F9 is the next value. You just learned that nine is followed by A, so the next address would be 3FA, then 3FB, 3FC, 3FD, 3FE, and finally 3FF. Why *finally*? Because the range is from 3F8 through 3FF, so when you get to the 3FF, you stop. Go back and count them up, and you'll see that a serial port uses eight I/O addresses.

What does it do with all of those addresses? Several things. First of all, a serial port can both transmit and receive bytes at the same time. One address holds received data and one holds outgoing data. Of the other addresses, some will be used for status information, such as, "Does the modem have a connection to another modem?" Some will be wasted—wasted because it's easiest for a circuit designer to take eight or 16 addresses, due to a peculiarity in the PC hardware. If you designed a board that required only seven I/O addresses, you'd still take eight of them.

Common I/O Address Uses

That's probably a bit more than you actually wanted to know. What you really need to know about addresses is "How do you know which ones are currently taken?" Well, you can start off with Table 6.1.

TABLE 6.1: Common I/O Address Uses in PCs

HEX ADDRESS RANGE	USER
00–0F	DMA Controller 8237 #1
20–21	Programmable Interrupt Controller 8259A #1 IRQs 0-7
40–43	Timer 8253
60–63	8255 Peripheral Controller
60–64	Keyboard Controller (8742)
80–8F	DMA page registers
A0–A1	Programmable Interrupt Controller #2 IRQs 8-15
A0–AF	NMI Mask Register
C0–DF	8237 DMA Controller #2
CF8–CFF	PCI bus I/O port
F0–FF	Math coprocessor (integrated into modern processors but still reserved)
170–177	Secondary hard disk controller, if present (present in most modern systems)
1F0–1F8	Primary hard disk controller
200–20F	Joystick controller
210–217	Expansion chassis
220–22F	FM Synthesis Interface (WAV device), Sound Blaster default
230–233	Common CD-ROM I/O port
238–23B	Bus mouse
23C–23F	Alternate bus mouse
274–277	ISA PnP I/O Port
278–27F	LPT2
2B0–2DF	EGA (usually *not* used by modern video)
2E8–2EF	COM4 serial port

Continued on next page

TABLE 6.1 CONTINUED: Common I/O Address Uses in PCs

HEX ADDRESS RANGE	USER
2F8–2FF	COM2 serial port
300–30F	Ethernet card (common location, not a standard)
320–32F	Hard disk controller (XT only)
330–33F	MIDI port (common location, not a standard)
370–377	Alternative floppy controller address
378–37F	LPT1 printer port
3B0–3BF	Monochrome adapter (also used on modern video)
3BC–3BF	LPT3 (uncommon)
3D0–3DF	Color/graphics adapter (also used on modern video)
3E8–3EF	COM3 serial port
3F0–3F7	Floppy disk controller
3F8–3FF	COM1 serial port
778–77F	LPT1 I/O port

Many devices have only one I/O address that they can use. Using the example of COM1 again, part of the very definition of COM1 is that it uses I/O addresses 3F8–3FF. Other devices may allow you to use any of a range of addresses. For example, most sound cards default to address 220, but will allow you to reconfigure them to use some other address if 220 is not available. Reconfigure a COM1 serial port, in contrast, and it's no longer a COM1 serial port.

The key to understanding why this information is important is to know that this address cannot be used by any other device: only one device is used per I/O address. To understand why this is so, I'll steal an old analogy.

I/O Address Conflicts

Think of I/O addresses as being like P.O. boxes. Say the keyboard has P.O. box 64. When the keyboard has data for the system, it puts the data in box 64. When the CPU wants to read the keyboard, it looks in box 64. Box 64 is, in a very real sense, a better definition of the keyboard from the CPU's point of view than the keyboard itself is. If you plug a new board into your system, and that board uses I/O address 64, then the new board won't work, and, in addition, the keyboard will cease to work as well—you can't run two devices off the same I/O address.

Now, in reality, no one's going to design a board that uses address 64, because that's the keyboard's. But what about a case where you have a conflict in optional boards?

For example, I recently installed a Sound Blaster 16 on a PC that was already equipped with an Ethernet card and a SCSI host adapter. The Sound Blaster 16 includes a circuit called a MIDI interface, and it happened to be set at I/O address 330. Unfortunately, 330 is the I/O address used by the SCSI host adapter, so I got a disk boot failure when I turned my system on. There actually was nothing wrong with the *disk*; it was the disk's host adapter board that couldn't work due to the conflict with the Sound Blaster 16. Checking the documentation, I found that the sound card's MIDI circuit offered either address 330, which it was currently using, or 300. I set the address to 300 (the Sound Blaster 16 uses a jumper to set its MIDI address), reinstalled the board, and had the situation shown in Figure 6.5.

FIGURE 6.5:

Sharing I/O addresses between an Ethernet card and a sound card

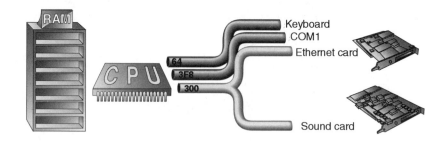

Now the CPU's I/O address 300—that particular "post office box"—is shared by the MIDI circuit on the sound card and the Ethernet card. The system didn't complain when I booted up, because my system doesn't need either the sound card or the Ethernet card in order to boot. But when I tried to configure the sound card, it failed. You can see why in Figure 6.6.

FIGURE 6.6:

I/O conflict between an Ethernet card and a sound card

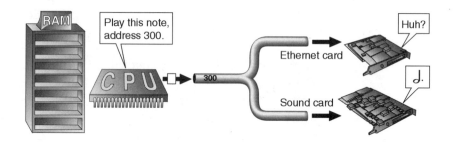

A "play this note" message went into I/O address 300. The Ethernet card has no idea how to respond to this request, and indeed may not be prepared for any requests at all. Worse yet, the electrical signal from the CPU gets split up two ways, so it may not be strong enough to actually get to *either* board.

Why did Creative Labs, the creator of the Sound Blaster 16, build a deliberate conflict into its card? The answer is, they did not. There is no official standard for SCSI host adapter I/O addresses; Adaptec uses 330 for some of their boards, Trantor uses 350, Iomega offers a range from 320 through 350, and I'm sure other SCSI vendors have other options. Ethernet cards *tend* to sit at address 300, but that's not cast in stone. What I'm saying is that the most common conflicts will be between the types of boards that appeared after the mid-'80s; since then, there's been no central coordinating force in the PC hardware industry.

How did I solve this, by the way? Well, the Adaptec board offered me 330 or 300 as my only choices, as did the sound card. The Ethernet board offered 300, 310, 320, 330, or 340. I didn't want to mess with the Adaptec board, because it was the hard disk interface, and if *it* became conflicted then I'd lose access to the hard disk—so I left the SCSI board at 330. That meant that the Sound Blaster 16 had to go to 300. The Ethernet board then played the peacemaker, as I set it to address 310.

More and more, I find that board manufacturers are moving from jumper settings to software settings, but in this case, the SCSI board and the sound card set their addresses with jumpers, and the Ethernet card set its I/O address with software. Which do I prefer? Well, software is, of course, nice. But suppose the sound card came preset to 330, as it did, and required that I run some software in order to get it to switch addresses? That would be a real pain. Think about it: I'd install the sound card at 330 initially, as I had no choice. That would disable my hard disk, requiring that I juggle floppies in order to run the program that would set a different address for the sound card. To add insult to injury, the setup program for the sound card works only after it's installed on the hard disk. I just might decide that getting past *that* gauntlet wouldn't be worth it and scrap the board altogether. In contrast, all I *actually* had to do was to move a jumper. So there are pros and cons to both sides.

I've already said this, but let me repeat: you probably won't have a clue which DIP switches do what without the documentation, so be sure to latch onto any switch-setting documentation you've got. Or hope the company that made the board whose DIP switches you're trying to set still has the switch settings on its Web site.

What would I have done, by the way, if the Ethernet card was set at 300 and wouldn't accept any other addresses? How would you resolve that problem? *You may not be able to resolve all I/O address conflicts*, as not all boards even give you the chance to change I/O addresses. It's hard to believe, but some boards are hardwired to use only one I/O address range. I had a LIM board that conflicted with a clock/calendar, but, unfortunately, neither board gave me a chance to change the I/O address. One board had to be removed—the conflict couldn't be resolved.

Programmed Input/Output (PIO)

Once a hard disk controller gets some data from the hard disk, that data's got to be stored in RAM. The same thing gets done when new data comes in on a local area network card. Big blocks of sound information must be zapped out to a sound card in a smooth, reliable fashion in order for that card to produce pleasant-sounding voice or music sounds. The data originates in the system's memory, and it has got to get to the sound card.

A fundamental problem in computer design is getting data from memory (RAM) to or from a hard disk controller, LAN board, video capture card, sound card, video card—in short, to transfer data between memory and a *peripheral*. (Peripheral is easier to write than LAN card, disk interface, etc., so I'll stick to that from here on in.)

The simplest way to move data between a peripheral and memory is through *programmed input/output*, or *PIO*. With PIO, the CPU sends commands to the peripheral through an I/O address or addresses; let's see how that gets done with a simple example.

Suppose the CPU wants some data from a part of one of the disk drives. Data on disks is, as you'll learn in the disk section of this book, organized into sectors, which are blocks of data than can be anywhere from 512 bytes to as long as 32K (actually, 32,768 bytes), depending upon the size and internal data organization of your hard drive. When a PC accesses data from a disk, it can't take it in 1- or 2-byte chunks; the smallest amount of data that the CPU can ask for is a sector of data (which, once again, can be from hundreds to tens of thousands of bytes long). Suppose the goal for the moment is to get sector 10 from the disk and to put it into RAM. The first step is for the CPU to tell the disk interface to get the data; it does that on I/O address 1F0 on many disk interfaces, as you can see in Figure 6.7.

FIGURE 6.7:

PIO part 1: Requesting data from the disk interface using I/O addresses

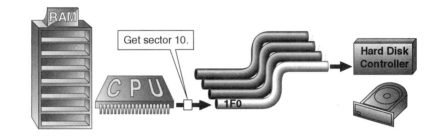

The disk interface then responds to the request, pulling all of the data in the selected sector off the disk drive. The interface then tells the CPU that it's ready, and the CPU now has the task of getting the data from the disk interface to the RAM. The CPU begins by requesting the first 2 bytes of data, as shown in Figure 6.8.

FIGURE 6.8:

PIO part 2: Requesting the first part of the data from the disk controller

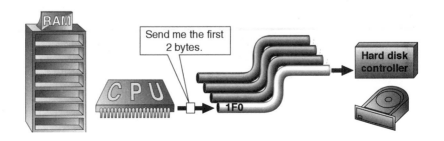

The CPU then stuffs that data somewhere in RAM, as you see in Figure 6.9.

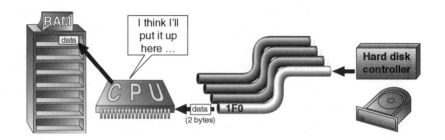

FIGURE 6.9:

PIO part 3: Putting the data into RAM

Moving those 2 bytes takes time, as does figuring out where to put the *next* 2 bytes. The CPU then requests 2 more bytes, puts them in RAM, figures out where the next bytes will go, and so on. Will this work? Yes, undoubtedly. Is it fast? Well, not always. Can we make this faster? Certainly, read on.

DMA (Direct Memory Access) Channels

Now let's take a look at how PC CPUs access floppy disk drives. Suppose I want to read sector 20 from a floppy disk. Things start out very much the same as before, as you can see in Figure 6.10.

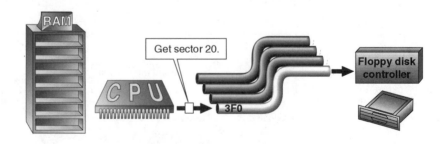

FIGURE 6.10:

DMA part 1: Requesting data from the disk controller

The floppy disk controller is at address 3F0, so the CPU sends the initial command out over that address. Ah, but when the floppy disk controller has the data ready, then it knows that having the CPU pick up 2 bytes and put them down and then pick up 2 more bytes and put them down (and so on) takes time. The idea is to get the data into the RAM, so why not cut out the middleman, as you can see in Figure 6.11.

FIGURE 6.11:

DMA part 2: Diversion of the CPU by the disk controller

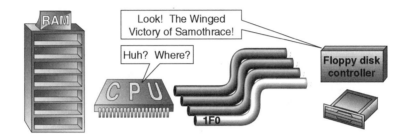

First, there's a diversionary tactic, allowing something other than the CPU to control the bus; then, as you see in Figure 6.12, the data gets delivered to the RAM directly.

FIGURE 6.12:

DMA part 3: Using the DMA channel to put data directly into RAM

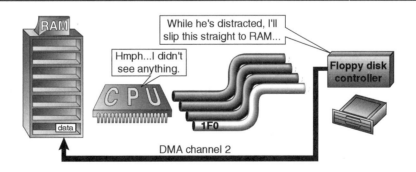

Okay, I admit that the floppy disk controller doesn't really distract the CPU; actually, it says to the CPU, "May I have direct

access to the memory?" Some of the wires on the bus are DMA request (DREQ) lines and some are DMA acknowledge (DACK) lines. A board requests direct access to the memory bus with a DREQ line, and the CPU responds with a DACK. The idea here is to allow only one peripheral at a time to control the bus. There are multiple DMA request/acknowledge lines, more commonly called DMA channels.

The original PC had a single DMA controller chip the 8237. It allowed up to four DMA channels, and to this day 8-bit ISA slots have only four DMA channels available numbered from zero to three.

The original PC used DMA channel 0 for "dynamic memory refresh." Briefly, here's how it worked. There are two kinds of memory: dynamic and static. Dynamic sounds better than static, but it isn't. When you tell a static RAM (SRAM) something, it remembers it until you turn off the power or change it. Think of memory as a container of liquid, and static RAM is a ceramic mug. You put water in it, and it stays there. Dynamic RAM (DRAMs), on the other hand, is like a water cup made out of a thin sheet of paper; it leaks. Put data into a DRAM and it will forget whatever you tell it within 4 milliseconds (ms).

As a result, old PCs had to drop everything and do a RAM refresh every 3.86 ms. This took 5 clocks out of every 72, or about 7 percent of the PC's time. Of course, if the CPU was doing a lot of INs, OUTs, internal calculations, or the like, then you would not notice the slowdown, as the whole idea of DMA is to work in parallel with the CPU. Wouldn't static RAM make a faster computer? Yes, in fact it would make it much, much faster, but it's also much, much more costly. In more modern PCs, the RAM refresh is handled by a separate circuit. DRAM still needs to be refreshed in modern systems, but the CPU isn't involved, so no DMA is required, and channel 0 is free on most modern PCs.

On those old PCs, the hard disk controller used DMA channel 1, but most modern disk interfaces don't use DMA, they use PIO for reasons I'll explain in a minute; as a result, channel 1 is available on modern PCs. The floppy disk controller has employed channel 2 since the old PC days, and it still does; don't assign anything else to channel 2. Channel 3 is unused in general.

Anything built after 1985 will have 16-bit ISA, MCA, EISA, PC Card, PCI, or VESA slots, all of which have *two* DMA controllers, and thus eight DMA channels to the XT's four.

Notice that this implies that you've got only *one* free DMA channel on an old XT-type machine, but seven available DMA channels on most modern PCs—just leave channel 2 for the floppy controller, and you're in good shape. PCs nowadays often require two DMA channels for the sound card, and many parallel ports can be configured to be an Enhanced Capability Port (ECP), which is basically just a parallel port with, uh, enhanced capabilities—it's bidirectional and faster than the standard parallel port—but ECP needs DMA.

To DMA or Not to DMA?

You're probably wondering by now what I left out of the story. I just got finished explaining that DMA allows for faster transfers of data between peripherals and memory, and modern machines basically don't use DMA. (You're supposed to go *"huh?"* at this point.)

DMA is pretty nifty, except for one thing. In order to assure backward compatibility, the AT's designers held DMA operations to 4.77MHz—the original PC's clock speed. Lest you skim over this because it sounds like a history lesson, *ISA bus machines still do DMA at 4.77MHz*. Honest. If you've got a shiny new 200MHz P6-based system on your desk and you do a DMA operation on it, the whole shootin' match slows down to just under *3 percent* of that

200MHz clock speed. The best the other buses do when DMA-ing is 8MHz on DMA. What's the answer? Bus mastering; but I'll get to that in a minute.

Anyway, that's why you'll see that some boards give you a choice about whether to DMA or not.

So, in summary, if you have an expansion board that needs a DMA channel:

- The only one available is generally DMA channel 3 on the old PCs.

- If you're installing a 16-bit board, try whenever possible to use the extra 16-bit-only DMAs, channels 4 through 7, to leave room for the 8-bit boards in your system.

- If you're out of DMAs, see if the board offers the option to disable DMA. It may be slower, or it may be faster. On computers above 25MHz, PIO will probably be faster than DMA. Try it both ways to see.

You can see common DMA uses in Table 6.2.

TABLE 6.2: Common DMA Channel Uses in the PC Family

CHANNEL	USE
0	Dynamic RAM Refresh (XT only)
1	Hard Disk Controller (XT only), or commonly used by sound cards in AT architecture
2	Floppy Controller
3	Unused, but also used on many 16-bit sound cards (they use two DMA channels) or ECP parallel ports
4–7	Available on modern PCs

Bus Mastering

This is a slight digression, but it's important, it fits in here, and I'll keep it short.

You just learned that DMA is a neat idea that is hampered by an historical error—4.77MHz. DMA actually has another problem, although it's not one that would be immediately apparent.

DMA can transfer data from a peripheral to RAM, or from RAM to a peripheral, with neither transfer requiring the CPU's intervention. But DMA can't transfer data from a peripheral to a peripheral; such an operation would actually be two DMA operations, peripheral to RAM, followed by RAM to peripheral.

Many boards built for the EISA, MCA, or PCI buses can do *bus master transfers*, allowing them to bypass not only the CPU, but RAM as well, transferring data between peripherals at the maximum speed that the bus supports. Bus mastering, then, can speed up a system in two ways. You see this diagrammed in Figure 6.13.

FIGURE 6.13:

Bus mastering

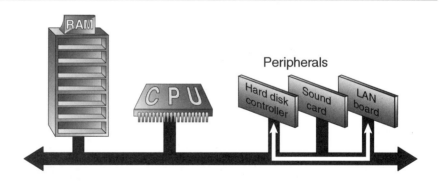

The ISA slots in your system support bus mastering, but allow only one bus master board in your ISA system. The PCI slots, in contrast (as well as EISA or MCA slots, if you're working with one of those systems) allow multiple bus masters. It's a feature worth exploiting. But bus mastering is useful for more than just peripheral-to-peripheral transfer, it's also terrific as a replacement for DMA. Designers of PCI-based boards use bus mastering to support fast peripheral-to-RAM transfers that aren't hobbled by the 4.77MHz limitation.

IRQ (Interrupt Request) Levels

In the DMA section, I was describing PIO. After the CPU made the request of the disk controller for the data, I then said, "The disk interface then tells the CPU that it's ready..."—which was a trifle sneaky on my part. As far as the CPU is concerned, it initiates all conversations with peripherals; they "speak when they're spoken to." A peripheral gets the CPU's attention in one of two ways: polling or interrupts.

Polling

Let's look at how DOS controls a parallel port in order to print data. The printer is massively slower than the CPU, so there's got to be some way to handshake the two. Things start off as you see in Figure 6.14.

FIGURE 6.14:

Printing data through the parallel port

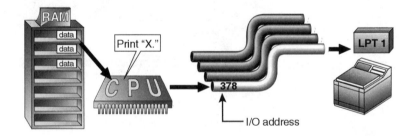

Data travels through I/O address 378, the address of LPT1, and is deposited from there into the printer. The CPU then keeps an eye on the printer, as you see in Figure 6.15.

FIGURE 6.15:

The CPU watches the printer

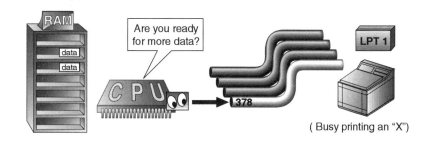

The CPU sits there at the "pneumatic tube" numbered 378, just waiting for the word from the printer, much as someone expecting a letter might run out to the mailbox every 10 minutes. (I'd include the lyrics for that song that goes "Wait a minute, Mr. Postman…," but then we'd have to get the copyright permission, and it's too much trouble. You might just want to hum along to get into the polling frame of mind.)

The CPU essentially sits on address 378, asking, "Are you ready now? How about *now*? How about NOW?…" It's a big waste of the CPU's time, but this polling method of waiting for an I/O device to finish its work is simple to design. Besides, in a single-tasking world like you see in DOS, the CPU doesn't have anything else to do anyway; it is singly focused on servicing the parallel port. Eventually, as you see in Figure 6.16, the port responds.

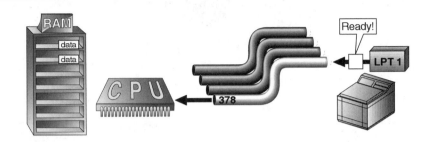

The CPU now sends another byte to the printer, and it begins all over again. As I've said, the process is wasteful but simple, and it works fine in the single-tasking DOS world.

Hardware Interrupts

But what about a multi-tasking world, such as most of us live in today? And even if you work in single-tasking mode, there are many peripherals on your PC, and the PC can't poll them all. That's why hardware interrupts are built into the PC.

You can see how interrupts work if we look back to the discussion of how the CPU gets data from the disk interface. Recall that the CPU stuffed a "get some data" request down I/O address 1F0. Now, it takes time for the disk to return the desired data. Why not let the CPU use that time to do other things? Take a look at Figure 6.17.

FIGURE 6.17:

The CPU works on
other things while
waiting for the disk
controller.

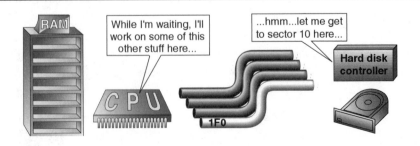

The disk interface is in its "own private Idaho," as the CPU is in its. But most modern disk controllers (I'm equivocating because some really high-performance SCSI host adapters don't do this) have a circuit running between themselves and the CPU, a circuit called an *interrupt request* level, or *IRQ* level. The disk interface wakes up the CPU, as you can see in Figure 6.18.

FIGURE 6.18:

Using IRQ levels to get the attention of the CPU

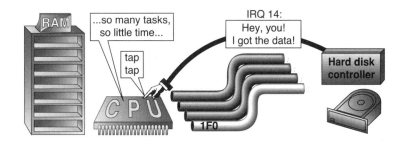

Once the CPU has been interrupted, it knows to start getting the information from the disk controller, as I described in the discussion of PIO a few pages back.

How Interrupts Work

PC interrupts were originally handled by an Intel 8259 prioritized interrupt controller (PIC); nowadays, there's no discrete 8259 on your system, it's just built into the motherboard's chipset. The interrupt controller is *prioritized* in that the interrupt levels it controls are numbered from zero to whatever (depending upon which computer you are using). Lower numbers get higher priority. That means that if interrupt 3 and interrupt 7 both ring at the same time, it's interrupt 3 that gets handled first (*serviced,* in PC hardware lingo).

When an interrupt occurs, the interrupt controller forces the CPU to put its current work "on hold" and immediately execute a program that allows it to handle the interrupt. Such a program is called, appropriately, an *interrupt handler* or an *interrupt service routine*. For example, in the disk drive example, when IRQ 14 occurs, then the CPU jumps to a small program that tells it how to grab the data from the disk controller. The computer then stuffs the data into some RAM, and returns to whatever it was doing before it was interrupted.

IRQs 2–7 in XTs (A Brief History)

The original PC had only one interrupt controller (the 8259), which had only eight interrupt lines. Interestingly, the 8259 implemented only lines 2 through 7. Lines 0 and 1 weren't even on the bus because they were preassigned. IRQ 8 (0 on the first 8259) was attached to a timer circuit that creates an interrupt about 18 times per second and IRQ 1 was attached to the 8042 keyboard controller.

Driving the keyboard interface using interrupts is a good idea, because the keyboard controller is pretty dumb. It has no memory to speak of, and so every time a keystroke arrives at the controller, it must hand off this keystroke to the CPU (which then puts it in the keyboard buffer) before another keystroke comes in. Essentially, once the keyboard controller gets a keystroke, it wants to say to the CPU, "Hey! Stop everything! Come service me *now* before the user presses another key!!!!" And so it "rings the bell"—okay, not really a bell, actually it just activates its interrupt line—and the CPU stops doing whatever it's doing and executes the program that moves the keystroke to the keyboard buffer. If it didn't do this, you would have a lot of dropped keystrokes. You can see a simple block diagram of how the bus, the CPU, and the 8259 interact in Figure 6.18. (I'm showing you how the XT did it because, as you'll see, IBM had to pull a bit of a trick to expand the number of interrupts on the AT, and—surprise!—that trick is still with us today, and sometimes causes mischief.)

Someone designing an expansion slot for the XT, then, could build a board to use IRQs 2 through 7; but couldn't use IRQ 0 or 1, as there simply weren't any wires running from IRQ 0 or 1 to the XT expansion bus slot connector.

Suppose a floppy disk controller wired to use IRQ 6 wants to interrupt the CPU to get serviced. Simplified a bit, here are the steps it would go through:

1. The floppy controller sends a signal through IRQ 6 on the bus.

2. The 8259 receives that signal on its input number 6.

3. The 8259 then looks to see if it is currently getting an interrupt signal from its higher-priority inputs—in other words, is the timer, keyboard, or anything attached to IRQs 2 through 5 demanding the 8259's attention?

4. Assuming there are no higher-priority interrupts, the 8259 then taps the CPU on the shoulder with the 8259's one "output" line, which is wired to the CPU's "incoming interrupt" line.

5. The CPU responds by putting a signal on the bus (not pictured) that says, "Okay, I'm willing to be interrupted; which interrupt number is it?"

6. The 8259 then seizes control of the *data* lines on the XT bus and uses them to transfer the value *6*, the interrupt number.

7. The CPU has a table of places where it keeps software to deal with different interrupts. There's a place there for servicing IRQ 6, the floppy controller, so the CPU jumps to that location and executes that program, called the "floppy interrupt service routine."

8. Satisfied that its work is done for the moment, the 8259 resets the IRQ 6 input line, and is ready for the next interrupt. See Figure 6.19.

FIGURE 6.19:

XT interrupt diagram

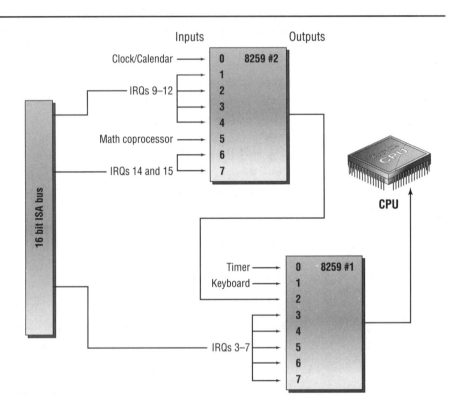

Choosing IRQs

Eight IRQ lines with two pre-allocated for the timer and keyboard made configuring XTs a bit tricky, so PCs since the AT have all been equipped with a second 8259, bringing the total of interrupts on most PCs up to 16. *How* they added that 8259 is another story, one I'll tell you in a minute. Before I do that, however, let's take a look at which IRQs are usually free or taken; you can see the common uses for IRQs in Table 6.3.

TABLE 6.3: Common IRQ Uses in the PC Family

INTERRUPT LINE	DEVICE	COMMENTS
0	Timer	Not accessible by peripherals.
1	Keyboard	Not accessible by peripherals.
2	Cascade to IRQs 8–15	Used by second 8259 to signal interrupts; not available except on XTs.
3	COM2	Can also be COM4, but only one of the two.
4	COM1	Can also be COM3, but only one of the two.
5	XT hard disk controller, LPT2	Free on most PCs. Hard disk interface used only on XTs, or alternatively for LPT2 on the unusual machine with LPT2.
6	Floppy disk controller	
7	LPT1	
8	Clock	Not accessible by peripherals.
9		Generally available, but can be confused with IRQ 2; see text.
10		Generally available.
11		Generally available.
12	"PS/2" type mouse port	If your PC/laptop has a built-in mouse port with a small circular connector, that port probably uses IRQ 12.
13	Coprocessor	Interrupt required even for modern processors with integrated numeric coprocessors.
14	Primary hard disk interface	Taken in virtually all machines as the "primary PCI EIDE interface."
15	Secondary disk interface	Taken on most post-486 systems as the "secondary PCI EIDE interface."

If you're installing a board and need an IRQ, then your best bet is to first look to IRQs 9, 10, 11, or 5, in that order (it's the order of descending priority, as you'll see in a minute). If they're not available, consider disabling your parallel port, if you're not using it, to recover IRQ 7, or perhaps one of your COM ports if they're idle. If you're *still* in need, and you have only one hard disk and one CD-ROM drive, then you might ensure that the drive and CD-ROM are on the primary EIDE interface (you'll read more about that in Chapter 14, "Recovering Data and Fixing Hard Disks") and then disable the secondary EIDE interface, freeing up IRQ 15. Be aware, however, that it can be a pain to consolidate a drive and a CD-ROM if they're not already on a single interface, *and* not all systems even *allow* you to disable the secondary port.

If you're configuring an XT (in a museum, perhaps?), then your best bet for a free IRQ is either 2 or perhaps 7, but 7 is available only if you disable or remove your parallel port. And if you're configuring an 8-bit card in a modern system, the card can use only IRQs 0 through 7. Typically, 8-bit cards can use only IRQ 5, because IRQ 2 is not available.

Whatever you set your boards to, *write it down*! You'll need the information later.

Earlier, I suggested taping an envelope to the side of a PC and keeping important floppies there. Here are some other things to put in there. Each time I install a board (or modify an existing board), I get a new piece of paper and write down all the configuration information for the board. For example, I might note, "Intel EtherExpress 16 card installed 10 July 1994 by Mark Minasi; no EPROM on board, shared memory disabled, IRQ 10 used, I/O address 310 set."

I hesitate to mention this, but sometimes device conflicts can be solved by doing surgery on the boards. Just lobotomize the chips that are performing the function that you wish to defeat. An example that I have seen a couple of times is in serial ports. A client wanted me to set up a multifunction board in a PC with clock, memory, printer, and serial ports. He already had a board installed that provided both serial ports COM1 and COM2. The jumpers on the multifunction board allowed me to set the multifunction board's serial port to either COM1 or COM2, but not disable it altogether. What to do? A chip called the 8250 UART (Universal Asynchronous Receiver/Transmitter) is the heart of most serial ports. I found the 8250 on the multifunction board and removed it. The problem was eliminated. *Please don't try this unless you understand what you are doing.*

IRQs 2 and 9: XT Problems That Live to This Day

Take a look at Table 6.3 and you'll notice that IRQ 2 is not available in post-1984 PCs, but it is available on XTs. Why did those old dinosaurs have an IRQ we don't have? Recall that I said earlier that IBM had to do some fancy designing to add more IRQs to their AT. Unfortunately, that designing built a few quirks into the AT's IRQ structure—and every PC since has been designed in the same way, even your new 433MHz Pentium II system.

Recall that the PC/XT systems had a single interrupt controller, an Intel 8259 chip. The 8259 could support up to eight interrupt channels, and the original PC/XT systems hardwired channels 0 and 1 to the system timer (a clock circuit that goes "tick" every 55 milliseconds) and the 8042 keyboard controller.

The system was wired with those interrupts because IBM wanted to make sure that the keyboard and the timer had high priorities; you recall that on an 8259, when two interrupts occur at the same time, the one with the lower number gets priority.

In 1984, the first 16-bit PC-compatible system was released—the IBM AT. The proliferation of add-in devices on the market made it clear that eight interrupt levels just wasn't enough. So, how to add another 8259? Just slapping the extra 8259 onto the motherboard might present some backward compatibility problems, so IBM decided to kind of slip the extra 8259 in "through the back door," as you can see in Figure 6.20.

FIGURE 6.20:

Adding an extra 8259
for more IRQ levels

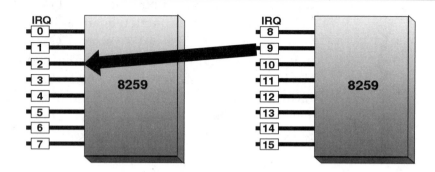

First, IBM added another 8259 and used its eight inputs to create IRQs 8 through 15. Just as the old 8259 had two IRQs that
never showed up on the system bus (0 and 1), so also the new
8259 had two IRQs that the system bus didn't see: IRQ 8 supported the clock/calendar, and IRQ 13 supported the math
coprocessor chip. But how to let the CPU know when one of the
second 8259's IRQs fired? By *cascading* the 8259s: the second
8259's output—its way of saying, "Hey, I've got an interrupt!"—
was connected as one of the *inputs* of the first 8259, IRQ 2 in fact.

So, if an IRQ between 8 and 15 triggers, the second 8259 activates its output line. That shows up in the first 8259 as an IRQ 2.
The first 8259 tells the CPU, "I've got an interrupt for you," and
the CPU of course asks, "Which IRQ?" When the 8259 replies,
"IRQ 2," the CPU knows that *really* means that it's now got to go
to the second 8259 and say, "I hear from the first 8259 that you've
got an interrupt. Which line is it?" The second 8259 replies and
the CPU services the second 8259's interrupt.

But now notice that IRQ 2 is dedicated, as were IRQs 0 and 1
before. There would be no point in leaving IRQ 2 available on the
ISA bus, so IBM removed the wires on the motherboard connecting the first 8259's input number 2 and the pin on the ISA bus
connectors. But, they reasoned, why waste that pin—so they recycled that bus pin, giving it to the newly created IRQ 9. That's fine,

in general, except for one thing—if you put an old 8-bit ISA board into a 16-bit ISA slot, the 8-bit board will think that pin is IRQ 2, as was the case in the 8-bit ISA days. Even the jumpers on the 8-bit board will tell you that you're using IRQ 2, but you're not—you're using IRQ 9. And generally software drivers written to go with 8-bit boards don't understand the IRQ 2/9 confusion, and don't even *give* you the option to choose IRQ 9. What to do? Well, avoid IRQ 2 on non-XT systems if you can; if you can't, then play around with the driver and jumper settings. In some cases, lying to the board and/or driver ("Sure, you're IRQ 2, trust me") will make it work. The best answer? Get those ancient 8-bit cards out of your system!

And here's one more thought about how this cascaded 8259 structure affects IRQs: priorities. In the vast majority of cases, you don't really care which IRQ you assign a board to, so long as the board has an IRQ. But sometimes you'll see two boards that won't work together—the system works with either one but not with both—even though they've got different IRQs. In that case, try swapping the IRQ levels. If that fixes it, then the problem was priorities.

But what is the order of priorities in IRQs? Well, you read earlier that back in the 8-bit XT days, IRQ 0 had the highest priority, IRQ 7 the lowest. But since IRQs 8 through 15 sneak in through IRQ 2, the priorities go from highest to lowest like so: 0, 1, 8, 9, 10, 11, 12, 13, 14, 15, 3, 4, 5, 6, 7.

So You Want a Third COM Port?

PCs were originally designed to support two RS-232 ports, which got the system names COM1 and COM2. But serial ports are so darn useful that many people find they need a third one—for example, on one of my PCs, I need a serial port for the mouse, another for my digital camera, one for my Palm Pilot, and a fourth for an external infrared port.

If the PC was designed to support just two COM ports, how can you have more than two? Basically, by going *outside* of the basic PC design. You can add as many COM ports as you like beyond the first two, but the system treats them like any other "unusual" device, like a network card, a SCSI board, or the like. What I mean is: whether you're running DOS, Windows 95/98, OS/2, or Windows NT, you don't need to load any drivers to configure your operating system to support things like a standard keyboard, LPT1, COM1, COM2, a floppy drive, or a hard disk. That's because those pieces of hardware are part of the "basic PC," so to speak. But add a network card, a sound card, or something else, and you take the PC beyond the bare minimum, requiring that you load drivers for the "unusual" hardware and perhaps configure those drivers. COM3 and beyond fall into the "unusual" category of hardware.

That means you'll need to do some more configuration to make a third or later COM port work. Each COM port needs an IRQ, so be sure you've got one free before trying to install an extra COM port. It also needs a range of I/O addresses, but there are usually enough of those around. Then you've got to get the operating system to play ball with your new port.

If you're running Windows 95 or 98, they do a pretty good job of detecting extra COM ports automatically. But if they don't, use the Control Panel to tell Windows that you've got a COM port. Open the System applet and choose Device Manager/Ports (COM and LPT), then choose the particular port and click on Properties. Click the Resources tab and uncheck Use Automatic Settings. You can then tell Windows 95/98 what I/O address and IRQ your serial port is using.

Windows 3.1 also has a Control Panel, but in it, you should open the Ports dialog box and choose Advanced. There you'll find the dialog box to tell Windows 3.1 what resources the serial port uses. Windows NT 4's Control Panel works similarly.

Note that if you have a mixed-bus system, like the PCI/ISA hybrids that most of us have on our desks, and ISA uses an interrupt, you can't share that through the advanced bus. If an ISA board uses IRQ 3, for example, then none of the PCI boards can use IRQ 3. On the other hand, if in that case no ISA board used IRQ 4, then any number of PCI boards could use IRQ 4—*if* the boards were designed to share IRQs, and *if* the drivers for the boards supported interrupt sharing. (How do you know? It'll be in the documentation. Unfortunately, there are very few add-in cards that support IRQ sharing.)

ROM Addresses and RAM Buffers

In addition to I/O addresses, DMA channels, and IRQ lines, there is a fourth source of conflict: ROM addresses. Some adapter boards require some ROM onboard to hold some low-level code; in particular, the most common examples are SCSI host adapters, video adapters, and some network cards. For example, the SCSI host adapters that I use the most are from Adaptec, and most of those have a ROM on them. A program stored in that ROM causes any computer equipped with the Adaptec adapter to show a message like "Press Ctrl+A to enter SCSI diagnostics." The diagnostics are a very useful set of utilities that you can access even if your hard disk isn't working (which is a good possibility, if you're installing a new SCSI adapter). Onboard ROM make sense on some adapters. Other boards have some RAM onboard to provide memory that is *shared* between the system CPU and the adapter's circuitry. But RAM and ROM can present a configuration problem because, as before, a possibility exists that two different boards may require some software onboard, and if the two boards *both* try to locate their ROM or RAM at the same location in the PC's memory address space, neither one will work.

Fortunately, some boards let you configure the start address of the ROM/RAM (through DIP switches, jumpers, or software).

Most of the major boards that include ROM/RAM, like the EGA, VGA, XT-type hard disk controller, and the like, should *not* have their ROM addresses changed (if it's even possible). Too many pieces of software rely on their standard addresses. The boards you'll see that typically include ROM are:

- Video boards, which have ROM addressed at either address C0000 (yes, more hexadecimal; memory addresses are, like I/O addresses, expressed in hex) or E0000. It's usually not a good idea to move these addresses around.

- High-performance disk interfaces, like some special EIDE host adapters or SCSI host adapters, have ROM on them, but those ROM can be safely moved if the board permits.

- Token Ring network adapters have some ROM on them; it is moveable.

- Any kind of LAN board can have ROM on it, if the PC boots from the network and not from its local hard disk. It's unusual, but some companies use this "diskless workstation" approach. Some have RAM as well.

- Some high-end sound cards may have ROM on them; the ROM contain images of prerecorded sounds, like pianos, violins, or flutes.

- All PCs have some ROM at the top 64K of the first megabyte, the memory range from F0000 through FFFFF. That ROM is called the BIOS ROM, which means Basic Input/Output System, as you read in the previous chapter.

There are two things to be concerned about when configuring memory on add-in cards. First is the obvious one: make sure that two different boards don't have memory configured to the same address.

The second thing you've got to be concerned about is the effect of adapter memory on your DOS memory manager, if you're using DOS. Memory managers must know exactly which areas of memory are already filled up with adapter RAM or ROM, or the memory manager will overwrite the RAM or ROM, causing lots of potential system failures.

Most adapter RAM and ROM ranges vary, so I can't document them for you here, but you can see the ranges that don't change in Table 6.4.

TABLE 6.4: Common ROM and RAM Buffer Addresses

FUNCTION	ADDRESS RANGE (HEX)	ADDRESS LENGTH
XT Hard Disk Controller	C8000–CBFFF	16K
EGA	C0000–C3FFF	16K
VGA	C0000–C7FFF or E0000–E7FFF	32K
LIM Boards (may vary)	D0000–DFFFF	64K

Another set of heavy users of onboard RAM is PC Card boards, which brings us to our next topic.

Configuring PC Card Boards

If you've got a laptop, it's probably got at least one expansion slot designed to support a credit-card sized adapter card called a PCMCIA or PC Card adapter. There are PC Card-format modems, network cards, hard disks, Global Positioning System sensors, memory cards, SCSI adapters, and sound cards, just to name a few. Under some circumstances, PC Cards offer no trouble—but in others you may have to struggle with them a bit.

PC Card Is Often PnP In theory, PC Card boards are PnP in that they set up their own interrupts, memory, and so on. The idea is that any system using PC Cards should have some software called a *card services manager* that examines the cards in the system and sets their resources appropriately, making sure that no IRQs, I/O addresses, or memory addresses conflict. (DMA is not a problem because PC Cards can't use DMA.)

Of the popular operating systems available, Windows 95/98 handles PC Cards the best.

Using a PC Card without Card Services   People running DOS on laptops without a card services manager and people running Windows NT on laptops will have a tougher time configuring software to use the PC Cards. Let's see how you'd configure a PC Card in a system that lacked a card services manager.

First, install the PC Card into the laptop; let's say for example that it's a network card. Then turn the laptop on and boot up the operating system, whether it's DOS or Windows NT. Next, load the driver for the network card. The driver's installation program will need to configure the driver, and it will ask you about the card—what IRQ is it using, what I/O address, and so on. Here's the hard part: *you have no idea what the answer is.* And the board ain't talking, at least not usually. You see, in the case where a PC Card powers up and there's no card services manager, the PC Card just picks its own resource values. That's the bad news, but it's not terrible news, as these boards are usually designed to default to some set of IRQ, I/O address, and so on.

The good news is that because the driver for the PC Card was written by the same folks who made the board, the driver usually *also* defaults to the same set of IRQ, I/O address, and the like as the board. So if you pop a PC Card into a laptop with no other PC Cards, chances are that (1) the PC Card's defaults will work just fine and (2) when you're installing the driver, you should just take the defaults. The card will then usually work. So even if you're working with a dumb operating system (one that isn't all that bright about PC Cards), a single PC Card in a system will usually work fine. If it doesn't, just be prepared to wait on hold with the PC Card's manufacturer.

Some PC Cards Make Life Easier Some cards work better than that, however. Given the choice, I buy 3Com's PC Card Ethernet boards when purchasing network cards for my laptop because they come with a traditional software setup program. This program lets me set their PC Card Ethernet board to whatever I/O address and IRQ that I want, and the board *stays* at that I/O and IRQ. It's way cool and I wish *everyone* did it, as it makes setting up a Windows NT laptop leagues easier.

The 3Com cards aren't perfect, however. Recently I tried to install two 3Com 10/100 Ethernet cards in the same laptop because I wanted to use the laptop as an Internet router (it *can* be done and it actually works quite well, in case you're wondering), but the 3Com setup program was unable to address *two* cards in the same laptop. This surprised me, because I'd installed multiple 3Com network interface cards (NICs) in a number of *desktop* systems, so I called 3Com tech support. The fellow on the phone laughed and admitted that no, the setup program *couldn't* distinguish multiple PC Cards in a single machine, but that they didn't get too many calls for that. I had no choice but to install a 3Com card and a Xircom card in the system. The Xircoms are a bit more of a pain to install—you can't pre-set IRQs and such for Windows NT installation—but with the help of Xircom tech support, I got them both working.

Handling Multiple PC Cards But what about a system with multiple PC Cards? Again, in Windows 95/98 you probably won't have a problem, as the integrated card services manager handles the conflicts if it can. But in a DOS environment without a card services manager, or in Windows NT, you *may* see a situation wherein two PC Cards clobber each other. You can easily test this: try the system with just the first card. If that works, pull out that card and insert just the second card. If *that* works, but they don't work together, then they're conflicting. What do you do about this?

Well, if one of the PC Cards is a well-designed one like the 3Com cards I mentioned a couple of paragraphs back, it's simple—just run the lame PC Card all by itself and note which IRQ, I/O, and possibly memory it uses. Then pull that card out and insert the well-designed one, the one that lets you configure it. Set its resources to give the lame PC Card's desired resources a wide berth, and all will be well. And remember that whenever you configure a card to use particular resources, *write it down*. Put a mailing label on the PC Card and note what I/O, IRQ, and memory you set the card to.

PC Cards and Docking Stations On a simple laptop with a single PC Card, PC Card configuration is usually pretty smooth. PC Card boards can pose a problem on *mixed-bus* systems, however, as the PC Cards can't PnP with ISA slots. When might this happen? On any modern laptop with a docking station, as the docking station typically has a different bus than the laptop.

Docking stations for laptops typically contain two ISA slots, usually used for a SCSI host adapter and/or a LAN adapter. Years ago, I once installed an IBM Voice Dictation PC Card into a laptop in a docking station, and installed its voice recognition software into Windows; it was an older version, 3.11. I started up Windows and everything froze.

I was running SystemSoft's CardSoft software. It includes a utility called CARD-INFO that I ran to find out what interrupt my PC Card board was using. According to the utility, the card used IRQ 5. "No wonder it's crashing," I thought. "My Ethernet card (an ISA card in the docking station) is also set to IRQ 5." But how to make it change?

As my PC Card board was automatically configured, there was no way to directly set it to particular interrupts. But you *can* tell it to avoid certain interrupts. On my SystemSoft software, there's a file called CSALLOC.INI, an ASCII configuration file used by the card services manager software. I just added this line to the file:

```
IRQEXCLUDE=3,4,5,6,7,8,9,A,C,D,E
```

This told the card services manager to avoid those hardware interrupts; the values are, of course, in hex. The only interrupts I allowed it to consider were B (11) and F (15). There are also MEMEXCLUDE and IOEXCLUDE commands. They might look like this:

```
MEMEXCLUDE=C000-CFFF,E000-EFFF
IOEXCLUDE=1F0-1FF,3F0-3F8
```

It's a kind of roundabout way to configure a board—by telling it what it *can't* use—but that's how these boards work. With the Windows 95/98 Device Manager, by the way, you'd have no problem, as the Device Manager would already *know* what IRQ the ISA card was set to, and Windows 95/98's card services manager would then just avoid those resources. The Voice Dictation software didn't work under Windows NT, so I never tried to make everything work under that operating system; my guess is that without a piece of third-party PC Card manager software, I probably *couldn't* make it all work, save to change the IRQ on the ISA card, if that were possible.

Resolving Installation Conflicts: An Example

I think the best way to get this configuration stuff across is with a lot of examples, so let me share a few war stories here. Years ago, I needed to put Ethernet cards in about a half-dozen computers running DOS and Windows 3.0. (Okay, it's an *old* war story, but it all could happen today.) Just about every one of those Ethernet cards gave me trouble, and seeing what *I* did wrong will save you some time later.

The first LAN card I installed was an Ethernet board that used everything we've discussed—an I/O address range, a DMA channel, an IRQ channel, and some shared RAM. I left the I/O address at 300 hex, as that wouldn't conflict with the computer into which I was installing the board. The IRQ I chose was IRQ 5, avoiding the more commonly used IRQ 2. I avoid IRQ 2 because it *can* be used in some systems, but the fact that it cascades to IRQs 8 through 15 makes me a bit nervous; in the past, using IRQ 2 has caused conflicts with Windows. I set the DMA to channel 1, and put the shared RAM between CC000–CFFFF, as I knew that it would not then conflict with the hard disk controller ROM between C8000 and CBFFF.

When I plugged the board in, however, it refused to function. A little fiddling around made me realize that the DOS memory manager I was using was placing its memory at the same addresses as the shared memory on my LAN board, which in turn was clobbering the LAN board. I told the memory manager to exclude the range of addresses from CC000 to CFFFF (consult your memory manager's documentation to see exactly how; for a complete discussion of DOS memory managers, read *Troubleshooting Windows*, available from Sybex.) The board worked fine after that.

I set the second board identically, and it refused to work. A quick check of my notebook reminded me that a sound card was using IRQ 5, causing a conflict. The LAN board offered only IRQs 2 through 7, and I didn't want to use any of them, as I wanted to avoid 2 if I could, and 3 through 7 were busy, so I needed an alternative approach. A quick look at the sound card showed that it could support any IRQ up to IRQ 10, so I reset the sound card to IRQ 10, leaving IRQ 5 free for the LAN board. Problem solved.

Trouble appeared on the next machine as well. After inserting the LAN board, not only did the LAN board not work, the video screen showed some odd colors upon bootup. It was a special Windows accelerator board, so I checked its documentation. The accelerator, as it turned out, employed the I/O address range 300–30F, causing a conflict with the Ethernet card. I reset the I/O address on the Ethernet card, and all was well with *that* machine.

The next computer booted up okay, but I got strange flickers on the video screen whenever I tried to test the Ethernet card with the test program supplied with the Ethernet board. The Ethernet card was also failing its tests, so I looked closer, and realized that I'd never opened this particular computer before.

This computer was equipped with a super VGA board. Almost all super VGA boards have an autoswitching feature that they'll optionally support, a feature whereby they automatically detect what video mode the currently running software needs, and then switch to that mode. This feature should be disabled for two reasons. First, it causes Windows NT to fail, as well as a number of other programs. Second, the autoswitch mode requires that the video board use a combination of interrupts 2 and 9, which is less than desirable because it steals a much-needed interrupt; in some cases, it causes a system to falsely report memory error. This super VGA card, as you can imagine by now, had the interrupt enabled, allowing for super VGA. I removed the interrupt jumper from the board—its location varies, so you must consult the documentation for your board before trying to remove the interrupt jumper. The Ethernet board ran without a hitch afterward. By the way, if you *are* planning to check your super VGA documentation to find out whether the interrupt is enabled, be aware that some manuals just refer to the interrupt and some refer to *autoswitching*. If you can't find one, look for the other.

By now, as I approached the final machine, I was trying to *anticipate* problems. The LAN board placed in this last machine, like its comrades, refused to work at first. I struggled with this for a while, idly running diagnostic programs on the entire system. As I've explained before, I reasoned that if I could figure out what *didn't* work on this system that had worked *yesterday*, I'd get a clue about what the board was conflicting with. (Of course, there was the possibility that the board just plain didn't work, but the earlier experiences of the day seemed to render that doubtful.) Then I realized that the diagnostic programs failed to notice that the PC had a mouse. Eureka! I recalled at that moment that this particular machine didn't have a serial mouse, unlike most machines in my office—it had a *bus* mouse. A bus mouse requires an interrupt-using circuit board of its own, and I was fairly sure that I'd set the interrupt on the bus mouse interface board to IRQ 5. Not wanting to remove the cover from the PC unless necessary, I tried loading the mouse driver, and got the error message "interrupt jumper missing." I opened up the PC, checked the mouse board, and sure enough, it was using IRQ 5. With its interrupt changed, I replaced the mouse board, and the last of the LAN boards was fired up and ready to go.

I don't want to discourage you with this story. I just want to underscore how important it is to keep documentation of what's installed in your current machines, and to share a war story with you that may give you an idea or two the next time you're having trouble making a new board behave.

Where Do You Find Diagnostic Programs?

Chapter 5, "Troubleshooting PC Problems," mentioned the names of several generic diagnostic programs, like the Norton Utilities or Windsor products. You could use those to test a board like, say, a motherboard, or a memory board. They're perfectly good for that. But don't do what some folks I've seen do. I know of a group who bought a lot of PS/2s. They loaded up the Reference Diskette that came with the PS/2, told the diagnostics to run over and over, and left the machine. Hours later, they came back to see if there were any errors reported on the screen. No errors, so they shipped the machine to users. But users complained that a lot of machines had malfunctioning video. It turned out that the VGAs on Model 50s had a higher-than-average failure rate: I myself saw a classroom with 30 Model 50s develop video problems in about 20 percent of the machines. (If you have this problem, you might like to know that it seemed most prevalent when the room was above 75 to 80 degrees F. Maybe you could turn up the air conditioning.) The support staff was puzzled. How did this slip by them? Simple. Video diagnostics often require a user to look them over. If your reds are greens and blues are blacks, the monitor doesn't know. The video board doesn't know. You need an operator to audit the video tests.

Here's a cheap memory test. Build a spreadsheet that fills memory. It just consists of a single cell A1 with the value 1, then a cell A2 with the formula A1+1. Copy that cell until you run out of memory. Set Recalculation to Manual. Then write a short macro that loops continuously, recalculating, and recalculating again. If you really want to add a level of elegance, calculate the sum of this large column of numbers, and check it against the actual value. (The sum of 1, 2, 3, 4,...N is equal to $N(N+1)/2$.)

If your board includes its own diagnostic testing programs, you should use them instead of the generic testing software, since they will be more likely to test the board more thoroughly. For example, Iomega supplies an RCDDIAG program that tests the controller. Alternatively, you can test a LAN board by putting a loopback connector of some kind on it to allow it to "hear" what it broadcasts.

Making Plug and Play Work

All of this fiddling-with-jumpers and rooting-around-for-setup-programs gets old quick.

I mean, *really* quick.

In a Perfect World, you'd just insert a board into your system, turn the system on, and the system would configure itself automatically, no muss, fuss, or greasy aftertaste. It would work something like this:

1. On bootup, the BIOS would recognize the board ("This is an Adaptec 2942W SCSI host adapter").

2. The BIOS would then ask the board what IRQs, DMAs, I/O addresses, RAM addresses, and ROM addresses it needs ("It requires an interrupt, a 256-byte block of I/O addresses, and a 16K ROM range").

3. *Then* the BIOS would ask the board what range of IRQs, DMAs, I/O addresses, RAM addresses, and ROM addresses it can *use* ("It can use IRQ 5, 7, 9, 10, 11, or 14, any 256-byte block from address 60K to 64K, and any ROM address from C0000 to E0000").

4. After that, the BIOS would set the resources (IRQ, and so on) so that they don't conflict with anything already in the system.

5. Once the board—and all others—were coexisting nicely, the operating system for the PC would load.

6. Early on, the operating system would note the existence of the new board and say, "Hey, this is an Adaptec 2940W, let's load a driver for it...ah, here it is, in D:\WINDRIVERS...ask the BIOS what IRQs and such it set the board to...configure the driver...done!" And the new board works like a charm.

Sounds cool, doesn't it? I mean, after all, that's what *you've* got to do to make a sound card, a SCSI host adapter, or a LAN adapter card work. Why not let the computer do it? Well, that's the whole idea behind Plug and Play (PnP).

Way back in 1993, Microsoft, Intel, and Compaq proposed a standard called PnP. The idea behind PnP was that board manufacturers would add circuitry to their add-in boards so that the automatic setup and resource query (resource here means IRQ, DMA, I/O address, ROM address, or RAM buffer address) capabilities of EISA and Micro Channel would become available to machines with ISA buses. In actuality, no one ever made a PnP system that included EISA, VESA, or MCA to my knowledge; every PnP system I've ever seen used either a hybrid of PCI and ISA or just PCI. Although PC Cards are not part of the PnP specification, most PnP systems can configure them. Laptops using just CardBus, the newer 32-bit bus, can be PnP.

PnP is a good idea, but it's a bit frustrating that you can't retrofit it on an existing system; it has to be built into a computer when you buy it. Today, fortunately, all new PCs are PnP-compatible, even if the expansion boards in them aren't. In fact, in some cases, you can install one or two non-PnP boards and the computer will build the rest of the system around them (as long as they don't conflict with themselves).

Booting on PnP Systems

Let's look into a bit more detail about how PnP works. PnP starts off with a PnP-compatible motherboard. This motherboard has a BIOS that understands PnP, and also contains about 16K of flash memory that is a part of the BIOS. Virtually all motherboards built in the past few years are PnP-compliant; I'd hazard a guess that anything since 1995 would be PnP-compatible.

You also must have add-in cards that are PnP-compatible. These cards are configured *every time you boot*, and that configuration is done by a routine called the Configuration Manager. The Configuration Manager is usually part of the BIOS. It's possible to build a PnP system that loads its Configuration Manager off disk, but I don't recommend it, as you end up with an only mildly PnP system. In addition to a PnP motherboard and expansion boards, you need, as I've noted a couple of times already, a PnP-compliant operating system.

In the ideal world (that is, everything is PnP), the system powers up and the Configuration Manager assumes control. It asks each board what resources it needs and what is the range of resources that it will accept. (For example, a board might say, "I need an IRQ, and I'll take either 2, 3, 4, or 5," in the same way that the Microsoft ISA bus mouse interface does; even though there are other interrupts, its circuitry for some reason will accept an IRQ only in the range of 2 to 5.) The Configuration Manager then assigns resources to cards, avoiding conflicts.

This means that potentially installing one new PnP card to a PnP system could cause all of the other cards to move their resources around. What does that mean for the network, SCSI, sound card drivers, and so on, that must know which resources those boards use? Well, it implies that device drivers must be a bit smarter than they are now.

For example, any DOS-based client on a Windows NT network has a file called PROTOCOL.INI on its hard disk. In that file are often references like IRQ=10, IOBASE=300, and so on. That DOS-based client doesn't work unless someone tells it what values to put in PROTOCOL.INI; in contrast, on a PnP system, the network software must take its cues from the Configuration Manager automatically, removing the need for operator intervention.

Once all boards are taken care of, then the system boots in the usual way. The main difference with PnP is that the hardware shuffling of resources (I/O addresses, DMA channels, RAM windows, and the like) happens every time you boot the system, and (one hopes) quickly and invisibly.

Oh, by the way, can you force a particular board to a particular resource? Yes—that's called *locking* the resource. The Configuration Manager on your system should allow that, or your operating system may; Windows 95/98 lets you do it with the Device Manager, which is in the Control Panel (Control Panel/System/Device Manager).

Configuring ATs and Beyond: Software Setup

Answering thousands of service calls that really just stemmed from incorrectly set DIP switches convinced IBM that they needed a computer that was easier to set up.

The main trouble with the XT and PC setup wasn't so much the switches, as it was the fact that the PC owner would have to take the top off the computer and pull out some boards in order to get to the switches. So IBM came up with software set up on the first AT, back in 1984.

The AT wasn't totally set up with software; it had one DIP switch to set that configured its video. The rest of its *motherboard* configuration information was retained in a battery-backed memory. The add-in boards were left to fend for themselves configuration-wise, as the bus was ISA and ISA does not support a standard method for doing software setup on a board.

Now, this isn't just an idle history lesson: *virtually every PC since then has used the same basic approach.* Let's see how it works.

PC Setup Memory: The CMOS Chip

The nice thing about switches was that they conveyed information—if switch number three was on, you had a monochrome video board, if switch number three was off, you had a color video board, that kind of thing. This information was "nonvolatile," meaning that when you turned the PC off, switch number three stayed where it was, so that the PC could read its state the *next* time you turned the PC on.

Software setup wouldn't be as easy, the IBM engineers reasoned, unless they could either (A) put little robotic fingers in the PC's case to flip the switches when the software told them to or (B) use some kind of memory structure to store the configuration information. Option B sounded like the better idea (I was just kidding about option A), so they decided to stuff the configuration data into a memory chip.

The problem with using a memory chip was that memory chips are volatile (as you recall from Chapter 3, "Inside the PC: Pieces of the Picture"), and as soon as you turned off the computer, the data in the chip would evaporate. So the AT engineers put a small low-power memory chip into the AT, and attached a battery to that chip to keep it powered when the system was turned off.

Like most memory chips, it was built around the Complementary Metal Oxide Semiconductor, or CMOS, technology. The chip also contained a crude time and date/clock/calendar circuit. For some reason, the chip got the nickname "the CMOS chip," and that name stuck. It's a silly name on its face, because *most* of the chips in modern machines are CMOS chips, but that's just what everybody calls it (and I'm surrendering and calling it that, since that's the term that others use).

The CMOS memory contains 64 bytes—not 64K, 64 bytes—of memory, as well as the clock/calendar. To read the data in the

CMOS, your PC pushes the value's address—zero through 63—into I/O address 70 hex, and then reads it back in I/O address 71 hex. The PC writes new data by storing the requested address to I/O address 70 hex, and then storing the new data to I/O address 71 hex.

The CMOS chip itself is often a Motorola 146818 24-pin chip. It is volatile, like all semiconductor memory, and so requires a battery to maintain the integrity of its data when the system is turned off. When the battery runs down, the computer starts acting aphasic (look it up, but it means what you expect it to). Most systems use non-rechargeable lithium batteries that claim to have lives of three to 10 years. Others use rechargeable NiCad batteries. Some systems use a memory and battery all-in-one chip from Dallas Semiconductor. It is distinguished by the alarm clock on its face, and contains a battery that Dallas Semiconductor claims is good for 10 years. When you replace it, you also replace its battery.

It's worth mentioning that, as time went on, 64 bytes just wasn't enough, so EISA, Micro Channel, and PCI machines usually have a different CMOS memory configuration.

Modifying the Setup Memory: Running Setup

The most important question in software setup is "How do you do it?" It depends. Since the AT's appearance in 1984, we've seen several approaches to setup programs:

- Early machines had a separate setup program on a floppy disk that you'd run to modify the CMOS chip's memory or to set the time and date.

- Later machines have a setup program in their BIOS, activated by a set of keystrokes.

- Micro Channel and EISA systems usually require a setup program on floppy, as the setup program must incorporate information about new boards.

- PCI-based systems are usually a hybrid of built-in setup programs and *automatic* setup, wherein a system sets up itself, or a part of itself, automatically with no operator intervention required.

Adjustable Bus Speeds

The standard ISA bus speed is, of course, 8MHz. Some clones allow you to increase the speed on that all the way up to 32MHz. It's a good idea to play with this feature, but carefully. I've found that most ISA cards can run just fine all the way up to 12MHz. On the other hand, if you want fast peripherals, then you should invest in a machine with a VESA or PCI bus, and use boards built for that interface.

Adjustable Memory Speeds

In contrast, here's something I *wouldn't* mess around with. If you've got memory that's significantly faster than the stuff that the documentation calls for, then go ahead and play around. But be sure that you know how to restore the settings to their default state—or your system may not be able to get far enough into the boot process to even let you restart the setup program.

Keyboard Settings

I prefer a machine that does not set the NumLock by default when powering up. (I'm old and inflexible, and the first PCs left the NumLock off by default.) Sometimes the BIOS lets you set this.

Passwords

Be careful with these, as well. Many machines, laptops in particular, include power-on passwords as options. If you manage to forget your password, then there's usually no way to get into the machine, short of disconnecting the battery (better hope it's not soldered, like the batteries on most modern machines…) and waiting overnight for the power to slowly drain out of the CMOS chip. Even more annoying, once you've set a password, there's usually no way to restore the machine back to "doesn't need a password" mode.

Power Management

As onboard power management becomes chic in PC design, control of that power management often goes into the built-in setup program. You can use this to control when the computer turns itself off to save power and how often it does it.

PCI Control

Many PCI bus machines come with no control and configuration program for the boards in the PCI bus. It's an incredible oversight, but it's the case for hundreds of thousands of machines that use the PCI bus but don't support PnP.

These settings usually control a few things about the bus, but they're a sign of a poorly designed PCI machine. PCI machines should all be PnP-compatible, and so should not require settings like PCI IDE interface enable/disable, or the like.

Replacing the Configuration Battery

If your AT-type system insists on being set up every day, you probably need a new battery. New batteries can be purchased in the $17–$30 price range. CompUSA and Radio Shack are two good places to find those batteries; so is your local PC hardware store. Alternatively, go to Radio Shack and get their Four AA Battery Holder (89 cents). Put four AA batteries in it and solder the wires from the holder to the AT battery contacts. This works, but it raises the question of where to put the battery holder (the power supply is a good place).

When you replace the battery, you will notice that it is connected to the motherboard with two wires, one red, and one white. If you didn't pay attention when you took the old battery off, you may wonder how the new battery is connected. In that case, remember RAP: Red Away from the Power supply.

Many modern motherboards have a lithium battery soldered onto the motherboard of the PC. When that battery runs out, you needn't solder a new one in place. Instead, these motherboards have a three-pin Berg connector that fits a standard battery. You usually have to find a jumper on the motherboard that tells the motherboard to stop trying to draw power from the soldered battery and instead pull from a battery attached to the Berg connector.

For laptop owners, there is often another type of rechargeable configuration battery, sometimes called a "standby battery." This item is actually designed to hold a charge while you replace the main battery pack, in order to preserve any data you have in RAM. It is recharged from your AC adapter, just like your main battery, and since it works only during the few moments when you are in the midst of a battery change, it should always have enough power. In the event that it should fail, however, you will not be able to replace it yourself. This is a "manufacturer-only" replacement item, and you should not try to work on this yourself.

Hey, Wait a Minute, My PC Doesn't Have a Battery!

Some PCs don't need a battery. Instead they use some kind of *EEPROM,* or *Electrically Erasable Programmable Read Only Memory.* These ROMs can be altered by the CPU. Newer systems use yet another kind of RAM that doesn't forget, yet can be altered by the CPU—called *flash RAM.* Flash RAM is sometimes referred to as *NVRAM* or *NRAM,* both of which are short for *NonVolatile RAM.*

Parallel Port Configuration Anomalies

Here's a real PC configuration brainteaser you'll see on older systems. I have a PC with *only one* parallel port I configured as LPT2. There *is* no LPT1 in this machine. I boot it up. Once the system is running, what LPT port do I have on my system?

Answer: LPT1.

PCs have a strange feature when it comes to parallel ports. On bootup, the BIOS checks the LPTs. If there's no LPT1, it looks for an LPT2 or LPT3. If you've got an LPT2 but no LPT1, it actually converts the LPT2 to an LPT1. This is, of course, a *software* adjustment. I'll repeat: it's flat-out impossible to have an LPT2 without an LPT1. If you *do* install an LPT2 without LPT1, the LPT2 gets made into an LPT1 on bootup time.

Nice feature. I just wish the documentation had *told* me about it. You see, it was late one night, and—oh, heck, I don't want to even talk about it. Now *you* know.

16-Bit Boards with ROM May Conflict with 8-Bit Boards with ROM

Here's an oddity you may see in older systems with a mix of 8-bit and 16-bit ISA boards.

If you have two boards in your system—one 16-bit, and one 8-bit, both with ROM on them—the 16-bit board may cause the 8-bit board to malfunction.

Why? It has to do with a characteristic of the 16-bit ISA bus. It recognizes that it must talk to some boards that are 8-bit and some that are 16-bit. It doesn't know which are which. So the extended part of the 16-bit slots have three *cheater* lines, lines that are duplicates of three lines on the 8-bit part of the slot. The way the extra lines work is this: every time a memory access is to occur, the CPU sends out a warning message on the three cheater lines, describing roughly where the upcoming memory request will be going. "Roughly" means within 128K of the desired memory address. If a board has memory that is addressed anywhere in that 128K area, it responds with an "Okay, I'm ready" signal. *But* only the 16-bit boards have the cheater lines—so if the upcoming memory access is to/from an 8-bit board, the CPU will receive no response to the warning. In that case, it just conducts 8-bit transfers.

If, on the other hand, the CPU *does* receive a response, it conducts the memory access using 16-bit transfers. To review:

- The CPU sends out a warning message: "I'm about to do a memory access. It will be somewhere in the following 128K memory area…"

- This message is audible only to 16-bit boards.

- If a 16-bit board contains any memory—RAM or ROM—in that 128K address range, it responds, "*I've* got some memory in that range—do the memory access as 16-bit transfers." Any other 16-bit boards that happen to have memory in that range reply likewise.

- On the other hand, 8-bit boards are deaf to the warning, so would make no response, even if they did have memory in that 128K range.

- If the CPU hears a 16-bit response, it conducts the memory access 16 bits at a time. Otherwise, it just transfers the data 8 bits at a time.

Where's the problem? What if there are *multiple* boards with memory in a given range? Well, if they're all 16-bit boards, that's no sweat. But what if, within a given 128K memory range, there were 8-bit *and* 16-bit boards? *Then* every time the CPU wanted to access the 8-bit board, it would send out a warning message that the 8-bit board, logically, would not hear or respond to—*but the 16-bit boards would*! Result: the CPU would send 16-bit data blocks to a board that could accept only 8-bit blocks—an apparent malfunction.

This sounds like a dire scenario, but it really only pops up in one area: the ROM reserve. The addresses from 768K to 896K are, you may recall, where the ROM is addressed: a 128K-sized memory area, notice. Every ROM access causes the CPU to issue a warning to the entire ROM area. If there are 8-bit boards and 16-bit boards with ROM on them, the 16-bit boards may respond to the CPU's attempts to access the ROMs on the 8-bit boards. This would result in the CPU again attempting 16-bit transfers to/from an 8-bit board. So if adding a 16-bit board kills an existing 8-bit board, that may be a reason why.

Well, some day you'll just buy a board, plug it into a system, and you *will* be able to "play" with it instantly. But that day is not here yet, at least not for most of us. But for now, master the concepts in this chapter, and you'll be an expert installer.

CHAPTER
SEVEN

Repairs with Circuit Boards and Chips

- Finding the problem board

- When to fix, when to replace

- The PC boot process

- How to find and replace bad chips

7

If the problem isn't software, if everything's plugged in, and it isn't something obvious like a burnt-out motor, a broken wire, a gummed-up printer, or an imploded display, then it's probably a circuit board. Step 1 is to identify the faulty part. I'll talk about diagnostic approaches in this chapter (they don't cost anything but time). Step 2 is repair. There are two levels of repair here: board level and chip level.

The more important, as well as the more difficult of these operations is the first, *identification*. How do you know which board is bad? There are several approaches we'll examine here. Next, should you fix or replace the bad board? You'll see the pros and cons. Further along, as some repairs can involve chip replacements, we'll examine diagnosing and repairing memory problems—the chips you're most likely to install and replace.

How Do You Find the Bad Board?

I've said as much as I need to say about "fix or repair?" Now let's hunker down to the tough part—figuring out which board is the problem child. Here's the overall roadmap.

1. Make *sure* you've checked steps 1 to 7 discussed in Chapter 5, "Troubleshooting PC Problems." You *know* by now that a switched outlet (or one with a tripped circuit breaker) isn't the culprit. You're not ripping the machine apart to figure out why it won't boot when the last thing you did was install a new expansion board (and the machine hasn't worked since you put the board in), without first removing the new board to see if the problem goes away.

    Again, just be lazy and follow the beaten path. Don't get original. Just make sure you've followed the seven steps.

2. Assuming the machine *does* boot, use the machine to help diagnose its own problems. Run the diagnostics to find out if it's the keyboard, video, and so on. That'll give you an indication of what's wrong.

3. Suppose the problem is clearly video. What now? Again, be lazy. Before you "remove the top and begin to swap," check the easy stuff. First swap the monitor or the video board.

4. Even lazier—is the problem specific to something like a time of day, or, more likely, a piece of software? If the video works well enough to boot the system, runs some applications but dies when you're running, say, PageMaker, the problem is likely software, not hardware. This may mean:

   - You've installed PageMaker incorrectly (easy to do), or

   - There's a bug in the PageMaker/Windows code that talks to your video board, or

   - Your video card is not compatible with PageMaker.

   In this situation, if you have a second, identical computer, I'd take the exact same copy of PageMaker and move it over to the identical system. But in order to find a problem like this, it's important that the second computer be identical, right down to the version of the operating system, add-in boards, and so on. If the problem shows up on the second machine, common sense tells us that it's a software problem with Page-Maker, an installation problem, or the brand of video board that both machines have is not 100 percent compatible. If it's the third problem, try using a different video card (in fact, if you have a lot of patience, you might even call the manufacturer and ask them which video cards work and which don't). If it's a problem with installation, try rereading the installation instructions. Maybe you made a wrong choice when you were installing the software. If you can't duplicate the problem by reinstalling the software, check the company's Web site. Most companies have troubleshooting page(s) that list dozens or even hundreds of things that can go wrong and are easily corrected—and all of the instructions are usually right there.

5. If the machine doesn't boot at all, consult the following section.

Night of the Living Data: Making a Dead Machine 'UnDead'

Suppose it's completely unresponsive. You can't run the diagnostics, because the machine won't talk at all. Here are two approaches to bringing your machine back from the dead, and a few other possibilities and solutions. (Do you then run an operating system called "DOSferatu"? Better quit while I'm ahead…)

Identifying the Problem Board I: Two Machines

First of all, assume that there is only one problem. Ideally, you have two machines, one sick and one well. A simple strategy here is to swap boards one by one. Each time you swap a board, turn on *both machines* and note which machines are currently well. Ideally, you would like to induce the problem from the originally sick PC to the originally well PC.

By the way, did you check the old "intensity turned down on the monitor" trick? I'll turn down the intensity on my monitor for some reason, leave the machine, come back to the machine after a while (forgetting I've turned down the intensity), and panic, thinking that (at best) I've got a bad monitor.

Ghost in the Machine (Contagious Components) Be careful here, however. Sometimes you end up with *two* sick machines. Why? I've seen components that, being damaged, damage other components. Suppose you've got a dead system, and you've stripped the system to the motherboard and power supply. You try to ascertain what's causing your problems, so you swap motherboards. Still no luck. So you try swapping power supplies. *Still* no response. What's happening?

You've got a "demon" in the power supply: not only is it not working, it destroys motherboards. Originally it "ate" motherboard number one, then you fed it another one. I've seen this in two situations: bad power supplies damaging motherboards and bad keyboard interfaces on motherboards damaging keyboards.

The moral is:

1. Swap the power supply before the motherboard.

2. Before swapping the keyboard, test the keyboard interface with a voltmeter, as described in Chapter 20, "Keyboards and Mice."

Identifying the Problem Board II: Just One Machine

If all you've got is one machine, here's a nice, minimalist approach. Some people call it the "min/max technique," short for "minimum/maximum."

Start with a machine that won't boot up at all and assume that there's only one thing wrong with it. We'll break it down to the bare essentials, then add pieces until the machine refuses to boot. *Once the machine refuses to boot, we'll know that the last item that we added is the trouble board.*

Start off by removing everything but the following:

- Power Supply
- Motherboard
- Speaker

Turn it on. You should observe several things:

- The fan on the power supply should start right up. If it doesn't, either the power supply isn't getting power, or the fan's burned out. If the fan is burned out, and it *has been* burned out, then the problem's easy—you cooked your PC the last time you used it.

- There is *one* other reason that the fan wouldn't start up. The power supply's pretty smart, and can sense short circuits on the motherboard. If it senses such a short, it will shut down and refuse to do anything until the short's resolved.

- You don't believe me? Try taking a board out while the power's on. If you do it just right, you'll create a short and the machine will shut down. (This is not a particularly smart idea, actually, and is not recommended. You might want to just trust me on this one.)

- The power supply should probably also produce a "click" on the speaker (you've probably never noticed it, but it happens each time you turn most PCs on). Another aspect of the "intelligent" power supply is that once it feels that it is up to the task of getting to work, it sends a signal to the motherboard that resets the system. The result is the "click." Once you hear that, you know that the power supply believes itself to be functional.

- Assuming that the two things listed above happened, you'll probably get one long and two shorts beep out of the speaker—the motherboard's way of saying, "I can't find the video card." You may hear a different beep combination—different BIOS configurations respond differently to the "no video" condition.

If the three things outlined here have happened, congratulations—the machine booted. (It didn't do that before, remember?) If it didn't, there are only three possible culprits: the motherboard, power supply, or speaker. It's child's play now to figure out which is the offending component: just swap the speaker, power supply, and/or motherboard. Remember what I said before about swapping the power supply first, in case it's got a demon. Remember that in the PC repair business *the cheapest and most effective piece of test equipment is a spare part.* At this point, it's a quick swap.

Assuming that the machine booted, the next step is to add the video card. Try to boot the machine. Again, if it doesn't boot, try another video card. If it boots, you'll get error messages complaining about the lack of keyboard and drives—errors 301, 601, and 1701 on an older IBM or Compaq machine, and messages in English on pretty much any current machine. Keep adding boards until the machine fails.

Whenever you assemble (or re-assemble) your computer and apply power, sometimes the system will respond with a series of beeps. (Be sure to attach the system speaker so you can hear them.) Depending upon the system, the beeps can mean a number of different things. For example, usually a single short beep or a couple of short beeps will mean "everything's okay." On the other hand, if you get a repeating pattern of not-so-short beeps, the computer is probably trying to tell you something.

Phoenix and AMI are the two primary BIOS manufacturers in the computer industry. The beep codes for the AMI BIOS are listed in Table 7.1.

TABLE 7.1: AMI BIOS Beep Codes

BEEP CODE	MEANING
1 beep	Refresh failure
2 beeps	Parity error
3 beeps	Base 64K memory failure
4 beeps	Timer not operational
5 beeps	Processor error
6 beeps	8042 - gate A20 failure
7 beeps	Processor exception interrupt error
8 beeps	Display memory read/write failure
9 beeps	ROM checksum error
10 beeps	CMOS shutdown register read/write error
11 beeps	Cache memory bad

The Phoenix error codes are a little different than AMI, in that the beeps occur in groups of three with pauses between the groups. So, for example, the first code would sound like this: BEEP (pause) BEEP (pause) BEEP-BEEP-BEEP (long pause) and then the pattern would repeat. Table 7.2 lists the Phoenix beep codes and their meanings.

TABLE 7.2: Phoenix BIOS Beep Codes

BEEP CODE	MEANING
1-1-3	CMOS write/read failure
1-1-4	ROM BIOS checksum failure
1-2-1	Programmable interval timer failure
1-2-2	DMA initialization failure
1-2-3	DMA page register write/read failure
1-3-1	RAM refresh verification failure
1-3-3	First 64K RAM chip or data line failure, multi-bit
1-3-4	First 64K RAM odd/even logic failure
1-4-1	Address line failure first 64K RAM
1-4-2	Parity failure first 64K RAM
2-1-1	Bit 0 first 64K RAM failure
2-1-2	Bit 1 first 64K RAM failure
2-1-3	Bit 2 first 64K RAM failure
2-1-4	Bit 3 first 64K RAM failure
2-2-1	Bit 4 first 64K RAM failure
2-2-2	Bit 5 first 64K RAM failure
2-2-3	Bit 6 first 64K RAM failure
2-2-4	Bit 7 first 64K RAM failure
2-3-1	Bit 8 first 64K RAM failure

Continued on next page

TABLE 7.2 CONTINUED: Phoenix BIOS Beep Codes

BEEP CODE	MEANING
2-3-2	Bit 9 first 64K RAM failure
2-3-3	Bit 10 first 64K RAM failure
2-3-4	Bit 11 first 64K RAM failure
2-4-1	Bit 12 first 64K RAM failure
2-4-2	Bit 13 first 64K RAM failure
2-4-3	Bit 14 first 64K RAM failure
2-4-4	Bit 15 first 64K RAM failure
3-1-1	Slave DMA register failure
3-1-2	Master DMA register failure
3-1-3	Master interrupt mask register failure
3-1-4	Slave interrupt mask register failure
3-2-4	Keyboard controller test failure
3-3-4	Screen initialization failure
3-4-1	Screen retrace test failure
3-4-2	Search for video ROM in progress
4-2-1	Timer tick interrupt test in progress or failure
4-2-2	Shutdown test in progress or failure
4-2-3	Gate A20 failure
4-2-4	Unexpected interrupt in protected mode
4-3-1	RAM test in progress or address failure > FFFFh
4-3-3	Interval timer channel 2 test or failure
4-3-4	Time-of-day clock test or failure
4-4-1	Serial port test or failure
4-4-2	Parallel port test or failure
4-4-3	Math coprocessor test or failure

Note that this isn't gospel—your machine, depending on the manufacturer, may do something different from these expected outcomes. *Try it* sometime on your functioning PC. Note the outcomes. Do it *before* your computer breaks down, so you'll have a reference.

NOTE   Again, I must stress this strongly: do this on a healthy PC so you can see what YOUR healthy machine looks like at various stages of reassembly. If you don't know what healthy looks like, you can't recognize disease.

Now, you may have gotten down to the last board, the machine may have been booting fine, and you insert that last board, thinking, "Aha! Gotcha. Now to prove it...." But then the machine boots fine. (Grrrr...) Why? One of the following may be true:

- It just wanted some attention.

- It fails when boards are hot, and the disassembly and reassembly cooled it to the point that it works.

- You didn't do the greatest job the first time you took it apart, cleaned it, and put it back together.

What Makes Boards Fail?

If you're reading this, you may already have a dead board. I've suggested just replacing it, but in case you're interested, here's what generally zaps boards.

Most component problems boil down to either environmental trouble, damage due to mishandling, or faulty manufacturing. The most common ailments are the following:

- Socketed chips creep out of their sockets due to expansion and contraction. (Push them back in.)

- Bad solder joints can disconnect or cause short circuits. (Resolder.)

- Weak components fail under heat. (Replace them, if possible.) By the way, one easy way to find a component that is failing under heat is to put a handful of cotton swabs in the freezer for an hour (keep them dry). Then put the tip of a swab on the suspected component(s). If they come back to life, you've found your culprit.

- PC board traces can be scratched. This is something you can usually see if you look carefully (or use a magnifying glass).

- Dirt and dust build up heat. (See Chapter 4, "Avoiding Service: Preventive Maintenance.")

- Edge connectors or chip pins corrode.

- RFI/EMI can cause impairment.

Other Problems and Solutions

The remaining chapters in the book cover peripherals in depth, but here are some ideas for solving some kinds of problems, and pointers to other sections in the book for more information.

Hard Disk Problems

If you seem to have a hard disk problem, look at the extensive discussions of drive recovery in the hard disk chapters (chapters 10 through 14).

Keyboard Problems

Keyboard problems are covered in detail in Chapter 20, but here are a few possibilities:

- The system board may be at fault. Test the keyboard test points (see Chapter 20 for more information).

- Is the keyboard plugged in?

- Is it a PS/2 keyboard plugged into the PS/2 mouse port?

- Are you leaning on the space bar (or any other key) accidentally, or is anything inadvertently resting on a key?

- Are any keys stuck?

Many Beeps when Booting, No Video

If you boot your PC and get one long beep and two short beeps, and then the drive A: light goes on, but no display, it's most likely the display board. Assuming you have a floppy diskette in drive A:, type **dir a:** and press Enter on the keyboard. If the drive A: light comes on, the system is responding—you just can't see it. Swap the video board. Take a look at Chapter 21, "Video Adapters and Displays."

Drive A: Light Stays On

You try to access drive A:, and the floppy light comes on and stays on. You probably put the floppy cable on backwards. Check Chapter 15, "Understanding, Installing, and Repairing Floppy Drives."

There's another possible reason—are you loading a program from a floppy? The problem could be insufficient memory to run your application. Try your backup disk also.

Parity Check Error (Memory Error)

See Chapter 8, "Semiconductor Memory."

Fix or Replace Boards?

Assuming (as we'll discuss presently) that you can find the bad board, do you just replace it, or do you try to fix it? Sure, it's macho to get out the soldering iron and fix an errant board. But, in general, you won't find it cost-effective to repair a circuit board. This is basically because (1) the inexpensive boards are far cheaper to replace than to repair, and (2) the more expensive boards require even more expensive equipment to repair.

Inexpensive boards, like one of those ubiquitous video or sound boards, can be had for a reasonable price. Chips on these boards are primarily soldered, not socketed, and so can only be fixed by someone trained to solder chips without destroying them. Add the hourly cost of this person to the cost of replacement chips, and the amount soon adds up to an amount in excess of the cost of a new $15 board. More and more boards are four-layer boards, which are tough to solder correctly. Four-layer means the board has not only printed circuit traces on the top and bottom, but two layers in the middle! Even if it is a simple two-layer board, don't forget that time is wasted inserting the board and powering up the computer after each chip replacement.

Maintenance Considerations for Integrated Motherboards

These days, most motherboards are of the all-in-one variety. The video, disk controllers, parallel and serial ports, mouse, and keyboard controllers all exist on proprietary chips (ASICs), mounted directly on the motherboard. Auggh! Worst-case scenario for troubleshooting! If one of the onboard controllers fails, you may have to replace the whole motherboard!

But it's not *all* bad news. Now there are fewer boards to worry about and fewer DIP switches to fuss with. Also, reducing chip count should produce a more reliable machine overall, and indeed it often does. But it can limit PC troubleshooting to an all-or-nothing matter, because there's just one board in the system, and, as I just said, it's just not reasonable to fix those kinds of surface mount components.

TIP

What can you do if one of the onboard subsystems fails? In many instances, the BIOS on newer boards give you the option of disabling one or more of the onboard circuits. So if, for example, your system board's IDE controller wanders off to the happy hunting grounds, you may be able to turn off the onboard circuitry and simply install a new IDE controller card in one of the available slots on your motherboard. Then all you have to do is move the data cable(s) (the flat, ribbon cables) to the new IDE card and you're back in business.

Understanding the PC Boot Process

Part of bringing a dead machine back to life is in understanding how PCs get started in the first place. In this section, you'll learn in great detail what steps a PC goes through to boot, from the time you flip the power switch to the time that the C:\> prompt appears. Basically, three things affect whether or not a PC will boot:

- First, the hardware must work.

- Second, the processor must start up and run a program in the BIOS called the Power On Self Test. (We'll discuss the BIOS shortly.)

- Third, the BIOS must load the operating system on the active partition.

Let's start from a quick overview, then we'll look at each step of the booting process in greater detail. First, the system needs power from the wall (at least until solar-powered PCs appear), and the power supply had better be able to use it; a faulty power supply means a useless PC. At least a few pieces of the motherboard itself must work: in particular, the CPU, the system's cache RAM, the clock circuit, and the bottom 64K or so of system RAM must be functional, or you don't get anything on the screen at all.

Then, assuming that the basic hardware can function, you'll recall that each PC has a set of software built into a ROM, called the Basic Input Output System, or BIOS. That BIOS is a collection of important programs—programs to control the video board, the disk controller, the keyboard, and the system clock, just to name a few—but perhaps the most important of those programs is the one that starts up the PC. That program determines what hardware is in the system, does a basic checkout of that hardware, and senses the presence of BIOS-like programs associated with expansion boards in the PC. If those programs exist on the expansion boards, the BIOS will yield control to them so that *they* can do the initialization.

Once the BIOS startup and checks work out all right, the BIOS then attempts to load the system software from the floppy or hard disk. Once the operating system gets loaded from disk into the computer's RAM, the BIOS passes control to the operating system, and the computer is ready to use.

That's the overview, now let's look at the details.

Step One: PC Power

The computer first requires power. I'll handle that in greater detail in Chapter 9, "Power Supplies and Power Protection," so I won't elaborate on the point here. But remember: the power supply in the PC can be the culprit, rather than the power coming from the wall.

Step Two: Check the Hardware

Once your system is getting power, there's got to be some functioning computing hardware to use that power. The familiarity of computers and CPUs sometimes makes us forget exactly how many microscopic components have to work together in order for the PC to get up and running...but the PC doesn't forget. What I mean by that is that the BIOS software's first job is to look at what hardware is in your system, and to check that it works.

The ROM and Bootstrapping

Why do we need BIOS? It has to do with how CPUs work. When a CPU powers up, it doesn't know how to communicate with anything—the keyboard, display, disk drives, you name it. Before it can communicate with, say, a hard disk, a CPU needs a program in memory that tells it *how* to communicate with a hard disk. Virtually all PC programs must be read from disk before the PC can run them. This kind of leads to a chicken-and-egg problem: the CPU needs a disk-reading program before it can read anything from disk, but it loads its programs from disk. From where, then, does the CPU read that first disk-reading program at the start of the day? It might seem like a good idea to just leave that program in memory in the first place, and that's the idea with ROM. Normal RAM chips lose their contents when you shut down power on a PC; ROM does not forget.

That means that an important use for the ROM is to contain low-level programs that control disks, keyboards, and the like—that's a big part of the BIOS, and it's used all throughout the day. The other part of the BIOS is the part that's used only when you first power up the computer, as seen in Figure 7.1.

All Intel chips have one feature in common: when they power up, they immediately start executing instructions located at an address 16 bytes below the 1024K level or, more specifically, at address FFFF:0000. That's why the main system BIOS chip gets a location up in the range of 960K through 1024K—so it can fill the need of the PC's CPU to have instructions to execute when it powers up. Take a look at Figure 7.2, which illustrates this concept.

FIGURE 7.1:

Step 1 of the BIOS process

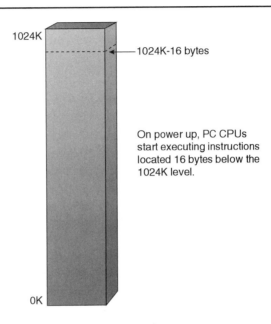

1024K

1024K-16 bytes

On power up, PC CPUs start executing instructions located 16 bytes below the 1024K level.

0K

FIGURE 7.2:

Location of BIOS in memory

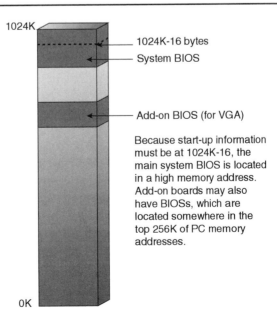

1024K

1024K-16 bytes

System BIOS

Add-on BIOS (for VGA)

Because start-up information must be at 1024K-16, the main system BIOS is located in a high memory address. Add-on boards may also have BIOSs, which are located somewhere in the top 256K of PC memory addresses.

0K

The BIOS's initial main job is to *inventory* and *initialize:* to figure out what's in your PC and then get it ready to do some work, testing it in the process. Now, this gets a little involved, so let's look at how BIOS does this in parts.

There are five steps to the BIOS initialization process:

1. Test some low memory.

2. Scan for other BIOS.

3. Yield to other BIOS.

4. Inventory the system.

5. Test the system.

Test Low Memory

In order for the BIOS to function, it needs some RAM to work with. So for most BIOS, one of the first things done is to test the bottom part of the system's RAM. Now, if that test crashes, then most BIOS can't recover. That leads to the following observation....

One major reason for a dead PC is that the lowest bank of RAM has failed. Therefore, one troubleshooting step is to replace the first bank of RAM. But that may not be possible, because some motherboards have their first bank of memory *soldered* in place.

Scan for Other BIOS

The BIOS in your PC can't support every possible piece of hardware—such as LAN boards, unusual video boards, you name it—and so the important functions of inventory and initialization have to go somewhere else. That is why many add-on boards have some ROM on them, as you may have noticed when installing boards. What you may not know is that those ROM chips contain some initialization code for those boards. For example, a hard disk controller ROM might do a quick read of the hard disk—kind of an "are you there?" test. A video board ROM might test the memory on the video board. A LAN board ROM might broadcast its network address over the LAN, testing that it has a unique network address.

Add-on ROM chips are supposed to be easy for the main BIOS to find, and should contain three signature bytes. The first bytes are hex 55, then AA, and then a number indicating how long the BIOS will be. That number is the length of the BIOS divided by 512. Take a look at the exercise at the end of this chapter for information on looking at a BIOS signature.

The main system BIOS allows the add-on boards to do *their* inventory and initialization first. Now, before that can happen, the main system BIOS must *find* those other BIOS.

The main system BIOS does that by examining memory in the ROM area— the addresses between 768K and 960K. Once it finds BIOS, it can go to the next step.

Yield to Other BIOS

Once it has found a BIOS on the add-on board, the main system BIOS passes control to that BIOS so that it can do whatever inventory and initialization the add-on BIOS requires.

The main system BIOS allows every add-on card's BIOS to initialize itself before doing its own inventory and initialization. Notice what that means: the software contained in the ROM on an add-in board gets to run before the system BIOS, and it also runs before DOS gets loaded—we haven't gotten near to loading DOS yet. For an example, consider a VGA board. As you saw in the exercise above, it's got a BIOS chip on it, one that contains a setup routine. That setup routine announces that the board is up and ready by putting a copyright notice on the screen.

When your PC is booting, the VGA message appears *before* the memory test occurs and before the PC checks for the drives. Again, the point here is that this VGA ROM assumed total control of the system fairly early in the boot process, as will each ROM on add-in boards. If anything goes wrong with a program in one of those ROM chips—and such things *do* happen—then a PC that functions properly before adding in the board will refuse to boot after that board has been installed. I'll come back to that notion in a minute, but let's finish up with the last two steps of this BIOS initialization.

Inventory and Test the System

Once all of the add-in ROM chips have gotten their time, and *assuming that their programs ran properly and returned control to the main system BIOS,* then the main system BIOS will now inventory the items that it will control, items that will vary from system to system. At minimum, one of the items that the system BIOS must inventory and initialize is the system memory.

What does "inventory and initialize" mean here? You've seen at least one example of it a million times—the memory test. Ever notice the quick flash of the drive lights on the floppy and hard disk drives? That's the inventorying of the storage devices.

Hard Disk Time Outs

Now let's put this information to use. Ever seen a computer do the memory test, then seem to lock up and not boot? It may be the disk drive. The simple "are you there?" test that the main system BIOS does every time you turn on the computer involves a quick disk read. But if the disk drive doesn't respond immediately, the BIOS doesn't give up—it waits, hoping that the drive will respond. The amount of time that it will wait is called the "time out period." I've seen more than one system BIOS with a timeout period of four minutes. That means that if the system has a bad hard drive, it could wait *four minutes* before reporting failure! The trouble is, most people aren't patient enough to wait four minutes—they just see the fact that their computer isn't doing anything. The logical verdict is that the computer is dead, and it's time for a new PC. So be *patient* when your computer doesn't respond on boot-up; give it a few minutes, literally, to report a disk drive timeout.

Inventory Lockups

Another manifestation of BIOS initialization problems, another manifestation that makes your PC look dead, is, as I've mentioned, the "inventory and initialize" function of add-on BIOS. I once installed an ESDI hard disk system in a computer, then powered up the computer to test the system, which consisted of a matching controller board and drive. I turned the system on and it did almost nothing: the fan whirred, but that's it—nothing on the screen. This, of course, panicked me, as the system that I tried the board in was a $5000 high-powered workstation that I was trying to make even faster: the client wouldn't be very happy if I smoked her computer. So I tried removing the new ESDI controller board, and the system booted up just fine. Restore the board, and the system won't boot. You know the problem: that high-speed ESDI board's initialization routine just wasn't written well and happened to crash on that particular system. Replacement ROM solved the problem.

You'll recall from Chapter 5 that the POST gathers a large amount of testing information about its PC that it never tells the PC's owner—*unless* the PC's owner has one of the POST boards that I mentioned in Chapter 5. If you're tracing a boot failure, don't overlook the POST board step.

CMOS Setup Information Read

I've seen people think that they have a bad hard disk because of a CMOS error, but what they *really* had was incorrect information in their CMOS. The CMOS has a battery that maintains startup information. If the battery dies, the system will not boot up.

Load MBR

First, the BIOS looks for a drive that's ready. The BIOS usually is set up to begin by first looking at A: (your primary floppy drive). If there is nothing in A:, the BIOS then looks at C:, your primary hard drive. This default setup allows you to use a bootable floppy disk to boot from drive A: if you want to run hard drive utility programs, install new operating systems, or run any program that needs to run before your installed OS boots up. While this may not actually be the greatest idea in this virus-plagued age, sometimes you just have to boot from your floppy. Anyway, we'll look at virus issues in Chapter 13, "Preventive Maintenance for Your Hard Disk." Of course, to boot from C:, just leave the floppy drive empty. Once the BIOS has detected a drive that's ready, it loads the first sector of data from that drive, the sector whose coordinates are cylinder 0, head 0, sector 1.

Things work slightly differently for floppies than hard disks, but the hard disk procedure is actually just the floppy procedure with a few steps added, so let's focus on hard disks. That first sector on a hard disk is called the Master Boot Record (MBR). It's just 512 bytes, so it should load easily into memory, although if it doesn't, the system won't boot and it probably will not show any error messages—it'll just lock up. Additionally, if the MBR is blank, then the system will also lock up, because it depends on that MBR to contain a meaningful program. If that happens, consult the troubleshooting procedure in Chapter 14, "Recovering Data and Fixing Hard Disks."

Find Bootable Partition, Load DBR, and Pass Control to DBR

Once the MBR is in memory, the BIOS passes control of the PC over to it. The MBR contains a very small program that is the next link in the chain of events that lead to a successful boot. As you may know, PC hard disks can be *partitioned*, allowing you to make one physical hard disk seem like several hard disks, or perhaps to put multiple operating systems on a single hard disk. The MBR program just finds a bootable partition, loads the first sector of that partition into memory, and then passes control to the newly loaded sector. The MBR finds the bootable partition using a small table contained in the MBR itself called the Partition Table. That program is created and maintained by the DOS FDISK program, so you've probably modified a few partition tables in your time if you've set up hard disks. Anyway, if the MBR can't find a bootable partition, it'll issue a message that says Missing Operating System. Assuming that it can find a bootable partition, it'll load the first sector from that partition into memory, and pass control to that sector.

By the way, you may know that the majority of computer viruses are called boot sector viruses. If your system is infected with one of these, then this is the point where the virus becomes active. That's why cold booting from a floppy bypasses a virus if one exists on the MBR.

The DBR Loads and Executes

The first sector of the bootable partition goes by different names for different operating systems, but in the DOS world it's called the DBR, or DOS Boot Record. The DBR is another very brief program whose sole job in life is to find the two so-called "hidden" programs, called IO.SYS and MSDOS.SYS for those of you who use MS-DOS, or IBMBIO.COM and IBMDOS.COM for those of you using PC-DOS.

Before loading the two hidden files, of course, the DBR must first check to see that they're on your disk in the first place. If it can't find them, or encounters problems while loading the two files, it issues the possibly familiar message `Non-system disk or disk error: insert boot disk and press any key when ready.`

Assuming that all is well, the DBR yields the stage to the two hidden files.

The Hidden Files Execute

Once the DBR loads the hidden files, the DBR passes control to the first hidden file (either `IO.SYS` or `IBMBIO.COM`) and disappears. The first hidden file then *double-checks* that it has been loaded properly, as well as checking the second hidden file. Once up and running, the first hidden file loads `CONFIG.SYS`.

CONFIG.SYS Loads and Executes

Assuming that you have a `CONFIG.SYS` file, the system executes the commands in `CONFIG.SYS` at this time. It first executes the `BUFFERS`, `FILES`, `STACKS`, `DOS`, `FCBS`, and `LASTDRIVE` commands, and then loads any device drivers.

Error information on drivers is fairly sparse, but if `CONFIG.SYS` can't load a driver, it will say something like `Bad or missing XXXX.DRV`. If you're using Windows 95/98 or Windows NT, you can slow down the process by pressing F8 on bootup; it forces the system to do one line at a time on the `CONFIG.SYS`, requiring a keystroke from you to continue to the next line. Some badly written drivers will just simply crash the system without any error messages.

COMMAND.COM Loads

The next step is to load something called the user shell; typically, it's the COMMAND.COM program. If CONFIG.SYS contains a SHELL statement, the hidden files will use that to locate a command shell, but, in the absence of a SHELL statement, the hidden files will next load COMMAND.COM from the root directory. Saying that COMMAND.COM is the "shell" of DOS means that it is the program that accepts user commands and loads programs at user request.

Your PC can run into trouble here if COMMAND.COM is missing, or if it's not of a version that matches the hidden files.

AUTOEXEC.BAT

Finally, COMMAND.COM loads and executes AUTOEXEC.BAT, executing any commands stored in there.

Where can these last few steps go wrong? Here are the most common places. First, CONFIG.SYS contains statements that can load device drivers, complete programs in their own right. Any bugs in a device driver can stop the system dead, so part of your troubleshooting approach might include temporarily renaming CONFIG.SYS to nullify its effects. If there's a SHELL statement in CONFIG.SYS, double-check that it makes sense: does it point to a bona fide copy of COMMAND.COM, and are all of the COMMAND.COM options correct? (Check your DOS manual to be sure.) If there's a SHELL statement, check to see if there is a corresponding SET COMSPEC statement in the AUTOEXEC.BAT file, as you see here:

CONFIG.SYS:

```
SHELL=C:\DOS\COMMAND.COM /E:512 /P
```

AUTOEXEC.BAT:

```
SET COMSPEC=C:\DOS\COMMAND.COM
```

Note in this example that the SHELL statement shows that the COMMAND.COM file is in the DOS subdirectory, and the SET COMSPEC agrees with it. If the two don't agree, you may see an error message like Cannot reload COMMAND.COM, system halted. That leaves AUTOEXEC.BAT as a source of troubles, and it's not without its share: load a buggy TSR program in AUTOEXEC.BAT, and the system will freeze at boot.

So, to review, you've seen how the PC starts up. A basic core of hardware must have power before anything can start. Then BIOS performs inventory and initialization. BIOS kicks off the DOS load process, and once DOS loads, your PC is ready to go to work. Now you understand the underlying mechanics, so you can recognize where the boot process is failing. That, in combination with some of the other techniques in this chapter, should help you get a dead PC up and running.

Finding and Replacing Bad Chips

Okay, you *insist* on trying to fix some boards? Sometimes you *can* be a real hero and actually fix a circuit board. Most maintenance shops do very little board repair, instead returning boards to the manufacturer or, more often, just disposing of them. Board repair can be time consuming and therefore expensive, not a great idea when most boards cost somewhere in the range of $100–$200 or even less. You'll spend a minimum of an hour and a maximum of forever fixing a board.

This is not to say that it should never be attempted. In fact, since the most expensive parts on your motherboard are usually socketed, the easiest chips you can troubleshoot are:

- Memory chip
- Replacement microprocessor

- Coprocessor

- ROM (Read-Only Memory)

If you're going to handle chips, please first take a look at the section on chip handling in Chapter 8. In general, bad chips are found in one of the following ways:

- Manufacturer notification

- Software identification of chip malfunction

- Temperature testing

- Digital probe and pulse testing

- Use of specialized (and expensive) signature analyzers

- Exhaustive chip replacement

Chip "Recall"

The most common method is the first: manufacturer notification. That is, the manufacturer will send you a replacement chip and a notice that "some boards built in 1996 malfunction due to a faulty 65X88 chip. Enclosed find a replacement 65X88…." Kind of like a car recall.

Software Chip Testing

Software identification is possible when the chip is not so vital to the system that the system can't run without it. For instance, if the 8088 or 80286 microprocessor goes on vacation, there is no way to run a diagnostic program to begin with. Many memory problems can be tested with software, however, as can some problems with some major chips, like the 8284 clock chip and the 8237 DMA controller. ROM often contains a checksum that can be used to verify that the contents of the ROM haven't been damaged.

You usually get the program that checks the checksum with the board that has the ROM in question. For example, most PC system diagnostics know where the checksum for the BIOS ROM is, and they check that as part of their routine.

Temperature Chip Testing

Some faulty chips can be traced through their temperature or lack thereof. A properly functioning chip should be slightly warm to the touch—warmer, at least, than after a night of deactivation. A completely cool chip, particularly a large one (large chips tend to run warmer) is probably dead. Similarly, a very hot chip—finger-burning variety—is probably dead or dying.

A worse situation is when the device works *sometimes*, then fails after a while. (Generally just before you were going to save your work.) Heat can make a marginal component stop working, and the marginal component may not seem unduly warm. In this situation, how do you locate the bad component? By controlled application of heat and cold.

First, start up the device—PC, modem, whatever—with the cover off. Then blow warm air (I *did not say hot*—100 degrees will do nicely; I mean, we're talking a burn *in* process here, not burn *up*) onto the circuit board: use a hair dryer. The intermittent chip will fail eventually. Now get a can of component coolant (Radio Shack Part No. 64-2321, for example) and direct the cold blast directly onto the suspect chip. If there is no suspect chip, start at the big ones. Now try to restart the device. If it starts, there's a good chance that the cooled chip is the bad one. If it doesn't restart, try another chip. As always, keep notes.

Finally, there is the brute force method. Get a digital probe and pulser and test each chip, one by one. Surefire, but slow.

Identifying Chips

As long as we're trying to replace chips, let's see how to find the silly things in the first place, and look at what those numbers atop the chip mean. A chip can be described by its function, its identification number, and its manufacturer.

Chip Function

A chip may be something as simple as just four NAND gates, each with two inputs (called a quad two-input NAND chip), or as complicated as a microprocessor. Physical size is some indication of a chip's complexity, but is not tremendously important. Memory chips are fairly small, but they are complex.

Identification Number and Manufacturer

When a manufacturer designs a new chip, it gives it an identification number. For example, an 8088 is a particular microprocessor chip, and a 7400 is a quad two-input NAND chip. Generally, chip designs are patented, so another manufacturer must be licensed before it can offer a chip that it did not design. For example, back in the XT days, Intel designed the 8088, but Advanced Micro Devices (AMD) probably made more of them than Intel ever did. I do not know who developed the first 256K x 1 dynamic RAM chip, but virtually everyone in the chip business makes them now.

Prefixes and suffixes may be added to a chip's ID number. The suffixes refer to the package that it is in (usually DIP—Dual Inline Pin, which is indicated by the suffix AN), or the temperature range (S is military specification, N is normal). Thus, 7400AN refers to a 7400 chip in a DIP package. A two-letter prefix refers to the manufacturer. Some manufacturer codes are HD for Hitachi, WD for

Western Digital, DM for National Semiconductor, and R for Rockwell. Another code may be present, like B9544. This means (ignore the B) that the chip was made in the 44th week of 1995. Some vendors, like Intel, do not put a date code on their chips. Instead, they put a serial number on the chip (for example, a motherboard in front of me has a chip with serial number L5450275). If you have an 80286- or 80386-based computer, it's probably a good idea to examine and write down your serial number. Periodically, bugs will pop up and certain serial numbers will be recalled. You should understand that there is no one single 8088 chip: it has gone through several revisions.

Other suffixes refer to performance, as in the 8088-1 and 8088-2 microprocessors. The -2 runs up to 8 MHz, and the -1 runs reliably only up to 5 MHz. In the case of memory chips, there are more specific speed codes, as we'll see in Chapter 8.

Soldering and Desoldering

If you're going to change chips, a few words about soldering.

It isn't hard, but it *does* take some practice. *If you have never soldered before, the place to learn is not on your PC!* Get some practice elsewhere, or just decide not to bother with soldering tasks. We PC fix-it people seek to minimize the amount of soldering required. More on sockets later.

The trick with soldering is to heat up *both* components to the desired temperature, then apply the solder. You want just enough heat to melt the solder, but not so much as to destroy whatever it is that you're soldering.

Soldering irons come in various powers or wattages. For PC work, you want a low-power iron, like a pencil iron fewer than 50 watts. Here are a few tips to remember when soldering.

- Use a pencil iron under 50 watts.

- Use a 60/40 solder with rosin core (*not* acid core), 1/32-inch width.

- Do not apply the tip for more than 10 seconds—this should be more than sufficient.

- For desoldering, *do not* use solder suckers or vacuum bulbs unless they have grounded tips. They can build up static charges. Use wire braid instead.

- Remove the board first. Don't try to solder things on/off boards that are installed in the PC.

- When replacing chips or transistors, socket them first (see next section).

- Buy a solder jig (sometimes called a "third hand") so that you have enough hands to hold the board, the soldering iron, the chip, and the desoldering tool. Many electronics stores sell different varieties of this product; Edmund Scientific (see Appendix A) sells a reasonably priced one called the Extra Hands Work Station.

NOTE   By the way, a techie student once claimed that I was dead wrong about this, as *true* techies scoff at solder jigs. To the true techies, I apologize. *I've* used the things, and *I* like 'em.

- If you are replacing a diode, transistor, or capacitor, draw a picture of how the original is installed. Memory (the human kind) gets faulty when faced with the normal frustration of soldering. It doesn't matter which way you insert a resistor.

- When desoldering a chip from a circuit board, don't desolder each pin in order. This builds up too much heat in one area. Jump around. Use a heat sink. Alternatively, use a solder tip designed for DIP packages.

- As mentioned before, many system boards are now four-layer boards. They are *very* tough to work on competently with the usual inexpensive equipment.

Chip Sockets and Chip Insertion/Removal

Chips need not be soldered directly to the motherboard. Chip *sockets* are available ("socket" as in light bulb "sockets"). As long as you're removing and replacing a chip, think about installing a socket for the replacement. Most chips are soldered directly onto the printed circuit board.

The advantages of socketed chips are that they are easy to remove and replace, and it's a lot easier to damage a chip while soldering it in place than to damage it while inserting it in a socket. On the other hand, a soldered chip saves money—no socket must be bought. Also, it can't creep out of the socket.

As mentioned before, a socketed chip's problem may simply be that it has crept far enough out of the socket to impair electrical connection. Recall that an early step in troubleshooting is to push all socketed chips gently back into their sockets.

Whether installing a socketed or directly mounted chip, you must be sure to install it with the correct side up. Chip pins are numbered with the furthest pin on the left side labeled 1, then counting down on the left side and finally up the right side (counterclockwise). You can see this in Figure 7.3.

FIGURE 7.3:

Chip numbering

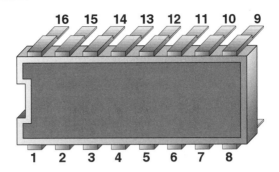

A chip can fit into a socket in one of two ways. Install a chip backwards, and you generally destroy the chip. So pay attention when installing. Figure 7.4 will guide you in correctly installing a chip. Consult the documentation for the chip if you cannot determine the correct alignment.

FIGURE 7.4:

Chip notches

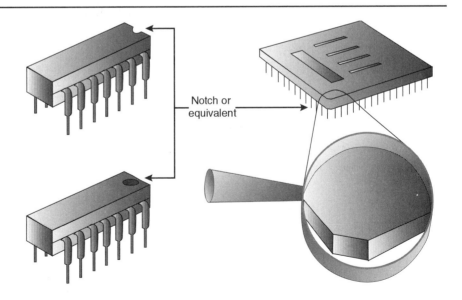

Notch or equivalent

The top of the chip generally has a notch to orient you when installing. To make things even easier, most circuit boards are designed so that all of the chips face the same way. This is *essential*: insert a chip with the notch facing the wrong way, and you may damage the chip.

Exercise: Dumping a BIOS Signature

You almost certainly have an EGA or later BIOS on your system. To see the signature for this, try the following:

1. From the DOS command line, type debug and press Enter.

2. You will see the prompt for DEBUG (-).

3. Your VGA ROM is either at hexadecimal address C000:0 or E000:0. To see it, type d C000:0 L 3 (and press Enter). If that doesn't yield a 55 AA xx code, try d E000:0 L 3.

CHAPTER

EIGHT

8

Semiconductor Memory

- Fast memory systems

- Memory banks and data widths

- Matching system memory to cache memory

- Causes of false memory errors

Removing and Installing SDRAM Modules

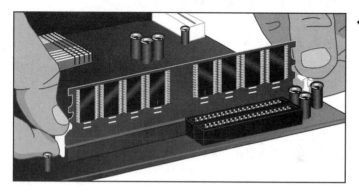

1 Pull the plastic clips at both ends of the slot away from the SDRAM module.

2 Gently pull the SDRAM module from the slot on the motherboard.

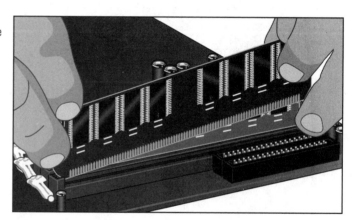

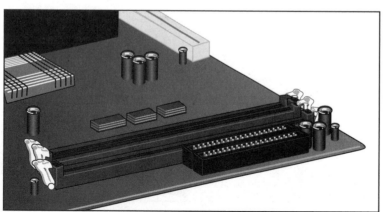

3 A motherboard with all of the SDRAM memory modules removed.

4 Carefully insert new SDRAM memory modules into the slot.

5 Press the SDRAM memory module into the slot until the plastic clips lock. (If it doesn't snap into place press the lever inward.)

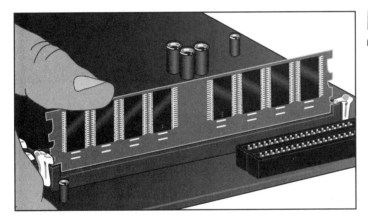

6 An SDRAM memory module properly seated in its motherboard slot.

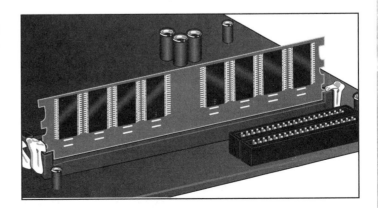

I said in the last chapter that you generally won't handle troubleshooting down to the chip level. There are, as I noted, exceptions. Memory is one of them. So let's talk about the chips that you *will* replace.

No discussion of circuit board and chip problems would be complete without some talk of memory chips. Memory (or RAM) chips are the chips that you are most likely to have to mess with. Generally, you'll handle *dynamic RAM (DRAM)*, but some computers use *static RAM (SRAM)*.

This chapter acquaints you with memory characteristics, how to read the numbers on the top of a chip, how to read memory error messages, what kinds of things can lead to false memory errors, and then provides some tips on handling and installing memory chips.

Introducing Memory Sizes, Speeds, and Shapes

You'll see memory referred to as "DIPs," "SIPPs," "SIMMs," "DIMMs," and so on. What do all these terms mean?

Chips are distinguished by their:

- Package type, which can be:
  - *Dual Inline Packages* (*DIPs*) look a lot like all the other standard chips in your computer. They are little black plastic bricks with two rows of metal legs, one on each of their long sides, hence the name "dual inline." *Single Inline Pin Packages* (*SIPPs*) are small circuit boards that contain several memory chips on them and have a single row of pins across the bottom.

- *Single Inline Memory Modules* (*SIMMs*) and *Double Inline Memory Modules* (*DIMMs*) are also small circuit boards containing several memory chips. They each have an edge connector across the bottom.

- PCMCIA cards or PC Cards are credit-card sized modules that plug into a special socket found mostly on notebook computers.

- Various proprietary, vendor-specific chip packages

- Access speeds, (how quickly the chip fetches data) are measured in nanoseconds. Common access times are 60, 70, and 80ns for normal memories, and as low as 8ns for expensive high-speed memories. Lower numbers are faster.

- Memory capacity ranges from 1MB to 256MB for memory modules.

Memory Package Types

Let's take a quick look at the kinds of packages in which you'll find memory supplied. DIPs are just simple memory chips. SIMMs look like Figure 8.1.

FIGURE 8.1:

SIMMs (30-pin SIMM & 72-pin SIMM)

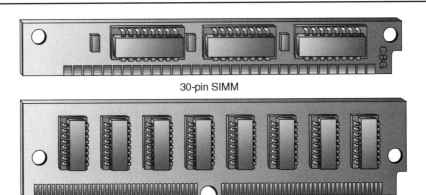

30-pin SIMM

72-pin SIMM

SIMMs come in 30-pin format and 72-pin format. The 30-pin format is the equivalent of about nine DIP chips. The 72-pin format is the equivalent of about 36 DIP chips. The actual SIMM itself may have three, eight, nine, or more chips on it—the actual number of chips on a SIMM is only loosely related to its memory capacity or type. I'll cover how to figure out which and how many SIMMs your system needs in the upcoming section, "Memory Organization." SIPPs look just like SIMMs except that they don't have an edge connector on the bottom; instead, they've got pins on the bottom. SIPPs enjoyed a brief popularity in the late '80s, but you won't find them around much anymore.

DIMMs, SIMMs, and SIPPs appear in a number of different sizes. Sizes that the PC market has seen include the ones seen in Table 8.1.

TABLE 8.1: Different Sizes of DIMMs, SIMMs, and SIPPs

MEMORY SIZE	DIMMS	SIMMs		SIPPs
		30-pin	72-pin	
256K (rare)		Yes	No	Yes
1024K (1MB)		Yes	No	Yes
4096K (4MB)		Yes	Yes	No
8192K (8MB)	Yes	No	Yes	No
16384K(16MB)	Yes	Yes	Yes	No
32768K (32MB)	Yes	No	Yes	No
65536K (64MB)	Yes	No	Yes	No
131072K (128MB)	Yes	No	No	No
262144K (256MB)	Yes	No	No	No

Modern computers use 72-pin SIMMs, DIMMs, or some kind or proprietary memory type. Laptops in particular make heavy use of proprietary memory modules, and there's no rhyme or reason to them. Some of these memory cards look like—but *aren't*—PC Cards. Others are just chip packages.

DIMMs are now replacing SIMMs, especially in laptops and notebooks where space is at a premium, since they can pack twice as much memory into the same space. They do so by mounting DRAM chips (which I'll discuss in another page or so) on both sides of the inline memory module and by using two sets of contacts, one on each side of the module board (SIMMs use only one set). And before you ask: No, you can't upgrade your computer simply by installing DIMM modules into your SIMM slots, because the actual package—the module board—has a different interface. Both the electronics and the connectors are different.

Will we need to keep boosting memory? Silly question. Speed and capacity largely drive the computer market. More is always better and memory sizes we thought really spiffy last year are called "brain dead" this year. Just stay tuned. Memory chips are a hot technology area and, other than CPUs, have the most influence on what you can do with your box.

Static versus Dynamic RAM

As computers are built faster and faster, all of the components must get faster and faster. Design a system around a 100 MHz chip, and you need a lot of 100 MHz components—including RAM.

Unfortunately, about the fastest type of common (that is, *cheap*) RAM doesn't come any faster than 20 MHz. This is where our story begins.

Static RAM (SRAM)

The simplest kind of memory to understand is called static RAM because when you put data into it, the data stays there.

Now, your response might be, "Big deal—isn't that the whole idea of memory? What good is memory that *doesn't* hold onto the data that you give it?" Well, to build that kind of memory, you've got to build about six transistors into each bit storage location. That kind of memory—SRAM—can be quite fast, but also quite expensive. If we used SRAM for our PC memory, then there'd be no trouble with getting memories that kept up with our CPUs; but, on the other hand, we wouldn't be able to *afford* those computers, because SRAM is about 10 times more expensive than the DRAM that we're used to buying. SRAM is also physically larger than DRAM and generally runs much hotter.

Dynamic RAM (DRAM)

The economical answer to SRAM was DRAM. Each DRAM bit is built of a single transistor and a capacitor, in contrast to SRAM's six transistors.

DRAM has two problems from the point of view of a PC designer. First, the "dynamic" in its name means that it forgets the data that you give it almost as fast as you can give it the data. That means that DRAM-based systems require refresh circuitry to get around this electronic amnesia that DRAM suffers from.

Second, the way that DRAMs are built to be cheaper is that DRAMs are organized not simply into a set of addresses; rather, each bit in a DRAM has a row address and a column address.

The slow part of accessing any part of a DRAM is in getting to its row. Once you're in a row, subsequent intra-row accesses can be quite fast. In fact, that's the area where we've seen the most advances recently, in DRAMs that can access data quite quickly, and this brings me to the next topic.

SDRAM

Synchronous Dynamic Random Access Memory (SDRAM) is a new variant of DRAM that includes an on-chip burst counter. This burst counter can be used to increment column addresses and helps increase the speed of memory access.

Aside from the facts that faster is generally considered better and speed is pursued for its own sake, the reason behind the SDRAM is that CPUs are getting faster. With their increasing speed, they demand ever faster memory, in order to function at their maximum potential. With SDRAM, the CPU and RAM are locked together by the same clock. Thus, the speed of the RAM and the CPU are linked, or synchronized.

(Another solution to the problem of speeding up RAM is cached RAM, which boosts the overall speed of the memory by adding a static RAM area on the dynamic RAM chip itself. This small amount of fast SRAM acts as a cache to the DRAM. More about that in a moment.)

Normally, memory chips answer data requests. Cache memory can anticipate the CPU's needs. When the CPU asks for data, the memory already has it waiting and ready to go. Some cache memory implementations also include a pipeline. The pipelined architecture has a design in which one stage can fetch an address while other stages present the data for output.

The cache memory idea has the advantage that it is a simple, elegant replacement for older chips; it just plugs into the system and goes. However, you can't just plug cache memory into any system and expect it to run faster. If the CPU is running at anything less than 66 MHz, it simply will not be able to accommodate the higher speed capabilities represented by SDRAM.

Cached RAM and EDRAM

Another method being devised to increase the speed of memory is adding a specialized cache area on the chip. This approach also goes by the name *Cached Dynamic Random Access Memory* (*CDRAM*). Some people also call it *Enhanced Dynamic Random Access Memory* (*EDRAM*), but it is still the same thing. The system works by adding a static RAM cache to the dynamic RAM chip. This cache area allows the whole chip to respond more quickly to requests from the CPU—as long as it has the right information already resident. Obviously, repetitive information requests will speed up. New or constantly changing requests, on the other hand, will not benefit, because the information already resident in the cache will not apply or be pertinent to the request.

The cached RAM also gains speed because the SRAM areas are able to fetch data from the slow DRAM in large blocks. When data is requested, the slow DRAM sends the entire block of data to the fast SRAM.

Error Correcting RAM (EC-RAM)

Information in your computer is nothing more than 1's and 0's. It's a very versatile system, and using just those two digits allows you to work with everything from word processors to stereo sound to high-quality graphics files. The limitation of the system of binary digits is that your computer has only two states to work with: data is either a 1 or it's a 0. There are no "maybes" and no gray areas where you can get the benefit of the doubt or "catch a break."

This brings us to the problem of errors. When data is moved around inside your system, there is always some chance that a mistake can be made; a 1 might accidentally be interpreted as a 0, or vice versa. This is especially true if you use your computer to communicate over the phone lines, where random static and poor-quality transmission lines can introduce an enormous amount of interference. Even within your computer, however, media defects, electronic noise, component failures, poor connections, and deterioration due to age can all cause a bit to be mistakenly interpreted and an error to occur.

Error correction is the process of detecting and correcting bit errors. For the kinds of high data rates you have inside your computer, error correction must be done on the fly, or at the same rate the errors occur, in special-purpose hardware (called *digital logic*).

Intel's Pentium Pro uses the 82450 chip set (a.k.a. Orion) to provide the *error-correction-code* (*ECC*) for data bus and system memory (up to 4GB), along with parity protection on the Pentium Pro address and control buses. It also provides four-way interleaving on a 256-bit memory bus.

With the P6, Intel has designed a system in which all internal registers are parity-checked, and the 64-bit path between the CPU core and level 2 cache uses ECC. Individual events and variables inside the chip, such as cache misses, register contents, and occurrences of self-modifying code can be counted and reported. Operating system or utility software then reads these values to gauge how well the processor is working.

The P6 and the Pentium both offer a *functional redundancy check* (*FRC*), in which two chips are physically joined and each constantly verifies the other's results. That way, they can signal an error if a conflict is found.

Uses of ECC

While error correcting RAM serves the primary purpose of making sure your data is correct, it also has some interesting side benefits for both the people who make computers and those who use them. For example, error correction is often used by vendors to decrease the price and increase the reliability of DRAM memory modules. Lower-grade DRAM components can then be used without sacrificing how well the computer operates.

If you have a laptop computer, error correction also can be used to extend the battery's life, by allowing a significant decrease in the DRAM refresh rate.

Putting Together a Fast Memory System

Besides buying the right size and package of memory, you need the right speed and memory type. To see how to make those choices, you've got to understand how PCs access memory. You've seen how dynamic and static memory differ. How, then, can a PC designer put together a system that uses predominantly economical but slow DRAM? There are three basic ways:

- Live with the slow DRAM, and just do a lot of waiting.

- Add a little bit of SRAM as a *memory cache*, increasing the price by only a bit.

- Instead of using normal DRAM, use fast page mode RAM, a DRAM that is still slow on the initial row access, but is extremely fast once inside a row.

DRAM-Only Systems and Wait States

On most modern PCs, memory must be able to respond to a CPU request in *two* clock ticks. Clock ticks are just the reciprocal of the clock rate: 8MHz means 8 million clock ticks per second, so each clock tick is 1/8,000,000 second. Punch 1 divided by

8 million into your calculator, and you'll get 0.000000125—0.125 microseconds, or 125 nanoseconds. You can do this for all the popular clock rates, as Table 8.2 shows.

TABLE 8.2: Common Clock Rates and Corresponding Clock Duration

CLOCK SPEED (MHz)	DURATION (ns)
25	40
33	30
40	25
50	20
60	17
66	15
90	11
100	10
120	8.3
133	7.5
166	6
233	4.3
300	3.3
333	3
400	2.5
450	2.2
500	2

The memory must be able to respond to a memory request in two of these clock ticks, so, for example, the memory for a 66 MHz computer must be able to respond in 2 × 15ns = 30ns.

Note, by the way, that I'm leaving out of the time calculation another factor, the DRAM charge time. DRAM needs a few nanoseconds to charge up the capacitors before reading them. That time was quite large in the past, and it's smaller in modern systems—but it still exists.

Anyone who's been DRAM shopping recently knows that nobody makes a 30ns DRAM; something around 50ns is the best you'll find. How, then, can we build a 66MHz computer with 50ns DRAMs?

By waiting around.

Instead of waiting two clock cycles—30ns—if the CPU waited for *four* clock cycles—60ns—then the DRAM could respond quickly enough for the CPU. Those two extra clock cycles are called *wait states*. It's a terrible answer to the memory speed problem, but it's the one that gets adopted most often for laptop computers. Is there a better way without going to a fully static system? Yes, there is a compromise.

Static RAM Caches

As you've seen, DRAMs are too slow, but there are faster memories: SRAMs. SRAMs are more expensive, but they can keep up with CPUs.

As has happened before, a leaf was taken from the mainframe's book, and *cache memory* was included in many PCs. Cache memory is a small amount of the expensive static RAM, RAM fast enough that the CPU can address it at no-wait-state speed. There is also a larger amount, usually megabytes, of the relatively slower 50-or-so ns dynamic memory. The last piece of hardware is a "cache controller" to manage the whole mess.

The cache controller tries to use the relatively small cache to speed up the much larger RAM by exploiting an assumption about computer use. The idea is that computer programs tend to stay within one area of code for a while, then move to another area and stay there for a while, and so on. The same phenomenon occurs with data. The cache controller gets an idea of what part of memory to work with, and guesses that the CPU will soon need the data that follows in that part of memory. Then it goes to that area in the slow dynamic memory and grabs a piece of it—not the whole cache amount, more commonly 4K or thereabouts—and transfers it into the cache. Now, if the cache controller guessed right, the next data that the CPU needs won't be in the slow memory: it'll be in the cache. The cache controller is fast enough to accept reads and writes at zero-wait-state speed.

That's *if the cache controller guessed right*. If not, the CPU must go all the way out to the slow dynamic memory, and endure two or more (depending on your computer) wait states. (Arggh!) That means the cache controller better be good, or you'll have a wait-state machine. In practice, cache controllers are right 80 to 99 percent of the time, so you end up with a machine that's zero-wait-state 80 to 99 percent of the time and two-wait-state the other 20 to 1 percent of the time.

Most 386 machines used the Intel 80835-cache controller to handle cache management. Since the 486, all *x*86 processors have had a built-in cache controller and a little RAM cache built in. It's only a *small* cache, at 8K or 16K. When buying systems, buy at least 256K of supplemental *external* cache. If you plan to put more than 32MB of RAM on your system, invest in 512K of static cache. If you're going to go for more than 128MB of RAM on your system, then get 1MB of static cache.

Fast Page Mode Systems

Static RAM is nice but expensive, dynamic RAM is cheap but slow. One compromise, as you just saw, is to mix a little static with a lot of dynamic. Another compromise is to create a version of dynamic RAM that's a bit faster than the average.

It's almost always been the case with DRAMs that initially accessing a row or page took the most time; access attempts after that within the page could happen much faster. An early version of that showed up in 16MHz 80386DX systems in a kind of RAM called *static column* RAM. As time has gone on, things have gotten even faster, leading to *fast page mode RAM*, followed by *Extended Data Out (EDO)* RAM and *burst EDO* RAM.

These are just three different kinds of RAM that have been created in the past few years. They have access times in nanoseconds, like all RAMs—but those access times are for the initial row accesses. Take a look at Table 8.3.

TABLE 8.3: Burst EDO RAM: Comparison of Key Specifications

Specification	Symbol	-5	-6	-7	-5	-6	-7	-5	-6	-7
		FAST PAGE MODE			**EXTENDED DATA OUT (EDO)**			**BURST EDO**		
Row access	t_{RAC}, ns	50	60	70	50	60	70	50	60	70
Column access	t_{CAC}, ns	13	15	20	13	15	20	10	11.6	15
Column address access	t_{AA}, ns	25	30	35	25	30	35	25	30	35
Page cycle time	t_{PC}, ns	30	35	40	20	25	30	15	16.6	20
Max page frequency	f_{max}, MHz	33	28.6	25	50	40	33	66	60.2	50
Relative page access performance		1.15	1	0.87	1.75	1.4	1.15	2.31	2.1	1.75

Take a look, for example, at the 50ns chips. Each of the three takes 50ns for the first access in a row. Compare the speeds of the *subsequent* row accesses, however.

Sounds like burst EDO is the way to go, then? Well, maybe. Prices for EDO and burst EDO change so fast (at the time that I wrote this, anyway) that it's hard to give you a hard-and-fast rule about which kind to buy. But bear a few things in mind.

First, EDO, burst EDO, and fast page SIMMs are all pin-compatible. That means that you could buy EDO SIMMs and plug them into your system, and they'd work—but they wouldn't make your system any faster. Systems built before 1995 definitely won't benefit from EDO, and you'll just spend more money (about 15 percent at this writing) for your SIMMs. But if you've got a system that can accommodate EDO or burst EDO, then you can see significant speed differences (up to 25 percent) with EDO RAM. So when you're examining systems, look for those built with EDO. EDO systems can offer decent speed without the need for static cache, although they *will* be slower than systems without any cache at all.

Interleaving

Designers can use EDO with or without cache to speed up a system, offering some flexibility in design options. Here's a *third* option that they can use to squeeze speed out of DRAMs.

Recall that I noted a few pages back that part of the access time of a DRAM is taken up in charging up a capacitor. Some systems attempt to minimize this by arranging memory into *interleaved banks*. The idea is this: memory is organized into banks, as you'll read in a few pages. With interleaving, memory subsystems always have an even number of banks. Memory addresses are then *interleaved* so that when one address (in the first bank) is being accessed, the following address (which is in the second bank) is being charged up. That way, when it's time to access the second bank, it needn't be charged, because the following address is ready to go. While reading that address in the second bank, its following address (back in the first bank) is being charged up, and so on.

Notice that this works only if the CPU's memory accesses tend to be in consecutive memory addresses. That's a pretty good assumption, but if the program running in the system jumps all around the RAM for data, then interleaving is defeated, and memory accesses slow down.

Interleaving is a good idea, but it's effective only for the first access in a row, and it requires an even number of memory banks.

Memory Banks and Data Widths

Once the designer of your system's motherboard has figured out how to arrange the static and the dynamic memory, the next concern is how to arrange the memory so that it can feed the processor data, as it needs it. Before, we were concerned with speed; now we're focusing on capacity. Memory chips have a storage capacity, as well as a kind of "delivery capacity," so to speak: their data path. You may recall from Chapter 3, "Inside the PC: Pieces of the Picture," that a chip's data path is the size of the "front door" of the chip. Once, a group or bank of memory consisted of nine small chips called bit chips. Now it's more likely to be SIMMs.

Data paths for memory chips are either 1 bit (as in the case of the 16K-bit, 64K-bit, 256K-bit, and 1024K-bit chips), 1 nibble—4 bits—as in the case of the 64K nybble, 256K nybble, and 1024K nybble. SIMMs are built up out of either nybbles and/or bits, and usually have a cumulative data path of 8 or 9 bits (for a 30-pin SIMM) or 36 bits (for a 72-pin SIMM).

Data path is more than just a techie side issue; it's vital to arranging banks of memory. For instance, consider a 64K-nybble chip and a 256K-bit chip. Notice that the 64K-nybble chips have 64K groups of 4 bits (nybbles), for an internal capacity total of 256K bits. A 256K-bit chip also has an internal capacity total of 256K bits, but it's arranged differently: the 64K-nybble chip can deliver 4 bits at a time, whereas the 256K-bit chip can deliver 256K separate bits only one at a time. A MB SIMM can provide 1024K of bytes—8-bit groups.

As you learned in Chapter 3, PC processors have appeared in three main families: the 8088, the 80286, and the 80386 families. The 8088 has an 8-bit data path, so it can read or write 8 bits at a time. The 80286 and 80386SX have a 16-bit data path, enabling them to transfer twice as much data in or out in one operation. The entire 486 family and all of the 386 family except the SX have 32-bit data paths, and the Pentium and Pentium Pro systems have 64-bit data paths. The sizes of those data paths will affect how memory banks are arranged.

Memory Banks on 32-Bit Computers

The 386DX and all of the 486 chips have a 32-bit data path. These 32 bits for data plus 4 bits for parity mean a 386 that uses bit chips requires 36 chips per memory bank—that's a lot of chip stuffing! While I've never seen a 386 with nybble memory, only nine nybble chips would be needed to create a 32-bit memory bank, and four normal 9-bit SIMMs would be required. The 72-pin SIMMs fit very nicely in a 32-bit architecture, and one single 72-pin SIMM can serve as a bank. Again, vendors using 16-bit SIMMs would only need two SIMMs to make a complete 386-memory bank. Room for eight 30-pin SIMMs is quite common for 386DX and 486 motherboards, so let's take a look at the possibilities there. There's room for eight SIMMs—how many banks is that? Just two, because the 32-bit data path of the CPUs we're discussing here demands four SIMMs per bank. The combinations are shown in Table 8.4.

TABLE 8.4: Different Memory Configurations for a 32-Bit Machine

BANK 0	BANK 1	TOTAL (MB)
256	0	1
1024	0	4
4096	0	16
256	256	2
256	1024	5
256	4096	17
1024	256	5
1024	1024	8
1024	4096	20
4096	256	17
4096	1024	20
4096	4096	32

Again, there are some "clunker" combinations; perhaps the worst of which is the 2MB arrangement—all of the SIMM sockets filled with 256K chips! Notice also that you've got a bit of a tough choice in the area of 8MB. You really need 8MB to make Windows 3.1 work well, and you will want 16MB eventually (or today, if you're running Windows 95, 98 or NT). But notice that to get 8MB you'll fill your motherboard with 1MB SIMMs, SIMMs that you'll have to throw away when you upgrade to 16MB—an upgrade that will require four 4MB SIMMs or two 8MB SIMMS.

Some 486 motherboards can take four 72-pin SIMMs. These 72-pin SIMMs come in the 4MB, 8MB, 16MB, 32MB, and 64MB sizes, so it's pretty easy to find a SIMM combination that'll meet your needs. A fair-sized minority, however, have room for only two 72-pin SIMMs, so choose wisely if you have a motherboard like that. Personally, I'd recommend that you start with 32MB; in the last half of the '90s, that's the ground floor for operating systems.

Most modern PC CPUs can accommodate quite a lot of memory. Unfortunately, many motherboards aren't designed well, so they cannot use very much memory. Therefore, when buying a PC, you should look closely at how much memory you can put on the motherboard. It's surprising how little memory motherboards from some big names can accommodate. Look for the ability to put at least 64MB on the motherboard, even if you're not going to use it immediately. Believe me, you'll get there eventually.

Memory Banks on 64-Bit Computers

Every Pentium or Pentium Pro-based motherboard I've seen either uses a proprietary memory module, or takes 72-pin SIMMs. You'll need two 72-pin SIMMs to make a bank on these computers. Many of these motherboards have four SIMM sockets, making two banks.

Matching System Memory to Cache Memory

All of the information mentioned earlier in this chapter on SDRAM and cache RAM points to one large problem in the personal computer industry: There is an increasing disparity in clock speeds between processors and DRAM. Combine this with an increasing degree of processor superscalability, and you get a situation in which effective cache management becomes a critical factor in obtaining optimal application performance. System main memory access now can take anywhere from tens to hundreds of CPU clock cycles. Hence, the difference between finding information in the on-chip cache instead of in main memory can completely dominate the effective speed of an application, or even an entire system. There are a variety of techniques that make more effective use of the processor caches.

Better Programs

A very important aspect in effective data cache management is how, and how well, an algorithm accesses the data that is in the cache. Since accessing memory whose addresses are adjacent or close together speeds up cache performance, structuring program code with the memory system in mind is often the best way to increase speed. Programmers can use a couple of design strategies to improve performance, such as making greater use of large element arrays instead of arranging data in multiple, individual structures. Additionally, code can be written to make use of processor-specific features. For example, most CPU instruction sets provide the user the ability to manage the data cache via software.

Better Processors

Although writing better programs is a good place to look for better matches between system memory and cache memory, what about something for those of us up in the cheap seats—those of us who aren't involved in program creation? The best thing (perhaps the only thing) we can do is look for systems that have already addressed this problem and look to the chip vendors to provide increasingly faster iron.

Some Pentium system designs use two or more processors with dedicated caches for each processor. The advantage of such a multiprocessor design is that each processor communicates freely with its own cache and thus provides highly efficient bus utilization. More efficient bus utilization equals more rapid cache access (equals a faster computer). Simple. The problem, of course, it that this kind of multiple processor design tends to be expensive and complex. Each dedicated cache requires an additional cache controller and SRAMs, and each cache also requires its own datapath, memory-bus, and interrupt-control circuitry. Big money. Big headaches.

A bit different is a design that uses two processors that share a single secondary cache. This design is simpler and less expensive. You need only one cache controller and some SRAM. It's not as fast as dedicated caches but according to Intel, it typically improves system performance by 50 percent to 80 percent with a secondary processor installed.

Causes of False Memory Errors

Memory often gets blamed for problems arising from other sources. In most cases, memory that has been working for a few weeks will work forever. While memory hardware failures were common up to the late '80s, the quality of memory chips has improved considerably since 1988.

Power Causes False Errors

Memory is often falsely accused for a simple reason: the memory is so demanding in its need for constant clean power. If the power drops out or surges for just a few millionths of a second, the memory loses its contents, causing a memory error. This wasn't an error caused by the memory—it was a power error that just *showed up* in the memory. Think of it as the canary in the coal mine of your PC.

Along the same lines, a static electric surge looks just like a power surge. Scuff across a shag rug on a dry day, touch your computer, and you're likely to cause a memory error—but please *don't* try this out, because you may cause permanent memory damage. A failing power supply may, in the same way, cause apparent memory failures. So will noisy power being fed to a perfectly good power supply.

The telltale signs in this case are the addresses reported by the memory errors. If you've truly got a memory error, you'll see the same address reported as bad over and over. But memory errors that always report different locations—locations that test fine when tested a few minutes later—likely point to power problems.

Is there *enough* power? Insufficient power can cause parity errors. This one can be a real pain, since it waits for some large disk access to trigger the parity error, like when you try to save your data to disk.

You see this one with underpowered clones: Lotus 1-2-3 works fine until you want to save the file, then you get a parity check. The problem is that you're running the power supply to the poor thing's limits and then want to fire up the hard disk. Not enough power, the memory gets shortchanged, and, BANG! A memory error happens.

And, while it's unusual, improperly shielded sources of RF noise can alter memory, causing parity errors. I remember a 64K chip made back in the early '80s that was built in a chip package that was accidentally built out of a ceramic material that was a very low-level emitter of alpha particle radiation. Once in while, an alpha particle would zip through the chip, causing a non-repeatable error. I'm glad I don't have to troubleshoot *those* chips any more.

Mismatched Chip Speeds and Manufacturers Cause Errors

If you need a chip that has an access speed of, say, 80ns, but you can get only a faster chip—say, one that runs at 60ns—can you use the faster 60ns chip to replace the slower 80ns chip? Yes, *but* you must replace the entire bank of chips when you do that. Putting a single 60ns chip into a bank of 80ns chips will often cause the 80s to appear to have errors.

Whenever possible, avoid mixing *manufacturers* in the same row. I flatly cannot explain this, but I have seen cases where it caused problems. For instance, I have two rows of chips—one entirely Mitsubishi, another entirely Toshiba—that work fine. Then I mix the rows. Errors occur. Restore the rows, and the problem disappears.

The little clips that hold the chips can also appear to be holding the chip correctly so be sure to check that the chip is held in place properly.

Test Memory

Modern RAM is pretty reliable, but you may come across a RAM failure of an odd sort on some SIMMs: *soft* failures. These are failures that show up only with very specific tests.

Walking Bit Errors

Years ago, an early edition of this book suddenly started growing typos. And odd typos they were, too: now and then, a letter would show up wrong for no reason. I first thought that the printer was failing, but checking in the file on the disk, I found that the typos were *there*, too. I thought this extremely odd, because I'd proofread the text—as had many others—and these obvious typos didn't appear. I began to be certain that the problem was machine-induced.

I suspected my mass storage device, a Bernoulli cartridge system, and so I started saving the document on my hard disk instead. Still, the errors were cropping up. That's when I also noticed that some files were being corrupted when I copied them.

It was starting to look like the problem was in the system's memory. Whenever a piece of data passed through the system's memory, it would sometimes—very rarely, actually—become corrupt. Finally, I ran a *walking bit* test.

You see, normal memory tests just go to a particular location and test the heck out of it, stuffing different combinations of ones and zeroes into a particular byte, and then reading them back. Tests of that kind were coming up zero for errors. But what about interactive problems? It turned out that there were two different memory locations, at roughly 560K and 600K, that were in cahoots with one another, so to speak. Test either location, and there was no problem. But put a 1 into the 560K location and, lo!, a 1 popped up in the 600K location.

This kind of error is called a *walking bit* error, and it's a problem on the memory address circuitry rather than the memory itself. It really doesn't matter where the error originates, however, because the answer is the same: replace the problematic memory units.

Mountain/Valley and Checkerboard Tests

Here's another example of memory problems that will never be detected by single-byte testing. Consider a set of bit memory cells, as you see in Figure 8.2.

FIGURE 8.2:

Set of bit memory cells

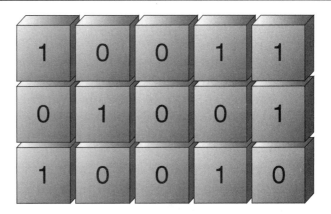

But suppose one kind of bit can "leak over" into another kind of bit, as you see in Figure 8.3.

FIGURE 8.3:

Set of bit memory cells with a "leak over" into another bit

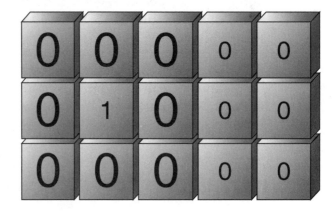

The effect is that the 0 bits leak over into the 1, eventually turning it into a 0. Filling each bit with a 0, and then surrounding it by 1s, and vice versa, is called the *mountain/valley* test. The *checkerboard* test lays out a pattern of 1s and 0s like the light and dark squares of a checkerboard.

All three of these tests are incorporated into the two memory tester programs (Checkit and QAPlus) that I recommended in Chapter 5, "Troubleshooting PC Problems." I strongly recommend running one of these programs overnight when you first install some new memory.

Tips on Installing Memory Chips

A lot of manuals include some really scary instructions for installing memory chips. I've probably installed a gigabyte or so myself (1MB chips have made it easier to get to the 1GB level), so here's what works for me.

First, as always, be aware of static electricity. Your acrylic sweater and the soles of your shoes are powerful producers of it.

If I'm worried about the static level of an area, and I'm not prepared with a ground strap, *I take my shoes and socks off*. I know it sounds a little bizarre, but I kill very few chips in my bare feet—probably less than a half dozen in all the time I've been installing memory.

Second, the memory chips go into sockets in a circuit board. As before, don't insert a memory chip into a board while the power is on. Orient it so that its notch is facing in the same way as the notches on other chips on the board. The legs of a new chip will be spread a bit too much to fit into the socket. Just insert one row of pins into their holes, then coax the other row into *their* holes. At this point, you've got some tension: the legs on both sides are eager to just spring out of the socket. Double-check that the legs are all positioned to slide into their holes, then push the chip into the socket firmly with your thumb.

If you make a mistake, or must remove old chips, use a small "tweaker" screwdriver. Use it to gently pry up one end of the chip, then work the screwdriver completely under the chip. It will come up easily. Make sure you put the screwdriver under the chip, not the socket. The socket will not come up easily, and if it does you will have damaged the motherboard.

Do not use one of the "chip remover" tongs that seem to be included in every PC toolkit these days. They work okay if you've had practice with them, but they scare me because they make it a lot easier to damage a chip taking it out. Stick with a small screwdriver, and remember that *patience* is the keyword here: look at what you're doing, and take your time if you're new to the process.

How about SIMMs? Between removing and installing, removing SIMMs is the harder task. Figure 8.4 shows you how to remove SIMMs.

FIGURE 8.4:

Removing SIMMs

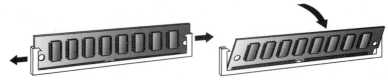

First, *gently* pull aside the plastic tabs that hold the SIMM in place. Be careful, as the tabs are easily broken.

Once the tabs have been pushed outward, rotate the SIMM forward. It then comes right out of its socket.

There is an unfortunately frequent occurrence in the classes that I teach on PC repair that concerns SIMM removal. In every class, I tell students, "Don't remove SIMMs until I show you how to do it." Now and then, I'll get some prize idiot who decides that he'd rather figure it out himself. So he grabs the SIMM and yanks it out—and sure enough, he *did* figure out how to remove a SIMM! Unfortunately, however, that SIMM socket will never again hold a SIMM, because he has broken off the little tabs that hold SIMMs in place. Even *more* unfortunately, that means that memory can't be installed on the motherboard, which means that someone—him—is going to have to buy a new motherboard. So, unless you plan to exercise the old MasterCard when you attack SIMMs, follow this procedure.

The key to removing SIMMs is to push the little tabs outward *gently.* They hold the SIMM in place. If you push too hard, you can break them off. Some SIMM sockets are better designed, and use metal spring tabs to hold the SIMMs in place—it's harder to break these off—but an unfortunate number of sockets use plastic tabs. Push the tabs outward either with the blade of a small screwdriver, or with your fingernails. Err on the side of caution. You'll feel the SIMM move a bit, and that will be your signal that you can try to pull it a bit forward. Once you've got one tab and one side free, work on the other side.

Reinserting SIMMs is similar. You place the SIMM angled forward in the SIMM socket, then push it back into place. As the

SIMM contacts the tabs, relieve the pressure on the tabs by helping them outward. The SIMM will snap into place—start over if it doesn't—and all will be well.

Memory is one of the most sensitive parts of your PC, both electronically and mechanically. Now that you know more about memory chips, your machine will run that much better. But let's see how to feed that memory with power—the subject of the next chapter.

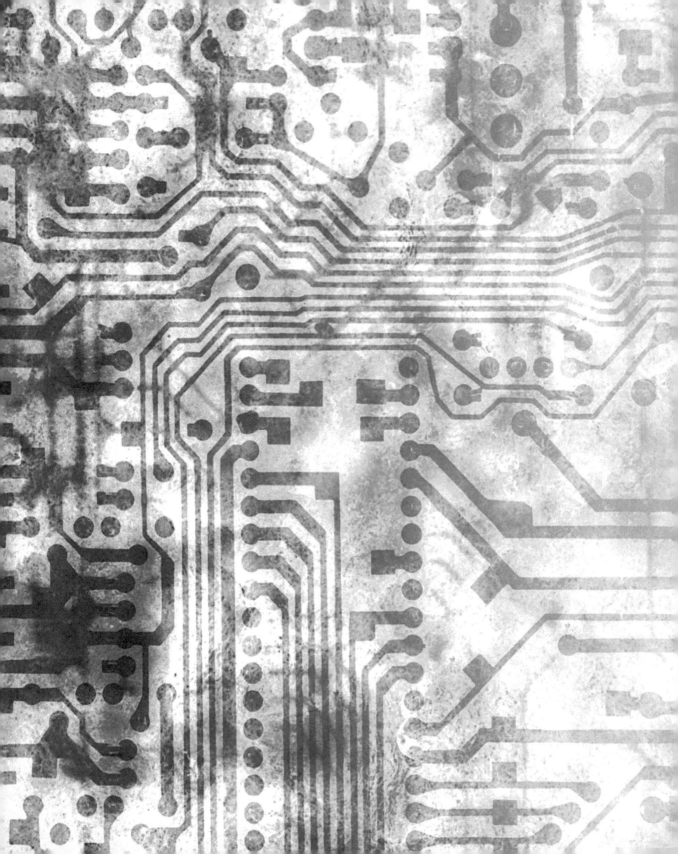

CHAPTER

NINE

9

Power Supplies and Power Protection

- ◼ Power supply components and connections

- ◼ Troubleshooting

- ◼ Protection from AC

- ◼ When lightning strikes

Installing a New Power Supply

1 Position the new power supply unit at the rear of the case.

2 Fasten the power supply to the chassis with four screws.

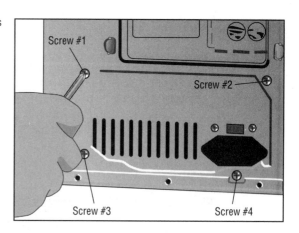

Screw #1

Screw #2

Screw #3

Screw #4

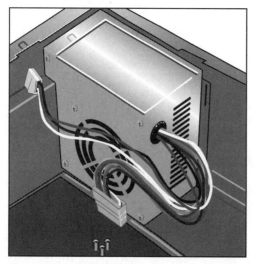

3 Connect the power supply's largest connector(s) to the motherboard. The connector(s) is keyed so that you cannot connect it incorrectly.

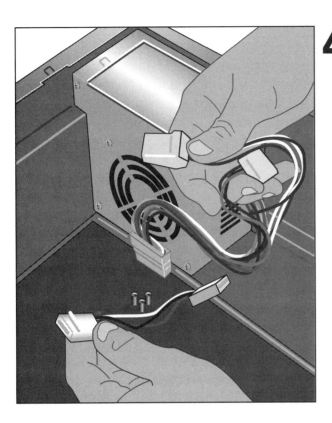

4 Connect the other Molex and Berg connectors to the fan, hard and floppy drives, CD-ROM drive, etc.

5 Plug the computer's power cord into the new power supply unit.

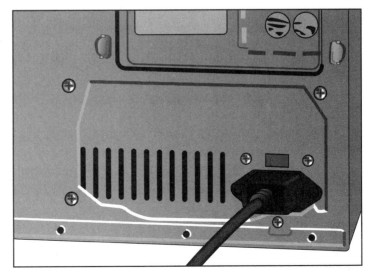

Personal computers (at least, desktop PCs) don't come with batteries included. You plug them into the wall socket and they work. But the PC itself does not directly use wall current, because this is 120-volt alternating current in North America, 220–240 in Europe and the UK. The PC doesn't need AC; it needs DC, usually 3.3 or 5 volts for its chips, 12 volts for the motors on older drives—newer drive motors run off 5 volts.

WARNING By the way, a word to European readers. Everything I say here applies to you *except* for references to the mains. As I just mentioned, your mains are not 120 volts, but more like 200+, and the power frequency is 50 cycles per second, not 60. *Do not* try any of the tests here that refer to the actual alternating current, unless you already know about working with the mains safely.

Anyway, I just said that the PC uses DC, but the wall sockets provide AC so how does the PC convert the juice? With the power supply. The power supply actually doesn't *supply* power—it *converts* it from AC to DC.

There are two kinds of power supplies, linear power supplies and switching power supplies. The PC's power supply is, in every PC *I've* ever seen, a switching power supply. Both linear and switching power supplies have their positive and negative aspects.

Linear power supplies are based on transformers. That makes them hot, heavy, and impervious to changes in current levels, while rendering them vulnerable to voltage swings. Linear power supplies are an older design than switching power supplies, and you still find them on monitors and some external drive cases. Even small linear power supplies generate a relatively large amount of heat, which is why you should never cover the holes atop a monitor; you can fry a monitor quickly that way.

Switching power supplies are digital in nature. They step down voltage by essentially "switching" it on and off, hence their name. Think of how they work in this way: suppose you had a 1000-watt bulb in a light, but you only wanted the lighting value of a 100-watt bulb. You could get 100 watts' worth out of the 1000-watt bulb by switching it on and off, but leaving it off 90 percent of the time. I know it sounds goofy, but if you could switch the light on and off quickly enough, then *you'd never see it flicker*. (In fact, that's how fluorescent lights work. They're actually very bright, but they flash off and on 60 times per second, too quickly for most eyes to register—and they're off over 90 percent of the time.)

Switching power supplies are less sensitive to fluctuations in input voltage, although they are still a problem. These power supplies generate heat, but a lot less of it than linear power supplies.

Why do we care about power supplies? Probably mainly because power supply troubles can be mysterious and annoying. Just as bad are similar-looking troubles with the supplied power itself. This chapter looks at both.

Components of the Power Supply

The power supply is the black or silver box in the back of the PC with the large yellow label telling you in five languages not to open the box up and warning you that it is dangerous. Despite the fact that I can only understand a few of the multilingual messages, I'm inclined to take them at their word.

The reason is mainly due to a thing called a *1000-microfarad capacitor*, which is inside the power supply. The capacitor is utilized to smooth out some power glitches. Big capacitors look like miniature soda cans, sized from about a couple of centimeters (about an inch) long to perhaps four times that size. Capacitors are kind of like holding tanks for electricity. If you've got some power that needs to go from point A to point B, but it tends to fluctuate a bit in the process, then an electronic designer can smooth it out a bit by putting a capacitor between A and B. The downside of a capacitor is that it's a part of a circuit that retains electricity even after you turn the circuit off. I once got a zap from a monster capacitor in a television that had been sitting unplugged in my family's attic for a few years, and I'm told that I'm lucky that I didn't do anything worse to myself.

The upshot of what I'm telling you is that the capacitors inside power supplies tend to argue against your trying to fix them. Power supplies can cost as little as $25, so just replace them if they're faulty. I recommend replacing and not repairing floppies just because it's a pain to repair them, but I recommend not repairing power supplies because they can hurt you.

Power Supply Connections

On the side of the power supply is the on/off switch for the computer. Sprouting out of the other side are the power connectors. Most power supplies have two connectors that are sometimes labeled P8 and P9 that connect to the motherboard; other non-standard power supplies use a single connector.

Looking at P8 connected to P9, you might wonder just why IBM designed a power supply interface to the motherboard that can so easily cause troubles; after all, if you reverse P8 and P9, as some of my friends have done in the past, then you irreparably smoke the motherboard. Why didn't IBM use a single larger connector?

Oddly enough, IBM *did*; the first prototype PC—which never saw production—had a single large connector from the power supply to the motherboard. But, in the final days of setting up the new microcomputer for production, the company supplying the connectors went out of business, and the only way to not get behind was to just use two connectors that were readily available from another vendor. Since then, some other companies have gone to a single-connector design, but that hasn't become part of the de facto PC standard, sadly.

Power supplies also sport from two to four identical Molex connectors for attaching to drives (hard disks, floppy disks, and tape drives), and most modern power supplies also include the smaller Berg connectors used to power 3.5-inch floppy drives.

The motherboard receives power through the power strip, which is often in the northeastern corner of the board near the keyboard cable connector. (This assumes that you are looking at the board so that the memory chips are closest to you and the expansion connectors and the keyboard connector are farthest from you.)

There are often two power connectors on current motherboards. One is a single, large connector that is used in ATX cases. The other is the older-style AT power connector that uses two connectors. One has only five wires, and connects above the other, which has six wires. See Figure 9.1 for a detail of a Pentium II motherboard. The power connectors are wired the same for even the newest Pentium Pro clone motherboard. When connecting these, the important thing to remember is to keep the black wires together in the center between the two connectors.

The power supply lines—the yellow, blue, and red wires—can be tested against a ground (any of the black wires). If you are actually testing a power supply, all of the black wires should be tested. Table 9.1 gives the specifications for these lines.

FIGURE 9.1:

Pentium II motherboard with power connectors

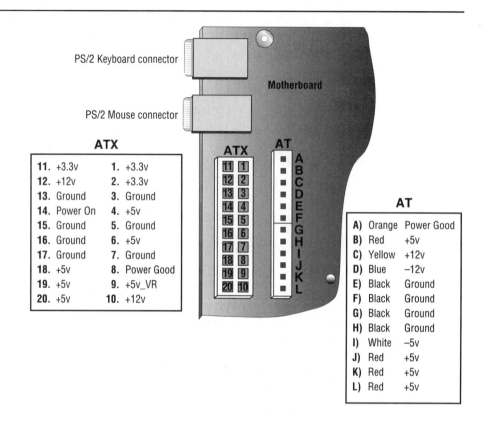

WIRE COLOR		ATX			AT	

ATX

11.	+3.3v	1.	+3.3v
12.	+12v	2.	+3.3v
13.	Ground	3.	Ground
14.	Power On	4.	+5v
15.	Ground	5.	Ground
16.	Ground	6.	+5v
17.	Ground	7.	Ground
18.	+5v	8.	Power Good
19.	+5v	9.	+5v_VR
20.	+5v	10.	+12v

AT

A)	Orange	Power Good
B)	Red	+5v
C)	Yellow	+12v
D)	Blue	−12v
E)	Black	Ground
F)	Black	Ground
G)	Black	Ground
H)	Black	Ground
I)	White	−5v
J)	Red	+5v
K)	Red	+5v
L)	Red	+5v

TABLE 9.1: Specifications for PC Power Supply Output

WIRE COLOR	RATED VOLTAGE (VOLTS)	ACCEPTABLE RANGE (VOLTS)	CURRENT RANGE (AMPS)
Yellow	+12	+8.5–+12.6	0.0–2.00
Blue	-2	-8.5– -12.6	0.0–0.25
Red	+5	+2.4– +4.2	2.3–7.00
Yellow	-5	-4.5– -5.4	0.0–0.30

You can then do a resistance test of the motherboard. The tests are conducted on the power supply pins. Table 9.2 contains the *minimum* resistance for each connection. If the measured values are less than this, the motherboard is definitely faulty.

TABLE 9.2: System Board Resistances

COMMON LEAD (BLACK PROBE)	VOM LEAD (RED PROBE)	MINIMUM RESISTANCE (OHMS)
8	10	0.8
8	11	0.8
8	12	0.8
5	3	6
6	4	48
7	9	17

The drive power connectors—*it doesn't matter which connector goes to which drive*—are interchangeable. You can use the larger Molex connectors for most internal drives: hard drives, CD-ROM drives, or whatever. The smaller power connectors are used primarily for 3.5" floppy drives.

You don't need to use all of the drive power connectors. Just because you've got four drive power connectors doesn't mean that you must have four drives. (I get asked that now and then.) Just make sure that the unused power connectors are tucked out of the way. I once saw a system freeze solid because one of the ground wires (the two black wires in the middle) on an unused drive power connector made contact with a test point on a motherboard.

Power Supply Maintenance

Good news here: there isn't any maintenance required. The fan and the power switch are the only moving parts. If you suddenly notice that the PC is very quiet, but still operating, then your fan may have died. If that happens, save everything and *shut down immediately!* The computer's own heat can quickly damage or destroy it if the fan isn't present to dissipate it.

This is a real concern. Twice in my PC experience, I've taken a floppy disk out of the PC's drive and realized that it felt too hot. In both cases, it meant that the power supply's fan had died. In the first case, it was an original PC packed to the gills with heat-producing devices, and even though I turned off the PC as soon as I realized the problem, I was too late. Over the next six months, things failed, one by one, inside the system. The next time, it was on a 50 MHz 486; the main casualty was a $1000 hard disk.

Don't block the vents that the PC uses for cooling. And take compressed air and blow the dust out of the fan now and then. Please remove the power supply first so the dust doesn't immediately settle on the inside of computer.

Saving Power

More and more of us are buying electronic things—from "smart houses" to microwave ovens to fax machines to…well, to *PCs*. All that electrical demand is not, sadly, matched by the corresponding electrical supply; we're not building power plants fast enough. That, in conjunction with a general concern for the Earth, has lead to a rating offered by the American Environmental Protection Agency called Energy Star. More generally, there is a lot of interest in power saving or "green" PCs.

We think that we're environmentally conscious here in the United States, but Taiwan's got us beat all kinds of ways. Everybody's building "green" monitors that drop power when not needed, but have you ever heard of a *green mouse*? They've got 'em in Taiwan.

The thesis of the green computer movement is that we need to design, build, and use computers that require less electrical power. Green PC research is good for consumers first because, obviously, less electricity used means lower power bills and a planet that's easier to live on. But it's got another side effect: we're building better *laptops*, PCs that run on their batteries for longer. Green PCs save energy in a few ways.

Turn Off Things When You Don't Need Them

One of the main sources of power savings for green PCs is just to turn off interfaces when they're not being used. Laptops spend a fair amount of power keeping parallel and serial ports active when they're not in use. Green machines shut down circuits that aren't doing anything. Unfortunately, that includes hard disks, but I'll have more to say on that in a minute.

Run Chips Slower

The power output of a circuit is related to its frequency. Run a CPU and its memories at a lower clock rate, and you use less power. Many green machines will slow down a CPU when the system is idle...or when the system *thinks* it is idle. One oddity of green PCs is that sometimes they go to sleep when you don't want them to, so when troubleshooting systems, turn off the power saving features first.

Build Lower Voltage Systems

Power is related to voltage as well, so lower voltage means less power. Older PCs used 12 volts for the fans and drive motors and used chips that ran at 5 volts. Newer systems have chips that run anywhere from 2.2 to 3.3 volts for the processor and 5 volts for the smaller logic chips, fans, and motors.

Green Cautions

Having said all that, I've got a few complaints about green PCs. First of all, I think the green PC technologists have missed the boat by focusing on hard disk and CPU power saves. The fact of the matter is that on your average desktop PC, the color monitor consumes two-thirds of the power. With the monitor, a desktop PC often consumes 150 watts, of which 100 are used by the monitor.

In contrast, consider the laptop that I'm writing these words on. It's got a color display, 20MB of RAM, a 75MHz processor, and 0.5GB of mass storage. All that power comes at a cost of no more than 15 watts for the whole thing, display and all. The answer seems easy: just move us away from energy-hungry CRTs and offer desktop LCD panels.

Further, it's a really bad idea to save a smidgen of power by turning the hard disk on and off when it's not used. You end up cycling the power on the hard disk dozens of times a day and saving a small amount of power, *but* you reduce the length of life of your hard disk. And if you're concerned about power use, consider how much power Seagate uses to forge the disk platters, build the semiconductors, solder them to the boards, make the shipping cartons, and send the drive to you...doesn't seem like much of a win, does it? Green PCs are a good idea. But don't play with the power settings for the hard disk.

Upgrading the Power Supply

Years ago, desktop PCs lacked the power to drive all of their peripherals. It was common to find a PC start to fail because it couldn't provide enough power to, well, *drive* its drives.

This experience led me to a preference for external peripherals, a preference that I retain to this day. Whenever I'm buying a CD-ROM, large hard disk, or backup device, I buy it in an external case when possible. That means that every peripheral has its own fan and, as a bonus, its own power switch. Sometimes it's convenient to have the ability to disable a drive without popping the PC's top. It also means that the peripheral doesn't heat up the inside of the PC, *and* it doesn't strain the PC's power supply.

Even if you don't have my "powernoia," however, you'll probably never have to worry about getting a larger power supply on your machine. *But*, if you're building a server with 256MB of RAM and a full height 23GB hard disk, as well as a couple of CD-ROMs, a SCSI host adapter, and two LAN cards, then you might think about one of the 300-plus-watt power supplies.

Better, however, is this advice: don't just get a *big* power supply. Get a *good* power supply, one of the ones made by the PC Power and Cooling people. I've referred to them in Chapter 4, "Avoiding Service: Preventive Maintenance," and the company's address is listed in Appendix A.

When buying a power supply, don't confuse "watts capacity" with "watts used." Will a 300-watt power supply use more power than a 150-watt power supply, if it's put in a PC that draws only 100 watts? No. While a 300-watt bulb uses more power than a 150-watt bulb—here, it's watts used. The description "300-watt power supply" means a power supply that can convert *up to 300 watts*. Notice the *up to*—putting a 300-watt power supply on a system that only requires 50 watts will only cause the power supply to convert 50 watts. A lot of folks misunderstand that—

even an IBM engineer in 1983 warned me that putting an XT's 130-watt power supply on an IBM PC would "burn up the motherboard." He was wrong, but I didn't know any better.

But pushing a power supply too far isn't a good idea. How do you know how much power your machine is using? One simple device is a Power Meter from PARA Systems. The Power Meter looks like a power strip with a gauge on it. You just plug it into the wall, then plug your system unit into the Power Meter. It has a wiring tester, so it tells you if your outlets are wired correctly. (See "Protecting the PC from the AC," coming up.) Then turn the system unit on, and look at the needle on the gauge. It measures amperes of current flowing. You'll get a value between 0.5 and 3. Then just multiply that ampere value by 58 and you'll get the number of watts that your system unit uses. If it is close to its rated power supply, it's time to get a bigger power supply.

Why 58? You may know that Power (Watts) = Volts × Amps, and that you ordinarily get 120 volts from the wall outlet. Why not multiply amps by 120? Simple—this isn't direct current, where amps and volts are always in phase. Instead, we're dealing here with AC, alternating current. In AC, current and voltage follow a sine-wave-like path, paths that can fall out of step. That means multiplying amps by 120 would overstate the total actual power requirements. To calculate the correct wattage we need to take a kind of "average" of the power used. This is called the RMS power.

When buying upgrade power supplies, consider the fan. I've seen far too many tower cases that put the drives and other hot things up above the fan. And for heaven's sake, don't buy those dumb plug-in boards that have a fan on them. Your PC is built to circulate air in a particular direction. Those fans may actually work *against* the system's fan!

Also avoid the newer power supplies with the fans that shut down "when they're not needed." They've got a thermocouple in them—a circuit that measures heat. If the heat in the system drops below some level, the fan shuts off. This is a terrible idea. PCs can suffer from "hot spots," areas that are considerably hotter than the average PC temperature. Just because the air going through the fan is, say 100 degrees F doesn't mean that there isn't a 130-degree section over the processor. (And speaking of processor fans, if you've got one, check it occasionally. They're made incredibly cheaply, and tend to die after nine months or so, leaving you with a useless fan that actually *increases* the heat on the processor.)

Speaking of replacement power supplies, remember the discussion of the power supply lines in the chapter on circuit boards? You may have noticed the first line on P8, called Power Good. This is a digital signal enabled by the power supply once it views itself as warmed up and ready. A flaky Power Good leads the computer to issue a long beep or short beeps or generally unusual noises. Some inexpensive replacement power supplies cause computers to emit a loud or long beep, then settle down to good service. I have experienced this myself, and can only account for the beeps if the power supply doesn't wait quite long enough to first enable Power Good. A little initial up and down activity on the line would induce the clock to issue a RESET command to the PC.

Troubleshooting the Power Supply

You turn the computer on and nothing happens at all. It is plugged in, so it's not that—where next?

The Power Supply Troubleshooting Trail

First, check the wall outlet. The outlet should be providing between 104 and 130 volts AC current. Just set the voltage-Ohmmeter (VOM) to read AC voltage and put one lead in each hole of the outlet.

Second, check the cables. The cables should be in place on the system board.

Third, is power getting to the power supply? The fan gets it first, so if it isn't turning then the power supply isn't getting power. When some power supplies are first turned on the speaker emits a low click.

Fourth, test the power supply with another.

Replacing a Power Supply

If you suspect the power supply, replace it. It's simple.

1. On the back of the PC, you will see four screws bolting the power supply to the chassis. Remove these.

2. Disconnect the power leads from the system and drives. Draw a picture and make notes of what connects to what. Note wire colors: the black wires on the connectors are always next to each other.

3. The only hard part of replacing the power supply is attaching the wires that go to the power switch at the front of the computer. Also, be sure to diagram the connectors by color. Putting the power wires in the wrong place can cause serious problems.

4. Install the new power supply by reversing the procedure.

5. To be extra careful, strip the PC down to the minimum circuit boards. Then power up and run whatever diagnostics you use.

Protecting the PC from the AC

You can control a lot of things in your environment, but you have little control over one aspect of the PC environment: the power delivered by the electric company. For various reasons, it may not come out clean and regular like it's supposed to. Worse yet, you can't always blame the power company—sometimes it's your fault or your building management's fault.

Do You Have Power Problems?

Power or wiring problems can show up as:

- The computer mysteriously "freezing up"
- Random memory errors
- Lost data on the hard disk
- Damaged chips on a circuit board
- Data transmission noise and peripheral errors

Years ago, I was at a hotel doing a presentation that involved a demonstration PC. The PC did the strangest things:

- Once, it stopped the memory test at 128K and froze.
- Another time, it gave a memory error message around 400K.
- The hard disk wouldn't boot about 30 percent of the time, despite a fresh format.
- It stopped talking to the keyboard a few times, requiring the "Big Red Switch" (the power switch).

What was the problem? The old "hotel power problem." When the coffee machine was on, the PC did strange things. Additionally, the PC shared an outlet with two 600-watt overheads in continuous use and a slide projector. I moved it to another outlet, and the problem disappeared.

Having said that, what can you do about power problems? The four steps to power protection are:

- Check that your outlets are wired correctly.

- Find out what else is on the power line.

- Provide a common ground for all devices.

- Protect against noise—surges, spikes, under- and overvoltage.

Following are the facts to "empower" you to solve your line problems.

Check Outlet Wiring

AC outlets have three wires: a large prong, a small prong, and a center cylinder. The cylinder is the safety ground, the prongs are the "hot" or *phase* line (the official term is "phase," but anyone who's ever accidentally touched it calls it the "hot") and the return, also called common, or neutral. The wires in the wall are supposed to be wired so that green is ground, white is return, and whatever's left (usually black) is phase.

It's not unheard-of for the hot and the return to be reversed. This actually isn't a problem so long as everything is wired backwards. But if you plug, say, the PC into a correctly wired outlet, and a printer into a wrongly wired outlet, and if one of the devices connects the ground and the common—again, not an unusual occurrence—*and* there is a break in the neutral, then you'll get 120 volts across the cable from the printer to the PC. Lots of destruction will follow. Worse yet, miswired outlets can hurt you: if you touch both the PC and the printer, then you are the electrical path.

You can buy circuit-wiring testers from most hardware stores. I got mine at Sears for $6 some years ago—they're probably a bit more now, but well worth it.

Check What Else Is on the Line

Ensure that there isn't any equipment on the same line as the PC that draws a lot of power. That includes:

- Large motors, like the ones you'd find in air conditioners, refrigerators, or machine tools

- Heating coils, such as in small space heaters or coffee makers—"personal coffee makers" are included here

- Copiers and their cousins, laser printers

Anything that draws a lot of current can draw down the amount of voltage being delivered to a PC on the same breaker or fuse. Worse yet, heating coil devices like coffee makers inadvertently create something called a *tank circuit* that can inject high frequency spikes into the power line, noise that can slip through your power supply and go straight to the chips on the circuit boards.

One simple solution is to just get a separate power circuit to the computer. Another is to get an isolation transformer such as we find in a power conditioner. A RF shield between the primary and secondary coils of the transformer removes the high frequency noise.

Some laser printers draw 15 amps all by themselves. That implies that, like it or not, you've got to put a 20 amp breaker in for *each* laser printer/PC combination. PCs *without* lasers don't draw much power and don't require a separate breaker.

Ensure Common Ground among Devices

Electrical ground is intended, among other things, to provide an electrical reference point, a benchmark value like sea level. A computer communicates ones or zeros to a modem, for instance, by varying voltage relative to ground: greater than +3 volts means 0, less than –3 volts means 1. Close to 0 volts means "nothing is being transmitted."

The problem arises when the two communicating devices don't agree on the value of ground. If, in the above example, the modem's ground is a 7 volts potential below the computer's ground, then the modem and the computer each think that the other is sending data when actually neither is.

Generally, it's not that bad. But if the computer's ground is 3 volts different from the modem, then the occasional bit will be lost or garbled.

The answer? Simple—just ensure that all devices plugged into your PC all share the same ground. A simple 6-outlet power strip will do this. There is one flaw in this approach, however: what about a Local Area Network (LAN)? Basically, a LAN is one big ground problem. Some people have suggested grounding the shield of the network cables every hundred feet or so. The only true solution is to use fiber optic LANs, but they're still a wee bit expensive.

NOTE   Ensuring that all equipment has a *common* ground has nothing to do with having a *good* ground. A proper ground is mainly for safety, not data protection. (If someone insists that you must have a good ground for proper data transfer, ask him how airplanes and spaceships manage it, hmmm?) We'll look at proper grounding soon.

Protect Against Power Noise

We've already discussed undervoltage, overvoltage, spikes, and surges in the chapter on Preventive Maintenance. Remember:

- *Undervoltage* is undesirable because the power supply reacts to too *little* voltage by drawing too *much* current. This heats up and may destroy components.

- *Overvoltage* can damage a chip because too much voltage destroys the circuits inside the chip.

When some outside force causes your power line to deliver more voltage than it is supposed to, this is called an overvoltage condition. Such conditions are, in general, dangerous to the computer.

The physics of it is this: the heart of the computer resides in its chips. The chips are a specially designed crystal. Crystals are highly structured molecules: many of them would be happier in a less structured environment. Applying electronic and heat energy to the crystals allows this breakdown in organization to occur. One spike might not do it, but it leaves damage that is cumulative. Even small spike damage is cumulative. Damage is proportional to energy. Energy is voltage, multiplied by current, multiplied by time.

Brief overvoltages of under a millisecond in length are called *spikes*. Longer ones—milliseconds to seconds—are called *surges*. *Spikes* may be of high enough frequency to introduce RFI-like problems.

You (or your boss) may be skeptical about the actual seriousness of power problems. This may all be, you suspect, a tempest in a teapot. If you don't think that you have power problems, spend $130 on a simple device that can monitor the quality of your power. Called the AC Monitor, it's from Tasco Ltd. in Colorado. They're listed in Appendix A.

It will continuously monitor the voltage that you are receiving at the outlet, and indicate power drops, surges, or spikes (no frequency variation, sadly) with a light and an audible warning.

The big three conditions that you wish to avoid are:

- Surges and spikes
- Low voltage
- No voltage (power outages)

Solutions to Power Problems

Solutions to power problems fall into three categories:

- Isolation
- Shielding
- Proper grounding

Isolation means isolating the noise (surge, spike, and so on) from the computer—draining it off harmlessly. This is done with filters, transformers, gas discharge tubes, and *metal oxide varistors* (*MOVs*). An MOV is an important part of a surge protector. When a surge comes in, an MOV shunts it off to ground. Unfortunately, the MOV is a kamikaze component—it "throws itself onto the grenade." Each MOV is only good for one big surge, or a bunch of little surges. (No, there's no easy way to test to see whether an MOV is still working or not, at least not without a $2000 tester.) Power conditioners and surge protectors provide isolation in varying quality.

Shields minimize high frequency noise. Shielding is evident in the filter capacitors in surge protectors, RF shields between the primary and secondary coils in a power conditioner, the metal case of the computer, and in the shield in shielded cable.

Some people view grounding as a magic answer to noise problems. Just run a wire from the device in question to a metal stake pounded into the ground (called a *ground stake*), and all of your ground problems go away! (Kind of like an electronic Roto-Rooter: "…and away go troubles down the drain.")

Nahhh.

First, having a proper ground *is* important. It makes electronic equipment safer (it keeps you out of the circuit), but, as we've seen, a *common* ground is important to minimize communication errors between devices. So the main reason for a proper earth ground is safety.

The idea behind a ground stake (ya know, years ago, I thought ground stake was just hamburger...) is to provide a nice electrical path to earth ground. It *doesn't* eliminate noise, however: two ground stakes a few yards apart will pass current and noise between themselves. Ground stakes are less effective when there's a drought. I once heard of a ground stake that provided a better connection to ground than others on a particular site because it was, err, "watered" by local fauna. (No, I'm not sure I believe it, but ground *is* magic, and magical stories accompany it.)

A final thought on grounding: some companies are extra careful to ground their computer rooms, thinking that this will somehow protect their data. They're not so careful about the other areas in the building, however, so you've got a computer room with a cleaner ground than the rest of the building. Step back for a moment and ask what effect would differential grounding have on lightning protection? If lightning were to strike the building, it takes the easiest path to ground. If the easiest path to ground is through your computers, so be it. Basically, if you ground your computer room well, and don't ground the rest of the building well, it's like putting a big "EAT AT JOE'S" sign on the computer room, as far as lightning is concerned.

Devices to Remedy Electronic Problems

Okay, now we've seen the problems and the approaches to solutions. Now let's look at what's available on the market to solve the problems.

If you're looking here for a recommendation, please understand that I haven't got good news. Electric power in the '90s in most of the Western world is getting worse and worse due to aging equipment and lack of new capacity being pitted against ever-growing energy demands.

The PC really needs cleaner power than the stuff that you feed your refrigerator, Mr. Coffee, or desk lamp. The only absolutely reliable way to get clean power is to rectify the power, put it in a battery, and then use the DC power in the battery to reconstruct the AC power. A device that does this is a *UPS* (*uninterruptable power supply*). A good one will cost you a few bucks, but in the long run will save hundreds on new computer components and lost data. On the other hand, there are some fairly effective alternatives like surge suppressors, *Standby Power Supplies* (*SPSs*) and power conditioners. Me? I'm building a Faraday cage for my office (just as soon as I get some time and money...).

Surge Suppressors and Spike Isolators

Many of us have purchased surge suppressors, or as they are also known, surge protectors or spike isolators.

The idea with suppression devices is that once they see a large surge coming they redirect it out to the electric ground—kind of like opening the floodgates. The most common redirection device is an MOV, which we talked about a few pages earlier. It is an impassable barrier between the supply voltage and protective ground *until* the voltage reaches a certain level. *Gas discharge tubes* and *pellet arrestors* are slower but beefier devices. *Coaxial arrestors* fit somewhere in the middle.

The best suppressors use several lines of defense: MOVs, coax arrestors, and gas discharge tubes, for example.

Of course, an overzealous surge suppressor can redirect *too much* power for too long and create a worse surge of its own.

Another important question is *what* voltage level triggers the surge suppressor? They're not waiting for 120.00001 volts to get going: some will pass 1000 volts before calling in the Marines. By then, your PC is toast.

PC Magazine started doing tests of surge suppression devices years ago and has published the results in the magazine. They created spikes and measured how much of the spike was allowed through. Some suppressors emitted smoke and flames when subjected to a real surge. Others died quietly, not informing the owner that they no longer protect the PC (they still pass electricity, so there's no way to know.) You can see a surge protector in Figure 9.2.

FIGURE 9.2:

Surge Protector

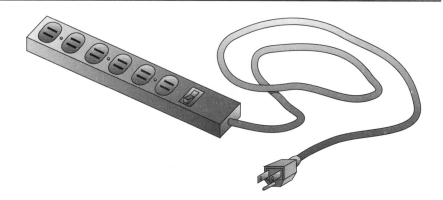

The Bad News about Surge Protectors

You see, I can't, in good conscience, recommend them to you.

The best suppressors use several lines of defense: MOVs, coax arrestors, and gas discharge tubes, for example. But the heart of surge protectors are MOVs. As we've said before, MOVs are one-time-only devices. One surge and they're history. Worse yet, they can't be tested.

Yes, some surge protectors come with a little light that goes out when the surge protector doesn't protect any more. But those little lights can't be trusted, either. The light is in series with a fuse, and the fuse is in series with the return from the MOV—it's called a *bleeder fuse*. Given a large enough surge, the fuse will blow (along with the MOV, you recall) and the light will go out. In that case, the case of a single large surge, the light *is* effective. But an MOV can also be destroyed by a number of smaller surges. In that case, the fuse would be unaffected, and the light would stay on.

Summarizing, there's no way to know whether or not your surge protector is still protecting. If you've got a light on your surge protector, and it goes out, you definitely have a dead surge protector. But if the light's on, that's no guarantee of surge protector effectiveness.

Another company has meanwhile built a renewable surge protector. The company's name is Zero-Surge, and their product is (likewise) called the ZeroSurge Protector. It's a good product, but be prepared to pay a bit for it, as you would for any quality device: models range from $150 to $200. Zero-Surge's address is in Appendix A.

Power Conditioners

Between a surge protector and a backup power supply is another device, also in-between in price, called a *power conditioner*. A power conditioner does all the things that a surge protector does—filters and isolates line noise—and more. Rather than relying on MOVs and such, the power conditioner uses the inductance of its transformer to filter out line noise. An isolation transformer is a far superior device for removing noise than a capacitor or an MOV. Additionally, most power conditioners will boost up undervoltage so that your machine can continue to work through brownouts.

Recall that the surge protector's MOVs fail with no sign, so there's no good way to know whether your surge protector is doing any good. Power conditioners don't have that problem—when a transformer fails, you know it—the power conditioner just plain doesn't provide any power.

Which power conditioner is right for you? I have used the Tripplite LC1800. I've seen it in mail-order ads for as little as $179. One firm that sells them cheaply is Altex Electronics, which is also listed in Appendix A.

The LC1800 even shows you your incoming voltage via some LEDs on its front panel. *Do not* plug your laser printer into the

LC1800, as it is only rated for 6 amps. (Remember that lasers draw up to 15 amps.)

Backup Power Supplies

In addition to protection from short power irregularities, you may need backup power. I have lived in a number of places in the northeastern U.S. where summer lightning storms will kill the power for just a second—enough to erase your memory and make the digital clocks blink. Total loss of power can be remedied only with battery-based systems. Such systems are in the range of $150 to $1200 and up. Figure 9.3 shows how UPS and SPSs work.

There are two types, *standby power supplies* (SPS) and *uninterruptible power supplies* (UPS). SPSs charge the batteries while watching the current level. If the power drops, they activate themselves and supply power until their batteries run down. A fast power switch must occur here, and it's important to find out what the switching time is—4ms or under is fine, and 14ms, in my experience, is not fast enough.

A UPS constantly runs power from the line current to a battery, then from the battery to the PC. This is superior to an SPS because there is no switching time involved. Also, this means that any surges affect the battery charging mechanism, not the computer. A UPS is, then, a surge suppressor also.

A UPS or SPS must convert DC current from a battery to AC for the PC. AC is supposed to look like a sine wave. Cheaper UPS and SPS models produce square waves. (See Figure 9.4.) Square waves are bad because they include high frequency harmonics, which can appear as EMI or RFI to the computer. Also, some peripherals (printers in particular) can't handle square-wave AC. So, when examining UPS, ask whether they use square wave or sine wave. Some produce a pseudo-sine wave. It has the stair step look of a square wave, but not as many harmonic problems.

FIGURE 9.3:

How UPS and SPS work

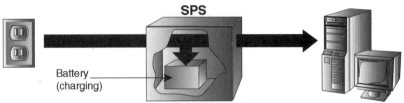

When power is normal, an SPS passes current through to the PC
– spikes and all – while siphoning off a bit of the power in order to keep the battery charged.

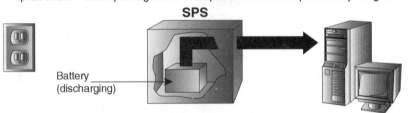

When the power is interrupted, the SPS supplies power to the PC from the battery for as long as the battery lasts. The SPS must also sense the power-down condition and get the battery on-line quickly enough that the PC can continue to work uninterrupted.

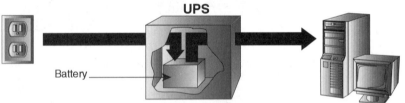

A UPS, on the other hand, sends power from the socket right into the battery, keeping it constantly charged. The computer draws the power from the battery instead of the line.

When power is interrupted, the UPS continues to supply power to the computer from the battery. Benefits: constant surge protection and zero switching time.

Ordinarily, the purpose of a UPS is to allow you enough time to save whatever you're doing and shut down gracefully. If you are in an area where the power may disappear for hours, and may do it regularly, then you should look for the ability to attach external batteries to the UPS so that you can run the PC for longer periods.

Remember that a sine-wave UPS is the only way to really eliminate most power problems. The reason *everyone* doesn't have one is cost.

A decent compromise can be found in a fast (4ms) square-wave SPS. I know I said that square waves are bad for your peripherals, but consider how often will the SPS actually be doing anything? Not very often—remember that it supplies power only when the line voltage drops out, which is not a common occurrence. The brief minute or two each month of square wave power that your peripherals end up getting won't kill them. And you'll save a pile over a UPS.

On the other hand, remember that a UPS is *always* on line, and so must produce sine-wave output. But UPS do have the benefit that they provide surge protection by breaking down and reassembling the power, and SPS *do not* provide this protection. You must still worry about surge protection when you buy an SPS, but not if you buy a UPS. So make the choice that your budget allows.

Something to look for in backup power supplies—either UPS or SPS—is a serial port.

A serial port? Yes, a serial port. Most other operating systems can monitor a signal from a serial-port-equipped UPS/SPS. When power fails, the operating system is informed by the backup power supply of that occurrence, and the operating system does a graceful shutdown in the battery time remaining. This function is also called a *heartbeat*. Table 9.3 summarizes what we've seen about power problems and solutions.

FIGURE 9.4:

UPS AC waveforms

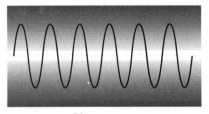

Sine wave

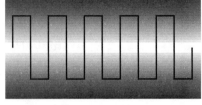

Square wave

TABLE 9.3: Power Problems and Solutions

PROTECTION METHOD	REMEDIES SURGES	REMEDIES LOW VOLTAGE	REMEDIES OUTAGES
Power Conditioner	yes	yes	no
SPS	no	no	yes
UPS	yes	yes	yes

Before buying an SPS or a UPS, however, be aware of just one more thing—many people are selling SPS under the name of "off-line UPS." Real UPS are nowadays being called "on-line UPS."

So What Should I Buy?

Sounds like you can spend a pile of money on power protection and, sadly, that's true: a real, honest-to- goodness UPS will set you back four figures. (Cheaper ones are SPSs that marketers call "off-line UPS." Kind of like calling a car "wingless ground-based airplane" or calling those sales people "honesty-challenged.") The best compromise that I've come up with is a neat little combination of a power conditioner and an SPS with, of course, a serial port attached. Called the Smart-UPS 450, it's made by American Power Conversion and I've found them for about $300. It's a complete power solution, and they've worked wonderfully for me for the past four years, through storms and power company screwups.

The Granddaddy of Power Problems: Lightning

When Thor's hammer falls near your site, you won't need any special equipment to note its passing. Curled-up, blackened circuit boards are pretty easy to spot.

I travel around North America and Europe teaching troubleshooting classes. You know what *everyone* tells me? No matter where we are, the natives tell me that they're in the "lightning capital of the world." (I know, hearing something *shocking* like that makes you want to *bolt*.) Take a look at Figure 9.5 to find out where you rate.

FIGURE 9.5:

Mean annual number of days with thunderstorms

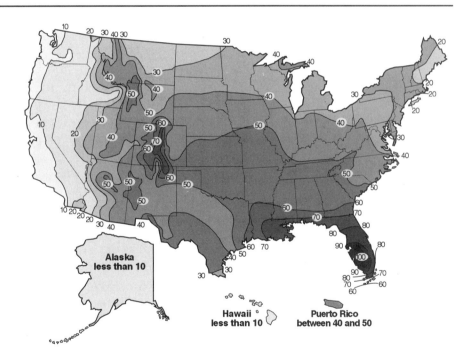

Looks like central Florida can lay claim to the "Thunderstorm Central" title. Here's what we know about thunderstorms:

- Lightning affects your system even if it doesn't strike your building.

- It is *good* to leave a machine plugged in—the lightning has an easy path to ground.

- As mentioned earlier, taking special care to ground the part of the building that the big computers are in just makes those computers more vulnerable. A better-grounded path is the one that lightning will take.

- Lightning arrestors can reduce the likelihood of lightning damage.

- Newer high-tech lightning rods are being used in some sites. They look like umbrellas built of barbed wire standing about 30 feet tall.

- A cheap lightning protection: overhand knots in the power cord.

Believe it or not, some researchers found this one out. It makes the lightning surge work against itself, and burn out the power cord, *not* the PC. And it works—Washington had the biggest thunderstorm it had had in years in the summer of 1989, and the stuff with knots in the cords rode it out without a hitch. The TV didn't have knots in the cord, so I did have to buy a new TV.

The following year, a bolt hit my *telephone line*. It literally toasted the line from the telephone pole to my house; little crispy brown bits flaked off at the touch. But once inside, the bolt hit my five knots, and nothing inside was fried. Why did I tie the knots? I got tired of losing a modem every summer to lightning. There are also surge suppressors for telephone lines—APC makes a good one, and they're not expensive, about $30, I think.

Power's not the sexiest part of PC hardware, but it sure can be the most troublesome. Get a Smart-UPS and a decent power supply, buy external peripherals, and you'll be electrified with the results.

Hard Disk Drive Overview and Terminology

- Hard drives and interfaces

- What's in a disk

- Disk performance characteristics

10

Hard disks are where most of a PC user's data lives. Since the data on your system is the most valuable part of the system, it stands to reason that the hard disk is, in some ways, the computer's most important part.

That's why this book has so many chapters on hard disks. In this one, we'll take a look at disk-ese and have an overview of disk technology.

Hard Drives and Interfaces

A hard disk subsystem consists of the hard drive itself, a disk interface, and the cable or cables connecting them. Disk interfaces are either host adapters or controllers, depending on the type of disk technology. Older drive technologies use controllers, newer ones use host adapters, and I'll cover the difference soon. You can see an example drive and a controller in Figure 10.1.

FIGURE 10.1:

Hard disk drive and controller

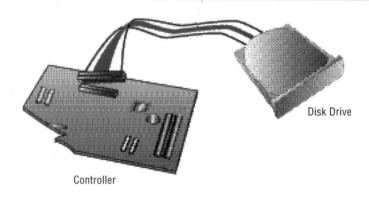

Disk Drive

Controller

Disk terms are relevant either to a hard drive or to a drive interface. For drives, you'll see the terms summarized in Table 10.1.

(Forgive the acronyms, by the way—I promise I'll define them later in the text, but I needed to keep the table tractable in size.)

T A B L E 1 0 . 1 : Hard Disk Terms

DRIVE CHARACTERISTIC	WHAT IT MEANS, WHY IT'S RELEVANT
Number of cylinders	Part of capacity determination. Hard drives store data on a stack of aluminum or glass platters. Each surface of each platter (top and bottom) is divided (magnetically) into circular tracks. A cylinder is a stack of corresponding tracks. For example, track 20 on each of the platters (tops and bottoms) would make up one of the cylinders of the hard drive.
Number of heads	Part of capacity determination. There are two heads for each platter of the hard drive (one on the top and one on the bottom). The heads read and write the data on the platters.
Number of sectors	Part of capacity determination. Each track on every platter is divided up into sections called sectors. In general, each sector contains the same number of bytes of data as every other sector on the drive.
Zone Bit Recording (ZBR)	Describes whether or not the number of sectors per track is constant. If the number of sectors per track remains the same on all of them, the tracks would divide up the platters more or less like slices of pie. This makes the center tracks more densely packed than the outer tracks. In order to make the data readable in the inner tracks, the data in the outer tracks is spread out more, compromising capacity. Therefore, most drives today vary the number of sectors per track to optimize the total disk area.
Head positioning mechanism	A drive design element, a tradeoff of speed versus cost. Older hard drives use a *stepper motor* to move the heads back and forth so they can access each of the tracks (cylinders). Today, virtually all hard drives move the heads using a *voice coil*.
Access time	Drive design characteristic. This is the amount of time it takes for the heads to locate a specific piece of data in the hard drive. Usually manufacturers specify the "average access time," since the actual seek time varies based upon where the heads are and where the next bit of data is located.
Data transfer rate	The data transfer rate is the speed at which the data is copied from the hard drive to the computer or from the computer to the hard drive.

Continued on next page

TABLE 10.1 CONTINUED: Hard Disk Terms

DRIVE CHARACTERISTIC	WHAT IT MEANS, WHY IT'S RELEVANT
Drive interface type	Configuration issues determine what kind of interface your computer will need to communicate with the hard drive. Most today are Enhanced IDE (EIDE). The other popular interface used today is Small Computer System Interface (SCSI).
Write precompensation cylinder	On older hard drives, the heads would require higher current output to write to the inner cylinders because the data was so close together that the heads switched on and off more quickly there. As a result, the platter would need more umph! to write the data reliably onto the inner tracks. The write precompensation cylinder specification told the computer when to boost the current to the write heads. Most current hard drives don't need the boost because they keep sector lengths constant.

Drive interfaces have characteristics, as well; they're summarized in Table 10.2.

TABLE 10.2: Drive Interface Characteristics

INTERFACE CHARACTERISTIC	RELEVANT TO CONTROLLER, HOST ADAPTER, OR BOTH?	WHAT IT MEANS, WHY IT'S RELEVANT
Logical Block Addressing (LBA)	Host Adapter	A method of allowing the computer to access all of the data on a large (more than 504MB) hard drive.
On-board cache memory	Both	Some controllers have some memory on them that they use to keep copies of frequently requested data.
Sector translation	Both	Alternate method of getting the computer to support larger drives.
Interface to system bus	Both	Which PC bus is this interface built for? Possible types are ISA, EISA, MCA, PC Card, VESA, PCI, and even parallel ports. Alternate method of getting the computer to support larger drives.

Continued on next page

TABLE 10.2 CONTINUED: Drive Interface Characteristics

INTERFACE CHARACTERISTIC	RELEVANT TO CONTROLLER, HOST ADAPTER, OR BOTH?	WHAT IT MEANS, WHY IT'S RELEVANT
Max error burst/ECC length Interface to system bus	Both	How many bad bits can this controller recover from? Which PC bus is this interface built for? Possible types are ISA, EISA, MCA, PC Card, VESA, PCI, and even parallel ports.
Max error burst/ECC length	Both	How many bad bits can this controller recover from?

We'll tackle everything in Table 10.2 in this chapter. Once you've gone through this, you'll be ready to see how to install, protect, and repair hard disk subsystems.

Disk Geometry: Heads, Tracks, Cylinders, and Sectors

If I wanted to tell you how to get to my house, I might say something like, "Travel west from Washington, D.C., for five miles on I-66 to Dreller Avenue, then turn left on Dreller and take it south for another mile until you reach Garner Drive. Take a right onto Garner and I'm two blocks up on the right." In order to understand what I'm talking about, you'd have to understand *west*, *south*, *block*, *left*, and *right*. In the same way, you can't even think about doing disk work without understanding terms like *cylinder*, *head*, *sector*, and *track*—words that are basic to disk discussions.

Data is stored on disks in bytes. The bytes are organized into 512-byte groups called *sectors*, and sectors are the minimum unit of data that you can read from or write to a disk. Sectors are grouped together into *tracks*; tracks on hard drives are conveniently arranged into groups called *cylinders*. A disk has at least two surfaces. You can see a cutaway view of a hard disk in Figure 10.2.

FIGURE 10.2:

Cutaway view of a
hard disk

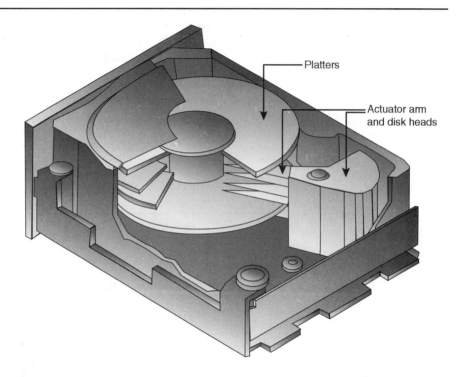

Before going into great detail about hard disks, however, it's easiest to explain hard disk structure with a very simple example, a simpler storage medium—a 1.44MB floppy diskette. We can describe a 1.44MB floppy diskette in this way:

- A floppy diskette has two *sides*, which require two *heads* to read them; these are sometimes called two *surfaces*.

- Each side contains data.

- Each side is divided into 80 concentric *tracks*. There is a related notion called *cylinders*, (we'll discuss them in a moment) so we say a 1.44MB floppy has 80 cylinders.

- Each track is divided, like pieces of a pie, into nine wedges called *sectors*.

- Each sector stores 0.5K (512 bytes) of information.

In contrast to a floppy diskette, a hard disk drive contains rigid metal or glass disks, called *platters*, stacked up inside an air-filtered enclosure. For example, the original XT 10MB drive had two platters. Other drives may have fewer, some others more. Again, a floppy diskette is like one "platter," but it's not rigid.

Disk Heads

Like a floppy diskette, the hard disk has an electromagnetic read/write *head* for each side of each platter. For example, some drives have four heads: two heads/platter (top and bottom) × two platters. Because the disk drive is sealed, you don't have to worry about aligning or cleaning these heads, and besides, you couldn't do those things even if you *wanted* to, because they're inaccessible.

Disk Tracks

Each side of each platter (sometimes called a *surface*) is divided into concentric tracks, like a floppy. A floppy like the 1.44MB example I'm using in Figure 10.3 typically has 80 tracks, but some of the oldest hard disks start at 305 tracks and go up from there; I've seen hard drives with over 16,000 tracks (cylinders). Today, although there are still a few hard drives made in the 5.25" size, 3.5" is the most widely used hard drive size. This means that the platters inside the drive are 3.5" in diameter. Most portable computers use 2.5" drives.

FIGURE 10.3:

A 1.44MB floppy diskette

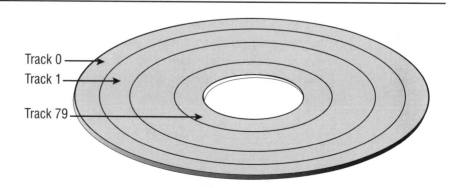

Track 0
Track 1
Track 79

Cylinders

Hard drives usually have more than one platter, so most hard disks have four or more read/write heads. All of a disk's heads—whether there are two heads or 16 heads—are attached to a bracket called an *actuator arm*. That means that when head 0 (as with most of the computer business, we count 0 to 3, not 1 to 4) is positioned over track 142 on surface 0 by the head actuator, head 3 is also positioned over track 142 on surface 3. Disk heads cannot be independently positioned, and that fact leads us to the notion of a *cylinder*. Here's how.

To read a particular sector, the disk hardware goes through two steps. First, it must move the read/write head over the desired track. Second, it must wait for the disk to rotate so that the desired sector is under the head, and then lastly, it must read. In general, moving the head takes the most time. This means that we'd most quickly read a file whose sectors were all on the same track, and *whose tracks lie above one another*—meaning that one head move reads a pile of data. Thus, if a large file starts out on, say, head 0, track 271, then it's a good idea to make sure that the next track that file uses is head 1, track 271, and then head 2, track 271, and so on. There's no need for a head movement, but the disk can suck up a lot of data.

There is, then, a relationship between all of the tracks labeled 271 in this example. Taken together, they become a virtual cylinder. (Tracks are circular, and if you pile a bunch of circles up on each other, you get a cylinder.) You can see the relationship of tracks and cylinders in Figure 10.4.

The number of tracks per surface is identical to the number of cylinders; therefore, most manufacturers do not report the number of tracks, they report the number of cylinders. Although the two terms mean different things, cylinders and tracks are used synonymously.

FIGURE 10.4:

The relationship of tracks and cylinders on a disk

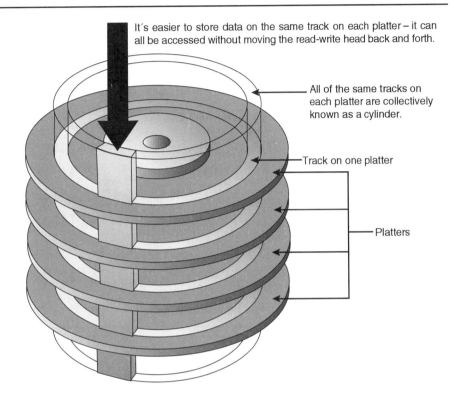

It's easier to store data on the same track on each platter – it can all be accessed without moving the read-write head back and forth.

All of the same tracks on each platter are collectively known as a cylinder.

Track on one platter

Platters

Sectors

Each surface is then figuratively divided up with cuts, like a pie. Floppies typically divide tracks up into 8 to 18 sectors apiece. Take a look at Figure 10.5.

FIGURE 10.5:

Tracks and sectors on a floppy

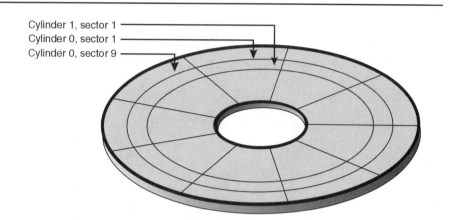

Cylinder 1, sector 1
Cylinder 0, sector 1
Cylinder 0, sector 9

Both hard and floppy disk devices typically store 512 bytes on a sector—0.5K of data, as 1K = 1024. (See Figure 10.6.)

FIGURE 10.6:

Each sector typically contains 512 bytes of data

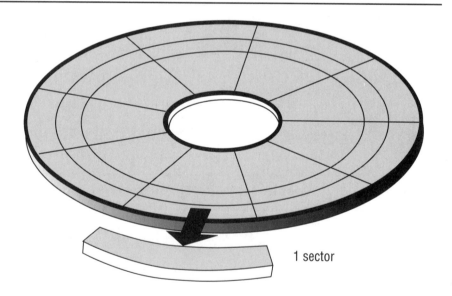

1 sector

Summarizing, then, a 1.44MB floppy is composed of:

- Two sides or surfaces (or heads)
- 80 tracks or cylinders per side
- 18 sectors per track
- 0.5K bytes per sector

So:

- $2 \times 80 \times 18 \times 0.5K = 1.44MB$ bytes

Now compare the specs on a 10MB XT hard disk, the simplest hard disk I've ever seen:

- Four surfaces
- 305 tracks on each surface
- 17 sectors to a track
- 0.5K bytes on each sector

So:

- $4 \times 305 \times 17 \times 0.5K = 10,370K$ bytes

As you examine other disks, you will find that the 512 bytes per sector is pretty constant. The number of tracks, the number of platters, and the number of sectors vary. Most manufacturers do not report the number of platters, but instead the number of heads, which equals the number of surfaces. For example, consider a more modern disk:

- 16383 cylinders
- 16 heads for storing data
- 63 sectors per track
- 512 bytes (0.5K) of data on each sector

Total all that up, and you get roughly a 8.4GB drive. (One costs about $100. Let me tell you about the 32MB drive that I bought for a thousand bucks in 1983...)

Zone Bit Recording (ZBR)

Before leaving the subject of sectors, it's worth mentioning that the diagrams that you've seen in this book so far have all depicted drives as having a constant number of sectors per track. That's not always the case.

Placing differing numbers of sectors per track on a disk surface is called *zone bit recording*, or *ZBR*. Consumer demand for greater and greater capacity on smaller and smaller drives, in combination with cheaper and faster electronics, has led to a growth in the use of ZBR.

Most software that you run on a computer won't know that your disk has ZBR. Because most computer software assumes that there are a constant number of sectors per track, ZBR drives keep that software happy by pretending that their drives contain a constant number of sectors per track.

One kind of disk that you'll run into that is *always* ZBR is a CD-ROM. Rather than concentric tracks, CD-ROMs are one long continuous spiral, like the grooves of a phonograph. CD-ROMs solve the "how does the hardware handle varying numbers of sectors?" problem by actually varying the speed of the drive motor depending on which part of the disk is being read; more on CD-ROMs in Chapter 24, "An Overview of CD-ROM."

Sector Translation and Logical Block Addressing (LBA)

The biggest problem with the BIOS-driven constraints for disks wasn't that it was hard to support drives with 500 heads, because there weren't any of those around. The bigger problem was that there are a *lot* of drives with more than 1024 cylinders.

Sector Translation

When you install a hard disk in a computer, as you'll learn in the next chapter, you've got to tell the computer how many cylinders, heads, and sectors that new drive has. Strictly speaking, you're putting that information into your system's CMOS chip. Some BIOS won't let you enter a value for cylinders above 1024. (Some newer systems allow you to enter larger numbers.) Now suppose you've got a drive that has 1600 cylinders and four heads. If you try to tell most systems that the number of cylinders is 1600, they'll just laugh. So some drive systems *lie* to the PC, saying that it's not 1600 cylinders and four heads, but rather 800 cylinders and *eight* heads. Do the math, and you'll see that the capacity is the same either way, but now the BIOS is happy. The BIOS then issues commands to an 800-cylinder, eight-head disk, and those imaginary coordinates get translated by the drive subsystem into a 1600-cylinder, four-head set of "true" coordinates. That's called *sector translation*.

Some SCSI and IDE systems take sector translation to new heights by internally keeping track of only total numbers of sectors on the entire drive. Ordinarily, system software would say to a disk interface, "Get me the sector on cylinder 100, head 3, sector 20," which is called a "three-dimensional" sector address. But for these SCSI and IDE systems, the system software would just say, "Get me the 143,292th sector on the disk." All sectors are numbered one after the other, with no concern for their head or cylinder location. Such a sector-addressing scheme is called a *linear addressing scheme*.

So why is this a problem? Usually, it's not. But if you're running a low-level disk fixer like SpinRite, the program may have to reformat particular tracks on the disk. When it requests the controller to low-level format, say, cylinder 10, head 5, the controller understands the request to mean, "Format the *real* cylinder 10 on the 1600-cylinder drive—not the *logical* 800-cylinder." In the process, the low-level format ends up destroying data that the disk fixer did not originally intend to destroy. SpinRite detects sector translation and thus avoids these problems, but not all disk utilities do.

Logical Block Addressing

Sector translation gets a bit stranger for larger drives.

If you look at the BIOS listings for some of the newer drives, you'll find that some have specs that don't seem to make sense. For example, some claim to have *64 heads*! How huge is *that* drive? Well, physically, it's about the size of a pack of playing cards. How do they fit all of those heads—let's see, 64 heads would be 32 platters—into a drive about an inch high? The answer, as you probably suspect, is that they *don't*. The drive claims to be 64 heads, 63 sectors, and 611 cylinders. That's a total of 1,231,776K, 1203MB, or 1.17GB. (Remember that a megabyte isn't 1,000,000 bytes, it's 1,048,576 bytes. Similarly, a gigabyte isn't 1,000,000,000 bytes, it's 1,073,741,824 bytes. Don't be surprised, however, if manufacturers conveniently redefine the definitions to 1,000,000 and 1,000,000,000.) I mentioned a page or two earlier that I had a drive with 2448 cylinders, 16 heads, and 63 sectors. Do the math on that one, and you get a drive of just about the same size, and it's no coincidence: it's the same drive.

Careful readers will be scratching their heads at this point and saying, "Hey, wait, 64 heads were definitely impossible for a drive that's one inch high, but *so are 16 heads*. What's the story?" It's true; the drive does not have 16 heads. But that's what I had to tell the computer when I set it up.

You see, this drive, like many modern high-capacity drives, uses ZBR encoding. That means that there are a variable number of sectors per track. The problem is, as I just explained, that your PC's BIOS will insist on knowing the number of cylinders, heads, and sectors per track on your drive, and will refuse to use any drive until you provide that information. But my technical specifications for my drive say that it's got 3854 cylinders, six data surfaces, and no information on sectors per track. There's no way for a modern BIOS to just say, "It's got 3854 cylinders, six data surfaces, and a variable number of sectors."

In response, my drive's on-board electronics are designed to make the PC happy, and to *appear* to provide a nice, consistent number of sectors per track. No problem, really it's a kind of sector translation.

The problem is that the regular drive geometry that's exposed to the CMOS is 2448 cylinders, 16 heads, and 63 sectors. Sixteen heads and 63 sectors are no problem; 2448 cylinders are a problem.

The problem is solved by my host adapter and my drive working together with another kind of sector translation called Logical Block Addressing, or LBA. In the case of this drive, LBA rearranged the apparent geometry of the disk. What it ended up doing was to produce an apparent drive with fewer cylinders and more heads than the system saw.

Usually, LBA is a feature supplied by the disk interface. Occasionally, however, I've seen jumpers on a drive that must be moved in order for LBA to work with that drive. LBA's main job is to bypass DOS's quirkiness with drives over 504MB.

But it's a good time to find out some things about your disk drive. Turn to the end of the chapter to do an exercise on disk geometry.

Disk Performance Characteristics

Some disk/controller combinations are faster than others are. We measure drive speed by looking at how long it takes to find a particular piece of data, and once the piece of data has been found, how quickly it can be read off the disk. The first is called the *access time* and the second is called the *data transfer rate*.

Seeks and Latency

Reading a particular sector involves two steps. First, move the head to the desired track. Then, once the head is over that track, wait for the sector to spin under the head, then read the sector. You see this in Figure 10.7.

FIGURE 10.7:

Reading a sector on a disk

Reading a particular sector involves two steps:

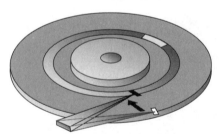 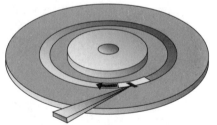

First, move the head to the desired track. That is called a *seek*.

Then, once the head is over that track, wait for the sector to spin under the head. The wait is called the *latency period*.

Now, moving the head takes a lot longer than waiting for the sector to come around. So low seek times (the time to move the head) are critical to good disk performance.

The formula to remember is seen in Table 10.3.

TABLE 10.3: Access Time Formula

ACCESS TIME	=	SEEK TIME	+	ROTATIONAL LATENCY PERIOD
Time to find a sector	=	Time to move to the sector's cylinder	+	Time to wait for the sector to rotate around and appear under the head(s)

The two components are called *seek time* and *latency period*. Seek time is the time required for the head to position over a track. Latency period is how long it takes for the desired sector to move under the head.

Typical Seek Times

Of the seek time and the latency period, the seek time is usually the longer wait. It varies according to how many tracks must be traversed. A seek from one track to the next track is usually quick—5 to 16ms, but most seeks aren't so convenient. A common measure of an average seek is the time required to travel one-third of the way across the disk. This is the one used in most benchmark programs. You might wonder, "Why not halfway across the disk, rather than one-third?" The reason is that most accesses are short seeks—just a few tracks.

Years ago, companies sold hard disks with seek times of almost 100ms; by the mid-'80s, seek times dropped to the high 30s, but IBM still considered it acceptable to deliver a system with a seek time of 84ms on its PS/2 Model 50. Nowadays, the range of acceptable seek times has narrowed considerably; the worst seek time you should accept from a new product is about 14 ms, but the best you'll find will probably be no better than about 8 ms. When I say that, I mean *all* computers; for example, my smallest laptop is a machine that wasn't built to be particularly fast; it was built to be three-point-something pounds, run a 486 chip, and include the largest 2.5-inch drive around at the time. The designers of this computer didn't care all that much whether the drive was 15ms or 10ms as long as it could fit into a small package. That drive is 13ms. In contrast, the high-speed Pentium that I keep on my desk has a Fujitsu SCSI-3 drive, a faster drive with a seek time of 10.2ms.

Seek times are built into a drive. There's no way for you to improve on a drive's seek time, short of getting a new drive. Seek times vary in part because there are two approaches to seeking: *band stepper* and *voice coil* head-positioning mechanisms.

Rotational Latency Period

Once a head is positioned over a track, the job's not done: now the head has to wait for the desired sector to rotate under the head. How *much* time is a matter of luck: if you're lucky, it's already there; if you're really unlucky, you just missed it and will have to wait an entire revolution. This waiting time, whether large or small, is called the *rotational latency period*. A common number cited is *average latency period*. This makes the simple assumption that, on average, the disk must make a half-revolution to get to your sector.

Many disks rotate at 3600 rpm. One-half revolution then takes 1/7200 of a minute = 60/7200 second = 8.33ms. This contributes to the amount of time that the system must wait for service. (Disks also rotate at speeds as high as 10,000rpm, depending on the model.)

The sum of the average seek time and the latency period is called the *access time*.

Today's hard drives use voice coils to move the heads back and forth. Named after the voice coil circuit used in telephone electronics, this is a coil with a cylindrical rod at its middle. When the coil is energized, the rod moves in or out of the coil, depending on how much energy is used. The rod is connected to the heads, so energizing the coil moves the heads in or out. You can see a voice coil in Figure 10.8.

FIGURE 10.8:

A voice coil

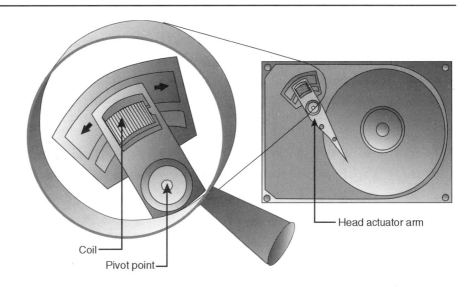

Coil

Pivot point

Head actuator arm

Electricity moves the heads, but how does the controller know how far to move the heads? Simple: head position information is encoded onto the disk *in addition to* the data. Some drives dedicate an entire surface to this information—which is why you'll see some drives report an odd number of sides. Such an approach is called a *dedicated servo* positioning mechanism. Other drives intersperse the head positioning information, allowing all surfaces to be used for data—that's called an *embedded servo*. One example of a dedicated servo drive was the old Seagate 4096. It claimed to have nine surfaces, but it actually had ten; the tenth was the dedicated servo surface used to position the heads, and as such was unavailable for data storage, hence the drive's under-reporting of surfaces.

Which is better? The voice coil seems more promising, because it is what engineers call a *closed control system*: it is self-correcting. The head moves, but it looks to the data on the disk to figure out exactly where to stop. In contrast, the stepper is an *open* system: it just assumes that cylinder 40 will always be 40 clicks away from cylinder 0. As time goes on, its position drifts further and further from the actual data (no self-correction). Also, the voice coil is faster. The voice coil is safer, too. As the head moves freely when the power is off, the heads would skitter all over the platter when the machine was turned off, but a spring holds the heads against the center of the disk. This means that whenever the computer is shut off, the drive parks itself!

Data Transfer Rates, Interleave Factors, and Sector Skew

Once a disk has found the desired data, how fast can it transfer it to the PC? This is called *data transfer rate*. Remember that there are only 512 bytes in a sector. This means that whenever an application requests, say, sector 1 of track 100 of side 2, it'll probably next need sector 2 of that track and side. In fact, most times when you need *one* sector from a track, you'll end up needing them all. So what's the best arrangement of sectors to allow them to be read at maximum speed? Read on to find out.

By the way, if you have a modern IDE or SCSI drive—which all of the new PCs have—then this discussion is irrelevant. All IDEs are arranged for maximum data transfer rate, and even if they *weren't*, you couldn't do anything about it anyway. This discussion *is* important, however, if you've got to maintain older PCs. For newer PCs, data transfer rate is determined by how much cache is on the drive, how fast the drive runs, and how quickly the disk interface can process the data, as you'll see in the end of this section.

When a disk—hard or floppy—is low-level formatted (more on this process later), milestones are laid down on each track called *sector IDs*. These IDs separate one sector from another, and are discussed in more detail in the section on low-level, or physical, formatting. What I *really* was asking earlier, then, is this: The IDs can be laid out in any order, so what order should the sectors be arranged in? The answer to this question is the optimal *interleave factor.*

On 1.44MB floppies, the 18 sectors are laid out like numbers on the face of a clock. Take a look at Figure 10.9.

FIGURE 10.9:

1.44MB floppy
interleave order

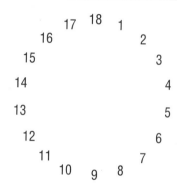

That's because reading all of the sectors on a 1.44MB floppy in one pass doesn't tax the controller, speed-wise. They have nine sectors on a track, and the disk rotates only five times per second. At maximum, the most burden a floppy could put on its controller would be to throw it 0.5K sector × 18 sectors/rotation × 5 rotations/second or 45K per second. Heck, the serial port on most PCs can run at almost that rate—consecutive sectors on a floppy is no big deal.

Hard disks usually don't work that way. The problem is that hard disks rotate a lot faster than floppies: hard disks spin at many times faster than that. In addition, you'll recall hard disks pack more sectors on a track. To see the problem, suppose we had a hard disk with the sectors in numerical order (called a *1:1 interleave*), as pictured in Figure 10.10.

FIGURE 10.10:

A 1:1 interleaved hard disk

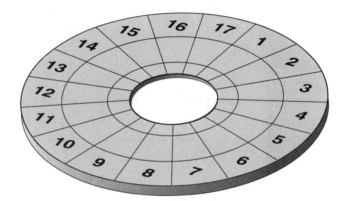

As the hard disk rotates, the minimum this disk will throw at the controller per second would be 0.5K/sector × 17 sectors/rotation × 60 rotations/second = 510K/second! Most hard disk controllers (and some computers) can't handle a half megabyte per second. You see, not only must the data be read, but also it must be checked for validity and then transferred to the computer's memory.

So let's look in detail at what happens when two sectors are read in succession on a 1:1 interleaved disk.

1. The operating system and BIOS request the hard disk controller to read a sector.

2. The controller instructs the disk head to move to the track and read the sector, as in Figure 10.11.

3. The head reads the data and transmits it to the controller.

FIGURE 10.11:

How interleaving
affects disk speed
(part 1)

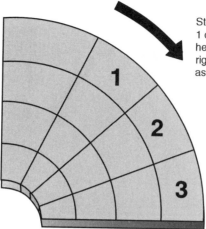

Step 1: An instruction to read sector
1 on a given track is executed. The
head has been positioned over the
right track, and now the data is read
as the disk turns under the head.

4. Because hard disks are fragile devices, the controller always includes *extra* data when it writes information to the disk. This information, when read back, enables the controller to detect whether or not errors have arisen in the data. The information is called the ECC (Error Correcting Code). It involves a mathematical function, and takes a little while to compute: see Figure 10.12. (The microprocessors on hard disk controllers aren't the fastest things in the world. I mean, you don't find too many Pentiums on disk controllers.) Meanwhile, the disk continues to spin, as in Figure 10.13.

FIGURE 10.12:

How disk error
correction works

Suppose these numbers have
been stored on a hard disk:

317
491
802

Now imagine that some of the
data has been obscured. Without
the extra information, we have no
hope of recovery:

317
1
802

An ECC (Error Correction
Code) adds redundant
information to the data on
disk so that in the event of
damage some data can be
recovered. A simple example
of redundant data is a sum:

317
491
802

1610

With the sum, however, the
controller can work backwards and
deduce the value of the lost data:

317
1
802

1610

<u>Must</u> be 491

FIGURE 10.13:

How interleaving affects disk speed (part 2)

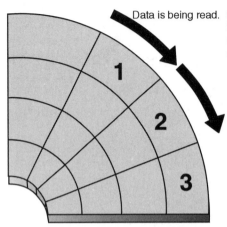

Data is being read. Step 2: The data has been passed from the disk head to the controller. The controller checks that the data was not corrupted while on disk. It does that check using a mathematical computation called an Error Correcting Code (ECC) test. Meanwhile, the disk keeps turning.

Data is being checked.

5. Once the controller has checked the data, it passes it to the BIOS and the operating system, which are also paranoid about hard disk data loss. The BIOS and the operating system have their own small amount of overhead—proportionately less than the controller's, but relevant nonetheless. Meanwhile, the disk continues to spin (See Figure 10.14).

FIGURE 10.14:

How interleaving affects disk speed (part 3)

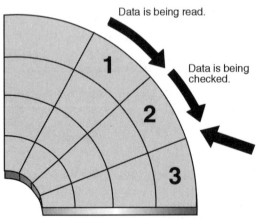

Data is being read.

Data is being checked.

Step 3: After the controller pronounces the data okay, the operating system and BIOS must be consulted again. Finally they're ready to request sector 2— but sector 2 has just passed by! We *are* in the perfect location, however, for sector 3. Why not, then, put sector 2 where sector 3 is now?

Request issued for sector 2.

6. Now that everyone is happy with the data, the operating system wants the next sector. *But*, while the controller, the operating system, and BIOS were taking so long with the last sector's data, the disk continued spinning. If we had put sector 2 right after sector 1, we would *always miss the subsequent sector*. That implies that we'd have to wait a whole rotation to get the next sector. This process would *always* occur.

Thus, with a disk with the sectors laid out clock-fashion, in numerical order, we'd always end up getting only one sector read per rotation. As the disk rotates at least 60 times per second, we read 60 or more sectors/second. Each sector holds at least 0.5K, so the "data transfer rate" from this disk is 30K/second, a rather poor transfer rate. (A 1.44MB floppy could outperform this disk, because it transfers data at 45K/second!)

But suppose we stagger the sectors, to give the controller time to get ready for the next sector. IBM did that on the XT, as pictured in Figure 10.15.

FIGURE 10.15:

A 1:6 disk interleave

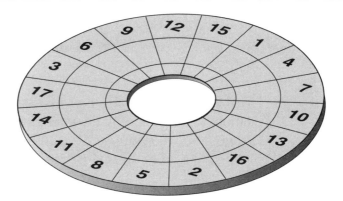

This is called a *1:6 interleave*. Start at 1, then count clockwise six sectors. You're now at 2. Count six more. You're now at 3. And so on. This then gives the XT time to do computations, and still catch the next sector. Inspection will show that the XT can read *three* sectors on the first rotation, or about 180 sectors/second. That means that we can get three times the throughput from an XT by changing from a non-interleaved disk layout to a 1:6.

As controllers get faster, they can compute error-correcting codes faster. IBM interleaved the AT disk more tightly, as illustrated in Figure 10.16.

FIGURE 10.16:

Hard disk with a 1:3 disk interleave

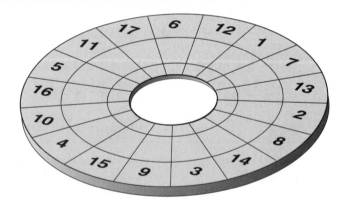

This is a 1:3 interleave factor. Six sectors can be read on a single rotation. Remember why the interleave must be a 1:3 disk—the sectors would be too close, and we'd always miss the next sector. The net effect would be, again, getting only one sector per rotation.

How important is the interleave factor? Take a look at Table 10.4.

TABLE 10.4: The Importance of the Interleave Factor

DRIVE TYPE	MAX DATA TRANSFER (K/SECOND)	SECTORS READ/ROTATION
HARD DISK (17 sectors/track)		
1:6	85	2.8
1:5	102	3.4
1:4	128	4.3
1:3	170	5.7
1:2	255	8.5
1:1	510	17.0

You can see that reformatting from IBM's default 1:6 interleave to a 1:5 interleave will improve disk throughput by 20 percent. Changing the interleave on an IBM AT from 1:3 to 1:2 will increase disk throughput by 50 percent. Other companies were guilty of the same thing: the AT&T 6386, for example, is formatted at 1:3, although it should be 1:2. The right interleave factor means that your controller, your computer, and your disk are right in step, pulling data off the disk as quickly as is possible.

So it's up to you to ensure that your machine disk is formatted to its optimal interleave factor. The optimal interleave factor is determined, again, by the kind of controller you have.

Recall that the interleave factor is set when you low-level format a hard disk. Some software writers have started offering interleave fixer programs. These both *measure* your disk's optimal interleave, then allow you to reset your disk's interleave factor without backing up, reformatting, and reloading. Their approach is really a simple one: just read a track, store it in memory, then reformat the track to the proper interleave factor and rewrite the original information.

Maximum Correctable Error Burst Length and ECCs

While this isn't really a disk performance feature, I mentioned this in passing a few pages back, and I want to give you the rest of the information on how disks can self-correct errors.

Disk systems are great as storage media, but they're volatile. From the first second after you lay a piece of data on a disk, it starts "evaporating." The magnetic domains on the disk that define the data slowly randomize until the data is unrecognizable. The disk itself and the media may be fine, but the image of the data can fade after X years. Put another image on, and it'll last for another X years. (If you're taking videotapes of your baby in the hopes that you can use them to embarrass her in front of her dates in fifteen years or so, you may be thwarted by physics, because the videotape is magnetic.)

Here's another way of looking at it. Suppose we stored data by writing it in the sand, at a beach. Write it today, and it's gone tomorrow: lost forever. Was the beach damaged—is that how the data was lost? No, the sand is just fine. It was the *relative positions of the grains of sand* that stored the data, and those positions are volatile. The same thing applies to magnetic domains recorded onto a disk surface.

Disk subsystems are aware of this, and so include some method of detecting and correcting minor data loss. (*Major* data loss can be detected but not corrected.) The controller includes *extra* data when it writes information to the disk. This information, when read back, enables the controller to detect whether or not errors have arisen in the data. The information is called the Error Correcting Code, or ECC. It was depicted in Figure 10.13. The basic idea is that the controller stores redundant information *with* the disk data at the time that the data is originally written to disk.

Then, when the data is later read from disk, the redundant information can be checked to verify data integrity.

The ECC calculations are much more complicated than the simple checksum depicted. They take time, so there's a tradeoff: more complex ECCs can recover more damaged data, but take more computation time. Some controllers let you choose to use an x-bit ECC. In this example, x refers to the number of consecutive bad bits that the ECC can correct. The original AT hard disk controller, for instance, could correct up to 5 bad consecutive bits. That meant that it had a "maximum correctable error burst length" of 5 bits. Newer controllers can usually correct up to 11 bits. They may be forced to stay at 5 bits, however, if used in an actual IBM AT—the IBM AT BIOS can support only 5-bit ECC. Newer AT-type clones can usually handle 11 bits (11 is better, if you can get it). Some of the newest drives are using special high-speed controller hardware to do *70-bit* error correction! They can correct 70 bad bits in a row—quite amazing. I discussed in passing a couple of pages ago the notion that a disk controller can reconstruct a small amount of bad data read from a disk.

Getting Good Data Transfer Rates on Modern Systems

I said earlier that interleave adjustment is of value only on older systems. How can you crank the maximum data rates out of your hard disk? Most of it boils down nowadays to choosing good hardware and, to a lesser extent, to tuning device drivers.

Modern SCSI-3 and EIDE host adapters can deliver megabytes and megabytes per second if they're set up right. The big things to look for follow:

- The drive must have a good data transfer rate. Unfortunately, most drives nowadays have a small amount of memory on them called *cache memory* (covered in the next section) that fool test programs into thinking that the drives are faster than they actually are.

- You've also got to have a fast disk interface. On IDE drives, you'd prefer to see a host adapter with the Enhanced IDE (EIDE) interface, because it can transfer data more quickly.

- The fastest disk interface in the world will run slowly if it's an ISA board. Fast disk interfaces must be built on top of fast buses. Get PCI- or VESA-based boards.

- *Don't* buy disk interface boards with tons of cache memory on them. Read the next section to see why.

Once you've got the hardware in place, you may have to tune a device driver on your PC. My EIDE system, for example, will run just fine without any special drivers, but the performance that it turns in isn't stunning. Add the drivers that came with the disk interface card, however, and you get the improved data transfer numbers.

Caches in Drive Subsystems

Disk drives are *slow*. I mean, *really* slow. Your computer uses RAM memory that responds to requests in tens of nanoseconds, but the disk responds to requests in tens of *milliseconds*—that's six orders of magnitudes difference in speed!

A disk cache seeks to use the speed of memory to bolster the effective speed of the disk. The cache is held in memory chips. Most drives nowadays have at least 64K of cache RAM right on them. Some disk interface cards supplement that with megabytes of on-board cache memory.

The three assumptions that disk cache programs are built on are:

- When you read or write something on a disk, chances are you'll read it again soon. This is the *principle of locality*— once you start working in an area, you tend to stay in that area. If you've ever noticed a quick flash of the hard disk light upon exit from a large program, you've seen the system reload a section of data from the hard drive's cache memory. Rather than firing up the disk and moving the head to reread a block of data in the same place again, the computer kept a copy of the file in memory, and reread it from *memory*, rather than from disk, which we've seen is so much faster.

- Another aspect of the principle of locality is that when you read one sector on a disk, you usually end up reading the next sector shortly thereafter. This implies that when we fire up the disk to read sector X, we might as well read X + 1, X + 2, and so on, because it's the seek time that takes the lion's share of the disk reading time. Those extra sectors that haven't been requested yet, but probably *will* be, go in the cache.

- Whenever you tell a program to read in a file, whether it's a word processing file, spreadsheet, or database, and you make changes, you'll soon thereafter tell the system to rewrite the file. But you probably haven't changed that much of the file, so rewriting the whole file is silly—but the system does it anyway. Some caches check a sector-to-be-written against the sector as it currently exists on disk. If there's no change, the cache tells DOS not to rewrite that particular sector.

Most computers nowadays have a disk caching *program* that uses these three principles to store data in some of the computer's memory set aside to do caching. In the DOS world, you use a program called SMARTDRV. Under Windows, a program called

VCACHE handles it, and other operating systems have their own cache programs.

But those are programs that you run like any other, programs that use your system's RAM. Why would disk drives include a little RAM? Why put RAM on controllers?

The amount of RAM on a disk drive is usually pretty small, between 32K and 1024K. The main *real* reason for it is to act as a holding area for a track or two worth of information. The point of buffering an entire track is simple: it would be just about impossible to manage one-to-one interleaving otherwise, and besides, the built-in sector translation that virtually every drive does nowadays requires some buffer space to juggle sectors around with.

There are two drives in this system, a high-performance EIDE drive and a lower-performance IDE drive. The EIDE drive turns in a buffered read value of 4688K/second, and the IDE transfers data at nearly the same rate, 4448K/second. Sounds like the two drives are pretty equal—but of course, they're not; it's just more likely that they both have 64K of similar-speed RAM chips on them.

You can see that when you compare the next transfer value, called the sequential read value. There, the EIDE drive transfers data at 3664K/second, but the IDE falls way behind to 1280K/second. Well, why not get a disk controller or host adapter with RAM right on it? There are some that offer that feature, but I'd caution you against it, for several reasons.

First, it doesn't do all that much, if anything at all, for computers running modern operating systems. They've got fairly efficient caching algorithms built into them, and so they've got the benefits of caching. On-board caches on disk interface boards just add another layer of data shuffling, and in my experience real-world tasks don't get done any faster with them. Think of it this way: buying 4MB of cache RAM for your disk interface card costs the same as buying 4MB more for your system, but buying 4MB for the system is general-purpose; you can use it for anything that computers need RAM for. Putting RAM on the controller, in contrast, means buying RAM that does only one thing.

The second reason is write caching. Interfaces with memory on them will delay actually writing data to the disk in order to make the disk subsystem seem faster. It's not a bad idea, *except* that sometimes your system resets itself without warning the disk interface. As the disk interface wasn't warned, it didn't write the data to the disk, and so you have the equivalent of turning off the computer in the middle of a disk write. This is *not* mere paranoia; every "version 1.0" of an operating system that I've ever installed on a controller with delayed writes caused major problems. That's why my bottom line recommendation on cached disk interfaces is: don't use them.

CHS and LBA

IDE drives are limited in size by a combination of requirements imposed by the BIOS and the IDE interface. IDE recognizes a drive and figures out its capacity by looking at the number of cylinders, heads, and sectors per track that it contains. These numbers are recorded in the *cylinder/head/sector* (*CHS*) bit field.

Two ways to circumvent this artificial limitation are to bypass the BIOS and to fool the BIOS during CMOS setup when it comes to accessing disk drives. The bypass method, proposed by Western Digital, is called auto-configure, and is designed for operating systems such as NetWare and UNIX. It uses the Drive Parameter Table instead of the BIOS to pass information about drive capacity from the IDE drive to the operating system.

The "fool the BIOS" method is called *auto-translate*, and can be used on DOS and Windows machines. When you choose this method during CMOS setup, you tell the BIOS to create an

Enhanced Drive Parameter Table during the power-on self-test. The initialization process fills this table with the appropriate values for all the drive characteristics, along with a checksum value to ensure the accuracy of the parameters.

The Enhanced Drive Parameter Table contains two groups of data relating to drive parameters. The first group comes from the Identify Drive command, while the second is information that comes from the BIOS. The information these two sources present to the operating system is a translation of information taken from the drive and is not dependent on how the CHS and IDE bit fields match up. The BIOS supports two types of translations based on information returned by the Identify Drive command:

- One provides a straightforward translation of BIOS CHS information to IDE CHS information.

- The other translates the CHS information that is passed to the BIOS into a 28-bit *logical block address* (*LBA*). The BIOS receives this LBA information and sends it to the drive's task-file register. It then sets bit 6 of the drive's select drive head register to indicate that the information in the task registers is LBA rather than CHS. From then on, the drive uses the LBA value to fetch the appropriate physical block from the disk.

The result of either of these translations is that the Enhanced Drive Parameter Table can now let the enhanced IDE interface access drives as big as 8.4GB. It doesn't require software or operating system changes, and the IDE CHS and the IDE LBA translations are mostly transparent to the operating system. The exception is with Windows 3.1, which has a 32-bit address-on mode and requires a new driver for either of the translations to work. Western Digital's IDE LBA-enabling driver is called FASTDISK.

Fortunately, virtually all newer systems have upgraded EIDE hard drive software, making it possible to use drives as large as 20GB with no modifications at all.

PIO

PIO stands for *processor input/output*. What it means is that data transfer is part of the CPU's job. The PIO data transfer method stands in contrast to the DMA data transfer method, which lets the drive take care of data transfer after the processor takes care of initial setup. The IDE interface usually employs PIO since, back when IDE first came on the scene, PIO was faster than DMA. DMA was slower because it was tied to bus speed, and the ISA bus of the time was quite slow indeed.

Buses are now faster; hence DMA is faster, too. The enhanced IDE interface supports these faster buses with Type B DMA (transfer rate of 4Mbps) and Type F DMA (for PCI local bus, transfer rates up to 8.33Mbps). Both Type B and Type F DMA require device drivers or BIOS changes.

The PCI interface also supports a new type of DMA transfer called Scatter/Gather. If your computer uses virtual memory management, you will find yourself in the situation that a requested block of memory is scattered across your hard disk in many different physical locations. The Scatter/Gather technique uses four 4KB blocks that make up a single 16KB block of memory, which can be fetched with a single I/O request instead of the four I/O requests and DMA instructions that would normally be required. Since you're using one request instead of four, you get faster response.

The VL-Bus uses both PIO and *block PIO* (*BPIO*). Block PIO deals in larger chunks of data but otherwise works the same way as standard PIO. For example, where PIO transfers a single block of 256 words (512 bytes), BPIO transfers *n* blocks of 256 words. (If you want to use BPIO, you need special drivers from Western Digital.)

ATA

Although your computer's processor controls both PIO and BPIO, local bus and enhanced IDE have made possible a method of PIO that the device controls. This is called ATA or AT Attachment. It relies on the I/O Channel Ready function, which was too fast for ISA but can now be handled by the newer VL-Bus. ATA pushes the data transfer rate up to 6.67Mbps, or 10Mbps for a cache-hit burst.

ATA is the protocol used to transfer data, status, and control information between a PC and a hard drive. ATAPI is an extension of the ATA protocol designed to let your computer recognize CD-ROMs and tape drives as though they were additional, ordinary hard disks.

Installing a Hard Disk

- Get compatible hardware

- Jumper and cable the drive

- Configure the system's CMOS

- Hard disk software installation and partitioning

- Setting up an EIDE drive

Installing a Hard Drive

1 Mount the new drive in the computer chassis (or removeable drive bay). Be sure to use two screws on each side!

2 If the computer has a removeable drive bay, mount it into the computer's chassis and lock it into place.

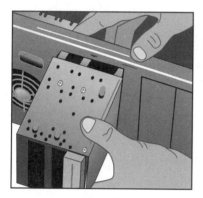

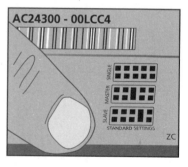

3 Check the drive's documentation (either in the manual or on the drive itself) for the drive's master/slave settings.

4 Set the jumper at the rear of the drive to signify either master or slave status.

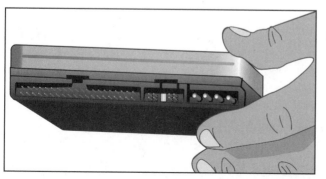

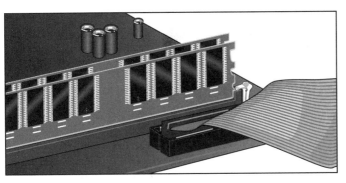

5 Connect the drive data cable to the EIDE connector on the motherboard (if you are installing the first or third EIDE in the computer).

6 Connect the free end of the EIDE data cable into the connector at the rear of the hard drive.

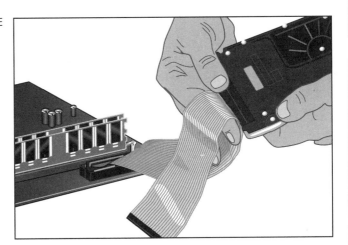

7 Connect the power supply's Molex plug into the power connector at the rear of the hard drive.

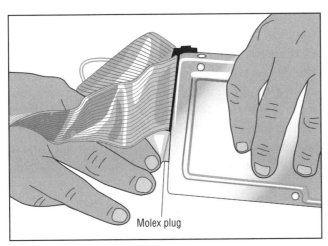

Molex plug

For as long as I can remember, hard disk prices have been in free fall. And that's good news for everybody—well, mostly. It's not entirely good news because just when I think I'm pretty happy with my computer, the drive prices go down, and I start eyeing a newer, larger, faster, cheaper (aargh!) hard disk. So, eventually, I give in, and I buy that new hard disk.

And then I've got to install it. Sound familiar? Then you've come to the right chapter. In this chapter, you'll learn how to do the software and hardware parts of putting in a hard disk.

Warnings and Apologia

Before we go on, however, let me warn you: hard disk installation has a lot of details to it. That's not because it's hard—it is not—but because of the radically different types of hard disk subsystems that have grown up and become popular over the years.

Even though we generically call them "hard drive subsystems," there are really two distinct kinds of disk installs that you might have to do, in roughly descending order of likelihood:

- IDE and EIDE drives
- SCSI drives

Although you may still find a few ESDI drives around, they are rare today and the older ST506 drives are so small in capacity that even if you do come across one, you'll most likely be obliged to replace it with a more current drive. These aren't as different as night and day, but there are significant enough differences that I was tempted to write a different chapter for each of these. That wouldn't have been practical, however, because the sheer amount of information that is common to each kind of drive installation would make the different sections too obviously repetitive. So I'll take a middle road, and I'll go through the generic steps to installing a hard disk, taking side trips as necessary to look at particular disk and hardware types.

Steps in Hard Drive Installation

Putting a hard disk in requires eight generic steps. Again, for any given drive type, a step may vary or may be left out altogether, but this is the common sequence:

1. Get compatible hardware to create a disk subsystem: a disk, a disk interface (host adapter or controller, depending on if it's SCSI, or IDE/EIDE), and a cable. Remember, if it's IDE or EIDE, chances are the drive will plug directly into the motherboard.

2. Jumper the drive (and, less often, the drive interface card) so that it can coexist with other drives, or jumper it to work alone.

3. Install, terminate (if it's SCSI), and cable the drive.

4. Configure the system's CMOS so that it knows that there's a drive there.

5. Partition the drive, whether you want the drive to act as one large drive or several smaller drives.

6. High-level format the drive to make it ready for your operating system.

As time has gone on, this process has gotten sometimes easier, and sometimes harder. Here's how to approach it.

Assembling Compatible Hardware

The hardest part about this step is just buying the right stuff. In the last chapter, you got some insights into what the main decision points are in choosing the right disk subsystem. Remember to stress compatibility, size, and speed in making your decisions.

Your disk subsystem should be based on EIDE or SCSI disk systems. The host adapter board should be built atop a fast bus, like PCI. Don't bother with cache memory on the host adapter; buy memory for your computer instead. When you're buying a drive, buy as much space as you can afford; believe me, you'll fill it up quicker than you can imagine. If the disk system is based on SCSI, then think about getting an external SCSI drive with its own fan and power connection; it'll help keep the inside of your PC cool.

When you buy a drive and interface, it's not a bad idea to check with the interface's manufacturer to ensure that it's compatible with the drive, and to check with the drive's manufacturer that the interface is okay. Despite the disk "standards," there are often quirks in particular drive/interface combinations. In the IDE/EIDE world, there are often problems when trying to interface two different drives.

Terminators

Disk systems usually support more than one drive on a single disk interface. Typically an IDE-based system can put two drives on a single interface card, and SCSI can usually put up to seven drives on a single SCSI interface. Most EIDE host adapters are actually a combination of an EIDE host adapter channel, which will support two drives, and an older IDE host adapter channel, which will support more drives.

Having two drives on a single cable talking to a disk controller is kind of like having three people on a telephone party line: you've got to have some etiquette to make sure that only one person talks at a time, and that everyone is identifiable (that is to say, everyone has a name, and so everyone knows whether or not a particular communication is directed to them).

This "how to share communications lines" problem is found throughout computer design. The answer is called a *bus*: for example, the expansion slots on your PC's motherboard share the PC bus, and the PC bus works equally well whether there are no boards in your bus slots or boards in every slot.

It's relatively difficult to build a circuit that works equally well with lots of load on it or no load on it. There are two common approaches to bus circuit design: open collector buses and tri-state buses.

The disk drives (floppy and hard) use an open collector bus. In order for the bus to work, it must have a resistor called a pull-up resistor at each physical end of the bus. These resistors are said to *terminate* the bus, so they are called terminators. One side of the bus is on the disk interface card, so we usually don't worry about it. For that reason, people usually only worry about one terminator—the one on the drive farthest from the disk interface card. (Farthest here means, again, the one on the end of the disk cable.) If you're installing a SCSI system, then you've got to be concerned about *both* terminators. (See? I told you that things vary from drive type to drive type.)

Even though the terminator is a resistor, it's not in a typical resistor package. It's in a chip-like package, so it often gets called the "terminator chip," although it isn't a chip. This bus circuit is designed to work best with a particular resistance value.

So one drive—the one on the physical end of the cable—must have a terminator chip. Any drive you buy will already have a terminator mounted on it, so you'll need to find it on the drive attached to the connector in the middle of the ribbon cable and remove the terminator from that drive. ("Remove the terminator" may mean just removing a jumper, or you may have to remove an entire chip on the drive.) If you leave both terminators on the drives, you cause *twice as much current* to run through the chips on the controller and the drive, slowly cooking them, so please attend to terminators. Leave both terminators off, and the bus is open and this makes signals float, introducing noise into the bus. So, either way, tend to your terminators—you want just *one* between the two drives, and that one should be on the drive that's on the physical end of the cable.

The only drives you'll have to be concerned about with are SCSI drives. There are no terminators to worry about in IDE or EIDE installations. You can find a drive's terminator location in the drive's documentation.

FIGURE 11.1:

Terminating a SCSI chain

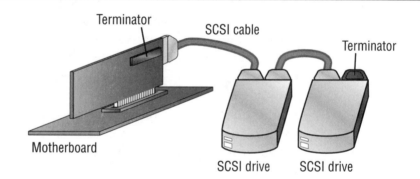

Drive Address Jumpers

You've read that most drive systems can support more than one physical hard disk. But if you put two identical hard disks into a system, how do the disk interface card and the operating system know which is which? Which is (for example) C and which is D?

SCSI drives have addresses, called *drive select* (*DS*) addresses. SCSI drives have three possible address lines labeled DS0, DS1, and DS2. Using combinations of jumpers or dip switches, you can assign the drive any address between zero and seven (see table 11.1). How do you address a drive? (No, not "Mr. Drive, *sir!*") On the *drive's* circuit board (not the controller board)— you'll see that there's a circuit board right on the drive, near the data connections—you will find a number of places to put a jumper or you'll find a dip switch. The places are generally labeled.

TABLE 11.1 Setting the SCSI Address

DS0	DS1	DS2	SCSI Address
0	0	0	0
1	0	0	1
0	1	0	2
1	1	0	3
0	0	1	4
1	0	1	5
0	1	1	6
1	1	1	7

Finding these things may take some study, and even when you've found them they're often not labeled. My experience is that you'll see at least four jumper positions, one for each drive address, although some drives offer six address choices.

For SCSI devices, you've got a choice of addresses zero through seven, but you'll use address zero for your C: drive. IDEs don't use address jumpers at all; instead, they use *master* and *slave* designations, which are explained in the next section.

Master/Slave Jumpers

What happens when you install a *second* IDE drive? Well, two IDE drives in a system would mean *two controllers in the same system*, which is, as you'd imagine, a prescription for trouble. (If you've forgotten why, look back to Chapter 6, "Installing New Circuit Boards (Without Creating New Problems)," for a reminder about circuit board conflicts.) Modern IDE drives are equipped for this problem, and have a provision to essentially shut off their onboard controllers. Installing two IDE drives in the same system, therefore, boils down to getting one of the controllers on one of the IDE drives to control *both* drives, and getting the other drive to essentially shut its controller off. In IDE terms, we say that one controller is the *master* and one is the *slave,* or that we must "slave" one controller to the other in order to make them work together.

When you've only got a single IDE drive, there's no question of master or slave, so you usually needn't do anything with jumpers. But once you add the second drive, you've got to configure both the old drive and the new, anointing one the master and the other the slave.

Careful readers will have noticed that I said "usually" in the last paragraph. That's because *not every IDE drive can be configured for mastering or slaving*. That's true mainly of older IDEs, but it's still something to look out for. I mention it in particular because the most common scenario for installing a second drive is one wherein you've already got a 40MB IDE drive from a computer that you bought in 1990, but now you've purchased a 500MB IDE to replace it. As you're going to install the 500, however, you say to yourself, "hey, why not keep the 40 in there; that way, I'll have *540MB* on line?" It's a good plan, but make sure that you *can* set one drive to slave and the other to master.

Cable, Jumper, and Terminate Drives

I'm going to combine two of my steps for discussion purposes, but they still happen in the order I originally described: first look at the drives and set their jumpers correctly, then install them in the machine.

Cabling methods vary among the different drive interface types; I'll start out with the ones you're more likely to see, and then move to the older, less likely ones.

IDE/EIDE Configuration

A typical IDE or EIDE hard disk has connections like the ones you see in Figure 11.2.

FIGURE 11.2:

Typical IDE/EIDE hard disk connections

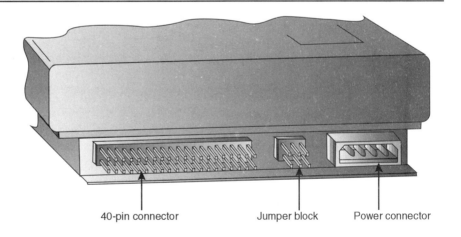

40-pin connector	Jumper block	Power connector

Like all drives, the hard disk needs a power connection. It uses the same old Molex connector that 5.25" floppies, tapes, and other hard disks use. There is only one cable for data and control information, a 40-wire cable. The jumper block on the back of the drive allows you to set whether this drive is a master or slave; usually, if there's only one drive, then there's a third setting—but check the drive's documentation to be sure. In Figure 11.3, you see an example from a 500MB drive.

FIGURE 11.3:

Configuring drive jumpers

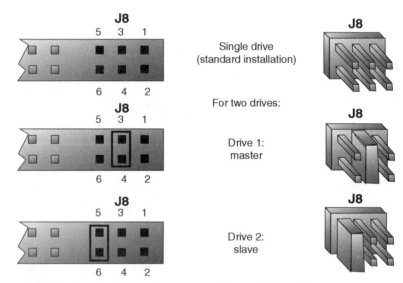

Configuring drive jumpers for a Western Digital AT-IDE 540MB hard disk drive

You don't put any jumpers on this drive at all if it's the only drive in the system, but put a jumper on the extreme left-hand position if it's the master, or jumper the middle if it's the slave. When installing a multiple-IDE system, try to use the newer and faster of the two drives as the master, and the slower one as slave. The reason I say "try" is because not every drive will "slave" to every other drive. If one way doesn't work, try it the other way. The only other jumper you might have to set on an EIDE drive would be an LBA jumper to enable or disable Logical Block

Addressing. Most drives don't require this, but I ran across it on an IBM machine once.

Once you've got the jumpers in place, then cable the hard drive to the host adapter. You'll see two kinds of cables, as shown in Figure 11.4.

FIGURE 11.4:

Types of hard drive cables

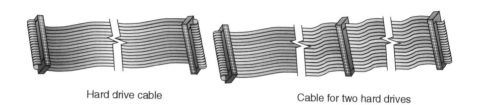

Hard drive cable   Cable for two hard drives

A multiple-drive configuration would look like Figure 11.5.

FIGURE 11.5:

Multiple IDE hard drives and a host adapter attached via a cable

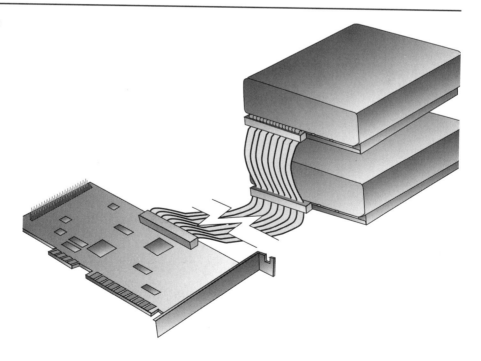

Note that it doesn't matter which connector the master or slave goes on. If you've put everything on right—no upside-down pin header connectors or forgotten Molex power connectors—then you're ready to proceed to CMOS configuration.

SCSI Cabling and Configuration

This is a topic all in itself that I take up in detail in Chapter 16, "Understanding and Installing SCSI Devices." I recommend that you read that chapter before installing a SCSI subsystem.

Summarized, however, here's how to do it. First, SCSI systems must be terminated. On a one-drive system, leave the terminator on the drive alone. On a two-drive system, take the terminator off the drive in the middle of the chain.

The back of a SCSI drive has a connector like the IDE connector, except that it has 50 pins (on SCSI-2) or 68 pins (on SCSI-3). Again, it doesn't matter which drive goes on what connector.

SCSI drives have address jumpers. Drive C: must be set to be SCSI ID 0 on most PCs. If you want to install a second SCSI drive, then you must set that to SCSI ID 1. If you want to install a third (or fourth or whatever) drive, then you can set those to whatever ID you want, but you'll need a special device driver in order for DOS to recognize that drive.

SCSI is a mite more complex to set up, but it's easier on the next step—the CMOS setup—and besides SCSI provides a platform for scanners, CD-ROMs, tapes, and other peripherals.

Configure the System's CMOS

Perhaps I should call this section "Introducing the Hard Disk to the Computer's Hard Disk BIOS." Your computer has low-level software, a set of machine language programs built into your computer whose purpose it is to control your hard disk hardware. That software *must* be on a ROM on your system.

Why must the disk startup software be in ROM?

Because if you want to boot from a storage device (like a hard disk), then the software to control that storage device must be already *built in* once you turn the computer on. Otherwise, the computer won't know how to access the storage device and load whatever operating system is on that device. It's kind of a chicken-and-egg problem: you need software in order to be able to read the hard disk, but you bought a hard disk in the first place so that you could put all of your software there. This software "vicious circle" is broken, of course, with ROM, because it allows a PC designer to ensure that a small amount of software is automatically present in the computer's memory just as soon as the computer powers up. All of that startup software is collectively called your computer's BIOS (basic input output system), as you've read earlier in this book.

The BIOS doesn't contain software to control every possible peripheral, simply because it doesn't *have* to. There's no need for the BIOS to support a scanner or sound card; you don't need them to boot. Most LAN boards have no need of BIOS, unless you have a diskless workstation and therefore need to boot from the LAN card itself.

Unfortunately, there's more to making a disk work than some generic software. The BIOS software must know some of those intimate details of hard disks that we've been examining for the past 50 pages or so: cylinders, heads, write precompensation, social security number, and the like. Which leads to another chicken-and-egg problem: where to store the details of a hard disk?

Well, one obvious answer would be to put the information into some kind of ROM. But that's not a very good answer, because ROMs were a pain to make in the early '80s. It would be ludicrous to tell a PC buyer that she'd have to go find somebody with a ROM burner to make her a configuration chip every time she bought a new hard disk. Nowadays, flash memory is cheap enough that someone could easily design a little flash memory into a system to keep track of disk characteristics, but nobody had ever heard of flash memory in 1982.

Personally, I think the best answer would have been to store the disk's hardware configuration information on the disk itself, on the first sector. There wouldn't be a chicken-and-egg problem because every hard disk has a first sector with coordinates "cylinder 0, head 0, sector 1." But that didn't occur to the first PC hard disk system designers, and, by now, you've probably figured out where the hard disk configuration information goes: into the system's CMOS. Most computers will store hard disk configuration information in the CMOS. *Most* computers? Sure. SCSIs don't need CMOS, and what about XTs?

The Evolution of CMOS Drive Tables

The first time I set up an AT-type system, I ran the SETUP program that came with the AT. Things started out pretty well, because it asked me easy stuff—"What day is it?" "How much memory does this computer have?" (Piece of cake—just count up the chips.) "What kind of floppy drives does this have?" (Still easy.)

Then it asked what kind of hard drive I had.

"Heck, no problem," I thought, and typed in Seagate ST225. (For the youngsters in the reading audience, that's a 21MB ST506 drive that was just the cat's pajamas in 1983. I told you, I've been at this for a long time.)

After I typed ST225, I *swear* snickering came out of the speaker. You see the AT wants a *drive type number,* a number from 1 to 47.

What's a drive type number? You read a page or two back that the XT world usually saw controllers that could only support a very small group of disks. In an effort to combat this, the original AT had a table in its ROM describing 14 common drives of the time. Remember, a big difference between the XT BIOS and the AT BIOS is that the XT BIOS didn't come with hard disk support; ATs, in contrast, were all built assuming that they'd have hard disks, and so their BIOS contains support for hard disks. The idea was that when you bought a hard disk for your AT, then the hard disk would look a lot like one of these 14 drives. If it didn't, then you couldn't use the drive.

Now, supporting 14 common drives sounded like a good idea; after all, 14 supported drives was better than four to eight supported by older XT controller boards. Of course, it only seemed like a good idea for a while, because drive types proliferated, so the next model of the AT had a BIOS that included descriptions of 25 common hard disks.

Do you suppose 25 drive types was enough? Nah, of course not, so the following generation of AT BIOS software included 47 drive types.

And then it stopped.

IBM's 1986 decision to use 47 built-in drive types has been adapted by most manufacturers to this day. And it has led to some troubles over the years. Since then, the market has split up, with different vendors taking a few distinct approaches to supporting different drive types. You'll see one of the two following situations on the computers that you work on:

- Some computers just have a fixed drive table; some have three entries, some have 60 or so, but 47 remains the most popular number.

- Some computers have a fixed drive table, but they add an extra drive type called the user-defined drive type. If the drive you're installing doesn't fit anything on the drive table, then you just select the user-defined type and then specify the number of cylinders, heads, sectors, and write precompensation on the drive.

The amazing variety of drive geometries today makes user-definable drive types a necessity, and most computers designed in the mid to late '90s include that option. Despite the clear usefulness of this feature, it was oddly enough the no-name clone vendors who embraced this option first; the big-name computers included this feature much later.

Today's computers generally identify new hard drives automatically and put the drive specs into the user-defined spot in the table for you.

What If Your PC Can't Match Your Drive At All?

Suppose you use the procedure outlined above to match your drive to your AT-type machine's drive table, and there's nothing on the drive table even remotely like your drive? It may be that even if you're willing to settle for a monstrous loss of cylinders, you still can't match write precompensation. Or suppose you're installing an RLL controller that formats 26 sectors/track: nothing in your drive tables will match that, as most of the drive tables out there are strictly MFM 17-sector entries.

In this case, you have three options:

- Get a new BIOS, one that includes your drive type, or a user-definable drive type, or get a BIOS custom-burned with your drive type. Again, that chip goes on your *motherboard*, not the disk controller board.

- Buy an add-on ROM in addition to the BIOS ROM.

- Use a device driver like SpeedStor or Disk Manager.

If you can't get a system BIOS ROM for your AT-type machine that allows user-defined types (not everybody offers them yet), you may just find that a newer system BIOS may be all you need. There are a lot of old IBM ATs out there that only have 14 drive types in their ROM: an upgrade to the more-common 47 types could do the trick. (Again, this is assuming that you need this particular computer; personally, I'd just spend $300 and get a bare-bones 386DX system, then move all the insides of the old AT over to the 386DX.) Or get a custom ROM. BIOS vendors will custom-burn a ROM for you with any drive you like. And while they're at it, they can change the sign-on message from "Golden Fountain AT 10 MHz" (or whatever you see when you turn the machine on) to "Jack The Hack's Personal Computer." A custom ROM will cost about $150—three times the cost of an off-the-shelf unmodified ROM. Most older 286- and 386-based AT-type machines have room for an extra pair of ROM. Some vendors sell add-on ROM solely to enlarge the AT drive table.

Finally, there *are* software answers, such as products called SpeedStor or Disk Manager. The way they solve the BIOS compatibility problem is to format most of your drive as something other than a hard disk, then require that you load a device driver to read the drive.

The idea behind these device drivers is that they only require a small DOS-compatible partition on the front of the drive, a partition just large enough to boot from. The rest of the drive is invisible to the system's BIOS, but that's okay: the device driver will handle that.

The strength of the device driver approach is that the device driver can present the remainder of the drive to DOS as a generic storage device. DOS is actually unaware that the device driver's space is a hard disk; all DOS knows is that there are lots of sectors that are available for storage. There's no limit on the number of sectors or tracks as far as the device driver is concerned.

The weakness of the device driver is that once you've installed the driver, the system must use the driver to access your hard disk. That can pose problems for alternate operating systems or even for games that stretch the limits of the PC a bit.

I'll discuss this in the next section, but let me say that in general I recommend against using a device driver to communicate with your hard disk. One reason is that it is *another* piece of software that must be functioning properly for your programs to use the hard disk and thus can complicate your troubleshooting hassles. Another is that a ROM is usable for any operating system, so you'll have no trouble going to Novell, Windows NT, or Unix in the future.

Well, now you've got the hardware end of the configuration out of the way. Next, let's look at the steps in a software installation.

Hard Disk Software Installation

Support for multiple operating systems has caused hard disk formats to become more complex than floppy formats. Where a floppy only requires FORMAT A:, a hard disk requires three steps. You may not have done all three, because the first one (or two) is often done before you get the drive. The three steps are:

- Low-level, or physical, format (this one's done during manufacturing)
- Partition creation
- Operating system (high-level) format (Windows 95/98, Windows NT)

Unfortunately, here again I must ask for your patience, because there's variation from drive interface to drive interface.

Partitioning

In 1983, IBM ushered in the era of hard disks in PCs with their XT. Nobody was surprised that IBM would introduce a computer with a hard disk, but we *were* surprised by the large size of the hard disk—*10MB*! That doesn't sound like much now, but it was twice as large as what most people were offering at the time.

Why did IBM put the large drive on the XT? Because they wanted to sell us *two* operating systems—DOS and *Xenix*. For those who don't know, Xenix was a UNIX variant that Microsoft was pushing for a while, back before they started selling OS/2, and *way* before Windows 95/98 or Windows NT.

The problem with having both DOS and Xenix on the system was that they didn't get along. Xenix didn't like DOS's file format, and vice versa. So the only way to get them to peacefully coexist was to draw a line down the center of the drive, saying in effect, "This is *yours*, DOS, and that's *yours*, Xenix."

So Microsoft and IBM came up with a way essentially to make a 10MB drive into two 5MB drives. (Or a 6 and a 4, or a 2 and an 8, or whatever; you can chop up a drive just about any way you like.) That "chopping up" became known as *partitioning*.

You must partition a drive in order to use it. Even if you're going to give it all to DOS, you've still got to create a partition. The program that we use most often to partition a drive is FDISK, which comes with DOS.

You don't just partition a drive to make more than one operating system happy. You can also do it to convert a single physical drive into multiple logical drives. For example, suppose you had a single 8GB drive. You could make it just one drive, named C: or you could divide it up into four logical drives named C:, D:, E: and F:. Their sizes could then be any combination that added up to 8GB—perhaps C: could be 2GB, D:, 2GB, E:, 1GB, and F:, 3GB.

Partitioning Options

Through the years, partitioning has fallen in and out of fashion. Originally, most of us just partitioned our 20MB drives as one big drive and thanked our lucky stars that we had such a large drive. Then, in the mid-'80s, people started buying drives bigger than 32MB, which caused problems because DOS 3.3 couldn't support partitions larger than that size. As a result, people with drives larger than 32MB had to partition the drives up into 32MB logical drives. Real power users in those days had 120MB drives that they had to divide up into a 32MB C:, 32MB D:, 32MB E:, and 24MB F:. It was a pain, but it was the only option.

Nowadays, people partition their drives for two reasons: to support multiple operating systems (history repeats itself, although this time it's Windows NT, Linux, Unix, and Windows 98 that are on the partitions, rather than Xenix), and to use disk space more efficiently.

Efficient Partitions: Clusters and Disks

What do I mean by "use disk space more efficiently?" Well, first of all, I'm talking about systems using Windows 95/98. Windows NT and OS/2 systems using their native file systems don't have the efficiency problem that I'm about to describe.

The name of the file system used in all versions of Windows is called the *file allocation table* (*FAT*) system. One of the cornerstones of FAT organization is the fact that a FAT-based system allocates space to files in units called *clusters*. A cluster is an area on a hard disk ranging from 2K to 64K. (Floppies can have smaller clusters.) The important part about clusters is this: when a program writes a file to disk, it gets the disk space allocated to it by the operating system. When a FAT-based operating system (again, like Windows) allocates space, it does it cluster by cluster. Each cluster is allocated to one, and only one, file. The *size* of a cluster on a logical drive is determined by the size of the logical drive, as you can see in Tables 11.3 and 11.4.

TABLE 11.3: Relationship between Logical Drive Size and Cluster Size: FAT16

SIZE OF LOGICAL DRIVE (IN MB)	CLUSTER SIZE (IN K)
0–16	4
16–127	2
128–255	4
256–511	8
512–1023	16
1024–2047	32
2048–4095	64

TABLE 11.4: Relationship between Logical Drive Size and Cluster Size: FAT32

SIZE OF LOGICAL DRIVE	CLUSTER SIZE (IN K)
> 260MB	4
> 8GB	8
> 60GB	16
> 2 Terrabytes	32

Using FAT16

Suppose, then, that you save a 400-byte file on an 80MB logical drive. Clusters on an 80MB drive are 2K in size, 2048 bytes, and so those 400 bytes are placed in this 2048-byte cluster, wasting 1648 bytes in the cluster. That's wasteful, but consider the greater amount of wasted space if you stored that 400-byte file on a logical drive 3GB in size, where clusters are 64K—65,536 bytes long. The cluster would have 400 useful bytes, and 65,136 bytes thrown away. Because cluster sizes are controlled by logical drive sizes, keeping logical drive sizes down keeps cluster sizes down, which leads to more efficient disk space usage.

Looking at Table 11.3, you see that the range of logical drive sizes that offer the smallest cluster is the range from 16MB through 127MB. If you had a drive that was 1024MB, then, you could divide it up into eight logical drives C:, D:, E:, F:, G:, H:, I:, and J:, each 127MB in size, and you'd even have a bit left on the end for a small logical drive K:. Table 11.4 shows similar information for FAT32 formatted drives (see the next section for more details).

Is that the right way to divide up a disk? Well, yes and no. If you make one big logical drive of it, then you'd end up with clusters 32K in size, and that's bad. On the other hand, one logical drive is easier to manage, search, and back up. So it's kind of a matter of temperament and taste. Years ago, I used a 660MB drive that I divided up into C:, D:, E:, F:, and G: partitions. I found the small partitions nice, in that I wasn't wasting a lot of space, but I found them annoying for several reasons:

- As you've probably found out by now, big drives are a blessing because they can store a lot of stuff, but small drives are a curse because they can store a lot of stuff—it's far too easy to forget where you put a file. If I know that I've got a file called THINGSTD.TXT somewhere on my C: drive, all I've got to do to find it is just type `dir c:\thingstd.txt /s` and DOS will search the entire C: drive. With C:, D:, E:, F:, and G:, there are five times as many things to do.

- I often found myself with 200MB free on C:, 300MB free on D:, 250MB free on E:, 400MB free on F:, and 350MB free on G:, but I wanted to load some software that required 600MB free. I had plenty of free space, but not enough in any one drive to load the software.

- Backing up the drives was a bit of a pain, because it took five separate backup statements rather than a single one.

Until 1995, I made heavy use of 500MB drives, so formatting them to a single logical drive didn't bring a heavy price, because 8K clusters aren't that baleful a prospect. Unfortunately, 1995 saw the introduction of cheap 1GB-plus hard disks, and the cluster size on a 1.2GB hard disk is *32K*. Wasting 32K for every little note I write to my assistant pained me, so I thought about it and realized that most of the stuff we do these days generates large files. In particular, as someone who assembles books like this, I've got a lot of diagnostic programs and graphics files. These files are all larger than 32K, and don't really cause that much wasted space, even on a system with 32K clusters. So I compromised by creating a smaller 250MB partition for small files, and kept larger file types (programs, graphics, and the like) on the remaining 950MB. As a side benefit, the larger 950MB partition is still big, but it's fewer than 1024MB, so it enjoys a 16K cluster size rather than 32K. It's a decent compromise, certainly, but the real answer is an operating system with a better file storage system. Of course, the answer to all these issues is to switch to the newer FAT32 file system that you'll find in Windows 95 OSR2 and Windows 98, or the NT File System that comes with Windows NT 4.

NT File System (NTFS) is a very powerful and system-intensive file system that provides many very awesome features for NT users and system administrators. It is, however, a high-level operating system file system, with management complexity to match. If it were to be converted for use with Windows 9*x*, it would consume most available base memory (640K) so that very few DOS-based games would be able to run and the system would be unstable. FAT32 is an abbreviated version of NTFS that works well within the requirements it has, primarily backward compatibility.

WARNING Windows NT 4 cannot recognize FAT32 partitions, so they will not be able to boot from a drive that has been converted from FAT16 to FAT32. Carefully consider your needs before proceeding.

Using FAT32

FAT32 makes it much easier to use a single partition on your drive because of its enhanced capacities and smaller cluster size, as seen in Table 11.4. In reference to that table, all new drives, with the exception of most consumer-grade laptop drives, are 4GB or greater in size. Consumer-grade hard disk drives are shipping in capacities from 2GB to 22GB in size and FAT32 is in a position to use that much space effectively. In fact, multiple partitions on a drive between 8GB and 13GB in size will not yield marked improvements in access performance.

The only real problem that may occur when converting a drive from FAT16 to FAT32 is if the target drive is compressed. FAT32 and Win98 do not do drive compression, so there could be problems. I've heard reports that existing compressed partitions or drives will continue to work under FAT32 and Win98, but I do not suggest you continue this trend. Very high capacity drives are readily available for very little money, so there should be nothing in the way of upgrading.

Other then that, there's nothing special about using FAT32. It is a very efficient and capable file system that offers many benefits to large and small drives alike. The only reason you should ever partition a large drive is if you want to. That's pretty nice.

How to Partition a Drive Formatted in FAT16

We've talked about the *why*, now let's look at the *how*. Suppose I've got that 1.2GB drive and I want to chop it up into some smaller drives. It might look like Figure 11.6.

FIGURE 11.6:

Partitioning of a 1.2GB drive

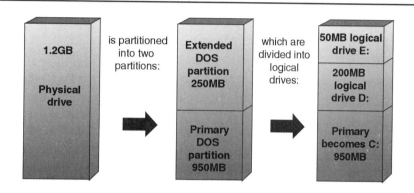

I'd use FDISK to do this. The disk gets divided into two partitions, a "primary DOS partition," and an "extended DOS partition." (You'll use a DOS partition even if you're using Windows 95 or Windows 98.) The first step is to divide the example 1.2GB drive into a primary DOS partition of 950MB and an extended DOS partition of 250MB.

Next, the extended DOS partition gets divided up into "logical" drives. You can have as many as you like, of any size. If you wanted, you could create drives D:, E:, F:, G:, H:, I:, and so on, each 1MB in size. (However, you should probably consider professional counseling if you'd really like to create piles of tiny logical drives.) For my example, I'll divide the 250MB extended DOS partition into a 200MB and a 50MB logical drive. Let's walk through actually doing this with FDISK.

Again, 1.2GB is a pretty big drive for DOS to be working with; but we ought to be trouble-free because I'm using an LBA host adapter, and DOS won't have any problems. There is another approach, the device driver approach that I'll examine later. My preference and my recommendation is that you use the LBA approach.

First I start up FDISK; it shows a screen like the one in Figure 11.7.

FIGURE 11.7:

Opening screen of FDISK

```
                      MS-DOS Version 6
                  Fixed Disk Setup Program
          (C)Copyright Microsoft Corp. 1983 - 1993

                       FDISK Options

   Current fixed disk drive: 1

   Choose one of the following:

   1. Create DOS partition or Logical DOS Drive
   2. Set active partition
   3. Delete partition or Logical DOS Drive
   4. Display partition information
   5. Change current fixed disk drive

   Enter choice: [1]


   Press Esc to exit FDISK
```

Your FDISK screen may look a little different from mine because I've got five options on my screen; the fifth option, Change current fixed disk drive, appears only if you've got two physical drives on the system. I want to create a partition, so I press **1** to create a DOS partition. The screen then looks like Figure 11.8.

FIGURE 11.8:

Create primary DOS partition screen in FDISK

```
              Create DOS Partition or Logical DOS Drive

Current fixed disk drive: 1

Choose one of the following:

1. Create Primary DOS Partition
2. Create Extended DOS Partition
3. Create Logical DOS Drive(s) in the Extended DOS Partition


Enter choice: [1]


Press Esc to return to FDISK Options
```

This is kind of a misleading screen. It seems to be indicating that you can create either a primary DOS partition, an extended DOS partition, or logical drives on an extended DOS partition. In reality, your only option is first to create a primary DOS partition. Try to create an extended DOS partition first, and it'll say Cannot create Extended DOS Partition without Primary DOS Partition on disk 1. The disk I'm working on is the master of an EIDE master/slave combination. The master becomes the first physical hard disk, and DOS requires that the first physical hard disk must have a primary DOS partition on it. It's perfectly acceptable for the second physical hard disk to only have an extended DOS partition without a primary, but the first disk must have a primary DOS partition. After I press 1 to create a primary DOS partition, the system thinks for a minute or two, and then I see a screen like the one in Figure 11.9.

FIGURE 11.9:

Create primary DOS partition screen in FDISK

```
                         Create Primary DOS Partition

        Current fixed disk drive: 1

        Do you wish to use the maximum available size for a Primary DOS Partition
        and make the partition active (Y/N)....................? [Y]




        Press Esc to return to FDISK Options
```

This question asks whether or not to just make the C: drive one big partition. We don't want to do that, so I press **N** and press Enter. Since I'm not going to do this all as one partition, I then see the screen shown in Figure 11.10.

FIGURE 11.10:

Defining partition size screen in FDISK

```
                         Create Primary DOS Partition

        Current fixed disk drive: 1


        Total disk space is 1203 Mbytes (1 Mbyte = 1048576 bytes)
        Maximum space available for partition is 1203 Mbytes (100%)

        Enter partition size in Mbytes or percent of disk space (%) to
        create a Primary DOS Partition................................: [1203]

        No partitions defined

        Press Esc to return to FDISK Options
```

I can then punch in either the target megabytes of the primary partition or a percentage, so I'll just enter **950** and then press Enter. The screen in Figure 11.11 then appears.

FIGURE 11.11:

FDISK screen after creating a 950MB partition

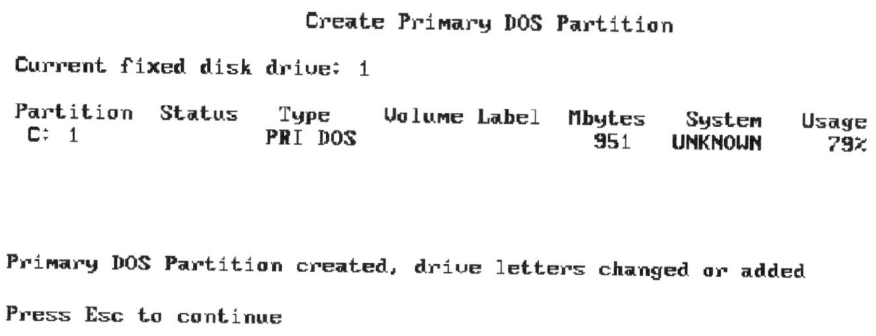

```
                              Create Primary DOS Partition

Current fixed disk drive: 1

Partition  Status   Type      Volume Label   Mbytes   System    Usage
  C: 1              PRI DOS                    951     UNKNOWN    79%



Primary DOS Partition created, drive letters changed or added

Press Esc to continue
```

Notice that it's already assigned the drive letter C: to the partition, because C: by definition is the primary DOS partition in the first physical hard disk. The System value is UNKNOWN because I haven't formatted it yet. As prompted, I press Esc to continue. That returns me to the original screen, but now it bears a warning message: WARNING! No partitions are set active - disk 1 is not startable unless a partition is set active. This means that while you're allowed to partition your drive into up to four partitions, you've got to tell the system which partition to boot from. That partition is called the active one.

I can remedy that by setting the newly-created partition to be active; just press **2**, and a screen appears like the one in Figure 11.12.

FIGURE 11.12:

Setting a newly
created partition
to be active

```
                              Set Active Partition

Current fixed disk drive: 1

Partition  Status    Type     Volume Label   Mbytes   System    Usage
   C: 1              PRI DOS                    951    UNKNOWN    79%


Total disk space is 1203 Mbytes (1 Mbyte = 1048576 bytes)

Enter the number of the partition you want to make active...........: [ ]



Press Esc to return to FDISK Options
```

Here's one of the all-time great dumb questions of PC history. Let's see now, there's only one partition on the hard disk, and the system needs to know which partition to set to active. Sometimes it's kind of hard to believe that Microsoft is the largest software company in the world, isn't it? I press **1** and Enter, and I get the confirmation Partition 1 made active; pressing Esc gets me back to the FDISK main menu.

Now let's create the extended DOS partition, and chop it up into two logical drives. Press **1** to get back to the Create Partition menu, and this time press **2** to Create Extended DOS Partition. You'll see the screen shown in Figure 11.13.

Take all of the space that it offers by pressing Enter. It confirms Extended DOS Partition created. Press Esc and you'll see a screen like Figure 11.14.

FIGURE 11.13:

Creating an extended DOS partition

```
                              Create Extended DOS Partition

Current fixed disk drive: 1

Partition  Status   Type    Volume Label  Mbytes   System    Usage
   C: 1        A    PRI DOS                  951    UNKNOWN    79%


Total disk space is 1203 Mbytes (1 Mbyte = 1048576 bytes)
Maximum space available for partition is  252 Mbytes ( 21%)


Enter partition size in Mbytes or percent of disk space (%) to
create an Extended DOS Partition.............................: [ 252]


Press Esc to return to FDISK Options
```

FIGURE 11.14:

Creating a logical DOS drive in the extended DOS partition

```
        Create Logical DOS Drive(s) in the Extended DOS Partition


No logical drives defined


Total Extended DOS Partition size is  252 Mbytes (1 MByte = 1048576 bytes)
Maximum space available for logical drive is  252 Mbytes (100%)

Enter logical drive size in Mbytes or percent of disk space (%)...[ 252]

Press Esc to return to FDISK Options
```

FDISK wants to create a single logical drive of 252MB, but I don't want to, so I replace the 252 with 200 and press Enter. The screen then looks like Figure 11.15.

FIGURE 11.15:

Creating a 201MB logical drive

```
                          Create Logical DOS Drive(s) in the Extended DOS Partition

Dru Volume Label  Mbytes  System  Usage
E:                 201    UNKNOWN   80%
```

```
Total Extended DOS Partition size is  252 Mbytes (1 MByte = 1048576 bytes)
Maximum space available for logical drive is   51 Mbytes ( 20%)

Enter logical drive size in Mbytes or percent of disk space (%)...[  51]

Logical DOS Drive created, drive letters changed or added

Press Esc to return to FDISK Options
```

Now you can see that our first logical drive has been created, at 201MB, and that it's got the drive letter E.

Hey, wait a minute! How come it's got drive letter E? Why not D? Because of the way that DOS names drives. I've got a second drive, and it has a primary DOS partition, so that gets the D: label. Look ahead to the next section to see the details.

FDISK shows that there's only 51MB left, so I press Enter to create the second logical drive. The screen looks like the one shown in Figure 11.16.

FIGURE 11.16:

Creating the second logical drive

```
                          Create Logical DOS Drive(s) in the Extended DOS Partition

Dru Uolume Label  Mbytes  System  Usage
E:                 201    UNKNOWN   80%
F:                  51    UNKNOWN   20%
```

```
All available space in the Extended DOS Partition
is assigned to logical drives.
Press Esc to continue
```

FDISK indicates that there's no space left. Press Esc three times, and the system will reboot; the partitioning is done.

How DOS Names Partitions

This one surprises people. If you have one physical drive with three logical drives defined on it, how are the drives named? Simple: the logical drive in the primary DOS partition is named C:, and the two in the extended partition are named D: and E:. But suppose you have *two* physical drives that are each divided into three logical drives? How are *they* named?

Answer: it depends on whether or not there's a primary DOS partition on the second drive. It is acceptable to DOS for the second physical drive to contain only an extended partition, unlike the first physical drive, which *must* have a primary DOS partition before it can have an extended partition. It is also acceptable to DOS if the second physical drive has both a primary and an extended DOS partition.

- **If the second drive has both a primary and extended partition:** then the primary partition on the first drive is C:, the primary partition on the second drive is D: (surprise!), the two (in our example) logical drives in the extended partition on the first drive are named E: and F:, and the two logical drives in the extended partition on the second drive are named G: and H:.

- **If the second drive has only an extended partition:** then the primary partition on the first physical drive is C:, again, and this time the logical drives in the extended partition on that first physical drive are named D: and E:.

The three logical drives in the extended partition on the second drive are named F:, G:, and H:. In my 1.2GB drive example, I ended up with three drives on my hard disk with names C:, E:, and F: because the second physical hard disk had a primary DOS partition, and so laid claim to the D: drive name.

Partitioning Large Drives with Device Drivers

As explained earlier, some vendors jumped in to solve the DOS disk size problem a while ago. It started with the 32MB barrier under DOS 3.3, but device drivers remain a small but significant part of the market. The way vendors originally got around the 32MB barrier was to format the drive to an alien, non-DOS format. They allocated a small area—a few cylinders—to a normal primary DOS partition. The rest was formatted to the alien partition. Again, this technique still works today; in fact, with a moderately sized drive like the 1.2GB drive I'm using for my example, a device driver would be the only option if LBA didn't exist. As a matter of fact, you may still have to use a device driver even if you have LBA, if your BIOS won't support LBA—and older computer BIOS software often doesn't.

Anyway, once you've run a device driver-type installer for a disk, then run DOS FDISK, and it'll report a small Primary DOS partition, and a large non-DOS partition. Reading the partition requires loading a device driver (Priam calls it EDISK.SYS, OnTrack calls it DMDRVR.BIN) at boot time. Then the alien partition shows up as drive D:, or whatever the next available drive letter is, so you've then got a small drive C:, and a large drive D:. The positive feature of this type of software is that if you are using an older system it allows you to support large drives without changing your version of DOS. (Another feature is that it allows you to make an ancient controller support drives it was never meant to support.) I have a few grumbles with the approach, however.

- Non-DOS operating systems, as I've mentioned before, cannot access these alien partitions. You would be unable to run OS/2 or Unix on your system.

- It's one more source of bugs. I'm not saying EDISK, DMDRVR, SpeedStor, Vfeature, or any program in particular is buggy. But the more software, the more bugs and potential software conflicts.

If the device driver or the `CONFIG.SYS` are corrupted, the partition is inaccessible. If the line `DEVICE=DMDRVR.BIN` is lost from `CONFIG.SYS`, the user's D: drive is gone. Again, although I avoid these drivers when possible, there are situations where they may be unavoidable, such as when handling a balky controller or when installing a 1024+ cylinder drive on a non-LBA compatible system.

What if the Drive is Larger than the System will Recognize

If you're using a system that has a motherboard that's a few years old, it may not be able to recognize a drive that's more than 2GB. Does this mean that you can't buy a new drive (there are few drives being made today that are smaller than 4GB)? Not at all.

You just need to trick your computer. Most new drives come with the tools you need to perform this little bit of magic. First, you need to get the BIOS to notice that you have a drive. Really large drives aren't even detected on some of the older motherboards.

To get the BIOS to identify the drive, first make it look smaller. This is usually done with a jumper near the IDE Master/Slave jumpers. It is usually called "sector limit" or something like that.

Once the BIOS acknowledges that your drive exists, you can run the utility diskette that came with the drive. As they all run differently, I won't go into the specifics of how to run the utility, but once you've run it, the drive will have it's full capacity (even though the BIOS doesn't know it) and you can use it. The only caveat you need to be aware of is when booting from a floppy.

Usually drives that are installed this way need to self-boot to load the drivers they need to access all of the space. Booting from a floppy can prevent this. So check the instructions on the driver. To boot from a floppy, you may need to press a key at boot time. This loads the driver and then returns you to a prompt that lets you run a floppy afterward.

Backing Up Partition Information

Having gone through all that work to create the DOS partition, you may wonder, *what happens if the partition information is destroyed?* This is a real problem: in this situation, the PC will refuse to even recognize that a disk exists. The data's not erased, but it might as well be. The way you solve this problem is with prevention: back up the partition information. There are several ways to do this, and I'll show you a number of them in the upcoming drive failure recovery chapter.

DOS Formatting

Finally, you run the DOS FORMAT program. It does not actually overwrite sectors and physically format hard disks. Disks have five areas, some of which we heard about earlier in this chapter and which you'll learn a lot more about in Chapter 12, "How The Operating System Organizes Your Disk." These are the five areas:

- **The *partition record* or *master boot record* (MBR).** This contains the disk partition information to divide the physical drive into logical drives. On auto-configure controllers, it also contains a few bytes that describe the disk. This resides on cylinder 0, head 0, sector 1. The remaining sectors on the first cylinder/head are unused.

- **The DOS boot record.** Originally, this contained only a snippet of code used to start booting up the system. In later versions of

DOS, other disk ID information was added. Among other things, the DOS boot record contains a pointer to the FAT, so if the boot record is damaged, the FAT will look strange to DOS. The boot record resides on DOS sector 0, which is cylinder 0, head 1, sector 1.

- **The FAT (file allocation table).** The FAT is a map of what clusters are associated with what files. DOS keeps two copies of the FAT, the primary, and the secondary.

- **The root directory.** The root directory is the basis of the tree-structured file system. There are 128 entries for a disk with a 12-bit FAT and 512 entries for a disk with a 16-bit FAT. *Entries* means room for directory information for a file. Twelve-bit FAT disks can only have 128 files in their root directories. Try to create a 129th, and you get a file creation error message.

  The root directory immediately follows the second copy of the FAT on the disk.

- **The data area (where the files go).** Actual user data goes here. It follows the root directory.

  - IBMBIO.COM or IO.SYS. If the disk is bootable, the first directory entry and the first cluster refer to the first "hidden file," IBMBIO.COM (for PC-DOS) or IO.SYS (for MS-DOS).

  - IBMDOS.COM or MSDOS.SYS. If the disk is bootable, the second directory entry will refer to the second "hidden file," IBMDOS.COM (for PC-DOS) or MSDOS.SYS (for MS-DOS).

The FORMAT command creates the DOS boot record, FATs, and root directory—it does not touch the MBR or the user data area. Since the FORMAT program does not destroy or overwrite data in the data area, this implies that *formatted hard disks can be recovered!* See Chapter 14, "Care and Feeding of Hard Drives," for more information.

There have been, incidentally, a few exceptions to this rule at various points in history. Earlier versions of AT&T, Compaq, and Unisys MS-DOS would actually torpedo the whole disk. There is no recovery from this.

A Note about Bad Areas

One of DOS's most important jobs is to ensure that unreliable, or bad, areas on a disk are not used. The FAT helps DOS avoid these bad areas.

Bad areas have either *hard* errors, or *soft* errors. Hard errors are problems in the disk surface itself, wherein it cannot record data at all. They are caused by manufacturing defects or later abuse. Soft errors occur when some data has faded on the disk to the point where it cannot be read. The idea is that if it faded once, it may again, so we'll cordon off the area and not use it again (kind of like a hazardous waste dump for your system). Programs like the Norton Utilities detect these things.

Hard errors are designated during manufacturing for newer drives. Soft errors, on the other hand, may allow FORMAT to read the sector just fine, so a cluster previously marked bad may not be re-marked on a subsequent format. Soft errors, recall, don't always show up when tested. The fact that FORMAT has not re-marked all of the bad areas as bad leads some people to think that they can get rid of bad sectors just by reformatting the drive. All *that* does is erase DOS's information about where bad areas exist, and it's not a great idea.

That's about it; you're now familiar with most of the general advice and methodology for installing a hard disk. In the remainder of the chapter, I present some reference information with notes on installing particular types of drives.

Reference: Setting Up an EIDE Drive

Historically, the PC was never designed to handle drives larger than about one-half a gigabyte. But since 1995, the price of 1GB and larger drives has become so cheap that most of us installing new drives will find ourselves installing "gig-plus" drives.

In this chapter I've touched on the problems of installing EIDE drives, but in the following section, I'll put it all together and take a step-by-step look into how to set up a typical EIDE drive.

Step 1: Get the Hardware

To make an EIDE storage system work, you need a few things:

- The EIDE host adapter. This is usually built into the motherboard.

- An EIDE disk *and its documentation*: there's not much to say here, except for the usual admonitions to have on hand:

    - Jumper settings to make the drive a master or slave

    - On some drives, the jumper to enable logical block addressing (LBA)

As you've learned, LBA is a kind of sector translation used by drives over roughly 500MB to slip past the BIOS's defenses. That means that *any* drive over 500MB destined for a DOS or Windows machine should have LBA enabled, and in fact most EIDE drives do. But some don't, and will never work in a DOS environment until you enable LBA.

Now, it may be just me, but I never seem to get documentation on a drive unless I do a lot of screaming at whoever sells the drive to me. The vendor always seems to assume that I can do some kind of Vulcan mind-meld with the drive and get it to surrender its secrets to me. Sadly, the closest I get to Vulcan mind-melds is when I create logical drives (sorry, couldn't resist), so I need documentation.

For some bizarre reason, drive manufacturers seem to have slipped into a consensus that they don't really have to supply documentation. Instead, they offer fax back documentation, put the documentation on bulletin boards, or sometimes use CompuServe forums or more often today, information at their Web sites. I'd recommend that you try to do enough yelling when you buy the drive that you get the documentation delivered with the drive, but if it's not in the box, then look for the vendor's Web site. (You can look in Appendix A for a list of drive vendors and Web site addresses.)

- Documentation for any existing drives that you'd like to keep. In many cases, I'm adding a 4.3GB drive to a system with an existing 1.2GB drive and I don't want to throw away the other drive. What I want to do in that case is to make the old (IDE) drive a slave, and the newer (EIDE) drive a master. But I can't slave the IDE unless I know how to set its jumpers to slave it.

- Cables. Many older IDE/EIDE cables (they're the same, just simple 40-wire ribbon cables) had connectors for only one drive. If that's all you were installing, then there was no trouble. But if you need to hang onto that older drive, then you'll need a cable with two connectors and, of course, enough slack to reach between the host adapter and the two drives. Alternatively, if your host adapter offers two separate circuits, one for the standard IDE drive and another for the EIDE, then all you need are two separate 40-wire cables. Given the choice, I'd rather run just one drive interface, and put the older IDE on the same drive channel as the new EIDE.

- A modern BIOS on your computer. Most LBA drives specify 16 heads and 63 sectors, which most BIOS software doesn't have a problem with, but also a total number of cylinders above 1024, which old BIOS programs don't like. Check that your BIOS has a user-defined mode which allows you to directly punch in a set of drive parameters—cylinders, heads, etc. Check also that the BIOS will accept more than 1024 cylinders for CMOS parameters.

With these ingredients, you're ready to continue.

Step 2: Install the Hardware

Installing an EIDE is the same as installing an IDE. As I mentioned before, some systems require that you enable LBA with a jumper; if the adapter documentation calls for it then set it up. Drives above 528MB always require LBA support.

Then figure out how you'll support the old drive, if you've got an existing drive to include in the system. As I said before, you'll either have a standard IDE connector and an EIDE connector, in which case you'll hook two cables and two drives to the two host adapter connectors, or you'll hang the IDE and the EIDE on the same cable.

Then you just plug the host adapter into the computer's bus, hook up the drive LED connector, screw the drive or drives in place, and put the top back on the PC.

Again, just to clarify: if you're using separate IDE and EIDE channels on a host adapter, then you probably won't have to do anything to the drives, because they are probably set to be masters already; that's the case if you've got two cables and two drives. On the other hand, if there are two drives on one cable, then one's got to roll over and play dead, and the other must assume the role of master.

Step 3: Set CMOS Values

Next, you've got to tell your system's hardware what kind of drive it's dealing with. (Note: With virtually all new SCSI and EIDE drives you never have to punch in drive geometry values, since the system gets them directly from the drive.)

User-Definable Drive Types without Restrictions

This is the best answer for older systems that don't autodetect hard drives. Here, you just punch in the cylinder, head, and sector combinations that the drive vendor tells you to.

Step 4: Partition and Format the Drive

In most cases, if you've enabled LBA on your host adapter and drive (again, recall that most drives don't require that you enable LBA, it happens automatically), then there's nothing more to say. You just use FDISK or whatever partitioning tool your operating system uses to create partitions, and then format the partition, again using whatever tool your OS supplies. Check the FDISK example earlier in the chapter for more information.

If you're using Disk Manager, then you'll use the tools that come with Disk Manager to do formats and partitions. EIDEs aren't that tough, they just require a few tricks—and now you know those tricks.

CHAPTER

TWELVE

12

How The Operating System Organizes Your Disk

- Absolute sectors and DOS sectors

- Clusters

- DOS boot record

- The FAT and the directory

- Logical drive structure

In the last two chapters, I've talked about the details of how your disk hardware works. But disk repair requires understanding disk software more than disk hardware. In this chapter, I'll show you how DOS (and Windows, for that matter) stores data on your disk.

In very simple disk-based systems, all you need to know about files is their location. In one early disk-based computer that I worked with, you'd keep track of files by noting their cylinder/sector/head location. It didn't have much of a user interface—you specified the address of a file, then the computer read it in and executed it. You'd generally start up the system by loading the word processor (not a great one, as you'd expect, but better than a typewriter). This was a bit cumbersome because, you see, if I lost the address of my word processor that meant I essentially lost the word processing program forever. I couldn't say "execute the program WP," which would have been preferable, but rather "execute cylinder 0, head 0, and sector 1."

Once the word processor loaded, however, things looked much nicer. You could pick out a text file by name, load it, and work with it—you didn't have to know its address. That was possible because the word processor just took a certain number of sectors for itself, sectors that it used to store documents. The reason you didn't have to know the document's address was that the word processor kept its own little "directory" to the sectors that it had taken over for documents. You'd ask for a file, say LETTER1.DOC. The word processor would look up LETTER1.DOC in its directory, see that LETTER1.DOC started in some cylinder/head/sector, and note how many sectors it was. Then the word processor would load up those sectors, and away you go.

That was a nice, simple system, but it had a few major drawbacks. The biggest problem was that only the word processor knew that the files existed. The BASIC interpreter or the simple database manager that came with the system was totally ignorant of the files, as they were totally ignorant of the directory that the word processor kept for its own personal uses. It also lacked most of the pieces of basic file maintenance. Space wasn't recovered well when files were erased, data recovery tools didn't exist, and if the disks hadn't been small floppies, the system probably would never have worked. Using such a system to manage a hard disk would be silly.

That's a major reason why we have DOS and Windows (despite the Microsoft claims, Windows and DOS pretty much store data in the same way). DOS provides a central space and file management unit. An area that Lotus-123 sees as a file named FINANCE.WK1 is the exact same area that WordPerfect sees as a file named FINANCE.WK1. That way any program can find any file and no program will inadvertently write over another program's files (unless something goes very wrong).

In this chapter, you'll learn that DOS manages files with a tree-structured directory and a construct called the File Allocation Table (FAT). You'll learn that space is managed with groups of sectors called clusters, a topic that we've discussed briefly already, but that I'll go into in more detail shortly. And you'll see how to use Norton Utilities to peek into your disk's structure and see how normal files are organized—so it's easy to restore normalcy when recovering data.

How DOS Organizes Disk Areas: Overview

You're now familiar with some terms: you know of tracks, cylinders, and such. Each OS organizes data in its own way. DOS sees data in the following way:

- Disks are divided into *absolute*, or *physical*, sectors.

- Absolute sectors map into *DOS* sectors.

- The DOS sectors are grouped into clusters.

- A file's *directory entry* includes the first cluster number in the file. That is the initial pointer into something called the file allocation table (FAT). The FAT keeps track of where files are located.

- Then the FAT contains information that DOS uses to locate the remaining clusters. There's a FAT entry for each cluster.

- A FAT entry can be:

    - A number, a pointer to another cluster

    - A 0, indicating an unused cluster

    - A bad sector marking

    - An end of file (EOF) indicator

Absolute Sectors and DOS Sectors

Identifying an area on a disk by its cylinder/head/sector refers to what DOS folks call its *absolute sector:* cylinder x, head y, sector z, this is illustrated in Figure 12.1. I have referred to this form of addressing as three-dimensional elsewhere in this book.

FIGURE 12.1:

Three-dimensional addressing: identifying an area on a disk by its cylinder/head/sector

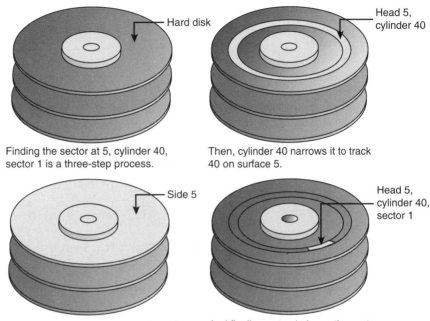

Finding the sector at 5, cylinder 40, sector 1 is a three-step process.

Then, cylinder 40 narrows it to track 40 on surface 5.

First, head 5 defines which surface the sector is on.

And finally, sector 1 shows the sector.

DOS doesn't directly use absolute sector locations. Instead, it refers to sectors with a single number called a *relative sector number* or *DOS sector number*. The number system is called relative rather than absolute because it numbers the sectors in order from front to back of a disk. There's no "cylinder 100, head 2, sector 1," instead there's "sector number 15,421."

When using relative sector numbering, DOS orders sectors by starting at cylinder 0, head 1, sector 1: this is "DOS sector number 0." (Note that cylinder 0, head 0, sector 1 does not have a DOS sector number designation: it is "out of bounds," so far as DOS is concerned.) The remaining sectors on the track are DOS sectors 2 through 16, assuming that there are 17 sectors on a track. DOS then moves to the next head, head number 2. The 17 sectors on cylinder 0, head 2 are the next 17 DOS sectors, number 17 through

33. DOS keeps moving up the heads until the cylinder is exhausted, and then moves to head 0 of cylinder 1. It continues in this fashion, moving further and further inward toward the center of the disk.

You can relate the absolute address of a sector to its relative sector if you know the following information:

DH = head that the *DBR* (*DOS Boot Record*) is located on, for a count of one

DC = cylinder that the DBR is located on

DS = sector that the DBR is located on, for a count of one

NS = number of sectors per track on this disk

NH = number of heads on this disk

Assuming that you have a C, H, and S (Cylinder, Head, and Sector) address for a sector, find its relative sector (let's call it RS) like so:

- $RS = NH \times NS \times (C - DC) + NS \times (H - DH) + (S - DS)$

For example, suppose we've got a logical drive D: whose DBR is on cylinder 100, head 1, and sector 1. The disk has 4 heads and 17 sectors per track. What is the relative sector number of the sector at cylinder 140, head 3, and sector 4?

DH = 1

DC = 100

DS = 1

NS = 17

NH = 4

Relative sector = $4 \times 17 \times (140 - 100) + 17 \times (3 - 1) + (4 - 1) = 2757$

The relative sector number is 2757.

How about computing the absolute location of a sector from its relative sector? Before we can do that, let me define some notation: DIV and MOD. *DIV* means do a division, but throw away the remainder: for example, 7 DIV 3 equals 2, not 2.33. MOD means do the division but *keep* the remainder—throw away the quotient. So 7 *MOD* 3 equals 1, because when you divide 7 by 3 you get 2 with a remainder of 1.

Given the same definitions of RS, DC, DH, DS, NS, and NH, we'd find the absolute cylinder, head, and sector like so. Remember this time we already know RS, NS, NH, DH, DC, and DS, but we're looking to find C (cylinder), H (head), and S (sector).

S = (RS MOD NS) + DS

Temp = RS DIV NS

Temp is a "temporary" variable we'll use and throw away. It makes writing the formulas easier.

H = (Temp MOD NH) + DH

C = (Temp DIV NH) + DC

Let's try it out on the example we've already done. We've got relative sector number 2757 on a disk with 4 heads and 17 sectors per track. The sector's logical drive has a DBR on cylinder 100, head 1, and sector 1. Collect what we know so far:

DC = 100

DH = 1

DS = 1

NH = 4

NS = 17

RS = 2757

And let's start calculating.

S = (2757 MOD 17) + 1 = 3 + 1 = 4

Temp = 2757 DIV 17 = 162

H = (162 MOD 4) +1 = 2 + 1 = 3

C = (162 DIV 4) + 100 = 140

So relative sector 2757 turns out to be at cylinder 140, head 3, sector 4.

This sector-numbering notation is also known as a *linear sector address*. Why use DOS (relative) sector numbers in the first place? One reason is that they are hardware-independent. All DOS assumes about the drive is that it consists of a bunch of sectors, and each sector contains 512 bytes. Another possible reason is that every 4 or 8 sectors are grouped into a cluster, and it's easier to divide up a nice one-dimensional number like a DOS sector than it would be to have to constantly figure out that cluster 200 is on cylinder 40, head 2, sectors 15–17 and cylinder 40, head 3, sector 1. (I just made those numbers up, so don't try to figure out where I got them from.)

Clusters

Next, as was mentioned previously, DOS sectors are grouped into clusters.

A *cluster* is the minimum space allocated by DOS when DOS gives space to a file. For example, if you create a file that is 1 byte long, you don't take up just a byte on the disk, but instead the minimum allocation—a cluster. Cluster size varies with the disk type and size, as you can see from Table 12.2. Floppy diskettes use clusters that are just one sector long, but a 10GB hard disk uses clusters that are many sectors long—4096 bytes (4K). That means that a 1-byte file on a single-sided floppy would take up 512 bytes on the disk, as would a 500-byte file. On the other hand, a 1-byte file would take up thousands of bytes on a 10GB disk drive.

TABLE 12.1: Cluster Sizes

DISK TYPE	CLUSTER SIZE (BYTES)	SECTORS/ CLUSTER
Single-sided floppy	512	1
Double-sided floppy	1024	2
3.5-inch 720K floppy	1024	2
3.5-inch 1.44MB floppy	512	1
5.25-inch 1.2MB floppy	1024	2
0MB–15MB logical drive	4096	8
16MB–127MB logical drive	2048	4
128MB–255MB logical drive	4096	8
256MB–512MB logical drive	8192	16
512MB–1024MB logical drive	16,384	32
1024MB–2048MB logical drive	32,768	64
2048MB–4095MB logical drive	65,536	128
4096MB–8GB	4096 (Fat 32 only)	* 64
9GB–16GB	8192 (Fat 32 only)	* 64
17GB–32GB	16,384 (Fat 32 only)	* 64
32GB and above	32,768 (Fat 32 only)	* 64
2048MB–4095MB	4096 (NTFS only)	8
4096MB–8GB	8192 (NTFS only)	16

Continued on next page

TABLE 12.1 CONTINUED: Cluster Sizes

DISK TYPE	CLUSTER SIZE (BYTES)	SECTORS/ CLUSTER
9GB–16GB	16384 (NTFS only)	32
17GB–32GB	32768 (NTFS only)	64
32GB and above	65,536 (NTFS only)	128

Think of the following analogy. There are two airline shuttles that operate out of National Airport, in Washington, D.C., where I live. They both promise a seat, with no reservation required, on a jet going from Washington, D.C. to New York every hour. Say you're the person running those shuttles and that the DC-9 jets that they use can accommodate 100 people. How many jets must you run this hour? If you've got 1–100 people, run one jet. Just one person—the 101st person—forces you to go to a second jet. There are no "half" jets.

Depending on what kind of storage medium DOS uses, different size "jets" are used. First the floppies appeared, then the 10MB disk drive, then the 1.2MB floppies, and the 16+MB drives. DOS versions 4.*x* and later support drives up to 512MB in size—they use a 16-bit FAT (65,536 entries) and clusters of size 8192. Today most new systems can support drives that contain many gigabytes of data.

You've seen that cylinders and heads are counted starting at zero, and sectors start at one, so it won't be *too* strange when I tell you that clusters start at number *two*. By the way, clusters start only in the data area, after the FAT and directory.

Note that the largest logical drives available are the 4GB drives. That's because DOS is built upon a processor architecture that can handle data objects up to only 64K in size, and the 4GB drive requires 64K-sized sectors. A bigger drive would require bigger sectors, and DOS can't handle sectors that big.

DOS Boot Record

The starting point in the DOS partition is the first sector, called, you will recall, DOS sector 0. That sector always contains an important piece of program code called the *DOS boot record* (*DBR*). That's the code that's actually used to boot up the system, in combination with the partition record and the so-called "hidden" files. I'll explain in greater detail what the DBR does a bit later, but for now understand that it resides in the first DOS sector.

As DOS has evolved into its various versions, the DBR has also taken another important role. There is a table in the beginning of the DBR that contains a bunch of disk ID information. Early versions of DOS pretty much ignored the table, but later versions need it. One byte on the table is actually pretty deadly—if set to a particular value, it keeps the system from booting from either the hard disk *or* the floppy. We'll see more about it in the chapter on bringing dead hard disks back to life.

The FAT and the Directory

As has been said, the directory and the FAT are a team in locating files. The directory tells you what the names of your files are, and the FAT tells you where the file is. Take a look at Figure 12.2.

The FAT immediately follows the DBR on the disk—it always begins on sector number 1. The operating system then stores two copies of the FAT—the primary FAT and one for backup—right next to each other. The FAT's size will vary according to how large the partition is.

The FAT is then immediately followed by the root directory. Directory entries are 32 bytes long, and the root contains space for 512 entries on a hard disk, and a lesser amount for floppies, depending on the floppy type. The exact number of root entries is stored in the DBR. Each root directory entry takes up 32 bytes. The data then follows the root on the disk.

FIGURE 12.2:

The file allocation table (FAT) and the directory work together to locate files

Each file has a directory entry telling DOS the file's name, size, last date altered, and the like.

The entry then includes a pointer to the FAT, which tells DOS exactly which sectors the file resides within.

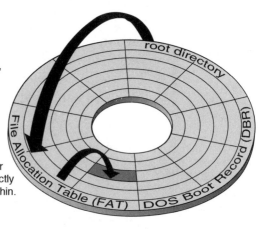

TABLE 12.2: FAT and FAT32

FAT and FAT32	NTFS
Cluster size determined by disk volume size	Cluster size determined by disk volume size and adjustable
Files are placed in first free location on disk	No special areas on disk requiring file placement
Supports only READ-ONLY, SYSTEM, ARCHIVE, and HIDDEN attributes	Supports FAT/FAT32 attributes and additional Time Stamp and compression
8 characters for a filename with 3 characters for file extension (255 for filename in FAT32)	Supports long filenames and FAT 8.3 filenames
Only one File Allocation Table (increased chance of corruption/lost data)	Multiple copies of Master File Table kept on disk

A file's name and extension are self-explanatory. Of course, while DOS and Windows 3.1 are limited to eight characters plus a three-character extension, Windows 95 and 98 can have file-names that are as long as 256 characters. You may not know about the attributes, however. The one-attribute byte is viewed by DOS as eight-attribute *bits*, six of which are used:

- *Archive* is set (= 1) if the file has not been backed up, reset (= 0) otherwise.

- If *hidden* is set, the file is invisible to most DOS functions.

- *Read-only*, if set, tells DOS not to allow changes or erasure of the file.

- *System* says, "Don't move this file."

- The *label* bit indicates that this directory entry is not a file entry at all, but the disk label. That's why disk labels can be up to 11 characters—the label name uses the space taken up by a file name and a file extension.

- The *directory* bit means that this directory entry does not point to a normal file, but rather to a subdirectory. Subdirectory information is stored in a file-like construct, hence the directory entry.

By the way, the "read only" and "archive" bits can be manipulated by DOS's ATTRIB command. Set a file to read-only with "attrib +r filename," and you won't accidentally erase it (–r removes the read-only status).

The starting cluster number tells DOS where a file begins; the FAT tells where the rest of the file is. The starting cluster number is vital, then, as it is our link into the FAT. Finally, the last 4 bytes contain the file size in bytes.

Each cluster on the disk has a corresponding FAT entry. Given an entry for cluster X, the entry must be one of the following:

- A 0, indicating that the cluster is unallocated.

- An EOF, (actually any value from hex FFF8 to FFFF) indicating that it is the last cluster in a file.

- A BAD, (actually hex FFF7) indicating that the cluster contains a bad sector or sectors, and should not be used.

- A non-zero cluster number, which is a pointer to the *next* cluster in the file that X is a part of.

Figure 12.3 adds to the ORDERS.DAT directory example an excerpt from the FAT with the entries relevant to ORDERS.DAT.

FIGURE 12.3:

Adding an excerpt from the FAT to the ORDERS.DAT directory

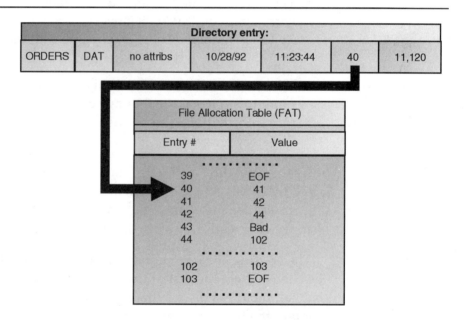

Reading this FAT excerpt, we see that cluster 39 is the end of some file—we don't know which file. We start looking for

ORDERS.DAT in cluster 40 because the directory entry *told* us to: entry 40 contains 41, meaning that 41 follows 40 as the next cluster in ORDERS.DAT. Entry 41 contains 42, meaning that 42 is the next cluster in ORDERS.DAT. Entry 42 contains 44, telling us to skip 43, which was skipped because it is a cluster with unusable areas in it—a bad cluster. Entry 44 tells us to skip up to cluster 102 for the next cluster, and 102 points us to 103, which is the end of the file.

Note that each cluster's FAT entry in a file links to the next cluster's FAT entry in that file. This is called a *one-way linked list*, one way because you can follow it in only one direction. (If this is unclear, look only at entry 103, the EOF for ORDERS.DAT. Looking only at the entry, what would tell you that 102 was the previous entry? Nothing. On the other hand, the FAT *will* tell you to go from 102 to 103.)

Subdirectories

Now let's add subdirectories to the above example.

The subdirectory structure in DOS is implemented with very little change over what we've said so far. Subdirectories look like files, as far as DOS is concerned, except (1) they have a size equal to zero and (2) their *directory* attribute bit is set. The subdirectory itself resides in a cluster or clusters, and is arranged identically to the root directory, *except* for the first two entries. You know the "." and ".." files that you see whenever you type DIR in a subdirectory? They actually have file entries. The "." and ".." are stolen from old Unix terminology. The ".." entry refers to the subdirectory itself, and the "." refers to the parent of the subdirectory. Those entries, like other subdirectory entries, do not have sizes. The entry for "." (the self-referencing one), reports *starting cluster* equal to the cluster that the subdirectory *itself* exists in. The entry for "`..`" reports the starting cluster of the parent directory. If the parent is the root, the cluster value is set to 0. I know that sounds complicated, so here are some pictures.

Suppose we have a subdirectory called `C:\JUNK`, and the subdirectory was created on December 31, 1998. Let's further suppose that the subdirectory itself is in cluster 5000. This does *not* mean that the files in the subdirectory are in cluster 5000—it means that the actual information about the names and such of the files in `\JUNK` can be found in cluster 5000. The root entry for `\JUNK` in the root directory would look like this:

Name	Ext	Size	Date	Time	Cluster	Attribs
JUNK		0	12/31/98	8:03 p	5000	directory

Suppose further that `\JUNK` contains only one file, `A.TXT`, created on January 1, 1999, that it starts in cluster 6000, and is 100 bytes long. If we looked in the contents of cluster 5000 to see the actual subdirectory structure of `\JUNK`, we'd see this:

Name	Ext	Size	Date	Time	Cluster	Attribs
.		0	12/31/98	8:03 p	5000	directory
..		0	12/31/98	8:03 p	0	directory
A	TXT	100	01/01/99	7:00 p	6000	no attribs

Silly though they seem, those two entries must be the first two entries in a subdirectory, or CHKDSK says that the subdirectory is invalid. (CHKDSK's "cure" is worse than the complaint, so when CHKDSK offers to convert the subdirectory to a file, tell it to take a walk. More on this later in the chapter on CHKDSK errors.)

`A.TXT` was a simple example, as it takes up only one cluster. (Why? Because it's 100 bytes long.) If the file were longer than one cluster, DOS would just follow the same procedure as with `ORDERS.DAT`—look in the FAT for entry 6000, read what's in there, and follow the FAT chain to the end of the file.

Let's summarize how a file in a subdirectory is read by DOS. Say we're reading file ORDERS.DAT from the subdirectory we've just examined, C:\JUNK.

1. DOS looks in the root directory for an entry with the name JUNK and whose directory attribute is set. It notes the starting cluster of JUNK—suppose it is 5000, as in our example.

2. DOS goes to the FAT and looks up entry 5000 to see if the subdirectory information extends over several clusters. Most subdirectories can fit easily in one cluster, so DOS probably sees EOF in entry 5000. (Why do most subdirectories fit in one cluster? Most hard disk clusters are 2048 bytes, and each directory entry is 32 bytes long. That's enough space for 2048/32 = 64 directory entries. Most subdirectories don't have more than 64 files in them.)

3. DOS reads cluster 5000, and assumes that the data is formatted as in the root directory. It looks for a directory entry called ORDERS.DAT and notes the starting cluster. Suppose the starting cluster is 40.

4. DOS returns to the FAT and examines entry 40. Suppose 40 contains 41; that means that the file is not only in cluster 40, but also 41.

5. Next, DOS continues examining the FAT, looking in entry 41. Suppose 41 contains 42; the file continues in cluster 42.

6. Assume that the remainder of the file search goes as in the earlier ORDERS.DAT example. Then DOS is done.

Notice that finding ORDERS.DAT in a subdirectory was the same as finding it in the root, except for the first two steps.

Logical Drive Structure

Ever since PC DOS 3.3 (MS 3.2), it's been possible to create multiple logical drives out of a single physical drive. This section explains how they are actually organized.

In the case of a simple disk system, the PC looks first to the partition table to find where a partition exists; the partition entry then points to the first sector of the partition, which, by the way, contains the code to boot from that partition. You've already seen how that works with the primary DOS partition. Suppose there were a 16384-cylinder, 16-head drive that contained a primary DOS partition in the first 8192 cylinders, and a Xenix partition in the last 8192 cylinders. That's one 4.2GB logical drive for DOS and one 4.2GB logical drive for Xenix. (NOTE: the drive has 63 sectors per track.) The disk structure would then look like Figure 12.4.

FIGURE 12.4:

Disk structure of a 16-head drive with a 4.2GB primary DOS partition and a 4.2GB Xenix partition

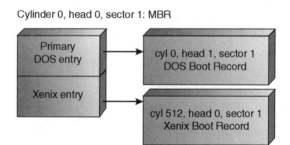

It would seem that a similar arrangement occurs with a logical drive (let's call it drive D: in this case) in an extended DOS partition: the partition points to the DBR of drive D: and everything is normal.

But it doesn't work that way. It *can't* work that way, as there can be *multiple* logical drives in the extended partition. We'd have a way to find the first logical drive, but how to find the others?

There's a one-to-one relationship between partition table entries and DBRs for primary partitions, but not for extended partitions.

DOS makes one extended partition look like multiple drives by creating a set of fake master boot records for the extended partition, one for each logical drive in the extended partition. The real MBR's partition table points to the extended partition. The first sector of the extended partition is not the DBR for a logical drive, but an extended partition table (EPT)—the first bogus MBR. Examining that EPT, we see a record pointing to the next track, where the DBR for drive D: (the first logical drive in the extended partition) resides. Let's use our 16384-cylinder drive again, but this time we'll make the second 8192 cylinders an extended DOS partition with a single logical drive. Take a look at Figure 12.5.

FIGURE 12.5:

Disk structure of a 16-head drive with a 4.2GB primary DOS partition and a 4.2GB extended DOS partition

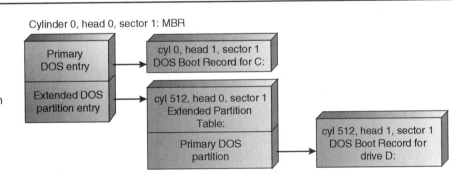

Note that, as in the case of the real MBR, the EPT wastes the rest of the track that the EPT is on. There is nothing in the sectors in cylinder 8192, head 0, sectors 2 through 17.

What if there are multiple logical drives in the extended DOS partition? Then there are a chain of EPTs. If the extended partition in our example were divided into two logical drives named D: and E:, the first EPT would contain two entries—the primary DOS entry for D: and an extended DOS entry pointing to the start of drive E. Examination of the sector pointed to would show *another*

EPT, this time with only one entry—a primary DOS partition for drive E: To illustrate this, assume that cylinders 8192 through 800 are used by logical drive D, and 801 through the end by logical drive E. Take a look at Figure 12.6.

FIGURE 12.6:

MBR to DBR relationship with three logical drives

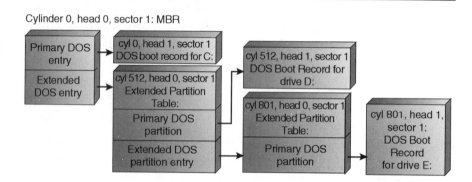

So the only way that DOS can find logical drives other than C: is to wend its way through the chain of EPTs on the disk. That's why FDISK shows a slight pause when moving from the Create extended partition function to the Create logical drives part—it's searching the chain. Once FDISK is done, the hard drive is partitioned, After that, all you have to do is format the partitions and it's ready to store data.

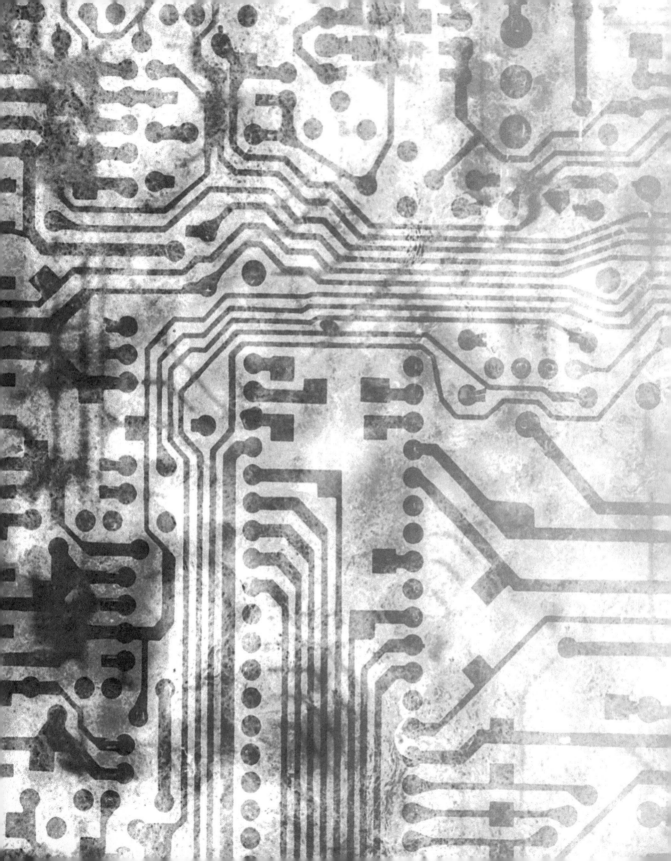

CHAPTER

THIRTEEN

Viruses

- What is a computer virus?

- How does a virus work?

- Suggestions to keep viruses away

- Virus attack procedures

- How to keep ahead of the game

13

Writing most of this book is a lot of fun. Fixing things is like putting together a puzzle—it's challenging and provides rewards in the end (a completed puzzle or a recovered hard disk). In either case, your only opponent is bad electrical power, buggy software, or (if you're supporting others) inattentive users.

Viruses are a whole different story.

With viruses, you actually have a human opponent and sometimes a competent one. Here's an overview of what viruses are, how they work, what they look like, and what to do to prevent them.

People often ask at this point, "Why do people write viruses?" I wish I didn't have to answer this question. The answer is, viruses are written by computer criminals. Some people just plain get their jollies making other people's lives difficult, and they think it's clever to write viruses. The fact is they're just childish. Virus authors exploit not cleverness but rather trust. Most viruses attack PCs via portals that exist because of *trust* in the computer community, not stupidity on the part of users. It's rather like this: suppose you lived in a community where everyone knew everyone else, so folks didn't lock their doors. How clever need one be in order to be a thief? Not very—the thief *knows* that it's easy to get into any house. Would you applaud or be impressed with the skill of such a thief? Of course not. That's what today's virus authors are—mere children screaming for attention.

There *are* people who get their kicks that way, however, and that's why antivirus software can be a nice support tool. It does the job that you and I have neither the time nor the knowledge for—monitoring the PC for common viruses and suspicious virus-like behavior. Good antivirus software should be able to prevent, detect, and remove viruses without destroying valuable data. It must also be easy to update, since new viruses are created every day, and software that can detect and clean every virus except the one you've currently got is less than useless. Good software, combined with educated users and regular backups, can make virus attacks less likely—and less serious.

What Is a Computer Virus?

Virus is the generic term that people are using these days to describe any of a group of willfully destructive computer programs. The three most common types of destructive computer programs are the *Trojan horse*, the *logic bomb*, and the *worm*. A virus is just a worm with a logic bomb or Trojan horse component.

Worms, Trojan Horses, and Bombs: Virus Components

A *worm* is a program that replicates itself. It creates an image of itself either in a file or at a particular location on the disk. Why bother duplicating itself? The original worm was intended only to be an experiment.

Worm Propagation

On mainframe and minicomputer networks, worms may use something like the electronic mail system to propagate. A famous "virus" (it wasn't a virus, it was just a regular old worm) in the early days of computing was the IBM Christmas message. Under IBM's worldwide network, mail messages used to include automatic "please forward to person X" commands. This Christmas greeting was sent to several users' electronic mailboxes with an added command: "When you (the message) get to an electronic mailbox, read that mailbox's list of known users and copy yourself to each of those users." So the Christmas message became a chain letter. The resulting exponential growth in messages (the first message went to five users, who each knew five users, who each knew five users, and so on) brought the system to its knees. The Internet "virus" is another example of a pure worm: all it did was copy itself on hosts on the Internet, dragging hundreds of computers to a halt. This kind of network propagation won't affect microcomputer users much.

When the first viruses were born, they were spread mostly through *bulletin board systems* (*BBSs*), electronic databases where people can log in and leave messages or communicate with others. Even though the Internet is a more popular communication forum nowadays, there are thousands of local BBSs still in operation throughout the world, typically run by amateurs out of their homes with a single modem line. Apart from public message areas, a BBS may provide archives of files, personal electronic mail, and any other services or activities of interest to the bulletin board's system operator ("sysop"). BBSs were a fairly obvious target early on for the spread of viruses, since most of the control was in the hands of the system operator, not the user.

The e-mail systems that we use today tend to require a fair amount of user intervention: to read mail with most Internet service providers (ISPs), I have to explicitly request messages. There's no way to send a message that can send other messages. It's the same thing with viruses spread over networks: you have to explicitly download an infected program and run that program in order for the virus to become active on your system. And note that I said program—you cannot transfer PC viruses in data files. Macro viruses are a different matter—they can be transported in data files. Although macros are not technically data (macros are programs), they can be attached to text files, so many users don't know that they are programs. You must be careful when you download Word, WordPerfect, and similar files, because they may have infected macros attached to them.

The major reason for including a worm component in a virus is to propagate the virus via floppy disks. The idea is that you infect your hard disk somehow (I'll explain the common ways a bit later), and a component of the virus becomes active, monitoring all floppy accesses. Whenever you do something with a floppy— read the directory, format it, copy files from it, whatever—the worm part of the virus "infects" the floppy, either by copying the virus to the floppy's boot sector, or by copying the virus into any

.EXE or .COM files that it finds. When you take the floppy to another machine and either copy infected .COM or .EXE files to the machine's hard disk or boot from the floppy with the infected boot record, the virus is transferred to the hard disk.

Trojan Horses

A *Trojan horse* program acts like the Trojan horse of Greek mythology. A malevolent program is hidden inside another, apparently useful, program. While the "useful" program is running, the malevolent part does something nasty, like erase your FAT and directory.

The earliest Trojans that I saw in the PC world were not viruses, but rather pure Trojans: there was no replication component. The first was called EGABTR. Uploaded to BBSs around the country, it promised to "show you neat stuff with your EGA." You ran it, and the screen cleared, then showed the message "Got you! Arf, Arf!," and the system froze up. When you rebooted, you found that the FAT had been erased from your hard disk. The only good thing about Trojans is that they're self-limiting: once an evil Trojan erases your hard disk, it has erased itself, also. Today, instead of running on private e-mail systems like BBSs, Trojans (which now typically do have a replication component) are finding their way to the Internet and the World Wide Web.

The next Trojan was rather crafty. Called STARS, it promised to show a moving starfield on the screen when run, and indeed it did. This Trojan was directed at BBS sysops. When a file was uploaded to a BBS, it was likely that the first person to run it would be the sysop of the BBS himself. When STARS was run on a BBS host machine, it surreptitiously located and copied the file containing the user's BBS passwords to another file. The sysop probably didn't notice the hard drive light come on while the copy operation was happening, so the new file sat on the BBS, waiting for the creep who uploaded STARS in the first place to call back and download the password file. Reasoning that people often use the same password for all their computer accounts, the criminal then had a bunch of names and passwords to try out on CompuServe or similar systems.

Pure Trojans seem to have gone out of style. Trojans instead show up in the virus world as the initial source of infection for some viruses. A virus that injects itself into .COM or .EXE files is also a Trojan, as it is waiting for you to run that formerly useful program: once you run an infected copy of dBase, you are waking the virus up.

Time Bombs and Logic Bombs

Third in this fell troika is the *bomb*. There are time bombs and logic bombs. It is a piece of code embedded in a program or the operating system itself that waits for a particular event to occur. When that event occurs, the logic bomb "goes off," doing some kind of damage.

Logic bombs have been around nearly since the beginning of computing. An early one showed up in a mainframe payroll program. The program's creator had inserted a clause in the payroll program that said, "If you find I'm not on the payroll, erase all payroll files."

Bombs show up as the more destructive part of viruses. They include instructions like, "If it's Friday the 13th, erase the hard disk," or "If the worm has succeeded in making 10 copies of itself, erase the hard disk."

Parasitic Viruses versus Boot Sector Viruses

In addition to classifying viruses as worms, Trojan horses, or bombs, you can classify them by their preferred habitat. Some viruses attach themselves to other programs, like lampreys; these viruses are known as *parasitic viruses*. Others, which prefer lodging in the boot sector of your floppy or hard disk, are known (not surprisingly) as *boot sector viruses.*

Parasitic Viruses or Program Infectors

Parasitic viruses begin their dirty work whenever the executable file to which they are attached is run. They may proceed directly to certain areas of the disk where specific files sit (like the partition tables or `COMMAND.COM`) or hide in memory for just the right moment. They are also called *program infectors.*

Another strain of program infector is made up of two split programs. One is the top program that will not register as a virus when a virus scanner runs, and one contains an algorithm that, once the first program is resident, changes part of the first program's code to make it a virus. It's sort of like a terrorist who gets through the security checkpoints at the airport, apparently unarmed, and then converts his umbrella to a shotgun once he's on the plane.

Boot Sector Viruses

Boot sector viruses generally prefer hard drives. A minority, including the "Stoned" virus, infects floppies. They are loaded into memory when the PC is booted from a drive that contains an infected disk. You're probably wondering, "What if the diskette is not really bootable (in other words, it has no `COMMAND.COM` file) and the screen displays the message `Non-system disk error?`" That doesn't stop anything, unfortunately. Once the computer boots from the infected disk, it's too late—the PC had to read the boot sector of the floppy to know it wasn't bootable. During the read, the virus woke up and sprang into action.

Multipartite Viruses

Just to make things maximally confusing, some viruses, like Ghost-balls, have a boot sector portion *and* a program infector portion.

Stealth Viruses

Some viruses are said to be "stealth" viruses. A stealth virus attempts to hide itself by keeping a copy of the parts of the disk that it infected, *before* it infected it. Then, when it detects that a virus scanner is looking for it, it shows the scanner the uninfected copy of the file, as if to say, "Nobody here but us chickens." Now, note that the stealth feature of a virus only works if the virus is active in memory, which will not be the case if you've first booted from a clean, write-protected DOS floppy. Always do that before running an important virus scan.

> **WARNING** Many program infectors (and all boot sector viruses) become "terminate and stay resident" (TSR) programs—which is a good reason to install a TSR scanner that can constantly monitor your system for viruses.

How Does a Virus Work?

Now you understand what a virus is and how it works. A simple virus might work in the following way.

1. The virus is introduced to your system with an infected .COM or .EXE file (an example is a Trojan horse), or you boot from a floppy with an infected boot record. Either this Trojan is hidden in an application program that has been doctored by the virus creator, or it is the Trojan portion of a virus that is injected into a program file or the boot record by the worm portion.

2. Once the program with the Trojan is activated, the virus is awakened. It installs itself in the operating system (a process

I'll explain a little later) as a logic bomb, waiting for an opportunity to (1) activate the worm and/or (2) activate the destructive portion of itself.

3. The logic bomb activates the worm portion whenever an acceptable host presents itself. Some viruses only replicate onto floppies from the hard disk. Other viruses infect any program file that gets activated, whether on the floppy disk or the hard disk. Every time the worm copies itself onto another disk or program, it activates a built-in counter that keeps track of how many copies it has made.

4. Eventually, the destructive part of the virus may be activated, either by an event, like running a program, a date occurring (such as Friday the 13th), or by a certain number of replications. When the destructive portion activates, the virus may do something as innocuous as flashing a message on the screen or as damaging as erasing the hard disk. I say, "may be activated," because some "viruses" are just pure worms—no dangerous part, except for the annoyance of their propagation.

Where Do Viruses Live?

Once people hear about viruses, they often get very paranoid. You must understand what a virus can and can't do, so you can understand how to avoid them and how to recover from them if you *are* hit.

A virus is just a computer program. The program doesn't run unless you let it run. Remember that the virus gets started through a Trojan horse process. Once started, the virus acts like a memory-resident program. Memory-resident programs (TSRs) live in memory, waiting to be activated.

The figure below illustrates how a normal memory-resident program works. The example memory-resident program is a keyboard enhancer program. Suppose you worked for a company called XYZ Manufacturing Industries. You get tired of typing the whole name out, so you buy a keyboard enhancer, and tell it that every time you type Alt+X, it should tell the system that you typed XYZ Manufacturing Industries. Look at Figure 13.1 to see how this works.

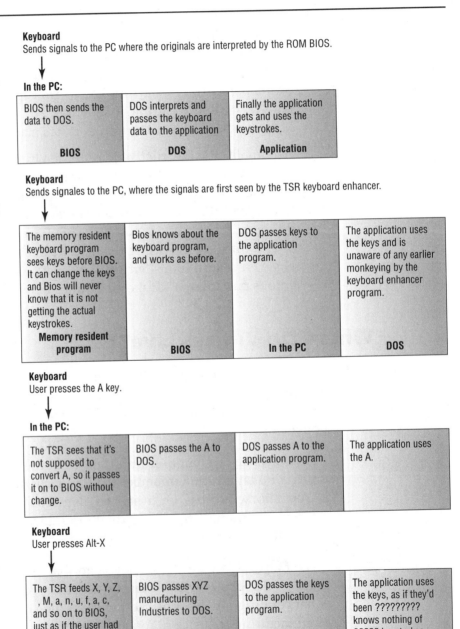

FIGURE 13.1:

How a normal memory-resident program works. The situation before a resident program (top). The memory-resident keyboard enhancer then installs before BIOS and filters any keyboard input (second row). In most situations, the TSR just passes keystrokes (third row), but when the user presses Alt+X, the TSR shows its stuff (bottom).

Keyboard
Sends signals to the PC where the originals are interpreted by the ROM BIOS.

In the PC:

BIOS then sends the data to DOS.	DOS interprets and passes the keyboard data to the application	Finally the application gets and uses the keystrokes.
BIOS	**DOS**	**Application**

Keyboard
Sends signales to the PC, where the signals are first seen by the TSR keyboard enhancer.

The memory resident keyboard program sees keys before BIOS. It can change the keys and Bios will never know that it is not getting the actual keystrokes.	Bios knows about the keyboard program, and works as before.	DOS passes keys to the application program.	The application uses the keys and is unaware of any earlier monkeying by the keyboard enhancer program.
Memory resident program	**BIOS**	**In the PC**	**DOS**

Keyboard
User presses the A key.

In the PC:

The TSR sees that it's not supposed to convert A, so it passes it on to BIOS without change.	BIOS passes the A to DOS.	DOS passes A to the application program.	The application uses the A.

Keyboard
User presses Alt-X

The TSR feeds X, Y, Z, , M, a, n, u, f, a, c, and so on to BIOS, just as if the user had typed them in herself.	BIOS passes XYZ manufacturing Industries to DOS.	DOS passes the keys to the application program.	The application uses the keys, as if they'd been ????????? knows nothing of ????? keystrokes.

Again, this is a useful, benevolent TSR program. Notice how it works: it installs itself in memory, then "goes to sleep" until something happens to awaken it. The kinds of things that awaken TSRs are typically:

- The keyboard (as in the above example): The Ctrl-Alt-Del combination will wake up some viruses, causing them to *fake a reboot*. This means that simply doing a warm boot will not de-install some viruses. When you suspect a virus, turn the machine off and then on again to reboot. Other viruses do bizarre things every certain number of keystrokes. One in particular is the Cascade or Italian virus, which causes letters to "drop off" the screen with each keystroke. Letters on the screen move from their current position to the bottom of the screen, making it look like they have fallen off the screen.

- The timer: Screen saver programs are TSRs that work off the timer, the mouse, and the keyboard. They monitor the keyboard, mouse, and timer, and shut off the screen if there hasn't been any activity after a certain number of timer ticks. A keystroke or a movement of the mouse tells the screen saver to reactivate the screen.

- The disk: TSR viruses are often activated by disk accesses. Every time a floppy is accessed, the virus may take a quick look to see if the floppy is infected and, if the floppy is not yet infected, the worm portion of the virus will copy the virus to the floppy. That's why you should always write-protect any floppy that you're not going to write data onto.

Just as you must explicitly load TSR programs in order for them to run, you must also run infected programs in order for viruses to operate. A virus lives in one of three places:

- The MBR or DBR, and so gets loaded at boot time.

- .EXE and .COM files, and so get loaded whenever those programs run. Of course, a virus that infects COMMAND.COM will get loaded every time you boot, as `COMMAND.COM` is a vital part of the boot process.

- A Microsoft Word (or other application) document, as a macro.

Macro Viruses

Until very recently, PC owners could relax in the knowledge that if they didn't boot from a floppy or run programs that weren't virus scanned, they were more or less safe from viruses. (Mac owners did not have this security, as Mac document files can be infected.)

This isn't true anymore.

There's now a new category of viruses to think about: *macro viruses.* As their name implies, these viruses are macros in a document. As a group, macro viruses have become far and away the most widespread viruses in the wild. You catch them simply by opening a document with a macro virus attached.

How do macro viruses work? Macro viruses are viruses written in the macro language of an application. Applications that currently permit the use of macros, such as word-processing programs and spreadsheet programs, are not only at risk from infection, but also for infecting others. Macro viruses are different from boot sector viruses, which are on the wane since they were spread mostly by people exchanging floppy disks. Macro viruses spread when infected documents are transferred. Most of the macro viruses around right now are designed to infect Microsoft Word (versions 6.x, 7.x, and 97) and Microsoft Excel. The names of some of the most common of today's macro viruses are Concept, Wazzu, NPad, and CAP.

Here's a relatively benign example of how a macro virus works. ShareFun is a Microsoft Word macro virus that attempts to spread over e-mail attachments. Every time somebody opens an infected file in Word, the chance of the virus becoming activated and spreading is one in four. You might open the document once, twice, or even three times and you might luck out, but open it a fourth time and the virus will activate. This means that if Microsoft Mail is running at the same time, the virus will try to send e-mail messages to three people randomly selected from the local MSMail alias list. (It's harmless if you're not running MSMail.) The subject of the messages is always the same: "You have GOT to see this!" The message is empty of text, but it contains a link to a file attachment called DOC1.DOC, which is infected by the virus. If the recipient double-clicks on the attachment, he or she will get infected by the virus and could spread the infection further with their own MSMail. As of this writing, the virus does nothing destructive; it merely propagates, and only when the circumstances are there for it. (Incidentally, this virus is not technically an "e-mail virus," because the recipients do not literally get infected from your e-mail; rather, they get infected by trying to open the attachment.)

ShareFun also has code to protect itself: if you try to analyze the virus in Word for Windows by looking at the "macro" using either Tools ➢ Macro or File ➢ Templates, the virus will execute and infect your Word NORMAL.DOT template.

As I mentioned earlier, many macro viruses do nothing or almost nothing: they spread, but that's about all. Some people believe that these relatively unobtrusive examples of macro viruses are not the product of hackers at all, but are mutations that first appeared as the result of random bit scrambling in somebody's download and wound up propagating, unseen and unnoticed, as time passed. On the other hand, there are destructive macro viruses that overwrite data, modify the contents of documents, and even send documents via e-mail.

As of this writing, there are four viruses of this type: Concept, DMV, Melissa, and Nuclear. The first two aren't bad, just annoying. Concept and DMV work pretty much the same way: they force you to save documents as templates and replicate themselves to your other documents. The main difference between the two is that DMV uses the AutoClose macro to install itself in the Normal template, while Concept uses AutoOpen. Nuclear can be destructive, however. On April 5, it deletes COMMAND.COM, and zeroes out MSDOS.SYS and IO.SYS, so that not only will your system not boot because it has no command shell, it won't tell you what the problem is because the .SYS files are missing.

That's the bad news. The good news is that Microsoft got on the ball and created the Word Macro Virus Protection Tool (available from their Web site) to alert you of the presence of macros in your documents (not macro viruses, just macros) and allow you to open documents without activating the macros. Once they're open, you can look at the list of attached macros. If you see anything called Insert Payload or Payload, you've got the Nuclear virus. AAAZAO and AAAZFS indicate the presence of the Concept virus. Other tools can clean the viruses from your system.

There are also a number of anti-virus packages that deal with macro viruses. Note, however, that since most of them come over the Internet, you need to make sure you get your anti-virus program from the vendor's home page and not from a user group. (And especially don't respond to any unsolicited e-mail offering an anti-virus program!)

How Much of a Threat Are Viruses?

Viruses aren't the sole instigators of data loss or corruption. Users can accidentally format hard drives, a programmer's extra code in a program could cause malfunctions, the software a user uses could be poorly written…viruses are only one of a number of threats to your data.

The nature of the threat is still a hot topic of debate. The National Computer Security Association (NCSA) estimated that six new viruses are written every day. Robert Bales, executive director of NCSA, feels that with the new tools for writing viruses available, less skilled people—and therefore more people—can create viruses. The increasing number of PC users alone is a good reason to assume that more viruses will appear. (See the section on "What's in Store?" later in this chapter for specific details.) On the other hand, other organizations (like USA Research Inc. of Portland, Oregon) estimated that the number of viruses attacking PCs and Macintoshes would decrease. The institute's report showed that the average damage incurred by viruses in the U.S. is just over $800 per infected computer.

How big a problem are viruses for *you*? You have to balance the cost of losing data against the costs of protecting it with backups, antivirus software, and user education. Considering the costs of antivirus software, regularly backing up all data files, and occasionally backing up application files, combined with a stringent no-unauthorized-foreign-disks policy, might end up being more cost-effective than buying tons of antivirus software and training all users on it. Don't forget—backups prevent data loss from other sources than viruses, while antivirus software is pretty helpless in the face of an accidentally formatted hard disk.

What Are the Most Common Viruses?

First of all, understand that we're on shaky ground here. There are really no totally reliable sources of data on virus prevalence. As I said earlier, the people doing most of the yelling about what a big danger viruses pose to life on Earth are generally the people who stand to gain the most from the panic—vendors of antivirus products. Personally, I am concerned about viruses, but I have not panicked and I do not advise panic on your part. I've been working with PCs for years, use shareware and ISP software all the time, work on corporate sites every week, and I have seen very few viruses; the highest number of infections came from Stoned and Joshi.

I spend a good amount of my travel time working in educational computer labs, supposedly a top source of viruses—students come in and out of the facility all the time, and bring possibly infected floppies with them. My company has run a computer BBS for the past five years, and has never had an infected program uploaded to us. So take the following with a grain of salt.

How common are viruses and which are the most widespread? The National Computer Security Association (a nonprofit group that supports itself by selling antivirus newsletters, seminars, and books—see what I mean?) reports that five viruses accounted for most of the virus incidents in 1989, (this data doesn't get updated very often, unfortunately) as Table 13.1 shows.

TABLE 13.1: The Most Common Types and Frequencies of Viruses, 1989

NAME	NUMBER OF INCIDENTS	WHERE VIRUS INFECTS	DAMAGE CAUSED
Jerusalem (a.k.a. Black Hole, Israeli)	115,000	.COM, .EXE	Blanks part of the screen, erases programs, formats disks, slows down PC.
Cascade (a.k.a. Falling Letters)	30,000	.COM, .EXE	Drops characters onto the bottom of the screen, or randomly reboots PC in the middle of operations.
Brain (a.k.a. Pakistani Brain)	20,000	Boot sector	Changes volume label, or "Chaos" strain may format hard disk.
Italian (a.k.a. Bouncing Ball, Ping-Pong)	18,000	Boot sector	Character bounces around the screen, may cause mismatch between FATs, may cause *false* Track 0 bad—disk unusable message.
New Zealand (a.k.a. Stoned, Dope)	12,000	Boot sector	Damages hard disk or 1.2MB floppy data, randomly flashes `Legalise Marijuana!` messages on bootup.

Those are the biggies, but there are lots more around. Here's a brief look at these top five. This section is derived from several sources, but the most significant are publications from the National Computer Security Association (you'll find the address in Appendix A), and VSUM, a document prepared by Patricia Hoffman, who is known as "the Virus Historian." VSUM is available on Network Associate's Web site (`www.nai.com`).

The Jerusalem Virus

This is a fairly widespread virus. It has lead to several variations, so you'll hear folks talking about "Jerusalem-A," "Jerusalem-B," and the like. It appears to have been targeted originally at Israeli computing institutions, as the original outbreak was reported in Israel, and the logic bomb was set to go off on Israel's 40th birthday on May 14, 1988. (Some birthday present!) It has since been modified to activate on any Friday the 13th, although I'm sure there are versions that have been set up for other dates. (One virus, "Century," waits for January 1, 2000, trashes your disk, and prints "Welcome to the 21st century." The author obviously didn't know that the 21st century starts on January 1, *2001*.)

Jerusalem infects `.COM` and `.EXE` programs as they are run, except `COMMAND.COM`. Once you turn the PC on, the virus is not loaded until you run an infected program. After the virus is active, it infects any `.COM` or `.EXE` files that are run, increasing their size by about 1800 bytes as it injects itself. The date, time, and attributes are unaffected, but the size is larger. Upon activation, part of the screen is blanked out, leaving a two-line black space—hence Jerusalem's other name, Black Hole. The timer is also hooked by the virus, slowing down the system by a factor of 10. These effects can occur on any day, not just Friday the 13th.

On the magic day—May 14, 1988, any Friday the 13th, or whatever—Jerusalem *erases* a program when you run that program. Some strains do not slow the computer down, and one (Jerusalem-D) does not erase program files, but instead destroys the FAT.

Remove the virus using the technique (described later in this chapter) for handling memory-resident viruses.

The Cascade Virus

Someone worked pretty hard on this one.

This virus activates randomly, so it's hard to pin down; activates seasonally—only in autumn, in most versions; and is encrypted using a random key. That means that the same file, infected by the same copy of the virus, will look different on two different machines. That makes it tougher for virus detection programs to find it.

This virus's main outward sign is the "falling letter" effect described earlier. It causes letters to "drop" to the bottom of the screen, and even make little dropping noises in the process. Nothing is happening to your data, but it's scary and annoying. There is a strain of the virus that, instead of doing the letter-drop, randomly reboots your machine.

Cascade is another memory-resident virus. It only infects .COM files and makes them 1701 or 1704 bytes longer. Disinfect by erasing the infected .COM and .EXE files and reloading from backups. (You do have backups, don't you?)

The Brain Virus

Brain originated in a computer shop in Lahore, Pakistan. There are different versions of the story, but basically Brain is a boot record virus that doesn't do much, except in the Chaos strain. When it infects the boot record, it makes a copy of the original boot record elsewhere on the disk and uses it to fool virus detection programs. Run a program like Norton, and try to look at the boot record, and you will see a perfectly fine boot record: Brain has intercepted Norton's read request and fed it false data. Of course, if you boot from an uninfected floppy and try to read the hard disk's boot record, you will see the true Brain boot record, because booting from a floppy never gives Brain a chance to install the "mirror" feature that fakes out Norton and the gang.

Brain may put the word BRAIN on your disk's volume label. The original Brain only infected floppies, but newer strains can transfer to the hard disk. NCSA says Brain is basically harmless, but other sources claim that it has a reformat logic bomb. The fix is easy: just reboot from a floppy and rebuild the hard disk's boot record.

The Italian, or Ping-Pong, Virus

Another boot record infector, this one puts a bouncing symbol (like the one from the old Pong games) on the screen. After a random amount of time, a character, or characters—a smiley face, a diamond, or a pair of parentheses—start bouncing around the screen. Some versions erase characters as they bounce around; others restore the character after passing through. The worst strain reports a format failure when you try to format a disk. There's really no great damage from this virus, but it is annoying. As it is a boot record virus, it is simple to remove.

The New Zealand, Stoned, or Dope Virus

First reported in New Zealand and Australia, this virus has become well traveled. One of my partners came across it in a PC learning lab in British Columbia. Another boot record virus, its main purpose was to flash a `Legalise Marijuana!` message about one out of every eight boots. A bug in the virus seems to cause unintentional damage to MBRs on some hard disks, and on 1.2MB floppies. The B strain stores a copy of the original MBR on cylinder 0, head 0, sector 7 of the hard disk, which I suppose could confuse some autoconfigure controllers.

Other Viruses

You wouldn't believe some of the viruses out there. A new one, Stealth, shows up as faked hardware errors—memory parity errors, boot failures, and the like. Fu Manchu monitors the keyboard buffer: type Reagan, Thatcher, Botha, or Waldheim, and you get a childish comment. Type one of two obscene four-letter words, and it disappears, as if it had never been typed. Den Zuk was originally designed as an *antivirus virus*—a virus killer, but it's buggy, and trashes any kind of floppy but 360K disks. Den Zuk even had a strain that would attack drive C: on September 13, 1991. (I guess that that's not a problem anymore.)

One company, the PC Cyborg Corporation, mailed out thousands of very professional-looking packages in March 1990 containing disks and a brochure on AIDS. The brochure claimed that the program on the disk would provide information on the AIDS disease. In the back of the manual was a warning that you shouldn't use this program unless you're prepared to pay for it. Boot the program and it shows that it means it: it tells you not to reboot until you've paid for the program. Reboot, and the system zaps the hard disk. PC Cyborg was apparently based in Panama. Was it retaliation for the U.S. invasion? Who knows? It turned out to be the work of an anthropologist in Ohio. As the Cyborg disks were mainly mailed out to European locations, several countries requested extradition.

The really annoying thing about viruses is that we can no longer trust our PCs. Several years ago, I received two generic floppies without labels. The only explanation was a piece of paper that said, "THANK YOU VERY MUCH FOR YOUR PATRONAGE. YOUR DISCS [sic] HAVE BEEN PROGRAMMED TO FACILITATE EASE OF USE. [signed] THANKS AGAIN, PUBLISHER SERVICE." I have no recollection of subscribing to a magazine that was offering disks. The programs are some games and a home accounting program, most of which lack any documentation. In the old days, I just would have popped the things into my system and tried them out.

Now? I don't dare, at least not until I've got the time to load my antivirus application, unpack the files to a quarantined machine, scan them, and so on. It's hardly worth it.

An Example Virus: New Zealand-B

The biggest fear that most people have about viruses is that they don't know how viruses infect their computers. Some people will start to visibly twitch just at the sight of an infected floppy on their desk—nowhere near the disk drive. To reiterate, a virus can't infect your machine unless you (a) run the program in which it resides (parasitic viruses) or (b) boot from a disk that has an infected boot sector (boot sector viruses).

Let's take a look at a virus infection. Suppose I'm doing some work for a client at the client's site. The client doesn't know it yet, but his PC has been infected with the New Zealand-B or "Dope" virus. I'm working on this machine, and pop a floppy—a data floppy—into drive A: to transfer some files to the client's machine. Everything goes well. I don't know it yet, but the memory-resident portion of Dope has now infected my DBR on the floppy.

That evening, I'm back home, writing up my report for the client. I put the floppy into my A: drive and read some files from the floppy onto my C: drive. I'm not infected yet.

As I'm busy, I forget to remove the floppy from drive A:. Eventually, I need to reboot, perhaps to change my configuration. As a floppy is in A:, I see the `Non-System disk or disk error` message, as the system has tried to boot from a non-bootable floppy. "Silly me," I chide myself, and flip the floppy drive door open and reboot.

Now I'm infected.

The boot from the floppy—even a non-bootable floppy—was all the virus needed. It was in the boot record, and it then copied itself to the MBR on the hard disk. At the next boot, the virus installed itself in memory. From now on, every floppy that I read will have its DBR infected. And, every now and then, I'll see the `Legalise Marijuana!` message when I boot. (Somehow, that message doesn't inspire me to write my congressional representative in support of legalization.)

Sample Virus Output

We've seen what the New Zealand virus does—it puts a simple message on the screen now and then at boot time. The Italian (or Ping-Pong) virus just bounces a dot around the screen, so there's not much to show. But how about the other biggies?

Cascade, or 1701/1704, will drop letters to the bottom of the screen. Here's a "before virus" shot in Figure 13.2.

FIGURE 13.2:

PC screen before Cascade virus detonation

```
C:\>dir/w

Volume in drive C has no label
Directory of  C:\

HIMEM    SYS    WP            WINOUT        DOS         UTILS
GRAPHICS        COMM          BATCH         LANG        GENERAL
UTSOS2          DELME         FRECOVER DAT  SS          AUTOEXEC BAK
CONFIG   BAK    PERSONAL      CONFIG   SYS  VENTURA     PCLFONTS
SFINSTAL DIR    IMAGE    DAT  AUTOEXEC BAT  TYPESET
         24 File(s)  15138816 bytes free

C:\>
```

After the virus is triggered, the screen looks like Figure 13.3.

```
: >  r/w
  \ di
 U    e in dr  e   h   n  la  l
 Dolu tor  of    :C
C i eм            \
H   Mc   Y    W              WINOU        DOS          UTILS
G   HICS y     C MMa         BATCH        ANG          GENERAL
  M S     S      LMEs         FRECOTER DAT  LS            EXEC  AK
    IZ   AK    D  SO  L       CONFIU   SYS  SENTURA    U  ONTS
 U   SG L SIR iuCPPRGENA oDATbe AUTOEGEC BAT  UYPESE       ACTO     B
       4 Fi e s      1 0 24  yte  f



     r
   I E
   RAP
   TSO             0
   CONF            E
   SFIN    B     IE              X
 C:\> TAZ D  1 < >MA15 3 6    b   s  ree         T    T      P LF
```

Cute, huh? I just can't wait until we catch the morons behind this one and set them to mining uranium. With their bare hands.

The most common virus, Jerusalem-B (the "A" strain couldn't infect hard disks) does a number of bad things, but one of its effects is to scroll part of the screen up and part down. At the same time, it slows the PC down. (Recall that there is also a particularly nasty segment of some strains that will erase any program that you try to run on some "trigger" date, usually Friday the 13th.) Here are "before" and "after" screens in Figures 13.4 and 13.5. Look toward the middle left of the screen to notice the difference.

FIGURE 13.4:

PC screen before Jerusalem-B virus detonation

```
RESTORE  COM     SHARE    EXE     SORT     EXE     SUBST    EXE     TREE     COM
FONTUS   F8      FONTUS   F14     FONTUS   F16     SYMDEB   EXE     BASICA   COM
BASICA   EXE     REPLACE  EXE     BATS                     CONFIGS          COMPFF   COM
ANSI     SYS
         51 File(s)   15122432 bytes free

C:\DOS>dir/w

Volume in drive C has no label
Directory of  C:\DOS

.                .               COMMAND  COM     DISKCOPY COM     DISKINIT EXE
DRIVER   SYS     FASTOPEN EXE     FDISK    COM     FORMAT   COM     GRAPHICS COM
MODE     COM     SYS      COM     VDISK    SYS     XCOPY    EXE     APPEND   EXE
ASSIGN   COM     ATTRIB   EXE     BACKUP   COM     CHKDSK   COM     COMP     COM
DEBUG    COM     DISKCOMP COM     EDLIN    COM     EXE2BIN  EXE     FIND     EXE
GRAFTABL COM     WIN              JOIN     EXE     HELP     COM     LABEL    COM
LINK     EXE     CHARSET  COM     MORE     COM     PRINT    COM     RECOVER  COM
RESTORE  COM     SHARE    EXE     SORT     EXE     SUBST    EXE     TREE     COM
FONTUS   F8      FONTUS   F14     FONTUS   F16     SYMDEB   EXE     BASICA   COM
BASICA   EXE     REPLACE  EXE     BATS                     CONFIGS          COMPFF   COM
ANSI     SYS
         51 File(s)   15122432 bytes free

C:\DOS>
```

FIGURE 13.5:

PC screen after Jerusalem-B virus detonation

```
RESTORE  COM     SHARE    EXE     SORT     EXE     SUBST    EXE     TREE     COM
FONTUS   F8      FONTUS   F14     FONTUS   F16     SYMDEB   EXE     BASICA   COM
BASICA   EXE     REPLACE  EXE     BATS                     CONFIGS          COMPFF   COM
ANSI     SYS
         51 File(s)   15114240 bytes free

C:\DOme in drive
       ctory of  C:
Volu             C has no label
Dire             .\DOS
    R    SYS     F
         COM     S.              COMMAND  COM     DISKCOPY COM     DISKINIT EXE
DRIVEN   COM     AASTOPEN EXE     FDISK    COM     FORMAT   COM     GRAPHICS COM
MODE     COM     DYS      COM     VDISK    SYS     XCOPY    EXE     APPEND   EXE
ASSIGABL COM     WTTRIB   EXE     BACKUP   COM     CHKDSK   COM     COMP     COM
DEBUG            ISKCOMP  COM     EDLIN    COM     EXE2BIN  EXE     FIND     EXE
GRAFT            IN               JOIN     EXE     HELP     COM     LABEL    COM
LINK     EXE     CHARSET  COM     MORE     COM     PRINT    COM     RECOVER  COM
RESTORE  COM     SHARE    EXE     SORT     EXE     SUBST    EXE     TREE     COM
FONTUS   F8      FONTUS   F14     FONTUS   F16     SYMDEB   EXE     BASICA   COM
BASICA   EXE     REPLACE  EXE     BATS                     CONFIGS          COMPFF   COM
ANSI     SYS
         51 File(s)   15114240 bytes free

C:\DOS>
```

Whom Should You Suspect in Case of Infection?

Everybody.

It's sort of like that grim statistic about how you're most likely to be murdered by a member of your own family: you're most likely to be infected by someone in your workplace. Who else would it be? The delivery person? The cleaning people? How often do you work late, look over, and see the UPS guy hard at work on the computer?

If, then, your coworkers are the most likely source of viruses in an office, how did they get the infected file or diskette? There are a number of potential sources:

- Games

- Pirated or "I-was-just-evaluating-it" software

- Internet service providers

- Customer/client diskettes

- E-mail attachments

- Public domain software

- Home PCs (is anyone in the household taking a computer course at a local college?)

- Networks

Sherlock Holmes would have appreciated the challenge of tracking a viral infection. Your best bet for tracking down the culprit? Be as low-key as possible. People may remember details of the past few days or hours under less intense pressure—if they think they are not a suspect they may be willing to talk more. (Of course, you should suspect *everyone* until the true virus source has been found.)

A colleague of mine had a heck of a time tracking down one virus infection. He was supporting a large organization's PCs and had reached the point of frustration with one user. That user's PC, despite having a TSR scanning antivirus program and being cleaned of viruses in the past, was constantly being reinfected. After much subtle questioning (the user was a senior staff member), the user admitted to playing his favorite game on his PC occasionally. The game diskette was self-booting and the virus was contained within the boot sector. Virus sleuths should keep asking probing but gentle questions until they get the right answer. Even the boss could be a virus carrier.

Suggestions to Keep Viruses Away

The most effective way to avoid catching viruses is to shut off your computer... permanently. Don't like that idea? How about just removing your floppy disk drives and disconnecting from your network?

Effective as those means are, they're not much good in the real world. Never using your floppy drives so as not to catch viruses is sort of like cutting off your hand so as not to get a hangnail. Sure, it prevents what you were trying to prevent, but it doesn't give you much good use of your hand—or your computer. In the real world, what can you do about viruses?

- **Run virus checker programs periodically.** There are some very good third-party virus checkers, like McAfee's Viruscan. Network Associates (the company that bought McAfee) is an organization that specializes in virus detection and eradication. They keep Viruscan very up-to-date. Viruscan is for home users (available for a $25 fee), or a "negotiated" price for commercial and government users. You can contact Network Associates through their Web site at www.nai.com. If possible, you should download current virus information on a regular basis to update your virus checker program so it will catch the latest viruses. One very important point: these programs are only completely reliable if run after you've cold-booted from a floppy. Some viruses have a "mirror" feature whereby they monitor attempts to locate them. They respond by telling the monitor program what it wants to hear. For example, .COM file infectors make .COM files larger. That means that one way to detect them is to watch for unexplained increases in file size, right? That's right for some viruses. But some change the file size back whenever any directory operations occur. So your virus scanner programs should be on a write-protected, bootable floppy, to be completely reliable. When you use them, cold-boot from the floppy.

- **Don't lose a lot of sleep about them.** I've already said this: viruses are scary, but not backing up regularly is scarier. Any of a large number of random external events—flood, fire, power surges, vibration—could destroy data on your hard disk, and it could happen at any time. Backing up regularly is more important than keeping up to date on the latest virus buster programs.

- **Get in the habit of leaving the floppy drive empty.** A sizable proportion of viruses are boot record viruses, and they can't get at your hard disk it you don't boot from an infected floppy. You can read and write data on a floppy with an infected boot record for years and never be infected. But boot from the floppy—even if it's not a bootable floppy—and you've got the virus. If you're not careful, you'll find that now and then you try to reboot the machine with a floppy in drive A:. Keep the drive empty and it won't happen.

- **Don't use pirated software, especially games.** First of all, it's not nice to use commercial software that you didn't pay for. Most software companies are fairly small operations, no more than 10 to 15 people. These are not large, faceless corporations that "deserve" (in the eyes of some people) being taken down a peg or two. Most software operations are Mom-and-Pop operations that just barely get by. Using copies of software you didn't buy is just plain theft. People who use illegal copies are thieves, plain and simple—and cowardly thieves, to boot. There's good cheap software in all areas, so "just say no" when someone offers you a copy of a program. More relevant to the present discussion, the majority of the virus attacks that I've heard of seem to have come from pirated software—another good reason not to use copies. A sad by-product of the virus scare is some misinformation about Web sites. People think that downloaded software is a major source of viruses, and that just isn't so. Downloaded pirate software may be, but not the shareware stuff. But if you're worried about using shareware Web sites, here are a few tips. If you want a shareware product, get it from a big Internet FTP site, or from the author. I used HDTEST, a shareware hard disk fixer program on the CD-ROM disc we include, for six months before I called to register (and pay for) my copy. I found that I had a very old version of HDTEST, and registration got me a much niftier version. At $30, it's a bargain. So call up the shareware author and get the most recent version. You'll end up getting the most up-to-date version, and it'll be virus-free.

- **Avoid Web sites that cater to self-proclaimed "hackers."** These tend to mainly have pirated games anyway, and the software generally isn't screened. The same idiots that think it's okay to crack the copy protection on a game and give it away free also think it's okay to insert a virus in the cracked game. In some odd Robin Hood manner, they view it as "just punishment" for anyone *else* who uses illegally copied software.

- **Be wary of shareware programs without documentation.**

- **Stick to big shareware download sites like Tucows or PC Magazine, and Web sites that register their users.** Most reputable Web sites these days ask that you register when you get on. Then they don't let you upload files until they've checked that you are who you say you are. That way, if you upload a virus, they can come after you. This makes people less likely to upload viruses.

- **Back up your data.** If the worst happens, you can always reformat and restore.

- **Write-protect any floppy that you put in your drive, if possible**. This is particularly important when installing a new piece of software: you don't want your master copy of a program to become infected. Some programs require that the disk not be protected while installing—I certainly hope that vendors move away from this practice.

An Ounce of Prevention...

Those of us who live in the real world have to compromise between utter safety and utility. Most computer experts suggest following these guidelines for preventing virus infection.

1. Install a scanning program on each computer to search the local drives immediately when powered on. This is the only way to spot a virus before it runs or is loaded into memory. To activate the scanning program at boot time, put a shortcut to your antivirus program in your Startup folder.

2. Educate and train users how and when to scan disks and new files. Some organizations put the scan option on all users' menus. Others have set aside a specific computer to be used for scanning disks and files. Though it might be more of an effort for everyone to use this computer, the organization can ensure that the most recent virus signatures are being used on at least one workstation. It also lessens the likelihood of an infection spreading over every machine in your office.

3. Write-protect all essential diskettes. Write-protection prevents any viruses from sneaking onto the disk. Keep in mind, however, that write-protection won't keep viruses already on a disk from infecting a computer.

4. Ensure that the floppy drives are empty before powering on or booting up the computer.

5. If you are a computer support person, scan your diagnostic and bootable disks regularly and write-protect them. Since the disks are used throughout the organization, they run a big risk of infecting or being infected by other PCs.

One senior MIS staffer at an insurance company was responsible for introducing a virus into his company. After much investigation, he discovered that it came from his home computer—his wife was taking a course at a local high school. Luckily, the company had backups, as thousands of files got knocked out by this nasty virus.

How Do Virus Scanners Work?

Virus scanners work by scanning for signatures or hex patterns. These patterns of hexadecimal codes are normally from 10- to 16-bytes long and are unique for each virus. This, for example, is the Disk Killer's code:

2EA1 1304 2D08 002E A313 04B1 06D3 E08E

This pattern *could* exist in a legitimate piece of software and set off a virus warning, but it's not likely. Given that, in a series of numbers only 10 digits long, there are 3,628,800 possible combinations, it's easy to see how one 32-character string written in hex will probably not be identical to another (hex uses the letters A through F in addition to all 10 numerals).

Using Anti-Virus Software

No anti-virus software can be completely effective, so the most important anti-virus software that you can use is your backup procedure, whatever that is.

We'll look at three kinds of anti-virus software in this section:

- File change monitors that detect viruses by examining unauthorized changes in a file's content.

- Program prescreening software that looks in a program's code for suspicious commands like Format.

- Virus detection programs that are actually programmed to recognize common viruses.

Remember that viruses live in one of two places: viruses either inhabit your hard disk's DBR or MBR, or viruses inhabit program files—.EXE or .COM files, generally. (There are a few kinds of program files that do not have the extension .COM or .EXE, such as .OVL overlay files. Some viruses attack these non-.COM, non-.EXE files also.) So some virus programs protect you by checking these areas for change periodically.

Checking for change could be a troublesome business—can you imagine having to drag out your backups and compare them to the programs on your hard disk every day? That's clearly impractical, so virus checkers take a different approach.

When you first install a virus checker, it computes a CRC for each executable file or "monitored" disk area. A CRC is just a mathematical function. The program treats all the data in the file as if it were all numbers, then runs the numbers through the function. The CRC function then returns a 16-bit or 32-bit value for each file. That original set of CRCs is then stored somewhere by the virus checker. Then, whenever you invoke the virus checker program, it recomputes CRCs for the files and compares them to the original CRCs. If a single byte on a file changes, the CRC changes also, and the virus checker warns you about the file.

This may sound like a lot of work, but it isn't really. Recall that the checker only has to compute CRCs on program files, and there can't be that many of them on a hard disk—just a couple hundred or so. And the fact that a CRC has changed doesn't necessarily mean that a program has been infected: you might have updated the program or reconfigured it. For example, I use the Q editor from Semware. Whenever I redefine the keyboard, the reconfiguration program directly modifies the program file for the Q editor. That causes a CRC change.

Viruses also must be loaded in the memory in order to do their dirty work. So other antivirus programs scan the memory, monitoring attempts to install TSR programs without authorization. The most common places for a virus to try to attach itself are INT 13 (the disk drivers) and INT 8 (used for the "random" effects that many viruses demonstrate). The virus checker's TSR keeps track of the status of these interrupts, and flags any changes.

Ross Greenberg's FluShot+ is a multitalented virus shield. It performs both of the above functions, and a bit more, for a mere $14.

- First, it computes checksums (checksums are like the CRC that the floppy uses to verify data) for any program file or files that you want it to. Then it compares the checksums *both at boot time and whenever you run the program*. It's fast, too, so you won't mind the time that it needs.

- It will also do checksums on the MBR and DBR, so it will protect you from boot sector viruses, as you'll be alerted to any changes to either of those areas.

- FluShot+ will advise you of any attempts on a program's part to directly modify the disk without the INT 13 calls. While this sounds nice, it is actually of little or no value. *Lots of programs*—friendly, helpful programs—use INT 13s. For example, in order for FORMAT.COM to work, it must repeatedly issue Format Track commands to the floppy. Running an antivirus package like FluShot+ and FORMAT.COM together is a painful process, as every single Format Track makes FluShot+ beep at you and ask if it's okay to proceed. On an 80-track floppy, this gets old quickly, and so you shut off FluShot+ just for the duration of the format operation.

- That's all the virus needs.

- Some of the newer viruses just behave themselves when monitors are running and only act in an antisocial fashion when no one's looking. Unfortunately, there's just no way to write the memory-resident portion so that it's all that effective.

A Simple Anti-Virus Program

No antivirus is able to protect your computers from every virus. With all the new viruses being written every day, you need to couple your antivirus software with a clear-cut program of safe practices. Here's a possible antivirus program that both individual users and office technical support people can implement. It's based on some suggestions from Dave Stang, who founded the NCSA. Understand that it is a set of compromises: you want good antivirus protection, but you don't want to spend all your time at it.

1. Scan all of your machines for viruses. Remember to prepare a write-protected bootable floppy and put a virus scanner on it. Then cold-boot the machine that you want to check from the floppy (put the floppy in A:, turn the machine off, and turn it back on), and run the scanner. Don't warm boot, as some viruses can survive that.

2. Don't tell people that they're not allowed to have shareware or bulletin board software. (They'll sneak it in if you forbid it

absolutely.) Tell them instead that all software must be screened. Screen software with a simple system:

- Keep a machine handy as the "quarantine" machine. Make sure you have a write-protected bootable floppy with whatever scanners you use and a CRC checker, as well as FDISK, and a copy of FORMAT so you can reformat the disk between tests.

- Keep a few program files (.COM and .EXE) on the hard disk of the quarantine machine—targets for the virus. I'd name them EXCEL.EXE, QUICKEN.COM, and so on—names of popular application programs. Some viruses only infect particular applications. Put a scanner program on the hard disk for convenience's sake, and run the CRC checker to get the initial checksums for the files on the disk.

- Boot from the hard disk (you know it's clean), and pop the floppy to be tested into drive A:—don't boot from it. Run the virus scanner against the files and boot record on the floppy in A:.

- Assuming the test floppy turned out okay, install its software to the hard disk. Reboot the system. Run the test software.

- Cold-boot the system from the write-protected floppy. Run the scanner and CRC checker. It won't take long, as there isn't much on the hard disk. If the disk comes up clean, the software is okay.

This process will take about two hours at the outside, and it's virus insurance. Yes, it's annoying, but that's the price of living in the '90s, I guess. For those of you with just one machine, you obviously cannot reserve a test machine. The best that you can do is back up regularly, keep several generations of backups, and run a virus scanner regularly.

Minimize Your Losses by Preparing for Them

Preparing backups and testing disks is an important part of the virus-recovery process, but there are other things that you can do as well. Never forget—the best way that you can minimize your losses from a virus attack is to assume that you will be attacked—today. That way, you won't be tempted to put off preparing for the attack.

- **Include boot sectors, partition table, and CMOS information:** We've already talked about this stuff. They are the basics you'll need to reassemble a computer whose software has been zapped.

Here are some other anti-virus protection measures:

1. **Centralize your applications:** Install all programs used in the department on one computer (preferably one not used as a workstation) and then back up all the application software from that computer. Protect this computer from virus infection with your life. If you get a virus, you can use either the files from the computer or backup floppies to restore applications to the newly cleaned computer.

2. **Write out procedures:** It might be hard to believe that you could forget important details, but under the stress caused by a virus attack anyone could be subject to bouts of amnesia. To keep from forgetting anything, make two damage control lists. The first list is for each user, detailing scanning procedures, and the steps to take if he or she encounters a virus. The second list is for you, the virus killer, detailing the steps *you* take. Isolating and destroying a virus with the minimum of damage to all files takes careful planning, so follow your preplanned procedure and take notes as you go. It's likely that you won't be done with the virus hunt immediately. To remember what you've done as the hunt continues, you will want to reread your notes for the next few days—or months.

Writing down what you are about to do also forces you to think about the next step. That mental pause may prevent you from taking an unnecessary step or making a dangerous error.

Your notes may be important in tracking a virus, as the case may last years. In one situation, an employee found the STONED virus on a disk and realized she had just finished formatting a number of disks for her coworkers. She tried to recall all of the diskettes but wasn't able to get all of them back. Despite having all the surrounding PCs and suspected diskettes scanned immediately, another coworker reported the same virus a few weeks later. Again, the PCs were scanned and cleaned.

About six months later, the same group of people got "Stoned" again. (You're probably wondering how they got any work done.) It turns out that two boxes of diskettes had been formatted originally. In frustration, the support people cleaned the diskettes and threw them away. But they missed one...and the infection started all over. The moral? Take notes, so that if you overlook something, you'll be able to tell later *what* you overlooked.

What to Do If Your PC Is Infected

All the preparation in the world won't help if someone slips up and gets a contaminated disk on their computer. If that happens, you may need to restore data, and you'll definitely want to know how to remove the virus. How do you do that? Your virus "disinfection" method will vary according the kind of virus.

Recall that, in the PC world, viruses are basically located in one of three places:

- Hard or floppy disk DBR
- Hard disk partition record
- Executable files

First, you should have a write-protected bootable floppy available. PC DOS is shipped on floppies that you *can't* write data on, so you can boot from your original DOS disks (remember to cold-boot—turn the machine off, insert the DOS disk in drive A:, and turn the machine on). You can then safely DISKCOPY the DOS originals onto floppies, write-protect the floppies, and use them for your disinfecting operation.

Some viruses announce their dirty work, with a message like "Do not turn off the PC or your data will be destroyed." *Turn off the PC immediately!* It's a matter of redirection: the virus buys time to destroy valuable data while you're reading the message and hesitating.

Recovering from a .COM or .EXE File Virus

This kind of virus puts itself into the code of a .COM or .EXE file. You will find the infected program files and replace them from the backups. I will warn you at the outset that it's a boring process.

Most .COM or .EXE viruses enlarge the program files and give themselves away by changing the file's size. Examine the sizes of .COM and .EXE files and compare them to the sizes of the programs on your backup disks. (Again, be sure to boot from a write-protected floppy first, and write-protect any backup diskettes that you're looking at before putting them in your drives.) If a file is a different size, reload from backups. Don't run "cleaner" programs.

You must be thorough with .COM or .EXE viruses. Check every .COM file and .EXE file: all it takes is one infected file to start the virus going again. As soon as you run the still-infected file, the virus is back in business, infecting any program files that it can find.

This works for Word macro viruses as well.

How Do Viruses Disguise Themselves?

With all these antivirus programs out to get them, viruses have had to get pretty smart about evading capture. To this end, they hide themselves in one of two ways: by pretending that they aren't there and by changing their appearance so that virus scanners can't recognize them.

Stealth

Stealth viruses install themselves in memory, concealing themselves from detection and defending themselves from being analyzed or removed. The code intercepts and redirects calls when needed. This could fool a user or program into missing a file that has been changed in size because the virus reports the original file size (which the stealth virus stored until it needed it to fool the checksum).

Polymorphic

Polymorphic viruses can change their appearance, thus evading virus-detection software that looks for recognizable character strings. The best-known Bulgarian virus author, known as the Dark Avenger, produced a Mutating Engine that is both a virus and a routine that virus authors can include in *their* viruses to make them polymorphic. The Mutating Engine causes the virus to which it is attached to continually change its appearance, thus evading detection. With the Mutating Engine, any amoral cretin can become a virus author—you don't even have to be a good programmer anymore!

Where Does the Virus Code Hide?

If you're a stealth virus, then you need a hiding place. You've got a few choices: you can tack your code onto the end of a program file and then substitute the original size of the program file whenever the virus scanner performs a checksum; you can lodge yourself in the extra bits of memory allotted to programs that the programs don't use; or you can insert your coding into the disk partition area or into some part of the disk that's marked as bad. Let's look at these hiding places in a little more detail.

Appended Code

A virus program may attach its additional code to the end of the program file. It usually needs a small line of code at the beginning of the program file to point out the address location of the rest of the virus program. As appended code increases the size of the entire file, most antivirus programs can detect changes in file sizes (remember, only data files should change size—Lotus 1-2-3 doesn't get bigger with use) by simply comparing it to its previous size or with the checksum method.

Unfortunately, not all viruses that use appended code can be detected with this method, as some are smart enough to conceal the true file size (by substituting the original file size as discussed above) when the program is scanned for viruses.

Inserted Code

To hide their extra bytes, some virus programs can cache themselves inside unused portions of memory that have been allocated to the legitimate program. The program does not appear to get any bigger because those spaces have already been accounted for. Since those empty spaces are limited, the functions of the viral code are limited as well. Because this method of avoiding detection limits the virus's size and complexity, it is not as popular among virus authors.

Redirection and Interception

More sophisticated virus programs insert some of their coding into the disk partition area or in a sector and either disguise themselves as a bad area or become a hidden file. This inserted code intercepts calls to the CPU (usually through the DOS interrupts), activates the virus, and then returns control to the CPU. This code can be as small as two bytes.

Part of these programs may also be resident in memory. You may not even notice the slight delay these interceptions cause. Even antivirus programs such as Norton Utilities may be fooled into checking viral decoys of program files.

Bad Sectors Reported on Floppies

When your disk drive suddenly can't read a floppy that recently worked fine, your disk may have lost clusters, or it may have been damaged. If you haven't exposed the disk to any undue physical conditions, run a CHKDSK against the floppy and look for lost clusters. (You should probably check for lost clusters even if you have baked the disk in a car, just on the off chance that that's not what the problem is.) If you subjected the floppy to heat, dust, dirt, or a magnetic surge since the last time it worked, it could be physically damaged and ruined.

Convert any lost clusters to files with the CHKDSK /F switch, then scan the disk for viruses. If you don't find any, monitor the disk for more lost clusters.

Cannot Execute XXXX

If a legitimate executable file is missing, a virus may have destroyed it (although I've seen more users than viruses delete executable files). Try any other executable files in that directory. If they are gone, it's time to check for viruses.

My Screen Is Acting Funny!

Some of the older, more common viruses may flash text messages, bounce a ball, show a black square, or cause letters to fall to the bottom of the screen. Such behavior is a pretty good indication that you have a virus.

Disk Drive Light Goes On

If a floppy disk drive light comes on when you are not trying to read from or save to that drive, it's time to check to make sure you haven't recently changed any configuration information (such as you might if you needed your B: drive to be the bootable drive). It's also possible that you (or someone) arranged to have temporary data files saved to one of the floppy drives.

Virus Attack Procedures

One day, you're merrily going along doing your job when the Help Desk telephone rings. A nearly frantic user is on the other end, crying, "Come quick! My computer's acting funny!" This might not be a virus attack (always remember that user errors and hardware problems happen more often than virus attacks), but it's still time to put on your deerstalker hat and Inverness cape and visit the scene of the crime.

After Infection

The following steps have been helpful to me in coping with a virus attack. I recommend that you make a form for yourself from this list, arranging the list in two columns so that you've got one side free for checking things off and for your notes.

1. Calm the user down.

2. If the user hasn't already powered down the computer, record all information being displayed on-screen inside the virus dialog box: the type of virus reported, in which files it is contained, the exact DOS or Windows message.

3. Ask the user about all his or her most recent actions and computer symptoms (leaving the screen on for this step may help the user's memory).

4. Note the names of all floppy disks lying around, and ask the user if he or she gave any disks to anyone else recently.

5. If the user's on-screen data must be saved, save it to an empty floppy and mark the disk *immediately* as "Potentially Infected."

6. Remove all floppies from drives.

7. Look up the virus on the most recent virus list. Compare the reported symptoms with those manifested by the computer.

8. Power down (just rebooting may not oust the virus).

9. Run your anti-virus software.

10. Write down all files reported as infected. If no backups or hard copies exist for infected files, consider making copies to another floppy. If you make backups, mark those floppies as "Potentially Infected."

11. Reboot from the hard drive.

12. Re-scan the hard drive with your anti-virus program.

13. Discard all the floppy disks that were around the infected PC. Although you can scan them all and reformat them, as inexpensive as diskettes are, it is generally not worth the trouble.

How to Keep Ahead of the Game

You can't buy a virus scanner, install it, and forget about it, no matter how good it is. There are new viruses all the time, and older scanners may not recognize the new viruses. Also, you should keep an eye on the projected seriousness of the virus threat, so you can budget your protection resources more easily.

Keeping Up to Date with New Viruses

All scanners work on the principle of scanning for already discovered viruses. There is no generic "There's a virus here" hex pattern. Since new viruses are discovered every day, it's in your best interest to keep current. Here, we'll review some of the places that you can pick up new virus information and help.

To obtain the signatures of new viruses, you can consult the Web sites operated by (for example) Symantec and Network Associates. The antivirus companies make frequent updates to the virus signature files, and you should always find and install the latest updates.

What's in Store?

Besides the run-of-the-mill viruses that are created daily, there are new strains of viruses that pose new challenges to the antivirus software. The Dark Avenger Mutation Engine (DAME) is a software program that you can attach to your favorite virus. With each execution, a new virus form is created (nice, eh?). This should make viruses ever harder to detect. Rogue programmers can also exploit new object-oriented technology with products like Mass Produced Code Generator, Virus Construction Set, and Virus Construction Laboratory.

On the other hand, it's in the interest of any organization that makes its living studying viruses and selling antivirus products to play up the virus scare. Normal caution should be enough protection. Remember: a virus can't get to your computer unless you let it.

Viruses don't have to be a big problem in your life. If you take the precautions detailed in this chapter, there's no reason why you should have a disastrous meeting with the Dark Avenger. Never forget: your data is far more valuable than that nice box (i.e., your computer) that you keep it in. Protect it accordingly.

Don't let fear of viruses destroy your use and enjoyment of your PC. The analogies between safe sex and safe computing, although now trite, are very accurate. Have a good time, but use protection. At the very minimum, back up regularly and run your scanner every month or so. Don't put original program floppies in your PC's drives unless they have write-protect tabs on them, and don't worry about data files, as they can't carry viruses.

On a final note: if you know someone who's a virus author, report him or her to the authorities. Viruses are computer terrorism, and terrorists should be caught and punished.

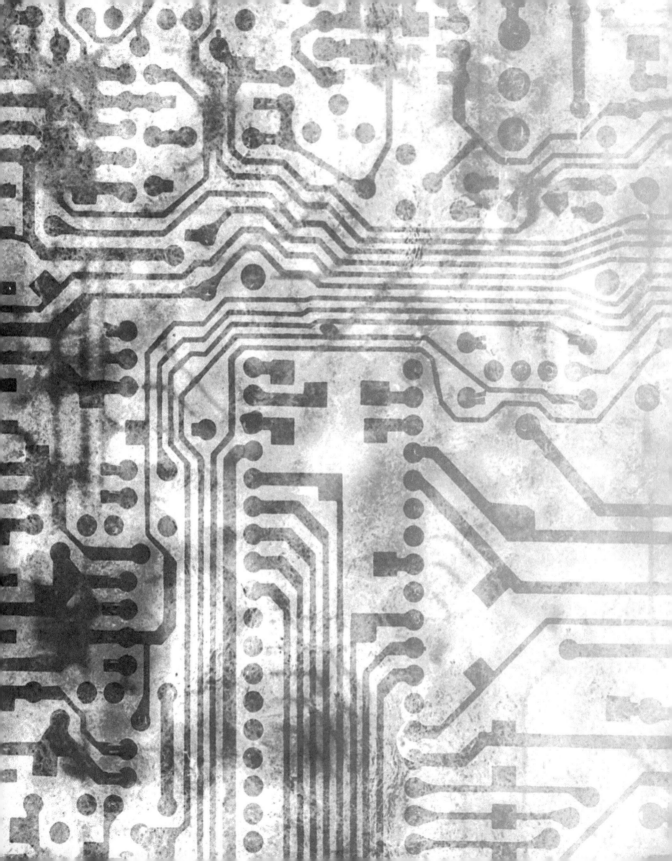

CHAPTER

FOURTEEN

Care and Feeding of Hard Drives

- Protecting your hard drive

- Backing up system files

- User data backup

- File defragmenters

- Recovering data and fixing hard drives

- Understanding and repairing media errors

I discussed some of these things earlier, but here's a summary of what you can do to make your disk hardware live longer. Some have either been covered earlier or are short enough that a line or two will suffice; for the others, I'll expand upon them in a few pages.

- As you read in Chapter 4, "Avoiding Service: Preventive Maintenance," leave your computers on all the time: it's easier on their drives not to have to start up every day.

- Get good power protection. You read in Chapter 9, "Power Supplies and Power Protection" about buying power conditioners, UPSs, and SPSs to protect your hardware—and the hard disk is no exception. Surges go through the *whole* system. Including the drive heads. And if the drive heads happen to be near the FAT or partition record…

- Don't smoke around drives. Smoke raises the particulate level in the air around you. Dust is, in general, not good for the hard disk.

- Use the proper mounting hardware for your drive, and mount it according to manufacturer's guidelines.

- Attend to squeaky drives. Not only are they annoying, they may be trying to tell you something.

Let's take a closer look at the last few items.

Most disk cases nowadays leave enough space for you to mount two 3.5-inch disk drives, meaning you've got enough room to put that second IDE drive into your system without having to get rid of the existing IDE drive. That's nice, except for the fact that there ends up being no space between the two drives. While smaller 3.5-inch drives don't generate as much heat as did the older drives, they still run warm, and stacking them one on top of the other isn't a good idea. Think about just drilling new holes, or finding a disk chassis that leaves some air space between the drives, or you may be able to mount the second drive in an extra floppy bay if you have one.

Protecting Your Hard Drive

There's not much to be done in the way of regular maintenance on the sealed Winchester drive: you can't clean the heads, you can't align them. If the drive itself is fried, then about all you can do with it is cut it open and leave it on your bookshelf as a conversation piece.

What kills hard disks?

- Dust and smoke

- Vibration

- Rapid temperature change

- Excessive heat

Even though there's an air filter on the drive, the filters aren't perfect, and dust can slip into a drive. When a dust or smoke particle sits on the disk, the head whips around and crashes right into it. Then it drags it around the platter, leaving scratches in its wake. On a 3.5-inch platter rotating at 5400 rpm, a particle on the outermost track would travel at 56 miles per hour. The outermost track is, by the way, the most important track, as it contains the directory information for the rest of the disk. The space between the head and the platter is infinitesimal compared to the size of dust, dirt, or hair, as you see in Figure 14.1.

FIGURE 14.1:

The space between
the disk head and the
platter

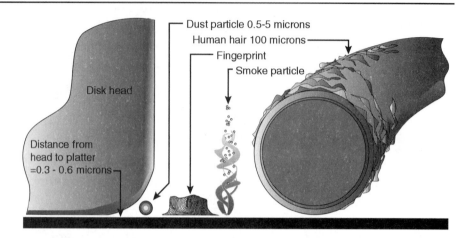

Ziplock Bags Keep Your Cool

Quick temperature changes aren't good for drives, either. A drive, while cold, may not respond properly. There is, of course, an easy fix for this—just let it warm up. But there's a related problem that's much worse. People leave a laptop with a hard disk in their car overnight on a cold night, then bring it into the office, and the hard disk dies. Even when heated up, the drive refuses to function. It's quite mysterious.

What killed this drive wasn't so much temperature change (although a lot of temperature change can kill a drive or make it appear dead), but condensation. The drive was sitting in cold, dry air. A quick transition to the warm, moist air inside a heated building in winter leads to condensation of water droplets on the platters.

The same thing happens with hard drives that are being transported. Suppose it's Friday, and you know that on Monday you must drive to another of your company's offices to install a hard disk. So you test the hard disk, see that it is okay, and put the disk in the trunk of your car. The weekend goes by too quickly, as always, and the hard disk spends it in the trunk of your car. Then, arriving at the PC's site on Monday, you install the hard disk— but it does not work. *Now* you know why it happened, but what can you do to keep it from happening again? Before you take the drive into the building on Monday, put it in a Ziplock bag and seal the bag. That will allow you to bring the drive into the building with its own bubble of dry air. Then let it warm up for about 30 to 45 minutes in the bag. Once the platters are no longer cold, it's safe to take the drive out of the bag, as no condensation will occur.

The other evil, vibration, is a problem because of the way in which the head travels above the disk platter. Recall that the head travels above the disk on a cushion of air. The distance between the platter and the head (called the *head gap*) is very small. Any bouncing around while the drive is running can cause the head to literally crash into the platter below. This plows a small furrow in the platter and grinds down the head.

Don't put your PC on the same table as your dot matrix or daisy wheel printer. All that shaking is no good for it. It's easier to lock the corral today than it is to explain to the boss tomorrow why all the horses are gone.

The essence of data protection is simple: back up data areas, as they can be lost in a number of ways, periodically re-write all information back onto your disks (as magnetism fades), and keep half an eye peeled for computer viruses. The different areas on your disk should be backed up at different intervals with different tools. A complete backup program consists of the following steps.

- Backing up:
  - The drive type (if you are using an older system or hard drive)The FAT and directory (daily)
  - The user data (regularly)

- Making an "emergency" boot floppy for each system.

- Taking whatever measures you can to minimize the probability of an accidental format.

- Testing and refreshing the disk media at least annually. This means you should, each year:

  - Back up, format, and rewrite your whole drive to refresh the sector IDs and data.

  - Test the disk media with a specialized media tester of some kind.

It also can't hurt if you:

- Periodically defragment the data to ease any data recovery problems.

- Utilize the verification features of the operating system and some applications.

- Understand the threat posed by computer viruses and know how to protect yourself from them. By the way, the best way to avoid computer viruses is to never download anything from the Web unless you are certain that the source computer is virus-free. Also, never, never copy programs from friends' disks. Not only is this illegal (unless the program is shareware or freeware) it's also one of the most common ways to contract a virus.

It looks like a lot, but it's not really: Let's take a look at each option.

Backing Up Your Hard Disk Drive Type

NOTE   Today, virtually all computers and hard drives auto-configure when they are installed. As such, you never need to set the drive type in CMOS and you can skip this section. If, on the other hand, you are using an older system then it's very important that you save the hard drive configuration data contained in your CMOS.

The most important part of that CMOS information is your hard disk's disk type. Not that the other information in your CMOS memory isn't important; it's that incorrect or missing hard drive data will crash your system. The other information (like the time and date) will be nothing more than an inconvenience. To look at your CMOS data, run your computer's BIOS setup program, and you'll see (among other things) the drive type displayed.

Looking at the list of information, in the BIOS you'll find a number of drive specifications (either two or four drives will be listed). Chances are that only one of the drives will have actual data. The others will generally say "not installed" or some other, similar note.

Your drive will either be a pre-built drive type, like drive type 15, or it will be a user-definable drive type. The user-definable drive type is usually numbered 47, although not all computers use type 47: the user-definable type in many older Compaq computers is a number in the low 60s.

If your drive is of a user-definable type, then be sure to write down not only its drive number, but also the number of heads, cylinders, sectors, and write precompensation. Some computers require that you note the ECC length, so take that down if it's shown by the Setup program.

Make a note of the drive type, or, better yet, stick a paper label on the drive with the drive number on it. If you ever move the drive to another computer, however, you may not be able to use the same drive type number in the new computer, because each computer's BIOS is different, and what is drive type 35 for one computer may be drive type 42 for another. But if you write down the specifications for the drive (heads, sectors, and so on) you'll always be able to enter the data into your new system and get the drive to work.

Backing Up and Restoring Your MBR with DEBUG

You may recall that the Master Boot Record (MBR) resides on cylinder 0, head 0, sector 1. Without your MBR, your computer will never boot. Unfortunately, because the head spends a lot of time there—the root directory and FAT are in that area, among other things, cylinder 0 is more prone to problems than most cylinders.

I have seen strange things kill cylinder 0, and when cylinder 0 is dead, the whole disk might just as well be dead. Lose the MBR, and the operating system has no idea how to communicate with the disk. So back it up.

As a matter of fact, it's a good idea to back up not only the MBR (which is the first sector of the first track), but the entire first track at cylinder 0, head 0. Various programs squirrel important information onto these otherwise-unused sectors: for example, a dual boot system relies on sectors 2 and 3 of the track, and Disk Manager stores information about a drive's geometry on sector 8.

Although DOS 5 included an MBR backup program, it was removed from DOS 6 and subsequent versions of DOS and all versions of Windows, so the chances are you won't have one. You can also back up the MBR with the Norton Utilities if you have a copy. But you can also back up your MBR if all you have is DEBUG (and that's available on even the most current systems). DEBUG is a very powerful utility and can damage a file. If it is not used correctly you will no longer be able to use the file. If you use DEBUG, it's a good idea to use it on a copy, not an original file. That way, if you make a mistake, you still have an undamaged original. Use a *bootable* floppy that contains DEBUG.EXE (MS-DOS users) or DEBUG.COM (PC-DOS users). If you're using Windows, put a copy of DEBUG onto a Startup floppy before you begin. You can make a Startup floppy from the control panel.

NOTE: Type the program lines into DEBUG as shown below. (The case doesn't matter, but I'm showing the words in caps for clarity's sake.) I've placed underscores where blanks should go. Line 1 starts DEBUG and creates a new file called MBR.DAT.

1. **DEBUG_MBR.DAT**. You will see a File Not Found message—because the file didn't exist before. Don't worry about the message.

2. **A**. This tells DEBUG that you want to assemble something.

3. **MOV_DX,9000**. This command tells DEBUG to move the value of segment 9000 to register DX. Since you can't write anything to a register, you have to move this information to an extra segment.

4. **MOV_ES,DX**. This command moves any information in register DX to the extra segment (called ES).

5. **XOR_BX,BX**. BX is the offset; xor is a programming trick to set it to zero.

6. **MOV_CX,0001**. This command stores the value of track 00 and sector 1 in register CX.

7. **MOV_DX,0080**. Here, you're storing the information at head 0 of drive 80 (your A: drive is drive 00, your B: drive is drive 01, your C: drive is drive 80, and your D: drive is drive 81—these are all physical drives, not logical drives) into register DX.

8. **MOV_ AX,0201**. This command tells DEBUG to read 1 sector.

9. **INT_13**. This is the BIOS disk call.

10. **INT_20**. This tells the BIOS, "I'm done!" and signals that it won't get any more commands and can leave memory.

11. Press **Enter** to stop entering commands.

12. **G** runs the program. When it's done, you should see a message that says Program terminated normally.

13. **R_CX**. This command asks DEBUG to show you the value of register CX, and lets you edit it.

14. **200**. This is the size of the file that DEBUG will write.

15. W_9000:00.

16. Press **Q** to exit DEBUG.

Congratulations! you have just created a file called MBR.DAT. You can see a sample screen of this operation in the next graphic.

The process of restoring your MBR is similar to that of saving it. To restore your MBR, first start from a bootable floppy that contains both DEBUG (.EXE or .COM) and the correct MBR.DAT— do *not* try restoring an MBR.DAT from one machine onto another machine unless the two machines are *identical!* Once you're set, change to the A: drive and type the following (again, under-scores should be typed as blanks):

1. **DEBUG_MBR.DAT**. This time, if you get a File not found message, *stop and exit* DEBUG (type **Q**) *immediately!* If you continue at this point, you could blast your MBR. (Seeing that message means that you didn't save it properly.)

2. Type **L_9000:0** to direct DEBUG to load the information to 9000:0, where we'll tell the program to look for it.

3. Assuming that all went well, now type **A** to let DEBUG know you want to assemble a file.

4. **MOV_DX,9000**.

5. **MOV_ES,DX**.

6. **XOR_BX,BX**.

7. **MOV_CX,0001**.

8. **MOV_DX,0080**.

9. **MOV_AX,0301**. This command tells DEBUG that you want to *write* 1 sector.

10. **INT_13**.

11. **INT_20**.

12. Press ENTER to stop entering commands.

13. **G** runs the program. When it's done, you should see a message that says Program terminated normally

14. Press **Q** to exit DEBUG. Your screen will look like Figure 14.2.

FIGURE 14.2:

Screen shot of
DEBUG data

```
A:\>debug mbr.dat
-l 9000:0
-a
25A4:0100 mov dx,9000
25A4:0103 mov es,dx
25A4:0105 xor bx,bx
25A4:0107 mov cx,0001
25A4:010A mov dx,0080
25A4:010D mov ax,0301
25A4:0110 int 13
25A4:0112 int 20
25A4:0114
-g

Program terminated normally
-q

A:\>
```

Backing Up System Files

It's no secret that operating systems are getting more and more complex these days. If you look in your Windows 95/98 directory, for example, you'll see a bunch of configuration files, called the Registry. Those system configuration files are what tells your operating system how to work and how your applications should work with it. Lose those files, and it's all over.

16-Bit Applications

To 16-bit applications, such as Windows 3.*x* and all applications created for it, the important files have the extension .INI. Each application that you run has its own "innie" file that defines the environment in which it operates. For example, my copy of Ami Pro has an initialization file called AMIPRO.INI, which defines the default document template used, the default location to which files are saved, and so forth.

The Windows operating system itself has several initialization files:

- SYSTEM.INI: Contains the hardware information for Windows.

- WIN.INI: Contains the Windows user environment.

- CONTROL.INI: Describes the color schemes and printers used with Windows.

- PROGMAN.INI: Defines the contents of all Windows program groups and how the Program Manager works.

- WINFILE.INI: Defines how objects appear in the File Manager.

This isn't the place for a complete discussion of the .INI files, but if you'd like to know more, the Windows Resource Kit has a very good description of all the .INI files and what they do.

NOTE   .INI files are generally kept in the Windows directory. You can view (and edit) an .INI file in a text editor such as Windows Notepad. It's not a good idea to open it in a word processor lest you save it as a word processor file.

What does all this mean in terms of rebuilding your system if necessary? When backing up, even if you normally only back up data rather than system files, it's a very good idea to back up all .INI files as well. This way, if you must reinstall the operating system you'll be able to restore your system exactly the way it was when you backed it up—application files and all. To restore .INI files, just copy them back to the Windows directory, replacing any existing files. (Of course, be very sure that the backed-up files are the ones that you want to use.) The only restrictions are that this will work best if you're restoring the system information to the same computer you took it from. Other computers may not work with the memory configuration or fonts that you set up on the original system.

Registry-Oriented Operating Systems (Windows 95/98 and Windows NT)

Windows 95, Windows 98, and Windows NT organize their configuration information differently. Rather than having a bunch of .INI files, all information relating to the operating systems and all 32-bit applications stored therein are stored in a central database known as the *Registry*. The exact files of which the Registry is composed depends on the operating system: to Windows 95, it's two files, USER.DAT and SYSTEM.DAT; for Windows NT, it's five *hive files*, each of which describes a part of how the operating system works. But whichever operating system you're talking about, all the files are combined to make one Registry. The only exceptions to this are any 16-bit Windows apps on your system. They don't know how to look in the Registry for configuration information, so they maintain .INI files and copy their contents to the Registry.

The good news about the Registry is that it's centralized: only one Registry to back up, not five or more individual text files. Most of the time, you make changes to the Registry in the same way that you most often make changes to .INI files: by changing the settings in the Control Panel.

Your method of backing up the Registry depends on the operating system you're using. If you're using NT and have a tape drive, then you can back up the Registry at the same time that you back up your other data. When you restore the data, you can choose to restore the Registry at the same time, so long as you restore it to the same drive that it came from. If you're using Windows 95, then you can export the Registry as a text file from the Registry Editor, and then import it as needed. Backing up the Registry on a regular basis is a *very* good idea, as it's required to boot the operating system.

NOTE   To learn more about the Windows 95 Registry, you can read *The Expert Guide to Windows 95*. For more about the Windows NT Registry, check out *Mastering Windows NT Server*.

Rebuilding the Operating System

Whichever operating system you're using, the process of rebuilding the system with its backed-up configuration is about the same:

1. Reinstall the operating system.

2. Install any patches (i.e., Service Packs) that were installed when you backed up.

3. If necessary, restore or reinstall any applications that were not backed up.

4. Restore the data and the configuration files.

This should put your system back to the way that it was when you last backed up.

User Data Backup

If you're concerned about data integrity, I shouldn't have to tell you to back up regularly, but...

Quick, now. How many of you have backed up your hard disk in the last seven days? Hmmm...not too many. How about in the last month? Last year? *Ever?*

There are two kinds of hard disk users: the ones who have had a disk failure and lost data that wasn't backed up, and the ones who are *going* to. (Actually, I first heard this as, "There are two kinds of dead pilots: the ones who have landed and forgot to lower their landing gear, and....")

You seek to stay in the latter category as long as possible.

I can't stress this strongly enough: at the first sign of unusual behavior, back up the entire disk.

Backup Options

When hard drives were smaller, it was semi-reasonable to back up an entire drive's data to floppies. These days, however, floppies just don't cut it for mass storage any more. Of my workstations, the one with the *small* disk has 1GB of storage space; one of the really monstrous systems has 17GB. For just a couple hundred dollars today you can buy a drive with 6GB or more. There's no way that I'm backing up one of those drives to 1.44MB floppies—it would take more than four THOUSAND floppies!

Over the years, backup options have improved dramatically. In the past you had three choices when it came to data protection: tape drives (controlled either by their own tape controller or from the floppy controller), removable drives such as Bernoulli boxes, or floppies. These days your options are:

- Tape drives

- Removable media drives such as Zip and Jaz drives

- Optical (MO) drives

- Writeable CDs

- A second hard drive (hard disks are cheap: why not?)

We'll discuss these options in more detail now.

Tape Drives

The traditional means of backing up a large hard disk is the tape drive. These devices are simple, they're a known quantity, and they're cheap. Although some tape drives still run off the floppy controller (which is bad, as it's slow), you can also buy SCSI or IDE models that can plug into your system's host adapter. When looking for a tape drive, keep the following in mind:

- An external tape drive may cost a little more, but you'll be able to use it to back up more than one system.

- Preformatted tapes save a great deal of time, since tapes can take up to an hour to format.

- The same tape software that works with Windows 95 may not work with other operating systems, such as Windows NT. Similarly, the data on those tapes may not be readable to NT-compatible tape software.

Tape drives come in a wide range of capacities and formats: models range in size from 250MB to 8GB and higher digital audio tape (DAT) format.

Removable Media Drives

Removable media drives are exactly what they sound like: they're magnetic storage units that look like other hard drives to your PC, but allow you to remove the media and put in a new set, giving you virtually unlimited storage capacity. They're not the fastest storage units out there, but they're cheaper than most and work pretty well. They've got other advantages as well. Because they can connect to your computer via the parallel port, you can use them to back up just about any system, even laptops. Plugging a removable drive into the parallel port doesn't mean that you can't use your printer, either: it goes between the parallel port and the printer.

TIP

Removable drives are a handy way of transferring data from a laptop back to your office workstation, if your laptop doesn't have a LAN connection to the other PC.

Iomega made the first popular removable drives for the PC in the form of the Bernoulli Box. Although I've still got my Bernoulli Box and like it, I find its cartridges to be a touch expensive, and it's bigger and heavier than the Zip drive without offering much more in the way of storage capacity (150MB as opposed to 100MB). The cartridges are physically bigger, too. Iomega now has some new offerings for backup: the Zip and Jaz drives.

For small systems, or for those who only want to back up part of a drive, there's the Zip drive. These units, which plug into your parallel or SCSI port, hold 25MB or 100MB cartridges. Zip drives are about as cheap as you'll find in the realm of largish-scale backups: the drives run for about $200 and the cartridges for $20. (I've seen them offered in five-packs for $150.) Even if 100MB doesn't back up most modern drives, backing up to five cartridges isn't too bad. The unit weighs about a pound, so you can even take it on the road. The cartridges are about the size of a 3.5-inch floppy disk, except thicker.

For larger systems, Iomega makes Jaz drives. These removable drives have cartridges that can hold up to 1GB—not too shabby. They're pricier than Zip drives, but they're fast (a Jaz drive backs up 1GB of data in about five minutes) and can back up most hard drives with only one cartridge.

CD-RW Drives

For those with larger storage needs, consider CD Read/Write (CD-RW) drives. They range in capacity from standard CD's (650MB) to DVD-RAM drives which can store up to 5.2GB. And unlike the older (and slower) optical drives, CD writers are quite inexpensive, starting as low as around $200 for the 650MB. The DVD drives are more expensive (around $700) but are well worth the expense if you are managing enough data to merit their use.

Another Hard Drive

Hard disk space has gotten so cheap that it's feasible to just get a second hard disk and keep a copy of your data on both disks. Depending on which operating system you're using, you'll need to do this by periodically XCOPYing your data to the second hard disk, or, if you're running Windows NT, you can use its Disk Administrator to set up the two disks as a mirror set.

NOTE A mirror set is a group of two physical drives that are set up so that when data is written to one, it is written to the second as well.

Of course, an extra hard drive isn't as portable as some of the other options that we've talked about in the previous pages. Unless it's an external drive, you can't switch it to another computer easily, and if it's part of a mirror set, you'll only be able to use it on a computer that has the compatible software installed. But for a high-speed and simple backup solution, it's very workable.

What Software Do You Need?

The answer to this question really depends on what you're installing and what operating system you're using. For example, if you're using Windows 95 or Windows 98 and decide to get a CD-ROM drive, the setup process is limited to telling Windows about the new hardware (you do this with the Add New Hardware utility in the Control Panel) and rebooting the machine.

Other hardware varies in its software requirements:

- **Tape drives:** You'll need to install the tape controller software. This may either come with the drive or be part of the operating system (like Windows 95 or Windows NT)

- **Removable drives:** They'll have installation utilities. The Zip drive, for example, works with Windows 95/98.

- **A second hard disk:** You'll need to set it up like you would any other hard disk.

- **CD-R drives and optical drives:** Like CD-ROM drives, they'll have setup software. Some operating systems will be able to detect compatible types, but you'll need to see what CD-R types are supported first.

Once the software is installed, you'll be able to back up files. When using devices such as CD-Rs, removable drives, or optical drives, you could use the DOS XCOPY command to copy files and directories from your hard disk. However, it's easier to take advantage of the graphical interface of today's operating systems. Just drag the icon for the drive you want to back up onto the icon for your removable media drive.

Backup Strategies

Having the tools to back up is only part of the solution. For complete data protection, you've got to make sure that you use them. I know it's a pain, but you've got to back up your data on a daily basis if you generate anything of importance at all. Even losing one day's work can be bad, so how would you re-create a week's worth?

First, centralize your data as much as possible. If you're responsible for backing up more than one networked computer, consider storing all data on a file server for backup. It's much easier to back up one computer than ten.

Second, create a schedule and stick to it. I've found that a rotating backup schedule that combines full and differential backups works quite well. On Monday, for example, you might do a full backup of the system. Then, the rest of the week, you can do a differential or incremental backup so that you only copy the files that have changed.

NOTE   A differential backup copies only those files that have changed since the last backup of any kind; an incremental one copies those files that have changed since the last full backup.

Name each backup tape, disk, or cartridge with its date, the machine it belongs to, and the type of backup it is. For example, a full backup of my workstation might be labeled **08/05/99 Full backup of INTEVA**.

Finally, don't rely on your memory. Make yourself a backup schedule and put it on the wall or someplace very visible. Posting your backup schedule in a prominent place has two advantages. First, you know at a glance when you last backed up (initial each backup after you've completed it). Second, it reminds you to back up, until it gets to be a regular habit.

Prepare Boot Floppies

Once you've got the important places backed up, make sure that you can get your computer up and running without the help of your hard drive: make sure you've got a boot floppy for each of your systems. That should be a bootable floppy with whatever device drivers you regularly use to boot your system. This is for emergencies when your PC won't boot from the hard disk. If you're running Windows 95, then you were given an opportunity to create a boot disk when you first installed the operating system. If you *didn't* create a boot disk, then all you need to do is to open the Control Panel, click Add/Remove Programs, and then choose the Startup Disk tab, and select Create Disk... option.

No matter what operating system you're using, you should be sure that you've got a boot floppy or some kind of recovery disk handy.

To make a boot (Windows calls it a Startup) disk, click the Start button, select Settings, choose Control Panel, and open Add/ Remove Programs. Once there, click the tab called Startup Disk and follow the directions.

Perform Media Tests Annually

No disk medium is perfect. Greater use of voice coil head positioning and sputtered media has greatly improved disks, but there's always the chance that a part of a platter isn't coated perfectly. Worse yet, there's the chance that all that bad treatment most PCs get has led to a disk scratch or two.

That's why there are so many "disk tester" programs around. A popular example is the Disk Doctor program that's been a part of the Norton Utilities for years. Basically, all these kinds of programs do is try to read your data, sector by sector. If there's a sector that they have trouble reading, they attempt to move the data elsewhere, then mark its cluster as bad in the FAT. Of course, once an area is marked bad, the operating system sidesteps it.

There are two problems with this approach. First—through no fault of their own—these programs miss most of the disk problems until they're just about disasters, and second, the way they mark bad areas (the FAT) is too transient. Take a look at Figure 14.3.

FIGURE 14.3:

How the operating system handles disk errors

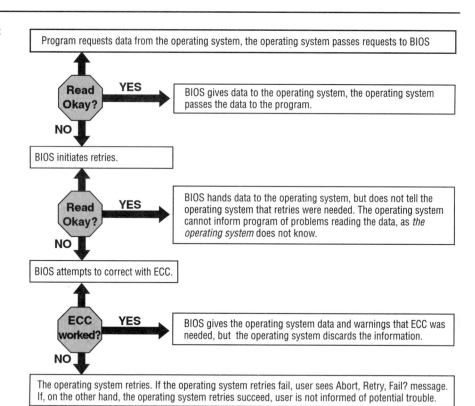

Program requests data from the operating system, the operating system passes requests to BIOS

Read Okay? — **YES** → BIOS gives data to the operating system, the operating system passes the data to the program.

NO

BIOS initiates retries.

Read Okay? — **YES** → BIOS hands data to the operating system, but does not tell the operating system that retries were needed. The operating system cannot inform program of problems reading the data, as *the operating system* does not know.

NO

BIOS attempts to correct with ECC.

ECC worked? — **YES** → BIOS gives the operating system data and warnings that ECC was needed, but the operating system discards the information.

NO

The operating system retries. If the operating system retries fail, user sees Abort, Retry, Fail? message. If, on the other hand, the operating system retries succeed, user is not informed of potential trouble.

You see, there are a lot of problems that the operating system doesn't tell us about with disks. If the operating system detects a read error, it performs several retries without informing the user. If the retries succeed, the user never knows there is a problem. Even *before* the operating system retries occur, however, BIOS can retry. When the BIOS sees errors, it will respond by executing retries of its own or, if the retries don't work, employing the error correction hardware. (You may recall that hard disk controllers use an ECC—Error Correction Code—that allows them to not only detect faulty data on the hard disk, but also correct it—or a short burst of bad data anyway.) If BIOS retries have been suffi-cient, the operating system discovers nothing of the problem. But if BIOS had to use ECC to reconstruct data, it informs the operat-ing system when it hands the data over. But believe it or not, the operating system actually has a small section of code whose job is to filter out these messages so that it can ignore the BIOS error messages.

"Ignore?" Yes. Upon bootup, the system sets up pointers to various important areas in the BIOS. These pointers are called "software interrupts"—different from hardware interrupts, they're basically "canned" utility programs easily available to any program running on the system. One of them, INT 13, points to disk routines. As provided by the BIOS manufacturer, read and write attempts with INT 13 will return messages that inform INT 13's caller of required error correction. Upon bootup, however, the operating system actually substitutes some of its *own* INT 13 code that ignores the fact that the sector had to be error corrected! That means that an application program can't even recover the error correction information if it *wants* to. This is dumb, as it would have been nice for Norton and the gang to be able to bypass the operating system and utilize INT 13 directly, employing the fact that there had to be an error correction to warn users of disk areas that are causing problems. This also means the operating system ignores the early warnings of data and reports nothing until disaster strikes. The operating system's approach seems to be "ignore any problems until they're disasters." It also means that it'll be tough for *any* tester program to do meaningful media tests, as both BIOS and the operating system seem to discard the early warning signs.

Pattern Testing Methods

In order to generate the problems that prompt retries and ECC corrections, a program's got to *do* something—read or write the disk. So disk tester programs write and read data to/from the disk. You wouldn't think it would matter exactly *what* a test program writes, just that it writes—it seems that a test program has only to write out "Mary had a little lamb" or the like zillions of times all over the disk, then read it back, and the disk's tested. Believe it or not, however, there's even science in the choosing of test patterns.

Recall that data are encoded on the disk using either MFM or some kind of RLL. Both encoding schemes seek to merge the clock and data signals into a stream of pulses on the disk. It turns out that not all patterns are equally simple to encode and decode: some are less reliable. A read/write test writes out these problem patterns that are encoding-method-specific.

Think of it this way. Suppose we wanted to test the degree of color definition of a TV picture tube. We might do this by displaying letters against a background on the tube, then measuring how far away the letters are readable. Would we display white letters on a black background? No, hopefully not—that would be cheating. It would be much better to use, say, blue on purple, or red on brown. Pattern testing is the disk equivalent.

Problems with Newer Controllers

As I'm writing this, changes are occurring in the disk world that may require another rewrite of the disk fixers.

We've already seen that it's common for a controller to automatically retry, and in fact to retry from eight to 30 times. Only if the retries haven't worked does the controller use the ECC information. So having to resort to an ECC correction is a fairly infrequent event, and one that should cause some worries.

That's changing as disks get smaller, physical size-wise, but larger, data capacity-wise. The original IBM specification for hard disks requires that the drives read no more than one bad bit in 10^{12} (an American trillion or a European billion). The smaller, denser disks, however, can see one bad bit in only 10^7, or one in ten million. To combat that, the disks are using a *76-bit* ECC! (You may recall that the old XT-type WD1002 controller gives you a choice between 5 and 11 bits. That's probably fine, for the older, more reliable drives.)

File Defragmenters

After running for a while, the files on your hard drive can become *fragmented* or *noncontiguous*. This means that a given file may be stored partly in clusters 30–40 (one contiguous group) and partly in clusters 101–122 (another contiguous group). A file is said to be noncontiguous if (logically) it has more than one contiguous block of disk space. Noncontiguous files are bad for two reasons, as demonstrated in Figure 14.4.

FIGURE 14.4:

A fragmented and unfragmented file

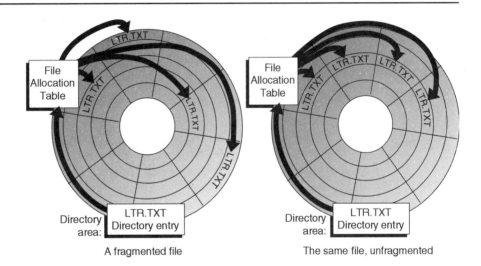

A fragmented file   The same file, unfragmented

First, noncontiguous files take longer to read. The fact that the disk head must go chasing all over the disk to read them slows down disk access. Putting the whole file together makes read operations quicker: move the head once and all of the data can be read.

Second, you have a higher probability of recovering a deleted file if it is not fragmented. Keeping disks defragmented just pushes the odds a little further in your favor. Think of it this way: suppose you've got to find and piece together a file on a disk whose FAT has been zapped. Would you rather have to find a file in clusters 100, 120, and 1521, or one in clusters 100 to 102? If the files are always defragmented, data recovery is easier.

How do files become fragmented? See Figure 14.5. When the operating system needs a cluster, it basically grabs the first one available. When the disk is new, only a few clusters have been taken, and the rest of the disk is one large free area. New files are all contiguous. But, as files are deleted, they create "holes" in the disk space. As the operating system looks for more clusters, it takes the first sector available. This can easily lead to a new file being spread out over several separate areas.

You can find fragmented files with Windows' built-in disk tools. The easiest way to access the disk tools is to put the mouse pointer somewhere in the desktop (no icons), click on the screen, and press the F1 key. This will bring up the search function in Windows Help. Type in **disk tools** and you can run them directly from there. Disk tools will allow you to perform a number of disk utilities in including defragmentation of your disk(s). Figure 14.5 shows how to access Windows Help and disk tools.

FIGURE 14.5:

Finding disk tools through Windows Help

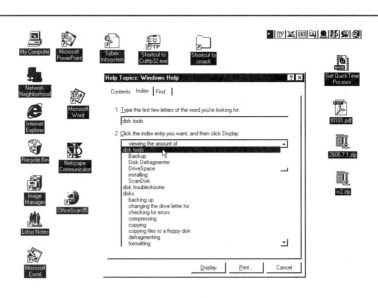

Recovering Data and Fixing Hard Disks

The simplest kind of problem (simplest to repair, that is) is one where the directory or the FAT has been damaged or modified in some way that you don't want. For example, if you delete a file, then it isn't really deleted, at least not at first; all that happens is that its entry in the disk's "table of contents" (the directory) is modified, and the areas that the disk sits in get marked "available." Another directory/FAT problem is something you've probably seen before, a *lost cluster*. Yet another is a formatted disk; believe it or not, you can often *un*format a hard disk! Again, you can repair all of these problems by manipulating the FAT and/or directory structure, leaving the data alone.

Somewhat harder to solve are the problems that come from actual disk damage in one part of the disk, the Sector not found errors. You usually fix them by telling the disk to avoid the affected area, then reloading backups on that area. Yes, I said backups; there's just no guarantee that you'll be able to recover data on an area that's been "cratered."

Toughest of all—but most rewarding to solve—are the "dead drive" problems, where the drive won't talk to you at all. At the end of this chapter, we'll look in great detail at how to resurrect dead drives and recover data.

Quickstart for the Panicked

As I said, I recognize that some of you are in a hurry, so here's a roadmap to the data recovery section. This is by no means a comprehensive list of the problems and solutions that you'll find in this book—just the biggies.

- **If your hard disk is not responding at all—no data, no boot.** Turn to the section "Resurrecting Your Dead Hard Drive."

There is a flowchart of things to do there, as well as a directory of messages and what they probably mean.

- **You get a strange error message from** Unerasing, Unformatting, and CHKDSK Messages: Fixing the FAT. The linchpin of the DOS (and Windows—everything here applies to Windows 95 as well) space allocation system is the File Allocation Table (FAT). The FAT and the directories allow DOS to keep track of the data you have and where it is.

Sometimes, however, the FAT and the directory "become confused," that is, they don't agree on what's going on with the disk. Such a thing may show up as an error from either the CHKDSK program or the SCANDISK program. One example is the familiar lost clusters message—quite dire-sounding, but actually fairly unimportant. (Surprised? Lost clusters aren't a big deal. Read on.) If CHKDSK squawks about something, you need to know whether to worry about it and how to fix it. Such problems are usually caused by software or operator error, as you'll see in this chapter.

There is also a class of FAT-related problems that are completely due to user error: accidental deletions and accidental reformatting of a disk. Both of these problems can be reversed. Believe it or not, if someone does a DOS FORMAT on your disk, all is not lost.

What CHKDSK Does

FAT troubles cause all of those cryptic CHKDSK woes. (Again, when I say CHKDSK, I'm also talking about SCANDISK, as it does basically the same thing, except with a prettier interface.) You see, CHKDSK *doesn't* check the disk, it checks the FAT. A lot of folks think that they're doing something good for their disk when they run CHKDSK. "I run CHKDSK now and then to look for bad areas on the disk," they say. That's totally wrong. CHKDSK just checks and reports on the state of the FAT. It doesn't do a new media check. The "bad sectors" report that CHKDSK gives is just a report of the clusters that have been marked "bad" in the FAT. Free space is just a tally of the clusters marked "free" in the FAT.

All CHKDSK does when it reports numbers of bad sectors is to just scan the FAT, counting up all the clusters marked as bad. Then it multiplies the number of bad clusters by the number of bytes per cluster and arrives at the number of bad bytes on the disk. Any new bad areas are *not* discovered by CHKDSK, but rather by one of the disk test programs that I've discussed in earlier chapters. CHKDSK does only a few things:

- It counts up the available clusters, used clusters, and bad clusters.

- It searches the directory structure to ensure that it makes sense: all subdirectories must have the proper format (for example, the "." and ".." files must be in place). It examines the entire subdirectory tree.

- It examines all files' directory entries and FAT chains. The directory entry, you will recall, records the file size in bytes. The FAT chain tells how many clusters a file uses. Those two numbers must agree: there have to be enough clusters allocated in the FAT to accommodate the number of bytes referenced in the directory.

- It checks that all FAT chains make sense.

Understand before we go any further that CHKDSK *errors do not point to hardware errors*. They either indicate bad software or dumb operators. Let's examine a few of the most popular messages briefly. For my examples, I'll use a very simple file called HAMLET.TXT. Figure 14.6 shows HAMLET.TXT when it doesn't have any problems.

HAMLET.TXT starts in cluster 100, and runs (contiguously) through cluster 104. Its file size implies that the file will be five clusters long, and indeed it turns out to be five clusters long.

FIGURE 14.6:

FAT and directory entries for a normal file

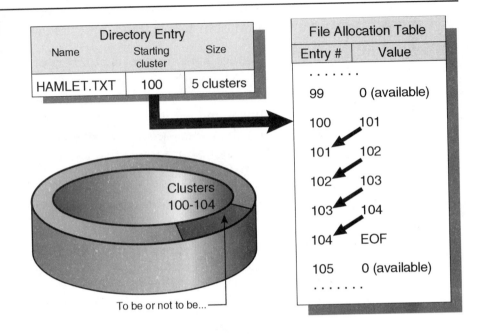

What Happens When a File Is Deleted

Sometimes carelessness and haste carry a painful price: accidental deletion of files. There are lots of ways to accidentally do this, and I need not dwell on them. Let's see how to recover from the problem.

Hold on a moment. Recover from *deletion*? Undeleting? Isn't that kind of like unpainting a house or unwatering a lawn?

Nope. First of all, understand that the operating system is lazy and doesn't really rub out much of *anything* when it deletes files.

Deletion is done not by blanking out clusters but instead by changing the first letter of the name of the file, as the name is kept in the directory. The operating system doesn't go to the trouble of erasing the clusters, so they just sit there, available for use the next time a new file is created (or an old file is expanded). *As long as you undelete before a new file is created, the file can be saved.* The following picture shows what HAMLET.TXT would look like if deleted. The first character is changed, and the FAT entries are changed to zero, making them available. Take a look at Figure 14.7.

FIGURE 14.7:

What happens when a file is deleted

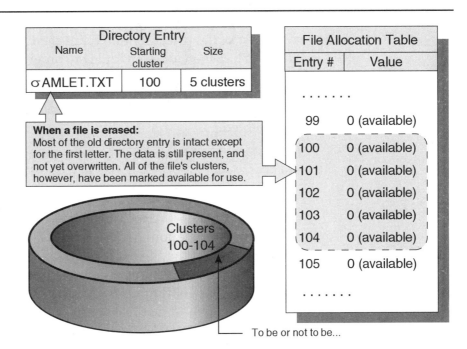

Basic Unerasing

The process could be done by hand, with a lot of patience and DEBUG, but fortunately there are products to do this. The best known one is, of course, the Norton Utilities. The original product included UnDelete, and since version 3.1 it has included Quick UnDelete (QU). For some reason, Windows 95 does not have any undelete facilities except for the Recycle Bin, which only allows you to undelete files if you deleted them by putting them in the Recycle Bin. If you deleted a file from a DOS command prompt, however, there are no undelete possibilities, unless you're using a third-party utility like the Norton Utilities.

No matter how you undelete, please understand that undeletion in this manner is not a guaranteed matter. Look back at the picture of what happens to HAMLET.TXT when deleted. The data's still there and so is most of the directory entry, but the FAT chain has been zeroed out. What, then, does an undelete program know?

- By looking at the old directory entry, it can see how large the file was, and so compute the number of clusters that must be reassembled.

- The directory entry also contains the number of the starting cluster. So we know, in the case of HAMLET.TXT, that it (1) occupied five clusters and (2) started in cluster 100.

- Looking at the FAT, we see that cluster 100 is available, so we can attempt undeletion. If QU found 100 occupied, that would mean that the file had been overwritten. Not only is 100 free, but the next four clusters are free, too. Assuming that the file was contiguous before it was deleted (as most files are), QU would just reassemble HAMLET.TXT out of clusters 100 through 104. On the other hand, if HAMLET.TXT had actually been in clusters 100, 200, 250, and 301, the unerasing program would have reassembled the file completely incorrectly based on its assumptions.

It should be obvious that there's some guesswork here. Can we reduce the guesswork? Well, we've seen now that undeletion is mainly a matter of manipulating the FAT. An even easier and more reliable approach to reassembling the FAT chain would be to back up the FAT every day so that if a file were deleted, the old FAT image would be around and available to assist the unerasing program. So, to summarize: when you've got a deleted file that you want to undelete, don't create any new files, undelete with a commercial program like Norton Utilities.

Here's a true story to underscore how important this is. I've got a friend who's a PC support person. He worked in a department with a woman that he *really* wanted to get to know better—I mean, he wanted her to suffer a data loss in a *big* way. One day, Fate offered him his chance. She called up, explaining that she'd accidentally deleted a couple of files on her hard disk. He assured her that he could help her, and raced over to her workstation with a copy of Norton Utilities. To make the program more convenient to work with, he (you guessed it) copied it to the hard disk. Arggh. The poor boy lost the data—*and* the date.

Unerasing Partially Overwritten Files

Someone calls you up. "I accidentally deleted a file," he or she says. "No problem," you reply, eager to don the cape and cowl and go save the day as Dataman, the finder of lost data.

"I'll be right over," you say. "Just be sure not to create any files until I get there." You arrive, and find him typing away at the keyboard. Dataman (that's you, remember) is aghast.

"I told you not to create any new files! What are you doing?" you cry.

"Oh, I lost a *WordPerfect* file. *This* is an *Excel* file I've just now created. That won't affect a deleted WordPerfect file, will it?"

"Users…," you mutter. No point in explaining now that there's only one FAT for the system and that it's not subdirectory-specific.

The previous is a true story. Let's see what we can do.

1. First, as the new file was created in a different subdirectory, the original WP file's directory entry was not overwritten. Pull it up with Norton, and we see (let us say) that the file

was five clusters long, and started in cluster 300. Thank goodness it's a file that contains text; partial text files are usually recoverable—partial spreadsheets often are not.

2. A look in the FAT shows that cluster 300 is, indeed, taken by the new Excel file. But 301 through 304 are open.

3. We are going to create a directory entry with Norton, and then string the FAT entries together by hand. Before we can do that, however, we've got to know which clusters used to contain the WP file. There are two approaches: one is to just assume that clusters 301 through 304 are the ones we're looking for. The other is to search the disk. Here's how.

Norton has a Text Search program that will search all of the disk (or just the deleted areas) for a string of characters. You give it some text to search for and tell it whether to search all of the disk or the deleted part of the disk. (Deleted here really means available areas. It will search just within a file, a range of sectors or clusters, or the whole disk, if you like.) In the WordPerfect case, I asked if there was a hard copy of the document around. There was, so I searched for random phrases that I typed in from the hard copy. Once the match is found, Norton shows you exactly what it found, and where it found it (cluster 20, sector 77). I kept notes on all the clusters that matched text from the hard copy, and found that in this case the text had probably been in cluster 300 (we know that from the directory entry), 301, 302, 310, and 311— it had been fragmented! Then I hand-assembled a file out of the remaining clusters.

Do be careful about using this search technique. There were also old versions of the document on the disk, and I kept finding them when trying to locate the remains of the deleted document.

So unerasing a partially overwritten file boils down to (1) finding out which clusters remain from the file and (2) building a directory and FAT chain by hand with Norton or the equivalent. At the end of the chapter are a couple of exercises that will show you how to reassemble a deleted file (and how to find that deleted file in the first place) and will show you an advanced undelete technique.

So you see that unerasing boils down to finding which cluster previously held data, hoping that the cluster hasn't been over-written, and stringing the clusters together into a file.

The way that most programs save files actually increases the chances that you can recover a lost file. Suppose I'm in my favorite word processor, Ami Pro, working on a document called BOOK.SAM. When I tell Ami to save the file, it goes through these steps:

1. First, it saves the file in its current state to a file called SAM-SAVE0.TMP.

2. It waits for the entire file to be written out safely.

3. Then it deletes the previous BOOK.SAM and renames SAM-SAVE0.TMP to BOOK.SAM.

The effect is that not only do I have the current BOOK.SAM on disk, I've also got a whole bunch of "free" space that actually con-tains the previous version of the file. What about the next time I save the file—will Windows overwrite the old BOOK.SAM? Proba-bly not. In order to minimize fragmentation, the operating system starts looking for free space after the cluster where it appeared previously. For example, suppose all of the disk's free space is contiguous. When I start up the PC in the morning, my BOOK.SAM might start at cluster 1000, and let's say that the free space starts at cluster 1500. Suppose also that BOOK.SAM is 50 clusters long. That means that the first time I save the file, the operating system will look for the first free cluster, which will turn out to be 1500. It will then save the file starting in clusters 1500–1549, and will mark clusters 1000–1049 as available.

The next time I save the file, the operating system won't put the new file at cluster 1000; instead, the way that the operating sys-tem looks for a free cluster is to remember the last free cluster that it saw, which would be cluster 1550, and to start from there. The net effect is that the space from 1000–1049 would be left alone, at least until you run out of space on the disk or until you reboot.

I've used this to my advantage. Once, I accidentally managed to destroy both this whole book *and* my backups. (Don't ask.) As I very rarely reboot, I had all of my work for the past week or so, all sitting in the "available" part of the disk. A little search and stitch work, and it was all good as new.

Recovering Accidentally Formatted Hard Disks

Formatting is kind of like erasing, only more so. Unformatting can be like undeleting, only a *lot* more so.

Accidental formats are a painful problem, as they zap the whole disk in one fell swoop. Remember that the DOS FORMAT command does not actually delete sector data, but only deletes the boot record, the FAT, and the root directory, creating a set of blank FATs and a root directory in their place.

So the sectors are all there, but how to sew them back together? (A 17GB hard disk has more than 16 million sectors.) There are two approaches, which I call Class I and Class II unformatters. Class I can recover an entire disk but requires some preparation *before* the format occurs. Class II, on the other hand, can't recover the entire disk but will work even if you've not prepared the disk prior to the format.

Class I Unformatters

The Class I approach is to keep a copy of the FAT, the directory, and the boot record in a specific physical location. As long as you keep it up to date, the disk can be easily restored.

Class II Unformatters

The alternative approach to unformatting, which I call the Class II approach, can only recover information in subdirectories, and even then there are no guarantees. Subdirectory information is maintained in files, recall, and those files are recognizable by their format: the "`..`" and "`.`" directory entries. Unformatting programs first locate these files, then use the information in them to reassemble data files.

The subdirectory files contain a link to the first FAT entry. Since the FAT is a blank FAT, it's only of use to tell us what the first sector was. It also tells us how many clusters the file used to take up. Unformatters just take a number of contiguous clusters and tack them together as the file. This means that fragmented files cannot be saved in their entirety, and garbage sectors may be tacked on the end of data files. But it's better than nothing, and your chances of success can be improved by running a defragmenting program now and then (discussed later in this chapter). The defragmenting program should be run *before* formatting the disk. Defragmenting a freshly formatted disk accomplishes nothing. It also means that any files kept in the root directory cannot be restored.

Understanding Lost Clusters

This is the CHKDSK message that, it seems, everyone has seen in the past. People confuse lost clusters with bad clusters, and so the lost cluster message strikes fear in users' hearts. It needn't, however: it generally just means some sloppy internal housekeeping on some program's part.

When CHKDSK reports lost clusters, it basically means loss of the pointer from the directory to the FAT. Recall that the *pointer* is just the "starting cluster" entry in a file's directory entry.

Lost clusters occur when the FAT entries for a file are written, but the starting cluster value for the file hasn't been put in the directory. Why would the FAT reflect a file's status while the directory would not? That happens generally because we can't report how large a file is until we've seen it and it's been stored on disk. Disk storage involves allocation of clusters, so as the clusters are allocated and filled, the FAT gets updated, little by little. The directory entry for a file, however, is the last part of the file to go on the disk, mainly because the directory contains the file's size, and the operating system can't know that until it's finished writing the file out.

As the directory entry, with the starting cluster value, is often the last thing written when the file is created, this means that a program that "died" in the middle of manipulating the FAT could easily have created some FAT chains, but not yet have written the directory entry. Why would a program "die"?

- The computer may be shut off by a user in the middle of a file operation, perhaps because the user thought that by turning the computer off, he would save himself from some mistake.

- Buggy software. It either tries to bypass DOS and handle the FAT and directory stuff itself (incorrectly), or just freezes up in the middle of the file write operation.

- Along the lines of buggy software, there are a fair number of programs that create "temporary" files for their own use. They're supposed to delete these files upon exit, but some don't do a very good job of erasing the files. Lost clusters result.

Fixing Lost Clusters

Lost clusters are a chain of FAT entries—allocated clusters—with no directory entry. A lost cluster is, then, a "file with no name." (Sounds kinda like there's a country-western song in there: "Ah wrote a letter to my babe/ but the disk went lame / an' now those purty words / are in a file with no name…" Okay, so I'm not Kenny Rogers.) You can see a chain of lost clusters in Figure 14.8.

FIGURE 14.8:

A chain of lost clusters

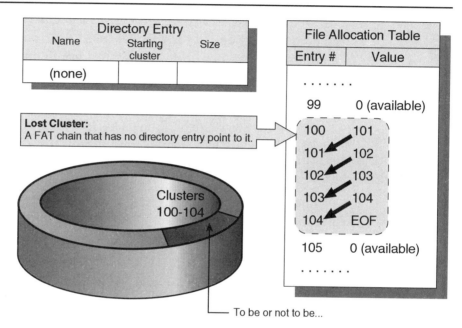

What do you do about lost clusters? First, remember that this is either a temporary file that's trash anyway or it's a file of some potential value whose write operation was never finished properly. In either case, there's probably nothing of value there. The main reason that you want to clean up lost clusters is to make CHKDSK happy and to get the space back on your hard disk that those lost clusters are wasting.

If you run CHKDSK on a disk with a lost cluster, you'll see a message like this:

```
Errors found, F parameter not specified. Corrections will not be
written to disk.
1 lost clusters found in 1 chain. Convert lost chains to files (Y/N)
```

Nobody ever knows what those first two lines mean, and they seem innocuous anyway. What gets people's attention, however, is the "lost clusters" part. First, CHKDSK is saying, "You have lost clusters." Most people are kind of panicky at this point, thinking, "Gee, I didn't even know I *had* clusters—much less that I could lose them." Lost gets confused with bad in most users' minds. They're not quite sure what's going on, but it seems that CHKDSK is offering to fix the problem with the "Convert lost chains to files?" question. So they say "Y" in response.

Those first two lines in the CHKDSK message *are*, in fact, important. CHKDSK, when run without the /F (Fix) option, does not actually do anything to the disk. What it's really saying is, "Even if I *say* I'm going to fix something, ignore me. I'm lying." If you tell CHKDSK to convert the lost chains to files, you'll get a response looking something like

```
XXXXX bytes total disk space
XXXXX bytes in XX directories...
2048 bytes would be in
1 recovered files...
```

You've got to read the fine print: 2048 bytes *would be* in 1 recovered files. It didn't actually *do* anything. Run it again, and you'll get the exact same response. Since it's not doing anything, it can easily *keep* doing nothing forever. I know this all seems pretty obvious when I explain it, but you'd be surprised how many users wonder why there are lost clusters every single time that they run CHKDSK. The answer is simple: they always run CHKDSK, not CHKDSK/F, and so the few lost clusters that they *have* never get fixed. How *would* you fix a chain of lost clusters? Just as CHKDSK says, it will convert the chain to a file. Lost clusters are just a file with no name, so CHKDSK creates a directory entry for the lost chain. The entry includes a bogus file name, FILE0000.CHK. If there's already a FILE0000.CHK, CHKDSK uses FILE0001.CHK, and so on. Those files are put in the root directory, by the way. For those people using DOS 6.2 and later, SCANDISK will do the same thing, and you don't have to bother with the /F parameter.

Here's a *very important point:* if, for some reason, you have loads and loads of lost clusters, you may see a File creation error message when CHKDSK is trying to convert the chains to files. That's because CHKDSK puts all the files in the root directory and the root, you may recall, only has room for up to 512 directory entries. So if you had 600 chains of lost clusters, CHKDSK would be able to create directory entries for the first 500-odd (depending on how many files you already have in the root), but would fail thereafter. The answer here is to handle the first 500-odd FILEXXXX.CHK files, then delete them, freeing up both their space and their directory entries. Then run CHKDSK again to handle their remaining lost clusters. Take a look at Figure 14.9.

FIGURE 14.9:

Fixing a chain of lost clusters

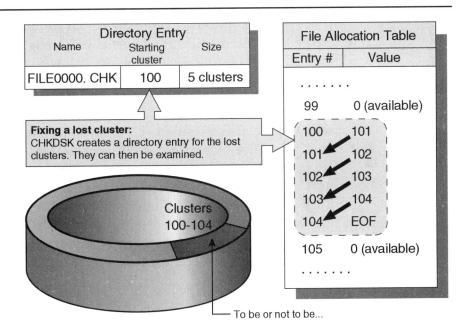

Once CHKDSK has put a file name on a chain, what can you do with this file? Generally, there's no value to the file. As I explained before, such files are usually temporary files and contain no valuable information. Data loss problems usually do not result in lost clusters.

On the other hand, it can't hurt to use a text editor or Norton to examine the file. There just may be some data that you thought you had lost.

Invalid Subdirectory Errors

As we've seen, a subdirectory's information is contained in a file. The subdirectory must have the "." and ".." files as its first entries. If they aren't there, CHKDSK assumes that the directory has been corrupted, and issues a message like this one:

```
C:\PCNET  Invalid sub-directory entry.
Convert directory to file (Y/N)?
```

CHKDSK is offering to take the actual subdirectory information and convert it to a file (not a particularly tough thing to do). The fact is, the operating system could work with the subdirectory without any trouble, even *if* the first two entries are corrupted.

CHKDSK, on the other hand, moves you from the frying pan into the fire. It is offering to *eliminate* the subdirectory as a directory. There are files in that subdirectory. Think about it: if we take away the directory, what do we have? FAT chains without directory entries, as their subdirectory has been zapped. You got it—files with no name: lost clusters. Allowing CHKDSK to convert the subdirectory to a file instantly converts all the files in that subdirectory (and any subdirectories *under* that subdirectory) to lost clusters. Sheesh! Nice job, CHKDSK. SCANDISK does the same dumb thing.

As I said, you can probably get to all the files even *if* the subdirectory is screwy. Try copying them elsewhere. Failing that, first print out the directory listing of the subdirectory.

Now CHKDSK sees a whole lot of FAT chains without directory entries, as their directory is gone. It then converts these to FILEnnnn.CHK files. Your problem is to match up the .CHK files with the former subdirectory contents. Your hints are the order and size of the files. The sizes may not match exactly, as CHKDSK just reports entire cluster size. The directory, with more specific file size information, is gone, so the best that CHKDSK can do is just to add up the number of bytes in the clusters and report that as the file size.

Here's an example. Imagine that we have the following files in an invalid subdirectory:

- ORDERS.TXT 2010 bytes

- NAMES.DBF   3000 bytes

Say that this is a hard disk, with 2048-byte sectors. After CHKDSK mauls the subdirectory, we find we have two new .CHK files:

- FILE0000.CHK 2048 bytes

- FILE0001.CHK 4096 bytes

Notice that the file sizes have been rounded up to the nearest 2048 multiple. To finish the recovery job first rename the files. Second, use Norton Utilities to revise the directory file size. *This is important*, as Lotus will refuse to read a file that has been completely recovered but has the wrong directory file size.

Or try to fix the subdirectory yourself. You know what the subdirectory is supposed to look like—recall the ".." and "." files. Load the damaged subdirectory file with NU and see if the damage is only minor. Perhaps you can do a little surgery and fix the problem without resorting to CHKDSK's extreme methods.

Allocation Error Message

Occasionally you will see CHKDSK complain about an *allocation error*. That means that the directory and the FAT do not agree about how large a file is. CHKDSK's response is to assume that the FAT has better information than the directory, and just set the directory's size entry equal to the number of clusters times cluster size—the total number of bytes that CHKDSK can find for the file in the FAT. Take a look at Figure 14.10.

FIGURE 14.10:

What an allocation error looks like

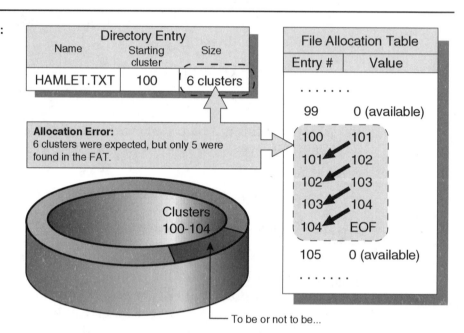

File Has Invalid Cluster Message

If a FAT chain leads to either a zero (an "available" cluster), or a "bad" marker, there's something wrong. CHKDSK responds by truncating the file at that point. For example, if a file were in clusters 100 through 104, a normal FAT chain would look like Table 14.1.

TABLE 14.1: Theoretical Normal FAT Chain

ENTRY NUMBER	ENTRY VALUE
100	101
101	102
102	103
103	104
104	EOF

If, through a software error, the value in entry 102 were converted to zero, the chain would look like Table 14.2.

TABLE 14.2: FAT Chain with a Value Converted to Zero

ENTRY NUMBER	ENTRY VALUE
100	101
101	102
102	0
103	104
104	EOF

This poses two problems. The first is that 101 points to 102, indicating that cluster 102 is "taken." There's a conflict, however, because 102 claims to be available, with a zero in its FAT entry. Further, 103 and 104 have now been cast adrift: there's a chain from 103 to 104, but nothing in the directory points to it. So CHKDSK would report both an allocation error (because 102 contains 0) and a chain of lost clusters.

When CHKDSK reports an allocation error, ask yourself: "When did I last modify this file?" That's when the problem was created. If you can nail down what program or, more likely, what *combination* of programs caused the bad FAT chain to be written, you can keep it from happening again.

Cross-Linked Clusters

Another CHKDSK complaint is *cross-linked clusters.* It refers to multiple pointers into the same cluster. It means that more than one file thinks it owns a disk area: cluster 14 (for example) is reported to be owned by more than one file. Figures 14.11 and 14.12 show a normal pair of files and a pair of cross-linked files.

FIGURE 14.11:

A pair of normal files

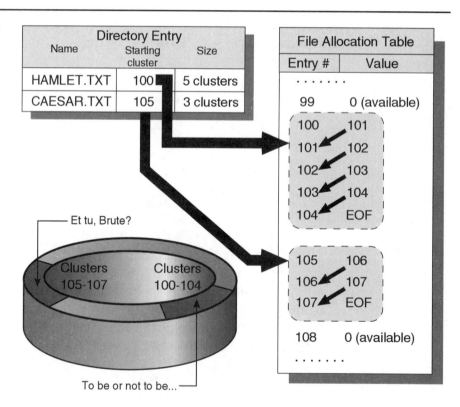

FIGURE 14.12:

A pair of cross-linked files

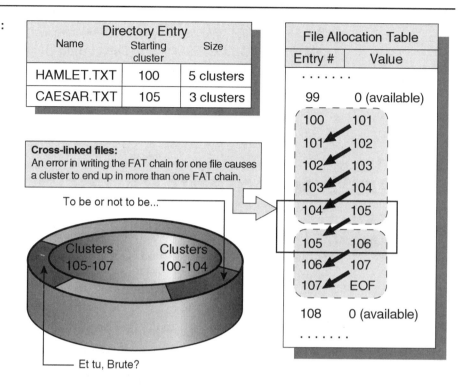

Directory Entry		
Name	Starting cluster	Size
HAMLET.TXT	100	5 clusters
CAESAR.TXT	105	3 clusters

Cross-linked files:
An error in writing the FAT chain for one file causes a cluster to end up in more than one FAT chain.

To be or not to be...

Clusters 105-107

Clusters 100-104

Et tu, Brute?

File Allocation Table	
Entry #	Value
. . . .	
99	0 (available)
100	101
101	102
102	103
103	104
104	105
105	106
106	107
107	EOF
108	0 (available)
. . . .	

Files become cross-linked generally because there is more than one program running on the PC at the same time, in some kind of multitasking mode, such as a LAN server or Windows. There are different ways to handle multitasking, but in one approach you run two programs simultaneously by modifying DOS so that you can run two DOS simultaneously and then run programs under these copies of DOS. Then program 1 asks DOS copy 1 to write out a file, and program 2 asks DOS copy 2 to also write out a file. As both copies of DOS are running simultaneously, each grabs for the same cluster. Result: cross-linked files. This will not necessarily happen with multitasking systems, but it does occasionally.

CHKDSK won't fix this for you; it'll just complain about it. The fix is to first copy all affected files to other files, and then delete the original affected files. In the example above there are two files, HAMLET.TXT and CAESAR.TXT, that are cross-linked. Copy them to HAMLET.BAK and CAESAR.BAK, respectively. Then delete HAMLET.TXT and CAESAR.TXT. The copied files will have as much data as can be recovered. In all probability, some data has been lost. Again, this is not a hardware error, but rather is caused by software.

Understanding and Repairing Media Errors

Some problems aren't solved so easily as just patching the FAT. Sometimes part of the drive just stops working. It could be that a part of the rusty coating on the drive that stores your data could have flaked off. Or perhaps the drive arm starts to wobble a bit and can't get to a particular part of the disk. Whatever the reason, you may find yourself with a dead—or dying—part of a disk.

There are two very different problems facing a user of a hard disk with a media problem. First and foremost is data recovery. There *is* such a thing as "too late" when it comes to disk media errors, so, as I've said before, I strongly counsel adopting a religious attitude to backups. Second is the question, "Can I continue to use this drive?" The answer is, "Maybe," and actually "probably," with some tricks you'll learn in this chapter.

Data Recovery: A Case Study and Some Tips

Late one night, I was working on the first edition of this book, concentrating on a fairly large chapter. I saved my document to my laptop's floppy disk drive (this was before laptops had hard disks), and tried to make a backup of my file (let's call it TEXT). The drive ran for a bit, then I heard a bone-chilling sound: the grinding noise of a mis-reading drive! Sure enough, seconds later I saw this:

```
Data error reading drive B:
Abort, Retry, Ignore?
```

What to do? I'd followed all the rules of good data integrity—I tried to back up as soon as I exited the application, but the dumb word processor hadn't verified the data when it wrote it out.

The first thing to try, of course, is *Retry*. It actually *does* work in some circumstances. Remember that your data doesn't actually disappear altogether, it just fades, albeit sometimes a *lot*. Before you get your hopes up, however, remember that Retry is almost always a wasted effort on hard disks, inasmuch as there may have been 90 retries even before you saw an error message. With floppies, it's a different story.

No luck. What now? Remember to go for the easy stuff first. Take the diskette out and reseat it in the drive. (It works sometimes.) Still no luck. Try another drive. Still no luck.

Now the chill begins to grow down my back. But I know what to do about this:

Get up and take a walk.

I'm serious. If you were in the position that I was at that moment, you'd be panicked at this point. Panic is a sure cause of problems.

Next, write-protect the diskette. Why? Simple. Most people do exactly the wrong thing at this point—they call in the big guns like Norton Disk Doctor. NDD is a nice program, but it's a surgeon. Surgeons get paid to *cut*. There's a time and place for surgeons, don't misunderstand me. But before you go to the surgeon, you get X-rays or MRIs, as a good doctor uses the most non-invasive techniques possible to figure out what the problem is before cutting.

And, for God's sake, *don't* run Norton SpeedDisk or Defrag! I have heard of no less than *five* cases in the last six months where someone wanted to recover data from a disk, so the "expert" first ran SpeedDisk. Arrgh. In case it's not clear why this is an incredibly stupid idea, go back and read the section that talks about defragmenter programs. (Do I sound harsh? If so, it's because few things annoy me more than "experts" who don't have the courage to say the magic three words "I don't know," and instead just blunder along in the hopes that they can solve the problem. That may work with some problems, but it sure doesn't work with data, believe me.) The job of these defragmenters is to move data that's in files so that each file is all in one place. That's data *in files*. In files means files that are good, readable, without problems. Delete data, and those areas that the data was once in are now available to be overwritten, and believe me, SpeedDisk will overwrite the data. Never, never, *never* run a disk defragmenter on a disk that you're trying to recover data from!

Now, try to make a copy to work from. There are two approaches to copying a file, each with its own pros and cons.

- COPY the file elsewhere. When it gets to the bad part, and asks `Abort, Retry, Ignore?`, tell it Ignore. As we've seen, Ignore says to take the data, warts and all. Better to have a file with a creepy cluster or two than to have no file at all.

- DISKCOPY the disk. DISKCOPY "Xeroxes" a disk—it copies the disk sector by sector. The problem is that when it hits a bad sector, it skips the whole track. It doesn't try to copy it at all, and in fact if there was data on the target disk before, DISKCOPY doesn't even bother to delete the track. But the resulting disk has the same structure as the problem disk.

Sometimes the DISKCOPY can get a few bytes that the COPY can't, and vice versa. Remember, these are the non-invasive techniques, so you can play to your heart's content without making things worse. Try the following techniques on the copies first. If that's no good, only *then* do you actually work on the *original* damaged disk.

Again, I wanted to affect the disk as little as possible, so I first "disconnected" cluster 612 from the file. It was simple: I just used Norton Utilities' NU program, and changed the FAT. The FAT previously said to go from cluster 611 to 612 and from 612 to 613. I changed it so that it went straight from 611 to 613, and I marked 612 as "bad," intending to look further at it later. Then I copied TEXT without a hitch. Terrific—most of the file's back, 1024 bytes to go.

Next, I went into NU and tried to read cluster 612. Now, as it turns out, clusters on a lot of floppy disks are just pairs of sectors—a sector on the bottom head and a sector on the top head of the floppy. No reason, therefore, to assume that the *whole* cluster was bad; it was quite unlikely that both sides would be damaged. So I asked NU to read the cluster, and sure enough, it got over half of it: one side (512 bytes) was totally undamaged, and some of the sector on the bad side was readable. Result: I got back about 800 bytes of the missing 1024 bytes, wrote them to another cluster, and again re-pointed the FAT to use the newly written cluster. Only 200 bytes remained of lost data, and 200 bytes is about a sentence or two, so it was a piece of cake to reconstruct. You'd nvr evn knw thr ws a prblem. (Just kidding.)

To summarize:

1. First choose Retry. If that does it, copy the data and throw away the problem disk.

2. Try another drive.

3. Stand up and walk around. Calm down.

4. Write-protect the problem disk before going further.

5. Try to DISKCOPY or COPY the file before going further. Do the surgery on the copy if possible. Remember that DISKCOPY throws out entire tracks and COPY only loses a bad cluster.

- *Do not* run invasive utilities like Norton Disk Doctor or Speed-Disk. If you *do* run Disk Doctor, don't let it make any of the "fixes" that it offers to do unless you've exhausted all other possibilities. *Under no circumstances* should you run Norton SpeedDisk on a disk with files that you're trying to recover.

6. Run SCANDISK or the like to determine where the bad clusters are. Then run DiskEdit and try to read these clusters. DiskEdit will read the good data as well as the bad. Copy the cluster to somewhere else and rearrange the FAT to use that cluster. Don't forget to modify *both* FATs.

It bears repeating: as soon as your hard disk starts showing spontaneous new bad sectors, back up the whole disk *immediately*, and get ready to replace it —it's on its way out.

What to Do with a Drive after a Media Failure

Assuming you've recovered your data, do you throw the drive away? Sometimes, sometimes not. Here's what you can do with a drive that demonstrates media errors.

Resurrecting Dead Hard Drives

Unerasing and Sector not found errors are really just the opening act for the big one—doing the Lazarus trick on your hard disk. Before you go further, you might review the information in Chapter 10, "Hard Disk Drive Overview and Terminology," on the details of how a PC boots.

Remember Your Priorities

Fixing a dead hard disk is really three different kinds of tasks, in order of importance:

- You seek to get your data off the hard disk.
- You must make the disk hardware respond to the system.
- You may want to make the disk bootable again and perhaps keep it in service.

Keep those priorities in mind. Many times, folks focus on the third and least important goal. Data recovery is the foremost goal, although you can't recover any data until the disk talks to the system in at least a minimal fashion.

The boot procedure is integral to the drive initialization process, the method whereby the system identifies the hard disk or disks in the PC. As I've already mentioned, look back to the boot description in Chapter 7, "Repairs with Circuit Boards and Chips," for more information on that. I'll build on that information immediately by presenting a flowchart of the drive recovery process. Large sections expand on each phase of the recovery process. Finally, I'll present disk troubleshooting from a different point of view, a "message-oriented" point of view. There's a large table that displays the various messages that you'll see if the disk doesn't boot and what they probably mean.

As I said in the previous chapter, this discussion assumes that we're talking about a drive that worked yesterday in the very same machine with the very same controller. You didn't drop it from the back of a truck, and you didn't add any new boards between then and now. If you're having installation problems, look back at Chapter 11, "Installing a Hard Disk," to find information on drive installation.

Tracing a Disk Failure

Understanding the boot process might lead us to try to first verify the hardware, then the partition, DBR, and so on—and that's how we'll do it, basically. But verifying the hardware involves popping the top and we'd like to avoid that if possible. So I've arranged the troubleshooting steps into a master hard disk troubleshooting flowchart designed for minimum effort. You can see it in Figure 14.13. It's an overview, and I'll frequently need to expand on one of the boxes, but it's still useful as a roadmap of the drive resurrection trail.

FIGURE 14.13:

A pair of normal files

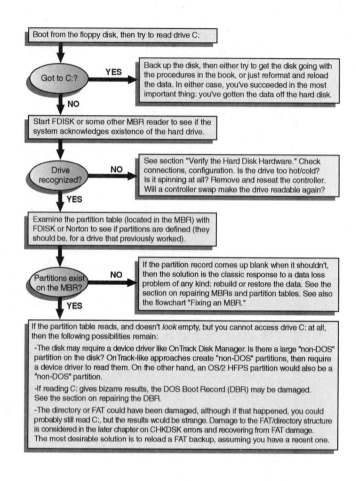

FIGURE 14.13:

A pair of normal files

There's a lot of detail in the following sections, so it's easy to get lost. If you do, come back to this flowchart to orient yourself.

Recovery Step 1: Boot from a Floppy

Get your "toolkit" floppy ("panic" floppy, some people call it) that I have suggested creating before. Boot from a floppy with whatever device drivers your system uses, and then try to read C: (or D: or whatever). If the drive is accessible, just copy all the data off the drive. Then you can figure out why it's misbehaving with less stress. You also don't need to go any further in this chapter: just reinstall the drive.

Recovery Step 2: Try to Read the MBR

The first and most important piece of data on the hard disk is the Master Boot Record (MBR), and the table that it carries within it, the Partition Table. Trying to read the MBR is a quick test of (1) the hardware's ability to recognize and read the drive and (2) the integrity of the MBR data itself.

There are a number of programs that will read an MBR on a disk. The DOS FDISK program is one such program, although a fairly limited one. The Norton Utilities' DiskEdit program will also read an MBR, as you saw in Chapter 13, "Viruses."

Whichever program you use, fire it up and try to read the MBR. If there's something seriously wrong with the MBR, you'll get a message along the lines of "you've asked me to read data off a disk, but the disk is not present," or the like. If you don't get that message, and it reads the MBR without complaint, skip the next subsection and go to "Recovery Step Three: Is the Partition Table Blank?"

Verify the Hard Disk Hardware

If a cable's loose, the controller's got a couple of cooked chips, or the drive motor doesn't want to start spinning, you've got a hardware problem. The BIOS generally detects that something is wrong during the initial POST (Power-On Self Test). You may see a message like one of the following. These messages are some of the first to appear when the system powers up, so watch carefully!

- 0 hard disk(s) found message on boot
- 1701, 1780, 1781, 1790, 1791, followed by an F1 to continue, and finally BASIC pops up on your screen
- Drive failure, Hard disk failure
- Invalid configuration—press F1 to continue
- Run SETUP—configuration lost

If you see one of these messages, don't panic. You can fix most hardware problems without a soldering iron and a schematic—a screwdriver and some patience will do the job in the majority of cases.

Try to resolve apparent hardware disk failures with the following steps:

1. Check that the PC has not lost its SETUP information.
2. Check that the drive has warmed to operating temperature: not too hot, not too cold.
3. Ensure that the cables are completely in place, or try swapping the cables.
4. Verify that the drive platters are spinning.
5. If it is a band-stepper, watch the stepper motor to see if the head moves on power-up.
6. Reseat the chips.
7. Swap the controller.

Details on the steps follow.

Check That the Drive Hasn't Lost CMOS

A drive won't work if it isn't recognized, as when an AT, PS/2, or 386 or later has lost its SETUP info, or the information is wrong.

Did you see a message like "Invalid configuration information—press F1 to continue"? If the battery's run down on your 286/386/486 or later computer, it may have forgotten that it has a hard disk or, worse, it may *misremember* what kind of hard disk it has. Run the SETUP program for your computer to check to see that the computer remembers correctly what kind of hard disk it has.

But what if you've lost the drive parameters? Well, you should look it up in your documentation. But if you don't have the documentation handy, check the exercises at the end of the chapter to see a trick that works many times to let you quickly retrieve drive parameters.

A 1790 or 1791 error almost always points to invalid configuration. AT-type systems first seek to cylinder 0, then out to the highest cylinder. If the seek to 0 fails, that's a 1780 or 1781, depending on whether it's the first or second hard drive. A 1780/1781 could be caused by a lot of things, so don't assume that the problem is configuration. If the seek to the highest cylinder fails, however, that's a 1790/1791—almost certainly a configuration problem. Why? Suppose a misconfiguration tells the system that the disk has 700 cylinders, when it actually has 500. The attempt to seek out to 700—200 cylinders further than the disk can handle—will fail, and 1790/1791 will result.

Is the Drive Too Hot or Cold?

The drive won't work normally if it is too cold, or, less likely, too hot.

Is it Monday morning? Did you just bring the drive in from the outside, if the computer is a laptop? Make sure the drive is warmed up to room temperature before you try to use it (this goes double if you're about to format it). Alternatively, could it be too hot? If a temperature probe indicates that your computer's insides exceed 110 degrees F (43 degrees C), your drive may be overheated.

One quick way to overheat the inside of a PC is if the PC's fan isn't working. Is air flowing through the chassis?

Check the Drive Cables

Perhaps the drive's cables have come loose or have been reconnected incorrectly, or they may just be bad.

Do you have another set of cables? Give them a try. Have you been inside the computer recently? I know, I know—you didn't touch the hard drive. But removing the case could accidentally move cables around. Just reach down behind the drive and make sure the cables are snugly in place. I taught a "hands-on" class recently where we used 10 identical machines. One of the machines kept experiencing hard disk failures. In each case, all that was needed to fix the drive was to just reach around behind the drive, and reseat the 34-wire edge connector, which kept slipping off.

Recovery Step 3: Is the Partition Table Blank?

If the previous steps worked, stop: you needn't continue. On the other hand, if they didn't, we'll now examine the partition table.

The previous step read the MBR mainly to see if the hardware was functioning in even a minimal way. Now we'll examine the

PT to see if the partition definitions are still intact. (In the next step, we'll see if they make sense.) If the PT is blank, *you will not see any error messages at boot time*. DOS just ignores a non-partitioned drive. If there isn't a bootable floppy in drive A:, the system will either go to Cassette BASIC (in the case of true-blue IBMs) or request that a bootable floppy be inserted in drive A: (in the case of the rest of the PC world); on some systems, you'll just get a Boot ROM not present message.

Returning to the master flowchart, we're now at "Examine the partition table…." You've got the MBR. Is the partition table blank—does FDISK report that there are no partitions?

The partition table should not be blank on a drive that was previously working, so something has deleted it. If it *isn't* blank, go to the next step. Perhaps the first thing you should do if you've got a blank partition table is to just reboot. I've got an old 32MB drive that's starting (after seven years) to misbehave. It doesn't quite spin up to 3600 RPM, and sometimes reports that the partition record is blank. A reboot or two gives it time to spin up to 3600, and the partition is read just fine. (Yes, I should throw it away, and I will eventually.)

You fix a blank partition table/MBR like any data loss problem. Try to restore the data from a backup (or rebuild, if you didn't make a backup). If the drive won't take the data, reformat cylinder 0, head 0 to restore the sector IDs on that track. And if the format won't work, there's physical damage on 0/0, and you need to get a new hard drive.

Recovery Step 4: Examine the DBR and BPB

Finishing up the large box at the bottom of the master flowchart, we come to the DBR, the DOS Boot Record. This is the first sector in the DOS partition. It contains a small program that loads the hidden files and boots the operating system.

We're not interested in that program right now, however, as the question of whether or not the hard disk is bootable is not important. What *is* interesting is a data structure inside the DBR called the BIOS Parameter Block (BPB). It describes the disk—how many FATs are on the disk, how large the clusters are, what the total number of sectors on the disk are, and so on: all very important information. If it's corrupted, the disk will be unreadable.

The Final Step: Send Your Drive to the Mayo Clinic

Still can't get it to talk to you? Hey, look—even Dr. Kildare lost a few. If you *really* need that data, there is a last hope. It ain't cheap—from $1,000 to $20,000—but you can send it to a service. They disassemble the disk and remove the data, then send it to you on floppies, or nowadays, often a CD. These services aren't inexpensive: they charge $200 to diagnose the problem, then you negotiate over the recovery cost. Expensive, yes, but cheaper than going out of business.

You'll find a list of data recovery services in the appendix. They may have specialties, so shop around a bit before sending your poor infirm hard disk to these wizards.

But I hope after getting through this chapter you needn't even contemplate bringing in outside help. That finishes the section of the book on hard disks; next, we'll take up floppies.

CHAPTER

FIFTEEN

15

Understanding, Installing, and Repairing Floppy Drives

- ■ The floppy subsystem

- ■ Preventative maintenance for floppies

- ■ Removing, configuring, and installing floppy drives

- ■ Troubleshooting and testing

Installing a Floppy Drive

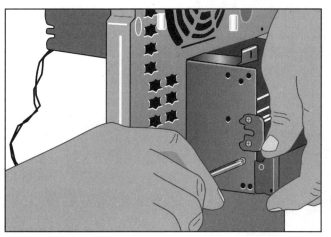

1 Mount the floppy drive into the computer's chassis or drive bay.

2 If you are installing the first floppy drive, connect the floppy data cable to the connector at the edge of the motherboard.

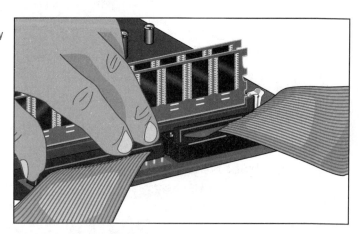

Berg connector

3 The power connector on the back of a floppy drive requires a Berg connector from the power supply unit.

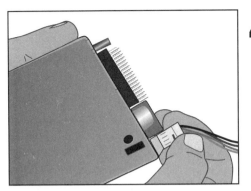

4 Connect the Berg connector from the power supply to the rear of the floppy unit.

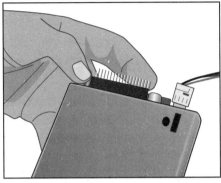

5 One of the other connectors on the floppy data cable will connect to the gold connector pins at the rear of the floppy drive.

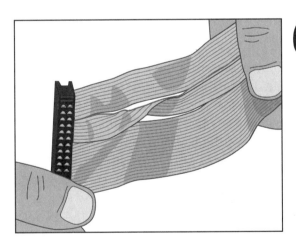

6 If you are installing floppy drive A:, use the connector with the twisted wires in the cable. If you are installing a second floppy drive, use one of the other data connectors on the cable.

7 Connect the floppy data cable to the connector pins at the rear of the floppy drive unit.

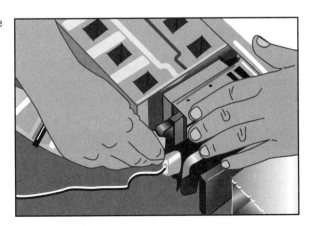

Now that we've covered hard drives, let's take a look at floppy drives.

In the Days before Floppies

I didn't buy my first four microcomputers (a Netronics Elf, a TRS80 Model I, an OSI Challenger 1P, and an IBM PC) with floppy disk drives. Floppies cost too much money at that time, so most of us micro users in those days used cassettes. *Cassettes?* Yup, cassettes. There was a standard interface called the "Tarbell interface" that let micros read and write data to standard $40 cassette machines at a rate of 600bps. They were a pain, and not very reliable, but there wasn't much else available.

Cassettes were so popular, in fact, that the IBM PC was shipped with a cassette port and the first PC I bought didn't have a floppy drive or floppy controller; I couldn't afford them at first, but eventually I could. When the system booted up without an attached drive, it defaulted to a version of the BASIC language stored in ROM. This was, again, no great innovation—most microcomputers shipped with BASIC in ROM in the late '70s and early '80s. That's why, to this day, if your PS/2 can't boot from the floppy or the hard disk, BASIC appears on the screen. You're seeing the same old cassette BASIC that's been part of PC system ROM since 1981.

The Post-Floppy Era

Today, however, virtually 100 percent of PCs have floppy drives. The few machines that do not have floppies lack them by design; some secure locations use "diskless" workstations that use a LAN for all mass storage needs. Never heard of them? A diskless workstation is a computer with no floppy drive and often no hard disk. How does it boot? Usually from the network. Why would you have such a machine? It's kind of the way that the boss tells his employees, "I don't trust you." There's no floppy on employee computers so that employees can't take data off of the job site on disk.

Floppies are a marvel of construction. The amount of moving parts that they possess makes it surprising that they are in the least bit reliable, but in fact they are fairly solid these days, with some exceptions. If you asked a PC repair person in the early '80s, "What's the least reliable part of the PC?" you'd be told that it was probably a toss-up between the floppy drive or the daisy wheel printer. But nobody uses daisies anymore, and their laser-based replacements are quite trouble-free. There's good news in the floppy department, as floppies are also less troublesome than they once were. This is partly because they are manufactured better and partly because they're used less: hard disks are the medium of choice for many home users and most corporate users. The floppy's role nowadays is mainly as a program distribution medium and an archival device. As most hard disks can't travel, most computers still rely on floppies to get information from the outside world. (By the way, ask that repair person what's the most troublesome part of *today's* PCs, and the answer will be the hard drive.)

Floppies Nowadays

Floppies are cheap enough these days that they're basically disposable—floppy problems can be fixed by someone with no troubleshooting ability at all by just replacing the bad drive. But there's more, and you'll first see in this chapter what the components of the floppy disk subsystem are and then how to test, replace, and adjust these components.

Floppies are again in a state of transition. Once, it was possible to ship commercial software on floppies. That's still happening, but having to load 30 floppies in order to install one's word processor is becoming a bit silly.

Furthermore, as floppy drives plummet in price, there's a concomitant drop in quality. Too often I install a package with 20 floppies, only to find that when I insert disk 16, the drive grinds a bit and finally says, "Please insert disk 16," another way of saying "I can't read this disk." How do you fix this, by the way? In almost every case, all I had to do was to go to another computer with disk 16 (or whatever number it was) and try to DISKCOPY that disk—the drive on the second computer was just different enough from the one on the original computer that it could read disk 16. I then try the disk created by the second computer, and the first computer takes it, so I can finish my software installation.

All of this is pretty much a thing of the past, however, because almost all PCs today have CD-ROMs, and most software loads from CD-ROM.

The Floppy Subsystem

The floppy disk subsystem is, like the rest of the PC, modular. That's useful because you will see that you can use this modularity to "divide and conquer" in order to solve problems. The subsystem consists of the drive, a controller board, the cable connecting the drive to the controller, and the floppy disks themselves.

Part 1: The Floppy Disk

A floppy, when extracted from its case, looks like a thin 45rpm record, only quite a bit smaller. It's a Mylar disk with iron oxide affixed to it. (Who would have imagined that we'd rely every day on a data storage medium made out of the same plastic that weather balloons are made of, with rust glued onto it? Maybe that's why I can't read my backups on rainy days.) We worry so much about dust getting on our hard disk surfaces that we seal up the disk drive. Should we have the same concern about floppies? Is there some way to "clean" a disk? You may recall, in your past (or present) audio buff days, getting out the Discwasher and cleaning the record prior to playing it. For some people, ritual like this is comforting. For those people, I must sadly report that no such thing occurs with floppies.

Floppies are stored inside their own Discwasher: a semi-rigid case lined with fleecy material. As the disk rotates inside the case, any dust is picked up by the material. The case has a hole cut in it so that the disk can be read/written without having to remove it from the case. In general, there is no need to clean a floppy disk. You can see floppy disks in Figure 15.1.

FIGURE 15.1:

Floppy disks

A reasonable life expectancy for a floppy disk is said to be about three to four years by disk manufacturers. There are, of course, better and worse disks. There are different coatings on higher density disks, generally incorporating less iron oxide (a cheap ingredient) and more cobalt (an expensive ingredient).

Part 2: The Floppy Drive

Almost everything available on disk nowadays comes on 3.5-inch disks, so there's no need any more to buy 1.2MB 5.25-inch drives on new PCs. When mounting a 3.5-inch drive, the data connections are the same as those used for a 5.25-inch drive. Power is connected via a smaller, 4-pin Berg connector, but the controller is now usually right on the motherboard.

Part 3: The Disk Controller

Whenever a computer wants to interface with an outside device, it needs a controller to act as a "go-between" to allow the outside device—a floppy, in this case—to talk with the CPU. XT-type machines generally had a separate controller board. AT-type machines usually put the floppy and hard disk controller function on the same board. Most motherboards today put the floppy controller function right on the motherboard.

Part 4: The Cable

The last piece in the floppy subsystem is the cable that connects the controller to the drive. Cables sound insignificant, but this one isn't: I've fixed a pile of floppy problems by swapping cables. The drive is connected to the controller by a 34-wire ribbon cable. Most of the cables have three edge connectors: one for the drive controller, one for drive A:, and one for drive B: (although very few computers nowadays have a second floppy drive). As the cable is 34 wires wide, you'd think that the interface between the floppy and the controller is a parallel interface—8 bits wide—but it's not. Floppy-to-controller interface is serial, transferring one bit at a time.

The connector from the drive controller to B: is a "straight-through" cable—i.e., pin 1 on the drive controller side is connected to pin 1 on the floppy side, 2 is connected to 2, etc. The connector to A: has a twist in it, however. It is this twist that identifies A: as different from B: and you can see this in Figure 15.2. The ribbon cable has three connectors: one on one end and two on the other end. The lone end goes on the controller. The one in the middle goes on drive B:. The one on the other end goes on drive A:. If you're likely to forget (as I am), get a magic marker and write "controller," "B:," and "A:" on the appropriate connectors before disassembling the whole thing.

FIGURE 15.2:

Floppy cable with twist for A: drive

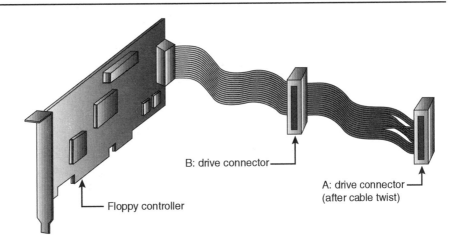

B: drive connector

Floppy controller

A: drive connector (after cable twist)

It never hurts to have a couple of extra cables around. The cables are inexpensive and are available from many mail-order houses or computer discounters, so it's easy to keep an extra one around. Swapping the cable is easy. Testing continuity is a pain.

Simple Preventive Maintenance for Floppies

Failure on the floppy could be a scary, potentially disastrous thing. What can you do to lower the probability of this disaster? Anyone who has a VCR and rents videotapes on a regular basis has probably learned of the need to clean the VCR's heads. Something like that can be done for the floppy as well, although you'll probably never need to. And a few diagnostic tests can point out upcoming floppy problems.

To Clean Heads or Not to Clean Heads?

Like your VCR, floppies have an electromagnetic read/write head that does most of the drive's work. In the process of accessing the disk, the head may rub some of the coating off the disk and onto itself. It seems reasonable, then, to assume that head cleaning kits are good things.

When you can't see something, you get superstitious about it. We can't see the junk on floppy heads (or data on magnetic disks, for that matter), so we play it safe and purchase a floppy head cleaner to ward off floppy evil spirits. Once procured, however, the first question is: how often should I clean the floppy heads?

The instructions on the head cleaner say to do it every week. That doesn't seem to be a good piece of advice, as shoving a floppy head cleaner in a drive could misalign a disk head. The floppy cleaner is a relatively thick piece of cotton shaped like a floppy. Worse yet, some floppy cleaners are *abrasive*—they wear away some of the floppy head with every use. (One has to look askance at this procedure. Scraping away some of the head to find a clean part seems somewhat like using sulfuric acid to clean one's teeth.)

Personally, I clean my heads only when the drive fails. I have some computers on which I've *never* cleaned the heads, and they work fine. My recommendation: clean the heads only when you start experiencing read/write errors.

As I hinted before, *be careful* in choosing a floppy head cleaner! Don't buy an abrasive cleaner—make sure it uses a cotton floppy and some cleaning fluid.

By the way, there's an issue related to cleaning the heads called *demagnetizing* them; it's done with some audio recording heads. People sometimes ask me if floppy heads need to be demagnetized—they don't.

Defending Disks

Did you ever notice the "do not" cartoons on the back of a disk jacket?

They lead you to believe that floppies are very fragile items. A little practical experience with disks teaches you that it isn't really true. Yes, disks must be taken care of, but you needn't get crazy about it. Don't put them on the radiator, or leave them on a shelf that gets three hours of direct sunlight every day. Don't store them under the roof leak. Given the choice, store them upright stacked left to right rather than on top of each other.

When it comes to temperature extremes, you've got to be concerned about something called *thermal shock*. If your portable computer has been sitting in the back of the car in freezing temperatures overnight, bring it in and let it warm up before using it. Just a little heat expansion/contraction can temporarily realign your drives or make the motors respond a little differently. More extreme temperatures can damage the disks: vendors claim that disks should never be stored below 50 degrees nor above 125 degrees. Cold isn't as much of a problem. I've ordered software through the mail and have had it sit outside in January in my mailbox for a week, and have had no problem reading the disks.

Dust, smoke, and dirt can cause damage to the head and/or to a disk. Everybody knows smoking is not good for you, but you may not know just how bad it is for your drives. If you're in a dusty environment, think about getting a power supply with a filtered fan. Running the air through a filter before pushing it through the system removes the vast majority of the dust particles.

As you read in Chapter 4, "Avoiding Service: Preventive Maintenance," magnets—both the permanent and electromagnetic type—can cause permanent loss of data on hard or floppy disks. Something I have yet to understand is the little plastic paper clip holders with the circular magnet near the opening. Why is the magnet there? Are people afraid the paper clips will get out if not magnetically restrained? (As Monty Python might say, "are you suggesting paper clips are *migratory?*") One day, you'll put a floppy on top of the paper clip holder. It'll be sad. Or you'll use one of the paper clips—now magnetized by their proximity to the magnet—to clip a document to a floppy. Arghh.

Removing, Configuring, and Installing Floppy Drives

You generally won't repair drives, but rather replace them. That means it's most important to be able to rip 'em out and slap 'em in.

Removing Floppy Drives

Floppy drives are removed in three steps:

1. Remove screws from mounting brackets.

2. Remove power connection.

3. Remove data connection.

I covered the physical extraction part pretty thoroughly in Chapter 2, "Disassembling the PC," so I won't repeat it here.

Installing Floppy Drives

Installing a floppy is just the reverse of removing one, except that the drive must be configured. To configure a new floppy, you must:

- Connect it to the twisted connector if it's drive A: or the non-twisted connector if it's drive B:.

- Attach a power connector.

Floppy Troubleshooting

The mechanical nature of floppy drives makes them prone to a host of ills.

A Disk Cannot Be Read

Pop a disk in the drive, try to read it, and the message says `Data error reading drive A:`, or `Sector not found reading drive A:`, or perhaps the dread `General failure reading drive A:`. Such a message is even better than your morning coffee to get the ole' blood pumping, particularly if the disk contains your only copy of the football pool.

What to do:

1. Press R for Retry. Sometimes it'll work. Ignore the painful grinding sounds.

2. Remove and replace the floppy. I've seen 3.5-inch drives that are unreadable until you take them out and put them back in. The hub centering is fairly critical.

3. Take the floppy out and try it in another drive.

4. A related question—does the drive read other disk? If so, either the disk's head could be misaligned, or the disk could have been written by a different disk drive, and that drive's head was misaligned. Try to find the drive that created the disk. (If it's the one you've been fooling with, obviously this advice isn't too useful.)

5. If you *still* haven't solved the problem, you're basically in the same boat as someone who's suffered a media failure on their hard disk. Look back in this book to the hard disk data recovery section.

The Drive Refuses to Function

When the drive won't read or write properly, there are a bunch of possible causes. I am assuming here that this is a drive that worked fine yesterday and that you haven't done anything that would obviously cause drive problems.

1. Did you see a floppy drive controller failure error on the screen when the system booted up? On Self Test (POST) an error message means that drive A: did not respond. The system no longer realizes you have a floppy drive. This means that your CMOS battery has failed, the controller has failed, drive A: has failed, or the cable is bad.

2. If there wasn't a POST error, try other disks. If only one disk gives the drive fits, the problem more likely lies in the disk.

3. Clean the disk heads. It's easy and takes only a minute.

4. Try to format a disk. If you can format a disk alright, but that disk is unreadable by other drives, your drive head is probably misaligned. If it's misaligned, toss it. New ones are about $15 today and realigning a floppy drive is not a project, it's a career.

5. Finally, if you get here, swap the relevant components: the controller, cable, and drive. Only swap one component at a time, and when swapping a component doesn't solve the problem, replace the component. If the problem goes away after you've swapped five components, you haven't really pinpointed the source of trouble. It could have been any of the five items that you replaced.

6. Again, don't overlook the lowly cable. Cables can get nicked when installing boards, replacing drives, or just removing the cover. How bad that is depends on which line gets nicked. One cable on an old laptop that I once owned kept the change line from working. A friend once had an AT that just plain wouldn't format the A: drive. We've got lots of drives

around, so we didn't worry much about it. One day he noticed a nick on the cable. He replaced the cable, and the problem went away, never to return.

It only takes a two-minute swap with another cable to find out for sure.

Intermittent Disk Errors Cannot Be Solved by Changing the Drive

Or the controller, for that matter. Suppose you get periodic data loss, and have changed the drive and controller—what next? The power supply. Malfunctioning power supplies show up as "gremlins" in the system. Try swapping the power supply.

Disk Rotation Speed

Small variations in disk speed (plus or minus 1 percent) are okay, but greater differences can make the floppy nonfunctional or dangerous.

Dangerous? Yes. Many years ago, I was asked to install a copy of a program I was using. It was a perfectly legal copy. When I went to install it, it informed me that it was an illegal copy and refused to load. I tried installing it on other machines. It didn't work. The software publisher first told me that I was lying or mistaken, and finally (after threats of violence) sent me another master disk.

What had happened was this: the floppy on the computer had a drive that was slightly out of correct speed. Not so different as to render it unusable for normal uses, but enough to upset the finicky copy protection system on the program disk. Worse, the copy protection system being used on the disk would permanently alter a disk that it saw as an illegal copy. Once the system thought a disk was bad, it would alter the disk so that it would always seem bad. That was why the disk wouldn't run on other computers. Copy protection is almost a quaint memory, but not quite yet.

Drive Shows Phantom Directories

The symptom here is that you do something, like a DIR command, on a floppy. Then you remove the disk and put a different disk in the drive. Do a DIR, and you see the *directory of the previous floppy, not the one in the drive now!*

If you see this on a computer, this is a RED ALERT! Don't use the thing until you get the problem fixed. Reason: say you put a floppy in the drive, and do a DIR on it. Then you put a different floppy in the drive, and write some data to the floppy. *The PC writes data to the new floppy using the old floppy's directory!* That means the newly written file is probably okay, but everything else on the floppy is trashed. (Let me tell you about how I lost four pages out of a chapter in a book I wrote many years back.) Where does this problem come from? It's something called the *change line signal*. Time for a little history.

Back in the old days, when floppies were the major storage medium for micros, software designers wanted to squeeze the most performance from those floppy drives, mainly because they were pretty low-performance. (I know, you were expecting one of those boring "old-timer" stories about how I used to have to write my own BIOS hacks and make cables using my teeth to bare the wires and so on. Not just now, but buy me a couple of Flowers' Bitters sometime, and I'll tell you about how I used a matchbook cover to repair a hard disk and saved the free world in the process.) One way to do that was to avoid, wherever possible, rereading information on a floppy. What information gets read the most? The directory and FAT. Way back before DOS even existed, there was an operating system called CP/M—Control Program for Microcomputers. To get better speed, some CP/M applications only read the directory when a disk was first inserted in a drive. That meant that if you were going to swap a floppy while in WordStar, you had to tell WordStar, or it would trash your floppy. It was a real pain.

The original PC guys remembered the CP/M experience, and (I'm guessing) decided that they'd sacrifice a little speed for reliability. So the PC and XT (not all XT clones) BIOS always read the disk directory and FAT prior to doing anything dangerous—they don't assume that the floppy stays in the same place. And all was well with the world.

But some makers of compatibles, looking to outdo IBM performance-wise, sold computers with slightly different floppies: these floppy drives had something called *change line support*. No big revolution: in fact, it had been around since the CP/M days. One of the signals from the drive to the controller was a "change line" signal—it signaled that the floppy door had been opened since DOS had last looked at the drive. If the change line was activated, DOS would reread the floppy; if not, it wouldn't bother. That meant that writes needn't be preceded by directory reads, as in the IBM XT case.

The IBM AT design team, looking to show the competition who was boss, added the change line feature to the AT. That means there is a minor difference between XT floppy drives and AT floppy drives: the XT drives don't really use line 34 on the floppy edge connector, but the AT drives use 34 as the "change line" line. To complicate matters, this question of whether or not change line support is really needed is determined by what BIOS your computer has. Some XT clones need it, some don't. Some AT clones need it, others don't. The IBM AT needs it. You really can't go wrong with a floppy with change line support, as a computer that doesn't need it will just ignore it.

If you have a computer that needs change line support, and you install a floppy drive that lacks it, the computer will display the phantom directory. (And possibly trash a floppy someday.)

Now you know what change line support is, and that some computers need it. Suppose you find yourself with a change line problem—phantom directories. What do you do?

Check the floppy cable. The aforementioned old XT (a clone) has a scratched cable. I haven't gotten around to replacing it yet, but that's the answer.

- **The other possibility "fools" the controller into thinking that there have been lots of change line signals.** One approach to this is simply to construct a cable that disconnects line 34 on the drive side, and cross-connects lines 34 and 20 on the controller side. As line 20 is activated with each head step, the controller will believe that it is seeing many change line signals.

- **Ctrl+C between disk accesses.** The last approach is to just remember to do a Ctrl+C keystroke when you're in DOS and you've changed the floppy. It forces DOS to reread the disk directories. Not great, but a good emergency measure.

The Future of Floppies

No discussion of floppies would be complete without a little look at where floppies are going, and going *soon*. Several companies are vying to set the next standard in floppies. Toshiba has put forth a ho-hum 2.88MB floppy disk that is a small increment in technology, but it has had a less than enthusiastic welcome. Today we have SuperDrives that can hold up to 120MB of data and still read our old 1.44MB floppies.

The Toshiba 2.88MB Floppy

Not much interesting here: an 80-track disk, as before, but this time with 36 sectors per track, rather than 18 as in the case of the 1.44MB floppy. Prices will probably end up around $90 per drive, and a box of 10 floppies will run around $40. At the normal 300-rpm rotation rate, the 2.88MB floppies would have a data transfer rate of 90K/second, about the same as the old IBM 10MB XT—not too shabby. It, like the other four drives, will read and write the older 720 and 1.44MB disks. Finally, the 2.88MB floppies can be formatted by a user's drive, unlike the other three.

CHAPTER

SIXTEEN

16

Understanding and Installing SCSI Devices

- SCSI overview and configuration

- SCSI physical installation

- SCSI software installation

- SCSI-1, SCSI-2, and SCSI-3

Installing a SCSI Card

1 SCSI cards have connectors for both internal and external devices.

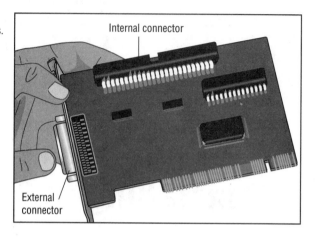

Internal connector

External connector

2 Connect an internal device to the connector at the top of the card.

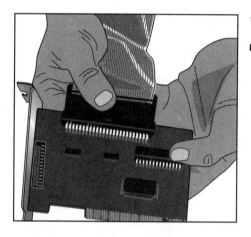

3 There are several types of external connectors for SCSI cards; be sure to match the correct cable to your card and device.

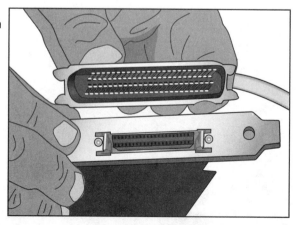

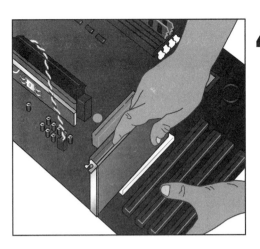

4 Insert the SCSI card into a PCI slot.

5 Insert the connector from an external device into the connector at the rear of the card.

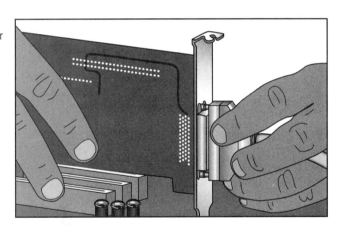

6 Set the target ID number for the external device (in this example, a JAZ drive). Be sure the last device on a SCSI chain is terminated (in this example, the JAZ drive has a switch on the back that sets the termination).

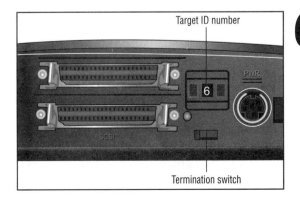

Target ID number

Termination switch

In this chapter, you'll learn about what SCSI does, how to physically install SCSI devices, and how to set up software to support SCSI devices. Once you know that, you will be better equipped to attack problems with SCSI.

SCSI Overview

Prior to the mid-'80s, every type of storage device had its own kind of controller. If you wanted to add a scanner, a hard disk, a tape backup device, and a CD-ROM to your computer, then you'd have to install one board into the system that would act as the interface for the scanner, another for the hard disk, one for the tape, and one for the CD-ROM. That meant not only four controllers, it also meant having to *configure* four separate boards. This is shown in Figure 16.1.

FIGURE 16.1:

Controllers and peripherals

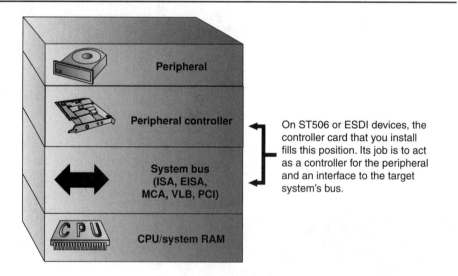

On ST506 or ESDI devices, the controller card that you install fills this position. Its job is to act as a controller for the peripheral and an interface to the target system's bus.

The computer industry responded to this with the following idea: build PC peripherals that have controllers built right in, so those peripheral/controller combinations are configured correctly, right out of the factory. The only interface problem that would remain would be interfacing the controller/peripheral pair to the bus of the target system—the PC, in this case, but it would be just as easy to interface (in theory) to a Macintosh, a UNIX workstation, or a PC. A new interface arose called the *Small Computer Systems Interface*, or *SCSI*. Take a look at Figure 16.2.

FIGURE 16.2:

SCSI

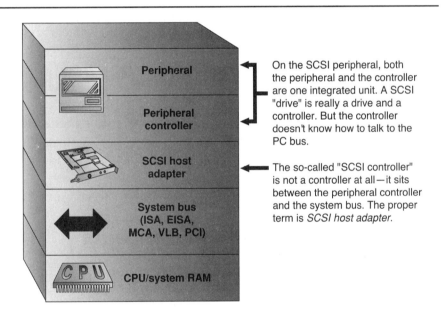

On the SCSI peripheral, both the peripheral and the controller are one integrated unit. A SCSI "drive" is really a drive and a controller. But the controller doesn't know how to talk to the PC bus.

The so-called "SCSI controller" is not a controller at all—it sits between the peripheral controller and the system bus. The proper term is *SCSI host adapter*.

SCSI Benefits

The benefit of putting a controller on each device in the SCSI world is that you know that the controller and drive are a matched set. In particular:

- The cables between the controller and the drive, which are a troublesome source of noise, can be extremely short, leading to much lower noise levels.

- The controller and drive (or peripheral) can be more closely matched. That means that built-in diagnostics can be included on the SCSI device.

SCSI peripherals can be focused to do a particular task, but they lack the ability to talk to any real-world bus. SCSI devices don't know what a Macintosh, a PC, or a Sun computer is. That's where the SCSI board that you install in your system comes in. The SCSI "controller," then, is not a controller at all; it's just a kind of "universal translator" that allows any SCSI device to communicate with a particular computer's bus. The SCSI *host adapter* (its true name) is, then, the "glue" that cements your SCSI devices and your computer.

The trick to SCSI is that it makes disk drives, all of which come in different shapes and sizes, into generic storage devices. That was the goal of the original SCSI. As time has gone on, SCSI has been expanded to include all kinds of storage devices, as well as printers and scanners.

Some Basic SCSI Concepts

SCSI includes a whole new bunch of terms. I'll describe some of them in a minute, as I take you step-by-step through planning and configuring a SCSI installation. But here's a quick introduction to some SCSI concepts.

SCSI-1, SCSI-2, and SCSI-3

The original SCSI specification appeared in 1980 as a hard disk interface. It lacked agreed-upon standards, leading to a plethora of different—and incompatible—SCSI implementations. SCSI-2 made some big steps toward standardizing SCSI, improved data transfer rate, and supported new types of devices. SCSI-3, or Ultra SCSI, increases the number of devices that a SCSI sub-system can support, their data transfer rate, and cable lengths, as well as providing for simpler cable schemes.

Single-Ended versus Differential SCSI

The vast majority of SCSI implementations use an electronic signaling system that is called "single-ended" in the SCSI world and is known as "unbalanced" in much of the data communications interface world. Single-ended SCSI systems will not work if the total length of their cables exceeds 6 meters. Differential SCSI uses a "balanced" approach that requires twice as many wires in a cable but can support up to 25 meters on a cable.

SCSI IDs

Because SCSI is a bus, multiple devices share it. One device is distinguished from another on the bus by its SCSI ID, a number from 0 to 7 on SCSI-1 or SCSI-2 systems, 0 to 15 on a single-channel SCSI-3 system, or 0 to 31 on a dual-channel SCSI-3 system.

Active and Passive SCSI Terminators

The electronics of SCSI require that both ends of the chain of SCSI devices contain a circuit that "terminates" the system. Older systems used a simple circuit called a *passive terminator.* Most systems nowadays require an *active terminator.* The problem is that many SCSI devices with "built-in termination" offer only passive termination, and that either means that you've got to buy an active termination device or put up with flaky SCSI performance.

I just defined those terms quickly so that we had a starting point. Let's dive into SCSI by setting up SCSI on a PC.

Defining a SCSI Configuration

Making SCSI work involves these items and issues. This is just an overview; we'll examine each of these issues in detail.

SCSI Host Adapters

Issues:

- The host adapter must be compatible with the system's bus.

- There are different versions of SCSI: SCSI-1, SCSI-2, and SCSI-3. The host adapter must be able to support the same level of SCSI as the peripherals.

- When you're buying a SCSI host adapter, you're buying the ambassador between all those expensive, fast peripherals you bought and your CPU and memory. Now, more than ever, bus mastering and 32-bit interface SCSI host adapters are preferable.

- The host adapter must be assigned a SCSI ID between 0 and 7, or 0 and 15 on a single channel SCSI-3 host adapter (most common for PCs).

- The host needs a SCSI driver that follows the same SCSI standard as the SCSI drivers on the peripherals. There are three standards here: ASPI, CAM, and LADDR. These are *not* related to SCSI-1, SCSI-2, and SCSI-3; this is a different dimension in SCSI compatibility.

SCSI-Compatible Peripherals

Issues:

- Each SCSI peripheral needs a SCSI driver that is compatible with the SCSI standard on the host's SCSI driver.

- All SCSI devices follow SCSI-1, SCSI-2, or SCSI-3 cable standards; it may be important to know which level the device follows when installing it.

- Each peripheral must be assigned a unique SCSI ID from 0 to 7, or 0 to 15 for single channel SCSI-3.

- Devices can be mounted internally or externally.

- Some devices have optional built-in termination (see below); others may have termination that's *not* optional (this is *very* bad, but more common than you'd hope), and still others do not include termination of any kind.

- Terminated devices should support active termination, but some will support only passive termination.

- Devices should be able to be daisy-chained, so they should have two SCSI connectors if they are external.

SCSI Cabling

Issues:

- There are several kinds of SCSI cables and even variations between SCSI-1, SCSI-2, and SCSI-3.

- You can't run cables more than a few feet, or the SCSI signal degrades and the peripheral doesn't work.

SCSI Termination

Issues:

- Each SCSI system needs two terminators, one on each extreme end of the chain of devices.

- There are two kinds of terminators: passive and active. You're supposed to be able to use either type for SCSI-1 or SCSI-2, but active is usually a better idea. SCSI-3 requires active termination.

- Some devices have built-in terminators, others require separate termination devices.

- The host adapter probably supports termination of some kind. This should be considered when terminating the system.

SCSI Drivers

Issues:

- The SCSI system will need a driver for each SCSI device, as well as a driver for the host adapter.

- SCSI hard disks may not require drivers; instead, they may have an on-board BIOS that serves that function.

SCSI Physical Installation

Actually putting SCSI adapters and peripherals into your system is pretty much the same whether you're using devices that are SCSI-1 or SCSI-2 or you're using the ASPI, CAM, or LADDR standards. (I know I haven't explained these yet; hang on for a minute and I'll get to them, I promise.) So let's look at physical installation first.

Installation Overview

Basically, putting a SCSI device into the PC involves these steps:

1. Choose a SCSI host adapter, if you don't already have one.

2. Put a SCSI host adapter into the PC.

3. Assign a SCSI ID to the peripheral. This is usually done with a jumper or a DIP switch.

4. Enable or disable SCSI parity on the peripheral.

5. If the peripheral is an internal peripheral, mount it inside the PC.

6. Cable the peripheral to the SCSI host adapter.

7. Terminate both ends of the SCSI system.

That's the physical end of a SCSI setup; software installation follows, but for the moment let's focus on the physical setup.

Choosing a SCSI Host Adapter

Many computers—more and more—have SCSI support right on their motherboards; others come with SCSI adapters in a slot as standard equipment. If this is true for you, then skip to the next section. But otherwise, just a few thoughts about choosing host adapters:

- There are host adapters for 8-bit ISA, 16-bit ISA, 16-bit Micro Channel, 32-bit Micro Channel, 32-bit EISA, VL-Bus, and PCI. The wider your interface, the better your maximum data transfer rate.

- Many SCSI host adapters use *bus mastering* to improve their performance. Bus mastering is very similar to Direct Memory Access (DMA) in that it allows the host adapter to transfer data straight into memory without having to involve the CPU. But DMA allows only high-speed transfer from peripheral to memory or memory to peripheral...not peripheral to peripheral. Bus mastering makes peripheral to peripheral transfers possible without CPU intervention, often leading to higher speed data access. Anyone who's heard of bus mastering has probably heard that the MCA and EISA buses support it. While it's not generally known, bus mastering is possible with ISA bus machines. Adaptec makes an AHA1542 controller that's almost jumper-free and that will do bus mastering on an ISA bus machine, providing some admirable data transfer rates.

- By the way, there's another benefit to bus mastering: it means that your host adapter doesn't need to use one of your precious DMA channels.

- Some SCSI devices come with *optional cache RAM*. While it sounds like it'll make your system really scream, what it mainly does is make the benchmarks look good. A system that provides no hurdles between the bits on the platter and the CPU's RAM will provide pretty good data transfer rates that are real data transfer rates, not bogus ones. Bus mastering should reduce or remove the need for cache RAM on the controller.

- Look for an adapter that supports SCSI-2, and potentially one that supports Fast SCSI, WIDE SCSI, and Fast-WIDE SCSI (I'll explain these toward the end of the chapter).

- If you need to support more than seven devices, or if you have a slow device that is monopolizing the bus and preventing faster devices from giving you the performance you need, consider a multichannel SCSI host adapter. That way you can put the faster devices on one channel and the devices that are slowing things down on a separate channel.

- Make sure that your adapter has drivers that support the ASPI standard. (See "SCSI Software Installation" for more information.)

Choosing the wrong host adapter isn't the end of the world, but it can mean more installation and troubleshooting headaches.

And if you're in a tight spot and need to interface a SCSI device with a computer that doesn't have slots, look into the MiniSCSI Plus from Adaptec. It costs around $79 and will convert your parallel port into a SCSI-2 adapter. The software provided with it is ASPI compatible, as well.

The MiniSCSI does suffer from one serious problem. It will not work unless the item at the end of the SCSI chain includes an active terminator. Most SCSI-1 devices don't provide termination power, but many SCSI-2 devices do. As a result, the MiniSCSI will work with only a subset of the SCSI devices. Try it before you buy it. (More information about termination later in this chapter.)

Installing the SCSI Host Adapter

Putting a SCSI host adapter into the PC is pretty much the same as installing any board. SCSI adapters are a bit more of a pain than the average board to install because they typically require DMA channels, IRQ levels, I/O addresses, and a ROM address.

It's usually possible to connect SCSI devices to a host adapter both internally and externally. In Figure 16.3, you see that there is a 50-pin header connector on the SCSI host adapter for internal connections, and an external connector, a Centronics 50-pin female connector, used to attach to external devices.

FIGURE 16.3:

SCSI connectors

More recent SCSI adapters will use a miniature 50-socket D shell connector. A note of interest here—some SCSI adapters with three interfaces (an internal WIDE 68-pin connector, a 50-pin connector, and an external connector) will only allow connection to any two of the three interfaces at the same time. Thus, if you have internal wide and narrow devices, the external connector cannot be used. You should consult your documentation for the particular adapter.

Assigning a SCSI ID to the Peripheral

Now consider the SCSI peripheral that you're going to install.

SCSI is a parallel interface. SCSI-1 (and most SCSI-2 implementations) defined eight wires to communicate data, an 8-bit data bus. Now, the SCSI designers needed a simple way for a number of devices on a SCSI bus to say, "I want to talk!" and they all needed a way to say that all at the same time—so they couldn't share a wire to signal that they wanted to use the bus. Every device needed a separate wire.

What, then, was the easiest way to let multiple devices signal that they wanted to use the bus? To let the data lines do double duty. Each data line is also a SCSI ID line, and, as the original SCSI design called for eight data lines, there are eight SCSI devices that can go on a SCSI bus.

A basic SCSI configuration assigns this identification number called a SCSI ID to each device on the SCSI system. The values for this ID range from 0 to 7, and the host adapter typically is set to 7. You typically can change the host ID from 7, but don't—you'll expose yourself unnecessarily to software incompatibilities.

Choosing SCSI IDs

Before installing a peripheral in your system, you should assign it a SCSI ID. You typically set a SCSI ID with a DIP switch, a jumper, a thumbwheel, or the like. There are just a few rules for setting SCSI IDs:

- Each device on the SCSI chain must have its own ID.

- The lower the SCSI ID, the higher the priority of the device. If two devices both want the bus at the same time, the one with the higher number wins.

- That means that you should give the slower devices, like tape drives and CD-ROMs, the higher numbers, and the faster devices, like the hard disks, lower numbers.

- Do not use ID 0 or ID 1 for anything but hard disks. If you plan to boot from a SCSI hard disk, make it ID 0.

- Check your system documentation to see if it expects a device at a particular ID. For example, my advice to put a hard disk on ID 0 or 1 is really DOS- and Windows NT-based advice. Other operating systems (SCO Unix, for example) may not care about which ID you use for a boot drive. At the same time, SCO must see any CD-ROMs at ID 5.

- Regardless of what I recommend, or what your documentation says, the only way to solve some SCSI problems is to just try out different ID combinations until something works. I've never fixed anything by fiddling around with the adapter's ID, but I've fixed things by messing with other IDs.

- IBM PS/2 machines with SCSI drives use ID 6 for bootable hard disks.

Does this sound a bit haphazard? Well, it is, to an extent: SCSI is still something of an evolving standard.

Something new to help us out is SCAM (SCSI Configure AutoMagically). With this newer functionality, devices and the host adapter configure SCSI IDs automatically. The hitch is that both the host adapter and devices need to support SCAM in order for this to work.

Targets, Initiators, LUNs, and LSUNs

So far I've been talking about SCSI IDs. But installing my Adaptec SCSI hardware—Adaptec is the SCSI market leader, and a manufacturer whose products I can recommend—I see a message upon bootup that says:

```
Host Adapter #0 - SCSI ID 6 - LUN 0: NEC CD-ROM DRIVE: 841 1.0
```

And a later message says:

```
Host Adapter #0, Target SCSI ID=6: NEC CD-ROM DRIVE:8411.0
```

First of all, "Target SCSI ID" is the same thing as "SCSI ID." Target refers to the fact that this device, a CD-ROM, is a "target" rather than an "initiator."

In the SCSI world, any communication is initiated by one device and acknowledged by another device. The device that starts the conversation is called an *initiator*. The device that responds is called a *target*. In general, it's the host adapter that acts as initiator and the SCSI peripherals that act as targets. It is possible, however, for the two to reverse roles in some communications, but the Target SCSI ID message references the fact that the CD-ROM is usually a target.

The *logical unit number* (*LUN*) refers to the fact that a SCSI device can have "sub"-devices. For example, consider the (now obsolete) Iomega 44 + 44 Bernoulli backup device. It is a metal case containing two 44MB cartridge drives, and it is SCSI compatible. If I connect an Iomega 44 + 44 cartridge device to one of my SCSI systems, I'll see a new SCSI ID, which refers to the 44 + 44 system. But the two drives will be distinguished not by different SCSI IDs, but instead by different logical unit numbers under the same SCSI ID.

This is actually fairly unusual in the SCSI world and as a result will probably give your system heartburn—that is, your drivers may not be able to address the second 44MB drive. But now you'll know what LUN refers to. Again, the vast majority of devices only include one LUN.

In theory, each SCSI device can have up to eight LUNs. If one of the SCSI IDs is taken by the host adapter, that leaves seven for peripherals. If each peripheral had eight LUNs, there could be 56 SCSI logical units on a single host adapter.

To make things even worse, each LUN can have a sub-sub-device called an LSUN, or Logical Sub-Unit Number, which can range from 0 to 255. Let's see, 56 logical units, each with 256 logical subunits…that's 14,336 devices on a single host adapter! Not bad, eh? Well, actually, this wouldn't work for several reasons. First, a standard PC SCSI host adapter wouldn't get too far having to keep track of 14,000 devices. Second, there's a maximum cable length of six meters that we'll discuss soon, with a minimum cable length of 10 centimeters. Third, I don't know of any PC SCSI software that supports LSUNs.

Notice also the "NEC CD-ROM…" information. That's actual descriptive information in English that the CD-ROM gives to the host adapter about what it—the peripheral—is.

Enable/Disable SCSI Parity

The SCSI bus can detect and use parity signals to detect errors in transmission over the SCSI cabling. Errors can and do occur, particularly as the cable gets longer from end to end.

To use SCSI parity, all devices must support it. If only one device does not support SCSI parity, then you must disable it for all devices on the chain.

Some operating systems, like Windows NT, will not work at all with a SCSI CD-ROM unless it supports SCSI parity. That implies that you should plan to support SCSI parity from the very beginning, and buy only devices that support SCSI parity (and SCSI-2, by the way.)

SCSI Daisy Chaining

Many of you will just end up putting only one or two SCSI devices on a PC, but SCSI can easily support seven peripherals off a single SCSI host adapter (15 for SCSI-3), or it could theoretically support hundreds of devices with a lot of rocket science. (The "hundreds of devices" concept works if you put eight SCSI adapters in a system, and each is connected in turn to eight SCSI adapters—that's possible; remember LUNs? The second-level SCSI adapters can be externally connected to other SCSI adapters, leaving the possibility of lots of devices. As I said a page back, it's impossible to find PC software that supports such a thing, so forget it.)

Multiple devices are attached to a single SCSI host adapter via daisy chaining. There are several kinds of cables in the SCSI world.

Types of SCSI Cables: SCSI, SCSI-1, SCSI-2, and SCSI-3 (Wide or Ultra Wide)

External SCSI devices tend to have two 50-pin female Centronics connectors, as you see in the view of the back of a SCSI device in Figure 16.4.

FIGURE 16.4:

Connectors for external SCSI devices

A 50-pin male connector, such as you'd see on a SCSI cable, looks like Figure 16.5.

FIGURE 16.5:

50-pin male connector for SCSI

Some external SCSI cables have a Centronics connector of this type on both ends of the cable. Such a cable is called a SCSI peripheral cable or SCSI cable and is pictured in Figure 16.6. Use it either to connect between SCSI-1 host adapters and SCSI devices or when daisy-chaining from SCSI device to SCSI device.

FIGURE 16.6:

SCSI peripheral cable

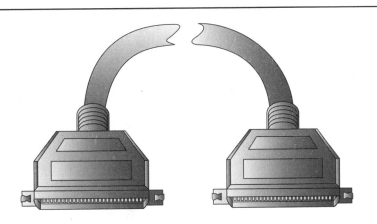

Other older SCSI cables have a male DB-25 connector on one side and a Centronics 50 conductor connector on the other side. Those are called Macintosh SCSI or SCSI-1 cables and are pictured in Figure 16.7.

FIGURE 16.7:

SCSI-1 cable

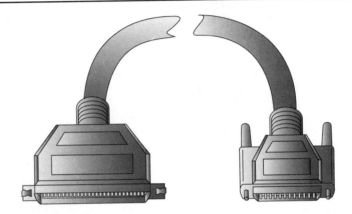

Newer SCSI adapters often do not employ a Centronics connector for external devices, but rather use a miniature 50-socket D shell connector; some people call it an "HP 50 connector." You can see the male version of that connector—the version that you'd see on a cable—in Figure 16.8.

FIGURE 16.8:

SCSI connector—
50-socket D shell (HP
50 connector)

The cable incorporates two buttons on either side that you must squeeze together in order to connect or disconnect the cable to or from the adapter. You will see this connector instead of the Centronics on some peripherals (more and more, as time goes on) and more commonly on the backs of SCSI adapters—since 1993 Adaptec has put them on the backs of their 1742 adapters in lieu of the more common Centronics 50. As a result, a common cable has a mini DB50 on one side and a Centronics 50 conductor connection on the other side. Such a cable—Centronics 50-conductor connection on one side, mini DB50-pin connector on the other—is popularly called a SCSI-2 cable. Take a look at Figure 16.9.

FIGURE 16.9:

SCSI-2 cable

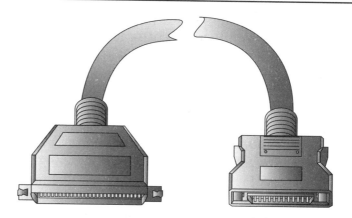

The names "SCSI-1 cable" and "SCSI-2 cable" are misleading. What I've called SCSI-1 and SCSI-2 cables are not universal terms. Whenever you buy a SCSI cable, be extremely careful to specify the kinds of connectors you want on either side. Be triple careful about the mini DB-50 or HP-50 connector; everyone seems to have a different name for it, so make sure you're getting what you want.

Note that there is a difference between the terminology used and the physical characteristics of the cable. Although "Wide"

SCSI has more pins (68 versus 50) the cable is not wider than a SCSI-2 cable. In fact, the SCSI-2 cable is the physically wider of the two. "Wide" refers to the data path—a 68-pin cable has 16 bits of data whereas a SCSI-2 has only 8 bits or pins devoted to the data path.

Through Thick and Thin: Not All Cables Are Equal

While we're discussing cables, let me relate a short war story that taught me an important lesson about cables.

I installed a CD-ROM onto a server so that I could install Windows NT on my LAN. The CD-ROM was an external drive that used the 50-conductor Centronics connector, so I walked over to my cable pile and pulled out a standard SCSI cable with 50-conductor Centronics connectors on both ends. I plugged the CD-ROM into the SCSI adapter's interface port on the back of my PC, and the problems started. My existing tape drive and hard disk drive—both internal SCSI—started acting up.

After an hour or two of playing around with the system, I found that if I downgraded the SCSI system from SCSI-2 to SCSI-1 (I did this by reconfiguring my SCSI host adapter, an Adaptec AHA1542C), the problems went away. I had vague forebodings about losing SCSI-2 compatibility—SCSI parity doesn't work under SCSI-1, recall—but everything seemed to work, so I figured that I'd live with it.

Then came time to install NT. The README file said, "The SCSI and CD-ROM support built into Windows NT require that CD-ROMs provide SCSI parity to function properly." Great, I thought, and started fussing with the SCSI devices to get the CD-ROM to support SCSI parity. I mean, there was a jumper specifically included on the CD-ROM to control whether SCSI parity would be used, so why wouldn't it support SCSI parity?

Just on the off chance that I had a bad cable, I went back over to the cable pile to see what else I had. I found another dual 50 Centronics cable identical to the cable that I was using, and another dual 50 Centronics cable that was about twice as thick as the first two. I tried swapping the original thin cable for the other thin cable—no difference. But when I used the thicker cable, everything started working! I got full SCSI-2 support, as well as SCSI parity functionality.

A few calls around to cable places brought the information that, yes, there were two kinds of dual 50 Centronics cables. The thin ones work fine for SCSI-1 but not for SCSI-2. The thick ones are good for both.

Internal SCSI Cabling

External devices, as you've read, tend to have two SCSI connections on them so that they can support the SCSI daisy chain. Internal devices, in contrast, only use a single 50-pin header connector. Internal SCSI cables are just ribbon cables with 50-pin IDC connectors, as you see in Figure 16.10.

FIGURE 16.10:

Internal SCSI cable

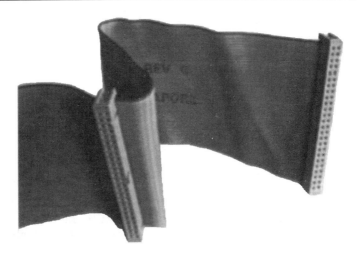

Because the connectors are sitting in the middle of the cable, one connector does the job for daisy chaining.

Terminating the SCSI Chain

Before popping the top back on your PC, there's one more thing that needs doing: you must terminate the SCSI chain.

NOTE   SCSI-1 termination was a simple resistor. SCSI-2 termination requires a small amount of power applied by the SCSI device (600 milliamps at 4–5.25 volts, exactly). Some devices do provide termination resistance, but not termination power, making them potential troublemakers in a SCSI-2 setting.

Whenever we discuss termination in class, people start referring to killer cyborgs, but it just means providing a voltage and resistance on either end of a cable, so that the entire bus has a particular set of electrical characteristics. Without this resistance, the SCSI cables cannot transport data around without significant error rates. (It will work sometimes, despite what some people claim, but it won't work reliably.)

Active and Passive Terminators

SCSI-1 specified two kinds of termination, active and passive. Active was pretty much ignored until SCSI-2 became popular. Passive terminators are just a resistor network; if you're interested in how they work electronically, you can see that in Figure 16.11.

If you don't speak schematic, don't sweat it: the jaggy-looking things are resistors, TERMPWR refers to a source of electricity, and the triangle standing on its head represents electrical ground, the place that the power from TERMPWR is seeking to go. The main thing to notice is that the only thing going on here is resistors; there are no chips, and no amplification is going on. Passive termination is basically an adaptation of the simple terminators found in ancient floppy disk or ST506 systems. Back in the SCSI-1 days, the designers figured that the major use for SCSI would be to hook up a couple of hard disks to a host adapter, all with no more than eight inches to a foot of cable.

FIGURE 16.11:

Passive SCSI terminators

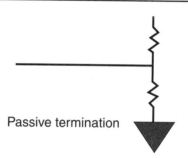

Passive termination

If, on the other hand, you intended to run longer cables and put a lot of stuff on them, then you need some kind of booster for termination power; that's active termination. It's represented schematically in Figure 16.12.

FIGURE 16.12:

Active SCSI termination

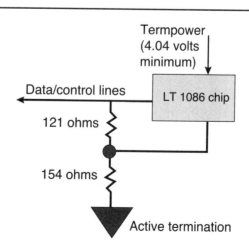

Termpower (4.04 volts minimum)

Data/control lines

LT 1086 chip

121 ohms

154 ohms

Active termination

The LT 1086 chip's job is to provide amplification power when necessary. Active termination is, then, a bit more expensive than passive, but there is no more than a few cents' difference.

So, in a modern setup, do you need active or passive? As in the old SCSI-1 configuration, if all you're going to do is to hang a single drive on a host adapter, then it probably doesn't matter. But if you want to use longer cables, external devices (they usually need longer cables), and more than one or two devices, then active termination is a good idea. The problem, as you'll see in the next section, is that termination is built into the SCSI devices themselves, and some vendors get cheap and simply add passive termination.

You can mix passives and actives on a SCSI chain, putting a passive on one end and an active on another.

Internal and External Terminators

You've seen that some SCSI devices are installed internally in the PC (and connect to the host adapter with a ribbon cable), and that other devices are installed externally (and connect to the host adapter with a SCSI cable of some kind). There are also internal and external terminators, as well as SCSI devices that have terminators built right in. As I mentioned a couple of paragraphs back, some vendors build active termination into their devices, some build passive termination in, and some don't build in termination of any kind, forcing you to buy a separate termination device of one kind or another. Most SCSI devices with termination let you disable that termination, but some are boneheadedly designed without any provision for disabling termination, forcing you to put those devices on one of the extreme ends of the SCSI chain.

If you've got to disable a terminator, you'll find that devices let you do that in one of these ways:

- An internal, *Single Inline Pin Package* (*SIPP*) terminator on the host adapter and/or a hard disk.

- Some host adapters, like the modern Adaptec adapters, let you enable or disable termination via software.

- Many devices adjust termination with a DIP switch or a jumper.

If you must buy an external terminator, then you'll need to choose the right one for whatever SCSI connector type you have. In Figure 16.13, you can see a Centronics terminator.

FIGURE 16.13:

Centronics terminator

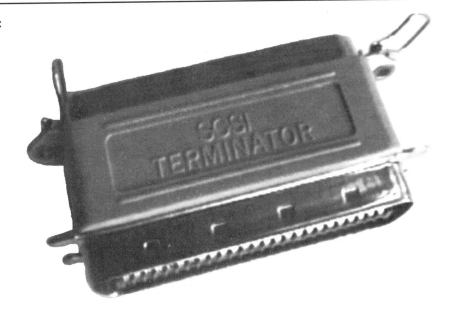

They clip onto one of the Centronics connectors on the back of the last external device on your SCSI daisy chain. I've also seen external SCSI terminators for the mini DB50/HP 50 connectors and the old Macintosh-style DB25s.

SIPP-type terminators often show up on the host adapter itself, as it needs termination and SIPPs don't take up too much space. You can see a SIPP in Figure 16.14.

FIGURE 16.14:

A SIPP-type terminator

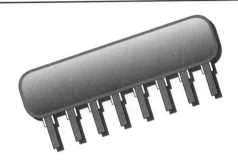

If you have a host adapter that uses SIPPs for its termination, then there are typically three of these SIPPs on a host adapter. You'll also find SIPPs on many internal SCSI hard disks. You just remove them (gently, as you may need to reinstall them one day) by working them out with needle-nose pliers. Once you've done that, put them in an envelope, seal it, label it "SCSI Terminators," and put it somewhere.

If you look at the back of the external SCSI device, you may notice a switch labeled "termination." It can be flipped on or off, so if this SCSI device is the last on the chain, then all I need do is to flip it on; otherwise, I flip it off.

Sample SCSI Setup: One Internal Drive

When I say, "Put terminators on the end of the chain," it's worthwhile taking a minute and making sure that you know what I mean. With that in mind, let's look at a few sample SCSI applications. Take a look at Figure 16.15.

In this setup, you've just got a SCSI hard disk. There must be terminators on each side, but there are only two sides, so it's simple to figure out where the terminators go. Both terminators are probably SIPP-type terminators. The host is ID 7, the hard disk is ID 0; this means that you're intending to boot from the hard disk.

FIGURE 16.15:

FIGURE 16.15:

SCSI setup: one
internal drive

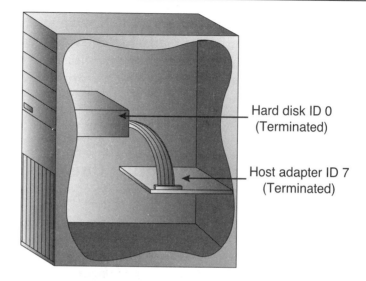

Hard disk ID 0
(Terminated)

Host adapter ID 7
(Terminated)

Sample SCSI Setup: Two Internal Devices

Now let's make it a bit more complex (see Figure 16.16).

FIGURE 16.16:

SCSI setup: two
internal devices

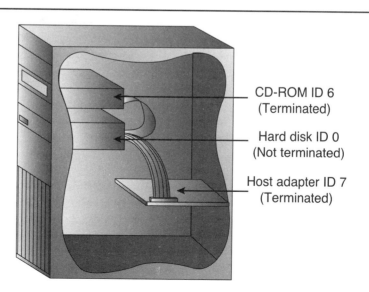

CD-ROM ID 6
(Terminated)

Hard disk ID 0
(Not terminated)

Host adapter ID 7
(Terminated)

Now we've added an internal CD-ROM. It needs to have a different ID, so ID 6 is good. Remember, I want to avoid ID 1 for anything other than a hard disk and, besides, the CD-ROM will be much slower than the hard disk, so I want it to have a higher number and therefore higher priority. The hard disk terminators must be removed, as the hard disk is in the middle of the chain, and the CD-ROM is terminated.

Sample SCSI Setup: One External Device

Now let's do the same things, but with external devices, as shown in Figure 16.17.

FIGURE 16.17:

SCSI setup: one
external device

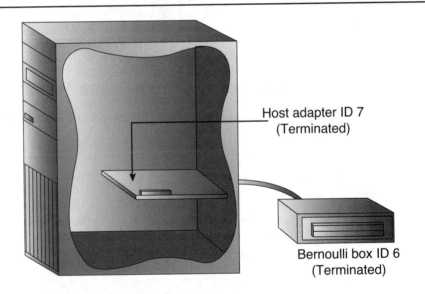

Host adapter ID 7
(Terminated)

Bernoulli box ID 6
(Terminated)

Now there's just one external device, a cartridge storage device that we won't try to boot from. I've set the Bernoulli box to ID 6 and terminated it, as it is the extreme end of the chain.

Sample SCSI Setup: Two External Devices

Continuing, I'll now add a second external device, as in Figure 16.18.

FIGURE 16.18:

SCSI setup: two external devices

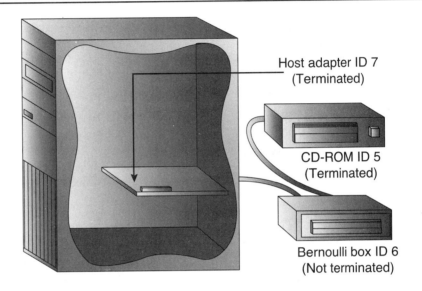

Host adapter ID 7
(Terminated)

CD-ROM ID 5
(Terminated)

Bernoulli box ID 6
(Not terminated)

This time, I'll make the CD-ROM ID 5, as ID 6 is taken. The Bernoulli box shouldn't be terminated, as it is now in the middle of the chain and the CD-ROM is terminated.

Sample SCSI Setup: Internal and External Devices

For the grand finale, let's put two external devices and two internal devices on this system (see Figure 16.19).

FIGURE 16.19:

SCSI setup: two external and two internal devices

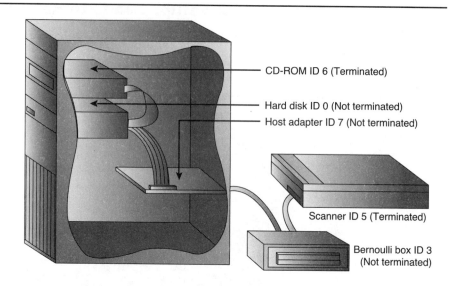

CD-ROM ID 6 (Terminated)

Hard disk ID 0 (Not terminated)
Host adapter ID 7 (Not terminated)

Scanner ID 5 (Terminated)

Bernoulli box ID 3
(Not terminated)

The thing to notice about this scenario is that the termination has been removed from the host adapter, as it is now (for the first time) in the middle of the chain. The external devices are attached to the external connector on the back of the SCSI host adapter (the Centronics or miniature D connector), and the internal devices are hooked to the internal 50-pin header connector. Every device has a unique SCSI ID, and there's termination on the ends of the chain. Additionally, I've assigned them SCSI IDs in roughly the order that their speeds warrant—the Bernoulli box is faster than the CD-ROM and scanner, and so it is of lower priority than they are.

Special Termination Issues for SCSI-3

There are some special termination issues that apply to SCSI-3. On the external connector of a SCSI-3 host adapter, you can daisy chain both 8-bit SCSI (SCSI-2) and 16-bit (SCSI-3) devices. This can present some unique termination problems.

For example, suppose I attach to the external connector a SCSI-2 CD-ROM with a standard Centronics type SCSI-2 connector. To do this, I get an adapter that converts the 68-pin SCSI-3 connector on the host adapter to the 50 pins the SCSI-2 device uses. What is the result?

Think about it this way: a SCSI-2 device has 8 data bits or pins plus ground wires and other assorted signals. A SCSI-3 device uses two sets of 8 data bits, or 16 data bits total. We can call these two sets a high order set of 8 data bits and a low order set. When I connect a converter to the SCSI host adapter, I pass only the low order data bits to the SCSI-2 devices that are attached. Remember that the last device is terminated. What does it terminate in this scenario? Only the low order data bits! For that reason, it is critical that the adapter connected to the external port of the host adapter not only converts the 68 pins to 50 but that it terminates the high order data bits and associated ground signals.

Installation Troubleshooting Notes

Now that I've drilled into your head the idea that you should have only terminators on either side of the chain, let me offer an exception.

NOTE   The sum total of your SCSI cables should not exceed 18 feet. In general, the shorter your cables, the better.

Sometimes a SCSI setup doesn't work. You check and recheck the SCSI IDs, but there are no duplicated IDs. You've terminated properly, but things still don't work. What do you do?

Remember that the sum total of cable lengths must not exceed six meters. Lower-quality cables mean that distance shrinks.

Things to try:

- Most SCSI host adapters display a sign-on message listing the recognized devices on the SCSI bus. Use that information as your first diagnostic. If the device is seen on the bus, but you can't get it to do tricks, then the problem is probably a driver problem rather than a hardware installation problem.

- If you encounter "phantom disks"—disks that you can see but cannot read or write—then you've probably put two devices on the same SCSI ID.

- Sometimes the ID-setting device is defective. I've seen a tape drive that, when set for ID 4, would show up as ID 6.

- Sometimes cables are defective, or combinations of cables don't get along.

To check whether it falls under the last item on this list, try this:

1. Install only the host adapter and its driver. Boot the system and make sure that the host adapter is working—no DMA/IRQ/IO address conflicts. It may even come with a host adapter diagnostic; run it.

2. Turn the PC off, add the first SCSI device and power it up before you reboot the PC. SCSI devices often must be active before the host adapter can recognize them. (Also be sure that everything is terminated correctly.)

3. Once you've got that device in place, power down the PC and the existing SCSI device (if it's external), and add the next SCSI device. Test it as you just tested the first SCSI device.

I find it most convenient to install the internal devices first, then the external devices. I usually remove the SIPP terminators from the host adapter, and just place an external SCSI terminator on the connector on the back of my host adapter if it's a Centronics-type connector. Otherwise, I get a SCSI cable, attach it to the back of the host adapter, and then terminate that.

And remember to power down all of the SCSI devices before adding or subtracting from the daisy chain.

SCSI Software Installation

Much of the SCSI installation process is like a normal hard disk's installation process: low-level format, partition, and high-level format. Doing those things isn't much different from doing them on non-SCSI hard disks, except that you may have to use a special program for the formatting and/or partitioning; check your SCSI software documentation for an example.

The tough part about SCSI software installation, however, is the drivers. There seem to be a million of them, and none of them appear to be on speaking terms with each another—and what do they do, anyway?

Until a few years ago, SCSI drivers were proprietary. You were crazy to buy a SCSI hard disk and host adapter unless you got them from the same vendor, a vendor that supplied drivers for the two of them. But since 1991, several "universal driver" standards have appeared. Figure 16.20 shows how they work.

FIGURE 16.20:

Universal SCSI driver standards

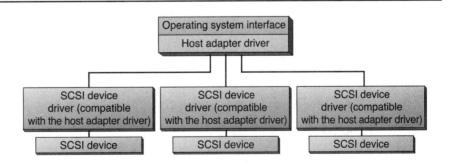

Rather than trying to create a hard disk driver, a CD-ROM driver, a scanner driver, and a tape driver that are all compatible with the operating system, a universal driver system defines an intermediate standard and supports that with a driver specific to the host adapter. The SCSI device drivers then need only be written to work with the intermediate standard defined by the host adapter's driver.

The three main competing universal standards are:

- ASPI (Advanced SCSI Programming Interface)
- CAM (Common Access Method)
- LADDR (Layered Device Driver Architecture)

Additionally, no discussion of drivers could fail to include:

- The INT 13 BIOS interface found on many SCSI host adapters

The idea here is that you buy a host adapter from anyone and get a driver for that adapter that supports one of these standards—for example's sake, let's use ASPI, as it's the most popular. You buy a SCSI tape drive that is advertised as being "ASPI compatible." That means that they include with it a driver that controls the tape drive via ASPI communication with the host adapter. Since the driver on your host adapter board speaks ASPI and your tape drive's driver speaks ASPI, everything will work out fine. And if you decide to replace your current SCSI host adapter board with one that's faster or better in some way, then all you need is an ASPI driver for that board—you don't even need to change the device driver for the tape drive. (It should be stressed that this is the idea; of course, ASPI compatibility is not a black-and-white thing in the real world.)

With Bootable Hard Disks, You Don't Need SCSI Software

I'm going to discuss this in detail in a few pages, but if you are in the process of installing a SCSI hard disk on device 0 or 1, and in a hurry, then I wanted to note here that you needn't worry about SCSI software; you don't need it. Hard disks on device numbers 0 and/or 1 have built-in BIOS support and don't need separate SCSI drivers. Hard disks above device 1 or removable hard disks do require separate drivers.

Installing SCSI Software

If your SCSI device didn't come with a driver, you can use the generic driver provided by Adaptec called EZ-SCSI, from Adaptec. Here's a section from a CONFIG.SYS file built with EZ-SCSI:

```
DEVICE=C:\ADAPTEC\ASPI4DOS.SYS /D
DEVICE=C:\ADAPTEC\ASPIDISK.SYS /D
DEVICE=C:\ADAPTEC\ASPICD.SYS /D:MSCD001
```

Taken in order, these three device drivers (1) load the base ASPI support for the host adapter, (2) provide an ASPI-to-hard-disk interface for a removable SCSI hard disk (a Bernoulli box), and (3) provide an ASPI-to-CD-ROM interface for a SCSI CD-ROM. If the first driver didn't load, then the second and third drivers could not load.

EZ-SCSI comes with drivers for CD-ROMs, removable cartridge hard disks (like Bernoulli boxes), and fixed hard disks. EZ-SCSI does not include drivers for scanners, WORM (optical Write Once, Read Many times) drives, WARM (optical Write And Read Many times) drives, scanners, and tape drives. If you get a device that supports ASPI later, then you can easily add it to a configuration that started out from EZ-SCSI. EZ-SCSI also comes with formatting and partitioning utilities for storage devices, a tape backup program, a scanning utility, and a benchmarking program.

SCSI Standards

The fact that there are three "universal" standards points out the truth that SCSI is still a standard in flux. Here's an overview of the three standards.

ASPI (Advanced SCSI Programming Interface)

ASPI was invented by Adaptec, and the first time I read anything about ASPI, the A stood for Adaptec. But ASPI has been adopted by other hardware manufacturers, and, as you've read, it is the home of two very fine suites of SCSI drivers. I'd personally recommend that you stay within the ASPI standard, as it's easiest to find drivers that are ASPI compatible.

Let me underscore that there is no such thing as an "ASPI-compatible SCSI hard disk." The compatibility question relates to the drivers, not the hardware. If someone wanted to—and she were technical enough—she could write an ASPI, a CAM, and a LADDR driver for a given SCSI device.

SCSI without Drivers: On-Board BIOS Support

After all this talk of mixing and matching drivers, you may be getting a bit queasy. But if all you're going to install is a hard disk or two, then you may never have to trouble with drivers.

Why SCSI Adapters Have BIOS

Using SCSI hard disks, if you think about it, can lead to a sort of chicken-and-egg problem. The SCSI device isn't accessible until the SCSI device drivers are loaded, and device drivers are generally loaded from the hard disk. But how can you load SCSI drivers from a SCSI hard disk? I suppose one answer would be to boot from a floppy and then not reboot, but it's a somewhat cumbersome answer.

The answer to the problem of, "How does my PC boot from a SCSI hard disk?" is that most SCSI adapters have an on-board BIOS that contains enough software to run the hard disk, even if there are no SCSI drivers loaded. That's a real lifesaver, allowing us to use SCSI hard disks without having to worry about drivers. However, they must be configured as SCSI IDs 0 and 1.

When to Disable a BIOS

Many SCSI installations that I do are not intended to support a hard disk. For example, installing a CD-ROM in an already running system means that I've already got a functional IDE drive in the system, so there's no point in replacing it with a SCSI drive.

In that case, I don't need the BIOS, so I disable it. You do that either with setup software or with some kind of physical setting, like a jumper or DIP switch. That's a real benefit, as it creates more space in my Upper Memory Area for larger Upper Memory Blocks. So disable your BIOS if you are not booting from a SCSI hard disk.

Bus Mastering Alerts

Many SCSI host adapters use a kind of "super DMA" called *bus mastering*. Again, it's a terrific feature, but be aware that it confuses Windows and SmartDrive unless you load SmartDrive with the double buffer option, or bypass loading SmartDrive into upper memory.

Now and the Future: SCSI-1, SCSI-2, and the Rest

I have referred to the different SCSI generations throughout this chapter. At this point, the different generations make little difference, as much modern software can't make full use of the modern SCSI generations. But some can, and that makes it worthwhile knowing about and purchasing more advanced SCSI. Here's a rundown on the different SCSI generations.

SCSI-1: The Beginning of a Good Idea

In 1981, Shugart Associates—the company that eventually became Seagate—developed a parallel block-oriented transfer protocol called the Shugart Associates System Interface, or SASI.

SASI became the Small Computer Systems Interface, or SCSI, in 1984, when the ANSI's X3T9 committee formalized the specification.

SCSI-1 Interface

SCSI is an 8-bit parallel interface between a SCSI host adapter and a SCSI device. ("Eight-bit" here has nothing to do—or very little to do—with your bus interface.) The standard runs at 5MHz, meaning a throughput of 8 bits, 5 million times a second, for a maximum data transfer rate of 5MBps. It incorporated a command set that could be only partially implemented by a vendor, but the vendor could still claim that its device was "SCSI compatible."

SCSI-1 Device Types

SCSI-1 defined several generic device types:

- Random access devices (hard disk)
- Sequential access devices (tapes)
- Printers
- Processors (host adapters)
- WORM optical drives
- Read-only random access devices

These types changed in SCSI-2, as you'll see later.

Asynchronous and Synchronous SCSI

SCSI-1 defined a SCSI notion that has remained with us, a set of rules for transferring data across the SCSI bus. You'll see references to it in some SCSI software, so let's take a minute and define asynchronous versus synchronous SCSI interfaces.

The most basic kind of data transfer over a SCSI bus goes something like this: the initiator requests a byte, the target responds by sending the byte over the SCSI bus, and the initiator says, "Got it," signaling to the target that the transfer went okay.

That "got it" message is called a *handshake* or an *acknowledgment*. Each handshake takes time, however, and introduces a fair amount of overhead; in fact, one of the main failures of SCSI-1 was the amount of time spent on overhead.

This method of handshaking every byte is called asynchronous SCSI. There's a faster method, where the initiator acknowledges big blocks of bytes, rather than every single byte. That's called synchronous SCSI. It's essential for high-speed disk access. Double-check that both your host adapter and your drives support synchronous access.

You can have both asynchronous and synchronous devices on the same SCSI bus, but nobody talks synchronous if the host adapter can't.

SCSI-1 left so much undefined that it was nearly inevitable that the actual SCSI-1 implementations on the market would be incompatible.

SCSI-2 Improves on a Good Thing

SCSI-2 was being developed even prior to formalization of the SCSI-1 standard by ANSI in 1986. The point at which SCSI-1 was finalized and SCSI-2 began was rather arbitrary and had more to do with simply deciding to get the standard published on a particular date than a quantum jump in specifications. The specification simply reflects where the state of progress was at the date of publishing. SCSI-2 enhancements include new command sets, wider data paths (16 and 32 bits), and command queuing.

Scripting and Disconnects

SCSI-2 incorporates scripting, where a series of transfers can be "batched" across the bus. For example, a hard disk could be backed up to an optical drive—with no processor intervention.

SCSI-2 also allows disconnects, where the host adapter sends a command to a slow device like a tape drive—a rewind command, for example—and then disconnects the drive from the SCSI bus, so that the whole bus doesn't have to remain idle while the tape rewinds.

Kinds of Devices

SCSI-2 defines a slightly different set of generic device types than did SCSI-1:

- Random access devices (hard disk)
- Sequential access devices (tapes)
- Printers
- Processors (host adapters)
- WORM optical drives
- CD-ROMs (replaced the "read-only" type)
- Scanners
- Magneto-optical drives

- Jukeboxes (the data storage type, not the music type)

- Communications devices

The first five are the same, the sixth changes, and there are four new types.

Fast and Wide SCSI

As originally defined, SCSI is an 8-bit parallel interface between a SCSI device and a SCSI controller. Several variations have been defined in SCSI-2.

Fast SCSI doubles the data transfer rate over the existing data path. If SCSI-1 8-bit transfers are 5MBps, then, Fast SCSI 8-bit transfers are 10MBps. Fast SCSI works on either single-ended or differential SCSI, but if you set up Fast SCSI on single-ended cables, your total cable length can only be three meters.

Wide SCSI uses an extra cable to increase the data path to 16 or 32 bits. Using non-differential cables and interface, Wide SCSI can increase data transfer rate to 20MBps.

Fast-Wide SCSI uses a greater data transfer rate over a wider cable to support a data transfer rate of up to 40MBps, but 20MBps is more common.

SCSI-3 or UltraSCSI

During the '90s, processor and data-transfer performance has increased by factors in the hundreds. Now the disk subsystem has become a real bottleneck. Ultimately, Fibre Channel, with its incredibly high speeds, will resolve this problem. However, the solution will take time, will not be backward compatible, and will likely prove too expensive for many situations. In the meantime,

Ultra-SCSI serves as an interim solution. It's twice as fast as SCSI-2, multi-channeled, and can use all that SCSI-1 and SCSI-2 hardware you have accumulated over the years.

For UltraSCSI, ANSI separated the single SCSI standard into a collection of standards that are extensions of the SCSI-2 interface standard.

More Devices

SCSI-3 will support up to 16 devices, rather than the current eight.

Device Types

The command set has been expanded. There are now device types for Digital Audio Tapes (DAT) and for file server-type devices as well.

Expanded Number of I/O Channels (MultiChannel)

Give an UltraSCSI drive an additional I/O channel, and you have MultiChannel SCSI, as it expands the number of I/O channels available to the system. For example, instead of a single channel supporting seven devices, the Adaptec 3940 has two channels, each with its own independent RISC processor. The 8-bit AHA 3940 UltraSCSI version can support up to 15 devices and move data at up to 40 MBps. The 16-bit AHA 3940 Wide UltraSCSI version doubles this to 31 devices, and it can move data at up to an incredible 80MBps.

Performance is greatly enhanced by this strategy (as well as by doubling the internal clock speed), since faster devices can have their own channel. Slower devices can use another channel, so they are no longer a bottleneck impeding the speedier peripherals.

Another advantage of having multiple channels is the ability to use only one of your valuable PCI slots for hardware mirroring.

Shorter Cables

As data transfer speeds are increased with UltraSCSI, transmission noise and signal quality become problematic over the entire length of the cable connecting the host and the device(s). To address this problem, the cable specification for UltraSCSI was shortened to 1.5 meters. Bus extenders can be added to increase the total cable length to 7.5 meters.

Mandatory Active Termination

SCSI-3, as I've already mentioned, also forces the termination circuits to get a bit more complex. Instead of simple passive resistors, SCSI-3 termination must include voltage regulation circuits that keep the bus voltage between 4 and 5.25 volts. That means a less noisy bus, but it also spells trouble for a SCSI-3 configuration with an old SCSI-1 or SCSI-2 that doesn't support active termination. Again, many SCSI-1 or SCSI-2 devices do support SCSI, but there's no guarantee. And, like SCSI-2, SCSI-3 requires SCSI parity.

Bridging into Serial and Fiber SCSI

SCSI-3 introduces a lot more wires with a 68-wire connector. That's because of the parallel nature of SCSI, in combination with the new 32-bit data bus. But there's another approach, as well—serial SCSI.

Serial SCSI is a six-wire version of SCSI. It's easier to cable and for greater distances; serial SCSI can run for over a kilometer of cable! Additionally, SCSI-3 is defined for optical fiber, paving the way for even faster systems. I'll talk more about Fibre Channel in a bit, but I mention it here because some aspects of this technology are included in the SCSI-3 standard.

Comparing SCSI-1, SCSI-2, SCSI-3

Table 16.1 compares SCSI-1, SCSI-2, and SCSI-3.

TABLE 16.1: SCSI-1, SCSI-2, and SCSI-3 Compared

Standard	Bit Width	Cable Name	Pin Cnt.	Max Transfer Rate MB/sec	Max SCSI-Devices	Description
SCSI-1	8	A	50	5	8	Asynchronous
SCSI-2	8	A	50	10	8	Fast
SCSI-2	16	A+B	50+68	20	8	Fast+Wide**
SCSI-2	32	A+B	50+68	40	8	Fast+Wide**
SCSI-3	16	A	50	10	8	Fast
SCSI-3	16	P	68	20	16	Fast+Wide*
SCSI-3	32	P+Q	68+68	40	32	Fast+Wide**

* with 1 cable
** with 2 cables

Fibre Channel

Hewlett Packard, IBM, and Sun Microsystems began the FCSI (Fibre Channel Systems Initiative) in 1993. The goal of this initiative was to create an industry standard for I/O interconnection that would increase I/O performance and allow for more configuration flexibility. This technology is so complex that an entire book could be devoted to it. Therefore, I will give only an overview here.

Fibre Channel Storage Area Networks

Imagine for a minute that your current SCSI cable connects to your computer in the same way your network cable does. The other end of the cable connects to a hub, which in turn connects to a 100MBps "network" of hard drives (or other peripherals). If you are using copper cables, these other devices may be located up to 30 meters away. If you use fiber optic, these devices may be in various buildings or even up to 10 kilometers apart. All your data I/O now travels through this cable rather than through the regular network. This configuration roughly defines a storage system implementation of Fibre Channel, illustrated in Figure 16.21.

FIGURE 16.21:

Storage system implementation of Fibre Channel

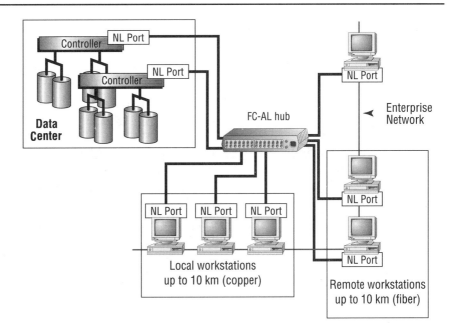

Terminology

Notice the rather strange new terminology used in Figure 16.22 for Fibre Channel. The concept of the interconnecting Fibre Channel network is called the fabric. Each point of connection, whether it be a hard drive or a server, is called an N-port or Node port. When Fibre Channel is used to network storage devices, the term *SAN* is used, meaning *Storage Area Network.* Fibre Channel implementations that use a dual loop configuration roughly analogous to Token Ring are called FC-AL, or Fibre Channel Arbitrated Loop.

Fibre Channel and Clusters

Clusters are groupings of servers that are accessed by a common group of clients. The main benefit of clustering is "fail-over" capabilities. If a client is running an application from a server that fails catastrophically, another server in the cluster will dynamically take over, with no disruption to the client. Some applications can also scale using clustering technology.

Fibre Channel complements clustering technology in several ways. Since it offers the ability to add more devices than other SCSI technologies, Fibre Channel offers the capability of creating larger clusters. Further, unlike older SCSI technologies, Fibre Channel can be configured not to give priority to any node, improving cluster performance.

Figure 16.22 shows Fibre Channel implemented with cluster technology.

FIGURE 16.22:

Fibre Channel implementation with cluster technology

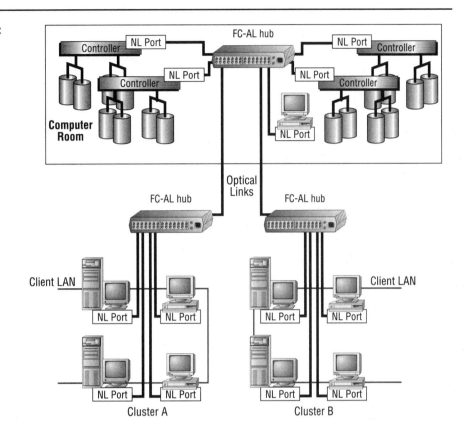

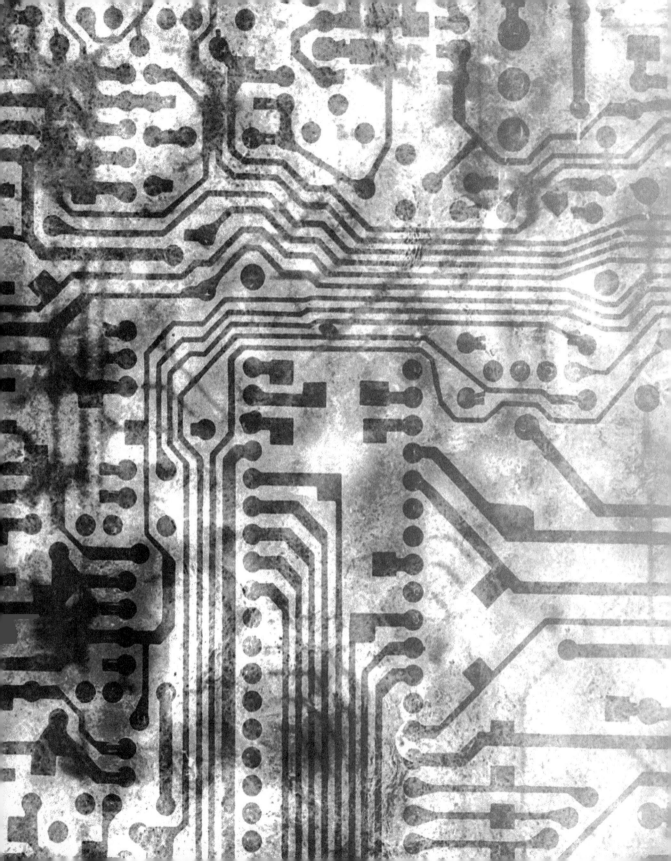

Troubleshooting Printers

- Components

- Parallel ports

- Maintenance

- Common problems and troubleshooting

Printers can be a real maintenance headache. As they produce tangible results (pieces of paper), malfunctions with printers can be more upsetting than their wholly electronic brethren. For example, try telling Windows that you've got a Hewlett-Packard laser printer configured as a PCL5 device when you actually have a PostScript HP printer, then print a graph. The printer will start spewing out pages, as if angry for being misrepresented.

Most of *my* printer problems—the vast majority—are software-related issues. The hardware problems more often seem to be cable or printer interface problems, now that the old daisy wheel printers are pretty much gone and forgotten. I use mainly laser printers, but the new ink jet printers can produce output that is as good as or better than some laser printers, at far lower initial cost.

Components

As with other peripheral troubleshooting, start your diagnosis from the three main pieces: a controller (the parallel or serial interface board), a cable, and a printer. The parallel port is simple enough that it is usually included right on the motherboard (although it has undergone some changes over the years).

Parallel Ports

The parallel port was originally devised as a high-speed, low-cost alternative to a serial port for printer interfaces. Until 1976, you'd connect a cheap (you know, under $10,000) printer to a minicomputer or a microcomputer via an RS-232 port.

The problem with doing that was that serial port hardware was expensive. Adding a serial port to a computer could raise the computer's price by $250 to $1,000. That got in the way of selling printers, and so a printer company, Centronics, decided to do something about it—they created the Centronics parallel interface. RS-232 allows cables of more than 50 feet in length; the Centronics interface is reliable for only 15 feet, actually less for modern ports. RS-232 is bidirectional and quite flexible as to the kind of things it can support. Originally, the Centronics parallel interface was designed to be unidirectional and really was aimed only at printers. RS-232 is serial, employing only two wires for data; Centronics is an 8-bit parallel interface, with eight wires for data. The circuitry required to implement a parallel port, however, is much simpler than that required to implement a serial port because data in your computer is also parallel so it simply transmits the data as it is, so the cost of making a parallel port is much lower. The result was a Centronics interface that was easy to cobble together for just a few dollars and offered terrific throughput, as much as 500,000 bits per second compared to RS-232's 20,000 bits per second.

Since then, the parallel port has continued to evolve. First, some laptops offered bidirectional parallel ports. Then those bidirectional parallel ports were further modified to become *Enhanced Parallel Ports* (*EPP*) and *Extended Capabilities Ports* (*ECP*). ECP is more commonly used for printers, while EPP is more common for other parallel devices such as scanners. These new port types let you print with the speed of the wind, between 500,000 and 1,000,000 bits per second. They also let printers form a lasting relationship with computers based on communication—the printer not only listens to the computer but also communicates its own problems, like being out of paper or having a paper jam. Using an ECP port, you don't need to go to the printer to discover that it didn't do its job—a message will pop up on your monitor telling you so.

To use an ECP port, you need four things: an ECP or EPP/ECP port, an ECP-capable printer, an IEEE 1284-compliant parallel cable, and Windows 95 or 98, which, at the time of this writing, are the only operating systems out there with ECP capability. Once you have installed these features, you will begin to print with unparalleled speed (excuse the pun).

The expanded capabilities of the parallel port have led to the parallel port's use in more areas than just printers. The parallel port now sees use as a file transfer interface (for removable media drives or external CD-ROMs), as a connection to a local area network adapter, or as a connection to a sound-producing device.

Windows 95/98 and Windows NT have support for up to three parallel ports, LPT1 through LPT3. Parallel port addresses are hex 3BC, 378, and 278. The PC has a peculiar process for relating I/O addresses to LPT addresses. First, it looks for address 3BC. If there is a port at that address, it assigns it LPT1. If not, it looks for 378 and, if it exists, assigns *that* to LPT1. If that's not available, it finally tries for 278. Once LPT1 is assigned, it looks (in the same order) for LPT2 and LPT3. This means that if you put a first parallel port into a machine, and the port has address 278, you'll end up with an LPT1, even though 278 is intended for LPT3. But install a second port at 378, and the next time you boot up, the 278 port will become LPT2.

Maintenance

A few things can be done to maintain printers of all types. Vacuum out the paper chaff periodically from the inside of the printer. You may find it unwieldy to use the same vacuum on the printer as you use on the living room carpet. Purchasing a tech vacuum of some sort may be best, because it is smaller and easier to use for tight areas and it won't suck key tops right off your keyboards. Determine if there is a belt tightening mechanism for the printer— usually a motor moves the print head via a belt. Find the correct tension values. Keep a replacement belt on hand. (Believe me, they're no picnic to find in a hurry).

WARNING　Some printers have ribbon cables that are used to carry the data to the print head. They often look like drive belts, but they are definitely not. Tighten these and they'll usually break. If they do, you can say good-bye to your printer.

Impact Printers

If you're still using an impact printer like a dot matrix or daisy wheel printer (and if you are, it's time to reevaluate your priorities in life), use a dry, soft cloth to clean both the paper path and the ribbon path. Most manufacturers suggest cleaning every six months, as the ribbon path can build up a film of inky glop that causes the ribbon to jam. To do this, go to a drug store and buy a dispenser box of 100 clear latex gloves. Use them when working on the printer (but not chips and boards—that latex can build up some mean static) so that you don't have to wash your hands for hours to remove the ink.

Most printers do not need to be lubricated in everyday use. In fact, oil can do considerable damage if applied to the wrong places. If you thoroughly disassemble the printer, then you will probably have to lubricate various points as you reassemble it. If you intend to do this, I strongly recommend that you get a maintenance manual from the manufacturer.

Here's a tip that will extend the life of both the ribbon and the head: put some WD40 lubricant on a used ink ribbon. Let it soak overnight. It'll produce good output the next day, and you won't damage the print head—WD40 is a good lubricant for print heads. Let me stress, however, that this only applies to ink ribbons. If you have a thermal-transfer printer, like an IBM Quietwriter or an Okidata 20, this will not work.

And here's a tip that will help you clean up after working on a printer. A friend once told me that hairspray will remove ink from fabric. So my girlfriend and I experimented with her hair mousse stuff—you know, the spray that you use to make your hair defy gravity? It did nothing. Then we tried some Aqua Net, a hairspray that hasn't changed since Jackie Kennedy used it in the White House. The result? We found that cheap hairspray works a lot better than the expensive stuff. Spray it on the fabric and rinse with cold water. A little soap will pick up the rest.

Daisy Wheel Printers

If you're cheap, or if you work for someone who's cheap, then you may have to keep a daisy wheel printer on life support systems way after its proper time. Depending upon how much you use them, daisy wheel printers require that the daisy wheels be replaced about annually. Some variations, like Spinwriter thimbles, last longer, but must also be replaced eventually. (The Spinwriter also needs a striker shield replaced every few months. It is a thin flat piece of plastic that sits near where the thimble strikes the paper.)

Be sure to replace the printing elements—daisy wheels and the like—before they wear out, as a worn daisy can damage a printer. You know when they're wearing because you'll see one of two symptoms. The first is fading on the more common characters first, the "e" and the "t"—between them these two letters constitute about 20 percent of the characters in typical English text. (Actually, the "space" character is the most common in English, constituting 20 percent of text. It's just hard to notice when the space has faded.) The other is tilted characters. This happens when the little plastic arms that hold the characters get worn out or if the printer timing slips a little.

And finally, the gap between the printing element and the paper must be aligned regularly—a little too regularly, actually. Assuming that you don't have to produce multi-part forms, get a laser or ink jet printer.

Dot Matrix Printers

The expensive part of a dot matrix printer that dies is the print head. Print for too long a time and the head just burns up. This is not as much of a problem for the newer printers as it was for the old Epsons and Okidatas. The models out today have a thermistor that shuts down the printer temporarily if the print head overheats. If the thermistor becomes ill, the printer shuts down regularly. Generally thermistors are pretty robust, but if such a thing happens, try changing the thermistor first; it's a lot cheaper than a print head.

On older Epson printers that didn't have a thermistor, when the print heads overheated they'd usually take the circuit boards with them when they burned up.

Replacing print heads is not economical on many printers because of the high price that manufacturers charge for replacements. My Okidata 92, which I purchased years ago for $370, would need a $125 print head if I needed to replace it. Fact is, in almost every case, it makes no sense to replace a dot matrix print head. Unless you have one of the very expensive, high-speed dot matrix printers. You can buy a brand new printer for about the cost of a replacement dot matrix print head.

Dot matrix printers are generally very reliable, but keeping the print head cool is vital. Don't stack things on or around the printer.

Ink Jet Printers

Ink jet printers have come a long way since their introduction back in the 70's. At one time they would clog pretty regularly because the ink would dry in the tiny holes in the heads. Today the jets are designed to resist drying and the heads are generally protected by a rubber boot that keeps the holes from drying out.

Also, the heads are built into the ink tanks so when you replace an empty tank, you're also getting new jets. This keeps the print on these printers looking like new.

By the way, many of the ink jet heads (called cartridges) can be refilled. This is an economical way of extending the life of the heads. But be aware that the heads will eventually wear and you'll lose some quality if you refill them too often. Also, some cartridges can't be filled effectively yet because the after-market inks that are currently available clog the high-resolution heads. This is true, however, only with the 1200 dot per inch (DPI) heads. Most of the other heads can be refilled.

Thermal-Transfer Printers

When you were a kid, did you ever make pictures by coloring with crayons onto a piece of heavy paper and then using an iron to transfer the colored wax to another piece of paper? (If not, then nod politely and keep reading—we'll get past the "when you were a kid" stories in a minute.) Thermal transfer printing works something like that. Very hot pins are pressed onto a wax- or wax/resin-coated ribbon and the wax or resin melts and is transferred to the paper beneath it. The difference is that the paper has to go through the process four times, once for each color (normally cyan, yellow, magenta, and black).

NOTE   One thermal-transfer printer, Pentax Technology's PocketJet, heats dye on special thermal paper supplied by the manufacturer. However, if you're talking about plain paper or transparency printing, this doesn't apply.

The issues involved with thermal-transfer printers are much like those with other printers: keep them cool and keep them plugged in. If you're having problems with print quality, such as smearing, you might try using another manufacturer's paper or ribbons.

Laser Printers

Laser printers are important enough that I'll devote the next chapter to them. As a result, I'll limit my discussion of them here.

The laser printer is very similar to a copy machine. Having said that, it's amazing that they are as reliable as they are.

The most common laser engine is made by Canon. Many of the HP LaserJets, Apple LaserWriters, and Canons (obviously), as well as the older QMS Kiss and others, are all built around the Canon engine. These need very little maintenance except for a new cartridge every 3,000 copies or so. The cartridges cost in the neighborhood of $70, and, according to HP, contain all that is needed for routine maintenance. So, every time that you change your cartridge, you'll perform routine maintenance like cleaning the corona wires and paper pickup pawls.

It's okay to recharge cartridges. Make sure your refill company completely rebuilds the insides, including replacing the photo-electric drum. Avoid the "drill and fill" vendors, as they don't replace the insides, and using that kind of refill will lead to a lower-quality print image and may damage the laser printer. If you don't refill them, many of the cartridge manufacturers provide a way to mail in the used ones for recycling.

Lasers require proper ventilation and a fair amount of power. Other than that, don't pour any Cokes in them and they last a long time. Never ship a laser with a toner cartridge in place. It can open up and cover the inside of the laser with toner.

An important thing to understand about laser printers is that they are *page printers*. This means that they won't do anything until the page is full. From an MS-DOS window, you can force a laser to eject a page with the following batch file.

When you create the batch file, you'll type or input the characters in bold below. The computer's prompts are shown in regular text.

```
C>copy con: eject.bat
echo ^L PRN
[F6]
1 file(s) copied
C>
```

Where you see ^L, generate this by holding down the Ctrl key and typing **L**. Where you see [F6], just press the F6 function key.

From this point on, you can just type **EJECT** from a DOS prompt and your printer will eject the current page.

Of course, if you are running an operating system like Windows, you should not have to worry about this since the printer driver will take care of filling the page for you.

Infrared Printers

For members of the "virtual office" who have no desk but only a laptop to carry around and plug in as needed, there's a way to eliminate at least one of the cables you need to plug in: printers with infrared ports are available. Rather than requiring a parallel cable to connect the printer to your computer, a ray of infrared light shines between a transceiver on the computer and one on the printer.

NOTE There's no reason why desktop computers couldn't use infrared printers as well, but for reasons that we'll cover in the course of this discussion, I think that they'll be more useful to laptop users.

Data travels between the computer and printer via an infrared connection. Light and electric impulses all pulse at a certain rate per second; this rate is called the *frequency*—the more pulses, the higher the frequency. Signals with higher frequencies can transmit data more quickly (each pulse can carry a bit of data). However, they have a shorter range and are more prone to interference than lower-frequency signals, because anything that interferes with the signal will affect more data than it would if there were fewer pulses per second. Infrared light has a high frequency. Thus, the computer sends a beam of infrared light to the receiver on the printer. The devices have a pretty good range, but it is usually limited to line of sight. (You can't print from an office around the corner.)

If you're having trouble with a wireless printer, check the following:

- Are the infrared ports on the printer and computer both clean and unblocked?

- Does it help to move the printer/computer to one side?

- Did someone stand between your printer and computer during the print job?

Other than that, troubleshooting an infrared printer is much like troubleshooting any other printer. The tricky thing about wireless printers is making the connections.

Network Printers

Most businesses today don't want to be tied down to using just a parallel port for their printers. You can imagine how annoying it would be if everybody in your department came to your desk to get their print jobs just because the printer was attached to your parallel port. Thus was born the network printer. HP's JetDirect card is a popular one that comes to mind; it just plugs right into the back of a number of their models. For the models that don't have a JetDirect slot, a special device will connect the printer to the network via the parallel port on the printer. Printers can be placed in convenient spots around the office without fear of being too far from a parallel port.

There are, however, a few caveats to using these marvels of technology. First, like any network device, you must be using the same protocols on your server as you use on the print card, since the printer driver is actually installed on a server, then shared. Standard protocols supported are TCP/IP, IPX/SPX, EtherTalk, and DLC. Unlike other protocols, DLC is used only for printing and mainframe access in the Windows environment, so you may not have it installed. You must also be sure that the protocols are configured correctly—if you are using TCP/IP, for example, you must have an IP address and a subnet mask for the printer. It is also a very good idea to be sure that your network cable is securely plugged into the card and hub.

Common Problems and Troubleshooting

It's hard to discuss printer troubleshooting without delving too deeply into the specifics of the thousands of models out there. I haven't got the space to do that (or, truthfully, the time to get to know all of those printers), but there are some generic pieces of advice that I can pass along.

Isolate the Problem

As always, try to isolate the problem. Something in the computer or its software? The printer interface? The cable? The printer? Is the printer plugged in, cabled, and *on-line*?

The steps I use are:

1. Check if it is on-line, is plugged in, has paper, and is turned on.

2. Cycle power switch on printer, reboot, and retry.

3. If it is a network printer, check the protocol configuration (i.e., the IP address and subnet mask on TCP/IP).

4. Use printer self-test mode to see if the test page prints correctly.

5. Check that the software is configured for the printer.

6. Swap cable to test it.

7. If it is a network printer, try printing from another machine.

8. Swap printer to test it. (Use the same type of printer.)

The first thing I'd try would be to cycle the power switch and restart the software. One time I was experimenting with graphics on a daisy wheel printer, setting the vertical and horizontal motion increment to a very small value, then using periods (.) for graphic points. (I got some impressive results, for a dumb daisy wheel.) Anyway, I forgot to reset the motion increments. Our word processor operator, Wally, came by about an hour later, saying, "Mark, were you messing with the printer?" She held out a letter that the printer had typed in a space of about 1 inch by 2 inches.

Some other things to check:

- Does the printer have paper? One of my favorite tricks is to check that the main paper tray is full, then accidentally and unwittingly select the empty alternate paper tray.

- Do a DIR from DOS, then try a screen print using the PRINTSCRN button.

- There's lots of buggy printer-driving software. Have you ever seen this software work on this printer?

- If you are dealing with a network printer, check the queue at the server to be certain there are no stuck jobs. If there are, then purge the queue.

Cable Lengths

The role of cable lengths in noise and interference has been discussed before in this text. But another problem is overly long cables. Serial cables aren't supposed to be longer than 50 feet, and older parallel cables should not exceed six feet. Newer IEEE 1284 (ECP and EPP) compliant cable can actually go to 15 feet. If you're using long cables and getting mysterious errors, the cables may be the culprits.

There are parallel port extenders—check the Black Box catalog to find them—which will let you run your parallel cable up to a kilometer.

Something I've noticed in recent years is that modern parallel port chips don't put out all that much power. I used to be able to share a printer between two computers with an A/B switch, but it's often the case that it won't work unless the A/B switch has amplification power. The moral seems to be to keep those parallel port cables as short as possible. It is also not recommended to use an A/B switch with laser printers unless you have a powered switch.

Setup DIP Switch Problem

A more and more common problem is emulation mode. Many printers nowadays will emulate a Hewlett-Packard LaserJet of some kind. Unfortunately, some vendors' idea of "Hewlett-Packard compatible" is a blend of fact and fantasy. Anyway, if you've got your Acme Laser Printer set up for HP emulation, don't tell your software you've got an Acme—tell it you've got an

HP. This sounds simple, but you'd be surprised at the number of people that get tripped up on that one.

This final option is an indication of how international the electronics business is. Many printers speak foreign languages. If you set up your printer for British, you may get the pounds sterling sign rather than a dollar sign. Oh, and by the way, most printers nowadays don't have DIP switches; they support some kind of software setup.

Port Problems

As you know, printers can have either a serial or parallel interface. On the PC, the only visible difference between the two is that the parallel port has a female connector and the serial port has a male connector.

Electronically, they are radically different, however. The parallel interface uses different voltages and handshakes than the serial interface. Printers can be bought with either serial or parallel interfaces. Given the choice, take parallel. It's a cleaner and faster interface. As laser printers get faster and, more particularly, support higher resolution, more high speed interfaces will appear. For example, Apple uses an AppleTalk 230,000bps interface to an Apple LaserWriter. Some printers interface with SCSI, and some use proprietary CPU-to-printer interfaces.

Remember to use the screws on the connector to secure your cable. I saw a situation where an Okidata printer printed consistently incorrect characters. I tried to understand the problem by comparing the ASCII codes of the desired characters to the codes actually printed. I found in each case that bit 6 was *always 1*. It turned out that the wire for line 6 was not fully seated. Securing the connector did the job.

I found a similar problem with a broken wire in a cable. Here's an example. Suppose I try to print "Hello" but get "Iekko." Compare the codes of the desired and actual characters in Table 17.1.

TABLE 17.1: An Example Printer Cable Problem

DESIRED CHARACTER	CODE	ACTUAL CHARACTER	CODE
H	01001000	I	01001001
E	01100101	E	01100101
L	01101100	K	01101101
L	01101100	K	01101101
O	01101111	O	01101111

The "E" and "O" aren't affected, but "H" and "L" are. Notice that in all cases the low bit is "1."

If you are using a serial interface, are the communications parameters set correctly? There are four:

- Speed (1200, 2400, 4800, 9600, 14400, or 19200)
- Parity (Even, Odd, or None)
- Number of data bits (7 or 8)
- Number of stop bits (usually 1 or 2)

You'll find the parameters in the technical manual of the printer. Then construct the DOS commands:

```
MODE COM1: speed,parity,data bits,stop bits,p
MODE LPT1:=COM1:
```

In the first case, an example would be:

```
MODE COM1:9600,N,8,1,P
MODE LPT1:=COM1:
```

Meaning "9600 bits per second, no parity, 8 data bits, 1 stop bit." The "P" means that it's a printer.

If you are using one of those new-fangled ECP ports for your printing needs, you may run into problems like garbled text or graphics. This is because some printers on the market haven't quite reached IEEE nirvana yet and therefore don't work so well with ECP. There are two things to do in this instance: in Windows, change the printer spooling properties from EMF to RAW; if that doesn't work, then change the port back to standard mode.

If you're having other port problems, did you install something recently? Could something be conflicting with the printer port? Recall the story of the 5251 emulation board. You'd never imagine it, but the terminal emulation board was killing the port. Is there another printer port? Are they both set for LPT1?

The Weather

Everyone talks about it, but…

A printer repairman told me about a day that he'd had the previous October. He said that all over town a particular model of printer was failing left and right. He couldn't figure it out. We thought about it. Around the middle of October, we turn on the heat in Washington. That dries out the air and, in turn, the items in the work area. Chips don't mind being dried, but what about capacitors? Could a paper-type capacitor be malfunctioning because it was drying beyond a certain point?

A repair memo came around from the manufacturer a couple of months later. Sure enough, a particular capacitor didn't like it too dry. The answer: either put a humidifier near the printer or change the capacitor to a similar, less dry-sensitive replacement. Moral: be suspicious when the seasons change.

That's an overview of printer troubleshooting in general. In the next chapter, we'll focus on laser printers.

CHAPTER

EIGHTEEN

18

Troubleshooting Laser Printers

- Parts of a laser printer and how it prints

- Common symptoms and solutions

- Basic and advanced testing

- Understanding error messages and fixing printer problems

- Maintenance and higher quality printing

Laser printers are actually pretty reliable. Most of the printer problems you'll see are not printer problems at all, but rather problems with the humans trying to use them. As I told you in Chapter 5, "Troubleshooting PC Problems," you should first check the part of the equation that walks and talks.

Once the human component has been checked and cleared, exercise a methodical approach to testing the rest of the system. Break the problem down into its possibilities/probabilities, testing and eliminating them, one by one. Start with the easy stuff first. It's always possible that the only thing the printer needs is more paper.

Parts of a Laser Printer

Let's start out understanding laser printers by looking at the parts of a laser printer.

The Data Interface

Much of a laser printer is actually a computer. Not the computer on your desk; instead, it's the computer *inside* the laser printer.

As would be expected, the largest printed circuit board in the printer has the most to do with receiving and modifying the data. This and other boards in the printer are referred to by Hewlett-Packard as PCAs. (PCA is HP-ese for Printed Circuit Assembly; you and I call them printed circuit boards.) This board in the HP Series II is called an Interface PCA and in the later printers is referred to as the Formatter PCA. We'll call the main board the *interface controller*.

The Interface Controller

The interface controller is the printer's motherboard. It contains several major and complex components. It has the following functions:

- Communicates with the host via one of four installed interface ports (parallel, serial, network, or direct video interface)
- Manipulates incoming data for translation to the print engine
- Monitors the Control Panel for user input
- Provides information on printer status at the display and through various LEDs
- Stores configuration and font information

The function that we'll consider first is a bus interface that allows input of data and communication with the host, the input interface.

The Input Interface

The input interface contains the familiar serial and parallel ports, and the not so familiar optional I/O port.

Serial Ports

Serial, as the name implies, is used to send data in a bit-by-bit fashion, using one wire to send and another to receive. This is a rugged and flexible interface when compared to the parallel port. It can be configured to change several parameters including speed and can be found on everything from mice to modems.

If a decent, shielded, twisted-pair cable is used in a quiet environment (one without lots of radio frequency or electromagnetic interference), it is possible to send and receive data through a serial port at distances of several hundred feet.

The serial port on the laser printer ends up being used less frequently than the parallel port.

Parallel Ports

Parallel, on the other hand, uses eight wires to transfer the data. A full byte (8 bits) of data at a time will travel the cable. Even though the interface connector on the printer is commonly referred to as a Centronics port, it really isn't. That's just a holdover name from a former port in a former time. The current interface was developed by Epson.

The Achilles' heel of the parallel port is the fact that it is quite limited in terms of distance. Most manufacturers want the parallel interface cable to be limited to about 15 feet for laser printer applications, but I have installed a 50-footer that worked—it was the best cable that we could buy, was installed in the floor rather than the ceiling of a new building, and we soldered the ends.

Optional I/O

The third interface is the optional I/O, or "video" port. The optional I/O port on HP printers is located at the back of the printer next to the standard serial and parallel ports. This is the receptor of many upgrades and emulation enhancements. One of the better known among them is the LaserWriter upgrade board that allows the printer to communicate with Macintosh computers.

This is also used as the interface for many other after-market enhancements such as printer sharing devices.

Network I/O

Network cards made specially for printers appeared in the last chapter and are of special note again here. This is a principal form of I/O in the business world today, since no one wants to keep the printer at their desk so it can be next to the parallel port. You can connect to Token Ring or Ethernet, 10 or 100MBps, coax, or twisted pair. This kind of flexibility makes these little doodads a must have.

The CPU

The interface controller also holds the main brain of the operation, the CPU. No matter which port receives the data, the CPU will control its processing. The one used on the earlier LaserJets was the Motorola 68000 series with the later LaserJet IIIs using the 68030. The LaserJet 4 and higher have the Intel 960 RISC-based processor.

Even though these processors are highly capable, you will often find them nearly abandoned by many after-market products in favor of the usually more powerful and faster CPU of the host computer. This occurs, for example, when you add an interface for background printing that takes over the chore of modulating the laser for higher resolutions.

Printer RAM

One of the areas that manufacturers have really paid a lot of attention to in the upgrades of their products is the amount and configuration of RAM. The LaserJet 4 and 5 have more standard RAM than the III (which had 2MB) and they are more easily upgraded by the owner/user using standard DRAM SIMMs. It's not that the old upgrades were all that hard to install, but being proprietary, they were just plain expensive.

RAM upgrades come in handy when one wants to do graphics and enable page protection as well as to speed up things in general.

As with the CPU, it is possible that the printer's RAM can be abandoned by an upgrade interface in favor of the host's memory.

System Bus

Like the PC, a laser printer has an internal bus. Think of this bus as a freeway; all of the pieces of information are the cars. When you want to drive on the freeway, you have to take an on-ramp and merge into traffic. The interface controller is the on-ramp to the printing freeway; it is where all of the information merges onto the main system bus.

How a Laser Printer Prints

Laser printing is a multi-step process. Understanding the process is more than just a techie exercise; it's essential to understanding what can go wrong and how to fix it.

I'll explain this in detail, but the overview on how a laser prints is roughly like this: the printing drum is cleaned, then an image is "painted" onto it with electrostatic charges, then print toner moves to the charged areas, then the toner is transferred to a piece of paper, and finally the toner is fixed onto the paper permanently with a heated metal roller. You can see this in Figure 18.1.

FIGURE 18.1:

How a laser printer works

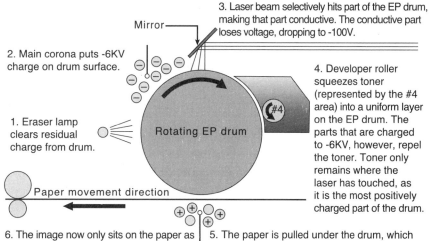

2. Main corona puts -6KV charge on drum surface.

Mirror

3. Laser beam selectively hits part of the EP drum, making that part conductive. The conductive part loses voltage, dropping to -100V.

1. Eraser lamp clears residual charge from drum.

Rotating EP drum

4. Developer roller squeezes toner (represented by the #4 area) into a uniform layer on the EP drum. The parts that are charged to -6KV, however, repel the toner. Toner only remains where the laser has touched, as it is the most positively charged part of the drum.

Paper movement direction

6. The image now only sits on the paper as fine, dust-like toner. The toner must be fixed to the page. The fuser roller actually melts the toner into the page with heat at a temperature of 180 degrees C.

5. The paper is pulled under the drum, which now contains the desired image written in toner. A second corona, the transfer corona, emits positive charge, drawing the toner from the drum to the paper.

Figure 18.2 shows a laser printer with paper ready to start running through the printing process.

FIGURE 18.2:

Laser printer beginning the printing process

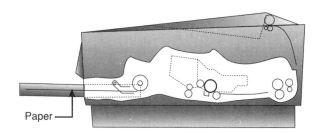

Paper

The paper feeds from the left. The rollers and the print cartridge are on the right.

Data Input

When an application has data ready to be printed, it establishes communication with the hardware services in the PC that are needed to obtain a door to the outside world. The PC then determines that there is indeed a data terminal device attached to the active I/O port and satisfies itself that the device is waiting for data.

The laser printer responds in a favorable manner to the overtures of the computer by signaling on the strobe line (pin 1) on the parallel interface or DTR (line 20) on serial. This indicates that the printer is inactive but receptive.

When the application begins to deliver the data, it will be received by the printer buffer.

In the case of an HP laser printer, the interface controller receives the data and offers it to anyone who might be interested in taking a shot at it. Candidates for such an action would be a hardware device in the optional I/O port or a program running in conjunction with a font cartridge or resident in the printer's memory.

If such a device or program exists, it will either manipulate the data directly or play around with the laser engine modulation to accomplish the desired end.

Once the data is ready for printing, the hardware will go through a preparatory process before the laser actually begins to define the image.

A significant percentage of the printing process involves the Electrophotographic Cartridge. There are several things that need to happen within the cartridge each time that the Interface PCA receives data.

Drum Preparation

The first of those steps is drum preparation. The heart of the print process is the photosensitive drum, an aluminum cylinder coated with a photosensitive material. The drum's job is to pick up laser printer *toner*—a fine black dust that is the "ink" of the laser printing process—and deposit it on the paper. Figure 18.3 points out the photosensitive drum.

FIGURE 18.3:

Photosensitive drum in a laser printer

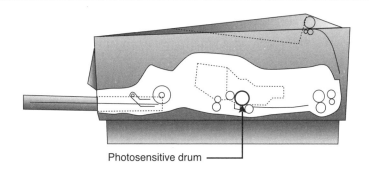

Photosensitive drum ———

Cleaning the Drum

Since the same photosensitive drum is used to print every image (it actually rotates almost three times during the printing of each letter-sized page), it must be prepared for the newer image by completely purging the previous one. If the drum weren't completely purged, then subsequent pages would have ghostly images from previous pages. You know how hard it is to completely clean a blackboard when you erase it, and so parts of what was on the blackboard previously kind of hang around? That's what we're trying to avoid in laser printing.

The cleaning process is accomplished in two parts. Physically, excess toner is constantly wiped from the drum by means of a rubber-cleaning blade.

The drum is then cleaned electrostatically by means of five erase lamps found in the hinged top cover on the early printers, and by means of another drum, a charged drum, in the later printer models. On the printers with lamps, the lamps can shine onto the photosensitive drum via one of the two narrow hinged covers on the top of the cartridge, which open automatically when the cover is closed. These lamps neutralize residual charges by illuminating the photosensitive component of the drum.

The photosensitive component can be permanently damaged by exposure to light; therefore, the illumination from the lamps is red filtered. Pop the top on your series II or III, and you'll see red plastic; those are the filters for the lamps.

Conditioning

After the original preparation, the drum requires conditioning for the next image. This process involves the application of a uniformly negative charge to the surface of the drum by the primary corona assembly (the one in the cartridge) in the early printers and a charged drum in the later ones. The high voltage power supply provides a −600VDC charge to the corona wire or charged drum, thus creating an electrical corona, kind of like some major-league static electricity. That −600v charge is applied by a very important thin wire called the *primary corona* located in the disposable laser cartridge. The corona must actually emit a −6000v charge in order to get the −600v applied to the drum.

Air is a natural insulator (it's true—in double-paned thermal windows, the air between the panes is as good an insulator as the glass panes are), and that could get in the way of transferring the charge from the corona wire to the drum. But when a corona wire produces a charge, it causes the air in the area of the wire to be ionized with the net effect that it no longer provides insulation between the drum and the corona. The −600v charge is therefore transferred to the entire surface of the drum.

The voltage buildup on the surface of the drum is uniform because it is filtered by a grid that is attached to a varistor in the high-voltage power supply. Take a look at Figure 18.4.

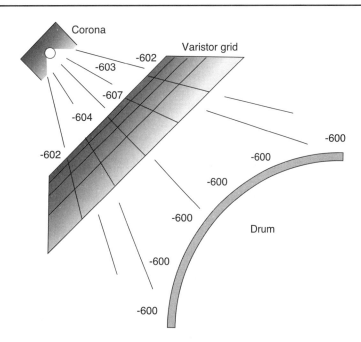

A varistor is so named because it is a variable resistor. It will not conduct electricity until a specific voltage level is achieved. This, of course, is the characteristic that allows it to be useful in this particular application.

Writing the Image on the Drum

Now that it's conditioned, the drum is ready for the image.

First, the photosensitive drum is scanned by the laser unit. This is done in a fashion similar to that of a CRT, with a repeated horizontal sweeping motion of the beam. (As a matter of fact, the interface cable on PostScript and optional I/O printer interfaces is referred to in HP technical documents as a video cable.)

Once a character definition has been determined by the interface controller, the laser light is provided by turning a laser diode on and off at the appropriate times in the current beam position, which in turn is determined by its reflection from the rotation of a polygonal mirror.

On the LaserJet III and earlier, the on/off status of the laser diode can be changed 300 times for each inch of the beam's progress across the drum, hence the 300-dpi resolution of that printer. This creates a map of the appropriate portion of the character on the drum by causing a discharge of the voltage potential in the affected areas, thus creating an invisible electrostatic image with the laser.

The laser access to the drum is through the second hinged door on the cartridge, as you see in Figure 18.5.

FIGURE 18.5:

Laser access to the printer drum

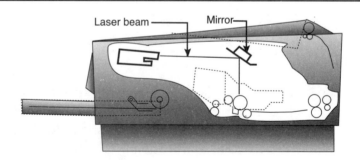

The beam continues its sweep in perfect synchronization with the rotation of the drum so that each incremental horizontal sweep of the beam is offset by 1/300 of an inch from the previous one. The process continues until the entire drum has thus been mapped.

The affected points of the drum are neutralized to about −100 VDC.

The fact that the drum rotates 1/300 of an inch with each horizontal sweep of the laser, and the laser diode is able to change states 300 times per inch, results in the 300 × 300-dpi resolution of the printer.

The Color Printing Difference

While color laser printers are very expensive, they are gaining a following due to the glorious graphics and text they produce. The professional-looking output produced by these printers makes them a boon to people who do their own advertising or graphics printing. Color lasers work in a similar manner to normal laser printers; they just charge more (from the corona, and the store where you bought it).

The color printing method that is gaining more popularity is the "Direct-to-Drum" method used by the HP Color Lasers. First in the transfer process is that the charging corona places the negative charge on the drum; the laser then gently sweeps over the drum and creates an image for the yellow toner (the first of four primary printing colors) to attach to. After the yellow toner has made itself at home, the drum is again charged by the corona, and the laser works its art on the drum and creates an image for the next printing color, magenta. This same process happens again for the final two colors, cyan and black. After all four colors have been applied to the drum, the image is transferred onto the waiting paper.

The Paper Feed

When the drum has been conditioned, the paper will be drawn into the printer by the paper sensor/feed roller assembly. You can see this in Figure 18.6.

FIGURE 18.6:

Paper sensor/feed roller assembly

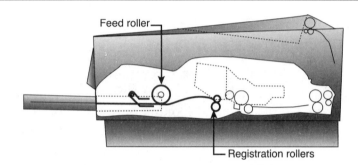

Feed roller

Registration rollers

Notice that the paper is bowed slightly upward. You might have also noticed at some time that the printer will draw the paper from the tray an inch or so and hesitate before continuing. Both occurrences are related to a procedure that ensures that the top edge of the paper will be perfectly aligned with the top of the image on the drum.

The paper is presented to the registration rollers, which impede its travel until a carefully timed release causes every part of the process to be synchronized.

Image Development

After the image is mapped on the photosensitive drum, there is then the simple application of a basic law of nature and of magnetic properties: opposites attract.

The developer component of the cartridge contains a rotating metallic cylinder with a permanent magnet running its length, a toner reservoir, and a toner height control mechanism. The height control is to regulate the amount of toner that may travel with the cylinder.

The metallic cylinder is situated adjacent to the photosensitive drum. Its sole purpose is to collect toner from the reservoir and present it to the drum in a usable form. This device is called the developing cylinder.

The developing cylinder rotates with a portion of its surface in contact with the toner in the toner reservoir of the cartridge. Its magnetic personality (not to mention the fact that its surface is given a highly negative –600VDC charge by the high voltage power supply) causes an irresistible attraction to the tiny neutrally charged particles of toner, which then cling to the cylinder.

The toner that adheres to the cylinder adopts its charge by the time it travels to the image area of the photosensitive drum.

The toner is made of plastic resin particles (the part that melts) bonded to iron oxide (the part that is attracted by the electrical charges).

While the toner-laden developing cylinder rotates toward the image-ready photosensitive drum, a scraping blade removes the excess toner, thus delivering a uniform supply of it to the image process.

The electrical properties of the magnetized developing cylinder are further enhanced by a DC bias and an AC potential.

The DC bias is adjusted by the user via the print density control knob. Its purpose is to regulate the density of the toner that ends up on the printed page. Counter-intuitively, selecting a higher number on the green wheel results in less toner being offered to the photosensitive drum, and therefore results in a lighter image being put on the page. As the developing cylinder presents the now highly negatively charged toner to the laser-affected areas of the photosensitive drum, they are attracted to the invisible electrostatic image because it, although still negative in charge, is much less negative than the toner itself.

The remainder of the drum, not having been struck by the laser, remains at a −600 VDC charge and effectively repels the similarly charged toner.

The AC component on the developer roller affects the DC potential, thus causing the toner, in a reciprocal process, to escape the negatively charged roller at the moment of highest potential, only to be re-attracted to it when the AC component swings high. This happens 60 times per second, effectively presenting a fog of toner to the laser-affected areas.

Those particles of toner that find their way to the electrostatically defined image are not drawn back to the developing cylinder.

The user has control of the magnitude of the DC bias at the green rotating knob (in most of the printers addressed), thus affecting the density of the toner that makes it to the paper. Take a look at Figure 18.7.

FIGURE 18.7:

Image processing (toner)

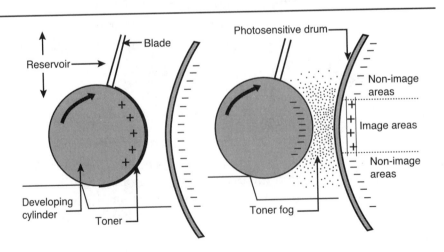

Image Transfer

The desired image now exists on the drum in the form of fine toner particles. Toner is about 50 percent iron oxide, 50 percent plastic: you can actually get toner out of material by rubbing a powerful magnet across the surface. Next, the laser printer transfers the toner to paper by giving the paper a strong (+600v) *positive* charge. That charge is applied by the *transfer corona*, another very important thin wire permanently mounted in the printer. The toner then jumps from the drum to the paper. Once the toner is on the paper, the paper runs past the *static charge eliminator*, which reduces the paper's charge. The image is now transferred to the paper. Take a look at Figure 18.8.

FIGURE 18.8:

Transfer corona

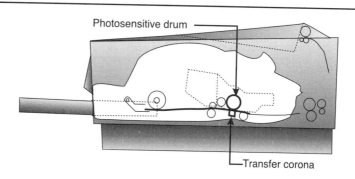

Photosensitive drum

Transfer corona

Once the drum has yielded the image, separation of the paper from it (the drum) is not a foregone conclusion. However, as the paper advances, its natural stiffness facilitates the separation due to the fact that the drum circumference is relatively small. It is likely that thinner papers could adhere to the drum, however, so separation is also assisted by the static eliminator, a row of teeth with a highly negative charge which aids in the neutralization of the potential between the positively charged paper and the negatively charged drum.

Fusing the Image to the Paper

The paper proceeds to the fusing station with its toner image in the precarious condition of being held to the paper by only gravity and a weak electrostatic charge.

The fusing station assembly is composed of a fuser roller, cleaning pad, thermistor, thermo-protector, and pressure roller.

The fuser roller is a Teflon-coated cylinder that has a high-intensity quartz lamp inside it to provide the heat for the fusing process. If the heat builds beyond acceptable levels, there is a detection/protection mechanism called a *thermistor*, located near the fuser roller, that will shut the printer down.

The temperatures of the LaserJet III's fuser were 165 degrees C (330 degrees F) when on but inactive, and 180 degrees C (355 degrees F) while printing. The temperatures are higher in the LaserJet 4. Given these temperatures, caution is advised in the insertion of any gummed, plastic-coated, inked, or raised image media (not to mention your fingers). I have had multiple reports of people inserting non-rated Mylar or acetate to make overhead projection display sheets. Put simply, if you try to print on something that melts below 180 degrees C, then you'll probably have to buy a new fuser roller.

The cleaning pad is positioned so as to remain in constant contact with the fuser roller. It collects any contaminants that seek to become part of the process and provides the already slippery fuser with a silicone film. This ensures that the paper with its now fused image will continue on as planned and not have a tendency to stick around (pardon the pun).

A critical part of the cartridge change is the replacement of this pad if the longevity and quality of the printer is deemed important. Without the silicone film, the hot fuser will be much more likely to receive permanent contamination.

The pressure roller is a rubber roller that is situated against the fuser roller in such a way that the paper is pressed between them as it passes through. The fuser roller is one of those strong personality types that leaves a lasting impression, so every few minutes the printer will rotate this assembly to keep the rubber roller from receiving a permanent indentation in the area where the rollers are being social. That's the odd noise that your laser printer sometimes makes for no obvious reason.

You could view the pressure roller on the LaserJet II and III by pushing back the felt-covered door that was located at the rear of the fuser assembly.

If you are unfortunate enough to get a paper jam prior to this point in the process, it will become immediately obvious that the image on the paper has not yet been fused. As you remove the affected sheet, liberal amounts of toner will remain on anything it gets in contact with.

As the paper proceeds along its path, it's very important that it not wobble off to the left or right, but instead cleave to the path of the straight and narrow. That is accomplished by the feed guide assembly.

As it passes between the fusing roller and the pressure roller, a combination of heat and pressure ensure that the deposited toner will not become random particles of plastic and iron at the slightest disturbance (see Figure 18.9).

FIGURE 18.9:

Fusing roller and pressure roller

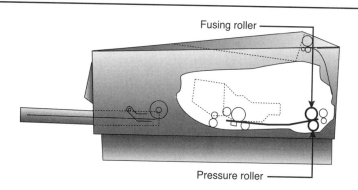

Fusing roller

Pressure roller

After the image is safely fused in place on the paper, the copy is ready for delivery utilizing the fuser roller and the exit delivery rollers. The paper will be guided by exit area paper guides for delivery to the face-down delivery tray at the top of the machine, or the face-up delivery tray at the rear of the machine. The face-up tray receives the paper only if the tray is released and lowered.

When you're printing with heavy stock or fragile items, you can spare them the final turn by using the delivery tray at the back; just open the door and the paper comes out the back.

I've noticed that my envelopes don't wrinkle quite as badly if I let them exit at the back. This is because the exit delivery area at the top of the printer has the most acute angle that the paper encounters in the entire process. Unfortunately, the LaserJet 4 doesn't offer an option in paper delivery. It can be made to deliver out the back but it can be tricky, particularly with older models. Take a look at Figure 18.10.

FIGURE 18.10:

Rear exit for paper on printers

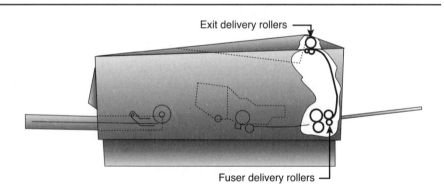

Exit delivery rollers

Fuser delivery rollers

During this whole process, the printer uses sensors located throughout it, which report to the CPU as soon as they see the paper. The printer knows how long it should take to get from one sensor to the next; if a sensor doesn't report "seeing" the paper within a particular window of time, then the printer's CPU assumes that the paper's jammed, and it stops the printing process and reports a jam.

Printer Disassembly Dependencies

Now that you've got some feeling for how laser printers operate, we'll move along to handling some common repairs. If you find yourself disassembling a laser printer, use Figure 18.11 to determine what you must disassemble before getting to a particular piece.

FIGURE 18.11:

Laser printer disassembly dependencies

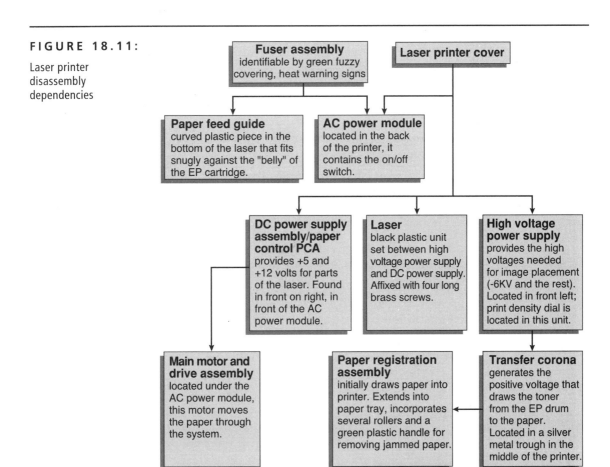

Common Symptoms and Solutions

Now that you know how a laser printer works, you can see what can go wrong. There are lots of *potential* problems with lasers, but I'll confine this to the most common problems only; then we'll take a look at the more rigorous testing you can do.

Vertical White Streaks on the Page

Since the paper is transported top-to-bottom through the laser printer, the paper also passes the coronas top-to-bottom. If a part of the corona were covered with toner, it couldn't transmit all of its charge, leaving either the drum (if it's the main corona) or the paper (if it's the transfer corona) with insufficient charge. That would lead to a vertical stripe with little or no charge, thereby leaving no toner—a white stripe. The answer: clean the coronas.

The main corona is, recall, in the toner cartridge, so if you are being barraged with support calls at the time and you need a quick fix, you can just change the cartridge. But there's a brush located inside your laser printer (HPs, at least, have them) that will clean your corona. Take a look at your HP manual for details.

The transfer corona is sitting in a metal trench inside the laser printer. To see it, open your laser printer (I'm talking the II, IID, III, IIID models here—you can't get directly at the transfer corona on a IIP or IIIP). Fairly close to the front of the printer, there's a metal trench that runs the width of the printer. It's protected with a webbing of monofilament threads. Shine a flashlight into the trench, and you'll see a hair-thin wire: that's the transfer corona. Dip a Q-tip into some rubbing alcohol, and carefully clean it end to end. (And as my friend Brock Meeks says, "Once you clean the Corona, it's Miller Time.")

Smearing on the Page

Well, what keeps the toner from smearing? The fusing roller. It is covered with a Teflon-like coating to keep stuff from sticking to it, but it can become scratched or junk can just get baked onto it. In either case, the heat doesn't get transferred to the page. Try cleaning the roller with a soft cloth and some alcohol, but *let the thing cool down before you mess with it!*

Another cause of smears is trying to print double-sided on lasers that are designed to print single-sided. It seems tempting to create double-sided documents by running paper through the laser twice, but it's not a good idea. For one thing, there are rubber rollers that grip the paper so as to pull it through the printer. Ordinarily, they grip the underside of the paper, and cause no trouble. But if you're printing on two sides, they end up gripping the underside of the paper—but the underside of the paper has printing on it. The rubber rollers smear the already printed side.

Horizontal Streaks on the Page

If you see a regular horizontal line on your output, it's more than likely caused by an irregularity in one of the many rollers that the paper must pass by on its journey from the paper cartridge to the output bin. The key to identifying *which* roller is in measuring the distance between the lines. If the horizontal lines are always spaced the same distance apart, then *that distance is the circumference of the bad roller*. Use the numbers shown in Figure 18.12 as a handy-dandy key: just measure the distance between the regular horizontal lines with a ruler, and then read off the name of the bad roller. Whether or not you want to try to *replace* the problem child is up to you: getting to some of those rollers is a bit hairy. In my experience, however, the most common distance is 3.75 inches—the circumference of the photosensitive drum.

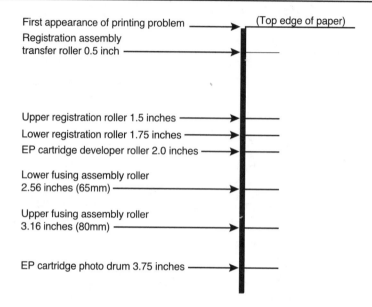

FIGURE 18.12:

Diagram of printer problems

Cloudy, Faded Output

This sounds like an ad for a laundry detergent; it's what you see when the whites aren't white and the blacks aren't black. The probable cause is either low toner or a dirty or damaged corona wire.

Recall that image creation and transfer requires two corona wires. The coronas attract toner, which can eventually get caked all over the wire and render it less useful. So you need to clean coronas now and then. How do you clean a corona? The main corona is in the cartridge, so you could just be lazy and replace the cartridge. But don't do that—use the brush right inside the printer. Open the printer and you won't be able to miss the green plastic brush. Note that one side of it has a gray suede-like feel. That's for cleaning the main corona. Now remove the cartridge.

Note the slot atop the cartridge. You'll see that the suede end of the brush fits nicely into the slot. Just run it across the slot once, and the corona's clean. You can't clean the corona on a LaserJet 4 cartridge.

The transfer corona is a permanent fixture in the laser, so it *must* be cleaned. Near the brush for the main corona, the transfer corona is a hair-thin wire set in a shallow trough below the paper path. You can't directly get at the transfer corona because there is a web of monofilament crisscrossing above it. The monofilament keeps the paper from accidentally feeding into the trough and getting crunched up and snapping the delicate corona. You can clean it a little bit at a time with a dry Q-tip and some patience. Reach the Q-tip between the monofilament and wipe the corona. Don't be too forceful, or you'll break the corona, and then we're talking tears and sadness. On a LaserJet 4, you'll also need to clean the teeth on the corona, a line of small, sharp black teeth just below the cartridge.

Black Line Down the Side of the Page

I don't know why this happens, but you'll see it when the toner is low. Replace the cartridge.

LJ Gives 20 MEM Overflow Error

The 20 means that you asked the LJ to do something that it doesn't have enough memory to do. One common reason for this is that you bought a LaserJet without a memory expansion.

The answer is generally to get more memory. But another possibility is that you've filled the printer's memory with *fonts*. They take up space in memory, too. I find that I can keep the printer from running out of memory under Windows 95/98 by doing these things (these are suggestions for a LaserJet 4):

- Print TrueType as graphics.

- Use raster graphics rather than HP-GL graphics.

Those are both settings you can control by clicking on a printer in your Printers folder. On earlier versions of Windows, just go to the Printers icon on the Control Panel.

55 Error on Startup

Sometimes you'll get a 55 error when you turn the system on. It's pretty scary, particularly when you get out the shop manual and look it up.

There are two circuit boards—oops, PCAs—in lasers that are relevant to this problem. The DC controller board handles charging and discharging the coronas, and the interface board controls the parallel and serial interfaces. If you smoke your interface with a switchbox, just replace the interface PCA. (In case you've never heard, HP says you can damage your LaserJet Interface PCA with a parallel port switchbox. If they catch you at it they void your warranty.)

Anyway, when powering up, the two boards do a communications test to ensure that they're talking all right. If there's noise in their communication, the 55 error pops up. The HP shop manual says that you must replace the cards if you see this error, but don't sweat it too much: this error can just crop up due to the normal inrush surge that you get when you turn the machine on. I had a series II that was giving me 55 errors about every other day on power up. I thought I'd have to do some surgery on the printer, but then I happened to move it to another outlet. Bingo! The error never returned. It seems that power noise of any kind on power up shows up as a 55 error.

Fonts Do Not Appear on Page

Once you become a desktop publishing maven, you dazzle others with your documents—documents replete with fonts galore. But one day you find that a *really* font-intensive page will not print. What's going on?

You've come up against a printer shortcoming, I'm afraid. Older HP lasers (the II and III) can print only 16 different fonts per page. Remember—Courier is not a font. *Font* refers to a combination of typeface, size, stroke weight, etc.

Actually, 16 fonts should not be a great hindrance. The strangest page in this book has no more than 10 fonts on it.

While we're on the subject, the series II can hold only 32 soft fonts in memory at any one time. That can be a real problem for a printer on a LAN, as it may have to serve *multiple* desktop publishing mavens. Can't you just hear it now? "I want four sizes of Helvetica, with italics and bold, and…" "But I *must* have Times Roman!" "*Times Roman*? You use *that* old woofer? You want to knock out my Palatino for Times Roman? Your name Gutenberg or something?" And the PostScript guys are just smiling in the corner…

Printer Picks Up Multiple Sheets

Believe it or not, this usually isn't the printer's fault. It's usually the paper. You need dry paper in order to get proper feed. Is the paper sitting in the tray for weeks at a time? Not good. When paper is removed from its ream wrapper, it's supposed to be dry. So how do you keep paper dry afterward? If it gets used in a day or two, there's no problem. But if it sits in the tray for longer, it could pick up some humidity. Here are two thoughts. First, keep the paper in a large Tupperware lasagna carrier. It'll keep it dry as long as you burp it when you put the paper in the Tupperware.

Another approach—if the paper is already damp—is to dry it out with a microwave oven. And make sure you've got the correct side of the paper up. (Look at the package for the arrow.)

Paper Jams

Trying to print double-sided can cause this. The first time you run the paper through the printer, the paper gets a slight curl imparted to it. Turn it upside down and run it through the printer again, and that slight curl translates to a paper jam. Another cause of paper jams is printing on the wrong side of the paper. There are, believe it or not, two different sides to a sheet of paper, called the *wax* and the *wire*. Paper will have a "print this side up" indication on the wrapper: pay attention to it. Paper can acquire a curl in humid environments, but the wrapper keeps the paper dry, so don't take paper out of the ream until you're ready to use it. Using cheap paper can also lead to paper jams. Old laser printers may have rollers that get out of round, leading to jams.

Basic Testing

If you've got a serious laser problem, then you may still be able to avoid taking the thing apart to fix it. Here are some tests to try before doing the heavy-duty screwdriver work.

Printer Power

Relative to your other office devices, laser printers are power hogs. Over seven amps of constant current draw puts this device in the same league as an entire well-equipped *kitchen*. Since the printer uses this much energy, it's critical that everything related to the electrical system be in top condition.

Outlet Wiring

We've discussed this one before. With lasers, however, it's doubly important because of all the power that they suck up. Ideally, you (as the technician) will have an electrical wiring diagram for each building you support, even if it's just your home. Then, when someone starts to plug a Mr. Coffee into an outlet on the same circuit as one of the workstations, you can offer appropriate and eloquent opposing arguments (all mainly consisting of "don't plug other things next to the laser unless you want to buy its replacement"), complete with documentation if necessary. You need to remember that it's a good idea to keep lasers on circuits of their own.

Device Interference

Again, I've mentioned this before. After you've established that wiring conditions are as they should be, find out what else is on the line. Although laser printers are arguably one of the bad guys when it comes to electrical line pollution, they can also be victims.

Reset

Like the PC, the laser printer can become confused—it is a very complex piece of equipment performing very complex operations. Things go wrong. On occasion, you may find it necessary to reset the printer.

As with the PC, there are different levels of reset for the LaserJet printer. The most severe reset of all for a PC is the power-down, or cold reboot. Cold reboots aren't usually the best way to handle PC problems, because you might be using an application that must be shut down a certain way in order to start up again without problems. Printers don't have the same problem. As a matter of fact, the power-down reset for the printer only clears the buffer. This can be a useful feature, but although it can temporarily get you past a difficulty, it won't always solve everything and you'll still have to address the cause of the initial problem.

You can also reset the LaserJet at the user interface panel. If you do this, however, you'll lose any fonts or macros that you've downloaded to the printer.

The Cable and Ports

Next, take a look at the cable and the I/O ports.

Secure Connection

If your printer and computer don't seem to be communicating, check the printer's power cable and the data cable to make sure that they're both snugly seated. Pay special attention to the connections at both ends of the data cable: if the little screws on the cable hood aren't screwed in all the way and securing the cable, it's very easy to dislodge the cable, even by doing something as minor as stretching your legs under your desk and knocking the data cable aside.

Cable Length

So long as it can reach from your computer to the printer, it's not possible for a data cable to be too short. It can easily be too long, however. HP recommends that a parallel cable be no longer than 15 feet. As with many manufacturer standards, I have found that to be quite conservative. I've seen printers work fine with parallel data cables well beyond twice that length.

A serial cable can be much longer than a parallel cable because the signal voltages are higher. Although slower, serial communication is more rugged and flexible than parallel.

What We Have Here Is a Failure to Communicate

If the printer is printing, but isn't printing what you sent it, try swapping the data cable for another one. Cables can have flaws that show up only after you've handled the cable a little. If a data pin in a parallel cable breaks, the results could be something like the "Iekko/Hello" example from the last chapter.

Ribbon Cable

Back in the old days, it was not uncommon to see ribbon cable hanging from the back of the PC on its way to the printer. One reason that ribbon cable has mostly gone the way of the horse and buggy is the fact that ribbon cable is a lot more susceptible to RFI (Radio Frequency Interference) than shielded twisted pair is.

Because ribbon cable is subject to this kind of interference, in many of the computers that use ribbon cable for drive interface you'll find a device, called a ferrite collar (or bead), encircling the cable. The ferrite collar effectively traps any signals that happen to be hitching a ride on the cable. For example, the IBM PS/2 model 55SX usually had a ferrite collar on the hard disk drive interface cable.

If you've got an environment not much troubled by RFI—no other cables, no fluorescent lights, no electric motors—you could make ribbon cable work for you. However, environments quiet enough to let you successfully use ribbon cable are rare enough that you'll probably be happier using the shielded twisted pair cables that are the norm for printers nowadays.

New Software Demands

The explosion of new, demanding software is straining the limits of all hardware. You know that you need a faster CPU to run Windows than you did to run WordPerfect, but did it ever occur to you that your parallel printer cable might not be up to the job?

Today's software takes advantage of system and device features that were previously totally ignored. Many of the programs and devices we use have features that are not exploited in their customary applications. For example, how many of us ever actually used the Format a Diskette feature of the IBM AT Advanced Diagnostics? Therefore, as cable manufacturers noted that some of the cable's features were going to waste, they started leaving some of them out. For example, until the advent of Windows 3.1, one of the least-addressed features of the parallel printer interface was the ability to use interrupt 0Fh–IRQ 7 to monitor task completion and errors. Since software was not utilizing all the conductors in the parallel cables, manufacturers began making cables without those particular conductors.

As programmers write software to take advantage of previously ignored features, the hardware's capabilities get pushed to new limits. A cable that has been getting it done for you with DOS may not be adequate when printing from Windows.

Environmental Considerations

You may not see these concerns on Greenpeace bumper stickers, but it's important that you consider them when setting up and using your printer.

Heat

The LaserJet can pump out some serious heat. This is one reason that it is important that it be placed in a well-ventilated area. Because of this, systems furniture, or any furniture that attempts to fit every part of your workstation into a neat little cubbyhole, can be bad news. It's sometimes built without regard for the fact that the equipment needs to breathe properly. While arranging a workstation, see to it that all your devices have air circulating around them, so that heat can dissipate. If you use your printer when it's in an unventilated area, its heat-sensitive components are likely to cook and fail prematurely.

Light

Always guard the toner cartridge from direct contact with strong light, as white light will shorten the useful life of the photosensitive drum. (The light that is used to bathe the drum for print preparation is red filtered, as in a darkroom.) Don't slide the toner cartridge's door open to see the photosensitive drum, unless, of course, you're planning to recycle the cartridge right away.

Ammonia

Ammonia can be detrimental to the laser printer's ability to neutralize ozone (discussed below) and can also permanently damage the toner cartridge. The chief source of ammonia in an office setting are the chemicals used for cleaning and those required in the blueprinting process. If you work in an office where blueprinting is done, keep a watchful eye on the fume hood fan and general ventilation in the area of the machine itself.

Ozone

In recent years, we've heard a lot about ozone and the ozone layer. Ozone is a pale blue gas naturally produced whenever a lightning bolt occurs. It's in the upper atmosphere as a by-product of the reaction of oxygen to solar ultraviolet rays. Ozone production doesn't require anything so dramatic as a lightning bolt, however. It's also a natural by-product of the ionization that takes place during the laser printing process.

Ozone is great stuff in the outer areas of the earth's atmosphere, but is not good for humans and can be anything from a minor irritant to downright dangerous in significant concentrations. If it is present in concentrations greater than one part in 20,000, it is irritating to the mucous membranes and is poisonous. You can't generally see it, but its odor is most often described as pungent. Most people can detect the presence of ozone at a concentration as low as one part of ozone per 10 million parts of air.

Not only can ozone be harmful to humans, but, as a super-effective oxidizer, it can also cause deterioration of components in the machine itself. Therefore, ozone buildup is one more reason to make sure that your printer is properly ventilated. You're more likely to have problems with ozone if:

- There are several active laser printers and/or copiers in a small, confined area.

- The relative humidity is very low.

- There is improper or nonexistent ventilation.

- The ozone filter is in need of replacement.

- Any combination of the above conditions exist.

You should replace the ozone filter in the laser printer after about every 50,000 prints. If office ventilation leaves something to be desired, or you've got a lot of laser printers in a small, enclosed area, I recommend that you replace the filters more frequently. Mind you, all of this only applies to printers that actually use a corona in the printing process; the LaserJet 4si, for example, would be exempt from this process.

Paper and Media Issues

Just think of this as an up-to-date version of "garbage in, garbage out."

Paper Type

Every kind of laser printer has its own paper type and quality requirements. If you follow those requirements, you'll be less likely to run into paper jams and distortion problems. In general, the better the quality of the printer, the better the quality of paper it will require. At the very least, higher quality paper may give you higher quality printouts. High humidity can also affect the performance of paper in a laser printer (not to mention the fact that it can cause the printer to seal your envelopes).

The Paper Feed

You'll need to inspect the feed assemblies periodically. Over time, the feed rollers become glazed and thus less efficient at picking up one sheet of paper at a time from the paper tray. Replacing the rollers is not a major production, but many people that I have talked to find immediate (but temporary—isn't that always the way?) gratification by abrading the feed rollers somehow. You might try rubbing pencil erasers or *very fine* sandpaper over the rollers.

The separation pad (it's just beneath the feed rollers) plays a major role in letting the feed roller pick up only one sheet at a time. Over time, however, it wears thin. It's a good idea to replace the feed rollers and the separation pad about every 100,000 prints. You can buy them in a kit of other like items for those heavy-duty printer maintenance sessions.

Contaminants

Laser printers are powerful, yet delicate, machines. Foreign objects in the printer can really affect its performance for the worse. Therefore, you must be very careful about what you feed your laser printer. No foreign objects, only the paper recommended by the manufacturer, and no labels or other printables not intended for laser printers.

One of the nastiest things I ever heard of anyone feeding the laser printer was a piece of paper that had a staple in place. This is almost certain to do damage to the fuser assembly. If the Teflon of the roller has scratches in it, your prints will have vertical white lines on them. There's nothing to be done about this; you have to replace the fuser assembly.

Another common contaminant is any printable not intended for a laser printer. If labels aren't specifically manufactured to be used in a laser printer, don't use them—this is one thing you really can't fudge on even if you've got extra plain labels. Also, letterhead that has raised ink may not fare well when run through the printer.

On a final note, there may be partial sheets of paper buried in the rest of the ream. They won't gum up your printer, but they could cause it to jam. Also, don't use textured paper since the toner does not stick to it.

Never Jam Today

There are several paper jam sensors in LaserJet printers. Some of them are timing sensors, which make it highly unlikely that a jam could occur anywhere in the process without the printer alerting you. One major cause of jams is improper media; stock that is thicker or thinner than the printer is prepared to handle can cause a fair amount of difficulty.

If a jam occurs before the paper reaches the fusing assembly, there are two things that you'll need to note:

- Any toner that has not gone through the fusing assembly will end up all over everything when the jam is fixed. The stuff is hard to get out of clothing or carpeting, so be careful when handling paper with loose toner on its surface.

- Carefully remove any paper jam in the area of the transfer corona, so as not to damage the wire or its attendant monofilament.

Paper Curl and Wrinkling

The major cause of curling is the effect that the fusion heat has on the paper composition—the amount of curl is generally directly proportional to the ash content of the paper. If you follow the manufacturer's recommendation for paper type, you're less likely to have problems with curling than otherwise.

Wrinkling will usually be the result of stiff paper negotiating the tight turn at the top of the printer near the facedown tray. It is most evident with heavy stock or envelopes. If the printer is equipped for it, you can avoid the problem by allowing heavy paper to feed from the face-up tray.

Advanced Testing

What you've already read are the easiest to fix and most common problems. Sometimes, however, the problem requires more work than a change in paper or a tap of the Reset button.

Voltage Tests

If, when you turn it on, the printer doesn't respond normally, the printer's power system is probably malfunctioning. To find out for sure, you'll need a voltage meter. A basic multimeter is a must for the printer technician, but a good digital unit is a good bit more accurate; you should be able to obtain one for about $30. Using a digital multimeter makes it possible to check for high and low AC and DC voltages, resistances, and continuity.

With a multimeter, you can check both the power source and the printer's supplies and regulators for proper voltages. There are three simple DC voltage levels that should be detected as output by the power supply. You don't need to rip the printer apart to check them; just snap off one cover and then unscrew one screw to be able to remove the other cover.

Location of DC Voltage Test Points

The DC power supply provides three different DC voltages to the system's components. All three can be checked at an interface labeled J210; it is a 20-pin female interface with pin 1 located at the lower left corner and the odd numbers along the bottom row, left to right.

Using the multimeter, check the indicated pins (every other pin along the bottom, left to right, starting at 1) for the following voltages (frame ground is the reference):

- pin 1 = + 5 VDC
- pin 5 = –5 VDC
- pin 9 = + 24 VDC
- If *none* of the voltages are present, check the fuse on the DC power supply.
- the AC power

If *one or more* of the voltages is missing, you'll need to do at least one of the following:

- Remove all optional devices, including memory.

- Replace the DC power supply assembly.
- Replace the DC controller PCA.

Testing the Host's Interface

When it comes to testing the host's I/O ports, a breakout box is a handy thing to have around. A breakout box is a diagnostic tool that will indicate with LEDs what the activity on the tested port happens to be. You can also use a breakout box to design a cable if you happen to be working with something that is non-standard.

Charting Printing Problems

You can sometimes tell which printer component is causing problems from where the problem appears on the page. Figure 18.12, shown earlier in this chapter, can help you track down errant components.

Diagnostic Software

If you're having output problems and want to see exactly what is going from the computer to the printer, you can capture printer output in a file by means of a utility package or shareware program.

Testing the Engine

There are many things that could be wrong if you send a print job to the printer and nothing happens; one of the worst is a problem with the laser engine. To determine whether the laser engine is functioning properly, you need to bypass the interface controller where data is received and force the printer to do a direct print from the engine itself.

On newer printers, like the LaserJet 4 or higher, the engine can be tested by using the Test Print menu on the printer (not the Print Test Page command from Windows). But if you still have one of those older models hanging around, then on the side of the printer that is opposite the memory upgrade socket there is a hole (exposed on the LaserJet II but with a plastic cover on the LaserJet III).

Push a ballpoint pen or the like into the hole. This will force a print direct from the laser engine circuitry. Try it now, while the printer's working, so you can compare it to tests you run when the printer is malfunctioning. Your good control test indicates:

- The laser engine and engine circuitry are functioning correctly.

- Laser alignment is correct (shown by side margins).

- Feed timing is correct (shown by top and bottom margins).

- There is sufficient toner.

- None of the major components is significantly damaged or contaminated in any way (there are no smudges or repeating anomalies).

Setting a Baseline

It's hard to get any information from a test print if you don't know what a good print looks like. Now, while the printer still works, you should print a test page using the Self-Test Menu on the printer itself. Some older models may not have menus to work with; in that case you should consult your manual to find the exact instructions, since they vary from printer to printer. Keep this test print somewhere, and you can compare it with your test prints later to see how the new print compares with the baseline test print. A self-test print shows various gray scales, text, horizontals, and verticals. The tightest horizontals and verticals will appear to the average viewer as single heavy lines, but, if you look at them closely, you'll see multiple lines in those areas.

Understanding Error Messages and Fixing Printer Problems

One sure way to know that you've got a problem is for your laser printer to *tell* you that you've got one. In Table 18.1, I explain what each printer error message is, what causes it, and what you should do to try to fix the problem that it describes. When the situation or the response required is not obvious (and sometimes even when it is), I have indicated the path to a (hopefully) happy ending.

TABLE 18.1: Printer Error Messages

MESSAGE	MEANING	SOLUTION (WHERE APPLICABLE)
00 READY	The printer is ready.	
02 WARMING UP		Wait a few moments for the printer to signal "ready."
04 SELF TEST	Continuous self test printing.	
05 SELF TEST	Self test in progress (on some printers, this will result in a print).	
06 PRINTING TEST	Self test printing.	
06 FONT PRINTOUT	Printing sample characters from all installed fonts. Or printing PS configuration pages.	
07 RESET	Returns all printer settings to Printing Menu settings and clears buffered pages, temporary soft fonts, and macros.	
08 COLD RESET	Returns both the Configuration and Printing Menu selections to the factory settings.	

Continued on next page

TABLE 18.1 CONTINUED: Printer Error Messages

MESSAGE	MEANING	SOLUTION (WHERE APPLICABLE)
09 MENU RESET	Returns all Printing Menu items to factory settings, clearing buffered pages, temporary fonts, and all macros.	
10 RESET TO SAVE (HP LaserJet only)		Press and hold Reset to confirm the acceptance of Printing Menu selections (you'll lose any temporary fonts, macros, or buffered data), or press Continue or On Line (no changes to selections will be made).
11 PAPER OUT (HP LaserJet only)		Add paper to the input tray.
12 PRINTER OPEN		Close the top cover assembly.
13 PAPER JAM	Sample jam codes (vary among printers): 13.1 internal jam 13.2 input jam 13.3 duplex jam 13.4 output jam	Open the printer, clear the jam, and press Continue or On Line to reprint the page.
14 NO EP CART		Install the toner cartridge.
15 ENGINE TEST	Engine test with printout preceded by pressing the Test Print button.	
16 TONER LOW		Replace cartridge (rotating the existing cartridge briskly can result in more prints even if the message remains).
17 MEMORY CONFIG (HP LaserJet III only)	Indicates memory configuration in progress (happens when Page Protection is set to On).	

Continued on next page

TABLE 18.1 CONTINUED: Printer Error Messages

MESSAGE	MEANING	SOLUTION (WHERE APPLICABLE)
18 SKIP SELFTEST (HP LaserJet III only)	Skips the ROM and RAM tests on startup, and is activated by holding down the minus key. Don't do this routinely.	
18 MIO NOT READY (LaserJet 4M or 4Plus)	The Modular I/O (network card) is not ready.	Power down the printer and make certain the card is seated properly in the socket. A new card may be needed if this persists.
20 ERROR	Indicates that memory capacity has been exceeded by the volume of data received.	
21 ERROR	Indicates that the memory received is too complex for the printer to process.	
21 PRINT OVERRUN		Enable page protection or reduce the complexity of the job (more printer memory may be required).
22 ERROR	Communication handshake was unsuccessful (rate of transmission or configuration may need changing).	
22 I/O CONFIG ERR	Wrong handshake protocol (XON/XOFF, DC1/DC3, and DTR handshake protocols are supported).	
40 ERROR	An error occurred during data transmission (an error occurs if you power down the computer while the printer is online or an attempted transfer uses unmatched rates).	

Continued on next page

TABLE 18.1 CONTINUED: Printer Error Messages

MESSAGE	MEANING	SOLUTION (WHERE APPLICABLE)
41 ERROR	A temporary page-creating error occurred.	Press the Continue key to repeat the page.
42 ERROR	Communications problem has occurred between the Interface/Formatter PCA and an optional interface device.	Reseat the optional I/O device and press Continue to resume printing.
43 ERROR	A communications problem has occurred between the Interface/Formatter PCA and an optional interface device.	
49 REMOVE PAGE	Paper was in the manual feed guides when the printer was turned on.	
50 SERVICE		Power off the printer for at least 10 minutes. If the problem persists, you may have to repair or replace the fuser assembly.
51 ERROR	Indicates loss of laser beam for more than two seconds.	
52 ERROR	Scanner motor unable to maintain appropriate speed.	
53-x ERRORUNIT	Error detected on optional memory card.	Verify that the correct revision level (B or greater) is installed.
54 ERROR	Problem with the duplex unit shift plate.	

Continued on next page

TABLE 18.1 CONTINUED: Printer Error Messages

MESSAGE	MEANING	SOLUTION (WHERE APPLICABLE)
55 ERROR	Communications problem between the DC Controller PCS and the Interface/Formatter PCA (do a test print to verify functional DC controller).	If the problem persists: check DC voltages at J210, replace the Interface/Formatter PCA, and replace the DC controller PCA.
61 SERVICE	A checksum error in the Interface/Formatter PCA's ROM was detected during self test.	
62 SERVICE	Checksum error occurred in the Interface/Formatter PCA's internal font ROM.	
63 SERVICE	Error was detected in either the Interface/Formatter PCA's dynamic RAM or in optional memory.	Remove any optional memory and retest.
64 SERVICE	Indicates a laser scan buffer error.	Turn the computer off and back on.
65 SERVICE	An error occurred on the dynamic RAM controller.	Turn the computer off and back on. If that doesn't work, replace the Interface/Formatter PCA.
67 SERVICE	A miscellaneous hardware or address error has taken place on the Interface/Formatter PCA.	Reseat all cables, font cartridges, and optional devices. If that doesn't work, replace the Interface/Formatter PCA.

Continued on next page

TABLE 18.1 CONTINUED: Printer Error Messages

MESSAGE	MEANING	SOLUTION (WHERE APPLICABLE)
68 ERROR	A recoverable error has occurred in NVRAM (non-volatile RAM).	Press Continue to clear, then verify the Control Panel menu settings; one or more items will have reverted to their factory defaults.
68 SERVICE	NVRAM failure has occurred.	Replace the Interface/Formatter PCA. You can temporarily operate the printer without VRAM, but all Control Panel volumes revert to their factory defaults and the 00 READY message becomes 68 READY/SERVICE.
69 SERVICE	Time-out error has occurred between the Interface/Formatter PCA and an optional I/O device.	Remove the optional device and retest. If the message persists, replace the Interface/Formatter PCA.
70 or 71 ERROR	Improper cartridge application.	Turn the printer off and back on. If the error persists, verify with the cartridge vendor that the cartridge was designed for that printer.
72 SERVICE	Font cartridge removal error. May also result from a malfunctioning font cartridge or poor connection.	Cycle the printer power.
79 SERVICE	Miscellaneous problem.	Turn printer off and back on. If the problem persists, remove the memory modules and any installed font, macro, and personality cartridges one at a time. If the problem still occurs, and the printer has an optional I/O device installed, try a different interface (parallel or serial) if possible. If the problem continues, replace the Formatter PCA. If the problem is intermittent, temporarily remove any non-HP hardware/firmware and test the printer. If it keeps failing, replace the Formatter PCA.

Continued on next page

TABLE 18.1 CONTINUED: Printer Error Messages

MESSAGE	MEANING	SOLUTION (WHERE APPLICABLE)
CONFIG LANGUAGE	This message is the result of holding down the ⏎ key while powering on the printer. Following the self test, you'll need to select a display language with the +, −, and ⏎ keys.	
EC LOAD (envelope size)	You've requested an envelope size not currently installed in the printer, or the tray is out of envelopes.	Load the correct envelope in the envelope tray. Insert a loaded tray and select the loaded envelope size from the Control Panel or press Continue to override. Envelope size may be COM10, MONARC, C5, or DL.
PC LOAD (paper size)	You've requested a paper size not currently installed. Same as above, only for paper. Paper size may be EXEC, LETTER, or LEGAL.	
PE FEED or MF FEED	You've requested to manually feed paper or envelopes of the indicated size.	
PE TRAY = (envelope size)	The printer wants to know the size of the paper or envelopes you're using.	Use the + and − keys to select one and then press ⏎. Press On Line or Continue to proceed.
FC (LEFT/RIGHT/BOTH)	You removed font cartridge(s) while the printer was offline and contained buffered data.	Reinsert cartridge(s) and press the Continue or On Line key.

Continued on next page

TABLE 18.1 CONTINUED: Printer Error Messages

MESSAGE	MEANING	SOLUTION (WHERE APPLICABLE)
NO FONT	The printer could not read the font cartridge(s).	Reinsert the cartridge(s) and try again.
FE CARTRIDGE	You removed a cartridge while the printer was online.	Turn the printer off, reinsert the cartridge, and turn the printer back on.
USER MAINTENANCE	Message on the 4si— has printed 200,000 pages.	
MENUS LOCKED	Administrator has a security lock on the Control Panel.	

Other Things to Consider

If you're still looking for the source of a problem, then one of these remedies may help.

The Toner Cartridge

If you install and maintain the toner cartridge properly, you shouldn't have problems with it. In these days of greenery, many people wonder whether they should use recharged cartridges. You're a lot safer using retreads than you used to be: the folks recycling them are either doing a better job or are using better components (or both); the recent efforts are far superior to many of the early ones. Still, keep an eye out for unscrupulous recyclers. If the life of an opened cartridge is specified as six months, how could anyone expect it to make it through yet another life cycle? A properly redone cartridge includes a new photosensitive drum.

While some of the earlier retreads sometimes used to distribute toner in the most inappropriate places, even first-time cartridges can cause print anomalies. If the cartridge is running out of toner, you might see vertical white streaks on your prints. Rocking the cartridge gently around its long axis usually lets you get about a hundred more prints out of the cartridge (depending on the amount of white space and toner density adjustment).

When new, toner cartridges sometimes make noises. Don't worry too much about them—incidental printing noises are quite common and are not usually a matter of concern. Just watch for any print anomalies that might be related to the sounds you hear.

Image Problems

There are several components that could cause image problems.

Mirror

There's a mirror in the lid assembly. If it gets dirty, your prints may have fuzzy edges. Tobacco smoke is the most common culprit, so use a good glass cleaner and lens-cleaning material to get it back in shape, and chase smokers away from the printing area.

Vertical Lines

We talked earlier about what scratches on the feed rollers do to your print jobs: they will almost always leave vertical lines on the print. Scratches don't just appear—they're generally the result of someone running things through the printer that don't belong there (staples, or labels, or transparencies not meant for laser printing). Since even running paper through the laser printer twice generally isn't a good idea, there's no reason why staples should be anywhere near the printer paper in the first place.

Distorted Images

If your printed images look stretched, the printer's feed components are probably slipping, or its gears are not functioning properly. The gears may not be gripping on the shaft, as they should be. To restore the printer's feed capability, get new feed rollers, separator pads, and assorted bushings in a kit, and replace the worn-out components.

Slipping feed components can also contribute to assorted...

Squeaking or Groaning Sounds

Laser printers can make some pretty bizarre sounds. Some of these sounds indicate developing problems, and should, therefore, receive appropriate attention, but a perfectly healthy and properly functioning printer can also make noises that sound as though the printer is malfunctioning. The most noticeable noises are generally part of the paper feed process.

A noise that I have been asked about more than any other is the one that comes every few minutes from an idle (but powered on) laser printer. This noise sounds like the printer's electric motor beginning, as though about to print, and then stopping abruptly. There's a good reason for that description: that's exactly what the sound is. Since the fuser assembly remains hot even when idle, the printer needs to rotate it every so often. Otherwise, the hot metallic fuser roller would burn a permanent depression into the rubber pressure roller, with which it is in constant contact.

Maintenance Issues

Here are a few things you should check to keep your laser printer in good working order.

Errant Toner

When, in the course of printer events, you are called upon to clean up toner the method will depend on the amount and location. You can clean up minute amounts on the inside of the printer along the paper's path with a slightly dampened cloth or a swab dipped in alcohol. If there are larger amounts of toner, more drastic measures are called for.

WARNING   Never, ever, ship a printer with a toner cartridge still inside.

If a cartridge is dropped or jostled improperly during shipment, it is possible that there will be larger quantities of toner to deal with.

WARNING   *Don't* get out the Electrolux! Toner is a plastic resin bonded to iron particles, a deadly combination to hot electric motors (like those in vacuum cleaners). If you try to vacuum up the runaway toner, it will blow straight through a normal vacuum cleaner bag and into the motor, where the plastic will melt and the iron will play havoc with the armature and brushes. The particles that don't stop in the motor will fly through the air and cover the vicinity (and you) with tiny black particles that are very difficult to wash out of clothing.

If you get toner on your clothing or skin, remember its properties; use only cold water and plenty of soap. You're likely to get toner on you if you have to clear a paper jam that happened before the paper got to the fusing assembly, so be careful. If you have a large toner spill in the printer, take it outside and use a compressed air canister to clean out the printer.

Cleaning

Like getting exercise and balancing your checkbook, printer cleaning rarely gets done as often as the manuals recommend. Each of the printer's components needs to be cleaned regularly, however.

The Clean Command

One of the kindest things you can do for your printer is to run the clean command from the software toolbox every time you change the toner cartridge. If you don't have a clean utility, then you should be able to download one from the manufacturer's Web site. The clean command will usually print a large black box on a piece of copier grade paper. This sheet of paper is then placed face down and sent through the process again. This is the only time you should refeed a piece of paper without the luxury of a duplex unit! Sending this sheet through again will reheat the toner that was placed on the paper the first time, causing it to become slightly adhesive. Any miscreant toner particles or small pieces of paper stuck to the innards of the printer will now be pulled out. The way to tell if the clean command has performed up to par is to check the black box that was printed on the first pass—if it is covered with shiny black specs, then you know it worked. You may need to do this more than once just to be sure you get all of the little varmints attached to your rollers.

Corona Wires

There are two corona wires in most printers. You should clean both of them regularly or whenever there is a problem with the print that might be caused by excess toner on the wire. Clean the primary corona in the toner cartridge once at the midpoint of the life of the cartridge—you've got no excuse to avoid doing so, as HP thoughtfully provides a plastic brush for the job, secured at the bottom of the inside of the printer beside the paper path. Insert the suede end of the brush into the slot in the cartridge and slide it from one end to the other.

The transfer corona is in the bottom of the printer beneath the paper path. Several monofilament lines protect it from damage in the event of a paper jam. Clean it with the cotton-tipped swab that comes with the cartridge, gently stroking it in each direction and on each side between the monofilament segments. I recommend that you do this in good light, so you can see how much pressure you are putting on the corona, as, if you break it, the entire corona assembly must be replaced.

Usually the products of your labor will be pretty innocuous: perhaps some toner or a little dust. The winner in the most-disgusting-corona-problem category, however, is the time one technician reportedly found several well-done roaches in the transfer corona channel. The only reason the users had discovered the cockroaches is because the insects' bodies were making the pages turn black.

The LaserJet 4 doesn't use a corona that you must clean; it actually uses charging rollers.

Registration and Feed Guide Assemblies

Here, maintenance is pretty easy: you need only occasionally wipe with a damp cloth to clean up that errant toner (unless, of course, some foreign object happens to stop in this area). You'll need to clear paper fragments away periodically, as it's here that paper fragments or partial pages will usually stop.

Fusing Assembly

I really can't overemphasize the importance of keeping the fuser roller free of contaminants. Because of the high temperatures at which it operates, this critical part of the printing process will have a tendency to hang onto a little bit of everything that touches it: paper curls up and stays with it, letterhead ink melts on it, etc. To keep this from happening, the roller itself is coated with Teflon and the brush that rides on top of it (underneath the fuzzy green lid) is permeated with silicone.

I've seen people leave the cotton tip on the silicone pad that cleans the fuser. This is not a good idea, as this causes the pad to fit its slot too tightly instead of floating easily on the roller.

Separation Pawls

Push back the lid behind the fuser assembly, and you'll see a set of four claw-like things called *pawls*. The pawls facilitate the separation of the paper from the fuser. Over time, however, they get a gradual buildup of contaminants that could eventually begin to scrape the Teflon from the fuser roller. If they scrape off the Teflon, the effect is the same as that of a staple fed to the printer: broad vertical lines will begin to appear on the print.

You can't repair scratches on the fuser roller; you'll need to replace the entire fuser assembly. To avoid having to make a habit of this, regularly use an alcohol-dipped swab to clean each of the pawls thoroughly.

Improving Print Quality

There are some amazing differences between the printers that are available today and the ones we started with a few years ago. The Lexmark R-Series printers do 1200×1200 DPI and use ultra-fine toner to produce some impressive printing. No matter which printer you use, however, there are things that you can do to improve the quality of its output.

Paper Quality and Feed Continuity

The type of paper and the quality of the toner can differ along a surprisingly wide range. A close inspection will reveal the difference. And, as you read earlier in this chapter, the wrong type of paper can cause paper jams.

Keep the paper-feed mechanisms in top condition to avoid paper slippage and, with it, image problems. The key items are the feed rollers and the separation pad, located just inside the printer and near the paper tray receptor.

Image Formation

The image formation components are the laser engine, beam mirror, toner, developer roller, primary and transfer coronas, and photosensitive drum. With all these items involved, you might worry that the imaging components of the printer will be a troubleshooting nightmare. It's not that bad, though: if you keep the cartridge changed and the coronas cleaned, that's usually all you'll need to do to keep the print sharp.

Lasers are in general very reliable, but when they go south, there's no mistaking it. Now you know how to attack the most common printer and printing problems. In the next chapter, you'll learn about a common interface for laser printers, and, in fact, a common interface for *lots* of things—the serial port.

A few last tips: use a fresh ream of paper, not one that's been sitting in your laser printer's cartridge for the last two weeks soaking up moisture and developing a curl. Distribute the toner in the cartridge. Take the cartridge out of the printer, and rotate it 15 times. Then shake it side to side 15 times. You can also help the laser's toner transfer process by "clearing its throat" and printing three to five *totally black pages*.

You can do that with a little LaserJet program. Here's the command sequence; keep it handy:

```
esc&10Eesc&10Lesc*p0x0Yesc*c2400a3300B esc*c0PescE
```

That'll print a black page. The "esc" stands for the ASCII escape code, ASCII 27.

Laser Printer Rumors and Truth

I wanted to leave this chapter with these rumors. I know they sound goofy, but I hear people ask this stuff in class, so here are the top laser rumors, and, where I can supply it, the Truth.

Font Cartridges in the Left Cartridge Have Priority over Those in the Right

Nope. In early LaserJets the software fonts, recall, establish priority on the basis of the order they were loaded, but the cartridges don't.

Toner Is Made of Powdered Chicken Bones

When I heard this one, I thought I'd make a million bucks organizing a chicken bone recycling center. No go, though. (I *did* mention it to some execs at a well-known fried chicken chain, however, so if you end up seeing separate trash cans for the bones, you know whose fault it is.)

Elvis Is in the Printer

If you press a certain set of keys on the laser panel, a full-page graphic of Elvis prints out, with the caption "The King Lives." So goes the tale.

HP swears it ain't so, and I believe them. Here's why: there aren't enough ROM on the laser circuit boards to store a bitmap of Elvis, even *before* he gained weight. I swear I heard this from someone in class, and others had heard of the rumor also. My guess is that HP brought it on themselves with the Secret Service Test Mode. (Why not tell everybody about it, anyway?)

Cartridges Are Designed to Self-Destruct

The rumor: there are pieces of glass in the toner of Canon-type cartridges that slowly chew up the print drum so it is completely unusable by about 8,000 copies. This supposedly is done to discourage rechargers.

I just don't know. HP denies it, but Canon's patent application for the toner includes "silica particles"—conceivably another name for pieces of glass. That's for the next book, I suppose.

The official HP spec sheet on toner says that toner is composed of the items listed in Table 18.2.

TABLE 18.2: LaserJet Toner Ingredients

COMPONENT	PERCENTAGE BY WEIGHT
Styrene acrylate copolymer	55–65
Iron oxide	30–40
Salicylic acid chromium chelate	1–3

Now, salicylic acid is *aspirin*. Maybe *that's* why it's no headache at all to set up a laser printer...

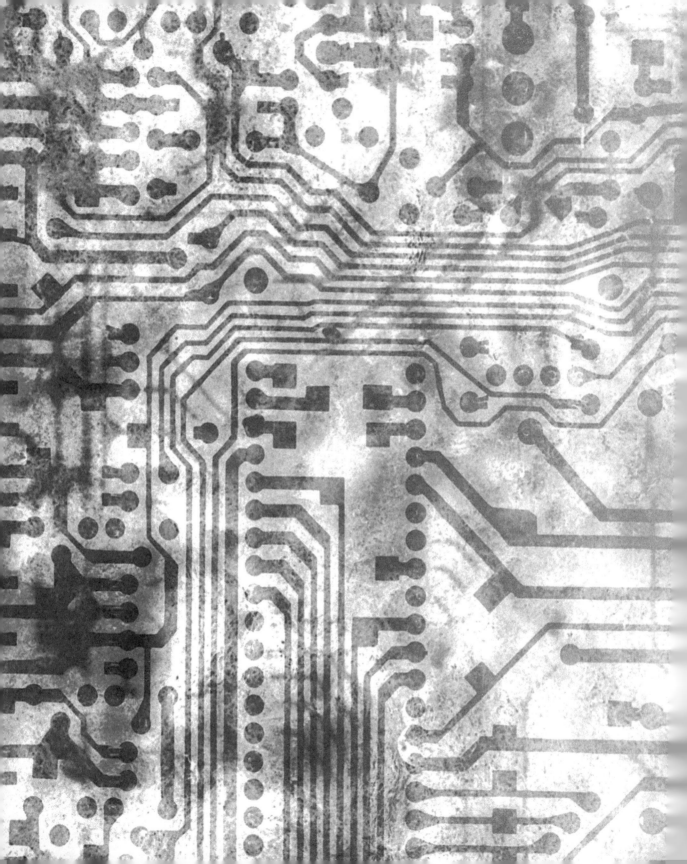

CHAPTER
NINETEEN

Modems and Serial Interfaces

- How a modem works

- Solving hardware and software problems

- Understanding RS-232

- Looking at digital modems

19

When computers first appeared on the scene, each was an island. But it didn't take us long to figure out how to dial up each other's machines, and soon the first computer bulletin board was born. Modems are the essential devices for getting digital data over phone lines, and low-priced modems made computer bulletin boards the craze of the mid-'80s.

In the late-'90s, we're still using modems, but now it's not just for bulletin boards. Many people need modems on their systems so that they can fax things back and forth right from the PC. Others use their modems to hook up to the biggest bulletin board of them all—the Internet.

In this chapter, I'll look at asynchronous communications: how they work, what goes wrong, and how to make things connect right.

A PC troubleshooter dealing with serial communications must understand:

- What RS-232 is
- How it's supposed to be used
- How it's actually used
- How to test its components

Components

Let's start off with a look at each of the pieces of the serial picture.

The Asynchronous Port

On the computer end, the computer must be able to speak the language of asynchronous communications. A device to allow this to happen is called an asynchronous port, asynchronous adapter, communications port, or RS-232C port. (RS-232 and RS-232C are the same thing. In fact, the "official" name nowadays is EIA 232D.)

The connector type used is generally the standard 25-pin DB-25 type connector, such as you would find on the back of most modems, or that you can see in Figure 19.1. Ever since the advent of the AT, some adapters have used a 9-pin connector. You won't miss the other 16 pins—asynchronous communication doesn't use them anyway. The signals are the same. You *may* have a cabling problem, however. We'll discuss cables later.

FIGURE 19.1:

Standard 25-pin DB-25 type connector

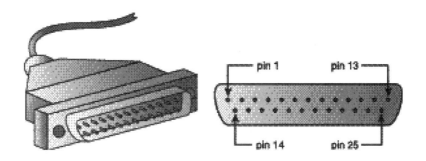

Most folks don't buy an asynchronous adapter on a board by itself. Instead, it usually appears as a connector (or two for COM1 and COM2) right on the motherboard.

The UART

This is going to sound like techie stuff, but it's important. You see, serial ports are not all created equal—even some of the newer serial ports.

Serial ports are based on a chip called a *Universal Asynchronous Receiver/Transmitter (UART)*. The original was a National Semiconductor 8250 designed back in the late '70s. It worked great on the slow XTs and PCs. Unfortunately, computer manufacturers kept on using them all the way through to the 486 compatible computers, and thereby hangs a tale.

One of the big performance criteria with a UART is how quickly it resets after an interrupt. Interrupts occur whenever data arrives in the serial port, so you can imagine that they're pretty common occurrences. The 8250 reset in 1000ns, which was no problem when it was used by the older PCs. The PCs would access the 8250 in *2000*ns, so the fact that the 8250 was taking forever to reset was no big deal from the PC CPU's point of view—it was a lot slower.

Problems began appearing as soon as turbo XTs appeared. At 10MHz, an XT could access the 8250 in just about the same amount of time that it took the 8250 to reset, leading to a potential "not ready" problem for the UART. To correct this problem, a new chip, the 16450, was built by National Semiconductor, with a reset time five times faster than the 8350—200ns. That basically solved the bottleneck problem between CPU and UART.

Multitasking and higher transfer speeds, however, posed another problem. The CPU can only be in one place at a time, and if you're running five programs, the UART might find itself full of data with no CPU to transfer the data to. By the time the CPU would say to the UART, "Whatcha got for me?" the UART may have been forced to discard some data. The 16450 UART can hold only 1 byte. If that space is full, and the CPU hasn't come around to get the byte, any incoming bytes get discarded due to "buffer overflow." (The 1 byte in the 16450 is the "buffer.")

Enter the 16550. It's got a 16-byte buffer. That may not sound like much, but have you done a file transfer under Windows 95/98 or Windows NT, and then opened up a new program? The resulting disk access to load the new program means that the CPU ignores the UART for hundreds of nanoseconds, and you usually drop a block or two of data. That's not the end of the world, as most communications software uses an error-checking scheme that detects the dropped block and resends it, but it still makes your system a bit slower and less reliable. And dropping a block at a critical time may mean losing your communications connection. The 16-byte buffer in the 16550 is the answer.

NOTE   As discussed in Chapter 3, "Inside the PC: Pieces of the Picture," the Universal Serial Bus (USB) is a potential challenger to the "of course the modem goes in the serial port" mindset. This new port type provides a single 4-pin connection for a number of devices (among them, compatible modems) to be daisy-chained from the computer, like a SCSI chain. For the moment, however, the modems that you buy are likely to require serial connections.

The Cable

Communications cables are the bane of a PC expert's existence. The problem is that no manufacturer follows the RS-232 standard exactly. Many manufacturers use a different connector or they rearrange the order of the pins. Neither is a fatal problem—just a pain in the neck.

Cables can get broken wires and loose pins, or they can be wired incorrectly. The end of this chapter includes wiring diagrams for common PC cables.

NOTE   There are now two (different) common internal serial cables being used by motherboards, and they are incompatible. In general, motherboards will include the internal (ribbon) serial cables, so all you need to remember is to keep the cables that came with the motherboard together with that motherboard.

The Modem

The most common use for a serial port is as an interface to a modem. Modems allow computers to communicate via regular phone lines. They've been around for decades. In the PC world, Hayes Microcomputer Products introduced the Smartmodem (now called the Smartmodem 300) in the early '80s, starting a whole new generation of communications devices. Now 56KBps modems are pretty much the norm.

Modems are designed to follow certain modem standards so that they can communicate with other modems. The one that you're likely to hear of is the V.90 standard. Why are some modems called "smart" modems? They're called smart because they're programmable. What does "programmable" mean? Well, back in the old days, you had to flip switches to do things like:

- Turn echo on/off
- Adjust speed, parity, data bits, or stop bits
- Turn a monitor speaker on/off

Additionally, you had to dial your calls by hand. You can send "programmable" modem commands via software in the computer. Thus, you could write a program to set some communications parameters, dial a number until it answers, log on to the computer at that number, download a file, and log off, all without the operator having to be present. This is the way that companies like Prodigy and America Online have automated email and Internet communications.

Also, it's important to understand that a 56KBps modem doesn't usually actually deliver 56KBps. High-speed modems adjust their speeds according to the perceived quality of the phone line. On a bad day, you might only get 10,000bps.

The Communications Software

If you have a programmable "smart" modem, as most of us do these days, be sure that your communications software understands the modem's language. Most smart modems claim to use the same language as the market leader, Hayes, but if you're using a clone modem of some kind it can't hurt to check with the software vendor. Most software has been checked out on the more popular clones, like the U.S. Robotics, Intel, or Practical Peripherals modems.

Maintenance

For the most part modems are solid state, and so have no moving parts. Modems can tend to run hot, as many are designed around one or two fairly dense chips, so don't pile books atop an external modem; make sure it's ventilated. I know the ads all show a phone perched on top of a modem, but I'm not sure it's such a good idea. I know for a fact that it's *not* a good idea to stack up modems. I've had a fair amount of heat-related modem trouble. Be sure that you know where the modem's warranty information is. (Most modems have two-year warranties, so don't throw that information out.)

The usual stuff applies: as they are large connectors with tiny pins, screw in the cables. Don't make the cables longer than they need to be: it increases the noise level in the cable, and if a loop of cable dangles down behind a table it may get caught in something or may be idly kicked. I know of a case where an analyst routinely braced his feet against the cable—just a nervous habit. The cable was even more nervous.

I mentioned power problems in the chapter on power supplies. *The same surge problems can appear on phone lines.* If the line from the phone company switching station to your computer is above ground at any point, think seriously about a phone line isolator (sometimes called a modem isolator). This sits between the modem and the phone. Another measure of prevention is an RS-232 isolator. It sits between the modem and the PC. I'd rather smoke a modem by itself than a modem and the rest of my system. Now, there used to be companies that offered optical isolators for RS-232, but they seem to have disappeared. I don't quite understand it, but it's certainly become difficult to find optical RS-232 isolators; they solve *all* communications power surge problems.

You may be wondering why I beat up on surge protectors before, in the power section, but am suggesting them now. Mainly cost. Surges really don't occur that often over the phone line, save in the event of lightning strikes. When that unlikely lightning strike occurs, you want something that'll take the brunt of the impulse and hopefully burn out in the process, cutting off the connection between your expensive equipment and the lightning. (I suppose you could also try knots in the phone cord.)

Troubleshooting

Communications troubleshooting can provide you with hours of mind exercising delight, *if* you're the kind of person who likes puzzles. Let's see how to deconstruct the problem and isolate the bad component.

The Software First: Common Communications Software Problems

If you are connecting to another PC by modem then you'll need to set up some parameters that you won't need to set up when you are connecting to the Internet. You must ensure that both parties in the communication have agreed on the *communication parameters*:

- Parity (can be even, odd, or none)
- Number of data bits (can be 7 or 8)
- Number of stop bits (generally 1, could be 2 or even 1.5)
- Local echo on/off

All direct communications packages, such as Windows Hyper-Term, have the ability to set these values. Don't worry about what the parameters mean—just be sure that they match. Common symptoms that may be software problems include the following:

Cannot Connect

Check the parameters. If you cannot connect, or you connect and see garbage ("{" characters in particular), you've probably got a speed or data bits mismatch.

Cannot See Input

You type, but you can't see what you're typing. Try a simple command, like whatever command you would use to get a file directory from the distant system. If the command gets a proper response from the other side, even though you can't see what you typed, the problem is that you must set your local echo to On. "Local echo" tells your PC whether or not to display the characters that you type. Sometimes you want to disable local echo, as the remote site will echo characters. In that case, you press a key, the key goes out to the remote site, the remote site echoes, and *then* you see the character that you typed. Whether or not you need local echo is determined by whether or not the other site provides echoes.

Input Is Double

You type a character and two appear on the screen. Output from the other computer is normal. Answer: set your local echo to Off.

Sometimes, there is no local echo command. In that case, the command has been misnamed (it's a common mistake) to "duplex." (Duplex is something completely different, an engineering concern in data communications.) Then:

- Half Duplex = Local Echo On
- Full Duplex = Local Echo Off

Again, it's incorrect terminology, but who cares as long as you can get the problem solved?

Is Your Software Set Up to Talk to Your Modem?

You instruct most modems to dial a number by sending the command ATD, followed by the phone number. Some modems *don't* do it this way, however. (IBM sold an internal modem for their luggable PCs for a while that used a strange command set.)

Simple Hardware Problems

Besides software problems, basic hardware incompatibilities can keep your communications from working successfully.

You set up to dial the distant computer, but the modem doesn't respond. There are lots of possibilities:

- Is it plugged into the phone jack? It's common to share the modem's phone line with a phone and forget to plug the modem back in before using it.

- Is the modem plugged into the computer? Did the serial cable fall out? (It won't if you screw the connectors in.)

- Is the phone line working? Plug in a phone. Is there a dial tone?

- Is it your phone system? If you have an in-house phone system, like a ROLM or Northern Telecom system, you may have to issue extra commands to dial out of your system (called a PBX). Check with your telecommunications manager.

Line Noise and Quality Problems

Sometimes it isn't hardware or software; it's the phone line itself. There are a few areas that you can reasonably check:

- Quality of the communications provider

- The in-house wiring

- Whether call waiting is interrupting modem sessions

Check the In-House Cable Plant

You may find that line noise is being created by the wiring in your building. Old wires don't transmit as well as they once did, or someone may have run the wires near the high-voltage lines in the elevator shaft, or any of a million things could go wrong with the in-house cable plant. Inspect your cable plant periodically. I had phone noise trouble in my building, so I restrung my phone lines and the problem went away. (I actually found that my termination block was made out of four wood screws driven into a rafter in the basement!)

Finally, did you check that the modem and the PC share a common ground? You may recall from the chapter on power protection that plugging the PC and a peripheral into different outlets can lead to slight differences in the value of "electrical ground," leading to noisy communications.

Solving Port and Cable Problems: Understanding RS-232

You know, for a "standard," RS-232 sure provides a lot of headaches. Buy a device from Vendor A with an RS-232 port on it, a device from Vendor B with an RS-232 port on it, and try to hook them up. When it doesn't work (a common outcome), you start calling people.

Vendor A: "Trouble with our unit? Gosh, we don't really ever get bad reports on…Wait! What are you trying to connect to? *Vendor B?* That's your trouble. That guy hasn't designed an interface that follows specs since the day he got into business."

So you, reasonably, are annoyed by the temerity of Vendor B, and call him. He is jolly.

Vendor B: "Vendor A? Is that old rapscallion (not the actual word used) still lying about me? His problem is that he builds 'em to the standard, all right—the *1964* standard. He's building RS-232-A ports. We follow the 1984 conventions, and..." (soothing noises follow).

If you could get these two guys in the same room, you know what they'd say?

"Your problem is the cable—it's the wrong one." You wait, expectant, for the solution. But they demur.

"Oh, no—we don't sell cables," they chorus, and then leave.

You see, you'll probably face about two big RS-232 compatibility problems per year, and you'll be a happier person if you can take a swing at fixing them. Look, if a simple country economist like myself can do it, so can you.

So here's the world's shortest course on what RS-232 is and how it works.

Why Is There RS-232?

RS-232 basically exists so that different vendors can offer equipment that can communicate with each other's equipment. I can buy a modem built before the PC was even designed, and it'll work with the PC just fine, as they use RS-232 to communicate. RS-232 is an example of a *physical interface*—an agreement among vendors about how to make equipment communicate.

For a simpler and more familiar example of a physical interface, think of the plug in your wall socket. It supplies 120 volts, 60 cycles per second, also called Hertz (Hz) alternating current. If you plug in something that uses, say, 220 volts, or 50 cycles per second, you'll get very unpleasant results, up to and including burning your house down. So when did you last check to be sure that something used 120 volt, 60Hz current? Probably never: you just figure that if you buy something with a regular power plug on it, it'll use the juice okay. And you're right. There's a standards agency—Underwriter's Laboratories—that concerns itself with power and safety, so you won't see a UL sticker on something that you could plug into a wall socket and damage yourself with.

So the plug itself seems important. Can I, for instance, use my U.S. microwave in London? Nope—they have different power. The first problem I'll run up against is, again, the plug—my plug won't fit into any wall sockets. Can I just snip off the plug, install a British-type power plug, and use the wall current? No again: it's 220 volts, 50Hz.

Why use different plugs, then? Simple: the plug is a *reminder* about where the equipment can and can't be used. The plug tells us something else, too: what devices *supply* power, and what devices *use* power. Female connectors indicate a device (like an extension cord) that supplies power. Male connectors indicate a device that uses power. This way, you don't plug a toaster into a microwave oven and think that something will come of the marriage.

Behind the plug lies a lot of information about an interface standard. Know what plug you've got, and you don't have to worry about things like how many volts or Hz the power is. RS-232 does something similar.

Just as there are two members of the power interface—the user and the supplier—so too are there two kinds of RS-232 interfaces. RS-232 was basically designed to allow computing devices, called *Data Terminal Equipment* (*DTE*), to talk to communications devices, called *Data Circuit-terminating Equipment* (*DCE*). So there's a DTE-type RS-232 interface and a DCE-type RS-232 interface. RS-232 is designed to allow DTEs to talk to DCEs. RS-232 uses DB-25 and

DB-9 connectors. Male connectors go on the DTEs; female connectors go on the DCEs.

DTE-type interfaces are most commonly found on PCs and printers. Devices with DCE-type interfaces include modems, mice, and scanners. Remember that RS-232 is defined to allow DTE-type interfaces to communicate only with DCE-type interfaces.

How RS-232 Works

The original specification for RS-232 is a digital interface with 25 separate wires, each with its own task. RS-232 is defined for both synchronous and asynchronous communication, so there are a lot of lines in the 25 that we'll never use in asynchronous communications. In fact, for the most basic RS-232 applications, all you need is three wires: transmit, receive, and ground. As mentioned before, lines are either "on" with a voltage level of +3 volts or more, "off" below –3, or "neither" in between. *Flow control* is an important part of RS-232's purpose. Flow control allows a receiving device to say to a sending device, "STOP! My buffers (a small amount of memory in the receiving device) are overflowing— hang on a second and I'll get right back to you."

There are 10 important asynchronous lines in RS-232, as shown in Table 19.1. It's important to understand that each line is controlled by either one side or another. Line 2, for example, is viewed as input by one side and output by the other side. If both viewed it as input, then both would be transmitting information that was never received. So each line (except grounds, which are just electrical reference points) is controlled by one side or another. Note, by the way, that there is also a 9-pin version of the RS-232 connector. When I refer to pin numbers, I'm referring to the 25-pin numbers, not the 9-pin.

T A B L E 1 9 . 1 : RS-232C Leads

DESCRIPTION	PIN # (25-PIN)	PIN # (9-PIN)	FROM	ABBREVIATION
Data Leads				
Transmit Data	2	3	DTE	TD
Receive Data	3	2	DCE	RD
Power On Indicator Leads				
Data set ready	6	6	DCE	DSR
Data terminal ready	20	4	DTE	DTR
Leads That Announce That an Outside Event Has Taken Place				
Data carrier detect	8	1	DCE	CD
Ring Indicator	22	9	DCE	RI
Ready to Send/Receive Handshake Leads				
Request to send	4	7	DTE	RTS
Clear to send	5	8	DCE	CTS
Ground Leads				
Signal ground	7	5		SG
Protective ground	1			FG

Here's the sequence of events for a normal RS-232 session.

1. Both devices are powered up, and indicate "power up" status. The DTE powers up line 20 (DTR, Data Terminal Ready). The DCE powers up line 6 (DSR, Data Set Ready). A well-designed RS-232 interface won't communicate further until these two lines are activated. The DTE waits to see a signal

on line 6, the DCE on line 20. Lines 6 and 20 are supposed to be "equipment check" signals that only indicate device power status, but they're sometimes used as flow control lines.

2. The modem connects with another modem. Data communication's no good without someone to communicate with, so next (in a modem/terminal situation, the situation envisioned by the RS-232 designers) a distant modem would be dialed up. The modems exchange carriers (the high-pitched whine that you hear when modems connect), and the modem (DCE, recall) tells the terminal (DTE, recall) about it over line 8, DCD (Data Carrier Detect). If you've got a modem with red lights, by the way, you see the preceding in the lights: line 6 is attached to the light labeled MR, Modem Ready, line 20 is attached to line 20, Terminal Ready, and line 8 is attached to the light labeled CD, Carrier Detect.

3. The terminal (DTE) asks the modem (DCE) if it's ready. The terminal activates line 4, RTS (Request To Send). The modem, if ready, responds with line 5, CTS (Clear To Send). Now the handshake process is complete. Lines 4 and 5 are flow control lines.

4. Data is exchanged. The terminal (DTE) passes information for the modem (DCE) to transmit along line 2. The modem passes information back to the terminal along line 3.

And that's all there is to RS-232.

A Note on Reality

The above description is nice and complete, so far as the standard goes, but most RS-232 interfaces aren't complete. Most PC software, for example, only looks at one handshake, such as 8 (Carrier Detect), 6 (Data Set Ready), or 5 (Clear To Send), and ignores the rest. Some software doesn't look at *any* control lines, so DTR, DSR, DCD, RTS, and CTS become irrelevant. That makes cabling easier, but ignores the question of flow control.

Flow Control

Flow control is implemented *either* in hardware or software. Software control uses signals that are sent as data to the receiving computer. Hardware control is implemented by sending control pulses along special wires (control lines) in the cable.

- Software flow control:
  - XON/XOFF
  - ENQ/ACK
- Hardware flow control is done with one or more of the control lines, usually:
  - DSR
  - CTS
  - DCD

The software approaches send "STOP!" characters back and forth when one side's buffers are overflowing. The hardware approaches just deactivate a line when the receiver needs a rest. Again, here's where your cable design is vitally important: if you neglect to include the particular handshake wire in your cable, there's no way for the computer to know that the printer is overflowing its buffer.

Another handshaking problem shows up when one side is using one method and the other side a different one, as when the PC is looking at CTS and the printer is using XON/XOFF.

You can test your handshake easily. Say you're hooking up a serial printer. Have the computer send a bunch of information to the printer to be printed and then do something like pulling the paper tray or taking the printer off-line. Once that's done, see if the computer figures it out—does it stop sending information to the printer? Then put the paper tray back in, or put the printer back on line, and see if it picks up where it left off.

The Port

Now that you know more about RS-232, you're equipped to look more closely at the port itself. The RS-232 port may be ill. As it is a bidirectional device (it talks as well as listens), you can use a *loopback* to allow it to test itself. Serial ports *do* become ill. I don't know why—I presume it's something to do with the plugging and unplugging that I do with the system that I have (I do a large amount of communications consulting, so I try a lot of equipment out on my system). For instance, years ago I bought two Toshiba 1100+ laptop computers and they both had something wrong with the serial port: Receive Data in the first one, Ring Indicate in the second. Probably 20 percent of the expansion boards that I've worked with had a serial problem. So it's worthwhile knowing how to diagnose such a problem.

To test the port, you need to see what is happening on the various control lines. I recommend that you get a *breakout box* to assist you in testing the communications port.

You can get an inexpensive breakout box from one of the electronic supply companies, such as Jameco, as shown in Figure 19.2.

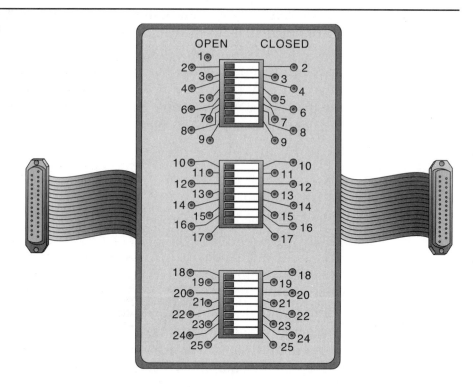

A breakout box allows you to prototype a serial cable without soldering or pin crimping (the two most common methods of cable assembly). That's nice because you can then figure out what the correct cable configuration should be even if you don't know how to solder or crimp, and then give that cable configuration to someone in your company or a technical service house to make up the cable for you. You see getting the cable made (soldered) isn't too hard, once you've settled on a cable design. But making sure that it's designed right *is*, so you want to do it yourself; a breakout box makes that possible.

Take a look at Figure 19.2. Regular 25-wire RS-232 type cables come in one side and go out the other. All 25 lines are represented on each side with large round metal posts. The breakout box comes with about a dozen wires that terminate in small plugs that mate with the posts. The way the box works is that you design a cable, then run wires from post to post to make the connections necessary for the cable, then plug in the breakout box (it serves as the cable) to the two devices that you want to interface, and the cable design either works or it doesn't.

Say I'm trying to design a cable to allow my laptop to transfer data to my PC. The cables on either end are too short to connect the two devices, so first run a couple of extension cables. I run a regular straight-through cable from the PC to one side of the breakout box, and a regular straight-through cable from the laptop to the other side of the breakout box.

Now we're ready to start prototyping. First, I figure I'll start my cable design with a cable that just connects 2 on the PC side to 3 on the laptop side, 3 on the PC side to 2 on the laptop side, and 7 on the PC side to 7 on the laptop side. (How did I know to try this? Hang on 'til the next section, when I describe how to design an RS-232 cable.) To set this up, I just run one of the wires from 2 on the PC side to 3 on the laptop side, and from 3 on the PC side to 2 on the laptop side. I actually don't have to run a wire from 7 to 7, as there are DIP switches for each of the 25 lines, and any time I want a "straight-through" connection all I need do is to close the DIP switch for that particular line. (Make sure the others are all set to "open," or you'll have lots of "wires" in your cable that you didn't intend to have.)

Some breakout boxes have red and possibly green lights to indicate activity levels for various inputs and outputs in the RS-232 connection. Red lights indicate the presence of voltage in excess of +3 volts (interpreted as 0) and green lights indicate the presence of voltage below −3 volts (interpreted as 1). The signal used to indicate "active" on the control leads is 0.

Cable Troubleshooting

To check out the serial cables, detach the breakout box from the computer, then connect the cable that you usually use to the computer. Connect the breakout box to the free end of the cable, and re-run the above tests. If one fails, you have a broken wire.

Remember that with cables, speed trades off for distance. If you have a 100-foot RS-232 cable, you won't be able to run it at 38,400bps. The exact same equipment and a two-foot cable might be able to do it. The only difference is in the length of the cable.

On the other hand, if you're reading this because the cable has never worked, turn to the later section on how RS-232 works and how to design cables.

The Modem

Some modems have loopback capabilities built right in. In that case, you can do simple loopback tests. If not, the best first procedure is just a modem swap. They're small and don't require much work to swap.

Do the front lights tell you anything? Put a breakout box in-line between the modem and the computer. You should see the correspondences as shown in Table 19.2.

TABLE 19.2: Modem Front Panel Light/RS-232 Line Correspondences

Modem Light	Red Light On Breakout Box
TR	20
MR	6
RD	3
SD	2
CD	8

When a specific modem light is on, the corresponding breakout box light should be on.

Are the connections correct? Many modems have two phone jacks—one to connect to the wall and one to pass through to the phone. Connect the "phone" one to the wall and you'll dial up okay, but disconnect as soon as the other side answers!

The Phone Line

The phone line has four lines, colored red, green, yellow, and black. Only the red and green are used. They should offer 48 volts DC power. If your phone varies greatly from this, call your repair office. Can you try the call on another line? Is it a multi-extension phone—could someone be picking up the phone as your modem tries to dial?

WARNING   The voltage on a normal phone line is enough to be felt. If you happen to measure the line while the phone is ringing, the voltage shoots up to almost 100 volts. Only do this test if you know what you're doing, please. We'd miss you.

Or you could try checking out the phone line with a phone line tester. IBM makes one called the Modem Saver for about $29; it's not the greatest thing in the whole world, but it does the job. You just plug it into the modular phone jack, and little lights tell you whether or not the line is working. You can find the information for this product in Appendix A.

The Other Side

Half of the possibility for problems comes from the folks that you're trying to communicate with. Double-check their parameters with them. Try calling out to another computer, if possible.

Have they recently installed a new revision of *their* communication software? Or installed a new, "completely compatible" modem?

Going Further

Devices exist, called *analog channel test units*, which will actually test the phone line between you and the other party. They are, however, quite expensive. An oscilloscope can help you measure the frequencies being produced by your modem to see if they are within specification. Again, you may not want to go this far, as the required investment in test equipment is not trivial.

Common Cables: A Configuration Cookbook

Well, that's the RS-232 overview. Hopefully you're an RS-232 expert by now. But whether you are or not, here are a few basic cable diagrams. On the following pages, I present cables to connect your computer.

- Serial DB-25 connector to a modem

- Serial DB-9 connector to a modem

- Serial DB-25 connector to another PC, or a printer

- Serial DB-9 connector to another AT or a printer

- Serial DB-9 to Serial DB-9 (computer to computer) or computer to printer

Take a look at Figures 19.3 through 19.7.

FIGURE 19.3:

25-pin DTE to 25-pin DCE cable description

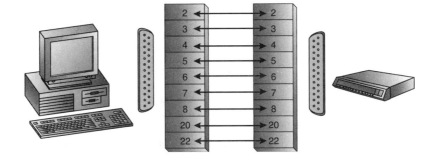

FIGURE 19.4:

25-pin DTE to 9-pin DCE cable description

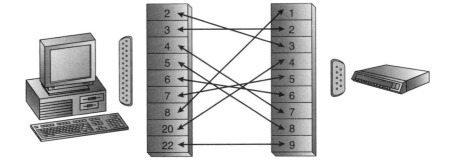

FIGURE 19.5:

25-pin DTE to 25-pin DTE null modem cable description

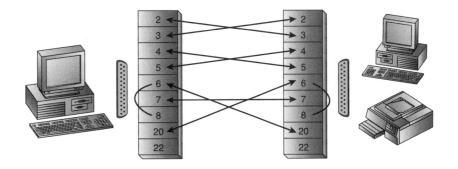

FIGURE 19.6:

25-pin DTE to 9-pin DTE null modem cable description

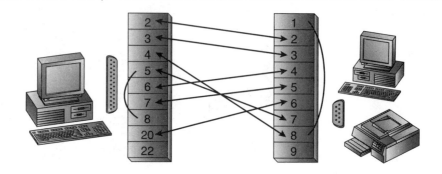

FIGURE 19.7:

9-pin DTE to 9-pin DTE null modem cable description

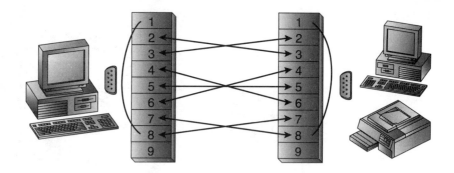

All About Digital Modems

To make a long story short, the combination of upper modem limits and too many graphics is beginning to make a faster modem connection look very attractive. Since modems are almost at the end of their rope, that faster connection is going to be digital—probably the *Integrated Services Digital Network* (*ISDN*).

What Is ISDN?

If you already know what ISDN is, you can skip this part. For the uninitiated, however, it's a high-speed digital telephone line with two data channels that can each transmit 64,000bps, or be combined for a single-channel throughput of 128,000bps. Not too shabby. If you keep the channels separate, then you can run two conversations via the same telephone connection. For example, you can talk on the telephone while using the modem.

Depending on two circumstances, you may be able to use ISDN to dial into the Internet or your favorite online service provider. The first circumstance is whether or not you can get an ISDN connection to your home or office. Depending on where you live, getting the connection can be mildly aggravating or just plain impossible. Washington, D.C., is one of the "mildly aggravating" areas, as ISDN has been offered there for several years now. Getting my ISDN connection up to connect my company's two offices three years ago was slightly less painful than having a root canal (the telephone installation guys were so new at it that they had to take the shrinkwrap off the ISDN installation kit before they used it), but the process has become somewhat less painful of late. Washington, D.C., is a big metro area, so it's had ISDN for years, but many smaller cities and towns are just getting it or don't have it at all, and they fall into the "impossible" category. If you're in an area that doesn't have ISDN, there's not much that you can do about it except complain to the local telephone company.

The cost of an ISDN connection varies significantly throughout the United States, so significantly that it's really impossible to quote usual charges with any amount of accuracy. Most often, the charges are based on a flat monthly fee plus a per-minute connection time charge. If you're connecting two places within the same calling zone or are able to wrangle a deal with your ISDN provider, you *may* only have to pay a flat monthly fee. If you can get such a deal, I highly recommend it, as it will probably save you money if you're the kind of person who goes online enough to need a high-speed connection.

The other circumstance that you'll need to get online with ISDN is an ISDN connection at your service provider. Just as you can't make a 56Kbps connection unless the modems on both ends of the connection support speeds that high, you can't dial up using ISDN unless there are ISDN devices on both ends of the connection. (Really, it's a bit more complicated even than that, as an analog modem wouldn't know what to do with a digital signal if you did call it, but the end result is still the same: unless your provider offers an ISDN connection to the Internet, you can't have one.) These can be a little tricky to come by even if you live in an area that offers ISDN, so you may have to shop around a bit for a provider.

ISDN-Capable Modems

Assuming that you've got an ISDN line and an Internet provider with an ISDN line, you'll need an ISDN adapter instead of a modem or device capable of letting your analog modem use a digital line. (Until fairly recently, you would have needed another device called an NT1 to plug the ISDN device into, but many new models are including the NT1 in the device itself.)

NOTE   This is true for telephones as well: If you intend to use an ISDN line, you'll either need a digital telephone or a converter.

If you've already got a modem and telephone and don't feel like getting new ones, then you can use a device such as Motorola's Bitsurfer to connect. This little box has two analog ports that you can plug devices into.

If you plan to upgrade, then you can replace your old modem with an ISDN model. These aren't cheap, but their cost is proportional to the increase in speed that you see. Some ISDN modems have more features than others do. For example, 3Com's IQ ISDN modem has user-controlled band allocation, so that you can combine the two data channels to get 128Kbps. If the telephone rings while you're connected, however, the channels will separate so that you can answer the telephone while keeping the original connection, and then re-combine once you hang up.

To recap, here's what you'll need to use ISDN:

- An ISDN telephone line

- Someone with an ISDN telephone line and associated equipment to call

- An ISDN modem and/or telephone, or a converter that you can plug analog equipment into

Once you've got all that, you can surf with speed, scoffing at the masses that you whiz by.

x2 Technology

x2 modem technology is a concept from U.S. Robotics that can let your Internet service provider increase the speed of downloads to you to approximately 56Kbps. It works by reducing the number of analog-to-digital and digital-to-analog conversions required to send computer data over the phone lines. x2 technology also makes more efficient use of the actual direction of transmission. Let me explain.

x2 technology speeds things up by making it possible to circumvent half of the conversion equipment at the telephone company.

It does this by relocating many of the analog-to-digital and digital-to-analog conversion operations that are required in communicating between your computer and the Internet, moving them to your local ISP instead of leaving them up to the nearest telephone company office. The fact that there will be fewer starts and stops at the telephone company for A/D and D/A conversion is what really provides most of the speed benefit of x2 technology. Since it's usually the case that ISPs already communicate with the telephone company over a digital-capable circuit, telephone companies will automatically have a much easier time sending data back and forth to your ISP.

As for the traffic between your computer and your ISP, it will still be the case that turning digital bits into analog waveforms (D/A conversion from the ISP to your modem) is easier and faster than turning analog waveforms into digital bits (A/D conversion from your modem to the ISP). The only slow part of the data flow is now the upload link from your computer to your ISP.

Uploads from your computer to your local ISP are at best only 33.6KBps. This is called "upstream" communication in telephone company jargon. It's slow not only because the translation is more cumbersome in this direction but also because our share of the telephone line is smaller. You and I communicate with our ISP over a "back channel" while the ISP to telephone company link goes over the main channel.

There are still a few shaky areas that should cause you to be cautious about buying a new x2 modem. For example, if you already have a 28.8KBps modem but you never seem to be able to connect at speeds higher than 14.4KBps, it either means that your local ISP doesn't yet have x2 capability or that your local phone lines are so lousy that a x2 modem won't work any better than what you've already got.

Asymmetric Digital Subscriber Line (ADSL)

The slow, "upstream" portion of the line between us and our local ISPs is the major hang-up encountered by x2 technology, as mentioned in the previous section. Now, along comes *Asymmetric Digital Subscriber Loop (ADSL)* which is meant to address just this issue. Upstream data flow (from computer users to the ISP) is a fraction of the data flow at the bottom of the data stream. Typically the upstream data flow is measured in kilobits per second while the downstream data flow is measured in megabits per second.

ADSL is able to transmit more than 6MBps downstream and 640KBps upstream, and all of it over existing twisted-pair telephone lines. ADSL is not here yet, but it is being tested by phone companies, and if it becomes a commercial reality it could increase capacity on the existing public information network by a factor of 50 or more without having to install new cabling.

ADSL is an ANSI standard. It specifies an ADSL circuit connecting two ADSL modems on each end of a twisted-pair telephone line, creating three channels. One would be a plain old telephone service channel (POTS), the second would be a medium-speed bidirectional channel, and the third would be a high-speed downstream data channel. Right now, the high-speed channels being tested can carry data at a rate from 1.5MBps to 6.1MBps, while the medium-speed bidirectional channel is running up to 640KBps. The POTS channel is split off to maintain secure telephone service even if the high-speed channels are inactive or incapacitated. Downstream rates of up to 9MBps are even thought to be possible.

ADSL is definitely a short- to medium-distance technology. The high-speed signal rates can be maintained only over cable spans ranging from 9,000 to 18,000 feet long (2.7km to 5.5km), and the faster you want to go, the shorter the distance has to be. Still, more and more people tend to be fairly close to their local Internet service provider and, if things shape up the way they're supposed to, ADSL could be used to get us out the door and down to the ISP, where we'd be handed over to fiber optic lines (or "fiber-quality" copper lines) and then the data would really accelerate.

ADSL is both faster and more versatile than ISDN. Its proponents point out that it is supposed to be capable of providing simultaneous telephone and data transmission service over the same single pair of copper wires. Furthermore, analog devices like fax machines can be used on the POTS channel, where in most cases ISDN requires digital devices.

There are already some companies, including Ericsson, Motorola, and AT&T, far along in ADSL development. Additionally, while early ADSL products are designed to offer T1/E1 and V.35 digital interfaces for signal transmission, there are also standard LAN interfaces slated for the future.

CHAPTER

TWENTY

Keyboards and Mice

■ How keyboards work

■ Maintaining mice and keyboards

■ What to do when a mouse doesn't work

■ The new wireless input devices

The design of the PC keyboard has apparently kept IBM fairly busy since the original PC's inception. Every time a new PC is released, a new keyboard follows. They're all the same to troubleshoot, however.

The near-universal acceptance of graphical user interfaces (GUIs) means that everybody needs some kind of pointing device. We've tried electronic stylus devices, light pens, (I wanted to call this chapter "Of Mice and Pens," but I couldn't really justify it) and even a "Headmouse" that tracks the way that you are facing, but the consensus pointing device seems to be the mouse. Mice can be, however, more of a pain than keyboards, so we'll look at how to handle them, too, in this chapter.

Keyboard Components

With all of its moving parts, the keyboard has many potential sources of problems. Understanding those sources means understanding the parts of the keyboard; here's a look at them.

Keyboard Interfaces

There are a number of IBM-type keyboard interfaces, but you're most likely to come across one of these three:

- Original PC or XT keyboard (generally called the "XT keyboard"). This had 83 keys on it, and had the benefit of a nice "clicky" feel to it. When you pressed a key, it offered some tactile feedback. Pretty much all of the IBM keyboards did that, but over the years many clone keyboards have adopted a mushy feel. The numeric keypad and the cursor control keys were integrated into one 5" × 3" area on the right side of the keyboard.

- Original AT keyboard (generally called the "AT keyboard"). This improved over the XT keyboard in that it had a larger Enter key, and added a SysReq (or SysRq) key intended for use with OS/2. It's still my favorite keyboard layout, but it's been largely superseded in the marketplace by the 101-key keyboard. It also had 10 function keys along the top of the keyboard (labeled F1 - F10).

- The 101-key PS/2 keyboard (generally called the "enhanced keyboard"). This appeared in 1987 and had the big benefit of being compatible with every other keyboard interface. The extra keys came from separating out the cursor and numeric functions from the numeric keypad, as well as adding two more function keys, F11 and F12.

The XT and AT keyboards are different mainly because the XT keyboard puts the keyboard microprocessor in the keyboard, and the AT keyboard assumes that the keyboard microprocessor is on the system board. They are generally incompatible: you can't use an XT keyboard on an AT or vice versa. Clone keyboards generally get around this by putting an XT/AT switch on the keyboard. The enhanced keyboard, on the other hand, will work on any machine without modification.

The "broken" keyboard designs (also called ergonomic keyboards) like the Microsoft Natural Keyboard, look like a 101-key keyboard to the PC hardware. Since they're compatible with the existing hardware, they're easy to install, and although they take a little getting used to, they're easier on the wrists than standard keyboards. Nice for those who do a lot of typing.

Switch/Contact Design

The hardest part of designing a keyboard is in designing in the right "action"—the right "touch." Anyone who learned to type on a keyboard expects the keys to move about a third of an inch when pressed, and some keyboards do that correctly—I find those kinds of keyboards preferable. Newer keyboards, on laptops in particular, don't move as much ("don't have as much travel," is the actual lingo), less than half that amount. Let's see…this book is about two million keystrokes…one sixth of a wasted inch per keystroke…comes out to almost five miles of extra finger work I'm doing with this old-fashioned keyboard! (And to think, they say writing isn't strenuous.)

You'll find two basic kinds of keyboards:

- Switch-based

- Capacitive

The switch-based keyboard uses, as you'd imagine, micro-switches for each key on the keyboard. The switches can become dirty. They can be cleaned sometimes, but often it's easier to just replace them. They're sufficiently cheap that perhaps when a problem of any magnitude occurs, one should just throw away the keyboard and buy a new one—I've seen them for as little as $6. Clones tend to use this switch-type approach.

The IBM and AT&T keyboards are capacitive: in the bottom of the keyboard is one large capacitive surface. Each keyboard key pushes a spring, which in turn pushes a paddle. The paddle makes an impression on the capacitive module. The capacitive module sends out signals, which are interpreted by the 8048 microprocessor in the keyboard. It then sends the key's ID, called a "scan code," to the PC. The PC then figures out what the key means.

This sounds more complicated (it is), but it involves one large capacitive module rather than a lot of prone-to-fail switches. Unfortunately, it limits you a bit as to what you can do to repair the keyboard. Truthfully, the most you can do to fix sticking keys is to clean them on most keyboards or just get a new keyboard.

The System Board Keyboard Interface

The interface between the keyboard cable and the system unit is the keyboard interface. This is a DIN (or mini-DIN if it's a PS/2) plug that has five pins, all numbered oddly. Figure 20.1 shows the connector *on the system unit side*. You can get adapters for DIN to Mini-DIN or Mini-DIN to DIN for a few dollars.

FIGURE 20.1:

An old style DIN keyboard connector with five pins (top) and a new style PS/2 mini-DIN keyboard connector with six pins (bottom)

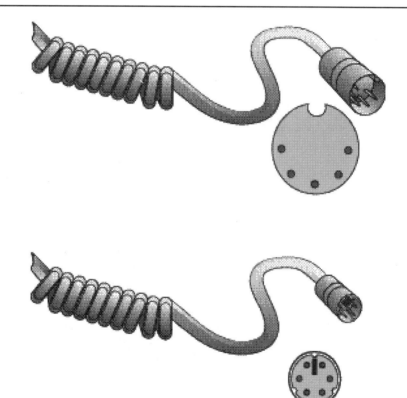

Test Voltages: voltage between all pins and pin 4 should be in the range of 2–5.5 volts DC. If any of these voltages are wrong, the problem probably lies in the PC—the system board in particular. If they're okay, the problem is probably in the keyboard. Check the keyboard cable next.

The Keyboard Connector

The keyboard cable runs from a DIN connector, which attaches to the system unit to a flat-jaw type connector inside the keyboard housing. The cable has five wires, and can be checked for continuity quickly with an ohmmeter: disconnect the cable inside the keyboard and test each line. On the other hand, once you're inside the keyboard, then you're kind of making a choice: do you really want to spend four hours playing around inside a keyboard, four hours that may be totally fruitless, or do you just spend a few bucks on a new keyboard?

Maintenance

The major aspect of maintenance for keyboards is *abstinence*. Abstinence, that is, from spilling things into the keyboard. The SafeSkin was discussed in the preventive maintenance chapter; this is one protection approach. Another is just to be careful.

Periodically disconnect the keyboard and remove it from the general area of the PC. Pull the key tops off of it (I hope this needn't be said, but I'll say it anyway: be sure you have a similar keyboard nearby so that you can put the key tops back in the right order, unless [heh heh] this is a keyboard for someone that you don't like). Then hold it upside down and blow it clean with compressed air. The key tops aren't that tough to remove—I use one of those "chip puller" tools that come with PC toolkits (recall that they're dangerous to use to actually pull *chips* with), and find it to be *just* the tool for the job. If things are particularly messy, you can use a spray cleaner. In extremis, you can soak a sticky keyboard in water overnight—but make sure it's completely dry before you try using it.

Troubleshooting

Since they are so inexpensive, you may want to view the keyboard as disposable. There are some simple things you can do before throwing out a keyboard, however.

Is It Plugged In?

On the back of computers that use PS/2 type connectors are two identical ports, the mouse port and the keyboard port. Make sure you've plugged the keyboard in to the correct port. You will get an error when turning on the computer if the mouse and/or keyboard are in the wrong port.

Is It One Key or All Keys?

If only one key is malfunctioning, check that key's spring. Remove the key by grabbing it with your fingers and pulling up. For the tough keys, fashion a hook from a paper clip or, again, use a chip puller. Under the key you will see a spring. Replace the key cap and see if the problem goes away. If not, try pulling the spring out *just a little*. Then replace the key cap.

Some keyboards use rubber cups instead of springs. Either way, the cup or spring is designed to keep the keys from being ON all the time.

Checking the Cable Continuity

Next, test continuity of the cable. Turn the keyboard upside down so that the cable is coming out of the back of the keyboard, to the right. Remove the two screws. The bottom plate will swing back and up to remove.

You will now see the cable splits to a single wire, which is grounded to the bottom plate and a cable with a flat-jaw connector. Push apart the jaws of the connector to release. You can then test each of the five wires for continuity with your ohmmeter.

Completely Disassembling the Keyboard

Not recommended for the fainthearted. You've got a good chance of making things even worse, so don't do it unless there's no other hope.

WARNING   It will take about four hours in total once you've taken the thing apart, put it back together wrong, figured out what you did wrong, taken it apart again, accidentally spilled all the pieces on the floor, etc., before you finally manage to reassemble the keyboard.

Remove the main assembly from the keyboard case. With a vise, or C-clamps, set up a support for the keyboard assembly on the sides. If you don't support it on the sides, you're in for a surprise when you remove the back metal plate. (Remember those springs on each paddle?)

Alternatively, you can make your life easier by removing all the key tops. But, again, don't do it unless you've got another keyboard around that you can use as a guide to replacing the key tops.

NOTE   One way to remember which keys go where is to put the keyboard (keys facing down) on a photocopier, and make a picture of the keys.

A printed circuit board with capacitive pads on it is held against a metal plate by 10 metal tabs—five above, five below—and a hex screw. You must use pliers to unbend the tabs enough to remove the plate. Position the assembly so that the plate is on top (not the printed circuit board), then remove the metal plate.

The plate has been holding dozens of plastic paddles against the printed circuit card, one for each key. These are small, flat, easily-broken pieces of plastic shaped like the outline of a castle turret, or the rook symbol in Chess. What you are looking for is a broken paddle. Replace any broken paddles and replace the metal plate.

The other reason to attempt this is if you've poured hot coffee into the keyboard. Very carefully remove all of the paddles and clean them as well as the bracket that they sit in. Then use alcohol to clean the capacitive PC board. Then reassemble and pray. I *have* seen this work, but only once.

Replacing the metal plate is a bit difficult. Position it correctly, then use clamps to hold one side together while you bend the tabs on the other side into place. Again, it is very easy to damage paddles at this point. Where do you get replacement paddles? No one that I know of sells them. Get them from the first keyboard that dies: it's good for 101 replacement paddles.

Replacement Keyboards

If you've gotten this far and have had no luck, don't despair. Many keyboard problems can't be fixed, and the things aren't that expensive anyway.

Keytronics, Datadesk, and Northgate make good replacement keyboards. Datadesk's are a bit cheaper, and they have one that is programmable. What that means is that you can move that annoying Esc key somewhere else, set up your keyboard as a Dvorak keyboard, and the like.

Keytronics offers a keyboard with an in-line bar code reader. Other software allows you to print out bar codes with a dot matrix or laser printer. One firm I know of uses bar codes at the top of their document tracking forms so that secretaries don't have to key (and sometimes miskey) a 12-digit document tracking ID every time they have to update the document tracking database.

Several companies are now offering "broken" keyboards, keyboard designs that are intended to lower hand and tendon stress. I'm using the Microsoft "Natural Keyboard," and if you're looking for advice, I'd suggest that you find someone with one of these and borrow it for a while before you buy it. It definitely feels easier on most of my hand, but my left index finger has to do enough reaching that it feels sometimes like it's going to separate from the rest of my hand.

Mice

Mice are in some ways simpler devices than keyboards; after all, they've only got two or three buttons, to the average keyboard's 101. But mice have some moving parts that can go seriously wrong.

Mouse Types

Basically, mice work in this way: you move them, they figure out somehow how much you've moved them, and then they transmit that information to the computer. The "how they figure out how much you moved them" and the "transmit the data to the computer" part is how mice vary.

Mouse Positioning Methods

Most mice are mechanical, meaning that they use some mechanical method for detecting motion. On most mice, the primary mechanical part is a ball on the bottom of the mouse. Take the mouse apart (there's a retaining ring; turn it over and the ball falls out, generally rolling under something), and you'll see three little wheels that turn when the ball moves against them.

Two of those wheels are monitored electronically; when they turn, they transmit how much they turned to the computer. The two wheels are perpendicular to one another, so one tracks X-axis motion and one tracks Y axis motion. The third wheel is just a wheel that balances the first two.

Another, less common, mechanical mouse manufactured by Rockwell uses two wheels that are on the outside of the mouse, They are positioned horizontally and are tilted slightly to detect the x and y movement. These mice are totally sealed and never need cleaning. Unfortunately, they are somewhat difficult to find.

The third kind of mouse positioning mechanism is the optical mouse. This has no moving parts. The mouse has optical sensors on the bottom of it, planted on a grid on a special mouse pad. As you move the mouse, its sensors see the grid lines running across the pad and report them to the PC.

And lastly, there is a new mouse design that is also optical but requires no special mouse pad. This mouse operates by taking 15,000 snapshots per second of the surface below it. By comparing the images dynamically, the mouse can determine speed, direction, and distance.

Mouse Interfaces

Most mice connect to a PC via a serial port. Some use a proprietary interface.

There have been several proprietary mouse interfaces over the years, but the most common are the Microsoft bus mouse interface and the IBM PS/2-type interface, which is very like yet another Microsoft interface, the InPort interface. All three interfaces use a miniature DIN connector as a plug.

The Microsoft bus mouse interface is a bit brain-damaged in that it only works with interrupts 2, 3, 4, or 5. The PS/2 type interface is typically integrated into a motherboard—I see it on a lot of laptops—and it's usually hard-wired to IRQ12.

Mouse Cleaning and Maintenance

On a mechanical mouse, the little wheels get gunk stuck to them or hair wrapped around them, so you must clean them. Just remove the mouse ball and examine the wheels. I've used rubbing alcohol, a toothpick, and a cotton swab to get the gunk off the wheels. You may also need to clean the ball with a bit of alcohol. Clean the mouse about twice a year, unless your desk is covered with dirt or dust, as dirt and dust are just gunk in its fetal stages.

On an optical mouse, just clean the sensors; you can often just polish them with a soft cloth. Keep the mouse pad clean as well so that the grid-lines are clearly visible to the sensors.

Mouse Troubleshooting

First, check the driver. Is the mouse driver set up correctly? Is it there in the first place?

Next, clean the mouse. Second, check the interface. If it's a serial port, then check the serial port. If it's a direct mouse port of some kind, then double-check that it's not installed with an interrupt conflict.

Pointing, typing, and clicking are important parts of getting computers to do what you want them to. But without video boards, we'd have no idea if they actually *did* what we wanted, and that's the topic of the next chapter.

Wireless Input Devices

This chapter discussed the issues involved with using cabled mice and keyboards. However, interest in wireless input devices has been picking up again. What is there to know about these devices?

They work like this: you get a receiver with the device (mouse or keyboard) that plugs into your computer, usually through the keyboard port. This cabled receiver then sits on top of your monitor or anywhere else handy that's within 45 degrees of the line-of-sight with the transmitter on your keyboard.

Most of these devices use infrared frequencies to transmit data, meaning that they've got high bandwidth (not really an issue with something that transmits as little data as a keyboard or mouse does) and are pretty much immune to outside interference. Use a cordless telephone or other infrared devices (such as a TV remote control) in the same room, and it will have no effect at all. Radio-controlled wireless keyboards are another matter. One such device operates at the 49MHz frequency, about where older cordless telephones operate (most new cordless phones operate in the 900MHz range). This means that if you use both devices at once then they'll interfere with each other. On the other hand, if you can get around the interference problem, radio waves are looser and thus much more flexible than infrared waves. If you've ever used a CB, you'll know that you don't have to be within line-of-sight to transmit data via radio. The radio-controlled keyboards have a range of around 30 feet under optimal conditions, as opposed to the 15 feet for most infrared devices. (Some manufactures claim a larger distance, but as you probably know from operating a TV remote control device, it's easier to point accurately from a short distance than from 20 feet away.)

Generally speaking, wireless devices are more expensive than wired devices, and input devices are no exception. Although one manufacturer's advertising extols wireless keyboards as a wonderful way to reduce cabling needs, the lack of one or two cables doesn't make up the price difference. You can find the cheapest keyboards for under $20 and the expensive wireless models are running in the $70 range.

If you're just interested in typing at a desk, I'd stick with the standard cabled keyboards. They're cheaper, you don't have to point them or keep the transmitter and receivers dust-free (a thick layer of dust causes a keyboard to stop working), and they're simple to use.

CHAPTER

TWENTY-ONE

Video Adapters and Displays

- How video boards work

- Resolution and interlacing

- Understanding and comparing monitors

- Fixing a failed monitor

21

Installing a Video Card

1 Never handle a circuit board by its edge connector; oils from your fingers can cause connectivity problems.

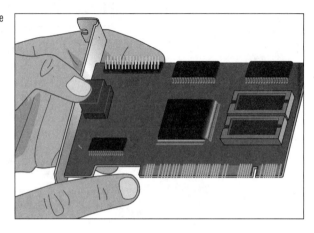

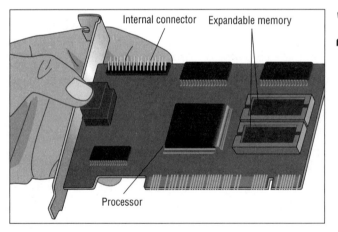

Internal connector   Expandable memory

Processor

2 Most video cards have expandable memory, a processor, and an internal connector.

3 The internal connector on a video card is called a feature connector; most commonly it is used to connect a television tuner or other video device to the computer's video card.

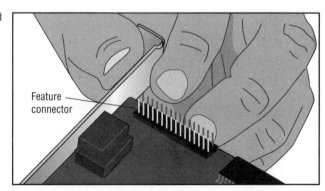

Feature connector

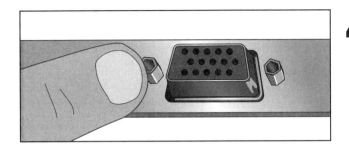

4 A video card's 15-pin, D-Shell connector is the standard plug for all computer video monitors.

5 Align the video card with the slot and press it down until it clicks into place.

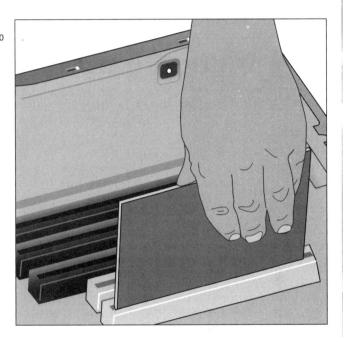

6 Mount the card securely by screwing the video card's rear plate into the computer's chassis.

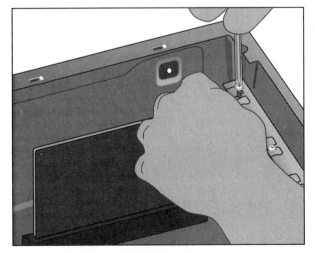

The display on a computer is the primary output device. Because of that, your personal comfort when using a PC is wrapped up in the display, and video taste tends to be a personal kind of thing. What's behind the screen, how can you choose the best equipment for you, and how much can you fix when it fails?

How a Video Board Works

The parts of the board that you must understand in order to see how video works and how it can be tuned up include:

- The system CPU
- The system bus and its interface to the video board
- The video memory on the video board
- The video imaging chip on the video board
- The digital-to-analog converter on the video board

Consider this: how does the CPU get an image onto the computer's display? I'll start from the CPU and end up at the monitor in this explanation.

A basic video board looks like the one shown in Figure 21.1.

FIGURE 21.1:

An AGP video board

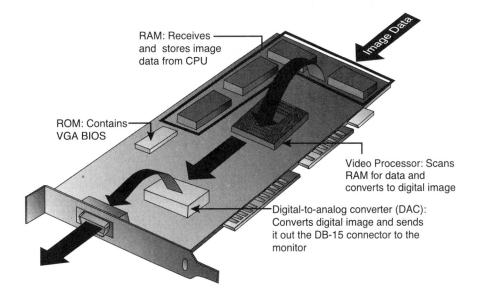

RAM: Receives and stores image data from CPU

Image Data

ROM: Contains VGA BIOS

Video Processor: Scans RAM for data and converts to digital image

Digital-to-analog converter (DAC): Converts digital image and sends it out the DB-15 connector to the monitor

The CPU and Video Images

The primary objective of a video board is to take information from the CPU and display it on a monitor. When a program wants to display data, it does so by telling the CPU to store data in the video board. Exactly *how* a CPU does that varies, as there are two basic kinds of video boards: dumb frame buffers and coprocessor/accelerator boards. I'll take up those two types in a bit, but for now just understand that the CPU controls the video board.

What that implies, for anyone trying to speed up a video subsystem, is that a faster CPU will make for faster video, all other things being equal.

The System Bus

Recall that in a system with an ISA bus, any board in a PC runs at a mere 8MHz. Spend all the money you like for a fast Pentium, but anything in an ISA (or EISA, for that matter) slot runs at 8MHz. Whenever Windows manipulates the video board, your "screamer" whispers at 8MHz.

The CPU is connected to the video board through the system's bus. The speed of that bus can be a constraint on how fast the video system can update. What's the fastest rate at which data might be zapped into a video board? Well, the video system need not update the picture on the screen more often than 72 times per second, as you can't perceive images faster than that. High quality video boards have 4MB of RAM on them, so the maximum amount of data that a video board might have to work with would be 72×4, or 288MB per second. The PCI bus runs at 33MHz and is 32 bits wide, so the maximum video data throughput for PCI video cards is 133MB per second. What does all that mean? Simply this: the faster your bus interface the better for your video board. That suggests that when you buy a video board, you should buy a video board that uses AGP bus. AGP runs at 66MHz and is 64 bits wide, providing a maximum video data throughput of 528MB per second!

In fact, the peripheral that probably benefits the most from a fast bus is the video board. How important is local bus? Well, a video card in a standard ISA bus slot can only transfer data 16 bits at a time, at 8MHz. That's only 16MB per second. A video card sitting in an AGP slot can potentially transfer video data 33 times faster!

The Video Memory

The video image is then stored in the video memory. Like all memory, faster is better and more is better. (Why is more better? I'll discuss video resolution and color depth later, but the answer is, briefly: the more dots you want to put on your screen and the more colors that you want to be able to use for them, the more memory your video board needs.) But video memory has some special needs in that it is usually addressed in blocks, and in that it is addressed simultaneously by several chips—in particular, the CPU and the video imaging chip.

Dual Ported Memory: VRAM

Lets look at that second characteristic first. Ordinarily, a RAM chip is addressed by the CPU and no other chip, unless there's a DMA operation going on—and when that happens, the CPU doesn't access the memory.

In contrast, memory on a video chip has no choice but to talk to two chips at the same time; the CPU shovels image data into the video memory, and the imaging chip pulls it out. On video boards with normal RAM, this presents a performance problem, as normal RAM can only address one chip at a time. Video boards with normal RAM just make the CPU and the imaging chip take turns, slowing things down.

Faster video boards use a special kind of memory originally called Dual Ported RAM, but which most people call VRAM, for Video RAM. There's nothing intrinsically video-ish about this RAM; it's just that its most logical application is in video boards.

Dual-Ported, Block-Addressable Memory: WRAM

But another thing about memory is its blocky nature. Modern graphical user interfaces tend to address memory in large blocks, rather than on a byte-by-byte basis. For example, to draw a colored background, the CPU must say to a whole large block of memory, "store value X," where X is the value that sets the desired background color. A CPU does that by arduously working on several locations one at a time.

A newer kind of RAM called Window RAM (WRAM) makes that easier by allowing blocks, or "windows," of memory to be addressed in just a few commands. WRAM is a bit more expensive, but it's a good buy in video boards.

Video Aperture

Some high-performance video accelerators (I'll discuss accelerators in a few pages) get their speed by mapping their video memory right into the computer's memory address space. This video is called the *video aperture*, and you've got to understand it to solve some configuration problems.

Let's see how a video board uses memory. In graphics mode, an EGA, VGA, or newer video board only uses the addresses between 640K and 704K for video memory. But think for a moment, and you'll see that this seems not to make sense. From 640K to 704K is just 64K, and even a simple VGA board has 256K of RAM on it. Super VGAs can have one to four *megabytes* of RAM on them. How does all that RAM fit into a 64K-address space?

Simple: a little bit at a time.

The VGA uses its 256K of RAM within a 64K constraint by taking the 256K and chopping it up into *four* 64K-sized areas. Most of the video memory is invisible to the CPU at any instant in time. To update the VGA, a VGA-aware program first asks the VGA to make the first 64K area visible to the CPU. The 64K is defined to describe the red part of the image. Once the red 64K is made visible to the CPU—"paged in" is the correct term—then the VGA-aware program can modify the red part of the VGA image. The red 64K—the "red page"—is then paged out, and the next 64K—the green page—is paged in, and modified. The same is done for the third page (the blue page) and the fourth page (the intensity page).

Stop and consider what had to happen just to update a single VGA screen: move in the red page, modify it, and move it out; then move in the green page, modify it, and then move it out; move in the blue page, modify it, and then move it out; and finally move in the intensity page, modify it, and then move it out. That's a lot of work. The reason why so much work must be done is because of the severe memory address constraints of DOS-based programs, which in general must live in the bottom 1024K of PC memory.

Now think about what happens with a super VGA board with 2MB of RAM. If the super VGA board is built like most super VGA boards, the 64K-page approach is still used. But 2MB is, however, *32 different 64K pages.* That means that a super VGA video driver for a 2MB-video board must page in and out 32 different pages in order to update the video screen just once. *Now* it should be obvious why high resolution super VGA screens can be so terribly slow.

Some super VGA boards take a totally different approach. They reason that they are being used not by DOS-based programs, but instead by Windows programs. Windows can easily rise above the 1024K address range, so some super VGA boards place the whole 2MB of RAM right into the PC's address space, just like the RAM that the system uses to run programs. The value of this approach is that now the video RAM can be updated in a straightforward, *fast* way, without having to wait around for 64K-sized blocks to be paged around. The range of addresses used for this 2MB block of memory is called the *video aperture.*

Mapping video memory right into extended memory is a good thing, in general, as it significantly speeds up video operations. But there's one catch. As you've learned in several places in this book, you can't have two things located at the same address. If the video RAM is directly mapped into the PC's extended memory address space, then you've got to be careful that it doesn't end up in the same address as some of the PC's installed extended memory. For example, if your PC has 8MB of memory, then be sure to put the video aperture above 8MB so that it will not conflict with your system memory.

Video aperture is usually an *option*; you can usually choose to just use the standard 64K-at-address-640K-page approach. While disabling video aperture and using the small page approach will slow you down, it might be the only way to get a system to work. IBM's accelerator board, the Extended Graphics Array (XGA), will optionally allow you to set its 2MB of video RAM to a video aperture—*but* that aperture must be somewhere in the bottom 16MB of memory addresses. That's a shame, as many Windows "power users" will have at least 16MB of system RAM. The video aperture must appear in the bottom 16MB of addresses, but those addresses are already filled with RAM, so the XGA user would have to disable video aperture. That's not a problem for *every* high performance board user, however. For example, the ATI mach32 system can use any address in the first four *gigabytes*—and I somehow suspect that before any of us puts 4GB on a computer, there will be some quite significant changes in video.

The bottom line is that you should:

- Look for video aperture as an option for high performance video systems.

- Make sure that the video aperture can appear *anywhere* in the address range of 0GB–4GB.

- When experiencing video troubles, check to see if the manufacturer has already enabled the video aperture, and has perhaps accidentally addressed it on top of some system RAM.

(I've seen that happen with an XGA system sold with 16MB of RAM and the XGA RAM addressed at the 8MB level. The system kept crashing Windows until the video aperture was disabled.)

The Video Imaging Chip

Once the image is in the video RAM, that image must be converted into a digital video image format. That's done by the "display chip," "video chip," or "imaging chip," depending on who's talking about it. Over the years, there have been many different imaging chips. Nowadays, however, the main question to answer when looking at video chips is this: is it a dumb frame buffer or an accelerator/coprocessor of some kind?

Frame Buffer Chips

Most video chips in the PC world before 1992 were frame buffers. *Frame buffer* means that the board is populated with memory chips, as you've just learned, and the memory chips hold an image that closely resembles what shows up on the screen. Each dot (*pixel*) on the screen has a corresponding location on the video memory. Set it to one numeric value, and one color appears on the pixel. Another value, and another color appears in its place.

The problem with frame buffers is that every one of those pixels must be arranged by the CPU. That can be a lot of work for one CPU—which is where accelerators and coprocessors come in.

Smarter Video Chips

Newer video chips take some of the burden off the main processor and put it on themselves. These kinds of chips are coprocessors called video accelerators.

Back in Chapter 3, you learned about numeric coprocessors, special-purpose CPUs that are particularly good at a small group of jobs.

Video coprocessors are just another kind of special-purpose CPU. As you'd expect, they're designed to shove pixels around quickly. Your math coprocessor is just a single chip, but video coprocessors are generally entire circuit boards. Coprocessors can be very fast, but unfortunately they're also expensive. It's not unusual to have to spend over $1000 on a coprocessor.

Related to a coprocessor is a less-expensive alternative called an *accelerator*. The difference is that a coprocessor is a full-fledged microprocessor, one programmable to do just about any task that the main CPU can do. An accelerator, on the other hand, is not a general-purpose CPU, but rather just a special-purpose chip that knows how to do a few particular graphical tasks quickly. Most accelerators are good at something called *bit blitting*. As you probably know, a term commonly used by GUI users for pictures is *bitmaps*. Windows wallpapers are bitmaps, screen captures are bitmaps, and any picture created with Paintbrush is a bitmap. Much of what slows Windows down is placing bitmaps on the screen, either transferring them from memory to screen, or in moving them from one part of the screen to another part of the screen. Moving a bitmap is technically referred to as a *bitmap block transfer,* which is abbreviated to *bitblt.* A number of inexpensive Windows accelerators are just VGA boards with a bitblitter chip on-board. The large number of bitblt operations that Windows does makes this combination of VGA and hardware bitblt support very cost-effective. Accelerators may also know how to build simple geometric shapes like lines or circles.

Accelerators typically include VGA circuitry on board; coprocessors typically complement a VGA, requiring that you have both a VGA board and a coprocessor in your system. Coprocessors require that you link them to a normal video board via a "feature connector," a pin header or edge connector you'll commonly see on video boards.

The fact that accelerators are a one-board approach in contrast to the video-board-and-coprocessor approach may make an accelerator a better buy. It's certainly a cheaper option, but be aware that an accelerator board's dual nature means that it has both generic VGA circuitry and accelerator circuitry, and the two circuits are unrelated. It's quite common to see incredibly fast accelerator chips paired with painfully slow VGA circuits, and the result is that running Windows is quite fast (the accelerator is at work) but that games run very poorly, as the slower VGA circuit is now active. When looking at benchmark results for an accelerator, look for times for both the VGA circuit and the accelerator.

Digital to Analog Converter (DAC)

The video board's work is almost done; the digital image has been produced by the imaging chip. Only one more thing to do—convert the image from digital to analog. That's done with a special chip called the Digital to Analog Converter, or DAC.

About all there is to say about the DAC is that it comes in varying abilities to produce color. The 15-bit DAC produces 32,768 colors; the 16-bit DAC produces 65,536 colors; and the 18-bit DAC produces 262,144 colors. The 24-bit and 30-bit DACs produce 16 million and 1 billion colors, respectively.

You usually can't upgrade DACs; whatever your vendor built in is what you're stuck with.

Video Board Characteristics

Now that you know the parts of a video board, how do you choose between video boards? RAM type, bus attachment, and video chip are all important, but so are image resolution, color depth, and vertical frequency. You'll learn about those in this section.

Resolution and Colors

Resolution on a video display is the number of horizontal and vertical dots that make up the picture. For example, the most basic resolution today is 640 × 480, which means that the image is 640 dots wide by 480 dots high. Most VGA boards nowadays are super VGA boards, even the cheap clones. You can pick up a no-name VGA board for about $15-$30, and in addition to standard VGA, it will probably support 800 × 600 mode. The more expensive VGA boards ($200–$300) will support 1024 × 768 or 1280 × 1024. More resolution means more dots on the screen, which means that the video board needs more memory.

A video board's memory requirements are determined by two things: its resolution and the number of colors that it can display. For instance, the basic VGA can display a resolution of 320 × 200 with 256 colors, but when in the higher 640 × 480 resolution, it can only display 16 colors. That has nothing to do with the constraints of the monitor, or even of the VGA board *except* for the amount of memory on the board. A normal VGA comes with 256K right on the board. Table 21.1 shows a summary of resolutions available for common video boards throughout PC history.

TABLE 21.1: Video Board Resolutions

Board Type	Resolutions Supported	Colors Supported
Color Graphics Array (CGA)	320 × 200	4
	640 × 200	2
Enhanced Graphics Array (EGA)	CGA resolutions	
	640 × 350	16
Video Graphics Array (VGA)	CGA and EGA	
	320 × 200	256
	640 × 480	16
Super VGA	CGA, EGA, VGA	
	640 × 480, 800 × 600, 832 × 624, 1024 × 768, 1152 × 870, 1280 × 1024, 1360 × 1024, 1600 × 1200	256, 32K, 64K, or 16 million+ (ranges from 4-bit to 32-bit color)

Resolutions like 1024 × 768 with 256 colors obviously require more memory—that's why you see ads for VGA cards with an option for 256K, 512K, or 1024K on the board. If all you're doing is regular old VGA, you need only 256K—there's no point in spending the extra money for 512K or 1024K. Table 21.2 shows the amount of memory that a video board needs for some example resolution/color combinations.

NOTE Note that cards can come with as much as 64MB of video RAM built-in, such as #9's 64MB digital video card especially built for SGI's 1600 × 1024 LCD monitor. Most PCI cards ship with 8MB of video RAM, but most AGP cards (a type of PCI that uses system RAM as well as it's own) come with 4MB and work just as well.

TABLE 21.2: Memory Required at Various Color Depths

VGA & Apple 13" - 640 x 480

Resolution and Color Depth	Minimum Memory Required
AT 16 Colors (4-Bit Color)	256K
AT 256 Colors (8-Bit Color)	512K
AT 32K Color (15-Bit Color)	1MB
AT 65K Color (Thousands) 16-Bit Color	1MB
AT 16.7M Colors (24-Bit Color) True Color	1MB

Super VGA (SVGA) - 800 x 600

Resolution and Color Depth	Minimum Memory Required
AT 16 Colors (4-Bit Color)	256K
AT 256 Colors (8-Bit Color)	512K
AT 32K Color (15-Bit Color)	1MB
AT 65K Color (Thousands) 16-Bit Color	1MB
AT 16.7M Colors (24-Bit Color) True Color	1MB

Non-standard SVGA - 832 x 624

Resolution and Color Depth	Minimum Memory Required
AT 16 Colors (4-Bit Color)	512K
AT 256 Colors (8-Bit Color)	1MB
AT 32K Color (15-Bit Color)	1MB
AT 65K Color (Thousands) 16-Bit Color	1.5MB
AT 16.7M Colors (24-Bit Color) True Color	2MB

Continued on next page

TABLE 21.2 CONTINUED: Memory Required at Various Color Depths

Extended SVGA (XGA) - 1024 x 768

Resolution and Color Depth	Minimum Memory Required
AT 16 Colors (4-Bit Color)	512K
AT 256 Colors (8-Bit Color)	1MB
AT 32K Color (15-Bit Color)	1.5MB
AT 65K Color (Thousands) 16-Bit Color	2MB
AT 16.7M Colors (24-Bit Color) True Color	2.5MB

Non-standard XGA - 1152 x 870

Resolution and Color Depth	Minimum Memory Required
AT 16 Colors (4-Bit Color)	512K
AT 256 Colors (8-Bit Color)	1.5MB
AT 32K Color (15-Bit Color)	2MB
AT 65K Color (Thousands) 16-Bit Color	2.5MB
AT 16.7M Colors (24-Bit Color) True Color	3.5MB

1280 x 1024

Resolution and Color Depth	Minimum Memory Required
AT 16 Colors (4-Bit Color)	1MB
AT 256 Colors (8-Bit Color)	1.5MB
AT 32K Color (15-Bit Color)	2.5MB
AT 65K Color (Thousands) 16-Bit Color	3MB
AT 16.7M Colors (24-Bit Color) True Color	4MB

Continued on next page

TABLE 21.2 CONTINUED: Memory Required at Various Color Depths

1360 x 1024

Resolution and Color Depth	Minimum Memory Required
AT 16 Colors (4-Bit Color)	1MB
AT 256 Colors (8-Bit Color)	1.5MB
AT 32K Color (15-Bit Color)	3MB
AT 65K Color (Thousands) 16-Bit Color	3MB
AT 16.7M Colors (24-Bit Color) True Color	4.5 MB

1600 x 1200

Resolution and Color Depth	Minimum Memory Required
AT 16 Colors (4-Bit Color)	1MB
AT 256 Colors (8-Bit Color)	2MB
AT 32K Color (15-Bit Color)	4MB
AT 65K Color (Thousands) 16-Bit Color	4MB
AT 16.7M Colors (24-Bit Color) True Color	6MB

Vertical Scan Frequencies: Interlacing and 72Hz

Your video monitor displays information by projecting a narrow beam of electrons onto a phosphor-covered glass panel—your monitor screen. Wherever the beam hits, the phosphor becomes excited ("excited" here is a relative term) and so the phosphor lights up for brief period of time (see, excitement *is* relative here), then fades out. Because it fades very quickly—in hundredths of seconds—the electron beam must retrace its path constantly to keep the image on the screen. How often must it travel across the screen? Well, the electron beam in the back of a video monitor must repaint or "refresh" the screen at least 60 times per second, or your eye will probably perceive flicker. (Why "probably"? Hang on for a sentence or two.) And that brings me to a story about the IBM 8514 video system.

Interlacing and the 8514

The 8514 was an early IBM high-resolution (1024 × 768) video system; as a matter of fact, the 8514 video system is important because it was the first mass-market PC-based video system to support a resolution of 1024 × 768. But, in order to save money on the monitor, IBM cut a corner on the system. Now, in order to get high-resolution images, you need a high-quality (read: expensive) monitor. One way to get higher resolution out of a cheaper screen is to refresh it less often. The 8514 does not refresh 60 times per second, but rather at 43 times per second.

This isn't the first time we've seen this less-than-60-refreshes-per-second approach to high resolution; it's called *interlacing*. What was significant was that *IBM* did it, so the practice of interlacing became acceptable.

But, you see interlacing is *not* acceptable, at least not from a quality standpoint. The result of interlacing is a flickering screen and eyestrain headaches. That's why you've got to be careful when buying a system with 1024 × 768 resolution. Check that it's *non*interlaced.

By the way, if you do have an interlaced monitor, there may be a few things that you can do to reduce the effects of flicker, because several factors affect flicker; that's why I said "probably" a few sentences back. First, you see flicker better with your peripheral vision, because the center of your vision is built around low-resolution color receptors called cones on your retina. Surrounding the cones are high-resolution monochromatic receptors called rods.

Peripheral vision images fall on the rods. Sailors know this because when searching for a ship on the horizon, they don't look right at the horizon—they look below it, so the horizon falls on the high-resolution rods. In any case, the closer you are to your monitor, the more of its image falls on the cones, which are less flicker-prone. You can demonstrate this with any monitor. Stand so that your monitor is about 60 to 80 degrees to your left: if the direction you're facing is 12 o'clock, the monitor should be at about 10 o'clock. Hold a piece of paper in front of you and read the text on it. You'll notice that you're seeing the monitor out of the corner of your eye, and that it's flashing. This also suggests that you should buy a small monitor, as a large image will end up falling more on your rods; but 1024×768 on a 12-inch screen is, well, sub-optimal. Glare screens will also reduce flicker. Another anti-flicker tactic is to keep your room bright. When the ambient light is bright, your pupils contract, which has the side effect of reducing the amount of light that gets to the peripheral rods. You'll also find that certain color combinations exaggerate the flicker—black and white is one problem combination—so play around with the Windows colors and you'll make the screen more readable.

72Hz Video

Since I've brought up the subject of video with low refresh rates, it's worthwhile looking at the opposite end of the spectrum—video systems that refresh at more than 60 screens per second. The more common use of larger monitors means that more people notice flicker on normal 60Hz VGA. Furthermore, people nowadays use their computers all day, so anyone who has even the slightest sensitivity to flicker will get some eyestrain. As a result, vendors nowadays are offering VGA and super VGA boards that put out a higher vertical refresh rate. The 72Hz is well worth investing in, in my opinion. My eyes rest much more easily on a 72Hz screen than a 60Hz screen. So, when buying your next video board, look for 72Hz vertical refresh.

There are, of course, a few caveats. First, you need a monitor that can handle a 72Hz vertical refresh; a basic cheap $200 VGA monitor can't handle a 72Hz signal. Before you buy a video board, find out what kind of monitor you currently have and ask the video board's vendor if your current monitor can use all of the video board's features. If not, either don't buy the board, or plan to buy a new monitor with your new board. (Don't you just love it when some computer expert tells you to go spend some money? Kidding aside, believe me, better video is worth it.)

The second caution is actually kind of funny or sad, depending on how you look at it. Every single computer I've set up in the past four years that has a video system that will handle both 60 and 72Hz video came out of the box configured for 60Hz. Now, reconfiguring the video for 72Hz usually isn't any harder than just running a short program that comes with the video board, so it's not like I unlocked some hidden feature of the video board. It's just plain inexplicable why a computer company would sell a superior video product as part of its PC, but wouldn't take the two minutes to utilize those features.

So, if you've got a recently purchased computer, take a close look at the video documentation that came with it. I've been able to bring more than a few surprised smiles to the faces of owners of PCs recently by running the video setup programs that were sitting right on their hard disks.

Video Monitor Characteristics

Now that you've got a board, what monitor goes with it? Monitors aren't as complex as video boards, but there are a few terms to work with.

Perhaps the most important thing to understand about the monitor/ board partnership is that the video board calls the tune, and the monitor dances—if it can. Virtually all modern computers (except for some laptops) have video circuitry that can produce 1024 × 768 signals, but most computers don't have monitors of a quality to actually *display* that signal. Having 72Hz is nice, but both the video board and the monitor must support it.

Monitor Mumbo Jumbo: Horizontal Scan Frequency

As I explained earlier, a monitor works by directing a beam of electrons against the inside of its screen. Phosphors on the inside of the screen become "excited" and glow. Making phosphors glow or not glow defines images on the screen. From a computer's point of view, a video display is just an array of pixels. *Resolution* is the number of dots that can be put on the screen. The electron beam sweeps across the tube, painting lines of dots. CGA used 200 lines top to bottom, EGA 350, and VGA uses 480. As it uses higher resolutions, super VGA does even more.

Consider the number of horizontal lines that a monitor must draw per second. In a basic VGA, each screen has 480 lines, and there are 60 screens per second. So 480 times 60 is 28,800 lines per second. That is called the *horizontal scan frequency*, as it is the number of times that the beam sweeps horizontally per second. It too is measured in Hertz, or kilohertz (kHz)—thousands of hertz. Actually, a VGA has a somewhat higher horizontal scan rate than 28,800Hz (28.8kHz), as the monitor has extra lines that you can't see (they're called *overscan*). How *many* extra lines a monitor has varies from video mode to video mode. A CGA has a horizontal scan frequency of 15,750Hz, or 15.8kHz. EGA uses 21.8kHz, and VGA 31.5kHz. So the horizontal scan frequency your monitor needs to serve your board is determined in part by two important factors: the number of horizontal lines on the screen and the screen's refresh rate.

Dot Pitch

Some monitor ads tout "0.28mm dot pitch." What are they talking about?

We've seen that more resolution means more dots (pixels) on the screen. The distance between the centers of the dots on the monitor is the monitor's *dot pitch*, and it's measured in millimeters (mm). The smaller the dots, the closer together they can be and the higher the resolution that a monitor can show in a crisp and readable manner. A larger monitor can have a larger dot pitch without sacrificing resolution, as its screen is larger.

In reality, you'll see four dot pitches for VGA monitors: 0.34, 0.31, 0.28, and 0.26 mm. Avoid 0.34 on 12-inch VGA monitors, but you may find it quite acceptable on 14-inch monitors—go take a look at one before you buy it. You'll find 0.34 on a 14-inch or 0.31 on a 12-inch monitor is fine for VGA only, but buy 0.28 if you plan to use a super VGA with 800×600 resolution, and 0.26 for a super VGA using 1024×768 resolution.

Multi-Frequency Monitors

The last monitor feature is *multisyncing*, the ability to handle multiple resolutions automatically. Recall that the horizontal frequency that you need to display an image is determined by the refresh rate (the vertical frequency) and the horizontal resolution. Until 1986, monitors were fixed-frequency in both the horizontal and vertical directions. When you bought a CGA monitor, it could only do one set of frequencies: 15.75kHz horizontal, 60Hz vertical. The EGA monitor had to be able to do double duty, as it could be attached to either CGA or EGA boards, and so had two sets of frequencies: 15.75kHz/60Hz for CGA boards and 21.8kHz/60Hz for EGA boards. The VGA knows of three sets of frequencies: one for CGA modes, one for EGA modes, and 31.5kHz/60Hz for its native standard VGA mode. So a "vanilla VGA" monitor is a fixed-frequency monitor that only supports CGA, EGA, and VGA—no super VGA modes.

In 1986, NEC changed that with its Multisync monitor. The Multisync could detect and synchronize with any horizontal frequency from 15kHz to 31.5kHz and with any vertical frequency from 50Hz to 70Hz. That meant that a single monitor could work on any kind of video board out at the time. More important, when IBM introduced the VGA in April 1987, the Multisync was ready—it could handle VGA's 31.5kHz horizontal frequency with no problem.

Now most video vendors offer their own Multisync-like monitors: they're generically called variable frequency monitors (VFMs). NEC doesn't sell the original Multisync any more, but they have Multisync models from the 3FGX (31.5–38kHz horizontal, 50–80Hz vertical) to the 6FGX (30–66kHz horizontal, 50–90Hz vertical). The competition is not asleep, however.

At the moment, my pick for the best reasonably priced monitor is the ViewSonic 17G. This is a terrific monitor for several reasons:

- It syncs up to a wide range of frequencies, including 1280 × 1024, and can do 1024 × 768 at 72Hz.

- It is crisp and clear.

- It automatically sizes itself. I don't have to play around with the size controls every time I change resolution or frequency.

- It's a 17-inch monitor, the smallest size I'd recommend for use day in and day out.

This is the monitor I'd pick for a new machine, without question.

Resizing Screens with Multisyncing Monitors

You'll notice on some of the cheap Multisync monitors that the screen size jumps around when you change resolution. Change from 640 × 480 at 60Hz to 640 × 480 at 72Hz, and the screen gets smaller.

That's due to the higher frequency of the beam writing the image on the screen. On those simple monitors, you must move size and position knobs in order to get the image just right.

This is normal, unfortunately. To combat it, you should buy "autosizing" monitors.

Video Troubleshooting

Once you have a system in place, how do you attack video problems? Here are a few suggestions.

Some of the dumbest monitor problems are the easiest to resolve.

- Is it turned on?

- Is the brightness or contrast turned down?

- Is everything plugged in? Is it plugged into the right place?

- Did you hear one long and two short beeps indicating a bad video card?

- There are non-video reasons for a display "malfunction." Such as when the power supply has killed the computer. If the display is dead, do you hear the power supply fan?

- If the computer is okay but the display is bad, you will see the drive light come on. Use a sound-emitting program to see if the computer is functioning.

The quickest test is a monitor swap. If that does nothing, swap the display cards. *Don't* try to service the monitor. As I've said before, you can hurt yourself doing that.

If the display is rolling and you can't see enough to check the video modes, restart the computer in Windows Safe mode (press the F8 key when you reboot and you'll be given a menu with Safe Mode as one of the options). This will start Windows in standard 640×480 in 16 colors, so you can use almost any card and monitor to test your system.

Speaking of drivers, sometimes you'll see a case where you reboot your operating system, only to lose synchronization—the screen turns into moving bands. That probably means that you told your video board to exceed the capabilities of the monitor, drop back a bit in resolution and you'll be okay.

Reference: Older Display Types

Before leaving this chapter, I wanted to finish up with some background on pre-1987 displays. You may need this information if you ever find yourself working on an old system.

Before 1987, video standards basically came from IBM. Big Blue controlled the market, and so whatever IBM did everyone else would follow. After 1987, however, the disastrous performance of the PS/2 in the market left the marketplace without a leader. The top-of-the-line video in 1987 was the VGA, which is the baseline standard today. But what preceded it?

There are several basic kinds of older monitors:

- Composite monochrome
- Composite color
- RGB
- EGA monitors
- Direct drive TTL monochrome

Table 21.3 offers one way to understand these monitors.

TABLE 21.3: PC Monitor Types

	Analog	**Digital**
Monochrome	Composite Monochrome	Monochrome TTL
Color	Color Composite	RGB:
		CGA (640 × 200), EGA (640 × 350), VGA (640 × 480)

Composite monitors are a step better than a television set. They offer greater resolution than a TV, but that's about it. They offer low expense and good quality.

RGB (Red, Green, Blue) monitors offer better resolution for color text than do color composite monitors. The IBM Color Display and the Princeton Graphics HX12 are RGB monitors. RGBs are more expensive, offer somewhat better quality than composite color, and attach to a display adapter with a 9-pin D shell connector. You see very few composite monitors in the PC world these days.

More expensive than regular RGB, EGA (Enhanced Graphics Adapter) monitors are RGB monitors with higher resolution. Characters are sharper and the display steadier. In addition, these monitors can display 43 lines of text on a screen rather than the usual 25. This isn't as great as it sounds: most programs won't support the 43-line mode. Notable exceptions are dBASE and the IBM Personal Editor, but more and more are joining the crowd: OS/2 even directly supports 43-line displays with the MODE command. An example of an EGA monitor is the IBM Enhanced Color Display. EGA has been supplanted by VGA, an even higher resolution display standard (it can display 50 lines of text where EGA can only do 43).

Direct drive TTL monitors are monochromatic (generally amber and black or green and black) and offer high resolution, steady images. An example of this is the IBM Monochrome Display. They are connected with 9-pin D shell connector like the RGB, but don't plug one of these in where RGB is expected or vice versa. You honestly will get smoke.

Fairly expensive, but most versatile, are the multiscan monitors. These can serve as an RGB or an EGA monitor—they sense at what rate data is coming in, and adjust their scan rates accordingly. Most modern monitors are multiscan monitors.

The second part of a display subsystem is the controller board. There are quite a few in use currently, and they all have their characteristics. Table 21.4 summarizes them.

TABLE 21.4: Common PC Adapter Types

Adapter	Maximum Resolution/ Colors	Char. Box Size	Monitors Supported	Graphics Supported?
Color/Graphics Adapter (CGA)	640 × 200/2	8 × 8	RGB	Yes
			Composite	No
Monochrome Display Adapter (MDA)	720 × 350/3	9 × 14	Mono TTL	No
Enhanced Graphics Adapter (EGA)	640 × 350/64	8 × 14	RGB	Yes
			EGA	No
			Mono TTL	No
Hercules Graphics Controller (HGC)	720 × 350/3	9 × 14	Mono TTL	Yes
Multi Color Graphics Array (MCGA)	640 × 480/2	8 × 16	Analog RGB	Yes
Video Graphics Array (VGA)	640 × 480/ 262, 144	9 × 16	Analog RGB	Yes
Super VGA	Up to 1024 × 768/256	9 × 16	Analog RGB	Yes
8514/A	1024 × 768/ 262, 144	9 × 16	Analog RGB	Yes
XGA	1024 × 768/ 262, 144	9 × 16	Analog RGB	Yes

Several display adapters were used throughout the late '80s:

- The IBM Monochrome Display Adapter (MDA)
- The Hercules Monochrome Graphics Adapter

- The IBM Color/Graphics Adapter (CGA)

- The IBM Enhanced Graphics Adapter (EGA)

- The IBM Professional Graphics Adapter

The PGA never really caught on, but it was the first real attempt in the PC world to add intelligence to a video board. That led eventually to the graphic accelerator boards that are becoming standard equipment on many modern PCs.

The IBM Video Graphics Array: Sporting PGA-quality graphics and a much more reasonable price (the PGA ran around $3000), the VGA made its appearance in 1987 with the PS/2s. This board is, as I've said, the baseline for video today.

The IBM 8514/A Very High Resolution Graphics Adapter: A video coprocessor in the tradition of the PGA. More successful than PGA, but still not a big smash hit. Replaced by the XGA.

The IBM XGA (extended graphics array): Built to do Windows and OS/2 quickly. Never really caught on, but if you buy a modern PS/2 then you'll have it built right into your motherboard.

There are details about these boards in Table 21.4.

Video is an important part of your PC, but its lack of moving parts means that the best medicine for video problems is to understand how it works, and how to attack its problems. The wide variety of so-called Super VGA boards has lead to a plethora of drivers and video setup programs. Make sure you've got the most up-to-date drivers, a monitor that matches your board, and all will be well.

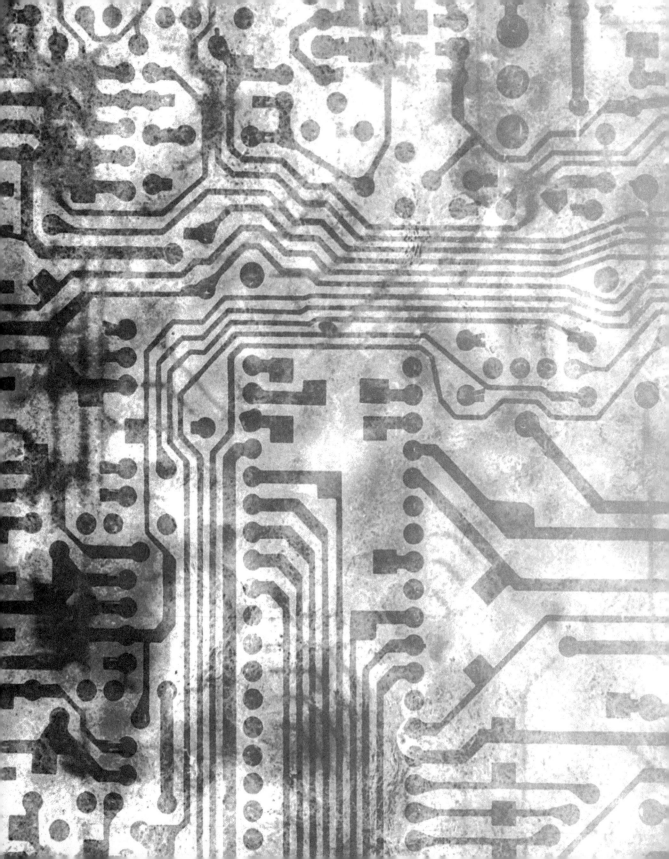

CHAPTER

22

Play It Loud: Sound Cards

- How sound synthesis works

- Sampling versus synthesis

- The characteristics of sound cards

- Choosing the right speakers

Installing a Sound Card

1 Sound cards have several internal and external connectors.

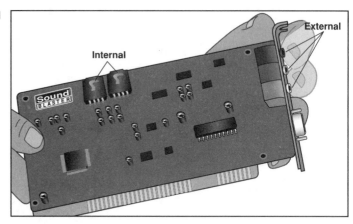

2 The rear of most sound cards has a joystick port in addition to mini-plug jacks for speakers, line in, and a microphone.

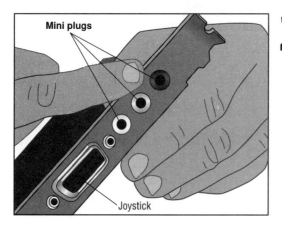

3 Insert the sound card into a free slot (ISA or PCI, depending on the type of card).

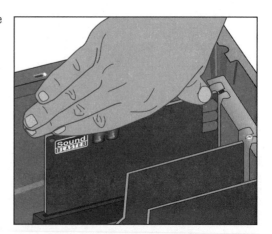

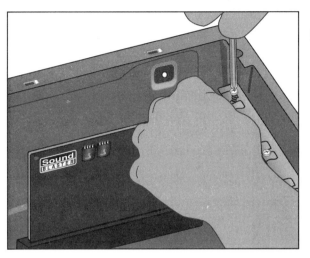

4 Screw the back plate of the card into the computer's chassis.

5 Connect one end of your CD-ROM's audio cable into the internal CD IN connector on the sound card.

6 Connect the other end of the audio cable to the AUDIO connector at the rear of the CD-ROM drive.

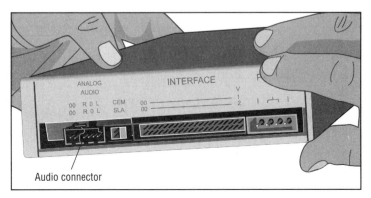

Audio connector

In the early days of PCs, the only way that a PC could make noise was with its built-in speaker. Even the best PC speaker is tinny, however, and the best we could hope for were squeaks, squawks, and the occasional "boom." One ambitious 1984 program called *PC Parrot* attempted to make the PC speak, but it was limited by the sound equipment possibilities.

That's not true any more. Sound equipment on the PC is so good that I didn't type much of this chapter; I spoke it, using a voice recognition product that allowed me to just talk and it typed what I said. Although that's an expensive system, sound's no longer expensive—basic sound cards can be had for under $50. And, as my voice dictation system shows, sound isn't only for games, either.

In this chapter, you'll learn how sound cards work, what features to look for when choosing one, and what you're likely to run into when you install a sound card.

Sound Synthesis

The goal of sound cards is to record and play back sound. How they do it varies considerably, however. There are three main methods of sound reproduction:

- Sampling
- FM synthesis
- Wavetable synthesis

We'll look at these three methods in this section.

Sound Characteristics

Sound consists of a set of waves of varying pressure created in the air by our vocal cords, musical instruments, or natural forces. A picture of a sound is called a *sonogram,* and you can see one in Figure 22.1. It's a sonogram of the word "hello" being spoken (by me, in this case).

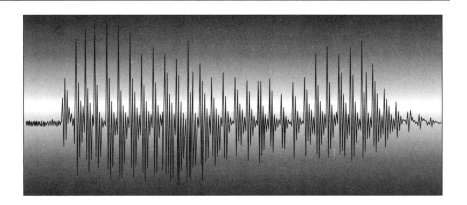

Understanding a bit about sounds requires understanding a bit about signals. The dimensions of this signal are just *amplitude* and *frequency*. Amplitude and frequency probably conjure up visions of trigonometry and physics, but—I promise!—there's nothing tough about this.

Sine Waves

In order to discuss signals in a bit more detail, I've got to talk about another potentially scary topic—sine waves. Take a look at Figure 22.2.

FIGURE 22.2:

Sine wave

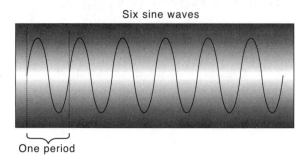

Six sine waves

One period

A wave starts anywhere, makes one upturn and one downturn (unless you start later in the signal, in which case it makes one downturn, *then* one upturn), and then ends up at the same height at which it started. That's one wave. But what does this have to do with data communications?

Talk of signals works around talk of waves just because of the up-and-down (*periodic* is the more exact term) nature of waves, and the sine wave turns out to be the building block of *all* waves.

NOTE   Sine waves are the "building blocks" of all signals. Understanding sine waves makes it possible to analyze (and better transmit) any kind of signal.

What do I mean by "building block?" A mathematician by the name of Fourier proved that *any* wave phenomenon could be built by adding together the right series of waves. *Finding* the right series of waves to build any one signal is not a simple task—it's called a "Fourier decomposition"—but it *can* be done with the right tools (read: computing power). We won't do Fourier decompositions in *this* book; I just wanted you to understand why sine waves are so important to any study of signals. To see an example of sine waves adding up to a signal, look at Figure 22.3, which shows a number of sine waves superimposed on one another.

Several sine waves
superimposed upon
one another

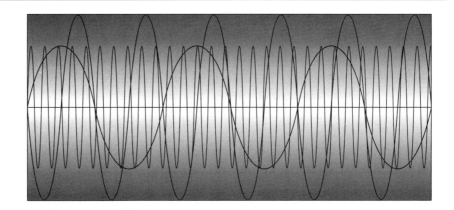

Notice that some jump up and down more quickly, some reach
higher or lower, and some stretch a bit further left and right,
but they're all sine waves. In Figure 22.4 we can add them all
together.

FIGURE 22.4:

Sum of all sine waves

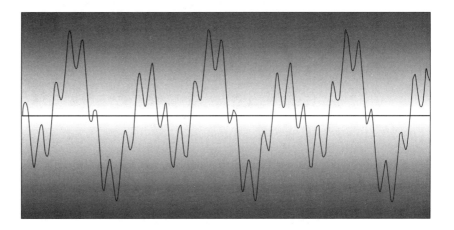

The sum is no longer anything *like* a sine wave. Any signal, no
matter how bizarre, can be broken down into sine waves...which

is why they're so important to a good understanding of signaling limitations. With that in mind, let's look at two aspects of a sine wave—amplitude and frequency.

Amplitude

This should be a familiar concept, as we talk about amplitude all the time—we just call it *loudness* or *volume*.

In human voice communications, volume carries meaning, such as urgency, or it may be used so that a voice will carry far. From a sine wave's perspective, amplitude means *height*. Take a look at Figure 22.5.

FIGURE 22.5:

Amplitude of a sine wave

Smaller amplitude

Greater amplitude

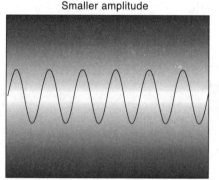 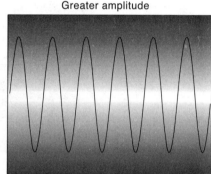

In signals, amplitude also relates to *power* used for transmission. When transmitting data, communications engineers must overcome the fact that transmitting data over a distance reduces a signal's amplitude, weakening it or *attenuating* it. You can partially restore a signal by *amplifying* it; all an amplifier does is to try to boost the amplitude of the signal.

Communications systems use power, or amplitude, to describe two things:

- The raw transmission power of the communications medium.

- Perhaps more important, the *clarity* of the communications medium—a ratio of the power of the *noise* to the power of the *signal*, known as the *signal-to-noise ratio.*

Frequency

The other sine wave characteristic is its *frequency*. Frequency describes how often a wave goes up and down in a given time and you can see this in Figure 22.6.

FIGURE 22.6:

Comparative frequency of two sine waves

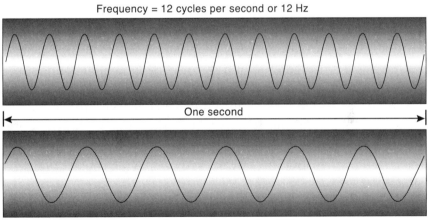

Frequency = 12 cycles per second or 12 Hz

One second

Frequency = 6 cycles per second or 6 Hz

In this figure, you see two waves diagrammed over the course of one second. The top wave goes up and down 12 times in that second, the bottom one, only six times. That means that the top wave has a higher frequency.

Frequency is measured in *cycles per second*, which is abbreviated CPS, or, more commonly, the term *hertz* is used. It's a unit just meaning, as you'd guess, "cycles per second," and is named after Gustav Hertz, a German physicist whose work on the nature of electrons won him a Nobel Prize. Hertz is usually abbreviated Hz. Look back to Figure 22.5, and you'll see that the two waves in that picture had the same frequency. Similarly, the two waves in Figure 22.6 have the same *amplitude*, but different frequencies.

We talk about frequencies when talking about sound; if you say that someone has a "high-pitched voice," then you mean that she has a voice that produces a range of frequencies whose average is somewhat high, as human voices go.

Signals to Bits: Sampling

In order for your sound card to use a sound, it's got to be converted from its analog self into a more bit-friendly format. The main method of converting analog sounds into digital is called *sampling*. (Before I learned how this was done, I called it "digitizing" the audio. I've since learned that expert types always say "sampling," so file "sampling" in your list of good-stuff-to-know-at-cocktail-parties, and *never* say "digitizing.") It's done with a method called PCM, or *Pulse Coded Modulation*.

Suppose we are trying to convert the following simple analog signal into digital, as in Figure 22.7.

Under PCM, the signal is sampled many times per second, and the height of the wave is recorded. (Actually, what is recorded is the *logarithm* of the height—remember that sound volume is perceived logarithmically.) You can see an example of sampling in Figure 22.8.

FIGURE 22.7:

Converting a simple analog signal into digital

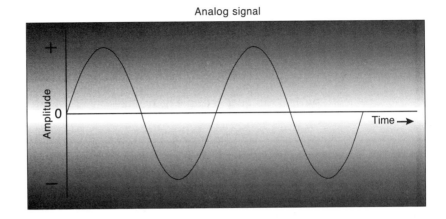

Analog signal

FIGURE 22.8:

Sampling a signal

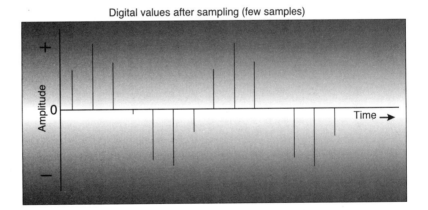

Digital values after sampling (few samples)

The lines represent the height of the signal at various times. It's impossible to measure the height of the signal at all times, so we can only measure a limited number of samples—hence the "sampling" name.

That doesn't seem like a lot of information about the signal, and it isn't. To get a better picture of how to reconstruct the original audio signal, we'd do better to get more samples in the same time period, as you see in Figure 22.9.

FIGURE 22.9:

Reconstructing an original audio signal by getting more samples

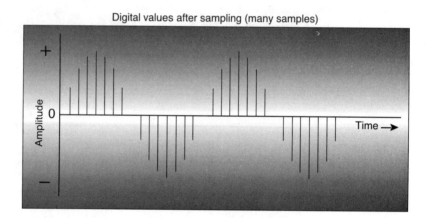

This underscores an important point, which is emphasized in the following diagram: more samples mean a higher-quality signal once reproduced. In Figure 22.10, you can see an original signal for a second's duration, then the result of sampling it 20 times in that second, and the result of sampling it 40 times per second.

There are more values in the more frequently sampled signal, and so the reconstructed signal will be of higher quality.

FIGURE 22.10:

More samples equal a higher-quality reproduction of the signal

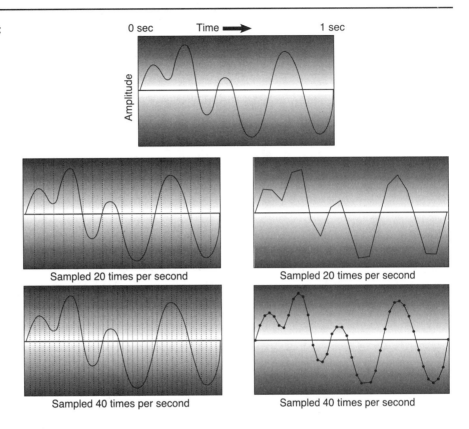

How many samples do we need per second? For the answer to that, we turn to Nyquist's Theorem. It says that to completely capture a signal, you've got to have N samples, where

- $N = 2 \times$ signal bandwidth

The bandwidth of our ears is considered to be well within a 22,050 Hz range. Twice that would be 44,100 samples per second, which is the sampling rate of a music CD. Higher sampling means more data must be stored per second.

But that's not all there is to sampling with PCM. Suppose the recorded values can range from –127 to +128, and they can be only integers. Since the total possible number of values is only 256, each signal value is encoded with 8 bits here.

Why not 16 bits per sample? Using 16 bits would allow for many more nuances of sound—65,536 values for 16 bits compared to 256 for 8 bits—but would double the amount of data needed to store a given audio signal. You can see the difference in bit sample sizes in Figure 22.11.

FIGURE 22.11:

The difference in bit sample sizes

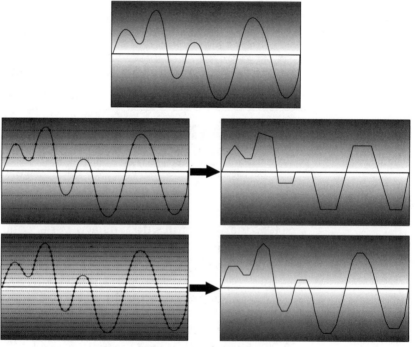

8-bit: ranges from -127 to +128
16-bit: ranges from -32707 to +32708

Music CDs sample 16 bits per sample, 44,100 samples per second.

The cheapest sound cards can only sample at 8 bits per sample; more expensive ones can sample up to 32 bits per second. For most voice and music uses, 16 bits is fine.

FM Synthesis

Sampling works well for recording sounds. But to assemble entirely new sounds, PC software authors need ways to tell a sound card, "play an 'A' as it would sound on a harpsichord." One method for that is with FM synthesis. It's usually implemented as a *MIDI* (*Music Instrument Digital Interface*) circuit.

I'm simplifying here, but the idea behind FM synthesis is that musical sounds follow a four-part cycle, as you see in Figure 22.12.

FIGURE 22.12:

The four-part cycle of musical sounds

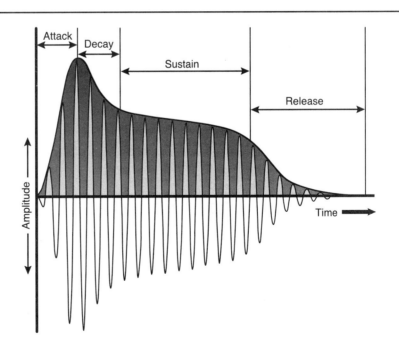

The notion in FM synthesis is to describe an instrument's waveform in terms of the size of the attack, decay, sustain, and release parts of the cycle.

Wave Tables

That's an easy model to encode, and it allows for some very compact music files, orders of magnitude smaller than sampled files. But the simplistic nature of the ADSR model limits musical fidelity.

Some sound cards get around that by storing entire instrument waveforms in a ROM on the board. That's called wavetable synthesis—and it isn't cheap. But if you want the best quality musical synthesis, it's the way to go. (Of course, you could alternatively just buy CDs and play them on your stereo; but that wouldn't be as fun.)

Sound Card Characteristics

Basically, sound cards vary in how they create sounds, how fine a resolution they use for it, and in what "extras" they carry on board, like a pass-through audio circuit or a CD-ROM interface.

8-, 16-, or 32-Bit Sound?

Thus far in this book, a "16-bit card" has meant one that has a 16-bit ISA slot connector on it. A 16-bit was good because of speed. When it comes to sound cards, however, this refers to sample types.

Eight-bit samples are good for very simple game sounds or music. You really need a board with the ability to play back and record 16-bit sounds, however, to do good multimedia. The Sound Blaster 16 from Creative Labs is a good example of a good 16-bit card. There are 32-bit cards, like the AWE32, but I'd recommend them only to someone who wants to do their own music composition on the PC.

Sampling, Synthesis, or Both?

Some sound cards will only do MIDI, and can only play back MIDI files; others can only play back sampled files, usually called WAV files because that's the name that Windows gives them. Most game music is MIDI and most multimedia sound is WAV, so you probably want both capabilities in your card.

IRQ or DMA Sound Recording?

Once you get a sound card up and running, you'll be eager to make a recording or two of your own. The Sound Recorder application in Windows is a good starter application for sampling audio. Just start it up and click on Record, and you can convert your silver throat into silicon bits.

When you try to capture sound in combination with video, however, you'll find that the lame multitasking structure of Windows makes total audio/video capture difficult. One good answer would be to capture with an OS/2- or NT-based product, but there are a scarce number of those. Here's another thought, however: most sound cards are driven by interrupts, which chew up CPU time when the CPU needs most to be able to just hunker down and pay attention to the video capture board. There are, however, some audio cards that aren't built to be interrupt-driven, but rather DMA-driven; the Turtle Beach cards are one good example. As they don't lean on the inter-rupts, you'll get smoother audio/video interleaving on your recordings.

Pass-through and/or CD-ROM Interfaces?

Many sound cards have a small Berg connector on them designed for a cable like the one in Figure 22.13.

FIGURE 22.13:

Berg connector on a cable

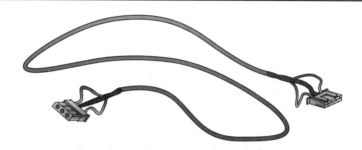

This is an audio pass-through cable. It lets you play music CDs from a CD-ROM in your PC, through the speakers on your sound card. The only problem with getting this audio cable is that there's a different cable for every CD-ROM/sound card combination, so be sure to get the right one.

In a pinch, you can always install a "poor man's (or woman's) pass-through cable": run a cable from the headphone output on the front of the CD-ROM to the LINE IN input on the back of the sound card.

Some sound cards have CD-ROM interfaces for proprietary CD-ROMs. I recommend that you avoid these, as they're a com-patibility headache. Even the sound cards with SCSI interfaces implement slow SCSI interfaces. If you have a SCSI CD-ROM, my advice is to just get a good SCSI host adapter and hang the CD-ROM off that.

Speaker Systems

All this sound stuff is of no value unless you've got some speakers so that you can hear it. You *can* run some sound cards through the internal PC speaker, but *don't*: it's monaural and of pretty low quality.

The speakers you'll likely get will be stereo speakers. They can either be externally powered or they will just run off the sound card's output; in general, a simple pair of speakers should not require power. More specialized woofer/speaker sets will pretty much always include an amplifier, so plan for a power outlet near the PC for the speakers if you can.

Make sure that the speakers are shielded, so that the magnetism they create is minimal. They'll be sitting near your PC, so it's quite likely that you'll end up putting floppies near them; an unshielded speaker can damage data on a hard or floppy disk if the disk is close enough to the speaker.

If you're a real computer music or game aficionado, then it might be worth the $100+ to pick up a speaker/woofer combination. We tend to think of PC sound as being kind of tinny, but that's mainly because of the $20 speakers that most of us buy: PC sound cards can put out CD audio quality sound, with the right speakers.

Installation Tips

There truthfully isn't much to say about installing sound cards that is special, except for two things.

First, I've mentioned it before, but please be careful where you put the speakers. I briefly mounted my Sony satellite-and-woofer system atop my monitor, and the picture looked like it was melting around the edges.

Second, when you install that sound card, now more than ever, document everything. The Sound Blaster 16, a popular sound card, requires *three* I/O addresses, *two* DMA channels, and an IRQ ("in a pear tree...") to top it all off. If you are clueless about what's in your machine before you install such a board, then it's high time that you do an inventory.

CHAPTER

TWENTY-THREE

23

You Oughta Be in Pictures: Video Capture

■ Video system components

■ Installing video boards

■ A look at video capture software

■ Compression techniques

Once, we transferred most of our technical knowledge through books. All you needed to receive information from a book was sufficient light to read, functional eyes, literacy skills, and the desire to learn. Computers could display the written word, but truthfully in a lower-quality manner than could books; it is considerably easier to read text from a book than from a video screen. Nevertheless, computers have been until recently little more than electronic books.

The pervasiveness of television and videotape has made non-written communications popular and, actually, *more* than popular—it's something of a requirement in some sectors. In response to this, moving video is being integrated more and more into PC software.

The word processor or spreadsheet of tomorrow will likely do the same things that it does today. What will be different will be how the program talks back to you. Instead of a dialog box that says, "Save file before exit?" it may pop up a video window containing an animation of Reddy Kilowatt (or his buddy Smarty CPU or whatever) saying (out of your speaker), "Hey, you don't want to lose this great stuff you've been doing, do you? Should I save this before the program closes?" Similarly, an online help file may incorporate a context-sensitive helper that pops up in a small video screen to explain how to do a mail merge, consolidate a bunch of spreadsheets, or whatever. All of the video clips of your online tutor will just be video captures of an actor/instructor.

E-mail can be affected by video: for less than a hundred dollars you can get a simple video camera that looks like a golf ball. You clip the camera to your monitor, hook the camera to your video capture board, Firewire, or USB port, and you record your message in full motion video and sound. Then you package the video clip into an e-mail message, and your recipient can hear your voice and see you. With a product like Intel's ProShare, you can hold interactive video conversations.

Just a few years ago, the state of the art in computer-assisted presentations was pretty color graphs. Now it's pretty color graphs with inserts of moving, talking figures. How do you accomplish all of these moving video feats? With video capture hardware and software. In this chapter, you'll learn what kinds of hardware and software you'll need, how to install it, and how to make it work.

Video Capture Overview

There's a lot to learn about doing video capture. Summarized, it looks like Figure 23.1.

FIGURE 23.1:

Creating video capture clips

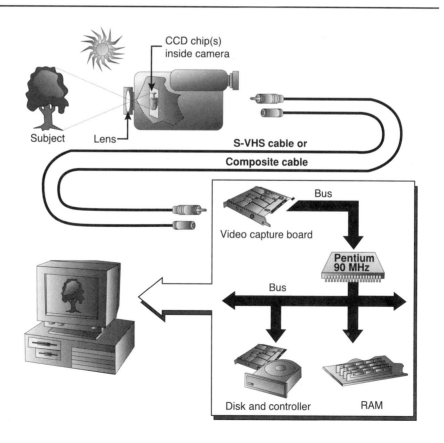

There's a lot to that; don't worry, I'll explain it all in this chapter. Briefly, however, creating video capture clips involves three main steps:

1. Connecting and configuring the video capture hardware and software.

2. Capturing the image with video capture hardware.

3. Running the resulting video file through an offline compressor for long-term storage.

The last step is useful because video compression software today will allow you to make your files much smaller and still maintain pretty good sound and image quality.

Video Capture System Components

Let's go shopping for video capture stuff. I'm not going to tell you what brands of things to buy—at the speed that this business moves, any brand-name specifics would probably be obsolete by the time you read this. Instead, I'll highlight the kinds of equipment you'll need.

There are four pieces to a video capture system:

- The video camera
- The cable connecting the camera to the video capture board
- The video capture board
- The rest of the PC doing the capture

These pieces are illustrated in Figure 23.2.

FIGURE 23.2:

The pieces of a video
capture system

To do video capture you need a camera, cable, video capture board, and your PC.

All four components rely on each other, making the whole thing like a chain, no stronger than its weakest link. Get a lousy camera, and you get lousy images. Great cables and the world's best video capture system will only ensure that you get really full-fidelity reproductions of the camera's lousy images. A million-dollar camera's super-high-quality images are useless if your capture board can't capture anything bigger than 160×120 pixel images. You're wasting your time unless you've got a good camera, good cables, a good capture board, and a powerful PC to back it all up.

The Camera

Video cameras come with a lot of options these days with names like Electronic Image Stabilization, autofocus, autoshutter, and tons more. Don't get distracted by the doodads; camera image quality boils down to three things:

- You've got to have good lighting and composition on your subject.

- You need good optics—that is, the lens or lenses—on the camera.

- The camera must receive the image with a high-quality imaging chip, an internal component in the camera.

The composition and lighting I leave up to you; but let's take a look at the optics and electronics end of image generation.

Lenses

The light from your image goes first through the camera's lens. Some lenses are plastic; some are glass. Although glass is better, I wouldn't worry much about a camera's lenses if you're doing video capture. Why? The low resolution of video capture (as compared to film) means that even the worst camera optics will deliver resolution beyond video capture's capabilities.

While plastic lenses can produce a credible video capture image, they are *much* easier to scratch than are glass lenses, so be sure to keep the lens cap on your camera when you're not using it, and clean the lens with a soft cloth and a lens cleaner. If you need to use special lenses for your video capture, then you might look into the higher-end camcorders that allow you to use normal camera lenses.

CCD Chip

The lens focuses the image onto the part of the video camera that records it. While most video images are stored and transmitted in analog formats (videotape is analog, and so are the two most common video interfaces), the image is originally recorded digitally, believe it or not. Modern cameras capture video images with a chip that's very similar to a memory chip, a chip called a *charge coupled device*, or CCD. A simplified version of how it works is something like this: a CCD is a memory chip that doesn't have a cover on it, just an array of memory cells. The camera electronics fill up all the memory areas, and then the lens applies the light to the exposed memory cells. Light affects how much data remains in the memory cells, so the camera circuitry figures out how much light is on various parts of the image by reading data in the various part of the memory array.

CCDs vary by how big they are, as measured by the total number of pixels that they detect. The total number of pixels on a camera's CCD ranges from about 250,000 to 570,000.

While that sounds like lots of pixels, it's really not. In order to store color information, the light from the lens is passed through a *stripe mask*, a colored filter that filters out all but red from some pixels, blue from some, and green from others. As a result, some of the pixels then become red-sensitive, green-sensitive, or blue-sensitive. Each complete *color pixel*, then, is composed of three of the chip's original pixels, so divide the original pixel count by three to get the total number of colored pixels that the camera truly has. Then, as the CCD is a square array of elements, take the square root of the resulting number to determine the CCD's horizontal and vertical resolution. You can see the composition of color pixels in Figure 23.3.

FIGURE 23.3:

Three pixels make up a single color pixel

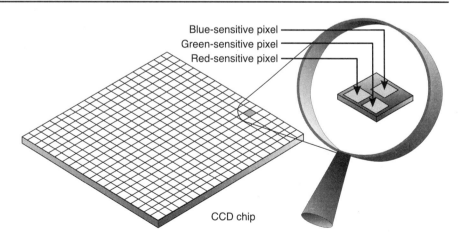

Blue-sensitive pixel
Green-sensitive pixel
Red-sensitive pixel

CCD chip

For example, a very common CCD has 270,000 elements. That becomes 270,000/3 = 90,000 color pixels. The square root of 90,000 is 300, so a 270,000-pixel CCD yields a color image with a resolution of 300 × 300.

Basic VHS cameras usually have 250,000–280,000-pixel CCDs, for resolutions of 300 to 306 pixels horizontally and vertically. If you're going to buy a VHS camera, then it really doesn't matter which one you buy, as the CCD on one will be about the same as any other.

Better cameras, in contrast, are equipped with an essential interface, the super VHS, also known as the S-VHS or Y/C interface. (I'll explain the details of the Y/C interface a little later.) When I surveyed the consumer camcorder market, I found that about one fifth of the camcorders are equipped with a Y/C interface. Those Y/C-equipped cameras have CCDs with pixel totals of 380K (356 × 356), 410K (370 × 370), 470K (396 × 396), and 570K (436 × 436), with the 470K chip most common.

My recommendation is that you purchase the cheapest Y/C-equipped camcorder that you can find; there's not all that much difference between the most common resolution, 396 × 396, and the highest I found, 436 × 436. If, on the other hand, you want much better quality, and can afford to spend more money, you can get cameras with *three* CCDs: one for red, one for green, one for blue; *each* CCD has a resolution of about 640 × 640. I don't recommend that because, as you'll see, about the maximum resolution you'll see out of a video capture system is 420 × 483.

No two chips and no two lenses are the same. Every year sees improvement in the CCD market. To find the best camera for your money, your best bet is to go to a showroom that sells lots of cameras. Connect different cameras viewing the same image to the same monitor, one at a time, to get the best idea of which camera produces the best image.

Don't presume that the most expensive camera is the best. Remember that it's not a camera—it's a *camcorder*. A camcorder is a camera *and* a VCR, so you're paying for both a camera and a VCR. In a VHS camcorder, S-VHS camcorder, and Hi8 camcorder, the terms VHS, S-VHS, and Hi8 do *not* describe the camera; they describe the videocassette recorder that is part of the camcorder— and *you really don't care what kind of VCR is part of your camera*. Why? Because I strongly advise you to do your video captures straight from the camera, not from tapes made with the camera.

The reason for capturing right from the camera is simple. The process of recording data to a VCR is an analog recording method, like photocopying a document. When you store an image to tape, you're losing some of the image quality, just as when you photocopy an original document. When you play that image back, you'll lose more quality as the image (1) is affected by electronic noise in the VCR and (2) is transported over a cable to the PC capture board. If, in contrast, you capture straight from the camera, then the only image loss is in the original digitization done by the capture board, and any cable-caused signal loss. Capturing from tape is something like making a photocopy of a photocopy.

Before I understood the general irrelevance of the VCR electronics in a camera, I went out and bought an S-VHS camera because I thought that it would give me a better picture. In retrospect, this was a pretty dumb thing to do, because the mere fact that the VCR on a camcorder was an S-VHS said nothing about the *important* thing—the camera's pixel count. It turned out later not to be a terrible buy, however, as there is an informal relationship between VCR quality and CCD quality in camcorders: as I mentioned before, camcorders with a Y/C interface, which every S-VHS has, tend to have better CCDs. But remember: the two things you're looking for are a Y/C interface and a pixel count of 470,000 or higher.

The VCR

As I've just said, part of a camcorder is a VCR. I've also just said that the VCR part of a camcorder is pretty much irrelevant to your needs. Having said that, however, let me amend it to add this one exception: you will sometimes have to capture to tape because whatever you're capturing can't come into your computer room, and you'd rather not drag your whole camera, PC, and cables to whatever you're capturing.

So, if you *must* capture to tape, use S-VHS or an 8mm format in preference to VHS. That's because of all of the recording formats in the video world, VHS is the absolute worst: it retains a low-resolution image. In fact, in ascending order of desirability, VHS is the worst; super VHS is better, and Hi8 is better yet.

What does "better" mean? Talk to TV people, and you'll find that they speak a different language than you and I when it comes to resolution. First of all, video formats—whether broadcast, S-VHS, VHS, Hi8, laser, or whatever, all share the same vertical resolution—483 visible pixels. The TV paints 483 horizontal lines as its electron beam travels from the top of the screen to the bottom of the screen. Actually, it paints *525* lines, but some of them get lost in TV overhead, making 483 the best number I can get for vertical resolution.

The difference in video products is, believe it or not, *horizontal* resolution. No one *ever* quotes vertical resolution because everything shows 483 lines top-to-bottom, at least in theory. But everyone quotes *horizontal* resolution. Horizontal resolution is defined something like this: if I were to point a camera at a piece of paper with a bunch of parallel vertical lines on it, how many of those lines could I fit on a screen before they blurred into each other?

The lowest answer to that question is VHS, which will show only about 200 lines. Therefore, VHS resolution in computer terms is around 200 pixels wide by 483 pixels deep. S-VHS is about 420 × 483. Broadcast video is around 360 × 483 in resolution. The composite interface can support around 240 × 483, and the Y/C (S-VHS) interface, like the tape format, is near 420 × 483 in resolution. The differences in resolution are illustrated in Figure 23.4.

FIGURE 23.4:

Comparing video resolution

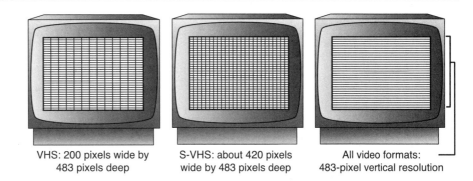

VHS: 200 pixels wide by 483 pixels deep

S-VHS: about 420 pixels wide by 483 pixels deep

All video formats: 483-pixel vertical resolution

I'm virtually certain that I'm going to get letters on this, so I'd ask that the video experts in the audience please note: no one in the video industry publishes vertical by horizontal pixel equivalents, at least not ones that can be tested and agreed upon as standard. I spoke to four people who were all undoubtedly experts on video, and got different resolutions—sometimes *very* different resolutions—from each. Please don't write to tell me that I'm all wrong unless you've got a repeatable, definitive reference for your resolutions.

The Camera/PC Video Interface

Once you've got the information in the camera, you've got to get it to the capture equipment. Cameras and VCRs tend to have one or more of three kinds of outputs:

- Some cameras and all VCRs have a radio frequency (RF) output, the kind that goes directly into a television's antenna connection. Your video capture equipment probably won't support this interface, and you wouldn't want it in any case.

- Most cameras and VCRs have an interface known as an NTSC, composite, or simply video interface. It's one of two common interfaces on a video capture board. It is the minimum quality interface that you'd use to connect a video source (a camera or a VCR) to a video capture board.

- As I mentioned earlier, better-quality consumer camcorders and VCRs have an output labeled S-VHS, known as a Super VHS or Y/C interface. It is the preferable interface between a video source and a capture board.

To understand these interfaces in detail, you've got to understand a bit about how video information gets shuttled around in the video and TV world. Explaining them will require that I take RF, composite, and Y/C a bit out of order.

Component versus Composite Interfaces Color signals all boil down to three simple or *primary* colors: red, green, and blue. You can describe any color as a combination of those three colors, as you can see in Figure 23.5.

FIGURE 23.5:

Primary colors combine to form other colors

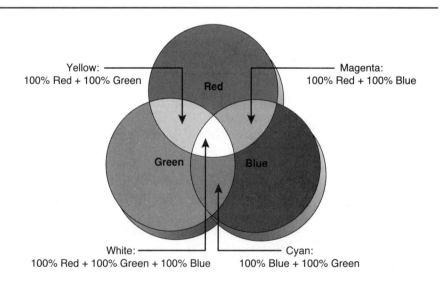

Yellow:
100% Red + 100% Green

Magenta:
100% Red + 100% Blue

Red

Green   Blue

White:
100% Red + 100% Green + 100% Blue

Cyan:
100% Blue + 100% Green

Basically, color video cameras record pictures by breaking a picture down into a grid of dots called picture elements or pixels. The camera senses the degree of red intensity, green intensity, and blue intensity of each pixel, transmitting that information to the recording equipment (the VCR, tape deck, or whatever). Figure 23.6 illustrates how this works.

FIGURE 23.6:

The camera records pictures as an array of pixels containing red, green, and blue color information

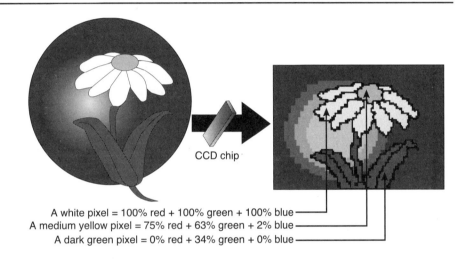

CCD chip

A white pixel = 100% red + 100% green + 100% blue
A medium yellow pixel = 75% red + 63% green + 2% blue
A dark green pixel = 0% red + 34% green + 0% blue

As a matter of fact, professional-quality video cameras connect to videocassette recorders of similar professional quality via an interface with *five* cables—one each for the red, green, and blue signals, and two more cables for synchronizing the signal. (Ever adjusted the "vertical hold" or "horizontal hold" knobs on a TV? That's what those cables transmit: vertical synchronization and horizontal synchronization information.) An interface of that type, a video interface that uses separate cables for each primary color, is called a *component* interface. Not all video interface types are component interfaces, however; alternative approaches blend the red, green, and blue signals together into a single-cable *composite* interface. Video interfaces are, then, either component or composite in nature. The two are contrasted in Figure 23.7.

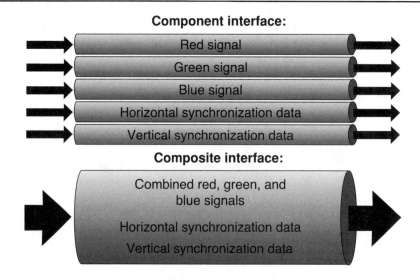

Component interfaces are preferable, because keeping the color signals separate allows higher-quality signal transmission. Composite video, on the other hand, is cheaper to build hardware-wise, and so most camcorders and VCRs in North America support only a composite-type interface called National Television System Committee, or NTSC. NTSC is the North American standard video interface format for broadcast color TV, developed in 1953 (an earlier black-and-white version of the NTSC standard was established in 1941). Y/C is an example of a kind of component interface. You see a variation of the RGB component interface on the back of some high-quality computer monitors; not only do they have the common 15-pin VGA D-shell connector, they may also have five BNC connectors for the professional RGB component interface that I described in the last paragraph.

From Black and White to Color Before getting any further into this, let me warn you: understanding video interfaces is a bit difficult because the video industry "just growed that way." If the video business were starting out now, every piece of video equipment would probably use the simple, intuitive five-cable RGB interface. Like the muddle of extended, expanded, and conventional memory, no one planned this—it just turned out this way.

As you know, video didn't start out with *color* transmission; the first TVs were black and white, or monochrome. Actually, neither term is really correct; it's better to describe colorless video images as *grayscale*. In grayscale, video images are represented as pixels, as in color video, except each pixel can only assume a shade of gray. But what is "gray?" Technically, gray is any color created by mixing equal amounts of red, green, and blue light. No red, green, or blue yields black; full intensity red, green, and blue yield bright white. Varying intensities in between create lighter or darker grays. Although we're used to a world of color, we can easily interpret grayscale images; we do it whenever we see a black-and-white TV show or movie, or most pictures in newspapers. The combinations of red, green, and blue that produce some various shades of gray are illustrated in Figure 23.8.

FIGURE 23.8:

Combinations of red, green, and blue produce various shades of gray

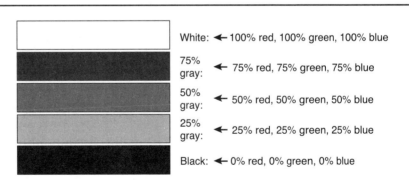

White: ← 100% red, 100% green, 100% blue

75% gray: ← 75% red, 75% green, 75% blue

50% gray: ← 50% red, 50% green, 50% blue

25% gray: ← 25% red, 25% green, 25% blue

Black: ← 0% red, 0% green, 0% blue

The original video equipment and TV broadcast equipment was designed in the grayscale-only days for grayscale-only signals. Basically, black-and-white TV signals consist of a series of information about the intensity of each pixel on the TV screen, information that tells the TV how much to light up each part of the screen, producing black and white images. A whole industry grew up in the '50s around grayscale TV: TV networks and studios invested millions of dollars in equipment that they obviously wouldn't want to see become obsolete. Millions of households invested hundreds of millions of dollars in TV sets that they wouldn't want to see become obsolete.

Which is why the advent of color TV in the 1960s posed a problem.

You see, everybody *wanted* color TV. Colorful pictures are more interesting than grayscale pictures to look at. But nobody wanted a new color system that would make the existing black-and-white TVs obsolete. NBC just couldn't say, "As of 1 January 1953, we're going to stop broadcasting old-style black-and-white signals and start broadcasting the new color signals. Now, the color signals won't work with your old TVs, so it's just too bad for all of you who've faithfully watched our network all this time—you'll have to go out and buy a new, expensive, color TV."

So the broadcast companies devised a method for transmitting color signals whereby the old grayscale signal still got transmitted, but with a separate color portion added. Old black-and-white TVs wouldn't look for the color information, and so they would still work fine, displaying grayscale images. But color TVs would know to look for that extra color information, and display it. As the color information got pasted on the back of the existing grayscale signal, there wasn't much room for the color information. As a result, NTSC color video isn't of a very high quality. That's why the television industry began broadcasting the new High Definition TV, or HDTV, this year. Remember that the color signal starts off as three pieces of information: its red value, its green value, and its blue value. Each of those values is measured in *lumens*, a measure akin in some ways to voltage; it actually measures the number of photons striking some small area. Black and white TV equipment converts the red, green, and blue values to a single grayscale value called the *luminance* of the pixel, or the Y value. (Y isn't an abbreviation of any word, it comes from a 1930s color model that described colors in terms of a set of X, Y, and Z axes, rather than red/green/blue.) The formula used to create the grayscale pixel (depicted graphically in Figure 23.9) looks like the following:

Luminance of the grayscale pixel (Y of a video signal) =

0.59 × (luminance of green) +

0.11 × (luminance of blue) +

0.30 × (luminance of red)

FIGURE 23.9:

Formula used to create the grayscale pixel

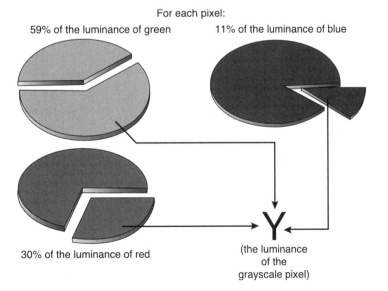

For each pixel:

59% of the luminance of green

11% of the luminance of blue

30% of the luminance of red

Y

(the luminance of the grayscale pixel)

You see that Y can be derived arithmetically from R, G, and B. Notice that green has the highest coefficient, 0.59—nearly 60 percent of the colors that you see depend on green! Of course, no one knows exactly *why* we see green so well, but one theory works something like this: most animals *lack* color vision, and see only in grayscale. Millions of years ago, however, our many-times-removed ancestors lived in trees as pre-primate, lemur-like creatures. Living in the green, leafy canopy of a jungle means having to detect predators who attempt to mimic the colors of the jungle, like the green of a tree-living python or the shadow-like stripes of a tiger. There are two ways to detect predators: by their movement and by color sense. Most animals detect other animals by motion. Our ancestors added a remarkable ability to see extremely fine differences in color, like the few-wavelengths difference in color between a green snake and the leaves that it hid in. Since a lot of their world was the green of leaves, green played a disproportionate role in their color sense, as it does today to *our* color sense. Notice also that you're most insensitive to blue; that's one reason why many people find blue to be a calming color. Looking at blues doesn't excite the optic nerve as much, which means that the ancient parts of our brains that are still looking out for predators can rest for a while.

Despite the fact that luminance contains red, green, and blue, it's not possible to deduce the original amount of red, green, and blue from a given luminance, any more than it's possible for me to ask you, "If I made $30,000 dollars this year, some from consulting and some from writing, then how much did I make from consulting and how much did I make from writing?" I haven't given you enough information to deduce the answer to my question. If you just transmit the luminance information, you haven't sent enough information to allow a color TV to reconstruct the R, G, and B.

But suppose I rephrase the question this way:

"I made $30,000 dollars last year from consulting and writing. I made half of my income from consulting and half from writing.

How much money did I make from consulting, and how much from writing?" You see, I asked you to derive two values—consulting income and writing income. But when I gave you only one piece of information—the sum of both incomes—I didn't give you enough information to compute the separate income amounts. When I added the second piece of information, however—the ratio of the two incomes—you had enough information to solve the problem. So, to solve for two values, you need two pieces of information.

In the same way, the color TV engineers knew that black and white TV was already using Y, so they wanted color TVs to *continue* to use Y (so that they'd be backward compatible with black-and-white signals). Y is derived from R, G, and B, but Y is only one piece of information. They'd need to add two more pieces of information onto the TV signal in order for a color TV to be able to reassemble the R, G, and B information.

Here's where it gets ugly: they decided to create two more signals composed of R, G, and B, but, unlike luminance, these two new signals, named I and Q, really don't correspond to anything in our experience. (Remember that Y corresponds to the grayscale part of the picture, the part you'd see if you turned down the color adjustment knob on your color TV set). For the curious, the formulas for I and Q are illustrated in Figure 23.10.

FIGURE 23.10:

Computing values for I and Q

$$I = 0.74 * (R - Y) - 0.27 * (B - Y)$$

$$Q = 0.48 * (R - Y) + 0.41 * (B - Y)$$

The I and Q signals are blended so that they can be easily broken apart with a technique called Quadrature Amplitude Modulation, or QAM. The entire process of QAM is a bit complex, but you'll get the idea of how it works if you think of it this way: with QAM, you start with a baseline signal called a *carrier wave*. Like all waves, it has an *amplitude*, a *frequency*, and a *phase*. QAM modifies the carrier wave's amplitude to match the I signal, and changes the carrier's phase to store the Q value. Phase and amplitude are different characteristics of a wave, like the height and weight of a person, so they can be modified somewhat independently of each other. The combined I/Q signal is called *chrominance*, which is usually abbreviated C.

So, to sum up where we've gotten so far: R, G, and B don't get transmitted as R, G, and B, because luminance or Y transmission has been central to television broadcasting since TV was invented. Color television tiptoes around the limits of Y-based black-and-white transmission by creating separate I and Q signals, then combining them with the Y signal in such a way that they're separable by the receiving TV. The combined Y, Q signal, and I is the composite video signal that I've discussed in this section and that is illustrated in Figure 23.11.

FIGURE 23.11:

The composite video signal

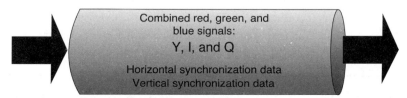

Composite interface:

Combined red, green, and blue signals:

Y, I, and Q

Horizontal synchronization data
Vertical synchronization data

Those composite signals are then converted into broadcast TV waves, where they are received by TVs, both color and black-and-white. Black-and-white TVs don't know to look for I and Q, so they see only Y, and are happy. Color TVs separate out (decode) Y, I, and Q, convert them to R, G, and B, and then display color on their screens.

As you've seen, the composite signal is also known as an NTSC signal. It blends Y, I, and Q. Separating them back out isn't a perfect process, which is one reason why a composite interface isn't the best available interface. The other kind of interface that you find on some video equipment is the S-VHS or Y/C interface, as I said before. Now you're in a better position to understand why it's called that: there are separate wires in the cable for the luminance (Y) signal and the chrominance (C) signal. Note that I'm going to call this interface the Y/C rather than the S-VHS because there are both an interface and a video tape format called S-VHS; there's only a Y/C interface, reducing any confusion.

The RF inputs and outputs that you see are for the broadcast TV signal, which is the messiest of all the interfaces: not only is it composite, but it also has been modulated onto a radio frequency carrier, adding even more noise. No video capture board that I know of accepts RF signals, although the PC-TV boards that allow you to view television in a window on your PC screen have RF inputs.

Before leaving this topic, there's another format to discuss. You've learned about RGB and YIQ, but there's one more format used in video capture—YUV. The Y in YUV is the same as in YIQ, but U and V are just two different ways to represent chrominance. Video capture boards may store the capture data as Y, U, and V data rather than R, G, and B data.

The Camera/PC Audio Interface

If you want to capture audio with your videos, you'll discover that most video capture boards do not capture sound. Instead, you'll have to have a PC sound card of some kind in order to make videos with audio included.

In order to capture video *and* audio, you'll probably have to limit the quality of your audio recordings to 8-bit, 11kHz monaural formats.

The Cables

Just one piece of advice: get good ones. The skinny S-VHS cables that come with the VCR or camcorder can't provide the noise resistance that a third-party cable like a Monster cable can (they're the company that makes what are probably the best audio and video cables; you can find their stuff in higher-end electronics stores).

There are composite cables and S-VHS or Y/C cables. They look like the ones in Figure 23.12.

FIGURE 23.12:

Video cables

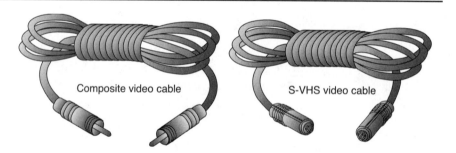

Even if you don't buy the really high-quality cables, buy *some* third-party cable. The cables that ship with video boards are usually of minimum quality, and a place like Radio Shack can sell you a better cable.

The shorter the cable, the less signal loss, so keep your cables as short as possible.

The Capture Board

The thing that makes your PC able to accept and record moving video is the video capture board. Video boards differ in a few ways:

- Some video boards support *overlay*, a feature whereby you can see video displayed in real time in a window on your computer.

- Most video boards support some kind of on-board real time compression hardware. The exact method for doing that compression varies, leading to more or less effective compression options.

- Some video boards can't save moving video and are only capable of grabbing still pictures.

- Most video boards have both a composite and a Y/C connector, but be sure that whatever board you buy has a Y/C S-VHS connector.

As always, a faster board would require a faster bus interface. Of the things that I just mentioned, let's get the important ones out of the way.

Avoid Still Capture Boards

First of all, make sure that the capture board can capture *moving* video. There are a few video capture boards out there in the $100 price range that sound like a good deal, but they capture only stills.

Do stills sound like all that you need? Then these boards are *still* (no pun intended) not a good deal. Unless your image is totally still, then your capture gets a visual side-effect that makes it look like you're viewing the image through venetian blinds.

Real-Time Compression Features

You've already seen why compression is so very important to video work. Those 320 × 240 windows are pretty small, but even at 15fps they produce about 3.5Mbps of data in a completely raw format. Shove that much data down most hard disks' throats, and you'll end up with a lot of lost data. While you *can* capture data to RAM, which is faster than disk by a good bit (see the upcoming section "Don't Drop Those Frames: Capture to Memory or Disk?"), most of us can't afford a few gigabytes of RAM with which to capture. How, then, to get high-volume video data onto a relatively low-speed drive? By pre-crunching the data down to size. Video capture boards do that with on-board compression hardware. For example, Intel's Smart Video Recorder Pro contains an i750 chip, a RISC chip that actually contains four pipelines!

Virtually all video capture boards do some kind of real-time compression as they capture the video data. Most offer the option of a compression technique called YUV9, which is pretty standard, and another technique, which can compress data better, but which is specific to that particular capture board.

The downside of the board-specific real-time compressor is that while it greatly improves your ability to capture long video sequences, it significantly reduces the video image quality. As I'll explain in an upcoming section, you usually *don't* want to capture data compressed by the video board, as the compression technique causes this degradation of image quality. If you can live with some image degradation, however, then the proprietary real-time compression support on most video capture boards will be useful; again, this will be clearer when I explain captures to memory versus captures to disk.

Overlay or Preview?

Video capture boards show you either the actual video signal as it arrives to the capture board, or the image that they're processing. In the first case—an overlay is the term—you see a window within your Windows screen (I'll assume that you're doing Windows, although there are a few tools around for other operating systems) and full-motion video. In the second case, you see the image that's been processed by the sound card, or the *preview* of the captured image. Previews will always be inferior in quality to overlays, as previews are limited by the color depth of your video board—if your video board shows only 256 colors, then you'll see a 256-color rendering of the 16-million-color image. As I've said before, today's computers and capture boards can't keep up with the 30 frames per second speed of broadcast video signals. In a preview window, the colors will look "muddier" because Windows attempts to take the millions of colors in the incoming image and convert them into combinations of its 256 colors, a process called *dithering*. For example, if you had a video screen that could show *only* red, green, or blue in one intensity—each color was just "on" or "off," instead of capable of varying intensities—then you could fool your eye into seeing yellow by displaying a lot of green pixels interspersed with an equal number of red pixels. That would be a dithered yellow.

It sounds like an overlay board is more desirable than a preview board, but I'd tend to disagree. Overlay boards show you a nice, colorful, smooth picture, but that's usually not the picture that you end up with, so it's not very helpful. Further, overlay boards are more difficult to install.

When I described overlays, you may have wondered just how an overlay board can display 16-million-color video on a Windows desktop with a video driver that only supports 256 colors; sounds too good to be true, eh? Overlay boards accomplish this by modifying the way your video board works. Most every VGA board has an edge or pin-header connector on it called the *feature connector*. An overlay board requires that you run a cable from the feature connector on the VGA to a similar connector on the overlay board, and that you then disconnect the monitor from the video port on the back of the VGA and connect it to a similar-looking connector on the video capture board. This means that now the video capture board can "process" the signals from the VGA board before they get to the monitor. It is the hardware on the video capture board that allows full-motion video and 16 million colors. Essentially, it makes a window on your screen into a TV set. In fact, there are some boards available that are not video capture boards at all, but simply overlay boards. Equipped with an antenna input and tuner circuit, they allow you to watch TV in a window on your Windows desktop. (Of course, they cost three times as much as a small portable TV would, so it's not clear why you'd want them.)

An odd side effect of the overlay is that the TV part of the window is not under the control of Windows (or whatever operating system is being used); it's just a kind of "hole" that the hardware fills. That means that if you try to capture an overlay window with the alt-Print Screen or Print Screen key, then you won't get the image. As the operating system doesn't control that portion of the screen, it cannot capture that part of the screen.

The CPU, Bus, and Disk Systems in Video Capture

I hope I've made clear by now that the whole name of the game in video capture is data transfer. There's lots of data to shovel around, and no room for your hardware to stop and "catch its breath," so to speak. That argues for a fast, wide bus.

Add audio capture, and you've got an extra problem: now there are two boards with real-time demands running simultaneously, throwing interrupts at the CPU, and, again, there's no time for either board to "catch its breath." That argues for bus mastering, so that both boards can transfer data to memory or disk without having to wait for the CPU.

It would seem, then, that the optimal bus for video capture would be PCI, offering speed, width, and bus mastering. Failing that, EISA or MCA make the most sense, and so you should look for a video capture board that uses one of those buses.

Installing a Video Capture Board

Installing a video capture board is just like installing any other board. Most video capture boards come with a software setup routine, and you must pick an I/O address, a hardware interrupt, and sometimes a memory "overlay" window.

Before you try to install the board, make sure that you've got a video source around that you can use to test the board. Every video capture board I've ever installed came with a self-test program; run it. The self-test will test for basic interrupt, memory, and I/O address conflicts. Then it will try to display the image coming in from the video source (the camera or the VCR). Now, if you pass the IRQ, I/O address, and memory test, then you still may not see an image. Here are some things to try if that happens:

- Check that the cable isn't loose or incorrectly connected. S-VHS cables in particular seem to need to be firmly pushed into their sockets.

- If the video source is a camera and the screen is black, don't forget that most video cameras will shut themselves off after a while if they're not actually recording. Perhaps it's better to just run a tape in a VCR as a video source so that you don't have to worry about whether or not there's a test signal.

- Most video capture boards have both composite and S-VHS inputs. They automatically figure out which input is active, but sometimes they guess wrong. The video capture software that comes with your board will usually allow you to force the board to use either the composite or the S-VHS input.

- Even if you pass the I/O address, IRQ, and memory tests, double-check that you don't have a conflict on one of those.

Once the board is up and running, it's time to try out the video capture software.

Running the Video Capture Software

The point of all your hard work so far was to grab a video. Now let's try it.

Start from a Known Video Source

The best bet for your first time around is to use a fairly good-quality video to practice with. I'd recommend that you hook up a VCR to your video capture board and just continuously run a commercial videotape. It's only VHS quality, granted, but it's going to be correctly color balanced, show decent brightness and contrast, and will serve as a good reference point.

You should be able to see the actual video image on a video monitor in addition to your PC's monitor. Set up the VCR and a

TV near the table. Most VCRs have both an antenna output and an NTSC composite video output—it's usually just labeled Video out, or the like. Connect the TV to the Antenna out connector, leaving the Video out connector available for you to connect to the video capture board.

Note that you should record off a VCR only while you're getting comfortable with video capture. Remember that you should do your captures straight off the camera into the capture board; saving to tape, then capturing from tape, adds a generation of the "photocopy" effect.

Use the Right Video Mode on Your PC

Before going any further, find a video mode that works well for your capture. You want a low-resolution driver, as high-resolution drivers must keep track of more pixels and so slow down the system. As video is very colorful, however, you want a 16-million color driver if possible. The best video mode is probably a 640×480 mode with 16 million colors. Whatever your options are, just pick 640×480 resolution and then choose the most colors that your board will support.

Adjust Contrast, Brightness, and Color

Now that you've got the TV showing you what the video *thinks* that it should look like, run the video capture software on your computer and take a look at the picture in the overlay/preview window. You're likely to see that the colors on the pictures are different. Use the video capture software's "video source options" command or the like (every program has a different name for it) to adjust brightness, contrast, and colors.

Some systems provide separate slider controls for red, green, and blue. Others offer sliders with names like saturation, tint, or hue.

Saturation refers to the purity of the color. Shine a red light on a white wall, and you'll see a red area on the wall. Shine a red light *and* a white light on the wall, and the resulting wall color changes; we'd say that it is "washed out." Adding white light *desaturates* a color. Pure colors are saturated; impure colors are desaturated.

Tint and *hue* are intended to mimic dials and knobs with similar names and functions on a TV set. They're compromises, and (in my opinion) not very good ones. As there are three things to adjust—red, green, and blue intensity—it's obviously impossible to provide all possible red/green/blue combinations on a single dial. Instead, then, these dials allow you to bias the colors between extreme red, extreme green, and anywhere in between. The bad news, then, about these controls is that they don't let you play with the blue setting. But, then, recall that blue is the least important of the three primary video colors.

Frame Size and Frame Rate

Next, you'll actually capture some moving images. You must choose frame size and frame rate. You'll usually have frame size options up to 320 × 240 for moving captures, and 640 × 480 for still captures. You can set any frame rate.

A 320 × 240 frame of 24-bit color will require 230,400 bytes to store. Using 15 frames per second would provide a raw data rate of 230,400 × 15, or 3,456,000 bytes per second, as I've said before. The relationship between frame size and data rate is illustrated in Figure 23.13.

FIGURE 23.13:

Relationship between
frame size and
data rate

1 frame (320 x 240 pixels, 24-bit color) = 230,400 bytes

|◄──────── 15 frames/second = 3,456,000 bytes/second ────────►|

That's a lot of data to shovel around. In contrast, 15 frames of size 160 × 120 at 24-bit color require only 864,000 bytes per second transfer. Assuming you had a high performance hard disk that could, say, capture data at about 1.7MB/second (not an impossible rate for a wide SCSI drive), then you'd be able to capture about 30 frames per second straight to disk. (You can capture to either RAM or disk; you'll learn about the details in the next section.)

The whole idea of 160 × 120 captures certainly sounds like it'll make your captures easy, and it will, because small frames don't require as much horsepower to record as do large frames. But you can't *see* small frames. My recommendation is that you do whatever is necessary to capture at 320 × 240 resolution, and at least at 15 frames per second.

Don't Drop Those Frames: Capture to Memory or Disk?

Depending on your capture program, you'll be asked whether to save the captured images to memory or disk. Neither option is perfect.

If you save to disk, then you'll find that it's likely that your disk drive won't be able to keep up with the stream of data. When that happens, the video compression software just plain *drops* any frames that the disk can't write out in time. You want to avoid dropped frames at all costs for two reasons:

- Dropped frames make the resulting video look jerky. The screen sits frozen for a few tenths of a second, waiting for the next frame to appear.

- Missing frames crash some video editors, like Asymetrix's Desktop Video Producer; DVP emits dozens of error dialog boxes if you try to do anything with a file containing dropped frames.

The way to avoid dropped frames is to capture the video data to *RAM*, not disk. As you know, CPU-to-memory transfers are quite fast, but are limited by the relative scarcity of RAM. For example, if you've got the Intel Smart Video Recorder Pro and 16MB of RAM on your system, and assuming that you're running a Windows-based video capture system, then you'll probably only have about 8MB available to receive the captured data. If capturing in 320×240 at 15fps in "raw" format, you'll end up with a data transfer rate of about 1.3MB/second data rate. (I know that number is different from the 3,456,000 bytes per second that I just computed, but the Intel board requires that you record using a basic compression technique called YUV9 that I'll cover later.) At that rate, you'll fill up your 8MB in about 6 or 7 seconds.

Once the physical RAM is filled, then Windows will keep capturing, because Windows supports the idea of virtual memory paging, wherein free disk space is used like RAM. That doesn't really help, however, as paging just uses disk space to stand in for actual RAM—and it was the relatively slow speed of disk that led to the original problem.

So RAM capture is preferable because you don't drop frames, but it's limited. Capturing to disk means that you've got more free space to play with, but you can't shove data at it too quickly. Which is the right answer? It depends; you'll use each method at a different time.

Captures to Disk

What this means is that, if you capture to disk, you'll have to reduce the flow of video capture data so that you don't overwhelm the maximum speed of the disk interface. You can do that in these ways:

- The capture process can't be slowed down by any extra DOS housekeeping. That means that it's much faster to allocate disk space on a defragmented disk drive, so defrag your disk before doing video capture.

- As I explained in the previous section, keep the frame rate low; 320×240 data at only five frames per second produces a raw data rate of about 1.2MB/second, which a fast hard disk can keep up with. Again, that's not the frame rate that I *recommend*, but if you must capture to disk, then it's one option.

- Again, use a smaller frame size; going from 320×240 to 160×120 cuts the data flow by a factor of four.

- Keep the audio sampling rate low, at 8 bits per sample and 11,000 samples per second.

- Capture data with a compressing codec (see the next section for more information about codecs), so that there's less data to have to store to disk. The downside of this is that the compression technique will lose some of the video capture data; again, see "Which Compression Format/Codec to Use with Capture?" later in this chapter for more information. Compression is a tradeoff, so different applications will have greater or lesser compression requirements.

- The CPU's speed is important as well. A Pentium can capture more data per second than can a 486.

Disk capture imposes limits that you'd rather avoid, but unless you've got lots of RAM, it may be your only option.

Captures to RAM

In contrast, if you capture to RAM, you won't have to worry about dropping frames until you run out of RAM. You can address that by buying more RAM. Many computers today can accept as much as 256MB of RAM or even more. In the final analysis, it is the best way to get captures done.

256MB can capture about 2 minutes of video data without data loss. 16MB lets you do about 7 or 8 seconds of capture without data loss. But what if you've got a longer video—one that exceeds the capacity of your memory?

In that case, just do a bunch of short captures, and then splice them all together with a video editor. For example, I recently wanted to capture a 15-second sequence off a videotape. I only had a 16MB system available, so I just divided up the 15 seconds into an 8-second and a 7-second capture, then used a desktop video program to splice them together.

Your system will, of course, be different from mine, and the 7 second/30 second numbers may be way off compared to your experience. Find out early on how much you can capture by just doing captures of different time lengths: try capturing 5 seconds. When the capture program is done, it will announce how many frames it dropped. Now, hopefully, a 5-second capture will show no dropped frames; if it does, then you're probably capturing 640×480 moving video, or have less than 16MB of RAM. Keep upping the length of time of the memory capture until you start dropping frames; you'll then know how long your captures can go.

Which Compression Format/Codec to Use with Capture?

You're almost ready to capture some video. You've got just one more decision to make: which codec to use.

Codec? That's another acronym, one that stands for Coder/DECoder. Its job is to compress the video data as it's captured, and decompress it as it's being viewed or edited. The program that supports the compression and decompression—the codec—is kind of like a driver. (Just to make things more confusing, some very simple codecs don't compress at all; they're called codecs for simplicity's sake.) Some codecs are specific to particular boards; some are generic.

Lossy and Lossless Compression

There are lossy and lossless compression methods. *Lossless* compression techniques allow you to compress data, and then decompress it without losing any information. For example, expressing a price of forty-nine dollars and ninety-nine cents as $49.99 takes up less space, and yet you don't lose any information in translating from the one format to the other. *Lossy* compression techniques don't exactly decompress back to the original data. Storing forty-nine dollars and ninety-nine cents as $50 yields a terrific amount of compression, and is probably fine for many uses, but it's not exactly right when decompressed into fifty dollars.

Most computer data cannot be subjected to lossy techniques; you certainly wouldn't want a spreadsheet to store your financial data "almost accurately." But image data withstands compression without corrupting its message terribly.

For example, on my hard disk I have an image of a forest. It is about 740K in size. Stored in the Windows BMP format, there's no compression, and so it ends up as a file that's 740K in size. The simplest kind of compression is *run length* compression, where you analyze the image for repeated bytes, and only store the pattern once. For example, if you've got a horizontal line of 500 blue pixels, you wouldn't store them as "blue, blue, blue…;" instead, a run length approach would store the information "repeat 'blue pixel' 500 times." Stored in a run length format, the file drops to a size of only 249K. A run length format is lossless, recall. A common *lossy* compression technique is called JPEG (after the group that invented it, the Joint Photographic Experts Group) compression. Stored as a JPEG file, the 740K file becomes 95K in size. Put the two images side by side and you don't really see the differences.

There are many techniques besides run length encoding and JPEG. One technique is *Variable Content Encoding* (VCE), where the codec scans the image for repeated patterns of bytes. For example, if the pattern "r,r,b,b,r,r,b,b,r,g,g,g,g,g,r" appeared several times in the image, then the codec would build a *dictionary* of that and other common patterns. It would give each pattern a short identifier, which it would then use in the stored file. I'm vastly oversimplifying here, but it would be kind of like if the codec stored an image of a flagpole, calling it "image01," and then encoded an image of the United Nations building. Instead of having to represent all the flagpoles in front of the UN building, the codec could skip all of the pixels devoted to representing flagpoles, storing just the one image of a flagpole and putting the instruction "insert image01 here" wherever a flagpole went. This is related to another lossless method called *Huffman encoding*. If you've ever used a file compression program like PKZIP or LHARC, then you've used Huffman encoding.

Yet another lossless technique is delta encoding. In delta encoding, video files are stored as groups composed of complete, or key, frames, followed by a series of "skeleton frames" that only record the differences from the previous frame. At 15 frames per second, most of the screen does not change from one frame to another. If the video is of a person sitting and talking to the camera—what is known as a "talking head," the phrase from which David Byrne took the name of his musical group—then the background remains unchanged perhaps throughout the entire video. That background can be three-quarters of the entire image, meaning that the delta frames need not store information about those three-quarters of the screen. The delta idea applies not only from frame to frame, but also within a frame. A codec could, for example, encode a horizontal line of the image, and then note that the next horizontal line of the image was almost identical; it wouldn't store the whole line, then, but just the changes—the deltas, in math and engineering terminology—for that line.

The idea of key frames matched with delta frames is common to many codecs, both lossy and lossless.

Codecs can do a lot of compression without loss, but the big gains are in lossy methods. Most lossy techniques rely on the fact that people are more sensitive to the grayscale image (the Y) than they are to the color (the C or the U and V, depending on the image encoding you're talking about).

The Intel Smart Video Recorder, for example, claims to record 24-bit data, but it doesn't; it uses a method whereby it captures and analyzes a four-by-four pixel area. Consider that 16 24-bit pixels are 48 bytes. The Intel capture board views each 3-byte pixel as having a byte that describes the Y (luminance) part of the pixel, and U and V bytes that describe the color, the chrominance. The raw Intel capture codec doesn't touch the Y byte, but scrutinizes the U and V bytes, compressing them to 1 bit! How? Well, a four-by-four pixel area is pretty small. As a result, you're not likely to see large color changes from pixel to pixel. For that reason, Intel can do a kind of compression called color sub-sampling. It just takes the U and V bytes for the entire four-by-four "pixel group," and averages them. The average of the 16 U bytes is 1 byte, and the average of the 16 V bytes is 1 byte. There is now 1 U byte and 1 V byte, or 16 bits, to spread out over the four-by-four area. The 16 pixels in the group each take 1 bit, and so each pixel has its untouched 8 bits of Y information, and 1 bit of the communal U/V information. This process is illustrated in Figure 23.14.

FIGURE 23.14:

Color sub-sampling

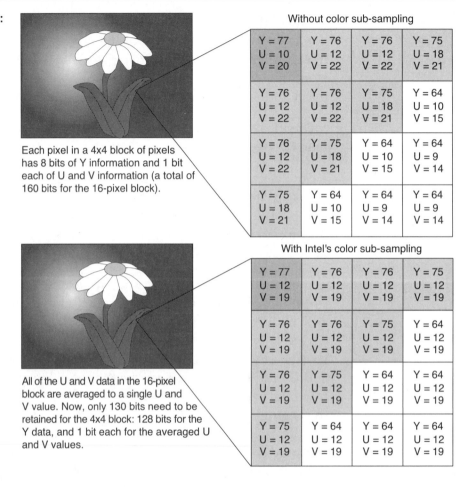

Without color sub-sampling

Y = 77 U = 10 V = 20	Y = 76 U = 12 V = 22	Y = 76 U = 12 V = 22	Y = 75 U = 18 V = 21
Y = 76 U = 12 V = 22	Y = 76 U = 12 V = 22	Y = 75 U = 18 V = 21	Y = 64 U = 10 V = 15
Y = 76 U = 12 V = 22	Y = 75 U = 18 V = 21	Y = 64 U = 10 V = 15	Y = 64 U = 9 V = 14
Y = 75 U = 18 V = 21	Y = 64 U = 10 V = 15	Y = 64 U = 9 V = 14	Y = 64 U = 9 V = 14

Each pixel in a 4x4 block of pixels has 8 bits of Y information and 1 bit each of U and V information (a total of 160 bits for the 16-pixel block).

With Intel's color sub-sampling

Y = 77 U = 12 V = 19	Y = 76 U = 12 V = 19	Y = 76 U = 12 V = 19	Y = 75 U = 12 V = 19
Y = 76 U = 12 V = 19	Y = 76 U = 12 V = 19	Y = 75 U = 12 V = 19	Y = 64 U = 12 V = 19
Y = 76 U = 12 V = 19	Y = 75 U = 12 V = 19	Y = 64 U = 12 V = 19	Y = 64 U = 12 V = 19
Y = 75 U = 12 V = 19	Y = 64 U = 12 V = 19	Y = 64 U = 12 V = 19	Y = 64 U = 12 V = 19

All of the U and V data in the 16-pixel block are averaged to a single U and V value. Now, only 130 bits need to be retained for the 4x4 block: 128 bits for the Y data, and 1 bit each for the averaged U and V values.

Other boards do similar things. For example, the Video Spigot has a YUV 4:2:2 option that also employs a four-by-four group, but that puts a bit more emphasis on the color information (2 bits for U, 2 bits for V) and a little less on the grayscale image (4 bits for Y).

The Intel Indeo codec takes things a step further by doing the four by four averaging not only on the U and V information, but on the Y information as well. If Indeo requires even greater compression, then it can average information over four-by-eight or eight-by-eight pixel groups. The Indeo codec also drops 1 bit of the 8 bits of Y information, so that what was YUV9 information becomes essentially YUV8 information.

Vector quantization is yet another lossy technique related to the delta encoding lossless technique. Under the delta encoding technique, you store delta frames that vary from a key frame, and deltas within a frame. But if you examined the patterns of deltas, you'd see that *they* had some common patterns, as well. For example, imagine a picture of a sunset. A codec encodes each line of video image as pixels. But if you examined each horizontal line of the image, you'd see a gradient pattern from midnight blue to blue to reds to the orange of the sunset. That's a smooth gradient; even as the sky gets darker, the relative change in darkness as you go from the top to the bottom of the sky is pretty constant. That gradient can be expressed as a table of deltas, and the Intel Indeo codec contains a number of these pre-built tables. The Indeo codec then tries to find one of these pre-stored delta tables that resembles whatever image it is working on, and essentially shoehorns the image into that delta table.

That's been a very quick look at compression. Here's what I want you to understand from all this: good compression involves a lot of analysis, and a lot of CPU time. Video capture boards just don't have the horsepower to do a really good job of compression in real time; heck, nothing short of a massively parallel computer could do a really good job of compression in real time. Now, most video boards come with a video editor program that will subject your video to *offline* compression, compression that can take an hour to compress one minute of video. I'll talk about offline compression in a minute, but understand for the minute that offline compressors can do a fairly good job of compacting your video data while doing the minimum damage to it; real-time compressors can't. It sounds like I'm saying that you shouldn't do any kind of compression when capturing, but that's probably not a realistic bit of advice.

Data transfer limitations on modern PCs mean that you'll probably have to accept *some* kind of real-time compression, but my advice is to play around a bit with the codecs that your system supports to find the one that does the least damage to the image as it compresses. As you'd expect, the codecs that reduce the data transfer rate the most also do the most violence to the original image. Start out with a no-compression codec, if that's an option. Record some reference data—something on a videotape, so you can assure that you're getting identical recording conditions—and see how much data you can record with each codec before you start dropping frames. Then go with the lowest compression codec that you can stand to work with, and get to work. (I say "that you can stand to work with" because slower codecs mean shorter captures, which mean more time spent editing and splicing.)

Offline Compression

Once you've got your video captured, you'll find that it's kind of huge. You may also want to trim off some needless intro and exit frames. That's where a video editor is useful: it lets you take a subset of a capture file, and then save it using some kind of offline compression. The things that you must choose at this stage are:

- The type of codec to use to compress the data
- Either the target data transfer rate of the output file, or an index of "quality"
- The audio/video interleave factor
- Whether or not to pad the data for CD-ROM storage

Offline compression uses a codec, just as capture does; it may even have the same name as the capture codec. But offline compression can compress at much greater ratios than capture compression. There's a price to pay, of course—two prices, in fact. First of all, really dramatic compression rates require lossy compression techniques, with all of their tradeoffs. Second, compression takes time, and ties up your computer. It only takes time once for each video, as you've only got to capture each video once, but it still takes time.

Let me revisit the reasons why you want to capture data in as pure a state as possible. The offline compression that you're going to do is lossy by nature. But if the data was first recorded with a lossy codec and you compress it further with an offline codec, then you end up with data that's been "smeared" twice. That's why you should either capture without compression, or with a codec that's as noninvasive of your data as possible.

Choosing a Codec: Don't Recompress Until You're Done!

After editing a captured video, you'll resave it to disk. At that time, the video editing software will use a codec to encode the video data, just as the capture software did. Choosing a codec is easy. The big question is: are you done working on this .AVI (audio/video) file? If you are, then use the codec that will give you the most compression. If not, then resave without any new compression. You'll compress even if you're not worried about the space that the file takes because of the data transfer rate required to play back the video clip. Playing back a raw Intel YUV9 video clip at full speed requires that the computer doing the playback read the file off its hard disk at about 1.3MB/second, so it's a good idea to compress the data so it can be played on slower systems if you want to.

Suppose you're building a video out of five smaller clips. Each time you splice one of the smaller clips into the master clip, you save the intermediate result. If you use a codec with lossy compression to save these intermediate videos, then you'll end up reapplying lossy compression to your video several times, resulting in an awful-looking video. *This is very important.* For example, suppose you'd captured several small clips using a 24-bit RGB codec. This codec stores the entire image to disk or RAM, meaning that you won't be able to save very long clips before frames start dropping, so you'll be doing lots of editing. Suppose you've got pieces A, B, and C that you want to splice together into video D, and suppose that your video editor only lets you splice together two files at a time. First, splice A and B, producing video IV1, for intermediate video 1. Also save it using the 24-bit RGB codec. Then splice IV1 to C, saving it to D. As D is the final product, it's fine to go ahead and use a lossy compression codec. The process is illustrated in Figure 23.15.

FIGURE 23.15:

Reserve the lossy compression for the last save.

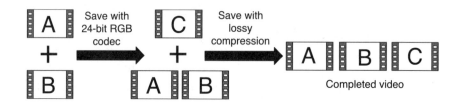

Setting Key Frames

Tell your video software that you want to set the compression type and options, and you'll probably see a dialog box something like the one shown in Figure 23.16.

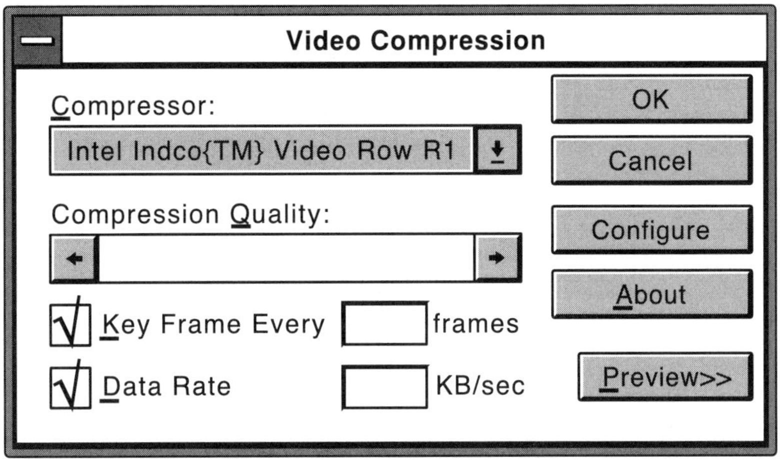

FIGURE 23.16:

Setting the compres-
sion type and options

FIGURE 23.16:

Setting the compression type and options

You can see the Compressor list box that lets you choose a codec. The compression software next lets you establish how often to set key frames, and whether or not you want to control the number of key frames. Tell the software that you do not want to control the number of key frames, and concentrate instead on the data rate. Key frame adjustment is just fine-tuning. When you've got your video just the way you like it, try saving it with slightly different frame rates, and you can sometimes adjust the picture quality and data transfer rate. In general, however, you can unselect the box and forget it.

Setting Data Rate and Compression Quality

The example dialog box also shows a slider bar for Compression Quality and a box for Data Rate. Actually, these options are the same thing. If you try to control one of them, you negate any control over the other.

Codecs have to make tradeoffs in order to compress data. Remember that less data means less data transferred per second.

Putting the same image into less data means, logically, getting a lower quality image; ergo, lower data rate equals lower compression quality.

The fact that the Compression Quality slider takes values between 0 and 100, and you can punch in any value that you like for the data transfer rate (from 10K/second to 16000K/second) makes it seem that codecs must have infinite options in crunching your data. In truth, that's not the case. The Intel Indeo codec basically chooses whether to do its pixel averaging on the basis of a four-by-four, four-by-eight, or eight-by-eight pixel group. That means that if you take the same video and save it with dozens of varying data rates, *you'll only end up getting two or three variations of the same file.*

This is important. If you tell a codec, "Make this a 405K/second file," then all the codec will do is to examine the file and say to itself, "Well, I could *really* compress this, and get it down to 100K/second, or do a kind of average job, and get it to 267K/second, or do a really basic job, and that'd probably work out around 624K/second. I guess I'd better do the 267K/second job, as that's less than or equal to what I've been asked to do."

Pad for CD-ROM

One option that you see in video editors is Pad output for CD-ROM, or something like that. This means to make sure that each frame's size is an even multiple of 2K. CD-ROM drives read data from a disc in sectors of 2K. For that reason, you'd like each video frame to come off right on a sector boundary. CD-ROM padding makes sure of that, writing enough zeroes at the end of each frame to ensure that it ends on a sector boundary, and so the next frame *starts* on a sector boundary. It's done to make the video play more smoothly.

Getting around Bugs in the Video Capture Software

This really isn't your job as a hardware fix-it kind of guy or gal, but you'll find that after you've done all the setting up, you'll have to deal with the worst part of video capture: software bugs.

Every programmer must grapple with memory when designing a program. Programs store all of their data in memory areas called heaps, arrays, or variables, all of which must be properly allocated and provided for by the programmer. For example, if the programmer of a financial analysis program knows that he's going to allow the program to track just 10 people's portfolios, then he's got to allocate enough space to store 10 portfolios. If the user tries to input an 11th, then the program should contain built-in safeguards that would intercept that attempt and reject the request. If the program *didn't* reject the request to create an 11th portfolio area, then it would end up creating that 11th portfolio area on top of some other program's memory space, "clobbering" the program.

In the Windows world, the word for "clobbering" memory space is a General Protection fault, or GP fault. GP faults happen when a program tries to utilize memory that it doesn't have the right to use, an area that may be in use by some other program. Similarly, a program may try to utilize memory that just plain doesn't exist, as in the case of a program trying to allocate the space from 16MB to 32MB on a 16MB system. Basically, GP faults happen because of sloppy programming.

NOTE   I bring this up because if you're running video capture software, you're going to run up against a lot of GP faults. Look at the kind of data rates that video can generate, and you can understand how the memory needs of video capture programs could easily exceed the amount of available memory. The GP fault may be caused by the video editing program, or it may be caused by the codec software, but no matter who's at fault, it still crashes your system.

How do you avoid GP faults in your video capture system? First of all, have as much memory as possible on your computer. If the program never exceeds physical memory, then it's less likely to GP fault. Second, allocate a big paging file, as that gives your video program a little "elbow room." Third, believe it or not, some Windows programs are sensitive about the amount of conventional memory available on your computer; they can't run unless you've got a certain amount of conventional RAM available. Finally, I've found that one way to reduce the number of GP faults created by the Microsoft Video 1 and Indeo codecs is by previewing a few frames. Most video editing programs have an option to allow you to select which compression codec to use, and in the resulting dialog box there's usually a Details button. Press it, and the dialog box unfolds, showing a Preview box and a slider bar that lets you control which frame you will see. Just let it build a few frames, and then the GP fault is less likely to occur. I have no idea why this works, but I've often found that it does.

Video capture can allow you to build some state of the art presentations and programs. Now that you know how to do it, go try it!

CHAPTER

TWENTY-FOUR

24

An Overview of CD-ROM

- The different types of CD-ROMS

- How CDs store data

- CD-ROM standards

- Installing and troubleshooting CD-ROMs

Installing a DVD Drive

1 Install an internal DVD drive into an open 5-1/4" drive bay in your computer.

2 Most DVD drives use a hardware decoder board that must be installed in an open PCI slot.

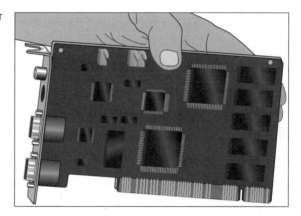

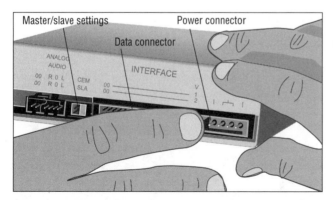

3 The rear of the DVD drive has several areas: the master/slave settings at the left; the data connector in the center; and the power connector at the right.

4 After setting the master/slave jumper, connect the IDE data cable to the drive. Then connect the power connector to the drive.

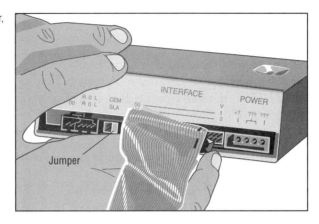

Jumper

5 The DVD decoder card has two video connectors: one for input and one for output.

Decoder Video In

System Video Out

Decoder Video Out

6 Attach a loopback cable from the computer video board's Video Out connector to the DVD decoder's Video In connector. Then connect your monitor's video cable to the DVD decoder board's Video Out connector.

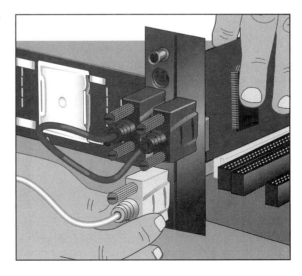

In the past, CD-ROM drives were considered a luxury item for your desktop computer. This changed in 1995, and today they are a necessity. In this chapter, you will learn:

- The differences between the various types of CD-ROM drives
- How CDs are recorded and read
- The associated technical standards
- The types of computer interfaces available for CD-ROMs
- How to install and troubleshoot CD-ROM drives

In discussions in this chapter, we'll use the term "CD-ROM" to refer to a drive and "CD" to refer to a disc.

Types of CD-ROM

Several different types of CD-ROM players and drives are available:

- CD-Recordable (CD-R) drives
- Photo CD players
- CD-Readable/Writeable (CD-R/W) drives
- DVD
- Computer-based CD-ROM drives

Each of these drive types is designed for a particular audience and application, and may require a particular operating environment and hardware platform. When choosing a CD-ROM drive, think about what it's for. Will the CDs display text, sound and graphics (mixed multimedia), just sound, or some combination of the three?

Photo CD Players

Kodak has taken the lead in developing Photo CD players. These drives are optimized for the manipulation of Photo CD images. Although many types of players can read and display the data on Photo CD discs, most are not customized for the manipulation of pictures, including such actions as zooming in, deleting sequences of pictures, and storing and retrieving changes to picture sequences.

CD-R

When they were first introduced, CD-R drives were recording devices that could write on special CD-ROM discs once only. Using a special kind of CD, you can use this device to make your own CDs for software distribution or data archiving. Today, most of the drives sold are actually CD-R/W drives, which can use either of two kinds of discs. One kind can be read and written many times, and the others can be written only once. We'll talk about how these two processes actually work later in this chapter.

DVD

Like CD, Digital Versatile Disk (DVD) is mostly known by its initials. Basically, DVD is a method of squeezing more data onto a single disc. CD-ROMs can fit about 630MB onto a disk, whereas DVD can fit as much as 17GB.

What's driving DVD technology? About the same things that drove CDs, really: the information that can be stored on it. While CDs are large enough to store about 76 minutes of audio data, DVDs can store enough data to hold an entire 2-hour movie. CDs really came into their own with the advent of applications and operating systems that were too big to fit onto a reasonable number of floppy disks. Nowadays, however, graphics-intensive games with built-in sound are becoming too big to fit onto a reasonable number of CDs. I've seen one game that fits on seven CDs, and, although I don't have anything in my personal library to match that, I've got Wing Commander III, which requires four. Unless you load all of that software on your hard drive, you'll end up swapping CDs in the middle of the game, which is annoying.

DVD is also being pushed by the home video market. DVD disks have the high quality of video disks (720 pixels on a horizontal line) combined with the high capacity of tapes. Today, DVD is becoming the new standard for distributing movies.

Computer-Based CD-ROM Drives

You'll see a CD-ROM drive in virtually every computer sold today.

The computer's operating system controls a computer-based CD-ROM drive and how it interfaces with the other computer components. The main difference between this type of drive and CD-R/CD-RW drives is that the computer-based CD-ROM cannot create CDs; it only reads them.

Cross-Platform Format Compatibility

Given the wide variety of drives that we've just discussed, it's probably no surprise that some of these drives will not work with each other's discs. For example, although you can read a CD-ROM on a DVD drive, you can't read a DVD disc on a CD-ROM drive.

The level of compatibility among the various kinds of discs and drives is determined by the physical interface and any software drivers that the drives require to run. The Red Book, the Yellow Book, the Yellow Book extension CD-ROM/XA, and ISO 9660 all define the standards that address how the various types of drives and discs will work together. We'll talk more about these standards later in this chapter.

How CD-ROMs Store Data

In order to understand how compact discs store data, you really have to understand several things about them: how the data is organized on the disc, what the disc is made of, and how discs are read and written. We'll cover that here.

The Anatomy of a Compact Disc

Compact discs are optical storage media that are read with laser light. The surface of the disc is arranged as a single spiral that begins at the inside of the disc and travels outward toward the edge of the disc. The commercially produced ones are made of injection-molded plastic formed from a stamper disc, are coated with an aluminum film to make them reflective, and are then lacquered to protect the surface. Compact discs aren't big (physically, only 4.72 inches in diameter) but from 527MB to 742MB will fit on a disc, depending on the number of sectors on the disc and the format used on it. Standard discs use the same size spiral as an audio CD (60 minutes) with 270,000 sectors and up to 99 tracks. The typical disc used in a computer-based CD-ROM drive stores 630MB using 333,000 sectors.

Compact discs are physically organized a little differently than hard disks. Whereas hard disks lay individual tracks in concentric circles, compact discs define a track by the length of a specific file; one file equals one track. The tracks on compact discs are laid sequentially on a continuous spiral. This spiral is a staggering three miles long, and can contain more than two billion pits (tiny holes burned into the disc to represent data).

CD Data Modes

The data written to the sectors on a CD is not homogenous and three different kinds of data may appear, each represented by a different mode. Each mode (0–2) includes a combination of some user data and some accessory data, such as error-checking or error-correction code.

The data in the modes gets more complex as the numbers get bigger. Mode 0 is empty data fields and zeroes. Mode 1 contains text and computer data with 288 bytes of Error Correcting Code (ECC) and Error Detection Code (EDC), plus 2048 bytes of user data per block. Mode 2 contains audio and video data.

There are actually two kinds of Mode 2 data: Form 1 and Form 2. Form 1 data has an additional third layer of EDC and ECC code for computer data. Form 2 data is used for compressed audio, video, and still pictures, and includes no error-checking or error-correcting information.

Reading and Writing to Compact Discs

Since tape recorders can both read and write to their media, you may be surprised to learn that you can't use a standard CD-ROM drive to both read and write data, and, in fact, the CDs used in read/write drives aren't even the same as standard CDs. First, we'll discuss how readable and writeable compact discs and disc drives are different, and then how the two processes work.

Physical Composition of Recordable Compact Discs and Drives

Recall from the beginning of this section that CD-ROMs are stamped from a mold and made of plastic (polycarbonate, if you're curious). The plastic disc is then coated with a very thin layer of aluminum, to make the surface reflective. Commercially available recordable CDs, on the other hand, are coated with Cyanine, Phthalocyanine or Azo dyes. The Cyanine discs are green, Phthalocyanine are yellow and Azo discs are blue.

Recording Compact Discs

It's easier to explain how CD-ROM drives read CDs if you understand how the data gets on the CD in the first place.

There are really two compact disc recording processes, the industrial one involving the aluminum-coated discs, and the writeable CD-ROM discs. First, the aluminum discs.

1. The technician records the data on 8mm DAT tape or on 9-track tape. The data is verified and then indexed so that it can be read from the CD. The tape is connected to the laser in the etching device mentioned in the next step.

2. The technician takes a glass plate called a *substrate* and covers it with a film of photo resist. Next, he runs a high-powered laser over the surface over the layer of photo resist. The laser alters the film, and when the substrate is placed in the developer, a chemical reaction takes place that leaves infinitesimal pits in the film in the places where the laser touched. The pattern of the pits corresponds to the data that the tape conveys to the laser. This developed substrate is called the *glass master*.

3. Next, the technician takes the glass master and coats it with a thin layer of silver. This silver-plated object is now called the *metal master*.

4. The technician electroplates the metal master with nickel to create a negative of the metal master. The negative, called the *father*, has bumps where the master had pits. Next, the father gets electroplated, and when the electroplating is removed, this is called the *mother*. When the mother is electroplated the final time and the coating is removed, the removed piece is called the *stamper*, and this is the piece that you work with.

5. The technician finishes the stamper by cutting the hole in the middle and trimming the edges so that it's the same size as a CD (the substrate was much bigger).

6. The technician puts the stamper into an injection-molding machine, and it presses the discs from polycarbonate. After the discs have cooled, the manufacturer then coats them with a thin layer of aluminum to make them reflective, lacquers them, and cools them quickly for protection, and that's the CD.

The process used for the write-once discs that you make with a CD-R drive is less complicated. Recall that the CD-R discs are coated with Cyanine, Phthalocyanine or Azo. While these three coatings have minor differences, they all operate in much the same way. They react to heat and light. To write to one of these discs, a laser beam is used to create microscopic pits in the surface of the coating. Once the pits have been written on the disc, it can be read by another laser, which detects the pits (or lack of pits) as 1's and 0's.

Read/write drives (CD-R/W) use a different coating and a special laser that can operate at different levels. They are coated with a Silver-Indium-Antimony-Tellurium alloy, which has the ability to change states when struck by a laser. If the laser is fired at high-intensity, the coating becomes amorphous in that spot and does not reflect light well. If a lower-intensity beam strikes the alloy, it crystallizes in that spot and becomes quite reflective. In this way it is possible to write to CD-R/W discs thousands of times.

Reading Compact Discs

Okay, we've got the data on the disc. How do we get it off?

When you insert a CD into the drive, the electronics within sense the disc and a controller tells the spindle motor to begin spinning. The laser device (which uses a low-intensity gallium arsenide laser mounted on a swing arm) is invoked and focus-control circuits adjust the optical beam to the size of the pits on the disc. The laser beam runs over the surface of the CD, reflecting light back to a photodetector that measures the reflected light and encodes it to a digital signal. This signal then transfers to the drive electronics, which give it to the computer.

The key part here is what's on the surface of the CD, because that affects how the light gets back to the photodetector. As you recall, the recorded CD has pits in it (or dots that looks like pits to a laser). To the CD player, however, the important part is not the pits, but the spaces between them, called the *land*. When the laser reads data, it senses the transitions between the lands and the pits. As you know, computers use the binary system (1s and 0s) to record data. A transition on a track is interpreted as a 1, and no transition is interpreted as a 0. The binary patterns are bounced back to the photodetector, which sends the data to a component that can interpret binary data back to its original format of sound, text, or graphics.

Standards: An Issue of Compatibility

If you've spent any time in the computing world at all, the concept of standards is not new to you. Parallel ports meet a standard, so that you can buy a parallel cable off the shelf and plug it into your printer. Data on your disks must follow the FAT format, so that your operating system and programs can read it. Internal hard drives fit into drive bays and so on.

Standards, both physical and logical, apply to compact disc technology as well so that the discs can be read and the user can find the data on them. In this section, we'll discuss some of the particulars of those standards and where they came from.

The Genesis of Standards

To make sure that all compact discs of a particular kind will work with its corresponding drive, data must be stored and indexed on all discs the same way.

The CD-ROM disc of today fared better than its forefather, the laser videodisc. Philips and Sony were early prominent developers of both videodisc and CD-ROM. They learned from their experiences with videodiscs that incompatibility can frustrate the user and subsequently restrict growth in the marketplace. Licking their wounds and vowing not to make the same mistake twice, they put their corporate heads together and developed a set of standards for CD-ROM discs. Since that time, technology has progressed, necessitating the creation of new standards and extensions to existing standards. Before we jump ahead, let's briefly review and define the original standards.

A color scheme was used to designate CD-ROM primary standards: red, yellow, orange, green, and white. To simplify matters, think of these standards in the following manner:

- Red Book = digital audio

- Yellow Book = data storage plus some

- Orange Book = write-once compact disc and CD-Magneto-Optical

The following discussion concentrates on those standards that are most important to computer-based CD-ROM users.

Red Book

The *Red Book* was the original specification defining how digital audio information is stored and indexed. It has a common base in the rest of the standards. Most music CDs conform to this standard.

Yellow Book

The *Yellow Book*, also named *ISO 10149* (ISO stands for the International Standards Organization), extends the Red Book audio specifications and deals specifically with the more interactive requirements of CD-ROM: random-access ability and multimedia. The specifications concentrate on storage and indexing of data and error correction. Data is broken down into two types. Mode 1 describes standards for writing computer data and text providing error detection code (EDC) and error correcting code (ECC). Mode 2 provides for video and audio using CRC for error correction.

This standard supports several file formats for the different computer platforms that use CD-ROMs. These include Native Macintosh hard disc format, DEC's (Digital Equipment Corporation) VMS, Apple's HFS (Hierarchical File System), and ISO 9660.

CD-ROM/XA: Extension to the Yellow Book

The CD-ROM/XA standard is an extension to the Yellow Book. The XA stands for extended architecture, and this standard does exactly that. By defining the way in which different data types may be interleaved on a CD, the XA standard really makes multimedia CD-ROMs possible.

A common application requiring the interleaving of sound and motion can be demonstrated through a multimedia presentation. Suppose you're running a presentation with pictures of a person speaking, and have sound to follow along. In order for the movement of the speaker's lips to match the spoken words, the sound and the pictures must be synchronized. To accommodate this, tracks on a CD-ROM/XA disc can contain interleaved video/picture, audio, and computer data.

A normal CD-ROM track contains only Mode 1 data type sectors. With CD-ROM/XA, a track contains only Mode 2 sectors. There are two form types within a Mode 2 sector. Form 1 contains user data (2048 bytes) and EDC (Error Detection Code) and ECC (Error Correction Code) data. Form 2 contains raw data (2324 bytes) such as audio or voice.

In order for a CD-ROM to be fully XA-compatible it must have the following capabilities:

- Read data from two differently defined data streams. These streams are Mode 2, Form 1, which is static information, and Mode 2, Form 2, which is time-dependent information.

- Allow data from each stream to be buffered and delivered to the CPU and video subsystem as required.

- Translate the ADPCM (adaptive differential pulse code modulation). ADPCM is a standard for audio compression, usually a 4:1 ratio. In other words, the CD-ROM must be able to send the audio signal to the speakers properly decoded and decompressed.

Be careful of manufacturer claims that their drives are XA compliant. XA-compatible drives are still evolving, and unless they are able to read Mode 2, Form 2, they are not compatible. In addition, ADPCM translation is not always embedded in drives listed as "XA-compatible." To get full compatibility, you may need to purchase a new interface board.

The increased visibility of multimedia CD-ROMs has increased customer interest in XA compatibility, but to date most manufacturers have concentrated on interpreting images, not standardization. Although this is not really an issue now, expect it to become so as more titles with full XA functionality become available.

High Sierra and ISO 9660

In 1985, CD-ROM companies formed an alliance to produce a standard CD-ROM file structure independent of the operating system. The result is commonly known as the High Sierra Standard. After some modifications, the standard was formally accepted by the ISO and is now named ISO 9660. It sets forth a standard file system with a hierarchical directory structure of eight levels. This file system is similar to the FAT architecture familiar to DOS users.

Theoretically, if a drive is an ISO 9660-compatible drive it can, for example, read the information whether it is a Windows-based system or a Macintosh. However, this alone does not ensure compatibility because applications may contain instructions which use the resources of a given computing platform and aren't available on another platform. Thus, reading data and executing the program code is not the same; you can't execute programs written for Windows on a non-Windows machine like a Macintosh, even if the Mac can detect the CD.

Standards to Use

At a minimum, you should purchase drives that have CD-Audio and ISO 9660 compatibility. Other format compatibility issues will be driven by specific applications and the requirements of a given CD-ROM title.

For example, today, there is considerable interest in accessing Photo-CD discs. Many Photo-CDs use the modified Mode 2 specified in CD-ROM/XA. In addition, if you plan to use Photo-CDs, a multi-session capability is also important. Multi-session refers to the recording events on a CD-ROM disc, which can be done as several different events. Standard CDs are recorded in a single-session or as a single event. Multi-session is the ability to read a disc that is recorded in more than one session.

Kodak's Photo-CD and CD-R are driving the need for multi-session drives. A standard CD-ROM drive would need modifications to both its firmware and software to read a second recorded session. In the corporate world, CD-R data discs are being used and recorded in multiple sessions for archiving purposes. In addition, the newer portable CD-ROM drives (such as Sony's MMCD portable) support XA format. If you intend to use a given CD on a portable and stationary drive, both should be XA-compatible.

Characteristics of Computer-Based CD-ROM Drives

Computer-based CD-ROM drives aren't all the same. They vary in terms of their hardware interface, speed, drivers used, access to additional hardware, and where they attach to the computer. So that you can select the right one for your needs, we'll go through the details of those characteristics now.

Multimedia Kits

Package deals that include a CD-ROM drive, sound card, speakers, and related hardware and software paraphernalia seek to avoid the compatibility problem altogether. They reason, not entirely incorrectly, that if they fulfill buyers' needs for multimedia hardware ahead of time, then the buyers won't replace the devices for a while. If you're not replacing the hardware, then you don't have to worry about the myriad options available.

These kits have a price, however. First, they tend to be more expensive than buying the components separately. Second, if they're built into the machine (as many are) and a single component goes bad, the entire machine goes into the shop. Third, many kits do not use the latest technology, or they include components not easily supported. Look carefully before purchasing a multimedia kit. If you're planning to upgrade in the life of your computer, then buying the pieces separately is a better idea.

Physical Characteristics

Physically, most CD-ROM drives look pretty much alike. The front panel typically has a power on indicator, CD busy signal, an eject button, a manual eject hole, an audio jack, and a volume controller of some kind.

Disc Loading

Not all computer-based CD players load discs the same way, as you may know from using the audio devices. Although they are becoming less and less common, some players require that you place the CD in a *caddy* (a protective storage case which minimizes exposure to contaminants) for loading, and then insert the caddy into the drive. If your drive uses caddies, get a separate caddy for each CD, rather than sharing a caddy between discs. This avoids the hassle of finding a caddy when you need it, and will keep the disc protected. Other drives have a tray in the drive that the disc goes directly into. Once you put the disc into the tray, it slides back into place in the drive and the CD starts spinning.

Although some caddy-style drives will play when the drive is on its side, so that the disc is positioned vertically rather than horizontally, many CD-ROM drives must be in a horizontal position to run. Do not attempt to run a CD player when it's on its side unless the drive is specifically listed as being able to support this position.

Internal or External?

Many CD-ROM models are available in both internal and external flavors. If you've got an empty drive bay and don't mind opening up your system to install the drive, internal drives are often the best choice. They tend to be less expensive than external drives, and more models are available. Additionally, some interfaces (like IDE, for example) aren't available at all in external models, so if you've got an IDE controller that you want to use with the drive, internal is your only choice.

External drives are good for those with a SCSI interface who don't like cracking the case, don't have an extra drive bay, or are running into a bit of a power crunch from too many devices making demands on the power supply (external drives have their own power supply). They do tend to be more expensive than comparable internal drives, but (assuming that you have a SCSI host adapter installed in your computer), they're much easier and faster to install. Plug an external drive into the SCSI chain and power, make sure it's terminated properly, reboot…and there's your drive.

Performance Characteristics

All CD-ROM drives look pretty much alike (within the limits of being internal or external drives), but looks are not the measure of performance. You can buy drives with various spinning speeds, access/seek times, data transfer rates, buffering techniques, and so forth. All of these things impact directly upon drive performance.

Some things external to the drive can also affect its performance, such as CPU speed, physical interface, and the video system, but unless you're planning to replace the entire system there's not much that you can do about system effects on CD-ROM performance except to be aware of them. A slow processor or inadequate video system will keep the fastest CD-ROM drive from maximizing its potential. The fastest drive will not perform well on a slow 486—best to save your dollars for your Pentium system.

Spinning Speed

If you're buying a CD-ROM drive, you've got several choices: the slowest drives available today are 32x and the fastest ones are more than 50x. Speeds are relative to the original (1x) CD-ROMs that were introduced back in 1981.

Data Transfer Rate

Data transfer rate, measured in kilobytes per second, is the measure of the quantity of data supplied to your computer at the onset of the first read operation. We talked about the specifics of data transfer rate in the hard disk chapter, and it works pretty much the same way on CD-ROM drives.

Access Time

Don't expect an access time from your CD-ROM that even approaches the access time you see from your hard disk. I've got one hard disk with an access time of 9ms, but a common CD-ROM access time is more than 100 ms. Generally speaking, most hard disks are 10 times faster than most CD-ROM drives.

Caching

Disk caching temporarily stores recently or frequently accessed data to the hard disk to take advantage of the higher access rates. Typically, the directory of the CD-ROM is cached. A cached directory makes it faster to navigate subdirectories and will make the CD-ROM drive appear to be faster. However, the actual reading of the data will still be slower.

Buffers

Cache uses some form of logic to figure out what to store: depending on how it's set up, it will temporarily store the most recently accessed or the most frequently accessed data on the hard disk. Buffering is similar to cache, except that there's no logic to how data goes there. Data is stored there until the CD-ROM drive is ready to send the data to the CPU for processing. Buffer sizes can vary from 32K to 1MB. Although bigger is always better, a minimum demand should be at least a 64K buffer on double-speed drives and 256K buffer for quad-speed (4x). Most newer drives provide at least a 256K buffer.

The efficiency of the use of the drive buffer is in part based on the firmware in the drive. Two different approaches for buffering are used, one to increase throughput to the CPU and one to reduce seek time. Circular buffer read-ahead allows the drive to continue reading with one interrupt to the CPU. As a result, the buffer is kept full and throughput is increased. In the other approach, the root directory of the drive is copied into buffer memory, which helps to reduce random-access time.

Interface Type

You can connect CD-ROM drives to the rest of your computer via an IDE, SCSI, EIDE, or parallel port. Although you should be familiar with these first three terms from earlier chapters, we'll briefly review them here.

Before we begin, however, I'd like to point out a couple of things about CD-ROM drive interfaces. First, they work in pretty much the same way as hard disk interfaces or floppy interfaces, so if you've got a handle on those, you're set. Second, most interfaces will do a credible job (with the exception of the parallel port, which is extremely slow). You can run into problems while installing CD-ROM drives with any of the interfaces, as illustrated in the section on installation and troubleshooting. Most conflicts will revolve around resource conflicts and outdated drivers.

SCSI drives have the best overall performance. However, the cost is higher, especially if you don't already own a SCSI controller. IDE drives cost less, and since most computers today have an integrated IDE interface, they are very simple to install. Proprietary interface drives are usually easy to install and comparatively cheap, but they won't work with all operating systems. Today, the push is toward EIDE, an interface that is similar to IDE but quite a bit faster.

IDE

Integrated Device Electronics (IDE) came into being around 1985. IDE uses the AT-Attachment specification (ATA). The ATA specification took form in 1984 due to the collaborative efforts of Western Digital and Compaq Computer Corporation, who developed the idea of building an AT-compatible controller directly into the drive electronics. More than any prior specification, IDE places drive and host-interface electronics directly into the drive. As a whole, this significantly reduced the price of the hard disk subsystem. It also allowed vendors to make improvements to the capacities and performance of drives with less risk of incompatibility.

Historically, IDE drives worked well with the host adapters from other vendors. Problems still arose when users mixed drives from different manufacturers in a master-slave configuration. The ATA specification standardized the communications between the master and slave drives. Most current drives now follow this standard.

The motherboards of most ISA bus PCs include an IDE interface, but the drive houses the controller logic. The 16-bit parallel interface can support two drives (either two hard drives or one hard drive and one CD-ROM). When attaching both a hard drive and a CD-ROM to the controller, the CD-ROM should be configured as the slave device. (On an IDE interface, one drive must be designated as master and the other as slave. This prevents the two drives from trying to "talk" over one another.)

Since IDE interfaces are already on most PC motherboards, many CD-ROM drives use IDE. IDE drives are a good, cost-effective solution for text and graphics applications. They don't work as well for CDs using multimedia, as IDE does not support multitasking. For multitasking, you need to move up to SCSI.

SCSI

If you're using a Mac or UNIX system, you probably don't have any choice about using SCSI, because the OS requires it. You can either take this time for a soda break or keep reading to learn more about the interface. For Windows users, however, SCSI is not a foregone conclusion unless one of the following applies to you:

- You already have SCSI-compatible peripherals attached to your system.

- You plan to install multiple peripherals.

- You are looking toward the high-speed CD-ROMs (which normally have a SCSI interface).

SCSI is a good choice for those who need high performance and system flexibility. One SCSI host adapter card can provide a system interface for up to seven devices (one or more of which can be the CD-ROM), and SCSI devices have a high data transfer rate.

EIDE

Enhanced IDE (EIDE) is a technology that can support one or two devices on a single cable. Since most computers have two EIDE connectors you can connect up to four EIDE devices in your computers at once. Most current CD-ROM drives use a subset of EIDE called ATAPI (AT Attachment Packet Interface). The same connector is used for IDE, EIDE, or ATAPI. Therefore, an IDE/ATAPI CD-ROM drive can be installed on a spare IDE connector.

Installation

The key to performing a smooth installation is to be aware of the resources being used currently within your system. Each component within the system has the potential to affect another.

Installation software can make changes to the `CONFIG.SYS` and `AUTOEXEC.BAT` files (and other system settings). Automated installation routines usually walk you through a series of questions allowing you to either accept a default setting or change it. These automated routines will not circumvent resource conflicts.

Document System Resources

The best way to set yourself up for a smooth installation is to start documenting. You can either keep tabs on your system as you add components to it, or you can use some of the many tools available to help you catch up.

Why Am I Doing This?

Regardless of how or what tools you use, compose a list of all system devices and required system resources. For example, record communication ports, parallel ports, internal modems, mouse, and expansion/controller/adapter cards. Record the IRQ number, DMA number, and base address of the software that controls each device.

The goal is to have enough information handy to circumvent potential resource conflicts. For example, for SoundBlaster compatibility the default IRQ assignment is IRQ 5. LPT2 (the second parallel port) also defaults to IRQ 5, although this is not usually a source of contention unless LPT2 is used.

It is easier to use the default settings on the sound cards and reconfigure other boards whenever possible. If the sound card needs to be changed, one will either need to change jumper settings on the board, use a software utility provided with the board, or some combination of the two. For an example of how you could configure a SoundBlaster 16, see Chapter 6, "Installing New Circuit Boards (Without Creating New Problems)."

Advanced knowledge of potential conflicts can lead to smoother installations. Troubleshooting and problem resolution will be easier to manage.

Physical Install

Installing the CD-ROM is basically the same regardless of the interface. Be sure you are prepared with documentation for the software drivers and switch settings for any boards with jumpers. Do not forget your handy list of in-use system resources.

1. Plug the adapter card into the slot on the motherboard (or connect the drive to the SCSI, ATAPI, or proprietary connection).

2. Install the drive into an open bay.

3. Attach the power cable.

4. Attach the interface cable.

5. (Optional) Attach the sound cable from the CD-ROM to the sound card.

Software

The next step of the installation process begins with drivers for your CD-ROM drive.

Drivers

CD-ROM drivers are supplied with most drives as required. If you have a problem with a driver and need a replacement, check with the manufacturer. In addition, CompuServe has a CD-ROM forum that has downloadable drivers. Most manufacturers can be located via the Internet, allowing you to download drivers directly from the source. Here are Web site addresses for a few of the major manufacturers:

NEC	www.nec.com
Philips	www.philips.com
Sony	www.sony.com

MSCDEX

The MSCDEX.EXE CD-ROM extensions initiate user-defined CD-ROM settings. This program is provided with Windows. MSCDEX does the following:

- Establishes a drive letter for the CD-ROM drive, allowing system commands to operate on the drive.

- Translates the ISO 9660 file system.

- Allows a CD-ROM installation or application to locate the drive letter associated with the CD-ROM drive. Some applications simply seek out the MSCDEX statement to report sensing of the CD-ROM drive.

- Supports the playback of audio tracks.

Table 24.2 provides a description of the various switch settings supported by the MSCDEX.EXE statement.

TABLE 24.2: Various Switch Settings Supported by MSCDEX.EXE

Mscdex Switch	Description
/D:xxxxxx	This is the device name used by the CD-ROM device driver used in the device table. This must match the /D:xxxxxx used in the device driver line of the CONFIG.SYS file.
/M:x	X represents the number of buffers used. Typically, eight are used for one drive with four added for each additional drive. Memory space can be freed if needed by setting to 1 or 2 in the current versions of MSCDEX. Avoid setting this too large as performance gains are not substantial compared to valuable free memory. If using SMARTDRV for caching, try setting this to 0 and see if you get a performance boost.
/L:x	This is the drive letter for the CD-ROM drive. It is optional and will default to the first available drive letter. A LASTDRIVE= is needed in the CONFIG.SYS to use letters beyond the next available drive. Be careful when making changes to the drive letter of a CD-ROM drive. Applications installed prior to the change may need to be reinstalled, as many packages will access only the specific CD-ROM drive letter used at the time of installation.

Continued on next page

TABLE 24.2 CONTINUED: Various Switch Settings Supported by MSCDEX.EXE

Mscdex Switch	Description
/V	Called the verbose option. When booting, the statistics for memory used by MSCDEX are shown on-screen.
/S	The share option that is used with networks (e.g. Windows for Workgroups).
/K	Called the Kanji option, it uses Kanji (Japanese) file types if present. Enables the Japanese character display. Sometimes this can cause a Not ISO or High Sierra error.
/E	This is the Expanded Memory option. It needs an expanded memory driver to support it.

The following illustrates some typical uses of the switch settings described above.

```
C:\DOS\MSCDEX.EXE /D:SONY_001 /M:0 /L:E
```

In this example, the /D: and the name of the device referenced (SONY_001) must match the name used by the device driver for the CD-ROM drive in the `CONFIG.SYS` file. Multiple /D: switches can be used as long as they conform to the device names used in the `CONFIG.SYS` file.

```
C:\DOS\MSCDEX.EXE /d:devicename1 /D:devicename2
```

Troubleshooting

Let's take a look at problems common to CD-ROM drives.

Common Reasons for Difficult Installations

Installations of CD-ROM drives can be fraught with challenges for a variety of reasons, but the most common problems stem from balancing the needs of the drive against the needs of other peripherals within the system. The following list identifies some common reasons for difficult installations:

- Problems with software drivers:

    - MSCDEX.EXE not installed or installed in the wrong directory.

    - Inaccurate syntax or information in the command line for loading the driver.

- Missing cables or forgotten cables:

    - Missing audio cable.

    - Inverting the cable so it is connected upside down (pin-1 rule).

- Improper SCSI termination or SCSI ID.

- Incompatible adapter devices or software drivers:

    - Wrong version of MSCDEX.EXE.

    - Many devices are shipped without the proper drivers. Verify the version in use with the manufacturer.

- I/O, DMA, and IRQ conflicts.

- CD-ROM drive and host adapter incompatibilities. Check with the adapter's manufacturer for a list of supported drives.

If you've checked all of the items in the previous list and the drive still doesn't work, it's possible that either the drive or the controller is dead. (Obviously, it's the drive if something else is plugged into the controller and the other device works.) Check the following:

- Is the controller board seated properly? Reseat it, and if that doesn't work, try swapping it with an identical working board.

- Does the drive unit even work? If you've got one, try connecting an identical working drive in its place.

Slow Initialization of the Drive

This error message can be symptomatic of having the buffer parameter in the MSCDEX.EXE statement set too high. Set the buffers to four or five for each CD-ROM drive attached to your system. Modify the /M: parameter in the command line. If using SMART-DRV, try setting this parameter to 0.

Maintenance

The majority of maintenance revolves around caring for your CD-ROM discs properly. By caring for your discs you are doing preventative maintenance on the CD-ROM drive, reducing the opportunity for contaminants to enter the drive.

Do's and Don'ts of Compact Discs

Here are a few pointers to keep your CD-ROM drive up and running.

- If a disc needs to be cleaned, use a soft, clean, *dry* cloth and wipe in a radial action from the inner hub to the outer hub. Do not use a circular motion as on a CD. Tracks are not recorded the same on a CD and if you scratch the CD on a circular arc, that may prevent a long set of pits from being read.

- Do not use cleaning agents, as many solvents used in them can damage a disc.

- Do not use a wet cloth.

- Avoid cleaning the label side of the disc.

- Use a caddy to transport discs.

- Avoid exposure to extreme heat or cold.

- Avoid excess humidity.

- Avoid direct sunlight and high-intensity UV light.

CHAPTER

TWENTY-FIVE

A Buyer's Guide to PCs

- The parts of a PC

- About proprietary PCs

- Generic versus proprietary PCs

- Where and how to buy PCs

If you're the kind of person who fixes your own or someone else's PC (and if you weren't, why would you be reading this book?) then you're likely to be the kind of person who's often looking to the next PC, the latest-and-greatest machine. Perhaps your palms itch when you see that someone else owns a dual processor Pentium III system, when all you can afford is a Pentium. You eye 18GB hard drives the way some teenage boys eye Corvettes.

Or maybe you're not that way. Maybe your computer is just a tool for you, a platform upon which to get some work done. But you've found that your current platform just isn't fast enough to support today's software: Windows 98 requires a Pentium with 32MB of RAM in order to be useful. And you need to know how to either upgrade your existing machines or buy new ones that won't offer as much trouble when it's time to upgrade again in a year or two.

It's a good time to upgrade; with prices these days, everybody can own some of the fastest PCs on the planet. Buyers with tons of money don't have much advantage over the rest of us currently. (Unless, of course, you've *got* to have a 550MHz Pentium III-based system with the digital, active matrix, flat panel screen and 18GB drive.)

But *which* one to buy? Well, I'm not going to tell you *that*: there are zillions of honest vendors out there who deserve your money. I'd just like to give you some advice on how to make sure that your vendor is one of the good ones.

I tell my clients that when they're going to buy a PC, they should consider four things: compatibility, upgradability (I know, it's not a word), serviceability, and price/performance.

Because I'm concerned about those things, I recommend that people avoid many of the big names in the PC business and buy a *generic* computer, rather than a *proprietary* computer.

Parts of a Generic PC

Now, I've discussed this before, but before I go any further, let me remind you about what I mean when I say "generic" and "proprietary." *Generic* refers to machines designed like the IBM AT, even if the machine is built around a Pentium. Generic machines are PCs consisting of a few separate industry standard parts. Those parts include:

- **Standard Case:** If you buy a computer with an unusually shaped case, as you'd see in the "slimline" PCs or the micro towers, then you'll find that all of the boards inside the computer may be unusually shaped as well. That means that you probably won't be able to easily locate affordable replacement parts, should you need them. It also means that you can't put an industry-standard ("generic") power supply in your system. That's undesirable because there are some very nice power supply alternatives these days, such as super-quiet fans or power supplies with built-in battery backup.

- **ATX Case:** This is a newer case style, which actually rotates the processor and expansion slots 90° inside the case, giving room to add more cards. A side-mounted fan on the power supply does a better job of cooling the system than the standard version. But the most visible difference is the double-height aperture in the back where the keyboard, mouse, and ports are located; these ports are all piled on top of one another. A standard motherboard will not fit in an ATX case, and vice versa.

- **Motherboard:** The largest circuit board in the case, the motherboard holds the CPU, memory, and expansion slots. On that motherboard there should be *eight* expansion slots, rather than the three that you find on some computers these days, so that you can add expansion boards to your PC now and in the future. Three slots just aren't enough.

- **I/O:** This used to be a separate entity, now it is built in to most motherboards. It's good to get a motherboard with two EIDE controllers. EIDE controllers allow your hard drives to talk to the CPU, and two of them let you have up to four hard drives or CD-ROMs. The parallel port resides here as well; get one that is ECP/EPP so that you can connect to a nice, fast printer. There should be a PS/2 port for your mouse so that you don't need to waste a perfectly good serial port. Speaking of which, serial ports and floppy drive connectors are considered I/O as well; not much to concern yourself with here, but just be sure you have the standard setup of one floppy controller and two communication (COM) ports.

- **Video Adapter Board:** This is the component that allows the PC to display images on the monitor. It will probably be a so-called "super" VGA board. VGA is Video Graphics Array, a common video standard. I'll recommend VGA accelerators a bit later.

That's just a generic overview. I'll zoom in on particular features you should be looking for in a few pages.

Problems with Proprietary PCs

How is one of these generic PCs different from a proprietary PC? Well, you find all of the same functions in a proprietary PC, but you find all of them on a single circuit board, a kind of "workaholic" motherboard. The big problem with proprietary computers is that you can't upgrade them easily, nor can you fix them for a reasonable price. Proprietary computer motherboards are typically shaped differently from each other and from generic motherboards, making it impossible for you to replace an old or damaged proprietary motherboard with anything but another motherboard of the exact same make and model. As motherboards of that particular make and model are only available from that particular vendor (by definition, since the motherboard is proprietary), it may be expensive or impossible to get a replacement. Likewise, it's almost certainly impossible to get an upgrade.

For more specific problems with proprietary designs, let's return to my four criteria.

Compatibility is at stake because if the vendor did anything wrong (for example, if the company chose a mildly incompatible video chip, as AT&T did for some of their systems), you must either throw away the computer or hope that the designer was farsighted enough to allow you to disable the built-in video function so you can go out and spend more money on a separate video board.

Upgradability is a concern because not all boards are built alike. Take, for example, the Compaq Deskpro systems. Although they work very well, they are difficult to upgrade (the motherboards especially, because they are not a standard shape). You must buy a new motherboard from Compaq, as opposed to running to your local vendor and picking up a newer, faster one when it comes out.

Serviceability is a problem for reasons touched on above. A generic design like a Gateway 2000 is a safe buy in many ways, not the least of which is that even if Gateway goes bankrupt tomorrow, the entire machine is composed of generic parts that can be bought at *thousands* of clone houses around the country. And this isn't brain surgery; you've seen in this book that you can break down and rebuild a PC in about 30 minutes, leaving it better than when you started.

And what about *price/performance*? First of all, notice that I put this last. That's because compared to what computers used to cost, *any* PC is a bargain, even if you pay list price for one made by IBM. In regard to the proprietary computers, in theory, a single-board design can be faster and cheaper for many reasons. You don't see that in actual fact because single-board designs tend to be embraced by the big-name companies that need to pay for four-page color spreads in *Byte* and *PC Magazine*.

You don't need to buy a big name to get big performance, reliability, or flexibility. Look in your local paper's business section for the names of companies near you that sell generic PCs. It couldn't hurt if the company offers service through a national service company like Wang or TRW. Then choose that fire-breathing 500MHz Pentium III you've been eyeing and put it to work for you and smile, knowing that you've bought the security of easy upgrades and independence from any single vendor.

Choosing a Market Niche

Where will you buy your PC? People in some companies are only allowed to buy from IBM or Compaq; others put machines together from parts. Computer dealers basically fall into three categories.

- **First Tier:** IBM and Compaq. The *definitions* of compatibility. The systems that these companies pump out are top of the line. It used to be that you could not upgrade them short of an act of Congress, but now they are much easier to work with; you can plop any old generic card in them. However, particularly with low-end systems, not all cards will work as well as you'd like them to. But they are quite easy to get serviced in the event of a problem, since just about every computer store in existence has technicians certified by one or more of these companies. The real drawback here is cost; they work well, but they cost quite a bit more than the other two tiers.

- **Second Tier:** Dell, Gateway 2000, and Micron. While the majority of these companies have seen the wisdom of generic architecture, some of them still use proprietary parts. You will find good price/performance with these companies, but there are some drawbacks. Both Micron and Gateway, for example, decided to experiment on me with some new motherboards that didn't work at all. Getting them to admit and then fix their mistakes was a hassle, but they did make it all better eventually, although it took longer than I would have liked. The moral of the story is this: don't let vendors experiment on you; ask for name brand parts if they are using a generic architecture.

- **Third Tier:** Also known as "box shovers" or "Three Guys and a Goat PCs." This group gets a scary reputation that's really not deserved. Yes, some of them are sleazy, deceptive, and unreliable, but then those are adjectives that have been aptly applied to some of the *big* names in the business, too. On the positive side, these companies are always aware of the fact that every sale is a significant portion of their total business, and they'll do just about anything to get a multi-machine contract with a large company or government client. You usually needn't worry about shoddy parts, as they're putting together pieces made by fairly big U.S., Taiwanese, Korean, and Japanese vendors. If you look at the sum total of all third-tier vendors, you'll see that between them they use only about three or four suppliers for any given part (drives, motherboards, controllers, etc.). That means that if you really look at the companies that are *supplying* those parts—Micronics, DTK, AMI, Chips & Technologies, Adaptec, and G2—you'll see that they're pretty large and reliable companies. The absolute best part about these machines is that they're the simplest to upgrade and maintain. And service is usually easier and faster, often at your own worksite (which beats having to pack up your machine and trust shipping services not to wreck it completely). They also have the best price/performance in the group, and compatibility is usually as good as the second-tier machines.

Your only real concern with such vendors is the need for a warranty *in writing*. If you have no warranty and your machine breaks, then you have no machine, just a large, beige paperweight.

Choosing PC Parts

In the process of choosing a PC, I look at what it's made of in order to decide if it's the kind of machine that I'm looking for. Let's look at the important parts of a PC and summarize what you should consider when buying a PC. All of these items are discussed elsewhere in the book; this is just a summary. Consult the index to find out where to read more about any given topic.

CPU

If you're buying today, consider the Pentium III. Pentium III chips are coming down in price and are quite fast. Most games written today are, in fact, written to take advantage of the Pentium CPU. If you go any lower than Pentium II (say Pentium Pro), look for MMX (Multimedia Extensions) as well, since a good number of programs are written to take advantage of it. MMX (which is built into the Pentium II and III) is actually just a set of extra commands in the CPU itself that allows it to process multimedia functions, like video and sound, faster. Make sure to get at least one fan with this too; Pentiums run a little warm and will not function for long without one.

The fact of the matter today is that CPUs are leveling out in speed. To explain: a 386 was twice as fast as a 286 at the same speed, thus a 386/20 was twice as fast as a 286/20. Same difference between the 386 and 486, and the Pentium and 486 again. Yet what about the difference between the Pentium II and the Pentium? Between the Pentium II and Pentium Xeon, or how about the Celeron? They are a little faster in clock speed only; the real difference is in the way these processors handle their work—Xeon, for example, gives access to more memory than a Pentium II, but it is not twice as fast. What's *not* getting faster, however, are the peripherals. CPUs today are hundreds of times faster than XT-level CPUs; modern peripherals, however, are only dozens of times faster than XT-era peripherals. Take the money you're saving by not buying the latest and greatest CPU and spend that on a faster bus and faster peripherals. (There are exceptions; some processes are very CPU-intensive and will benefit from a faster processor.)

Additionally, there is a lot of evidence that Pentium architecture chips require some kind of special cooling hardware for the CPU itself. That includes heat sinks and fans mounted on the CPU, much like the faster 486 chips required. If you get a CPU with a built-in heat sink, this may not be a problem for you, so check with the vendor when you buy.

"Upgradable" PCs

What about modular "upgradable" PCs? The idea *sounds* good, but the upgrades are proprietary and can be quite expensive. Generic PCs are the original "upgradable" PCs.

Bus

You need a fast bus to drive fast peripherals. You want a *smart* bus so that your system works with Plug and Play and so that you can set up new boards easily. There's really only one smart and fast bus: PCI.

Unfortunately, most PCI implementations sport only three or four PCI slots and supplement with EISA slots. Most new boards also include an AGP slot, which is currently reserved for high-speed video. Which brings me to my next bus requirement: Plug and Play. Make absolutely sure that your new machine will support Plug and Play as implemented by Windows 98; I say "as implemented by Windows 98" because a good number of vendors have a kind of loose interpretation of what Plug and Play means. The simplest hard-and-fast test is "Does it work with Windows 98?"

Not every board you plug into your system needs to be a PCI board, although that is preferable. You should be pretty sure, however, that the following adapters are PCI:

- SCSI host adapter

- Any LAN cards

- Any video capture or sound capture hardware

RAM

Remember this simple mathematical equation to help you buy the right amount of RAM: More = Better. Today's operating systems like RAM (especially so with NT). Get a system with at least 32MB of RAM. Be certain to get enough cache memory as well. Cache memory is used by the processor to access frequently used pieces of data and can speed up your system. It is fairly standard to find 256K of cache on the board already; you may want to consider upgrading that to 512K or even 1MB since Windows operating systems use this much cache quite well.

ROM BIOS

This is an important part of compatibility. Buy from one of the big three—Phoenix, Award, or AMI. That way, it's easy to get upgrades. Nice BIOS features include:

- User-definable drive types

- Bus speeds that can be set in the setup
- Processor cache enable/disable

Motherboard/System Board

This board contains the above items. If you're buying from a first- or second-tier company, you'll end up with their board. From a third-tier place, look for motherboards from Acer, Micronics, DTK, Mylex, ASUS, and FIC.

Disk Drives

You're probably going to end up buying EIDE-type drives mainly because they're so amazingly cheap, fast, and reliable. Just back the silly things up *regularly*, because there's only a limited array of repair options open to you.

Floppy Disks

I've seen too many problems with Mitsubishi drives to recommend them; TEACs seem the most trouble-free. I would recommend getting an Iomega Zip or Jaz drive also, if you need a lot of data storage space. Don't bother with the 2.88MB floppies; nobody else uses them.

Video Board

Get an AGP bit-blitting video accelerator board to support modern graphical operating systems. (See Chapter 21 for more about video.) Any accelerator based on the S3 chip set will be easy to support, as S3 drivers are common for any operating system. Alternatively, look at one of the two market leaders: either an accelerator card from Diamond, or one from ATI.

Video Monitor

Buy a monitor based on the resolution you'll use it at. If you're doing regular old VGA (with a resolution of 640 dots across the screen by 480 dots down the screen), buy a 15-inch fixed frequency VGA monitor; it'll cost around $120. For the super VGA 800 × 600 resolution, get a 15-inch multisyncing monitor that can handle that resolution. For 1024 × 768, buy a monitor that's at least 17 inches diagonally. And *do not* buy interlaced 1024 × 768: sure it's cheaper, but the lawsuits from your employees going blind will be expensive. Buy non-interlaced. And only worry about it at 1024 × 768: Nobody I know of tries to interlace 640 × 480 or 800 × 600. My favorite for a 17-inch monitor is the Viewsonic 17G.

Mice

Although I hate to put more money in Microsoft's pocket, any of the Microsoft mouses (meese, mice?) seem the best of all the ones I've worked with. But $30 for a mouse? Arggh. If you have that PS/2 port I mentioned earlier, then don't forget to make the little guy a PS/2 mouse instead of serial.

Printers

Although laser printers used to be the standard for high-quality output, today's ink jet printers are excellent. In fact some like the Lexmark 7000 series printers, actually support up to 1200 × 1200 dpi. Additionally, these printers can produce photo-quality color. And ink jet printers are usually only a couple hundred dollars, while color laser printers can cost upwards of thousands of dollars.

Serial Ports

Look for serial ports based on the 16550 UART chip. It's built for multi-tasking.

Parallel Ports

Make sure that your parallel ports are Enhanced Parallel Ports, or ECP/EPP interfaces. They're faster and bi-directional. Bidirectional parallel ports are essential for modern printers, which send status information back to the PC over those ports.

Universal Serial Bus (USB)

How many things do you currently have attached to your computer? A modem, monitor, sound card, etc.? Eventually, on a standard system, you'll run out of room for more additions. USB is designed to solve this problem—you can have up to 127 devices attached to a USB port. Not only that, you can simply plug in the device and forget it, no messy configurations, or even reboots. When you get a system, look into one with USB ports on the motherboard, since so many people are coming out with compatible add-ons.

From Whom Should You Buy?

When I ask this question, I don't mean whether you should buy from Dell, IBM, or Jeff and Akbar's House of Clones; instead, I mean, "Should you buy direct from the manufacturer, via mail order, or at a store?"

Well, if you're a really large company, then it probably makes sense to go straight to Compaq or whomever and negotiate a specific deal. But if you're a hobbyist or a SOHO (small office/home office) shop, then you'll have to examine your strategies.

You can probably buy cheapest from mail order. *But* if you do that, then returning defective merchandise involves shipping things around, getting RMA (Return Merchandise Authorization) numbers, etc. That can be a hassle.

Going to a big computer retailer is just a fast way to waste money, so I'm not intending to shove you into the arms of Computerland or the like. But there are many small businesses whose main line of work is to sell computer parts, software, supplies, and systems at a reasonable price. These local vendors often offer prices that aren't much more expensive than mail order. (Besides, the nice thing about local stores is that I like my vendors within choking distance....) And patronizing your local PC store means that when you need that disk drive on Saturday, you need only run down the street to get it, rather than waiting a week for it to ship.

That's not to say that mail order doesn't make sense. Mail order firms are more likely to have the latest and greatest software and hardware. Their prices will, again, sometimes be lower than the local store's. They may even know more about the product than a local vendor might. But take it from a veteran, there are a few things to be sure of.

- First, use a credit card. It's your first line of defense when mail order companies get nasty. If you didn't get what you wanted, then just box it up, ship it back, and cancel the charge. Years ago, Dell used to charge a 15 percent "restocking fee." (They may still, but I refuse to do business with them, so I wouldn't know.) They sent me a hard disk that had clearly been dropped. When it worked, it registered seek times in the hundreds of milliseconds, despite what their ad promised. They tried to convince me that the drive was just what I wanted, but I knew better and sent it back. They tried to charge me a restocking fee, so I just complained to Citibank, and Dell backed off.

- Second, find out whom you're talking to. If the person responds, "operator 22" (I suppose his friends call him "22"), ask to speak with a supervisor. You're about to give this guy your name, address, phone, and credit card number, and he won't even tell you who he is? Write the name down. Also get a confirmation number or order number.

- Third, only buy the product if it's in stock. Back-ordered things can take months to arrive, and by the time they do, you'll be charged the older (and higher) price. Get the salesperson to check that it can ship today. If not, don't place the order.

- Ship it overnight or second day. By default, mail order companies use UPS ground, which can take anywhere from one week to a millennium to arrive. Second day is usually only a few dollars more, and then you can get a guaranteed delivery date out of the salesperson.

- Once you have the product, keep the carton that it came in for 30 days. That way, if a problem arises, it's easy to ship it back. And if you do have to ship something back, then by all means insure it.

- Another new way of buying computers is over the Internet. Many computer manufacturers will sell directly from their Web sites. Some of those that do are Compaq, Dell, and Gateway. What's nice about these sites is that you can custom-design your own system right online choosing your CPU, memory, video display, and so on. Once ordered (usually with a credit card) the company builds your system to order and ships it to you within days.

Just follow those rules, and you'll have some great luck getting things through the mail.

Now that you have a beautiful new desktop machine, you are ready to get to work. But what happens if that work requires you to travel? It's not too easy to take that desktop model with you, so let's look at something a little easier to carry around, a notebook computer.

CHAPTER
TWENTY-SIX

Notebook/Laptop Computers

- Upgrading your CPU

- Upgrading your memory

- Upgrading your hard disk

- Recharging and replacing batteries

- Laptop maintenance and protection issues

In some respects, upgrading and maintaining your laptop or notebook computer is much simpler than taking care of a desktop machine. On the one hand, usually the things you can deal with on your own are plainly indicated in your owner's manual, and often involve nothing more than unplugging an old module and plugging in a new one. On the other hand, there are things you must leave in the hands of experts with specialized equipment. Again, your task is simple: put your laptop in a box, ship it off, and pay the nice people who are taking care of you.

In between these two clear extremes are upgrades and fixes that involve taking the laptop apart and doing the kind of minor surgery that, with a little instruction, the typical readers of this book can usually handle on their own. In this chapter, we'll identify which types of upgrades and fixes fall into each of the above-mentioned categories, and give you instructions for accomplishing them. Here are some examples of all three classes of upgrade.

- Say you want to add a modem. For most laptops the process is simple: you locate the PCMCIA slot on your laptop, open the cover, and slide in your new credit-card sized modem. Okay, you'll need to install the drivers too, but with PC Cards (the other name for PCMCIA) it's almost automatic.

- Say you've decided to install a larger hard disk or more memory. These are two things you *can* handle yourself, but both involve opening a system that was not really designed to be taken apart easily. If you're adventurous, handy with small tools, and want to save some money, you can do the job on your own. If you have a lot invested in your laptop and don't feel that experimenting is such a good idea, companies that specialize in laptop upgrades will do the job quickly and for relatively little money, and will usually guarantee their work.

- Say you want to upgrade your 486 laptop to a Pentium processor. This you cannot do on your own. Reason: Laptop CPUs are generally surface mounted rather than socket mounted. You cannot remove a surface-mounted laptop CPU on your own. It takes special tools and expert skills.

We'll be spending most of our time in this chapter on the first and second categories in the previous list. However, I don't want to give you the feeling that I'm simply blowing off category three, so I'll take a little time to explain *why* CPU upgrades are done by outside experts. I'll also try to give you some information on what you need to know before you send your system off to have its brain replaced.

Let me also reiterate that such items as hard drives and memory modules, while designed to be easily replaced, do involve opening your system. Whenever you do your own upgrading, be mindful of several important factors:

- Depending on what brand of laptop you have, opening the system could mean removing the screen and/or the keyboard before you can get to the object of your replacement tasks. Getting from point A to point B in a laptop usually involves a detour or two, so don't get frustrated. Plan your moves carefully, but expect to be sidetracked.

- Refer to your owner's manual early and often. If you've lost it, write to the manufacturer and get a new one.

- In all cases be even more aware than usual of cleanliness and antistatic precautions. Real estate inside a laptop is very cramped; loose bits of dust, crumbs, and cat fur really need to be kept out. Not only can they cause components to not fit right, they can cause electrical shorts and can trap and hold excess heat. In a big desktop box you can get away with a little dust; there's usually enough room to let the system fan work and enough space to dissipate the heat. Laptops don't give you that luxury.

- Always assume that there is no slack in cables and connectors. Again, things are so tight inside a laptop that everything has been measured down to the last millimeter. Never tug, bend, or twist anything.

- Never handle new parts anywhere but along the edges if at all possible (and, if there's a choice, along the plastic edges instead of the metal edges). Latex hospital gloves are really handy, as well as cheap; consider wearing one glove for basic moves like picking things up and taking things out of a bag, and keep your other hand free for performing the moves that require more dexterity.

- Go out and buy the correct tools if you don't already have them. A set of jeweler's screwdrivers with rotating barrel bodies will save you more grief than you can even guess at, and for five or ten dollars a set you don't have to break the bank to add them to your toolbox.

Modern laptops have been purposely designed to keep those of us who love to tinker firmly in the back seat. The parts we can mess with are clearly marked. The parts that are off-limits should be scrupulously avoided. In a lot of respects, these are delicate, precision instruments and the best way to really screw one up is to start hacking around with the assumption that you can make something fit by pushing just a *little* bit harder.

CPU Upgrades

I've already told you that you cannot do a CPU upgrade on a laptop on your own. Briefly, the reasons have to do with the way CPUs are attached to the system board in a laptop. The method is called surface mounting and involves attaching each of the CPUs I/O channels directly to the appropriate circuit traces on the system board. In a desktop machine the task of lining up the CPU's

I/O circuits with the system board's circuit traces is taken care of by the CPU *socket*. The socket permanently aligns things on both sides, so that when you insert the CPU into the socket, the system's brain and nervous system hook up the way they're supposed to. The only problems with this approach, as far as laptops are concerned, are that the socket consumes space and the CPU has to be built with pins that can be inserted into the socket. The total effect is a structure that is relatively tall, and would entail lots of wasted space inside the laptop, thereby ruining the sleek, sexy lines of the whole laptop package.

Surface mounting eliminates the socket and the requirement for pins on the CPU. The CPU simply lies flat on the system board with its bare I/O points exactly aligned with the board's circuit-trace ends. There are three basic methods for surface mounting. One is called wire bonding, the second is called tape-automated bonding, and the third is called solder bumping.

Each one of the points where an I/O point and a circuit trace meet has to be joined in such a way as to allow electrical conductivity, meaning that each point is usually bridged with a minute glob of solder. In each of the methods a robotic arm positions the chip precisely over the motherboard and gently lowers it until the wire or tape comes into contact with the traces or until the terminations on the chip come into contact with the solder balls sitting on top of the traces. Hot air is blown into the space between the chip and the motherboard, melting the solder. The hot air is turned off, the solder solidifies, and you have a new CPU. The whole process is completely automated. The only place humans get involved is inspecting the solder joints under a microscope to make sure the solder hasn't bled from one trace to another. Getting all that connectivity exactly right, with each point simultaneously soldered, with no variation in the thickness of the joints, and all done in a space only a couple of microns thick, is a job for a surface mounting machine…and is the real reason we can't do this type of upgrade ourselves.

Your CPU Might Not Be Upgradable

Nevertheless, there are a few things we can do to make sure our upgrade goes smoothly. Primarily, we need to find out whether or not we have the kind of laptop that can be upgraded at all. With surface mounting, remember, the I/O point on the CPU must mate directly with the circuit traces on the system board. If the system board doesn't have the proper traces to accept, for example, a Pentium processor, you simply can't force the issue. Here are some examples:

- **286:** Sad to report, but the 286 chip has finally made its appointment with obsolescence. If you want to upgrade a 286 notebook computer, buy a new one.

- **386SX:** Can be upgraded to a 486, but you may have to upgrade to a Cyrix processor, assuming that you can find one. Most of these are also obsolete and the replacement chips hard to find.

- **386SL:** Cannot be upgraded to a 486 processor of any type.

- **486SL:** Cannot be upgraded to any other speed.

- **486DX** and **486SX:** Generally have no problem being replaced by Pentium chips, but the speed of the Pentium chip will be directly related to the speed of the 486 chip you're replacing.

- **Pentium Overdrive:** Cannot be upgraded. (Even though it's possible to upgrade a desktop machine that's using a Pentium Overdrive chip, you can't upgrade a similarly equipped laptop.)

There are also a number of Pentium upgrades available to make some of the earlier Pentiums faster. But once again, upgrading a portable computer's CPU is not generally something you can do yourself.

Table 26.1 shows some of the 486 upgrades that are possible, depending on the type of system you currently have.

TABLE 26.1: Upgrades for 486 Processors

Current CPU	Upgrades Available
486SX-25	586-75, 586-100, and 586-133
486DX-25	586-75, 586-100, and 586-133
486SX2-50	586-75, 586-100, and 586-133
486DX2-50	586-75 and 586-133
486DX4-75	586-75 and 586-133
486DX-33	586-100 and 586-133
486SX2-66	586-100 and 586-133
486DX4-100	586-100 and 586-133

Determining Your System's Current CPU

You want to upgrade your CPU and you now know from what we've said in the previous section that what you've *already* got will determine what you *can* get. Thus, you want to make sure of exactly what type of CPU you have in your laptop before you send it off. You can usually rely on the information in your owner's manual. If it says you have a 486SX, that's probably what you've got. However, if you bought the system from your cousin, or you've lost the owner's manual, or simply want to double check (highly recommended), there's a very simple way to do it, using a utility that is included with DOS, called Microsoft Diagnostics, or MSD.EXE. To run it, simply do the following:

NOTE   MSD cannot identify many of the newer processors. On the other hand, it's not included with the newer systems, so it's an easy decision: If you have MSD, it'll probably work. If not, it probably won't, so don't go looking for a copy.

1. Reboot your system so it comes up in DOS mode. (Do not run MSD.EXE from a DOS window in Windows 95 or 98, because MSD's results will be unreliable and might hang up your system, forcing you to do a hard reboot and causing you to lose any and all unsaved data.)

2. Change to the DOS directory.

3. Type **msd** and press Enter.

Your system will pop up a screen with various information (see Figure 26.1), the first item of which will be your type of processor.

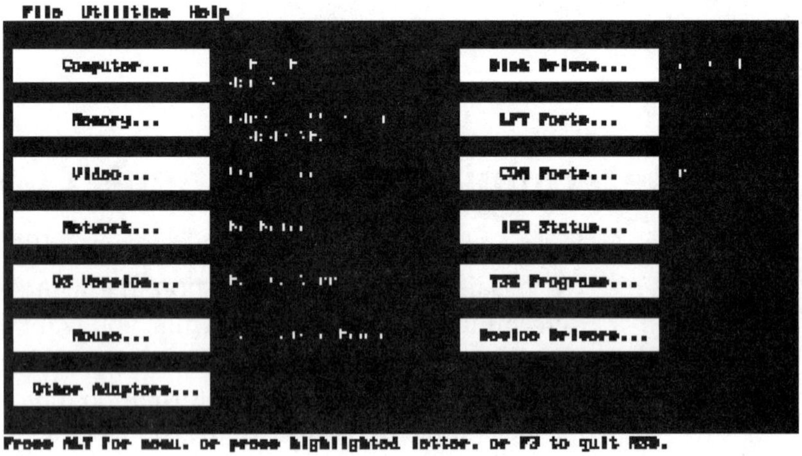

FIGURE 26.1:

MSD screen providing information about your system

To get more detailed information on your processor, press **p** on your keyboard or click the word "Computer" with your mouse. You will see a screen similar to the one shown in Figure 26.2.

MSD screen showing
detailed information
about your processor

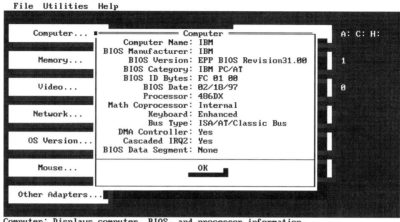

```
 File  Utilities  Help

   Computer...  ■═══════════ Computer ═══════════        A: C: H:
                   Computer Name: IBM
                 BIOS Manufacturer: IBM
   Memory...        BIOS Version: EPP BIOS Revision31.00       1
                    BIOS Category: IBM PC/AT
                    BIOS ID Bytes: FC 01 00
   Video...            BIOS Date: 02/18/97                     0
                       Processor: 486DX
                 Math Coprocessor: Internal
   Network...           Keyboard: Enhanced
                        Bus Type: ISA/AT/Classic Bus
                   DMA Controller: Yes
   OS Version...    Cascaded IRQ2: Yes
                 BIOS Data Segment: None
   Mouse...                      OK

   Other Adapters...■
```

Computer: Displays computer, BIOS, and processor information.

The information on this screen is important primarily because it gives you BIOS data. Many companies that specialize in replacing CPUs will also replace your BIOS chip at the same time, all the better for the whole system to work together. They may ask you on the phone what kind of BIOS you have, and it's good to have this information handy.

This is where you need to get on the phone with one of the upgrade companies and discuss your options. The best way to find an upgrade house is on the Internet:

1. In your browser, go to a search engine (such as Yahoo, Web Crawler, HotBot, or Excite).

2. Type **laptop + upgrade** and press Enter.

3. You will get a screen listing everything that particular search engine could find on the subject. The higher the item is on the list, the more likely it will provide the information you seek.

You can usually find answers to most general questions, including price, shipping information, and how long an upgrade will take, by just browsing through a particular subject area. For specific questions, look for a customer support telephone number; you will usually find that the tech support people are both knowledgeable and happy to help.

Memory Upgrades

Upgrading the computer's memory is probably the most frequent improvement that people make, as well as one of the easiest to accomplish. Most laptops come with specific instructions on how to do it and provide the specifications to show you exactly what kind of memory to buy. By this I mean the type and speed of the RAM and the specific increments you have to buy.

As far as speed is concerned, you can usually use faster RAM than what you've already got, but not slower. Slow RAM just won't be able to keep up, and you'll be wasting your time and money to even try. The best thing to do is always get new chips that match the speed of your current ones.

NOTE   As far as the type of RAM to get, most notebooks use proprietary memory modules instead of the more generic SIMMs or DIMMs.

If you do have a proprietary memory system, you have no option but to buy a single module in the exact size needed because proprietary memory modules are only replaceable, and there is generally room for only one module in such machines.

Preparing for the Upgrade

As long as you follow some basic, preliminary precautions there is little you should worry about when it comes time to upgrade the memory on your laptop.

Back Up Your Hard Disk

It's always a good idea to make sure you back up your hard disk before you do any work on your computer. The chances that you'll do some damage are slight, but you only have to lose everything one time to understand the value of backups.

Prepare Your Workspace

Before you start, clear off your workspace. The kitchen table will do just fine (wipe it down first). Have a flat surface to work on with plenty of room to lay things out. You don't want your screwdriver rolling onto the floor just when you need it. I like to work on a clean white towel (not a terry cloth towel, though—you don't want to introduce lint). The color provides contrast, and the softness reduces ricochets and adds a little traction for fast moving small items such as screws. Lay out your tools (a small flat-blade screwdriver, a small- and large-head Phillips screwdriver, and maybe small needle-nose pliers just in case). Some systems require little hex-head screwdrivers, but most do not. The tools will vary; just make sure you've got your toolkit close at hand. You may want a grounding strap that you can wrap around your wrist or ankle to keep static from building up while you work, but for a short job like this you probably won't need one.

Disconnect Everything

When installing any kind of internal components in your laptop, including memory modules, always double check that the computer is turned off and disconnected from the AC adapter. Remove the battery pack from the computer. Remove all cables to such things as printers and external modems, and so on.

Ground Yourself

Make sure that you are well grounded and always touch something metal before you touch the delicate stuff inside the laptop. That way, if you've collected any static you'll discharge it onto the metal object instead of into your computer. Those little blue sparks that come off your fingers can have hundreds or even thousands of volts and that's definitely not good for electronic components that run on 2.2–5 volts. Filing cabinets, light fixtures, co-workers, and doorframes are good things to touch to see if you're sparking.

Also, please make sure that none of your tools are the magnetized kind that come in so handy in other situations around the home. They're good for fishing lost screws out of the sink, but you don't want them anywhere near your computer.

Keep It Clean

So, touching some things is good to get rid of static. On the other hand, there are other things you never want to touch at all. For example, do not touch the metal conductors on the memory modules. Even minute amounts of dust, grit, skin oils, and sticky crud left over from lunch can be a real problem. Also, try not to touch cables, wires, and other components you're not working on. Maybe it's picky, but the fewer things you mess with, the fewer things you'll have to check later if the system doesn't work the way it's supposed to. Remember the latex gloves we talked about earlier? This is a good time to take them out and put them on.

Make a Map

With some laptops, you may need to unplug something else (such as a hard drive or a battery) before you can get to the memory module adapter or slot. If you do, sit back for a minute, grab a pencil and paper, and make a sketch of what plugs into what before you start pulling things apart. Don't worry about making it pretty or exactly to scale, just make sure everything in the sketch is accurately identified and labeled. This is especially important for any wires you need to move out of the way. You can't rely on your remembrance of things past to make sure they all go back exactly they way they need to go back. With bigger machines, like desktop computers or car engines, you can get away with tagging wires with masking tape. You won't have that kind of room inside a laptop and you really don't want gummy tape glue inside your system. Lastly, don't worry if the other kids in the class laugh at you—read what your manual says about installing new memory.

Get Motivated!

At this point, you may be asking yourself if you really want to get involved in doing this kind of upgrade on your own. You may think that all of these precautions signal something very difficult or dangerous. That is really not the case. All I'm trying to do is point out that you need to take your time and proceed in a careful, well-planned manner. Look at it this way—installing memory in your laptop will take you 10 to 15 minutes. These things are made to be upgraded, after all. Now, if you pay someone at the local computer store to do the upgrade for you, it will take them the same 10 or 15 minutes to do the job. It will also cost you about $85. That's the going hourly rate for most PC repair jobs and you'll pay for a full hour regardless of how little time the upgrade really takes. At the very least, you should try doing the installation yourself and, if you get to a place where you really don't want to go any farther, then take it down to the shop. But give it a shot yourself, first. You'll be surprised at how easily most of these systems come together and you can use the $85 you save to treat yourself to dinner and a movie.

Doing the Installation

Increasing the memory on your laptop is probably the easiest upgrade option available. The following sections detail the steps involved.

Access

The first thing you have to do is open up the computer so you can get at the memory modules. Most laptops have access hatches that you open from the bottom, so close the screen, turn the laptop over, and work from the bottom of the laptop system unit. Sometimes you have to unscrew a cover plate to open the memory hatch; with other laptops you push small locking tabs and lift the cover plate away from the body of the machine. In either case, the correct hatch should be marked with something that indicates which is the correct one. It might say "memory," it might have a stylized drawing of a memory module, it might have something arcane, like the word "exp," but it will usually have something to indicate that this is where the memory lives. If there are other hatches, they too will be marked. You're smart, you'll figure it out.

Some laptops require you to remove or simply lift up the keyboard in order to access the memory area. For these systems, open up the screen, unlatch the keyboard (by sliding the unlocking latches on the side or at the back), and work on the system from the top.

The top-access systems usually still have the memory modules down at the bottom of the system, so you may also have to move the diskette drive or hard drive to get at the memory. If you have to move a drive, it will usually come equipped with a plastic tab that you use as a handle. Always use the tabs or handles they give you. Do not put a screwdriver under the drive and try to lever it out. Look before you pull. There may be little plastic or metal devices that the manufacturer used to hold the drive in place. There may be small screws that hold it down. Refer to your owner's manual to see if you need to remove any of these things or if the whole unit should slide out as a single piece.

Even on systems you access from the bottom, you may still have to move something else out of the way before you can get to the memory area. Some laptops, for example, require that you remove the hard drive by sliding it out of its socket and removing it from the machine.

Look Around

Once you have exposed the memory area, you'll want to stop for a minute and study what's in front of you. Does your system have slots that accept SIMM or DIMM memory modules, or is it the kind that uses prepackaged proprietary memory modules?

If you have the latter, you'll simply insert the new, two-plug memory module into the sockets that are provided. These machines are usually limited to accepting only one upgrade module, so if there is already something in the upgrade sockets you'll have to remove it before you can add the new module.

Even if you have the kind of laptop that accepts ordinary SIMMs or DIMMs, you need to see what kind of room you have. Such systems as Toshiba's or IBM's have slots that accept SIMM or DIMM modules, and they can accept more than one module before the system is fully loaded.

Do you have empty slots or are all of them filled? If you have empty slots you can go ahead with the addition of your new memory. If your slots are all filled you'll have to empty one or more of them so you have a place to put your new memory.

Out with the Old

If you have to remove memory, look for something that indicates which slot has the highest number (for example, there might be a small 0 or 1 printed on the board next to the slot). You will usually want to replace existing memory starting with the highest numbered slot. (This is where your owner's manual or the company's tech support people can be most helpful, by giving exact instructions if you can't find a clear indicator just by looking at the slots.)

To remove any memory modules you have to get rid of, look for the locking latches on both edges of the socket. Unhook the latches from the module by pressing them away from the module. These latches can sometimes be fairly tight, but don't get carried away and apply too much force; you don't want to snap them off. Just a gentle push outward should be enough. Once the latches are released from the edges of the module, you can tilt the module upwards and slide if out. Do not touch the gold or tin connectors.

Set aside any modules you've removed and save them for possible future use. You never know when they might come in handy. You may be able to sell your old memory. My local computer store has a bulletin board for people to advertise when they want to buy or sell old parts, including used chips. Failing that, try giving them to a school. Taxpayer revolt being what it is, the school's probably pretty desperate for any charity you care to offer, and you can probably take a tax break by deducting the value (or a percentage of it) when April rolls around. (Ask your tax preparer, just to be sure.)

In with the New

If you have empty slots and don't have to take anything out before you add the new memory, or if you've freed some room by following the instructions above, pick up your new module by the edges and slide it into the socket. It will go in at an angle and then pivot down until it locks into place. Make sure it's fully seated in the slot before you pivot it down.

Most memory modules are keyed by having little notches cut into the side so that they will only fit into the slot one way. If you have any doubts, such as if the module seems really hard to fit into the connector, take it out and try it the other way. (This is also why you took a few minutes to make a sketch of what things looked like before you started.) Never try to cram something into a place where it doesn't seem to want to go. It might be misaligned, there may be something blocking the way, or it might be upside down. These things slide in easily. If yours doesn't, it's the wrong way around. Turn it and try again, dust it off, line it up and make sure it goes in straight; just don't force it.

Put Everything Back

Once you have the new memory correctly installed, by whichever method your laptop requires, replace whatever you took out, or off in exactly the same way you removed it. Replace the drives, battery packs, and access covers in reverse order from the way they came off. Reconnect any cables you disconnected, and turn the machine on. It will go through its normal boot cycle, only this time you should see a bigger number on your screen when it does the memory check. If all goes well, you're done. For example, if you installed two 16MB DIMMs to a computer that already had 8MB of memory, the boot sequence should confirm that all went well by showing you that you now have 40MB of memory.

If you get an error message or if the amount of memory the computer recognizes does not match the amount you should now have, you'll have to turn off the machine and go through the installation process again. If you have to reopen the computer and do it all again, it'll probably be because the new memory module isn't fully inserted into the slot. Make sure that it's straight and fully seated, so the locking tabs snap into the notches on the module. And if that doesn't fix it, send the memory back because it's defective.

Upgrading the Hard Disk

The capacity of your laptop's hard disk drive can be increased by installing compression programs, like Microsoft's DriveSpace, that will effectively double the amount of space you can use. But it won't work if you're using one of the newer versions of Windows that uses FAT 32. At some point, however, you may decide that you've compressed everything as far as you can and you still need more room. You have a number of options:

- You can attach a removable media drive, such as a Zip drive, via your laptop's parallel port.

- You can slip a PCMCIA hard drive into your laptop.

- Some laptops will let you replace the floppy disk drive or CD-ROM drive with a second hard disk.

- You can remove your current hard drive and completely replace it with a new, higher-capacity model.

The last of these options is the one most people choose. The others have certain drawbacks. External removable media drives force you to carry extra gear and, while they're good for special occasions such as hauling around huge graphics files, they tend to be cumbersome and somewhat slow. PCMCIA hard drives are handy and work quite well but using one means giving up, at least temporarily, access to PCMCIA modems and other devices that use the same slot or slots. Replacing your floppy drive or CD-ROM with a second hard drive is a tempting solution, and some people are happy to trade off their floppy for something bigger. However, others rely on their floppies to allow them to load new files and programs, or need to keep their CD-ROMs for the large reference works they have in their CD libraries. Additionally, not all laptops have controllers capable of supporting a second hard drive. If you have one that will, such as an IBM ThinkPad, we'll go into that upgrade option shortly. For now, though, let's take a look at what you need to do to replace your current hard drive with a new one.

Finding the Right Hard Disk

The only real trick in replacing your hard drive is getting a new one that will work with your laptop and that isn't really much of a trick. Almost all laptop computers use 2.5 inch hard drives. If your laptop was made before 1996, it probably has a *full-height* hard drive, about 18 millimeters high. If your laptop was made after 1996, it probably has a *slim-line* hard drive, about 11 millimeters high. A slim hard drive will usually work in an older (pre-1996) laptop but a full-height drive won't fit in a laptop made for the 11mm drives. If you find a really good deal on a full-height drive but aren't sure if it will fit into your newer laptop, the best way to check is to remove your current drive (see "Taking Out the Old Hard Drive" later in this chapter) and take a ruler to its height. Just measure the height of the drive, not its supporting brackets. If it's 18mm, you can use a new drive that is either 11mm or 18mm. If it's 11mm, you need to specify the same (a slim-line model) for your new drive, too.

Verifying the BIOS

Another thing you have to watch out for is what kind of BIOS you have. Some older BIOS chips will not let you have a hard drive larger than 540MB. If this is the kind of BIOS you have, you will need a software BIOS *extender* (software that allows the BIOS to recognize larger hard drives) for your notebook/laptop, or you will need to send your laptop to an upgrade company that will update your firmware BIOS. The good news is that most mail-order sources will either include the BIOS upgrade software as part of the price, or will upgrade your firmware BIOS if you send them the computer. The bad news is that, if you have to send your laptop away to be upgraded, you're going to be without it for a few days. Generally speaking, however, most laptops will do just fine with a software BIOS extender and you won't have to send your machine out into the cold cruel world on its own.

Mounting Hardware

Finally, some laptop hard drives are manufactured in such a way that their supporting brackets are built right into the drive itself. If you have this kind of hard drive, you will need to get new mounting hardware along with your hard drive, and you may have to hunt to find it. A lot of retailers don't carry a large variety of brackets. Your best bet in such a case will be to call your laptop's manufacturer, or the hard drive vendor, and find out where you can get the hardware you need to attach the new drive to the laptop. Seems like such a minor item, but things like these can give you the biggest headaches.

NOTE   Need some pointers on how to locate a source for laptop hard drives? Again, the best way to find one quickly is to use one of the search engines on the Internet. Just run a search for **laptop + hard drive**.

Backing Up Your Data

Things can go wrong—remember Murphy's Law? It's always better to be safe than sorry when messing around with your hard-earned data. Do not remove your old hard drive until it is entirely backed up, either on the new hard drive or by some other means.

To back up your data you have a number of options, as presented in the following paragraphs.

Network Backup

If you have access to a network, the easiest way to back up your hard disk is to copy everything from your laptop to the server and keep it there until you are done installing your new hard drive. You will need to make sure you have all of your configuration software on a floppy disk, however, or your machine won't be able to access the network to let you download all of your files when you are ready for them.

External Drive

If you have an external tape drive or a Zip drive, you can use MSBackup to move all of your files to the external drive and then restore them to the new hard drive after you finish installing it.

Second Laptop or Desktop Computer

You can use a commercial program like LapLink to copy all of your files to another machine and then restore them to the new hard drive after you finish installing it.

Second Hard Drive

If you have a laptop that will accommodate two hard drives (by removing the floppy disk drive or CD-ROM, for example) you can install the new hard drive, XCOPY everything from the old drive to the new drive, remove both drives, install the new drive in place of the old drive, and finally, re-install the floppy drive or CD-ROM. This is a lot of work, but sometimes you have to get creative if you want to get anything done.

Alternatively, you can use the Seagate FileCopy program. File-Copy will make an exact, bootable duplicate of the original hard drive on another hard drive that's as large or larger capacity.

Preparing for the Hard Drive Upgrade

You've got the hard drive and mounting hardware. You've backed up all of your files. You have a bootable floppy disk at hand and another floppy with all of your network access software. If you've backed up your old hard drive to a server, and removed all boisterous children and kittens to another room, you're all set to begin. Before you start, however, check to make sure you have all the necessary tools handy. You won't need many, but here are some you should have on hand:

- Small Phillips and flathead screwdrivers, to remove screws on access plates (if necessary) and mounting hardware (if necessary).

- A hex or Torx type screwdriver on some computers, to remove screws on access plates (if necessary) and mounting hardware (if necessary).

- Needle nose pliers, in case you drop something into the system and need to fish it out.

- Pencil and paper, to write or sketch the current physical layout of cables and connectors.

- Software to partition and format the new drive, if you have bought what is known as a "bare" drive, which has not been partitioned and formatted by the manufacturer.

Installing the New Hard Drive

You're all ready to go. You have your hard drive. You have your laptop. You have a flat, clean surface on which to work. Your tools are all laid out where you can reach them. You have grounded yourself. Let's get started.

Opening the Laptop

In order to get to the hard drive, some laptops may need to be completely opened up. With others, you may just have to lift off the keyboard by unsnapping it. And some have drives that simply slide out (my favorite).

First, make sure you know the location of the hard drive.

You may be lucky and have a drive caddie that slides out from the computer, no screws required. Another easy replacement job is for machines in which the keyboard or other piece unsnaps or lifts up to reveal the hard drive.

Only slightly more involved are laptops in which a top or bottom piece is unscrewed and removed to get to the hard drive.

More difficult are the laptops that have a top or bottom piece that is unscrewed and removed, and then require that one or more components be removed to get to the hard drive

The hardest type is the kind of laptop in which a top or bottom piece is unscrewed and removed, and most components including the system board are removed to get to the hard drive.

If you have a compnuter that comes with a hard drive caddie, you can ignore most of this information since you just slide out the old drive and slide in the new one.

Work slowly and carefully. Don't try to pry apart your computer once the screws are removed. Many of the notebook computers have extremely thin plastic snaps that align the top and bottom and help to hold them together. In addition, some types of notebooks also require you to remove a keyboard mask, while others may have this keyboard mask built into the top cover piece. Slowly pull the plastic cover away while carefully looking for connecting cables. If you find any, they will need to be disengaged before you can completely open the system.

Finally, with many laptops there will be quite a bit of mounting hardware, which has to be removed before you can gain access to the drive.

Taking Out the Old Hard Drive

Once you can see the hard drive, find the proper screwdriver among the tools you have thoughtfully laid out within reach and unscrew the mounting bracket. Remove the mounting bracket along with the drive.

Make sure to carefully detach the drive interface from the interface connector and remember which way the drive was positioned. Consider drawing a sketch to help you remember the proper position.

Remove the hard drive from its mounting bracket. It will probably just slide out, but you may have to push it a little. Make sure you're not pushing at an angle and be careful not to push too hard. If you don't detect any movement while applying moderate force, check it for small screws or plastic tabs that may be holding it in place.

WARNING Do not apply excessive force to the hard drive.

Putting In the New Hard Drive

First, install the new hard drive in the mounting bracket. Next, carefully place the new hard drive (in its mounting bracket) into the same spot where the old one was positioned. Pull out the sketch you made when removing the old drive and make sure you're putting the new one in the same way the old one came out. Also, be extra careful that the drive interface pins are properly aligned with the cable or connector to which they attach. These things are really small and often quite delicate and it's easy to wind up with the top row of pins in the bottom row of the connector.

That's really all there is to it. Carefully align and replace any covers, keyboard masks, plastic snaps, and so on, in the same order you removed them, but don't try to permanently close up the system just yet. Make sure any screws you do install go in all the way, but don't over-torque them. Make sure you don't have any pieces left over. If you drop a screw and it rolls down into the system, get it out before you do anything else. These are small machines. It didn't go very far. Pick the system up and roll it from side to side (like one of those kid's toys with little ball bearings that you try to roll into the clown's nose). The little screw will eventually rattle into a place where you can see it and grab it with your non-magnetized needle nosed pliers. Dental picks and hemostats are also handy for this kind of work but are usually not things most people have in their tool boxes and are too expensive unless you do this kind of thing a lot. Finally, while you have everything open, you could spray it with a can of compressed air to get out any dust. Don't try to wipe away the dust with a cloth or a paper towel, though, as you'll likely scratch something or leave lint or paper fibers behind. Also, don't blow on the inside of your laptop. Your breath may be minty fresh, but it's also very humid.

Testing the New Hard Disk

Now before you put the system completely back together, put the battery pack back in and turn the laptop on. If the system runs through its memory test you can breathe a sigh of relief. If the system won't run the memory test the most likely culprit is the hard drive interface or one of the other connections. Check everything. If you don't find anything obvious, try replacing the old drive and try again. If this works, something is wrong with the new hard drive.

If the memory test succeeds, you'll probably get an error message like `HDD Configuration Error`. Don't worry. You want it to say this. Your CMOS is looking for the hard drive you took out and just doesn't recognize the new one yet. Get into your CMOS Setup routine (with the Setup disk, or by pressing one or more keys while the system is booting) and set the hard drive to the correct type as indicated by the information that came with the new unit. You may have to identify it by number, you may need to fill in several parameters, such as number of heads, number of cylinders, number of sectors, etc. All of this information should be in with the packing slip and the bubble wrap in the new drive's shipping box. On the other hand, you may not need to do anything except reboot.

Now that there is nothing on your hard drive, you'll need to boot your computer from your bootable floppy disk (a floppy with `COMMAND.COM` on it). After you've formatted the drive, you should be able to boot right from the new hard drive.

If you've transferred your `CONFIG.SYS` and `AUTOEXEC.BAT` files from your old hard drive your system may not boot from the new hard drive because something in these files is not configured correctly for your new drive. Turn to Chapter 11, "Installing a Hard Disk." From here, dealing with a laptop hard disk is the same as with any other computer.

Closing Up

Once everything seems to be working, you can close-up your computer. Put the keyboard back in place. Screw down any access hatches you had to remove. Connect your laptop to the network,

Zip drive, external tape drive, or whatever you used to hold all your backup files, and copy everything onto your new drive.

Installing a Second Hard Drive

With some laptops, such as the IBM ThinkPad 760, you can replace the floppy drive or CD-ROM drive with a second hard disk. Often, however, you will need to buy a second hard disk holder since you can't just let the new hard drive rattle around in there.

Make sure, when you put your secondary hard drive into its caddie, that any slots, connectors, or projections on the hard drive match the corresponding slots, connectors, and projections on the caddie. Then press it firmly into the caddie until you hear it click into place. If it doesn't seem to be going in after you've applied a moderate amount of force, don't keep pushing. It's probably not lined up right. Take it out and re-insert it. You may have to wiggle it a little to make sure everything is lined up correctly.

Next, remove the disk drive or CD-ROM drive. On laptops that have removable keyboards, this involves the following steps:

1. Make sure there are no disks or CDs in the drive you're taking out.
2. Turn the power off.
3. Disconnect the AC adapter.
4. Unplug any cables that attach to printers and modems.
5. Unlatch the keyboard and swing it up out of the way.
6. Remove the battery.
7. Use the attached handles, tabs, or straps to remove the CD-ROM drive or disk drive.

If you're replacing a disk drive with a hard drive you will have a hole in the front of the laptop where you used to insert disks. You can cover this over with a shaped piece of plastic called a bezel. Remember the baggie with all that unidentifiable stuff from when you brought your laptop home and unpacked it? Your bezel's in there. If you saved the box, go rummage around in the closet until you find it. If you threw it away you can usually get one at your local computer store. Generally, they are shipped with new hard drives but you might make a note to ask just to be sure. Some bezels are made to be installed from the inside of the computer while the drive bay is empty. Others are designed to be pushed into place from the outside. Either way, make sure you cover the hole in the front or side of your laptop. Holes like that are invitations to all sorts of problems.

If you're replacing a CD-ROM drive with a hard drive, you can usually just slide the new hard drive into the space vacated by the old, unwanted CD-ROM. If that space was previously unoccupied, you may have to remove a bezel so the front of the hard drive can be seen from the outside (so you can see the drive's activity light) and then finish up with the following steps:

1. Firmly press the new hard drive holder until it clicks into the connector.

2. Replace the battery.

3. Re-attach the keyboard and re-connect the AC adapter and whatever cables you just took off.

PCMCIA Drive Cards

PCMCIA hard drives, sometimes also called drive cards or credit card hard drives, offer an extremely simple way to add storage capacity to your laptop. They generally come in the size known as Type III PCMCIA, which means that they take up two card slots in your laptop. You can get Type I and Type II PCMCIA hard drive cards, which take up only one slot, but they tend to be quite small in terms of capacity.

Installing a PCMCIA hard drive involves nothing more that making sure you have installed the device driver software that comes on a disk with the card and that you have the card pointed the right way. Make sure the notched edge on the card goes in first. Press the card firmly into the connector. Usually, there will be an eject button either inside the PCMCIA opening or on the side of the computer next to the card slot. You'll know when the card is fully installed because the Eject button will pop out. On some laptops, the IBM ThinkPad for example, you then pull the eject button out a little bit and fold it towards the front of the laptop.

Drive cards are in short supply since Compact Flash (CF) cards are dirt cheap and getting huge (32MBs for $90). There is a smattering of Type II HDD cards, but they are few and far between. CF is by far the most popular mass storage format for portable devices, as they can be used in CF-enabled devices and, with an adapter, be used in Type II slots. Table 26.2 lists some of the PCMCIA cards currently available. As you can see, they come in a wide variety of capacities and, aside from using up those jealously guarded PCMCIA slots, offer absolutely the simplest way to make sure you never have to get rid of old files.

TABLE 26.2: PCMCIA Hard Drives

Vendor	Product ID#	Contact information
3M COMPANY	44409-2	www.mmm.com
EPSON AMERICA, INC.	Notebook70-004502	www.epson.com
EPSON AMERICA, INC.	Notebook70-004546	www.epson.com
EPSON AMERICA, INC.	Notebook70-004843	www.epson.com

Continued on next page

TABLE 26.2 CONTINUED: PCMCIA Hard Drives

Vendor	Product ID#	Contact information
CALLUNA TECHNOLOGIES	Type II-260MB; Type III-520MB, 1GB	www.calluna.com
TOSHIBA AMERICA, INC.	NWHD340	www.toshiba.com
TOSHIBA AMERICA, INC.	NWHD262M3	www.toshiba.com
XEROX CORPORATION	97K15370	www.xerox.com
XEROX CORPORATION	97K22280	www.xerox.com

Other Kinds of Upgrades

Now that we've covered upgrading CPUs, memory, and hard drives, what if you want to upgrade your laptop in different ways? Say you want to increase its utility in the office instead of just using it at home or on the road. The following sections go into some of the other things you can do to put more life in your laptop.

Laptop LAN Adapters

Connecting your laptop to the company network is accomplished by connecting a LAN adapter to the parallel or SCSI port of your laptop or inserting a LAN adapter card into your PCMCIA card slot. Some have telephone-jack type connectors (RJ45) for 10BaseT connections and some have coax cable connections (BNC). You'll need to find out which kind you need, as well as making sure your laptop is configured with the correct software for networking. Prices can range from around $75 to several hundred dollars, depending on the type of network you have and which vendor you choose. Also, prices change very rapidly, as with everything else involving computers, so be sure to get the most recent price quotes from whomever you choose.

There are dozens of resources on the net that make information about LAN adapters very easy to find. Computer Shopper has a wonderful set of utilities that allow a person to select, compare, and choose which system they want peripherals for. C | Net has similar information, as does ZDNet and dozens of other sites, both retail and editorial.

PCMCIA LAN Adapter Cards

A different type of LAN adapter is the PCMCIA type. Instead of plugging a cable with an attached adapter into a port on your laptop, you insert the PCMCIA LAN adapter card into the PCMCIA slot in the side of your laptop and connect to the network by means of attaching the network cable to it. There are many different kinds, from many different manufacturers. Lots of current information about them is available online.

Wireless LAN Cards

If you're the type of person who thinks it's more than a little pointless to have a walkabout computer that's shackled to a desk by its LAN connection, you can upgrade to a wireless LAN card. These are more expensive than the ones discussed in the preceding sections, but they do give you more mobility.

As mentioned earlier, your best source for current and accurate information about wireless LAN cards is the Internet, since technology and pricing changes so rapidly.

Battery Upgrades & Replacements

Battery replacement is usually not a problem for most laptop users. Many laptops now have power-management functions, either built in or available by using special drivers. These functions monitor whether the system is on, and whether anybody is using it. After prescribed periods of no input from the keyboard or mouse, the laptop "goes to sleep." It doesn't turn itself off but it slumbers until you wake it up. The advantage is that power-consuming features of the unit, such as the screen display, are no longer drawing down the charge in the battery. Preserving the life of the battery is obviously preferable to replacing it, so there are a number of things you can do to make sure you get the most use out of yours.

First, new batteries and those that have not been used in a long time will not take a full charge the first time you connect them to the AC adapter. With some types of batteries, such as the lithium-ion battery pack that IBM uses in the ThinkPad, you will have to fully discharge and then recharge the battery up to a half-dozen times before the battery is operating at peak performance.

Second, batteries do not like to be recharged until they are completely empty. You might think you're helping the battery to a longer life by keeping the laptop connected to the AC adapter all the time but just the opposite is true. They wear out a lot quicker. Always run them down before you plug them in again.

Third, with some laptops you are advised not to run them while their batteries are charging. The competing demands of accepting a new charge while simultaneously losing charge as part of normal operation cause internal problems that shorten the battery's life.

Fourth, some batteries need to be completely discharged and then recharged from time to time. It cleans them out, so to speak, the same way you sometimes drain and refill the radiator on your car. Some power management utilities that come with the laptop, or that you can buy at your local computer store, have discharging functions as part of the program. For example, the discharging program for the IBM ThinkPad works like this: 1) Connect the AC adapter to the computer. 2) Click the Discharge button on the Fuel-Gauge program. 3) The battery automatically drains. 4) When it hits bottom, it starts to charge up again automatically.

Finally, even if your laptop has a sleep mode, turn it off when you're not going to be using it for a while, like when you go to lunch.

Replacing the Battery

Regardless of how well you care for your battery, there will come a time when you have to take it out and put in a new one. Since this is one of the things most people will actually have to do fairly routinely, most laptops make it pretty easy.

1. Turn the computer off.

2. Disconnect it from the AC adapter and remove any cables to printers, modems, networks, etc.

3. Find out where your battery is located. On some laptops you will access it through a hatch on the bottom of the computer. Generally the hatch will simply slide out but in some cases you will need to take out some screws or release a locking mechanism. On other laptops you reach the battery from the top by first lifting off the keyboard. Check your owners' manual if you're not sure how the keyboard comes off.

4. The battery is usually right on top. Once you get the hatch or access panel off, the battery is the first thing you see. Make sure, however, that you don't need to remove something else before you go to work on the battery. If your laptop has a

CD-ROM, for example, you may have to remove it before you can pull the power pack.

5. Some batteries have plastic tabs or handles that you use to pull them away from their sockets before lifting them out. Others are unplugged simply by sliding them out of the connectors by hand. If yours has tabs or handles, use them.

6. Don't pull out the battery and then go home for the evening. Put the new one in right away. Some laptops depend on their batteries to hold their CMOS configurations for more than a few minutes or seconds.

7. Close up the laptop in the reverse order you opened it.

8. If this is a brand new battery, keep the machine off and connect the AC adapter. Fully charge the battery before you turn on the computer. Also, you may have to completely discharge and then recharge the battery a few times before the battery will operate at maximum capacity.

Buying a New Battery

From time to time, no matter how well you take care of your laptop, you'll need to get a new battery, and sometimes the information printed on the side of the battery itself can be confusing or obscure. The Internet has a plethora of information about batteries for just about every laptop and notebook available.

NOTE   There are several good online sources available on the Internet for finding more information about batteries for your laptop. Just run a search on **laptops + battery**.

If you still can't find a battery for your machine, the technical support people who work for the online supply houses will generally be able to locate the information (and the battery) you need. For some of the more obscure or older makes, you may have to send your old battery to the supplier and have it rebuilt. Doing so can sometimes take a week or more.

Laptop Maintenance Issues

While keeping your laptop in good condition involves many of the same considerations as a desktop machine (for instance, keep it clean and dry, and feed it high-quality electricity), the fact that it's portable adds a few factors to the equation and makes some of the ordinary things especially important.

The Case for Cases

One of the most important things you can do to keep your laptop in good shape is to make sure you have a good carrying case. Sounds trivial, maybe, but it's not. Your laptop is a traveling companion and, as with any situation where you leave a secure, controlled environment, it will be subject to the same bumps and knocks as you.

Modern carrying cases are especially designed to save you and your notebook lots of grief and it's well worth the investment to get one you can count on. I don't necessarily mean you have to spend hundreds of dollars for one of those aluminum suitcases, either. A good padded shoulder bag will give you all the protection you'll normally need, will make it easier for you to get through doors, into cars, and onto airplanes, and will keep you from having to reinvest in new laptops.

So, don't carry your laptop outside without a case. It may look power-chic in a TV commercial, but it's probably the worst thing you can do. People drop things, even important things, and no ordinary laptop will survive a tumble onto concrete.

When you're looking at carrying cases, check to make sure that it's made of a non-porous material. Even if you like the look of a canvas-type bag, make sure there's some kind of inner liner that will keep it from transferring moisture to the inside. Raindrops on the outside are OK. When they soak through and fizzle your laptop, they're not OK.

Check the hardware between the bag and the carrying strap. If the connection is a simple spring latch, never pick up the bag with the computer inside without first making sure the "tongue and groove" pieces are straight before pulling on the strap. Sideways pressure on many of the latches that I've had experience with will cause most of them to release. You will get to find out how much a new case (or perhaps a new computer) costs when the case opens and the computer lands on one of its corners or slams into something hard (like airport steps).

You also want to make sure the case you get has separate compartments for things you carry with you. Pens, pencils, mice, and modems rattling around and bumping into your machine can cause damage.

Make sure the outer walls of the case are well padded. It doesn't have to be extremely thick but you want something between the case walls and your computer to distribute the shock of accidental bumps.

Finally, don't put anything in your case that doesn't belong there. I know people who have packed socks, toothbrushes, and candy bars into their carrying cases and treated them as overnight bags for emergency business trips. These people also tend to buy rather more new laptops than my other acquaintances. Putting anything in the bag that is damp, pointy, or crumbly is always a bad idea.

Battery Care

Most laptops come with specific instructions on how to deal with their batteries. They are not all the same. In general, however, you will have a recharger and/or AC adapter you can use when your battery power runs low. The AC adapter will recharge the battery at the same time that it provides power to keep your laptop running. Some batteries will fully recharge no matter when you plug in the AC adapter. Others will not. The IBM ThinkPad, for example, carries this warning: "Repeatedly charging a battery pack that has not been completely discharged shortens the battery operating time. To preserve battery operating time, discharge the battery pack completely, then recharge it."

Always be especially careful that the adapter you use with your laptop is the one that came with the computer, or a replacement that is specifically recommended by the manufacturer. The plug from your cordless electric drill's adapter may very well fit your computer, but there is very little chance that the voltage and amperage requirements will match as well and you'll be really sorry if you use it to recharge your laptop.

WARNING A battery is not just something that can hurt your computer. It is something that can hurt you. Batteries can and do explode if you handle them carelessly.

- Keep the battery away from fire.
- Keep the battery away from water.
- Never try to take it apart.
- Don't drop it, throw it, or bang it on the table.
- Always use only the battery designed especially for your particular make and model.

On a less urgent note, keep your battery healthy by following the manufacturer's guidelines for first use and for when and how to recharge it. For example, the battery pack in many computers will be low or "dead" when you first buy it. You have to plug in the AC adapter and let it take a charge before you can use it. Further, many batteries will require that you charge them, drain them completely, and charge them again (sometimes repeatedly) before they will accept and hold their maximum charge.

Something else to pack into your carrying case is a small, one or two socket surge protector. If you're going to be using your laptop from hotel rooms, conference centers, airport lounges, and other such places, you'll need one. You can't be any more confident of the quality of the electricity out there than you can back in the office—and you've got a surge protector on the floor under your desk, right?

Finally, it's a good idea to have more than one battery for your laptop. This is not just to let you keep working when you're out of reach of electricity. Many batteries need to be completely depleted before being recharged, so an extra battery lets you completely drain a battery, swap it out, and plug it into a recharger while you use the laptop with the backup battery. Completely draining a battery before recharging it often adds significantly to it useful life.

Physical Considerations

The weakest link on your laptop is the hinge that flips the screen up and down. It's not that the hinges are designed badly, it's just that they get the most exercise and, unlike people, exercise makes them weaker instead of stronger. Unfortunately, the only thing you can do to keep a hinge from croaking before its time is just don't fool with it too much.

- Never pick up the laptop by the open screen.

- Don't slam it shut because you're in a hurry.

- Don't yank it open and bend it too far.

- Don't open and close it repeatedly as a way to ease nervous tension.

Generally, you should not oil the hinges. They really weren't made for that kind of maintenance, and oil is a tremendous attractor of dust, grit and pollen, all of which will only gum things up even worse.

The other areas you have to watch are the openings in your laptop's case. The floppy drive has a latch, flap, or door that closes when there's no disk in the drive. If this gets stuck in the "open" position you'll collect lots of dust and your floppy drive, at least, could be ruined. On a lot of laptops, the floppy drive flap is pretty flimsy and can be quite easily pushed aside (which makes another good reason to have a laptop carrying case that gives you separate compartments for business cards, paper clips, and pencils). You don't want a stick of chewing gum wedging into your floppy drive after you've packed up your laptop for a business trip.

The other area that exposes the inside of your laptop to the outside world is the bay with your PCMCIA (PC Card) slot openings. Your computer probably came with plastic covers to seal up any slots that are not in use. Or it may have hinged flaps that come down when the slot is empty. Make sure these slots are closed or sealed. The connectors inside the slots are especially tiny and even minute amounts of foreign material can cause big problems.

When it comes to the monitor screen, there are really only a couple of precautions you have to keep in mind. First, when you clean it, use a soft, lint-free cloth. Dry is best; very slightly damp is okay if you have really sticky garbage caked onto the screen; wet is never recommended. Try not to use paper towels since the cheap kind can scratch. Second, don't twist the monitor, which means don't grab it when you want to swivel the computer around to show somebody what's being displayed. You can damage the screen as well as the hinges that hold it to the computer. If your computer uses one of the film technologies for display (such as a thin-film transistor or TFT display), then pushing, hitting, or twisting the screen can warp the film. Screens are not repairable items. If yours gets broken, you have to replace it.

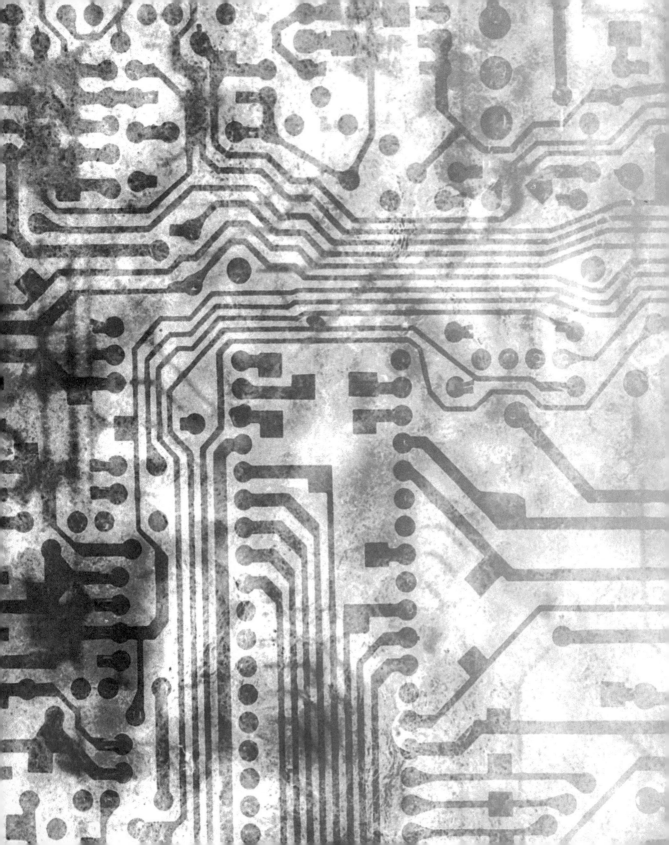

27

Using the Internet and Online Services

■ Exploring online services

■ Techniques for moving quickly around the Internet

■ How to find information online

■ Where to get the help you need

Keeping up with PC technology can be an exhausting task. You've got problems to solve, new drivers to track down and acquire, newer and fancier hardware to install, and new software versions to learn about. Many good trade magazines are available, and some of them are free to computer professionals, but the problem with them is that they give you too much to look at. It's easy for me to accumulate a dozen magazines and journals in a week while I'm out of town, between the weeklies and the monthlies. How can I read all of that and pull out the information that I need in time to get through the next lot when they show up the following week?

Some problems can't be solved by magazines, either. A lot of very knowledgeable people read them and write for them, but the problem is the time lag. If I'm installing a new board and it's not working no matter what I do, I want to know how to make it work *now*, not weeks or months from now. It's not going to help me if I write a letter to an advice columnist at my favorite computer magazine, wait for the letter to be published, and then wait for a reply. Calling the board manufacturer's tech support line might work, but then it's on my nickel (ever notice how few tech support lines are 800 numbers?) and I might not get the right answer anyway.

Then there's the problem of acquiring updated drivers, software patches, hardware documentation that the maker assumed that I wouldn't need, and just plain new product information. Working with computers often involves a fair amount of isolation and not a lot of free time, and it's hard to keep up with all that stuff. What I need is a way to throw questions into the ether for anyone and everyone to answer, to acquire drivers without waiting for the manufacturer to get around to sending me a disk, and to learn about new products.

Problems with Traditional Methods

We touched on the subject of how it can be difficult or impossible to get the information you need through traditional means, but here are some examples of the frustrating situations you can run into when trying to get information you need *now*. At the very least, these are some reasons why *I* learned to use online services for tech support and getting software.

Journey into Faxback Hell

In concept, faxback services are a nice way of answering common customer questions. Why hire staff to run a telephone line when 75 percent of the people who call have the same question? It's much simpler to prepare documents that answer the most frequently asked questions, and then make those documents available via fax to those who request them.

The catch is that you usually have to know exactly what you want before these services work, and be able to provide a document number for it. No document number, no fax. Even if you get one of the rare faxback services in which real people handle telephone questions, that real human probably doesn't know which document you need. Usually, the only way to get a document number is to order the catalog from the faxback service, at which point you have a list of titles with document numbers next to them. In other words, you still can't be sure that you're ordering the document that you need.

Facing the Muzak: Technical Support Lines

I don't want to pick on those who man tech support lines. That's got to be one of the most thankless jobs around. Everyone they talk to is stressed out from worrying about their problem, callers are probably snappish from being kept on hold, and many are prone to ask what sound like stupid questions because the tech support rep has answered that same one six times already that day. (See where faxback services come from?)

But tech support lines aren't usually any fun for the caller, either. Many people have a hard time explaining a particular chain of events to someone who they can't see. Others wait on hold for twenty minutes to hear a tech support guy tell them, "Gee, I've never heard of that problem before. Can you hold on a minute (or two, or ten) while I get my supervisor?" Unlike sales, the lines to tech support are often not toll-free, which means that if you're at work you may have to explain to the business manager where all those long-distance charges on your code came from, or if you're at home, you have to swallow the long-distance bill yourself. (Far too many tech support lines are 9–5 propositions, which means that weekend warrior types can be stuck until Monday if they have a problem.) And then there's that period of being on hold. I'm never sure whether it's more annoying to hear violin renditions of "Purple Haze" or a comforting male voice repeatedly assuring me that my patience is appreciated. (How do they know that I'm being patient? Maybe I'm grinding my teeth smooth while waiting to get back to something productive.)

Then there are the tech support lines (such as Microsoft's Windows NT support line) that won't even talk to you until you've given them $150, whether or not they can help you.

The *idea* of tech support lines is wonderful—that a company will provide a team of experts to answer your questions on demand. The reality is often less wonderful, for both the caller and the tech support person.

Making Friends and Influencing People

Often, one of the best ways to answer a question is to find someone who's got more experience than you do. Unfortunately, this is sometimes easier said than done. You may not have anyone around to ask (often the case for home PC-ers), or you may be the person with the most experience. Sometimes, your circle of personal resources just doesn't have experience where you need it. If you've been a NetWare person all your life, and all the people you know are NetWare people, then you could be stuck when setting up that Windows NT Server machine and something obscure goes wrong. At this point, you need more friends and work associates.

Then, too, friends don't always give you written instructions when answering your questions. Either you try to remember what they told you or you write it down yourself, but there's always the possibility of misinterpreting or disremembering what they told you. I leave it to your imagination to envision how ugly *that* can get.

Read All about It

As I noted in the introduction to this chapter, there's just too much for one person to keep up with—hundreds of pages show up on my doorstep every week. Then there's the problem of money. Not all of these magazines come cheap, especially if you can't demonstrate that you work in the industry (not difficult to do, but a consideration) and therefore warrant a professional courtesy rate. And for some magazines, such as *PC Week*, you pay full price no matter who you are. Even if the subscriptions are tax-deductible for you, it adds up.

What's Out There?

So what help can you get from cyberspace? Let's take a look at a few things you can expect to find.

New Product Information

Unsurprisingly, there's lots of new product information on the Web, as people try to make the idea of the marketplace on your desk a reality. Sometimes it can be difficult to get cold hard facts about how something actually works, but at least you can learn that a product exists.

White Papers and Background Information

Not quite the same thing as product information, which can be just a marketing tool, a white paper provides you with some in-depth information about a product or technology. Other sources of background information are not official (as white papers are) but are assembled by those with experience in the field.

Product Documentation

This is not *always* available in cyberspace, but sometimes it will be there when you need it. Some hardware is sold without its documentation (like we didn't need the documentation to set up the hardware?), and, if available, this is the easiest way to get it.

Device Drivers and Utilities

Lots of these. Device drivers are crucial to getting your old hardware to work with your new software. For instance, when Windows NT originally came out, the HP scanners wouldn't work with the old drivers, so we eagerly awaited the arrival of new NT drivers for the scanner. Shareware and freeware PC utilities are also common.

Advice

As we'll discuss in this chapter, advice comes in two flavors, interactive (via user groups) and static (via information papers and Web documents). There are a lot of very knowledgeable people out there who are willing to help you out—all you've got to do is ask!

WARNING   Advice that you'll get from other users of online services is not any more universally accurate than advice that you get from other people. Check your sources before doing anything drastic based on anyone's posting!

The Advantages of Gathering Information Online

We've discussed earlier some of the disadvantages of gathering information with traditional means. Information culled from cyberspace has some advantages over information gathered via traditional means, too. Let's take a look at a few of those.

It's Often Cheaper

Cost comes in two main categories: money that you spend and money that you lose—or, as we old country economists would have it, explicit and implicit costs. Let's assume that you've got both a telephone and a modem, and that you live in an area that has local access to the Internet (in case you're not sure what this means, we'll be discussing it later in this chapter). If you call tech support with your problem, the process goes like this:

1. Call the tech support line (almost certainly long distance), probably between 8:00 a.m. and 5:00 p.m. when telephone rates are highest.

2. Wait on hold.

3. Talk to the tech support person.

4. Possibly wait on hold again while they look up the problem or consult with someone.

5. If all goes well, get the answer.

Every bit of that process occurs while the meter is ticking.

If you post the question, on the other hand, the process looks more like this:

1. Create a forum/newsgroup message.

2. Connect to your online service.

3. Post the message in the appropriate forum or newsgroup.

4. Close the connection.

5. Periodically, dial in to see whether you have waiting messages. (Some forums even will email you alerts that an answer or comment has been posted to your question.) Download the messages.

6. Close the connection.

7. Read your messages.

None of this costs you anything above the monthly service charge (usually about $20). And at no time do you have to sit on hold, listening to elevator music or some inane greetings.

It's Convenient

One of the biggest hassles of tech support lines is the time spent on hold. If you've got something else that you could be doing, it's annoying to have to wait, tied to the telephone, for someone to answer your call. If instead you post your question to a newsgroup or forum, then you can write your question as clearly as possible, upload it, and then do something else while waiting for an answer. Check back in a couple of hours, and you may already have an answer. If you need an answer *now*, posting a question to a newsgroup may not be good enough—you may get the answer you need in ten minutes, tomorrow, next week, or never. But if it's something that you want to know but don't have to know right this second, newsgroups and forums are great.

Another aspect to the convenience of online services and the Internet is that they run on a 24-hour clock. I've found that one of the best times to post a question to a newsgroup is after the normal workday. This may have something to do with geography—I live on the East Coast, so 5:00 p.m. comes earlier to me than it does to most of the country. But it's also due to the fact that a lot of techies check into their newsgroups when they get home from work, or late at night. If I post a question at 5:00 p.m. EST, then by morning I often have a collection of answers.

For example, I once posted a message about a problem that I was having with installing Windows NT Server on a new machine. All of the hardware conformed to NT's compatibility requirements, but on reboot the dratted installation would just tell me that it couldn't find NTLDR, one of the required components for starting the system. NTLDR was on my hard disk—I could see it when booting from a DOS floppy—but darned if the installation program saw it. I gave up late that night (trying to fix things when you're tired can be a great mistake), posted a message that outlined the problem and described the error messages that I saw, and resolved to check in the following day. When I returned, I discovered that three people had posted responses to my original posting, and one of those responses did the trick. I updated the system BIOS, and the installation worked just fine.

The convenience isn't limited to question-and-answer sessions, either. Want to see what applications are out for Windows 95, but it's 3:00 a.m.? How about looking up the technical specs on AMD's latest CPU? You can use a search engine (more on those in a minute) to search the Web for sites containing information about the subject. Once you've found them, you can review them to see which one you want, then copy it to your computer. If you've got an unlimited-access account, then you can even read at your leisure on the Web without filling up your hard disk with information you won't need past that minute. You can also download drivers and evaluation software at your convenience, not at the convenience of someone else.

Follow Up Is Often Better

One of the best parts of the interactive parts of newsgroups and forums is that those who answer your questions are generally doing it not because they're getting paid for it, but because they're trying to help you out. I've found that that translates to good follow-up. Until you post a message saying that all is well with your problem, you can almost certainly count on people trying to help you through the process, if you're polite and respond to messages posted to you.

For example, on one occasion I was helping a friend figure out how best to get PowerPoint 95 (a PC application) to people in a largely Unix-oriented office. We were deciding whether it would be better to provide the users with individual machines that could run the application, set up a PowerPoint workstation or two for those times when they needed it, use some kind of PC emulation on the Sparc 5s and 20s that the users already had, or what. (For those raising their eyebrows at the thought of buying users a second computer just to run an application, this office was an intelligence shop that had some money to spend on the project.) I posted a message outlining the situation on a couple of relevant forums, one for the PowerPoint side of the problem and one for the organizational side of the problem. The answers that I received about the organizational aspects of the problem sparked some new questions, which I asked, and then some other people got into the question and raised some more issues. By the time things wound down a couple of days later, I not only had the answer to the original question, but some other issues had been brought up and those helping me out had tried to make sure that I'd got all the information that I needed.

Internet Choices

You can access information on the Internet using either a local Internet service provider (ISP) or a national service provider. Local ISPs usually provide only access to the Internet, in varying degrees of reliability and speed. National ISPs such as CompuServe, America Online, and Netcom often provide special forums and other amenities in addition to Internet access.

Parts of the Internet

For purposes of research today, the Internet has three important parts: the World Wide Web, newsgroups, and FTP sites. ("Gopher holes," or sites that held information on a variety of topics, have been more or less superseded by the Web as sources of new information, although they still maintain a small following.)

The World Wide Web

Originally a method devised by a Swiss think tank to make its papers on physics available to other scientists, the Web has become one of the most hyped aspects of the Internet over the past couple of years. The graphical side of the Internet, it offers papers that can be read online, files to download, and links to related sites. Search engines make it possible to easily find information on a particular topic.

Right now, the Web is at a crossroads of sorts. On the public side, it's becoming a favorite marketing ploy, much to the disgust of many people who've been involved with the Internet for a long time and like its ideals of shared information for the public good. (Ever notice all the television advertisements nowadays that close with invitations to visit the product's Web site?) In many circles, electronic commerce exhibits the same kind of bad taste as handing out business cards at a private barbecue. On the other hand, there are thousands of Web sites run by people who create Web pages for the sake of information-sharing, not to sell anything. (Then there are the "vanity pages" created by people who assume that the rest of the planet wants to know what they're doing that week, but those aren't really relevant here.) I'm hoping that the marketing side of the Web doesn't drown out the information side, as it's a good place to do preliminary research and I'd hate to see it become more of a shopping mall than a library.

FTP Sites

Before the Web became so popular, the easiest way for a hardware or software manufacturer to get new drivers, utilities, or patches to its customers was to set up a server that customers could dial into and download the files with the *file transfer protocol*, or FTP. Servers set up this way are called *FTP sites*. Even though Web pages are often the method of presenting files for download, the sources for some of those files are FTP sites that are available to the Web page via a link created by the page's author.

Usenet Newsgroups

Newsgroups are discussion groups that are part of a service called Usenet. They cover all kinds of topics, from bicycle maintenance to cat stories to problems associated with configuring hard drives to...you name it. If you haven't found a group that covers exactly the topic that you want to discuss, either you should look a little harder or one will probably pop up soon enough. Most newsgroups are unmoderated, meaning that no one's watching the message content to ensure that subject discussions stay on track, or that people are polite (or even not downright obscene) to each other, or that people don't post totally irrelevant messages in the wrong forums (called *spamming*, and considered to be very impolite). Although there's a lot of garbage in newsgroups on the order of offers of nude celebrity pictures, newsgroups have been around for a long time and are good places to find people with lots of technical experience. Technical newsgroups, after all, are frequented by those interested enough in talking shop to do it online.

NOTE   Because thousands of newsgroups exist, a server that holds traffic for all of them may be able to keep only a few days worth of traffic at a time. To keep current with a newsgroup, you may want to check in fairly regularly.

Normally, your access to newsgroups works like this: your ISP maintains a news server that stores as many of the postings in all or selected newsgroups as possible. (Note that this means that you may not have access to all newsgroups—if it's not on your news server, you can't reach it.) Rather than connecting directly to UseNet, then, you dial into the news server and read the messages posted there. Any messages that you post to a newsgroup will be uploaded from the news server to UseNet itself.

What Is UseNet?

UseNet, also called NewsNet and NNTP, is similar in many ways to e-mail with one major difference: you don't need a UseNet address. UseNet is a collection of topic-related messages that are stored on special NNTP servers. You access the messages using an NNTP-compliant client, like Outlook Express. UseNet groups have names similar to Web site domain names but they are often longer and hence, more descriptive. An example of a UseNet group address is `comp.os.ms-windows.apps.compatibility.win95`, a group dedicated to discussing application compatibility issues with Windows 95. Other UseNet addresses can get quite silly, such as the obvious dislike for a beloved purple dinosaur shared by the list members of `alt.barney.dinosaur.die.die.die`.

Beware, however, as UseNet is also used by unscrupulous individuals to pass illicit and illegal information and/or material with mature content, including child pornography. Groups that carry this type of information often have descriptive names such as `alt.sex.pictures` or as a sick turn to the above mentioned strong dislike group, `alt.sex.beastiality.barney`. If you are careful you'll never see such material, but be aware that it is out there (the Internet is anonymous, especially UseNet). Also remember that many people cross-post (distributing the same message to a number of other groups) and send such material to groups that do not dwell on such things.

Of course, newsgroups can be a powerful tool if used properly, and there are a number of ISPs and other organizations that offer smut-free NNTP access. You need merely make the choice.

CompuServe

CompuServe is an online service that's been around for quite a while. Like the Internet, it was originally mostly technical in nature, and although its social membership has expanded in recent years (helped by its dropping connect charges and easier interface software), it's still a good place to get technical help.

CompuServe has scads of well-attended technical forums. AOL is good for socializing, but not as good as CompuServe for technical support, and Prodigy's membership has fallen off so much that it's not the best place to look for active forums and lots of people to help you with problems. Recently, AOL acquired CompuServe, so it now also provides Internet access as one of its services.

Basic Service and Structure

The base service is organized into subject areas called forums. Forums are similar to newsgroups, in that they're a place for people to post messages pertaining to a particular topic, but they are different in several ways:

- CompuServe forums are moderated for consistency and message content (some more heavily than others—the rules change when you move from forum to forum)

- Forums are subdivided into sections that deal with a particular aspect of the general topic. For instance, in a PC Utilities forum, you find sections devoted to categories of PC Utilities, such as file management utilities, virus checkers, and the like. If you post a message, you should try to post it into its appropriate section (if you miss, a sysop moderating the forum may move it for you).

As you can see in Figure 27.1, messages are only half the content of most forums, however. The other half is the forum library, where binary files are stored.

The contents of a library depend on the forum's character; for example, in a vendor forum, you might find drivers or patches related to that vendor's products; in a more social forum, you might find essays that forum members had written or pictures of their dogs. Some forum sysops create files for particularly useful series of posts (called *threads*) that may be useful or interesting to people who weren't around for the original conversation. For example, when researching a networking question at one point, I found an archive thread that had started with one member's post regarding the best way to network his school's computers, but had evolved into a discussion of practical uses and limitations of network hubs. Before the Web took off like it has, CompuServe forums were a common way for vendors to make drivers and patches available to their customers, and some still serve that purpose.

FIGURE 27.1:

You can download both messages and binary files from CompuServe forums.

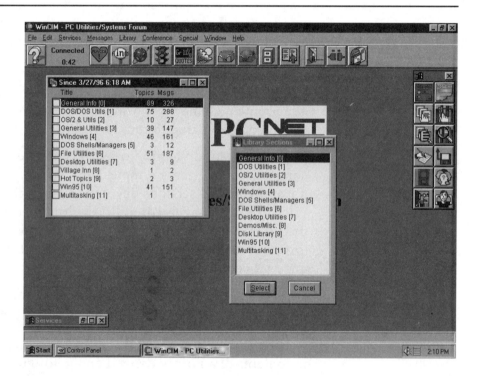

Additional CompuServe Services

Since about 1994, CompuServe has extended the scope of their services to include access to the Internet: the Web, newsgroups, and FTP sites. As this Internet access includes PPP (as we'll discuss in a minute, this is a good thing when it comes to Internet access), it's not bad if you don't have any other way of connecting. But if you've got a direct Internet account as well, I'd recommend using it instead. WinCIM, CompuServe's GUI interface, isn't bad to work with for ordinary CompuServe use, but the Internet connection is an annoying combination of too many graphics (which eat up connect time) and an ugly interface when you finally do get to the Internet.

Except in the most rudimentary way, this chapter does *not* explain how the Internet or CompuServe works—this is a discussion of how to use the technology, not of the composition of a packet or how a transport protocol works.

Getting an Internet or CompuServe account isn't the only way to do online research, however. In the past couple of years, online packages have become another way to get connected.

All-in-One Online Services

What about all-in-one online services such as the Microsoft Network (MSN), America Online (AOL), and Netcom? The options that they offer are similar to those available from an Internet connection or CompuServe, the main difference being that these online services come to you—you don't have to go out of your way even a little bit to get access to cyberspace. Microsoft Network comes with Windows 95 and Windows 98, America Online will mail you their startup software, and startup software for Netcom is available at Netcom's page on the Web (www.netcom.com).

The Basics

These online services are designed to offer you universal (or, at least countrywide) access to both the Internet (chat groups, Usenet newsgroups, and the Web) and to special forums that they operate. They've got some advantages: no negotiating with a provider, easy acquisition of software (Microsoft Network software comes with Windows 95 and Windows 98, and AOL software comes through the mail), and you can set it up either as you install the operating system or from the Add/Remove Programs utility in the Control Panel. Netcom's NetCruiser software is available from their Web site at `http://www/netcom.com`.

Using Netcom

Using Netcom is pretty straightforward: once you've installed the software and set up an account, every aspect of the Internet (FTP sites, gopher holes, Usenet) is open to you from one screen. Rather than moving between folders, you can choose the option that you want from the toolbars on the main screen, as shown in Figure 27.2. Netcom does not offer a separate forum area distinct from the Internet, although you can filter the display of newsgroups to show only those concerned with Netcom.

Part of the attraction to Netcom is that the direct connection was faster at the place in which I initially got connected, but I also found it less graphic than the Microsoft Network. Everything's available from the main screen, so you don't have to flip through folders to find what you want. Essentially, getting a Netcom account gets you the same thing as getting an Internet account, without having to go get any communications software such as newsreaders or Web browsers. It all comes in the package.

FIGURE 27.2:

All of the Netcom tools are available from the toolbar and menus on the main screen.

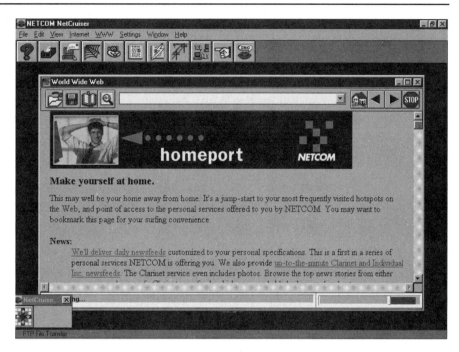

Netcom should be out as well, since it is now owned by Mind-Spring. Should discuss ways in reaching MindSpring support for installation assistance, which assumes that the user has never had access to the Internet before. Some slightly more advanced material on what needs to be set to access an ISP from an existing dial-up and application suite would also be helpful (DNS, etc…).

So Which Should I Choose?

To clarify some differences between the options we've discussed, CompuServe is a specialty content provider that also gives access to the Internet. Their system is entirely TCP/IP-based, so a good quantity of their content is available through secure connections in a Web browser. The Microsoft Network (MSN) is an ISP with content for its members, but Microsoft has chosen to make most of that content available free to everyone with access to the Internet. This greatly reduces the amount of MSN specialty content that members of AOL or CSI typically enjoy (you can't get AOL content on the Web). Netcom was the first national ISP, and at one time did provide customers with their own content and custom software to access their systems. NC was recently purchased lock, stock, and barrel by MindSpring, a national ISP. They now have no specialty content that is not available to the general public.

The best way to choose an Internet service is to request information and decide which service provides the features and options you need or want. The quickest way to access such information is through the Internet itself. Every ISP has a Web site detailing the services they provide; borrow a friend's computer and go exploring before you make any decisions.

The Tools You Need

What do you need to explore cyberspace? Not much: a PC (since you're reading this book, I'll assume that you've got that much), a modem, an account with an Internet Service Provider (ISP), and some communications software.

Modems

Modems were discussed in detail in Chapter 19, "Modems and Serial Interfaces," but they're worth a little attention here. Most systems nowadays come with a modem already installed. If you're just gearing up for exploring cyberspace, you may be wondering just how fast a modem you should get. Really, it depends on what's available. Almost all new modems today support 56K, theoretically. Unfortunately, almost none can really run at that speed. In almost every case you'll be lucky if you get more than 33K using a dial-up modem.

If you can't get a 56K connection, should you look for a lower-speed modem or go with the best available? I'd do the latter. First, it's often hard to find modems that aren't the latest and greatest unless you're looking in a place that sells used hardware. Second, modems aren't expensive equipment. Third, many online connections are increasing in speed, as providers realize that they've got to give their customers a faster path to cyberspace. If you can't get a high-speed connection now, you may be able to do so in the near future—particularly if you're talking about Internet access, in which case several companies in the area may be competing for your online dollars.

You may have seen or heard of Winmodems and wondered why they are so much cheaper than other modems. Winmodems are designed to work only with Windows, so if you try to use a non-Microsoft operating system with a Winmodem, you'll find that there are no drivers for it and the modem won't work. Although Winmodems can be considerably cheaper than other modems, their limitations and unreliability make them a poor choice.

What about internal versus external modems? Although they're a touch more expensive, I like external modems. First, their position outside of the PC means that you can watch the status lights, so if a problem occurs you may be able to tell the point at which the problem occurred. External modems are also much easier to swap out if you're using the swap method for troubleshooting. Second, using an external modem saves that slot in your PC for something else, such as another board, or just for air circulation. The only real downside to using external modems is that they usually use up a serial port.

Besides, modems that beep and flash make you feel that they're *doing* something. Most techies I know get warm fuzzy feelings from status lights of any kind.

Onramps to the Information Highway

The question of the connection you get depends a great deal on what you're planning to connect to, so we'll break this discussion down slightly.

Connecting to the Internet

To connect to the Internet, whether you want to reach the World Wide Web, FTP sites, or newsgroups, you'll need to be running a number of communications programs. In the early days of the Internet you would have to install and set up all of them yourself. These days, however, most connection software automatically installs and sets up all of them for you. In this section we'll take a look at what each of the communications programs is and what it does.

TCP/IP is the transport protocol used by the Internet. It's actually two protocols working in tandem: the Internet Protocol shuffles data between source and destination, and the Transmission Control Protocol makes sure that the data gets to its destination in one piece and in the proper order.

The Serial Line Interface Protocol (SLIP) and the Point to Point Protocol (PPP) are two ways of doing the same thing: making the Internet think that your system has its own IP address, so that it can receive images directly instead of having to view them on the connection server at the ISP. If you can get it, go with PPP—it's faster than SLIP and has some features (such as data compression and error correction) that SLIP does not have. It's also easier to use, as it doesn't require you to create a login script to negotiate your connection to the Internet.

TIP If PPP isn't available, see if you can get CSLIP, a compressed version of SLIP. It doesn't have all the features of PPP, but it's a little faster than regular SLIP.

How much will the connection cost you? It depends on where you are in the country and what kind of connection you get. Many ISPs offer two classes of Internet connection: one in which you pay a flat monthly rate for a certain number of connection hours, and then a per-hour charge for any hours beyond that; and one in which you pay a somewhat higher rate for an unlimited access account. At $25 per month, the unlimited Internet dial-up access account I was able to get seemed a bargain. When browsing the Web or reading newsgroups online, it's easy to stay up longer than you actually meant to. For those offline readers that don't disconnect you when they're done downloading messages, it's nice to know that you haven't blown your entire free connection time allotment because you forgot that the line was still open.

TIP When choosing an ISP, be careful to choose one that has a local access number. Otherwise, you'll run up long distance charges while connected.

What about Connecting with ISDN?

ISDN connections to the Internet are beginning to be available in some areas of the United States. Getting an ISDN connection can speed up your connection more than fourfold (potential 128KBps versus 28.8KBps), significantly reducing your connection time when downloading large files or browsing graphics-intensive

Web sites. Rather than waiting for images to slowly develop on your screen, they appear instantly. I use it and like it very much.

ISDN is faster than dialing in with a regular modem, but it's also much more expensive, both in terms of startup costs and monthly charges. ISDN rates vary across the country (I've heard of prices that range from about $20/month to *$800*/month). It's impossible to say how much it will cost you, but think about this: to connect to the Internet requires a modem, a telephone line that you've already got, and an account with an ISP. Connecting via ISDN can require some or all of the following:

- ISDN line (outside) installation fee
- Measured service connection charge
- Site-specific fee for additional inside wiring
- Terminal adapter/NT1 equipment
- Ethernet Network Interface Card with 10Base-T connector for your computer, if it does not already have one

None of these items come cheap: one ISP offering ISDN in central Virginia estimates that your startup costs will be between $200 and $1000.

Communications Software

Once you've got the connection, you'll need some communications software to go with it to get to the resources out there. The software you need depends on the type of connection you choose to go with. For example, if you've got CompuServe and you're using the latest version of their software, you'll have a newsreader and Web browser in addition to a forum reader. On the other hand, if you've got an Internet connection through an ISP, you may have to get your own newsreader and browser (many ISPs provide you with an e-mail client).

NOTE   When you sign up for Internet access with an ISP, they'll usually include an e-mail package in the deal.

As we've already discussed in this chapter, some of this software can overlap. For example, if you like you can also use your CompuServe interface or Web browser to FTP and browse newsgroups. None of this software is expensive, some of it's available free on the Web, and some of it comes with the connection you get.

Tucows (`www.tucows.com`) is the ultimate resource for Internet software for all platforms. Each item is rated and accompanied by a short description of what it does.

Navigating CompuServe Forums and Getting Mail

When you subscribe to CompuServe, you'll get an interactive CompuServe browser in the mail called WinCIM. This software works fine to begin with: it's easy to understand, and has some useful tools that can help you locate the forum you need for a particular situation. (All of CompuServe is organized into groups called *forums*; these forums contain both message traffic from forum members and libraries of downloadable files that pertain to the forum's content.) Once in a forum, the software lets you download messages to read offline, and it also collects all mail sent to your CompuServe address, whether from other CompuServe subscribers or via the Internet.

Once you've been using CompuServe for a while, however, it's a good idea to get an offline reader such as Dvorak Development's NavCIS, shown in Figure 27.3. CompuServe has been getting increasingly graphical and glitzy over the past couple of years, and I for one don't like waiting for all the graphics that I can't skip.

FIGURE 27.3:

Offline CompuServe navigators reduce your connect time.

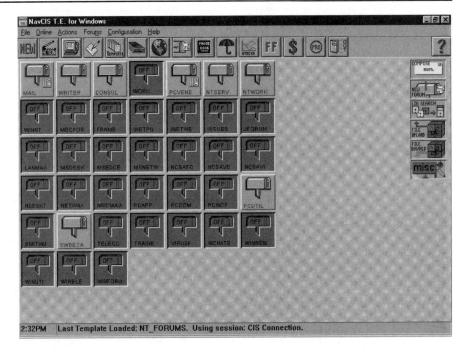

You run into the most graphics when you're browsing around, so once you're familiar with your surroundings, the process becomes less graphics-intensive. But once you're that familiar it might be time to use an offline reader and *really* save some time and money. An offline reader gets and sends your mail, goes to the forums and downloads the messages that you instruct it to gather (either only ones to you, all messages, or some subset of the messages that you specify), and then closes the connection. Although offline readers are *not* free (but fairly cheap—less than $100), they'll end up paying for themselves in connect charges that you didn't have while waiting for unsolicited graphics.

The only catch to NavCIS? You can't use it to read newsgroups via CompuServe.

Browsing the Web

If you're a Windows user, it's getting hard *not* to have a Web browser these days. Windows 95 comes with a built-in version of Microsoft Internet Explorer. There are many other browsers (such as Netscape) that you can download from the Web, for Windows 95/98 and Windows NT 4.

You can buy Netscape or other browsers as part of an Internet starter kit.

The aforementioned Tucows Web site (`www.tucows.com`) provides free downloads of most available browsers.

Reading Newsgroups

You've got a lot of different options when it comes to reading newsgroups:

- AOL
- CompuServe
- Netcom
- Web browsers
- Third-party newsreaders

America Online (AOL) To get to the newsgroups on AOL, all you need to do is select keyword "newsgroups." When you first sign on, it will walk you through the steps needed to enable junk mail filtering. You can change the settings any time you like afterward.

CompuServe First, as we've already discussed, you can connect to the Internet via CompuServe and from there access the Usenet newsgroups. I don't like this choice much. It's slow (when connecting to the Internet via CompuServe, you must navigate through a myriad of graphical forms), the interface is not nearly as nice as the one CompuServe created for reading forum mail, and it's hard to download messages and inconvenient to read them once they're down. If you read newsgroups while connected, on the other hand, you'll run through your free hours in no time at all. Unless this is the only possible option you have for Usenet access, I don't recommend it.

Netcom If you subscribe to Netcom, you'll get a newsreader as part of the package. It's not bad; it lets you sort newsgroups by topic (it takes a little practice to figure out how Netcom categorized some topics, but it's easy to get to the computer newsgroups). You can choose how many messages to download at once and which ones, and the reader handles threads pretty well so you can follow a discussion. The only catch? You must read and reply to postings online. You can see the opening screen of the Usenet reader in Figure 27.4.

FIGURE 27.4:

Netcom organizes its newsgroups by topic, rather than by group name or keyword.

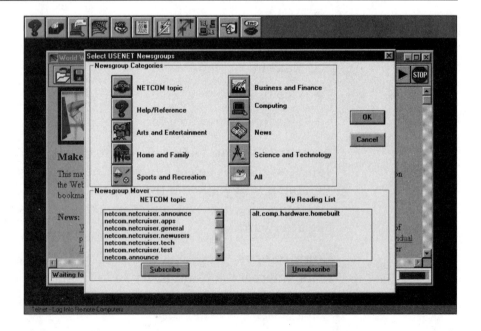

Web Browsers You may also be able to read newsgroups with your Web browser. This is better than using CompuServe, but still leaves some things to be desired. The biggest problem I have with this method is that some browsers (such as version 2 of Internet Explorer) do not allow you to sort newsgroups, but instead lists them all alphabetically. To find a newsgroup on a particular subject, then, you must either scroll through the thousands of groups out there, or, as illustrated in Figure 27.5, use the Find function to search for text that may help you find a group. Once you're *in* a newsgroup, however, the interface is fairly straightforward and it's easy to move between messages and back to the main list. When performing a page text search in a Web browser to find a particular newsgroup, be as specific as possible. For example, the Find tool in Internet Explorer will locate every instance of the text string you specify on that page, whether it's a whole word or not.

FIGURE 27.5:

When using Internet Explorer to read newsgroups, you can search for text strings to find newsgroups covering a specific topic.

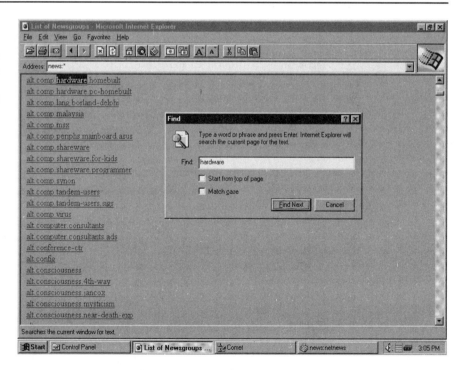

If you want to use Internet Explorer to read newsgroups, it's a good idea to eschew the menu item altogether and run the DejaNews service, available at `http://www.dejanews.com/`.

This service won't allow you to browse the available news-groups, but if you're interested in a particular topic it does one better. You can enter keywords for the service to locate in all mes-sages posted to all newsgroups. Once it has completed the search, it lists the hits it found with links to the messages, and you can read and answer messages (even moving up and down in the sub-ject thread) from there.

Third-Party Newsreaders If you've got access to the Web, how-ever, you've also got access to dozens of freeware and shareware newsreaders. The Tucows Web site contains links to many of these, including descriptions, licensing information, and file sizes. I picked up Microsoft's freeware Internet News (shown in Figure 27.6) to try out, and I like it fairly well. It doesn't provide you with many setup options, and its sort function for helping you find relevant news-groups is limited, but it's small, the interface is easy to use, and the software is easy to set up. (Another freeware newsreader that I experimented with had more options and a better search function, but also made me feel really intelligent for having gotten it to work successfully.)

FIGURE 27.6:

You can download a free copy of Microsoft's Internet News from the Internet.

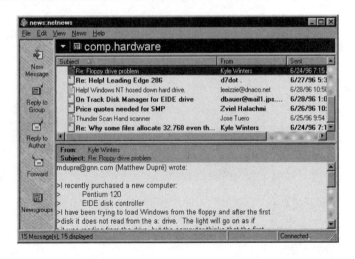

If you don't have an unlimited access Internet account, you may want to consider using an offline newsreader, such as Free Agent, TIFNY, and X News, which are available from the Tucows Web site. One newsreader that's been around for a long time is Dvorak Development's Offline Usenet Interface (OUI), which is shown in Figure 27.7. It works like NavCIS for CompuServe—you identify the newsgroups that you want to browse, then start the connection and wait for the automated navigator to search the active newsgroups for the messages that you've specified. OUI does have one major flaw, however: it does not download the subject headers attached to the postings, so that everything you download is listed as "no subject." Not very helpful, but you can search messages for relevant text—just make the text strings you specify as specific as possible. You can read more about OUI v1.5 online at www.cnet.com/Content/Reviews/Hands/073096/oui.html.

FIGURE 27.7:

Dvorak Development's Offline Usenet Reader lets you download messages from selected newsgroups.

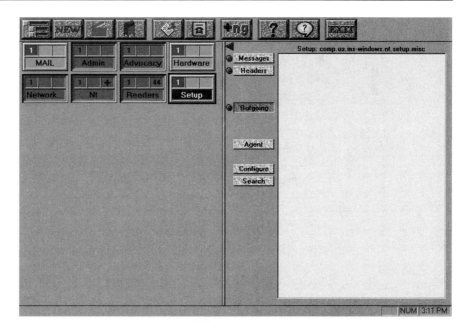

So many newsreaders are available for downloading from the Web that you can experiment with them to see which one you like best. Using one of the search engines discussed later in this chapter, try searching for "newsreader." With so many options, it's worth spending a little time finding the one that will make researching easiest for you.

Finding and Getting What You Want

First of all, what do you want? Help solving a problem? Utilities? Background information? What you want drives where you go to look for it.

Getting Advice

Due to their interactive nature, forums and newsgroups are the best places to get problem-solving advice. Sometimes, you can get lucky and someone's asked the question before you did, but most of the time it's easiest if you go ahead and ask anyway.

TIP　　If the forum or newsgroup in which you plan to post a question has a FAQ (list of frequently asked questions), read the FAQ before posting to make sure that your solution isn't in it.

Reading and Posting in Newsgroups

Earlier in this chapter, we discussed some of the places in which you can find newsreaders and some of the nice features you can look for. When you're first using a newsreader, one of the features that you'll *definitely* want is a good sort mechanism that makes it easy for you to find newsgroups to post to or read.

Why? I just updated the list of newsgroups that one of my newsreaders knows about. Guess how many newsgroups it knows about? 500? 2000? 5000? I lost track at 28,000.

Browsing more than 28,000 newsgroups takes more time and energy than I have, so there's got to be a way to organize them. There is, in the form of the newsgroups' prefix. Many (not all) newsgroups are sorted by domain:

- `alt.` newsgroups are "alternative"—the discussions here are probably a little weird, as just about anything goes in these groups.

- `comp.` newsgroups are, broadly speaking, computer-based. They may be computer-related humor or Sound Blaster installation hints. The exact nature of the discussion depends on which group you're talking about, but the discussions should in some way touch on computers (even if it's about how evil they are).

- `misc.` newsgroups are hard to fit into any particular category. These groups might cover topics such as good techie books, militia activity, and home schooling.

- `news.` newsgroups generally cover network and newsgroup-related technical issues.

- `rec.` groups are recreation-oriented, covering just about any topic that you could think of for recreation.

- `soc.` groups deal with social and cultural issues.

- `talk.` groups are for those who like debate. Whatever you feel like arguing about, it's probably covered here.

There's a lot of crossover. You can probably start a flame war on a `comp.` newsgroup that would do credit to an `alt.` newsgroup by posting an "NT is better than Linux!" message if you're so inclined, but that's more or less how the usual domain breakdown shakes out. Not all newsgroups fall into one of these domains, however. Thus, it's useful to have a newsgroup reader that sorts groups not only by domain, but by topic. For example, as shown in Figure 27.8, the Offline Usenet Interface (OUI) from Dvorak provides a place for you to enter keywords by which to sort newsgroups.

FIGURE 27.8:

Some readers let you sort newsgroups based on keywords.

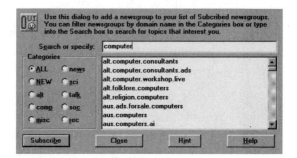

As you can see, a search for "computer" gets newsgroups not in the comp or news domains. Note, however, that this list does *not* include some newsgroups that I know (from personal experience) are computer-related, because those newsgroups don't have the word "computer" in their names. In other words, don't assume that if the keywords you supply to find information about your SuperSender modem don't net anything, then no one is talking about your SuperSender modem. You just need to start surfing the groups themselves to see what people are talking about, or use DejaNews on the Web to search the last two weeks worth of Usenet postings for messages about SuperSender.

When you need help with a problem and you don't know where to start looking, think about keywords associated with your difficulty. In your newsreader, you can see the way that newsgroups are named. Based on that naming scheme, identify the parts of your problem that might be in the name of a newsgroup. For instance, if you want to ask advice about choosing a

SCSI controller to work with your system running NT Workstation, that gives you several good potential keywords: *SCSI*, *NT*, and *configure*. In this case, I'd probably start with SCSI, since that's really what the problem is about. You can see one result of this search in Figure 27.9.

FIGURE 27.9:

Results of search for "scsi" in newsgroup names

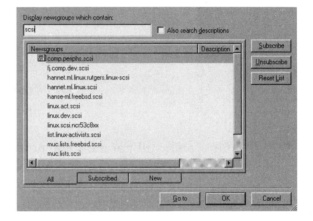

From this, I can choose a newsgroup that looks likely (perhaps `comp.periphs.scsi`), go to it, and read a little of the message traffic already posted to see if it looks like people are talking about subjects related to my problem.

If no SCSI newsgroups seem to fit the bill, I can try NT instead. There's a trick to this one, though: newsreaders aren't case-sensitive, and most don't let you distinguish between searching for whole words only and searching for part of a word. Therefore, if I search for "nt" only, I'll get the NT hits, but I'll also get any other newsgroups with names that have *nt* in any form. (Obviously, this point doesn't apply to just NT, but to any combination of letters that have significance on their own but can also be part of a word.) So this time I'll search for ".nt" and I'll get results like the ones in shown in Figure 27.10.

FIGURE 27.10:

Results of search for ".nt" in newsgroup names

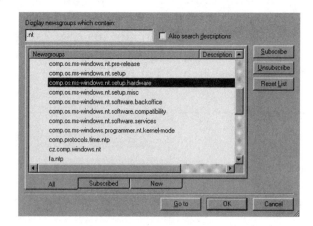

This search still got me some newsgroups not focused on Windows NT, but it's better than the results that I would have gotten by searching for "nt" by itself. Scrolling down the list, I notice that there's a newsgroup called `comp.os.ms-windows.nt.setup .hardware`. That looks more promising, so I go to it, read some of the messages already posted, and post my question if it doesn't look like my question has already been asked recently. Then, I can check back into the newsgroup at intervals to see if anyone has replied to my posting.

WARNING   There isn't much that you can do about this, but be advised that if you post to a newsgroup you're likely to get on the mailing list for get-rich-quick schemes—even ones having nothing to do with what you posted about.

Reading and Posting to CompuServe Forums

There are really two parts to the process of finding useful information on CompuServe. First, you've got to figure out where to look. I can't just log onto CompuServe and tell the system to give me all postings, binary files, and text files that exist in CompuServe related to virus checkers; I have to go where the information might be (such as security or utilities forums) and look there. Second, once you've found a likely place to look, you've got to search that likely place to find out what's there. This second process involves a lot of inspired guesswork that gets easier the more often you do it.

The methods you'll use to find information in each of the media we've been discussing depend on which media you're talking about. As there's several different kinds of software out there with which you can access CompuServe, I can't tell you which keystrokes and mouse-clicks will net the results that you want, but after reading this section you should have a good idea of how to find the information that you need. That said, when you subscribe to CompuServe, you get a CD with the connection software called WinCIM. As Windows is so ubiquitous, any references that I make to the interface over the course of the next few pages will be in terms of WinCIM; if you're using another interface, or an offline navigator like NavCIM, translate the commands according to the actions described.

The Find Tool   The first step in getting advice on CompuServe is to find a forum that discusses that topic, based on certain keywords. CompuServe forums are not perfectly indexed (it's possible to enter keywords that won't identify a forum even if that topic is frequently discussed in that forum), but for the more technical topics the Find tool works pretty well. To use Find, choose that option from the Services menu or choose the Find icon on the toolbar. You'll see a dialog box like the one shown in Figure 27.11.

FIGURE 27.11:

The Find tool can help you find forums that discuss a certain topic.

Don't worry about case; the index is not case-sensitive. You can enter more than one word to refine the search. For example, *hard drive* works fine. Boolean operators (*and*, *not*, and so on) don't work, however. You may have to try some different parameters before CompuServe finds a matching forum. Your dialup connection to CompuServe will start and the search will begin.

When it finds a match, you'll see a dialog box showing the matches, as shown in Figure 27.12.

FIGURE 27.12:

When the Find tool locates forums that match the keywords you used in a search, it displays them for you.

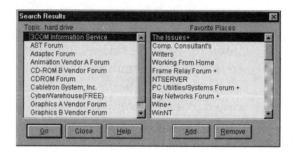

> **TIP**
>
> If you're looking for information about a particular manufacturer's hardware or software, try searching for the name of the manufacturer, not the product. In other words, look for *Creative Labs* rather than *sound card* if you're having trouble installing Sound Blaster 16.

You may have to run a search more than once to get the right results, as sometimes apparently logical combinations of keywords net very odd results. For example, I tried the combination of *fix PC* to try to locate hardware support forums. Nope—instead, I got three gaming forums; nice, but not quite what I was looking for. If you're having trouble with a particular component, try searching for the manufacturer's name. Not all vendors have official forums with tech support on CompuServe, but you may be able to find people with experience in the particular problem you're having.

NOTE   Once you've got a list of possible sites, you can move to a forum from this dialog box. The column on the right side of the dialog box shown in Figure 27.12 is a list of forums that I previously designated as "Favorite Places," or forums that I use a lot. If a forum in the Found list is in your Favorite Places list, then it will have a check mark next to it. Double-click the forum, and you'll move there. If you've never been to a particular forum before, you'll have to join it, just like subscribing to a newsgroup before reading its posts. This almost never costs anything extra; if it does, the message box on the Join dialog box will tell you. You'll have the option of just visiting a forum before joining, but when the message warns you that your abilities in the forum will be limited, they're not kidding—you can do almost nothing in a forum unless you're a member. Go ahead and join if you think that there's any chance that you'll want to use the forum.

Searching a Forum   Once you're in the forum, you can either scan the subject headers of the messages posted in the forum, or you can perform a search for particular topics that interest you. To search the posted messages for a particular subject, choose Search… from the Messages menu, or click the icon on the right side of the screen that shows the yellow pages with a magnifying glass held over it. You'll see a dialog box like the one in Figure 27.13.

FIGURE 27.13:

You can search the contents of a forum's message board according to any one of several criteria.

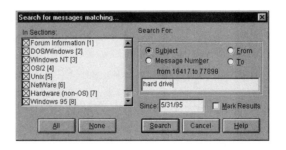

In Figure 27.13, notice that you've got the option of searching a forum not just by keyword, but by the identity of the person who posted the message. This won't help you much when you've first joined a forum and don't know who posts there, but it can be very helpful once you're more familiar with the lay of the land. For example, if you learn over time that Joe Blow frequents the forum and gives good advice on a variety of topics, you can search for uploads done by Joe Blow and make sure that you don't miss anything.

As we discussed earlier, forums are set up in sections, with each section covering a particular topic. For example, in a Windows NT forum, you might find one section on printers, another on communication devices, and another on IDE drives. When you're searching, you can restrict the search to only sections, or look through the entire thing. When the search is complete, you'll see a dialog box like the one in Figure 27.14 that shows the results.

FIGURE 27.14:

Messages are assigned keywords to make it easier to find a message on a particular subject.

At this point, you've got messages to review. Now to get them back to your machine so that you can read them offline.

Downloading Files At this point, you can either browse the results to find the exact subject thread you want, or just mark what's there and download them to your system to review offline.

If you're looking for messages pertaining to a certain subject, I'd strongly recommend that you download them to read offline—it's easy to start reading and use up all your free connect time. (Binary files are another matter. Most of them have been uploaded to the library with short descriptions, and all have dates, so it's easy to tell which file you want.) If you mark a thread for downloading, you don't have to retrieve it right away: when you leave the forum, any messages that you've marked will be downloaded to your system by default. As they're downloading, you'll be able to watch the process. Once they're down and you're disconnected, you can open the section of the File Cabinet corresponding to that forum and read the messages in it. (The ones that you haven't read yet have black arrows next to them.)

TIP   By default, CompuServe will disconnect you from the service after downloading messages. Unless you're planning to search another forum immediately after leaving the one you're currently in, it's a good idea to disconnect automatically—it will keep you from accidentally reading online.

Netiquette   This chapter is about research, not manners, but manners can play a significant role in determining whether your research results pay off. Remember, no one *has* to answer your questions.

- DON'T WRITE IN ALL CAPITAL LETTERS. THIS IS CONSIDERED SHOUTING AND IS RUDE.

- The more traffic a newsgroup or forum experiences (that is, the more new messages are posted each time you visit), the more likely it is that someone will see your posting and reply to it.

- Be specific in message headers. "Help!" is too vague to grab my attention; "Need to restore hard disk configuration information" is more effective.

- Explain your situation briefly but completely, at the beginning of the message. If it's a troubleshooting question, describe what you've done so far and any relevant parts of your configuration. People are more likely to reply to your posts if they know the background.

- Don't make posts longer than they need to be. First, reading onscreen is harder than reading hard copy, and paging through messages is wearisome. Second, people are paying to download and read your messages—don't give them junk.

- In CompuServe, don't post a question in more than one section in a forum. If it's in the wrong section, the forum sysop will move it to the correct one. (Posting a question in more than one forum at a time is sometimes appropriate, however, if you're trying to get different points of view.) Posting the same question to more than one newsgroup is sometimes acceptable if the groups are not too similar in topic and the question fits into more than one category, but keep it to a minimum.

- Be polite. The people who are replying to your posts are doing *you* a favor. For heaven's sake, don't be rude to them, even if you disagree with their conclusions. Everyone can see your posts, not just their intended recipient.

- If you encounter anyone breaking these rules, don't lecture them about it. If the forum or newsgroup is moderated, the moderator will do so. If it isn't, I assure you that someone else will take care of it and you won't have to look like a scold.

Getting Patches, Drivers, or Utilities

Web sites, CompuServe forums, MSN forums, FTP sites, and newsgroups devoted to binary files may have drivers, utilities, or patches available for downloading.

NOTE   Newsgroups actually aren't a terrific source of utilities. Many of the groups devoted to binary files have names such as `alt.binaries.pictures.hamster`, and the ones devoted to computer-related binary files don't get much traffic.

As always when downloading files, keep these things in mind:

- Shareware is not freeware. If you use a shareware product, then you're implicitly agreeing to pay the shareware's author for the software once the evaluation period has expired.

- Downloading large files can take a long time, and if there's an error on the line during the download you may have to repeat it. If the telephone line that you're using for your modem has call waiting, disable it before connecting to CompuServe.

TIP   To disable call waiting before connecting to CompuServe or the Internet, preface the telephone number to dial with *70, without the quotes. For example, if the number to your local CompuServe node was 555-1234, you'd configure your system to dial *70,555-1234.

- It's rare that a virus is uploaded to a moderated forum, but it can happen. Before running any program on your system, it's a good idea to virus-check it first. (PC viruses, recall, can only exist in executable files, so other binary files and message threads don't need to be virus checked.)

- Copyright laws apply to electronic documents. You can't, for example, download a white paper that someone's written, remove their name, and substitute your own.

Web Sites

Unless you know the exact URL for the Web site that has the file you want to download, it's usually easiest to use one of the many Web search engines to search for the *type* of file that you want (see "Web Search Engines" later in this chapter). If you want benchmark tools, search for "benchmark"; for newsreaders, search for "newsreader," and so forth. For drivers, try searching for the vendor's name plus the word "driver." The parts of the Web are so interlinked that many utilities and drivers are available from more than one site.

Once you find a site with files for downloading, click the link to the file and choose to save it to your machine.

Sometimes the official product Web site isn't the best place to look for documentation. For instance, on one occasion I was looking for the documentation for an Adaptec SCSI host adapter, the AHA-2490. Intrepidly, I searched first for *AHA-2490 documentation* with Alta Vista. When that engine produced no useful-looking sites, I tried the same search with Excite (if I don't find anything that looks close in the first ten, I tend to assume that I need to change either the query parameters or the search engine). Bingo! Six Adaptec sites topped the list! (Of course, number seven is a site for ordering skin-care products, but I resisted temptation and didn't check it out to see how in the world the name of a SCSI host adapter netted me an online beauty salon.) So, after entering Adaptec's personal space and moving to the Support section, I used the site's internal search engine to search for the word "documentation" to see where I should be looking for the files I needed. Unfortunately, this is what I saw when I got the results back:

```
Q. Is technical documentation available for Adaptec hardware and
software products? How do I get it?
A. You can call Adaptec's Literature Hotline at (800)-934-2766, and
request Technical Reference manuals or User's Guides for our
hardware. Software manuals are available with the purchase of Adaptec
software.
```

Hmm. This wasn't exactly the answer that I wanted—I wanted this documentation *now*, not after it was mailed to me. (Internet access really encourages instant gratification.) As it happened, using a slightly different search I found the documentation at Memory Lane Computers site, but the point is that Adaptec's site didn't contain the documentation with jumper settings that I required—a third-party site did.

FTP Sites

FTP (file transfer protocol) sites are servers that hold collections of files available for downloading. Although Web sites and CompuServe forums are now the most common places to find files for downloading, some FTP sites are still good resources for information, software, and drivers.

Unless you've got an account on the FTP server that you're trying to reach—if you're not sure, you probably don't—you'll have to log in anonymously, providing your e-mail address for a password. (It isn't always necessary, but it is polite because that lets the FTP administrator know who's been there.) Not all sites support anonymous login, but most of the ones that you're likely to need do.

How can you get to FTP sites? Internet access is widely available these days; if you've got it either directly or via CompuServe, try one of the methods described below.

FTP via the World Wide Web   In the address space where URLs are displayed in your Web browser, type the address of the FTP site you want, starting with FTP instead of HTTP. For example, the address might look like this: `ftp://ftp.megatrends.com`. (For the curious, you can pull down utilities and NT information from this site.)

TIP

If you don't know the address you want, you can check out an FTP Web site (such as Tile.Net at `http://tile.net/ftp-list`) that indexes FTP sites by subject and provides links to them.

When you use a Web browser to FTP, you are automatically connected to FTP sites with anonymous login—no extra steps required. If a site does not support anonymous login, then you'll know it: you'll be prompted for a password that you won't have and have to cancel out in disgrace.

By the way, it's easy to find drivers on the Web. There are a number of driver sites that maintain complete listings of all available and updated drivers. Two that come to mind are Driver-Guide (`www.driverguide.com`) and a C|Net site called WinFiles (`www.winfiles.com`). DriverGuide offers a free membership in the "users helping users" system of driver collection. WinFiles maintains a very large database of driver information from practically all the vendors that exist. Plus, almost all vendors that have a Web site have a Support link on their home page and a relatively easy way to locate driver downloads.

FTP via CompuServe Using an interactive navigator, connect to the Internet. (If you're using WinCIM, the Internet connection is annoyingly graphics-intensive—apparently designed in one of CompuServe's misguided attempts to look like America Online— and thus slow to appear.) Once you've made the connection, choose File Download (FTP) from the list, then click the Proceed button when you see a warning message.

From here, you'll have the option of opening CompuServe's list of commonly accessed FTP servers (including 3Com, IBM, and Microsoft), or opening a dialog box to type in the name of the FTP server that you want. Whichever you choose, you'll next see a dialog box from which you'll be able to log in anonymously to the server.

Once you're at the site, you'll see a list of folders; in most cases, "pub" will hold the files that you're looking for. Open the pub folder or one of its subfolders and select the file that you want. Folders on an FTP server normally have very cryptic names, so you may have to do a bit of exploring to find the file you want.

CompuServe

To find the probable location of a particular file on CompuServe, you've got two options. First, you can use the Find option described earlier in this chapter, then search within the forum library for that file. (Like the message areas, forum libraries are divided into sections, so you can narrow the search based on the kind of file you're looking for.) Your other option is to use the CompuServe File Finder (GO FILEFINDER), if you have fairly specific information about the file you're looking for. Unless you know the name of the file you want, it's easiest to search by keyword, according to what you want to be able to do. You can specify up to three keywords for your search, and the more keywords you specify, the more exact the search will be. For example, on one occasion I searched first for *compress*, and second for *compress* and *encrypt*. The first search netted 148 matches; the second 53.

When you review the search results, you can download the file directly (without going to the associated forum) by selecting it and then choosing Proceed in the following dialog box. If you're not positive about whether a file is the one you want, read the description that's posted in the Proceed dialog box.

Cautions about Online Troubleshooting

Throughout this chapter we've been talking about how online services and the Internet can be a marvelous help to you when you're trying to research something related to your computer or to get help with a problem. They can help, but now it's time for some cautions to go along with the cheerleading. (Most of this stuff will probably seem really obvious, but bear with me.)

Don't Believe Everything You Hear

There's a lot of misinformation in the PC world. It's not actual lying, but it's stuff that's misheard, or corrected later and the person telling you missed the correction, or misunderstood because the listener didn't have enough background to remember the information correctly. The trouble is that a lot of this misinformation gets repeated until it has a life of its own. Some is harmless, such as an assertion that I saw repeated that Microsoft was responsible for changing the PCMCIA card's name to the PC Card (they weren't), but some is not. If someone suggests a drastic measure in response to a problem that you've posted a question about, I suggest that you hang on for a little while and see if you get any other responses. Surely you've met people in person who claim to know more than their experience covers; they exist in cyberspace, too—and they're harder to strangle when you followed their suggestion and something went desperately wrong.

When in Doubt, Check for Viruses

First, a dose of reality: viruses aren't a problem for most sites. FTP sites rarely allow anonymous logins to upload files to their sites, and CompuServe forums check all files uploaded to forum libraries before making them publicly available. No company wants the public relations nightmare of being responsible for a virus infection.

That said, you might just be careful of sites that are not representative of a particular company and cater to those who might enjoy a little rule breaking before breakfast. If you come across a site that offers to let you download games and (possibly) pirated software, or quite openly caters to hackers, it's a good idea to check the files that you download before running them. Once again, only executable files can contain PC viruses, so you needn't worry about document files (with the exception of Word documents that have macros in them) or messages.

NOTE   Word macro viruses represent the first cross-platform virus and the only PC virus that can be contained in a document. This class of virus is discussed in more detail in Chapter 13, "Viruses."

Don't Give Out Personal Information

When posting in public areas such as newsgroups or forums, don't give out any personal information that you don't want the world to know about, such as your home address, your telephone number, credit card or checking account information, or the like. This information isn't impossible for anyone to figure out who's got a little time on their hands and nothing better to do, but that doesn't mean that you have to make it easy for them.

Places to Go, People to See

In the course of this chapter, I've identified some of the ways in which you can find what you're looking for in the far reaches of cyberspace. However, in the course of my travels I've found some useful places (or keywords to places) that I'll include here, to perhaps save you a little time.

Note, however, that in all of these online services groups and sites come and go (especially when you're talking about Web sites). Also, the character of existing groups or Web sites may change. This information is not guaranteed.

NOTE I've probably left out dozens of useful sources of information, but this is meant to be a starting point, not a definitive guide to researching online. If you know of a newsgroup, forum, or Web site that I haven't mentioned here but you think could be helpful for those repairing or upgrading their PCs, please *don't* e-mail me with the information. I'll find it.

Finding Helpful Usenet Newsgroups

As we've discussed, there are tens of thousands of newsgroups out there. Not all of them will be available from your news server (some only subscribe to a limited number, and there's not much that you can do about that), but there's enough that you should be able to get help with almost anything.

The best troubleshooting groups seem to have the word "hardware" in them. This keyword nets you a plethora of useful newsgroups:

- If you're building a computer from scratch, you might be interested in checking out `alt.comp.hardware`. The discussions that I've seen there tend to focus on what components will work together and pricing, with some postings advertising components for sale.

- An even better "how-to" site in terms of traffic (more traffic means more people to see your posts) is `alt.comp.hardware.homebuilt`. (An apparent offshoot of this one, `alt.comp.hardware.homedesigned`, gets less traffic, some of which is cross-posted from `alt.comp.hardware.homebuilt`.)

NOTE `alt.comp.hardware.homebuilt` is a good source of advice for those building or repairing homemade machines, but not those upgrading store-built machines. If you've got questions about IRQ settings on a sound card you're installing, better to stick with `alt.comp.hardware` or `comp.hardware`.

- Finally, `comp.hardware` is an active newsgroup and covers many repair and installation issues.

Why "hardware" and not more specific words? Traffic levels, mostly. More specific groups devoted to particular hardware questions (such as I/O transfer) seem to have too little traffic to do any good. I recommend checking out the newsgroups discussed above, as the IBM and Microsoft sites generally don't look as good as the generic sites in terms of response rates and relevant material.

Oddly enough, some seemingly computer-related keywords really don't net you much help in the hardware department:

- The groups with the word "setup" in their name seem to be software-related, particularly operating systems. (Then again, if you've got the PC trouble taken care of and you're ready to move on to software, these newsgroups might be able to help you after all.)

- Typing "boot" gets you music and video bootleg groups. Not much good there.

- "computer" nets computer-oriented newsgroups, but so many newsgroups—technical or not—have the word "computer" in their name that the results of a search are a bit overwhelming. Searching for "comp." has a similar problem—even though the comp. domain is computer-oriented, the hundreds of newsgroups that have comp. in their name are not necessarily so. Try being more specific about what aspect of the computer you want to talk about.

- "CPU" nets hardly any results (and of three on my news server, one is in Chinese, and one is a newsgroup currently holding nothing but a get-rich-quick scheme—you can tell how little traffic the group sees because no one has bothered to tell off the poster yet, and it's a week old.)

TIP

If you've got access to the Web, you can use DejaNews to search Usenet for messages concerning a particular topic. Go to http://www.dejanews.com and enter your search criteria (including a custom filter, if you like). You'll get a list of every message in every newsgroup that has that word in the text, and you can then jump to that particular message or thread.

Useful CompuServe Forums

Use any online service long enough, and you're bound to find favorite places to get information. Now that Microsoft is no longer directly represented on CompuServe, you have to go to the forums to find useful information and files for downloading. My favorite CompuServe forums are listed in Table 27.1.

NOTE

Many of the members of the Computer Consultants' forum are very good at what they do and very helpful. However, this forum caters to those who make a living contracting out their services or providing specialty services. If you've got simple questions, find an answer before posting here, or you'll likely get brushed off—reserve this forum for the questions that you can't answer otherwise.

T A B L E   2 7 . 1 : Useful CompuServe Forums

What's Available	Forum	How to Reach It
Utilities for Windows, W95, W98, and Windows NT	PCUTIL	PC Utilities/Systems Forum
Benchmark utilities, diagnostics	BENCHM	Benchmark & STDS
Windows support	WUGNET	Windows User Group Network
General PC hardware help	PCHW	PC Hardware
Advanced PC hardware and connectivity help	CONSULT	Computer Consultants' Forum

Web Search Engines

Keeping up with the Web sites out there (and listing every Web site that might be potentially interesting to you) is an impossible task. The most important thing that you need to know about researching on the Web is which search engine will make researching easiest. These aren't all of the search engines available, but these are some of the ones that I've used most or like best.

NOTE   Before deciding that a particular topic isn't referenced on the Web, try a few different search engines. For example, a search for "cyrix" under Yahoo! netted 12 hits; the same search under WebCrawler netted 434. One of the reasons for this is that not all search engines work the same way. Some, for example, list hits by the number of times that your query criteria appear in a document; others by how early the hit appears in a document.

Yahoo! I find Yahoo! (http://search.yahoo.com) to be less useful for technical topics than social ones. Its indices are limited and it puts too much extra text in the search results for my taste. If you're not quite sure what you're looking for and just want to browse, Yahoo's browse function is pretty good. Skip the word search function altogether, and choose Browse to move to the Computers section. (If you're using the Explorer's all-in-one search page, you'll have to move to Yahoo!'s page to do this.)

The Open Text Index The Open Text Index (`http://search.opentext.com`) has a nice feature that not all search engines have: it provides a See Matches on the Page Link that allows you to scan the parts of the document in which your search criteria appears. It also shows the URL and size of a found page in an easy-to-read format—something that not all search engines do (even the ones that provide this information). Knowing the size of Web pages before visiting them is nice for those of us who don't like waiting for unnecessary graphics.

WebCrawler I like the WebCrawler (`http://www.webcrawler.com`) quite a bit. First, it shows you more hits per page by default than most other search engines do: the usual number is about ten, but WebCrawler shows 25. This is possible because, by default, the search engine only shows the titles of pages that meet your criteria, not a summary. (Because many search engines use quotes from the page text as summaries, they usually aren't very helpful, so I don't find this to be a drawback.) Like most other engines, WebCrawler also lists the total number of hits that your search produced.

Excite! When researching, I tend to use Excite! (`http://www.excite.com`) fairly frequently, mostly because it turns up the more technical topics rather than marketing-oriented ones. Excite! also comes with a fair text-searchable newsreader—you can search for messages with certain words in the text, but the reader does not do thread handling, so you can't read messages before or after the one that came up in the search. However, even this limited capability can help you identify newsgroups that you'd like to visit. Excite! can also search Internet classifieds—nice if you're interested in picking up used hardware.

For me, the main faults of this search engine are twofold. First, it doesn't report the total number of hits generated from a search (a nice feature of many search engines that helps you determine whether perhaps you should refine your search a little). And although it provides you with useful information about the size of a page, this information is hard to pick out of the entries because of the font used and the way that the entries are structured. On the plus side, however, the search logic tends to come up with useful hits.

Alta Vista Digital Equipment Corp's Alta Vista (`http://altavista.com`) is another very useful search engine. First, it's one of the most complete search engines available. Second, it tells you not only about how many hits your query found, but also (if you queried using more than one word) how many hits each of the words found. Best yet, you can use the advanced search techniques to use a limited set of Boolean operands (AND, OR, NOT, and NEAR) to refine your search. Alta Vista also does Usenet searches as well as Web site searches.

That's a flying look at some of the search engines available on the net. If none of these do the trick, try Infoseek, HotBot, or Lycos. Or, to have access to a number of search engines all at once, check out Microsoft's search page at `http://www.msn.com/access/allinone.asp`.

How to Pick a Search Engine

In general, these are the features that I find desirable in a search engine:

- A report of the total number of hits generated from a search

- A large number of hits displayed simultaneously (I find it faster to scroll down a page than to move to another page to see the next ten hits)

- As little extraneous text surrounding the hits as possible, so that the links are easy to see, or the ability to customize the query results to show more or less surrounding information

---

TIP   It's often quicker to go to non-official Web sites that link to the official ones, rather than going to the opening page of an official site and wandering through a maze of linked documents. For example, if you need HP scanner drivers, go first to a third-party site that contains links to a bunch of different manufacturers' scanner download sites. When you activate the HP link there, you'll move immediately to the part of the HP site where drivers are stored.

FTP Sites

Like Web sites, FTP sites are sufficiently numerous that it's easier to suggest ways in which you can find the one you want than to provide a list of all sites that hold files pertaining to a particular topic.

FTP with CompuServe

If you're connecting to the Internet from CompuServe and you're not sure where to look, first try the list of sites available from the FTP window, or choose from the list of CompuServe's popular FTP sites. Although these lists aren't very descriptive, it may at least get you pointed in the right direction, as in, "Ah, 3Com. *Those* are the drivers that I need." If you know the name of a site, you can enter it directly by choosing "Access a Specific Site" from the list. CompuServe does not offer a complete list of all anonymous FTP sites, so if you don't know the address of a particular site and it's not on CompuServe's lists, you're out of luck.

FTP with the World Wide Web

It's easy to find FTP sites from the Web: just look for one of the many index pages with links to them. Following are two that I've found to be helpful—both of them incorporate a search engine, so you're not dependent on the (limited or nonexistent) search abilities of your Web browse.

The best way to get access to public FTP servers is by downloading a copy of CuteFTP from Tucows. The free version is advertiser supported, but it includes a complete list of public and corporate FTP servers. A complete list of anonymous FTP servers can be found at `bmews.snu.ac.kr/ftp_serv.html`. The freeware FTP/2 from Kaufman Software does not have a list of servers but it also has neither the overhead nor the advertisements that CuteFTP does.

Microsoft Network Forums

For the purposes of researching how to upgrade and maintain your PC (check the title), the Hardware Forum on MSN is probably your best bet. It's got an active membership, a variety of question topics and skill levels are represented (I haven't seen anyone laughed at for asking a newbie question yet). In fact, one very basic question about what RAM was got some people out of the woodwork admitting that they didn't know either; thanks for asking. The traffic there is not as heavy as some hardware-related Usenet newsgroups and CompuServe forums, but it's not bad.

If you're looking for more product-specific information, you might want to check out one of the vendor forums. The easiest way to find a forum that discusses the topic in which you're interested is to use the Find tool (discussed earlier in this chapter) to search for instances in MSN of a particular keyword.

Summary

That's about all there is to researching online. At this point, you should have a good idea of how you can get connected to the outside world, the tools available to you, and how to find what you need. I'll see you out there.

Whether you're connecting to CompuServe, the Internet, or the Microsoft Network, the rules are much the same:

- The answer is probably out there somewhere. Don't give up too easily.

- Most people like nothing more than to give advice, so never be afraid to ask.

CHAPTER

TWENTY-EIGHT

28

This Old Computer

- How and why computers evolved

- What to keep from your old computer, and what to toss

- Saving your data

- Upgrading a home computer

I've been working with computers in one way or another now for the better part of 37 years. As a result, I've seen computers evolve from giant, room-filling monsters like the Univac that predicted the presidential election results in the early days of television, all the way to computers so small that they fit easily in the palm of a hand. And in all that time, one thing I've learned has been universally true. Every new computer is faster, smaller, and cheaper, and has greater capacity than the last.

What does this mean to you? Well, for starters:

- Any computer you buy today will already be becoming obsolete while you're taking it home.

- The options you buy for your computer today will be cheaper tomorrow.

- No matter what your computer can do today, you'll want it to do something new tomorrow.

What can you do? The answer is actually pretty simple: *never buy anything for your computer that you won't be using now.* Why? Because (as I just mentioned) the thing you want today will be faster, cheaper, and generally better tomorrow. So if you won't need it until tomorrow, wait until tomorrow to buy it.

Okay, okay, I understand that this can be taken too far. If you've got your computer open and you really think that you're going to need something SOON, go ahead and install it now. Unless you really love taking your computer apart and putting it together again.

The March of Technology

Back in the "good old days," personal computers were not a business at all. They were a hobby. They were the hobby of people who loved technology. They dabbled in electronics. Actually a lot of us did much more than dabble. Most of us were also engineers. Engineers who designed and built radios, TVs, and just about any kind of electronic test equipment that you might be able to think of.

We were engineers because we loved the technology. So when Intel produced the 4004 chip, the first microprocessor (they originally called it a microcomputer), back in the mid-'70s, it opened the door to a new world for us. Interestingly, Intel really didn't know what they'd done at first. What happened was that they developed the 4004 processor to solve a problem for one of their customers. Figure 28.1 shows the 4004 processor, the first ever made.

FIGURE 28.1:

Intel's 4004
Microprocessor Chip

The problem Intel needed to solve was that their client, Busicom, was competing with several companies that were producing new versions of their circuits very quickly. Busicom needed a new way to bring their new designs to market faster. Intel found a way.

At that time, whenever a company developed a new circuit design, it took them months to lay out new circuit boards and manufacture them. It was a process that had been refined and refined, but they had hit a wall. They couldn't get any faster.

Intel proposed something revolutionary. To understand what they did, you need to know that electronics firms were beginning to use components called Programmable Array Logic (PAL) integrated circuits. They were devices that contained small arrays of logic circuits that could be customized to perform specific tasks by burning certain circuit paths in the chip. The PAL allowed companies to bring new products to market faster because they could include a number of these customizable parts in the design and make changes to the circuit without redesigning the board.

Trouble was, the PALs were limited. First of all, they were small and contained only a few logic gates. And second, they could only be customized once. After that, they were as unchangeable as any other chip, so if you wanted to make another change, you had to get new PALs. (Today's PALs are a *lot* more powerful than the ones we had back in the old days.)

Intel's idea was to use a programmable device that could perform many tasks based upon programming. And that device could be reprogrammed at any time, even when it was running another program. They had developed a part that was designed to replace a lot of logic chips. In fact, though, what they had invented was the first single-chip computer. (Well, not quite, since it required some support chips, but it was amazing nonetheless.)

The 4004 was programmed in products to couple the processor with a ROM chip. The program was stored in the ROM and the computer did whatever task was programmed into the ROM. Later, EPROM (Erasable/Programmable Read Only Memory) chips were developed. To erase one of the EPROMS you exposed the logic wafer inside the chip through an open window on the top of the chip to ultraviolet (UV) light.

Intel's programmable chip (the 4004) was a great idea, but in the end Busicom backed out and Intel was left with a part that was developed, but had no customers.

What could Intel do?

They sold it to hobbyists, engineers, and anyone with the "bug." Remember the people we were talking about before? The ones who loved technology? They became the first real customers for Intel's 4004 chip. But it wasn't long before they wanted more. You see Intel never intended to make computers—just a chip that allowed for making circuits faster and easier. Now they were being asked to take their relatively simple, 4-bit processor and turn it into something that hobbyists could use to make a real computer...a *personal* computer.

So Intel made the 8008—the first 8-bit microprocessor—and the rest is history.

Hobbyists who were passionate about technology were initially Intel's primary customers for this new class of product. Intel sold parts faster than they could make them, because they had customers who were obsessed. Their own engineers joined in the frenzy, which resulted in newer, faster, more capable parts streaming out of the new technology. Computers doubled and tripled in speed and power in a heartbeat. Initially, it was passion for technology that drove the market. But in the end, it was money that drove the market.

More and more people in the computer business were becoming multi-millionaires, and soon the drive was on to make better, faster, and cheaper parts because it meant making more money.

That's why the computer industry moves so quickly. It's designed to make the makers rich. But it also makes the end users confused. In the early days of computing, most people had no interest in computers. In fact, most people were only barely aware of them. But with the introduction of a single computer program—VisiCalc, the first "killer app"—people found themselves compelled to buy computers. A company, noticing that its competitors had computers, felt compelled to buy them so as to compete more effectively. And once again, the rest is history.

The whole point of this history lesson is to show how (and why) computers got here as they are, and to explain why things move so quickly. About twenty years ago, I was a part of the team designing one of the first video game systems. One day we were sitting around a work bench discussing the crazy business we'd found ourselves in, and we all agreed then that this was a business in which the only way you could stand still was to "run as fast as you could." So grab your hat, your checkbook, and your old computer—we're going to start running.

Worth Their Weight in Chips

Okay, so now you have a decision to make. Is your computer an old computer?

C'mon, didn't you read the previous section? If you have a computer, you have an old computer. The question is *how* old is your computer. There's a saying I used to hear when I was a kid. "Worth its weight in gold." It meant that something was very valuable. Nowadays, gold is worth about $400 an ounce. That's about the weight of a silver dollar. Today, we have a new measure of value: silicon. Well, not exactly silicon, but the circuits that we implant onto the surface of silicon. Figure 28.2 shows a microprocessor on the tip of a finger, weighing maybe a 50th of an ounce. Depending upon the actual part, one of these can be worth more than $1,000! And sometimes much, much more.

Computers are made of these chips of silicon—integrated circuits. How much they're worth is dependent upon a lot of factors, but with microprocessors, nothing has more influence on their value than their age. For example, when they were first introduced, 80286's were worth hundreds of dollars. Today they are worth only a few cents.

FIGURE 28.2:

Microprocessor on the tip of a finger

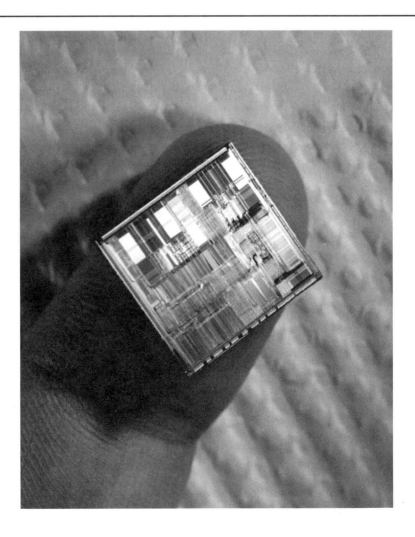

What to Keep and What to Toss

The fact that a computer is old doesn't necessarily mean that you should throw it away lock, stock, and barrel. Let's take a look at which components you can salvage, and which ones you should consider replacing.

New Life for a 286?

Let's take a look at an old 286 system. It includes a 286 motherboard, 640K of "DIP chip" memory, an expansion board, a 1.2MB, 5.25" floppy drive, a 32MB RLL hard drive, a 300 baud modem with an audio telephone coupler, a 14" monochrome monitor, a Qume WideTrack daisy wheel printer, a 5MB Iomega 8" cartridge drive, a multifunction serial/parallel I/O card, an RLL hard drive, a hard/floppy controller board, and a multi-function I/O card.

Why did I start with a 286? Because anything older wouldn't be worth upgrading, and there are almost no parts that you can use to upgrade them. And everything newer can be upgraded. Of course, the newer they are, the easier they are to upgrade.

Getting back to the 286, the motherboard is one of the old-style boards that contains 640K of memory in a huge bank of little memory chips called dual inline packages (DIPs) and lots of small logic chips. The 286 processor is socketed, so it might be possible to upgrade it—but there are no processor upgrades available for 286s anymore. You can still find 386 and 486 processor upgrades (although the 386s are getting rare). Unfortunately for 286 owners, manufacturers stopped making 286 processor upgrades years ago.

The memory expansion board was custom made to work with this system only. It contains 1.5MB of memory. The 1.2MB, 5.25" floppy drive uses the older, large-style floppy diskettes.

So what can we do to make this system more current? Here's the list, but be aware that upgrading all of these components will cost about the same as putting together a totally new system, will be more trouble, and will not work as well.

"All right," I hear you asking, "if it's a bad idea to upgrade a 286, why should I even read this information?"

Because you don't need to replace all of these components. The best advice I can give you for a computer as old as a 286 is to keep using it, as it is, for as long as it does what you need and as long as the parts keep working. This, by the way, is good advice for any computer that you have. If you need a faster computer, save your data and get a new system. In Chapter 29, "Building the Ultimate Computer," we'll talk about the benefits of buying a new computer versus building one yourself.

If you decide to keep using your old computer but things start to fail, you can replace some of the parts one or two at a time to keep it alive. So if your old 286 is still adequate for your needs but something is broken, here's what you can replace:

Video Card

If your old monochrome card bites the dust, you can replace it with a new card, but most of the new ones are SVGA color cards. Some will support monochrome monitors, but not the old digital monochrome displays. So if the card goes (or the monitor goes), you'll need to replace them both.

Floppy Drive

I haven't seen a new, 5.25" floppy drive in quite a while. If yours stops working, you may be able to find an old drive in a surplus store, but otherwise, plan on upgrading it to a 1.44MB 3.5" drive. In fact, this is a fix you should probably do before the old floppy dies. That way you can make 3.5" backups of all your old 5.25" diskettes. Then, if the 5.25" drive fails, you can still read your old floppy files.

Hard Drive

There are no new RLL or MFM drives or controller cards being made, but you can replace them with an IDE drive and controller. One problem you may run into is that many of the older 286 motherboards won't support the drive tables that allow you to set the drive type or parameters. Fortunately, you can use one of the hard drive setup programs like EZMax or OnTrack to install these drives on older systems. Most new drives have the software bundled with them.

Serial and Parallel Ports

Actually these are generally a part of the IDE controller we looked at above. If you replace the hard drive and controller, you should just pull out the old I/O card and use the ports on the new IDE card. If you only need the I/O ports (serial and/or parallel) but don't need the hard drive functions, you can usually use jumpers on the board to disable the functions you don't need.

Power Supply

This is the component that fails more often than any other in older systems. This is primarily because the power supplies that came with the systems were often designed to meet the needs of the basic system but had very little to spare. So when users added boards or drives, they exceeded the capacity of the supply. If the power supply on one of the older systems dies, you may need to get a new case as well, since many of the new power supplies won't fit in older cases—they're too small.

Motherboard

This is it. The big upgrade. When you're done with this one, your faithful old 286 will have a new brain. It can become a 386, a 486, or even a Pentium. But since you'll probably want to replace a lot more than the motherboard if you do this upgrade, (putting old, slow parts with a new, fast motherboard is a bad idea) before you perform this upgrade, you should probably read the next chapter. There we'll look at how to build your ultimate computer from scratch.

Save Your Data!

When people think of a computer, they generally think of the actual physical equipment—the CPU, monitor, keyboard, and so on. But the fact is the most important part of your computer is the information that it contains. You can always replace the CPU, the keyboard, or the mouse. But once data is lost, the only way to get it back is to reconstruct it. The process of reconstruction can be, by far, more expensive than the entire computer. It's the information in the computer that makes it YOUR computer. It has your bookkeeping, your addresses, your letters, your taxes, and your games—everything that you do with your computer that *makes* it your computer lives in the data.

So when you upgrade your system, make sure that your data follows you. Here's how you do it.

Backing Up to Removable Media

There are a few kinds of removable computer media. There are cartridge hard drives like the Zip and Jaz drives (shown in Figure 28.3), tape drives like HP's Colorado drives, and CD Writers (and Read/Write CDs). All of these have their upsides and their downsides. The real benefit to removable media is that you can easily transport your data from one place to another. The only real downside to removable media is that it loads more slowly than it does from your primary hard drive.

FIGURE 28.3:

Removable Media Drives

To move your data to a removable drive like a Jaz or Zip drive, install the drivers for the unit you have and reboot with the drive connected and powered up. In Windows, it will appear as another drive in your "My Computer" window. Once installed, every removable drive behaves essentially like another hard drive. You can copy files in Windows using the standard click-and-drag technique pictured in Figure 28.4.

FIGURE 28.4:

Using click-and-drag in Windows to copy files to a removable drive

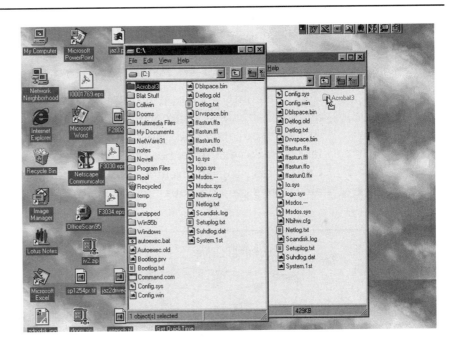

You can also use Windows' Backup Wizard to save your data to a backup drive. To access Backup from Windows 95 or 98, choose Programs from the Start menu. Then choose Accessories, System Tools, and Backup. Make sure that you have your backup drive plugged in and ready to go before you begin. Once there, the Backup Wizard will guide you through the process.

Backing Up to Tape

Backing up to a tape drive is similar to backing up to removable media but since it's a serial device, not random access, it has some subtle differences. You can't just drag and drop files with most tape backup systems. You have to use a backup program to manage the process. Most tape drives come with some kind of backup software. If you don't like the features of the backup program that came with your drive, there are plenty of alternative programs out there to select from.

Direct Backup to Another Hard Drive

If you're going to be upgrading to a new hard drive, the fastest and probably best approach is to copy files directly from your old drive to your new one. Most new drives include software to facilitate this. For example, Seagate drives have a program called File-Copy. This program creates an exact, runnable duplicate of your old drive's data on your new drive.

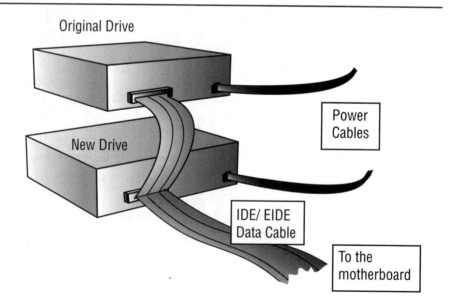

FIGURE 28.5:

Hooking up both your new and old hard drives to the same system is probably the best way to transfer files from the old drive to the new drive

When you install a new drive without removing the old one first, you need to run a program that tells your computer which drive is the old one and which is the new one. Then you set up the drive parameters (it's mostly automatic), partition and format the new drive, and go into Windows. From there, run FileCopy or a similar program, and the computer automatically transfers the files.

Once you're done, you can either remove your old drive or leave it in as a secondary drive. Either way, you switch the new drive to primary (since the newer one is usually both larger and faster), and off you go. If you remove the old drive, you can hold onto it as it is and you'll have an image backup of your system for emergencies. Remember though, that magnetic data is not ever-lasting—it needs to be renewed every few years if you want it to maintain its integrity. To do this with your old hard drive, just plug it in as your secondary drive and run ScanDisk. Then put it away for another five years or so. Whatever you do, don't wait 10 years like I did with one system drive. The drive read once and then the data became unreadable (yes, reading does remove a tiny bit of the signal strength). Under normal circumstances, this is inconsequential, since you read and write data regularly so your data is always relatively current. But on a drive that's been sitting around for years, you can't read it to check what's there before you copy the data, since you may get only one read out of the drive.

Choosing an Upgrade Path

There are many reasons why you might want to upgrade your computer system. A very common reason many people upgrade is because they learn about a tool or program and decide that they must have it, for one of these reasons:

- Their friend has it
- They saw it in an ad
- A salesman said it was cool

These, by the way, are all the wrong reasons to upgrade. If you find yourself considering an upgrade because you want another "thing" on your computer, you're asking for trouble. The more "things" you have attached to your system, the slower it will perform and the more likely it is to crash. Every time you add another device driver or use up another IRQ or address line, there's a chance that all the other stuff on your system will stop working. (By the way, this is also true of any software you install.)

Most people add software and peripherals to their computers much as they would add a new CD to their music collection. Trouble is, unlike a music CD, programs actually alter the way your system works. Before you add another program (or anything else) to your system, make sure you really want it and will have a good use for it.

The right way to choose a peripheral or a new program is to find that you need your computer to be able to do something that it can't, then do some research to be sure that the new item will actually provide your computer with that new ability. For example, let's say that you have a 33K-baud modem. Your system connects at 33K but you have been reading that 56K baud modems are available. So you decide to get a new modem. Not because you're unhappy with the speed at which you connect, but because you just want the latest and greatest modem. So you go out and buy one. But when you hook it up, you find that you're still connecting at the same old 33K speed.

After tediously waiting on hold and then finally talking with tech support, you find out that none of the phone numbers in your local calling area support 56K baud. So now you have a choice. Go back to the old modem, keep using the new modem at the old connection speed and take your chances, or start paying toll rates to get the faster lines.

If you choose the toll rates, you'll find out that even with the right modem at the receiving end, most 56K-baud modems connect at 33K. Yours actually seems to drop down to 28K most of the time. Much of this is due to the fact that most phone lines just can't support that much speed most of the time.

If you choose to go back to your old modem, you need to uninstall the new modem drivers and reinstall the old ones. Do you have copies of the old drivers? No? No problem, you can go online and download them from the manufacturer's Web site. What's that? You can't go online because you just uninstalled the new modem. So you decide to just reinstall the new modem and use it, even though your connection speed isn't any faster than it was with the old modem. (And you may run into problems if you try to connect to a 56K-baud modem that requires V.90 and yours doesn't support it—it may actually not work at all.)

Getting the picture?

In the above scenario, you went to a lot of trouble just to wind up in the same place you began. You logged lots of wasted time and maybe some lost money as well. If you had done a little research up front, you could have saved yourself all that time and effort, not to mention the cost of a new modem that you couldn't use anyway.

If you really need an upgrade, then it's worth it. But if you don't *really* need it, look out—you may be asking for a lot of trouble for nothing. So be careful not to upgrade your computer just because you see or hear of something that sounds interesting. The best decision making process to use for upgrading your computer is:

1. Decide whether or not you need new functionality.

2. Research products/tools/techniques to determine which one(s) best meet your needs, and be sure they will integrate easily with your existing system to provide the functionality you seek.

3. Acquire new products/tools/techniques and install necessary components.

Ready to start upgrading? Okay then, let's go.

Upgrading a Home Computer

Before you begin any type of upgrade to your system—even installing a new software program—be sure that you've backed up all necessary data on your hard drive. If you haven't, stop reading and do it now. Skipping this step would be a terrible mistake.

Planning Your Upgrade

Computer owners usually have one of two basic types of computer systems—a home PC or a business PC (or a combination of the two). While these two categories often involve basically the same hardware, they tend to do different kinds of things. One is optimized to do home applications and the other is optimized for business applications. When planning for an upgrade, the decisions you make should be based on the type of system you have.

First, make a checklist of what you need the computer to do. Should it be faster? I know the answer to this is always "yes." But you need to ask yourself how much you're willing to pay for increased speed. Do you need new capabilities? This would include modems, networks, printers, scanners, and video cameras...you get the idea.

The following list includes most traditional computer hardware and peripherals; use it as a guide to create your own checklist for planning your upgrade. You may choose to add other unusual or esoteric components to your own list.

- Motherboard
- Microprocessor
- Memory

- Hard Drive
- Floppy Drive
- Removable Media Drive
- Tape Drive
- Modem
- Home Networking
- Scanners
- Printers
- Cameras
- TV Tuners

The sections that follow discuss some of the individual components that you might consider upgrading.

Motherboards

Although your microprocessor is really the heart of your computer, virtually everything plugs into the motherboard. And today's motherboards have most of the I/O circuits on them as well. Current motherboards have:

- EIDE controllers for your:
  - Hard drive(s)
  - CD-ROM drive(s)
  - Internal removable media drive(s)
- Floppy controller
- Serial Ports

- Parallel Port
- USB Port(s)
- PS/2 keyboard port
- PS/2 mouse port
- Video chipset (on some boards)
- Sound chipset (on some boards)
- PCI Expansion Slots
- ISA Expansion Slots
- AGP Video Slot (on some boards)
- Cache Memory
- Memory slots
- Microprocessor socket and support circuits
  - ZIF socket (on some boards)
  - Variable voltage circuitry
  - Variable processor bus speed

Although some of these items are pretty obvious, some are not so obvious. Let's take a look at what each of these does.

EIDE Adapter

Most motherboards have two of these, labeled "Primary" and "Secondary." Figure 28.6 shows a typical pair of EIDE connectors. By the way, as you may recall from earlier in the book, EIDE adapters will talk to both IDE and EIDE drives. In fact, some older boards actually have one EIDE (the primary) and one IDE (the secondary) instead of two EIDEs.

Make sure, when you connect the data cables to the EIDE/IDE connectors, that you align pin 1 of the cable with pin 1 of the connector.

FIGURE 28.6:

Typical EIDE/IDE connectors on a motherboard.

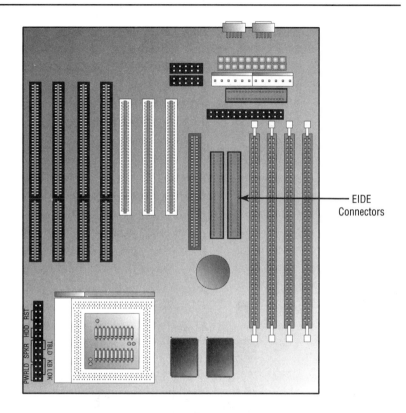

EIDE Connectors

The other end of the data cable goes into the connectors on the appropriate drive. They are also labeled, usually on the bottom of the drive.

When you connect your drives, connect your boot hard drive to the primary connector. Also, be sure to set it to Master. There's a jumper that determines whether a drive is the Master or the Slave drive. Every drive has a host adapter built into it that has the ability to control two drives. This allows two drives to share a single data cable. So when you set one of the drives to Slave, it turns its host adapter off. Setting it to Master sets it up to control two drives. On some drives you need to remove all jumpers for a single drive. Others can control one or two drives if they are set to Master. Figure 28.7 shows the jumper settings for Master, Slave, and Single.

FIGURE 28.7:

Jumper settings for IDE drives: Master, Slave, and Single

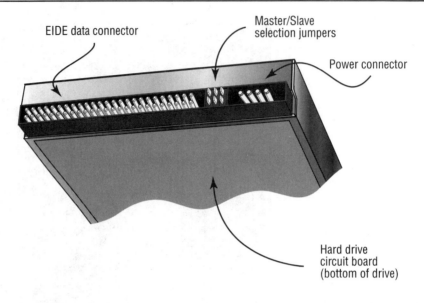

EIDE data connector

Master/Slave selection jumpers

Power connector

Hard drive circuit board (bottom of drive)

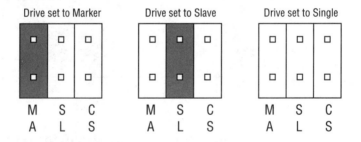

Drive set to Marker

Drive set to Slave

Drive set to Single

M S C
A L S

M S C
A L S

M S C
A L S

Microprocessor

Choosing an upgrade microprocessor can be a tough decision. At any given moment, a variety of processors are available from several manufacturers. The top three are Intel, AMD (Advanced Micro Devices), and Cyrix. Intel, of course, is the market leader. They invented the microprocessor and they lead the pack. That is, they set the standards. Everyone else has to follow the leader. AMD traditionally makes compatible processors that are almost always a little (or sometimes a lot) faster in one way or another than comparable Intel processors. Cyrix is usually the fastest of the pack for a given part, but they often sacrifice total compatibility for speed.

Another thing to be aware of is that the newest, fastest processors are almost always much more expensive than those that are just a bit slower. For example, recent pricing for a 500MHz Intel Pentium (which was the fastest processor at the time this book was being written) was about $800. The AMD K6-III/450, which is rated at 90% as fast as the 500MHz Intel Pentium, is currently about $250—less than a third the price.

Floppy Controller

The floppy controller on the motherboard can control up to two floppy drives. The floppy drives also use a single cable, but instead of setting jumpers on the drives to select which is drive A: and which is drive B:, the cable itself is modified. The A: drive must be plugged into the connector that has a twist in the middle (see Figure 28.8).

FIGURE 28.8:

The twist in the floppy cable selects drive A:

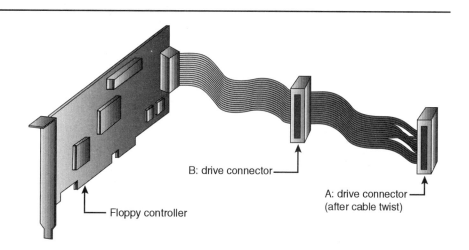

B: drive connector

Floppy controller

A: drive connector (after cable twist)

Serial and Parallel Ports

The serial and parallel port cables should be plugged into the motherboard in the same way as the EIDE/IDE connectors are plugged in (be sure to align pin 1). The trick to installing these connectors is that most are supplied on a metal bar that most people attach to a slot in the back of the computer, in a slot that could hold an expansion card. To avoid losing a potential slot, take the connectors off the metal bar and mount them in the mounting holes in the back of the case, as shown in Figure 28.9.

FIGURE 28.9:

Installing the serial and parallel port connectors in the back of the computer

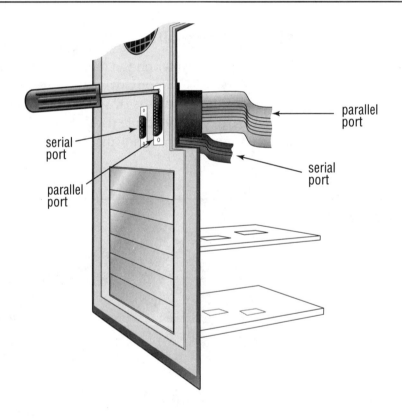

USB Ports

Two varieties of USB ports are available. For motherboards that have the USB circuitry onboard, you'll get a pair of connectors, mounted on a metal bar just like the serial and parallel ports described earlier. In this case, however, leave the connectors on the metal bar—there's no place to attach the USB ports individually on a standard case.

For motherboards that don't have USB circuitry onboard, you can get a USB adapter card that will plug right into a PCI slot (see Figure 28.10).

FIGURE 28.10:

Installing USB Ports

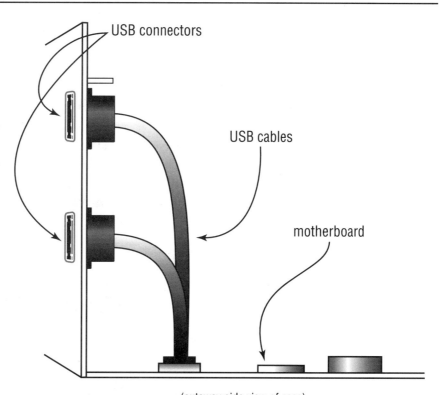

USB connectors

USB cables

motherboard

(cutaway side view of case)

Keyboards, Mice, PS/2, and DIN

Now this is a confusing bunch of connectors. Depending upon your motherboard, either you will have a single large DIN connector or you'll have two mini-DIN (PS/2) connectors. The older style keyboards use the larger DIN connectors and new ones use the smaller PS/2 style connectors. The main problem you may run into is that the PS/2 keyboard and mouse connectors look almost exactly the same, so look for the labels before you plug anything into them. And NEVER, NEVER force them!

Video and Sound

Years ago, personal computers were text-based and had no sound. Then one day Mr. Sim came to America. He brought with him the first Sound Blaster card and he, not Steve Jobs, changed computers forever. In essence, he created multimedia. Today almost every application uses some kind of sound and graphics. Even Microsoft uses multimedia. People understand sound and graphics, and if your system doesn't have it, you should probably consider getting it. Lots of motherboards today actually have sound and video right on the board. If they do, then all you need to do to set them up is plug them in. Windows 95, 98, and NT will identify these ports automatically and prompt you for the included driver disk(s).

PCI, ISA, and AGP

These are the expansion slots that you'll find on your motherboard. Most new boards are PCI boards. They are the new standard for expansion slots because they are much faster than the older-style ISA slots. On the other hand, even new motherboards include at least a few ISA slots so that you can still use some of the older ISA expansion boards. The AGP slot on newer motherboards is a high-speed expansion slot that you can use for the new fast video cards. Figure 28.11 shows the PCI sockets, the ISA sockets, and an AGP connector on a motherboard.

FIGURE 28.11:

PCI, ISA, and AGP connectors

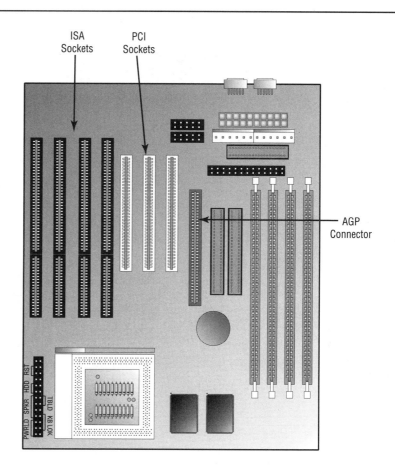

ISA Sockets

PCI Sockets

AGP Connector

Most new motherboards have several kinds of memory and memory slots, such as the DIMMs, SIMMs, and cache memory shown in Figure 28.12. Most boards have at least 256K of fast cache memory. In most cases you can increase that to as much as 1MB, and sometimes even 2MB.

FIGURE 28.12:

DIMM sockets and cache memory on the motherboard

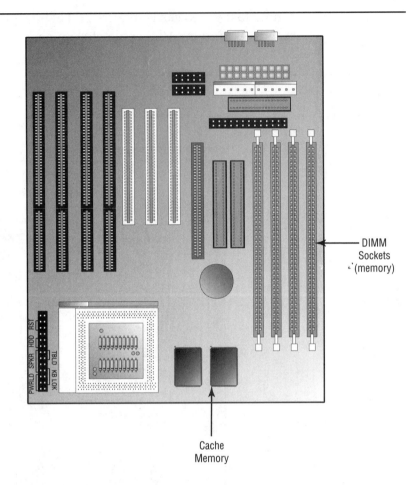

NOTE If you have the option of using DIMMs or SIMMs, choose the DIMMs if you can. They are available in faster speeds, and some motherboards that will run at only 66MHz using SIMMs will run at 100MHz with DIMMs.

The Microprocessor Slot and Control Circuitry

The microprocessor socket is very special. It's called a Zero Insertion Force (ZIF) socket, and it's shown in Figure 28.13. It allows you to insert or remove your expensive microprocessor in the socket without putting any stress on its leads. If you look at it closely, you'll see that there's a lever on the side of the socket. When the lever is in the up position, the holes in the plastic top align with the electrical connections below them so the socket will slide in easily. Once the chip is in place, move the lever to the down (locked) position and the top of the socket slides over and presses the leads of the processor tightly against the electrical contacts inside the socket.

FIGURE 28.13:

ZIF Socket with microprocessor out and lever up

Near the ZIF socket you'll find a few groups of jumpers. By putting the jumpers in the right places, you can set both the voltage and the frequency for the processor. Details are printed in the motherboard manual and often on the motherboard itself.

Final Decisions

Okay, so now you're familiar with your motherboard, you know what goes where, and you know how to plug things in. Time to make the final decisions. What new capabilities do you want to add to your system? In this section, we'll take a look at the choices you have and what each does for you.

Communication Options

No matter what kind of computer you have today, you're almost certainly going to want to have communications capabilities. This includes Internet access, e-mail, perhaps a home network, and possibly even video conferencing. All of these things are forms of communication.

For the most part, computer communications consists of sending and receiving digital information between computers. In addition to the fact that both computers must be compatible, there are two other limiting factors when it comes to digital information. First, can the computers both handle the type and speed of the data being sent? Second, can the medium used to connect the computers support the data speed? The medium, by the way, is the vehicle that carries the data, such as phone lines, cable, or satellite.

Modems

The most basic kind of communications today is modem to modem. Modem, by the way, is a word that was created from the term "*mod*ulator/*dem*odulator," which describes what a modem does. What happens during modem communication is that the signal is initially digital information. The modem receives data from your computer, and converts that data into a series of tones (which, by the way, are what we hear as screeches and beeps when the modem is connecting—sometimes referred to as *white noise*). Once the modem connects, the speaker is usually programmed to shut off. It only makes that lovely sound so we know it's trying to connect.

Choosing a modem is pretty easy if all you want to do is connect to your ISP. There are basically two kinds of modems: internal and external. Internal modems plug into a card slot in your motherboard and external modems connect to a serial port on the outside of your computer. That is, unless you have a USB modem (not common yet). Actually, if I were choosing an external modem, I'd get the USB kind since they won't use up any of my precious COM ports. But frankly, I almost always choose internal modems because they are more convenient. No extra wires to fall over, no extra power connectors to deal with.

Home Networks

Home networks are getting more and more common these days. Quite a few homes today have more than one computer. A home network will allow you to share data as well as resources. For example, with a home network everyone can print using the same printer. And if you do have more than one printer, any computer connected to the network can print to any printer connected to the network. So if you have a laser printer in your home office, for example, then your son could write a report on his own computer and print it on your laser printer (if you'll let him). Similarly, if you want to print some color photos, you could load glossy paper into junior's color inkjet printer and print your photos on that printer.

There are a couple of kinds of home networks. One connects your computers via standard Ethernet cables. The other, which is gaining more acceptance these days, is the phone line network.

Ethernet networks connect computers together via special cables and sometimes hubs. There are two popular Ethernet cabling systems, *twisted pair* and *coaxial*. Twisted pair cabling looks like phone wires with a gland problem. The wires are thicker and the connectors are the same basic shape only larger. Coaxial cabling is similar to the cable used for cable TV, and uses bayonet-type screw-on connectors. (Coaxial cabling is not often used for computer networking because it is not upgradable and it cannot provide network redundancy.) For most home installations, twisted pair or phone line networks are the best choice. They are far easier to install, and generally are quite a bit less expensive.

Setting Up a Phone Line Network

Phone line networks use your existing telephone wiring. The assumption is that you already have telephone wiring to the same places that your computers will be located. Each computer in your network will need a phone line adapter card. The cards transmit and receive data over the same lines as your phone without interfering with phone service, because they operate at a different frequency than the phones.

For this example, we'll look at Diamond's Home*Free* Phone Line Network. The package comes with two network adapters (one for each of two computers), phone cords, and all the software you need to set it up. (Actually, you may need to use your Windows 95 or 98 setup CD to load some of the network protocols, so keep it handy.)

To set up the network, all you need to do is plug the cards into the system, use the cables to connect the cards to a nearby telephone jack, and run the setup software. Once the network's installed, you can share files, resources (like printers and modems), and even drives (including removable media drives). One very useful feature of Diamond's phone line modem is its ability to let up to three users each log onto the Internet from a single account.

Playing Games

Did you know that game playing is the second most popular reason that people buy computers? (The top reason is Internet access.) What do you need to have in order to really get the most out of game play on your computer?

You need a high-performance computer. In fact, video games are really "pushing the envelope" of multimedia. So if you're planning to play games, get a fast video card with at least 4MB of video RAM. You should also get a great sound card like Creative Labs' "Live" card and speakers, the best monitor you can afford, and whatever game controllers you will need to make your game playing more realistic.

The Next Step

Well, that's about it. If you have an older system and you want to convert it to a new system, go through your checklist and replace the parts you want to upgrade. But choose carefully. Remember never buy more computer than you expect to need right now. Buying parts that you think you may need in the future is usually a waste of money, since those parts will probably be faster, smaller, and less expensive in the future. And by the way, when it comes to computers, the future can be as soon as tomorrow…or even later on today.

And one final note: If, after reading this chapter, there's more you want to do to your system, read on. In the next chapter we'll look at building the ultimate computer. Of course that, too, is a moving target. So all I can really do is give you the basics, since by the time you get this book there's almost certainly going to be yet another generation of components.

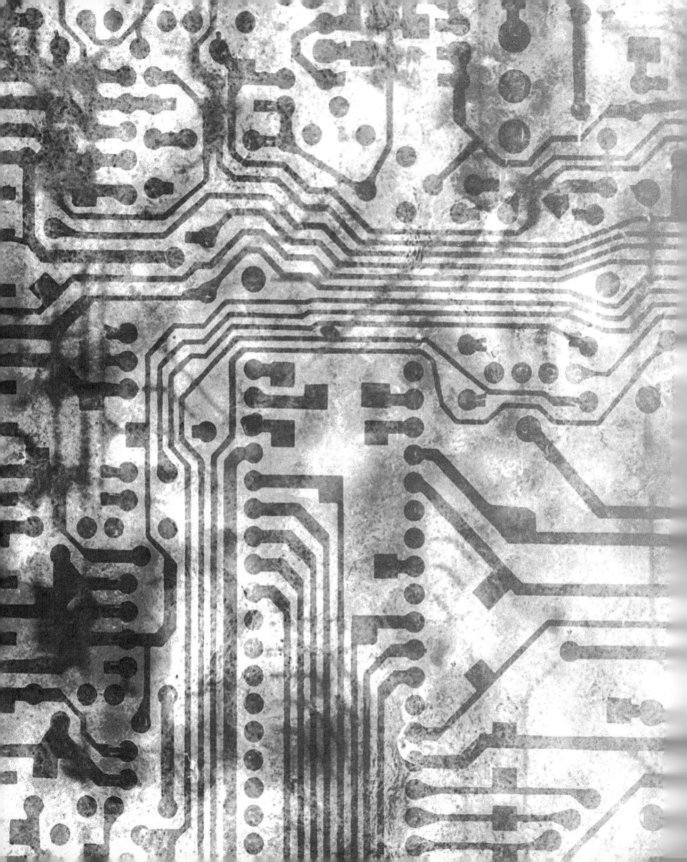

CHAPTER

TWENTY-NINE

Building the Ultimate Computer

- Assembling all the parts

- Installing the video board and testing the system

- Installing the drives and the operating system

- Installing the sound card and the rest of the boards

- Setting up the motherboard

Well folks, this is it. In this chapter we're going to build the ultimate computer. Sounds like a tall order? All right, I'll admit that building any system from scratch is a big project. But by now, you've already done the toughest part: figuring out what to put into your ultimate system. (You have decided, haven't you?)

On the "outside chance" that you're still not sure, stick around, 'cause in this chapter we're putting one together from beginning to end. So grab your parts, clear a big table and let's get started.

Step 1: Assembling All the Parts

The first thing to do is look over all the parts you have, just to make sure that you've got everything you need. I'll briefly recap what you should look for when you go out to buy the items discussed in this section, but almost everything listed here has already been covered in more detail earlier on in the book. So if you want more information, check the index or table of contents for pointers to more detailed information.

Computer Case

There's more to this important item than meets the eye. The case provides a framework for your whole system. It's the main part of the computer that you'll see, and it includes the power supply that will run your computer. So choose one that looks nice (if that is important to you), has lots of room to work in, and is sturdy and solidly built. Figure 29.1 shows an excellent case. The power supply is up out of the way of the rest of the system, and the metal frame that holds the drives is removable, which is very important.

FIGURE 29.1:

Computer case with removable drive frame

Notice that the power supply is at the top of the case. Always make sure that the power supply is near the top if you are getting a tower case. This is important because heat rises, and the fan in the power supply pulls air out of the case. Therefore, all of the hot air produced by the computer will be drawn out of the top and cooler air will be pulled in through the bottom of the computer. A power supply near the middle or bottom of the case would draw heat from the top of the computer across the CPU, drives, or whatever is between the fan and the top of the case.

Motherboard

Over the years there have been so many changes in motherboards that it's almost impossible to say exactly what will be on one and not on another. Also there's some disagreement about what things you should want built into your motherboard. For example, virtually every motherboard today has built-in controllers for floppy drives hard drives, serial ports, and parallel port. Some also have circuitry for USB ports, SoundBlaster-compatible sound, and VGA video.

So what do you do, then, if your motherboard already has (for example) a video board, and you want to install your own, faster video board later? What you need to do is make sure that your motherboard allows you to disable the conflicting on-board circuitry. You can usually do this from the BIOS setup program. But be sure that you check this before you buy it and take it home.

Video Board

Since I was already talking about video cards, let's finish up that subject here. Video cards are one of the hidden bottlenecks in computers. You can have the fastest system (we are building one), but if you use a slow video card, it'll still perform like it's on vacation in the Bahamas.

For our ultimate system, we'll use an AGP video card with lots of built-in video RAM. When you go to buy a video card, the kinds of basic things you should look for initially are things related to speed, color depth, and resolution. Speed on video cards is measured in lots of different ways. One is a measurement of "millions of polygons per second." Polygons are the shapes used to create 3D graphics. The more polygons per second, the faster the card can produce images.

Another speed measurement that is often listed is something called the "frame rate." A frame in computer graphics terms is the same as a single frame on movie film. To get smooth, realistic, full-motion video, you should have a frame rate of at least 30 frames per second. As the frame rate goes down, the image gets jumpy. While a rate of 15 frames per second is acceptable, anything slower is not.

Color depth is the number of colors that can be displayed on screen at one time, and resolution is the number of dots that are displayed on screen at one time. Although there's a certain amount of circuitry behind these two functions, both of them are limited by the amount of video memory you have. The more memory you have, the more colors you can display at a higher resolution.

I should tell you, though, that there are limits to how high you may want to go with colors and resolution. For example, one survey of 100 users showed that the vast majority of users couldn't see any significant difference between high color (16-bit) and true color (24-bit). By the way, 16-bit color is 2 to the 16th power, which is 64K colors (65,536). 24-bit color is 2 to the 24th power, which is 16M colors (16,777,216).

Oh, and by the way, if anyone ever offers to sell you a video card that displays more than 16 million colors, turn and run. The human eye can't discern more colors than that. And unless you have a HUGE display, resolutions higher than 1024 x 768 produce icons and text so small that you'll be working too hard to see them if you have higher resolution.

Another thing you need to think about with video cards are inputs and outputs. The basic function of a video card is to accept data from a computer and output images to a video display. But many video cards today do a lot more. Some accept video input from video cameras and output to television sets and others will output to the new digital flat-panel displays.

Sound Cards

Back in the early days of computing, the only sounds computers made were the whirring, chungging, zizzing, and clicking of equipment running. Sometimes you might get an urgent beep if something jammed or broke. But otherwise, nothing. In fact, the loudest sound I remember was the huge air conditioner the lab needed to keep the computer cool enough to operate within its temperature limitations.

Today, computers are a lot more tolerant of heat, and the equipment operates much more quietly. So instead of the computer support equipment making a lot of sound, it's the movies, music CDs, and video games that make them loud.

People love this kind of loudness. And whom can we thank for it? Mr. Sim and his amazing Sound Blaster cards. Okay, there are other sound cards out today. But the Sound Blaster was the first, and for a long time, it's been the best. They made the rules for sound cards, much as Hayes made the rules for smart modems. So today, even though Hayes is long gone, their modem's AT instruction set is still the standard (along with a lot of new extensions). And as far I can see, Creative Labs (Mr. Sim's company) will be with us for a long time to come, and the Sound Blaster's standard will continue to be the template for all other sound cards.

When you go out to buy a sound card, the first thing to look for is Sound Blaster compatibility (unless, of course, you're getting a genuine Sound Blaster of some sort). If you get a card that isn't Sound Blaster compatible, then there's a chance it won't work with some of the programs you may want to run.

The next thing to look for is the card's specifications. Sound cards have several sections. One circuit plays wave (.wav) files. These are digital audio, similar to the data that's on CDs. They are sampled audio data that's been converted into numbers.

The other kind of sound file that your sound card can play is called a midi (`.mid`) file. Midi files don't contain any actual audio information. Instead, they specify a sound from a built-in table and, among other things, how long and how loud the sound will play. Sound cards play sounds for midi files based upon tables of sampled sounds kind of the way electronic pianos play sounds based upon buttons you select.

Better sound cards have more and better-sampled sounds to use in their midi players. Also, better sound cards have more bits per sample (giving you better sound quality). And by the way, just in case you were wondering where you might get a joystick adapter, most sound cards have a built-in joystick port like the one shown in Figure 29.2.

FIGURE 29.2:

Joystick port on the sound card

Modems

Want to connect to the Internet? To get on, you need a device that will connect your computer to it. For most of us, this is going to be some kind of modem. Of course there are all sorts of modems. The most common modems connect to your computer on one side and to a phone line on the other. Your computer tells the modem to dial a number and, once connected, the modem handles all of the electronic details.

There are, of course, other kinds of modems. Some, called cable modems, connect to the Internet via cable lines. Others connect to the Internet via ISDN lines. Incidentally, the last ones aren't really modems, but they're still called modems. The thing to remember with modems is that the kind you get is determined by the kind of connection you'll be using. For our computer, we'll stick to a standard phone line, since that's the most widely available kind of connection.

If you're getting a standard phone line modem, the things you should look for are the speed (almost all are 56K), data translation capability (these days you should get V.90), and any extra features you may want to have, such as voice and fax. Most modems today do faxing, but not all have voice capabilities. This allows you to hook up a speaker and microphone so the computer will operate as a speakerphone. You may also want to get a modem that can handle a low-cost video camera so you can have two-way videophone communications.

The final decision you need to make regarding your modem is whether or not to get an internal or external one. External modems have LEDs on them (see Figure 29.3) that let you see what the modem is doing from one moment to another. They also don't use any of the system power or system slots. On the other hand, most of us don't need to know exactly what the modem is doing and we rarely use up every slot in our systems. Also, an external modem uses up either a serial port (there are only two of them) or a USB port, which will cost you more money.

FIGURE 29.3:

External modem showing indicator lights

For these reasons, and because I don't like to have so many extra things hung on the outside of the computer, I usually recommend internal modems. For this system, that's what we'll use.

Hard Drive

The hard drive holds the most valuable thing in your computer—your data. Choose your new drive carefully. The drive should be fast, reliable, and large enough to handle more than double the data you'll need to store.

"Double?" you say? Yep, double. Fact is once a drive gets half full, it starts to slow down. So (for example) if you think you'll need 10GB, get a 20GB or larger drive.

When you get a hard drive, buy it as a complete kit. That way you'll get all of the extra bits and pieces you'll need to install it easily.

The kinds of features you should consider are UDMA (Ultra Direct Memory Access) capability and a good spindle speed. UDMA means that the drive can access memory more efficiently, thereby increasing the speed of the drive. The spindle is the shaft in the center of the platters inside the hard drive. The higher the speed, the higher the data rate can be (in theory). Of course, you also need to look at the average access time, data transfer rate, and burst rate. Oh, and if you can't remember what these terms mean, just remember this: you want the highest possible data transfer rate and burst rate (which is a kind of data transfer rate) because this is how quickly the information goes from the hard drive to the computer and back. And you want the shortest possible access time because that's how long it takes for the hard drive to find your information once the computer asks for it.

Floppy Drive

Although getting a floppy drive should be a simple thing, it turns out that there are a few choices. First of all, I feel I should tell you that if you haven't already done so, it's time to get rid of your old 5-1/4" drive. We're making the ultimate computer here, and the 5-1/4" drive isn't a part of that picture. If you still have some sentimental attachment to the old drive (like there are some old programs you still run from it), don't consider building a brand new computer; go back to the last chapter and perform an upgrade.

I say this because newer systems can actually develop problems if you run some types of older software on them. Also, many older programs won't run at all, or will run so poorly on newer systems that it's just not a good idea to use them. Most of the problem software dates back to the old 5.25" drives. So, if you have a lot of software that you really want to keep that's on those disks, don't build a new computer—you may make the old software effectively unusable.

For this new computer, we're getting a SuperDrive. This is a floppy that can read and write to the old 1.44MB floppies but also can read and write to the new 120MB floppies! So with one drive you've got compatibility and high capacity. After all, the reason we use floppy drives is because we want to be able to exchange data with computers that aren't connected to our computer. 1.44MB floppies are the standard. Virtually every computer today has one. But we also know that 1.44MB isn't very much space today. So the SuperDrive provides a reasonable upgrade that's built-in. The SuperDrive includes all of the hardware you'll need to install the drive, as well as some software and usually at least one of the 120MB disks. If you happen to purchase one that doesn't include a disk, be sure to purchase a disk separately when you get the drive so you can test your installation.

Zip Drive

Okay, I hear you. You asking, "...since I've already got a Super-Drive (120MB drive), why should I also get a Zip drive?"

Although the Zip drive is more of a marketing achievement than an engineering achievement, it is, nevertheless, useful for transferring large files. When you buy your Zip drive, I recommend getting at least one 10-pack of disks. First of all, most dealers will give you a deal if you buy them when you're getting the drive. And second, you'll want them later. I usually get the ones that come in a variety of colors. This makes it easy for me to see which disk I want quickly.

So I guess that if your budget will only allow you to get one or the other, I'd suggest getting a standard floppy (which you can now get for about $10 if you look around) and get the Zip drive. I like the SuperDrive better, although it's not the standard at this time. But, hey, we can put one into this system because it's the dream machine...the ultimate computer! So grab your drives and let's move on.

CD-ROM/DVD Drive

Now this is something that always gets me excited. Don't ask me why. I guess that I'm still a kid when it comes to movies, but the technology of DVD movies is just plain incredible.

DVD drives can hold more than two hours of high-quality, full motion picture—video as well as CD-quality, 3D stereo sound! And I can watch it on my computer (my own personal movie theater) or I can connect it to a big-screen TV and hi-fi stereo system and share it with my friends.

Like SuperDrives, DVD drives are backward compatible to audio CDs and CD-ROMs. So if you get a DVD drive, you can use any of the standard format CDs or DVDs. The kinds of things to look for when you go out to buy a DVD drive are speed and features.

Now when I say "features," I'm not kidding. DVD drives can be purchased as a drive only or they can be purchased as a kit. You should definitely buy the kit, as it contains some items that you'll definitely be glad to have. Notice the small circuit board? This is something that you really, really want. It provides you with hardware decoding. You see when the DVD image is put onto the disc the information is compressed so that the manufacturer can fit more stuff on it. These include things like alternate languages (yes, Kermit the Frog speaks Cantonese on some DVDs); different screen proportions, like standard and wide-screen (also called letterbox). They also usually include the promos, trailers, and sometimes extra goodies like a director's cut of the movie, or a film of the director(s) commenting on what they were doing or other behind the scenes information.

Anyway, the data on the DVD disc has to be decoded. There are two kinds of decoders available: software and hardware. The software decoders are slower than the hardware decoders are, so they produce an image that's not as sharp as it can be. The hardware decoder produces an image that is razor sharp. Remember that this is the ultimate computer, so we're getting the kit with the hardware decoder.

Networking

You may think that just because you have a home system or a small office system, you don't need networking. Well, you may want to think again.

The only people who don't really need a local area network are people with just one computer. Everyone else will benefit from it. This is true even if the other computer is your kid's computer. A second system can really save you if you ever crash. One of the best things you can do with your network is back up the data from one computer onto another. Or better yet, onto a removable media drive that's connected to another computer. Then, if one of the systems goes down (I should say *when* it goes down, since eventually they all do), you can go over to the other computer, download the files you need from the removable media drive, and continue working while the sick one is being revived. And by the way, make sure that the removable media drive can be run from either computer by installing the drivers for it on both machines.

Now, getting back to networking. There are a lot of options available for networking (as you may recall from the last chapter). The fastest of these today is Ethernet. So as you probably guessed (ultimate computer, you know the routine)...we're getting Ethernet.

With Ethernet, the thing to look for is speed and expandability. Speed should be 100MHz (10MHz is cheaper, but we're not after cheaper). You should also check to see what kind(s) of cables and connectors the network interface cards (NICs) will accept. Some will take several cables; others will accept only one kind. And by the way, once again, I recommend getting a complete kit if you can, since that will have all of the necessary parts.

Extra Interfaces

The idea of extra interfaces might surprise you. Don't worry, we'll use them later—for now, just get them. They're pictured in Figure 29.4. One is USB, which you may actually have built into your motherboard. It's getting to be another standard interface like serial and parallel, and most of the new motherboards have them. If yours doesn't, get it. A lot of new devices are being offered with USB connections, and they make adding devices very simple. No IRQs or other complications to consider. Just plug it in and the system recognizes it.

The other connection I'm recommending is Firewire, also known as IEEE 1394. This new interface is quite fast and for now, it's the only way to get (for example) full motion, digital video from a DV camera. If you aren't concerned about getting the video as a digital signal, you can use a standard NTSC or S-video interface, but neither is as sharp as digital.

FIGURE 29.4:

USB card and cables

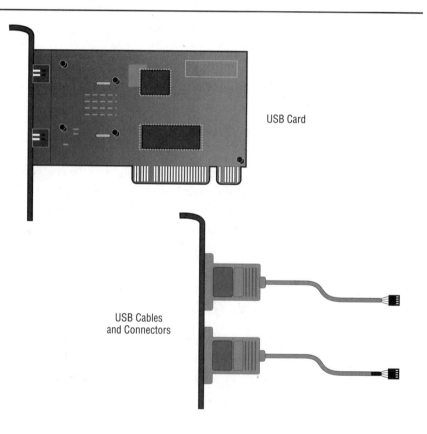

USB Card

USB Cables
and Connectors

Step 2: Start with the Case

Now that you have everything you need and you're ready to roll, you need to find a large, open space that's big enough for you to open the case and work on any side of it easily. The most ideal situation would be to get a large lazy Susan that's big enough to hold the entire case and put the case. Make sure that the base is stable—some lazy Susans are a bit wobbly. But if you don't have a lazy Susan, just be sure that you allow plenty of room around your work area so that you can get to all sides of the case as you work.

> **TIP** One thing you need to be careful of when using a lazy Susan is to make sure that you don't start winding any wires around the system or the turntable.

Get a couple of cups, an egg carton, or some other convenient containers to hold all of the loose screws that you'll be taking out of the computer case. Typically there are at least two sizes of screws used in computers. If you get more than one container, then you can keep them separated.

We're using a tower case for the ultimate computer (see Figure 29.5). Find the cover screws and take them all out. Leave the screws for the power supply in place for now.

> **TIP** The power supply screws will generally be only in the back panel of the case, while the case screws will go through the cover and the back panel and will be nearer the outer perimeter of the back.

Once the cover is off (put it somewhere you won't trip over it), you can see inside the cabinet. Find the screws (and possibly latches) that hold the drive chassis on. Take out the drive chassis and set it aside in a spot where you won't trip over it. While the cover may hurt you if you trip on it, the drive chassis will probably be ruined if it has an unexpected encounter with your shoe.

FIGURE 29.5:

Removing the cover
screws from a tower
case

Now take out the power supply. This may require removing the front panel of the case as well as removing the screws on the back of the power supply. Be sure not to remove the screws that hold the power supply together.

Once the power supply is out, set aside the computer case and replace the lazy Susan (if you're using one) with a book or box that is about 2 inches high and roughly 9 × 11 inches. This will allow you to work easily on your system without any of the boards popping out from their mounting brackets.

Step 3: Setting Up the Motherboard

Now get out your motherboard. Carefully put it on the box and open up the motherboard manual that came with it. This is an extremely important document. When you're done here, put it in a safe place. It contains information that you must have to be able to use the motherboard.

Installing the CPU

Take a look at your CPU. Engraved on the top of the processor itself you'll find a lot of important information. Figure 29.6 shows the top of the processor. This one is an AMD (Advanced Micro Devices) K6-III/450. It uses a core voltage of 2.4 volts and an I/O voltage of 3.3 volts. It also says it was designed to work with Windows NT and Windows 95. In fact, I've found that none of the new motherboards will work on Windows 95 reliably if they are running faster than 333MHz. They all develop strange anomalies. So if you're running a processor faster than 333MHz (like this one), plan on upgrading to Windows 98. Besides, it has much better support for USB.

FIGURE 29.6:

The AMD K6/III 450 processor

Open up the motherboard manual to the page that shows a diagram of the motherboard layout. It should be labeled with all of the locations of the various control jumpers, interface connectors, and components. Find the jumpers that control the CPU and system voltage. The motherboard we're using in this chapter looks like the one shown in Figure 29.7.

FIGURE 29.7:

The motherboard layout showing all of the major components, connectors, and jumper locations

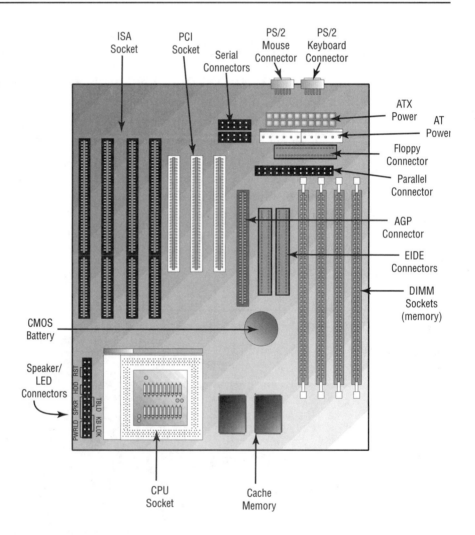

Setting the Voltages

Now take a look at the page that shows the jumper positions for different voltages on the motherboard. If you look closely at the CPU above, you'll notice that the CPU uses two different voltages. The *core voltage* is the voltage that the CPU uses for its internal operation. The *I/O voltage* is the voltage it uses to communicate with the rest of the system. Depending upon your motherboard, you will need to set either one or the other of these voltages.

To set the voltages, you'll need to put some jumpers in the right places on the motherboard. You should find a table in your motherboard manual that looks a lot like the one in Figure 29.8. Placing or removing these jumpers sets the correct voltages for the CPU and system I/O. Set them incorrectly, and you can say goodbye to your expensive CPU—so set the jumpers carefully.

FIGURE 29.8:

The motherboard's voltage settings table

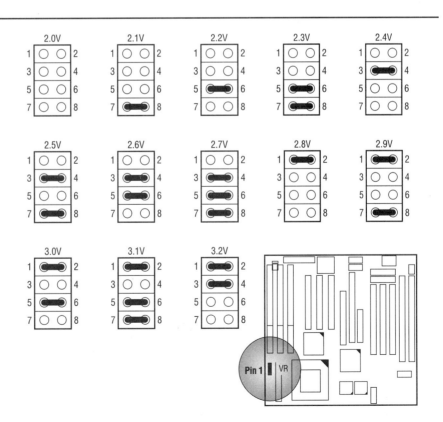

Setting the Clock Speed

Before we go any further, on the outside chance that your CPU isn't imprinted with the information on what frequency to set it up, the motherboard manual usually contains a table that covers that information for most current processors. Table 29.1 is an example of such a table. (This is just an example; you should use information relevant to your CPU.)

TABLE 29.1: Operating Frequencies and Multipliers for CPUs

CPU Type	Frequency (MHz)	System Bus Clock (MHz)	Multiplier
INTEL			
Pentium 166 MMX	166	66	2.5x
Pentium 200 MMX	200	66	3x
Pentium 233 MMX	233	66	3.5
AMD			
K6-166	166	66	2.5
K6 -200	200	66	3.5
K6-233	233	66	3.5x
K6-266	266	66	4x
K6-300	300	66	4.5x
K6/II-300	300	66	4.5x
"	"	100	3x
K6/II-333	333	95	3.5x
K6/II-350	350	100	3.5x
K6/II-366	366	66	5.5x
K6/II-400	400	100	4x
K6/III-400	400	100	4x
K6/III-450	450	100	4.5x

Setting the clock speed is very similar to setting the voltages. Let's say that the CPU runs at 450MHz (like the one we have). If the motherboard manufacturer tried to make the all of the components operate at 450MHz using today's technology, we'd either have a system too expensive to buy or one that would work only if it were all on a single chip. Bottom line: the rest of the system has to run slower. In general, we have two choices today for the system bus speed: 66MHz and 100MHz. Needless to say (but I'll say it again anyway), we're making the ultimate computer here, so we're going with a 100MHz bus.

On this motherboard, the settings allow you to choose frequencies ranging from 66MHz to 124MHz. Although there are no external components currently manufactured that claim to operate as high as 124MHz, the board provides the capability for future (and hopefully) faster parts. Also, for people who like to live on the edge, you can overclock the parts (run them faster than they say will run) and some will actually run at the faster speeds. For this you have to experiment. Just be aware that running the parts a lot faster than they were designed to run can make them fail prematurely, because they're likely to run hot. This also will void your warranty on the processor should it fail on you, so do this at your own risk.

The Multiplier

Now take a look at Figure 29.9. This shows the table of multiplier factors. The way you set the CPU's internal speed is by making it run some multiple faster than the system bus speed. The options on this board are 2x, 2.5x, 3x, 3.5x, 4x, 4.5x, 5x and 5.5x. So if you've set the system bus clock to 100MHz, then setting the multiplier to 4.5x will make the CPU run at 450MHz. If I chose the 5x or 5.5x, I'd be overclocking the processor as mentioned earlier. But for this PC I won't take any risks, so the 4.5x multiplier will do fine.

FIGURE 29.9:

The motherboard's CPU clock multiplier settings table

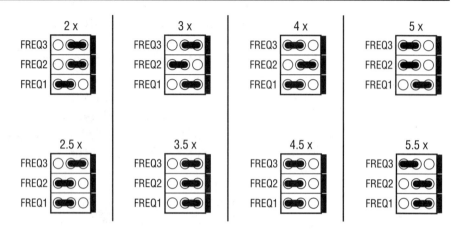

Plugging in the CPU

All your CPU settings should be complete now, so get ready to install the CPU. First, get your CPU fan and put it nearby. Lift the lever on the CPU's ZIF (Zero Insertion Force) socket as shown in Figure 29.10. Then carefully align the pins on the CPU with the holes in the socket.

WARNING   Be sure to align the holes correctly. One corner of the CPU has a pin missing and one corner of the socket has a hole missing. Make sure that you align the CPU correctly or it won't go in correctly, and you may damage one or more of the delicate pins, making the CPU unusable.

The CPU should fit into the socket with absolutely no resistance. If it's tight, check the locking lever to make sure it's not partly locked. It should be up and back as shown in Figure 29.11.

FIGURE 29.10:

Aligning the CPU pins with the holes in the ZIF socket

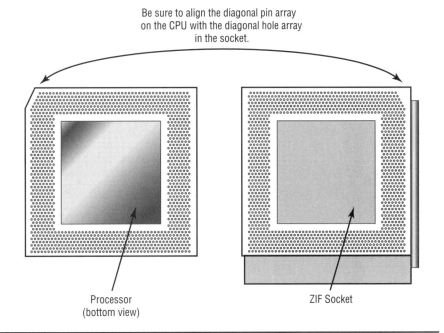

Be sure to align the diagonal pin array on the CPU with the diagonal hole array in the socket.

Processor
(bottom view)

ZIF Socket

FIGURE 29.11:

Opening the locking lever fully

Once the CPU is fully seated in its socket, lower the lever and lock it into place. It should click into position behind a molded clip in the socket's side.

Next, squeeze a bit of heat sink compound from its tube into the center of the metal top of the CPU and put the heat sink/fan on top of the CPU as shown in Figure 29.12. Finally, clip the heat sink/fan on both sides, and you're done installing the CPU.

FIGURE 29.12:

Installing the heat sink/fan on the CPU

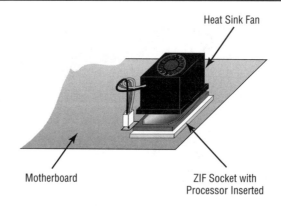

Heat Sink Fan

Motherboard

ZIF Socket with
Processor Inserted

Installing Main Memory

The next thing you need to do is plug the memory into the motherboard. Today there are two kinds of memory available, SIMMs and DIMMs. To get maximum system speed we'll use DIMMs, since there are DIMMs that can run at the 100MHz bus speed. The fastest SIMMs can handle only 66MHz.

Following the rule that you should never buy more computer than you know you'll need immediately, we'll install 64MB of RAM in this system. Although there are 128MB and 256MB DIMMs available, nothing this computer is doing will require that much memory. So, ultimate system or not, 64MB is all it'll get. If the need arises, we can always put another 64MB DIMM in the other DIMM slot.

To install the DIMM, first take a look at the DIMM and then take a look at the DIMM socket.

Although it's not initially obvious, there are small notches in the edge connector of the DIMM that align with mating plugs in the DIMM socket. Turn the DIMM so it lines up correctly and press it straight down into the socket until the latching levers on either side start to lock into position. Once the DIMM is fully seated, pull the latches up the rest of the way to lock in the DIMMs.

Step 4: Installing the Video Board and Testing the System

At this point, I feel I should tell you about a good friend of mine. This friend, we'll call him Jim, loved to build computers. Trouble is, most of the time they didn't work...well not at first, anyway. I don't know if it was the parts he bought, a negative attitude or what, but if he ever assembled a computer right into the case without testing the parts first, it never...I mean *never* worked.

I can't tell you why. He'd take the same parts, lay them out on the test bench, and plug them together first, and they'd work just fine. But skip the test, and the system would be doomed. Oh, he'd get it running eventually, but in the end, he always wound up taking it apart and putting it together again piece by piece on the test bench first.

So let me give you some advice: put the whole thing together first outside of the case. Once you're sure everything is working, then assemble it into the case. This, by the way, is good advice even if you don't have the same little black cloud following you around that my friend had.

Plug In the Video Card

The next step in building our computer is to plug in the video card. Although the philosophy at this point is to plug the system in and test it with as close to nothing plugged into it as possible, without a video card you'll have a real hard time telling what's going on in the computer. This system has an AGP video card so find the AGP port.

Notice that when you plug in the card, there's a stem that goes down below the edge of the motherboard. This would normally engage in the bottom of the computer case to help secure the card. Here, however, we've got the motherboard up on a box, so it won't get in the way.

Now plug the video monitor's cable into the video card, plug in the monitor's power cord and…no, hang on a minute, I didn't tell you to plug in the computer yet, did I? I strongly suggest that you read the next section before you do anything else.

Checking Out the Power Switch

Get the power supply, plug in the power plug—AT or ATX, whichever you have (in this case it's AT) —and plug it into the motherboard. Then take a close look at the power switch that's hanging off the end of the long, thick wire coming out of the power supply.

| NOTE | This is important! Make sure the wires going to the power switch are well insulated before you switch it on for the first time! Skip this step and your friends could wind up scraping you off the ceiling. There's 120V—at more amps than you want to meet face to face—in there. |

If there are no insulators, or if the insulators aren't covering the connectors properly, you could get one heck of an electric shock when you grab that switch. So if you need to, get some electrical tape and wrap the exposed connectors before you plug in the power supply!

The First System Test

Take a look at the monitor. Did the system messages come up? Did it count up as much memory as you installed? (NOTE: 64MB comes up to about 65 million, and 128MB reaches about 131 million.) If the system got that far, it's doing well. Move on to the next step. If it didn't make it, you need to recheck all of the steps we took so far.

Step 5: Installing the Drives

Now that you're sure the motherboard, memory, and video card are all working, the next thing you need to do is (as you may have guessed from the rather large lettering above) install the drives. Well, okay, not all the drives, just the floppy drive, hard drive (we're only using one in this system), and the CD-ROM or DVD.

All these drives need to go in next because it takes all of them to install the operating system. Actually, on some systems you can do without the floppy drive, but in this case we'll use it too.

Installing the Floppy Drive(s)

Figure 29.13 shows a floppy drive and its data cable. See the dark stripe along one edge of the data cable? This marks the wire that goes to pin #1 on the connectors. Another thing you should look for is a twist in the cable. The twist is positioned just before the connector for drive A:. The floppy drive controller is wired to detect this twist and assigns the drive nearest the twist to drive A:. Except for the cabling, there's no difference between an A: drive and a B: drive unless one is a (shudder) 5.25" drive.

FIGURE 29.13:

Floppy drive and cable (notice the twist near one of the connectors)

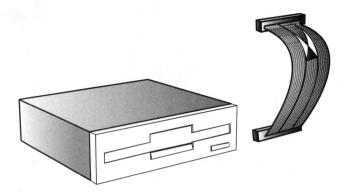

If you look at the back of a floppy drive you'll see that there are two connectors back there. One is the data connector and the other is the power connector. Although many drives print where pin 1 is on the circuit board, some don't. When that happens, just plug the data cable so that the dark stripe (usually red) is nearest the power connector.

Installing the Hard Drive(s)

Like floppies, two hard drives can also share a single flat ribbon data cable. These, however, are not twisted to define the drives. Instead, they are set up as Master and Slave. Figure 29.14 shows the back of a typical IDE/EIDE hard drive. There are three connector areas. The largest is for the data cable, the one with large pins is the power connector and the center one is the control block where you place the jumpers for the Master and Slave settings.

FIGURE 29.14:

Location of the connectors on a hard drive

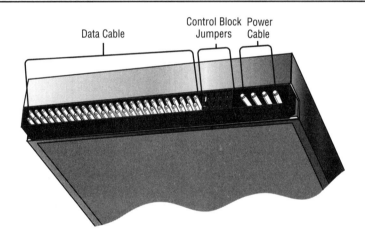

Data Cable   Control Block Power
Jumpers   Cable

There are usually two IDE/EIDE connectors on the motherboard. One is called Primary and the other is called Secondary. To specify a hard drive as drive C: (also called the boot drive), plug its data cable into the Primary connector and set its control block jumper to Master.

Now plug in the data cable and the power cable. Be sure to position pin 1 of the data cable nearest to the power connector (as shown in Figure 29.14) and align the angled corners of the power plug with the angled corners of the power connector.

Setting Up the BIOS

As you may recall, there are a number of different ways to get the computer to go to the BIOS setup screen. Since this one has an AMI BIOS, it's very easy. Shortly after the computer begins to boot up, it displays a message on the screen like the one shown in Figure 29.15.

FIGURE 29.15:

The main BIOS setup screen

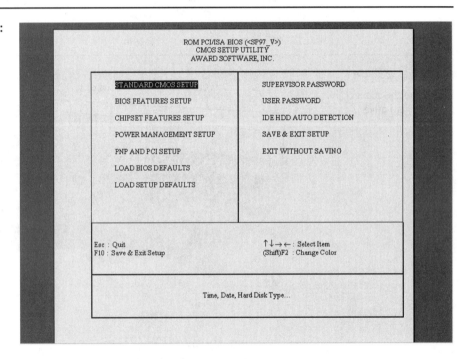

If you're like me, you're probably thinking that there are way too many options in the BIOS. But don't let it intimidate you. The first screen is just a table of contents. Every listing in the table of contents takes you to another page of options in the BIOS. Once you get into it, you'll find changing the BIOS options pretty easy.

In fact, some people get so comfortable with the BIOS setup that they start to change things they don't understand. *Don't do this.* If you don't know what you're doing, making changes to the BIOS can get you into more trouble than you even want to think about. Fortunately, there really aren't that many things that you'll need to do in the BIOS under normal circumstances. So let's move on to the things we need to do.

The BIOS: Setting the Time, the Date, and a Few Other Essentials

The settings we program into the BIOS will be saved by CMOS memory so the computer will know how to boot up each time you start it. The BIOS contains information on your hard drive, your built-in peripheral controllers like the floppy, COM ports, and so on.

If you're using an AMI BIOS like the one pictured in Figure 29.15, the first place you should go is to the "Standard CMOS Setup" page. To do this, just highlight it with the up or down arrow on the keyboard and press Enter. The Standard CMOS Setup page looks like the screen in Figure 29.16.

Take a look at the bottom of the screen. There you'll find the basic controls for the BIOS setup. Since it's text-based, you'll need to press different keys to make changes. To move from one item to the next, use the arrow keys on the keyboard. This moves the highlight around the screen. Once the item you want to change is highlighted, press the "Page Up" or the "Page Down" key to change the value in the highlighted area. To get an idea of how it works, move the highlight to the month and press Page Up.

FIGURE 29.16:

The Standard CMOS
Setup screen

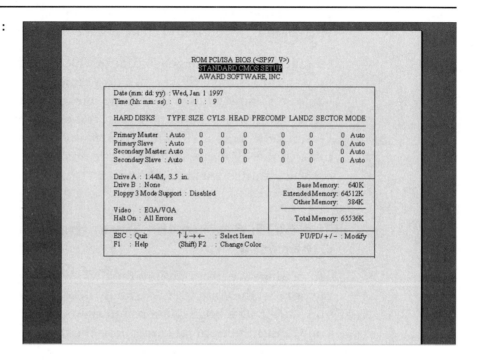

One thing that you should be aware of as you set the time is that the computer uses military time. This means that 12:00 (twelve hundred hours) is noon and 0:00 is midnight. Hours between 0:01 and 11:59 are A.M. hours. Hours between 12:01 to 23:59 are P.M. hours.

Another thing you may notice is that many of the items in the list are already filled in for you. This computer is set up to automatically detect quite a few devices. It found the 1.44MB floppy drive, the VGA display, and the memory. What you may also notice is that the hard drive is not listed. The BIOS, however, can automatically detect the hard drive. You just need to tell it you want it to. Once you're satisfied with all of the other settings on this screen, exit by pressing the "Esc" key on your keyboard to go back to the main screen.

Now move the highlight to "IDE HDD Auto Detect" and press "Enter." The computer will immediately begin to auto-detect your drives. Once it finds one, it will display the drive's parameters in the box near the bottom of the screen. Sometimes it will give you two or three options for how you may want the drive set up. Generally, it's best to just press the Enter key to accept the default settings.

Once the system has detected your drives, exit the auto-detection screen by pressing the Esc key and go back to Standard CMOS Setup to confirm that your drives match what you have in the system. Finally, check the time and date. If everything checks out, press Esc to get back to the main menu, move your cursor over to the item that says "Save & Exit Setup," and press Enter.

This will reboot your system. Of course, it won't be able to boot up unless you already have a system on your hard drive, and we don't. But you're still not quite ready to install Windows. Remember that Windows is generally supplied on a CD-ROM, and so far you don't have a CD-ROM drive in the system. So let's do that now.

Installing the CD-ROM (or DVD) Drive

Installing a CD-ROM or DVD is pretty much the same as installing a hard drive. In fact, it's almost identical. You set the control block to Master or Slave (in this case, since there's only one other IDE-type drive, we'll make it Slave), plug in the power and data cables (remember, red stripe nearest the power connector), and you're done. We'll install the little audio cable later when we put everything into the case. To help you visualize the whole thing, Figure 29.17 shows a picture of the back of a typical IDE DVD drive (CD-ROMs look essentially the same).

The connectors on the
back of a DVD drive

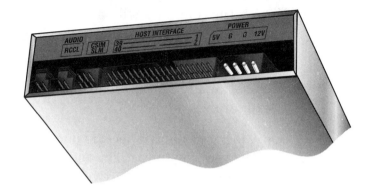

Okay, there's one more thing you need to do before you fire up
the computer to install the operating system. You need to attach
a mouse and keyboard. If you have a PS/2 type mouse, just plug
it into the motherboard's mouse connector. If you have a serial
mouse, get the serial connector. It's usually attached to a metal
bracket like the one pictured in Figure 29.18, along with the parallel port connector. Plug the 10-pin header connector at the end
of the serial data cable into the motherboard's COM1 connector.
Then plug your mouse into the 9-pin D connector.

FIGURE 29.18:

9-pin and 25-pin
serial ports

Step 6: Installing the Operating System (Windows 98)

Ready to install Windows? It'll take between 30 and 60 minutes…at least that's what Microsoft claims. Of course, as fast as this system is, we should be able to cut off quite a bit of that time. So get out your stopwatch and let's get started.

For this installation, we'll use a floppy boot disk to launch the system and a CD containing Windows 98 (be sure you are using the newest version of Windows 98, the second edition—the CD may even be labeled "Windows 98 SE").

00:00:00 - Insert the boot disk into the floppy drive, and the Windows 98 SE CD into the DVD drive. Power up the system.

This, by the way, is why we needed to install the floppy before this step. If you prefer (or if you don't have a boot floppy), you can set up the CD-ROM or DVD drive as the boot device. Just make it the Master and make the CD-ROM the boot device in the BIOS by going to the BIOS Features page.

Anyway, if you don't make the CD-ROM your boot device, then you need to install MSCDEX (which means Microsoft Compact Disc Extensions). Once the system boots and has the extensions installed, then control is turned over to the CD-ROM.

One thing that can happen with this method is that the CD-ROM isn't found because you have more than one drive. The startup program is looking for the CD-ROM to be on drive D: but your second hard drive is there. The CD-ROM is assigned to drive E:. So if you get an error, don't panic, just switch to the correct drive by typing the drive letter and a colon (like E:), press Enter, type **setup**, press Enter again, and you'll be on your way.

One of the first things Windows startup does is to check the integrity of your hard drive by running SCANDISK.

03:19:12–The Windows 98 terms agreement screen appears.

After about three minutes of testing (this will vary, depending upon the size of your hard drive), you'll be presented with Microsoft's terms and copyright notice. You'll have to accept these to continue. If you like, you can even read them all. On the other hand, almost no one ever does read them. Boiled down, they're telling you that you're not allowed to make extra copies of the program, and that you may not modify it and distribute it or transfer the copy you have without deleting it from all your systems. In other words, if you have it installed on a computer and you sell the computer, you have to include all the disks and documentation that came with it. You can't keep a copy for yourself. There are a few other details, but that's basically it.

03:30:17–Enter the Product Key.

Once you've agreed to abide by Microsoft's copyright, you need to prove that you are the rightful owner of the program. To do this, you need to enter the excessively long product code that is on the original sleeve or on a sheet of paper that came with the CD. You should have very little trouble identifying it—it's 25 digits long! (Five groups of five letters and numbers.)

04:58:32–Accept the Windows directory.

After you enter the product key, the computer buzzes and whirrs for a little while and after about another minute and a half it asks you where you want to put the Windows files. It offers you the opportunity to put them into a subdirectory called Windows. Personally, I recommend you use that one. All of the programs you get for the system will expect it to be there. And besides, what would be a better name to store it under? Basketball? Watermelon? Take my advice, accept the default name and press Enter.

05:32:46–Make a startup disk.

For this step, you'll need a blank 3½" disk. You'll use this to boot up your system if, for some reason, you can't get your hard drive to cooperate some day. Think of it as a little insurance policy. It takes only a few minutes to make it, but it could really bail you out some day.

If you decide to make a startup disk, put on a blank label, write "Windows 98 SE Boot Disk" on it, put it into the floppy drive, and press Enter.

Now you can go grab a cup of coffee, you'll have about five minutes to kill before you need to check the screen again.

10:42:23–Load files from the CD.

After completing all of the basic housekeeping stuff, the installation program starts loading Windows onto your hard drive from the CD. Now you can really take a break, this will take almost seven minutes.

When it's done loading, the system reboots so you'll know it's time to pay attention again.

17:17:13–Find Plug and Play devices.

Now Windows goes through your system, searching for any Plug-and-Play devices. Of course, many of the things that you'll be adding are still lying on the table a few feet from the system, so it won't detect those. Don't worry, it'll notice them when we put them in later. For now, just relax.

Oh, and watch out for another reboot which will happen when the computer's done with this step too.

19:38:22–Finish up

After the second reboot, the computer sets up your desktop, the Control Panel, puts the programs on the Start menu, installs Windows help, configures Windows, sets the time and date, and guess what...?

You guessed it...it reboots again!

24:21:26–Done!

Here we are. It only took a little more than 24 minutes to install. This is one fast computer! By now you deserve a break. So if you'd like, you can take the Windows Tour and play with some of the programs or whatever pleases you. But once you're done, don't forget that you still have a few more parts to check out and install.

Step 7: Installing the Sound Card

For this system we're using the Creative Labs' Sound Blaster Live! Sound card. It provides 3D sound and 64 voices—it can play up to 64 sounds at once, and can handle up to eight speakers!

It's a PCI board, so it needs to go into one of the PCI slots. This, by the way, is very important. It's actually possible to plug a PCI board into an ISA slot, so do not do this! You can fry both the board and/or the entire system, motherboard and all, if you are unlucky.

The PCI plugs are short and they are white or light colored. The ISA slots are much longer and are generally black or a dark color.

Now plug the sound card into one of the PCI sockets and plug in at least one set of powered speakers. These are speakers that have a built-in amplifier. They're necessary because the output from the Sound Blaster Live! Card is not amplified. If you tried to play it through unpowered speakers you would have a hard time hearing anything.

Turn on the computer and wait for it to start Windows. This time you'll probably get a lot of messages as you boot up, telling you that Windows has detected motherboard resources, the video card, and your sound card. It will also ask you for the disk(s) or CDs that came with the boards. Go ahead and install the drivers by putting in the disks it asks for, and let it continue booting up.

Once the system has finished booting, you should hear the Microsoft sound. If you don't, then open the Control Panel by selecting it under Settings in the Start menu. Then double-click the Sounds icon and you'll get a window.

This window has a large area near the top labeled "Events." This is a list of the different things that can trigger a sound in Windows. Beside the events that have sounds associated with them are little yellow speaker icons. If you click one of the little speakers, the name of the sound associated to it will appear in the text window below the Events window (these items are all labeled in Figure 29.19).

Once you've selected one of the events, you can hear the sound it'll make by clicking the right arrow button to the right of the Preview window. Do that now.

Did you hear a sound?

If you did, the sound card is working correctly. Now, make sure the CD that came with the sound card is in its drive and run the setup program that came with it. This will install some additional drivers and a number of sound applications on your hard drive.

FIGURE 29.19:

The Sounds Properties window

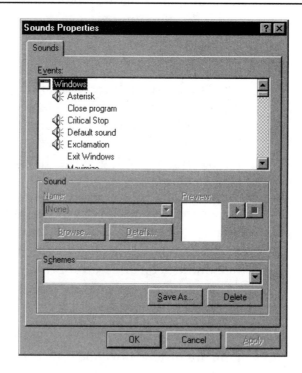

Step 8: Installing the Rest of the Boards

Now you can pat yourself on the back and take a deep sigh of pleasure—you're almost halfway through building the ultimate computer! There are only a few more things to install and test, and we'll get to those right now.

Installing the Modem

If you haven't already done it, power down the computer and plug in the modem. It also goes into a PCI slot.

Now power up the computer again and wait for the system to detect your modem and request the driver disk. Insert the disk into the floppy drive and press Enter. This will install the drivers for your modem and prepare it for connection to the Internet.

Installing the DVD Decoder Board

Shut down the system again and plug in the DVD decoder card. To understand what this card does, it's important to understand how movies are digitized and put onto a disc. Moving video images produce huge data files, and to make matters worse, they must be read at an incredibly fast rate to provide smooth full motion video on the screen.

As big as they are, DVD discs would not be large enough for a full two-hour movie if the video data were not compressed. DVD movies are compressed using a method called MPEG (Moving

Picture Experts Group, the folks who created this method of compression). This compressed data is then stored on the disc and must be decompressed (also called decoded) before it can be viewed.

The computer has two methods of decoding the MPEG data, hardware and software decoding. The DVD decoder card we're installing will do hardware decoding, which produces an image that is much sharper than that produced by software decoding.

The DVD decoder card works in conjunction with the video card. To install the DVD decoder card, plug the card into another open PCI slot. A special video feed-through cable is included in the package with the video card. Connect the mini-DIN connector at one end of the special cable to the DVD decoder card (pictured in Figure 29.20). Then connect the end with a 15-pin D-connector to the video output of the video board (you'll need to remove the monitor's cable first). Finally, connect the monitor to the video output on the back of the DVD decoder board.

FIGURE 29.20:

The DVD decoder card and its cable connections

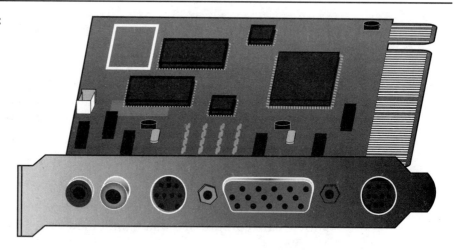

Power up the computer one more time. This time the system should recognize the new DVD decoder board. Install the software that come with the board and then, as a final check, insert a DVD movie into the DVD drive and check it to make sure the video plays correctly.

Step 9: Putting It All Together

Now it's finally time to put all of the pieces into the computer case. Take the system apart, put all of the cards, cables, and connectors aside, and get out the lazy Susan and put the computer case right on top. (If you're not using a lazy Susan, put the computer case on a table with good access all the way around.) The first thing you should put in the case is the motherboard. It's easiest to do this when the case is empty.

Installing the Motherboard

The motherboard is held in the case by a couple of small brass nuts and screws and some small white plastic standoffs like the one pictured in Figure 29.21.

FIGURE 29.21:

A motherboard standoff

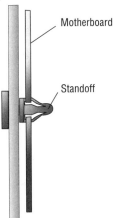

Cross-sectional view (magnified)

Motherboard

Standoff

One thing you may notice is that there are more metal clip locations than there are holes in the motherboard. This is so that one case design can accommodate a number of different board designs.

Holding the motherboard at an angle, make note of the locations of the clips and holes in the case that line up with holes in the motherboard. Some of the locations on the motherboard that line up will correspond to threaded holes in the case bottom. Screw the nuts into those holes (usually only one or two per case).

NOTE   Use a nut driver to make sure the nuts are tight, but do not tighten them so much that you strip their threads or break them off.

Next, insert the white standoffs into the clips that aligned with holes in the motherboard. Then, very carefully, put the motherboard over the standoffs, making sure they all are showing through their respective holes, and gently press the motherboard down onto the standoffs. They should all snap into place.

Once the motherboard has been clipped to the standoffs, get a couple of the smaller screws and screw them into the nut(s) you installed earlier.

Installing the Power Supply

Once the motherboard is in, you can reinstall the power supply. The box itself goes in the same bracket it came out of near the top of the case and the power switch needs to be reinstalled in the front of the case. You'll probably need to take the plastic front piece off first so you can get to the screws that hold the switch on. This is all illustrated in Figure 29.22.

FIGURE 29.22:

Installing the power
supply

Attaching the Add-on Boards

If you look at the rear of the computer case, you'll see that there
are a number of metal covers that line up with the various slot
positions of the motherboard. You need to remove the covers that
line up with the places you'll be installing boards into the motherboard as shown in Figure 29.23.

NOTE   When you unscrew the covers, be sure to keep the little screws that
come out so you can use them to attach the new boards you'll be
installing.

There are three kinds of board connectors on the motherboard: AGP (for your video card), PCI (for all the other boards), and ISA (which we won't need now, but can be used to add legacy boards later if you want).

> **NOTE** Ideally, the boards should fit straight down into the connector in the motherboard. Some, however, will be tight. There are a few tricks you can use to get these boards to cooperate. First, try rocking the board back and forth along its length as shown in Figure 29.24. *Never* rock it across its length; that could break the connector (see Figure 29.25).

FIGURE 29.24:

The right way to rock an expansion card

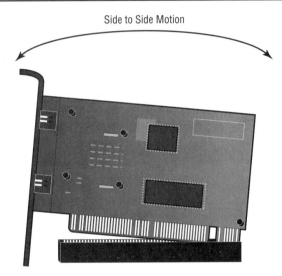

Install the video card into the AGP slot (it's the one that's a bit back of the other slots). Be sure to line up the metal tab at the bottom of the bracket so it goes between the motherboard and the case. Then, using one of the screws that came out of one of the cover plates, secure the board into the computer case.

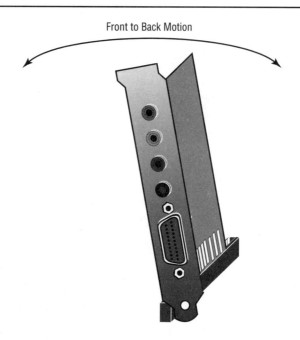

Front to Back Motion

The one rule you should never break when you're installing
boards is **don't force it!** If it doesn't go in easily, look around.
You'll eventually find the culprit. Once I was installing a board
and didn't know about the "don't force it" rule. So I leaned into
the board to make it go in. Two things happened: (1) The connector cracked (this not a replaceable part) and (2) I cut the wire that
was under the board, between it and the connector—but not
before jamming the board and wire into the connector so tightly
that I couldn't get the board out of the connector without a pair of
pliers. So, needless to say, I had no choice but to buy a new board
and start all over again.

Once you've installed the video card, plug the power connectors into the motherboard. I know I've said this before, but I think
it's important to remind you, just in case you've forgotten—be
sure you're plugging connectors into the correct spots.

TIP	Since there are two plugs on an AT power supply, it's possible to plug them into the wrong places. So remember this rule: the black wires go together near the center of the two connectors as shown in Figure 29.26.

FIGURE 29.26:

Plugging the AT power connectors into the motherboard

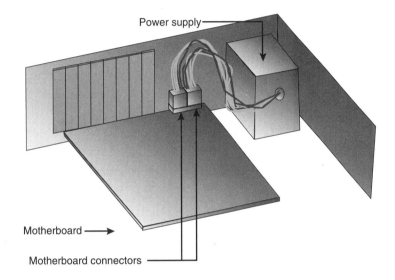

Power supply

Motherboard

Motherboard connectors

Okay, now it's time to test the system again. Plug in the mouse and keyboard. Also, if you have a serial mouse, you'll need to plug in the serial adapter before you can attach the mouse. Don't worry about mounting the adapter in the case, just plug it into the motherboard for now.

Now plug in the power cord and monitor, and switch on the system. After a few seconds you should see some activity on the display. If you do, then you're ready to put in the rest of the boards and the drives.

Installing the Drives

Although there are several different arrangements you can use for the drives, I usually suggest that you put the CD-ROM (or DVD) in the topmost position in the drive. This makes it easy to see and easy to reach over and put in CDs, since there's nothing on top of it. Next item down should be the Zip drive, then the floppy drive, and finally, the hard drive.

Whichever drive arrangement you choose, be sure to reattach the smaller drive frame before you install any of the drives. Then grab the CD drive. Since the space at the top of most tower cases is a bit cramped, I suggest you plug the data and audio cables into the drive while it is still outside of the case. Then feed the loose ends of the cables through the front opening of the drive bay, followed by the drive itself (as shown in Figure 29.27).

FIGURE 29.27:

Installing the CD drive

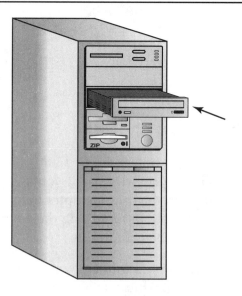

Once the CD drive is in the case, plug its power connector into its power receptacle, plug the end connector on the data cable into the motherboard, and screw the drive into the mounting.

Make sure that the audio cable is routed into the computer so you can plug it into the sound card later.

The next drive to install is the Zip drive. The Zip drive is a 3.5" drive, so either you can put it into the top 3.5" drive bay, or you can put it into a 5.25" adapter and put it right under the CD drive as shown in Figure 29.28.

FIGURE 29.28:

The Zip drive can go in the location shown or in the bay above (shown with floppy drive)

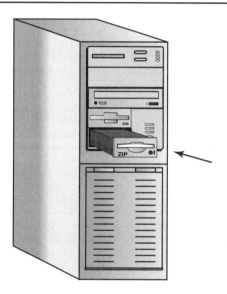

In this case, we'll put it in the 3.5" bay. It should be installed just like the CD drive. First set the Master/Slave jumper to Master (it'll be the first drive on the secondary IDE connector). Then connect the data cable to the drive while it's still outside the case and feed the data cable through the open bay. Then slide the drive in behind it. Push the drive most of the way in and attach the power cable to its connector. Then push it in the rest of the way and screw the drive into the side frames like you did with the CD drive. Oh, and don't forget to plug the other end of the data cable into the Secondary IDE connector on your motherboard. Also, check to make sure that pin 1 (the side of the data cable with the red stripe) is connected to pin 1 on both the drive and the motherboard connectors.

Now get the floppy drive and attach the twisted end of its data cable to the back of the floppy drive. Since there won't be a second floppy drive in this system, the second connector will be empty. Feed its cable through the open floppy bay and plug the far end of the floppy cable into the floppy connector on motherboard as shown in Figure 29.28.

Installing the hard drive is similar to installing the other drives, but there is one small difference: it's installed from the inside of the computer. It doesn't show on the front of the system.

Unlike the other drives, do not install the data cable yet. You'll be installing the connector in the center of the cable you used to connect the CD drive. Put the drive into the lowest position in the drive bay and push it forward into position, as shown in Figure 29.29.

FIGURE 29.29:

Installing the hard drive

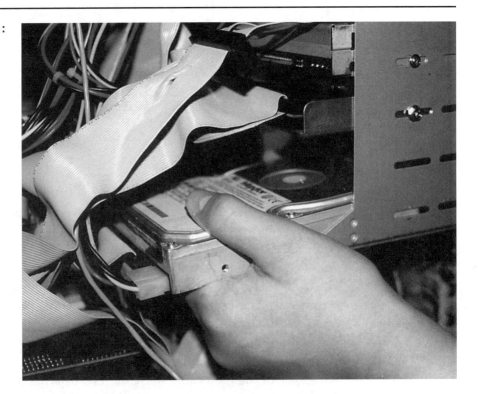

Next, find the middle connector of the data cable you used to connect the CD drive. Plug it into the data connector of the hard drive, aligning pin one on the drive with the red stripe on the data cable. Then plug the power connector into the hard drive and screw the drive into the drive frame.

Another System Check

Before you go any further, it's a good idea to test out the system again. This will confirm that you installed all of the drives correctly. So make sure the video cable is plugged into the monitor, your mouse and keyboard are connected, and your power plug is in. Then turn on the system.

The computer should boot up, read the hard drive, and go right into Windows. When it's finished booting, double-click My Computer and make sure that all of your drives appear in the window.

Install the Rest of the Boards

Once you know that the system works with the drives, you can install the remaining boards. Insert them, one at a time, and then screw them down.

After you've installed all the boards, you should see one or more little wires dangling down from the back of the CD drive. This is the audio cable that feeds sound from the audio portion of the CD drive to the sound card, so you can play audio CDs and the sound from video games that use audio tracks (like Riven or Heroes of Might and Magic).

Parallel and Serial Port Connectors

Getting tired of connecting wires? Well hang on, we're almost done. Remember the serial and parallel cables? They're usually attached to one of those metal mounting brackets like the ones at the edge of the add-in boards. Get a small nut driver and remove the two cables from the mounting bracket. Now take a look at the back of the case. Notice the D-shaped recesses. These are mostly already cut out from the case. All you need to do is get a pair of pliers and push them back and forth a few times. They should pop out easily after that.

But wait! Don't start popping yet. Take a close look at that figure again. Notice that one of the cutouts is larger than the others? The larger one is for the parallel port and the smaller one is for the serial port. I've had a few overzealous students pop out two large or two small cutouts. Do this and you'll find yourself taping a cutout back into the case.

Front Panel Lights and Speaker

Okay, that's it! Only one more, tiny task left: connecting the LEDs and the system speaker. The front panel LEDs tell you if the system has power, when the hard drive is reading or writing, and so on. And the speaker beeps at you when the computer wants your attention.

The LED and speaker connections on the motherboard are all labelled—in tiny, almost unreadable letters. Unfortunately, there's always stuff around them that makes them hard to read. And of course, it's dark down in there. And to keep things interesting, the motherboard manufacturers change the positions of the connectors periodically, just to keep us on our feet (so to speak).

So get out your flashlight and magnifying lens, pull up close to the motherboard, and let's dive in.

In most cases, the bundle of little black connectors is rubber-banded together near the front of the case. Take off the rubber band (if it's there) and look closely at the connectors. Most of the time they'll also have labels. The following list tells you what wires you should have and what they are labeled.

HDD: This is the hard disk drive activity light. The circuit that runs the hard drive turns this on whenever it writes/ reads to/from the hard drive.

TBLD: This is the Turbo LED, a holdover from the old days. Originally, a lot of video games' motion was controlled by the computer's system clock. As computers got faster and faster, some games got so fast that no human could possibly play them. So motherboard manufacturers added a Turbo switch. In Turbo mode, a game ran at the system's native speed (fast). In non-Turbo mode, it ran at the older compatibility speed so users could play their old games. Today we don't generally use this function since the speed of a game is now based on the timer, which runs at a constant speed regardless of the processor speed.

SPKR: The speaker beeps once when you boot, and many times if there's an error. It also provides the sound for some applications, although more and more programs use the real sound card found in most systems today.

KEYLOCK: The keylock is also not commonly used, because it is so easy to overcome. The keylock prevents the keyboard from entering data if the key is not in and turned. Trouble is, all anyone needs to do is remove the cover and pull off this connector.

PWR: This is often grouped together with the keylock connector. It lights when the system has more than 5 volts of power available.

How do you plug these in? Simple, just shove the connector onto the pins. There is, however one minor thing you need to look out for. Since they're LEDs, the connectors are polarized. That is, they need to go on one particular way. And the way is almost never labeled. So you may need to experiment until you get it right.

Well, that's it—we're finished building the ultimate computer! All you need to do now is put the cover on and secure it with screws. Be sure to hang onto all the documentation that came with your components, both for future reference and in case you need them for warranty service or replacement.

CHAPTER

THIRTY

30

Software Solutions: Using the Control Panel

- Setting Accessibility options

- Adding new hardware

- Adding and removing programs

- Changing the date, time, or display

- Configuring a modem and system options

One of the most useful features of Windows is the Control Panel. The Control Panel gives you access to utility programs that can make the difference between finishing an installation and total frustration. (Trust me; I've been there.) In this chapter, we'll take a short tour of the utility programs you'll find in the Control Panel. We'll look at what they do and how to use them. To open the Control Panel, click the Start button, click Settings, and then click Control Panel. By the way, since there are some applications that produce their own items in the Control Panel, yours may look a little different from the one in Figure 30.1. Don't worry about it. We'll look at the most common utilities you'll need (or at least find useful).

FIGURE 30.1:

The Control Panel

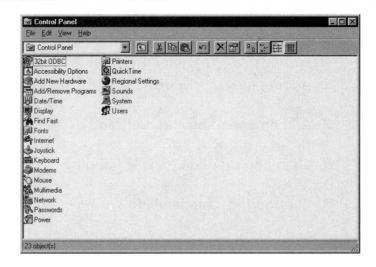

Setting Accessibility Options

The Accessibility Options are a set of controls that can make it easier for people with special disabilities to use their computer. Double-click this icon and you'll see a window that looks like the one pictured in Figure 30.2.

FIGURE 30.2:

Accessibility Properties

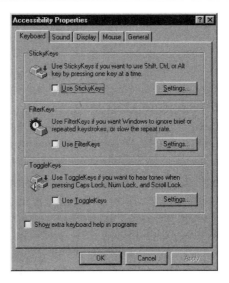

This control window contains a number of pages that are accessible through the tabs along the top of the pages. Each tab is labeled according to the options it provides.

Keyboard Functions

Use the Keyboard tab of the Accessibility options to manage the settings for keyboard functions. Keyboard functions let you control your interaction with the keyboard, and its interaction with your computer.

StickyKeys

StickyKeys are keys that stay in effect until you press them again. This is useful for people who find it difficult to press two keys at once. For example, if you turn on StickyKeys and then press and release the Alt key, the system will behave as though you were holding down the Alt key, until you press it again. In Microsoft

Word, this would have the affect of accessing menu options instead of typing characters. To cancel the sticky key, just press the control key a second time.

You can specify whether or not StickyKeys will make a short tone when you turn on a function key and when you turn it off again. To change this setting, press the Settings button for Sticky-Keys to open the Settings window. There are quite a few options you can adjust in this window; they're pictured in Figure 30.3.

FIGURE 30.3:

StickyKeys Settings

You can turn StickyKeys on by selecting it from the icon in the control panel, or, if you enable it, by pressing the shift key five times.

FilterKeys

Take a look at the FilterKeys option in Figure 30.2. If you press its Settings button (Figure 30.4) you'll see that this feature has two functions. First, it can be programmed to ignore multiple key-strokes of the same key. This is useful if you tend to press some keys twice or more accidentally when you type.

FIGURE 30.4:

FilterKeys Settings

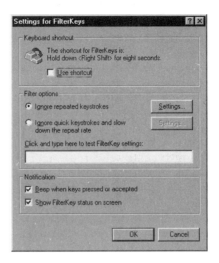

Second, FilterKeys can ignore quick keystrokes and slow down the keyboard's key repeat rate. This is an especially useful setting if you find that as you're typing, you often get several repeats of a character when you only intended to type one.

You can even choose the repeat rate and the rate at which multiple keys are detected by clicking the settings buttons in the Filter options box and setting the rate on the slider (Figure 30.5).

FIGURE 30.5:

The FilterKeys Control Slider

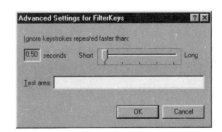

NOTE   Once you've chosen a new rate, it's a good idea to test the repeat speed by typing in the Test area below the slider.

As with the other Accessibility Options, you can tell the system to beep or flash the screen (or both) when the computer activates the function by choosing that option under Notification.

ToggleKeys

This simple function makes a sound whenever the Caps Lock, NumLock, or Scroll Lock keys are pressed. It's useful for beginning typists who may accidentally press one of these without realizing it initially. If you enable it, you can then use a shortcut to turn ToggleKeys on or off as you work. To enable the function, click the box under settings in ToggleKeys. Once the feature is enabled, you can turn on ToggleKeys by pressing and holding the NumLock key for five seconds.

Sound

The Sound tab of the Accessibility Properties window contains options for controlling sounds (see Figure 30.6).

FIGURE 30.6:

The Sound tab of Accessibility Properties window includes the Sound Sentry and ShowSounds options for controlling the sound of your computer

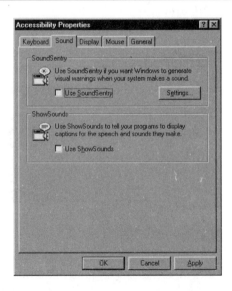

SoundSentry

This feature is very useful for hearing impaired users. It flashes parts of the screen when the computer would normally generate a sound. If you click the Settings button in the SoundSentry box it will open a window like the one in Figure 30.7.

FIGURE 30.7:

Settings for
SoundSentry

The controls in this window allow you to choose which part of the screen will flash when the system generates a sound. For windowed programs (those that aren't full screen) you can select the caption bar, the window itself, or the entire desktop.

NOTE   In general it's better to choose the active caption bar (the colored bar across the top of the active window) because the desktop can be obscured by the active window in some cases.

ShowSounds

ShowSounds is an add-on function for SoundSentry that displays short text messages describing warnings that might have audio messages or signals.

Display

The Display tab of the Accessibility Options window contains options for controlling the display (see Figure 30.8).

FIGURE 30.8:

The Display tab of Accessibility Properties window includes the High Contrast option for controlling the display of your computer

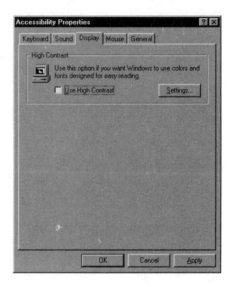

Use High Contrast

This page has only one option: Use High Contrast. Actually though, there's more to this setting than meets the eye (so to speak). Click on the settings button and you'll see what I mean (or look at Figure 30.9).

FIGURE 30.9:

High Contrast color schemes

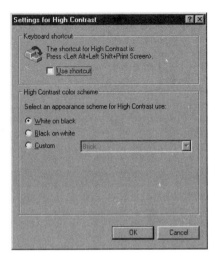

If you use one of the two primary default options (White on Black or Black on White) you'll get a display that can be more easily seen by people with visual problems. But look at the Custom button. Custom lets you choose any of the standard Windows color schemes. This allows you to switch between two color schemes (as your mood dictates) just by pressing the Left Alt, Left Shift, and Print Screen buttons at the same time.

NOTE   In High Contrast mode, some system fonts may appear larger.

Mouse

The Mouse tab of the Accessibility Options window doesn't really control mouse functions. Instead, it allows you to control the mouse pointer with the keyboard (see Figure 30.10). It's designed to help people who have trouble with (or are unable to use) a mouse.

FIGURE 30.10:

The Mouse tab of Accessibility Properties window inlcudes the MouseKeys option that allows you to control the mouse pointer using the keyboard

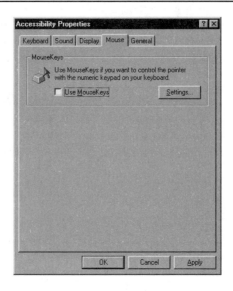

Selecting this option will allow you to move the mouse pointer by pressing the arrow keys on the keyboard. Click the Settings button (Figure 30.11) and you can control the way the mouse behaves. The options let you control the speed and acceleration of the mouse pointer. You can also specify whether you want to be able to change the pointer speed "on the fly" by pressing the Ctrl key to speed up and the Shift key to slow down.

FIGURE 30.11:

The MouseKeys settings window

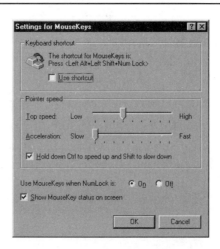

General

The General tab of the Accessibility Options window has three functions: Automatic Reset, Notification, and SerialKey (see Figure 30.12).

FIGURE 30.12:

The General tab

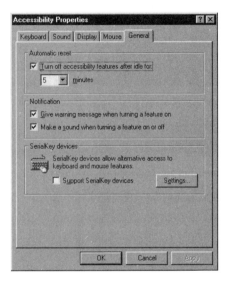

Automatic Reset turns off the accessibility features if you don't use the computer for a while. The default time is 5 minutes, but it can be set to any time you like (in 5-minute increments) up to 30 minutes.

Notification gives you a warning message and/or a sound when one of the accessibility features is turned on or off.

SerialKey allows you to use special add-on devices through one of your serial ports as an alternative interface to the mouse and keyboard. Because of his degenerative nerve disease, Dr. Stephen Hawking, the famous physicist, uses one of these controls (among other things) to control his computer.

Adding New Hardware

When you install a Plug and Play board in your system, Windows will generally detect it automatically and either install its drivers from those already in your system, or ask you to insert a driver disk from the manufacturer.

Some boards need a little help, however. You'll find that help in the Add New Hardware control. If you've installed a new board in your system and Windows didn't notice, double-click Add New Hardware and it'll open a Wizard that will walk you through the process of getting it installed (Figure 30.13).

FIGURE 30.13:

The Install New Hardware Wizard

Click the "Next" button to go on to the next window. Here, the wizard will examine your system to determine what's there, what's installed and what isn't.

NOTE   By the way, if you run the wizard and there are drivers installed for things that you want but are not currently connected, it could possibly delete them—although usually you will see an exclamation point warning icon next to the device in the Control Panel. It's best to be sure all of your external devices are connected before you run the Install New Hardware wizard.

Running this wizard can take a while, since the computer will check every possible hardware configuration. Once it's done, though, it will usually find any new things that have been added.

But of course, like anything, there will always be exceptions. Sometimes the hardware wizard will find the wrong things. And sometimes it still won't find a new board because there is some kind of conflict. For example, if you have a new board that is designed to use IRQ15 and you already have a device using IRQ15, the wizard may be unable to install it.

In this case, there's a trick you can do that will often solve the problem. Temporarily remove the existing device from your system. Our hope here is that the first device will then be a bit more cooperative in choosing a different IRQ.

Once you've taken the device out of the system, you need to go to the Device Manager in the Control Panel.

To get to the Device Manager, double-click System in the Control Panel and the System Properties window (shown in Figure 30.14) will open.

FIGURE 30.14:

The General tab of the System Properties window

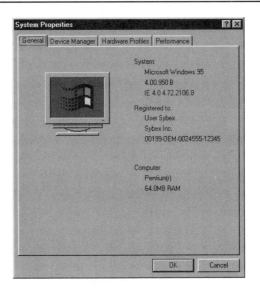

This is another one of those windows that has a number of tabbed pages. The first page, called General, shows a brief list describing the computer, listing your operating system version, owner's name, manufacturer, processor, and installed memory.

Click the second tab (labeled Device Manager) and you see a window that looks like Figure 30.15.

The Device Manager shows all of the devices that are installed in your computer. Since every computer is a little different from others, chances are your list won't look exactly like this one. But it will have most of the same devices. The information in the list is organized like an outline with main items and the things in them listed as subcategories below them. For example, the top item in the list is always "Computer."

FIGURE 30.15:

The Device
Manager tab

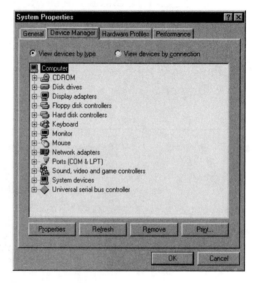

Under "Computer" you'll find categories for your drives, controllers, keyboard, and so on. And under those categories you'll find the specific devices themselves. For example, under modem you might find "US Robotics 56K V.90." To see the subcategories, click the plus sign beside the category.

We'll take a closer look at the Device Manager a little later on in this chapter. Right now we're here to do one thing: delete one of the items from this list. The reason we want to delete the item is because once it's out, the computer can assign the conflicting resource to the uncooperative device we're trying to install. So go down the list and find the first device. In this case it's a scanner. Fortunately, the scanner can use several different IRQs, so we go down the list until we find the scanner, click it, then click the Remove button near the bottom of the window. Click OK to close the System Properties window.

Windows should ask if you wish to reboot, but if it doesn't you need to shut down the system (choose Shut Down from the Start menu) and power the system down. Physically remove the older board, but leave the new board in.

Now power up the system again. This time the system should have little trouble installing the new board and its driver(s). Once the new board is installed, shut down the system again, plug in the old board, and let the system redetect it. It should find a new IRQ for it and you'll have installed both boards.

Installing Boards that the System Can't Find

Sometimes you'll want to install a legacy board that the system just can't find at all. To do this, choose "No" on the page that shows the found devices in the Hardware Installation Wizard (Figure 30.16). (To access the Hardware Installation wizard, click the Add New Hardware icon in the Control Panel.)

FIGURE 30.16:

The Add New
Hardware Wizard

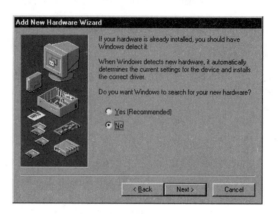

Now when you click the Next button you'll get a page that asks you if you want Windows to search for devices that are not Plug and Play. The default is "Yes" and in general, it's better to let Windows try. Windows is pretty good at finding and identifying many non-Plug and Play devices.

If Windows finds the device (after what is usually a pretty long wait), it'll either inform you of what it is and automatically install the drivers if it has them on hand, or it'll ask you to insert your Windows installation disk or the manufacturer's driver disk.

Getting the Drivers Online

At one time, if you needed a driver and you didn't have it, you had only one recourse—call the manufacturer. Sometimes, if you were lucky, they would be able to send you the driver(s) you needed within a short period of time (a week or so). But all too often, it took longer...much longer. And you'd have to wait and wait to install your board. And sometimes, if you were really unlucky, the manufacturer was out of business or simply didn't support that board any more.

Today, things have improved a lot because of the Internet. If you need a driver, generally all you need to do is go to the manufacturer's Web site, find their support page, and download any drivers you need on the spot.

What's really amazing, though, is that not long ago, I needed a driver for a board that was made by a company that had gone out of business. In the old days I'd have been out of luck. With the manufacturer gone, my chances of finding the driver were about zero.

But with the Internet, I was able to get the driver with almost the same ease I would have had if the company was still around. Once I found out that the company had disappeared, what I did was go to a search engine (like Lycos, Alta Vista, or Yahoo), entered the name of the device I was looking for (I used its actual part number), and waited a few minutes.

I got about a thousand hits! (Hits, by the way are items that match your search criteria.) I looked down the list of hits and found a Web site that was operated by a users group that maintained a file of what they called "Obsolete Drivers."

They had exactly what I was looking for. Within minutes I had downloaded the driver and installed it in my system. Thanks, Internet!

NOTE   One thing you should know when you are downloading anything from a site: it's a good idea to run a virus check on any file you download before you install it in your system. Even the best-intentioned Web site operators can inadvertently use files that have become infected.

If Windows Still Can't Find Your Board

If, after all these steps, Windows still can't find your board, you can try one more thing. At the page that asks if you want Windows to search for boards that aren't Plug and Play (see Figure 30.17), click "No, I want to select the hardware from a list." Then click Next.

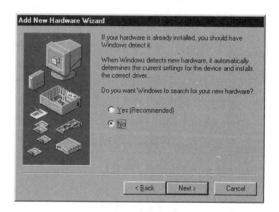

This will display a window that looks like the one in Figure 30.18.

This window lists every kind of board that Windows can install. Here you need to select the kind of device you'll be adding by clicking the category and then clicking the Next button.

The next window you'll see is split into two sections (Figure 30.19).

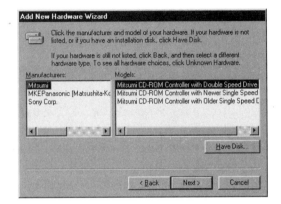

From here, you first need to select your manufacturer in the left-hand list box. When you do that, the various supported models will appear in the right-hand list box. Click your model and the Next button to continue. By the way, if you already have the driver disk, click the "Have Disk…" button instead and you will be prompted to insert and run the disk to install your drivers.

If the manufacturer isn't listed and you don't have a driver disk, choose the top item, "Standard types," and click the item in the right-hand list box that most closely matches the device you're installing (good luck). This will install a driver that we hope will do an adequate job of running your device. Sometimes you'll get lucky and it'll work. Sometimes you won't be so lucky and…well, you may need to spend some time finding the right drivers.

Adding and Removing Programs

Like the Add/Remove Hardware feature in the Control Panel, the Add/Remove Programs feature has multiple tabbed pages (see Figure 30.20). The top page lists all of the programs that are currently in your Registry. The Registry is a file that contains a record of all the programs in your system that are Windows 95/98 compliant. These programs use an assortment of resources, and the Registry keeps track of them.

Why have a Registry? Well, in the old days of computing, you just copied programs into your computer and it ran them. Some programs were a little large, so they might be broken into modules that did certain tasks for ease in maintaining them. Later, some programmers found that they could maintain a library of certain modules that did certain tasks that they could use over and over in different programs.

FIGURE 30.20:

The Install/Uninstall tab of the Add/Remove Programs Properties window

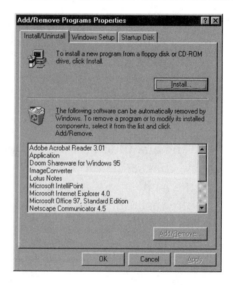

Eventually this led to the concept of object-oriented programming where each object in a program had a set of qualities or capabilities that defined it. An object could have an image or an icon that was connected to it. It could use special kinds of windows and so on. These resources are maintained in different places. The Registry keeps track of all the pieces of your programs so it can find them when it needs them.

So if you try to delete an installed program, you're very likely to wind up leaving a lot of the program behind to just take up space on your hard drive. By using the Add/Remove Programs utility, you can get rid all of the parts of a program when you delete it.

Removing (Uninstalling) a Program

To remove a program, select it from the list box in the Install/Uninstall page and click Remove. The program will prompt you for confirmation as shown in Figure 30.21.

FIGURE 30.21:

Selecting a file to remove

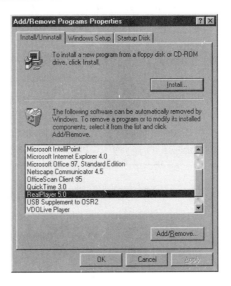

Once you click the "Yes" button, the Uninstall wizard (Figure 30.22) will delete the program and all of its related components.

FIGURE 30.22:

The Uninstall Wizard

Sometimes there are pieces to a program that the Uninstall wizard can't delete because they are in use or have other active components in them. In that case, it will tell you that there were pieces left behind and tell you to remove them manually. To see the pieces that were left behind, click the "Details" button.

Installing a Program

To install a program, click the install button on the Install/Uninstall page. This will prompt you to install the CD or diskette that contains your program.

NOTE   Some CDs will autoplay. This means that as soon as you put them into the drive, they are read and begin their installation process. If you insert a program CD and it offers to install itself, go ahead and let it. You can always abort the process in Install/Delete.

If your program doesn't start automatically, click the "Install" button and the wizard will look for a setup program to install. Once it finds one, it will ask you if that's the one you want to use to install (Figure 30.23).

FIGURE 30.23:

The Install window, asking if this is the program you want to install

If it is, click the "Finish" button and it will install your program.

Windows Setup

Windows Setup lets you install additional Windows components that were not installed when you initially loaded Windows. When you select the Windows Setup tab, you'll get the page shown in Figure 30.24.

FIGURE 30.24:

The Windows Setup tab

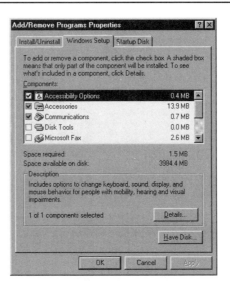

The list box near the top of the page shows all of the components available to install or delete. The ones with check marks in the boxes beside them are already installed. Those with check marks that are grayed out are partially installed…that is, they have some parts installed and other parts that may not yet be installed.

If you want to get more information about one of the items in the list, all you have to do is single-click the item to highlight it. When you do, a brief description of the item will appear in the gray box below the list box.

To install an item, click its check box and click the OK button. (You can check more than one item before clicking OK.) To delete an item, uncheck its box by clicking it. The check will disappear and Windows Setup will remove those items when you click OK.

Startup

The last tab in the Add/Remove window opens the Startup Disk page (Figure 30.25). Creating a diskette is pretty simple—put a blank disk into your floppy drive and click the "Create Disk" button.

FIGURE 30.25:

The Startup Disk tab used to create a boot disk

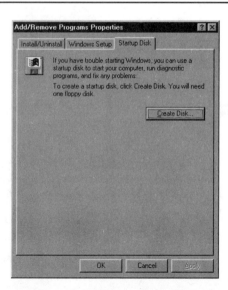

Date/Time

Up until last year, the Date and Time functions on personal computers were rarely considered an important issue. However, since many people are worried about the so-called "Millennium Bug," it's something that is attracting a lot more attention.

Setting the Date and Time

This control has two tabs. The first is used to adjust the time and date of your computer. When you first open the control, you'll see the window shown in Figure 30.26.

FIGURE 30.26:

The Date/Time
Properties tab

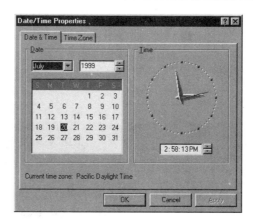

There's a calendar on the left and a clock on the right. To set the date, choose the month and year you want from the selection lists and click the day you want from the calendar. To change the time, click the item you want to change in the numeric list box and either type in a new time or click the up/down arrows to scroll to the correct time.

> **NOTE** If you want to see if your computer will operate correctly in 2000, all you have to do is change the year to 2000, click the Apply or OK button, and use your computer. If it's going to have problems, you'll find out now. A word of caution though: While it's unlikely that you'll have any serious problems with your system, it's best to back up your files first and only do this test over a weekend, so you'll have time to restore your files if something does go wrong.

Time Zone

The Time Zone adjustment tells your computer where it is so it can tell you the time and date of other countries accurately. To change time zones, just click the world map in the approximate area where you are located (Figure 30.27).

FIGURE 30.27:

The Time Zone tab

You can also tell the computer whether or not it should adjust the time for daylight saving time changes from this window by clicking the small box at the bottom of the map.

Display

The Display icon does far more than we need to cover in an upgrade and maintenance book. But there are a few things that we should look at. Double-click the icon and you'll see a window that looks like Figure 30.28.

FIGURE 30.28:

The Background tab of the Display Properties window

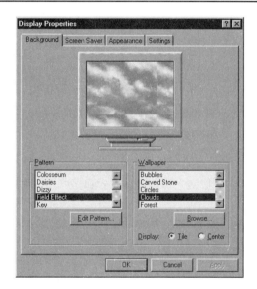

Display Properties lets you change your screen saver, background, and quite a few other items that can be fun, but the only thing that we'll need to look at is the Settings tab. This is where you can change the resolution of your screen, the number of colors displayed, and the type of display adapter and monitor you use (Figure 30.29).

FIGURE 30.29:

The Settings tab

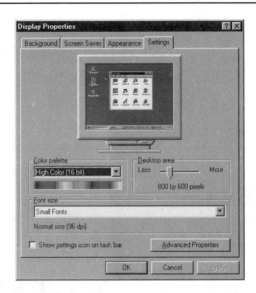

Directly under the picture of a monitor you'll find a description of the current display adapter and monitor. Below that are two windows that let you change the color depth and screen resolution. Depending upon the display adapter and monitor you're using, you'll be able to choose anything from 16-color to True Color, which may be either 24-bit or 32-bit, depending, once again, upon your display adapter and monitor.

Advanced

Although there are usually lots of tabs in the Advanced section of the Settings window, most video boards have extra tabs that they add to the basic four tabs as shown in Figure 30.30: General, Adapter, Monitor, and Performance. Here, we'll look at only the four basic tabs, since there's no way I can guess what extra tabs you have.

FIGURE 30.30:

The General tab of
the advanced display
properties window

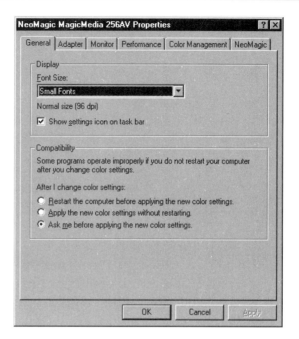

General

The General tab (Figure 30.29) lets you change the system font
size and whether the system restarts after you change any of the
display parameters.

Display (Font Size)   You can choose small, large, or custom
font sizes. Large fonts are 125% the size of the Small (normal)
fonts. If you select Other, a window like the one in Figure 30.31
will open.

FIGURE 30.31:

Custom font size
control

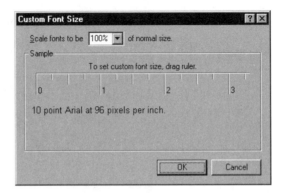

You can change the font size by typing a percentage value in the
text box at the top of the window or by dragging the ruler in the
graphic below it to the left or the right. Dragging to the right
makes the font larger and dragging it to the left makes it smaller.
You can choose any size between 20–0 and 500–0.

Once you've chosen a size, a sample of the text size will appear
in the graphic window below the ruler (Figure 30.32).

NOTE   Changing the font size can have a profound effect on the appearance
of your computer display and the programs you run.

FIGURE 30.32:

Viewing the new
font size

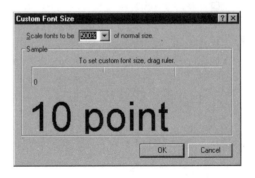

Modems

Now skip down to the Modems control. This is used to configure and test your modem. When you double-click this icon you'll see the Modems Properties window as shown in Figure 30.33.

There are two tabbed pages in this control window, General and Diagnostics.

FIGURE 30.33:

The Modems Properties window

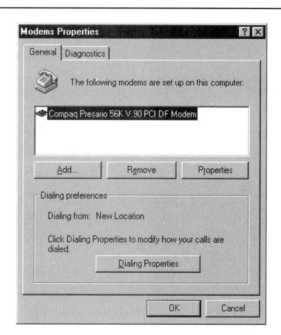

General

The first tabbed page, General, shows you the modems that are connected to your computer. Although most people never have more than one, you can actually connect several if, for example, you wanted to use your system as a dialup e-mail server.

From this window you can also logically add or remove modems in your system. If you do, you'll also need to physically install or remove the modem from the motherboard or connect/disconnect them from the system.

The third button on this page allows you to look at the properties of the modem. This includes the connection (COM port), speaker volume, and maximum data speed.

Connection

This tab controls the connection and call preferences. Connection preferences control the number of data bits transmitted, as well as the parity and stop bits. Of course, most modem programs automatically set these parameters for you, so you'll rarely have to make any changes here.

Call preferences control how the modem dials. The default values (which you shouldn't change unless you really know what you're doing) are "Wait for dial tone before dialing" and "cancel the call if you can't get connected within a minute (60 seconds)." If you're ever in a foreign country that has a lot of trouble connecting, you might want to increase this value to give the modem a chance to connect eventually.

Diagnostics

The Diagnostics tab of the Modems window lets you communicate with your modem and try a few of the standard commands to see if it will respond correctly. Although the test isn't conclusive, it does tell you if the modem is connected and can receive commands. Figure 30.34 shows the Diagnostics tab.

FIGURE 30.34:

The Diagnostics tab

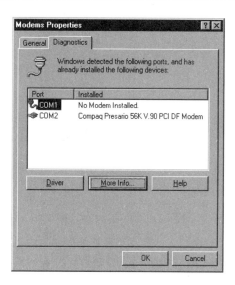

System

Although I mentioned the System feature of the Control Panel earlier, we really only touched on its capabilities. This is where you can look at and change any of the devices in your computer. Double click the System icon and you'll see the System Properties window, which is shown in Figure 30.35.

FIGURE 30.35:

The System Properties window

Device Manager

Click the Device Manager and you'll see the list of all your devices (Figure 30.36). Click any of the listed devices that has a + (plus sign) beside it, and it will display a list of all the devices that are in that category. For example, click the tab marked Ports. This displays all of the ports on your system, including your serial ports and parallel ports. The serial ports are called Communications ports and the parallel ports are called Printer ports.

There are two ways you can organize the devices in the Device Manager—by device type, or by connection. Generally it's easier to organize them by type because it organizes the devices by what they are, not where they are.

FIGURE 30.36:

The Device Manager tab

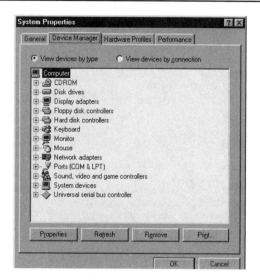

To look at the properties of a device, you can double-click the device or you can select it and then click the Properties button. If you do this, you'll open a window that shows the device specifications and the driver that's running it. And for some devices, you can look at and set which port, IRQ, and memory it uses. However, generally it's a bad idea to mess with those settings because it prevents Windows from reassigning resources should you decide to add or remove devices later.

APPENDIX
A

Vendors Guide

- Computers, peripherals, and components manufacturers

- Data recovery and memory vendors

- BIOS upgrade and storage device vendors

- Miscellaneous products vendors

The vendor listing that follows is divided into the following categories:

- Manufacturers of Computers, Peripherals, and Components

- Data Recovery Vendors

- Memory Vendors

- Storage Device Vendors

- Miscellaneous Computer Products Vendors

- Older PC Repair and Exchange

- Computer Recycling Centers

Wherever possible, I have included non-800 numbers, as I recognize that my non-American readers cannot use 800 numbers.

Products, prices, and addresses change, so you may find some vendors listed here no longer exist or cannot be reached given the information below. I am not endorsing these particular vendors, but merely providing the information as a useful resource to you, the reader.

Manufacturers of Computers, Peripherals, and Components

The following are names, addresses, and phone numbers of various manufacturers of computers, peripherals, and components:

3Com Corporation

5400 Bayfront Plaza
Santa Clara, CA 95052-8145
(800) 638-3266, (408) 326-5000
http://www.3com.com

3DTV Corporation

1863 Pioneer Parkway East #303
Springfield, OR 97477
voicemail/fax (415) 680-1678
http://www.3dmagic.com

Hardware and software for 3D (stereoscopic) video, computer graphics, and virtual reality

4Q Technologies

14425 Don Julian Road
City of Industry, CA 91746
(626) 333-6688
http://www.4qtech.com

Speakers

A4 Tech Corporation

20256 Apseo Robles
Walnut, CA 91789
(909) 468-0071
http://www.a4tech.com

Scanners

ABS Computer Technologies, Inc.

9997 Rose Hills Road
Whittier, CA 90601
(800) 876-8088
fax (562) 695-8923
http://www.buyabs.com

Abstract R&D, Inc.

120 Village Sq., Suite 37
Orinda, CA 94563
(510) 253-9588

Palmtop PCs

Acecad, Inc.

791 Foam St.
Monterey, CA 93940
voice (831) 655-1900
fax (831) 655-1919
http://www.acecad.com

Acecat III mouse replacement

Acer America Corporation

2641 Orchard Parkway
San Jose, CA 95134
(800) 733-2237
fax (408) 922-2933
http://www.acer.com

Acer Sertek Inc.

128 S. Woolfe Rd.
Sunnyvale, CA 94086
(408) 733-3174
www.ussertek.com

CD-ROMs, MPEG cards, sound cards

ACL/Staticide

1960 E. Devon Avenue
Elk Grove Village, IL 60007
(800) 782-8420
http://www.aclstaticide.com

Anti-static equipment & cleaning kits

ACT-RX Technology Corporation

10F, 525, Chung Cheng Road
Hsin Tien, Taipei, Taiwan ROC
(886) 2-218-8000Booth I9025

CPU coolers

Action Electronics Co., Ltd.

198, Chung Yuan Road
Chung Li, Taiwan, ROC
(886) 3-4515494

Axion monitors

Action Well Development Ltd.

Rm. 1101, 1103 and 4 Star Center
443-451 Castle Peak Road
Kwai Chung, NT, Hong Kong
(852) 2422-0010

Fax modems, sound products, controller and VGA cards, and computer cases

ActionTec Electronics, Inc.

760 N. Mary Avenue
Sunnyvale, CA 94086
technical support (408) 752-7714
main (408) 752-7700
fax (408) 541-9003
http://www.actiontec.com

PC card (PCMCIA) products

Actown Corporation

8F, 527, Chung Cheng Road
Hsin Tien, Taipei, Taiwan ROC
(886) 2-2184612Booth S2050E

Opto-electronic products, including handheld scanners, flatbeds, and sheet-fed scanners

Adaptec, Inc.

691 S. Milpitas Boulevard
Milpitas, CA 95035
(800) 934-2766, (408) 945-8600
http://www.adaptec.com

Addonics Technologies

48434 Milmont Drive
Fremont, CA 94538
(510) 438-6530, (800) 787-8580
http://www.addonics.com

Addtronics Enterprise Co.

No. 66, Chen-Teh Road
Taipei, Taiwan ROC
(886) 2-5591122

An integrated computer case manufacturer

ADI Systems, Inc.

2115 Ringwood Avenue
San Jose, CA 95131
(800) 228-0530, (408) 944-0100
fax (408) 944-0300
http://www.adiusa.com

Multi-scanning color monitors

Adobe Systems Inc.

345 Park Avenue
San Jose, California 95110-2704
(408) 536-6000

(800) 833-6687
fax (408) 537-6000
http://www.adobe.com

ADPI (Analog and Digital Peripherals, Inc.)

P.O. Box 499
Troy, OH 45373
(937) 339-2241
(800) 758-1041

www.adpi.com

Backup devices

Advanced Digital Systems

13909 Bettencourt Street
Cerritos, CA 90703
(800) 888-5244
http://www.adstech.com

Multimedia specialty audio/video hardware

Advanced Gravis Computer Technology Ltd.

World Headquarters
2855 Campus Drive
San Mateo, CA 94403
(650) 572-2700, (800) 535-4242
fax (610) 231-1022
http://www.gravis.com

PC game interfaces

Advanced Integration Research, Inc.

2188 Del Franco Street
San Jose, CA 95131

(408) 428-0800

http://www.airwebs.com

Manufacturer of 486 and Pentium system boards based on ISA, EISA, PCI, and VL-bus architectures

Advanced Matrix Technology, Inc.

747 Calle Plano

Camarillo, CA 93012-8598

(805) 388-5799

Dot matrix, laser, and inkjet printers and plotters

Advantage Memory

25A Technology Drive, building 2

Irvine, CA 92718

(800) 266-0488

http://www.advantagememory.com

Agfa (Bayer Corporation)

200 Ballardvale Street

Wilmington, MA 01887

(508) 658-5600

http://www.agfa.com

Scanners, film recorders, color management software, digital cameras

Ahead Systems, Inc.

44244 Fremont Boulevard

Fremont, CA 94538

(510) 623-0900

3D multimedia surround-sound, accelerator, and 3D stereo vision products

AITech International Corporation

47971 Fremont Boulevard

Fremont, CA 94538

(510) 226-8960

http://www.aitech.com

Multimedia and desktop video products

Aiwa America, Inc.

800 Corporate Drive

Mahwah, NJ 07430

(800) 920-2673

http://www.aiwa.com

Tape backup products

Alaris, Inc.

47338 Fremont Boulevard

Fremont, CA 94538

(510) 770-5700

http://www.alaris.com

Graphics acceleration and scalable full-motion video playback products

Alfa Infotech Co.

46600 Landing Pky.

Fremont, CA 94538

(510) 252-9300

Multimedia and communication products

ALi (Acer Laboratories, Inc.)

4701 Patrick Henry Drive, Suite 2101

Santa Clara, CA 95054

(408) 764-0644

ICs for personal computers and embedded systems

Alpha & Omega Computer

101 S. Kraemer Boulevard, Suite 116
Placentia, CA 92670
(714) 577-7688

486/Pentium CPU coolers

Alphacom Enterprise, Inc.

1407 Englewood Street
Philadelphia, PA 19111
(215) 722-6133

Joysticks, mice, trackballs, CPU cooling
fans with built-in heat sink, and removable hard disk drive kits

ALPS

3553 N. First Street
San Jose, CA 95134
(408) 432-6000
http://www.alpsusa.com

GlidePoint input devices, drive products

AMCC (Applied Micro Circuits Corporation)

6195 Lusk Boulevard
San Diego, CA 92121
(800) 755-2622
http://www.amcc.com

AMD (Advanced Micro Devices)

One AMD Place
P.O. Box 3453
Sunnyvale, CA 94088
(800) 538-8450, (408) 732-2400
http://www.amd.com

CPUs

American Cover, Inc.

102 W. 12200 S
Draper, UT 84092
(801) 553-0600

Computer accessory products

AMI (American Megatrends, Inc.)

6145F Northbelt Parkway
Norcross, GA 30071
(770) 246-8600
sales (800) 828-9264
fax (770) 246-8791
http://www.ami.com

Motherboards and AMIDiag software

Amptron International, Inc.

1239 Etcher Ave.
City of Industry, CA 91748
(626) 912-5789
http://www.amptron.com

System boards

Amrel Technology, Inc.

11801 Goldring Road
Arcadia, CA 91006
(800) 882-6735
http://www.amrel.com

Modular notebook computers

AMS, Inc.

12881 Ramona Boulevard
Irwindale, CA 91706
(800) 886-2671

Ana Precision Co., Ltd.

Suite 694, Kumjung-Dong, Kunp'O-shi
Kyunggi-Do, 435-050, Korea
(0343) 53-0813

Inkjet and dot matrix printers

Angia Communications

441 East Bay Boulevard
Provo, UT 84606
(800) 877-9159
fax (801) 373-9847

PCMCIA fax modem

AOC International

311 Sinclair Frontage Road
Milpitas, CA 95035
(408) 956-1070

Visual display products

APC (American Power Conversion)

132 Fairgrounds Road
West Kingdom, RI 02892
(800) 800-4APC, (401) 789-5735
fax (401) 789-3710
http://www.apcc.com

UPSs, phone line surge protectors

Apex Data, Inc. /SMART Modular Technologies, Inc.

4305 Cushing Parkway
Fremont, CA 94538
(800) 841-APEX
tech support (510) 249-1605
fax (510) 249-1600

tech support fax (510) 249-1604
email: sales@smartm.com
support@smartm.com
BBS (510) 249-1601 (8 data bits, 1 stop
bit, and no parity)
http://www.apexdata.com

Apple Computer, Inc.

1 Infinite Loop
Cupertino, CA 95014
(408) 996-1010
http://www.apple.com

APS Technologies

6131 Deramus, Suite 4967
Kansas City, MO 64120
(800) 235-2753, (816) 483-1600
fax (816) 483-3077

Arcada Software

Seagate Software
920 Disc Drive
Scotts Valley, CA 95067
(408) 438-6550
fax (408) 438-7612
http://www.arcada.com

Data protection and storage management software products

Archtek America Corporation

18549 Gale Avenue
City of Industry, CA 91748-1338
(818) 912-9800
http://www.archtek.com

Voice/data communications and network products

Arco Computer Products, Inc.

2750 N. 29th Avenue, Suite 316
Hollywood, FL 33020
(305) 925-2688
http://www.arcoide.com

IDE busless, slotless, operating system-independent mirroring adapter

Arkenstone, Inc.

1390 Borregas Avenue
Sunnyvale, CA 94089
(800) 444-4443
http://www.arkenstone.org

Products to aid individuals who are blind, visually impaired, or learning disabled to better access written information

Artek (Asicom, Inc.)

46716 Fremont Boulevard
Fremont, CA 94538
(510) 354-0900

High-end PC subsystems

Artisoft, Inc.

2202 N. Forbes Boulevard
Tucson, AZ 85745
(520) 670-7100
http://www.artisoft.com

Networking products Suited to small businesses and workgroups

ArtMedia

2772 Calle del Mundo
Santa Clara, CA 95050
(408) 980-8988
http://www.artmedia.com

ASK LCD, Inc.

100 West Forest Ave, Suite. E
Englewood, NJ 07631
(201) 541-2424
tech support (888) 307-2561
fax (201) 541-2391
http://www.asklcd.com

LCD presentation products

Ask Technology Ltd.

Unit 1, 4/F., Henley Ind. Ctr.,
9-15 Bute Street
Mongkok, Kowloon, Hong Kong
(852) 2398-3223

System boards, VGA cards, and sound cards

Askey Communications USA

162 Atlantic Street
Pomona, CA 91768
http://www.askey.com

PCMCIA, external, and internal modem cards and pocket models

Asolid Computer Supply, Inc.

(Biostar Manufacture Group)
4044 Clipper Court
Fremont, CA 94538
(510) 226-6678

Motherboards

Aspen Systems Inc.

4026 Youngfield Street
Wheat Ridge, CO 80033-3862
(303) 431-4606

RISC systems

Aspen Technologies

400 Rogers Street
Princeton, WV 24740
(304) 425-1111

Internal, external, and PCMCIA fax
modems

Assmann Data Products

1849 W. Drake Drive, Suite 101
Tempe, AZ 85283
(877) ASSMANN (1-877-277-6266)
fax (602) 897-7255
http://www.usa-assmann.com

Ergonomic mice

AST Computer

AST Research, Inc.
16225 Alton Parkway
Irvine, CA 92618
or
P.O. Box 57005
Irvine, CA 92619-7005
(949) 727-4141
tech support (800) 727-1278
http://www.ast.com

ATI Technologies

33 Commerce Valley Drive East
Thornhill, Ontario, Canada L3T 7N6
tech support (905) 882-2626

tech support fax (905) 882-0546
faxback (905) 882-2600 (press #2)
CompuServe: GO ATITECH
http://www.atitech.com

Graphics accelerators

Atlantic Technology

343 Vanderbilt Avenue
Norwood, MA 02062
(617) 762-6300

Speakers

ATronics International, Inc.

44700-B Industrial Drive
Fremont, CA 94538-6431
(510) 656-8400
fax (510) 656-8560
http://www.ati1.com/

Advanced external storage products

ATTO Technology, Inc.

40 Hazelwood Drive, Suite 106
Amherst, NY 14228
(716) 691-1999

VantagePCI-Multi Channel SCSI accelerator card

AuraVision Corporation

47865 Fremont Boulevard
Fremont, CA 94538
(510) 252-6800
http://www.auravision.com

Multimedia IC devices

Autumn Technologies

11705 69th Way N
Largo, FL 34643
(800) 837-8551

Test Bed Pro, a commercial PC testing, assembly, and repair workbench

AVerMedia, Inc.

47923A Warm Springs Boulevard
Fremont, CA 94538
(510) 770-9899
http://www.aver.com

PC-Video multimedia hardware

AVM Technology, Inc.

9774 S. 700 East
Sandy, UT 84070
(801) 571-0967

Professional MIDI wavetable modules

Avnet Technology Co., Ltd.

6F-1, No. 102, Sung Lung Road
Taipei, Taiwan ROC
(886) 2-7607603

Audio-Visual Network Card

Award Software International

777 E. Middlefield Road
Mountain View, CA 94043
(650) 237-6800
fax (650) 968-0274
http://www.award.com

Desktop plug-and-play BIOS for 486, 586, Pentium, and P6-based PC platforms

Axonix Corporation

844 S. 200 East
Salt Lake City, UT 84111
(801) 521-9797

CD-ROMs

Axxon Computer Corporation

3979 Tecumseh Road E
Windsor, ON N8W 1J5, Canada
(519) 974-0163
http://www.softio.com/

Jumperless I/O cards

Aztech Labs, Inc.

45645 Northport Loop East
Fremont, CA 94538
(510) 623-8988
fax (510) 623-8989
BBS (510) 623-8933
tech support (510) 623-9037
tech support fax (510) 353-4327
http://www.aztechlabs.com
http://www.aztechca.com
ftp://ftp.aimnet.com/pub/users/aztech

CD-ROM drives

Belkin Components

501 West Walnut Street
Compton, CA 90220
(310) 898-1100
(800) 2-BELKIN (223-5546)
fax (310) 898-1111
http://www.belkin.com

Standard and custom computer cables, printer sharing devices, surge protectors, and LAN cabling-related products

Benwin Inc.

345 Cloverleaf Drive, Suite B
Baldwin Park, CA 91706
(818) 336-8779

Multimedia products, specializing in speakers

Best Data Products

21800 Nordhoff Street
Chatsworth, CA 91311
(818) 773-9600

Best Power

General Signal
P.O. Box 280
Necedah, WI 54646
(800) 356-5794
http://www.bestpower.com

UPSs and shutdown software

BIS Technology

13111 Brooks Drive, Suite A
Baldwin Park, CA 91706
(818) 856-5800

High-speed voice/fax/data modems

Boca Research

1377 Clint Moore Road
Boca Raton, FL 33478
(407) 997-6227
fax (407) 994-5848
http://www.bocaresearch.com

Borland International

100 Borland Way
Scotts Valley, CA 95066
(408) 431-1000

http://www.borland.com

Products and services for software developers

Bose Corporation

The Mountain
Framingham, MA 01701
1 (800) 999-2673 (1-800-WWW-BOSE)
http://www.bose.com

Brooks Power Systems, Inc.

1400 Adams Road
Bensalem, PA 19020
(800) 523-1551

Power Systems' SurgeStopper surge and noise suppressors

Brother International Corporation

100 Somerset Corporate Boulevard
Bridgewater, NJ 08807-0911
(908) 704-1700
fax (908) 704-8235
http://www.brother.com

Multi-function products and laser printers

BRYSiS Data, Inc.

17431 Gale Ave.
City of Industry, CA 91748
(818) 810-0355

Touch screen monitors

BSF Components Inc.

420 Third Street
Oakland, CA 94607
(510) 893-8822

Molded and assembled computer cables

C-Cube Microsystems

1778 McCarthy Boulevard
Milpitas, CA 95035
(408) 944-6361
http://www.c-cube.com

MPEG and JPEG decoders and encoders for personal computers

California PC Products

205 Apollo Way
Hollister, CA 95023
(408) 638-9460

Computer chassis and power supplies

Calluna Technology Ltd.

1 Blackwood Road
Eastfield, Glenrothes
Fife KY7 4NP, Scotland, UK
(44) 1592-630-810

PC card hard disk drives

Canon Computer Systems

2995 Redhill Avenue
Costa Mesa, CA 92626
(800) 848-4123, (714) 438-3000
http://www.ccsi.canon.com

Canon U.S.A., Inc.

1 Canon Plaza
Lake Success, NY 11042-1113
(516) 488-6700

Bubblejet CJ10 desktop color copier, scanner, and printer

Canopus

2010 N. First Street, Suite 510
San Jose, CA 95131
(408) 467-4000

High-performance multimedia products for PCs

Cardinal Technologies, Inc.

1827 Freedom Road
Lancaster, PA 17601
(770) 840-2157
tech support (770) 840-2157
http://www.cardtech.com

Fax modems

Casco Products, Inc.

3850 River Ridge Drive
Cedar Rapids, IA 52402
(800) 793-6960
fax (319) 393-6895
http://www.casco.com

LightLink infrared, cordless keyboard

CD Technology, Inc.

766 San Aleso Avenue
Sunnyvale, CA 94086
(408) 752-8500

CD-ROMs

Centon Electronics, Inc.

20 Morgan
Irvine, CA 92718

(714) 855-9111

http://www.centon.com

Manufacturer of memory upgrades for desktops, workstations, laptops, notebooks, portables, and printers

Cerwin-Vega, Inc.

555 E. Easy Street
Simi Valley, CA 93065
(805) 584-9332

Digital audio-quality multimedia speaker systems

CH Products

970 Park Center Drive
Vista, CA 92083
(619) 598-2518
http://www.chproducts.com

Joysticks, F-16 sticks, throttles, rudder pedals, flight yokes, trackballs, and gamecards

Chaintech Computer U.S., Inc.

12880 Lakeland Road
Santa Fe Springs, CA 90670
(310) 906-1698

Mainboards, VGA cards, multi I/O cards, SCSI interfaces, and sound cards

Chaplet Systems USA, Inc.

252 N. Wolfe Road
Sunnyvale, CA 94086
(408) 732-7950

Notebook computers

Chartered Electronics Industries

210A Twin Dolphin Drive
Redwood City, CA 94065
(415) 591-6617

PC PrimeTimeTV add-on board

Chase Advanced Technologies

500 Main Street
Deep River, CT 06417
(203) 526-2400

Computer peripheral products

Cheer Electronics (USA)

9740 N. Seymour
Kansas City, MO 64153
(816) 891-0050

Monitors

Cherry Electrical Products

3600 Sunset Avenue
Waukegan, IL 60087
(708) 662-9200

PC/POS keyboards, low-cost 101-key data entry keyboards

Chinon America, Inc.

615 Hawaii Avenue
Torrance, CA 90503
(310) 533-0274

Digital cameras, CD-ROM drives

Cirque Corporation

433 W. Lawndale Drive
Salt Lake City, UT 84115

(800) 454-3375, (801) 467-1100
http://www.cirque.com
GlidePoint trackpad

Cirrus Logic, Inc.

3100 W. Warren Avenue
Fremont, CA 94538
(510) 623-8300
http://www.cirrus.com

Citizen America Corporation

831 South Douglas Street, Suite 121
P.O. Box 1021
El Segundo, CA 90245-1021
(310) 643-9825
fax (310) 725-0969
http://www.citizen-america.com/

Printiva 600C near-photo-quality color
printer

Clary Corporation

1960 S. Walker Avenue
Monrovia, CA 91016
(800) 442-5279
http://www.clary.com/onguard/
UPSs

CMD Technology, Inc.

1 Vanderbilt
Irvine, CA 92718
(714) 454-0800
http://www.cmd.com

SCSI RAID and PC host adapters

Colorgraphic

5980 Peachtree Road
Atlanta, GA 30341
(770) 455-3921

COM2001 Corporation

4350 La Jolla Village Dr., Suite 930
San Diego, CA 92122
(619) 638-2001
http://www.com2001.com

Video and audio conferencing software

ComByte, Inc.

4424 Innovation Drive
Fort Collins, CO 80525
(970) 229-0660

Doubleplay dual-mode drive, reads and
writes both floppy disks and minicar-
tridge tapes

Comdial Corp.

1180 Seminole Trail
Charlottesville, VA 22906-7266
(800) 347-1432, (804) 978-2200
faxback (800) COMDIAL
http://www.comdial.com

PC and telephone interfaces

Command Software Systems

1061 E. Indiantown Road, Suite 500
Jupiter, FL 33477
(800) 423-9147
http://commandcom.com

F-Prot Professional anti-virus software

Compaq Computer Corporation

P.O. Box 692000
Houston, TX 77269
(800) 345-1518, (281) 370-0670
product information (800) 345-1518
http://www.compaq.com

Computer Connections America

19A Crosby Drive
Bedford, MA 01730
(617) 271-0444

Peripheral equipment for backup and
data storage

Computer Fun

8250 Valdosta Avenue
San Diego, CA 92126-2130, USA
e-mail: garyo@computerfun.com
http://www.computerfun.com/

Manufacturer of mouse pads & computer toys

Connectix Corporation

2655 Campus Drive
San Mateo, CA 94403
(800) 950-5880, (415) 571-5100
fax (415) 571-5195
http://www.connectix.com

QuickCam video camera

Conner Peripherals, Inc.

1650 Sunflower Avenue
Costa Mesa, CA 92626
(800) 4-CONNER
http://www.conner.com

Copam Dynamic Systems, Inc.

46560 Fremont Boulevard, Suite 409
Fremont, CA 94538
(510) 770-0149

CPU cooling kits and memory-related
components

Copper Leaf Technology

2233 Paragon Drive
San Jose, CA 95131
(408) 452-9288

Motherboards

Cornerstone Imaging, Inc.

1710 Fortune Drive
San Jose, CA 95131
(408) 435-8900
http://www.corimage.com

Creative Labs, Inc.

1901 McCarthy Boulevard
Milpitas, CA 95035
(800) 998-1000, (408) 428-6660
fax (408) 428-6631
http://www.creaf.com

Creatix Polymedia, L.P.

3945 Freedom Cir., Suite 670
Santa Clara, CA 95054
(408) 654-9300
http://www.creatix.com

Multimedia products, high-speed
modems, and PCMCIA cards

Crystal Semiconductor

3100 W. Warren Avenue
Fremont, CA 94538
(510) 623-8300

CTX International, Inc.

748 Epperson Dr
City of Industry, CA 91748
(626) 839-0500
customer service (800) 888-2012
fax (626) 810-6703
http://www.ctxintl.com

Monitors

CyberMax Computer, Inc.

133 North 5th Street
Allentown, PA 18102
(800) 443-9868, (610) 770-1808
from Canada (800) 695-4991
http://www.cybmax.com

Cyrix Corporation

P.O. Box 853923
Richardson, TX 75085-3923
(800) 462-9749, (800) 340-7971
email: tech_support@cyrix.com
BBS: (214) 968-8610
http://www.cyrix.com

Daewoo Electronics

120 Chubb Ave.
Lyndhurst, NJ 07071
(201) 460-2000
http://www.daewoo.com

Monitors

DarkHorse Systems, Inc.

Tanisys Technology
12201 Technology Blvd., Suite 130
Austin, Texas 78727-6101
(512) 335-4440, (800) 533-1744
fax (512) 257-5310
http://www.tanisys.com

Memory test systems

Data Depot, Inc.

1710 Drew Street, Suite 1
Clearwater, FL 34615
(813) 446-3402

PC diagnostic test products, including
hardware and software products

DataLux Corp.

155 Aviation Dr.
Winchester, VA 22602
(800) DATALUX, (703) 662-1500
fax (540) 662-1682
faxback (540) 662-1675
email: info@datalux.com
http://www.datalux.com

Space-saving PC hardware

Datasonix Corporation

5700 Flatiron Pky.
Boulder, CO 80301
(303) 545-9500

Portable gigabyte storage devices

Dell Computer Corporation

Dell Computer Corporation
One Dell Way
Round Rock, TX 78682

(888) 560-2384
http://www.dell.com

Delrina Corporation

Symantec Corp.
175 West Broadway
Eugene, OR 97401
(541) 334-6054 (outside the U.S. and
Canada)
(800) 268-6082
fax (541) 984-8020
http://www.delrina.com

PC fax, communications, and electronic
forms software

Delta Products Corporation

3225 Laurelview Ct.
Fremont, CA 94538
(510) 770-0660

Video display products

Deltec

2727 Kurtz Street
San Diego, CA 92110
(619) 291-4211
http://www.deltecpower.com

Uninterruptible power systems and
power management software

Denon Electronics

222 New Road
Parsippany, NJ 07054
(201) 575-7810

CD-ROM jukebox that houses 200 discs

DFI (Diamond Flower, Inc.)

Exide Electronics
8609 Six Forks Road
Raleigh, NC 27615
(800) 554-3448, (919) 872-3020
fax (800) 75-EXIDE
http://www.exide.com

Motherboards, video cards, notebooks,
desktop systems, and multimedia
components

DiagSoft, Inc.

5615 Scotts Valley Drive, Suite 140
Scotts Valley, CA 95066
(408) 438-8247

Diagnostic software

Diamond Multimedia Systems, Inc.

2880 Junction Avenue
San Jose, CA 95134-1922
(408) 325-7000
customer service (800) 468-5846
fax (408) 325-7070
http://www.diamondmm.com

Digital Equipment Corporation (DEC)

20555 State Hwy 249
Houston, TX 77070
(281) 370-0670
http://www.compaq.com

PCs, servers, and workstations for 32-
and 64-bit computing

DPT-Distributed Processing Technology

140 Candace Drive
Maitland, FL 32751
(407) 830-5522
http://www.dpt.com

SmartCache SCSI host adapters

DTC Data Technology, Inc.

1515 Centre Pointe Drive
Milpitas, CA 95035
(408) 942-4000
technical support (408) 262-7700
fax (408) 942-4027
faxback (408) 942-4005
BBS (408) 942-4010
http://www.datatechnology.com

Drives and SCSI devices

DTK Computer, Inc.

770 Epperson Drive
City of Industry, CA 91748
(818) 810-0098

Pentium-based systems

Edek Technologies, Inc.

Div. of Elite Computer, Taiwan
1212 John Reed Ct.
City of Industry, CA 91745
(818) 855-5700

Manufacturer and distributor of computer mainboard and VGA card products

ELSA, Inc.

2041 Mission College Boulevard
Suite 165
Santa Clara, CA 95054
(408) 565-9669

2D and 3D graphics accelerators and ISDN products

Enhance Memory Products, Inc.

18730 Oxnard Street, Suite 201
Tarzana, CA 91356
(818) 343-3066

Memory systems

Ensoniq

155 Great Valley Parkway
Malvern, PA 19355
(610) 647-3930
http://www.ensoniq.com

EPS Technologies

10069 Dakota Avenue
Jefferson, SD 57038
(800) 447-0921, (800) 526-4258,
(605) 966-5586
fax (605) 966-5482
http://www.epstech.com

Epson America, Inc.

20770 Madrona Avenue
Torrance, CA 90509
(800) 463-7766, (310) 782-0770
http://www.epson.com

ESS Technology, Inc.

46107 Landing Pky.
Fremont, CA 94538
(510) 226-1088

ES689 Wavetable Music Synthesizer,
ES938 3D Audio Effects Processor

Evergreen Technologies, Inc.

915 N.W. 8th Street
Corvallis, OR 97330
(503) 757-0934
http://www.evertech.com

CPU upgrades for 386- and 486-based
computers

Exabyte Corporation

1685 38th St.
Boulder, CO 80301
(800) 445-7736, (303) 417-7511,
(303) 417-7792
fax (303) 417-7890
EXAFAX (fax-on-demand system)
(201)946-0091
support@exabyte.com
http://www.exabyte.com

EXP Computer, Inc.

141 Eileen Way
Syosset, NY 11791
(516) 496-3703

Memory and PCMCIA products for
notebooks and palmtops

Expert Computer International, Inc.

129 166th St.
Cerritos, CA 90703
(310) 407-1740

Generic and name-brand VGA cards in
DRAM/VRAM ISA, VL-bus, and PCI
configurations

Fast Electronic U.S., Inc.

393 Vintage Park Drive
Foster City, CA 94404
(415) 345-3400

FPS60 video compression board for
multi-media production

Focus Computer Products, Inc.

35 Pond Park Road
Hingham, MA 02043
(617) 741-5008

Anti-glare glass screen filters, anti-
radiation glass screen filters, wrap-
around screen filters, cleaning products
for screen filters

Focus Electronic Corporation

21078 Commerce Pointe Drive
Walnut, CA 91789
(909) 468-5533

Signature Series keyboards

Formosa USA, Inc.

9400 Lurline Avenue, Suite B
Chatsworth, CA 91311
(818) 407-4956

MPEG decoding cards, video capture boards, TV tuners, video conference products, 16-bit sound cards, wavetable modules

Fujitsu Personal Systems, Inc.

5200 Patrick Henry Drive
Santa Clara, CA 95054
(408) 982-9500

Fujitsu Computer Products of America

2904 Orchard Parkway
San Jose, CA 95134
(408) 432-6333
http://www.fujitsu.com
http://www.fcpa.com

Peripherals including hard disk drives, optical disk drives, tape drives, laser and dot matrix printers, document imaging scanners

Fujitsu Microelectronics, Inc.

3545 N. First Street
San Jose, CA 95134
(408) 922-9000
tech support (800) 626-4686
http://www.fujitsu.com

Memory cards, LAN cards, multimedia, and communications cards

Gateway2000

610 Gateway Dive
N. Sioux City, SD 57049-2000

(888) 888-0244, (605) 232-2000
from Canada (800) 846-3609
fax (605) 232-2023
faxback (800) 846-4526
http://www.gw2k.com

GVC Technologies

376 Lafayette Road
Sparta, NJ 07871
(800) 289-4821

Modems

Hayes Microcomputer Products, Inc.

P.O. Box 105203
Atlanta, GA 30348-5203
(800) 377-4377, (770) 840-9200
fax (770) 441-1213
http://www.hayes.com

Modems

HEI

1495 Steiger Lake Lane
P.O. Box 5000, Victoria, MN 55386
(612) 443-2500

Fast Point light pens

Hercules Computer Technology, Inc.

3839 Spinnaker Court
Fremont, CA 94538
(800) 323-0601, (510) 623-6030,
(510) 623-6050
fax (510) 623-1112

tech support fax (510) 490-6745
faxback (800) 711-HERC (800-711-4372)
e-mail: support@hercules.com
CompuServe: GO HERCULES,
71333,2532
BBS (510) 623-7449
http://www.hercules.com

Hewlett-Packard

Personal Information Products Group
5301 Stevens Creek Boulevard
Santa Clara, CA 95052
(800) 762-0900
http://www.hp.com

Hewlett-Packard Co.

Information Storage Group
800 S. Taft Avenue
Loveland, CO 80537
(970) 679-6000
http://www.hp.com

HP Colorado tape products, HP DAT
tape products, and HP optical products,
disk drives, and disk array systems

Hewlett-Packard Co.

North American Hardcopy Marketing
16399 W. Bernardo Drive
San Diego, CA 92127
(800) 752-0990
customer information
center (800) 752-0990
http://www.hp.com

Printers

Hilgraeve, Inc.

111 Conant Avenue, Suite A
Monroe, MI 48161
(313) 243-0576
http://www.hilgraeve.com

32-bit communications software,
including HyperTerminal

Hitachi America, Ltd.

50 Prospect Avenue
Tarrytown, NY 10591-4698
(800) HITACHI, (914) 332-5800
fax (914) 332-5555
http://www.hitachi.com
http://www.internetworking
.hitachi.com

Computer peripherals and components,
including storage products

HTP International

1620 South Lewis Street
Anaheim, CA 92805
(714) 937-9300

Hyundai Electronics America

1955 Lundy Avenue
San Jose, CA 95131
(408) 232-8000
fax (408) 232-8146
http://www.hea.com

Components including memory devices
for DRAM, SRAM

I/OMagic Corporation

6B Autry
Irvine, CA 92618

(949) 727-7466
customer support (949) 597-2462
fax (949) 727-7467
customer support fax (949) 380-0696
http://www.iomagic.com

IBM PC Co.

1 Orchard Road
Armonk, NY 10504
(800) 772-2227, (914) 766-1900
fax (800) 426-4323
http://www.ibm.com
http://www.pc.ibm.com

Iiyama North America, Inc.

650 Louis Drive, Suite 120
Warminster, PA 18974
(215) 957-6543
http://www.iiyama.com

Integrated Technology Express, Inc.

1557 Centre Pointe Drive
Milpitas, CA 95035
(408) 934-7330

PC core logic chip sets, I/O peripheral chips, and custom ASIC design services on x86 and PowerPC architectures

Intel Corporation

2200 Mission College Boulevard
Santa Clara, CA 95052
(408) 765-8080
customer service (800) 321-4044

fax (408) 765-9904
http://www.intel.com

Interact Accessories, Inc.

(formerly STD Entertainment)
10945 McCormick Road
Hunt Valley, MD 21031
(410) 785-5661

Multimedia gaming products such as joysticks, control pads, game cards, speakers, woofers, mice, storage cases, and cleaning kits

Iomega Corporation

1821 West Iomega Way
Roy, UT 84067
(800) MY-STUFF, (801) 778-3010
http://www.iomega.com

IPC Peripherals

48041 Fremont Boulevard
Fremont, CA 94538
(510) 354-0800

Sound cards, 24 and 32 speed CD-ROM drives, three- and seven-disc changers, PCMCIA sound and Ethernet cards, audio/fax/modem telephony products, and multimedia upgrade kits

IPC Technologies, Inc.

Austin Computer Services, Inc.
10300 Metric Boulevard
Austin, TX 78758
(512) 339-3500
http://www.ipctech.com

J-Mark Computer Corporation

13111 Brooks Drive, Suite A
Baldwin Park, CA 91706
(818) 856-5800
http://www.j-mark.com

Motherboards, fax modems, SVGA cards, PCMCIA devices, and network cards for notebooks and PCs

Jazz Speakers

1217 John Reed Ct.
Industry, CA 91745
(818) 336-2689

JBL Consumer Products, Inc.

Harmon Consumer Group
80 Crossways Pk. W
Woodbury, NY 11797
(516) 496-3400, (800) 336-4JBL
www.jbl.com

Multimedia speakers, both satellites and subwoofers

Joss Technology Ltd.

No. 20, Lane 84, San Min Road
Hsin Tien City
Taipei Hsien, Taiwan ROC
(886) 2-9102050

Motherboards, 4MB/16MB 72-pin SIMM modules

JVC Information Products of America

#2 JVC Road
Tuscaloosa, AL 35405
(205) 556-7111
authorized service centers (800) 537-5722
http://www.jvc.com
http://www.jvcdiscusa.com

CD-ROM products and software

KeySonic Technology, Inc.

A Div. of Powercom America
1040A S. Melrose Street
Placentia, CA 92670-7119
(714) 632-8887

MPEG video and audio decoding cards

Kinesis Corporation

22121 17th Avenue SE, Suite 107
Bothell, WA 98021-7404
(206) 402-8100
fax (206) 402-8181
http://www.kinesis-ergo.com/

Ergonomic keyboards

Kingston Technology Corporation

17600 Newhope Street
Fountain Valley, CA 92708
(800) 435-0640, (714) 435-2639
fax (714) 424-3939
http://www.kingston.com

Konica Business Machines U.S.A., Inc.

500 Day Hill Road
Windsor, CT 06095
(203) 683-2222
http://www.konica.com

Multifunctional printers

Koss Corporation

4129 N. Port Washington Boulevard
Milwaukee, WI 53212
(800) USA-KOSS, (414) 964-5000
http://www.koss.com

Stereo audio accessories for computers

Labtec Enterprises, Inc.

3801 109th Ave., Suite J
Vancouver, WA 98682
(360) 896-2000
http://www.labtec.com

Lava Computer Mfg., Inc.

LSMI Division
28A Dansk Ct.
Rexdale, ON M9W 5V8, Canada
(800) 241-5282

High-speed I/O boards

Leverage International, Inc.

46704 Fremont Boulevard
Fremont, CA 94538
(510) 657-6750

Memory modules and other semiconductor products for IBM, Compaq, PC compatibles and other computers

Lexmark International, Inc.

2275 Research Boulevard
Rockville, MD 20850
(301) 212-5900
(800) LEXMARK or (800) 539-6275
http://www.lexmark.com

LG Electronics

1000 Sylvan Avenue
Englewood Cliffs, NJ 95131
(201) 816-2000

Goldstar monitors

Liberty Systems, Inc.

375 Saratoga Avenue, Suite A
San Jose, CA 95129
(408) 983-1127

CD-ROMs, hard drives, backup devices

Lion Optics Corporation (Likom Sdn BhD)

1751 McCarthy Blvd.
Milpitas, CA 95035
(408) 954-8089
http://www.likom.com.my/

CD-ROM drive products

Logicode Technology, Inc.

1380 Flynn Road
Camarillo, CA 93012
(800) 735-6442, (805) 388-9000

Logitech, Inc.

6505 Kaiser Drive
Fremont, CA 94555

(510) 795-8500

http://www.logitech.com

Pointing devices

MAG InnoVision Co., Inc

2801 South Yale Street

Santa Ana, CA 92704

(800) 827-3998, (714) 751-2008

fax (714) 751-5522

http://www.maginnovision.com

Monitors

Magnavox

Philips Consumer Electronics Company

One Philips Drive

Knoxville, Tennessee 37914-1810

(800) 531-0039, (423) 521-4316

http://www.philipsmagnavox.com

Matrox Graphics, Inc.

1025 St-Regis Boulevard

Dorval, Quebec, Canada H9P 2T4

(514) 969-6320

http://www.matrox.com

Video boards

Maxell Corporation of America

Multi-Media Division

22-08 Rt. 208

Fair Lawn, NJ 07410

(800) 533-2836

http://www.maxell.com

Data storage media

Maxi-Switch

2901 East Elvira Road

Tucson, AZ 85706

(520) 294-5450

Keyboards

Maximus Computers

710 East Cypress Avenue, Unit-A

Monrovia, CA 91016

(800) 888-6294, (818) 305-5925

fax (818) 357-9140

http://www.maximuspc.com

MaxTech Corporation

400 Commons Way

Rockaway, NJ 07866

(800) 9-FORMAX

fax (201) 586-3308

http://www.maxcorp.com

Maxtor Corporation

510 Cottonwood Dr.

Milpitas, CA 95135

(800) 2-MAXTOR, (408) 432-1700

fax: (408) 922-2050

tech support fax: (303) 678-2260

http://www.maxtor.com

McAfee Associates

2710 Walsh Avenue

Santa Clara, CA

(408) 988-3832

tech support (972) 278-6100

http://www.mcafee.com/

VirusScan anti-virus software

Media Vision

47900 Bayside Pky.
Fremont, CA 94538
(510) 770-8600
http://www.mediavis.com

Semiconductor products, audio products

Mediatrix Peripherals, Inc.

4229 Garlock Street
Sherbrooke, PQ J1L 2C8, Canada
(819) 829-8749
fax (819) 829-5100
http://www.mediatrix.com

Audiotrix Pro 16-bit sound board

Megahertz Corporation

3COM Corporation
Great America Site
5400 Bayfront Plaza
Santa Clara, CA 95052
(408) 326-5000
fax (408) 326-5001
http://www.megahertz.com

Memory Card Technology

10235 S. 51st Street, Suite 180
Phoenix, Arizona 85044
(602) 785-7800
fax (602) 785-7500
http://www.memory-card-
technology.com/

Memory upgrades and PCMCIA
products

Micro 2000, Inc.

1100 E. Broadway, Suite 301
Glendale, CA 91205
(818) 547-0125
tech support (800) 864-8008
http://www.micro2000.com

Universal Diagnostics Toolkit

Micro Accessories, Inc.

Blue Earth Research, Inc
1416 N Riverfront Drive
Mankato, MN 56001-3253
(507) 387-4001
fax (507) 387-4008
http://www.blueearthresearch.com
/macess.html

Computer interface cables and
terminators

Micro Solutions

132 West Lincoln Hwy
DeKalb, IL 60115
(815) 754-4500
sales (800) 890-7227
fax (815) 756-4986
faxback (815) 754-4600
BBS (815) 756-9100
http://www.micro-solutions.com

MicroClean, Inc.

2050 S. Tenth Street
San Jose, CA 95112
(408) 995-5062
http://www.microclean.com

Computer care cleaning products

MicroData Corp.

3001 Exec. Dr.
Clearwater, FL 34622
(813) 573-5900

PC diagnostic hardware and software products for technicians, system integrators, and computer service professionals

Microlabs

204 Lost Canyon Court
Richardson, TX 75080
(214) 234-5842

Micron Electronics, Inc.

8000 S. Federal Way
P.O. Box 6
Boise, ID 83707-0006
(208) 368-4000
tech support (888) FIX-MYPC or
(888) 349-6972
sales (800) 9-MICRON
fax (208) 368-4435
http://www.micron.com

Computer systems, WinBook notebook computers

Micronics Computers

221 Warren Avenue
Fremont, CA 94539
(510) 651-2300, (800) 577-0977
http://www.randomc.com/~dperr/mi
cronics/microntac.htm

Orchid series graphics accelerators

Microsoft Corporation

One Microsoft Way
Redmond, WA 98052-6399
(206) 882-8080, (800) 426-9400
http://www.microsoft.com

MicroStar International

45500 North Point Loop West
Fremont, CA 94538
(510) 623-8818
http://www.msicomputer.com

PC-based mainboards, Ethernet cards, and video accelerators

Microtek Lab, Inc.

3715 Doolittle Drive
Redondo Beach, CA 90278
(800) 654-4160, (310) 297-5000
tech support (310) 297-5100
fax (310) 297-5050
BBS (310) 297-5102
AutoTech faxback (310) 297-5101
CompuServe: GO GRAPHSUP, library 6
http://www.mteklab.com

Mindflight Technology, Inc.

4-608 Weber Street North
Waterloo, Ontario N2V 1K4
(519) 746-8483
fax (519) 746-3317
http:// www.mindflight.com

Portable data products that connect to a PC parallel port or a SCSI port

Minolta Corporation

101 Williams Drive
Ramsey, NJ 07446
(201) 825-4000
http://www.minolta.com

Graphics-specific input and output
devices

Miro Computer Products, Inc.

Pinnacle Systems, Inc.
280 N. Bernardo Avenue
Mountain View, CA 94043
(650) 526-1600
fax (650) 526-1601
faxback (650) 237-1973
http://www.miro.com

Multimedia products

Mita Copystar America, Inc.

225 Sand Road
P.O. Box 40008
Fairfield, NJ 07004-0008
(800) ABC-MITA, (201) 808-8444
tech support (800) 652-6482
fax 201-882-4415

Multifunctional printers

Mitsuba Corporation

1925 Wright Avenue
Laverne, CA 91750
(800) 648-7822

tech support (888) 999-2186
http://www.mitsuba.com

Custom file servers, PCs, and notebooks

Mitsubishi Consumer Electronics America, Inc.

Americas Corporate Office
Washington, D.C. Office
1150 Connecticut Avenue, N.W.
Suite 1010
Washington, D.C. 20036, U.S.A.
(202) 223-3424
fax: (202) 775-0116
http://www.mitsubishielectric-usa.com/

Mitsumi Electronics Corporation

6210 N. Beltline Road, Suite 170
Irving, TX 75063
(800) 648-7864, (800) 801-7927,
(214) 550-7300
BBS (415) 691-4469
http://www.mitsumi.com

Keyboards, mice, floppy disk drives,
and CD-ROM drives

Motorola ISG

5000 Bradford Dr.
Huntsville, AL 35805
(205) 430-8000
faxback (800) 221-4380
outside of North America (205) 430-8894
http://www.mot.com/mims/isg/

Modems

Motorola PCMCIA Products Division

50 East Commerce Drive
Shaumburg, IL 60173
(800) 4A-PCMCIA
http://www.mot.com

MP Computer Parts Supply Co., Ltd.

150 Commercial Street
Sunnyvale, CA 94086
(408) 738-3388

Cables, switches, connectors, computer accessories, and data communication accessories

MTC America, Inc.

2500 Westchester Avenue, Suite 110
Purchase, NY 10577
(800) MTC-CDRS

Mitsui Gold CD-R device

Multi-Tech Systems, Inc.

2205 Woodale Drive
Mounds View, MN 55112
(800) 328-9717
tech support (800) 972-2439
fax (612) 785-9874
http://www.multitech.com

Multiwave Technology, Inc.

15318 Valley Boulevard
City of Industry, CA 91746

(800) 234-3358, (800) 587-1730,
(818) 330-7030
fax (818) 333-4609
http://www.mwave.com

Mustek, Inc.

121 Waterworks Way, # 100
Irvine, CA 92618
(949) 788-3600
fax (949) 788-3670
http://www.mustek.com

Scanners

Nanao USA Corporation

EIZO NANAO Technologies, Inc.
5710 Warland Drive
Cypress, CA 90630
(562) 431-5011
fax (562) 431-4811
http://www.nanao.com

Monitors

National Semiconductor

Personal Systems Div.
2900 Semiconductor Drive
Santa Clara, CA 95052
(408) 721-5000
http://www.nsc.com

Silicon products and systems for personal computers and peripherals

NCE Storage Solutions

9717 Pacific Heights Blvd.
San Diego, CA 92121

(619) 658-9720, (800) 767-2587
fax (619) 658-9733
Web: http://www.ncegroup.com

Emerald System backup devices

NCR Corp.

1700 South Patterson Blvd.
Dayton, OH 45479
(937) 445-5000
fax (937) 445-4184
http://www.ncr.com

NEC Technologies, Inc.

1414 Massachusetts Avenue
Boxborough, MA 01719
(508) 264-8000, (800) 338-9549
pre-sales information (800) 632-4636
http://www.nec.com

New Media Corporation

One Technology Park, building A
Irvine, CA 92718
(714) 453-0100, (800) CARDS-4-U
fax (714) 453-0114
http://www.newmediacorp.com

NewCom, Inc.

31166 Via Colinas
Westlake Village, CA 91362
(818) 597-3200
fax (818) 597-3211
http://www.newcominc.com/

Internal and external fax modems,
high-fidelity stereo sound cards, and
multimedia kits

Nokia Display Products

1505 Bridgeway Boulevard
Sausalito, CA 94965
(800) 396-6541, (415) 331-0322
http://www.nokia.com

Nokia Mobile Phones

Corporate Communications
6000 Connection Drive
Irving, Texas 75039
(972) 894-4573
fax (972) 894-4831
http://www.nokia.com

NSA/Hitachi

100 Lowder Brook Drive
Westwood, MA 02090
(800) 441-4832, (617) 461-8300
tech support (800) 536-6721
http://www.nsa_hitachi.com/

Number Nine Computer Corporation

18 Hartwell Avenue
Lexington, MA 02173
(781) 869-7214, (800) GET-NINE
fax (781) 869-7222
http://www.nine.com

Ocean Information Systems Inc. (Octek)

688 Arrow Grand Circle,
Covina, CA 91722
(818) 339-8888
fax (818) 859-7668
http://www.ocean-usa.com/ocean
http://www.oceanhk.com

PC computer systems, motherboards, cases, power supplies, multimedia products, and peripherals

Okidata Corporation

532 Fellowship Road
Mt. Laurel, NJ 08054
(609) 235-2600
(800) OKIDATA or (800) 654-8326
http://www.okidata.com

Olivetti Office USA

765 US Highway 202
Bridgewater, NJ 08807
(908) 526-8200
http://www.olivettilexicon.com/
http://www.olivetti.com/

Orchestra MultiSystems, Inc.

12300 Edison Way
Garden Grove, CA 92841
(800) 237-9988, (714) 891-3861
fax (714) 891-2661
http://www.orchestra.com

Orchid Technology

221 Warren Avenue
Fremont, CA 94539
(800) 577-0977, (510) 651-2300,
(510) 661-3000
fax (510) 651-6692
Fax-on-demand (510) 661-3199
BBS (510) 651-6837
CompuServe: GO ORCHID
http://www.orchid.com

Orevox USA Corporation

248 N. Puente Avenue
P.O. Box 2655
City of Industry, CA 91746
information (626) 333-6803
orders (800) 237-0700
fax (626) 336-3748
www.dynavox.com

Computer cases and multimedia speakers

Pacom Data, Inc.

1257 B Tasman Drive
Sunnyvale, CA 94089
(408) 752-1590

Monitors and multimedia products

Padix Co. Ltd.

Rockfire
18F-3, No. 75, Sec. 1, Hsin Tai Wu Road
Hsih-Chih, Taipei, Taiwan ROC
(886) 2-6981478

PC-compatible game controllers and joysticks

Panasonic Communications & Systems Co.

2 Panasonic Way
Secaucus, NJ 07094
(787) 750-4300, (800) 742-8086
fax (787) 768-2910
http://www.panasonic.com

Pantex Computer, Inc.

10301 Harwin Drive
Houston, TX 77036
(713) 988-1688, (888) PANTEX-1
fax (713) 988-2838
http://pantexcom.com/

Motherboards, bare-bones systems

Pathlight Technology, Inc.

9 Brown Road
Ithaca, NY 14850
(800) 334-4812, (607) 266-4000
fax (607) 266-4010
http://www.pathlight.com

Storage I/O and networking interface
technologies and products

PC Cables and Parts

One-Up Computer
2331 NE 50th Court
Lighthouse Point, FL 33064
(954) 418-0817
fax (954) 418-0835
http://www.pccables.com

PC Concepts, Inc.

10318 Norris Avenue
Pacoima, CA 91331
(800) 735-6071

Computer accessories including color-
coded cables, manual and auto data
switches, printer network devices,
surge protectors, and multimedia
products

PC Power & Cooling, Inc.

5995 Avenida Encinas
Carlsbad, CA 92008
(619) 931-5700

CPU cooler for Intel's P6 processor

PCMCIA (Personal Computer Memory Card Int'l. Association)

4529 Lillian Ct.
La Canada, CA 91011
(408) 433-2273

Pengo Computer Accessories

16018-C Adelante Street
Irwindale, CA 91702
(888) PENGO99, (626) 815-9885
fax (626) 815-9964
http://www.pengo.com/

Floppy disks, dust covers, keyboard
drawers, disk file boxes, tool kits, and
various workstation accessories

Phillips Consumer Electronics Co.

1 Phillips Drive
Knoxville, TN 37914
(423) 521-4316, (800) 531-0039
http://www.philipsmagnavox.com

Phoenix Technologies, Ltd.

411 East Plumeria
San Jose, CA 95134
(408) 570-1000
fax (408) 570-1001
http://www.ptltd.com

PhoenixBIOS for desktops, NoteBIOS for notebook computers, and PhoenixPICO for handheld and embedded systems

Pioneer New Media Technologies, Inc.

Multimedia & Mass Storage
2265 E. 220th Street
Long Beach, CA 90810
(310) 952-2111, (800) 527-3766
fax (310) 952-2990
http://www.pioneerusa.com

CD-ROM and CD-R products for multimedia and mass storage applications

Pionex Technologies, Inc.

3 Riverview Dr.
Somerset, NJ 08873
(732) 764-5680
fax (732) 563-2661
http://www.phoenix.com

Pixie Technologies

46771 Fremont Boulevard
Fremont, CA 94538
(510) 440-9721
fax (510) 440-9356
http://www.pixie.com

Monitors

PKWare, Inc.

9025 N. Deerwood Drive
Brown Deer, WI 53223
(414) 354-8699
http://www.pkware.com

PKZIP compression utilities

Play, Inc.

2890 Kilgore Road
Rancho Cordova, CA 95670-6133
(916) 851-0800, (800) 306-PLAY
fax (916) 851-0801
http:www.play.com

Snappy Video Snapshot software

Plextor USA

4255 Burton Drive
Santa Clara, CA 95054
(800) 886-3935, (408) 980-1838
http://www.plextor.com

CD-ROM drives

Portrait Display Labs

5117 Johnson Drive
Pleasanton, CA 94588
(510) 227-2700
fax (925) 227-2705
http://www.portrait.com

Monitors

Powercom America, Inc.

1040A S. Melrose Street
Placentia, CA 92670-7119
(714) 632-8889
fax (714) 632-8868
http://www.powercom-usa.com/

Modems and UPSs

PowerQuest Corporation

1083 North State Street
Orem, UT 84057
(800) 379-2566
http://www.powerquest.com

Manufacturer of Partition Magic, software utility for creating and managing disk partitions

Practical Peripherals

P.O. Box 921789
Norcross, Georgia 30092-7789
(770) 840-9966
http://www.practinet.com

Princeton Graphic Systems

2801 South Yale Street
Santa Ana, CA 92704
(800) 747-6249, (714) 751-8405
fax (714) 751-5736
http://www.prgr.com

Monitors

Procom Technology

2181 Dupont Drive
Irvine, CA 92715
(714) 852-1000, (800) 800-8600
fax (714) 852-1221
http://www.procom.com

Hard drives, backup devices

Professional Technologies

21038 Commerce Pointe Drive
Walnut, CA 91789
(800) 949-5018, (909) 468-3730
fax (909) 468-1372

Computer systems

ProLink Computer

15336 East Valley Blvd.
City of Industry, CA 91746
(626) 369-3883, (800) 686-8110
fax (626) 369-4883
http://www.prolink-usa.com/

QLogic Corporation

3545 Harbor Blvd.
Costa Mesa, CA 92626
(714) 438-2200, (800) 662-4471
fax (714) 668-5008
http://www.qlc.com

Quadrant International, Inc.

269 Great Valley Parkway
Malvern, PA 19355
(800) 700-0362
tech support (610) 251-9999
fax (610) 695-2592
email: qi-tech@quadrant.com
http://www.quadrant.com

Video editing and capture products

Quantex Microsystems, Inc.

400B Pierce Street
Somerset, NJ 08873
(800) 864-9022
fax (732) 563-9262
http://www.quantex.com

Quantum Corporation

500 McCarthy Boulevard
Milpitas, CA 95053
(800) 624-5545, (408) 894-4000
fax (408) 894-5217
http://www.quantum.com

Quarterdeck Select

13160 Mindanao Way
Marina del Rey, CA 90292-9705
(800) 225-8148
fax (813) 523-2331
http://www.quarterdeck.com

Troubleshooting tools

Quatech, Inc.

662 Wolf Ledges Pky.
Akron, OH 44311
(330) 434-3154, (800) 553-1170
fax (330) 434-1409
http://www.quatech.com

Communication, data acquisition,
industrial I/O, and PCMCIA products

QuickPath Systems, Inc.

46723 Fremont Boulevard
Fremont, CA 94538
(800) 995-8828, (510) 440-7288
fax (510) 440-7289
email: qpinfo@quickpath.com
http://www.quickpath.com/

QuickShot Technology, Inc.

QuickShot Technology, Inc.
950 Yosemite Drive
Milpitas, CA
(408) 263-4163
fax (408) 263-4005
http://www.quickshot.com

QVS, Inc.

2731 Crimson Canyon Drive
Las Vegas, NV 89128
(800) 344-3371

Computer cables, computer electronic
products

Regal Electronics, Inc.

4251 Burton Drive
Santa Clara, CA 95054
(408) 988-2288, (800) 882-8086
fax (408) 988-2797, (800) 345-2831
http://www.regalusa.com/

Plug-and-play CD-ROM changers and
multimedia speakers

Relisys (Teco)

320 S. Milpitas Boulevard
Milpitas, CA 95035
(408) 945-9000
http://www.relisys.com

Video monitors, scanners, and multifunctional facsimile products

Repay Trading, Inc.

3345 Wilshire Boulevard, Suite 901
Los Angeles, CA 90010
(213) 385-2580

CD-ROMs and CD-R drives

Reveal Computer Products, Inc.

CNM Corp
(900) 225-3000
http://www.reveal.com/

Rockwell Telecommunications

Multimedia Communications Division
4311 Jamboree Road
Newport Beach, CA 92658

(714) 833-4600, (800) 854-8099
fax (714) 221-6375
http://www.nb.rockwell.com

Modems

Roland Corporation U.S.

Desktop Media Production
7200 Dominion Cir.
Los Angeles, CA 90040
(213) 685-5141
http://www.rolandus.com

Sound cards, PCMCIA cards, MIDI keyboards, powered speakers, and music software

Rose Electronics

10707 Stancliff
Houston, TX 77099
(281) 933-7673, (800) 333-9343
fax (281) 933-0044
http://www.rosel.com

Keyboard and video control products, print servers, and data switches

S & S Software International

17 New England Executive Park
Burlington, MA 01803
(617) 273-7400, (888) 377-6566
fax (781) 273-7474
http://www.drsolomon.com

Dr. Solomon's Anti-Virus Toolkit

S. T. Research Corp.

8419 Terminal Rd.
Newington, VA 22122
(703) 550-7000

Palmtop computers

S3, Inc.

2841 Mission College Blvd.
P.O. Box 58058
Santa Clara, CA 95052-8058
(408) 588-8000
fax (408) 980-5444
http://www.s3.com

Graphics acceleration products

Sager Computer

18005 Cortney Court
City of Industry, CA 91748
(800) 669-1624, (818) 964-8682
fax (818) 964-2381

Notebook computers

Sampo Technology, Inc.

5550 Peachtree Ind. Boulevard
Norcross, GA 30071
(770) 449-6220
fax (770) 447-1109
http://www.sampotech.com

Monitors

Samsung America, Inc.

14251 E. Firestone Boulevard
La Mirada, CA 90638

(310) 802-2211
http://www.samsung.com
CPU cooler for the Pentium and P6

Samsung Electronics America, Inc.

Information Systems Div.
105 Challenger Road
Ridgefield Park, NJ 07660
(800) 933-4110, (201) 229-4000
http://www.samsung.com

Notebook PCs, color monitors, hard disk drives, and laser printers

Samtron

A Div. of Samsung Electronics America
18600 Broadwick Street
Rancho Dominguez, CA 90220
(310) 537-7000

Monitors

Sanyo Energy (USA) Corporation

2001 Sanyo Avenue
San Diego, CA 92173
(619) 661-6620

Batteries and amorphous solar cells

Sanyo Fisher (USA) Corporation

Office Automation Products
21350 Lassen Street
Chatsworth, CA 91311
(818) 998-7322
http://www.sanyo.com

Multifunctional fax machines, CD-ROM drives, notebooks, desktop personal computers, monitors

Seagate Software

1098 Alta
Mountain View, CA 94043
(650) 335-8000
http://www.seagatesoftware.com

Seagate Technology

920 Disc Drive
Scotts Valley, CA 95066-6550
(831) 438-6550
(831) 936-1687
fax (831) 936-1685
http://www.seagatesoftware.com

Hard drives

Seattle Telecom & Data, Inc.

18005 N.E. 68th, Suite A115
Redmond, WA 98052
(208) 883-8440

Manufacturer of PS/2-compatible accelerator boards for most Micro Channel models

Sempro L.L.C.

2459 SE. T.V. Highway, Suite 133
Hillsboro, OR 97123
(503) 693-7894

PC gaming peripherals

Sharp Electronics Corporation

Sharp Plaza
Mahwah, NJ 07430
(201) 529-8200, (800) BE-SHARP
fax (201) 529-8425
http://www.sharp-usa.com

LCDs and LCD-based products

Shining Technology, Inc.

10533 Progress Way, Suite C
Cypress, CA 90630
(714) 761-9598

Parallel I/O products to EIDE (supporting HDD and CD-ROMs)

Shuttle Computer International, Inc.

1161 Cadillac Ct.
Milpitas, CA 95035
(408) 945-1480

Pentium 75-180MHz PCI motherboards with pipeline SRAM, EDO, and DRAM support

Shuttle Technology

43218 Christy Street
Fremont, CA 94538
(510) 656-0180

Parallel port interfacing technology

Sicos Products

SICOS Computer
Vertrieb Deutschland GmbHAn den Hirtenäckern
9 - 63791 Karlstein
06188/95999-0

fax 06188/95999-59
http://www.sicos.com

Scanners

Sigma Interactive Solutions Corporation

46515 Landing Parkway
Fremont, CA 94538
(510) 624-4928

Simple Technology

3001 Daimler Street
Santa Ana, CA 92705
(714) 476-1180
(800) 4-SIMPLE or (800) 474-6753
http://www.simpletech.com

Memory and PC card products

SL Waber

520 Fellowship Road
Mount Laurel, NJ 08054
(800) 634-1485, (609) 866-8888
fax (609) 866-1945
http://www.waber.com

Uninterruptible power supplies

Smart and Friendly

20520 Nordhoff Street
Chatsworth, CA 91311
(800) 542-8838, (818) 772-8001
fax (818) 772-2888
http://www.smartandfriendly.com/

CD recording devices

SMART Modular Technologies, Inc.

4305 Cushing Pkwy.
Fremont, CA 94538
(510) 623-1231, (800) 956-7627
fax (510) 623-1434
http://www.smartm.com

DRAM, SRAM, and Flash memory modules and upgrade cards

Smile International, Inc.

175 Sunflower Avenue
Costa Mesa, CA 92626
(714) 546-0336, (800) USMILE-2
fax (714) 546-0315
http://www.smilekfc.com

Sony Corporation

1 Sony Drive
Park Ridge, NJ 07645
(201) 930-1000
sales (800) 352-7669
tech support (800) 326-9551
http://www.sony.com

Digital technologies for computers, communications, audio, and video

Spider Graphics, Inc.

580 Charcot Avenue
San Jose, CA 95131
(408) 526-0535

Graphics and multimedia accelerators

SRS Labs, Inc.

2909 Daimler Street
Santa Ana, CA 92705
(714) 442-1070, (800) 243-2733
fax (714) 852-1099
http://www.srslabs.com

3D sound technology

Stac Electronics

12636 High Bluff Drive
San Diego, CA 92130-2093
(619) 794-4300, (800) 522-7822
fax (619) 794-4575
http://www.stac.com

Backup and disaster recovery products

STB Systems, Inc.

1651 North Glenville, Suite 210
Richardson, TX 75085
(214) 234-8750, (214) 669-0989
fax (214) 234-1306
tech support fax (214) 669-1326
BBS (214) 437-9615
email: support@stb.com
http://www.stb.com

Storage Technology Corporation

2270 S. 88th Street
Louisville, CO 80028-4341
(303) 673-5151, (800) STK-2217
fax (303) 673-5019
http://www.storagetek.com

StorageTek storage products

Stracon, Inc.

1672 Kaiser Avenue
Irvine, CA 92714
(714) 851-2288

Memory upgrades for PCs, laptops, and workstations

Supra Corporation

Diamond Multimedia
2880 Junction Avenue
San Jose, CA 95134-1922
(408) 325-7000, (800) 468-5846
fax (408) 325-7070
http://www.diamondmm.com

Modems

Swan Instruments

Drive Div.
3000 Olcott
Santa Clara, CA 95054
(408) 727-9711

Ultra High-Capacity (UHC) Flexible Disk Drives

Symantec Corporation

175 West Broadway
Eugene, OR 97401
(800) 441-7234, (541) 334-6054
outside the U.S. and Canada (541) 334-6054
tech support (541) 465-8420
fax (541) 984-8020
http://www.symantec.com

Norton Utilities, Norton Anti-Virus software

Synnex Information Technologies, Inc.

3797 Spinnaker Court
Fremont, CA 94538
(510) 656-3333, (800) 756-9888
http://www.synnex.com

SyQuest Technology

47071 Bayside Pky.
Fremont, CA 94538
(510) 226-4000, (800) 245-2278
fax (510) 226-4108
http://www.syquest.com

Removable storage products

Tagram System Corporation

1451-B Edinger Avenue
Tustin, CA 92680
(800) TAGRAMS, (714) 258-3222
tech support (800) 443-5761
fax (714) 258-3220
http://www.tagram.com

Tahoe Peripherals

999 Tahoe Boulevard
Incline Village, NV 89451
(800) 288-6040
fax (702) 832-3611

Tandberg Data

2685-A Park Center Drive
Simi Valley, CA 93065
(805) 579-1000, (800) 826-3237
fax (805) 579-2555
http://www.tandberg.com

SCSI QIC tape backup drives and kits

Tanisys Technology Corporation

12201 Technology Boulevard, Suite 160
Austin, TX 78727-6101
(800) 533-1744
http:// www.tanisys.com

Memory products

Tatung Company of America, Inc.

2850 El Presidio Street
Long Beach, CA 90810
(310) 637 2105, (800) 827-2850
fax (310) 637 8484
http://www.tatung.com

Monitors

TDK Electronics Corporation

12 Harbor Park Drive
Port Washington, NY 11050
(516) 625-0100, (800) TDK-TAPE
fax (516) 625-0171
http://www.tdk.com

Optical and magnetic recording media

TEAC America, Inc.

Data Storage Products Div.
7733 Telegraph Road
Montebello, CA 90640
(213) 726-0303
tech support (213) 727-4860
tech support fax (213) 727-7674
http://www.teac.com

CD-ROM, tape, and floppy drives

Techmedia Computer Systems Corporation

7345 Orangewood Avenue
Garden Grove, CA 92641
(800) 379-0077, (714) 379-6677
fax (714) 379-6688

Monitors

Tektronix, Inc.

P.O. Box 7000 MS 63-580
Wilsonville, OR 97070
(800) 835-6100, (503) 682-7377
fax (503) 682-2980
http://www.tek.com

Tempest Micro

375 N. Citrus Avenue #611
Azusa, CA 91704
(800) 818-5163, (800) 848-5167,
(818) 858-5163
fax (818) 858-5166

Texas Instruments, Inc.

P.O. Box 650311
M/S 3914
Dallas, TX 75265
(800) 848-3927, (214) 917-6278
http://www.ti.com

ThrustMaster, Inc.

7175 NW Evergreen Parkway, #400
Hillsboro, OR 97124
(503) 615-3200
fax (503) 615-3300
http://www.thrustmaster.com

Thunder Max Corporation

15011 Parkway Loop, Suite A
Tustin, CA 92680
(714) 259-8800

TMC Research Corporation

631 S. Milpitas Boulevard
Milpitas, CA 95035
(408) 262-0888

Windows 95-compatible motherboards
and SCSI host adapters

Toshiba America Information Systems, Inc.

9740 Irvine Boulevard
Irvine, CA 92718
(800) 457-7777, (714) 583-3000
sales (888) 598-7802
http://www.toshiba.com

CD-ROMs, hard drives

TouchStone Software Corporation

2124 Main Street
Huntington Beach, CA 92648
(800) 531-0450, (714) 969-7746
fax (714) 969-4444
http://www.checkit.com

CheckIt Pro, WinCheckIt 4 diagnostic
software

Trend Micro Devices

10101 N. DeAnza Blvd. Suite 400
Cupertino, CA 95014
(408) 257-1500, (800) 228-5651

fax (408) 257-2003
http://www.trendmicro.com

PC-cillin anti-virus software

Trident Microsystems, Inc.

189 N. Bernardo Avenue
Mountain View, CA 94043
(415) 691-9211
http://www.trid.com

32- and 64-bit integrated graphics and
multimedia video processing controllers for PC compatibles

Truevision, Inc.

2500 Walsh Avenue
Santa Clara, CA 95051
(800) 522-TRUE, (408) 562-4200
fax (408) 562-4200
tech support fax (317) 576-7770
BBS (317) 577-8777
email: support@truevision.com
CompuServe: GO TRUEVISION
http://www.truevision.com

Tseng Labs, Inc.

6 Terry Drive
Newtown, PA 18940
(215) 968-0502
http://www.tseng.com

Graphics and video controllers

Turtle Beach Systems

5690 Stewart Avenue
Fremont, CA 94538
(510) 624-6200

tech support (510) 624-6265
fax (510) 624-6291
tech support fax (510) 624-6292
faxback (510) 624-6296
BBS (510) 624-6279
email: support@tbeach.com
CompuServe: GO TURTLE, GO TBMIDI
http://www.tbeach.com

Tyan Computer

3288 Laurelview Court
Fremont, CA 94538
sales (510) 651-8868
tech support (510) 440-8808
fax (510) 651-7688
http://www.tyan.com

High-end motherboards and add-on cards

U&C AMERICA

5931 N. Reno Avenue
Temple City, CA 91780
(818)287-4488
fax: (818)287-4499
http://www.superpen.com

Makers of SuperPen

U.S. Robotics Corp.

3Com Corp
Great America Site
5400 Bayfront Plaza
Santa Clara, CA 95052
(408) 326-5000
fax (408) 326-5001
http://www.3com.com

UMAX Technologies

3353 Gateway Boulevard
Fremont, CA 94538
(800) 562-0031, (510) 651-9488
fax (510) 651-8834
http://www.umax.com

Unisys Corporation

Personal Computer Div.
2700 N. First Street
San Jose, CA 95134-2028
(800) 448-1424
http://www.unisys.com

Notebook and desktop systems

Valitek

100 University Drive
Amherst, MA 01102
(413) 549-2700, (800) 825-4835
fax (413) 549-2900
http://www.valitek.com

Backup devices

Verbatim Corporation

1200 W.T. Harris Boulevard
Charlotte, NC 28262
(704) 547-6500, (800) 538-8589
http://www.verbatimcorp.com

Optical discs, tape products, floppy disks, CD-R and CD-ROM, and imaging products

Video Electronics Standards Association (VESA)

2150 N. First Street, Suite 440
San Jose, CA 95131
(408) 435-0333

ViewSonic Corporation

20480 East Business Parkway
Walnut, CA 91789
(800) 888-8583, (909) 869-7976
http://www.viewsonic.com

ViewSonic and Optiquest monitors

VLSI Technology, Inc.

VLSI Technology, Inc.
1109 McKay Dr.
San Jose, CA 95131
(408) 434-3000
http://www.vlsi.com

64-bit+graphics controller supporting
SGRAM

Voyetra Technologies

5 Odell Plaza
Yonkers, NY 10701
(914) 966-0600
sales (800) 233-9377
http://www.voyetra.com

Multimedia sound products

WACOM Technology Corporation

501 S.E. Columbia Shores Blvd., Suite 300
Vancouver, WA 98661
(800) 922-9348, (360) 750-8882
fax (360) 750-8924
BBS (360) 750-0638 (300 to 14400 baud, 8
bis, no parity, 1 stop bit)
email: sales@wacom.com,
support@wacom.com
http://www.wacom.com

Pen tablets

Weitek Corporation

1060 E Arques Avenue
Sunnyvale, CA 94086
(408) 738-8400
http://www.weitek.com

Processors

Western Digital

8105 Irvine Center Drive
Costa Mesa, CA 92718
(714) 932-5000
tech support (800) 275-4932
http://www.wdc.com

IDE hard drives, integrated circuits,
and board-level products for the microcomputer industry

Wetech Electronics Inc.

14704 South Redburn Ave.
Santa Fe Springs, CA 90670
(562) 802-5960
fax (562) 802-3158
http://iready.com/wetech/

Monitors

Willow Peripherals

190 Willow Ave.
Bronx, NY 10454
(718) 402-0203, (800) 444-1585
fax (718) 402-9603
email: peripherals@willow.com
http://www.willow.com

Manufacturer of video output and
video capture products

Winner Products (USA) Inc.

21128 Commerce Pointe Drive
Walnut, CA 91789
(909) 595-2490
fax (909) 595-1483
http://www.joystick.com

Joysticks and other peripherals

Wyse Technology

3471 N. First Street
San Jose, CA 95134
(408) 473-1200, (800) GET-WYSE
http://www.wyse.com

Advanced video display terminals

Xerox Corporation

80 Linden Oaks Pky.
Rochester, NY 14625
(800) ASK-XEROX
tech support (800) 821-2797
http://www.xerox.com

Printers

Xircom

2300 Corporate Center Drive
Thousand Oaks, CA 91320-1420
(800) 438-4526
tech support (805) 376-9200
fax (805) 376-9311
http://www.xircom.com

Yamaha Corporation of America

CBX Group
6600 Orangethorpe Avenue
Buena Park, CA 90620

(714) 522-9011
http://www.yamaha.com

Computer sound products

Zenith Data Systems

2455 Horse Pen Road, Suite 100
Herndon, VA 22071
(703) 713-3000
http://www.zds.com

Desktops and wireless technology

Zoom Technologies

207 South Street
Boston, MA 02111
(800) 631-3116
fax (617) 423-3923
http://www.zoomtel.com

Data Recovery Vendors

The following vendors specialize in products for recovering data from damaged hard drives:

AA Computech

28170 Avenue Crocker #105
Valencia, CA 91355
(800) 360-6801, (805) 257-6801
tech support (805) 257-6804
fax (805) 257-6805
http://www.scvnet.com/~bobs

AMS (American Micro Solutions)

15461 Redhill Avenue, Suite E
Tustin, CA 92680
(800) 580-2525, (714) 258-8818

fax (714) 258-8918
email: ams@calypso.com
http://www.calypso.com/ams

Aurora Electronics

1101 National Drive
Sacramento, CA 95834
(800) 767-9281, (916) 928-1107
fax (916) 928-1006
email: sacrepair@aur.com

Data Recovery Labs

1315 Lawrence Avenue East
Unit 502-503
Don Mills, Ontario, Canada M3A 3R3
(800) 563-1167, (416) 510-6990
fax (416) 510-6992
email: admin@datarec.com
http://www.datarec.com

Data Recovery Labs, Inc.

24705 US 19 North, Suite 312
Clearwater, Florida 34623
(813) 725-3818
fax (813) 712-0800
http://webcoast.com/drl/

Data Retrieval Services

1040 Kapp Drive
Clearwater, FL 34625
(813) 461-5900, (800) 952-7530
fax (813) 461-5668

Disk Drive Repair, Inc.

863 Industry Drive, Bldg. 23
Seattle, WA 98188
(206) 575-3181
fax (206) 575-1811

Disktec

5875 W. 34th Street
Houston, TX 77092
(713) 681-4691
fax (713) 681-5851

Drive Service Company

3303 Harbor Blvd., Suite E-7
Costa Mesa, CA 92626
(714) 549-DISK (714-549-3475)
fax (714) 549-9752
email: jimc@driveservice.com
http://www.driveservice.com

DriveSavers Data Recovery

400 Bel Marin Keys Blvd.
Novato, CA 94949
(800) 440-1904, (415) 382-2000
fax (415) 883-0780
email: recovery@drivesavers.com
http://www.drivesavers.com

Electric Renaissance

105 Newfield Avenue
Edison, NJ 08837
(908) 417-9090
fax (908) 471-9099

Excalibur Data Recovery, Inc.

101 Billerica Avenue, Bldg. #5
N. Billerica, MA 01862-1256
(800) 466-0893, (508) 663-1700
fax (508) 670-5901
email: brnonteer@excalibur.ultranet.com
http://www.excaliburdr.com

Lazarus

381 Clementina Street
San Francisco, CA 94103
(415) 495-5556, (800) 341-DATA
fax (415) 495-5553
http://www.lazarus.com

Micro Com

19011 Ventura Boulevard
Tarzana, CA 91356
(800) 469-2549, (818) 881-7417
fax (818) 881-8015

OnTrack Data Recovery, Inc.

6321 Bury Drive
Eden Prairie, MN 55346
(800) 872-2599, (612) 937-5161
fax (612) 937-5750
http://www.ontrack.com

Total Peripheral Repair

(a division of Technical Parts, Inc.)
4204 Sorrento Valley Blvd., Suite A
San Diego, CA 92121-1412
(800) 890-0880, (619) 552-2288
fax (619) 552-2290
email (sales): sales@recoverdata.com
email (service):service@recoverdata.com
http://www.recoverdata.com/

Valtron Technologies, Inc.

28309 Avenue Crocker
Valencia, CA 91355
(800) 2VALTRON, (805) 257-0333
fax (805) 257-0113

VANTAGE Technologies, Inc.

4 John Tyler Street, PO Box 1570
Merrimack, NH 03054
(800) ITS-LOST or (800) 487-5678,
(603) 429-3019, (603) 883-6249
fax (603) 883-1973
email: recovery@vantagetech.com
http://www.vantagetech.com

Memory Vendors

Here are a number of computer memory dealers. Many will also buy your old memory; however, call and check first before sending anything.

Avalon Micro

688 #D Wells Road
Boulder City, NV 89005
(800) 610-1215, (702) 293-2300
fax (702) 293-4453

The Chip Merchant

World 1580 Oakland Rd #C208
San Jose, CA 95131
(408) 441-1477
fax (408) 441-1463
http://www.chipmerchant.com/

DMS (Data Memory Systems)

24 Keewaydin Drive
Salem, NH 03079
(800) 662-7466, (603) 898-7750
fax (603) 898-6585
email: datamem@aol.com
http://www.datamem.com

H&J Electronics International, Inc.

2700 West Cypress Creek Road
Ft. Lauderdale, FL 33309
(800) 275-2447, (954) 971-7750
fax (954) 979-9028

Laptop, printer, and PC memory for name-brand computers

McDonald and Associates: The Memory Place

2544 South 156th Circle
Omaha, NE 68130
(800) 694-1307, (800) 306-8901, (402) 691-8548
fax (402) 691-8548
email: buymemory@aol.com
http://www.buymemory.com

Memory 4 Less

2622 West Lincoln, Suite 104
Anaheim, CA 92801
(800) 821-3354, (714) 826-5981
fax (714) 821-3361

Memory and CPU Warehouse

8361 East Evans Road, Suite 105
Scottsdale, AZ 85260
(800) RAM-7091, (602) 443-0696
fax (602) 443-0918

The Memory Man

7225 NW 25th Street
Miami, FL 33166
(800) 854-0067, (305) 418-4149

fax (305) 418-4277
http://www.memory-man.com

Worldwide Technologies

437 Chestnut Street
Philadelphia, PA 19106
(800) 457-6937, (215) 922-0050
fax (215) 922-0116
http://www.worldwidetechnologies.com

They carry motherboards and drives, too.

BIOS Upgrade Vendors

These are vendors who sell upgrade BIOS ROM to support new hard and floppy drive types, solve some compatibility problem, or add a new feature (such as built-in SETUP).

If you've got a clone, your clone may have a compatible BIOS written by Phoenix Technologies. Phoenix periodically updates their BIOS to speed them up, support new devices, and fix bugs. The person whom you bought the clone from, however, may have gone on to selling land in Florida. You can buy upgrades for your Phoenix ROM from Wholesale Direct.

Alltech Electronics Co.

1300 E. Edinger Avenue, Suite D
Santa Ana, CA 92705
(714) 543-5011
fax (714) 543-0553
email: allelec.com
http://www.allelec.com

TTi Technologies, Inc.

1445 Donlon Street #9
Ventura, CA 93003
(800) 541-1943
email: mike@ttitech.com

Unicore Software

1538 Turnpike Street
N. Andover, MA 01845
(800) 800-2467, (508) 686-6468
fax (508) 683-1630
http://www.unicore.com

Storage Device Vendors

In case you're looking specifically for a new hard drive or tape drive, here are a few vendors who specialize in storage devices:

AA Computech

28170 Avenue Crocker #105
Valencia, CA 91355
(800) 360-6801, (805) 257-6801
fax (805) 257-6805
http://www.scvnet.com/~bobs

Hard drives and data recovery

Ashtek, Inc.

2600-B Walnut Avenue
Tustin, CA 92680
(800) 801-9400
fax (714) 505-2693

Buy and sell hard drives and memory SIMMs

Bason Hard Drive Warehouse

(800) 238-4453, (818) 727-9054
fax (818) 727-9066
http://www.basoncomputer.com

Dirt Cheap Drives

3716 Timber Drive
Dickinson, TX 77539
(800) 786-1170, (713) 534-4140
fax (713) 534-6452

Hard drives, CD-ROMs, optical drives, tape backup units

Drive Outlet Center

3412 Milwaukee Avenue #445
Northbrook, IL 60062
(800) 260-5930
fax (847) 419-0705

Hard drives, CD-ROMs, optical drives, tape backup units

MegaHaus Hard Drives

2201 Pine Drive
Dickinson, TX 77539
(800) 786-1185, (713) 534-3919
fax (713) 534-6580
http://www.MegaHaus.com/

Drives, controller cards, drive accessories

Storage USA

101 Reighard Avenue
Williamsport, PA 17701
(800) 538-DISK, (717) 327-9200
fax (717) 327-1217
http://www.storageusa.com

Miscellaneous Computer Products Vendors

Many manufacturers also sell their own products. Here, however, are the dealers who sell a wide range of useful computer parts and peripherals:

1st Compu Choice

740 Beta Drive - Unit G
Cleveland, OH 44143
(800) 345-8880, (216) 460-1002
fax (216) 460-1066

A Matter of Fax

65 Worth Street
New York, NY 10013
(800) 433-3FAX, (212) 941-8877

Fax machines, printers, scanners, other components and peripherals

A+ Factory Outlet

526 S. Coralridge Pl.
City of Industry, CA 91746
(800) 717 7060, (818) 937-3090
fax (818) 937-3091
email: info@datatrend.com

Computers and parts; a liquidator of computer products

A2Z Computers

701 Beta Drive, Unit 19
Mayfield Village, OH 44142

(800) 983-8889, (216) 442-9028
fax (216) 442-8891
http://www.a2zcomp.com

Computer components and peripherals

ABC Drives

8717 Darby Ave.
Northridge, CA 91325
(818) 885-7157
http://www.abcdrives.com/

Specializes in the sale and service of most major storage devices, including hard-to-find or obsolete drives

ACIS Corporation

2381 Philmont Avenue, Suite 219
Huntingdon Valley, PA 19006
(800) 223-9493, (215) 938-4288
tech support (215) 938-6482
fax (215) 938-4290

Motherboards, sound cards, video cards, RAM, hard drives, CPUs, CD-ROMs

AllMicro, Inc.

18820 U.S. Hwy 19 N, #215
Clearwater, FL 34624
(800) 653-4933, (813) 539-7283
fax (813) 531-0200
BBS (813) 535-9042
email: allmicro@ix.netcom.com

Many computer products, including the AlertCard (power supply and temperature monitoring card)

Allsop Computer Accessories

4201 Meridian
Bellingham, WA 98226
(800) 426-4303
http://www.allsop.com

Ergonomic enhancements (drawers and glare filters)

Alpha Systems, Inc.

47000 Warm Springs Blvd, #455
Fremont, CA 94539-7467
(510) 249-9280
fax (510) 259-9288
email: compu@alphasys.com
http://www.alphasys.com

American Computer Products (ACP)

Mercantile Medical Plaza
4015 SW Mercantile Drive, Suite 200
Lake Oswego, OR 97035
(503) 526-3551, (800) 623-7489
fax (503) 646-7631
http://www.acp1.com

American Computer Resources, Inc.

88 Long Hill Cross Road
Shelton, CT 06484-4703
(203) 944-7333
fax (203) 944-7370
http://www.the-acr.com/

American Micro Professionals

Corporate Center
5351 Naiman Parkway
Solon, OH 44139
(800) 857-3223, (216) 498-9564
fax (216) 349-6170

American Ribbon and Toner Co.

2895 West Prospect Road
Ft. Lauderdale, FL 33309
(800) 327-1013

Printer ribbons, toner cartridges, etc.

American Wholesale Center

817 New Churchman's Road
New Castle, DE 19720
(302) 845-4962

AMP Tech (American Micro Products Technology)

5351 Naiman Parkway
Solon, OH 44139
(800) 619-0508, (216) 498-9499
fax (216) 349-6170
email: amptech@icgroup.net
http://www.amptech.com

Computers, motherboards, cases, drives, memory

Arlington Computer Products

851 Commerce Court
Buffalo Grove, IL 60089
(800) 548-5105, (847) 541-6583
fax (847) 541-6881

ARM Computer Inc.

1637 South Main Street
Milpitas, CA 95035
(800) 765-1767, (408) 935-9800
fax (408) 935-9192

email: arm@armcomputer.com
http://www.armcomputer.com

ASI

48289 Fremont Boulevard
Fremont, CA 94538
(510) 226-8000

Distributor of computer hardware, peripherals, and private-label Nspire personal computers and multimedia kits

Aspen Imaging International, Inc.

1500 Cherry Street, Suite B
Louisville, CO 80027-3036
(800) 955-5555(303) 666-5750
fax (303) 665-2972

Computer printer supplies including printer ribbons, printbands, and laser toner and inkjet supplies

Associates Computer Supply Co., Inc.

275 West 231st Street
Riverdale, NY 10463
(718) 543-8686
fax (718) 548-0343
http://www.associatescomputer.com

Motherboards, cases, video cards, hard drives, keyboards, memory, CD-ROMs

Astra Computer Corporation

7786 Metric Drive
Mentor, OH 44060
(800) 800-6047, (216) 974-7933
fax (216) 974-7939

Atlantic Logic

41 Canfield Road
Cedar Grove, NJ 07009
(201) 857-7878

ATronics International Inc.

44700-B Industrial Drive
Fremont, CA 94538
(800) 488-7776, (510) 656-8400
fax (510) 656-8560
http://www.atronicsintl.com

Parallel port CD-ROM adapter, BIOS enhancement card for IDE hard drive controllers

Aura Industries, Inc.

6352 N. Lincoln Avenue
Chicago, IL 60659
(312) 588-8722

CPUs, hard drives, memory, multimedia products, and computer accessories

Automated Tech Tools

851B Freeway Drive
Macedonia, OH 44056
(800) 413-0767

Autotime Corporation

6605 S.W. Macadam Avenue
Portland, OR 97201
(503) 452-8577
http://www.teleport.com/~autotime/

Memory recycling services and products

Barnett's Computers

417 Fifth Avenue
New York, NY 10017
(212) 696-4777

Battery Network

50 Tannery Road, Unit 2
North Branch, NJ 08876
(800) 653-8294
http://www.battnet.com/

Assembly, sales, and service of
rechargeable batteries

Battery Technology, Inc.

5700 Bandini Boulevard
Commerce, CA 90040
(213) 728-7874

Battery products for laptop computers
and portable peripherals

Battery-Biz Inc.

31352 Via Colinas, Suite 104
Westlake Village, CA 91362
(800) 848-6782, (818) 706-2767
http://www.battery-biz-br.com/

Distributes batteries for desktops, laptops, and notebooks, as well as for UPS
systems and utility meters

Black Box Corporation

1000 Park Drive
Lawrence, PA 15055
(412) 873-6564

http://www.blackbox.com

Networking and data communication
products

BNF Enterprises

134R Rt.1 South Newbury St.
Peabody, MA 01960
(508) 536-2000
fax (508) 536-7400
http://www.bnfe.com

Bulldog Computer Products

851 Commerce Court
Buffalo Grove, IL 60089
(800) 438-6039, (847) 541-2394
fax (847) 541-6988

Cable Connection

102 Cooper Ct.
Los Gatos, CA 95030
(408) 395-6700

Manufacturer of cable products and
interconnect accessories

Cables America

(800) 348-USA4
fax (800) FAX-USA4

Cables To Go

1501 Webster Street
Dayton, OH 45404
(937) 224-8646, (800) 826-7904
fax (937) 496-2666, (800) 331-2841
http://www.cablestogo.com/

Cables, test equipment, toolkits

CAD & Graphics Warehouse

8515-D Freeway Drive
Macedonia, OH 44056
(216) 487-0485

CAD Warehouse

1939 East Aurora Road
Twinsburg, OH 44087
(216) 487-0485
http://www.cadwarehouse.com

Century Microelectronics, Inc.

4800 Great America Parkway, Suite 308
Santa Clara, CA 95054
(408) 748-7788
http://www.century-micro.com/

Memory upgrades, with products ranging from industry-standard SIMMs and DIMMs to proprietary modules and memory cards

Chemtronics

8125 Cobb Centre Drive
Kennesaw, GA 30144
(800) 645-5244, (404) 424-4888
fax (800) 243-6003, (404) 423-0748

Ozone-safe compressed gas for cleaning inside PCs

CIRCO Technology Corporation

222 South 5th Avenue
City of Industry, CA 91746
(800) 678-1688
http://www.circotech.com

Cases, power supplies, removeable hard drive kits, motherboards

CMO Corporation

101 Reighard Avenue
Williamsport, PA 17701
(800) 417-4580, (717) 327-9200
fax (717) 327-1217
http://www.cmo.newmii.com

Compaq DirectPlus

P.O. Box 692000
Houston, TX 77269-2000
(281) 370-0670
http://www.compaq.com

CompUSA Direct

15167 Business Avenue
Addison, TX 75244
(800) COMPUSA
http://www.compusa.com

ComputAbility

P.O. Box 17882
Milwaukee, WI 53217
(800) 554-9950, (414) 357-8181
fax (414) 357-7814
http://www.computability.com

Computer City

P.O. Box 2526
Tempe, AZ 85280-2526
http://www.computercity.com

Computer Discount Warehouse (CDW)

1020 East Lake Cook Road
Buffalo Grove, IL 60089
(800) 726-4239
fax (847) 465-6800

http://www.cdw.com

Computers, parts, memory, monitors, printers

Computer Gate International

2960 Gordon Avenue
Santa Clara, CA 95051
(408) 730-0673
fax (408) 730-0735
email: cgate@aimnet.com
http://www.computergate.com

Testers, cleaning products, cables, switches, computer assembly products

Computer Parts Outlet, Inc.

33 S.E. First Avenue
Delray Beach, FL 33444
(800) 475-1655

Buys all types of memory, including large or small quantities of working or non-working modules

Computer Products Corporation

1431 South Cherryvale Road
Boulder, CO 80303

Computer Things

27 Melken Court
Baltimore, MD 21236-3011
(410) 661-8613
http://www.computerthings.com

Inkjet printer supplies

Computers Direct

3613 Lafayette Road
Portsmouth, NH 03801

CompuWorld

24441 Miles Road
Cleveland, OH 44128
(800) 666-6294, (216) 595-6500
fax (216) 595-6565
http://www.compuworld.com

Core Components

9728 Alburtis Avenue
Santa Fe Springs, CA 90670
(888) 267-3266, (310) 654-2866
fax (310) 801-5630

Motherboards, controllers, video boards, memory

Corporate Raider

1449 39th Street
Brooklyn, NY 11218
(718) 453-3555

Dalco Electronics

275 S. Pioneer Boulevard
P.O. Box 550
Springboro, OH 45066
(800) 445-5342, (513) 743-8042
fax (513) 743-9251
BBS (513) 743-2244
CompuServe: GO DA
http://www.dalco.com

Data Impressions

13180 Paramount Blvd
South Gate, CA 90670
(310) 630-8788
fax (310) 634-5033
http://www.di-wave.com

Computer supplies, printer supplies

DataVision

445 Fifth Avenue
New York, NY 10016
(800) 771-7466
http://www.datavis.com

Computers and multimedia
components

DC Drives

1110 NASA Road One, Suite 304
Nassau Bay, TX 77058
(800) 473-0960, (713) 333-9602

Dee One Systems

1550 Centre Point Drive
Milpitas, CA 95035
(408) 262-8938

DellWare Direct

2214 West Baker Lane, Building 3
Austin, TX 78758-4053

Digital Micro, Inc.

901 S. Fremont Avenue, Suite 118
Alhambra, CA 91803

Diskette Connection

P.O. Box 1674
Bethany, OK 73008
(800) 654-4058, (405) 789-0888
fax (405) 495-4598

Disks, tapes, drive cleaning kits

Diskettes Unlimited

6206 Long Drive
Houston, TX 77087

(713) 643-9939
fax (713) 643-2722

Disks

DTP & Graphics

1175 Chess Drive, Suite C
Foster City, CA 94404
(415) 387-9945

Edmund Scientific Corporation

101 E. Gloucester Pike
Barrington, NJ 08007
(609) 573-6250
fax (609) 573-6295

Dual Function Digital Lab Thermometer

ELEK-TEK

7350 North Linder Avenue
Skokie, IL 60077
(800) 395-1000, (708) 677-7660

Envisions Solutions Technology, Inc.

47400 Seabridge Drive
Fremont, CA 94538
(800) 365-SCAN, (510) 661-4357
fax (510) 438-6709
http://www.envisions.com

Scanners, printers, graphics/OCR
software

Expert Computers

2495 Walden Avenue
Buffalo, NY 14225
(716) 681-8612

FairFax

145 West 45th Street, Suite 1010
New York, NY 10036
(800) 932-4732, (212) 768-8300

First Computer Systems, Inc.

6000 Live Oak Parkway, Suite 107
Norcross, GA 30093
(800) 325-1911, (770) 441-1911
fax (770) 441-1856
email: sales@fcsnet.com
http://www.fcsnet.com

Motherboards, computers, peripherals

First Source International

7 Journey
Aliso Viejo, CA 92656
(800) 348-9866, (714) 448-7750
fax (714) 448-7760
email: sales@firstsource.com
http://www.firstsource.com

Fry's Electronics

600 E Brokaw Rd
San Jose, CA 95112
(408) 487-4500

Galaxy Computers, Inc.

423 South Lyndhaven Road, Suite 109
Virginia Beach, VA 23452
(814) 486-8389
http://www.galaxyusa.com/

Motherboards

GIFI Inc.

20814 Aurora Road
Cleveland, OH 44146

(216) 662-1910
http://www.gifi.com

Global Computer Supplies

2318 East Del Amo Boulevard, dept. 73
Compton, CA 90220
(800) 829-0785, (800) 227-1246
fax (516) 625-6683

Global MicroXperts

6230 Cochran Road
Solon, OH 44139
(800) 676-0311, (216) 498-3330
http://www.microx.com

Graphics Warehouse

8515 Freeway Drive, unit C & D
Macedonia, OH 44087
(216) 487-0485

Harmony Computers

1801 Flatbush Avenue
Brooklyn, NY 11210
(800) 441-1144, (718) 692-3232
http://www.shopharmony.com/

Hartford Computer Group, Inc.

1610 Colonial Parkway
Inverness, IL 60067
(800) 617-4424, (847) 934-3380
fax (847) 934-9724
http://www.awa.com/hartford

HDSS Computer Products

2225 El Camino Real
Santa Clara, CA 95050

Hi-Tech Component Distributers, Inc.

59 S. La Patera Lane
Goleta, CA 93117
(800) 406-1275, (805) 967-7971
fax (805) 681-9971

Hi-Tech USA

1582 Centre Pointe Drive
Milpitas, CA 95035
(800) 831-2888, (408) 262-8688,
(408) 956-8285
fax (408) 262-8772
BBS (408) 956-8243

HyperData Direct

809 South Lemon Avenue
Walnut, CA 91789
(800) 786-3343, (800) 380-1899,
(909) 468-2933
fax (909) 468-2954
BBS (909) 594-3645
http://www.hyperbook.com

Laptops, accessories

Insight Computers

6820 South Harl Ave.
Tempe, AZ 85283
(602) 902-1176
http://www.insight.com

InterPro Microsystems, Inc.

46560 Fremont Boulevard, Suite 417
Fremont, CA 94538

(800) 226-7216, (510) 226-7226
fax (510) 226-7219
http://www.interpromicro.com

Jade Computer

18503 Hawthorne Boulevard
Torrance, CA 90504
(800) 421-5500, (310) 370-7474
fax (310) 371-4288

Parts and peripherals

Jinco Computers

5122 Walnut Grove Avenue
San Gabriel, CA 91776
(800) 253-2531, (818) 309-1108
fax (818) 309-1107
email: jinco@wavenet.com
http://www.jinco.com

Cases and power supplies

Kahlon, Inc.

22699 Old Canal Road
Yorba Linda, CA 92687
(800) 317-9989, (714) 637-5060
fax (714) 637-5597
email: kahlonmem@aol.com

IBM and Compaq parts and memory

Kenosha Computer Center

2133 91st Street
Kenosha, WI 53143
(800) 255-2989, (414) 697-9595
fax (414) 697-0620

KREX Computers

9320 Waukegan Road
Morton Grove, IL 60053
(800) 222-KREX, (847) 967-0200
fax (847) 967-0276
http://www.trcone.com/krexcom.html

Laitron Computer

1550 Montague Expressway
San Jose, CA 95131
(408) 888-4828

Lamberth Computer Services

3837 Northdale Blvd, #113
Tampa, FA 33624
fax (800) 876-0762
email: john-lcs@intnet.net

Legend Micro

5590 Lauby Road, Suite 70B
N. Canton, OH 44720
(800) 366-6333, (33) 497-2444
fax (330) 497-3156

Motherboards and components

M.B.S.

7466 Early Drive
Mechanicsville, VA 23111
(804) 944-3808

Macro Tech Inc.

23151 Verdugo Drive, Suite 102
Laguna Hills, CA 92653
(714) 580-1822
http://www.macropc.com/

Magic PC

5400 Brookpark Road
Cleveland, OH 44129
(800) 762-4426, (216) 661-7218
fax (216) 661-2454

Motherboards, systems, components

Main Street Computer Co.

1720 Oak Street
Lakewood, NJ 08701-9885
(800) 333-9899
fax (908) 905-5731

Marine Park Computers

3126 Avenue U
Brooklyn, NY 11229
(719) 262-0163

Megacomp International, Inc.

261 N.E. 1st Street, #200
Miami, FL 33132
(888) 463-4226, (305) 372-0222
fax (305) 374-5040

Megatech Inc.

3070 Bristol Pike
Bensalem, PA 19020

Merritt Computer Products, Inc.

5565 Red Bird Center Drive, Suite 150
Dallas, TX 75237
(800) 627-7752, (214) 339-0753
fax (214) 339-1313

SafeSkin keyboard cover

Micro Assist

50 Harrison Street
Hoboken, NJ 07030
(888) 97-MICRO, (201) 459-0233
fax (201) 459-0283

Micro Time, Inc.

35375 Vokes Drive, Suite 106
Eastlake, OH 44095
(800) 834-0000, (216) 954-9640
fax (216) 954-9648

CPUs, memory, motherboards,
peripherals

Micro X-Press

5646-48 West 73rd Street
Indianapolis, IN 46278
(800) 875-9737, (317) 328-5780

MicroniX USA, Inc.

23050 Miles Road
Cleveland, OH 44128
(800) 580-0505, (216) 475-9300
fax (216) 475-6610

Motherboards, memory, and other
hardware

MicroSense, Inc.

370 Andrew Avenue
Leucadia, CA 92024
(800) 544-4252, (800) 246-7729,
(909) 688-2735
fax (619) 753-6133
email: docdrive@microsense.com
http://www.microsense.com

MicroSupply, Inc.

(800) 535-2092
http://www.microsupply.com

Midland ComputerMart

5699 West Howard
Niles, IL 60714
(800) 407-0700, (847) 967-0700
fax (847) 967-0710
email: sales@midlandcmart.com
CompuServe: 102404,327

Midwest Computer Works

180 Lexington Drive
Buffalo Grove, IL 60089
(800) 86-WORKS, (847) 459-9410
fax (847) 459-6933
http://www.mcworks.com

Midwest Micro

6910 US Route 36 East
Fletcher, OH 45326
(800) 537-1426, (513) 368-2309
fax (513) 368-2306
http://www.mwmicro.com

Midwestern Diskette

509 West Taylor
Creston, IA 50801
(800) 221-6332
fax (515) 782-4166
email: salesinfo@mddc.com
http://www.mddc.com

Bulk disks

Millenium Technologies

35 Cherry Hill Drive
Danvers, MA 01923
(800) 251-3448

Motherboards, additional components

MMI Corporation

2400 Reach Road
Williamsport, PA 17701

Motherboard Discount Center

1035 N. McQueen, Suite 123
Gilbert, AZ 85233
(800) 486-2026, (602) 813-6547
fax (602) 813-8002

Motherboards, video boards, other
hardware

Motherboard Express

333-B West State Road
Island Lake, IL 60042
(800) 560-1195, (847) 487-4639
fax (847) 487-4637
http://www.motherboardx.com

Motherboards and drives

Motherboards International (Shambis Corporation)

8361 East Evans Road, Suite 107
Scottsdale, AZ 85260
(800) 574-4000, 499-3970
(602) 596-5226
fax (602) 596-1554
http://www.motherboards.com

Motherboards & cases

Nationwide Computers Direct (NWCD)

110A McGaw Drive
Edison, NJ 08837
(800) 747-NWCD, (908) 417-4455
fax (800) 329-6923

Notebook computers, PCMCIA cards,
printers, modems, scanners

NCA Computer Products

1202 Kifer Road
Sunnyvale, CA 94086
(800) NCA-1115, (408) 522-5066
fax (800) NCA-1666

NECX Direct

4 Technology Drive
Peabody, MA 01960
(800) 961-9208
http://www.necx.com

Network Express

1720 Oak Street
P.O. Box 301
Lakewood, NJ 08701-9885
(800) 333-9899
fax (908) 905-5731
email: netexp@netline.net

Computers, peripherals, and test
equipment

Next Generation

6230 Cochran Road
Solon, OH 44139

Next International

13622 Neutron Road
Dallas, TX 75244
(800) 730-NEXT, (214) 404-8260
fax (214) 404-8263
email: next@fastlane.net

North American CAD Company

4A Hillview Drive
Barrington, IL 60010
(800) 619-2199, (847) 381-8834
fax (847) 381-7374
http://www.nacad.com

Graphics-related peripherals, including printers, monitors, video boards, digitizers, and scanners

Nova Computers, Inc.

1420 Lloyd Road
Wickliffe, OH 44492
(800) 461-5535, (216) 516-3035
fax (216) 516-3040

Computers, parts, accessories, motherboards

Odyssey Technology

5590 Lauby Road, Suite 70B
Canton, OH 44720
(800) 683-2808, (330) 497-2444
fax (330) 497-3156

PC Connection

6 Mill Street
Marlow, NH 03456
(603) 800-1111

PC Impact

(800) 853-9337, (800) 698-3820
fax (216) 487-5242

PC Importers

290 Lena Drive
Aurora, OH 44202
(800) 886-5155
fax (216) 487-5242

PC Importers

8295 Darrow Road
Twinsburg, OH 44087

PC International

290 Lena Drive
Aurora, OH 44202
(800) 458-3133
fax (216) 487-5242

Parts, systems, and components

PC Universe

2302 North Dixie Highway
Boca Raton, FL 33431
(800) 728-6483, (407) 447-0050
fax (407) 447-7549
email: sales@pcuniverse.com
http://www.pcuniverse.com

Computers, peripherals, accessories

PCL Computer, Inc.

636 Lincoln Highway
Fairless Hills, PA 19030
(215) 736-2986

Cases

PComputer Solutions

130 West 32nd Street
New York, NY 10001
(212) 629-8300

Peripherals Unlimited, Inc.

1500 Kansas Avenue, Suite 4C
Longmont, CO 80501
(303) 772-1482

Supplies computer-related hardware
and software products, specializing in
mass storage and connectivity

Power Pros, Inc.

105 Cromwell Court
Raleigh, NC 27614
(800) 788-0070, (919) 782-9210
http://www.powerpros.com

Power protectors, UPSs

Price Pointe

3 Pointe Drive
Brea, CA 92621
(800) 840-7860
fax (800) 840-7861

Computers, peripherals, and software

Publishing Perfection

P.O. Box 307, dept. CS9608
Menomonee Falls, WI 53052-0307
(800) 716-5000, (414) 252-5000
fax (414) 252-2502
email: cs9608@perfection.com

Digital cameras, scanners, multimedia
hardware

Quark Technology

5275 Naiman Parkway
Solon, OH 44139
(800) 443-8807, (216) 498-7387
fax (216) 498-8857

Quick-Line Distribution

26001 Miles Road, Unit 8
Warrensville Heights, OH 44128
(800) 808-3606, (216) 514-9800
fax (216) 514-9805

Royal Computer

1208 John Reed Court
Industry, CA 91745
(800) 486-0008, (818) 855-5077
fax (818) 330-2717

Multimedia/graphics monitors

Seattle Data Systems

746 Industry Drive
Seattle, WA 98188
(206) 575-8123
fax (206) 575-8870
email: sdsinc@seadat.com
http://www.seadat.com

Sky 1 Technologies

437 Chestnut Street
Philadelphia, PA 19106
(800) 294-5240, (215) 922-2904
fax (215) 922-6920

Motherboards, memory, drives,
peripherals

Starquest Computers

4491 Mayfield Road
Cleveland, OH 44121
(800) 945-0202, (216) 691-9966

Systems, parts, peripherals

Sunshine Computers

1240 East Newport Center Drive
Deerfield Beach, FL 33442
(305) 422-9680

Sunway Inc.

(715) 483-1179
fax (715) 483-1757

Ergonomically designed computer
accessories

Swan Technologies

3075 Research Drive
State College, MA 01680

TC Computers

P.O. Box 10428
New Orleans, LA 70181-0428
(800) 800 723-8282, (504) 733-2527
http://www.tccomputers.com

Motherboards, cases, peripherals

TDN Inc.

1000 Young Street, Suite 270
Tonawanda, NY 14150

Technological Innovations, Inc.

26 Main Street
East Haven, CT 06512
(800) 577-1970, (203) 488-7867

Technology Distribution Network

1000 Young Street, Suite 270
Tonawanda, NY 14150
(800) 420-3636, (716) 743-0195
fax (716) 743-0198

Motherboards and components

The PC Zone

15815 SE 37th Street
Bellevue, WA 98006-1800
(206) 258-2088

Tiger Software

800 Douglas, Executive Tower
Coral Gables, FL 33134

Top Data

574 Wedell Drive, #5
Sunnydale, CA 94089
(800) 888-3318, (408) 734-9100

Tri-State Computers

650 6th Avenue
New York, NY 10011
(800) 433-5199, (212) 633-2530
fax (212) 633-7718

USA Flex

444 Scott Drive
Bloomingdale, IL 60108
(800) 944-5599, (708) 582-6206
fax (708) 351-7204

Vektron

2100 N. Highway 360, Suite 1904
Grand Prairie, TX 75050
(800) 725-0009
http://www.vektron.com

Older PC Repair and Exchange

For those of you with older PCs, there are vendors who will repair and/or exchange parts for these PCs. Many vendors will not service all brands, so call to confirm that the vendor actually services your specific model of hard drive, motherboard, floppy drive, etc., before sending it off. Typically, vendors will not exchange damaged parts (i.e., the board is in two pieces or is water or fire damaged).

Computer Commodity, Inc.

1405 SW 6th Court, Suite B
Pompano Beach, FL 33069
(305) 942-6616
fax (305) 946-7815
email: computer@gate.net
www.commodityinc.com

A full service dealer/broker/distributor of new, used and refurbished computer hardware

Computer Recycle Center, Inc.

303 East Pipeline
Bedford, TX 76022
(817) 282-1622
fax (817) 282-5944
email: bert@recycles.com
http://www.recycles.com/

A world wide trading site and recycling center for used and surplus computer equipment and materials; provides upgrades for users of older equipment

Computer Recycler

670 West 17th Street
Costa Mesa, CA
(714) 645-4022
email: maurer44@wdc.net
http://www.computerrecycler.com/

Buyer, seller, and trader of new and preowned Mac and PC equipment

Computer Recyclers

4119 Lindberg Road
Addison, TX 75244
(214) 774-0366
fax (214) 774-1161
http://www.comp-recycle.com

CPAC (Computers, Parts, and Commodities)

22349 La Palma Ave, #114
Yorba Linda, CA 92687
(800)778-2722, (714) 692-5044
fax (714) 692-6680
email: cpac@wavenet.com
http://remarketing.com/broker_
html/cpac/

Crocodile Computers

240 West 73rd Street
New York, NY 10021
(212) 769-3400
http://www.crocs.com/

DakTech

4025 9th Ave. SW
Fargo, ND 58103
(800) 325-3238, (717) 795-9544
fax (717) 795-9420

email: daktech@ix.netcom.com
http://www.gndi.com/shwcs/
daktech.htm
Specializing in IBM and COMPAQ parts

Data Exchange Corporation

3600 Via Pescador
Camarillo, CA 93012
(800) 237-7911, (805) 388-1711
fax (805) 482-4856
http://www.dex.com/dexhome/

A leading full-service company specializing in contract manufacturing, end-of-life support, depot repair, logistics services and worldwide inventory management services for all high-technology industries; has an extensive inventory of spare parts for sale

Eritech International, Inc.

(800) 808-6242, (818) 244-6242
fax (818) 500-7699

Buyers of old CPUs and memory

NIE International

3000 E. Chambers
Phoenix, AZ 85040
(602) 470-1500
fax (602) 470-1540
email: nie@nieint.com
http://www.nieint.com/

A leading supplier of micro-computer parts and systems to companies that maintain and support PC installations

Northstar

7101 31st Avenue North
Minneapolis, MN 55427
(800) 969-0009, (612) 591-0009
fax (612) 591-0029
http://www.northstar-mn.com/

A complete PC repair service

Oak Park Personal Computers

130 South Oak Park Avenue, Suite #2
Oak Park, IL 60302
(708) 848-1553
fax (708) 524-9791
email: mlund@oppc.com
http://www.oppc.com/

OnLine Computing

3550-L SW 34th Street
Gainesville, FL 32608
(352) 372-1712
fax (352) 335-8192
email: online@gnv.fdt.net

The Used Computer Marketplace

(part of the Affiliated ReMarketing Web)
http://www.remarketing.com

A place where you can list for-sale or wanted items for free in their confidential classifieds, which are then accessed by subscribing dealers

United Computer Exchange

2110 Powers Ferry Road, Suite 307
Atlanta, GA 30339

(800) 755-3033, (770) 612-1205
fax (770) 612-1239
fax info line (770) 955-0569
email: united@uce.com
CompuServe: 73312,1224
America Online: UnCoEx
info on demand: uce-info@uce.com
http://www.uce.com/

A global clearinghouse for buyers and sellers of new and used microcomputer equipment

Computer Recycling Centers

After upgrading your PC, you might prefer to donate the older parts to needy organizations rather than sell them. Here are some organizations that help with the redistribution:

Computer Re-use Network (CoRN)

P.O. Box 1078
Hollywood, SC 29449
(803) 889-8247
email: corn2000@juno.com
http://www.awod.com/gallery/probono/corn/

Computer Recycling Project, Inc.

http://www.wco.com/~dale/list.html
email: dale@wco.com

A listing of additional organizations that deal with accepting old computers and funnelling them to nonprofit groups/individuals in need

Lazarus Foundation, Inc.

East Coast:
10378 Eclipse Way
Columbia, MD 21044
Donald Bard, President
(410) 740-0735
email: lazaruspc@aol.com
West Coast:
30 West Mission Street, #4
Santa Barbara, CA 93101
Kenneth M. Wyrick, Western Regional Director
(805) 563-1009
email: Recycle@west.net

This is a computer recycling center that accepts donated computers which they, in turn, refurbish. These computers are then donated to individuals, schools, and other non-profit organizations.

APPENDIX
B

A Short Overview on Reading Hexadecimal

Throughout this book, and in other technical publications, you see numbers expressed not in *decimal*, the numeric system that we're all accustomed to, but rather in *hexadecimal*, a somewhat different system. This appendix is a quick guide to what you need to know about hexadecimal.

The decimal system is based on the number 10 as we know it—the number of fingers on most people's hands. *Dec-*, a word root, permeates the language: *decathlon* refers to a contest with 10 sporting events, *decimate* literally means to kill every 10th man, and *December* is the name of what once was the 10th month. We write "ten" as "10," but that's really only correct if we base the numbering system on 10. Strictly speaking, the number that I wrote is "one zero," and it means different things in different number systems.

Look at the sequence of how we write the first 11 numbers: 0, 1, 2, 3, 4, 5, 6, 7, 8, 9, 10. Why is "ten" written with two digits, not with one digit, as with all the numbers before? Because the system is based on 10. So ten is written 10, pretty much by definition once you decide that you're using 10 as your number base. Next, look at 10 times 10, or 100: it is written 100—the first number with three digits. Ditto for the first number with four digits—1000, which is 10 times 10 times 10. Why'd we pick 10 as a basis for a number system? No one knows, but the obvious guess is that 10 is, again, the number of fingers that most people have.

For reasons that aren't really worth pursuing here, it's easiest to talk about numbers in a computer system (memory or I/O addresses, for example) not in a number system based on 10, but rather on 8 or 16. A base-8 system is called *octal*, and a base-16 system is called *hexadecimal*, or *hex* for short. PCs tend to use hex, so I'll discuss that here. You don't even have to know hex in its entirety, just a few salient points.

Counting in Hex

Recall that a base-10 system uses ten single-digit numbers up to, but not including, the number 10 (0-9). A base-16 system, similarly, has sixteen single-digit numbers up to, but not including, 16 (0-9 and A-F). You can see a base-16 system in Table B.1.

TABLE B.1: Hex Digits and Decimal Equivalents

Hex Digit	Decimal Value
0	0
1	1
2	2
3	3
4	4
5	5
6	6
7	7
8	8
9	9
A	10
B	11
C	12
D	13
E	14
F	15
10	16

As you can see, the next number after F is 10, (which is 16 in decimal), then 11 (which is 17 in decimal). With any numbering system, you count from 0 to the highest number in the system, and then you go to 10. In decimal, the two-digit numbers increase up to 99, the last two-digit number. Hex goes up to FF. One hundred in hex is not 10 times 10, but 16 times 16—100 in hex, 256 in decimal.

Reading Memory Hex Addresses

You will recall that the typical PC, when running DOS, can address 1MB of memory—640K for user data and programs and 384K of reserved area for video memory, ROMs, and buffers. Let's look at how to read memory addresses in hex.

First, understand that to a computer, 1MB is a binary number equivalent to decimal 1,048,576. It's composed of sixteen 64K (65,536 decimal) *segments*. Conveniently, 10000 in hex equals 64K. And 640K is ten 64K segments, so the low 640K is the address range from 00000 to one short of A0000, or 9FFFF. All of the addresses in 64K increments are shown in Table B.2.

TABLE B.2: Memory Addresses in Decimal and Hex

Decimal Address	Hexadecimal Address	Preceding Hex Address
0K	00000	N/A
64K	10000	0FFFF
128K	20000	1FFFF
192K	30000	2FFFF

Continued on next page

TABLE B.2 CONTINUED: Memory Addresses in Decimal and Hex

Decimal Address	Hexadecimal Address	Preceding Hex Address
256K	40000	3FFFF
320K	50000	4FFFF
384K	60000	5FFFF
448K	70000	6FFFF
512K	80000	7FFFF
576K	90000	8FFFF
640K	A0000	9FFFF
704K	B0000	AFFFF
768K	C0000	BFFFF
832K	D0000	CFFFF
896K	E0000	DFFFF
960K	F0000	EFFFF
1024K	100000	FFFFF

So when you see that a VGA display adapter puts memory in addresses A0000–BFFFF, you know that the board is using the addresses starting just above 640K and going up to just short of 768K. And when you see that the BIOS ROM is addressed from FC000 to FFFFF, you know that it's using addresses right up to the top of the first megabyte.

You've endured enough theory for the moment. Right now, let's put it to good use. Here are a couple of examples.

Example 1: Counting in Hex—Determining the Size of a Range

If COM1 uses I/O addresses 3F8 to 3FF, how many I/O addresses does that mean that it uses?

Count 'em up: 3F8, 3F9, 3FA (remember that A comes after 9), 3FB, 3FC, 3FD, 3FE, 3FF—eight addresses.

Example 2: Comparing Overlapping ROM Address Ranges

Let's look at a hypothetical example concerning the installation of a ScanJet interface card. When installing this card, you should be concerned that the address of the ROM on the ScanJet card doesn't conflict with the addresses of any other ROM in the system.

Now let's say that the only thing in the system with ROM is a VGA, but what is its ROM address...C0000–C5FFF. The scanner interface has a factory default of C4000–C7FFF. That would be okay for an EGA, as the EGA's ROM ends at C3FFF, just short of C4000. But the VGA's ROM, note, goes all the way up to C5FFF, which tromps all over the range C4000–C7FFF....

You may have had some trouble following it, so let's review exactly what the quandary was:

1. The factory default address for the scanner is C4000–C7FFF. Note that this is a range of values: C4001, C4002... C7FFF, and there are lots of them—16K of addresses, in fact.

2. The address range of the EGA ROM (if there were an EGA in the system) is C0000–C3FFF, and that range does not conflict with the ScanJet's range. The last value in the EGA range is C3FFF. C4000 comes after C3FFF in hex. You compare numbers in hex just like you do in decimal. If they've got the

same number of digits, just compare the left-most one. In this case, they've both got hex digits "C" in the left-most position, so there's no difference. If the leftmost are the same, look immediately to the right. The number 4 comes after 3, so C4000 is after C3FFF.

3. The address range of the VGA ROM is C0000–C5FFF, and that conflicts with the ScanJet ROM range of C4000–C7FFF. The top of the VGA ROM range is C5FFF. The bottom of the Scan-Jet ROM range is C4000, which is below C5FFF. Again, how do I know? Compare them: The C in the left-most position is the same, the 4 and 5 are different. The C5FFF, then, is above C4000—the starting point for the ScanJet ROM—and so the VGA range overlaps the ScanJet ROM range.

So we've briefly looked at how to use hex when looking at I/O address ranges and memory address ranges. If you'd like to get into the nitty-gritty details, like actually converting hex to decimal and back, read on. But you don't need to know any more.

Converting Hex to Decimal

This isn't tough, and you may also live your whole life without having to know how to do it. This is especially true since the Windows calculator can do the conversions for you if you're in a hurry. But for those of you pioneers who want to know how it's done, here's what you do.

First, look back at Table B.1. Use it to convert each of the hex digits to decimal. For example, F in hex is 15 decimal, 8 in hex is 8 decimal, and so on. For this example we'll use the hex number C801F—how do I convert it to decimal?

1. **Write the hex number on a piece of paper. Create a column labeled "Subtotal" on your paper. Put a zero in it.** We'll

work from left to right, crossing out hex digits as we convert them. Subtotal is where we'll accumulate the decimal value. So we write down C801F, and put a zero under Subtotal.

2. **Examine the hex number.** If there are no digits left, stop: Subtotal contains your converted decimal value. Otherwise, remove the leftmost digit from what remains of the hex number, convert it to decimal, and add it to the subtotal. So we remove the C and convert it to decimal—12, in this case—and add it to the subtotal. The subtotal becomes 12 for the moment. Cross out the "C" in the hex number, so we've got "801F" left.

3. **Go back to step 2.** Step 2 says to first see if there are any hex digits left. There are, so continue: Multiply the subtotal (12) by 16 so it becomes 192. Take the left-most digit—8—from the hex number, convert it to decimal (8 hex equals 8 decimal), and add it to the subtotal (192 + 8 = 200). Cross out the 8 on the hex number, leaving 01F.

- Hex digits remain, so back to step 2 again. Subtotal times 16 makes the subtotal equal to 3200 (200 × 16). The next hex digit is 0; subtotal plus zero leaves it unchanged. Cross out the 0 on the hex number, leaving 1F.

- The subtotal times 16 is 51,200 (3200 × 16). The next hex digit is 1, which equals 1 decimal. Add it to the subtotal, making the subtotal 51,201. Cross 1 from the hex number, leaving F.

- Subtotal (51,201) times 16 is 819,216. The next hex digit is F, which equals 15 decimal. Add it to the subtotal (819,216 + 15), and you get 819,231. Cross out F from the hex number, leaving nothing.

- There's nothing left in the hex number, so the subtotal is the desired result. C801F hex equals 819,231.

For those of you who prefer a simpler approach, open the Windows Calculator (choose Start, Programs, Accessories and Calculator). Then choose Scientific from the View menu. Make sure the Hex (hexadecimal) button is selected and enter the number you want to convert. Then click the Dec (decimal) button and the calculator will display the converted number.

Converting Decimal to Hex

This involves just about the reverse process. Let's convert 75,000 from decimal to hex.

1. **Divide the decimal number by 16. Convert the remainder to a hex digit and make that the *rightmost* hex digit.** That's the first digit in the subtotal. The number 75,000 divided by 16 yields a quotient of 4687 and a remainder of 8. Because 8 decimal is just 8 hex, the rightmost hex digit is 8.

2. **Divide the quotient by 16. Make the remainder the next hex digit—put it to the left of the Subtotal.** Dividing 4687 by 16 yields a new quotient of 292 and a remainder of 15. As 15 decimal is F hex, the next hex digit is F, so the subtotal is now F8.

3. **If the new quotient is zero, stop.** Otherwise, just keep dividing the quotient by 16 and putting the hex remainder to the left of the subtotal. Dividing 292 by 16 yields a new quotient of 18 and a remainder of 4, so 4 goes on the subtotal. It's now 4F8.

4. **Divide 18 by 16** and you get a quotient of 1 with remainder 2, so the subtotal becomes 24F8.

5. **Finally, divide 1 by 16** and you get quotient 0, remainder 1, so the subtotal is now the final total—124F8. 124F8 hex equals 75,000 decimal.

To convert decimal to hex using the Windows' Calculator, open the Scientific Calculator again. This time, make sure the Dec (decimal) button is selected and enter the number you want to convert. Then click the Hex (hexadecimal) button and the calculator will display the converted new number.

Complete Hardware Dictionary

A: In DOS, *Windows*, and *OS/2*, the identifier used for the first *floppy disk drive*; the second floppy disk is designated as drive B:, while the first *hard disk* is known as drive C:. Unless instructed differently in the ROM-BIOS settings, the *operating system* always checks drive A: for startup (or *bootstrap*) instructions before checking the hard disk, drive C:.

a-b box A switching box designed to share a *peripheral* between two or more computers. It can be switched manually or under program control.

ABIOS Acronym for Advanced Basic Input/Output System. A set of *firmware* service routines built into the IBM PS/2 series of computers that use the Micro Channel Architecture (MCA) to support *multitasking operating systems* such as *OS/2*.

accelerator board An add-in *printed circuit board* that replaces the main processor with a higher-performance processor, so you can upgrade your system without replacing monitor, case, keyboard, and so on.

Using an accelerator board can reduce up-grade costs substantially. However, there are other factors to consider, such as disk access time, in determining the overall performance of your system.

access mechanism In a *floppy* or *hard disk drive*, the component that positions the *read/write* head over the surface of the disk, so that data can be read from or written to the disk.

access time The period of time that elapses between a request for information from disk or *memory*, and the information arriving at the requesting device. Memory access time refers to the time it takes to transfer a character from memory to or from the processor, while disk access time refers to the time it takes to place the *read/write* heads over the requested data. *RAM* may have an access time of 60 nanoseconds or less, while *hard disk* access time could be 10 milliseconds or less.

active-matrix screen An *LCD* display mechanism that uses an individual transistor to control every *pixel* on the screen. Active-matrix screens are characterized by high contrast, a wide viewing angle, vivid colors, and fast screen refresh rates, and they do not show the streaking or shadowing that is common with passive matrix LCD technology.

active partition That part of the *hard disk* containing the *operating system* to be loaded when you start or restart the computer.

You can install two different operating systems (perhaps *DOS* and *OS/2*) on your hard disk, but each must be in its own separate area, or partition. Only one partition can be active at any given time, and to change from the DOS to the non-DOS partition, you may have to use the DOS *FDISK* command.

ActiveX The name given by Microsoft to a set of object-oriented programming technologies. The main product of this technology is the ActiveX control, a piece of code that programmers can use over and over again in many different applications.

adapter A *printed circuit board* that plugs into a computer's *expansion bus* to provide added capabilities. Common adapters for the PC include display adapters, memory expansion adapters, input/output adapters that provide serial, parallel, and games ports, and other devices such as internal *modems*, *CD-ROMs*, or network interface cards. One adapter can often support several different devices; for example, an input/output adapter may support one parallel port, a games or joystick port, and several serial ports. Some PC designs incorporate many of the functions previously performed by these individual adapters on the *motherboard*.

address

1. The precise location in *memory* or on disk where a piece of information is stored. Every *byte* in memory and every *sector* on a disk has their own unique addresses.

2. To reference or manage a storage location.

address bus The electronic channel, usually from 20 to 32 separate lines wide, used to transmit the signals that specify locations in *memory*. The number of lines in the address bus determines the number of memory locations that the processor can access, as each line carries one bit of the address. An address bus of 20 lines (used in early Intel 8086/8088 processors) can access 1MB of memory, one of 24 lines (as in the Intel 80286) can access 16MB, one of 32 lines (as used by the Intel 80386, 80486, and later processors, or the Motorola 68020) can access over 4GB, and one of 36 lines (used by the Pentium II Xeon) can access up to 64GB of RAM.

advanced run-length limited encoding Abbreviated ARLL. A technique used to store information on a hard disk that increases the capacity of *run-length limited* (RLL) storage by more than 25 percent, and increases the data-transfer rate to 9 megabits per second.

AGP Short for Accelerated Graphics Port, AGP is a video specification that enhances and accelerates the display of three-dimensional objects.

algorithm A formal set of instructions that can be followed to perform a specific task, such as a mathematical formula or a set of instructions in a computer program.

Altair 8800 The first commercially successful microcomputer, based on the *Intel 8080*, introduced in 1975 by Micro Instrumentation Telemetry Systems of New Mexico. Over 10,000 were sold, mostly in kit form, and the Altair was packaged with the Microsoft MBASIC interpreter, written by Paul Allen and Bill Gates. The Altair 8800 had 256 bytes of memory, received input through a set of switches on the front panel, and displayed output on a row of LEDs.

alternating current Abbreviated AC. An electrical current that reverses its polarity or direction of flow at regular intervals. AC is usually represented by a sine wave. In the United States, domestic wall plugs provide AC at 60 hertz, or 60 cycles per second.

alt newsgroups A set of *USENET newsgroups* that often contain *articles* on controversial subjects usually considered to be outside of the mainstream.

These newsgroups were originally created to avoid the rigorous process required to create a normal USENET newsgroup. Some alt newsgroups contain valuable discussions on subjects that range from agriculture to wolves, others contain sexually-explicit material, and still others are just for fun. Not all service providers and *online services* give access to the complete set of alt newsgroups.

American National Standards Institute Abbreviated ANSI. A nonprofit organization of business and industry groups, founded in 1918, devoted to the development of voluntary standards. ANSI represents the USA on the International Standards Organization (ISO). In the PC world, ANSI committees have developed recommendations for the C programming language, as well as the *SCSI* interface and the *ANSI.SYS* device driver.

America Online One of the most popular and fastest-growing of the commercial *online services*, often abbreviated as AOL.

America Online provides a well-designed and easy-to-use service that includes a wide range of content, *e-mail* services, and basic Internet-access services. Many hardware and software vendors maintain software libraries and well-moderated technical-support *forums*, news and weather information is available through Reuters and UPI, and sports, hobbies, games, and online shopping are also available.

analog Describes any device that represents changing values by a continuously variable physical property such as voltage in a circuit, fluid pressure, liquid level, and so on.

An analog device can handle an infinite number of values within its range. By contrast, a *digital* device can only manage a fixed number of possible values. For example, an ordinary mercury thermometer is an analog device and can record an infinite number of readings over its range. A digital thermometer, on the other hand, can only display temperature in a fixed number of individual steps.

analog-to-digital converter Abbreviated ADC or A-D converter. A device that converts continuously varying *analog* signals into discrete *digital* signals or numbers by sampling the analog signal at regular intervals. Once analog signals have been converted into digital form, they can be processed, analyzed, stored, displayed and transmitted by computer. The key to analog-to-digital conversion lies in the amount of digital data created from the analog signal. The shorter the time interval between samples, and

the more data recorded from that sample, the more closely the digital signal will reproduce the original analog signal. Many modern *sound boards* can sample and playback at up to 44.1 kHz using a *16-bit* analog-to-digital converter.

anonymous ftp A method of accessing an *Internet* computer with the *ftp* (*file-transfer program*) that does not require that you have an account on the target computer system. Just log in to the Internet computer with the user name anonymous and use your *e-mail* address as your password.

anonymous posting In a *USENET newsgroup*, a public message *posted* via an anonymous *server* in order to conceal the identity of the original author. This server removes all the information from the message that could identify the sender and forwards the message to its destination. If you ever use an anonymous server, don't forget to remove your *signature* from the bottom of your posting.

anti-virus program An *application* program you run to detect or eliminate a computer *virus* or *infection*. Some anti-virus programs are *terminate-and-stay-resident* programs that can detect suspicious activity on your computer as it happens, while others must be run periodically as part of your normal housekeeping activities.

applet A small *application* program, limited in scope to one small but useful task. A calculator program or a card game might be called an applet.

AppleTalk A suite of protocols used by Apple computers to communicate with one another over a network.

application layer The seventh, or highest, layer in the International Organization for Standardization's Open Systems Interconnection (ISO/OSI) model for computer-to-computer communications. This layer uses services provided by the lower layers, but is completely insulated from the details of the *network* hardware. It describes how *application* programs interact with the *network operating system*, including *database management*, *e-mail*, and *terminal emulation* programs.

application program interface Abbreviated API. The complete set of *operating system* functions that an *application* program can use to perform tasks such as managing files and displaying information on the computer screen.

An API is a complete definition of all the operating system functions available to an application program, and it

also describes how the application program should use those functions.

In operating systems that support a *graphical user interface*, the API also defines functions to support *windows*, icons, pull-down menus, and other components of the interface.

In *network operating systems*, an API defines a standard method application programs can use to take advantage of all the network features.

application-specific integrated circuit Abbreviated ASIC. A computer chip developed for a specific purpose, designed by incorporating standard cells from a library, rather than designed from scratch. ASICs can be found in VCRs, microwave ovens, automobiles, and security alarms.

arbitration The set of rules used to manage competing demands for a computer resource, such as *memory* or *peripheral* devices, made by multiple processes or users.

Archie A system used on the *Internet* to locate files available by *anonymous ftp*. Archie was written by students and volunteers at McGill University's School of Computer Science in Montreal, Canada and is available worldwide.

Once a week, special programs connect to all the known anonymous ftp sites on the Internet and collect a complete listing of all the publicly available files. This listing is kept in an Internet Archive Database, and when you ask Archie to look for a file, only this database is searched rather than the whole Internet; you can then use anonymous ftp to retrieve the file.

architecture   The overall design and construction of all or part of a computer, particularly the processor *hardware* and the size and ordering sequence of its *bytes*. Also used to describe the overall design of *software*.

array processor   A group of special processors designed to calculate math procedures at very high speeds, often under the control of another central processor. Some computers use array processors to speed up video operations or for fast floating-point math operations.

ASCII   Pronounced "askee." Acronym for American Standard Code for Information Interchange. A standard coding scheme that assigns numeric values to letters, numbers, punctuation marks, and control characters to achieve compatibility among different computers and peripherals.

In ASCII each character is represented by a unique integer value. The values 0 to 31 are used for non-printing control codes, and the range from 32 to 127 is used to represent the letters of the alphabet and common punctuation symbols. The entire set from 0 to 127 is referred to as the standard ASCII character set. All computers that use ASCII can understand the standard ASCII character set.

The extended ASCII character set (from code 128 through code 255) is assigned variable sets of characters by computer hardware manufacturers and software developers, and is not necessarily compatible between different computers. The IBM extended character set includes mathematical symbols and characters from the PC line-drawing set.

ASCII file   A *file* that only contains text characters from the ASCII character set. An ASCII file contains letters, numbers, and punctuation symbols, but does not contain any hidden text-formatting commands. Also known as a *text file*, and ASCII text file.

Association for Computing Machinery   Abbreviated ACM. A membership organization, founded in 1947, dedicated to advancing computer science through technical education of computing professionals and through technical publications. ACM also sponsors several *special interest groups (SIGS)*.

Association of PC User Groups

Abbreviated APCUG. A nonprofit affiliation of local PC User Groups, dedicated to fostering communications between *personal-computer user groups*, and acting as an information network between user groups and software publishers and hardware manufacturers.

asynchronous transmission In communications, a method of transmission that uses *start* and *stop bits* to coordinate the flow of data so that the time intervals between individual characters do not have to be equal. *Parity* may also be used to check the accuracy of the data received.

ATA The first IBM PC had no hard disk storage capability. When the 80286-based AT was developed, it included a hard disk as a major feature, and the hard disk *controller* interface (ATA or AT Attachment) became a *de facto* industry standard from that day to this. As PCs have grown up, however, the controller interface has also evolved, and we do mean evolution rather than revolution. Everything still leads back to that original interface, in one way or another. The children of

ATA are now quite various, and the family tree currently looks like this:

- **ATA** (Advanced Technology Attachment) is the original interface and is the same as the Integrated Drive Electronics Interface (IDE) for disk drives. ATA (thus IDE) was designed as a way to integrate the controller onto the hard disk drive itself and to lower manufacturing costs, as well as making firmware implementations easier.

- **ATA-2** is an extension of ATA that was beefed up to include performance enhancing features such as fast PIO (programmed input/output) and DMA (Direct Memory Access) modes. The ATA-2 interface also got an improved Identify Drive command. This particular feature lets a hard drive tell the software exactly what its characteristics are and is the basis for both Plug and Play hard drive technology and compatibility with any new version of the standard that may come down the road in the future.

- **ATAPI** (ATA Packet Interface) is a standard that is still being worked out. It has been designed for devices such as CD-ROMs and tape drives that plug into an ordinary ATA (IDE) port. The major benefit of ATAPI hardware is that it's cheap and works on your current adapter. For CD-ROMs, ATAPI also uses fewer CPU resources than proprietary adapters, but is not otherwise any faster. For tape drives, ATAPI could potentially be both faster and more reliable than interfaces that are driven by the floppy drive controller.

• **Fast ATA** is what people are calling the technology and products that support the high-speed data transfers specified by ANSI-standardized Programmed Input/Output (PIO) Mode 3 and multi-word Direct Memory Access (DMA) Mode 1 protocols. Fast ATA enables the drive to transfer data at speeds as high as 13.3 MB/s.

• **Fast ATA-2** is like Fast ATA, but is a standard that will allow manufacturers to create products that support ANSI PIO Mode 4 and multi-word DMA Mode 2 protocols. With Fast ATA-2, we should be able to get data transfers as high as 16.6 megabytes/second.

AT command set   A set of standard instructions used to activate features on a *modem*. Originally developed by Hayes Microcomputer Products, the AT command set is now used by almost all modem manufacturers.

The code AT is short for ATtention and precedes most of the modem commands. On a Hayes or Hayes-compatible modem, the ATDP (ATtention Dial Pulse) command initiates pulse (rather than touch-tone) dialing, while the ATDT (ATtention Dial Tone) command initiates touch-tone (rather than pulse) dialing.

attenuation   In communications, the decrease in power of a signal transmitted over a wire. Attenuation is measured in *decibels* and increases as the power of the signal decreases. In a *local area network*, attenuation can become a problem when cable lengths exceed the stated network specification; however, the useful length of a cable can often be extended by the use of a *repeater*.

ATX   A type of computer case that uses a different power connector and rotates the processor 90 degrees on the motherboard, physically placing it and the slots in a different position. The ports on the motherboard (i.e., the keyboard, serial, and mouse ports) are all stacked on top of one another. An ATX motherboard will not fit in a standard case and vice versa.

A20   The A20 line is a *microprocessor address* line on Intel processors that controls access to the 64K of address space known as the *high memory area*. This is managed automatically by Windows and OS/2 operating systems; however, if you are still using DOS, then this area is managed by *HIMEM.SYS* on IBM AT and compatible computers. You specify the A20 handler you want to use on your computer with the appropriate code value for the HIMEM.SYS /MACHINE switch in *CONFIG.SYS*; the default setting for IBM ATs and compatible computers is AT or 1.

AUTOEXEC.BAT A contraction of AUTOmatically EXECuted BATch. A special DOS batch file, located in the *root* directory of older DOS systems that would run automatically every time the system was booted up or rebooted.

B: In *DOS, Windows,* and *OS/2*, the identifier used for the second floppy disk drive; the first floppy disk is designated as drive *A:*, while the first hard disk is known as drive *C:*.

backbone In communications, that portion of the network that manages the bulk of the *traffic*. The backbone may connect several different locations or buildings, and may also connect to other, smaller networks.

back-end processor A secondary processor that performs one specialized task very effectively, freeing the main processor for other, more important work.

background noise In communications, any unwanted signal that enters a line, channel, or circuit.

backplane A *printed circuit board* containing slots or sockets, into which *expansion boards* are plugged.

backup An up-to-date copy of all your *files* that you can use to reload your *hard disk* in case of an accident. It is an insurance against disk failure affecting the hundreds or possibly thousands of files you might have on your system hard disk or on your local area network hard disk.

backward-compatible Fully compatible with earlier versions of the same *application* program or computer system.

bad sector An area on a *hard disk* or *floppy disk* that cannot be used to store data, because of a manufacturing defect or accidental damage. One of the tasks an *operating system* performs is finding, marking, and isolating bad sectors. Almost all hard disks have some bad sectors, often listed in the *bad track table*, as a result of the manufacturing process, and this is not usually anything to worry about; the operating system will mark them as bad, and you will never even know that they are there. If you see these appear regularly during routine maintenance, usually running Scandisk, then you may need to consider replacing your hard drive.

bad track table A list of the defective areas on a *hard disk*, usually determined during final testing of the disk at the factory. Some disk-preparation programs ask you to enter information from this list to reduce the time that a *low-level format* takes to prepare the disk for use by an *operating system*.

bandwidth In communications, the difference between the highest and the lowest frequencies available for transmission in any given range.

In networking, the transmission capacity of a computer or a communications channel, stated in *megabits* or *megabytes per second*; the higher the number, the faster the data transmission takes place.

bank switching A method of switching between two sets (or banks) of memory in a computer, only one of which can be active at a time. Because of the overhead involved in switching between banks, memory-intensive tasks can take much longer to perform using bank-switched memory than when using contiguous memory.

batch file An ASCII text *file* containing operating system commands and possibly other commands supported by the batch processor. The commands in the file are executed one line at a time, just as if you had typed them at the system prompt. You can include program names, operating system commands, batch language commands, and other variables in your batch files. Batch files are used to automate repetitive tasks; almost all DOS users place regularly-used setup commands in a batch file called *AUTOEXEC.BAT*, which executes every time the computer is started.

A DOS batch file must have the *filename extension* .BAT, while an *OS/2* batch file has the extension .CMD.

baud A measurement of data-transmission speed. Originally used in measuring the speed of telegraph equipment, it now usually refers to the data-transmission speed of a *modem* or other *serial* device.

baud rate In communications equipment, a measurement of the number of state changes (from 0 to 1 or vice-versa) per second on an *asynchronous* communications channel.

Baud rate is often mistakenly assumed to correspond to the number of bits transmitted per second, but because in modern high-speed digital communications systems one state change can be made to represent more than 1 data bit, baud rate and *bits per second* are not always the same. A rate of 300 *baud* is likely to correspond to 300 bits per second, but at higher baud rates, the number of bits per second transmitted can be higher than the baud rate as one state change can represent more than one data bit. For example, 2400 bits per second can be sent at 1200 baud if each state change represents two bits of information.

On the PC, the *MODE* command is used to set the baud rate of a serial device, perhaps a modem or a printer. Both the sending and the receiving devices must be set to the same baud rate, and in times past, mismatched baud rates were one of the most common reasons for communications failures. These days, intelligent *modems* can lock onto one of a range of rates, and can even change rates in response to changing line conditions during the course of a transmission.

benchmark A test that attempts to quantify hardware or software performance—usually in terms of speed, reliability, or accuracy. One of the major problems in determining performance is deciding which of the many benchmarks available actually reflects how you plan to use the system. For best

results, you should evaluate performance using the same mix of *applications* and system commands that you expect to use in your day-to-day work.

Bernoulli box A high-capacity data-storage device featuring a removable cartridge, developed by Iomega Corporation.

beta software Software that has been released to a cross-section of typical users for testing before the commercial release of the package.

B-Channel Two of the three channels that comprise an ISDN line. The B-Channels (or bearer channels) are used for sending data and use 64Kb of bandwidth each. Each B-Channel can be used as a separate connection or combined to give a full 128Kb connection.

binary Any scheme that uses two different states, components, conditions or conclusions. In mathematics, the binary or base-2 numbering system uses combinations of the digits 0 and 1 to represent all values. The more familiar decimal system has a base of 10 (0–9).

Computers and other digital devices are designed to work with information (internally) in the form of binary numbers, because it is relatively simple to construct electronic circuits that generate two voltage levels ("on" and "off," corresponding to 1 and 0).

Unlike computers, people find binary numbers that consist of long strings of 0s and 1s difficult to read, so most people who work at this level use *hexadecimal* (base-16) numbers instead.

binary-coded decimal Abbreviated BCD. A simple system for converting decimal numbers into *binary* form, where each decimal digit is converted into binary and then stored as a single character.

In binary numbers, the largest value that can be stored in a single *8-bit byte* is 255, and this obviously represents a severe limitation to storing larger numbers. BCD is a way around this limitation that stays within the 8-bit storage format. For example, the decimal number 756 can be broken down so that the numbers 7, 5, and 6 are represented by one byte each. In BCD, each decimal digit occupies a byte, so three bytes are needed for a three-digit decimal number. There is no limit to the size of the stored number; as the number increases in size, so does the amount of storage space set aside to hold it.

BIOS Acronym for basic input/output system, pronounced "bye-os." In the PC, a set of instructions, stored in read-only memory (ROM), that let your computer's hardware and operating system communicate with *application programs* and peripheral devices such as hard disks, printers, and video adapters. These instructions are stored in non-volatile memory as a permanent part of your computer. They are always available at specific addresses in memory, so all programs can access them to perform their basic input and output functions.

IBM computers contain a copyrighted BIOS that only their computers can use; however, other companies such as *Phoenix*, *Award*, and *American Megatrends* have developed BIOSs for other manufacturer's computers that *emulate* or mimic the IBM instructions without using the same code. If you use a non-IBM computer, the BIOS company's copyright message and BIOS version number are displayed every time you turn on your computer.

BIOS extensions In the PC, extensions to the main *BIOS* (basic input/output system) that enable the computer to work with add-on devices such as hard disk controllers and EGA or VGA adapters. The *ROM* chips containing these extensions do not have to be located on the *motherboard*; they can also be on *expansion boards* plugged into the *expansion bus*. Any BIOS extensions needed to run these expansion boards are loaded automatically when you *boot* your computer.

BIOS parameter block   Abbreviated BPB. In the PC, a part of the *boot record* contained on every formatted disk that contains information about the disk's physical characteristics. This information includes the version number of the operating system used to format the disk, the number of bytes per sector, the number of sectors per cluster, per track, and per disk, and is provided for use by *device drivers*.

bit   Contraction of BInary digiT. A bit is the basic unit of information in the *binary* numbering system, representing either 0 (for off) or 1 (for on). Bits can be grouped together to make up larger storage units, the most common being the 8-bit *byte*. A byte can represent all kinds of information including the letters of the alphabet, the numbers 0 through 9, and common punctuation symbols.

bit-mapped font   A set of characters in a specific style and size, in which each character is defined by a pattern of dots. The computer must keep a complete set of bitmaps for every font you use on your system, and these bitmaps

can consume large amounts of disk space.

bit-mapped graphic   A graphic, created using a *paint program* like Mac-Paint or PC Paintbrush, composed of a series of dots, or *pixels*, rather than a set of lines or vectors. Resizing a bit-mapped image without distortion or *aliasing* is very difficult, and bit-mapped graphics consume large amounts of disk and memory space. Color bit-mapped graphics often require many times the amount of control information that a monochrome bit-map needs. *Scanners* and screen-capture programs may also produce bit-mapped images.

bits per inch   Abbreviated bpi. The number of *bits* (binary digits) that a tape or disk can store per inch of length.

bits per second   Abbreviated bps. The number of binary digits, or bits, transmitted every second during a data transfer. A measurement of the speed of operation of equipment such as a computer's data bus, or a modem connecting a computer to a transmission line.

BNC connector   A small connector with a half-turn locking shell used with coaxial cable.

boot The loading of an operating system into memory, usually from a hard disk, although occasionally from a floppy disk. This is an automatic procedure begun when you first turn on or reset your computer. A set of instructions contained in ROM begin executing, first running a series of power-on self tests (POST) to check that devices such as hard disks are in working order, then locating and loading the operating system, and finally, passing control of the computer over to that operating system.

The term is supposed to be derived from the expression "pulling yourself up by your own bootstraps."

bootable disk Any disk capable of loading and starting the operating system, although most often used when referring to a floppy disk. In these days of larger and larger operating systems, it is less common to boot from a floppy disk. In some cases, all of the files needed to start the operating system will not fit on a single floppy disk, which makes it impossible to boot from a floppy.

boot record That part of a formatted disk containing the operating system loading program, along with other basic information needed by the computer when it starts running.

bridge A device working at the data-link layer of the Open Systems Interconnect model used to connect local area networks to each other, thus forming one larger network. A limitation of bridges is that they rely heavily on broadcast traffic, meaning that all traffic goes to all computers on all networks connected by a bridge.

broadband network In communications, a technique for transmitting a large amount of information, including voice, data, and video, over long distances.

The transmission capacity is divided into several distinct channels that can be used concurrently, normally by using *frequency-division multiplexing*, and these individual channels are protected from each other by guard channels of unused frequencies. A broadband network can operate at speeds of up to 20 megabits per second and is based on the same technology used by cable television.

brouter In networking, a device that combines the attributes of a *bridge* and a *router*. A brouter can route one or more specific protocols, such as *TCP/IP*, and bridge all others.

brownout A short period of low voltage often caused by an unusually heavy demand for power. A brownout may cause your computer to crash, and if your area experiences frequent brownouts, you should consider purchasing an *uninterruptable power supply* (UPS).

browser

1. An application program used to explore *Internet* resources. A browser lets you wander from node to node without concern for the technical details of the links between the nodes or the specific methods used to access them, and presents the information—text, graphics, sound, or video—as a document on the screen.

2. In networking, a service that keeps a list of all available resources on a network and disseminates that list to clients.

buffer An area of memory set aside for temporary storage of data, often until some external event completes. Many peripherals, such as printers, have their own buffers. The computer transfers the data for printing from memory into the buffer, and the printer then processes that data directly from the buffer, freeing the computer for other tasks.

bug A logical or programming error in hardware or software that causes a malfunction of some sort. If the problem is in software, it can be fixed by changes to the program. If the fault is in hardware, new circuits must be designed and constructed. Some bugs are fatal and cause the program to hang or cause data loss, others are just annoying, and many are never even noticed. The term apparently originates from the days of the first electro-mechanical computers, when a problem was traced to a moth caught between two contacts inside the machinery.

bug-fix A release of hardware or software that corrects known *bugs* but does not contain additional new features. Such releases are usually designated only by an increase in the decimal portion of the *version number*; for example, the revision level may advance from 2.0 to 2.01 or 2.1, rather than from 2.0 to 3.0.

bulletin board system Abbreviated BBS. A computer system, equipped with one or more modems, acting as a message-passing system or centralized information source, usually for a particular special interest group. Bulletin board systems are often established by software vendors and by different PC *user groups*. For the most part, BBS has been replaced by the World Wide Web.

bus An electronic pathway along which signals are sent from one part of a computer to another. In the PC, several buses are available:

- ISA
- EISA
- VL bus
- PCI

Because you may want to add a new function to your computer, most PC buses allow for this through one or more *expansion slots*; when you plug an *expansion board* into an expansion slot, you are actually plugging the board into the bus and making it part of the system.

bus mastering A technique that allows certain advanced bus architectures to delegate control of data transfers between the central processing unit (CPU) and associated peripheral devices to an add-in board. This gives greater system bus access and higher data-transfer rates than conventional systems.

More modern buses such as *MCA*, *EISA*, *VL bus*, and *PCI* all support some form of bus mastering, but older systems such as *ISA* do not.

bus mouse A *mouse* connected to the computer using an *expansion board*

plugged into an *expansion slot*, instead of simply connected to a serial port as in the case of a *serial mouse*.

byte Contraction of BinarY digiT Eight. A group of 8 bits that in computer storage terms usually holds a single character, such as a number, letter, or other symbol.

Because bytes represent a very small amount of storage, they are usually grouped into *kilobytes* (1,024 bytes), *megabytes* (1,048,576 bytes), or even *gigabytes* (1,073,741,824 bytes) for convenience when describing hard disk capacity or computer memory size.

bytes per inch Abbreviated bpi. The number of *bytes* that a tape or disk can store per inch of length.

C: In the PC, the drive designation for the first *hard disk*.

cache Pronounced "cash." A special area of memory, managed by a *cache controller*, that improves performance by storing the contents of frequently accessed memory locations and their addresses. When the processor references a memory address, the cache checks to see if it holds that address. If it does, the information is passed directly to the processor; if not, a normal memory access takes place instead.

A cache can speed up operations in a computer whose RAM access is slow compared with its processor speed, because the cache memory is always faster than normal RAM.

cache controller   Pronounced "cash controller." A special-purpose processor, such as the Intel 82385, whose sole task is to manage *cache memory*. On newer processors, such as the *Intel Pentium*, cache management is integrated directly into the processor.

cache memory   Pronounced "cash memory." A relatively small section of very fast memory (often *static RAM*) reserved for the temporary storage of the data or instructions likely to be needed next by the processor. For example, the *Intel Pentium II* has a 16K code cache as well as a 16K data cache built into the processor.

caddy   A flat plastic container used to load a *compact disc* into older *CD-ROM drives*.

Canon engine   The combination of laser mechanism and toner cartridge, first produced by Canon, used as the heart of Hewlett-Packard's popular line of laser printers.

card   A *printed circuit board* or *adapter* that you plug into your computer to add

support for a specific piece of *hardware* not normally present on the computer.

cardcage   An enclosure designed to hold *printed circuit boards* or *cards*. Most PCs have an area with edge connectors and mounting plates designed to receive *expansion boards*. The term originally referred to an external box that held rack-mounted cards.

card services   Part of the software support needed for *PCMCIA* hardware devices in a *portable computer*, controlling the use of system *interrupts, memory,* or power management.

When an application wants to access a *PC Card*, it always goes through the card services software and never communicates directly with the underlying hardware. For example, if you use a PCMCIA modem, card services establishes which communications port and which interrupts and I/O addresses are in use, not the applications program.

carpal-tunnel syndrome   A form of wrist injury caused by holding the hands in an awkward position for long periods of time. A narrow tunnel in the wrist—the carpal tunnel—contains tendons and the median nerve, which conducts sensation from the thumb, index, and middle fingers and parts of the hand up the arm to the central nervous system. Burning sensations and tingling occur when the median nerve is compressed as it passes through the narrow tunnel of bone and ligature at the wrist. Keyboard operators, musicians, dental hygienists, meat packers, and other workers who perform repetitive motions for long periods of time may be prone to this sort of injury. Improvements in the work environment, more frequent breaks, and even job modification can all help alleviate this problem, which is costing industry $805 million each year, according to National Institute for Occupational Health figures.

carrier signal In communications, a signal of chosen frequency generated to carry data, often used for long-distance transmissions. The data is added to this carrier signal by *modulation*, and decoded on the receiving end by *demodulation*.

CBIOS Acronym for Compatibility Basic Input/Output System. Firmware service routines built into the IBM PS/2 series of computers with the Micro Channel Architecture (MCA), generally considered to be a super-set of the original IBM PC BIOS.

CCITT Acronym for Comité Consultatif Internationale de Téléphonie et de Télégraphie. An organization, based in Geneva, that develops world-wide data communications standards. CCITT is part of the ITU (International Telecommunications Union).

Three main sets of standards have been established: *CCITT Groups 1–4* standards apply to facsimile transmissions; the *CCITT V series* of standards apply to modems and error detection and correction methods; and the *CCITT X series* standards apply to local area networks. Recently, the trend has been to refer to these standards as ITU standards rather than CCITT standards; you will see both.

Recommendations are published every four years, and each update is identified by the color of its cover; the 1988 edition was known as the Blue Book, and the 1996 version has green covers.

CCITT Groups 1–4 A set of four *CCITT*-recommended standards for facsimile transmissions.

Groups 1 and 2 defined analog facsimile transmissions and are no longer used. Groups 3 and 4 describe digital systems, as follows:

• **Group 3** specifies a 9600 bps modem to transmit standard images of 203 dots per inch (dpi) horizontally by 98 dpi vertically in standard mode, and 203 dpi by 198 dpi in fine mode.

• **Group** 4 supports images up to 400 dpi for high-speed transmission over a digital data network like *ISDN*, rather than a dial-up telephone line.

CCITT V Series A set of recommended standards for data communications over a telephone line, including transmission speeds and operational modes, issued by *CCITT*.

CCITT X Series A set of recommended standards issued by *CCITT* to standardize protocols and equipment used in public and private computer networks, including the transmission speeds, the interfaces to and between networks, and the operation of user *hardware*.

CD-I Acronym for Compact Disc-Interactive, pronounced "see-dee-eye." This older *hardware* and *software* standard disk format encompasses data, text, audio, still video images, and animated graphics. The standard also defines methods of encoding and decoding compressed data, as well as displaying data.

CD-R Abbreviation for CD Recordable. A type of CD device that brings *CD-ROM* publishing into the realm of the small business or home office. From a functional point of view, a CD-R and a CD-ROM are identical; you can read CD-R disks using almost any CD-ROM

drive, although the processes that create the disks are slightly different. Low-cost CD-R drives are available from many manufacturers, including Kao, Kodak, Mitsui, Phillips, Ricoh, Sony, TDK, 3M, and Verbatim.

CD-ROM Acronym for Compact Disc—Read-Only Memory, pronounced "see-dee-rom." A high-capacity, optical storage device that uses *compact disc* technology to store large amounts of information, up to 650MB (the equivalent of approximately 300,000 pages of text), on a single 4.72" disk.

A CD-ROM uses the *constant linear velocity* encoding scheme to store information in a single, spiral track, divided into many equal-length segments. To read data, the *CD-ROM disk drive* must increase the rotational speed as the read head gets closer to the center of the disk, and decrease as the head moves back out. Typical CD-ROM data access times are much slower than *hard disk* data access times.

CD-ROM drive A disk device that uses *compact disc* technology for information storage. CD-ROM drives designed for computer use are much more expensive than audio CD players; this is because CD-ROM drives are manufactured to much higher tolerances. If a CD player misreads a small amount of data, the human ear will probably not detect the difference; if a CD-ROM drive misreads a few bytes of a program, the program simply will not run. Many CD-ROM drives also have headphone jacks, external speaker jacks, and a volume control because they can also read audio CD disks. CD-ROM drives come in a variety of transfer speeds from the most common 32× up to 50× used in large networks. The two most popular CD-ROM drive interface cards are IDE/EIDEand SCSI. Other CD-ROM drives may use the computer's *parallel port* or a *PCMCIA* connection.

CD-ROM Extended Architecture

Abbreviated CD-ROM/XA. An extension to the *CD-ROM* format, developed by Microsoft, Phillips, and Sony, that allows for the storage of audio and visual information on compact disc, so that you can play the audio at the same time you view the visual data.

CD-ROM/XA is compatible with the *High Sierra specification* also known as ISO standard 9660.

Celeron The Intel Celeron processor is a *Pentium II* processor with the L2 *cache* shut off, access only to a 66 MHz systems *bus*, and a *clock speed* of 266 to 300 MHz. It is specifically designed for the sub $1200 PC range and for users who do not require the high performance of the Pentium II.

central processing unit Abbreviated CPU. The computing and control part of the computer. The CPU in a *mainframe computer* may be contained on many *printed circuit boards*; the CPU in a *mini computer* may be contained on several boards; and the CPU in a PC is contained in a single extremely powerful microprocessor.

Centronics parallel interface A standard 36-pin *interface* in the PC world for the exchange of information between the PC and a *peripheral* such as a printer, originally developed by the printer manufacturer Centronics, Inc. The standard defines 8 *parallel* data lines, plus additional lines for status and control information.

CGA Acronym for Color/Graphics Adapter. A *video adapter* introduced by IBM in 1981 that provided low-resolution text and graphics. CGA provided several different text and graphics modes, including 40- or 80-column by 25 line 16-color text mode, and graphics modes of 640 horizontal *pixels* by 200 vertical pixels with 2 colors, or 320 horizontal pixels by 200 vertical pixels with 4 colors. CGA has been superseded by later video standards, including *EGA*, *VGA*, *Super-VGA*, and *XGA*.

charge-coupled device Abbreviated CCD. A special type of memory that can store patterns of changes in a sequential manner. The light-detecting circuitry contained in many still and video cameras is a CCD.

checksum   A method of providing information for error detection, usually calculated by summing a set of values.

The checksum is usually appended to the end of the data that it is calculated from, so that data and checksum can be compared. For example, *Xmodem*, the popular *file* transfer protocol, uses a 1-byte checksum calculated by adding all the *ASCII* values for all 128 data bytes, and ignoring any numerical overflow. The checksum is added to the end of the Xmodem data packet. This kind of checksum will not always detect all errors, and in later versions of the Xmodem protocol was replaced by a *cyclical redundancy check* (CRC) for more rigorous error control.

circuit   A communications channel or path between two devices capable of carrying electrical current. Also used to describe a set of components connected together to perform a specific task.

Class A certification   An *FCC* certification for computer equipment, including mainframe and mini computers destined for use in an industrial, commercial, or office setting, rather than for

personal use at home. The Class A commercial certification is less restrictive than the *Class B certification* for residential use because it assumes that most residential areas are more than 30 feet away from any commercial computer equipment.

Class B certification   An *FCC* certification for computer equipment, including PCs, laptops, and portables destined for use in the home rather than in a commercial setting. Class B levels of radio frequency interference (*RFI*) must be low enough so that they do not interfere with radio or television reception when there is more than one wall and 30 feet separating the computer from the receiver. Class B certification is more restrictive than the commercial *Class A certification*.

clock-multiplying   A mechanism used in certain chips that allows the chip to process data and instructions internally at a different speed from that used for external operations. For example, the Intel *80486DX2* operates at 50 MHz internally, but at 25 MHz externally and when communicating with other system components; this is known as clock doubling. The Intel *DX4* chip uses clock-tripling technology, and the *PowerPC* 601 can run at 1, 2, 3, or 4 times the speed of the bus.

clock speed Also known as clock rate. The internal speed of a computer or processor, normally expressed in *MHz*.

The faster the clock speed, the faster the computer will perform a specific operation, assuming the other components in the system, such as disk drives, can keep up with the increased speed. Current clock speeds vary with processor type. The Pentium II is capable of running at 400 MHz while the DEC Alpha RISC processor is able to run at 533 MHz.

clone *Hardware* that is identical in function to an original. Usually used in the sense of, for example, an "AT clone," a PC that uses an 80286 microprocessor and functions in the same way as an IBM PC/AT computer. Although most clones do perform as intended, minor internal differences can cause severe problems in some clones that can only be solved by the intervention of the manufacturer.

Companies have offered clones of IBM-compatible computers for many years, but Apple waited until early 1995 to announce that they too would license the Macintosh operating system and related technology to other manufacturers.

cluster The smallest unit of *hard disk* space that *DOS* can allocate to a file, consisting of one or more contiguous *sectors*. The number of sectors contained in a cluster depends on the hard disk type.

CMOS Acronym for Complementary Metal-Oxide Semiconductor, pronounced "see-moss." A type of integrated circuit used in processors and for memory. CMOS devices operate at very high speeds and use very little power, so they generate very little heat. In the PC, battery-backed CMOS is used to store operating parameters such as *hard disk* type when the computer is switched off; in the *Macintosh* PRAM performs this same function.

coaxial cable Abbreviated coax, pronounced "co-ax." A high-capacity cable used in networking. It contains an inner copper conductor surrounded by plastic insulation and an outer braided copper or foil shield. Coaxial cable is used for *broadband* and *baseband* communications networks. Coax is also used by cable television because the cable is usually free from external interference, and it permits very high transmission rates over long distances.

cold boot The computer startup process that begins when you turn on power to the computer. A cold boot might be needed if a program or the *operating system* crashes in such a way that you cannot continue. If operations are interrupted in a minor way, a *warm boot* may suffice.

color printer A general term for all printers, including *dot-matrix*, *ink-jet*, thermal-transfer, and *laser printers* that can create color as well black and white output.

command processor Also called the command interpreter. The command processor is that part of the *operating system* that displays the command prompt on the screen, interprets and executes all the commands and *file names* that you enter, and displays error messages when appropriate.

The command processor also contains the *environment*, a memory area that holds values for important system definitions or defaults that are used by the system, and which can be changed by the user.

compact disc Abbreviated CD. A non-magnetic, polished, optical disk used to store large amounts of digital information. A CD can store approximately 650 MB of information, equivalent to more than 450 *floppy disks*. This translates into approximately 300,000 pages of text or 72 minutes of music, all on a single 4.72" disk.

Digital information is stored on the compact disc as a series of microscopic pits and smooth areas (called lands) that have different reflective properties. A beam of laser light shines on the disk so that the reflections can be detected and converted into digital data.

compatibility The extent to which a given piece of *hardware* or *software* conforms to an accepted standard, regardless of the original manufacturer.

In hardware, compatibility is often expressed in terms of certain other widely accepted models, such as a computer described as IBM-compatible, or a modem as Hayes-compatible. This implies that the device will perform in every way just like the standard device.

In software, compatibility is usually described as the ability to read data file formats created by other vendors' software, or the ability to work together and share data.

complex instruction set computing Abbreviated CISC, pronounced "sisk." A processor that can recognize and execute well over 100 different *assembly-language* instructions. CISC processors can be very powerful, but there is a price for that power in terms of the number of clock cycles these instructions take to execute.

This is in contrast to *reduced instruction set computing* processors, where the number of available instructions has been cut to a minimum. RISC processors are common in *work-stations*, and can be designed to run up to 70 percent faster than CISC processors.

COM port The device name used to denote a *serial communications* port. Modems, mice, and printers are commonly connected to these ports.

composite video A method of combining all the elements of video information, including red, blue, and green components, horizontal synchronization, and vertical synchronization, into one signal. Televisions and video recorders require an *NTSC* composite-video signal.

CompuServe An online PC information service, CompuServe (a subsidiary of America Online) provides a tremendous range of information and services, including online conferences, hundreds of vendor-specific *forums*, file downloading, weather and stock market information, *e-mail* and other messaging services, and travel and entertainment information. CompuServe also offers *Internet* access, as well as access to *USENET newsgroups*.

computation bound A condition where the speed of operation of the processor actually limits the speed of program execution. The processor is limited by the number of arithmetic operations it must perform.

CONFIG.SYS In *DOS* and *OS/2*, a special *text file* containing settings that control the way that the *operating system* works. CONFIG.SYS must be located in the root directory of the default *boot* disk, normally drive C, and is read by the operating system only once as the system starts running.

Some *application* programs and *peripheral* devices require you to include special statements in CONFIG.SYS, while other commands may specify the number of disk-read buffers or open files on your system, how the *disk cache* should be configured, or load any special *device drivers* your system may need.

configuration The process of establishing your own preferred setup for an *application* program or computer system. Configuration information is usually stored in a *configuration file* so that it can be loaded automatically next time you start your computer.

configuration file A file, created by an *application* program or by the operating system, containing *configuration* information specific to your own computing environment.

Application program configuration files may have a *file-name extension* of CFG or SET; older Windows configuration files use the INI file-name extension (newer programs use the Registry). If you accidentally erase an application's configuration file, the program will return to using its default settings and so will continue to function, but these settings may not be suitable for your use.

connectivity In networking, the degree to which any given computer or *application* program can cooperate with other network components, either hardware or software, purchased from other vendors.

constant angular velocity Abbreviated CAV. An unchanging speed of rotation. *Hard disks* use a constant angular velocity encoding scheme, where the disk rotates at a constant rate. This means that *sectors* on the disk are at the maximum density along the inside *track* of the disk; as the *read/write heads* move outwards, the sectors must spread out to cover the increased track circumference, and therefore the *data transfer rate* falls off.

constant linear velocity Abbreviated CLV. A changing speed of rotation.

CD-ROM disk drives use a constant linear velocity encoding scheme to make sure that the data density remains constant. Information on a *compact disc* is stored in a single, spiral track, divided into many equal-length segments. To read the data, the CD-ROM disk drive must increase the rotational speed as the read head gets closer to the center of the disk and decrease as the head moves back out. Typical CD-ROM data access times are in the order of 0.3 to 1.5 seconds; much slower than a *hard disk*.

conventional memory The amount of memory accessible by *DOS* in PCs using an Intel processor operating in *real mode*, normally the first 640K. The Intel *8086* and *8088* processors can access 1MB of memory; the designers of the original *IBM PC* made 640KB available to the *operating system* and *application* programs, and reserved the remaining space for internal system use, the *BIOS*, and video buffers. 640KB may not seem like much memory space now, but it was 10 times the amount of memory available in other leading personal computers available at the time. Since that time, operating systems have broken through the conventional memory barrier, and we no longer need worry about configuring our systems to surpass it.

convergence The alignment of the three electron guns (one each for red, blue, and green) in a monitor that create the colors you see on the screen. When all three of the electron guns are perfectly aligned and used at full power, the result is pure white. Deviation from this alignment gives poor convergence, leading to white *pixels* showing some color at the edges and to a decrease in image sharpness and resolution.

cooperative multitasking A form of *multitasking* in which all running *applications* must work together to share system resources. *Microsoft Windows* 3.11 and lower supports cooperative multitasking by maintaining a list of the active applications and the order in which they execute. When Windows transfers control to an application, other applications cannot run until that application returns control to Windows once again. Windows' cooperative multitasking system differs from a *preemptive multitasking* system such as that used in *OS/2, Windows NT*, and Windows 95/98, where the *operating system* executes each application in turn for a specific period of time before switching to the next application, regardless of whether the applications themselves return control to the operating system.

coprocessor A secondary processor used to speed up operations by taking over a specific part of the main processor's work. The most common type of coprocessor is the math or *floating-point coprocessor*, designed to manage arithmetic calculations many times faster than the main processor.

crash An unexpected program halt, sometimes due to a hardware failure, but most often due to a software error, from which there is no recovery. You will probably have to *reboot* your computer to recover after a crash.

cross posting In *USENET*, to post the same *article* to more than one *newsgroup*. Sometimes it may make sense to post the same message to more than one newsgroup, but in general, the practice is frowned upon as it wastes network resources.

CRT Acronym for cathode-ray tube. A display device used in computer monitors and television sets. A CRT display consists of a glass vacuum tube that contains one electron gun for a monochrome display, or three (red, green, and blue) electron guns for a color display. Electron beams from these guns sweep rapidly across the inside of the screen from the upper-left to the lower-right.

The inside of the screen is coated with thousands of *phosphor* dots that glow when they are struck by the electron beam. To stop the image from flickering, the beams sweep at a rate of between 43 and 87 times per second, depending on the phosphor persistence and the scanning mode used—*interlaced* or *non-interlaced*. This is known as the *refresh rate* and is measured in Hz. The Video Electronics Standards Association (VESA) recommends a vertical refresh rate of 72 Hz, noninterlaced, at a resolution of 800-by-600 *pixels*.

cyberspace A descriptive term for the virtual geography of the online world. This term first appeared in print in William Gibson's novel *Neuromancer*, published in 1984, where it describes the online world of computers and the elements of society that use these computers.

cylinder A *hard disk* consists of two or more *platters*, each with two sides. Each side is further divided into concentric circles known as *tracks*; and all the tracks at the same concentric position on a disk are known collectively as a cylinder.

daisy-wheel printer An *impact printer* that uses a plastic or metal print mechanism with a different character on the end of each spoke of the wheel. As

the print mechanism rotates to the correct letter, a small hammer strikes the character against the ribbon, transferring the image onto the paper. Changing to a different font is a matter of changing the daisy wheel; this means that you cannot change fonts in the middle of a document as you can with a *laser printer.* Daisy-wheel printers have two main drawbacks; they are relatively slow in printing, and they can be very noisy.

data Information in a form suitable for processing by a computer, such as the *digital* representation of text, numbers, graphic images, or sounds. Strictly speaking, "data" is the plural of the Latin word "datum," meaning an item of information; but it is commonly used in both plural and singular constructions.

data area In *DOS*, that part of a *floppy disk* or *hard disk* that is available for use after the *boot record, partition table, root directory,* and *file allocation table* have been established by the *formatting* program. This area is the largest part of a disk and is where programs and *data files* are located.

data bits In asynchronous transmissions, the *bits* that actually comprise the *data;* usually seven or eight data bits make up the data word.

data compression Any method of encoding *data* so that it occupies less space than in its original form. Many different mathematical techniques can be used, but the overall purpose is to compress the data so that it can be stored, retrieved, or transmitted more efficiently. Data compression is used in facsimile and many other forms of data transmission, CD-ROM publishing, still image and video image manipulation, and *database management systems.*

data encoding scheme The method used by a *disk controller* to store digital information onto a *hard disk* or *floppy disk*. Common encoding schemes used in the PC world include *modified frequency modulation* (MFM) encoding, *run-length limited* (RLL) encoding, and *advanced run-length limited* (ARLL) encoding.

Data Encryption Standard Abbreviated DES. A standard method of encrypting and decrypting *data*, developed by the U.S. National Bureau of Standards.

DES is a block cipher that works by a combination of transposition and substitution, and was developed after years of work at IBM, rigorously tested by the National Security Agency, and finally accepted as being free of any mathematical or statistical weaknesses.

This suggests that it is impossible to break the system using statistical frequency tables or to work the algorithm backwards using standard mathematical methods. DES has remained unbroken despite years of use; it completely randomizes the information so that it is impossible to determine the encryption key even if some of the original text is known. DES is used by the federal government and most banks and money-transfer systems to protect all sensitive computer information.

data-link layer The second of seven layers of the *International Standards Organization*'s Open Systems Interconnection (ISO/OSI) model for computer-to-computer communications. The data-link layer validates the integrity of the flow of *data* from one node to another by synchronizing blocks of data, and by controlling the flow of data.

data packet In networking, a unit of information transmitted as a discrete entity from one node on the network to another. More specifically, in *packet-switching networks*, a *packet* is a transmission unit of a fixed maximum length that contains a header, a set of *data*, and error control information.

data transfer rate The speed at which a *disk drive* can transfer information from the drive to the processor, usually measured in megabits or megabytes per second. For example, a *SCSI* drive can reach a transfer rate of about 40 megabytes per second.

data type

1. The kind of *data* being stored or manipulated. In Paradox for Windows, for example, data types include numeric (numbers), *alpha*numeric (text characters), date, logical (true or false), memo (used for larger pieces of text), formatted memo, short number, currency, *OLE*, graphic, and *binary* (all other types of data). Once the data type has been specified for a *field*, it cannot be changed to another data type, and the type also determines the kind of operation that can be performed on the data. For example, you cannot perform a calculation on alphanumeric data, or separate the digits in a numeric field.

2. In programming, the data type specifies the range of values that a *variable* or *constant* can hold and how that information is stored in the computer memory. For example, the *floating-point* data type can hold a different range of values from the *integer* data type, and should be manipulated differently; and the character or *string* data type is different again.

daughter board A *printed circuit board* that attaches to another board to provide additional functions. For example, a multimedia PC *video adapter* may accept a *frame grabber* daughter board to add *freeze-frame* video processing.

DB connector Any of several types of cable connectors used for *parallel* or *serial* cables. The number following the letters DB (for data bus) indicates the number of pins that the connector usually has; a DB-25 connector can have up to 25 pins, and a DB-9 connector up to 9. In practice, not all the pins (and not all the lines in the cable) may be present in the larger connectors. If your situation demands, for example, that all 25 lines of a serial cable be present, make sure you buy the right cable. Common DB connectors include DB-9, DB-15, DB-19, DB-25, DB-37, and DB-50.

DCE Abbreviation for Data Communications Equipment. In communications, any device that connects a computer or terminal to a communications channel or public network, usually a *modem*.

D-Channel One of three separate channels that comprise an ISDN line. The D-Channel uses 16Kb of bandwidth and is used for control and signaling information.

DCI Abbreviation for Display Control Interface. A device-driver specification from Intel and Microsoft intended to speed up video playback in Microsoft Windows.

For this device driver to work, your hardware must support DCI; if it does, a Windows application can send video information directly to the screen and so bypass any holdups in the Windows *graphics device interface* (GDI).

Multimedia applications and programs that manage digital video can benefit from using DCI.

DC-2000 A quarter-inch tape mini-cartridge used in some tape backup systems with a capacity of up to 250 MB when some form of *data compression* is used.

DEC Alpha A 64-bit *microprocessor* from Digital Equipment Corporation (DEC), introduced in 1992. The Alpha is a *superscalar* design, which allows the processor to execute more than one instruction per clock cycle. The fastest Alpha runs at an incredible 533 MHz.

decibel Abbreviated dB. One tenth of a bel, a unit of measurement common in electronics that quantifies the loudness or strength of a signal.

decimal The base-10 numbering system that uses the familiar numbers 0–9.

dedicated line A communications circuit used for one specific purpose. Like the phone line in your house, your neighbors do not use the same line that is dedicated to you.

defragmentation The process of reorganizing and rewriting *files* so that they occupy one large continuous area on your hard disk rather than several smaller areas.

When a file on your hard disk is updated, especially over a long period of time, it may be written into different areas all over the disk. This *file fragmentation* can lead to significant delays in loading files, but its effect can be reversed by defragmentation. Windows 95 and 98 come with defragmentation programs and the *Norton Utilities* package contains an excellent defragmentation program.

defragmenter Any *utility* program that rewrites all the parts of a *file* into contiguous *clusters* on a hard disk. As you update your *data files* over time, they may become fragmented, or divided up into several widely-spaced pieces. This can slow down data retrieval if the problem becomes severe.

Using a defragmenter (such as the Windows 98 utility *DEFRAG*) can restore that lost performance.

demand paging A common form of *virtual memory* management where pages of information are read into memory from disk only when required by the program.

desktop In a *graphical user interface,* an on-screen version of a desktop containing *windows,* icons, and dialog boxes that represent *application* programs, *files,* and other desktop accessories. As you work, you open files, then put them away again, move items around on the desktop, and perform other day-to-day tasks. The analogy to a real desktop breaks down fairly quickly, but it is useful in understanding how the graphical user interface helps you to organize your activities.

device A general term used to describe any computer *peripheral* or *hardware* element that can send or receive *data.* For example, modems, printers, serial ports, disk drives, and monitors are all referred to as devices. Some devices may require special software, known as a *device driver,* to control or manage them.

device-dependence The requirement that a specific hardware component be present for a program to work.

Device-dependent *software* is often very difficult to move or *port* to another computer due to this reliance on specific hardware.

device driver A small program that allows a computer to communicate with and control a *device.* Each *operating system* contains a standard set of device drivers for the keyboard, the monitor, and so on, but if you add specialized *peripherals* such as a *CD-ROM disk drive,* or a *network interface card,* you will probably have to add the appropriate device driver so that the operating system knows how to manage the device. In *DOS,* device drivers are loaded by the *DEVICE* or *DEVICEHIGH* commands in *CONFIG.SYS.*

device-independence The ability to produce similar results in a wide variety of environments, without requiring the presence of specific hardware.

The *Unix operating system* and the *PostScript page-description language* are both examples of device-independence. Unix runs on a wide range of computers, from the PC to a Cray, and PostScript is used by many different printer manufacturers.

device name The name used by the *operating system* to identify a computer-system component. For example, LPT1 is the *DOS* device name for the first *parallel port.*

DHCP An acronym for Dynamic Host Configuration Protocol. On a network using the TCP/IP protocol suite, computers must have settings such as an address and default gateway to communicate. Ordinarily you would have to configure this manually at each machine, but with the Windows NT Server program DHCP or its Unix counterpart BootP, this information can be assigned to a computer automatically each time it starts.

diagnostic program A program that tests computer *hardware* and *peripherals* for correct operation. In the PC, some faults, known as "hard faults," are easy to find; the diagnostic program will diagnose them correctly every time. Others, such as memory faults, can be difficult to find; these are called "soft faults" because they do not occur every time the memory location is tested but only under very specific circumstances.

Most PCs run a simple set of system checks when the computer is first turned on; in the IBM world these tests are stored in *ROM,* and are known as the *power-on self-tests* (POST). If the POST detects an error condition, the computer will stop, and you will see an error message on the screen. AMIDiag from American Megatrends is an excellent diagnostics program.

digital Describes any device that represents values in the form of *binary* digits.

digital audio Analog sound waves stored in a digital form; each digital audio file can be decomposed into a series of samples.

digital audio tape Abbreviated DAT. A method of recording information in digital form on a small audio tape cassette, originally developed by Sony and *Hewlett-Packard.* Over a gigabyte of information can be recorded on a cassette, and so a DAT can be used as a backup media. Like all tape devices, however, DATs are relatively slow.

digital-to-analog converter Abbreviated DAC or D-A converter. A device that converts discrete digital information into a continuously varying *analog* signal.

Many modern *sound boards* can sample and play back at up to 44.1 kHz using a *16-bit* digital-to-analog converter that produces spectacular stereo sound. *Compact disc* players use a digital-to-analog converter to convert the digital signals read from the disc to the analog signal that you hear as music.

Digital Video Interactive Abbreviated DVI. A proprietary technique from

Intel Corporation used to store highly compressed, *full-motion video* information onto compact discs. DVI is usually available as a chip set, and uses a form of compression that saves only the changes between images, rather than saving each individual frame. This form of *data compression* can reduce memory requirements by a factor of 100 or more.

On a CD-ROM, DVI provides over 70 minutes of full-screen video, 2 hours of half-screen video, 40,000 medium-resolution images, or 7000 *high-resolution* images.

DIP switch A small switch used to select the operating mode of a *device*, mounted as a *dual in-line package*. DIP switches can be either sliding or rocker switches and are often grouped together for convenience. They are used on *printed circuit boards, dot-matrix printers, modems*, and other *peripherals*.

direct access storage device Abbreviated DASD, pronounced "daz-dee." A storage device such as a *hard disk*, whose *data* can be accessed directly, without having to read all the preceding data (as with a sequential device such as a tape drive).

direct current Abbreviated DC. Electrical current that travels in one direc-

tion only and does not reverse the direction of flow. The PC's *power supply* converts AC line voltage from a wall outlet into the various DC voltages that the internal components of the computer need to operate.

direct memory access Abbreviated DMA. A method of transferring information directly from a mass-storage device such as a *hard disk* or from an adapter card into *memory* (or vice versa), without the information passing through the processor. Because the processor is not involved in the transfer, direct memory access is usually very fast.

DMA transfers are controlled by a special chip known as a DMA controller; the 8237A (or its equivalent) is used in most PCs. Generally, most PCs use two of these chips to provide eight DMA channels numbered 0 through 7; only seven of these channels are available, as channel 4 is used to connect—or cascade—the two controllers together. Channels 0 through 3 are 8-bit channels, and can manage up to 64K of data in a single DMA operation; channels 5 through 7 transfer data 16 bits at a time and can manage up to 128K of data. Channel 3 is reserved for the floppy disk drive controller, and channel 5 is used by the hard-disk controller in PS/2 systems.

DirectX A set of predefined code, called an Application Programming Interface, written by Microsoft. Programmers can use it to create graphic images or other multimedia effects in their applications. It is divided into five distinct parts: DirectDraw manages two-dimensional images, Direct3D manages three-dimensional images, DirectSound coordinates sound with images, DirectPlay speeds game play, and DirectInput manages input devices such as a joystick.

disable To turn a function off or prevent something from happening. In a *graphical user interface*, disabled menu commands are often shown in gray to indicate that they are not available.

discrete component Any electronic component or *hardware device* that can be treated as a separate and distinct unit.

disk cache An area of computer memory where *data* is temporarily stored on its way to or from a disk.

When an *application* needs *data* from a hard disk, it asks the operating system to find it. The data is read and passed back to the application. Under certain circumstances, such as when updating a database, the same information may be requested and read many times over. A disk cache mediates between the application and the hard disk, and when an application asks for information from the hard disk, the cache program first checks to see if that data is already in the cache memory. If it is, the disk cache program loads the information from the cache memory rather than from the hard disk. If the information is not in memory, the cache program reads the data from the disk, copies it into the cache memory for future reference, and then passes the data to the requesting application.

A disk cache program can significantly speed up most disk operations. *DOS* contains the disk cache driver *SMART-DRV.SYS*, and *OS/2* provides *CACHE* if you are using the *high performance file system*, or *DISKCACHE* if you are using the *file allocation table* system. Disk cache programs are also available from other third-party sources.

disk capacity The storage capacity of a *hard* or *floppy disk*, usually stated in kilobytes (KB or K), megabytes (MB), or gigabytes (GB).

disk controller The electronic circuitry that controls and manages the operation of *floppy* or *hard disks* installed in the computer.

A single disk controller may manage more than one hard disk; many disk controllers also manage floppy disks and compatible tape drives. In the *Macintosh*, the disk controller is built into the system. In IBM-compatible computers, it is part of the hard disk drive itself as in the case of an *IDE* drive.

disk drive A *peripheral* storage *device* that reads and writes magnetic or optical disks. When more than one disk drive is installed on a computer, the *operating system* assigns each drive a unique name—for example *A:* and *C:* in *DOS, Windows,* and *OS/2.*

Three types of disk drive are in common use; *floppy-disk* drives, *hard-disk* drives, and compact-disc drives. Floppy-disk drives accept removable 5.25" or 3.5" media. Hard-disk drives usually have much greater capacity and are considerably faster than floppy-disk drives, and they are contained inside a protective sealed case. Compact-disc drives can be either internal or external to the system unit; they contain a great deal more than a floppy disk yet less than a hard disk and are generally used for read-only files.

disk duplexing In networking, a *fault-tolerant* technique that writes the same information simultaneously onto two different *hard disks*. Each of the hard disks uses a different *disk controller* to provide greater redundancy. In the event of one disk or disk controller failing, information from the other system can be used to continue operations. Disk duplexing is offered by most of the major *network operating systems* and is designed to protect the system against a single disk failure; it is not designed to protect against multiple disk failures, and is no substitute for a well-planned series of disk *backups*.

diskless workstation A networked computer that does not have any *local disk* storage capability.

The computer boots up and loads all its programs from the network *file server*. Diskless workstations are particularly valuable when very sensitive information is processed; information cannot be copied from the file server onto a local disk, because there isn't one.

disk mirroring In networking, a *fault-tolerant* technique that writes the same information simultaneously onto two different *hard disks*, using the same *disk controller*. In the event of one disk failing, information from the other can be used to continue operations. Disk mirroring is offered by most of the major *network operating systems* and is designed to protect the system against a single disk failure; it is not designed to protect against multiple disk failures and is no substitute for a well-planned series of disk *backups*.

distributed processing A computer system in which processing is performed by several separate computers linked by a communications network. The term often refers to any computer system supported by a network, but it more properly refers to a system in which each computer is chosen to handle a specific workload, and the network supports the system as a whole.

DLC An acronym for Data Link Control. This is a point-to-point protocol that functions at the *data-link layer* of the Open Systems Interconnect networking model. On the *Windows* operating system, DLC is used to connect printers and mainframes to PCs over a network.

DLT An acronym for Digital Linear Tape, DLT is a tape storage medium that is used to back up 20 to 40GB of data at speeds of up to 800KB per second.

DMI Abbreviation for Desktop Management Interface. A standard method of identifying PC hardware and software components automatically, without input from the user.

At minimum, DMI will identify the manufacturer, product name, serial number, and installation time and date of any component installed in a PC.

DMI is backed by Digital Equipment Corporation, IBM, Intel, Microsoft, Novell, Sun, and more than 300 other vendors.

DNS Abbreviation for Domain Name System. The method used when naming Internet *host* computers, and the directory services used when looking up those names. Each of these host names (such as pd.zevon.com) corresponds to a long decimal number known as the IP address (such as 199.10.44.8). These *domain names* are much easier to remember than the long IP addresses.

docking station A hardware system into which a laptop computer fits so that it can be used as a full-fledged desktop computer.

Docking stations vary from simple port replicators that allow you access to parallel and serial ports and a mouse, to complete systems that give you access to network connections, CD-ROMs, even a tape backup system or *PCMCIA* ports.

domain
1. The general category that a computer on the Internet belongs to. The most common high-level domains are:

- **.com**: a commercial organization

- **.edu**: an educational establishment

- **.gov**: a branch of the U.S. government
- **.int**: an international organization
- **.mil**: a branch of the U.S. military
- **.net**: a network
- **.org**: a non-profit organization

Most countries also have unique domains named after their international abbreviation. For example, .UK for the United Kingdom and .CA for Canada.

2. In networking, this is a logical grouping of users and resources grouped together for ease of administration and security purposes.

domain name The easy-to-understand name given to an *Internet* host computer, as opposed to the numerical IP address.

DOS
1. Acronym for Disk Operating System, an *operating system* originally developed by *Microsoft* for the *IBM PC*. DOS exists in two very similar versions; *MS-DOS*, developed and marketed by Microsoft for use with *IBM-compatible* computers, and *PC-DOS*, supported and sold by IBM for use only on computers manufactured by IBM. A third version, originally developed by Digital Research and called *DR-DOS*, is now owned by Novell and is called Novell DOS.

2. A DOS *CONFIG.SYS* command that loads the *operating system* into *conventional memory*, *extended memory*, or into *upper memory blocks* on computers using the Intel *80386* or later processor. To use this command, you must have previously loaded the *HIMEM.SYS device driver* with the *DEVICE* command in CONFIG.SYS. This command is not used on Windows 95 or later since Windows configures the high memory area for you.

DOS prompt A visual confirmation that the *DOS operating system* is ready to receive input from the keyboard. The default prompt includes the *current drive* letter followed by a greater-than symbol; for example, C>. You can create your own custom prompt with the PROMPT command.

dot-matrix printer An *impact printer* that uses columns of small pins and an inked ribbon to create the tiny pattern of dots that form the characters. Dot-matrix printers are available in 9-, 18-, or 24-pin configurations, but they are very noisy and produce relatively low quality output. They are especially useful when you must print on carbon duplicates.

dot pitch In a monitor, the vertical distance between the centers of like-colored phosphors on the screen of a color monitor, measured in millimeters (mm). As the dot pitch becomes smaller, the finer detail appears on the screen; straight lines appear sharper and colors more vivid. Today's monitors often have a dot pitch of between 0.31 mm and 0.28 mm.

dots per inch Abbreviated dpi. A measure of resolution expressed by the number of dots that a device can print or display in one inch. *Laser printers* can print at up to 1200 dpi, while *Linotronic* laser imagesetters can print at resolutions of 1270 or 2450 dpi.

drift In a monitor, any unwanted motion or undulation in a line drawn on the screen.

drive bay An opening in the *system unit* into which you can install a floppy disk drive, hard disk drive, or tape drive. Modern computers usually accommodate *half-height drive* bays.

drive letter In *DOS, Windows,* and *OS/2,* a designation used to specify a particular hard or floppy disk. For example, the first floppy disk is usually referred to as drive A, and the first hard disk as drive C.

DSL Short for Digital Subscriber Line, DSL is a remote access connection technology that will eventually allow users to download at speeds of up to 6Mbps as opposed to the current 56Kbps limitations seen with standard modems.

To do this, phone companies have started to upgrade their systems to handle digital data instead of the analog data that modems send. Because phone companies can use more bandwidth to send digital data, transmission speed will increase dramatically.

DSP Abbreviation for Digital Signal Processor. A specialized high-speed chip, used for data manipulation in sound cards, communications adapters, video and image manipulation, and other data-acquisition processes where speed is essential.

DSR Abbreviation for data set ready. A *hardware* signal defined by the *RS-232-C* standard to indicate that the device is ready.

DTE Abbreviation for Data Terminal Equipment. In communications, any device, such as a terminal or a computer, connected to a communications channel or public network.

DTR Abbreviation for data terminal ready. A *hardware* signal defined by the *RS-232-C* standard to indicate that the computer is ready to accept a transmission.

dual in-line package   Abbreviated DIP. A standard housing constructed of hard plastic commonly used to hold an *integrated circuit*. The circuit's leads are connected to two parallel rows of pins designed to fit snugly into a socket; these pins may also be soldered directly to a *printed-circuit board*. If you try to install or remove dual in-line packages, be careful not to bend or damage their pins.

dual in-line memory module Abbreviated DIMM, it is actually best described as a double SIMM. SIMMs are small circuit boards that contain RAM chips and can be snapped into SIMM slots on a motherboard. One drawback is that they use a 32-bit data-path, which means that SIMMs must be installed in pairs on newer systems. DIMMs use a 64-bit data-path, and therefore only one DIMM is needed where two SIMMs would ordinarily be used.

dumb terminal   A combination of keyboard and screen that has no local computing power, used to input information to a large, remote computer, often a minicomputer or a mainframe. This remote computer provides all the processing power for the system.

duplex   In asynchronous transmissions, the ability to transmit and receive on the same channel at the same time;

also referred to as full duplex. Half-duplex channels can transmit only or receive only.

One popular use for this is in a Fast Ethernet network. Some 100MBps hubs are not capable of transmitting at 100MBps and full duplex. If you have such a network configuration, then configure your network cards to transmit at half duplex.

duplex printing   Printing a document on both sides of the page so that the appropriate pages face each other when the document is bound.

DVD   Acronym for Digital Versatile Disk or Digital Video Disk. A type of CD that is capable of holding up to 4.7GB of data as opposed to the standard 600MB. DVD can also be used to store video or audio recordings.

Dvorak keyboard   Pronounced "di-vor-ack." A keyboard layout invented by August Dvorak in 1936 as a faster alternative to the *QWERTY* typewriter keyboard. The Dvorak keyboard groups all vowels and punctuation marks on the left side of the keyboard and common consonants together on the right. Studies have shown that typists make 70 percent of all keystrokes on the second or home row on the Dvorak keyboard compared with 32 percent on the

QWERTY keyboard. The Dvorak keyboard, in spite of its advantages, has not found wide acceptance, mostly because of the retraining costs involved in switching.

DX4 A 32-bit chip, based on the *80486*, from Intel. Despite the name, the DX4 is not a clock-quadrupled chip; it is a clock-tripled chip. For example, the 75-MHz version of the chip completes three CPU cycles for each cycle of the 25 MHz motherboard. The DX4 is available in 75, 83, and 100 MHz versions, and fills the performance gap between the existing chips in the 80486 set and the Pentium processor.

dynamic link library Abbreviated DLL. A program module that contains executable code and *data* that can be used by *application* programs, or even by other DLLs, in performing a specific task.

The DLL is linked into the application only when you run the program, and it is unloaded again when no longer needed. This means that if two DLL applications are running at the same time, and both of them perform a particular function, only one copy of the code for that function is loaded, making for a more efficient use of limited memory. Another benefit of using dynamic linking is that *.EXE* files are not as large, since frequently used routines can be put into a DLL rather than repeated in each EXE that uses them. This results in saved disk space and faster program loading.

DLLs are used extensively in *Microsoft Windows*, *OS/2*, and in *Windows NT*. DLLs may have *file-name extensions* of .DLL, .DRV, or .FON.

dynamic RAM Abbreviated DRAM, pronounced "dee-ram." A common type of computer memory that uses capacitors and transistors storing electrical charges to represent memory states. These capacitors lose their electrical charge, and so need to be refreshed every millisecond, during which time they cannot be read by the processor.

DRAM chips are small, simple, cheap, easy to make, and hold approximately four times as much information as a *static RAM* (SRAM) chip of similar complexity. However, they are slower than static RAM. Processors operating at *clock speeds* of 25 MHz or more need DRAM with access times of faster than 80 nanoseconds (80 billionths of a second), while SRAM chips can be read in as little as 15 to 30 nanoseconds.

edge connector A form of connector consisting of a row of etched contacts along the edge of a *printed circuit board* that is inserted into an *expansion slot* in the computer.

EEPROM   Acronym for Electrically Erasable Programmable Read-Only Memory, pronounced "ee-ee-prom," or "double-ee-prom." A memory chip that maintains its contents without electrical power, and whose contents can be erased and reprogrammed either within the computer or from an external source. EEPROMS are used where the application requires stable storage without power, but where the chip may have to be reprogrammed.

EGA   Acronym for Enhanced Graphics Adapter. A *video adapter* standard that provides medium-resolution text and graphics, introduced by IBM in 1984. EGA can display 16 colors at the same time from a choice of 64, with a horizontal resolution of 640 *pixels* and a vertical resolution of 350 pixels. EGA has been superseded by *VGA* and *SVGA*.

EIDE   An acronym for Enhanced Integrated Drive Electronics, EIDE is an interface between your computer and your mass storage devices, such as a hard drive or CD-ROM. The EIDE standard allows access to drives larger than the standard IDE limitation of 528MB. It is also faster than IDE and allows up to four drives to be connected as

opposed to the standard IDE two-drive limit.

8-bit color   A method of representing a graphical image as a bitmap containing 256 different colors.

80286   Also called the 286. A 16-bit *microprocessor* from *Intel* first released in February 1982 and used by IBM in the IBM PC/AT computer. Since then it has been used in many other IBM-compatible computers.

The 80286 uses a 16-bit *data word* and a 16-bit *data bus*, uses 24 bits to address memory, and has the following modes:

• *Real mode* effectively limits performance to that of an 8086 microprocessor and can address 1MB memory.

• *Protected mode* prevents an *application* program from stopping the operating system due to an inadvertent error and can address 16MB of memory.

The 80286 is equivalent to approximately 134,000 *transistors* and can execute 1.2 million instructions per second. The *floating-point processor* for the 80286 is the *80287*.

80287   Also called the 287. A *floating-point processor* from *Intel*, designed for use with the *80286 CPU* chip. When supported by *application* programs, a floating-point processor can speed up floating-point and transcendental math operations by 10 to 50 times.

The 80287 conforms to the *IEEE 754-1985* standard for binary floating-point operations, and is available in clock speeds of 6, 8, 10, and 12 MHz.

80386DX   Also called the 80386, the 386DX, and the 386. A full 32-bit *microprocessor* introduced by *Intel* in October 1985, and used in many IBM and IBM-compatible computers. Available in 16-, 20-, 25-, and 33-MHz versions, the 80386 has a 32-bit *data word*, can transfer information 32 bits at a time over the *data bus*, and can use 32 bits in addressing memory. It has the following modes:

• *Real mode* effectively limits performance to that of an 8086 microprocessor and can address 1MB of memory.

• *Protected mode* prevents an *application* program from stopping the operating system due to an inadvertent error and can address 4GB of memory.

• *Virtual 8086 mode* allows the operating system to divide the 80386 into several 8086 microprocessors, all running with their own 1-megabyte space and all running a separate program.

The 80386 is equivalent to about 275,000 *transistors*, and can perform 6 million instructions per second. The

floating-point processor for the 80386DX is the *80387*.

80386SX   Also called the 386SX. A lower-cost alternative to the *80386DX microprocessor*, introduced by *Intel* in 1988. Available in 16-, 20-, 25-, and 33-MHz versions, the 80386SX is an *80386DX* with a 16-bit data bus. This design allows systems to be configured using cheaper 16-bit components, leading to a lower overall cost. The *floating-point processor* for the 80386SX is the *80387SX*.

80387   Also called the 387. A *floating-point processor* from *Intel*, designed for use with the *80386 CPU* chip. When supported by *application* programs, a floating-point processor can speed up floating-point and transcendental math operations by 10 to 50 times.

The 80387 conforms to the *IEEE 754-1985* standard for binary floating-point operations, and is available in speeds of 16, 20, 25, and 33 MHz.

80387SX   Also called the 387SX. A *floating-point processor* from *Intel*, designed for use with the 16-bit data bus of the *80386SX CPU* chip only. When supported by application programs, a floating-point processor can speed up floating-point and transcendental math operations by 10 to 50 times.

The 80387SX conforms to the *IEEE 754-1985* standard for binary floating-point operations, and is available only in a 16-MHz version.

80486DX Also called the 486 or i486. A 32-bit *microprocessor* introduced by *Intel* in April 1989. The 80486 represents the continuing evolution of the *80386* family of microprocessors and adds several notable features, including on-board *cache*, built-in *floating-point processor* and *memory management unit*, as well as certain advanced provisions for *multiprocessing*. Available in 25-, 33-, and 50-MHz versions, the 80486 is equivalent to 1.25 million *transistors*, and can perform 20 million instructions per second.

80486DX2 Also known as the 486DX2. A 32-bit *microprocessor* introduced by Intel in 1992. It is functionally identical to, and 100 percent compatible with, the 80486DX, but with one major difference; the DX2 chip adds what Intel calls speed-doubling technology— meaning that it runs twice as fast internally as it does with components external to the chip. For example, the DX2-50 operates at 50 MHz internally, but at 25 MHz while communicating with other system components, including memory and the other chips on the

motherboard, thus maintaining its overall system compatibility. 50- and 66-MHz versions of the DX2 are available. The 486DX2 contains 1.2 million transistors and is capable of 40 million instructions per second.

80486SX Also called the 486SX. A 32-bit *microprocessor* introduced by *Intel* in April 1991. The 80486SX can be described as an *80486DX* with the *floating-point processor* circuitry disabled. Available in 16-, 20-, and 25-MHz versions, the 80486SX contains the equivalent of 1.185 million transistors and can execute 16.5 million instructions per second.

80487 Also called the 487. A floating-point processor from *Intel*, designed for use with the *80486SX CPU* chip. When supported by *application* programs, a floating-point processor can speed up floating-point and transcendental math operations by 10 to 50 times.

The 80487 is essentially a 20 MHz 80486 with the floating-point circuitry still enabled. When an 80487 is added into the coprocessor socket of a *motherboard* running the 80486SX, it effectively becomes the main processor, shutting down the 80486SX and taking over all operations.

The 80487 conforms to the *IEEE 754-1985* standard for binary floating-point operations.

8080   An 8-bit *microprocessor*, introduced by *Intel* in April 1974, that paved the way for the *8086* family of microprocessors that followed. The 8080 contained 6000 transistors and was capable of 0.64 million instructions per second.

8086   A 16-bit *microprocessor* from *Intel*, first released in June 1978, available in speeds of 4.77 MHz, 8 MHz, and 10 MHz. The 8086 was used in a variety of early IBM-compatible computers as well as the IBM PS/2 Model 25 and Model 30. The 8086 contains the equivalent of 29,000 transistors and can execute 0.33 million instructions per second.

8087   A *floating-point processor* from *Intel*, designed for use with the *8086* and *8088 CPU* chips. When supported by *application* programs, a floating-point processor can speed up floating-point and transcendental math operations by 10 to 50 times.

The 8087 conforms to the *IEEE 754-1985* standard for binary floating-point operations, and is available in speeds of 5 MHz, 8 MHz, and 10 MHz.

8088   A 16-bit *microprocessor* from *Intel* released in June 1978 that was used in the first IBM PC, as well as the IBM PC/XT, Portable PC, PCjr, and a large number of IBM-compatible computers. The 8088 uses a 16-bit *data word*, but transfers information along an 8-bit *data bus*; the *8086* uses a 16-bit data word and a 16-bit data bus. Available in speeds of 4.77 MHz and 8 MHz, the 8088 is approximately equivalent to 29,000 *transistors* and can execute 0.33 million instructions per second.

8514/A   A *video adapter* from IBM, providing up to 256 colors or 16 shades of gray, on an interlaced display of 1024 by 768 *pixels* in the highest resolution mode. The IBM monitor used with this adapter is also known as an 8514/A.

88000   A family of 32-bit *RISC* microprocessors from *Motorola*, introduced in 1988 and used in *workstations*. The 88000 chip set includes one 88100 *CPU*, and usually two 88200 *cache memory management units*. One of the units is used to cache *data*, the other to cache instructions. The 88100 CPU also includes a *floating-point processor*.

The 88000 is a true *32-bit computer*, with 32-bit internal registers, and a 32-bit data *bus*. Up to four chip sets can be configured to work together in a *multiprocessor* system.

EISA   Acronym for Extended Industry Standard Architecture, pronounced "ee-sah." A PC *bus* standard that extends the traditional *AT-bus* to 32 bits and allows more than one processor to share the bus.

EISA was developed by the so-called Gang of Nine (AST Research, *Compaq Computer Corporation*, *Epson*, *Hewlett-Packard*, NEC, Olivetti, *Tandy*, Wyse Technology, and Zenith Data Systems) in 1988 in reply to IBM's introduction of their proprietary *Micro Channel architecture* (MCA).

EISA maintains compatibility with the earlier *Industry Standard Architecture* (ISA) and also provides for additional features introduced by IBM in the MCA standard. EISA accepts ISA *expansion cards*, and so, unlike the Micro Channel architecture, it is compatible with earlier systems.

EISA has a 32-bit data path, and, at a bus speed of 8 MHz, can achieve a maximum throughput of 33 megabytes per second.

electromagnetic interference
Abbreviated EMI. Any electromagnetic radiation released by an electronic *device* that disrupts the operation or performance of any other device.

e-mail   Also called electronic mail. The use of a network to transmit text messages, memos, and reports. Users can send a message to one or more individual users, to a predefined group, or to all users on the system. When you receive a message, you can read, print, forward, answer, or delete it.

emoticon   A set of characters commonly used in *e-mail* and *USENET newsgroups* to signify emotions. An emoticon can be as simple as including <> or <grin> in the text, meant to indicate that the writer is joking, to some of the complex smiley faces, such as the wink ;-) or the frown :-(which are all meant to be read sideways.

emulator   A *device* built to work exactly like another device, either *hardware*, *software*, or a combination of both. For example, a *terminal emulation* program lets a PC pretend to be a terminal attached to a *mainframe computer* or to certain of the online services or *bulletin boards* by providing the *control codes* that the remote system expects to see.

Encapsulated PostScript   Abbreviated EPS. The *file* format of the *PostScript page description language*. The EPS standard is *device independent*, so that images can easily be transferred between different *applications*, and they can be sized and output to different printers without any loss of image quality or distortion. Many high-quality *clip art* packages store images in EPS form.

The EPS file contains the PostScript commands needed to recreate the image, but the image itself cannot be displayed on a monitor unless the file also contains an optional preview image stored in *TIFF* or *PICT* format.

The EPS file can only be printed on a PostScript-compatible *laser* printer, and the printer itself determines the final printing resolution; a laser printer might be capable of 1200 *dpi*, whereas a *Linotronic* printer is capable of 2450 dpi.

encryption The process of encoding information in an attempt to make it secure from unauthorized access. The reverse of this process is known as decryption.

One of the most popular encryption programs is Pretty Good Privacy (PGP), written by Phil Zimmermann, available at no charge from certain Internet sites.

end user During the mainframe computer era, the end user was always a person who received output from the computer and used that output in their work. They rarely, if ever, even saw the computer, much less learned to use it themselves.

Today, the term more often refers to the person who uses the *application* program to produce their own results. End users today often write *macros* to automate complex or repetitive tasks and sometimes write procedures using command languages.

Enhanced Expanded Memory Specification Abbreviated EEMS. A revised version of the original Lotus-Intel-Microsoft *Expanded Memory Specification* (LIM EMS), that lets DOS *applications* use more than 640KB of memory space.

enhanced keyboard A 101- or 102-key keyboard introduced by IBM that has become the accepted standard for PC keyboard layout. Unlike earlier keyboards, it has 12 *function keys* across the top, rather than 10 function keys in a block on the left side, has extra *Ctrl* and *Alt* keys, and has a set of *cursor control keys* between the main keyboard and the numeric keypad.

Enhanced Small Device Interface Abbreviated ESDI. A *hard disk, floppy disk*, and tape drive interface standard, capable of a *data transfer rate* of 10 to 20 megabits per second.

enterprise A term used to encompass an entire business group, organization, or corporation, including all local, remote, and satellite offices. Most often used with reference to large networked systems.

entry-level system A computer system that meets the basic requirements for a specific task. As computers become both cheaper and more capable, the definition of an entry-level system changes. Also, *application* developers continue to create new and more complex programs, which in turn demand more capability from the *hardware*.

EPP/ECP An acronym for Enhanced Parallel Port/Enhanced Capabilities Port. EPP/ECP is a parallel port standard defined in IEEE standard 1284 that allows computer systems to communicate with parallel port devices at faster speeds than standard parallel ports. It also allows for bidirectional communication. EPP ports are for non-printer devices, like scanners, while ECP ports are suited for printers. The two technologies can be combined into one port called an EPP/ECP port.

EPROM Acronym for erasable programmable read-only memory, pronounced "ee-prom." A memory chip that maintains its contents without electrical power, and whose contents can be erased and reprogrammed by removing a protective cover and exposing the chip to ultraviolet light.

erasable CD A standard format for an erasable CD that allows users to store and revise large amounts of data.

The standard is supported by Sony, Phillips, IBM, Hewlett-Packard, and other leading companies. One of the major advantages of this new standard is that it is completely compatible with existing compact discs, and makers of *CD-ROM disk drives* only have to make minor manufacturing changes to existing drives to meet the standard.

error The difference between the expected and the actual. In computing, an error is not necessarily the same as a mistake, but is often the way that the computer reports unexpected, unusual, impossible, or illegal events. Errors range from trivial, like a disk drive that does not contain a disk, to fatal, as when a serious operating system bug renders the system useless.

error detection and correction A mechanism used during a *file* transfer to determine whether transmission errors have occurred and to correct those errors, if possible. Some programs or transmission protocols request a retransmission of the affected block of *data* if such an error is detected. More complex protocols attempt to both detect and correct transmission errors.

error message A message from the program or the operating system, informing you of a condition that requires some human intervention to solve.

Error messages can indicate relatively trivial problems, like a disk drive that does not contain a disk, all the way to fatal problems, as when a serious operating system bug renders the system useless and requires a system restart.

Ethernet A widely use local area networking technology defined in IEEE standard 802.3. Ethernet uses the Carrier Sense Multiple Access with Collision Detection (CSMA/CD) protocol to ensure that data can move between computers without getting in an accident on the wire (called a collision). Standard Ethernet will transmit at speeds of 10Mbps while Fast Ethernet will transmit at speeds of 100Mbps.

exa- Abbreviated E. A prefix meaning one quintillion, 10^{18}. In computing, this translates into 1,152,921,504,606,846,976; the power of 2 closest to one quintillion (1060).

exabyte Abbreviated EB. 1 quadrillion bytes, or 1,152,921,504,606,846,976 bytes.

expandability The ability of a system to accommodate expansion. In *hardware*, this may include the addition of more memory, more or larger disk drives, and new adapters, and in *software* may include the ability of a network to add users, nodes, or connections to other networks.

expanded memory A *DOS* mechanism by which *applications* can access more than the 640KB of *memory* normally available to them.

The architecture of the *8086* and *8088* processors restricted the original IBM PC to accessing 1MB of memory, 640KB of which was available for application programs, and the remaining 384KB was reserved for system use, the *BIOS*, and the video system. At that time, 640KB was more than 10 times the amount of memory available in other *personal computers*. However, as both applications and DOS grew larger, they began to run out of room.

expanded memory manager Abbreviated EMM. A *device driver* that supports the *software* portion of the *expanded memory specification* in an IBM-compatible computer.

Expanded Memory Specification Abbreviated EMS. The original version of the Lotus-Intel-Microsoft Expanded Memory Specification (LIM EMS), that lets DOS applications use more than 640 KB of memory space.

expansion bus An extension of the main computer *bus* that includes *expansion slots* for use by compatible *adapters*, such as including memory boards, video adapters, hard disk controllers, and SCSI interface cards.

expansion slot One of the connectors on the *expansion bus* that gives an *adapter* access to the system bus. You can add as many additional adapters as there are expansion slots inside your computer.

expansion unit An external housing available with certain portable computers designed to contain additional *expansion slots* and maintain a connection to the main *expansion bus* in the computer's system unit.

extended ASCII character set The second part of the *ASCII character set* from decimal code 128 to decimal code 255. This part of the ASCII character set is not standard, and will contain different characters on different types of computer. In IBM-compatible computers, it includes special mathematical symbols and characters from the PC line-drawing set. The Apple extended ASCII character set uses a different set of characters.

extended DOS partition A further optional division of a hard disk, after

the *primary DOS partition*, that functions as one or more additional *logical* drives. A logical drive is simply an area of a larger disk that acts as though it were a separate disk with its own *drive letter*. Creating an extended partition allows you to install a second operating system, such as OS/2; in early DOS versions it is the only way to use disk space above 32MB.

DOS partitions are created and changed using the *FDISK* command.

extended memory Memory beyond 1MB on computers using the Intel *80386* and later processors, not configured for *expanded memory*.

Computers based on the Intel *8086* and *8088* processors can only access 1MB of memory, of which 640KB is available for application programs, and the remaining 384KB is reserved for *DOS*, the *BIOS*, and video settings.

Later processors can access more memory, but it was the *80386* with its ability to address 4GB of memory that really made extended memory usable, along with the DOS memory manager *HIMEM.SYS* that lets DOS use all of the extended memory installed in your computer. Modern operating systems do not require HIMEM.SYS because memory management is built into the operating system.

extended memory manager A *device driver* that supports the *software* portion of the *extended memory specification* in an IBM-compatible computer in older operating systems like DOS.

extended memory specification Abbreviated XMS. A standard developed by Microsoft, Intel, Lotus, and AST Research that has become the preferred way of accessing *extended memory* in the PC running older operating systems like DOS. *DOS* and Windows 3.*x* include the extended memory *device driver* HIMEM.SYS, and this command or an equivalent must be present in your *CONFIG.SYS file* before you can access extended memory successfully.

external hard disk A *hard disk* packaged in its own case, with cables and an independent power supply, rather than a disk drive housed inside and integrated with the computer's system unit.

extremely low-frequency emission Abbreviated ELF. Radiation emitted by a computer monitor and other very common household electrical appliances such as televisions, hair dryers, electric blankets and food processors.

ELF emissions fall into the range from 5 Hz to 2000 Hz, and decline in signal strength with the square of the distance from the source. Emissions are not constant around a monitor; they are higher from the sides and rear, and weakest from the front of the screen. Low-emission models are available, and *laptop computers* with an *LCD* display do not emit any ELF fields.

FAQ Pronounced "fack," a document that answers frequently asked questions. If you have just purchased new hardware or software and have some questions, check the manufacturer's Web site for a FAQ before calling tech support.

fatal error An *operating system* or *application* program error from which there is no hope of recovery without rebooting (and thus losing any unsaved work).

fault tolerance A design method that ensures continued system operation in the event of individual failures by providing redundant elements.

At the component level, designers include redundant chips and circuits and add the capability to bypass faults automatically. At the computer system level, they replicate any elements likely to fail, such as processors and large disk drives.

Fault-tolerant operations often require backup or *UPS* power systems in the event of a main power failure, and may imply the duplication of entire computer systems in remote locations to protect against vandalism, acts of war, or natural disaster.

fax Abbreviation for facsimile. The electronic transmission of copies of documents for reproduction at a remote location.

The sending fax machine scans a paper image and converts the image into a form suitable for transmission over a telephone line. The receiving fax machine decodes and prints a copy of the original image. Each fax machine includes a scanner, fax modem, and printer.

fax modem A modem that includes fax capabilities providing many of the functions of a full-sized *fax* machine In addition to standard modem operation.

There are three main classes of fax modems:

• **SendFax:** originally developed by Sierra Semiconductor, these fax modems are send-only, and date from the days when a single-function fax modem was much cheaper than one that could both send and receive.

• **Class 1**: an early fax-modem standard which specified that most of the processing of the fax document should be performed by the application software.

• **Class 2**: a more recent standard that shifts the task of preparing the fax document to the fax modem itself. In this standard, the modem hardware manages all data-compression and error-correction functions.

FCC Acronym for Federal Communications Commission. A U.S. government regulatory body for radio, television, all interstate telecommunications services, and all international services that originate inside the U.S.

All computer equipment must be certified by the FCC before it can be offered for sale in the U.S. to ensure that it meets the legal limits for conductive and radio frequency emissions, which could otherwise interfere with commercial broadcasts.

FCC certification Approval by the FCC that a specific computer model meets its standards for *radio frequency interference* emissions.

There are two levels of certification. *Class A* certification is for computers used in commercial settings, such as mainframes and minicomputers, and the more stringent *Class B* certification is for computers used in the home and in home offices, such as PCs, laptops, and portables.

female connector Any cable connector with receptacles designed to receive the pins on the male part of the connector.

fiber distributed data interface (FDDI) Abbreviated FDDI. A specification for fiber-optic networks transmitting at a speed of up to 100 megabits per second over a dual, counter-rotating, *token-ring* topology. FDDI is suited to systems that require the transfer of very large amounts of information, such as medical imaging, 3-D seismic processing, oil reservoir simulation, and full-motion video.

fiber optic cable A transmission technology that sends pulses of light along specially manufactured optical fibers. Each fiber consists of a core, thinner than a human hair, surrounded by a sheath with a much lower refractive index. Light signals introduced at one end of the cable are conducted along the cable as the signals are reflected from the sheath.

Fiber optic cable is lighter and smaller than traditional copper cable, is immune to electrical interference, and has better

signal-transmitting qualities. However, it is more expensive than traditional cables and more difficult to repair.

file A named collection of *data* stored on disk, appearing to the user as a single entity. A file can contain a program or part of a program, may be a *data file*, or can contain a user-created document. Files may actually be fragmented or stored in many different places across the disk; the *operating system* manages the task of locating all the pieces when the file is read.

file allocation table Abbreviated FAT, pronounced "fat." A table maintained by the *operating system* that lists all the *clusters* available on a disk. The FAT includes the location of each cluster, as well as whether it is in use, available for use, or damaged in some way and therefore unavailable.

Because files are not necessarily stored in consecutive clusters on a disk, but can be scattered all over the disk, the FAT also keeps track of which pieces belong to which *file*.

FAT comes in two sizes, 16 and 32 bit. FAT16 is capable of supporting a 2GB drive while FAT32 is capable of supporting up to 2TB on a single drive.

file compression program An *application* program that shrinks program or *data files*, so that they occupy less disk space. The file must then be extracted or decompressed before you can use it.

Many of the most popular file compression programs are *shareware*, like *PKZIP*, LHA, and StuffIt for the *Macintosh*.

file fragmentation The storage of a *file* in several noncontiguous areas of a disk, rather than as one single unit.

When you store a file on a disk, the operating system looks for the first available free cluster on the disk, and stores the file there. If the file is too large for one cluster, the operating system looks for the next free cluster, and stores the next part of the file there. These clusters may not be next to one another and may be widely scattered over the disk.

This fragmentation can slow down data retrieval if the problem becomes severe, but by using a *defragmenter*, you can restore that lost performance. The defragmented program removes file fragmentation by rewriting all files and *directories* into contiguous areas of your disk.

file recovery The process of recovering *deleted* or damaged *files* from a disk. In many operating systems, a deleted file still exists on disk until the space it occupies is overwritten with something else. A file can be deleted accidentally, or it can become inaccessible when part of the file's control information is lost.

Many utility packages offer excellent file recovery programs that guide the user through the recovery process, including the *Norton Utilities* from Symantec, *PC Tools* from Central Point Software, and the Mace utilities from Fifth Generation Systems. In cases where damage is extreme, the program may only be able to recover some of the damaged file, and substantial editing may be necessary before the file can be used; indeed the best way to recover a damaged program file is to restore it from a *backup* copy. You must, of course, recover the deleted or damaged files before you add any new files or *directories* to the disk.

file server A networked computer used to store *files* for access by other *client* computers on the network. On larger networks, the file server may run a special *network operating system*; on smaller installations, the file server may run a PC operating system supplemented by *peer-to-peer* networking software.

file sharing In networking, the sharing of *files* via the network *file server*. Shared files can be read, reviewed, and updated by more than one individual. Access to the file or files is often regulated by password protection, account or security clearance, or file locking, to prevent simultaneous changes from being made by more than one person at a time.

filespec A contraction of file specification, commonly used to denote the complete drive letter, path name, *directory* name, and file name needed to access a specific *file*.

file system In an *operating system*, the structure by which *files* are organized, stored, and named.

Some file systems are built-in components of the operating system, while others are installable. For example, *OS/2* supports several different file systems, including the FAT file system, the high-performance file system, and the CD-ROM file system, which is installed by the ISF command when you attach a CD-ROM to your system.

finger A Unix utility program found on many Internet systems and online services that displays information about a specific user, including full name, login time, and location.

Finger may also display the contents of the user's .plan or .project file, and there are many users who exploit this in a rather novel way, in order to display such varied information as instructions for using a university's computerized Coke-vending machine, sports scores, and earthquake information.

firewall A method of preventing unauthorized access to a computer system, often found on networked computers.

A firewall is designed to provide normal service to authorized users, while at the same time preventing those unauthorized users from gaining access to the system; in reality, they almost always add some level of inconvenience to legal users, and their ability to control illegal access may be questionable. The Internet community has long favored unrestricted access to information, but as more and more commercial use is made of the Internet, the need for stricter controls is becoming increasingly apparent.

FireWire Apple Computer Corporation's implementation of IEEE standard 1394 for High Performance Serial Bus. It is supposed to function a great deal like Universal Serial Bus. FireWire will allow up to 63 devices chained together on a single serial tp communicate at up to 400Mbps.

firmware   Any *software* stored in a form of read-only memory—*ROM*, *EPROM*, or *EEPROM*—that maintains its contents when power is removed. The *BIOS* used in IBM-compatible computers is firmware.

first in, first out   Abbreviated FIFO, pronounced "fi-foe." A method used to process information in which the first item in the list is processed first. FIFO is commonly used when printing a set of documents; the first document received in the queue is the first document to be printed.

5.25" disk   A *floppy disk*, enclosed in a flexible 5.25" jacket, used in IBM and IBM-compatible computers.

The 5.25" disk can contain either 360KB or 1.2MB of information, depending on the type of disk used. Because the disks are flexible, and because part of the recording surface is exposed through the read/write slot, 5.25" floppy disks should be handled with care and always stored in their paper jackets when not in use.

These are no longer in general use because they have been replaced by the 3.5" floppy disk.

fixed-frequency monitor   A monitor designed to receive an input signal at just one frequency. This is in contrast to a *multisynch monitor*, which can detect and adjust to a variety of different input signals.

flame   A deliberately insulting *e-mail* message or *post* to a *USENET newsgroup*, usually containing a personal attack on the writer of an earlier post. Flames are often generated by established newsgroup members when a *newbie* posts a question which is answered in the newsgroup's *FAQ*.

flame war   A prolonged series of *flames* in a *USENET newsgroup*, which may begin as a creative exchange of views but which quickly degenerates into personal attacks and crude name-calling.

flash memory   A special form of non-volatile *EEPROM* that can be erased at signal levels normally found inside the PC, so that you can reprogram the contents with whatever you like without pulling the chips out of your computer. Also, once flash memory has been programmed, you can remove the *expansion board* it is mounted on and plug it into another computer if you wish.

flatbed scanner   A device used to transfer paper copies of documents or pictures into a file that can be stored and used on a computer.

flat-panel display In laptop and notebook computers, a very narrow display that uses one of several technologies, such as electroluminescence, *LCD*, or thin film transistors.

flicker On a monitor, any form of unwanted rapid fluctuation in the image that occurs when the refresh rate is too slow to maintain an even level of brightness.

floating point calculation A calculation of numbers whose decimal point is not fixed but moves or floats to provide the best degree of accuracy. Floating point calculations can be implemented in *software* or they can be performed much faster by a separate *floating point processor*.

floating point processor A special-purpose secondary processor designed to perform *floating point calculations* much faster than the main processor.

Many processors have matched companion floating-point processors; the 80386 and the 80387 for example, although a modern trend in processor design is to integrate the floating-point unit onto the main processor, as in the 80486 and the Pentium.

floppy disk A flat, round, magnetically coated plastic disk enclosed in a protective jacket.

Data is written on to the floppy disk by the disk drive's read/write heads as the disk rotates inside the jacket. The advantage of the floppy disk is that it is removable, and so can be used to distribute commercial *software*, to transfer programs from one computer to another, or to *back up files* from a *hard disk*. But compared to a hard disk, floppy disks are also slower, offer relatively small amounts of storage, and can be easily damaged.

Floppy disks in personal computing are of two physical sizes, 5.25" or 3.5", and a variety of storage capacities. The 5.25" floppy disk has a stiff plastic external cover, while the 3.5" floppy disk is enclosed in a hard plastic case. IBM-compatibles and Macintosh computers generally use 3.5" disks capable of storing 1.44MB of information.

floppy disk drive A device used to read and write *data* to and from a *floppy disk*.

floptical disk A removable optical disk much like a compact disc with a recording capacity of between 20 and 25 megabytes.

font cartridge A plug-in module available for certain printers that adds new fonts to those already available in the printer. The font information for *bit-mapped* or *outline fonts* is stored in *ROM* in the cartridge.

footprint The amount of desktop or floor space occupied by a computer or display terminal.

foreground In an *operating system*, a process that runs in the foreground is running at a higher level of priority than a *background* task.

Only *multitasking* operating systems support true foreground and background processing; however, some *application* programs can mimic background and foreground processing; many word processors will print a document while still accepting input from the keyboard.

formatting
1. To apply the page-layout commands and font specifications to a document to produce the final printed output.

2. The process of initializing a new, blank *floppy disk* or *hard disk* so that it can be used to store information.

form feed Abbreviated FF. A printer command that advances the paper in the printer to the top of the next page.

This can be done by pressing the form feed button on the printer, or an *application* can issue the command. In the *ASCII character set* a form feed has the decimal value of 12.

forum A feature of *online services* and bulletin boards that allows subscribers to post messages for others to read, and to reply to messages posted by other users.

Most forums are devoted to a specific subject such as working from home or photography, while others are run by hardware and software vendors providing what amounts to online technical support.

free memory An area of memory not currently in use.

Free-net Sometimes Freenet. An organization that provides free Internet access, usually through public libraries or local universities.

freeware A form of *software* distribution where the author retains copyright of the software, but makes the program available to others at no cost. Freeware is often distributed on Web sites or through *user groups*. The program may not be resold or distributed by others for profit.

frequency modulation encoding

Abbreviated FM encoding. A method of storing digital information on a disk or tape. FM encoding is inefficient in its use of disk space and has been replaced by the more efficient method *advanced run length limited (ARLL) encoding.*

friction feed A paper-feed mechanism that uses pinch rollers to move the paper through a printer, one page at a time.

Friction feed is usually available on those printers that use paper with *pin-feed* holes or that use a *tractor feed*, so that they can also print on single sheets of paper. Manually loading more than just a few sheets of paper using friction feed can become tedious very quickly.

front-end processor A specialized processor that manipulates *data* before passing it on to the main processor. In large computer-to-computer communications systems, a front-end processor is often used to manage all aspects of communications, leaving the main computer free to handle the data processing.

ftp Abbreviation for file transfer protocol. The protocol used to access a remote *Internet host* and then transfer files between that host and your own computer. Ftp is also the name of the program used to manage this protocol.

Ftp is based on *client/server architecture*; you run an ftp client program on your system and connect with an ftp server running on the Internet host computer. The ftp program originated as a *Unix* utility, but versions are now available for almost all popular operating systems. The traditional Unix ftp program starts a text-based command processor; modern versions use a graphical user interface with pull-down menus instead. The general consensus seems to be that the graphical versions are easier to use, but once you get the hang of things, the command processor versions, while not as pretty, are usually faster.

full backup A *backup* that includes all the *files* on your *hard disk*. If you have a large hard disk, this process can consume a lot of time and a large number of floppy disks, and one way to speed up the process is to use a tape drive system to help streamline and automate the process.

function keys The set of programmable keys on the keyboard that can perform special tasks assigned by the current *application* program.

Most keyboards have 10 or 12 function keys, and they are used by an application as shortcut keys. For example, many programs use F1 to gain access to the help system; in other programs the use of function keys is so complex that special plastic key overlays are needed just so you can remember how to use them.

G Abbreviation for *giga-*, meaning 1 billion, or 10^9.

gateway In networking, a shared connection between a *local area network* and a larger system, such as a mainframe computer or a large *packet-switching network*. Usually slower than a *bridge* or *router*, a gateway typically has its own processor and memory and can perform protocol conversions. Protocol conversion allows a gateway to connect two dissimilar networks; data is converted and reformatted before it is forwarded to the new network.

gender changer A special intermediary connector for use with two cables that both have male or both have female connectors.

general purpose interface bus Abbreviated GPIB. A 24-pin parallel interface bus that conforms to the IEEE 488 interface definition standard, often used to connect scientific instruments together or to a computer. Originally developed by *Hewlett-Packard*, GPIB is also known as the Hewlett-Packard Interface Bus (HPIB).

genlocking A contraction of generator lock. The synchronization and superimposition of computer-generated text or graphics onto a video signal, so that the two images can be combined onto the same signal and displayed at the same time.

In the PC, a board containing the circuitry required for genlocking often plugs onto the display adapter. It converts the *VGA* signal into a standard *NTSC* video signal, which it then synchronizes with an external video signal.

giga- A prefix meaning 1 billion, or 10^9.

gigabyte Pronounced "gig-a-bite." Strictly speaking, a gigabyte would be one billion bytes; however, bytes are most often counted in powers of 2, and so a gigabyte becomes 2^{30}, or 1,073,741,824 bytes.

GPF Short for General Protection Fault, this occurs in an operating system when a program tries to use Random Access Memory that it is not supposed to use.

graphical user interface Abbreviated GUI, pronounced "gooey." A graphics-based user interface that allows users to select files, programs, or commands by pointing to pictorial representations on the screen rather than by typing long, complex commands from a *command prompt*.

Application programs execute in *windows*, using a consistent set of *pull-down menus*, *dialog boxes*, and other graphical elements such as *scroll bars* and *icons*. This consistency among interface elements is a major benefit for the user, because as soon as you learn how to use the interface in one program, you can use it in all other programs running in the same *environment*.

graphics accelerator board A *video adapter* that offloads most of the graphics processing from the CPU. By offloading most of the graphics processing tasks from the main processor onto the graphics accelerator board, you can improve the performance of your system considerably, particularly if you are a Microsoft *Windows* user.

graphics coprocessor A fixed-function graphics chip, designed to speed up the processing and display of high-resolution images. Popular graphics coprocessors include the *S3 86C9xx* accelerator chips.

gray-scale monitor A monitor and *video adapter* that uses a set of gray shades from black to white instead of using colors. Gray-scale monitors are expensive and are used in medical and photographic imaging systems.

half-height drive A space-saving drive bay that is half the height of the 3″ drive bays used in the original IBM PC. Most of today's drives are half-height drives.

hand-held computer A *portable* computer that is small enough to be held in one hand.

hand scanner An optical device used to digitize a relatively small image or artwork.

hard card A single *expansion board* that contains a small *hard disk* and associated controller circuitry. A hard card allows you to add another hard disk, even when all your drive bays are occupied, as long as there is still a single *expansion slot* available. Hard cards were brought to prominence by Plus Development Corporation.

hard disk controller An old-technology *expansion board* that contains the necessary circuitry to control and coordinate a *hard disk drive*. Many hard disk controllers are capable of managing more than one hard disk, as well as floppy disks and even tape drives.

hard disk drive   A storage device that uses a set of rotating, magnetically coated disks called *platters* to store data or programs. In everyday use, the terms "hard disk," "hard disk drive," and "hard drive" are all used interchangeably, because the disk and the drive mechanism are a single unit.

A typical hard disk platter rotates at up to 3600 rpm, and the read/write heads float on a cushion of air from 10 to 25 millionths of an inch thick so that the heads never come into contact with the recording surface. The whole unit is hermetically sealed to prevent airborne contaminants from entering and interfering with these close tolerances.

Hard disks range in capacity from a few tens of megabytes to several gigabytes of storage space; the bigger the disk, the more important a well-thought out *backup* strategy becomes. Hard disks are very reliable, but they do fail, and usually at the most inconvenient moment.

hard disk interface   A standard way of accessing the data stored on a hard disk. Several different hard-disk interface standards have evolved over time, including IDE, EIDE and SCSI.

hard reset   A system reset made by pressing the computer's reset button or by turning the power off and then on again. Used only when the system has crashed so badly that a Ctrl-Alt-Del *reboot* doesn't work.

hardware   All the physical electronic components of a computer system, including *peripherals*, printed circuit boards, displays, and printers.

hardware-dependence   The requirement that a specific *hardware* component be present for a program to work. Hardware-dependent *software* is often very difficult to move or *port* to another computer.

hardware-independence   The ability to produce similar results in a wide variety of environments, without requiring the presence of specific *hardware*.

The *Unix operating system* and the *Post-Script page-description language* are both examples of hardware independence. Unix runs on a wide range of computers, from the PC to a Cray, and Post-Script is used by many printer manufacturers.

hardwired   Describes a system designed in a way that does not allow for flexibility or future expansion. May also refer to a device or computer connected directly to a network.

Hayes-compatible modem Any modem that recognizes the commands in the industry-standard *AT-command set*, defined by Hayes Microcomputer Products, Inc.

head The electromagnetic device used to read and write to and from magnetic media such as *hard* and *floppy disks*, *tape drives*, and *compact discs*. The head converts the information read into electrical pulses sent to the computer for processing.

head crash An unexpected collision between a hard disk *head* and the rapidly rotating magnetic recording surface of the disk resulting in damage to the disk surface, and in some severe cases resulting in damage to the head itself.

A head crash in the *file allocation table* (FAT) area of a disk can be especially devastating, because the FAT contains instructions for the *operating system* on how to find all the other *directories* and *files* on the disk, and if it is damaged, the other files and directories may become completely inaccessible.

Recent hard disk design has done much to eliminate this problem.

hertz Abbreviated Hz. A unit of frequency measurement; 1 hertz equals one cycle per second.

hexadecimal Abbreviated hex. The base-16 numbering system that uses the digits 0 to 9, followed by the letters A to F (equivalent to the decimal numbers 10 through 15).

Hex is a very convenient way to represent the binary numbers computers use internally, because it fits neatly into the 8-bit byte. All of the 16 hex digits 0 to F can be represented in four bits, and so two hex digits (one digit for each set of four bits) can be stored in a single byte. This means that one byte can contain any one of 256 different hex numbers, from 0 through FF. Hex numbers are often labeled with a lower-case h (for example, 1234h) to distinguish them from decimal numbers.

HGC Abbreviation for Hercules graphics card. A *video adapter* for DOS computers, introduced by Hercules Computer Technology. HGC provides monochrome graphics with 720 horizontal *pixels* and 348 vertical pixels.

high-density disk A floppy disk with more recording density and storage capacity than a *double-density disk*. In the *Macintosh*, high-density disks contain 1.44 MB. In IBM-compatible computers, high-density 5.25" floppy disks contain 1.2 MB, while high-density 3.5" floppy disks contain either 1.44 MB or 2.88 MB of storage space.

high-level format   The process of preparing a *floppy disk* or a *hard disk partition* for use by the *operating system*. In the case of *DOS*, a high-level format creates the *boot sector*, the *file allocation table* (FAT), and the *root directory*.

high memory area   Abbreviated HMA. In an IBM-compatible computer, the first 64K of *extended memory* above the 1MB limit of 8086 and 8088 addresses. Programs that conform to the *extended memory specification* can use this memory as an extension of *conventional memory* although only one program can use or control HMA at a time; *DOS*, *Microsoft Windows*, or an *application*. If you load DOS into the HMA, you can recover approximately 50K of conventional memory for use by your *applications*.

high performance file system   Abbreviated HPFS. A *file system* available only in *OS/2* that supports long, mixed-case *file names* of up to 256 characters, up to 64K of *extended attributes* per *file*, faster disk access with an advanced *disk cache* for caching files and *directory* information, highly contiguous file allocation that eliminates

file fragmentation, and support for hard disks of up to 64GB in size. You cannot use the HPFS on a floppy disk.

high-persistence phosphor   In a monitor, a phosphor that glows for a relatively long time after being energized by electrons. This can lead to ghost images on the screen.

high resolution   In monitors and printers, a description of high-quality output; resolution refers to the sharpness and detail of the image.

What actually constitutes high resolution is in the eye of the beholder; high resolution to one person represents a bad case of the *jaggies* to another. On a 12-inch monitor, a realistic-looking display requires a grid of approximately 1000 by 1000 *pixels*. *Laser printers* can manage a resolution of 1200 *dpi*, but Linotronic typesetters can print at up to 2540 dpi.

HIMEM.SYS   The *DOS* and *Microsoft Windows 3.x device driver* that manages the use of extended memory and the high memory area on IBM-compatible computers. HIMEM.SYS not only allows your *application* programs to access extended memory, it also oversees that area to prevent other programs from trying to use the same space at the same time.

HIMEM.SYS must be loaded by a *DEVICE* command in your *CONFIG .SYS* file; do not use *DEVICEHIGH*.

home computer Any computer designed or purchased for home use. Originally, home computers were often used for games, educational purposes, and financial management, and they were less powerful than their business counterparts. This gap has narrowed considerably in recent years as home users continue to demand the same level of power, speed, and convenience that they find in office systems. Often the home computer is used as an extension to an office system for after-hours work.

home page On the *Internet*, an initial starting page. A home page may be related to a single person, a specific subject, or to a corporation, and is a convenient jumping-off point to other pages or resources.

horizontal scanning frequency In a monitor, the frequency at which the monitor repaints the horizontal lines that make up an image. Horizontal scanning frequency is measured in kHz, and is standardized at 31.5 kHz for a *VGA*. For *SuperVGA*, this frequency ranges from 35 to 85 kHz, depending on the refresh rate of the *video adapter*.

host The central or controlling computer in a networked or *distributed processing* environment, providing services that other computers or terminals can access via the network.

Computers connected to the *Internet* are also described as hosts, and can be accessed using *ftp*, *telnet*, *Gopher*, or a *World Wide Web browser*.

HP LaserJet A family of very popular desktop *laser printers* launched in 1984 and manufactured by Hewlett-Packard Company.

HTML Abbreviation for Hypertext Markup Language. A standardized *hypertext* language used to create *World Wide Web* pages and other hypertext documents.

When you access an *Internet* HTML document using a *World Wide Web browser*, you will see a mixture of text, graphics, and *links* to other documents. When you click on a link, the related document will open automatically, no matter where on the Internet that document is actually located. Normally, you don't see the individual elements that make up HTML when you view a document, although certain browsers have a special mode that displays both the text and the HTML in a document.

HTTP Abbreviation for Hypertext Transfer Protocol. An application layer protocol included with the TCP/IP protocol suite on most operating systems. Used to transfer HTML documents, files, sound, graphics and anything else linked to the web page.

hub In networking, a hub is the junction for all of the cables coming from the networked computers, thus allowing the systems to communicate with each other.

hypertext A method of presenting information so that it can be viewed by the user in a non-sequential way, regardless of how the topics were originally organized.

Hypertext was designed to make a computer respond to the nonlinear way that humans think and access information—by association, rather than the linear organization of film, books, and speech.

In a hypertext *application*, you can browse through the information with considerable flexibility, choosing to follow a new path each time you access the information. When you click on a highlighted word, you activate a *link* to another hypertext document that may be located on the same *Internet* host or can be on a completely different system thousands of miles away.

IAB Abbreviation for Internet Architecture Board. The coordinating committee for the management of the *Internet*. Previously, the abbreviation IAB stood for Internet Activities Board.

IBM-compatible computer Any personal computer compatible with the IBM line of personal computers. Also referred to as a clone.

IBM PC A series of *personal computers* based on the *Intel 8088* processor, introduced by IBM in mid-1981.

The specifications for the IBM PC seem puny in comparison to current computer systems; the PC was released containing 16K of memory, expandable to 64K on the *motherboard*, and a monochrome *video adapter* incapable of displaying *bit-mapped graphics*. The floppy disk drive held 160K of data and programs. There was no hard disk on the original IBM PC; that came later with the release of the *IBM PC/XT*.

In 1983, IBM released an improved version of the PC, the IBM PC-2, which came with 64K of memory, expandable to 256K on the motherboard, and a double-density floppy disk drive capable of storing 360K of programs and *data*. The Color/Graphics Adapter (*CGA*) and an *RGB* color monitor were also introduced at the same time.

IBM PC/AT A series of *personal computers* based on the *Intel 80286* processor, introduced by IBM in 1984.

The AT represented a significant performance increase over previous computers, up to 75 percent faster than the PC/XT, and the *AT bus* standard is used in many *clones* or *IBM-compatible computers*.

IBM PC/XT A series of *personal computers* based on the *Intel 8088* processor, introduced by IBM in 1983.

The PC/XT was the first IBM personal computer to offer a built-in hard disk and the capability to expand memory up to a whopping 640K on the *motherboard*. The original PC/XT used an Intel 8088 running at a *clock speed* of 4.77 MHz—very slow when compared with today's 66 and 100 MHz clock speeds.

IBM PS/2 A series of personal computers using several different *Intel* processors, introduced by IBM in 1987.

The main difference between the PS/2 line and earlier IBM personal computers was a major change to the internal *bus*. Previous computers used the *AT bus*, also known as *industry-standard architecture*, but IBM used the proprietary *micro channel architecture* in the PS/2 line instead. Micro channel architecture *expansion boards* will not work in a computer using ISA.

IBM RS/6000 A set of seven or nine separate 32-bit chips used in IBM's line of *RISC* workstations. With up to 7.4 million transistors depending on configuration, the RS/6000 uses a *superscalar* design with four separate 16K data cache units and an 8K instruction cache.

The joint venture announced between IBM, Apple, and Motorola in late 1991 specified the joint development of a single-chip version of the RS/6000 architecture called the *PowerPC*.

IBM ThinkPad A series of innovative and popular notebook computers from IBM.

The ThinkPad first introduced the touch-sensitive dual-button pointing stick or TrackPoint, the pencil-eraser-like device between the G, H, and B keys that replaces the mouse, which is now found on many different portable computers.

The ThinkPad 701C, also known as "the Butterfly," introduced another innovative concept, that of the expanding keyboard. When the 701C case is closed, the TrackWrite keyboard is completely concealed inside the case; the right half sits above the left. When the case is opened, the two parts of the full-sized keyboard automatically unfold and overhang the edges of the case. The 701C, based on the *Intel DX2 50 MHz* processor, also contains an internal 14,400 bps fax/data modem with built-in speaker phone and digital answering machine, infrared wireless file transfer, and two *PCMCIA* Type I or Type II *PC cards* or one Type III card.

IBM 3270 A general name for a family of IBM system components—printers, terminals, and terminal cluster controllers—that can be used with a *mainframe computer* by an *SNA* link. *Terminal emulation software* that emulates a 3270 terminal is available for both *DOS* and *Microsoft Windows*, as well as for *OS/2*.

imagesetter A large, professional-quality typesetter capable of *high-resolution* output on paper or film.

Linotronic imagesetters can print at resolutions of 1225 to 2450 dpi; compare this to the 300 to 600 dpi produced by most desktop laser printers.

impact printer Any printer that forms an image on paper by forcing a character image against an inked ribbon. *Dot-matrix*, *daisy-wheel*, and *line printers* are all impact printers, whereas *laser printers* are not.

impedance An electrical property that combines capacitance, inductance, and resistance. Impedance can be described as the apparent resistance to the flow of alternating current at a given frequency; mismatches in impedance along a cable cause distortions and reflections.

incremental backup A *backup* of a hard disk that consists of only those *files* created or modified since the last backup was performed.

infection The presence of a computer virus.

Information Superhighway Sometimes abbreviated I-Way. An imprecise albeit popular term often applied to the *Internet* or to the National Information Infrastructure.

ink-jet printer A printer that creates an image by spraying tiny droplets of ink from the printhead. While many *dot-matrix printers* have 9 to 24 pins, most ink jets have printheads with somewhere between 30 and 60 nozzles, and this allows them to create *high-resolution* images in a single pass over the paper. Both color and black-and-white ink-jet printers are available.

input/output Abbreviated I/O. The transfer of *data* between the computer and its *peripheral* devices, disk drives, terminals and printers.

input/output bound Abbreviated I/O bound. A condition where the speed of operation of the I/O port limits the speed of program execution; getting the *data* into and out of the computer is more time-consuming than processing that same data.

install To configure and prepare *hardware* or *software* for operation.

Many application packages have their own install programs—programs that copy all the required files from the original distribution floppy disks or CD into appropriate *directories* on your hard disk, and then help you to configure the program to your own operating requirements. *Microsoft Windows* programs are usually installed by a program called SETUP.

installation program A program whose sole function is to install (and sometimes configure) another program.

The program guides the user through what might be a rather complex set of choices, copying the correct files into the right *directories*, decompressing them if necessary, and asking for the next disk when appropriate. This program may also ask for a person's name or a company name so that the startup screen can be customized.

Some older IBM-compatible installation programs may change your *CONFIG .SYS* or *AUTOEXEC.BAT* files without letting you know; others will ask your permission and add their statements to the end of the existing commands.

Institute of Electrical and Electronic Engineers Abbreviated IEEE. Pronounced "eye-triple-ee." A membership organization, founded in 1963, including engineers, students, and scientists. IEEE also acts as a coordinating body for computing and communications standards, particularly the IEEE 802 standard for the physical and *data-link* layers of *local area networks*, following the *ISO/OSI model*.

integer Also referred to as INT, an integer is a whole number, one in which there is no decimal portion.

integrated circuit Abbreviated IC, also known as a chip. A small semiconductor circuit that contains many electronic components.

integrated drive electronics interface Abbreviated IDE. A popular *hard-disk interface* standard, used for disks in the range of 40MB to 1.2GB, requiring medium to fast *data transfer rates*. IDE gets its name from the fact that the electronic control circuitry needed is actually located on the drive itself, thus eliminating the need for a separate *hard-disk controller* card.

Intel OverDrive The original Intel OverDrive *microprocessor* was designed as a user-installable upgrade to an *80486SX* or *80486DX*-based computer, while the Pentium OverDrive chip is designed as a replacement for 486-based systems. OverDrive chips boost system performance by using the same *clock multiplying* technology found in the Intel *80486DX-2* and *DX4* chips. Once installed, an OverDrive processor can increase *application* performance by an estimated 40 to 70 percent.

interface That point where a connection is made between two different parts of a system, such as between two *hardware devices*, between a user and a program or *operating system*, or between two *application* programs.

In hardware, an interface describes the logical and physical connections used, as in *RS-232-C*, and is often considered to be synonymous with the term "port."

A *user interface* consists of all the means by which a program communicates with the user, including a command line, menus, dialog boxes, online help

systems, and so on. User interfaces can be classified as *character-based*, *menu-driven*, or *graphical*.

Software interfaces are *application program interfaces*; the codes and messages used by programs to communicate behind the scenes.

interface standard Any standard way of connecting two *devices* or elements having different functions.

Many different interface standards are used in the PC world, including *SCSI*, *integrated drive electronics*, and the *enhanced small device interface* for hard disks, *RS-232-C* and the *Centronics parallel interface* for serial devices and parallel printers, and the *ISO/OSI model* for computer-to-computer communications over a network.

interlacing A display technique that uses two passes over the *monitor* screen, painting every other line on the screen the first time, and then filling in the rest of the lines on the second pass. *Non-interlaced* scanning paints all the lines on the display in a single pass. While more expensive, interlacing reduces unwanted *flicker* and eyestrain.

interleave factor The order in which the *sectors* were arranged on your hard disk by the initial *low-level format*.

Introduced as a compensation for slow computers, interleaving eliminates the delay that results when a drive is not ready to read or write the next sector as soon as it has read or written the previous one. With a 3:1 interleave factor, sequentially numbered sectors are located three sectors apart on the disk. An interleave that is either too high or too low can lead to a severe degradation in performance, because the computer spends its time waiting for the next sector to arrive at the read/write heads. Thanks to increases in PC speed, interleaving is obsolete, and most modern disks use a 1:1 interleave factor (which actually indicates a non-interleaved drive).

interleaved memory A method of speeding up *data* access by dividing *dynamic RAM* (DRAM) memory into two separate banks so that the processor can read one bank while the other is being refreshed. DRAM requires that its contents be updated at least every thousandth of a second, and while it is being refreshed it cannot be read by the processor; interleaving memory speeds up access times. Of course, if the processor needs to read from the same bank of RAM repeatedly, it must wait for the full DRAM cycle time.

The introduction of *static RAM* (SRAM) has removed the need for interleaved memory, because SRAM memory can retain its contents without the need for refreshment.

internal hard disk A *hard disk drive* housed inside the computer's system unit and integrated with it, rather than an external drive packaged with its own case, cables, and independent power supply.

International Standards Organization Abbreviated ISO. An international standard-making body, based in Geneva, that establishes global standards for communications and information exchange. ANSI is the U.S. member of ISO.

The seven-layer International Standards Organization's Open Systems Interconnection (ISO/OSI) model for computer-to-computer communications is one of the ISO's most widely accepted recommendations.

internet Abbreviation for internetwork. A set of computer networks, made up of a large number of smaller networks.

Internet The world's largest computer network, consisting of over 2 million computers supporting over 20 million users in almost 200 different countries. The Internet is growing at a phenomenal rate—between 10 and 15 percent per month—so any size estimates are quickly out-of-date.

The Internet was originally established to meet the research needs of the U.S. Defense industry, but it has grown into a huge global network serving universities, academic researchers, commercial interests, and government agencies, both in the U.S. and overseas. The Internet uses *TCP/IP* protocols, and many of the Internet *hosts* run the *Unix* operating system.

Internet access can be via a permanent network connection or by dial-up through one of the many service providers.

Internet address An *IP* (i.e., 131 .107.2.200) or *domain* (i.e., www .microsoft.com) address which identifies a specific node on the Internet.

interprocess communication Abbreviated IPC. A term that describes all the methods used to pass information between two programs running on the same computer running a *multitasking operating system*, or between two programs running on a network, including pipes, *shared memory*, *queues*, the Clipboard, DDE (Dynamic Data Exchange), and OLE (Object Linking and Embedding).

interrupt A signal to the processor generated by a device under its control (such as the system clock) that interrupts normal processing.

An interrupt indicates that an event requiring the processor's attention has occurred, causing the processor to suspend and save its current activity, and then branch to an interrupt service routine. This service routine processes the interrupt, whether it was generated by the system clock, a keystroke, or a mouse click; and when it's complete, returns control to the suspended process. In the PC, interrupts are often divided into three classes; internal *hardware*, external hardware, and *software* interrupts. The Intel 80×86 family of processors supports 256 prioritized interrupts, of which the first 64 are reserved for use by the system *hardware* or by *DOS*.

interrupt controller A chip, used to process and prioritize *hardware interrupts*. In IBM-compatible computers, the Intel 8259A Programmable Interrupt Controller responds to each hardware interrupt, assigns a priority, and forwards it to the main processor.

interrupt handler Special *software* invoked when an *interrupt* occurs. Each type of interrupt, such as a clock tick or a keystroke, is processed by its own specific interrupt handler. A table, called the *interrupt vector table*, maintains a list of addresses for these specific interrupt handlers.

interrupt request lines   Abbreviated IRQ. Hardware lines that carry a signal from a device to the processor.

A *hardware* interrupt signals when an event has taken place that requires the processor's attention and may come from the keyboard, the input/output ports, or the system's disk drives. In the PC, the main processor does not accept interrupts from hardware devices directly; instead interrupts are routed to an Intel 8259A Programmable Interrupt Controller. This chip responds to each hardware interrupt, assigns a priority, and forwards it to the main processor.

interrupt vector table   A list of addresses for specific *software* routines known as *interrupt handlers*. In a *DOS* computer, the interrupt vector table consists of 256 pointers located in the first megabyte of memory.

intranet   An interconnected collection of networks that is contained within an enterprise. Intranets can be connected to the Internet, with people from the outside being given limited access to the intranet.

IP   Abbreviation for Internet Protocol. The underlying *communications protocol* on which the *Internet* is based. IP allows a data packet to travel across many networks before reaching its final destination.

IPSEC   Most current methods of securing network transmission work at the application layer of the Open Systems Interconnect networking model. IPSEC is a developing security standard that is designed to work at the network layer of the OSI model where the packets are actually processed. At this layer, it is possible to encrypt the packet and digitally sign the packet so that its origin can be verified.

IPv6   The next revision of IP, IPv6 lengthens the IP address from 32 to 128 bits, thereby creating a much larger address pool. IPv6 is faster than IP and allows for security as well as other enhancements.

IPX/SPX   A suite of networking protocols created by Novell Corporation to allow Novell Netware systems to communicate over local and wide area networks.

IRC   Abbreviation for Internet Relay Chat. An Internet client/server application that allows large groups of users to communicate with each other interactively. Specific channels are devoted to one particular topic, from the sacred to the profane, and topics come and go regularly as interest levels change.

ISA Abbreviation for industry-standard architecture. The *16-bit bus* design was first used in *IBM's PC/AT* computer in 1984. ISA has a bus speed of 8 MHz, and a maximum throughput of 8 megabytes per second. *EISA* is a *32-bit* extension to this standard bus.

ISDN Abbreviation for Integrated Services Digital Network. A worldwide digital communications network emerging from existing telephone services. Computers and other devices connect to ISDN via interfaces called terminal adapters or ISDN modems. ISDN systems are capable of transmitting voice, video, music, and data.

ISO/OSI model Abbreviation for International Standards Organization/Open System Interconnection. In networking, a reference model defined by the ISO that divides computer-to-computer communications into seven connected layers, known as a "protocol stack."

ITU Abbreviation for International Tele-communications Union. The United Nations umbrella organization

that develops and standardizes telecommunications worldwide. The ITU also contains the *CCITT*, the International Frequency Registration Board (IFRB), and the Consultative Committee on International Radio (CCIR). Popular usage is starting to refer to the CCITT standards as ITU standards.

JAVA An object-oriented programming language designed specifically for use in large distributed networks like the Internet. It is designed to look and feel like C++ and yet be easier to use. Programs written in JAVA are portable, which means that they can run on any computer with any operating system that has a JAVA virtual machine.

joystick A popular multidirectional pointing device, used extensively in many computer games, as well as in certain professional applications such as computer-aided design (CAD).

Jughead An *Internet* search mechanism used to construct an index of high-level Gopher menus. Once a search is complete, you interact with the Jughead-built menu in the same way that you use a Gopher menu.

jumper A small plastic and metal connector that completes a circuit, usually to select one option from a set of several user-definable options. Jumpers are often used to configure older pieces of hardware that do not support *Plug and Play*.

kernel The most fundamental part of an *operating system*. The kernel stays resident in memory at all times, often hidden from the user, and manages system memory, the file system, and disk operations.

keyboard The typewriter-like set of keys used to input *data* and control commands to the computer. Most keyboards use a *QWERTY* layout, and may also have a calculator-like numeric keypad off to one side, as well as a set of *cursor-movement keys*.

keyboard buffer A small amount of system memory used to store the most recently typed keys, also known as the type-ahead buffer. Some utility programs let you collect a number of keystrokes or commands and edit or reissue them.

keyboard layout Most computers use a keyboard based on the traditional *QWERTY* typewriter-like keyboard.

In the *IBM PC* and *DOS* computers, the most common keyboard currently used has 101 keys, with 12 function keys in a row above the other keys.

keyboard template A plastic card that fits over certain keys (usually the *function keys*) on the keyboard to remind you how to use them. These templates are specific to an *application* and can be very useful if you are an occasional user or are learning to use the program.

kilo- A prefix indicating 1000 in the metric system. Because computing is based on powers of 2, in this context kilo usually means 2^{10}, or 1024. To differentiate between these two uses, a lowercase k is used to indicate 1000 (as in kHz), and an uppercase K to indicate 1024 (as in KB).

kilobit Abbreviated Kb or Kbit. 1024 *bits* (binary digits).

kilobits per second Abbreviated Kbps. The number of *bits*, or binary digits, transmitted every second, measured in multiples of 1024 bits per second. Used as an indicator of communications transmission rate.

kilobyte Abbreviated K, KB, or Kbyte. 1024 *bytes*.

L1 and L2 cache *Cache* memory is much faster for a processor to access than Random Access Memory. Level one cache, which is built right into the processor, is checked first for required data, and if it is not present then the processor checks level two cache, which is usually on a separate chip or chips.

LAN Manager A *network operating system*, developed by *Microsoft* and 3Com, that runs on *80386, 80486* (and better) computers. The *file-server software* is a version of *OS/2*; client PCs can be OS/2-, *DOS-, Unix-,* or *Macintosh*-based. *Disk mirroring, disk duplexing,* and *UPS*-monitoring functions are all available, and the operating system supports *IPX/SPX, TCP/IP* and *NetBEUI* communications protocols.

laptop computer A small *portable computer* light enough to carry comfortably, with a *flat screen* and keyboard that fold together.

Laptop computers are battery-operated and often have a thin, backlit or sidelit *LCD* display screen. Some models can even mate with a *docking station* to perform as a full-sized desktop system back at the office. Advances in battery technology allow laptop computers to run for many hours between charges, and some models have a set of business applications built into ROM.

laser printer A *high-resolution* non-impact printer that uses a variation of the electrophotographic process used in

photocopying machines to print text and graphics onto paper.

A laser printer uses a rotating disc to reflect laser beams onto a photosensitive drum, where the image of the page is converted into an electrostatic charge that attracts and holds the toner. A piece of charged paper is then rolled against the drum to transfer the image, and heat is applied to fuse the toner and paper together to create the final image.

latency The time that elapses between issuing a request for *data*, and actually starting the data transfer.

In a *hard disk*, this translates into the time it takes to position the disk's read/write *head* and rotate the disk so that the required *sector* or *cluster* is under the head. Latency is just one of many factors that influence disk access speeds.

layout In *printed-circuit board* design, the arrangement of the individual components on the circuit board.

LCD monitor A *monitor* that uses *liquid-crystal display* technology. Many *laptop* and *notebook computers* use LCD displays because of their small size and low weight.

LDAP An acronym for Lightweight Directory Access Protocol, LDAP is used to search for individuals, companies, and the like on large networks and display e-mail address, phone number, city, state, zip code, and just about any other information that the systems administrator has seen fit to include in their directory.

letter quality A printer mode that produces text higher in quality than *draft mode*. As the name suggests, letter quality printing is supposed to be good enough to be used in business letters and therefore comparable to typewriter output. *Laser printers*, some *ink-jet printers* and all *daisy-wheel printers* produce letter-quality output; certain high-end *dot-matrix printers* can produce letter-quality output, but most do not.

light-emitting diode Abbreviated LED. A small semiconductor device that emits light as current flows through it. LEDs are often used as activity lights on computer peripherals such as hard disk drives and modems.

light pen A light-sensitive input device shaped like a pen, used to draw on the computer screen or to make menu selections. As the tip of the light pen makes contact with the screen, it sends a signal back to the computer containing the x,y coordinates of the *pixels* at that point.

line adapter In communications, a device such as a *modem* that converts a digital signal into a form suitable for transmission over a communications channel.

line printer Any printer that prints a complete line at a time, rather than printing one character at a time (as a *dot-matrix* or *daisy-wheel printer* does), or one page at a time (as a *laser printer* does). Line printers are very high-speed printers and are common in the corporate environment where they are used with *mainframe computers, minicomputers,* and networked systems.

line sharing device A small electronic device that allows a fax machine and a telephone answering machine to share the same phone line. The device answers the call and listens for the characteristic high-pitched fax carrier signal. If this signal is detected, the call is routed to the fax machine; if it is not present, the call is sent to a telephone or answering machine instead.

Linux A Unix-style operating system developed by Linus Torvalds at the University of Helsinki. Linux is free, or very low cost, and extensible by anyone who feels like doing some programming. Linux has a reputation of being a stable and efficient operating system.

liquid crystal display Abbreviated LCD. A display technology common in *portable computers* that uses electric current to align or misalign crystals, allowing light to pass or not to pass as needed.

The rod-shaped crystals are contained between two parallel transparent electrodes, and when current is applied, they change their orientation, creating a darker area. Many LCD screens are also back-lit or side-lit to increase visibility and reduce the possibility of eyestrain.

local area network Abbreviated LAN. A group of computers and associated *peripherals* connected by a communications channel capable of sharing files and other resources between several users.

local bus A PC bus specification that allows peripherals to exchange data at a rate faster than the 8 megabytes per second allowed by the ISA (Industry Standard Architecture), and the 32 megabytes per second allowed by the EISA (Extended Industry Standard Architecture) definitions. Local bus can achieve a maximum data rate of 133

megabytes per second with a 33 MHz bus speed, 148 megabytes per second with a 40 MHz bus, or 267 megabytes per second with a 50 MHz bus.

To date, the *Video Electronics Standards Association (VESA)* video cards have been the main peripheral to benefit from local bus use.

local disk In networking, a disk attached to a *workstation* rather than to the *file server*.

local printer In networking, a printer attached to a *workstation* rather than to the *file server* or a *print server*.

logical drive The internal division of a large *hard disk* into smaller units. One single *physical drive* may be organized into several logical drives for convenience; *DOS* supports up to 23 logical drives on a system. On a single-floppy system, the disk drive can function as both logical drive A and logical drive B, depending on the exact circumstances.

long filename The ability of a file system to take advantage of multiple-character file names. Several operating systems are not limited to the DOS "8.3" file-naming convention of eight characters before a period and three more optional characters forming the *file-name extension. Unix, Windows 95/98, Windows NT, OS/2,* and the Macintosh file systems can all manage long file names, even those containing spaces, more than one period, and mixed upper- and lowercase letters.

lost chain   A part of a *file*, consisting of one or more *clusters*, that no longer has an entry in the *file allocation table* and so cannot be reconnected to the rest of the file. The Windows program Scandisk detects these lost chains, converting them into files so that you can delete them and recover the disk space they occupy. You can also examine the contents of these lost chains after Scandisk has recovered them, but the chance of the contents being usable is very slim indeed.

lost cluster   A *cluster*, originally once part of a *file*, for which there is now no *file allocation table* entry. Use the Windows program Scandisk to convert lost clusters into files. You can then examine the contents of the cluster, and decide if you want to keep it or delete it and recover the disk space that it occupies.

low-level format   The process that creates the *tracks* and *sectors* on a blank *hard disk* or *floppy disk*; sometimes called the physical format. Most hard disks

are already low-level formatted; however, floppy disks receive both a low- and a *high-level format* (or logical format) when you use the *Windows, DOS* or *OS/2* command *FORMAT.*

low resolution   In monitors and printers, a description of low-quality output, lacking sharpness or definition. *Resolution* is determined by the technology used to create the output.

What actually constitutes low resolution is in the eye of the beholder; what one person may consider to be low resolution may be quite acceptable to another.

LPTx ports   An acronym for Line Printer Terminal, LPT is the device name used to denote a parallel communications *port*, often used with a printer. DOS supports three parallel ports: LPT1, LPT2, and LPT3, and *OS/2* adds support for network ports LPT4 through LPT9. Windows 95/98 supports up to 128 parallel ports; of course, this is actually limited to the number of physical ports in the system.

lurking   The practice of reading an *Internet mailing list* or *USENET newsgroup* without *post*ing anything yourself. In the online world, lurking is not considered to be particularly antisocial;

in fact it is a good idea to lurk for a while when you first *subscribe* so you can get a feel for the tone of the discussions in the group, and come up to speed on recent history.

magneto-optical drives Abbreviated MO. An erasable, high-capacity, removable storage device similar to a *CD-ROM drive*.

Magneto-optical drives use both magnetic and laser technology to write *data* to the disk, and use the laser to read that data back again. Writing data takes two passes over the disk, an erase pass followed by the write pass, but reading can be done in just one pass and, as a result, is much faster.

mailing list On the Internet, a group of people who share a common interest and who automatically receive all the mail posted to the listserver, or mailing-list manager program. Contributions are sent as *e-mail* to the listserver and then distributed to all subscribers. Most listserver programs include a command that will send you a complete list of all the subscribers' e-mail addresses by return e-mail.

mainframe computer A large, fast *multi*-user computer system, designed to manage very large amounts of *data* and very complex computing tasks.

Mainframes are normally installed in large corporations, universities, or military installations, and can support hundreds, even thousands, of users.

maintenance release A software upgrade that corrects minor *bugs* or adds a few small features, distinguished from a major release by an increase in only the decimal portion of the version number—for example, from 3.0 to 3.1, rather than from 3.1 to 4.0.

male connector Any cable connector with pins designed to engage the sockets on the female part of the connector.

Maltron keyboard An alternative keyboard designed to eliminate *carpal tunnel syndrome* that arranges the keys in two concave areas conforming to the shape of the hand, allowing better alignment of the forearm and wrist.

MBONE Abbreviation for Multicast Backbone. An experimental method of transmitting digital video over the *Internet* in real time.

The TCP/IP protocols used for Internet transmissions are unsuitable for real time audio or video; they were designed to deliver text and other files reliably, but with some delay. MBONE requires the creation of another backbone service with special hardware and software to accommodate video and audio transmissions; the existing Internet hardware cannot manage time-critical transmissions.

MCA Abbreviation for Micro Channel Architecture. A *32-bit* proprietary *expansion bus* first introduced by IBM in 1987 for the *IBM PS/2* range of computers and also used in the RS/6000 series.

MCA is incompatible with expansion boards that follow the earlier *16-bit* AT bus standard, physically because the boards are about 50 percent smaller, and electronically as the bus depends on more proprietary integrated circuits.

MCA was designed for *multiprocessing*, and it also allows expansion boards to identify themselves, thus eliminating many of the conflicts that arose through the use of manual settings in the original bus.

MCGA Acronym for Multi-Color Graphics Array. A *video adapter* included with certain *IBM PS/2* computers, that provides 64 gray shades with a palette of 16 colors at a resolution of 640 by 350 *pixels*.

MDA Acronym for Monochrome Display Adapter. A *video adapter* introduced in 1981 that could display text but not graphics, in one color, at a resolution of 640 *pixels* horizontally by 350 vertically. MDAs were replaced in many cases by the Hercules Graphics Card (*HGC*).

mean time between failures Abbreviated MTBF. The statistically-derived average length of time that a system component operates before failing.

mean time to repair Abbreviated MTTR. The average length of time that it takes to repair a failed component.

Media Control Interface Abbreviated MCI. A standard *interface* used for controlling *multimedia* files and devices. Each device has its own *device driver* that implements a standard set of MCI functions such as stop, play, or record.

meg A common abbreviation for *megabyte* or *megahertz*.

mega- Abbreviated M. A prefix meaning one million in the metric system. Because computing is based on powers of 2, in this context mega usually means 2^{20} or 1,048,576; the power of 2 closest to one million.

megabit Abbreviated Mbit. Usually 1,048,576 binary digits or bits of *data*. Often used as equivalent to 1 million bits.

megabits per second   Abbreviated Mbps. A measurement of the amount of information moving across a network or communications link in one second, measured in multiples of 1,048,576 bits.

megabyte   Abbreviated MB. Usually 1,048,576 bytes. Megabytes are a common way of representing computer *memory* or *hard-disk* capacity.

megahertz   Abbreviated MHz. One million cycles per second. A processor's *clock speed* is often expressed in MHz. The original IBM PC operated an *8088* running at 4.77 MHz, the more modern *Pentium* processor runs at speeds of up to 400 MHz.

membrane keyboard   A pressure-sensitive keyboard covered by a protective plastic sheet used in a hostile environment where operators may not always have clean hands. Since it is very difficult to type quickly and accurately on a membrane keyboard, they are most often used for occasional *data entry* in factories or in fast-food restaurants. They do not work well for touch typing.

memory   The primary random-access memory (*RAM*) installed in the computer.

The operating system copies *application* programs from disk into memory, where all program execution and *data* processing takes place; results are written back out to disk again. The amount of memory installed in the computer can determine the size and number of programs that it can run, as well as the size of the largest data *file*.

memory address   The exact location in memory that stores a particular *data* item or program instruction.

memory board   A *printed circuit board* containing *memory* chips. When all the sockets on a memory board are filled, and the board contains the maximum amount of memory that it can manage, it is said to be "fully populated."

memory cache   An area of high-speed *memory* on the processor that stores commonly used code or *data* obtained from slower memory, replacing the need to access the system's main memory to fetch instructions.

The Intel 82385 cache controller chip was used with fast *static RAM* on some systems to increase performance, but more modern processors include cache management functions on the main processor. The Intel *80486* contains a single 8K cache to manage both *data* and instruction caching; the *Pentium* contains two separate 8K caches, one each for data and instructions. The Pentium II has two 16K caches built into the chip.

memory chip A chip that holds *data* or program instructions. A memory chip may hold its contents temporarily, as in the case of *RAM*, or permanently, as in the case of *ROM*.

memory management The way in which the computer handles memory. In the PC, you may find the following kinds of memory:

• **Conventional memory.** This is the area of memory below 640KB.

• **Upper memory.** Also known as reserved memory. The 384KB of memory between 640KB and 1MB. This space is used by system hardware such as your *video adapter*. Unused portions of upper memory are known as *upper memory blocks* (UMBs), and on an *80386* (or later) processor, you can use these UMBs for loading device drivers or terminate-and-stay-resident programs.

• **Extended memory.** That memory above 1MB on 80386 (or later) processors. Extended memory needs an extended-memory manager such as *HIMEM.SYS*.

• **High memory area.** The first 64K of extended memory.

• **Expanded memory.** Memory above conventional memory that can be used by certain *DOS* applications.

The accompanying diagram shows the memory configuration of a computer with 640KB of *conventional memory*, 4MB of extended memory, and 2MB of expanded memory on an additional expanded-memory board.

Many of the design decisions made in the original PC, and in early versions of *DOS*, define these apparently random memory boundaries. While these descriptions are still accurate, modern operating systems hide this from the user and require no configuration on the user's part.

memory management unit Abbreviated MMU. The part of the processor that manages the mapping of virtual memory addresses to actual physical addresses.

In some systems, such as those based on early Intel or Motorola processors, the MMU was a separate chip; however, in most modern processors, the MMU is integrated into the *CPU* chip itself.

memory map   The organization and allocation of memory in a computer. A memory map will give an indication of the amount of memory used by the *operating system* and the amount remaining for use by *applications*.

message channel   A form of *inter-process communication* found in *multi-tasking operating systems*. Interprocess communications allow two programs running in the same computer to share information.

metafile   A *file* that contains information about other files, particularly those used for *data* interchange. For example, a graphics metafile contains not only a graphical image of some kind, but also information on how the image should be displayed. This allows the image to be output to a variety of different display devices. Metafiles often have the *file-name extension* .MET.

metropolitan area network
Abbreviated MAN. A public high-speed network, operating at 100 megabits per second, capable of voice and *data* transmission over a distance of up to 50 miles. A MAN is smaller than a wide area network (WAN) but larger than a local area network (LAN).

microcomputer   Any computer based on a single-chip processor. Many modern microcomputers are as powerful or even more powerful than *mainframe computers* from a few years ago.

microkernel   An alternative *kernel* design developed by researchers at Carnegie-Mellon University and implemented in the Mac and now Windows NT *operating systems*.

Traditionally, the kernel has been a monolithic piece of the operating system, resident in memory at all times, taking care of operations as varied as *virtual memory* management, *file* input/output and task scheduling. The microkernel, on the other hand, is a kernel stripped down to the point where it is only concerned with loading, running, and scheduling tasks. All other operating system functions (virtual memory management, disk input/output, and so on) are implemented and managed as tasks running on top of the microkernel.

micron   A unit of measurement. One millionth of a meter, corresponding to approximately 1/25,000 of an inch. The core diameter of *fiber optic* network cabling is often specified in terms of microns, 62.5 being a common size.

microprocessor   Abbreviated processor. A *CPU* on one single chip. The first micro-processor was developed by *Intel* in 1969. The microprocessors most often used in PCs are the Motorola 680 × 0 series (in the *Apple Macintosh* computers), and the Intel 80 × 86 family (in IBM and *IBM-compatible* computers).

Besides computers, microprocessors are used in applications ranging from microwave ovens, VCRs, and automobiles to pocket calculators and *laser printers*.

Microsoft Diagnostics A PC diagnostic and technical information program first released along with *MS-DOS* 6.

MIDI Pronounced "middy." Acronym for musical instrument digital interface. A standard *protocol* that describes communications between computers, synthesizers, and musical instruments.

Instead of transcribing a composition by hand, a musician can play the piece at a piano-style keyboard and record it on a computer as a series of musical messages. These messages include the start of a note, its length, tempo, pitch, attack, and decay time. Once this information is recorded on disk, it can be edited very easily using appropriate software; for example, transposing a piece from one key to another is an easy task for a computer, but a long, laborious task to perform manually.

MIDI port A port that allows the connection of a musical instrument digital interface (*MIDI*) device to a personal computer.

The three types of port described in the standard are MIDI In, MIDI Out, and MIDI Thru. A synthesizer receives MIDI messages via its MIDI In port, and forwards messages to other devices using the MIDI Thru port. A synthesizer can send its own messages to the computer using the MIDI Out port.

MIDI ports are standard on the Atari ST personal computer, but have to be added to the *IBM-compatible* and *Macintosh* computers.

milli- Abbreviated m. A prefix meaning one thousandth in the metric system.

millisecond Abbreviated ms or msec. A unit of measurement equal to one thousandth of a second. In computing, *hard disk* and *CD-ROM* drive *access times* are often described in terms of milliseconds; the higher the number the slower the disk system.

millivolt Abbreviated mv. A unit of measurement equal to one thousandth of a volt.

MIME Abbreviation for Multipurpose Internet Mail Extensions. A set of extensions that allows *Internet e-mail* users to add non-ASCII elements such as graphics, PostScript files, audio, or video to their e-mail. Most of the common e-mail client programs include MIME capabilities.

minicomputer A medium-sized computer system capable of managing over 100 users simultaneously, suitable for use in a small company or single corporate or government department.

minihard disk A hard disk mounted on a Type III *PCMCIA* card.

MIPS Acronym for million of instructions per second. A measure of the processing speed of a computer's *CPU*.

MIPS R4000 and R4400 A family of 64-bit *microprocessors* from MIPS Computer Systems. The R4000 has a 1.3 million *transistor* design, with both an 8K data *cache* and an 8K instruction cache, as well as a *floating point processor*. Internally, the R4000 runs at 100 MHz, double its external 50-MHz clock output. The R4400, with 2.2 million transistors, is based on the R4000, but has larger cache units (16K data cache and 16K instruction cache) and runs internally at 150 MHz, externally at 75 MHz. Silicon Graphics acquired MIPS in June of 1992.

MMX A series of 57 commands built into the Pentium II and higher processors from Intel that accelerate processing of multimedia applications.

modem Contraction of modulator/demodulator, a device that allows a computer to transmit information over a telephone line.

The modem translates between the *digital* signals that the computer uses, and *analog* signals suitable for transmission over telephone lines. When transmitting, the modem modulates the digital *data* onto a carrier signal on the telephone line. When receiving, the modem performs the reverse process and demodulates the data from the carrier signal.

Modems usually operate at speeds ranging from 2,400 to about 53,000 bits per second over standard telephone lines, and can use even faster rates over leased lines. A suitable communications program is needed to operate the modem. Modems come in internal and external versions; the internal version plugs into an expansion slot inside the computer while the external is connected via a serial cable and sits outside the system.

moderated newsgroup On the Internet, a *USENET newsgroup* or *mailing list* that is managed by one or more people in an attempt to maintain standards for the newsgroup. All *posts* to the newsgroup are reviewed by the moderator to make sure that they meet the standards the newsgroup has set for subject and commercial content before being passed on to the whole group. Moderation is not censorship, but an attempt to avoid some of the more extreme antics of those who enjoy *flaming* and *flame wars.*

moderator A person or small committee of people who review the contents of all *posts* to a *USENET newsgroup* or *mailing list* in an attempt to ensure that the postings meet the standards set by the group. Moderators are almost always volunteers.

modified frequency modulation encoding Abbreviated MFM encoding. An obsolete method of storing *data* on a hard disk. Based on an earlier technique known as frequency modulation (FM) encoding, MFM achieves a two-fold increase in data storage density over standard FM recording, but it is not as efficient a space saver as *run-length limited encoding.*

modulation In communications, the process used by a *modem* to add the *digital* signal onto the *carrier signal*, so that the signal can be transmitted over a telephone line.

The frequency, amplitude, or phase of a signal may be modulated to represent a digital or *analog* signal.

monitor A video output device capable of displaying text and graphics, often in color.

monochrome monitor A *monitor* that can display text and graphics in one color only. For example, white text on a green background, or black text on a white background.

motherboard The main *printed circuit board* in a computer that contains the *central processing unit*, appropriate *coprocessor* and support chips, device controllers, *memory*, and also *expansion slots* to give access to the computer's internal *bus.*

mouse A small input device with one or more buttons used as for pointing or drawing.

As you move the mouse in any direction, an on-screen mouse cursor follows the mouse movements; all movements are relative. Once the mouse pointer is in the correct position on the screen, you can press one of the mouse buttons to initiate an action or operation; different user interfaces and *file* programs interpret mouse clicks in different ways.

MS-DOS Acronym for Microsoft Disk Operating System, pronounced "emmess-dos." MS-DOS, like other *operating systems*, allocates system resources such as hard and floppy disks, the monitor, and the printer to the applications programs that need them.

MS-DOS is a *single-user*, single-tasking operating system, with either a *command-line interface*, or a *shell* interface.

multilayer A *printed circuit board* that contains several different layers of circuitry. The layers are laminated together to make a single board, onto which the other discrete components are added.

multimedia A computer technology that displays information using a combination of *full-motion video*, animation, sound, graphics and text with a high degree of user interaction.

multimedia personal computer Abbreviated MPC. The Multimedia PC Working Group, formerly the Multimedia PC Marketing Council, consisting of several hardware and software vendors, including Micro-soft, Zenith Data Systems, Video Seven, Media Vision, and NEC Technologies, sets standards for multimedia PCs and the software that runs on them.

The Council's original Level 1 minimum requirements for a multimedia PC included an *80386SX* running at 16 MHz, 2MB of memory, a hard disk with 30MB of free space, a *CD-ROM* capable of a 150K/second transfer rate and an *8-bit sound card*.

Level 2 requirements specify an *80486SX* running at 25 MHz, 8MB of memory, a hard disk with 160MB of free space, a double-speed *CD-ROM* capable of a 300K/second transfer rate, and a *16-bit* sound card.

Level 3 requirements, released in February 1996, require at least a 75 MHz Pentium processor, 8MB RAM, 3.5" floppy drive, 540MB hard disk, CD-ROM with 250-millisecond access time, 16-bit stereo sound card with 44.1 sample rate, 3-watt speakers, and a video card capable of 30 frames per second with MPEG playback capabilities.

multiplexing In communications, a technique that transmits several signals over a single communications channel.

Frequency-division multiplexing separates the signals by modulating the *data* into different carrier frequencies. *Time-division multiplexing* divides up the available time between the various signals. *Statistical multiplexing* uses statistical techniques to dynamically allocate transmission space depending on the traffic pattern.

multiplexor Often abbreviated mux. In communications, a device that merges several lower-speed transmission channels into one high-speed channel at one end of the link. Another multiplexor reverses this process at the other end of the link to reproduce the low-speed channels.

multiprocessing The ability of an *operating system* to use more than one *CPU* in a single computer. Symmetrical multiprocessing refers to the operating system's ability to assign tasks dynamically to the next available processor, whereas asymmetrical multiprocessing requires that the original program designer choose the processor to use for a given task at the time of writing the program.

multisync monitor A monitor designed to detect and adjust to a variety of different input signals. By contrast, a *fixed-frequency monitor*

must receive a signal at one specific frequency.

multitasking The simultaneous execution of two or more programs in one computer.

multithreading The *concurrent* processing of several *tasks* or *threads* inside the same program. Because several tasks can be processed in parallel, one task does not have to wait for another to finish before starting.

multiuser Describes a computer system that supports more than one simultaneous user.

DOS, OS/2, Windows, and *Windows NT* are all *single-user operating systems; Unix* and its derivatives are all multiuser systems.

nano- Abbreviated n. A prefix meaning one-billionth.

nanosecond Abbreviated ns. One-billionth of second. The speed of computer memory and logic chips is measured in nanoseconds.

Processors operating at *clock speeds* of 25 MHz or more need *dynamic RAM* with access times of faster than 80 nanoseconds (60 nanoseconds is the current speed of choice), while *static*

RAM chips can be read in as little as 10 to 15 nanoseconds.

narrowband In communications, a voice-grade transmission channel of 2400 bits per second or less.

NetBEUI Abbreviation for NetBIOS Extended User Interface. A network *device driver* for the *transport layer* supplied with *Microsoft operating systems*.

NetBIOS Acronym for Network Basic Input/Output System. In networking, a layer of software, originally developed in 1984 by IBM and Sytek, that links a *network operating system* with specific network hardware. NetBIOS provides an *application program interface* (API) with a consistent set of commands for requesting lower-level network services to transmit information from node to node.

netiquette A contraction of network etiquette. The set of unwritten rules governing the use of *e-mail*, *USENET newsgroups*, and other *online services*.

network A group of computers and associated peripherals connected by a communications *channel* capable of sharing files and other resources between several users.

A network can range from a *peer-to-peer network* connecting a small number of users in an office or department, to a *local area network* connecting many users over permanently installed cables and dial-up lines, or to a *wide area network* connecting users on several different networks spread over a wide geographic area.

network file system Abbreviated NFS. A distributed file sharing system developed by Sun Microsystems, Inc.

NFS allows a computer on a network to use the files and peripherals of another networked computer as if they were local. NFS is platform-independent, and runs on mainframes, minicomputers, *RISC*-based *workstations*, *diskless workstations*, and personal computers. NFS has been licensed and implemented by more than 300 vendors.

network interface card Abbreviated NIC. In networking, the PC expansion board that plugs into a personal computer or server and works with the *network operating system* to control the flow of information over the network. The network interface card is connected to the network cabling (*twisted pair*, *coaxial* or *fiber optic cable*), which in turn connects all the network interface cards in the network.

network layer The third of seven layers of the International Standards Organization's Open Systems Interconnection (ISO/OSI) model for computer-to-computer communications.

The network layer defines protocols for data routing to ensure that the information arrives at the correct destination node.

newsgroup A USENET e-mail group devoted to the discussion of a single topic. Subscribers post articles to the newsgroup which can then be read by all the other subscribers. Newsgroups do not usually contain hard news items.

newsreader An application used to read the articles posted to *USENET newsgroups.*

Newsreaders are of two kinds; threaded newsreaders group the newsgroup posts into threads of related articles, while unthreaded newsreaders just present the articles in their original order of posting. Of the two types, threaded newsreaders are much more convenient to use.

NeXT A *Unix*-based *workstation* from NeXT Inc. using a 24 MHz *Motorola 68040* processor, a high-resolution color display, stereo sound, and an erasable optical disk.

NeXT computers had the reputation for being well manufactured and providing good value for money; however, the hardware part of the company was sold to Canon in 1993, and NeXT now concentrates on marketing the software development environment known as NeXTStep, a windowed, *object-oriented,* programming environment for creating graphics-based *applications.*

9-track tape A tape storage format that uses 9 parallel tracks on half-inch reel-to-reel magnetic tape. Eight tracks are used for data, and one track is used for *parity* information.

node In communications, any device attached to the network.

noise In communications, extraneous signals on a transmission channel that degrade the quality or performance of the channel. Noise is often caused by interference from nearby power lines, from electrical equipment, or from *spikes* in the *AC* line voltage.

nonimpact printer Any printer that creates an image without striking a ribbon against the paper.

Nonimpact printers include *thermal printers, ink-jet printers,* and *laser printers.* These printers are all much quieter in operation than *impact printers,* and their main drawback is that they cannot use multi-part paper to make several copies of the same printout or report.

non-interlaced Describes a *monitor* in which the display is updated (*refreshed*) in a single pass, painting every line on the screen. *Interlacing* takes two passes to paint the screen, painting every other line on the first pass, and then sequentially filling in the other lines on the second pass. Non-interlaced scanning, while more expensive to implement, reduces unwanted *flicker* and eyestrain.

non-preemptive multitasking Any form of multitasking where the operating system cannot preempt a running *task* and process the next task in the queue.

The *cooperative multitasking* scheme used in *Microsoft Windows 3.x* is non-preemptive, and the drawback to this method is that while programs are easy to write for this environment, a single badly-written program can hog the whole system. By refusing to relinquish the processor, such a program can cause serious problems for other programs running at the same time. Poorly-written non-preemptive multitasking can produce a kind of stuttering effect on running *applications,* depending on how well (or badly) programs behave.

nonvolatile memory Any form of *memory* that holds its contents when power is removed. *ROM, EPROM,* and *EEPROM* are all nonvolatile memory.

Norton Utilities A popular package of small *utility programs* from the Peter Norton Computing Group of Symantec Corporation that run on *DOS* computers, the *Macintosh,* and *Unix*-based systems.

The utilities include UnErase, the famous file-recovery program; Speed Disk, the disk *defragmenting* program; and Norton Disk Doctor, a program that finds and fixes both logical and physical problems on hard and floppy disks.

notebook computer A small *portable computer*, about the size of a computer book, with a *flat screen* and a keyboard that fold together.

A notebook computer is lighter and smaller than a *laptop computer,* and recent advances in battery technology allow them to run for as long as 9 hours between charges. Some models use *flash memory* rather than conventional hard disks for program and data storage, while other models offer a range of business applications in *ROM.* Many offer *PCMCIA expansion slots* for additional *peripherals* such as *modems, fax modems,* or network connections.

NTSC Abbreviation for National Television System Committee, founded in 1941 to establish broadcast-television standards in North America.

NTSC originally defined a picture composed of 525 horizontal lines, consisting of two separate interlaced fields of 262.5 lines each, refreshed at 30 Hz, or 30 times a second. The modern broadcast signal carries more information including multichannel television sound (MTS) and second audio program (SAP). Many personal computer video controllers can output an NTSC-compatible signal in addition to or instead of their usual monitor signal.

null A character that has all the binary digits set to zero (*ASCII* 0) and therefore has no value.

In programming, a null character is used for several special purposes, including padding fields, or serving as delimiter characters. In the *C* language, for example, a null character indicates the end of a *character string*.

null modem cable A short *RS-232-C* cable that connects two personal computers so that they can communicate without the use of *modems*. The cable connects the two computers' serial ports, and the send and receive lines in the cable are crossed over so that the wires used for sending data by one computer are used for receiving data by the other computer, and vice versa.

numeric keypad A set of keys to the right of the main part of the keyboard, used for numeric data entry.

object-oriented A term that can be applied to any computer system, *operating system*, programming language, *application program*, or *graphical user interface* that supports the use of *objects*.

octet The *Internet's* own term for eight bits or a *byte*. Some computer systems attached to the Internet have used a byte with more than eight bits, hence the need for this term.

OEM Acronym for original equipment manufacturer. The original manufacturer of a *hardware* subsystem or component. For example, Canon makes the print engine used in many laser printers, including those from Hewlett-Packard; in this case, Canon is the OEM and HP is a value-added reseller (*VAR*).

offline Describes a printer or other *peripheral* that is not currently in ready mode and is therefore unavailable for use.

offline reader An application that lets you read postings to *USENET newsgroups* without having to stay connected to the *Internet*.

The program downloads all the newsgroup postings you have not read into your PC and disconnects from your *service provider*. You can then read the postings at your convenience without incurring online charges or tying up your telephone line. If you reply to any of these postings, the program will automatically upload them to the right newsgroup the next time you connect to your service provider.

off-the-shelf Describes a ready-to-use hardware or software product that is packaged and ready for sale, as opposed to one that is proprietary or has been customized.

online

1. Most broadly, describes any capability available directly on a computer, as in "online help system"; or any work done on a computer instead of by more traditional means.

2. Describes a *peripheral* such as a printer or modem when it is directly connected to a computer and ready to operate.

3. In communications, describes a computer connected to a remote computer over a network or a modem link.

online service A service that provides an *online* connection via *modem* for access to various services. Online services fall into four main groups:

- **Commercial services**: Services such as *America Online*, *CompuServe*, and Prodigy charge a monthly membership fee for access to online *forums*, *e-mail* services, software libraries, and online conferences.

- **Internet**: The *Internet* is a worldwide network of computer systems containing a wealth of information that is easily accessible to most computer users today. To gain access, all one needs is an account with an Internet Service Provider and an Internet *browser*.

- **Specialist databases**: Specific databases aimed at researchers can be accessed through online services such as Dow Jones News/Retrieval for business news, and Lexis and Nexis, the legal information and news archives.

- **Local bulletin boards**: There are thousands of small, local *bulletin board systems* (BBS), often run from private homes, by local PC *Users Groups*, or by local schools. Some BBS offer software libraries, e-mail, online conferences, and games, while others may be devoted to a specific subject. Look for listings in local computer-related publications, or ask at your local PC Users Group.

Exploring the world of online services is a fascinating pastime that can eat up all your spare time; it can also quickly increase your phone bill.

open architecture A vendor-independent computer design that is publicly available and well understood within the industry. An open architecture allows the user to configure the computer easily by adding expansion *cards*.

operating system Abbreviated OS. The software responsible for allocating system resources, including memory, processor time, disk space, and peripheral devices such as printers, modems, and the monitor. All *application* programs use the operating system to gain access to these system resources as they are needed. The operating system is the first program loaded into the computer as it *boots*, and it remains in memory at all times thereafter.

Popular PC operating systems include *DOS*, *OS/2*, *Windows 95/98,* and *Unix*.

optical character recognition Abbreviated OCR. The computer recognition of printed or typed characters. OCR is usually performed using a standard optical *scanner* and special software, although some systems use special readers. The text is reproduced just as though it had been typed. Certain advanced systems can resolve neat hand-written characters.

OS/2 A *32-bit multitasking operating system* for *Intel 80386* (or later) processors, originally developed by Microsoft and IBM, but now wholly supported by IBM.

Originally, OS/2 was developed jointly by Microsoft and IBM as the successor to DOS, while Windows was developed as a stop-gap measure until OS/2 was ready. However, Microsoft chose to back Windows, placing considerable resources behind the breakthrough release of Windows 3. IBM took control of OS/2 development, and in spring 1992 released OS/2 version 2.

output Computer generated information that is displayed on the screen, printed, written to disk or tape, or sent over a communications link to another computer.

packet Any block of data sent over a network. Each packet contains information about the sender and the receiver, and error-control information, in addition to the actual message. Packets may be fixed- or variable-length, and they will be reassembled if necessary when they reach their destination.

packet switching A data transmission method that simultaneously sends data packets from many sources over the same communications channel or telephone line, thus optimizing use of the line.

paged memory management unit Abbreviated PMMU. A specialized chip designed to manage *virtual memory*. High-end processors such as the Motorola *68030* and *68040*, and the Intel *80386*, *80486*, and later, have all the functions of a PMMU built into the chip itself.

page-mode RAM A *memory-management* technique used to speed up the performance of *dynamic RAM*.

In a page-mode memory system, the memory is divided into pages by specialized dynamic RAM chips. Consecutive accesses to *memory addresses* in the same page result in a page-mode cycle that takes about half the time of a regular dynamic RAM cycle. For example, a normal dynamic RAM cycle time can take from 130 to 180 *nanoseconds*, while a typical page-mode cycle can be completed in 30 to 40 nanoseconds.

pages per minute Abbreviated ppm. An approximation of the number of pages that a printer can print in one minute. This number often represents the rate that the printer can reach when printing the simplest output; if you combine text with complex graphics, performance will fall.

palmtop computer A very small battery-powered portable computer that you can hold in one hand. Many palmtop computers have small screens and tiny keyboards. A growing number of these come with the Windows CE operating system and scaled-down versions of Microsoft software like Word and Internet Explorer.

parallel communications The transmission of information from computer to computer, or from computer to a peripheral, where all the bits that make up the character are transmitted at the same time over a multiline cable.

parallel port An input/output port that manages information 8 bits at a time, often used to connect a *parallel printer*.

parallel printer Any printer that can be connected to the computer using the *parallel port*.

parallel processing A computing method that can only be performed on systems containing two or more processors operating simultaneously.

Parallel processing uses several processors, all working on different aspects of the same program at the same time, in order to share the computational load. Parallel processing computers can reach incredible speeds; the Cray X-MP48 peaks at 1000 million floating point operations per second (1000 MFLOP) using just four extremely powerful processors, while parallel-hypercube systems first marketed by Intel can exceed 65,536 processors with possible speeds of up to 262 billion floating point operations per second (262 GFLOPS). What is this mind-boggling speed used for? Applications such as weather forecasting where the predictive programs can take as long to run as the weather actually takes to arrive, 3D seismic modeling, ground-water and toxic flow studies.

parameter RAM Abbreviated PRAM and pronounced pee-ram. A small part of the Macintosh random-access memory (RAM) that holds information including the hardware configuration, the date and time, which disk is the startup disk, and information about the state of the Desktop. The contents of PRAM are maintained by a battery, and so the contents are not lost when the Mac is turned off or unplugged at the end of your session.

parity In communications, a simple form of error checking that uses an extra, or redundant, bit, after the *data bits* but before the *stop bit(s)*.

Parity may be set to odd, even, mark, space, or none. Odd parity indicates that the sum of all the 1 bits in the byte plus the parity bit must be odd. If the total is already odd, the parity bit is set to zero; if it is even, the parity bit is set to 1.

In even parity, if the sum of all the 1 bits is even, the parity bit must be set to 0; if it is odd, the parity bit must be set to 1.

In mark parity, the parity bit is always set to 1, and is used as the eighth bit.

In space parity, the parity bit is set to 0, and used as the eighth bit.

If parity is set to none, there is no parity bit, and no *parity checking* is performed.

The parity setting on your computer must match the setting on the remote computer for successful communications. Most *online services* use no parity and an eight-bit data *word*.

parity bit An extra or redundant bit used to detect transmission errors.

parity checking   A check mechanism applied to a character or series of characters that uses the addition of extra or redundant bits known as *parity bits*. Parity checking is used in situations as diverse as asynchronous communications and computer memory coordination.

parity error   A mismatch in *parity bits* that indicates an error in transmitted data.

park   To move the hard disk read/ write heads to a safe area of the disk (called a landing zone) before you turn your system off, to guard against damage when the computer is moved. Most modern hard disks park their heads automatically, and so you do not need to run a special program to park the heads.

partition   A portion of a *hard disk* that the *operating system* treats as if it were a separate *drive*.

In *DOS*, a hard disk can be divided into several partitions, including a *primary DOS partition*, an *extended DOS partition*, and a non-DOS partition:

• The primary DOS partition contains important DOS files needed to start the computer running, and is generally assigned the drive letter C.

• The extended DOS partition can help organize that part of the hard disk not occupied by the primary DOS partition.

• The non-DOS partition is only needed if you want to use more than one operating system at a time on your computer; if you only plan to use DOS, you don't need to reserve disk space for a non-DOS partition.

Information about these partitions, including which of them is the *active partition*, is contained in the *partition table*. Partitions are created or changed using the *FDISK* command. Floppy disks cannot be shared between different operating systems, and so do not have partitions.

partition table   In *DOS*, an area of the *hard disk* containing information on how the disk is organized.

The partition table also contains information that tells the computer which *operating system* to load; most disks will contain DOS, but some users may divide their hard disk into different *partitions*, or areas, each containing a different operating system. The partition table indicates which of these partitions is the *active partition*, the partition that should be used to start the computer.

passive-matrix screen   An *LCD* display mechanism that uses a transistor to control every row of *pixels* on the screen. This is in sharp contrast to *active-matrix screens*, where each individual pixel is controlled by its own transistor. Passive-matrix displays are slower to respond, have weaker colors, and have a narrower viewing angle, but they are much cheaper to make than active-matrix displays.

PC Acronym for personal computer. A computer specifically designed for use by one person at a time, equipped with its own *central processing unit*, *memory*, *operating system*, *keyboard* and display, *hard-* and *floppy disks*, as well as other *peripherals* when needed.

When written in capital letters, the acronym usually indicates a computer conforming to the IBM standard rather than a *Macintosh* computer. The spelled-out capitalized form, Personal Computer, indicates that the computer was made by IBM.

PC Card A term describing add-in cards that conform to the *PCMCIA* (Personal Computer Memory Card International Association) standard.

PC Card slot An opening in the case of a *portable computer* intended to receive a *PC Card*; also known as a *PCMCIA* slot.

PC-DOS The version of the *DOS operating system* supplied with PCs sold by IBM.

PC-DOS and *MS-DOS* started out as virtually identical operating systems, with only a few very minor differences in device driver names and file sizes, but after the release of MS-DOS 6, the two grew much further apart.

PC-DOS 7 was released by IBM in early 1995, and includes the *REXX* programming language, enhanced *PCMCIA* support, *Stacker* file-compression, and FILEUP, an application used to *synchronize* files between portable and desktop PCs.

PCI Abbreviation for Peripheral Component Interconnect. A specification introduced by *Intel* that defines a *local bus* that allows up to ten PCI-compliant expansion cards to be plugged into the computer. One of these ten cards must be the PCI controller card, but the others can include a video card, network interface card, SCSI interface, or any other basic input/output function.

The PCI controller exchanges information with the computer's processor as 32- or 64-bits, and allows intelligent PCI adapters to perform certain tasks concurrently with the main processor by using *bus mastering* techniques.

PCI can operate at a bus speed of 32 MHz, and can manage a maximum throughput of 132 megabytes per second with a 32-bit data path or 264 megabytes per second with a 64-bit data path.

PCMCIA Abbreviation for PC Memory Card International Association. A non-profit association formed in 1989 with over 320 members in the computer and electronics industries that developed a standard for credit-card size plug-in adapters aimed at *portable computers*.

A PCMCIA adapter card, or *PC Card*, uses a 68-pin connector, with longer power and ground pins, so they always engage before the signal pins. Several versions of the standard have been approved by PCMCIA:

• **Type I:** The thinnest PC Card, only 3.3 mm thick; used for memory enhancements including *dynamic RAM*, *static RAM*, and *EEPROM*.

• **Type II**: A card used for *modems* or LAN adapters, 5 mm thick.

• **Type III**: A 10.5 mm card, used for *mini-hard disks* and other devices that need more space, including wireless LANs.

In theory, although space is always a major consideration, each PCMCIA

adapter can support 16 PC Card sockets, and up to 255 adapters can be installed in a PC that follows the PCMCIA standard; in other words PCMCIA allows for up to 4080 PC Cards on the same computer.

The majority of PCMCIA devices are *modems*, *Ethernet* and *Token Ring* network adapters, dynamic RAM, and *flash memory* cards, although mini-hard disks, *wireless LAN* adapters, and *SCSI* adapters are also available.

PDA Abbreviation for Personal Digital Assistant. A tiny pen-based *palmtop* computer that combines fax, *e-mail*, *PCMCIA* support, and simple word processing into an easy-to-use unit that fits into a pocket. PDAs are available from several manufacturers, including Apple, Casio, Tandy, Toshiba, Motorola, Sharp, Sony, and AT&T.

pen-based computer A computer that accepts handwriting as input. Using a pen-like stylus, you print neatly on a screen, and the computer translates this input using *pattern recognition* techniques. You can also choose selections from on-screen menus using the stylus.

Pentium A 32-bit *microprocessor* introduced by *Intel* in 1993. After losing a courtroom battle to maintain control of the *x*86 designation, Intel named this member of its family the Pentium rather than the 80586 or the 586. The Pentium represents the continuing evolution of the *80486* family of microprocessors and adds several notable features, including 8K instruction code and data *caches*, built-in *floating-point processor* and *memory management unit*, as well as a *superscalar* design and dual *pipelining* that allow the Pentium to execute more than one instruction per clock cycle.

Available in a whole range of clock speeds, from 60 MHz all the way up to 200 MHz versions, the Pentium is equivalent to an astonishing 3.1 million *transistors*, more than twice that of the 80486.

Pentium Pro The latest microprocessor in the 80*x*86 family from Intel. The 32-bit P6 has a 64-bit data path between the processor and cache, and is capable of running at clock speeds up to 200 MHz. Unlike the Pentium, the Pentium Pro has its secondary cache built into the CPU itself, rather than on the motherboard, meaning that it accesses cache at internal speed, not bus speed. The Pentium Pro contains the equivalent of 5.5 million transistors.

Pentium II The Pentium II is a *Pentium Pro* with *MMX* technology built in, as well as a 512KB L2 *cache* and 32KB L1 cache (16KB data and 16KB instruction). The *clock speed* is currently at 333 MHz.

Pentium II Xeon Same as the *Pentium II* with the ability to access 64GB of RAM and a 100 MHz system bus. The *clock speed* is currently at 400 MHz.

peripheral Any hardware device attached to and controlled by a computer, such as a monitor, keyboard, hard disk, floppy disk, CD-ROM drives, printer, mouse, tape drive, and joystick.

permanent swap file A *swap file* that, once created, is used over and over again. This file is used in *virtual memory* operations, where *hard disk* space is used in place of random-access memory (*RAM*).

A permanent swap file allows *Microsoft Windows* to write information to a known place on the hard disk, which enhances performance over using conventional methods with a *temporary swap file*. The Windows permanent swap file consists of a large number of consecutive contiguous *clusters*; it is often the largest single file on the hard disk, and of course this disk space cannot be used by any other *application*. If you have plenty of unused hard disk space, consider a permanent swap file to boost performance. If disk space is at a premium, use a temporary swap file to conserve disk space, at the cost of a slight loss in performance.

peta- Abbreviated P. A prefix for one quadrillion, or 10^{15}. In computing, based on the binary system, peta has the value of 1,125,899,906,842,624, or the power of 2 (250) closest to one quadrillion.

petabyte Abbreviated PB. Although it can represent one quadrillion bytes (10^{15}), it usually refers to 1,125,899,906,842,624 bytes (250).

phosphor The special electrofluorescent coating used on the inside of a *CRT* screen that glows for a few milliseconds when struck by an electron beam. Because the illumination is so brief, it must be refreshed constantly to maintain an image.

Photo CD A specification from Kodak that allows you to record and then display photographic images on CD. Originally, only single-session recordings could be made. However, several CD-ROM players are now compatible with multi-session Photo CD, where images can be loaded onto the CD several times over several different recording sessions.

physical drive A real device in the computer that you can see or touch, rather than a *logical drive,* which is a part of the *hard disk* that functions as if it were a separate disk drive but is not. One physical drive may be divided into several logical drives.

physical layer The first and lowest of the seven layers in the International Standards Organization's Open Systems Interconnection (*ISO/OSI*) model for computer-to-computer communications. The physical layer defines the physical, electrical, mechanical, and functional procedures used to connect the equipment.

pica A unit of measure used to measure type size. One pica (twelve points) is equivalent to 1/6".

pincushion distortion A type of distortion that usually occurs at the edges of a video screen where the sides of an image seem to bow inwards.

pipelining
1. In processor architecture, a method of fetching and decoding instructions that ensures that the processor never needs to wait; as soon as an instruction is executed, another is waiting.

2. In parallel processing, the method used to pass instructions from one processing unit to another.

pixel Contraction of picture element. The smallest element that display software can use to create text or graphics. A display *resolution* described as being 640 × 480 has 640 pixels across the screen and 480 down the screen, for a total of 307,200 pixels. The higher the number of pixels, the higher the screen resolution.

A monochrome pixel can have two values, black or white, and this can be represented by one bit as either zero or one. At the other end of the scale, *true color*, capable of displaying approximately 16.7 million colors, requires 24 bits of information for each pixel.

platter The actual disk inside a *hard disk* enclosure that carries the magnetic recording material. Many hard disks have multiple platters, most of which have two sides that can be used for recording data.

plotter A *peripheral* used to draw high-resolution charts, graphs, layouts, and other line-based diagrams, and often used with CAD (*computer aided design*) systems. Plotters generally print very large documents up to 36 inches wide as opposed to 11 inches wide for a laser or deskjet printer.

Plug and Play (Plug 'n Play)
Abbreviated PnP. A standard from Compaq, Microsoft, Intel, and Phoenix that defines automatic techniques designed to make PC configuration simple and straightforward. Currently, ISA and PCI expansion boards are covered by the specification, but the standard may soon also cover *SCSI* and *PCMCIA* buses.

PnP adapters contain configuration information stored in non-volatile memory, which includes vendor information, serial number, and checksum information. The PnP chipset allows each adapter to be isolated, one at a time, until all cards have been properly identified by the operating system.

PnP requires *BIOS* changes so that cards can be isolated and identified at boot time; when you insert a new card, the BIOS should perform an auto-configuration sequence enabling the new card with appropriate settings. New systems with flash BIOS will be easy to change; older systems with ROM BIOS will need a hardware change before they can take advantage of PnP.

Plug and Pray What most of us will do when our *Plug-and-Play* systems do not work automatically.

plug-compatible Describes any hardware device designed to work in exactly the same way as a device manu-factured by a different company.

For example, external *modems* are plug-compatible, in that you can replace one with another without changing the cabling or connector.

POP3 A protocol used for receiving e-mail on a TCP/IP network. In a POP3 environment, your mail is received at a POP3 server and held there until you connect and download the mail.

port
1. A physical connection, such as a *serial port* or a *parallel port*.

2. To move a program or *operating system* from one hardware platform to another. For example, *Windows NT* portability refers to the fact that the same operating system can run on both *Intel* and *RISC* architectures.

3. A number used to identify a specific *Internet* application (location).

post An individual article or *e-mail* message sent to a *USENET newsgroup* or to a *mailing list,* rather than to a spe-cific individual. Post can also refer to the process of sending the article to the newsgroup.

posting The process of sending an individual *article* or *e-mail* message to a *USENET newsgroup* or to a *mailing list.*

PostScript A page-description lan-guage developed by Adobe Systems, Inc., used for designing and printing one kind of high-quality text and graphics. Desktop publishing or illus-tration programs that create PostScript output can print on any PostScript printer or imagesetter, because Post-Script is *hardware-independent*. An *inter-preter* in the printer translates the PostScript commands into commands that the printer can understand. This means that you can create your docu-ment and then take it to any print shop with a PostScript printer to make the final printed output.

PostScript uses English-like commands to scale outline fonts and control the page layout; because of this, users have a great deal of flexibility when it comes to font specification.

PostScript printer A printer that can interpret *PostScript* page-description language commands. Because the Post-Script page-description language is complex and computer intensive, Post-Script printers often contain as much computing power as the PC you origi-nally used to create the output, and they are often much more expensive than standard printers.

power-on self test Abbreviated POST. A set of *diagnostic programs,* loaded from *ROM*, designed to ensure that the major system components are present and operating. If a problem is found, the POST software writes an error message in the screen, sometimes with a diagnostic code number indicating the type of fault located. These POST tests execute before any attempt is made to load the operating system.

PowerPC   A family of *microprocessors* jointly developed by Apple, Motorola, and IBM. The *32-bit* 601 houses 2.8 million transistors, runs at 110 MHz, and is designed for use in high-performance, low-cost PCs. The 66 MHz 602 is targeted at the consumer electronics and entry-level computer markets. The low-wattage 603e is aimed at battery-powered computers, the 604 is for high-end PCs and workstations, and the top-of-the-line 620 is designed for servers and very high performance applications. The 620 is a 64-bit chip.

PCs based on the PowerPC chip usually include a minimum of 16 MB of memory, a 540 MB hard disk, PCI bus architecture including a local-bus based graphics adapter, and a CD-ROM.

power supply   A part of the computer that converts the AC power from a wall outlet into DC in the lower voltages, (typically 5 to 12 volts DC), required internally in the computer. PC

power supplies are usually rated in watts, ranging from 200 watts at the low end to 300 watts at the high end. The power supply is one of the main sources of heat in a computer and usually requires a fan to provide additional ventilation; it is also a sealed unit with no operator-serviceable parts, and you should make sure it stays that way.

power surge   A brief but sudden increase in line voltage, often destructive, usually caused by a nearby electrical appliance such as a photocopier or elevator, or when power is reapplied after an outage.

power user   A person who is proficient with many software packages and who understands how to put the computer to work quickly and effectively. While not necessarily a programmer, a power user is familiar with creating and using *macros*, and other command languages.

PPP   Abbreviation for Point-to-Point Protocol. One of the most common protocols used to connect a PC to an *Internet* host via high-speed modem and a telephone line.

PPP establishes a temporary but direct connection to an Internet host, eliminating the need for connecting to an interim system. PPP also provides a method of automatically assigning an IP address, so that remote or mobile systems can connect to the network at any point.

preemptive multitasking A form of *multitasking* where the operating system executes an application for a specific period of time, according to its assigned priority. At that time, it is preempted, and another task is given access to the *CPU* for its allocated time. Although an application can give up control before its time is up, such as during input/output waits, no task is ever allowed to execute for longer than its allotted time period. *OS/2, Unix, Windows 95/98,* and *Windows NT* all use preemptive multitasking.

presentation layer The sixth of seven layers of the International Standards Organization's Open Systems Interconnection (*ISO/OSI*) model for computer-to-computer communications. The presentation layer defines the way that data is formatted, presented, converted, and encoded.

primary DOS partition In *DOS,* a division of the *hard disk* that contains important *operating system* files.

A DOS hard disk can be divided into two partitions, or areas; the *primary DOS partition,* and the *extended DOS partition.* If you want to start your computer from the hard disk, the disk must contain an active primary DOS partition that includes the three DOS system files: *MSDOS.SYS, IO.SYS,* and *COMMAND.COM.* The primary DOS partition on the first hard disk in the system is referred to as drive C.

Disk partitions are displayed, created, and changed using the *FDISK* command.

printed-circuit board Abbreviated PCB. Any flat board made of plastic or fiberglass that contains chips and other electronic components. Many PCBs are *multi-layer* boards with several different sets of copper traces connecting components together.

printer A computer *peripheral* that presents computer output as a printed image on paper or film.

Printers vary considerably in price, speed, *resolution,* noise level, convenience, paper-handling abilities, printing mechanism, and quality, and all of these points should be considered when making a selection.

printer emulation The ability of a printer to change modes so that it behaves just like a printer from another manufacturer.

Many *dot-matrix printers* offer an Epson printer emulation in addition to their own native mode. This means you can use the printer as an Epson printer just by changing some switches—a useful feature if the software you are using does not have a *device driver* for your printer, but does have the appropriate Epson driver. Many non-HP laser printers support an HP LaserJet emulation.

PRINTER.SYS A *DOS device driver* that lets you use *code-page* switching with printers that support this capability. To activate it, load PRINTER.SYS using *CONFIG.SYS*.

printhead That part of a printer that creates the printed image. In a *dot-matrix printer*, the printhead contains the small pins that strike the ribbon to create the image, and in an *ink-jet printer*, the printhead contains the jets used to create the ink droplets as well as the ink reservoirs. A laser printer creates images using an electrophotographic method similar to that found in photocopiers and does not have a printhead.

privileged mode An operating mode supported in protected mode in *80286* (or later) processors, that allows the operating system and certain classes of *device driver* to manipulate parts of the system including memory and input/output ports.

PRN In *DOS* and *OS/2*, the logical device name for a printer, usually the first parallel port, which is also known as LPT1.

process In a *multitasking operating system*, a program or a part of a program. For example, in *OS/2* there are really no such things as programs; they are known as processes instead. All EXE and COM files execute as processes, and one process can run one or more other processes. Indeed, all full-screen *sessions* contain at least two processes, the *command processor* and the *application* running in that session.

program A sequence of instructions that a computer can execute. Synonymous with *software*.

programmable Capable of being programmed. The fact that a computer is programmable is what sets it apart from all other instruments that use microprocessors; it is truly a general-purpose machine.

PROM Acronym for programmable read-only memory, pronounced "prom." A chip used when developing firmware. A PROM can be programmed and tested in the lab, and when the firmware is complete, it can be transferred to a ROM for manufacturing.

protected mode In *Intel 80286* and higher processors, an operating state that supports advanced features.

Protected mode in these processors provides hardware support for *multitasking* and *virtual memory* management, and prevents programs from accessing blocks of memory that belong to other executing programs.

In *16-bit* protected mode, supported on 80286 and higher processors, the *CPU* can directly address a total of 16 MB of memory; in *32-bit* protected mode, supported on *80386* and higher processors, the CPU can address up to 4GB of memory.

OS/2, Windows, and most versions of *Unix* that run on these processors execute in protected mode.

protocol In networking and communications, the specification that defines the procedures to follow when transmitting and receiving data. Protocols define the format, timing, sequence, and error checking systems used.

protocol stack In networking and communications, the several layers of *software* that define the computer-to-computer or computer-to-network *protocol*. The protocol stack on a Novell *NetWare* system will be different from that used on a Banyan *VINES* network, or on a *Microsoft LAN Manager* system.

public-domain software Software that is freely distributed to anyone who wants to use, copy, or distribute it.

Pulse Code Modulation Abbreviated PCM. A method used to convert an *analog* signal into noise-free *digital data* that can be stored and manipulated by computer. PCM takes an 8-bit sample of a 4 kHz bandwidth 8000 times a second, which gives 16K of data per second. PCM is often used in multimedia applications.

QEMM 386 A memory-management program from QuarterDeck Office Systems for IBM-compatible computers.

QEMM 386 moves *terminate-and-stay resident programs* and *device drivers*, including network drivers, into *high memory*, leaving more *conventional memory* available for running *application* programs.

QEMM 50/60 is a special version of the program designed for use on *IBM PS/2* Model 50 and 60 computers.

quadrature amplitude modulation A data-encoding technique used by modems operating at 2400 bits per second or faster.

Quadrature amplitude modulation is a combination of phase and amplitude change that can encode multiple bits on a single carrier signal. For example, the CCITT V.42 bis standard uses four phase changes and two amplitude changes to create 16 different signal changes.

quarter-inch cartridge Abbreviated QIC. A set of tape standards defined by the Quarter-Inch Cartridge Drive Standards, a trade association established in 1987.

queue Pronounced "Q." A temporary list of items waiting for a particular service. An example is the print queue of documents waiting to be printed on a network print server; the first document received in the queue is the first to be printed.

QWERTY keyboard Pronounced "kwer-tee." The standard typewriter and computer keyboard layout, named for the first six keys at the top left of the alphabetic keyboard.

quoting To include a relevant portion of someone else's article when posting a followup to a *USENET newsgroup* or online *forum*. It is considered to be very poor *netiquette* to quote more of the original post than is absolutely necessary to make your point.

radio frequency interference Abbreviated RFI. Many electronic devices, including computers and *peripherals*, can interfere with other signals in the radio-frequency range by producing electromagnetic radiation; this is normally regulated by government agencies in each country.

RAID Acronym for Redundant Array of Inexpensive Disks. In networking and truly critical applications, a method of using several hard disk drives in an array to provide *fault tolerance* in the event that one or more drives fail catastrophically.

The different levels of RAID, 0 through 5, are each designed for a specific use; each having its own advantages in a particular situation. The correct level of RAID for your installation depends on how you use your network.

RAM Acronym for random access memory. The main system *memory* in a computer, used for the *operating system*, *application* programs, and *data*.

RAM chip A semiconductor storage device, either dynamic RAM or static RAM.

RAM disk Used in older operating systems like DOS, a RAM disk is an area of *memory* managed by a special *device driver* and used as a simulated disk.

Because the *RAM* disk operates in memory, it works very quickly, much faster than a regular *hard disk*. Remember that anything you store on your RAM disk will be erased when you turn your computer off, so you must save its contents onto a real disk first. RAM disks may also be called *virtual drives*.

RAMDRIVE.SYS   The *DOS* device driver used to create a *RAM disk*. You must load this device driver using a *DEVICE* or *DEVICEHIGH* in your *CONFIG.SYS file*.

random access   Describes the ability of a storage device to go directly to the required *memory address* without having to read from the beginning every time *data* is requested.

There is nothing random or haphazard about random access; a more precise term is direct access. Unfortunately, the word "random" is used as part of the abbreviation RAM, and is obviously here to stay. In a random-access device, the information can be read directly by accessing the appropriate memory address. Some storage devices, such as tapes, must start at the beginning to find a specific storage location, and if

the information is towards the end of the tape, access can take a long time. This access method is known as "sequential access."

raster device   A device that manages an image as lines of dots. Television sets and most computer displays are raster devices, as are some electrostatic printers and plotters.

read   To copy program or *data* files from a floppy or a hard disk into computer memory, to run the program or process the data in some way. The computer may also read your commands and data input from the keyboard.

README file   A *text file* placed on a set of distribution disks by the manufacturer at the last minute that may contain important information not contained in the program manuals or online *help* system. You should always look for a README file when installing a new program on your system; it may contain information pertinent to your specific configuration.

The file name may vary slightly; READ.ME, README.TXT, and README.DOC are all used. README files do not contain any formatting commands, so you can look at them using any *word processor*.

read-only Describes a *file* or other collection of information that may only be read; it may not be updated in any way or deleted.

Certain important *operating system* files are designated as read-only files to prevent you from deleting them by accident. Also, certain types of memory (*ROM*), and certain devices such as *CD-ROM* can be read but not changed.

read-only attribute In *DOS, Windows*, and *OS/2*, a *file attribute* that indicates the file can be read but cannot be updated or changed in any way; nor can you delete the file.

read/write head That part of a *floppy-* or *hard-disk* system that reads and writes *data* to and from a magnetic disk.

reboot To restart the computer and reload the *operating system*, usually after a *crash*.

Red Book audio The standard definition of compact disc digital audio as a *16-bit* stereo *pulse code modulation* waveform at 44.1 kHz. So called because of the cover color used when the definition was first published.

reduced instruction set computing Abbreviated RISC, pronounced "risk." A processor that recognizes only a limited number of *assembly-language* instructions.

RISC chips are relatively cheap to produce and debug, as they usually contain fewer than 128 different instructions. *CISC* processors use a richer set of instructions, typically somewhere between 200 to 300. RISC processors are commonly used in *workstations* and can be designed to run up to 70 percent faster than CISC processors.

reformat To reinitialize a disk and destroy the original contents.

refresh
1. In a *monitor*, to recharge the phosphors on the inside of the screen and maintain the image.

2. In certain memory systems, *dynamic RAM* must be recharged so that it continues to hold its contents.

refresh rate In a *monitor*, the rate at which the phosphors that create the image on the screen are recharged.

registry In *Windows* 95, 98, and NT systems, the Registry is the heart of the system. It is a database that contains all user, software, and machine settings. Everything that is done on the computer requires the Registry for configuration.

relative addressing In programming, the specification of a memory location by using an expression to calculate the address, rather than explicitly specifying the location by using its address.

removable mass storage Any high-capacity storage device inserted into a drive for reading and writing, then removed for storage and safekeeping. This term is not usually applied to floppy disks, but to tape- and cartridge-backup systems, and *Bernoulli boxes*.

rendering In computer graphics, the conversion of an outline image into a fully-formed, three-dimensional image, by the addition of colors and shading.

repeater In networking, a simple hardware device that moves all *packets* from one local area network segment to another. The main purpose of a repeater is to extend the length of the network transmission medium beyond the normal maximum cable lengths.

Repetitive Stress Injury Abbreviated RSI. A common group of work-related injuries. Computer operators performing repetitive tasks can suffer pins-and-needles and loss of feeling in their wrists and hands, and pains in their shoulders and necks. *Carpal-tunnel*

syndrome, common among people who use a keyboard all day, is one form of RSI.

reserved memory In *DOS*, a term used to describe that area of memory between 640 K and 1 MB, also known as upper memory. Reserved memory is used by DOS to store system and video information.

reserved word Any word that has a special meaning and therefore cannot be used for any other purpose in the same context. For example, the words that make up a computer language (if, printf, putchar), and certain device names in an *operating system* (COM1, LPT1), are all different kinds of reserved word.

reset button The small button on the front of many computers used to *reboot* the computer without turning off the power.

resolution The degree of sharpness of a printed or displayed image, often expressed in *dpi*.

Resolution depends on the number of elements that make up the image, either dots on a laser printer or *pixels* on a monitor; the higher the number per inch, the higher the resolution of the image appears.

resource Any part of a computer system that can be used by a program as it runs. This can include memory, hard and floppy disks, and printers.

In some programming environments, items like *dialog boxes*, bit maps, and *fonts* are considered to be resources, and they can be used by several different *application* programs without requiring any internal changes to the programs.

response time The time lag between sending a request and receiving the *data*. Response time can be applied to a complete computer system, as in the time taken to look up a certain customer record, or to a system component, as in the time taken to access a specific cluster on disk.

reverse engineering The process of disassembling a hardware or software product from another company to find out how it works, with the intention of duplicating some or all of its functions in another product.

reverse video In a monochrome monitor, a display mode used to highlight characters on the screen by reversing the normal background and foreground colors; for example, if the normal mode is to show green characters on a black background, reverse video displays black characters on a green background.

RGB Abbreviation for red-green-blue. A method of generating colors in a video system that uses the additive primaries method. Percentages of red, blue, and green are mixed to form the colors; 0 percent of the colors creates black, 100 percent of all three colors creates white.

RGB monitor A color monitor that accepts separate inputs for red, blue, and green color signals and normally produces a sharper image than composite color monitors, in which information for all three colors is transmitted together.

ring network A network topology in the form of a closed loop or circle.

RJ-11/RJ-45 Short for registered jack, RJs are commonly used modular telephone connectors. RJ-11 is a four or six pin connector used in most connections destined for voice use. RJ-45 is the eight-pin connector used for data transmission over *twisted-pair wiring*.

ROM Acronym for read-only memory. A semiconductor-based *memory* system that stores information permanently and does not lose its contents when power is switched off. ROM is used for *firmware* such as the *BIOS* used in the PC; and in some *portable computers, application* programs and even the *operating system* are being stored in ROM.

root directory   In a hierarchical *directory* structure, the directory from which all other directories must branch.

The root directory is created by the FORMAT command and can contain files as well as other directories. It is wise to store as few files as possible in the root directory, because the number of entries (files or directories) that the root directory can hold is limited to 512 in most operating systems. Also, you cannot delete the root directory.

The *backslash* (\) character represents the root directory, and you can use this character to make the root directory the current directory in a single step, if you type **CD** \ from the system prompt.

roping   In a *monitor*, a form of image distortion that gives solid straight lines a twisted or helical appearance. This problem is caused by poor *convergence*.

ROT-13   A simple *encryption* scheme often used to scramble *posts* to *USENET newsgroups*. ROT-13 makes the article unreadable until the text is decoded and is often used when the subject matter might be considered offensive.

Many newsreaders have a built-in command to unscramble ROT-13 text, and if you use it, don't be surprised by what you read; if you think you might be offended, don't decrypt the post.

router   In networking, an intelligent connecting device that can send packets to the correct local area network segment to take them to their destination. Routers link local area network segments at the network layer of the International Standards Organization's Open Systems Interconnect (*ISO/OSI*) model for computer-to-computer communications.

RS-422/423/449   In *asynchronous transmissions*, a recommended standard interface established by the Electrical Industries Association for distances greater than 50 feet, but less than 1000 feet. The standard defines the specific lines, timing and signal characteristics used between the computer and the *peripheral* device.

RS (recommended standard) 449 incorporates RS-422 and RS-423; serial ports on *Macintosh* computers are RS-422 ports.

RS-232-C   In *asynchronous transmissions*, a recommended standard interface established by the Electrical Industries Association. The standard defines the specific lines, timing and signal characteristics used between the computer and the *peripheral* device, and uses a 25-pin or 9-pin *DB connector*.

RS-232-C is used for *serial communications* between a computer and a peripheral such as a printer, *modem*, *digitizing tablet*, or *mouse*. The maximum cable limit of 50 feet can be extended by using very high quality cable, line drivers to boost the signal, or *short-haul modems*.

RS is the abbreviation for recommended standard, and the C denotes the third revision of that standard. RS-232-C is functionally identical to the CCITT V.24 standard.

RTS Abbreviation for request to send. A hardware signal defined by the *RS-232-C* standard to request permission to transmit.

run-length limited encoding
Abbreviated RLL encoding. An efficient method of storing information on a *hard disk* that effectively doubles the storage capacity of a disk when compared to older, less efficient methods such as *modified frequency modulation* encoding (MFM).

RXD Abbreviation for receive *data*. A *hardware* signal defined by the *RS-232-C* standard to carry data from one device to another.

save To transfer information from the computer's *memory* to a more permanent storage medium such as a *hard disk*.

As you work with your computer, you should save your work every few minutes. Otherwise, if you suffer a power failure or a severe program error, all your work will be lost because it is stored in memory, which is volatile, and when the power is removed, the contents of memory are lost.

scan code In *IBM-compatible computers*, a code number generated when a key on the keyboard is pressed or released. Each key and shifted key is assigned a unique code that the computer's *BIOS* translates into its *ASCII* equivalent.

scanner An optical device used to digitize images such as line art or photographs, so that they can be merged with text by a *page-layout* or *desktop publishing program* or incorporated into a *CAD* drawing.

SCSI Acronym for small computer system interface, pronounced "scuzzy." A high-speed, system-level *parallel interface* defined by the *ANSI* X3T9.2 committee. SCSI is used to connect a *personal computer* to several peripheral devices using just one *port*. Devices connected in this way are said to be "daisy-chained" together, and each device must have a unique identifier or priority number.

SCSI is available on the IBM RS/6000, and the IBM PS/2 Model 65 and higher computers. It can also be installed in an IBM-compatible computer as a single *expansion board*, with a special connector extending through the back of the computer case. Today, SCSI is often used to connect *hard disks*, *tape drives*, *CD-ROM* drives, and other mass storage media, as well as scanners and printers.

There are several different SCSI interface definitions:

• **SCSI-1**: A 1986 definition of an *8-bit* parallel interface with a maximum data transfer rate of 5 megabytes per second.

• **SCSI-2**: This 1994 definition broadened the 8-bit data bus to *16-* or *32-bits* (also known as Wide SCSI), doubling the data transfer rate to 10 or 20 megabytes per second (also known as Fast SCSI). Wide SCSI and Fast SCSI can be combined to give Fast-Wide SCSI, with a 16-bit data bus and a maximum data-transfer rate of 20 megabytes per second. SCSI-2 is backward compatible with SCSI-1, but for maximum benefit, you should use SCSI-2 devices with a SCSI-2 controller.

• **SCSI-3**: This definition increased the number of connected peripherals from 7 to 16, increased cable lengths, added support for a *serial interface* and for a *fiber optic* interface. Data transfer rates depend on the hardware implementation, but data rates in excess of 100 megabytes per second are possible.

• **SCSI FAST:** Refers to a derivative of SCSI-2 that allows data transfer rates of 10 MegaTransfers per second. (A "MegaTransfer" is the term used to describe the speed of the signals on the interface regardless of the width of the bus. For example, 10 MegaTransfers per second on one-byte-wide bus produces a data transfer of 10 megabytes/second. On a two-byte-wide bus, 10 MegaTransfers per second produces a data transfer of 20 megabytes/second.)

• **SCSI FAST-20:** Follows the SCSI standard and can ship data back and forth at 20 MegaTransfers per second (see definition in the bulleted item directly above), which is twice as fast as SCSI FAST rates.

• **SCSI FAST-40:** The same as SCSI FAST-20, except that it handles data at 40 MegaTransfers per second.

• **SCSI WIDE:** is technically the term used to describe the two-byte-wide connector (68-pin) specified in the SCSI-3 Parallel Interface standard.

• **SCSI FAST-WIDE:** simply means a combination of FAST transfer rate with two-byte-wide connector, producing a data transfer rate of 20 megabytes/second.

SCSI bus Another name for the *SCSI* interface and communications *protocol*.

SCSI terminator The *SCSI* interface must be correctly terminated to prevent signals echoing on the *bus*. Many SCSI devices have built-in terminators that engage when they are needed; with some older SCSI devices you have to add an external SCSI terminator that plugs into the device's SCSI connector.

sector The smallest unit of storage on a disk, usually 512 bytes. Sectors are grouped together into *clusters*.

seek time The length of time required to move a disk drive's *read/write head* to a particular location on the disk. The major part of a hard disk's *access time* is actually seek time.

segmented addressing An addressing scheme used in *Intel* processors that divides the address space into logical pieces called segments.

To access any given address, a program must specify the segment and also an offset within that segment. This

addressing method is sometimes abbreviated to "segment:offset" and is used in Intel processors in *real mode*; most other processors use a single flat address space.

semaphore In programming, an *interprocess communication* signal that indicates the status of a shared system resource, such as *shared memory*.

Event semaphores allow a *thread* to tell other threads that an event has occurred and it is safe for them to resume execution. Mutual exclusion (mutex) semaphores protect system resources such as files, data, and peripherals from simultaneous access by several processes. Multiple wait (muxwait) semaphores allow threads to wait for multiple events to take place, or for multiple resources to become free.

semiconductor A material that is halfway between a conductor (which conducts electricity) and an insulator (which resists electricity), whose electrical behavior can be precisely controlled by the addition of impurities called dopants.

The most commonly used semiconductors are silicon and germanium, and when electrically charged they change their state from conductive to nonconductive, or from nonconductive to conductive. Semiconductor wafers can be manufactured to create a whole variety of electronic devices; in personal computers, semiconductors are used in the processor, memory, and many other chips.

Easily the most significant semiconductor device is the *transistor*, which acts like an on/off switch, and is incorporated into modern *microprocessors* by the million.

serial communications The transmission of information from computer to computer, or from computer to a *peripheral*, one bit at a time.

Serial communications can be synchronous and controlled by a clock, or asynchronous and coordinated by *start* and *stop bits* embedded in the data stream. It is important to remember that both the sending and the receiving devices must use the same *baud rate*, *parity* setting, and other *communication parameters*.

serial mouse A *mouse* that attaches directly to one of the computer's *serial ports*.

serial port A computer input/output *port* that supports *serial communications*, in which information is processed one bit at a time.

RS-232-C is a common serial *protocol* used by computers when communicating with modems, printers, mice, and other peripherals.

serial printer A printer that attaches to one of the computer's *serial ports*.

server In networking, any computer that makes access to *files*, printing, communications, or other services available to users of the network. In large networks, a server may run a special *network operating system*; in smaller installations, a server may run a personal computer *operating system*.

service provider A general term used to describe those companies providing a connection to the *Internet* for private and home users. Several of the online services such as CompuServe and America Online are providing access to the Internet as a part of their basic services.

session layer The fifth of seven layers of the International Standards Organization's Open Systems Interconnection (*ISO/OSI*) model for computer-to-computer communications. The session layer coordinates communications and maintains the session for as long as it is needed, performing security, logging, and administrative functions.

settling time The time it takes a disk's read/write head to stabilize once it has moved to the correct part of the disk. Settling time is measured in milliseconds.

setup string A short group of text characters sent to a *printer*, *modem*, or *monitor*, to invoke a particular mode of operation.

SGML Abbreviation for Standard Generalized Markup Language. A standard (ISO 8879) for defining the structure and managing the contents of any digital document. *HTML*, used in many *World Wide Web* documents on the *Internet*, is a part of SGML.

shadow memory In PCs based on the *80386* (or later) processor, the technique of copying the contents of the *BIOS ROM* into faster *RAM* when the computer first boots up; also known as shadow RAM or shadow ROM.

RAM is usually two to three times faster than ROM, and the speedier access cuts down the time required to read a memory address so the processor spends more time working and less time waiting.

shared memory An *interprocess communications* technique in which the same *memory* is accessed by more than

one program running in a multitasking *operating system*. *Semaphores* or other management elements prevent the applications from "colliding," or trying to update the same information at the same time.

shareware A form of software distribution that makes copyrighted programs freely available on a trial basis; if you like the program and use it, you are expected to register your copy and send a small fee to the program creator. Once your copy is registered, you might receive a more complete manual, technical support, access to the programmer's bulletin board, or information about upgrades. You can *download* shareware from many *bulletin boards* and *online services* including *CompuServe*, and it is often available from your local PC *user group*.

silicon A *semiconductor* material used in many electronic devices. Silicon is a very common element found in almost all rocks and in beach sand that, when "doped" with chemical impurities, becomes a semiconductor. Large cylinders of silicon are cut into wafers, and then etched with a pattern of minute electrical circuits to form a silicon chip.

Silicon Valley A nickname for the area around Palo Alto and Sunnyvale in the Santa Clara Valley region of Northern California, noted for the number of high-technology hardware and software companies located there.

single-density disk A floppy disk that is certified for recording with *frequency modulation encoding*. Single-density disks have been superseded by double-density disks and high-density disks.

single in-line memory module Abbreviated SIMM. Individual *RAM* chips are soldered or surface mounted onto small narrow circuit boards called carrier modules, which can be plugged into sockets on the *motherboard*. These carrier modules are simple to install and occupy less space than conventional memory modules.

single in-line package Abbreviated SIP. A plastic housing containing an electronic component with a single row of pins or connections protruding from one side of the package.

16-bit color A method of representing a graphical image as a bitmap containing 65,536 different colors.

68000 A family of 32-bit *microprocessors* from Motorola, used in the Macintosh computers and many advanced workstations.

The 68000 uses a linear addressing mode to access memory, rather than the segmented addressing scheme used by popular microprocessors from *Intel*; this makes it more popular with programmers.

6845 An early programmable video controller chip from *Motorola*, used in IBM's *Monochrome Display Adapter (MDA)* and *Color/Graphics Adapter (CGA)*. Because of the extensive use of the 6845, later and more capable video adapters like the *EGA* contained circuitry to emulate the functions of the 6845.

SLIP Abbreviation for Serial Line Internet Protocol. A communications protocol used over serial lines or dial-up connections. SLIP has been almost entirely replaced by PPP because it lacks a great deal of the functionality that PPP provides.

SMARTDRV.SYS The *DOS device driver* that provides compatibility for *hard-disk controllers* that cannot work with EMM386 and Windows 3.x running in enhanced mode. Use the *DEVICE* command to load this device driver in *CONFIG.SYS*.

This command does not load the DOS *disk cache*; use the *SMARTDRV* command for that. Neither SMARTDRV.SYS or command files are used with Windows 95 or later operating systems.

socket services Part of the software support needed for *PCMCIA* hardware devices in a *portable computer*, controlling the interface to the hardware.

Socket services is the lowest layer in the software that manages PCMCIA cards. It provides a BIOS-level software interface to the hardware, effectively hiding the specific details from higher levels of software. Socket services also detect when you insert or remove a PCMCIA card and identify the type of card it is.

software An *application program* or an *operating system* that a computer can execute. Software is a broad term that can imply one or many programs, and it can also refer to applications that may actually consist of more than one program.

SOHO Abbreviation for small office/home office. That portion of the market for computer services occupied by small offices and home-based businesses rather than the large corporate buyers. SOHO is a small but growing market sector characterized by very well-informed buyers.

Over 13 million Americans run a small business from home, and more than 40

million work at home either full or part time. This is a result of many factors in the economy, including corporate downsizing, and cheaper and more capable computers and office equipment, and is a trend that is likely to continue.

Solaris A *Unix*-based *operating system* from SunSoft that runs on *Intel* processors and supports a *graphical user interface*, *e-mail*, the *Network File System*, and Network Information Service. Solaris brings a common look-and-feel to both *SPARC* and Intel platforms.

sound board An add-in *expansion board* for the PC that allows you to produce audio output of high-quality recorded voice, music, and sounds through headphones or external speakers. In the *Macintosh*, digital stereo sound reproduction is built into the system.

Almost all *multimedia* applications take advantage of a sound board if one is present; the *MPC* Level 2 specification requires the inclusion of a *16-bit* sound card.

source The disk, file, or document from which information is moved or copied.

source code The original human-readable version of a program, written in a particular programming language, before the program is compiled or *interpreted* into a machine-readable form.

spaghetti code A slang expression used to describe any badly designed or poorly structured program that is as hard to unravel (and understand) as a bowl of spaghetti.

SPARC Acronym for Scalar Processor ARChitecture. A *32-bit RISC* processor from Sun Microsystems.

SPARCstation A family of *Unix work-stations* from Sun Microsystems, based on the *SPARC* processor. SPARC-stations range from small, *diskless* desktop systems to high-performance, tower SPARCservers in *multiprocessor* configurations.

special interest group Abbreviated SIG. A group that meets to share information about a specific topic; *hardware, application software, programming languages*, even *operating systems*. A SIG is often part of a larger organization like a *users group* or the *ACM*.

stack A reserved area of *memory* used to keep track of a program's internal operations, including functions' return addresses, passed parameters, and so on. A stack is usually maintained as a "last in, first out" (LIFO) *data structure*, so that the last item added to the structure is the first item used.

stand-alone Describes a system designed to meet specific individual needs that does not rely on or assume the presence of any other components to complete the assigned task.

standard mode The most common *Microsoft Windows* 3.x operating mode, in which *application* programs run in *16-bit protected mode* on *80286* (and later) processors. Standard mode supports *task switching* and provides access to 16 MB of memory. It does not allow the *multitasking* of non-Windows *applications* found in *386-enhanced mode*.

star network A network topology in the form of a star. At the center of the star is a wiring *hub* or concentrator, and the *nodes* or *workstations* are arranged around the central point representing the points of the star. Wiring costs tend to be higher for star networks than for other configurations, as very little cable is shared; each node requires its own individual cable.

start bit In *asynchronous transmissions*, a start bit is transmitted to indicate the beginning of a new data *word*.

static RAM Abbreviated SRAM, pronounced "ess-ram." A type of computer *memory* that retains its contents as long as power is supplied; it does not need constant refreshment like *dynamic RAM* chips. A static RAM chip can only store about one fourth of the information that a dynamic RAM of the same complexity can hold.

Static RAM, with access times of 15 to 30 nanoseconds, is much faster than dynamic RAM, at 60 nanoseconds or more, and is often used in *caches*; however, static RAM is four to five times as expensive as dynamic RAM.

S3 86Cxxx A family of fixed-function graphics accelerator chips from S3 Corporation. These chips, the 86C801, 86C805, 86C924, and 86C928, are used in many of the accelerated graphics adapters that speed up *Microsoft Windows*' video response.

stop bit(s) In *asynchronous transmissions*, stop bits are transmitted to indicate the end of the current *data* word. Depending on the convention in use, one or two stop bits are used.

streaming tape A high-speed tape *backup* system, often used to make a complete backup of an entire *hard disk*.

A streaming tape is designed to optimize throughput so that time is never wasted by stopping the tape during a backup; this also means that the computer and backup software also have to be fast enough to keep up with the *tape drive*.

stylus A pen-like pointing device used in *pen-based* systems and *personal digital assistants*.

substrate The base material used in the construction of a disk, tape, *printed circuit board*, or *integrated circuit*.

supercomputer The most powerful class of computer. The term was first applied to the Cray-1 computer. Supercomputers can cost over $50 million each. They are used for tasks such as weather forecasting, complex three-dimensional modeling, and oil reservoir modeling.

superscalar A microprocessor architecture that contains more than one execution unit, or pipeline, allowing the processor to execute more than one instruction per clock cycle.

For example, the *Pentium* processor is superscalar, and has two side-by-side pipelines for integer instructions. The processor determines whether an instruction can be executed in parallel with the next instruction in line. If it doesn't detect any dependencies, the two instructions are executed.

SuperVGA Abbreviated SVGA. An enhancement to the Video Graphics Display (*VGA*) video standard defined by the *Video Electronics Standards Association* (VESA).

SuperVGA *video adapters* can display at least 800 pixels horizontally and 600 vertically (the VESA-recommended standard), and up to 1600 horizontally and 1200 vertically, with 16; 256; 32,767; or 16,777,216 colors displayed simultaneously. Most SuperVGA boards contain several megabytes of *video RAM* for increased performance.

surface mount technology Abbreviated SMT. A manufacturing technology in which *integrated circuits* are attached directly to the *printed circuit board*, rather than being soldered into pre-drilled holes in the board. This process also allows electronic components to be mounted on both sides of a board.

surge A sudden and often destructive increase in line voltage. A regulating device known as a *surge suppressor* or surge protector can protect computer equipment against surges.

surge suppressor Also known as a surge protector. A regulating device placed between the computer and the AC line connection that protects the computer system from power *surges*.

swap file On a *hard disk*, a file used to store parts of running programs that have been swapped out of *memory* temporarily to make room for other running programs.

A swap file may be permanent, always occupying the same amount of hard disk space even though the *application* that created it may not be running, or is temporary, and only created as and when needed.

swapping The process of exchanging one item for another. In a virtual memory system, swapping occurs when a program requests a virtual memory location that is not currently in memory; the information is then read from disk, and displaces old information held in memory.

Swapping may also refer to changing floppy disks as needed when using two disks in a single floppy disk drive.

synchronization The timing of separate elements or events to occur simultaneously.

1. In a *multimedia* presentation, synchronization ensures that the audio and video components are timed correctly, and so actually make sense.

2. In computer-to-computer communications, the hardware and software must be synchronized so that file transfers can take place.

3. The process of updating files on both a portable computer and a desktop system so that they both have the latest versions is also known as synchronization.

synchronous transmission In communications, a transmission method that uses a clock signal to regulate *data* flow. Synchronous transmissions do not use *start* and *stop bits*.

system area That part of a disk which contains the *partition table*, the *file allocation table*, and the *root directory*.

system attribute The *file attribute* that indicates that the file is part of the *operating system*, and should not appear in normal directory listings. There are also further restrictions on a system file; you cannot delete, copy, or display the contents of such a file.

system date The date and time as maintained by the computer's internal clock. You should always make sure that the system clock is accurate,

because the *operating system* notes the time that files were created; this can be important if you are trying to find the most recent version of a document or spreadsheet.

system disk A disk that contains all the files necessary to *boot* and start the *operating system*. In most computers, the *hard disk* is the system disk; indeed, many modern operating systems are too large to run from floppy disk.

system file A file whose *system attribute* is set. In IBM's PC-DOS, the two system files are called IBMBIOS .COM and IBMDOS.COM; in Microsoft's MS-DOS, they are called IO.SYS and MSDOS.SYS. These files contain the essential routines needed to manage devices, memory, and input/output operations.

SYSTEM.INI In Microsoft *Windows*, an *initialization file* that contains information on your hardware and the internal Windows operating environment. These files are used primarily in Windows 3.*x* and are used in Windows 95 or later for backward compatibility only.

Systems Application Architecture Abbreviated SAA. A set of IBM standards, first introduced in 1987, that define a consistent set of interfaces for future IBM software. Three standards are defined:

• **Common User Access (CUA)**: A *graphical user interface* definition for products designed for use in an *object-oriented* operating environment. The OS/2 desktop follows CUA guidelines in its design; Microsoft Windows implements certain CUA features, but by no means all of them.

• **Common Programming Interface (CPI)**: A set of *Application Programming Interfaces (APIs)* designed to encourage independence from the underlying *operating system*. The standard *database query language* is *SQL*.

• **Common Communications Support (CCS)**: A common set of *communications protocols* that interconnect SAA systems and devices.

system software The programs that make up the *operating system*, along with the associated utility programs, as distinct from an *application program*.

system time The time and date maintained by the internal clock inside the computer.

This internal clock circuitry is usually backed up by a small battery so that the clock continues to keep time even though the computer may be switched off. The system time is used to date-stamp files with the time of their creation or revision, and you can use this date stamp to determine which of two files contains the latest version of your document. The system time can also be inserted into a document as the current time by a *word processor* or a *spreadsheet program*.

system unit The case that houses the processor, *motherboard*, internal *hard-* and *floppy disks*, *power supply*, and the *expansion bus*.

tap
1. A connector that attaches to a cable without blocking the passage of information along that cable.

2. In communications, a connection onto the main transmission medium of the network.

tape cartridge A self-contained tape storage module, containing tape much like that in a video cassette. Tape cartridges are primarily used to back up *hard disk* systems.

tape drive A computer *peripheral* that reads from and writes to magnetic tape. The drive may use tape on an open reel, or may use one of the small, enclosed *tape cartridges*. Because tape-management software has to search from the beginning of the tape every time it wants to find a *file*, tape is too slow to use as a primary storage system, but tapes are frequently used to back up *hard disks*.

T-connector A T-shaped connector, used with coaxial cable, that connects two *thin Ethernet* cables and also provides a third connector for the *network interface card*.

TCP Abbreviation for Transmission Control Protocol. The connection-oriented, transport-level protocol used in the *TCP/IP* suite of communications protocols.

TCP/IP Acronym for Transmission Control Protocol/Internet Protocol. A set of computer-to-computer communications protocols first developed for the Defense Advanced Research Projects Agency (DARPA) in the late 1970s. The set of TCP/IP protocols encompass media access, packet transport, session communications, file transfer, e-mail, and terminal emulation.

TCP/IP is supported by a very large number of hardware and software vendors, and is available on many different computers from PCs to mainframes. Many corporations, universities, and government agencies use TCP/IP, and it is also the foundation of the *Internet*.

telnet That part of the *TCP/IP* suite of protocols used for remote login and *terminal* emulation; also the name of the program used to connect to *Internet* host systems.

Originally a Unix utility, telnet is available these days for almost all popular operating systems. You will find that most versions of telnet are character-based applications, although some contain the text inside a windowed system.

temporary swap file A *swap file* that is created every time it is needed. A temporary swap file will not consist of a single large area of contiguous hard disk space, but may consist of several discontinuous pieces of space. By its very nature, a temporary swap file does not occupy valuable hard disk space if the *application* that created it is not running. In a *permanent swap file* the hard disk space is always reserved, and is therefore unavailable to any other application program. If hard disk space is at a premium, choose a temporary swap file.

tera- Abbreviated T. A prefix meaning 10^{12} in the metric system, 1,000,000,000,000; commonly referred to as 1 trillion in the American numbering system, and one million million in the British numbering system.

terabyte Abbreviated TB. In computing, usually 2^{40}, or 1,099,511,627,776 bytes. A terabyte is equivalent to 1,000 gigabytes, and usually refers to extremely large hard-disk capacities.

terminal A monitor and keyboard attached to a computer (usually a *mainframe*), used for data entry and display. Unlike a personal computer, a terminal does not have its own *central processing unit* or *hard disk*.

terminate-and-stay-resident program Abbreviated TSR. A *DOS* program that stays loaded in memory, even when it is not actually running, so that you can invoke it very quickly to perform a specific task.

Popular TSR programs include calendars, appointment schedulers, calculators and the like that you can invoke while using your word processor, spreadsheet, or other application. TSRs occupy *conventional memory* space that becomes unavailable for use by your applications programs; however, if you have a recent version of DOS and an *80386* (or later) processor, you can load your TSRs into *upper memory blocks*, and therefore recover that conventional memory for other uses.

TSRs are no longer in general use thanks to the onset of Windows 95, which allows multiple programs to run at the same time without being preloaded into memory.

terminator A device attached to the last *peripheral* in a series, or the last *node* on a network.

For example, the last device on a *SCSI bus* must terminate the bus; otherwise the bus will not perform properly. A resistor is placed at both ends of an *Ethernet* cable to prevent signals reflecting and interfering with the transmission.

text editor In computer programming, software used to prepare program *source code*. Text editors do not have all the advanced formatting facilities available in word processors, but they may have other features that particularly relate to programming like complex search and replace options, and multiple windows.

text file A *file* that consists of text characters without any formatting information. Also known as an *ASCII* file, a text file can be read by any word processor. The *README* file, containing late-breaking news about an *application*, is always a text file.

thermal printer A *nonimpact* printer that uses a thermal *printhead* and specially treated paper to create an image. The main advantage of thermal printers is that they are virtually silent; the main disadvantage is that they usually produce poor quality output that is likely to fade with time. They are used in calculators and in terminals to provide a local printing capability.

thick Ethernet Connecting *coaxial* cable used on an *Ethernet* network. The cable is 1 cm (approximately 0.4") thick, and can be used to connect network *nodes* up to a distance of approximately 3300 feet. Primarily used for facility-wide installations.

thin Ethernet Connecting *coaxial* cable used on an *Ethernet* network. The cable is 5 mm (approximately 0.2") thick, and can be used to connect network *nodes* up to a distance of approximately 1000 feet. Primarily used for office installations.

thrashing An excessive amount of disk activity in a *virtual memory* system, to the point where the system is spending all its time *swapping* pages in and out of memory, and no time executing the application. Thrashing can be caused when poor system *configuration* creates a *swap file* that is too small, or when insufficient memory is installed in the computer. Increasing the size of the swap file and adding memory are the best ways to reduce thrashing.

thread

1. A *concurrent* process that is part of a larger *process* or program. In a *multitasking operating system*, a program may contain several threads, all running at the same time inside the same program. This means that one part of a program can be making a calculation, while another part is drawing a graph or chart.

2. A connected set of *postings* to a *USENET newsgroup* or to an online *forum*. Many newsreaders present postings as threads rather than in strict chronological sequence.

386 enhanced mode In Microsoft *Windows 3.x*, the most advanced and complex of the different operating modes. 386 enhanced mode lets Windows access the *protected mode* of the *80386* (or higher) processor for extended *memory management* and *multitasking* for both Windows and non-Windows application programs.

3.5" disk A *floppy disk*, originally developed by Sony Corporation, that encloses the recording media inside a rigid plastic jacket.

TMS34020 A graphics chip from Texas Instruments used in *high-end* PC graphics adapters. The older 34010 uses a 16-bit data *bus* with a 32-bit data *word*, while the 34020 uses 32 bits for both.

Both are compatible with the Texas Instruments Graphical Architecture (*TIGA*) used in some IBM-compatible computers. TIGA video adapters and monitors display 1024 *pixels* horizontally, and 786 pixels vertically, using 256 colors.

token-ring network A *local area network* with a ring structure that uses token-passing to regulate traffic on the network and avoid collisions.

On a token-ring network, the controlling computer generates a "token" that controls the right to transmit. This token is continuously passed from one node to the next around the network. When a node has information to transmit, it captures the token, sets its status to busy, and adds the message and the destination address. All other nodes continuously read the token to determine if they are the recipient of a message; if they are, they collect the token, extract the message, and return the token to the sender. The sender then removes the message and sets the token status to free, indicating that it can be used by the next node in sequence.

Token Ring network IBM's implementation of the *token-ring network*

architecture; it uses a token-passing protocol transmitting at 4 or 16 megabits per second.

Using standard telephone wiring, a Token Ring network can connect up to 72 devices; with shielded *twisted-pair wiring*, the network can support up to 260 nodes. Although it is based on a closed-loop ring structure, a Token Ring network uses a star-shaped cluster of up to eight nodes all attached to the same wiring concentrator or MultiStation Access Unit (MSAU). These MSAUs are then connected to the main ring circuit. See the accompanying diagram.

A Token Ring network can include *personal computers, minicomputers,* and *mainframes*. The IEEE 802.5 standard defines token ring networks.

T1 A long-distance, point-to-point 1.544-megabit per second *communications channel* that can be used for both digitized voice and data transmission; T1 lines are usually divided into 24 channels, each transmitting at 64 kilobits per second.

toner cartridge The replaceable cartridge in a *laser printer* or photocopier that contains the electrically charged ink to be fused to the paper during printing.

touch screen A special *monitor* that lets the user make choices by touching *icons* or graphical buttons on the screen.

Touch-screen systems are popular for interactive displays in museums and in automatic teller machines, where input is limited. They never achieved much popularity in the business world, because users have to hold their hands in midair to touch the screen, which becomes tiring very quickly.

tower case A vertical *system unit* case designed to have more *drive bays* and *expansion slots* than the desktop units.

track A concentric collection of *sectors* on a *hard-* or *floppy disk*.

The outermost track on the top of the disk (or *platter*) is numbered track 0 side 0, and the outermost track on the other side is numbered track 0 side 1. Numbering increases inwards towards the center of the disk. Tracks are created during the disk *formatting* process.

On tapes, tracks are parallel lines down the axis of the tape.

trackball An input device used for pointing, designed as an alternative to the *mouse*.

A trackball is almost an upside-down mouse; it stays still, and contains a movable ball that you rotate using your fingers to move the mouse cursor on the screen. Because a trackball does not need the area of flat space that the mouse needs, trackballs are popular with users of *portable computers*; Apple PowerBook computers include a trackball as part of the keyboard case, and Microsoft has released a small trackball that clips onto the side of a laptop computer.

tracks per inch Abbreviated TPI. The number of tracks of sectors on a hard or *floppy disk*. TPI is an indication of the density of data that you can store on any given disk; the larger the TPI, the more data the disk can hold. Among floppy disks, *high-density 5.25" disks* have 96 TPI, while most *3.5" disks* have 135 TPI.

track-to-track access time An indication of *hard disk* speed; the amount of time it takes the disk's *read/write heads* to move from one track to the next adjacent track.

transistor Abbreviation for transfer resistor. A semiconductor component that acts like a switch, controlling the flow of an electric current. Transistors are incorporated into modern *microprocessors* by the million.

transport layer The fourth of seven layers of the International Standards Organization's Open Systems Interconnection (*ISO/OSI*) model for computer-to-computer communications. The transport layer defines *protocols* for message structure, and supervises the validity of the transmission by performing some error checking.

Trojan horse A type of *virus* that pretends to be a useful program, such as a game or a utility program, when in reality it contains special code that will intentionally damage any system onto which it is loaded.

true color A term used to indicate that a device, usually a video adapter, is capable of displaying 16,777,216 different colors; you will also see this number abbreviated to simply 16 million.

T3 A long-distance point-to-point 44.736-megabit per second communications service that can provide up to 28 *T1* channels. A T3 channel can carry 672 voice conversations, and is usually available over *fiber-optic cable*.

TWAIN Generally thought to be an acronym for Technology Without An Important Name, TWAIN is the name given to the technology that allows you to scan images directly into any application without the use of a dedicated scanning program.

24-bit color A method of representing a graphical image as a bitmap containing 16,777,216 different colors.

24-bit video adapter A video adapter that uses 24 bits to define the color used for an individual *pixel*. Each of the three color channels (red, green, blue) is defined by one 8-bit byte; this means that each channel can be defined in terms of 256 different intensities for each of the three primary colors. This adds up to a total of 16,777,216 different gradations of colors; probably at least as many as the human eye can distinguish.

twisted-pair cable Cable that comprises two insulated wires twisted together at six twists per inch. In twisted-pair cable, one wire carries the signal and the other is grounded. Telephone wire installed in modern buildings is often twisted-pair wiring.

TXD Abbreviation for transmit data. A *hardware* signal defined by the *RS-232-C* standard that carries information from one device to another.

UART Acronym for Universal Asynchronous Receiver/Transmitter. An electronic module that combines the transmitting and receiving circuitry needed for *asynchronous transmission* over a serial line.

Asynchronous transmissions use *start* and *stop bits* encoded in the data stream to coordinate communications rather than the clock pulse found in *synchronous transmissions*.

Ultra DMA/33 A protocol that allows a hard drive to transfer information directly to random access memory at up to 33.3Mbps without passing the information through the central processor.

undelete To recover an accidentally deleted *file*. *DOS* 5 (and later) provides the UNDELETE command, but many of the popular utility program packages also contain similar *undelete programs*, which often have a much better user interface and are therefore easier to use.

undelete program A utility program that recovers deleted or damaged *files* from a disk. A file can be deleted accidentally, or it can become inaccessible when part of the file's control information is lost.

Many utility packages offer excellent file recovery programs, including the *Norton Utilities* from Symantec. DOS 5 (and later) also offers undelete programs. These programs guide the user through the recovery process or, if

damage is extreme, attempt to recover as much of the damaged file as possible. In this case, substantial editing may be necessary before the file can be used; the best way to recover a damaged file is to restore it from a backup copy.

unformat The process of recovering an accidentally formatted disk. *DOS* 5 (and later) provides the UNFORMAT command, but many of the popular utility program packages also contain similar programs, which often have a much better user interface and so are easier to use.

unformat program A utility program that recovers files and directories after a disk has been formatted by accident.

Many utility packages offer excellent unformat programs, including the *Norton Utilities* from Symantec. DOS 5 (and later) and Windows 95 (and later) also offer unformat utilities. These programs guide the user through the recovery process, offering advice and assistance as they go. You must, of course, recover the original information on the disk before you add any new files or directories to the disk.

uninterruptible power supply Abbreviated UPS, pronounced "you-pea-ess." An alternative power source, usually a set of batteries, used to power a computer system if the normal power service is interrupted or falls below acceptable levels.

A UPS can often supply power for just long enough to let you shut down the computer in an orderly fashion; it is not designed to support long-term operations.

Unix Pronounced "you-nix." A *32-bit, multiuser, multitasking, portable operating system* originally developed by AT&T.

Unix was developed by Dennis Ritchie and Ken Thompson at Bell Laboratories in the early 1970s. It has been enhanced over the years, particularly by computer scientists at the University of California, Berkeley.

Networking, in the form of the *TCP/IP* set of protocols, has been available in Unix from the early stages. During the 1980s, AT&T began the work of consolidating the many versions of Unix. In January 1989, the Unix Software Operation was formed as a separate AT&T division, and in November 1989, that division introduced a significant new release, System V Release 4.0. In June 1990, the Unix Software Operation became known as Unix System Laboratories (USL), which was bought by Novell in 1993.

Unix is available on a huge range of computational hardware, from a *PC* to a Cray, and is also available in other, related forms. For example, *AIX* runs on IBM *workstations*; *A/UX* is a graphical version that runs on powerful *Macintosh* computers, and *Solaris* from SunSoft runs on *Intel* processors. Many of the computers that make up the *Internet* run Unix.

unmoderated newsgroup A *USENET newsgroup* or *mailing list* in which *posts* are not subject to review before distribution. You will find the discussions in unmoderated newsgroups to be wildly spontaneous, but they will also contain more than their fair share of *flames* and *flame wars*.

upgrade
1. The process of installing a newer and more powerful version; for example, to upgrade to a newer and more capable version of a *software* package, or to upgrade from your current *hard disk* to one that is twice the size. In the case of *hardware*, an upgrade is often called an upgrade kit.

2. A new and more powerful version of an existing system, either hardware or software, is also known as an upgrade.

upgradable computer A computer system specifically designed to be upgraded as technology advances.

Upgradable computers differ in how much of the PC's circuitry must be changed when you make the upgrade, and also in how you actually make the upgrade. At minimum, you must replace the processor; at most, some upgrades come close to changing all the circuitry installed in the computer.

upload In communications, sending a *file* or files from one computer to another over a network or using a *modem*. For example, a file could be uploaded to a *bulletin board*. In this case, the remote computer stores the uploaded file on disk for further processing when the transmission is complete. Files can also be uploaded to a network *file server*.

upper memory blocks Abbreviated UMB. The memory between 640 KB and 1 MB in an IBM-compatible computer running *DOS* was originally reserved for system and video use; however, not all the space is used, and the unused portions are known as upper memory blocks.

If you have an *80386* (or later) processor, you can gain up to 120K of additional memory by accessing these UMBs, and you can use this space to load *device drivers* and *terminate-and-stay-resident* programs.

upward compatibility The design of *software* so as to function with other, more powerful, products likely to become available in the short term. The use of standards makes upward compatibility much easier to achieve.

URL Abbreviation for Uniform Resource Locator, pronounced "earl." A method of accessing *Internet* resources.

URLs contain information about both the access method to use and also about the resource itself, and are used by *Web browsers* to connect you directly to a specific document or page on the *World Wide Web,* without you having to know where that resource is located physically.

The first part of the URL, before the colon, specifies the access method. On the Web, this is usually *http* (for hypertext transmission protocol), but you might also see file, *ftp,* or *gopher* instead. The second part of the URL, after the colon, specifies the resource. The text after the two slashes usually indicates a *server* name, and the text after the single slash defines the directory or individual file you will connect to. If you are linking to a document, it will usually have the filename extension .html, the abbreviation for hypertext markup language.

URLs are always case-sensitive, so pay particular attention to upper- and lowercase letters, and to symbols as well. One example of a URL is www.sybex.com.

USB An abbreviation for Universal Serial Bus, a peripheral bus "standard" that was jointly developed by Compaq, DEC, IBM, Intel, Microsoft, NEC, and Northern Telecom to allow computer peripherals to be automatically configured as soon as they are physically attached. USB will also allow up to 127 devices to run simultaneously on a computer, with peripherals such as monitors and keyboards acting as additional plug-in sites, or hubs. USB was specified to have a 12 megabit/second data rate and to provide a low-cost interface for Integrated Services Digital Network (ISDN) and digital PBXs.

One of the benefits of having Microsoft as part of the development effort is that Windows 95/98 can already let your PC recognize USB peripherals. Once you get the drivers installed for the new drive or whatever, Windows will take care of the rest. Almost all new PC designs from major vendors shipping today already have USB connections on the motherboard and the correct Win OS to make them work.

USB and FireWire (IEEE 1394) may appear similar in their goals of automatic configuration of peripherals (what FireWire calls "hotplugging") without the need to reboot or run SETUP, but they are not really the same, and the developers point out that they have different applications. USB is slower than FireWire but is supposed to address traditional PC connections, like keyboards and mice. Conversely, FireWire targets high-bandwidth consumer electronics connections to the PC, like digital camcorders, cameras, and digital videodisc players. The two technologies target different kinds of peripheral devices and are supposed to be complementary. USB proponents feel that future PCs probably will have both USB and FireWire connection ports.

USENET Contraction of USEr NETwork. An international, non-commercial network, linking many thousands of *Unix* sites.

Although there is a very close relationship between the *Internet* and USENET, they are not the same thing by any means. USENET predates the Internet; in the early days, information was distributed by dial-up connections. Not every Internet computer is part of USENET, and not every USENET system can be reached from the Internet.

Like the Internet, USENET has no central governing body; USENET is run by the people who use it. With well over 10,000 different newsgroups, USENET is accessed by millions of people every day, in more than 100 countries.

USENET newsgroups The individual discussion groups within *USENET*.

USENET newsgroups contain articles posted by other Internet and USENET subscribers; very few of them contain actual hard news. Most newsgroups are concerned with a single subject; the range of subjects available through USENET is phenomenal—there are over 10,000 different newsgroups from which to choose. If people are interested in a subject, you are sure to find a newsgroup for it somewhere.

Newsgroups are like the online forums found on CompuServe or America Online; you can post your own articles and browse through similar items posted by others. When you reply to a post, you can reply to the newsgroup so that other subscribers can read your reply, or you can respond directly to the originator in a private e-mail message.

user group A voluntary group of users of a specific computer or *software* package, who meet to share tips and listen to industry experts. Some PC user groups hold large, well-attended monthly meetings, run their own *bulletin boards*, and publish newsletters of exceptional quality.

utility program A small program, or set of small programs, that supports the *operating system* by providing additional services that the operating system does not provide.

In the PC world, there are many tasks routinely performed by utility programs, including *hard disk* backup, *disk optimization*, *file recovery*, *safe formatting*, and *resource* editing.

uudecode Pronounced "you-you-de-code."
1. To convert a *text file* created by the *Unix uuencode* utility back into its original *binary* form. Graphical images and other binary files are often sent to USENET newsgroups in this form, because the newsgroups can only handle text and don't know how to manage binary files.

2. The name of the utility program that performs a text-to-binary file conversion. Originally a Unix utility, uudecode is now available for most operating systems.

uuencode Pronounced "you-you-en-code."

1. To convert a *binary file* such as a graphical image into a *text file* so that the file can be sent over the *Internet* or to a *USENET newsgroup* as a part of an *e-mail* message. When you receive a uuencoded text file, you must process it through the *Unix uudecode* utility to turn it back into a graphical image that you can view.

2. The name of the utility that performs a binary-to-text file conversion. Originally a Unix utility, uuencode is now available for most operating systems.

vaccine An *application* program that removes and destroys a computer *virus*.

The people who unleash computer viruses are often very accomplished programmers, and they are constantly creating new and novel ways of causing damage to a system. The *antivirus* and vaccine programmers do the best they can to catch up, but they must always lag behind to some extent.

vaporware A sarcastic term applied to a product that has been announced but has missed its release date, often by a large margin, and so is not actually available.

VAR Acronym for value-added reseller; a company that adds value to a system, repackages it, and then resells it to the public. This added value can take the form of better documentation, user support, service support, system integration, or even just a new nameplate on the outside of the box. For example, Canon makes the print engine used in many laser printers, including those from Hewlett-Packard; in this case, Canon is an original equipment manufacturer (*OEM*) and HP is the value-added reseller.

VDT Acronym for video display terminal. Synonymous with *monitor*.

vendor The person or company that manufactures, supplies, or sells computer hardware, software, or related services.

Veronica A search service built into the *Gopher Internet* application. When you use Veronica to search a series of Gopher menus (files, directories, and other items), the results of the search are presented as another Gopher menu, which you can use to access the resources your search has located. Veronica supposedly stands for Very Easy Rodent-oriented Net-wide Index to Computer Archives.

version number A method of identifying a particular *software* or *hardware* release.

The version number is assigned by the software developer, and often includes numbers before and after a decimal point; the higher the number, the more recent the release. The number before the decimal point indicates the major revision levels (DOS 5, DOS 6), while the part after the decimal indicates a minor revision level (DOS 6.1, DOS 6.2), which in some cases can produce a significant difference in performance.

vertical scanning frequency In a *monitor*, the frequency at which the monitor repaints the whole screen; sometimes called the vertical refresh rate.

Vertical scanning frequency is measured in *Hz* (cycles per second), and higher rates are associated with less *flicker*. *VGA* has a vertical scanning frequency of 60 or 70 Hz, and *SuperVGA* rates vary from the *VESA* guidelines of 56 Hz (which is about the minimum tolerable) and 60 Hz, to the official recommended standard of 72 Hz or higher.

very low-frequency emission Abbreviated VLF. Radiation emitted by a computer monitor and other very common household electrical appliances such as televisions, hair dryers, electric blankets, and food processors. VLF emissions fall into the range from 2 kHz to 400 kHz, and decline with the square of the distance from the source. Emissions are not constant around a monitor; they are higher from the sides and rear, and weakest from the front of the screen.

VGA Acronym for Video Graphics Array. A *video adapter* introduced by IBM along with the *IBM PS/2* line of computers in 1987.

VGA supports previous graphics standards, and provides several different graphics resolutions, including 640 *pixels* horizontally by 480 pixels vertically. A maximum of 256 colors can be displayed simultaneously, chosen from a palette of 262,114 colors.

Because the VGA standard requires an *analog display*, it is capable of resolving a continuous range of gray shades or colors, in contrast to a digital display which can only resolve a finite range of shades or colors.

video adapter An *expansion board* that plugs into the *expansion bus* in a *DOS* computer, and provides the text and graphics output to the monitor.

Some later video adapters, such as the *VGA*, are included in the circuitry on the *motherboard*, rather than as separate plug-in boards.

Video CD A compact disc format standard developed by Sony, Phillips, JVC, and Matsushita that allows up to 74 minutes of video to be stored on one compact disc.

Compact discs recorded in Video CD format can be played on *CD-I*, Video CD, and *CD-ROM drives*, and CD players that have digital output and an add-on video adapter.

videodisk An optical disk used for storing video images and sound. A videodisc player can play back the contents of the videodisc on a computer or onto a standard television set. One videodisc can contain up to 55,000 still images, or up to 2 hours worth of *full-frame video*.

video RAM Abbreviated VRAM, pronounced "vee-ram." Special-purpose *RAM* with two data paths for access, rather than just one as in conventional RAM. These two paths let a VRAM board manage two functions at once—refreshing the display and communicating with the processor. VRAM doesn't require the system to complete one function before starting the other, so it allows faster operation for the whole video system.

virtual DOS machine Abbreviated VDM. A *DOS emulation* that takes

advantage of the *virtual 8086 mode* of *80386* (or later) processors.

Both *OS/2* and *Windows NT* use this feature of the processor to create multiple *multitasking* DOS and Windows sessions, and each VDM runs as a single-threaded, *protected-mode* process.

virtual 8086 mode A mode found in the *80386* and later processors that lets the processor *emulate* several *8086* environments simultaneously.

The *operating system* controls the external elements, such as *interrupts*, and input and output; and *applications* running in this mode are protected from the applications running in all the other virtual 8086 environments, and behave as though they have control of the whole 8086 environment. To the user, this looks like several 8086 systems all running side-by-side, but under the control of the operating system.

virtual machine An environment created by the operating system that gives each executing *application* program the illusion that it has complete control of an independent computer, and can access all the system resources that it needs.

For example, the Intel *80386* (and higher) processor can run multiple

DOS applications in completely separate and protected address spaces using a processor mode known as *virtual 8086 mode*.

virtual machine boot Abbreviation VMB. A feature found in the *OS/2 operating system* that lets you boot a native, non-emulated version of *DOS* into a *virtual DOS machine*.

Support is provided for versions of DOS other than the *OS/2* emulation, including DOS 3.3, 4.0, 5.0, 6.0, *DR-DOS*, Concurrent DOS, and indeed, any other 8086 operating systems. Applications running in this mode are protected from the applications running in all the other *virtual 8086* environments, and behave as though they have control of the whole 8086 environment. To the user, this looks like several 8086 systems all running side-by-side, but all under the control of the OS/2 operating system.

virtual memory A memory-management technique that allows information in physical memory to be swapped out to a *hard disk*. This technique provides *application* programs with more memory space than is actually available in the computer.

True virtual-memory management requires specialized *hardware* in the processor for the operating system to use; it is not just a question of writing information out to a *swap file* on the hard disk at the application level.

In a virtual memory system, programs and their data are divided up into smaller pieces called pages. At the point where more memory is needed, the operating system decides which pages are least likely to be needed soon (using an algorithm based on frequency of use, most recent use, and program priority), and it writes these pages out to disk. The memory space that they used is now available to the rest of the system for other application programs. When these pages are needed again, they are loaded back into real memory, displacing other pages.

virtual reality Abbreviated VR. A computer-generated environment that presents the illusion of reality. The user wears a head-mounted display (HMD) that displays a three-dimensional image of the environment, and uses an instrumented glove to manipulate objects within the environment.

A whole range of applications are emerging to exploit VR; architects can present clients with a VR walk through of a proposed structure, and biologists can seem to get inside a human cell. Undoubtedly, the most lucrative avenues for VR will be computer games.

virus A program intended to damage your computer system without your knowledge or permission.

A virus may attach itself to another program, or to the *partition table* or the boot track on your *hard disk*. When a certain event occurs, a date passes, or a specific program executes, the virus is triggered into action. Not all viruses are harmful; some are just annoying. An example is the Israeli or Jerusalem virus, also known as Friday the 13th, first seen on a computer at the University of Jerusalem in July 1987. This virus slows down your system and draws black boxes on the lower-left portion of the screen. If the virus is in memory on any Friday the 13th, every program executed is erased from your hard disk.

VL bus Also known as VL local bus. Abbreviation for the *VESA* local bus, a bus architecture introduced by the Video Electronics Standards Association (VESA), in which up to three adapter slots are built into the motherboard. The VL bus allows for *bus mastering*.

The VL bus is a 32-bit bus, running at either 33 or 40 MHz. The maximum throughput is 133 megabytes per second at 33 MHz, or 148 megabytes per second at 40 MHz. The most common

VL bus adapters are video adapters, hard-disk controllers, and network interface cards.

voice recognition Also known as speech recognition. Computer recognition and analysis of human language is a particularly difficult branch of computer science. Background noise, different voices, accents and dialects, and the ability to recognize and add new words to a computer vocabulary all contrive to complicate the problem.

Systems that work with only one speaker must be trained before they can be used, and systems that can work with any speaker have extremely restricted vocabularies. In the future, voice recognition will find wide applications from the phone companies to credit card authorizations to automatic voice-mail systems.

volatile memory Any memory system that does not maintain its contents when power is lost. Normal computer memory, whether *dynamic RAM* or *static RAM*, is volatile; *flash memory* and *ROM* are not volatile.

volume
1. A unit of physical storage, such as a floppy disk, a hard disk, or a tape cartridge. A volume may hold a number of complete files, or may just hold parts of files.

2. In networking, a volume is the highest level of the *file server directory* and file structure. Large hard disks can be divided into several different volumes when the *network operating system* is first installed.

volume serial number In *DOS* and *OS/2*, a unique number assigned to a disk during the formatting process, and displayed at the beginning of a directory listing.

In the *Macintosh*, System 7 assigns a similar number, known as a "volume reference number," that programs can use when referring to disks.

VRML Short for Virtual Reality Modeling Language, VRML is used to design three-dimensional, interactive worlds on the Internet. In a VRML world, it is possible for a user to interact with objects just as if they were in real space.

wafer A flat, thin piece of *semiconductor* material used in the construction of a chip. A wafer goes through a series of photomasking and etching steps to produce the final chip, which has leads attached and is finally packaged in a ceramic, plastic, or metal holder.

wait state A clock cycle during which no instructions are executed because the processor is waiting for data from a device or from memory.

Static RAM chips and paged-mode RAM chips are becoming popular because they can store information without being constantly refreshed by the processor and so eliminate the wait state. A computer that can process information without wait states is known as a *zero wait state* computer.

warm boot A *reboot* performed after the operating system has started running.

Web browser A *World Wide Web* client application that lets you look at *hypertext* documents and follow links to other *HTML* documents on the Web. When you find something that interests you as you browse through a hypertext document, you can click your mouse on that object, and the browser automatically takes care of accessing the Internet host that holds the document you requested; you don't need to know the IP address, the name of the host system, or any other details.

wideband In communications, a channel capable of handling more frequencies than a standard 3 kHz voice channel.

window In a *graphical user interface*, a rectangular portion of the screen that acts as a viewing area for *application* programs.

Windows can be tiled or cascaded, and can be individually moved and sized on the screen. Some programs can open multiple *document windows* inside their *application window* to display several word processing or spreadsheet *data files* at the same time.

Windows accelerator An expansion card or a chip containing circuitry dedicated to speeding up the performance of PC video *hardware* so that *Microsoft Windows* appears to run faster. Standard display adapters do not handle the throughput required by Windows particularly well, and rapidly become *input/output bound*. An accelerator card specifically "tuned" for Windows can improve overall performance considerably.

Windows application Any *application* program that runs within the Microsoft *Windows* environment and cannot run without Windows. All Windows applications follow certain conventions in their arrangement of menus, the use and style of dialog boxes, as well as keyboard and mouse use.

Windows 95/98 The replacement for the DOS and Windows 3.1 operating systems, from Microsoft Corporation.

Windows 95/98 is a *32-bit*, *multitasking*, multithreaded operating system capable of running DOS, Windows 3.1, and Windows 95/98 applications, supports *Plug and Play* (on the appropriate hardware), and adds an enhanced FAT file system in the Virtual FAT which allows *long file names* of up to 255 characters while also supporting the DOS 8.3 filenaming conventions.

Applets include WordPad (word processor), Paint, and WinPad (personal information manager), as well as System Tools such as Backup, ScanDisk, Disk Defragmenter, and DriveSpace. Access to Microsoft Network is available directly from the Windows 95/98 desktop. A Start button and desktop Taskbar make application management easy and straightforward.

Windows NT A *32-bit multitasking portable operating system* developed by Microsoft, and first released in 1993.

Windows NT is designed as a portable operating system, and initial versions run on Intel *80386* (or later) processors, and RISC processors such as the MIPS R4000, and the DEC Alpha.

Windows NT contains the *graphical user interface* from *Windows* 3.1, and can run Windows 3.1 and *DOS* applications as well as *OS/2* 16-bit character-based applications, and new 32-bit programs specifically developed for Windows NT.

Multitasking under Windows NT is *pre-emptive*, and applications can execute multiple *threads*. Security is built into the operating system at the U.S. Government- approved C2 security level. Windows NT supports the DOS *FAT file system*, installable file systems such as *CD-ROM* systems, and a native file system called *NTFS*. Windows NT also supports *multiprocessing*, *OLE*, and *peer-to-peer* networking.

WIN.INI In Microsoft *Windows 3.x*, an *initialization file* that contains information to help customize your copy of Windows.

When Windows starts, the contents of WIN.INI are read from the *hard disk* into memory so that they are immediately available. WIN.INI contains sections that define the use of colors, fonts, country-specific information, the desktop, and many other settings.

word A computer's natural unit of storage. A word can be 8 bits, 16 bits, 32 bits, or 64 bits in size.

workgroup A group of individuals who work together and share the same files and databases over a local area network. Special *groupware* such as *Lotus Notes* coordinates the workgroup and allows users to edit drawings or documents and update the database as a group.

workstation
1. In networking, any *personal computer* (other than the *file server*) attached to the network.

2. A high-performance computer optimized for graphics applications such as *computer*-aided design, *computer-aided engineering*, or scientific applications.

World Wide Web Abbreviated WWW, W3, or simply the Web. A huge collection of *hypertext* pages on the *Internet*.

World Wide Web concepts were developed in Switzerland by the European Laboratory for Particle Physics (known as CERN), but the Web is not just a tool for scientists; it is one of the most flexible and exciting tools in existence for surfing the Internet.

Hypertext links connect pieces of information (text, graphics, audio, or video) in separate *HTML* pages located at the same or at different Internet sites, and you explore these pages and links using a *Web browser* such as Netscape Navigator or Microsoft Internet Explorer.

You can also access a WWW resource directly if you specify the appropriate *URL* (Uniform Resource Locator).

worm A destructive program that reproduces itself to the point where a computer or network can do nothing but manage the worm. Eventually, your computer *memory* or *hard disk* will fill up completely.

WORM Acronym for Write Once Read Many. A high-capacity optical storage device that can only be written to once, but can be read any number of times. WORM devices can store from 200 to 700MB of information on a 5.25" disk, and so are well-suited to archival and other non-changing storage.

write To transfer information from the processor to memory, to a storage medium such as a *hard* or *floppy disk*, or to the display. In the PC world, the term usually refers to storing information onto disks.

write-back cache A technique used in *cache* design for writing information back into main memory.

In a write-back cache, the cache stores the changed block of data, but only updates main memory under certain conditions, such as when the whole block must be overwritten because a newer block must be loaded into the cache, or when the controlling algorithm determines that too much time has elapsed since the last update. This

method is rather complex to implement, but is much faster than other designs.

write-protect To prevent the addition or deletion of *files* on a disk or tape. *Floppy disks* have write-protect notches or small write-protect tabs that allow files to be read from the disk but prevent any modifications or deletions.

Certain *attributes* can make individual files write-protected so they can be read but not altered or erased.

write-through cache A technique used in cache design for writing information back into main memory.

In a write-through cache, each time the processor returns a changed bit of data to the cache, the cache updates that information in both the cache and in main memory. This method is simple to implement, but is not as fast as other designs; delays can be introduced when the processor must wait to complete write operations to slower main memory.

XGA Acronym for Extended Graphics Array. A high-resolution *video adapter* introduced by IBM in 1991 to replace the *8514/A* standard.

XGA is available as a microchannel architecture expansion board or in certain laptops; it is not available in *ISA* or *EISA* form. XGA supports resolution of 1024 horizontal *pixels* by 768 vertical pixels with 256 colors, as well as a *VGA* mode of 640 pixels by 480 pixels with 65,536 colors, and like the 8514/A, XGA is *interlaced*. XGA is optimized for use with *graphical user interfaces*, and instead of being very good at drawing lines, it is a bit-block transfer device designed to move blocks of bits like windows or dialog boxes.

Yellow Book The definition of the standard storage format for compact disc data, also referred to as the *CD-ROM* format. So called because of the cover color used when the specification was first published.

zero wait state Describes a computer that can process information without *wait states*. A wait state is a clock cycle during which no instructions are executed because the processor is waiting for data from a device or from memory.

Static RAM chips and *paged-mode RAM* chips are becoming popular because they can store information without being constantly refreshed by the processor, and so they eliminate the wait state.

ZIF socket Abbreviation for Zero Insertion Force socket. A specially designed chip socket that makes replacing a chip easier and safer.

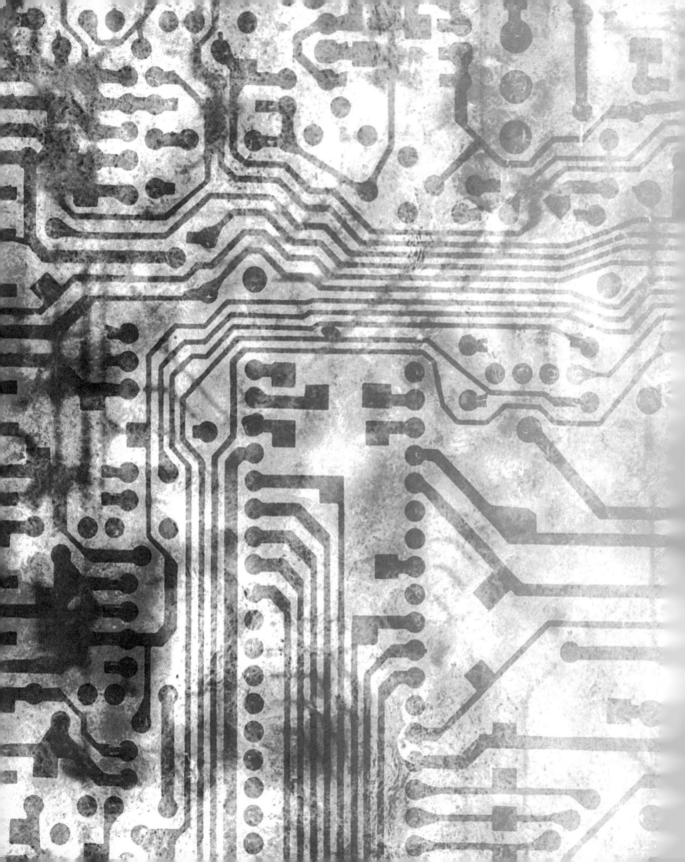

Sample A+ Core Module Exam Questions

The A+ Certification testing program is sponsored by the Computer Technology Industry Association (CompTIA) and backed by major computer hardware and software vendors, retailers, and distributors. The A+ Certification provides employers with a benchmark for evaluating employee's knowledge.

NOTE For detailed information about the A+ certification program, visit the CompTIA Web site at **www.comptia.org.**

In order to attain A+ certification, candidates must pass two exams: the Core Module and the DOS/Windows Module. The Core Module exam is designed to test an applicant's knowledge of basic PC troubleshooting and repair techniques. This appendix contains a sample of the type of questions you could expect to find on the A+ Core Module exam.

NOTE While many of the topics included in the Core Module exam are covered in this book, I recommend it only as supplemental A+ study material. Sybex also publishes comprehensive study guides for the A+ certification. Check out your local bookstores or online book sellers for *A+ Complete Study Guide* written by David Groth and published by Sybex, 1999.

Sample A+ Core Module Exam Questions

1. Which of the following is *not* a consideration when upgrading the RAM on a common PC?

   A. Number of pins

   B. Parity

    C. Speed

    D. Number of clusters

2. What primary precaution should you take when replacing a keyboard?

    A. Completely power down the system

    B. Turn off the keyboard

    C. Wear an ESD strap

    D. Use a screwdriver

3. What is the standard I/O address for COM2?

    A. 2F8–2FF

    B. 3F8–3FF

    C. 2E8–2EF

    D. 3E8–3EF

4. What is the standard I/O address for COM3?

    A. 2F8

    B. 3F8

    C. 2E8

    D. 3E8

5. What is the standard I/O address for COM4?

    A. 2F8

    B. 3F8

    C. 2E8

    D. 3E8

6. Where is IDE hard disk drive configuration information kept?

    A. Hard disk controller

    B. CMOS

    C. CONFIG.SYS

    D. AUTOEXEC.BAT

7. Which of the following is an invalid DMA channel in a machine that contains an ISA bus?

    A. 0

    B. 1

    C. 5

    D. 8

8. What is IRQ 6 used for in most PCs?

    A. Hard disk controller

    B. PS/2 mouse

    C. Floppy controller

    D. LPT1

9. How many pins does a standard serial port contain?

    A. 9

    B. 15

    C. 20

    D. 40

10. An IDE hard disk drive cable has how many pins?

    A. 10

    B. 34

    C. 40

    D. 50

11. Standard bidirectional parallel ports use which standard?

    A. RS-232C

    B. RS-241

    C. RJ-45

    D. IEEE 1284

12. Where are ROM BIOS routines stored?

    A. Hard disk 0

    B. Floppy disk

    C. CMOS

    D. Hard disk controller

13. Which component is activated first in a normal boot sequence?

    A. CPU

    B. Floppy disk

    C. Hard disk

    D. Memory

14. On ISA buses, which IRQ gets cascaded to IRQ 9 to provide additional IRQ addresses?

    A. 1

    B. 2

    C. 3

    D. 4

15. A 25-pin D shell connector is most often used for:

    A. Serial port

    B. Parallel port

    C. SCSI port

    D. Mouse port

16. A 15-pin, 2-row D shell connector is most often used for:

    A. Parallel port

    B. Serial port

    C. Video port

    D. Game port

17. What may have to be upgraded when installing an EIDE drive?

    A. Memory

    B. BIOS

    C. Case

    D. Monitor

18. ATAPI provides which major benefit?

    A. Attach up to four devices

    B. Add a larger monitor

    C. Add a MIDI component

    D. Compress data

19. MSCDEX provides what function for DOS?

    A. Data caching

    B. File copying

    C. Enables CD-ROM use in DOS

    D. Not used in DOS

20. Each device on a wide SCSI bus must have its own, unique, SCSI ID.

    A. True

    B. False

21. What is the maximum bus length of a SCSI-2 Fast/Wide SCSI bus?

    A. 1 meter

    B. 2 meters

    C. 3 meters

    D. 4 meters

22. You have just installed a sound card. You now notice both your printer and your new sound card don't work. What is the most likely source of the problem?

    A. Your printer is broken.

    B. You've damaged the sound card during installation.

    C. Your motherboard is faulty.

    D. The sound card is set to the same IRQ as the printer port.

23. Your computer was accidentally shut off during the boot process. After turning it back on, you receive an error: "Bad or Missing Operating System." What is the most likely cause of the error?

    A. Corrupt master boot record (MBR)

    B. Power failure

    C. Bad RAM

    D. Bad monitor

24. Which component is *not* tested by the POST routines?

    A. RAM

    B. Power supply

    C. CPU

    D. Motherboard

25. You are trying to figure out what is wrong with your computer. When you turn on the computer, no video appears on the monitor, and the hard disk isn't making any noise. The only noise you hear is the power supply fan. Which of the following could be eliminated as a possible cause?

    A. Keyboard unplugged

    B. Power supply unplugged

    C. Monitor unplugged

    D. Hard disk failed

26. What voltage range should your multimeter be set to when measuring household AC voltage?

    A. 50

    B. 100

    C. 200

    D. 500

27. Which AT command will cause a modem to hang up?

    A. ATDT

    B. ATH

    C. ATDP

    D. AT

28. After downloading a new game from the Internet, your computer experiences strange, non-reproducible errors. What is the most likely cause?

    A. A virus

    B. Modem failure

    C. Motherboard failure

    D. Monitor failure

29. You are on the phone with a user who is trying to get a CD-ROM to work. They just finished installing it. What should you ask them first?

    A. Is the cardboard insert still in the drive?

    B. Can you change the IRQ to 5?

    C. What did you mess up?

    D. How much RAM do you have?

30. What should you use to clean a computer's case?

    A. Emery cloth

    B. Contact cleaning solution

    C. Jeweler's cloth

    D. Silicon carbide

31. What can you install to protect your computer against power spikes?

    A. Power supply

    B. Surge suppressor

    C. Lightning rod

    D. SPS

32. Store laser printer OPC drums in what kind of environment?

    A. Warm, light

    B. Warm, dark

    C. Cool, light

    D. Cool, dark

33. You should always wear an ESD grounding strap, except under what conditions?

    A. When servicing a printer

    B. When servicing a monitor

    C. When servicing a PC

    D. When servicing electronic equipment of any kind

34. What component is installed in an ESD strap to prevent shock?

    A. Resistor

    B. Capacitor

    C. Wire

    D. SIMM

35. What conditions promote ESD?

    A. Cool, dry

    B. Cool, wet

    C. Warm, dry

    D. Warm, wet

36. Memory locations are called ports.

    A. True

    B. False

37. Which of the following is a feature of EDO RAM?

    A. Intelligent data recovery

    B. Faster data transfer

    C. Support for more processor types

    D. Permanent storage

38. Which of the following is *not* a common PC bus expansion type?

    A. ISA

    B. OSB

    C. VLB

    D. PCI

39. Which of the following is *not* stored in the CMOS?

    A. Disk geometry

    B. Time

    C. Modem speed

    D. Memory configuration

40. A system that keeps losing the time and date could be most likely caused by:

    A. System battery going dead

    B. Clock going bad

    C. Motherboard failing

    D. Bad sectors on the hard disk

41. Where is the boot sequence changed?

    A. BOOTCFG.EXE

    B. CMOS setup

    C. MSD

    D. ESD

42. Which EP printer component moves toner from the EP drum to the paper?

    A. Pickup roller

    B. Fuser roller

    C. Printhead

    D. Corona wire

43. Which of the following are impact printers?

    A. Dot matrix

    B. Daisy wheel

    C. Ink jet

    D. Laser

44. You just bought a new ink jet printer. After unpacking it, installing the ink cartridge, and installing the printer driver, the printer only produces blank pages. What is the *most likely* cause of the problem?

    A. The ink cartridge is plugged.

    B. You are using the wrong paper.

    C. You forgot to remove the sealing tape from the ink cartridge.

    D. The printer isn't plugged in.

45. A laser printer is printing all black pages. What is the *most likely* cause of the problem?

> **A.** Primary (charging) corona wire is broken or malfunctioning.
>
> **B.** Transfer corona is broken or malfunctioning.
>
> **C.** Laser is broken or malfunctioning.
>
> **D.** Fuser is broken or malfunctioning.

46. A "shifting" margin on a dot matrix printer might be caused by:

> **A.** Overheating print head
>
> **B.** Misadjusted paper guide
>
> **C.** Wrong paper type
>
> **D.** Wrong ribbon

47. Which PC Card type is most often used for hard disks?

> **A.** Type I
>
> **B.** Type II
>
> **C.** Type III
>
> **D.** Type IV

48. To use resources on a network, you need:

> **A.** A print server
>
> **B.** Rights
>
> **C.** A file server
>
> **D.** A hard disk

49. Rules used to govern network communications are called:

    A. IEEE

    B. Laws

    C. Standards

    D. Protocols

50. Which type of communication allows both sender and receiver to "talk" at the same time?

    A. Full duplex

    B. Half duplex

    C. Simplex

    D. Suplex

51. To override PnP and configure an expansion card manually, which of the following must you disable?

    A. RJ-45

    B. IRQ 6

    C. Plug and Play

    D. DMA

52. Which setting is important to set on a Token Ring NIC before installing it in a computer?

    A. Lobe length

    B. Ring speed

    C. Ring size

    D. Token length

Answers

1. D
2. A
3. A
4. B
5. C
6. B
7. D
8. C
9. A
10. C
11. D
12. C
13. A
14. B
15. B
16. D
17. B
18. A
19. C
20. A
21. C
22. D
23. A
24. B
25. A

26. C
27. B
28. A
29. A
30. C
31. B
32. D
33. D
34. A
35. C
36. B
37. B
38. B
39. C
40. A
41. B
42. D
43. A, B
44. C
45. A
46. B
47. C
48. B
49. D
50. A
51. C
52. B

INDEX

Note to the Reader: Throughout this index **boldfaced** page numbers indicate primary discussions of a topic. *Italicized* page numbers indicate illustrations.

NUMBERS

A

C

D

E

F

G

H

J

K

L

M

O

P

Q

R

S

T

V

W

X

CD #1: The Upgrader's Toolbox

The CD at the front of the book contains A+ Preparation Software, useful utilities, and a bonus appendix listing hard drives available on the market today.

A+ Preparation Software

Direct from David Groth's best-selling *A+ Complete Study Guide* are two test engines designed to get you up-to-speed for CompTIA's challenging A+ certification tests.

- **199 Core Module practice questions**
- **175 DOS/Windows practice questions**

Utilities

The CD includes several valuable utilities that will assist you in your day-to-day computer activities, including:

EasyClean 32, from EDV-Beratung, is an uninstaller that will keep both your system registry and drives clean and tidy.

Extreme System Manager, from Chin Cheung Lun, provides you with additional settings for Windows 95/98 including making changes to the file system, hiding icons on the desktop, hiding hard drives, and password protecting your entire system.

Norton AntiVirus, from Symantec, is a leading anti-virus program that allows users to quarantine infected files and protect against viruses, as well as ActiveX and Java applets.

Norton Speed Disk, from Symantec, is a disk defragmenter for Windows NT that supports both NTFS and FAT drive systems.

PACT JumpReg, from PACT Software, is a new list technology that allows you to get current keys, jump keys in clipboard, close upon jump, and jump to keys and values.

PACT Profile Copy, also from PACT Software, allows you to save Windows profiles and restore settings easily on new user accounts, computers, notebooks, or installations of Windows 95/98/NT.

ProtectZ, from H&H Soft, is a utility to protect your files and folders, as well as edit some system policies of Windows 95/98.

Registry Crawler, from 4Developers, allows you to find and configure registry settings quickly and easily.

SysFix, from JCL Developments, takes a snapshot of your Windows/System folder before you install a program, which allows you to compare it later to other snapshots of your system folder and check for errors when your system has problems.

Web Seeker 98 Demo, from Blue Squirrel Software, lets you combine in a single search the knowledge base of more than a hundred Internet search engines—from Alta Vista to Lycos to Yahoo!—pinpointing the exact info you need.

WebWhacker 2000 Demo, also from Blue Squirrel Software, provides a complete facility for browsing Web pages offline.

WinZip 7, from Nico Mak Computing, Inc. This is a shareware evaluation version of WinZip 7 SR-1. WinZip is a Windows 95/NT utility for zipping and unzipping files.

Bonus Appendix: Characteristics of Available Hard Drives

Forty pages of nitty-gritty information. Find the capacity, interface, data transfer rate, and more for the hard drives that are available today. (You can view this appendix using Adobe Acrobat Reader, also included on this CD.)